THE WORLD'S BEST BOOK ON THE WORLD'S GREATEST G...

Here it is, sports fans, the Big Book of Golf! With a broad and in-depth approach that other golf books just can't match, *Inside Sports Golf* gives you:

- In-depth tournament histories

- Hundreds of player profiles — from Bobby Jones to Annika Sorenstam and Tiger Woods

- Golf lesson with Kip Puterbaugh

- 100 magic moments in tournament play

- 200 great public courses

- Celebrities on the links — with Ann Ligouri

- 200 photos

- And more!

No matter how you tee it up, *Inside Sports Golf* is the definitive guide to the game (and by far the most fun)!

1997 • paperback
• ISBN 1-57859-007-8
• $19.95 U.S.

INSIDE SPORTS MAGAZINE

GOLF

Your Ultimate Tour Guide

Roger Matuz

VISIBLE INK PRESS

BUD COLLINS'
TENNIS
encyclopedia

(Peter Mecca)

BUD COLLINS'
TENNIS
encyclopedia

Edited by Bud Collins and Zander Hollander

an Associated Features book

Detroit • New York • Toronto • London

BUD COLLINS' TENNIS ENCYCLOPEDIA

Published by Visible Ink Press ®
a division of Gale Research
835 Penobscot Building
Detroit, MI 48226-4094

Visible Ink Press is a trademark of Gale Research.

Most Visible Ink Press books are available at special quantity discounts when purchased in bulk by corporations, organizations, or groups. Customized printings, special imprints, messages, and excerpts can be produced to meet your needs. For more information, contact Special Markets Manager, Gale Research, 835 Penobscot Bldg., Detroit, MI 48226. Or call 1-800-776-6265.

Art Director: Michelle DiMercurio
Typesetting: The Graphix Group
Front cover photos of Pete Sampras and Steffi Graf: AP/Wide World Photos
Back cover photo of Andre Agassi: AP/Wide World Photos
Back cover photo of Bud Collins: John Russell

Library of Congress Cataloging-in-Publication Data

Bud Collins' tennis encyclopedia / edited by Bud Collins & Zander
Hollander. – [3rd ed.]
        p.   cm.
  "Formerly published as Bud Collins' modern encyclopedia of
tennis."
  Includes index.
  ISBN 1-57859-000-0 (pbk.)
  1. Tennis–History. 2. Tennis–Records. 3. Tennis players–
Biography. 4. Tennis players–Rating of. I. Collins, Bud.
II. Hollander, Zander. III. Bud Collins' modern encyclopedia of
tennis.
GV992.B78 1997
796.342--dc21
                                97-13215
                                CIP

DEDICATION

For the extraordinary Tim Gullikson (1951–1996), small-town guy who made the big time, yet never forgetting that being kind, helpful and understanding embodied life's mission.

And for Tom Winship, my go-get-'em commander-in-chief for many years as editor of the *Boston Globe*, whose verve and imagination lifted it to eminence among newspapers.

And Joan Hildebrand "Biz" Jensen, my original editor, who encouraged my scribbling for the Bera High *Focus*.

Also for my kids from various liaisons: Suzanna, Betsy, Danielle, Gretchen, Karl, Rob, Kristin, Sharon.

—*Bud Collins*

CONTENTS

PREFACE

Fifty-five years before a handful of Londoners saw the possibilities of getting high on tennis at the introductory Wimbledon, Thomas DeQuincey took the town on a trip with his autobiography, *Confessions of an English Opium-Eater*. Sadly, DeQuincey, though assuring himself a place as a literary champ in 1822, didn't last long enough to try to smoke the Big W's grass. But he did talk about addiction. And I knew what he meant. Opium, tennis . . . what's the difference?

Did Leo Tolstoy wield a racquet when he wrote *War and Peace*? Did dour Karl Marx sneak away from his pondering (and ponderous) writing at the British Museum months before his death to watch the first significant champion, Willie Renshaw, win Wimbledon in 1882? Might he have attended specifically to scowl and hiss at Renshaw, playboy and *scion of capitalism*? Probably not. Otherwise, Marx might have written that tennis is the opiate of some of the people.

I'm one of those people. A tennis degenerate. Hooked as hopelessly as DeQuincey was on opium, Marx on communism. But don't send me to rehab, please. I don't want to get clean. I can't "just say 'no'" when there's a game in town—to be played, watched, scribbled/babbled about.

Deal me a racket, a typing machine, a microphone, and let the fix begin.

If this is a hallucinatory confession of a tennis devourer, so be it. True, there can be bad trips. But more often transporting, stimulating, captivating—even sublime. Hardly ever bland. The cast changes. So does the scene, the circumstances, the tensions, the stakes, the human drama and comedy.

Lasting visions flash through this junkie's neural mush. Not just the great victories and performances, but—

• Long forgotten Al Stitt, on the way to his outer court match in the 1958 U.S. Doubles at Boston's Longwood Cricket Club, is distracted by unusually frantic screams of children at the club

Russian novelist and social thinker Leo Tolstoy dabbled in tennis. Bud Collins Collection

• Over a stretch of 21 days of grace, loose and lambasting, Arthur Ashe wins the 1968 U.S. Amateur title in Boston, then the initial U.S. Open Championship in New York, a dual feat certain never to be repeated. Beneath the Forest Hills Stadium his father secludes himself to sob openly, joyfully, almost unbelievingly: "That boy, that boy . . . it's a miracle . . . he came so close to dying as a sickly baby. . . . "

• Suzanne Herr Feldman, one of the world's top juniors, eventually becomes a housewife, and is talked into entering the U.S. Indoor Championships by a friend. She shows up with her three-year-old daughter, saying, "Somebody has to babysit or I can't play." She is looking at me. It isn't that hard to cover a match while trying to restrain a child from shrieking, "Mommy! Mommy!," making bathroom runs and amusing her in general. But why didn't I even get 75 cents an hour for my time?

• Rod Laver completes his second Grand Slam, beating Tony Roche at Forest Hills, accepts a check for $16,000 (untold riches in 1969), and has to borrow a dime—"to call my wife to see if she's had our baby yet."

• At the Roman Colosseum revisited—a.k.a. Houston's Astrodome in 1973—Billie Jean King, in spangles and spiffy volleys, polishes off an aged gladiator named Bobby Riggs, as womankind whoops it up and turns thumbs down on His Piggishness. "The broad beat me fair and square. She was too good," says reprobate Bobby, winking, "but I saved their tour by losing, didn't I?"

pool. Seeing that an infant has tumbled in, Al dives to the rescue. He hands the child to the hysterical, thankful mother, plods squishily onward to arrive late and dripping for his match to disapproving stares and comments of partner and foes.

• Statuesque Pat Stewart, a top-twenty American player in the amateur days, remarks, "I'd rather have my numbers than be No. 1." She is 36-26-36, a lingerie model who sometimes sighs when she loses, "That's the way the strap snaps."

• A nineteen-year-old Swede, on a high of his own, is pitched toward the ceiling of the Kungligahallen in Stockholm again and again by his elated teammates as the crowd of usually reserved countrymen go wild. This rite of flying is called a *hissening*, in this case honoring Bjorn Borg for virtually single-handedly beating Czechoslovakia, 3-2, to give Sweden its first Davis Cup in 1975. Diligently—fortunately—the hisseners catch him each time, so that more will be heard from him.

• Kathleen Horvath, moderately regarded but highly motivated for one Parisian afternoon, decides to beat Martina Navratilova at her own game: going to the net. She does, and becomes the answer to a trivia question: Who gave Navratilova her only loss in 86 matches and 17 tournaments in 1983?

• "I'm out of here!" cries Ivan Lendl, deserting the smoke-inundated Grandstand at Flushing Meadow. "Come back!" commands Umpire Adrian Clark. "No way!" replies Lendl, sprinting for the exit—leaving behind fans, opponent Mark Vines and smoldering Umpire Clark—because he thinks the joint is burning down. Too bad, perhaps, but it isn't and doesn't. Firemen quell the blaze in a trash compactor just beyond the wall, and future champ Lendl returns to resume his march to the 1981 fourth round.

• A man watching two women play tennis at Flushing Meadow in 1986 is sitting on a dilemma so sharp it could be a saber. How can he cheer for either? The man, named John Wilkerson, a teaching pro at an inner city playground in Houston, raised both of them—Zina Garrison and Lori McNeil—from girls to Top Ten women. McNeil wins an excruciating third set tie-breaker on a net-cord trickler, and will continue, depriving a startled Chris Evert of her seemingly God-given place in the U.S. Open semis. Tears trickle down the man's face.

• Sudden, terrible explosions in the neighborhood cause a terrified me to belly flop onto the concrete court. After all, it is 1969 and this is a war zone: Saigon, South Vietnam. My doubles partner at Cercle Sportif, an aged Vietnamese, looks down at me impatiently. "Only a few rockets," he says as casually as Jim Bowie at the Alamo declaring, "Just a few Mexicans, fellows." He suggests, "Please get up and play. We don't let rocket attacks interfere with our tennis." Sound outlook. Meekly I obey.

• " . . . I know it was wrong, a lousy thing to do . . . and I'm sorry . . . it'll never happen again. . . . " This is John McEnroe, contrite at innumerable post-match press conferences that stretch from 1977 to this very day. He makes reporters wonder if they are surrogate priests at confessionals or Freudians who should be charging John a standard fee for listening.

Why do I delight in Jana Novotna? Because she just keeps coming back for more, like a hard-luck blackjack addict, demanding, "Hit me! Hit me! Hit. . . . " How could she blow the 1993 Wimbledon final to Steffi Graf? Clutching a third-set lead of 4-1, 40-30, with serve, wasn't she a lock like the one on the door at Fort Knox? Or the 1995 French Open match against Chanda Rubin when Rubin sagged 0-5, 0-40 in the last set and was pinned by a total of nine match points? How? Did the Duchess of Kent ask as Jana blubbered all over her at that wet Wimbledon presentation? Unlikely. Too polite. Too polite, probably, to even send Jana a dry-cleaning bill.

But what is Jana supposed to do—play in a designer hair shirt? Make a pilgrimage on her knees to the grave of St. Suzanne Lenglen? Get a lobotomy?

She doesn't have the Teutonic resolve of Steffi Graf, constantly playing through emotional and physical stress; the buzz and relentlessness of the Barcelona Bumblebee, Arantxa Sanchez Vicario; the fierceness of purpose of Monica Seles and Thomas Muster; the "glitzkrieg" style of Andre Agassi; the nonchalant thunder of Pete Sampras and Stefan Edberg; the power of Lindsay Davenport and Boris Becker; the perpetual motion of Jesus-driven Michael Chang. But who does?

Like everybody else she just goes out there to see what happens the next time, without any deep psychological ruminations, self-flagellation or apologies. Plays the game. Because that's what it is: a game, a wonderful game and diversion, and sometimes a drama. But not life or death. Either the ball goes over the net or it doesn't.

That's the essence of tennis, the simple and obvious requirement. Take a racket, an instrument that looks like an oversized skillet—but with a network of strings for a bottom—and hit a rubber ball over a wall of webbing merely three feet in height (though it can seem like Gibraltar). Hit the ball over the net within a rectangular court one more time than your opponent and you win a point. Win enough points and you defeat that opponent.

Few do it more gloriously than Novotna, a nimble gunner with a full arsenal of shots, a risk-taker, a builder of seemingly invulnerable leads. Mostly shoe-ins. Her bank account attests to that. But few can lose as spectacularly as on those occasions when she comes apart like Raggedy Ann with sawdust pouring from her head. The monumental lead collapses like a sand castle as the tide comes in, and she is washed away with it, as human as we hackers.

Jana was eminently human after that lovely July afternoon in Centre Court, after divinely playing champ Graf out of her sneakers, poised on the delicate balance between glory and . . . gulp . . . tight-fisted acquisitiveness and philanthropy. You know what happened, which way she went: Mother Teresa was never more generous. Some of us felt for her in the heat of championship-interruptus more than we ever did for a champion installed. However, Graf, the gazelle in gorgeous human form, got the ball over the net one more time.

At best, tennis does deliciously evoke Kipling's iffy impostors, Triumph and Disaster. Obviously a Borg-McEnroe, Agassi-Sampras, Evert-Navratilova, Graf-Seles epic does—but a first-rounder between nobodies can be just as gripping.

My heart never beat quicker for tennis than on a rainy May afternoon in Prague, 1971, as obscure Frantisek Pala, the homeside guy, and Vladimir Korotkov of the Soviet Union went at each other in an insignificant early-round Davis Cup struggle.

Insignificant? Not to the tormented folk of Czechoslovakia, under the thumbs of the USSR. Tuned in to TV over a tense, capricious weekend, they prayed and cursed against the white-costumed athletes representing the black-hearted invader whose tanks had echoed across those ancient streets only three springs before.

"Politics!" wailed Jan Kodes, the Czechs' main man, fresh from winning the French Open. "It isn't sport, it's politics, and my head aches from it because people want me to win so bad." Those expectations made Jan tighter than Scarlett O'Hara's corset, and he was beaten by Alex Metreveli, who could feel the hatred directed at him by the jammed-in crowd of 5,000, most of them standing for hours.

Dank silence greeted Metreveli's every point, no matter how brilliantly he might hit the ball. It was eerie. Wild, delighted cheers followed his errors plus anything good Kodes could do. Barbed whistles assailed the Soviets whenever they disputed a line call, many of which were very patriotic—against the Soviets—in other words, and well worth disputing.

"Yes, we screwed them on some calls," Kodes conceded, "but not as bad as they screwed us last year in Moscow."

Kafkaesque gloom descended after Metreveli beat Kodes, but Pala saved the first day with his curlicue spins to defeat Korotkov. So-called journalistic objectivity vanished in the drizzle. Sitting and soaking there, I became a Czech, chanting "Doe-tuh-hoe!"—"Come on!"—over and over as a member of the all-encompassing chorus.

Back and forth it went for three sodden days of nerve-quaking play wrapped around rain interruptions, days of hopes dashed and revived, dashed and revived again. "They don't like me much, do they?" Metreveli observed with a wry smile. "Too much politics. I have nothing to do with that. I just do my job: play tennis."

But there was an unexpectedly happy ending. Kodes pulled himself together, and the Czechs won. The hall porter at my hotel was ecstatic. "Tiny Czechoslovakia . . . " he held his hands about two inches apart. "Tiny Czechoslovakia . . . " and then he spread them a far as possible, "beat giant Soviet Union!"

Momentary bliss.

Tennis can do that, although not often so plaintively. But it remains a game, albeit at the professional level one that has been refined and polished, commercialized and subsidized well beyond the 19th-century imagination of the original champion, Spencer W. Gore, triumphant at Wimbledon in 1877. Gore, unseated the following year by the impromptu sky-high tactic of the lobfather—his "arc" rival, P. Frank Hadow—remarked in 1880 that any gamesplayer worth his sweat wouldn't find tennis a satisfactory exercise for very long.

In today's world, bad-mouthing the game that put him in history books would gain Gore a severe censure from his agent: "Don't bite the sport that feeds us, Spence."

But the champ's doubting statements had as much impact as the *Titanic* on its frosty foe. Gore sank from view quickly. However, the game has flourished and spread across the planet so incessantly that even I, the hopeless lover, am pleasantly startled. In my fifth decade as a two-way journalist (scribbler/babbler) following the bouncing ball, I must admit that it does beat working for a living.

Ed Costello, my sports editor at the now deceased *Boston Herald,* would never have believed it. He was actually apologetic in sending me out to my first tennis assignment, a local CYO tourney, taking pains to let me know I wasn't being punished. "Clubby types running around in their underwear, chasing a little white ball" weren't high on his list of sports to be covered.

But Tom Winship, editor-in-chief of the *Boston Globe*, where I moved in 1963, encouraged me to give readers a world-wide view of this rising game. It was the same year that my TV career was launched by Boston's PBS station, WGBH, specifically by producer/director Greg Harney. Harney (who started such people as Mary Carillo, Frank Deford, Sean McDonough, Donald Dell, Vic Braden, Kim Prince, Kathryn Switzer, Larry Rawson and, yes, Michael Dukakis at the microphone), pioneered the Public Broadcasting Service's thoughtful and thorough telecasting of tennis well ahead of the commercial networks. It would have been hard to find two more inspiring bosses than Greg and Tom.

Soon enough I began babbling for CBS, thanks to Jack Dolph and Bill MacPail, then NBC, courtesy of Carl Lindemann and Chet Simmons. And anybody else who'd hire me.

Although my Uncle Studley swears that I covered the seminal Wimbledon with a quill pen, he's off by a few years. Still, I guess I could give you, treasured reader, a digest of the 127 years of tennis history, and it wouldn't take long.

1874—English gentleman with time on his hands, Major Wingfield, devises and patents the game, makes small change selling sets, and somebody—take your pick of claimants and candidates—starts it off in the U.S.

1877—Wimbledon is launched (first, still foremost), and even shows a profit of a few pounds.

1881 and 1887—Inaugural U.S. Championships for men, then women. The world will follow.

1900—Harvard rich kid Dwight Davis donates sterling punch bowl for an international team competition, eventually known as Davis

Cup. Davis and college pals beat Brits in leadoff finale. Only two countries interested then; more than 100 now.

1905 and 1907—Californian May Sutton and Aussie Norman Brookes, respectively, are first alien winners of Wimbledon, a place no longer safe from barbarians for the English homebodies.

1919—France's Suzanne Lenglen wins Wimbledon, scandalously, showing thighs and unbeatable strokes, vanquishing corsets and everyone opposing her. English are so shocked by her flaunting of female assets that the "new" [present] Wimbledon must be built in 1922 to accommodate increasing hordes of disapproving ticket purchasers.

1920—Big Bill Tilden, arrogant, artistic, all-conquering Philadelphian, takes over, dominates game in the twenties, makes U.S. tennis-conscious, inspires construction of Forest Hills Stadium for championships, keeps Davis Cup at home.

1923—Unflappable "Little Miss Poker Face," Helen Wills, wins first of seven U.S. titles, succeeds Lenglen as dominatrix, wins eight Wimbledons from baseline.

1926—Lenglen goes for the dough, signs as first to tour professionally, opens new avenues, job opportunities in an infant sport.

1927—Four hands are finally better than one: the Four Musketeers—René Lacoste, Henri Cochet, Jean Borotra, Jacques Brugnon—bring down Tilden and Co., carting Davis Cup to France, necessitating the building of Stade Roland Garros in Paris.

1932—English Davis Cupper Bunny Austin liberates male legs by showing up in shorts.

1933—Last known Englishman—as far as many are concerned—to play tennis, Fred Perry, lifts Davis Cup from French, wins Wimbledon 1934–36, turns pro, joining Tilden, who did so in 1931.

1938—Don Budge, having retrieved Davis Cup, wins Australian, French, Wimbledon, U.S. titles, thus doing the never-before-done Grand Slam.

1946—World War II over, Jack Kramer spearheads recovery of Davis Cup from Australia. In 1947 he's first to win Wimbledon in shorts, also captures U.S., turns pro to swipe that crown from Bobby Riggs.

1950—Frank Sedgman and Ken McGregor heist Davis Cup from U.S., the beginning of the Australian Dynasty that will make Wimbledon and Forest Hills hostage to such Down Undertakers as Lew Hoad, Ken Rosewall, Rod Laver, Neale Fraser, Roy Emerson, Fred Stolle, John Newcombe, Tony Roche for a quarter-century.

1953—Maureen "Little Mo" Connolly, 18, navigates first female Grand Slam.

1961—Billie Jean King, 17, wins Wimbledon doubles with Karen Hantze, the first of B. J.'s record 20 titles at the Big W, 6 in singles.

1962—Laver, after following Budge and Connolly as third member of Grand Slam club, turns pro.

1965—Jimmy Van Alen, father of tie-breaker, shows it off at small Newport, R.I., pro tourney, but it won't be accepted until 1970.

1968—Open tennis dawns. Prize money is out on the table. Commercialization blooms and tennis begins metamorphosis from sort-of-amateur sport to big-business game. But amateur Arthur Ashe stuns the tennis world by winning first U.S. Open, leads U.S. to Davis Cup success and five-year hold. Back from isolated life as outcast professionals, Rosewall at French, Laver at Wimbledon, win first major opens.

1969—Laver repeats as Grand Slammer, this time a pro.

1970—Aussie Margaret Smith Court, all-time winner of major titles, 62 (24 in singles), goes Grand Slamming, fourth member of club.

1971—Schoolgirl Christine Evert, 16, arrives at Forest Hills, coolly goes to semis, and the Chrissie craze is on.

1973—Labor problems. ATP boycotts Wimbledon. Most top men don't play, including Open-era champs Laver, Newcombe, Stan Smith. Show goes on but ATP becomes a force. Billie Jean King beats Bobby Riggs in mixed singles schlockathon.

1974—"Lovebirds Double" at Wimbledon. Then affianced Chris Evert and Jimmy Connors triumph, begin cutting long championship swaths, pay 33-to-1 with London bookies. Bjorn Borg, 18, wins French, and the three of them change the game, guiding the world to two-fisted backhandedness.

1976—High-tech rackets are here to stay, supplanting wood, as Howard Head puts the Prince Classic oversized club into play, drawing initial laughs, but commencing serious alteration of the game.

1977—Borgiastic period is under way at Wimbledon's Centenary celebration as Bjorn wins second of five straight. But show is stolen by last known Englishwoman—or so it seems—to play tennis. Virginia Wade, 32, accepts championship prize from the other queen in the house, Elizabeth II.

1978—Martina Navratilova beats Evert to win first of record nine Wimbledons, the last in 1990.

1979—John McEnroe, 20, wins first of four U.S. titles while Tracy Austin, 16, becomes youngest to rule her country.

1980—Borg holds off McEnroe to win a wowser of a Wimbledon, highlighted by the Battle of 18-16 (fabulous fourth-set tie-breaker). McEnroe will win 1981 rematch.

1983—Yannick Noah sets off rejoicing across France as first citizen in 37 years to win French men's title.

1984—Ivan Lendl, from two sets back, beats McEnroe for French title, establishes himself as major figure who will win three U.S. titles.

1985—Blasting Boris Becker, 17, is youngest and first unseeded Wimbledon victor.

1988—Steffi Graf, 19, not only crashes Grand Slam club as fifth member, but embellishes it with a gold medal as tennis returns to the Olympics.

1989—Drought-buster Michael Chang, 17, seizes French, first American man to do so in 34 years.

1990—Cool summer for the callow: Monica Seles, 16, youngest winner of a major in this century, takes French; Pete Sampras, 19, is youngest U.S. champ.

1993—Seles, stabbed by loony Guenther Parche during match at Hamburg, will lose 26 months of a career already embracing seven major titles.

1995—Seles resurfaces to win Toronto, almost beats Graf in splendid U.S. Open final, but Steffi, with fourth title, becomes only one to hold all four majors four times.

1996—Winning a fifth French and seventh Wimbledon, Steffi eclipses Evert and Navratilova (18), and Helen Wills (19), in major singles, and with her 20th is hot on the track of Margaret Court's 24.

Brisk enough? There's much more to it on the following pages. As the opium-loving Thomas DeQuincey would have said—and I second in my own form of dependency—once you've started, it's hard to stop.

I hope that, like tennis itself, the reading is a lot more fun than Karl Marx's *Communist Manifesto*, and maybe, at times, as much fun as Groucho Marx. Groucho was no stranger to tennis, in fact. In 1941 his son, Arthur Marx, was ranked No. 6 in Southern California, the world's strongest neighborhood of that day, not far behind Frank Parker, Jack Kramer and Ted Schroeder.

Disappointingly, Arthur didn't move in a loping crouch or blow cigar smoke in opponents' eyes.

I also hope you keep on hackin' as a player, and harkin' to the lore of this marvelous pastime/pleasure/passion.

—*Bud Collins*

ACKNOWLEDGMENTS

Words, words, words . . . , " Eliza Doolittle wailed in *My Fair Lady*, and we know how she felt.

In pulling together the 123 years since the magnanimous Major—Walter Clopton Wingfield—gave us lawn tennis by patenting the game in London, we've used more words than ever in this third edition of "Our Fair Labor." More years, more characters on the rectangular stages throughout the world, more results and events have found their way into print. Talk about the expansion of tennis—this tome has expanded along with it, although we hope not so excessively as to induce hernia, valued reader.

Lawn tennis—just plain tennis to most of us—has been written about voluminously, first in England, enthusiastically by our favorite sportswriter, Henry Jones. Why are we so fond of Henry? Because he helped launch the All England Club, pushing tennis onto its lawns that had been devoted to croquet, and was the guiding light in organizing the fountainhead tournament, The Lawn Tennis Championships (a.k.a. Wimbledon), at the club. We also applaud the fact that Jones, a physician by training, like the patriarch of American tennis, James Dwight, was of similar outlook: neither man let medicine interfere with his tennis.

Though the literature of tennis stretches a long way, impressively, writers such as Jones were not overly concerned with facts and figures in chronicling the game. Compared with golf or baseball, tennis is woefully short on history, authoritative data and records. You can easily find out how many times sharp-eyed Joey Sewell of the 1920 champion Cleveland Indians struck out during his career. But how many matches did a contemporary champion, Bill Tilden, win during his? Nobody had any idea until our nonpareil researcher/historian Frank V. Phelps painstakingly dug it out for the *Tennis Encyclopedia.*

Gentleman though he is, and respectful of reputations, Frank nevertheless had to report catching the popular Molla Mallory in a fib. Molla, uh, shall we say, misannounced her age when she arrived in the U.S. from her native Norway in 1914. Winning the U.S. title in 1915, she said she was 23. She was actually 31—but what are eight years among friends? So when she won the last of her record eight in 1926, the dossier stated that she was 34. It stayed that way for decades, until Phelps' double-checking revealed her to be 42, the elder among major champs. But that only makes her an even more remarkable lady, doesn't it?

Although much remains to be ferreted out, we are confident that this is the most informative Encyclopedia yet, and are grateful that when we often cried "Help!" we got a lot of it from our willing friends. It's impossible to repay them fully, but we hope they'll settle for sincere acknowledgments.

We hail the memory of extraordinary contributors, those good men so devoted to the game, Hall of Fame journalists Allison Danzig of the *New York Times* and Lance Tingay of the *Daily Telegraph* of London. Both have died since the first edition in 1980, but their fine work lives on in these pages.

We're also indebted to historian George Alexander, who not only was responsible for fleshing out the life of Major Wingfield, but found the first documented account of tennis in the U.S. (1874), locating the game at a most unlikely site: a remote Army post in Arizona.

Applause goes also to matchless contributors Barry (Orso) Lorge of *Tennis Magazine*, Steve Flink of *Tennis Week* and CBS Radio, Marty Lader, formerly of UPI and Stan Isaacs, formerly of *Newsday*. Also to Joe Gergen of *Newsday*, Ram Ramnath, distinguished academician at MIT, and peerless Phyllis Hollander of Associated Features, who smoothly chaperoned the manuscript through many prickly passages. You've heard of labors of love. But the best is laboring with love, which this opus was for Collins and roommate Anita P. Ruthling Klaussen. Her tireless triple threat performance—digging, organizing, sustaining—kept it moving at the end.

From across the planet, generous assistance poured in from such talents as David Studham at the Melbourne Cricket Club Library; John Treleven and Barbara Travers at the ITF in London; Robert Geist, the Vienna visionary; Alan Little at the Wimbledon library; the omnivorous Shark of Ponte Vedra, ATP's Greg Sharko.

Honorable mention goes as well to various people at Visible Ink Press and Gale Research: Judy Galens, Becky Nelson, Leslie Norback, Jim Craddock, Jeff Hermann, Christa Brelin, Dean Dauphinais, Maria Franklin, Edna Hedblad, Margaret Chamberlain, Pam Hayes, Mikal Ansari, and keyer extraordinaire Kathy Dauphinais; Jane Brown, Linda Johnson, Melissa Mulrooney, Mark Stenning, Mark Young of the International Tennis Hall of Fame; Art Campbell, Page Croslan, Bruce Levy, Randy Walker of the USTA; Debbi Edwards, Jim Fuhse, Liz Holloway, Susan Vosburgh, Toni Waters of the WTA; Joe Lynch of the ATP; Helen, Harold and Josh Zimman plus Adam Scharff and Jay Donahue of H. O. Zimman, Inc.

Plus Russo Adamo, Glenn Adamo, Neil Amdur, Arthur Ashe, Dick Auerbach, Roberto Basche, Bob Beach, Ron Bookman, Mary Carillo, Giovanni Clerici, Donald Dell, Bob Dunbar, Dick Enberg, Ed Fabricus, Igor Federovsky, John Feinstein, the Furgal-ivanters, Mimi Harney, Julie Hatfield, Gladys and Julius Heldman, Ed Hickey, David N'g Ives, Joe Johnson, Elizabeth and David Kahn, Bob Kelleher, Harry Kirsch, Karl H. R. Klaussen, Larry Lawrence, Timothy C. A. Leland, Michelino Lupica, C. Gene Mako, Suzanna Collins Mathews, Geoff Mason, Steve Mayer, Paul Metzler, Pop Merrihew, Mother Morris, Murray the

Wrench, Ted Nathanson, Dennis Phillips, Warren Pick, Elizabeth Pratt, Ron Sampson, Jimmy Scalem, Ubaldo Scanagatta, Pancho Segura, Fred Sharf, Bill Talbert, Rino Tommasi, Alan Trengove, Candy Van Alen, Visser & Stockton, Hazel Wightman, Bryan Williams, R. B. D. H. Wogan and indexer Terry Murray.

Thank you all. We couldn't (and shouldn't) have done it without you.

(If, treasured reader, you should find any errors or questions or have suggestions to offer, please notify Collins, c/o Sharf Marketing, P.O. Box 67197, Chestnut Hill, Mass., 02167)

—*Bud Collins and Zander Hollander*

INTRODUCTION

Like other professional sports that have succeeded with the public since World War II, tennis has come to be regarded as an entertainment and a business as much as a game. As the 1997 campaign began, the 29th anniversary of the advent of "open" tennis—the integration of amateurs and pros with cash payments offered on the basis of winning performance—more than $125 million was available throughout the world to male and female professionals. The total for the dawning season of opens, 1968, was about $400,000.

Grandest financially of the first open championships in that inaugural year was the U.S. Open at Forest Hills. A $100,000 pot held $14,000 and $6,000 as first prize for man and woman, respectively. By 1996 the pot had sweetened to $10,893,890 and the singles first prize (the same for men and women since progressive 1973) amounted to $600,000.

Despite all the gold, this diversion is yet a game that is sometimes raised to an art form—a competitive ballet—by the splendor in movement of such acrobatic zephyrs as Maria Bueno, Rod Laver and Ken Rosewall, Evonne Goolagong and Ilie Nastase, Martina Navratilova and John McEnroe, Steffi Graf, Martina Hingis and Pete Sampras.

Often it is sublime drama. Never more so than on a chilly, grim October afternoon in Bucharest in 1972 when nationalism and personal pride, strength of character, and moral outlook were all wrapped up in a game of tennis between an American, Stan Smith, and a Romanian, Ion Tiriac. Smith was the best player in the world that year, but he was out of his element. Slipping on the slow, salmon-hued European clay, he was assaulted by a canny, dark-maned lion, while a feverish crowd and unfailingly patriotic officials gave him a thumbs-down treatment. Never mind the tennis match, Smith sometimes wondered whether he'd get out of town alive.

At stake was the Davis Cup, that huge silver basin from which world conquerors have swilled victorious champagne since 1900. It is the most difficult prize to win in tennis, a reward for the team title, pursued each year by more than 120 countries. In 1972 the United States and Romania were the finalists. The Cup would be decided by the Smith-Tiriac match, and this fact made a boiling tea kettle of an intimate 7,000-seat wooden stadium that was hastily hammered together for what amounted to a state occasion in Romania. Though Tiriac, a deceptively plodding and unstylish player, wasn't in Smith's league, he lifted himself as high as his native Carpathians with one thought: His tiny homeland, producer of few world-class players besides himself and teammate Ilie Nastase, could score a fantastic victory over the mighty U.S. if he beat Smith. "I know only one way to play—to win. If I lose," Tiriac said, "then it is nothing. We don't win the Cup."

Ion orchestrated the chanting crowd and deferential line judges into a united front for himself and against Smith. He stalled, he emoted—and he played like a madman, forcing the excruciating match all the way into a fifth set. It seemed a morality play in short pants: the exemplary sportsman Smith, tall and fair-haired, against the scheming Tiriac, hulking and glaring. Somehow Smith held together amid chaos to play to his utmost, too, and win the last set in a run of six games, 4-6, 6-2, 6-4, 2-6, 6-0. Considering the adverse conditions and the magnitude of the prize, Smith's triumph was possibly the most extraordinary in the history of the game. "I concentrated so hard I got a headache," he said.

While Tiriac was chastised outside of Romania for a pragmatic approach to tennis, avoiding the accepted behavior, he was merely doing the best he could to seize a rare day for his homeland. It was only a game of tennis, but it had assumed a far greater significance for a few hours that afternoon.

The significance was global, and this internationality is a source of much of the appeal of tennis. By this, of course, I mean the established worldwide tournament game to which this encyclopedia is primarily devoted. The advance of the game since the tennis court was patented in London in 1874 by Major Walter C. Wingfield has been so complete that all continents are routinely represented in any tournament of consequence. Australians, Asians, Europeans, Africans, and North and South Americans populate a family of tournament players who work their way around the globe on an unending trek among the continents. They flit between Melbourne and Munich, Bombay and Buenos Aires, Johannesburg and Jacksonville as casually as commuters, aware that jets have made it possible to compete on one continent today and another tomorrow.

Tennis players have been ocean-hoppers almost since the beginning, but the year 1900 is set apart: A British team showed up in Boston to launch the Davis Cup by challenging the U.S. Five years later a robust Californian, May Sutton, became the first foreigner to win Wimbledon. Two years after that Norman Brookes journeyed all the way from Melbourne to London to win the singles, showing the way to the Big W for Australians, who would one day be more awesome there than any other aliens. The next year, 1908, an American, Fred Alexander, was the first outsider to win the Australian title.

The game may have been restricted to a 78-by-27-foot plot, but the players were operating on a planetary playground. Don Budge presented striking evidence in 1938 when he circumnavigated the initial Grand Slam by winning the Australian, French, Wimbledon and U.S. titles all within that year. Budge traveled more leisurely, by ocean liner, but players would become winged rugbeaters in a few years, and no tournament was too far off the beaten path.

Major Wingfield's attempt to fire a tennis boom and cash in on it by patenting a set of equipment and instructions in 1874 is a convenient event in marking the start of the game we know as tennis—lawn tennis to sticklers (mostly Britons), who wish to distinguish this game from its parent, real (court or royal) tennis. Real tennis, a complex and beguiling indoor game, is played with lopsided rackets in an erratically walled concrete court where the balls—hard as baseballs—rattle around on sloping roofs and disappear into arcane apertures. The game is still to be found in a few private clubs (eight in the U.S.) where members presumably have to pass a blood test: blue-positive required.

Real tennis dates back to the Middle Ages, called *jeu de paume* in France because the hand was used to smack the ball before the instrument called racket was conceived. Numerous kings, who had the court-building wherewithal and leisure time, were enthusiastic players, the first probably Louis X of France (1314–16). Poor Louis may have been a mite too enthusiastic. The story is that he became overheated at play, drank cold water immediately, developed a chill and died. Where was Gatorade when he needed it?

A more famous playboy monarch, old London Fats (a.k.a. King Henry VIII of England), made his reputation in amorous mixed doubles. Reportedly, in a game at Hampton Court, he employed a reliable chop stroke while an executioner at the Tower of London was doing same to the neck of Anne Boleyn, breaking his service on Henry's second wife.

The King obviously took his tennis seriously and sanctioned the kind of edge players of today would envy by employing his personal scorekeeper, one Anthony Angeley. What opponent would question a call by the royal umpire on the King's behalf?

If you think John McEnroe was the champ at unleashing passions on court, he was really a pussycat compared with another master stroker, the Italian painter Caravaggio. Enraged during a match in Rome in 1606, he killed his opponent, Ranucci Tommasoni (thus winning by default?), and had to leave town for a while.

According to Shakespeare, yet another English tennis-playing king, Henry V, also had a temper. He was not amused by a gift of tennis balls from the Dauphin of France.

Taking it as a "Balls to you, pal!" message, Henry declared: "When we have matched our rackets to these balls, we will, in France, by God's grace, play a set. . . . " He proceeded to invade France to backhand the locals at the Battle of Agincourt in 1415.

Since kings and millionaires aren't numerous enough to carry a popular sport, real tennis never came very far out of its curiously constructed closet. Actually, Major Wingfield wasn't the originator of an outdoor version. He was among several who tried their hands at fresh-air tennis prior to 1874, but it was Wingfield who codified a game and envisioned commercial possibilities. When he set out to market equipment and rules for his game, Wingfield realized that a profitable volume of sales would rest on attracting a broader public than that involved in real tennis and very expensive indoor courts: not the masses, certainly, but the affluent with property large enough for one of the courts detailed in his rules.

It was natural enough in England to raise a net and outline a court on a croquet lawn—thus lawn tennis. Regardless of how far tennis would stray from a grass surface—to such exotic footing as cow dung in India, ant bed in Australia, and plastic carpets for indoor play everywhere—the game was once and forever lawn tennis to the Brits, who would rather break their necks than tradition.

Although grass courts hold firm at Wimbledon as well as at a few other pro tournaments in Britain, the Netherlands and Germany, they are scarce in number elsewhere. Steadfastly resisting the trend away from the sacred sod is Newport Casino at Newport, R.I., birthplace of the American tournament game. The world's oldest tournament-active tennis patch, the Casino (1880) is a hardy survivor, a gingerbread architectural gem, scene of the first recognized American tournament, the men's U.S. Championships of 1881. Staged on grass, Newport—now an annual pro tour stopover as the Hall of Fame Championships—remains on grass, the last such American tourney. Like Wimbledon, Newport has no intention of forsaking God's own greenery.

Lawn tennis or just-plain-tennis—whatever it is called, however the ball bounces on whichever surface—has caught on in the U.S. more widely than anywhere else. Shortly after Wingfield started peddling tennis, it reached the U.S. In 1876, Dr. James Dwight, a Bostonian, won a baptismal tourney of sorts, a sociable get-together he arranged in the yard of the Appleton estate at Nahant, Mass.

Americans were swinging rackets in numerous locales in 1874, and Dr. Richard Dwight of Boston, the son of "The Father" and an active player himself in his 90s, had this to say in 1992:

"In 1874, just after Major Wingfield patented the game, and the first tennis sets were sold in London, a Sears relative named Beebe brought one to Nahant. There was a good lawn at the Appleton place and Father and his cousin, Fred Sears, set up a court. They didn't care much for the game the first time they played. But the second time—ah, they were caught."

However, nobody declared that tennis had landed in America. Or much noticed. For many years afterwards, it was assumed, and written in numerous histories, that one Mary Outerbridge, of a prominent Staten Island (N.Y.) family, in bringing a set of tennis equipment home from Bermuda in 1874, had planted the game in the United States on Staten Island. Feminists may have been dismayed in 1979 when an English historian, Tom Todd, asserted that it was Dwight—not Outerbridge—who introduced tennis to the States earlier that year. Founding mother or father? Both Outerbridge, longer hailed, and Dwight have their backers.

A century later (1974), an American historian, George Alexander, uncovered evidence of the first recorded play in the U.S. Not in New York or Massachusetts, but—holy half-volleys!—in the wilds of Apache country in the Arizona Territory, also 1874. And a brand new name enters the game's literature: Ella Wilkins Bailey. Was Ella, wife of a U.S. Army officer, the champ of Camp Apache? Unknown. But it has been documented that she played on the court there that year, possibly with her sister, Caroline Wilkins.

Fair Ella may or may not have been the first American player—Doc Dwight and Sears, his cousin, get this guesser's nod—but according to the thorough Alexander, Ella Wilkins Bailey is the first for whom a reliable reference has been found.

While some may keen, "Say it ain't so, Doc!" and charge Alexander and Todd with revisionism, Dr. Dwight the younger is, as ever, gracious. "Even my father got mixed up as to the date when he later wrote about it," he says. "The main thing is that people did start to play and Mary Outerbridge was important in giving the push in New York. The fact seems to be that both my father and Outerbridge imported sets at about the same time, and nobody can be quite sure who was first."

Papa Dwight, however, has a much more solid position in tennis annals than Mama Outerbridge. A graduate of Harvard Medical School, he was not one to let his profession stand in the way of something as important as tennis. Dwight didn't work as a physician, excusing himself on the grounds of "poor health." Instead he devoted himself to tennis, teaching the game to the first U.S. singles champion, a fellow Bostonian, Dick Sears, and accompanying Sears to the U.S. doubles championship five times between 1882 and 1887.

Although tennis drifted across the country from Staten Island and Nahant and probably Newport, San Francisco, and New Orleans, the power remained in the Northeast. Three decades after Sears began his American championship dynasty in 1881, the American men's championship was still the property of an Ivy League crowd. Exceptions popped up among the women. Best known were Californians May Sutton, champ in 1904 (a year prior to butting into the homebodies' monopoly at Wimbledon), and Hazel Hotchkiss, 1909. But the Northeast's early stranglehold had actually been broken by Irishwoman Mabel Cahill (1891–92) and defied by Californian Marion Jones (1899 and 1902) and Myrtle McAteer from Pittsburgh in 1900.

At least, in 1912, the men's U.S. Championships began to go truly national on the tail of the California Comet, hyper-aggressive Maurice "Red" McLoughlin, and the general sporting public would soon become aware of tennis.

It was too good a game to be cloistered at Newport as an amusement of the swells, and in 1915 the U.S. Championships for men moved to the metropolis, New York, and the West Side Tennis Club at Forest Hills. There would be a country-club tinge right up to the present day of heavy money and professionalization, but at Forest Hills tennis gained exposure to larger, more diverse crowds, and a national press.

Once peacetime arrived, following World War I, the press had a tennis hero to hype—and a heroine. Big Bill Tilden, the gangling Philadelphian with a blowtorch serve, and Suzanne Lenglen, a flying Frenchwoman, worked their respective sides of the Atlantic with irresistible flair and shotmaking. Not only were Tilden and Lenglen virtually invincible champions, they were also regal figures and somewhat mysterious. Theirs was a magnetism that pulled crowds and sold tickets, and tennis became a commercial venture. With Tilden as strong man, the U.S. went on a record rampage of seven straight Davis Cups, and it was necessary to construct a 13,000-seat stadium at Forest Hills to hold the throngs following Davis Cup matches and the U.S. Championships.

Because of Lenglen, never beaten in singles at Wimbledon, the place seemed to shrink. It became too small for all the customers who wanted in. Thus the All England Lawn Tennis & Croquet Club, needing more space and seats, moved in 1922 to the present Wimbledon grounds with a Centre Court accommodating nearly 14,000.

Tennis joined other sports as a business game, but, unfortunately, not as a profession. By 1926 it was apparent that the athletes who sold the tickets deserved to be paid. It was not apparent, however, to those volunteer officials who controlled the game, and for generations past its

Dr. James Dwight: Father of U.S. tennis. (USTA)

time they would keep alive the fiction of "amateurism" at the upper level of tennis. Instead of prize money, the subsidy for careerists was "expenses," paid beneath the table in proportion to a player's value as a gate attraction. During the 1920s Tilden made more real income out of tennis as an amateur than some of the better pros today. He earned it. But Tilden, a supreme individualist, showed neither gratitude nor obeisance to the amateur authorities and was eventually driven to the wilderness of outright professionalism in 1930, to take his place brilliantly on the treadmill of one-nighters.

Until 1926 the only professionals were instructors, ineligible for customary tournaments. Occasionally they played small tournaments among themselves for pin money. Even though open tennis was discussed wistfully by progressives among players, officials and aficionados, such a sensible arrangement was well in the fu-

Early action at the Seabright (N.J.) Tennis Club. (Fischer Collection/SPS)

ture—1968. From time to time a motion to approve open tennis was even introduced within the International Tennis Federation, but the governing body was much too narrow and steeped in the so-called gentlemanly tradition of "amateurism." The motion always failed, and "shamateurism" was maintained until 1968. Amateurs who traveled the world swinging at tennis balls, living and eating well, were nicknamed "tennis bums."

However, those who decided to accept their money above the table were considered outlaws traveling under that dirty label, "professionals." At least that was the view of amateur officials who barred pros from traditional championships.

Forced to scrape for their living outside of the usual framework of private clubs, the pros appeared mainly in public arenas, moving constantly as nomads, folding their canvas court and jaunting to the next night's location.

This way of life began in October 1926 when La Belle Suzanne Lenglen defected from amateurism to roam North America with a troupe that included her nightly foe, Mary K. Browne, the U.S. champion of 1912–14, and Vinnie Richards, the American second to Tilden. Their stopovers were regarded as exhibitions, but the pay was all right. Lenglen reportedly collected at least $75,000—a fortune in 1927 dollars—for her four months on the road.

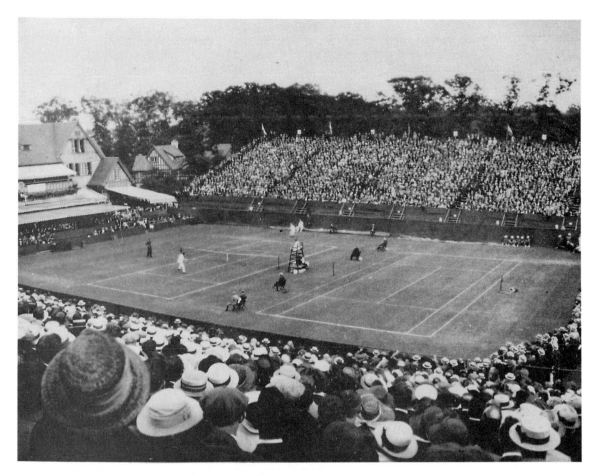

The U.S. National Championships at Forest Hills, N.Y. in 1920. (Fischer Collection/SPS)

A few months after the debut of the original wandering pros, the first U.S. Pro Championships for men was thrown together at a small club in Manhattan in the summer of 1927 and won by Richards, whose reward was $1,000 from a purse of $2,000. His 1994 successor, at Boston's Longwood Cricket Club, Ivan Lendl, won $50,000, and the tournament was worth $400,000, another startling piece of inflationary evidence in men's pro tennis.

The U.S. Pro Championships went along year after year, precariously and unprosperously, the longest-lasting of a few tourneys, but life as a pro meant barnstorming, and there wasn't enough money to support more than a handful of outlaws.

The tournaments that mattered were restricted to amateurs, whose game had structure, continuity, and the attention of the press and tennis public. Interest in amateur sport was high during the 1920s and 1930s, as a reader of newspapers preserved from that time quickly ascertains.

But after World War II that interest declined. The emphasis shifted to professional sport, particularly in the U.S., and tennis, stocked with phony amateurs, didn't keep pace. While other sports gleamed in television's red eye, tennis languished away from the cameras. Three events maintained an eminence: Wimbledon, Forest Hills, and the Davis Cup finale, which became the postwar preserve of the U.S. and Australia.

The legendary Bill Tilden early in his career. (Fischer Collection/SPS)

As the 1950s dawned, a tidal wave swept from the Antipodes at the bottom of the world: It was the Aussies, the most dynastic force ever in tennis. Their muscle lasted for more than two decades, between the Davis Cup seizure spearheaded by Frank Sedgman in 1950 and John Newcombe's U.S. Open triumph of 1973. In between were 16 Davis Cups and 14 Wimbledons for the men, two Grand Slams by Rod Laver, and a male record of 28 Big Four titles by Roy Emerson, as well as the rise and fall of Lew Hoad, and the rise and rise of ageless Kenny Rosewall.

Directed by a martinet named Harry Hopman, the Aussies were hungry and superbly conditioned, and they gave the impression that the primary occupations at home were tennis and beer drinking. They were world champs at both. Their women were not as pervasive successes as American females, but one of them, Margaret Smith Court, outdid everyone else: Mighty Maggie rolled up 62 major titles in singles, doubles and mixed (24-19-19), bracketing the singles championships of Australia, France, Wimbledon and the U.S. in 1970 for her Grand Slam. Only Martina Navratilova with 56 majors (18-31-7) has come close to Court's accomplishments, but Steffi Graf is creeping close in singles with 21.

Midway through the 1960s, a period of rising acclaim for sport in general, tennis was sagging at both the amateur and professional levels. The best players were pros, but the best tournaments were amateur. Agitation for open play increased, especially in England, where Wimbledon officials, tiring of exorbitant "expense" payments to amateurs, sought to present the finest tennis. This was impossible as long as the professional elite—Rod Laver, Ken Rosewall, Pancho Gonzalez, Lew Hoad, Butch Buchholz and Andres Gimeno—were off in limbo as outlaws.

An impetus for the decisive move toward opens was provided startlingly in 1967 by a man unknown within tennis—Dave Dixon of New Orleans. Buoyed by Texas money supplied by Dallas petrocrat Lamar Hunt, his partner in a wildcat tennis venture, Dixon, late in the summer, signed up amateurs John Newcombe, Tony Roche, Roger Taylor, Cliff Drysdale and Nikola Pilic plus pros Butch Buchholz, Pierre Barthes and Dennis Ralston as his World Championship Tennis troupe. Since another promoter, George MacCall, had enlisted amateur Roy Emerson to blend with pros Laver, Gonzalez, Rosewall, Gimeno, Fred Stolle, Rosie Casals, Billie Jean King, Ann Jones and Françoise Durr in his National Tennis League, the amateur game was abruptly depleted of its top resources, the 10 best players.

Aware that Dixon was lurking, Herman David, the Wimbledon chairman, realized that he and Wimbledon must follow their desire to open up the game. Even with the players that Dixon and MacCall would pluck, Wimbledon '67 had been dull. Now the outlook for this, the ultimate championship, in 1968 was downright barren.

Suzanne Lenglen was the wonder woman of the Golden Twenties. (UPI)

First, David organized a test run, a three-day, pros-only tournament in August on the august Centre Court. Would the venerated turf wither beneath the feet of out-and-out outlaws (Laver, Rosewall, Gonzalez, Gimeno, Hoad, Stolle, Ralston, Buchholz)? Would the Big W's clientele even show up, pay to watch the banished bad boys jousting for a then-record purse of $35,000?

The temple didn't crumble—it rumbled with applause for this preview of better days, amounting to the world championship of 1967. Starved

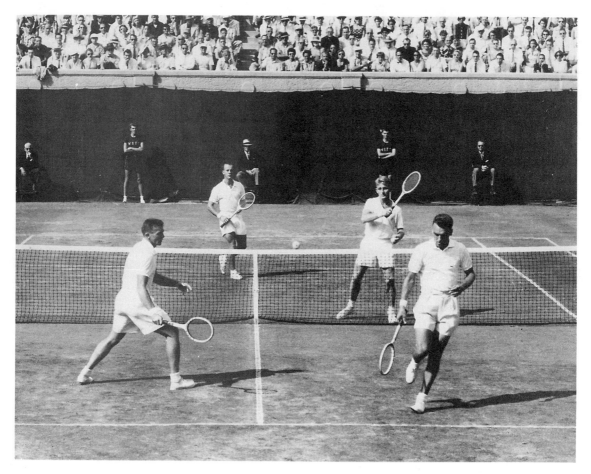

Australia's Lew Hoad (right) has just slammed the ball en route to a clinching doubles victory (with Rex Hartwig) over Tony Trabert (left) and Vic Seixas in the 1955 Davis Cup challenge round at Forest Hills. (UPI)

patrons made it a success by filling Centre the second and third days, and David and confreres came as close as All England Clubbies can come to grinning as Laver beat Rosewall in a terrific final, 6-2, 6-2, 12-10. David Gray wrote in *The Guardian*: "Having grown used to margarine, it was good to be reminded of the taste of butter."

There was no turning back. Confident of the British public and press's support, and with the backing of the nation's influential LTA (Lawn Tennis Association), Wimbledon announced that in 1968 it would be open to all players regardless of their status, amateur or pro. The best were welcome. When that shot was fired, the rest of the

world—the membership of the International Tennis Federation, led by the USTA and its enlightened president, Bob Kelleher—fell into line.

Bournemouth, England, was the scene of the first open, the British Hard Court Championships in April 1968. Kenny Rosewall won the men's title, Virginia Wade the women's. And curly-headed Englishman Mark Cox wrote his footnote in sporting history as the first amateur to beat a pro at tennis. Cox, a left-hander, knocked off Pancho Gonzalez and Roy Emerson on successive afternoons to upstage all else on Britain's front pages.

The Tennis Epidemic to come in the 1970s had been set in motion, along with the venture into high-tech tennis that would make wooden rackets obsolete. Arthur Ashe won the U.S. Amateur and Open titles in 1968 with a split-shaft Head aluminum racket that he called "the snowshoe." Billie Jean King and Rosie Casals, as well as teenager Jimmy Connors, were waving "steelies," the Wilson T2000, in the late '60s. In 1971 financial pioneer Rod Laver crossed the million-dollar mark in prize money after nine years as a pro. But by 1979, 15 other men and three women had followed, making their millions in shorter spans. And in 1977 Guillermo Vilas had a year that would seem a splendid career for most athletes: $800,642.

This was just walking-around money, as the upward-and-onward finances of the '80s and '90s would show. In 1990, 19-year-old Pete Sampras carted off a flabbergasting first prize of $2 million for winning the newly minted Grand Slam Cup tournament, and wound up the season with men's record winnings of $2,900,057. That mark wouldn't last long. He'd soon be in the $5 million-season class. In 1992 an 18-year-old Monica Seles set the female season record, $2,622,352, also quickly perishable as Arantxa Sanchez Vicario was a few dollars shy of $3 million in 1994, and Steffi Graf surpassed it in 1996. Ivan Lendl retired in 1994 with the staggering prize-money record of $21,262,417, since hurdled by Sampras. Martina Navratilova went out at about the same time with $20,337,902, a momentary record representing 22 years of labor, eclipsed by Graf in her 14th professional season. While career millionaires weren't quite a dime a dozen, more than 200 men and 75 women had earned that appellation by the close of 1996.

It is to smile, looking back at Rod Laver's victory in the 1964 U.S. Pro tournament in Boston. The wobbling event had gone bust the year before in New York, with Laver and Ken Rosewall receiving nothing from their final-round labors but a mutual, warm handshake. The U.S. Pro was rescued by Longwood Cricket Club and a sponsoring Boston bank.

Australia's Rod Laver serves against Arthur Ashe as rain falls in the semifinals of the U.S. Championships in 1969. Laver won the match and then beat Tony Roche for the title. (UPI)

Laver, in his sophomore year as a pro, got $2,200 as first prize and would say only a few years afterwards, "It seemed like a million then."

At first the boom in prize money benefitted principally the men. As in so many areas of life, the women were left behind. However, the tennis-playing women refused to stand at the back of the game. Guided by brainy Gladys Heldman, publisher of *World Tennis* magazine, and inspired by the liberation-minded firebrand, Billie Jean King, the women divorced themselves from the conventional tournament arrangement that had been shared unequally by the sexes. Top billing (and top dollars) had always gone to the men. Carrying the banner of Virginia Slims cigarettes, the women crusaded on a separate tour and made good artistically and economically. The Slims tour began haltingly in 1970 and picked up steam in 1971, when Billie Jean won $117,000, the first woman to earn more than 100 grand in prize money. The tour was solid by 1972, when ingenue Chrissie Evert won the first eight-woman playoff at the climax. In 1973 the women demanded and got equal prize money at Forest Hills, one of the few remaining tournaments staging both men's and women's events.

Television didn't rush to hug tennis when the open era began, although network interest picked up. Two telecasts in particular aided in lifting the game to wide public notice: Rosewall's sensational 4-6, 6-0, 6-3, 6-7 (3-7), 7-6 (7-5) victory over Laver for the World Championship Tennis title of 1972 in Dallas, and Billie Jean King's 6-4, 6-3, 6-3 put-down of 55-year-old Bobby Riggs in the bizarre "Battle of the Sexes" in 1973.

Creating one of the greatest matches, Laver and Rosewall flailed away at each other brilliantly for three-and-a-half hours. It came down to a fifth-set tie-breaker where the 37-year-old Rosewall, seemingly beaten as Laver served at 5 points to 4, took the last three points and the championship in the closest finish of a significant tourney until Boris Becker beat Ivan Lendl in a 7-5 fifth-set tie-breaker for the 1988 Masters title. Rosewall won $50,000, the richest prize in tennis at the time.

Bobby Riggs, well past his prime—"one foot in the grave" was one of the lines amid his con and corn—had challenged and beaten a nervous Margaret Court in what he termed the "Mother's Day Massacre" earlier in 1973. Glowing with hubris and newfound celebrity, Riggs then challenged 29-year-old Billie Jean King. "Nobody knew me when I was the best player in the world in 1939, when I won Wimbledon," he said. "Now I'm over the hill but I'm a star. Everybody recognizes me—the old guy who can beat the best women."

Publicity was tremendous. Super schlock blanketed the Astrodome in Houston, where a record tennis crowd, 30,472, assembled for the oddest couple's encounter. Though a meaningless match in one sense, it seemed to mean everything to millions everywhere: mankind against womankind. Billie Jean was the defender of her sex against His Piggishness, Bobby. She won easily. Tennis was the beneficiary. Laver and Rosewall had showed a television audience how majestically the game could be played. King and Riggs lured a much larger audience because their gimmick caught the fancy of many unaware of the existence of tennis.

Tennis began to appear regularly on television, prize money accelerated for the stars, equipment sales and participation accelerated for the hackers. Construction of public courts as well as private clubs increased, particularly in the United States, where the proliferation of indoor courts was a sporting phenomenon.

Tennis was big business, and the professional performers involved, following the example of brethren in other sports, unionized to gain a stronger position in the management of their business. The male ATP (Association of Tennis Pros) and female WTA (Women's Tennis Association) were formed as player guilds, and two new governing bodies were also formed: the International Professional Tennis Councils for men (MIPTC) and women (WIPTC), containing representatives of the unions, the ITF, and the tournament promoters. Each IPTC set down codes of professional conduct.

Those who thought the war was over when the forces of open tennis triumphed over those upholding amateurism in 1968 soon realized that strife would become a way of life in this sport. Revolution and evolution continued to change the face of the professional game. Though for a long time the U.S. was the financial base, the stronghold for pro tennis, Europe has taken the lead, holding more events, offering greater incentives.

Interestingly it was another non-tennis figure, Hamilton Jordan, who launched a revolution on behalf of the ATP as Dave Dixon had done in founding WCT. Taking over as chief executive of the ATP in 1988, Jordan, former chief of staff for President Jimmy Carter, performed a political tour de force in bringing all the men's tourneys (except the four majors) under the umbrella of the ATP Tour in 1990, sponsored first by IBM, then Mercedes.

This maneuver destroyed the MIPTC and the Grand Prix structure, which had embraced and administered the men's game for almost two decades, and WCT as well. WCT, which had led the way into professionalization, operated its own circuit until absorbed by the Grand Prix. Nevertheless, WCT continued its annual championship playoff in Dallas, the event that had electrified the game with the $50,000 payoffs to Rosewall for his 1971 and 1972 victories over Laver. But after John McEnroe beat Brad Gilbert in the last of those in 1989, WCT sadly expired.

As the brainchild of Hall of Famer Jack Kramer, the Grand Prix commenced in 1970, a points scheme linking men's tourneys and leading to a year-end showdown, the Masters, for the tour leaders. Although the Masters continues in format, it has been billed as the ATP Championship since the Grand Prix's takeover and renaming at Jordan's instigation.

Feeling threatened by the ATP's increased muscle, the ITF, principally Britain, the U.S., France and Australia, raised extraordinary prize money for their "Grand Slams"—the majors: Wimbledon and the U.S., French and Australian Opens. Furthermore, in 1990, the ITF added to the usual confusion and overcrowded calendar by instituting the $6-million Grand Slam Cup, admitting the top finishers in those four tourneys, as the season's closing event. The obvious attempt was to upstage the ATP/Masters Championship by amassing a substantially richer purse.

Considerably more orderly have been the women. Their tour, generally easier to follow, has been underwritten by several sponsors (originally Virginia Slims, then Avon, Colgate, Toyota, back to Slims/Kraft and, since 1996, Corel), climaxing with the WTA's season-ending Chase Champi-

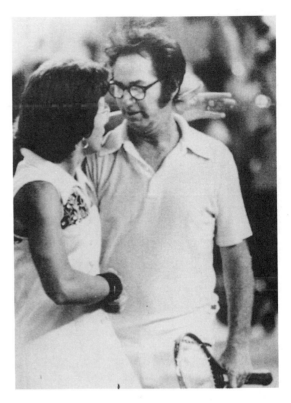

Billie Jean King consoles Bobby Riggs after defeating him in straight sets in their $100,000 "Battle of the Sexes" at the Houston Astrodome in 1973. (UPI)

onships at New York's Madison Square Garden. Since 1990 the WTA, unlike the ATP, has cooperated with the ITF so that the four majors are part of the women's tour.

The increasingly popular Lipton Championships at Key Biscayne, Fla., and the Newsweek at Indian Wells, Calif., embracing both men and women, may have started a trend back to an increasing number of dual sex events, showing the complete face of the game as at the majors, recapturing the flavor of—of all things!—the amateur days.

In 1974 an ill-starred venture called World Team Tennis began in the U.S., a league of city franchises comprising teams of men and women. Most of the leading women took part, and once more the crusader, Billie Jean King, was a driving force. She was the player-coach of Philadel-

Martina Navratilova serves to Gigi Fernandez during the women's semifinal match at Wimbledon in 1994. (AP/Wide World/Dave Caulkin)

phia in 1974, another first: a woman in charge of a team containing male professionals. As a player she led New York to the 1976–77 titles. General lack of television and spectator interest, coupled with unrealistically high payrolls, caused the league to fold after the 1978 season.

Unwilling to accept the defeat, the resilient King revived the concept under the banner of Team Tennis in 1981, and it continues today (as World Team Tennis again) with a shorter schedule and lesser-known players, although Jimmy Connors, Martina Navratilova and John McEnroe have played during the '90s.

The U.S. has led in all facets of the game's development, but tennis is truly universal and well received in pro tournament locations in more than 30 countries. Growth continues, and Forest Hills was finally outgrown after 63 years. In 1978 the U.S. Open was relocated a few miles away, in Flushing Meadow, where the U.S. National Tennis Center is the largest of all tennis playgrounds. The main court, Louis Armstrong Stadium, surrounded by 20,000 seats, enabled the Open to set a tournament attendance record of 505,666 in 1996. But a $300 million-plus renovation of the Center was to be complete for the 1997 Open. This includes a new principal stadium, seating 23,500 and replete with today's "necessities," fantastically high-priced luxury boxes. The Armstrong arena was to be reduced in size, but the question remained: would the USTA also cater to non-affluent tennis loyalists by providing daily seating for kids and families at reasonable prices to help perpetuate the game and elevate interest?

Luxury box denizens are seldom concerned with the game's well-being or growth, the factors that motivated W. E. "Slew" Hester, that rare and resourceful USTA president who in 1978 drove the move to Flushing and the Center's construction in the hope of making the Open "the people's tournament." That should still be the goal. Hester's move produced a third level in the evolution of the Championships' game: hard courts of asphalt base.

The Championships, begun in the grass period in 1881, switched to clay in 1975 as tennis lawns vanished as an American tournament surface. For a while, clay was predominant on the summer circuit. But the paving of Flushing Meadow led to regrettable conformity and a stony greentopping of America. By 1988, Australia had gone the way of the U.S., forsaking the greensward for hard courts at the splendid new center for its Open, Flinders Park, a retractable-roof stadium in Melbourne. Of course, then the Aussie circuit's grass also gave way to the bulldozers and pavement.

The Grand Slam route, once three-quarters turf and one-quarter clay (at Paris), was now more diverse. But more than 50 percent of professional tournaments are currently contested indoors on thin green or blue toupees—artificial plastic rugs—covering bare floors.

Whatever the surface and wherever it is played, will the game ever be at peace? Probably not, particularly with player agents behind the scenes, guiding the greed and cluttering the calendar with exhibitions and pseudo tournaments called "special events."

The unending season is simply, obviously, too long for the game's good and the players' physical and emotional welfare. A genuine off-season (October, November, December) is badly needed, but who will have the sense and guts—through an unselfish ATP-WTA-ITF bonding on behalf of the game—to bring it about?

Despite all the conflict and obfuscation, I believe the comment of Hall of Famer Bill Talbert, onetime director of the U.S. Open: "Tennis will survive in spite of itself. It's too good a game not to."

—Bud Collins

1

R O O T S :

1 8 7 4 - 1 9 1 8

W here does our present game come from? Surely it's a descendant of the ancient and original tennis that yet exists—known variously as real tennis, royal tennis or court tennis—and dates to 12th-century France. Its precise origins are shrouded in mystery, as are the name—tennis—and the scoring terms, passed down from real tennis to our game which is properly named lawn tennis. This much is clear: it began on an English lawn—and remains there for its most exalted occasion, Wimbledon.

Love? How can you take seriously anything in which love means nothing? Probably it derives from the French, *l'oeuf:* the old goose egg. The quartered face of a clock seems the likely source of the game, and point scores—15, 30—but why 40 instead of the original 45? Was it a cuckoo clock? Probably modified over time. Nobody really knows. Deuce is the clearest, from the French *a deux.*

"Tennis" itself? There are many theories which historian George Alexander discusses, and have appeared elsewhere before, not conclusively. George has his own idea, on "tens" from the German, different from all the rest, as will be seen.

Lawn tennis reached an early high point of national prestige during the presidency of Theodore Roosevelt (1901–09), who formed a "tennis cabinet." The players, headed by the vigorous president, were drawn from the younger administrators of just below the cabinet rank and from the foreign diplomats. The diplomats were led by the French ambassador, J. J. Jusserand. He was small, wiry and quick, and often the match of "Teddy, the hero of San Juan Hill."

The ambassador was a serious player of both court tennis and lawn tennis and a student of the history of those games. Among the studies he undertook was the derivation of the English word "tennis." His was not the first search for the origin of the word, nor was it the last. Then, as now, the usual explanation was that "tennis" was derived from the French *tendere* meaning "to hold." The etymologists rationalized that the server called out tendere as a warning to his opponent just prior to serving. At first glance this has an authentic ring, for it carries the approval of scholars of repute. The problem was that it did not make sense to Jusserand.

Jusserand made an extensive study of old French literature and he found much shouting by players, mostly profane, but no one ever seemed to have called out *tendere* or anything like it. The several studies on the subject made before and since the French ambassador have come to the same findings.

In 1878 Julian Marshall in his monumental *Annals of Tennis* addresses the matter and he lists 10 spellings of tennis through the years, but he leaves the decision as to the origin of the word "tennis" to others, finding no answer that satisfied him.

Tennis historians E. B. Noel and A. E. Crawley wrote on the subject but they offered no additional information. In *Bailey's* magazine of August 1918, C. E. Thomas offered a slightly more logical explanation. According to him, the derivation is from the French *tenez,* meaning "take it." Again a call of warning from the server. No one has come forth with evidence of such ever being done, let alone ever having been the custom.

Tennis Origins and Mysteries, by Malcolm Whitman, U.S. champion (1898–1900), devotes a chapter to the subject and covers most of the theories that have been put forth through the years by tennis players with an interest in etymology. Most of these theories have a common root in French words that have "ten" as the start of words meaning variously "hold," "taut," "tense," "tendon," and several other similar words. Another idea was that tennis like the name Tennyson was derived from Saint Denis.

Two towns, widely separated, one on the Nile River in Egypt, the other in Northern France,

having "Tennis" as their name, are thought to be possible origins of the name. Tennis in France was known for its lace, Tennis in Egypt for its fine long staple cotton. Since balls were often cloth bound, some have thought that was connection enough.

Alexander offers a more logical derivation. First, why was a new name for the game necessary when it came to England (some evidence indicates it came earlier to Scotland)? The French name then and now is *jeu de paume* (hand ball). By the time it reached the British Isles (the date not known with certainty), implements such as battledores and forerunners of rackets were replacing the hand. Some of the French was retained such as "deuce" and "love," so no strong aversion to French words existed. The game needed a name to differentiate the game of playing across a net from those played against a wall.

The root stem of "tens" has given us many words including those such as *tendere,* which is the often listed parent of "tennis." One of the meanings of "tens" is the "weaver's shuttle" and other to-and-fro motions. Whitman had previously come across this, but he chose not to pursue it and he dropped it short of the shuttle meaning.

The naming of the game with a descriptive word is more logical than one requiring a tortured explanation. The logic of naming the game after some "shout" or ball material would have us call golf "fore" and the games of football "pigskin" and baseball "horsehide." The back-and-forth motion further lent its name to the missile that we know as the shuttlecock in badminton.

While the explanation may satisfy a few, more evidence is needed to support the theory, even though none has been offered to support the usually accepted *tendere.* It is like the unauthenticated story of Mary Outerbridge introducing the game to the U.S.: Once in place and repeated a few times, it takes on the position of presumed fact.

But this is part of the intrigue of tennis. We aren't quite sure of the origin and meanings of many aspects—even the name.

Even though the beginnings of tennis and many other sports and games are unknown and lost in the distant past, the history of modern (lawn) tennis is clearly documented. Its arrival was publicly announced on March 7, 1874, in two papers, the *Court Journal,* read by almost all of the British upper class as well as those who aspired to join, and the *Army & Navy Gazette,* read by the military, which was stationed worldwide; for then the sun truly never set on the vast British Empire.

These notices followed the British patent office issuing Major Walter Wingfield provisional letters of patent (No. 685) for "A Portable Court of Playing Tennis" dated Feb. 23, 1874. English-speaking sportsmen around the world who read *The Field* of March 21, 1874 were informed in detail of the new game, for it reproduced much of the Major's game of lawn tennis. It contained a short history of tennis, instruction and notes for the "erection of the court," and the six rules of the game.

The game was an immediate success and spread throughout Great Britain and Ireland in a matter of weeks and around the English-speaking world soon thereafter. The necessary equipment to play was sold by the inventor's agents, Messrs. French and Co., 46, Churton Street, London, S.W. The price: five guineas.

Sales literature noted that "the game is in a painted box, 36 x 12 x 6 inches and contains poles, pegs, and netting for forming the court, 4 tennis bats, by Jeffries and Mallings, a bag of balls, mallet, and brush and the instructive *The Book of the Game.*"

The daily sales book for almost a year, July 6, 1874 to June 25, 1875, has a following notation of July 15, 1874 that Major Rowan Hamilton settled his account for tennis sets he purchased in May "for Canada." Sets were bought for India and China. Sets were sold to Russia's royalty and to, of course, the Prince of Wales and many others, including 42 Lords, 44 Ladies and members of Parliament, among them agriculturist Ward

Major Walter Clopton Wingfield pioneered the game.
(Fischer Collection/SPS)

Hunt, First Lord of the Admiralty, renowned for his girth which caused a semicircle to be cut from the Admiralty board table.

The records of French and Co. are not the complete list, for many sales went to unnamed parties and the company did much wholesale business with several London retailers and, as so often happens, competing sets were soon on the market despite patent protection.

There were several reasons for this great and widespread success. There was a need for a game which afforded vigorous exercise for both sexes and all ages. That was how Wingfield described his new game. Croquet had been the fad during the 1860s and it inspired the construction of many well-rolled, level courts with close-clipped grass. The least standard croquet court measured 30 yards by 20 yards. Such courts were ubiquitous and were ready-made for lawn tennis, and "The ground need not even be turf; the only condition is that it must be level."

This was not today's marvelous game, for it was quite simple. It used the scoring of 1,2,3, etc. of the game of rackets, but it bore the more refined name "tennis" rather than "rackets," which was associated with taverns and prisons. The game could also be played without buying the set, for items were sold separately. Rackets were 15 shillings, balls were 5 shillings a dozen, and *The Book of the Game* was 6 pence. People with rackets of other sports could easily try out the new game at little or no expense.

Wingfield learned, as have most inventors, to their dismay, that rather than receiving the thanks of grateful sportsmen, he was belittled. "Anyone could have invented his game," said numerous skeptics. Others came forth with claims for earlier games. Inventions almost always are based on other inventions, and (lawn) tennis obviously was based on (court) tennis. This was acknowledged by Wingfield, as even the title of his patent and the game indicate.

Outdoor racket, ball and net play go back to the time of Queen Elizabeth I. Earlier in England and France, a game called long tennis (*longue paume*) was played, and it is still played in France. The other previous such games, at best neighborhood games, were without formal rules and they never traveled, soon dying out. The name Harry Gem is associated with just such a game. He wrote in *The Field* of Nov. 28, 1874: "He (J. B. Perera) first introduced the game fifteen years ago, and it recently has received the name of Pelota. . . ." After (lawn) tennis arrived, Gem wrote rules for "Pelota," which he sent to *The Field* and to his club, the Leamington Club, which added "Lawn Tennis" to it name.

Wingfield wrote to Gem in the fall of 1874 that he had worked on the game for a year and a half. After Wingfield's death an acquaintance wrote that Wingfield's thoughts of a game went back to his service in India. He wrote in *The*

Book of the Game that the game was "tested practically at several country houses during the past few months."

Since all five editions of the book are "dedicated to the party assembled at Nantclwyd [in Wales] in December 1873," it has been assumed that was where it was introduced. There is no evidence that it was, for that party was a house-warming given by the new owner of the estate Nantclwyd, Major Naylor-Leyland, for his friends in the area. It featured the presentation of two plays and a grand ball. The three-day affair was covered in detail by the *Wrexham Guardian* and makes no mention of lawn tennis or any athletic activity. Wingfield, his host and hostess and a great beauty of the day, Patsy Cornwallis-West, performed in the plays.

It would be reasonable that Onslow Hall, the main estate of his branch of the family, would be one of the test sites. It is more likely a test site than Wingfield's own Rhysnant Hall, which was at that time leased. The one country house which has a written record as a test site is Earnshill in Somerset. In May 1881, Wingfield's first cousin, R. T. Combe of Earnshill, wrote to the *Daily Telegraph,* "It is now some seven or eight years since Major Wingfield first put up a lawn tennis court here."

Several other places have been put forth as being sites of early play but confirming evidence is lacking. The first public exhibition occurred the Saturday following *The Field* announcement of May 4, 1874, which read in part, "It (lawn tennis) may be seen and played next week, on and after the opening of the Princes Cricket Ground, and also at the Polo Club, Lillie-bridge."

In the *Whitehall Review* (Nov. 14, 1896), Wingfield's good friend, Clement Scott, wrote in his column, "Wheel of Life," that the exhibition was in 1869. Such is an example of how fallible the human memory is and how important "the palest ink" is to true history.

The closing of the Haymarket court tennis courts and the outdoor racket courts at taverns in several neighborhoods undoubtedly caused

A.D. 1874, 23rd February. Nº 685.

A Portable Court for Playing Tennis.

LETTERS PATENT to Walter Clopton Wingfield, of Belgrave Road, Pimlico, in the County of Middlesex, for the Invention of "A NEW AND IMPROVED PORTABLE COURT FOR PLAYING THE ANCIENT GAME OF TENNIS."

Sealed the 24th July 1874, and dated the 23rd February 1874.

PROVISIONAL SPECIFICATION left by the said Walter Clopton Wingfield at the Office of the Commissioners of Patents, with his Petition, on the 23rd February 1874.

I, WALTER CLOPTON WINGFIELD, of Belgrave Road, Pimlico, in the
5 County of Middlesex, do hereby declare the nature of the said Invention for "A NEW AND IMPROVED PORTABLE COURT FOR PLAYING THE ANCIENT GAME OF TENNIS," to be as follows:—

The object and intention of this Invention consists in constructing a portable court by means of which the ancient game of tennis is much
10 simplified, can be played in the open air, and dispenses with the necessity of having special courts erected for that purpose.

(Fischer Collection/SPS)

Wingfield to bring forth the new game. It was also helped by the development of the thin-wall rubber ball in Germany.

Besides private homes with croquet lawns becoming places to play tennis, it immediately became a game played at public parks and other common lawns and the great clubs. Among the London clubs to take up the sport quickly were M.C.C.—The Marylebone Cricket Club (Lords)—Hurlingham Club and Princes Club, as well as many others throughout the land. A club that waited until 1875 to accept a rival sport was the then five-year-old, All England Croquet Club, which was located off Worple Road in the London suburb, Wimbledon.

Henry Jones, the editor of the Pastimes section of *The Field,* which covered card games, Jones' forte, as well as lawn tennis, was a founder, along with his publisher, John Walsh, of the All England Croquet Club. Jones introduced lawn tennis to the club. He wrote under the *nom de plume* of "Cavendish." Jones and Walsh were both doctors who had given up the practice of medicine to pursue their greater love, games and sports. Jones earned Wingfield's enmity by presuming to take over his game. It was Jones' nature to assume he had greater knowledge of all matters concerning games, and this included lawn tennis.

To Wingfield the remarkable success of the game was evidence of the rightness of it, and that you should not change a winning game. However, in the fall of 1874 he issued a second edition of *The Book of the Game.* There were now twelve rules and a larger court, and it also made more use of the alternate name of *Sphairistike,* Greek for ball games. These changes and complications could be added, for now the game had taken root. By that time some confusion existed, at least on the pages of *The Field,* because Perera's game, pelota, and a rival game, Germains Lawn Tennis, by J. H. Hale, with Jones' help, had been put forth. In reality nothing came of either; they were more complicated with no added redeeming features.

Through the winter, there was continued confusion. J. M. Heathcote, who with his wife had introduced the Melton cloth-covered ball, wrote to Fitzgerald, secretary of M.C.C., suggesting a meeting of the factions. With the cooperation of Wingfield, the other interested parties agreed to a general meeting with the M.C.C.'s rules committee to establish rules for lawn tennis as they recently had done for court tennis. This was done and the rules were announced in *The Field* of May 1875. There were now 25 rules and they appeared in subsequent editions of Wingfield's book.

Before the M.C.C. rules came out on May 2, 1875, Wingfield wrote Fitzgerald that he would execute any legal document "for the public good," canceling "en masse" his rules. A similar letter appeared in *The Field* a week after *The Field* published the M.C.C. rules. With the letter agreeing to the M.C.C. rules, Wingfield withdrew from the tennis scene.

In the spring of 1877 under the leadership of Henry Jones, the All England Club decided to hold a tennis tournament. *The Field* carried the announcement and a call for competitors and the promise "if entries are sufficiently numerous, prizes: Gold Champion Prize and the Silver Prize. . . . Also a Silver Challenge Cup, value 25 guineas. . . ."

The tournament committee worried about infringing on Wingfield's patent. This was unnecessary, for Wingfield had allowed his patent to expire on Feb. 23, 1877, the patent's third anniversary, by not paying the £50 fee to extend the patent seven years. It was public information, being published in the *Official Journal (Patents).* This was to the game's long-term benefit for it caused new rules to be drawn. These were written by a committee of Jones, Julian Marshall and C. G. Heathcote. They established much of our present game. The tournament—the original Wimbledon—was a success. There were 22 entries. Spencer Gore, a rackets player, beat William Marshall, a court tennis player, in the final, 6-1, 6-2, 6-4.

The new rules used tennis scoring and a rectangular court (78 x 27 feet), abandoning Wingfield's hourglass shape with baselines wider than the net and tapering to the net posts. The service lines were 26 feet from the net and the 33-foot wide net extended 3 feet on each side and was 5 feet on each side, 5 feet at the posts and 3½ feet at the center.

The championships became an annual fixture with Jones as referee. For several years he adjusted the net height and the service line according to the total of points won and lost on service until 1882, when the net heights arrived at today's 3½ feet at the posts and 3 feet at center with the service line at 21. The rules then became essentially today's rules except for two rules which were troublesome for several years. The changing-of-ends rule went through many alterations until the simple and fair changing sides after each odd game of each set was established in the rules of 1890. Foot-faulting has been more difficult to control and may still be further changed. Through the years the policy has been to make legal the past infringements, only to have the aggressive servers take that and a little more.

In the matter of tournament control, two improvements were brought forth. R. B. Bagnal-Wild of Bath in 1883 proposed the present system of having byes in the first round so as to have the number of remaining players be of a power of two. This prevented three players arriving in the semifinals as happened in the first Wimbledon. This was accepted for the 1885 Championships.

The hourglass court, as illustrated in Major Wingfield's book. (Fischer Collection/SPS)

The other improvement took longer. In 1883 Charles L. Dodgson, a mathematician who wrote under the name of Lewis Carroll (*Alice in Wonderland*), wrote a pamphlet, *Lawn Tennis Tournaments*—"The true method of assigning prizes, with proof of the fallacy of the present method." It was seeding that he envisioned, but he died before it was first permitted in the 1922 tournament.

In 1880 a Northern Lawn Tennis Association (of England) was founded and in 1883 the formation of a Lawn Tennis Association was attempted, but it failed for want of All England Club cooperation. The All England Club became the premier organization in tennis, supplanting the M.C.C. in those matters, and has remained a powerful tennis body, as witness its ability to lead the world to open tennis. The game owes much to the M.C.C. for its guidance and lending its name and prestige to the infant tennis during its early critical years.

On the courts, tennis made great strides in the 1880s. This progress in the level of play was led by the Renshaw twins. They had grown up with the game and were not handicapped with styles formed for rackets or court tennis. Willie Renshaw won the Wimbledon championships of 1881 through 1886 and 1889. Ernest won in 1888. Herbert Lawford won in 1887 when Willie did not defend his title. The Renshaws also dominated the doubles, winning in 1880, '81, '84, '85, '86, '88 and '89.

Doubles was introduced in 1879 and ladies' singles made the scene in 1884. Ladies' doubles and mixed doubles began in 1913. The draws were small, only 16 players in 1887 for the men's tournament and six ladies in 1888. Attendance grew from 200 in 1877 to 3,500 in 1885. This growth of tennis ended in 1890 with interest switching to bicycle activities which were much enhanced by the invention of the modern bicycle. The 90s were also a time of recession in the business world.

With the cooperation of the A.E.C. (All England Club) the L.T.A. (Lawn Tennis Association) was formed in 1888. It was agreed the A.E.C. and the L.T.A. would share the funds raised by the Championships. However, the fall of popularity of tennis brought small draws and reduced attendance. The tournament of 1895 had a £35 loss. By the turn of the century tennis regained its popularity and went on to greater crowds and more players.

It was natural that tennis would come quickly to North America for there were close relationships, both social and commercial, with the motherland. British periodicals, including *The Field*, came to many in the United States and Canada. The date the first set arrived is not known but its arrival was inevitable. The earliest found recorded play is Oct. 8, 1874 in the then remote Camp Apache, Arizona Territory, north of Tucson.

In Martha Summerhayes' book, *Vanished Arizona*, she reports tennis being played by an Army officer's wife, Ella Wilkins Bailey. The date is confirmed by her husband's records. The trip to Apache began in San Francisco on Aug. 6, 1874. Based on Major Hamilton's purchase in May 1874, Canada may have had its first taste of the game soon after he unwrapped his "unpainted box."

Tennis certainly was on the East Coast in the summer of 1874, and who was first is of no importance, for it arrived independently at several places: Boston, Newport, New York and Philadelphia as well as New Orleans and San Francisco. The game did not spread from only one center.

While both Miss Mary Outerbridge of Staten Island, N.Y., and Dr. James Dwight of Boston have their adherents as "the introducer" of the game to the United States, there is no clear-cut certainty for either. It is certain that neither was trying to be first, and made no claim to that effect. However, leadership of the game in the U.S. clearly fell to Dr. Dwight, who became known as "the father of American lawn tennis."

He may also have been a "first" player, but regardless he was associated with almost all important tennis events during the first quarter-century of tennis in the United States. Dr. Dwight, while summering at Nahant, Mass., outside of Boston, organized a tournament in 1876. With his cousin, Fred Sears, he held a formal and handicapped round-robin tournament for 15 entries, Dwight beating Sears in the final.

In 1878 the Nahant tournament used the A.E.C. rules. In 1880 Dr. Dwight and cousin Richard Sears played in the so-called "Nationals" at Staten Island Cricket and Baseball Club. Dwight's questioning of the balls used as not being proper was turned aside by the tournament officials by showing the "Regulation" marked on each ball.

That unsatisfactory tourney caused the formation of the U.S. National Lawn Tennis Association in 1881. This country's governing tennis body, it was the first of such sport organizations, evolving in name from USNLTA to the present USTA (the organization will hereafter be referred to as USTA). Dr. Dwight followed the first president, R. S. Oliver, as president and was president for 21 of the association's first 31 years.

Under the direction of the new association, the first national tournament was held at Newport and a 19-year-old Harvard student, Dick Sears, another Dwight cousin, was the winner, retaining the title through 1887. The "other guy" in that original final was an Englishman, William E. Glyn, who was 20 or 21, summered at Newport, and has pretty much been lost in history, not even being accorded celebrity as the first flop. Did he choke?

In the 1881 doubles, Sears and Dwight were surprised losers in the third round to Philadelphia's team of Clarence Clark and Fred Taylor, who went on to win the championship. Sears and Dwight won the doubles five of the next six years. In 1883, following matches between Dwight and Sears versus the winning Clark brothers—Clarence and Joe—the Clarks went off to England. There in an exhibition they lost to the Renshaws 6-4, 8-6, 3-6, 6-1, and a week later the Renshaws won in straight sets.

Later that year, following the U.S. Championships, Dr. Dwight went abroad and spent the fall, winter and spring competing against the best English players, including the Renshaws, playing indoors at Maida Vale and outdoors at Cannes. In 1885 he lost in the Wimbledon semifinals to Herbert Lawford in straight sets. As the most successful of the first Americans to play Wimbledon in 1884, Dwight was beaten in the second round of singles, 6-1, 2-6, 6-3, 3-6, 7-5, by the ambidextrous Herbert Chipp. Dick Sears, kept out of the singles by injury, then joined him to reach the doubles semifinals where they lost to the champion Renshaws, 6-0, 6-1, 6-2.

Dwight won the Northern England Championship in 1884, and with Willie Renshaw the 1885 Buxton doubles Tournament. During these years he ranked just below the very best of England. He was much respected and through his instructional articles and two books, *Lawn Tennis* in 1886 and *Practical Lawn Tennis* in 1893, did much for the level of play in the U.S. His books were the standard instruction until 1920 when Bill Tilden's *The Art of Lawn Tennis* was published. The 1890s found tennis losing players to both the bicycle and to the newly arrived game of golf. Dwight saw the game and the USNLTA through those lean years. It was through his contacts with English players that the Davis Cup was launched in 1900, for which he drew up the rules. This helped restore the game to popularity.

As the 20th century came, tennis had weathered its first recession and had come back stronger than ever. It would not be the last time the sports taste of some would stray to the newest fad. But a faithful band of lovers of this exquisitely fair and always challenging game of a lifetime would remain true. The game was firmly attached to sportsmen and sportswomen in all the English-speaking countries and making inroads throughout the rest of the world.

By 1900 all the strokes, tactics and strategies had become part of the game. The Renshaws brought the net game, Lawford topspin, and Holcombe Ward and Dwight Davis the American twist serve (kicker). All these have been improved, but a few, like the reverse twist serve, are no longer used.

Then as now most of the play took place on the public courts. This is not to gainsay the importance of the great tennis clubs. In the mid-1880s Prospect Park in Brooklyn, N.Y., had over 100 clubs using its facilities. Sports clubs have often been targets as havens of snobs and bigots. Clubs, as other groups of people, have their share, but they have done much good for tennis

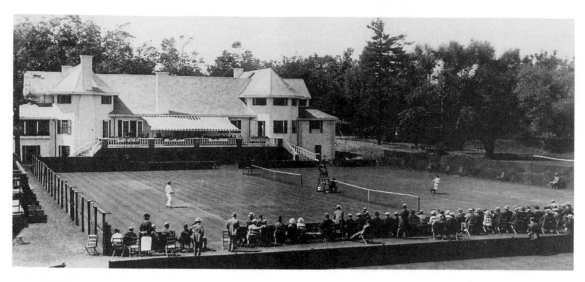

The Longwood Cricket Club had lawn tennis as early as 1878 at its original site in Boston, moving to this, its present site, in 1922. (Fischer Collection/SPS)

and other sports. They established standards of play, deportment, and facilities which elevated the game everywhere. Almost all the greats of the game have started on the public courts, but they refined their games at clubs and colleges.

The year of that seminal tournament at Nahant, 1876, with Dr. Dwight free-forming the format and rules, was also that of the founding of the first tennis club in the U.S., the New Orleans Lawn Tennis Club.

Founded in 1877, Boston's Longwood Cricket Club, then situated at the corner of Brookline and Longwood Avenues, near the plot where Fenway Park would rise in 1912, adopted lawn tennis in 1878. An older institution, the Merion Cricket Club, in Philadelphia, which was founded in 1865, took up the new game in 1879. In that year a concrete court, making the name "lawn tennis" less than descriptive, was built in Santa Monica, Cal. The Orange Lawn Tennis Club in New Jersey had its beginnings in 1880, as did the Newport Casino and the Cincinnati Tennis Club.

The inaugural Wimbledon embraced only one event, the men's singles. An entry of 22 was received, and on Monday, July 9, 1877, a fine, sunny day, The Lawn Tennis Championships began. One

entrant, C. F. Buller, was absent, so there were only 10 instead of the expected 11 matches.

The 11 survivors were reduced to six on Tuesday, then to three on Wednesday. The notion of restricting byes to the first round was still eight years off. On Thursday William Marshall had a free passage into the final while Spencer W. Gore beat Charles Heathcote, 6-2, 6-5, 6-2. Advantage sets had been adopted but only for the final.

The title match was held over until the following Monday. Such delay had been indicated in the prospectus to allow for the Eton and Harrow cricket match at Lords. This was the ultimate sporting event so far as the fashionable London world was concerned, and lawn tennis, itself a fashionable sport, did not dream for many years of coming into conflict with that important fixture.

Monday turned out wet, and the final was postponed until Thursday, July 19. That day was also damp, but rather than disappoint 200 spectators, each of whom had paid one shilling (then about 25 cents) to see Wimbledon's baptismal final, Gore and Marshall sportingly agreed to play. Gore came up to the net and volleyed. Whether this was entirely sporting was a matter of some debate, as was his striking the ball before it had crossed the net. He won, 6-1, 6-2, 6-4.

Gore, an old Harrovian of 27, had played rackets at school and was a keen cricketer. He did not think much of the new game. He defended his title the next year, losing in the challenge round to Frank Hadow, another old Harrovian on leave from coffee planting in Ceylon, who circumvented the volleyer by lobbing. Gore later wrote:

"That anyone who has really played well at cricket, tennis, or even rackets, will ever seriously give his attention to lawn tennis, beyond showing himself to be a promising player, is extremely doubtful; for in all probability the monotony of the game as compared with the others would choke him off before he had time to excel at it."

Those were the views of the world's first champion. Gore died in 1906, still a keen cricketer.

Competing in 1878 was a former Cambridge court tennis player, A. T. Myers. He was an innovator. He served overhand. Yet it is clear that at the time there was more of the vicarage lawn than athleticism about the infant game. In 1879 the Wimbledon champion was in fact a vicar. He was the Reverend John Hartley, yet another old Harrovian. He kept his title in 1880, and his ability to endlessly return the ball was notorious.

In 1881 the game took on a new dimension. Two wealthy young twins from Cheltenham, in the west of England, initiated a dominance that endured for nearly a decade. They were Willie and Ernest Renshaw. In that year Willie won the first of his seven singles titles at Wimbledon. In the challenge round he beat Hartley, 6-0, 6-1, 6-1, in an extraordinarily brief and devastating 37 minutes.

Its brevity is partly explained by the fact that at that time players changed ends only after each set. It is also explained by the difference in style. Hartley was a gentle retriever. Renshaw served hard, volleyed hard, smashed hard and went for fast winners all round. He and Ernest created modern lawn tennis. Crowds flocked to see them play.

Overshadowed Ernest took only one Wimbledon singles title, 1888, but he might have had another in 1889 if win-happy Willie hadn't made the first extraordinary comeback at the Big W—maybe the most extraordinary—in the all-comers final to beat Harry Barlow, 3-6, 5-7, 8-6, 10-8, 8-6. Willie resurrected himself from 2-5 in the fourth through six match points, and 0-5 in the fifth. Exhilarated by that, Willie beat Ernest in the fratricidal four-set challenge round for his seventh and last title. Not to be outdone that year, Blanche Bingley Hillyard made her own exciting Wimbledon comeback to beat Lena Rice for the second of her six titles, 4-6, 8-6, 6-4, brushing aside three match points as Rice served at 5-3 in the second.

The Scottish Championships in Edinburgh was inaugurated in 1878. The Irish Championships in Dublin began in 1879 and was notable for initiating a women's singles as well as a mixed doubles event. The women's events, however, were restricted in some degree. While the main part of the tournament was played on courts prepared in Fitzwilliam Square and open to the public, the women were confined to the relative privacy of the Fitzwilliam Club itself. Only members and their guests were permitted the sight of well-turned ankles on display. The game's first woman champion of the world was 14-year-old May Langrishe.

The men's singles champion in the game's first Irish Championships was Vere "St. Leger" Goold. In the same year he became finalist in the all-comers' singles at Wimbledon, losing to the gentle Hartley. Many years later Goold wrote a unique chapter for himself in the history of the game by being convicted of murder by a French court and getting sent to Devil's Island, where he died.

A "Championship of America" was staged in 1880. It began on Sept. 1 on the courts at the Staten Island (N.Y.). Cricket and Baseball Club. The prize was a silver cup valued at $100. Rackets scoring was used, with the results turning on the aggregate number of aces.

An Englishman, O. E. Woodhouse, wrote from Chicago asking if he could enter. He was a member of the West Middlesex Club, Ealing, England. He had played that year in the Wimbledon Championships and reached the all-comers' final before losing to Herbert Lawford. Woodhouse's overhand service was a novelty to American players. With this advantage he reached the final, where he beat a Canadian, J. F. Helmuth, 15-11, 14-15, 15-9, 10-15, victory based on a score of 54 points to 50.

In October 1880 there was a tournament played in Beacon Park, Boston. The winner was Dick Sears. Tennis scoring was used. The nonstandardization of the game, both in its equipment and scoring, brought increasing difficulties as it grew. There was controversy about the correct way to play lawn tennis.

With the need for standardization in mind, a meeting was arranged at the Fifth Avenue Hotel in New York on May 21, 1881, in the name of three prominent clubs: the Beacon Park Athletic Association of Boston, the Staten Island Cricket and Baseball Club of New York, and the All Philadelphia Lawn Tennis Committee.

There were 33 clubs represented, and the U.S. National Lawn Tennis Association, as it was then named, came into being. A constitution was drawn up. The rules of the All England Club and the M.C.C. were adopted. R. S. Oliver of the Albany Lawn Tennis Club was elected president, and Clarence Clark was elected secretary and treasurer. A vice president and an executive committee of three were also chosen.

This was the first national association in the world. It is the doyen of such bodies. Apart from its standardization of the game, where the British example was followed, its other major decision was to inaugurate the National Championships of the United States (hereafter called the U.S. Championships), men's singles and men's doubles. As a venue it settled on the Newport Casino, Newport, R.I., probably without equal at that time as the resort of wealth and fashion.

It began on August 31, 1881, with a singles entry of 26. Except for the final, the best of three sets, not of five, was played. Dick Sears won without losing a set. He was 19 years, 10 months, and the first U.S. champion would have a remarkable career. He won seven times in all, playing through in both 1882 and 1883 without losing a set. In 1884 the challenge round was instituted, and in the title match Sears yielded a set for the first time, to Howard Taylor. After three further victories he did not defend in 1888. Sears' singular singles record: matches played, 18; matches won, 18. From 1882 through 1887 he also won the doubles six times—five with James Dwight and once with Joseph Clark.

Sears learned to volley in 1881, the same time that the Renshaw twins were introducing their arts of aggression in England. They did so independently of each other.

In 1884 the Wimbledon meeting was enlarged to include a women's singles and a men's doubles. The doubles cups were passed on from the tournament that had been staged, albeit with failing interest, at Oxford since 1879 and where originally the distance was over the best of seven sets.

The other new Wimbledon event, the women's singles, was staged at the same time. The first winner, 1884, from a field of 13 ambitious and progressive-minded young ladies, was Maud Watson. She was 19 years old and in the final she faced her 26-year-old sister, Lilian. They were the daughters of the vicar of Berkswell, a village in the heart of England. Maud won a tough match, 6-8, 6-3, 6-3.

The losing semifinalist to Maud Watson, Blanche Bingley (later Mrs. George Hillyard), became one of the most indefatigable champions of all time. She won the singles six times between 1886 and 1900 and played for the last time in 1913 when she was 49 years old.

Before winning at Wimbledon in 1884, Watson beat the first woman champion in the world, May Langrishe, the Irish winner of 1879, in

Dublin. There was coincidence in the deaths of the two women players, who have enduring fame as pioneer champions. Langrishe died at a house called "Hammersmead" in Charmouth, a small seaside resort in Devonshire, England, in 1939. Seven years later Watson died in the same house.

The women, recognized first by the Irish in 1879, made their early efforts in England and Ireland in concert with the men. In the U.S. the women came forward independently, at least in the beginning.

In 1887 the first U.S. Women's Championship, held at the Philadelphia Cricket Club, was an outgrowth of the first (1886) Chestnut Hill Tennis Club Ladies Open. The second "open" became the first U.S. Championship when the Wissahickon Inn offered the Wissahickon Cup as the singles prize. Arrangements for the 1886–87 tournaments were conducted by the Chestnut Hill T.C., and play was at the Philadelphia C.C. In 1888 the Cricket Club took over sponsorship of the national championships, and continued until the 1921 move to Forest Hills.

Seven women entered the singles in 1887, all from the greater Delaware Valley area, and the champ, Ellen Hansell, a 6-1, 6-0, victor over Laura Knight, represented Philadelphia's Belmont Cricket Club. The 1888 tourney included New Yorkers Adeline Robinson and the Roosevelt sisters, Ellen and Grace, but was won by another Philadelphian from the Belmont Club, Bertha Townsend, over Hansell, 6-3, 6-5, in the challenge round.

On February 9, 1889, the USNLTA carried a motion that "its protection be extended to the Lady Lawn Tennis players of the country."

Ireland's Mabel Cahill won in 1892 and again one year later. She beat Elisabeth Moore in 1891, 5-7, 6-3, 6-4, 4-6, 6-2. For eight of the next nine years the women played the best of five sets, but only in the all-comers finals and challenge rounds. It was not unknown in Britain, though the women at Wimbledon at no time competed over such a distance.

The growth of lawn tennis round the world was fast. Clubs were founded in Scotland, Brazil and India in 1875. It was played in Germany in 1876. In 1877 the Fitzwilliam Club was started in Dublin, Ireland, and the Decimal Club was the first in France, in Paris. Australia, Sweden, Italy, Hungary and Peru had lawn tennis courts in 1878, and the first tournament in Australia was the Victorian Championship meeting in 1879. Denmark and Switzerland date their beginnings from 1880, Argentina from 1881. The first club in the Netherlands was in 1882; in Jamaica in 1883; and in 1885 in both Greece and Turkey. Lawn tennis came to Lebanon in 1889, to Egypt in 1890 and to Finland in the same year. South Africa's first championship was staged in 1891.

Wealthy Russian landowners were setting up courts in the late 1870s. One of them was the great author, Leo Tolstoy, whose 1878 novel, *Anna Karenina,* includes a tennis scene. An enthusiastic player himself, he was photographed playing as early as 1896 on his court at Yasnaya Polyana. Founded as the first Russian club in 1888 was the Lakhta Lawn Tennis Club outside of St. Petersburg.

In 1879, two years after the original Wimbledon, a prize-money tournament was held at Duke Kinski's castle at Chocen, Bohemia (a sector of Czechoslovakia). That year another Bohemian tourney was played on grass at Nove Benatsky involving a thirsty cast: first prize was a barrel of wine. The hungry were involved in the same area in an annual team match between the towns of Zbraslov and Rakovenic: first prize, a gigantic cucumber. Like those remarkable cukes, the game just kept growing.

After the successful intervention of Britain's O. E. Woodhouse, in the unofficial American championship of 1880, an Irishman, J. J. Cairnes, was refused entry to the 1881 Championships at Newport. But he was permitted to play in the Ladies Cup tourney there immediately afterwards, and Cairnes, a semifinalist in the initial Irish Championships of 1879, won the event easily, beating the newly crowned U.S. champ, Dick Sears, in the final.

In 1889 E. G. Meers, a top British player, was one of the first overseas challengers at Newport. He lost in five sets to Oliver Campbell, 18. The following year Campbell became champion for the first time and, at the age of 19 years, six months, was the youngest to do so until Pete Sampras, 19 years, 1 month, won at Flushing in 1990.

It was evidently a time that favored youth. One year later, in 1891, Wilfred Baddeley won the men's singles championship at Wimbledon at 19 years, 6 months, a record lowered by 17-year-old Boris Becker in 1985.

A "pro tour" of sorts even took brief form in 1889. George Kerr, billed as the Irish professional champ, came to the U.S. to battle Tom Pettit of Boston, the teaching pro at Newport Casino and regarded as the New World's leading professional. They played at Springfield, Mass., Boston and Newport, and Kerr was the victor in three of four matches.

Manliffe Goodbody, one of the many Irishmen prominent in the game in the British Isles, gained notable success at Newport in 1894. He beat Clarence Hobart and Bill Larned, both players of championship ilk, and failed only in the challenge round, to Robert Wrenn.

In 1895 what almost amounted to a representative contest between the Americans and the British took the form of a round-robin tournament at the Neighborhood Club, West Newton, Mass. The British were from Ireland, Joshua Pim, the Wimbledon champion of 1893 and 1894, and Harold Mahony, destined to become the champion in 1896. The Americans were Larned, who later became a seven-time U.S. singles champion, Hobart, Fred Hovey and Malcolm Chace. Pim lost only to Hobart, while Mahony, unbeaten by Americans, lost only to Pim. The first prize went to Pim, the second to Mahony.

The British challenge at Newport in 1897 was formidable, comprising Mahony, Harold Nisbet and Wilberforce Eaves, who was Australian-born but living in England. The British spectators, if there were any among the wealthy and fashionable who came to the Newport Casino, must have held their heads high. Eaves and Nisbet made an all-British final in the all-comers' singles. Eaves was the winner and challenged Wrenn. American pride was restored. Wrenn won in five sets as he took the title for the fourth time. It was the second occasion he had to thwart a cross-Atlantic challenge.

Anglo-American rivalry was channeled into a team instead of an individual exercise in 1900. Dwight Davis put up his famous Davis Cup for competition in that year. He had been inspired 12 months earlier by a tennis-playing tour he undertook with Holcombe Ward, Malcolm Whitman and Beals Wright, all keen players in their early 20s. Accompanied by George Wright, the father of Beals, they traveled some 8,000 miles, from the Atlantic Coast to the Pacific and up to British Columbia.

The USTA accepted Davis' offer and the International Lawn Tennis Challenge Trophy was offered to the world. They had the British primarily in mind and the British, despite the Boer War then taking place in South Africa, took up the challenge.

Davis was named as the U.S. captain for the inaugural. He was then 21 and had reached the all-comers' singles final at Newport in 1899. Whitman, 23, the champion of 1898, and Ward, 22, doubles partner of Davis, were the other members, Harvard men all. The venue chosen was the Longwood Cricket Club, still at its original Boston site, and the matches were arranged for early August, well before the Newport meeting at the end of the month.

The British team comprised Arthur Gore, Ernest Black, and Herbert Roper Barrett. The 32-year-old Gore still had a lot of tennis life in him and had not yet won any of his three Wimbledon singles titles. The Scot, Black, did not achieve the

Dwight Davis (right), donor of the Davis Cup in 1900, won the U.S. Doubles Championship with Holcombe Ward in 1899, 1900 and 1901. (Fischer Collection/SPS)

distinction of reaching the last eight at Wimbledon. Barrett was noted as a player of subtle abilities. It was not the best British team—the preeminent Doherty brothers were unavailable—since it was selected not only on playing ability but also on a capacity to spare both the time and the money for the trip.

After the British arrived in New York, they took the opportunity to pay a visit to Niagara Falls and eventually turned up at the Longwood Club in the best of spirits, though without having had much practice.

They found the courts too soft, the grass too long and the Americans unexpectedly too tough. Barrett would later complain that the net "was a disgrace, the balls awful—soft and mothery—and when served with the American twist come at you like an animated egg-plum. We never experi-

enced this service before and it quite nonplussed us." The kicking serves, particularly those of Holcombe Ward, bounding to the receiver's left, confounded them. But—saving graces—Barrett thought the spectators "impartial" and "the female portion thereof not at all unpleasant to gaze upon."

The first two singles were played side by side on adjoining courts. Whitman beat Gore in three easy sets. Davis beat Black after losing the opening set. Black and Barrett could not take a set in the doubles against Ward and Davis the following day. On the last day Davis was one set up and 9-9 each in the second against Gore when it rained and further play was abandoned. The U.S. had won by a mile.

Later, by the sea at Newport, Gore and Black made an effort to retrieve British honor. They clashed in the quarterfinals and Gore survived, only to lose to George Wrenn in the next round. Whitman revealed the temper of his steel. He thrust back the challenge of Larned to keep his title.

Anglo-American rivalry continued to be the international aspect of tennis for some years. There was no challenge for the Davis Cup in 1901, but in 1902 the British renewed their effort, sending Reggie and Laurie Doherty, the finest British players of the time, with Joshua Pim. They played against Whitman, Davis and Larned at the Crescent Athletic Club in Brooklyn, N.Y. As in 1900 the two singles were played at the same time on adjacent courts. Fearful of Laurie's fitness, the British played Pim with Reggie Doherty in the singles. The doubles was scheduled to take place on the third day. By that time it was over, for Pim lost both his singles and Reggie was beaten by Whitman. The British plan to reserve Laurie's strength for the doubles had lost its point.

The classic powers of the Dohertys, which had captivated the crowds at Wimbledon and elsewhere in Britain, were again displayed to American audiences later in the month at Newport. The brothers reached the semifinals and should have played one another. Laurie gave a walkover to his elder brother and Reggie went on to beat Whitman in the final. Reggie, though he had beaten Larned in the singles in the Davis Cup, could not repeat his success when the U.S. title was at stake.

The year 1903 was a turning point and the British challenge in the United States was as effective as it was formidable. In the Davis Cup, where the British Isles was again the only challenger, the venue was again Longwood in Boston. Reggie and Laurie Doherty were put forward as a two-man side and made a gambling start, giving a match away. Because Reggie was the weaker physically and feeling unwell with a sore right shoulder, the Brit defaulted his opening singles to Larned while Laurie beat Robert Wrenn. Then providence butted in—two days of rain. Reggie felt better, accompanying his brother to doubles victory over the brothers Wrenn, Robert and George.

Thrilling but screwy was the decisive third day when both Dohertys won tight five-set matches, played side by side, that could have gone the other way. Larned's probably should have. In the confusion and tension of witnesses whose cheers for one match might interrupt the other as they tried to follow both, as well as the anxiety of the players, the two contests were neck-and-neck in the fifth: 3-3 between Reggie and Wrenn, 4-4 between Laurie and Larned. But Larned, up 15-40 against Laurie's serve, knocked a winning return and was announced as the leader, 5-4. Hold on. Laurie thought his serve had been a fault, long, and queried umpire Fred Mansfield. The umpire turned to the service linesman and . . . beheld only an empty chair! That judge had disappeared. Referee James Dwight ruled the point replayed. Laurie won the point, the game, and the next two—thus the Cup, 7-5. Having paused to monitor the discussion, Reggie proceeded to finish off Wrenn, 6-4, and the Cup was to leave its homeland for the first time.

It stayed away, in London, as the Dohertys backboned their country's four-year run, with help from Sid Smith, through 1906. That was

their cutoff date as a dominant duo. Then Australasians—Aussie Norman Brookes and New Zealander Tony Wilding—spirited the Cup to the Antipodes, 3-2, and kept it until 1912 when Brits Jim Cecil and Charles Dixon, taking advantage of Wilding's absence, scored a shocking 3-2 win.

After snatching the Cup in 1903, the Dohertys achieved something more in raiding the U.S. In the U.S. Championships at Newport, they were again cast against one another in the quarterfinals. This time Laurie was given the walkover. He went on to reach the challenge round, where he dispossessed Larned of his title, 6-0, 6-3, 10-8, rather more easily achieved than his win in the Davis Cup, where his measure had been 7-5 in the fifth set.

Laurie Doherty, the first man to take the U.S. Championship in singles overseas, was then 27 and perhaps at his peak. Reggie, three years older, won four straight Wimbledon singles, 1897–1900. The more robust Laurie followed with a five-year sequence, 1901–06. Their classic skill became a British legend and their impeccable sportsmanship a byword. In doubles there was only one year between 1897 and 1905 when they were not Wimbledon champions. The U.S. title fell to them in 1902 and 1903.

If 1903 was a momentous year for the U.S. Championships, that of 1905 was equally so for Wimbledon. An American woman had entered for the first time in 1900. Marion Jones, then the U.S. champion, got as far as the quarterfinals. Five years later a chubby, robust 18-year-old from California with an intimidating forehand made a memorable appearance. She was May Sutton and she, too, was the U.S. title-holder. She was, as it happened, English-born, having seen the light of day at Plymouth, Devonshire, as the daughter of a British naval captain who later took his family to the U.S.

The staunch Sutton penetrated a citadel where the names of some women players were already being spoken of reverently. Most venerated at that time was Lottie Dod. She won the first of

The British-born May Sutton, the first American to win at Wimbledon, in 1905 and again in 1907, won the U.S. Singles in 1904. (Fischer Collection/SPS)

her five championships when only 15 years old, the youngest ever to win a major singles. There was Blanche Hillyard, six times the champion. Dorothea Douglass (later Mrs. Lambert Chambers) had, when the uninhibited Sutton appeared, already won twice and was on the way to making herself a legend.

Sutton carved through all opposition and had the temerity to stop Douglass from winning for the third time. Sutton was the first overseas player to take a Wimbledon championship. This was in a year of the biggest invasion to date, for in 1905 there were among the men five Americans, two New Zealanders, three Australians, three Belgians, two Danes and a South African.

Tennis was in fact assuming an international role. The Davis Cup in 1905 enlarged to six nations. With the British Isles as holders, Belgium and France had challenged in 1904. So did Austria, only to withdraw before taking the court. The United States, in the position of challenger for the first time, did not then do so, for the difficulties of finding a team to cross the Atlantic proved overwhelming.

But in 1905 teams from the U.S., France, Austria and Australasia converged on London.

Belgium should have done so but in the event conceded a walkover to the U.S. At Queen's Club in July, after the Wimbledon meeting was finished, the four nations played a knock-out competition to decide the best fitted to challenge the British Isles for the trophy. The U.S. beat France, 5-0. Australasia beat Austria, 5-0. The U.S. then beat Australasia, 5-0. In the challenge round the Doherty brothers and Sid Smith beat the U.S.— Larned, Ward, Beals Wright—5-0. It all took place in 12 days, July 13-24.

The Australasian side (until 1924 New Zealand and Australia functioned as a single entity for tennis) included Norman Brookes and Tony Wilding. Each was to impress himself deeply in the history of the game. New Zealand's Wilding combined athletic skill, good looks, and a personality that made him a teen-age idol.

In 1907 the men's singles at Wimbledon was won by Brookes. He was one of the world's all-time great volleyers, a left-hander of consummate skill. Brookes and Wilding took the men's doubles. May Sutton, who had lost her women's singles in 1906 to Dorothea Douglass, won it back again. All three championship titles at Wimbledon—at that time the women's and mixed dou-

New Zealand's Tony Wilding (foreground), representing Australasia, vanquishes Melville Long of the U.S. in 1909 Davis Cup play at Sydney, Australia. (Fischer Collection/SPS)

bles did not have the same high status—went overseas. A contemporary wrote that a new epoch had begun in the history of lawn tennis.

In the U.S., the championship meeting at Newport settled back after the Doherty sortie of 1903 to control its own destinies. The outstanding player of the first decade of the century was Larned. In 1892 this Cornell man won the Intercollegiate Championship, a title established in 1883. A New York stockbroker, he won the U.S. singles for the first time in 1901 when he was 28. He equaled the record of Dick Sears taking it seven times, the last in 1911.

He played 73 singles in all and won 61. Tilden, the other seven-time winner along with Sears, did better (69-7), and Jimmy Connors (98-17), Ivan Lendl (73-13) outdid both while John McEnroe is up there (65-12). Larned had an unbroken sequence of 11 victories from 1907, when he played through and won, to his success in his last challenge round of 1911.

The popularity of the Newport singles reached unprecedented heights during his career. The entry passed 128 for the first time in 1908. It peaked at 202 in 1911, and this was the last year of the challenge round.

The winner in 1912 was a red-headed Californian, Maurice McLoughlin. His dynamic serving brought a new dimension to the game and so, perhaps, did his background. He was the first public parks player to take a title that had been dominated by club men from wealthy families. With McLoughlin's game, serve-and-volley came first. "The California Comet," as he was known, electrified tennis prior to the First World War.

He was a precociously skilled player. He took the Pacific Coast Championship, an event dating from 1889, in 1907, when he was 17. His first international experience, at 19, was invaluable, if painful. He and fellow San Franciscan Melville Long, 18, were sent to Sydney in 1909 as sacrificial lambs—the greenest U.S. team ever—to challenge for the Davis Cup against Brookes and Wilding because none of the higher-ranked Americans such as champion Bill Larned and runnerup Bill Clothier cared to make the long boat trip. They lost, 5-0, in 16 sets, McLoughlin taking one from Wilding. His triumph at Newport in 1912 came after losing the all-comers' final to Bill Clothier in 1909, after yielding in the quarterfinal to Beals Wright in 1910 and after taking the all-comers' event and losing to Larned in the challenge round of 1911.

He repeated in 1913, the year McLoughlin made his only appearance in Europe. Wimbledon spectators were awestruck by his serving, and the word "cannonball" was used for the first time. His reputation preceded him and he did not disappoint. Before record crowds he came through the all-comers' singles and challenged Wilding, the title-holder since 1910, for the crown. "The history of the match," it was written at the time, "may be succinctly stated by saying that McLoughlin ought to have won the first set and was very near to winning the third. He lost both of them, and the second into the bargain, and so Wilding retained the honors." The score: 8-6, 6-3, 10-8.

Nevertheless it was a jubilant visit because McLoughlin, scoring the decisive victory over Charles Dixon, 8-6, 6-3, 6-2, joined with Dick Williams and Harold Hackett for a 3-2 victory over the Brits to bring the Davis Cup back home.

Wilding's invincibility at Wimbledon was brought to an end in 1914 by his Davis Cup colleague, Norman Brookes. The great Australian was 36 years old when he won his second Wimbledon singles championship. Later that year he and Wilding were in America challenging the U.S. for the Davis Cup. They played at the West Side Tennis Club, Forest Hills, a few days after the start of World War I. (Wilding was killed, at 31, on May 9, 1915, at Neuve Chapelle on the Western Front.)

McLoughlin won both his singles against Australasia. In the first, he beat Brookes, 17-15, 6-3, 6-3, and the strength of his serve and volley had never been so devastatingly displayed. Nonetheless, Australasia won, 3-2. The International Team trophy had been in contention 13 times, with three successes for the U.S., five for the British and five for Australasia.

The West Side Tennis Club staged its first Davis Cup in 1911 when America beat the British Isles, 4-1. The famous club was founded in 1892, when 13 founder members rented three clay courts on Central Park West between 88th and 89th Streets, Manhattan. By the end of that sea-

Maurice McLoughlin (left) won his first U.S. Singles title against Bill Johnston in 1912. (Fischer Collection/SPS)

son there were 43 members, five courts, and the initiation fee was $10, with a yearly subscription of the same amount.

A move was made to a site near Columbia University at 117th Street between Morningside Drive and Amsterdam Avenue in 1902. Six years later a further move took the club to 238th Street and Broadway, where there was room for 12 grass and 15 or more clay courts. The shift to Forest Hills in Queens was made in 1913. Until the building of the concrete stadium in 1923 the main courts were in front of the clubhouse, flanked by temporary stands.

The West Side Tennis Club became the host of the U.S. Men's Singles Championship in 1915. In 1914, the last year at Newport, Dick Williams reversed the outcome of the final of the preceding year and beat McLoughlin to take the title. In the

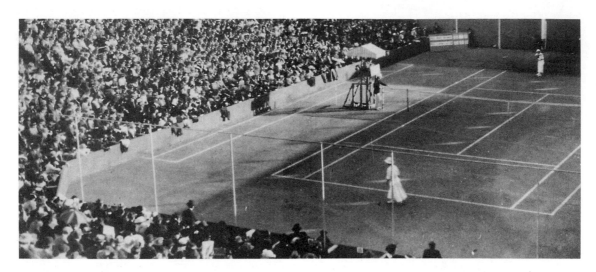

May Sutton and Molla Bjurstedt play this 1914 match on the Hotel Virginia Courts at Long Beach, Cal. (USTA)

first meeting at Forest Hills, McLoughlin was again the losing finalist, this time to Bill Johnston.

The Newport Casino, after 34 years as the home of America's most prestigious event, had outlived that purpose, though it remains in the game as a tourney site and home of the International Tennis Hall of Fame. The age it represented, of wealth and fashion and leisure, was passing. The victory by McLoughlin, the public parks player, had been significant.

In due course—1921—the West Side Tennis Club became the home of the U.S. Women's Championships as well. Until that time the Philadelphia Cricket Club was the site. The champion of 1908, Maud Barger Wallach, took a special place in the roll of winners. She was 38 when she won the title, having taken up the game as late as 30. When she was 45 she still ranked No. 5 in the U.S.

The successor to Mrs. Wallach was Hazel Hotchkiss, who became Mrs. George W. Wightman in 1912 and in the course of her career the winner of 45 U.S. titles. Her name would have survived as a valiant and stalwart champion even without the Wightman Cup she later founded.

Hazel Wightman was succeeded as national singles champion in 1915 by the Norwegian-born Molla Bjurstedt. As Mrs. Franklin Mallory she took the fame of the American women's game into the postwar years. Her record, though, was not exclusively as an American. When the Olympic Games was staged in Stockholm in 1912 she represented Norway and won the bronze medal for the women's singles on indoor courts.

Tennis was featured as part of the Olympic Games from the first in Athens in 1896 to the Paris event of 1924, then restored in 1988. At the prewar Games, British players predominated except for those at St. Louis in 1904. Only men took part and the gold medalists were exclusively American, Beals Wright taking one for the singles and, with Edgar Leonard, the doubles.

In international administration 1913 was an important year. It marked the founding of the ILTF (International Lawn Tennis Federation), today (and hereafter referred to as) the ITF. Prior to this time the world governing body, so far as there had been one, was the Lawn Tennis Association of Britain. Its membership included clubs and associations from all around the world.

In 1913 the LTA members included the associations of Australasia, Belgium, Bohemia, Ceylon, Chile, Finland, Hungary, Ireland, Jamaica, Mauritius, Netherlands, Norway, the Riviera, Russia, South Africa, Spain and Switzerland, as well as 26 individual clubs from 15 countries.

The ITF had its inaugural meeting in Paris on March 1, 1913. Its founder members were Australasia, Austria, Belgium, the British Isles, Denmark, France, Germany, Netherlands, Russia, South Africa, Sweden and Switzerland. The U.S. was voteless and was only informally represented—by one of the British delegates, H. Anthony Sabelli, secretary of the LTA.

The absence of the U.S. resulted in the Davis Cup organization developing along different lines from ITF, parallel but separate. (The merger between the two international bodies did not take place until 1978, and even then the difference of voting procedure was left to mark the original reluctance of the U.S. to yield any of its independence to the world's governing body.)

This reluctance to join the ITF was occasioned by the allocation of various "World Championship" titles. The Wimbledon meeting was granted ("in perpetuity") the description of "The World Championships on Grass." There was a "World Championships on Hard Court," (clay) which was staged mainly in Paris, and also a peripatetic "World Championships on Covered Courts." When these grandiose titles were abolished soon after World War I, the U.S. found its way clear to become a member of the ITF.

An early winner of the women's singles in the World's Hard Court Championships in Paris was a promising French girl only 15 years old. She won the women's doubles with an American, Elizabeth Ryan. She was from Picardy and her name was Suzanne Lenglen, perhaps the greatest player in the history of the women's game.

Ryan's name was also to echo reverberatingly in the annals of tennis. Even before 1914 this Californian had laid the foundation of her career as an assiduous, effective competitor.

The doubles events at Wimbledon, the women's and mixed, became full championship

Mary K. Browne (left) was U.S. Singles champion in 1912, 1913 and 1914, and with Louise Williams won the doubles in 1913, 1914 and 1921. (Fischer Collection/SPS)

competitions in 1913 when officially the World title on grass belonged to it. In 1914, the indefatigable Ryan partnered Agnes Morton to win the women's doubles, the first of 19 titles she was to gain at Wimbledon, a record that stood until 1979 when Billie Jean King won her 20th, the doubles, with Martina Navratilova.

The Riviera season was by then a well-established feature of the game, reflecting the world of fashion, wealth, and leisure of which tennis had become as much a part in Europe as it had in the U.S., where Newport had been for so long a center.

Immediately prior to World War I, however, it was perhaps Imperial Russia that represented the high point of tennis in its smart social context. A party of British men who played in St. Petersburg in the Russian Championships of 1913 recorded

Tennis players in World War I (left to right): Lt. Col. Dwight Davis, Maj. Bob Wrenn, Maj. Bill Larned, Capt. Watson Washburn, Capt. Dick Williams, Capt. O. S. Walters, Lt. Dean Mathey, Col. Wallace Johnson. (USTA)

that the ball boys were footmen in ornate uniforms who passed the balls on silver salvers. Ryan was the last women's champion of Imperial Russia, a title she was never able to defend.

Ryan was overshadowed at this time, like all other women, by Mrs. Lambert Chambers, as Dorothea Douglass had become. She made 13 attempts to win the Wimbledon singles between 1902 and 1920, and was beaten only six times. At the age of 24 she won for the first time, in 1903. Her seventh success was in 1914. She was the precursor of great, near-invincible players.

Yet at this period it was still possible to be near invincible and excel at other sports. Mrs. Chambers was one such, for she was a champion at badminton and a top-class field hockey player.

The Davis Cup strongly helped boost tennis as an international sport. Prior to 1914, when the war brought the competition to a temporary halt, there were nine entries: the U.S., the British Isles, Belgium, France, Australasia, Austria, Germany, Canada and South Africa.

The Australian Championships was staged first in 1905. Four years earlier the former British colonies of Victoria, New South Wales and others united in a federal government.

A notable woman champion of New Zealand was K. M. Nunneley. She took the title first in 1895 and for the 13th successive year in 1907. Rodney Heath won the first Australian title in 1905; the women's event didn't begin until 1922, Mall Molesworth the victor.

The French, prior to the war, made an impact on the world with men of high caliber, Andre Gobert and Max Decugis most notably. They won the men's doubles at Wimbledon in 1911, but it was not until 1925 that the French Championships was open to non-citizens. A German pair, Heinrich Kleinschroth and Friedrich Rahe, were runners-up for the Wimbledon title in 1913. In 1912 Kleinschroth competed in the U.S. Championships at Newport but did not survive the opening round.

The German Championships was an event favored by British players and among the fashionable happenings of the season. They were staged in Hamburg from 1892.

Canada's first championships was held two years earlier, in 1890. The first tournament staged was on the turf of the Montreal Cricket Club in 1878. Like those in the U.S., the first official championships followed the founding of the

Canadian Lawn Tennis Association in Toronto in 1890. The first women's championship was in Toronto in 1892.

In Europe the outbreak of the war in 1914 brought a halt to competitive tennis. Australia, more remote, staged its championships for the 1914–15 season, and a Brit, Gordon Lowe, was the winner.

In the United States the game was affected to a lesser degree. Inevitably the international field dried up. In 1917, when the U.S. became directly involved in the war, there was a break. The U.S. Championships was not staged as such that year, though the continuity of the events was not broken. The events were known as "Patriotic Tour-naments," with the winners eventually taking full championship status.

In 1918 a tall, somewhat ungainly man from Philadelphia, William Tatem Tilden II, did well on his third attempt in the U.S. singles at the West Side Tennis Club. He reached the final, where he was beaten by R. Lindley Murray, a left-hander with a big serve. Murray had revealed his aggressive qualities by taking the "Patriotic" event the year before.

Tilden was not all that young to make his mark. He was, in fact, 25 years old. He was a late developer. His record was to surpass, by far, those of Larned and Sears.

2

WAS IT REALLY GOLDEN?

1919–45

It was called "The Golden Age of Sport." Hyperbolic, probably, considering the purple language of the sports pages of the past, although there was some truth to it. Sport came on strong in the Roaring Twenties as never before, held high by such highly publicized stars as Babe Ruth in baseball, Jack Dempsey in boxing, Red Grange in football, Bobby Jones in golf, Man o' War in horse racing. Tennis was right up there, too, with players whose names had a broad public impact: Big Bill Tilden, Suzanne Lenglen, Helen Wills Moody. World War I was over, the trenches silent, and a prosperous period, with more leisure, seemed ripe for games-playing heroes and heroines who could be colored gold.

1919

This was the year of the arrival of Suzanne Lenglen on the world tennis stage she would dominate until she turned pro in 1926. A product of constant drilling by her father, Charles Lenglen, a well-to-do Frenchman, she had style as well as ability and would come to be ranked with Helen Wills Moody among the greatest women players of all time.

Lenglen appeared in her first tournament at age 12 and won the singles and doubles in the World Hard Court (clay) Championships at 15, so she was not an unknown when she came to Wimbledon upon the resumption of play following World War I. Playing on grass for the first time, Lenglen won the title in a match that is still regarded as one of the greatest Wimbledon women's finals.

Although the stocky Lenglen was no conventional beauty, and never married, she had a captivating allure and numerous love affairs, an appeal that was dynamite at the box office. Her magnetism and invincibility made the original Wimbledon too small, leading to the construction of the "new" (present) complex in 1922. Her long Gallic nose and prominent chin were complemented by a fiery disposition, a chic appearance and dancer's movements. She was 20 and advanced to the challenge round to play the seven-time champion, Britain's Mrs. Dorothea Douglass Chambers, who had won her first Wimbledon in 1903, and was two months from her 41st birthday.

Lenglen's dress created a sensation. The British had been accustomed to seeing their women in tight-fitting corsets, blouses and layers of petticoats. When Suzanne stepped onto Centre Court in a revealing one-piece dress, with sleeves *daringly* just above the elbow, her hemline *only* just below the knee, reaction ranged from outrage on the part of many women spectators—some reportedly walked out during her matches, muttering "shocking"—to delight among most of the men.

But everybody was also impressed by the young Frenchwoman's grace and disciplined shot-making as she won the title, 10-8, 4-6, 9-7, the 44 games amounting to the longest female final until Margaret Court's 14-12, 11-9, victory over Billie Jean King topped it by two games in 1970.

Future champ Kitty McKane, an eyewitness in the full-house crowd of 8,500 that included King George V and Queen Mary, wrote: "It was a very hot afternoon, and I think Suzanne wanted to quit when she was behind, 4-1, in the second. But her father would have none of it, shaking his umbrella furiously at her, and tossing her sugar cubes soaked with brandy. After losing the second set, she seemed back in control with a 4-1 lead in the third. But Mrs. Chambers, who'd missed out on two set points in the first, at 6-5, came back to win five games straight to 6-5 and 40-15 on her serve, on the verge of her eighth championship with two match points.

"Suzanne was lucky on the first. Reaching for a lob she hit in barely, on the frame, and the ball hit the net cord, dropping over. But the second she saved with a backhand down the line. She was unstoppable after that."

In the Wimbledon men's championship, tall Australian Gerald Patterson, on his first visit, advanced to the challenge round by beating Britain's Algernon Kingscote and then met coun-

"Little Bill" Johnston was the first post–World War I U.S. champion. He defeated "Big Bill" Tilden in the 1919 final. (UPI)

tryman Norman Brookes, who'd won the title in 1914, the last Wimbledon before the war. As champion, Brookes did not have to play until the challenge round. Patterson beat him, 6-3, 7-5, 6-2.

In the 1919 resumption of Davis Cup play after a four-year hiatus, Australasia, a combination of Australia and New Zealand, retained the Cup it had won in 1914, beating the British Isles, 4-1. The U.S. did not enter. Patterson was the dominant player, winning both singles and combining with Brookes to win the doubles. The Australian title went to Kingscote.

The U.S. final at Forest Hills between the 1915 champion, 5-foot-8, 120-pound William "Little Bill" Johnston, and 6-foot-2, William "Big Bill" Tilden, was billed in *The New York Times* as the battle for the title, "William the Conqueror."

It was the first of six meetings between the two Bills in the Championships final, the only one Johnston would win. Tilden had first played in the Championships in 1916 and lost in straight sets in the first round to Harold Throckmorton. In 1918 he lost the final to R. Lindley Murray. By 1919 he was already being called the greatest player of all time. Johnston, however, spotted a weakness in Tilden, a backhand that was totally defensive, hit invariably with underspin. Johnston pounded away at the weakness and won relatively easily, 6-4, 6-3, 6-3.

Tilden would go to the indoor court of a friend, Arnold Jones, in Providence, R.I., later in the year, work for months to correct the flaw, and come away with an improved backhand that would enable him to become the dominant tennis figure over the next decade.

For the women's championship the challenge round was abolished and Mrs. Hazel Hotchkiss Wightman won the title, interrupting a seven-year reign by Molla Bjurstedt of the United States, who had won in 1915, 1916, 1917 and 1918 and who would, as Mrs. Franklin Mallory, win in 1920, 1921, 1922 and then again in 1926. Marion Zinderstein eliminated the defending champion in the semifinals and was beaten 6-1, 6-2, in the final by Wightman, the first mother to win the title.

1920

William Tatem Tilden II, born in 1893, the son of a Philadelphia wool merchant and prominent civic figure, came of age at 27 when he won at Wimbledon and Forest Hills and helped the United States win the Davis Cup for the first time since 1913.

In the all-comers final at Wimbledon against the Japanese Zenzo Shimidzu, Tilden fell behind in all three sets, 1-4, 2-4, 2-5, but rallied in each and won the match, 6-4, 6-4, 13-11. It became the mark of Tilden to put on a show and entertain the crowd as well as win at tennis. In his remarkable biography of Tilden, *Big Bill Tilden,* Frank Deford

Bill Johnston (left) and Bill Tilden set sail for Auckland, New Zealand, where they swept Australasia for the Davis Cup in 1920. (Fischer Collection/SPS)

wrote, "Nobody realized it at the time, but it was one of Tilden's amusements, a favor to the crowd, to give lesser opponents a head start." Tilden had whipped Shimidzu, 6-1, 6-1, in a tournament prior to Wimbledon. In the challenge round final, Tilden defeated the defending champion, Australian Gerald Patterson, 2-6, 6-3, 6-2, 6-4. The Associated Press reported that "Tilden in the first set opened with experiments all around the court and then settled down mercilessly to feeding his opponent's backhand, and, as the game progressed, Patterson got worse and worse. . . . Tilden exploited his famous cut-stroke to his opponent's backhand again and again."

The British marveled at Tilden, acclaimed him the greatest of all time, and one observer rhapsodized, "His silhouette as he prepares to serve suggests an Egyptian pyramid king about to administer punishment."

In the U.S. Championships, Tilden beat Bill Johnston in a dramatic five-set final, 6-1, 1-6, 7-5, 5-7, 6-3, that was regarded as the greatest championship final up to that time. During the match a Navy photographic plane crashed while making passes over Forest Hills and disrupted the match momentarily. The pilot and the photographer were killed.

It was the first of six straight national titles for Tilden, a flamboyant, controversial figure who dominated any match, win or lose.

Tilden, who would not lose an important match until 1926, teamed with Johnston in a 5-0 Davis Cup sweep of Australasia. He and Johnston each took a pair of singles matches and a doubles over Norman Brookes and Gerald Patterson.

In the women's championship at Wimbledon, Dorothea Douglass Chambers defeated Elizabeth Ryan and Molla Mallory of the United States on the way to a return match with Suzanne Lenglen in the challenge round. Lenglen beat her, 6-4, 6-0. Mallory won the American title, defeating Marion Zinderstein, 6-3, 6-1.

1921

Suzanne Lenglen, who hadn't lost a match to anyone since the end of the war, came to the United States for the first time, and lost a match on a default. It was one of the most stunning results in tennis up to that time, and was long talked about and cited whenever Lenglen was discussed.

The position occupied by Lenglen at the time of the great default was described by Al Laney, the eminent tennis writer: "She probably did more for women's tennis than any girl who ever played it. She broke down barriers and created a vogue, reforming tennis dress, substituting acrobatics and something of the art of the ballet where decorum had been the rule. In England and on the Continent, this slim, not very pretty but fascinating French maiden was the most popular performer in sport or out of it on the postwar scene. She became the rage, almost a cult. Even royalty gave her its favor and she partnered King Gustav of Sweden in mixed doubles more than once."

Lenglen was beaten by the defending champion, Molla Mallory, in the second round of the

first U.S. Women's Championships played at Forest Hills, six years prior to the advent of seeds. Lenglen lost the first set, 6-2, seeming weak and nervous, coughing from time to time, causing some concern to those who had seen her play before. Then, when she lost the first point of the second set and double-faulted to trail, 2-6, 0-30, she started weeping. She went to the umpire's chair and, speaking French, said she was too ill to go on. As she and the disappointed Mallory walked off the court, there was a faint hissing sound in the stands from the crowd of 8,000, the largest ever to witness a women's match in the United States.

The newspapers reported she told the umpire that she was unable to breathe and that she coughed the night before. Others recalled her saying she did not feel like playing and had been listless in a practice session. If she was suffering from menstrual cramps, that was not mentioned because it was a taboo subject in the public prints at the time. It was also pointed out that she had arrived in the United States only four days before her first scheduled match. Her opponent, Eleanor Goss, defaulted, so she did not have a warmup before her match with Mallory.

Lenglen incurred criticism because she appeared at Forest Hills the next day in good spirits, continuing to attend parties. Despite her signs of physical distress in the match, it was not considered acceptable to default, and there arose speculation about whether Lenglen could accept defeat. For some time the phrase "to cough and quit" was in vogue in New York; in France there were accusations of mistreatment by the Americans and the charge that her first-round opponent had purposely defaulted to help set up Lenglen for defeat.

Mallory went on to win the U.S. Championship, her sixth, with a 4-6, 6-4, 6-2 victory in the final over Mary K. Browne. Lenglen had breezed to her third Wimbledon title with a 6-2, 6-0 victory over Elizabeth Ryan of the United States.

Bill Tilden retained his Wimbledon Championship, coming out of a sickbed to defend against South African Brian "Babe" Norton in the chal-

Molla Mallory (left) won her sixth U.S. Singles title in 1921. Along the way she ousted Marion Zinderstein Jessup (right). (UPI)

lenge round. Tilden won, 4-6, 2-6, 6-1, 6-0, 7-5. It was the third successive five-setter for 21-year-old Norton, who had beaten Frank Hunter and Manuel Alonso on the way. In the quarters the Japanese Zenzo Shimidzu plus considerable champagne took their toll on tippling Randolph Lycett. Too many refreshing pauses for Lycett, who at least was able, barely, to stagger to the distant finish line, 10-8 in the fifth. In the windup, after losing the first two sets to Norton, Tilden gave up his normal hard-hitting game, took to chops and slices, and turned the match around. This displeased the crowd, which booed Tilden despite the remonstrations of the umpire that he was playing quite fairly and within the rules. Norton recovered in the last set, led 5-4 with two match points, but Tilden rallied to hold serve, and prevailed, serving an ace on match point. F. P. Adams wrote: "He is an artist, more of an artist than nine-tenths of the artists I know. It is the beauty of the game that Tilden loves; it is the chase always, rather than the quarry."

Still not fully recovered from his illness in England, Tilden registered one of his more difficult and dramatic victories in the 5-0 defense of the Davis Cup at Germantown Cricket Club. Johnston opened with a swift 6-2, 6-4, 6-2 win over Ichiya Kumagae, but the clever, unorthodox little Zenzo Shimidzu took the first two sets and was within two points of winning with a 5-3, 30-15 lead in the third. Groping on a boiling 100-degree afternoon and hobbled by a boil on his foot, Tilden somehow reeled off four games to get through the set. A physician lanced the boil during the intermission, and Bill charged back to win, 5-7, 4-6, 7-5, 6-2, 6-1.

Remaining at Germantown for the U.S. Championships, Tilden, through the luck of the unseeded draw, faced foremost foe and 1920 finalist Johnston in the fourth round, winning 4-6, 7-5, 6-4, 6-3. He didn't lose another set, taking his second straight title in an all-Philadelphia final over chop-and-slice maestro Wallace Johnson, 6-1, 6-3, 6-1. Rhys Gemmel won the Australian.

1922

Having outgrown the Worple Road site in the London suburb of Wimbledon, occupied since 1877, the All England Club moved to its present site in a picturesque hollow at the foot of Church Road near Wimbledon Common. King George V and Queen Mary attended the opening on June 22 at the new Centre Court holding 14,750 seats (the previous arena had 8,500) and saw the first match, played by Leslie Godfree and Algernon Kingscote of Great Britain.

The challenge round was abolished. Bill Tilden did not choose to make the Atlantic crossing to defend his title, and it was won by Australian Gerald Patterson, whom Tilden had dethroned in 1920. Patterson defeated Great Britain's Randolph Lycett in the final, 6-3, 6-4, 6-2.

Suzanne Lenglen avenged her controversial default to Molla Mallory at Forest Hills the year before when she trounced Mallory in the Wimbledon final, 6-2, 6-0. Lenglen's appeal was such that before her first-round match with Kitty McKane, "a line stretched more than a mile and a half from the underground station to the entrance to the All England Club," Wimbledon official Duncan Macaulay wrote. "People used to call it the 'Leng-len trail a-winding' after the famous war song of those days ['a long, long trail . . .']."

Australia's Gerald Patterson won Wimbledon for the second time in 1922. (Fischer Collection/SPS)

Lenglen won three Wimbledon titles for the second time. She teamed with Pat O'Hara Wood to win the mixed doubles and with Elizabeth Ryan to take the doubles.

After her loss to Lenglen at Wimbledon, Mallory, 38, returned to Forest Hills to win her seventh U.S. title, defeating 16-year-old Helen Wills in the final, 6-3, 6-1. It was the greatest disparity in ages for any major final.

The meeting between perennial rivals Bill Tilden and Bill Johnston in the U.S. Championships at the Germantown Cricket Club was called "a match for the Greek gods." They played for a coveted championship bowl, which each had won twice and which would be retired permanently by any three-time winner. Tilden advanced to the final, beating Wimbledon champion Gerald Patterson, while Johnston defeated a

Helen Wills, right, defeats Kitty McKane in the inaugural match at the new stadium in Forest Hills in 1923. (UPI)

promising newcomer, 19-year-old Vincent Richards. Tilden lost the first two sets, then came back to win the match 4-6, 3-6, 6-2, 6-3, 6-4. The trophy gained by Tilden had on it the names of such previous winners as William Larned and R. Lindley Murray, Maurice McLoughlin, Dick Williams and Johnston.

In the Davis Cup, Australasia advanced past Spain to the challenge round, to be beaten by the United States, 4-1. In those days of unusual interest in Davis Cup, something of a stir was created by the loss of the doubles by the U.S. team of Tilden and Richards to Gerald Patterson and Pat O'Hara Wood. Tilden and Johnston swept Patterson and James Anderson in the singles.

1923

A new stadium was constructed at the West Side Tennis Club grounds in Forest Hills, but the men's U.S. Championships wouldn't return from Philadelphia until 1924. Built at a cost of $250,000, the concrete bowl that would eventually seat 14,000 opened on August 10 with the inauguration of the Wightman Cup matches.

The competition was the brainchild of Hazel Hotchkiss Wightman, a champion in pre–World War I days who would compete until she was past 70, winning the last of her 45 U.S. titles (senior doubles) at the age of 67. She had conceived the idea of a women's competition equivalent to the Davis Cup in 1920 and donated a silver vase. But

Flanking the Wightman Cup won by the U.S. in 1923 are (left to right): Helen Wills, Molla Mallory, Capt. Hazel Hotchkiss Wightman (the donor), Geraldine Beamish and M. H. Clayton. (UPI)

the idea lay fallow until it was seized upon by Julian Myrick, a USTA official, as a way of launching the new Forest Hills stadium.

The competition between Great Britain and the United States consisted of five singles matches and two doubles, and though Wightman hoped to make it an international tournament by bringing in France, that never came to pass. With Wightman as captain, the U.S. team of Molla Mallory, Helen Wills and Eleanor Goss scored a 7-0 sweep, starting with an inaugural match before 5,000 in which Wills beat Kitty McKane, 6-2, 7-5.

Wills won the first of her seven U.S. titles, defeating Mallory, 6-2, 6-1. Suzanne Lenglen

breezed through the Wimbledon field, losing only 11 games in the 12 sets she played defeating McKane in the final 6-2, 6-2.

With Bill Tilden, universally regarded as the kingpin of tennis, absent again from Wimbledon, Bill Johnston won for the only time. In straight sets he swept past countryman Vincent Richards, South Africa's Babe Norton and then Frank Hunter of the United States in a final that was completed in 45 minutes. Johnston's success at Wimbledon could not carry over to the U.S. Championships where he was crushed by Tilden in the final, 6-4, 6-1, 6-4. Pat O'Hara Wood won the Australian title.

Bill Tilden won the U.S. crown for the fourth year in a row and led the Americans' Davis Cup triumph in 1923. (UPI)

The Crocodile, René Lacoste, one of the Four Musketeers, lost to fellow Frenchman Jean Borotra in an all-French Wimbledon final in 1924. (Fischer Collection/SPS)

In a Davis Cup field increased to 17 entries from 11, Australasia beat France to challenge the U.S. The U.S. won, 4-1, with Tilden winning both singles and Johnston losing one of his singles to James Anderson. In the doubles, Tilden and Dick Williams won the first set, 17-15 (longest set for a Davis Cup finale), lost the second, 11-13, and the third, 2-6, before winning the final two sets from Anderson and John Hawkes, 6-3, 6-2.

It is hard today to realize how significant the Davis Cup used to be before open tennis, when there were not so many tournaments that players could choose to skip Cup play to chase big money. After World War I an atmosphere of international good fellowship took hold and the Davis Cup acquired tremendous significance, partly because of the U.S. dominance of the competition. It was front-page news then and controversies

such as Tilden's threats to quit were looked upon as almost national calamities.

1924

In the latter part of the 1920s, when the French would dominate men's tennis, each of the three great Frenchmen would win two Wimbledon championships, and it started this year with the French final (French nationals only) in which 25-year-old Jean Borotra defeated 19-year-old René Lacoste, 6-1, 3-6, 6-1, 3-6, 6-4.

Borotra, the colorful "Bounding Basque" who wore a beret while playing, and Lacoste, the "Crocodile," were two of the Four Musketeers along with 22-year-old Henri Cochet and 29-year-old Jacques "Toto" Brugnon, who was es-

President Calvin Coolidge makes the 1924 Davis Cup draw at the White House. (Fischer Collection/SPS)

sentially a doubles specialist. Wimbledon Secretary Duncan Macaulay wrote in *Behind the Scenes* at Wimbledon: "They were all very different in style and temperament, and they sometimes clashed bitterly with one another on the courts. But whenever they felt they were playing for France . . . they always put France first. Thus it was the combined pressure of Lacoste and Cochet which began to rock the great Bill Tilden on his pedestal, and which finally toppled him off it."

Tilden, increasingly at odds with the tennis establishment, sent a letter of resignation to the USTA, bowing out of the Davis Cup because of a proposed ban on his writing for newspapers about tennis. That was a conflict with amateur rules. The threat of not having Tilden's gate appeal in the Davis Cup competition forced the tennis body to cave in. Tilden and Bill Johnston swept the Australian team of Gerald Patterson and Pat O'Hara Wood, 5-0.

Underdog rooters hopeful that Little Bill Johnston would break the spell held over him by Tilden had reason to believe that Johnston would crash through in the U.S. Champi-

onships, the first played in the new West Side Tennis Club Stadium at Forest Hills. Tilden's feud with the USTA and the increased time he was devoting to a theatrical career led to charges that he was out of shape. He came to the final with a desultory five-set victory over Vincent Richards, while Johnston routed Australia's Gerald Patterson. In the final, however, Tilden crushed Johnston, 6-1, 9-7, 6-2, in a stunning display that tennis savant Al Laney later called "Tilden at his absolute peak, and I have not since seen the like of it." Patterson said, "Tilden is the only player in the world—the rest of us are second-graders."

Suzanne Lenglen, a five-time winner at Wimbledon, weakened by an attack of jaundice earlier in the year, was forced to drop out after winning a quarterfinal match over Elizabeth Ryan of the United States in which Lenglen was extended, 6-2, 6-8, 6-4. That was the first singles set she lost—except the one to Molla Mallory in her great default at Forest Hills in 1921—since 1919. Britain's Kitty McKane got a walkover in the semifinals and then defeated Helen Wills in the final, 4-6, 6-4, 6-4, from 1-4 in the second, Helen's lone loss in 56 Wimbledon matches.

They had met only a few days earlier in Wightman Cup play at Wimbledon, McKane winning, 6-2, 6-2. The British evened the series at one-all, winning the competition, 6-1. The United States' only point came on a doubles triumph by Wills and Hazel Wightman over McKane and Evelyn Colyer. The 18-year-old Wills won her second successive U.S. title, defeating Molla Mallory, 6-1, 6-2.

In Australia, the men's championship was won by James Anderson, the women's by Sylvia Lance. Norman Brookes, the 47-year-old Australian immortal who had first played at Wimbledon 20 years before, highlighted early-round Wimbledon play with an upset victory over Frank Hunter, who had been a finalist in 1923 and was ranked No. 5 in the world.

Helen Wills made it three in a row in U.S. Singles in 1925. (Fischer Collection/SPS)

1925

The French dominated Wimbledon as it never had been dominated before. They scored almost a clean sweep of the championships, winning the men's singles and doubles, the mixed doubles and women's singles—and half of the women's doubles.

Suzanne Lenglen, reaching the zenith of her career, lost only five games in sweeping through five opponents. She scored a 6-0, 6-0 semifinal triumph over Kitty McKane, who had won the title when Lenglen was incapacitated the previous year, and defeated another Englishwoman, Joan Fry in the final, 6-2, 6-0. Lenglen combined with American Elizabeth Ryan to win the women's doubles for the sixth time, and Lenglen won the mixed doubles with Jean Borotra for Lenglen's third Wimbledon triple crown.

The men's final was a rematch of the previous year. This time, René Lacoste scored a 6-3, 6-3, 4-6, 8-6 victory over Borotra, who was troubled by foot-fault calls. In the quarterfinal round Henri Cochet began to gain a Tilden-like reputation for comebacks, losing the first two sets to American John Hennessey, then sweeping the last three. In the first year that the French Championships was opened to players from all countries, Lacoste triumphed. James Anderson won his second straight Australian title, 11-9, 2-6, 6-2, 6-3, this over Gerald Patterson, who served 29 aces and 29 double faults; and Daphne Akhurst the first of her five Australian championships.

Bill Tilden achieved the distinction of winning 57 straight games during the summer. The stage was set for another Big Bill–Little Bill confrontation in the U.S. Finals at Forest Hills after semifinals in which Tilden beat Vincent Richards and Bill Johnston advanced past Dick Williams. Despite an injured shoulder, which prevented him from holding hardly more than half his service games in a long, five-set match, Tilden defeated Johnston, 4-6, 11-9, 6-3, 4-6, 6-3.

Johnston said immediately afterward, "I can't beat him; I can't beat the sonofabitch, I can't beat him." It was the last of Tilden's six straight U.S. titles and the last time he and Johnston would contest the title. Tilden, like most tennis people, admired Johnston greatly, and after Johnston's premature death from tuberculosis in 1946, dedicated his memoirs to him.

The French made their first breakthrough into the Davis Cup challenge round. Though the Four Musketeers—Lacoste and Borotra in singles, and Cochet and Jacques Brugnon in doubles—were swept by Tilden and Johnston in singles and Dick Williams and Vincent Richards in doubles, both Frenchmen extended Tilden to five sets. Borotra came within two points of shocking Tilden and the U.S. at the outset, serving for victory at 6-5 in the fourth set (and leading 2-0 in the fifth), but Big Bill called on all his wiles to win, 4-6, 6-0, 2-6, 9-7, 6-4. On the third day, the outcome already decided, Tilden had to save four

Spectators unable to purchase tickets for the 1926 Lenglen-Wills match in Cannes found a view from the ladder. (UPI)

match points to beat Lacoste, 3-6, 10-12, 8-6, 7-5, 6-2—65 games—the longest of all the master's 30 Cup singles.

Helen Wills won her third straight U.S. Championship, defeating Kitty McKane of Great Britain, 3-6, 6-0, 6-2, in the final. Wills won both her matches in Wightman Cup play at Forest Hills, but Great Britain won the competition for the second straight year, 4-3. Dorothea Douglass Chambers, 46, who lost an epic singles confrontation with Suzanne Lenglen in the 1919 Wimbledon final, won a singles match over No. 5 American Eleanor Goss, 7-5, 3-6, 6-1, and participated in one of Britain's two doubles victories.

1926

Suzanne Lenglen and Helen Wills met in what would be the only confrontation between the women generally recognized as two of the greatest players of all time. One writer called this match "the most important sporting event of modern times exclusively in the hands of the fair sex"—this five decades before two of the fair sex met Bobby Riggs.

Wills took off early in the year for a trip to southern France to participate in invitation tournaments on the Riviera and what some observers regarded as a chance for a showdown with Lenglen. "This girl must be mad," Lenglen told a

Football immortal Red Grange (left) and promoter C. C. "Cash and Carry" Pyle welcome Suzanne Lenglen as she turns pro in September 1926. (UPI)

close friend. "Does she think she can come and beat me on my home court?"

Chaotic and dramatic was the scene as they collided in the final of the normally insignificant Carlton Club tourney at Cannes that became a magnet for press from across the globe. Ticket scalpers abounded, carpenters barely completed auxiliary stands before the match began. Those shut out at the game commandeered ladders, rooftops and trees for a glimpse of the two goddesses of the game squaring off in the limited arena, crammed with about 3,000 witnesses. Lenglen won, 6-3, 8-6, in 63 minutes, though given a fright, pushed as never before or after,

falling apart in tears after Wills erred on a fourth match point.

Confusion took over as Lenglen served at double-match point, 6-5, 40-15, and a spectator called "Out!" though a Wills forehand sped along the line for a winner. Thinking she'd won, Lenglen relaxed, basking in the cheers of compatriots who felt she'd turned back the California invader. However, the no-nonsense Wimbledonian, umpire George Hillyard, restored order after ascertaining that Wills' shot was good. Play resumed. Frazzled, Lenglen lost serve to 6-6. Then she turned on her greatness again, perhaps for the last time, and seized the remaining two furiously

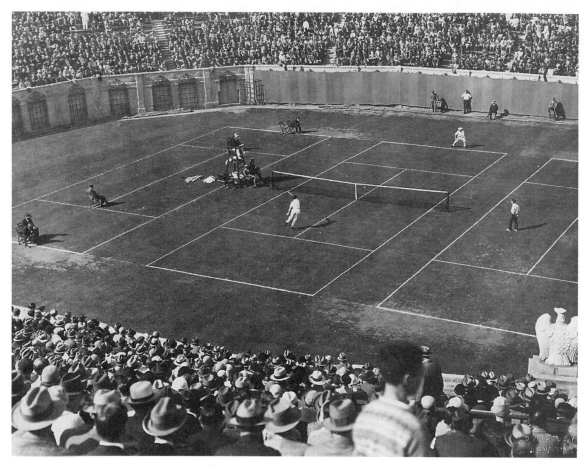

In an all-French final at Forest Hills, René Lacoste (far court) won the U.S. crown in 1926 in straight sets over Jean Borotra. (Fischer Collection/SPS)

contested games, both going to deuce twice. "She's terrific," lauded Wills. "It was one of my greatest matches."

Lenglen's brilliant amateur career came to a sad end amid controversy at Wimbledon when she failed to show up on time for a women's doubles match at which King George V and Queen Mary were present. Due to a mixup after a scheduling change, Lenglen arrived at Centre Court after the King and Queen had left. This drew a reprimand and she became hysterical. She never quite recovered, though the officials agreed to postpone her match. Meeting hostility from the crowds and in the press, Lenglen lost her doubles

match. She won a first-round singles match and an opening mixed doubles, but then withdrew from the tournament. She never played amateur tennis again, signing on as a pro with American promoter Charles C. "Cash and Carry" Pyle. She went on a North American tour, winning nightly (38-0) over ex-U.S. champ Mary K. Browne, 35.

Unable to entice Bill Tilden to professionalism, Pyle settled for the next best American, Vinnie Richards, 23. He completed the troupe with Americans Howard Kinsey and Fred Snodgrass, and Frenchman Paul Feret—the original touring pros.

After debuting at New York's Madison

Square Garden on Oct. 9, where they drew 13,000 and grossed $40,000, they traveled the U.S. and into Canada by train. Lasting four months over the winter of 1926–27, the tour was a success. It was reported that Lenglen was paid a $25,000 bonus beyond her $50,000 guarantee, and that Pyle, who had no interest in tennis as such, made about $80,000 while putting pro tennis into operation.

With Lenglen out of Wimbledon, the title was won by Kitty McKane Godfree of Great Britain over Lili de Alvarez of Spain, 6-2, 4-6, 6-3. The U.S. title, which had been the property of Helen Wills, was opened to others when Wills was sidelined after an appendicitis operation. Molla Mallory came back to win the championship for a record eighth time. Molla was 42, the oldest of all major singles champs. The sentimental favorite of the crowd, she defeated Elizabeth Ryan, 4-6, 6-4, 9-7, after trailing, 4-0, in the third set, and saving a match point.

The six-year reign of Bill Tilden came to an end in the U.S. Championships when he was eliminated in the quarterfinals by Henri Cochet, 6-8, 6-1, 6-3, 1-6, 8-6. This stopped Tilden's record U.S. run at 42 matches.

In many ways Tilden came to be more popular in defeat than he had been as the kingpin of the sport. Allison Danzig wrote of the Tilden-Cochet match: "The climax of the match, the point at which the gallery broke into the wildest demonstrations, was during the final set when Tilden, trailing at 1-4, rallied to volley Cochet dizzy with one of the most sensational exhibitions he ever gave at the net and pull up to 4-all. Every winning shot of the American was greeted with roars of applause. Tilden, 33, then led, 15-40, on Cochet's serve, but fell back."

Bill Johnston also lost in the same round, to Jean Borotra in five sets. Borotra advanced to make it an all-French final by eliminating Vincent Richards. René Lacoste eliminated Henri Cochet in the semifinals and then beat Borotra for the title, 6-4, 6-0, 6-4.

Henri Cochet overcame two-set deficits against Frank Hunter, Bill Tilden and Jean Borotra to capture Wimbledon in 1927. (UPI)

It was the first time since 1917 that Tilden did not make the U.S. final, the first time since 1920 he didn't win; it was the first of three years in which Forest Hills and Wimbledon would be swept by the French.

Although Lacoste was ill, unable to defend, a third straight all-French final was the Wimbledon prospect as Borotra eluded a set point in the second while squeezing past Cochet, 2-6, 7-5, 2-6, 6-3, 7-5, and Jacques Brugnon held five match points in the fifth against American Bob Kinsey. But Kinsey escaped, 6-4, 4-6, 6-3, 3-6, 9-7, only to fall to Borotra's volleying that overcame his defense and clever lobs. Kinsey lost, 8-6, 6-1, 6-3. He carried on to make a rare "cripple," losing the doubles and mixed finals as well, with Vinnie Richards and Mary K. Browne, a last splash before turning pro with the Lenglen tour.

Uncommon attention focused on a men's doubles first-rounder as the left handed 31-year-old Duke of York (later King George VI) played alongside Louis Grieg. They were soundly beaten, 6-1, 6-3, 6-2, by a couple of commoners, old crocks and ex-champs, Roper Barrett, 52, and

Arthur Gore, 58. Embarrassed, His Royal Highness, the lone member of the royal family ever to compete, abstained as Big W entrant thereafter. Kitty McKane Godfree and her new husband, Leslie Godfree, became the only married couple to win the mixed.

A record seventh straight Davis Cup was taken by the U.S., a 4-1 defeat of the ever-advancing French at Germantown Cricket Club. Johnston and Tilden's opening-day sweep of Lacoste and Borotra respectively with only Little Bill losing a set, and Vinnie Richards and Dick Williams's straight-set putdown of Cochet and Brugnon, made the third day meaningless. Except that Tilden, showing signs of wear, was beaten by Lacoste, 4-6, 6-4, 8-6, 8-6. It was Big Bill's first loss in an important match since 1919, ending his Cup singles streak at 16, a record not broken until 1975. Then Bjorn Borg eclipsed it, extending the record to 33 in 1980, his last year.

The French title went to Cochet, 6-2, 6-4, 6-3, over Lacoste, the second all-domestic finale after the tournament welcomed aliens in 1925. Outsiders were becoming more interested, and New Yorker Richards was a semifinal loser to Cochet. Lefty Jack Hawkes took the Australian.

Though playing without Helen Wills, the U.S. tied the Wightman Cup competition at 2-all, defeating Great Britain at Wimbledon, 4-3, with a pair of doubles and singles triumphs. Elizabeth Ryan split in singles and won her doubles match teamed with Mary K. Browne. She and Browne also won the Wimbledon women's doubles, and Ryan teamed with Eleanor Goss to win the U.S. crown.

1927

One of the most astounding turnarounds in the history of tennis occurred in the semifinals at Wimbledon. Bill Tilden at 34 was no longer the supreme tennis player in the world, but he was a legendary figure, imposing and formidable still, seeded second (seedings had just been introduced) only to Lacoste in his first appearance at

Helen Wills (left), with Lili de Alvarez, her victim in the Wimbledon final, also won the U.S. and French titles in 1928. (UPI)

Wimbledon since he won there in 1921. Playing fourth-seeded Henri Cochet, Tilden won the first two sets, reached 5-1, 15-all in the third set and then lost, probably as great a collapse as any outstanding tennis figure would ever experience.

Big Bill had beaten Cochet in a straight set semi at the French. He may have felt he needed to do the same this time, remembering that he'd lost the three-hour Paris final in five, 6-4, 4-6, 5-7, 6-3, 11-9, to Lacoste—61 games, the longest French title match—after holding two match points on serve (9-8, 40-15). So Tilden went for winners with big forehands, missing three, and Cochet was off on a 17-point binge that lifted him to 5-5, 30-0. Even though Tilden got back in it on a break to 3-2 in the fifth, the inexorable force was with Cochet, roaring to perhaps the most remarkable of Wimbledon championships. His finishing off of Tilden, 2-6, 4-6, 7-5, 6-4, 6-3, was only the appetizer, as it turned out.

Tilden later wrote: "I have heard many interesting, curious, quite inaccurate accounts of what happened. One ingenious explanation was that King Alfonso of Spain arrived at 5-1 in the third set and I decided to let him see some of the match. . . . Ridiculous! I didn't even know he was there. Another was that a group of Hindus hypnotized me. If they did, I didn't know it, but they certainly did a swell job. Personally, I have no satisfactory explanation. All I know is my coordination cracked wide open and I couldn't put a ball in court."

Before ambushing Tilden, Cochet had also come out of the 0-2 pit to beat Bill's doubles partner, Frank Hunter, 3-6, 3-6, 6-2, 6-2, 6-3. But he saved the most exciting for last, overcoming Borotra (a 6-2 in the fifth winner over Lacoste in the semis) through six match points at the climax, 4-6, 4-6, 6-3, 6-4, 7-5. Cochet dodged one bullet on his own serve to 3-5, then five more with Borotra trying to serve it out in the next game. From the sixth match point (Borotra missing a volley), Cochet pounced, grabbing 15 of the remaining 18 points.

Wallis Myers, the game's foremost critic, declared Cochet "was favored by the gods." Obviously. Wimbledon secretary Duncan Macaulay wrote, "Cochet was incredibly cool in a crisis— so much that I sometimes wondered whether he really knew what the score was." Footnote: In the doubles final, Cochet and Jacques Brugnon led Tilden and Frank Hunter, two sets to love, 5-3, 40-15, on Cochet's serve for the match, only to be up-ended, 1-6, 4-6, 8-6, 6-3, 6-4.

René Lacoste (the Crocodile) won three great matches over Tilden this year to establish his own supremacy in the sport. He won the French and U.S. Championships in extraordinary finals and also beat Tilden in a crucial Davis Cup match, saving two match points. In the Forest Hills final, Lacoste may have played the best tennis of his life, defeating Tilden, 11-9, 6-3, 11-9.

"It was a match," Allison Danzig wrote, "the like of which will not be seen again soon. On one side of the net stood [Tilden], the perfect tactician and most ruthless stroker the game probably has ever seen, master of every shot and skilled in the necromancy of spin. On the other side was the player who has reduced defense to a mathematical science; who has done more than that, who has developed his defense to the state where it becomes an offense, subconscious in its workings but nonetheless effective in the pressure it brings to bear as the ball is sent back deeper and deeper and into more and more remote territory."

Lacoste, whose career was cut short by illness and who became famous for his sports-shirt line with the crocodile emblem on the chest, never played at Forest Hills again.

America's record seven-year reign came to an end in the Davis Cup. France broke through in its third challenge with a 3-2 victory over the U.S. team that included the two men who had brought America the Cup in 1920, Tilden and Johnston. Lacoste beat Johnston, then Tilden beat Cochet, and the Americans took a 2-1 lead on a doubles victory by Tilden and Frank Hunter over Jean Borotra and Jacques Brugnon. Tilden could not come through with another victory, however. He fell to Lacoste, 6-3, 4-6, 6-3, 6-2, and the Cup moved to France when Johnston was beaten by Cochet, 6-4, 4-6, 6-2, 6-4 in a dramatic match. The overflow crowd of 15,000 at the Germantown Cricket Club was so carried away in loudly pulling for an American victory that, a report said, "it broke all bounds of tennis etiquette and cheered madly both Johnston's winning shots and Cochet's mistakes."

With Suzanne Lenglen off in the professional ranks, Helen Wills (called Little Miss Poker Face because of her lack of expression on the court) assumed complete dominance of the women's ranks at 22. She began a string of four Wimbledon titles with a 6-2, 6-3 victory over Spaniard Lili de Alvarez. Wills won her fourth straight U.S. Championship, defeating 19-year-old Helen

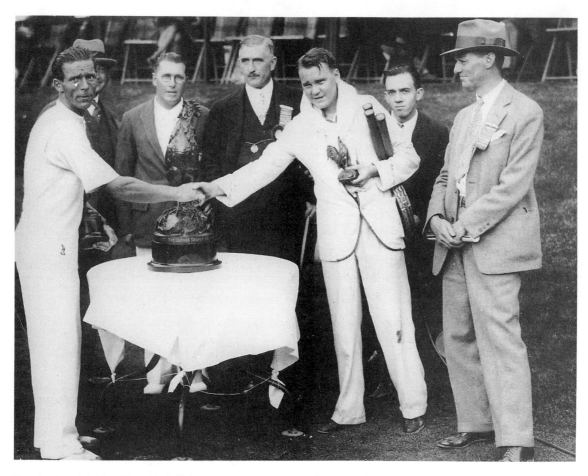

Czechoslovakia's Karel Kozeluh (left) is congratulated by Vinnie Richards after Kozeluh won the U.S. Pro championship at Forest Hills in 1929. (UPI)

Jacobs in the semifinal and 16-year-old Betty Nuthall of England in the final, 6-1, 6-4.

The United States went ahead in Wightman Cup play, 3-2, beating the British, 5-2, at Forest Hills. Wills and Molla Mallory both won a pair of singles matches, and Wills teamed with Hazel Wightman for a doubles triumph.

A new concrete horseshoe stadium seating 13,000 at Kooyong in Melbourne, in the style of Forest Hills, was opened for the Australian Championships and remained the focal point of tennis Down Under for six decades until the 1988 unveiling of Flinders Park. The title matches were suitably grand. In high 90s heat for 3½

hours Gerald Patterson fought off Jack Hawkes, 3-6, 6-4, 3-6, 18-16, 6-3. He served his way off the ledge of four match points at 12-13, and another at 15-16. Runnerup five straight years, Esna Boyd revived to snap out of it and beat Sylvia Lance, 5-7, 6-1, 6-2.

The first U.S. Pro Championships was played in New York, Vinnie Richards winning over Howard Kinsey, 11-9, 6-4, 6-3.

1928

Controversy raged much of the year between Bill Tilden and the USTA over Tilden's writing newspaper articles about tennis, a violation of

Time marches on: An electric scoreboard was installed at Wimbledon in 1929. (UPI)

Tilden then went out and played what teammate George Lott called his greatest match of all time. He defeated Lacoste on clay—the first time grass hadn't been the surface for the Cup deciding round—1-6, 6-4, 6-4, 2-6, 6-3. Afterward, Lacoste said, "Two years ago I knew at last how to beat him. Now, he beats me. I never knew how the ball would come off the court, he concealed it so well. I had to wait to see how much it was spinning—and sometimes it didn't spin at all. Is he not the greatest player of all time?"

That victory was not enough. Tilden lost to Henri Cochet. Both Lacoste and Cochet beat John Hennessey, and the Cochet-Jean Borotra team beat Tilden and Frank Hunter for a 4-1 French triumph. The ranks of the Davis Cup, which was contested for by six countries in 1920, had now swelled to 33 participants.

French supremacy carried to the major championships where, for the first time, one country's representatives swept all four major championships, a "Gallic Grand Slam." Cochet won the U.S. and French crowns, Lacoste his second Wimbledon title and Borotra the Australian Championship.

With Tilden and Lacoste missing from Forest Hills, Cochet won by beating Frank Shields in the semifinal and Frank Hunter in the final, 4-6, 6-4, 3-6, 7-5, 6-3. It was the third straight victory by a Frenchman at Forest Hills, and it would turn out to be the last. Except for Cochet, who would be runner-up in the 1932 U.S. final, there would be no outstanding Frenchman to play in the United States, let alone win, after the retirements of Lacoste and Borotra, until Cedric Pioline lost the 1993 final to Pete Sampras. At Wimbledon, a Lacoste-Cochet final was set up when Lacoste scored a five-set victory over Tilden, 2-6, 6-4, 2-6, 6-4, 6-3 and Cochet beat countryman Christian Boussus. Lacoste won, 6-1, 4-6, 6-4, 6-2.

In the Wightman Cup matches Great Britain evened the series again, 3-all, with a 4-3 victory gained on two doubles triumphs. The American victories came as Helen Wills won both her sin-

amateur rules. Tilden was suspended, missing the interzone Davis Cup defeat of Italy. As the finale with France approached, other members of the American team threatened to strike. René Lacoste announced he would not defend his title at Forest Hills. He said, "We would rather lose the Davis Cup than retain it where there may be some excuse in the absence of Tilden."

Having built Stade Roland Garros for the Cup defense (and subsequent French Championships), and needing Tilden's presence to fill the seats, French tennis officials protested the suspension, along with the press and public. To the rescue, U.S. Ambassador Myron T. Herrick defused a potential Franco-American crisis by suggesting to State Department superiors that they lean on the USTA to restore Tilden to the lineup. The USTA diplomatically bowed for the moment, although presently barring Big Bill again, keeping him out of the U.S. Championship.

Bill Tilden's valedictory as an amateur in 1930 included his third Wimbledon title in singles, over Wilmer Allison (right). (UPI)

gles and Helen Jacobs won in Wightman Cup play for the first time. Both lost in separate doubles matches, and 44-year-old Molla Mallory lost twice in the singles.

Wills became the first to hold three majors in one year, and convincingly: 6-1, 6-2, over Englishwoman Eileen Bennett at the French; 6-2, 6-3, over Spaniard Lili de Alvarez at Wimbledon; 6-2, 6-1, over Helen Jacobs at the U.S., first of the intriguing battles of the Helens from Berkeley. (Wills never journeyed to Australia). As much was made of her reserved manner as her skills. W. O. McGeehan wrote in the New York *Herald Tribune*, "She is powerful, repressed and imperturbable. She plays her game with a silent, deadly earnestness, concentrated on her work. That, of course, is the way to win games, but it does not please galleries. Of course, there is no reason

why an amateur athlete should try to please galleries." Daphne Akhurst won the Australian.

Vinnie Richards succeeded C. C. Pyle as a promoter of professional matches and imported Karel Kozeluh, a Czech who was being acclaimed as a great player even though he had never played on the amateur circuit. In a head-to-head duel with Richards, Kozeluh proved superior on clay and hardwood, winning a majority of the matches (13-7), but he lost on grass to Richards in the second U.S. Pro Championships.

1929

In the years the French were dominating Wimbledon and Forest Hills, Tilden was still the most dynamic figure in the sport. René Lacoste wrote, "He seems to exercise a strange fascination over his opponents as well as his spectators. Tilden, even when beaten, always leaves the impression on the public mind that he was superior to the victor."

The French had broken Tilden's six-year dominance at Forest Hills, and now Tilden ended the three-year French reign. He won the U.S. title for the seventh time, coming back from 2-1 set deficits against John Doeg in the semifinals and against Frank Hunter in a 3-6, 6-3, 4-6, 6-2, 6-4 final triumph. At 36, he was the second oldest man to win the U.S. crown. Bill Larned won in 1910 and 1911 at 37 and 38.

After Lacoste gave way to illness following his French championship, Henri Cochet became the No. 1 Frenchman. He won the last all-French final at Wimbledon, beating Jean Borotra, 6-4, 6-3, 6-4, after defeating Tilden in the semifinals, 6-4, 6-1, 7-5. Great Britain's future great, Fred Perry, 6-4, 6-1, 7-5, made his Wimbledon debut, losing in the third round to John Olliff.

France was extended in winning a third successive Davis Cup competition over the United States. Cochet beat Tilden, 6-3, 6-1, 6-2, then Borotra beat American newcomer George Lott, 6-1, 3-6, 6-4, 7-5. The U.S. doubles team of John

Van Ryn and Wilmer Allison beat Cochet and Borotra, 6-1, 8-6, 6-4, and then Tilden beat Borotra, 4-6, 6-1, 6-4, 7-5, tying the competition at 2-all. In the deciding match, Cochet defeated the 22-year-old Lott, 6-1, 3-6, 6-0, 6-3.

Helen Wills, now Mrs. Fred Moody, was never more supreme. She swept Wimbledon and Forest Hills for the third straight year and the French Championship for the second, 6-3, 6-4 over Simone Mathieu. In the first of four Wimbledon finals she would win over Helen Jacobs, she romped, 6-1, 6-2. At the U.S. Championships, Jacobs was eliminated in the semifinals by Britain's Phoebe Watson, and Wills shut out 45-year-old Molla Mallory, 6-0, 6-0. Wills then beat Watson, 6-4, 6-2. South African Billie Tapscott caused an echoing wave of criticism by being the first female player to be seen at Wimbledon without stockings.

Wills led the American team to a 4-3 Wightman Cup victory on the strength of singles superiority. Wills beat Watson and Betty Nuthall, Jacobs beat Nuthall, and Edith Cross beat Peggy Michell. The English won two doubles matches, and Watson beat Jacobs in the other singles. The U.S. led in the series, 4-3, no team having taken a more than one-match lead since the Wightman Cup inaugural in 1923.

Colin Gregory of Britain and Australian Daphne Akhurst won the Australian singles titles.

In what still was a minor aspect of the sport, the U.S. Pro Championships was contested for again by Vinnie Richards and the Czech Karel Kozeluh. This time Kozeluh won a squeaker, 6-4, 6-4, 4-6, 4-6, 7-5.

1930

Bill Tilden's magnificent career as an amateur came to an end on the last day of the year when he officially announced he was turning professional. He bowed out after one of the most glorious victories of his career. He won his third Wimbledon, becoming at 37 years, five months,

Nineteen-year-old Sidney Wood made history when he won Wimbledon in 1931. (UPI)

the second oldest man to win the Wimbledon singles title. Arthur Gore won at 41 in 1909.

Tilden, seeded second, beat unseeded 25-year-old Texan Wilmer Allison 10 years and six days after winning his first Wimbledon over Gerald Patterson. Before defeating Allison, 6-3, 9-7, 6-4, Tilden survived a tough one, 7-5 in the fifth over Borotra, who led 3-1 in the stretch. Allison, who had removed first-seeded Henri Cochet in the quarters, also scored, 7-5 in the fifth over countryman Johnny Doeg.

Tilden had his most successful European tour, winning the Austrian, Italian and Dutch Championships, losing to Cochet in the French final, 3-6, 8-6, 6-3, 6-1. Ranked No. 1 in the United States for the 10th time, Tilden wanted badly to break a tie with Bill Larned and Richard Sears by winning the U.S. title for an eighth time. He came a cropper against 21-year-old Californian Doeg, a big left-hander with a powerful serve, a formidable opponent when he had control of his ground game. Eighth seed Doeg made 28 aces, 12 in the final set, losing his serve only once in 29 games, and beat Tilden, 10-8, 6-3, 3-6, 12-10. Doeg hit his serve so hard, it was reported that he turned the ball into an ellipse; it was called his "egg ball." The loss marked the first time Tilden had been beaten by a countryman in a U.S. Championship since Bill Johnston 11 years earlier. Doeg then beat 19-year-old Frank Shields in the final, 10-8, 1-6, 6-4, 16-14. Shields, seeded eleventh, had a set point at 13-14 cancelled by an ace.

Tilden's record in U.S. Championships showed 78 matches, at least one every year since 1916, except for 1928, when he was suspended. He won 71, lost seven. He won 210 sets and lost 56.

Tilden, who had a long love-hate relationship with crowds that admired his gallant efforts in the face of defeat and his sportsmanship, but didn't like some of his showboating, now had no great goals to achieve as an amateur. Frank Deford wrote in his biography of Tilden:

"Frustrated by the reductions of age, appearing more effeminate in his gestures (Tilden would die a lonely, broken figure at 60 after two convictions on morals charges), he became testier, even petty, on the court. Once, on the Riviera, in a match of no consequence, the umpire, an Englishman, finally just got up and departed when Tilden kept fussing. Once, at South Orange, New Jersey, he rudely informed the tournament chairman that Big Bill Tilden was not accustomed to competing on grass that had the texture of cow pasture, and had to be coaxed back onto the court."

Earlier in the year, Tilden played in his 11th consecutive and last Davis Cup final round. Despite an injured ankle, he came back from a slow start to beat Jean Borotra in four sets. He then lost to Henri Cochet in four sets, his final Davis Cup appearance. George Lott, who would make his

mark as a doubles player, was beaten in both singles by Cochet and Borotra, and the French doubles team of Cochet and Jacques Brugnon beat Wilmer Allison and John Van Ryn for a 4-1 victory, France's fourth in a row.

The year marked the first appearances in the U.S. Top Ten rankings of Sidney Wood, No. 4; Ellsworth Vines, No. 8; and Bitsy Grant, No. 10.

Queen Helen, now Mrs. Helen Wills Moody, won Wimbledon for the fourth straight year without working up too much of a sweat in a 6-2, 6-2 final triumph over Elizabeth Ryan. Moody and Ryan teamed to win the doubles over Edith Cross and Sarah Palfrey, making her Wimbledon debut at 17. Moody did not play at Forest Hills, and Britain's 19-year-old Betty Nuthall won. Daphne Akhurst won the Australian women's title for the third straight year and Gar Moon defeated Harry Hopman for the men's crown.

For the fifth time in the eight-year rivalry, Wightman Cup competition ended in a 4-3 score, Great Britain evening the series at 4-all. Moody won her two singles matches, Helen Jacobs split her two matches, and the pair suffered one of the two doubles defeats when they played together in a loss to Phoebe Watson and Kitty Godfree. Watson and Phyllis Mudford won singles matches over Jacobs and Palfrey, respectively.

Women's dress continued to be less cumbersome. Lili de Alvarez was wearing a pagodalike trouser dress. Eileen Bennett and Betty Nuthall showed up at Wimbledon with open-backed tennis dresses, and necklines continued to drop.

1931

Sidney Wood first appeared at Wimbledon as a 15-year-old wearing white knickers on the Centre Court and losing to René Lacoste. Wood returned at 19, became the youngest player in this century (until 17-year-old Boris Becker in 1985) to win and the only one ever to win an unplayed Wimbledon final in a walkover.

Wood, who was seeded seventh, advanced to the final, 4-6, 6-2, 6-4, 6-2, over 22-year-old Fred Perry, a winner in an early round over a promising young German, Gottfried von Cramm.

Facing top-seeded Borotra, fresh from winning the French, Shields managed to win their semi, 7-5, 3-6, 6-4, 6-4, although twisting an ankle near the end. Frank was ordered by the U.S. Davis Cup committee to default to teammate Wood in order to recuperate for a Cup meeting against Britain the following weekend in Paris, where the winner would meet France for the Cup in the challenge round. "Frank wanted to play me, and it was an insult to Wimbledon and the public that he didn't," recalls Wood. "But it gives you an idea of the importance of Davis Cup then, and the USTA's tight control of American amateurs. Can you imagine a player today abandoning a Wimbledon final to save himself for Davis Cup? But, as amateurs, we had no say. Frank played well against the Brits, beating Fred Perry, but we lost, 3-2."

Ellsworth Vines, who had been ranked No. 8 in 1930 and hadn't been picked for the Davis Cup team early in the year, came into his own at 19 when he won the United States Championship in September. Vines, from Pasadena, Cal., was a lanky 6-foot-1, weighing only 145 pounds, who had a great cannonball serve. Analyst Julius Heldman wrote, "He had the flattest set of ground strokes ever seen and they were hit so hard, particularly on the forehand, that they could not clear the net by more than a few inches without going out."

Fred Perry scared Vines in the semis winning the first two sets, but the champ served his way out (4-6, 3-6, 6-4, 6-4, 6-3) and concluded by beating George Lott for the title, 7-9, 6-3, 9-7, 7-5, despite trailing 5-3 in the third and 5-2 in the fourth. Lott, who came from two sets down to outlast Johnny Van Ryn in the quarters, next knocked out the defender, Johnny Doeg, 7-5, 6-3, 6-0. At Sydney, uniquely among the majors, a husband and wife took shots at the Australian singles titles. All-timer Jack Crawford made it, the first of his four, 6-4, 6-2, 2-6, 6-1, over Harry Hopman, but

The U.S. Championship and Wimbledon were 20-year-old Ellsworth Vines' conquests in 1932. (UPI)

Marjorie Cox Crawford couldn't bring in a spouses double, falling to Coral Buttsworth, 1-6, 6-3, 6-4. Still, the Crawfords won the mixed, starting a three-year run of success.

Playing without Bill Tilden, the U.S. failed to appear in the challenge round of the Davis Cup for the first time since 1914. It appeared the U.S. would have a crack at the French in the challenge round when, in the inter-zone final, after a loss by Sidney Wood to Great Britain's Bunny Austin, the U.S. took a 2-1 lead as Shields beat Perry, and the American doubles team of Lott and John Van Ryn beat George Hughes and Perry. Britain prevailed, however, as Perry beat Wood, and Austin defeated Shields in the decider, 8-6, 6-3, 7-5.

In the challenge round, France won, 3-2, for the fifth straight time, on a doubles victory and two singles triumphs by Henri Cochet, the second over Perry in the climactic match, 6-4, 1-6, 9-7, 6-3.

With Helen Wills Moody choosing not to play at Wimbledon, it appeared that Helen Jacobs would have an excellent opportunity to win, particularly after she beat Betty Nuthall, the 1931 Forest Hills winner, in a quarterfinal. Jacobs lost, however, in the semifinal to Hilde Krahwinkel, and in the only all-German Wimbledon final five-foot Cilly Aussem defeated Krahwinkel, 6-2, 7-5. Aussem had beaten Nuthall in the French final, 8-6, 6-1.

Arriving at Forest Hills after missing the 1930 tourney, and without a major title for 1931 (having skipped Wimbledon and the French), Moody rectified that by taking her seventh (and last) U.S. title in 35 minutes over Eileen Bennett Whittingstall of England, 6-4, 6-1. By the end of 1931 Moody had gone four years without losing a set!

As the U.S. and Great Britain prepared for the Wightman Cup matches, they were tied at 4-all. The U.S. won 5-2, with both Moody and Jacobs winning a pair of singles. This was the start of a 21-year string of U.S. Wightman Cup victories that would not be broken until 1958.

Bill Tilden made his long-awaited debut as a professional in the midst of the Depression. Co-promoter of his tour with entrepreneur William O'Brien, Tilden opened against Czech Karel Kozeluh at Madison Square Garden on Feb. 18 before a crowd of 13,000 paying $36,000. Tilden won, 6-4, 6-2, 6-4, then ran off 16 straight victories and went on to beat Kozeluh before big galleries at almost every stop (27-6) of a cross-country tour that grossed $238,000.

Frank Hunter, Robert Seller and Emmett Pare played subordinate roles on the tour. Other professionals at the time were Hans Nusslein and Roman Najuch of Germany, the three Irish Burke brothers—Albert, Thomas, Edmund—living in France; and Major Rendell of England. At Forest Hills during the summer, the U.S. Pro Championships drew a field of 39, Tilden trouncing Vinnie Richards, 7-5, 6-2, 6-1 in the final.

1932

Ellsworth Vines became the first man since Bill Tilden in 1921 to win both the Wimbledon and U.S. Championships. Competing in his first Wimbledon at 20, Vines was so impressive that some English reporters were calling him the greatest player of all time.

He defeated Australia's Harry Hopman in an early round and sailed through Australia's Jack Crawford and Britain's Bunny Austin, 6-4, 6-2, 6-0, in the last two rounds in straight sets. Vines scored 30 service aces against Austin, who broke his serve only once. Vines' match point was a service ace and Austin said, "I saw him swing his racket and I heard the ball hit the back canvas. The umpire called game, set and match, so I knew it was all over, but I never saw the ball." Vines' serve was timed at 121 miles per hour (Pancho Gonzalez' serve was later measured at 118 miles per hour).

Crawford, the winner of the Australian Championship, had beaten Fred Perry in the quarterfinals. An oddity of the tournament was top-seeded Henri Cochet losing in the second round to Ian Collins, then entering and winning the All England Plate competition for also-rans eliminated in the first two rounds. He became the first ex-champion to win the Plate.

Americans were so impressed with Vines at Wimbledon that hopes were high the U.S. would win back the Davis Cup after the U.S. had advanced past Great Britain in the inter-zone final. Vines showed himself to be less than invincible, however, losing to Jean Borotra in the first singles, 6-4, 6-2, 3-6, 6-4. When Cochet beat Wilmer Allison in the second singles, it looked as if France would win easily. A doubles triumph by Allison and John Van Ryn over Cochet and Jacques Brugnon, however, tightened things and set up one of the most controversial episodes in Davis Cup history: The Great Cup Theft.

First, the groundskeepers heavily watered the clay at Stade Roland Garros in the hope of slowing the court down to hamper Vines in his final

Helen Wills Moody's default to Helen Jacobs (left) in 1933 marked Moody's last appearance in a Forest Hills final. *(New York Herald Tribune)*

match. The slow court served instead to bother Borotra in the third singles against Allison. But Borotra, only days from his 34th birthday and reluctant to join the team, had one last gallant Cup thrust within him. Despite losing the first two sets to Allison, he rode the roars of a chauvinistic jam-packed crowd of 10,000 and volleyed his way back to parity. With gestures he called for their help, and thrice the Bounding Basque bought revival time in the fifth set by changing his flimsy espadrille-style shoes, once during a game. Still, Allison worked his way to a 5-3 lead with serve, 40-15, then advantage—but squandered the three match points, one a net cord shot by the Frenchman. The final blow came at a sub-

sequent match point on Borotra's serve at 4-5. Borotra netted his first serve. The second was long, so long that a relieved Allison, who had performed so well over the three days, hit the ball aside, making no attempt to play it. He moved to the net to shake hands.

"We were cheering," recalls Van Ryn, "thinking it was all tied up at 2-2. But then the umpire [Morin] announced, 'Egalite'—deuce—and we couldn't believe it. The service linesman [Gerrard le Ferrier, thereafter considering himself a notable patriot] had stolen the win. He made no call and indicated the serve was good. The umpire backed him up. That was too much for

Wilmer, and he lost the last three games [10 of the remaining 12 points]. Dwight Davis, who sat next to me, was so mad that he withheld us from attending the official dinner that night. It was an incredible rebuke to the French from such a great sportsman. I only heard him cuss once, and it was then. He said, 'I'm sorry I ever gave the goddam Cup!' " Most newspaper accounts, including the French, agreed that Borotra's second serve was clearly long.

Fans were left to debate whether Cochet, who won the first two sets and then lost the final match to Vines, would have been able to pull through if France needed that point. This was the sixth straight Davis Cup for France, and her last—until 1991.

Vines, who often wore a white cap, had a curious windmill stroke in which the racket made an almost 360-degree sweep. Starting on high as though he were going to serve, he brought the racket head back almost to the ground and swept up to the ball. He put no spin on it, however, thereby hitting a flat shot with tremendous force that made him unbeatable when he was on.

Opponents came to realize that the way to beat Vines was to keep the ball in play, hitting him soft stuff until he started making errors. A harbinger of all that came in one of the memorable U.S. semifinals at Forest Hills. Cliff Sutter, the National Intercollegiate champ from Tulane, won the first two sets, and twice came within two points of victory (5-6, deuce in the third set; 5-6, 30-all in the fourth), but Vines persevered in the exhausting 75-game, 2 1/2-hour struggle, 4-6, 8-10, 12-10, 10-8, 6-1. That left little time for the Cochet-Allison semi, and they were chased by darkness at two sets apiece. It meant finishing a semi the same day as the final, the lone such incident in the Championships history. Beating Allison in the 45-minute fifth, 7-5, Cochet, almost 31, was given about two hours to rest for the final against Vines, who wouldn't be 21 until the end of the month. He complained, justifiably, about having to play again that day, but the USTA wasn't going to turn away an overflow

crowd of 15,000. Henri had a point in saying that American officiating in treatment of a foreigner was no better than that received, and bemoaned, by the Americans in the recent Davis Cup contest in Paris. He was plainly weary in the 6-4, 6-4, 6-4 defeat.

Twice he was unable to move out of the way in time to avoid being hit by Vines' blinding serve. The last two aces of the match by Vines were so hard that they bounced into the stands. Cochet never returned to Forest Hills.

Helen Wills Moody returned to Wimbledon after a one-year absence and won her fifth title. She lost only 13 games in the 12 sets she had to play. For the second time in the final she met Helen Jacobs, and won, 6-3, 6-1. Moody also won her fourth French Championship. Jacobs raised eyebrows playing in what now are regarded as Bermuda shorts.

With Moody absent from Forest Hills, Jacobs won the U.S. Championship for the first time, defeating third-seeded Carolin Babcock in the final, 6-2, 6-2. Alice Marble made her first appearance in the U.S. rankings at No. 7 and was a finalist in the women's doubles at Forest Hills. Mrs. Coral Buttsworth won her second successive Australian title.

The U.S. took a 6-4 lead in Wightman Cup play on a 4-3 victory. Moody won two singles matches, Jacobs and Anna McCune Harper one each. Bill Tilden continued to dominate the thin professional ranks with a mixture of tennis skill and theatrical showmanship. He, Vinnie Richards and the German, Hans Nusslein, were the tour's standouts. Tilden faced Nusslein 100 times, winning 60, and was 12-1 over Richards, but Karel Kozeluh beat Nusslein, 6-2, 6-2, 7-5, for the U.S. pro title.

1933

Helen Wills Moody and Suzanne Lenglen are regarded by many long-time observers as two of the greatest women players of all time. It is an

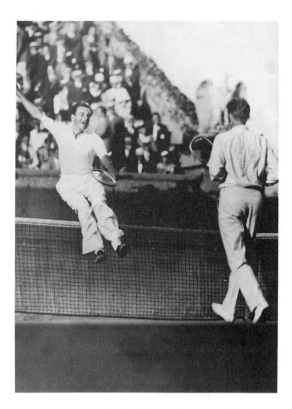

His leap says it all for Fred Perry, winner over Jack Crawford in the 1933 U.S. final. (New York Herald Tribune)

irony that both are also remembered for matches they lost—in which they defaulted and walked off the court. Lenglen defaulted to Molla Mallory at Forest Hills in 1921, and Moody quit in the middle of her U.S. final with Helen Jacobs in 1933.

The two Helens—Moody, almost 28, tall, dark-haired, and coldly methodical, and Jacobs, 25, stocky and outgoing—were natural rivals. They both came from the San Francisco Bay area. Both had the same coach, William "Pop" Fuller. When they met for the second time in this U.S. final, Moody had long been the dominant figure. She had won her sixth Wimbledon title earlier in the year, over Dorothy Round, 6-4, 6-8, 6-3. She had won seven U.S. titles and had never lost to Jacobs after trouncing her, 6-0, 6-0, the first time they played. She beat her in two Wimbledon finals and the 1928 Forest Hills finale. Ja-

cobs had won Forest Hills in 1932 when Moody did not compete.

Though Jacobs insisted there was no feud, she wanted badly to beat Moody. She went to none other than Lenglen, who drilled her in hitting crosscourt so that she would avoid giving Moody the backcourt dominance she liked best. Jacobs, the faster, was determined to play the net as often as possible.

In the semifinal Moody had lost her first set in seven years at Forest Hills to Betty Nuthall. Jacobs proceeded to take her first set ever from Moody, 8-6. Moody won the second, 6-3, using drop shots to tire her opponent. Given a respite in the intermission, Jacobs broke Moody's service in the opening game and then again for a 3-0 advantage. In his history of tennis, Will Grimsley wrote: "At this point Moody strode to the umpire's chair and put on her sweater. 'I am sorry, my back pains me. I cannot go on,' she said tersely. That was all she said. Wearing a long coat, her familiar eyeshade pulled low, she strode to the dressing room. She declined an interview."

It was reported that Jacobs pleaded with her to continue. Jacobs denied this, saying she merely inquired if she would like to rest. Moody said no and walked away without shaking hands. The fans were stunned. The press lambasted her for not trying to finish the match. She was accused of being a poor sport, a quitter, ungracious. Later she said, "I feel that I have spoiled the finish of the U.S. Championships and wish that I had followed the advice of my doctor and returned to California. I still feel I did right in withdrawing because I was on the verge of collapse on the court."

The loss was her first since she had been beaten by Lenglen in 1926, ending a 27-tournament, 158-match winning streak.

Lining up without Moody (due to her back injury that would precipitate her walk-out at Forest Hills) and Alice Marble (heat exhaustion) in singles, the U.S. still won the Wightman Cup over Britain, 4-3, as Jacobs beat Round, then Peggy Scriven (5-7, 6-2, 7-5), Sarah Palfrey beat

Scriven and Jacobs-Palfrey won the decisive doubles over Round and Mary Heeley, 6-4, 6-2.

But the ordeal of Marble just days before in the compressed tournament at Easthampton, N.Y., not only kept her out of Cup singles but diminished her at Forest Hills (fourth-round loss despite three match points to Nuthall), and may have contributed to her physical collapse and absence from tennis for most of 1934 and 1935. Playing singles and double semis and finals during one oppressive 104-degree day, Alice labored a total of 108 games over a period of 8 ½ hours, suffering sunstroke. She had asked to play only doubles in the three-day event, but was told by USTA official Julian Myrick that she had to play both to be considered for the Wightman team. "I was heartbroken," she wrote, "when a doctor told me I was too weak to play singles. I'd never been on the team and worked so hard to make it."

Before Don Budge was to come along and popularize the notion of the Grand Slam—victories within a calendar year in the Australian, French, Wimbledon and U.S. Championships—Australia's Jack Crawford came within a set of achieving that sweep, missing out only at Forest Hills in a five-set loss to Fred Perry.

Wimbledon Secretary Duncan Macaulay wrote in *Behind the Scene at Wimbledon:* "Jack Crawford was one of the most popular champions who ever appeared at Wimbledon. Although he was only 25 when he won the title, he always seemed much older. Perhaps it was the effect of his hair, parted in the middle, the sleeves of his cricket shirt buttoned at the wrist (though he was known to roll them up in moments of crisis) and, most of all, the old-fashioned square-headed racquet with which he always played. In a long match he liked to have a pot of tea, complete with milk and sugar, and reserves of hot water, by the umpire's chair, instead of the iced beverages and other revivers favored by the moderns."

English authority Max Robertson wrote in 1974 that if a poll were taken about the best men's singles final at Wimbledon, "the Crawford–

Ellsworth Vines match in 1933 would probably head it; certainly it would have to be included in the top six." Vines' service earned him 13 aces and he ran out 11 service games at love. Crawford played a defensive game against Vines' power, concentrating on Vines' relatively weak backhand. They split the first two sets, then the next two. Then Crawford changed tactics, rushing the net. He broke Vines at the end, winning the last game at love on Vines' serve. The score: 4-6, 11-9, 6-2, 2-6, 6-4.

The crowd exulted over the first victory by a player from the British Empire since another Australian, Gerald Patterson, won 10 years earlier. Macaulay wrote, "The cheering of the spectators went on and on, and their enthusiasm was so great there appeared to be a distinct danger that the sacred turf of the Centre Court would be invaded by the multitude."

There were two innovations at Wimbledon. Vivian McGrath, an Australian, showed his two-handed backhand. Brit Bunny Austin wore shorts for the first time on the Centre Court. (He had previously worn them at Forest Hills in 1932.) Henri Cochet put on a pair, but only for the mixed doubles, and his opponent, Norman Farquharson, rolled up his trousers.

A big disappointment at Wimbledon was fourth-seeded Fred Perry, who lost in the second round to Farquharson, a South African. Perry finally achieved his first major title, at Forest Hills, when he outlasted Crawford in a grueling match, 6-3, 11-13, 4-6, 6-0, 6-1. Defending champion Vines lost in the fourth round in straight sets to 5-foot-4 Bitsy Grant in what was called a Mutt & Jeff match.

The term "Grand Slam" didn't exist as Crawford began his circumnavigatory journey toward the undone by winning his homeland's title a third time in succession, this one over Californian Keith Gledhill, 2-6, 7-5, 6-3, 6-2, on a soggy court at Melbourne where 19-year-old Joan Hartigan unseated champ Coral Buttsworth, 6-4, 6-3. Crawford had to share plaudits with a countryman, "the freak"—17-year-old Vivian McGrath, who knocked off favorite Ellsworth Vines with his unconventional two-fisted backhand drives, the first both-handed stroke to be seen in the upper class.

Stricken by an asthma attack in France, Crawford nevertheless recovered in time to dethrone Henri Cochet, 8-6, 6-1, 6-3, the first alien male to win the French. Completing the distress of the locals was another dethroning, that of Simone Mathieu by unseeded 20-year-old Brit lefty, Peggy Scriven, 6-2, 4-6, 6-4.

Next for Crawford came his glorious Wimbledon deposing of Vines (although he was pressed in the opening round, running four games from 2-4 in the fifth to beat Spaniard Enrique Maier). But by the time Jack arrived, against his wishes, in New York, he was bushed, anxious to go home after almost five months on the road. Having won 13 straight tournaments, troubled by insomnia and asthma, he wanted to skip the U.S. However, the Australian Association got a $1,500 payment from the USTA guaranteeing his presence at Forest Hills, and he had no choice. People were beginning to talk of an unprecedented "clean sweep of the Big Four titles," and *New York Times* columnist John Kieran, a bridge player, wrote: "If Crawford wins, it would be something like scoring a grand slam on the courts, doubled and vulnerable."

It looked as though he would make it, getting to the final on the loss of two sets, and leading Perry 2-1 in sets at the intermission. But Jack was through, and would win only one more game. While Perry showered and changed, returning to the court refreshed, Crawford, drained, unwisely remained at the court, sitting in wet clothes. Unknown to him, his friend Vinnie Richards had spiked Jack's tea with bourbon as a pick-me-up. No help. Perhaps a hindrance. But no alibis. There never were from Crawford. And Perry—"I just went mad!"—came on like a firehorse to win eight games on a gallop, and his first major, 6-3, 11-13, 4-6, 6-0, 6-1. No sweep/grand slam. Not for five years.

After his early Wimbledon loss, Perry began making his move to greatness. It started in Paris with the heist of the Davis Cup. After Perry spearheaded Britain's first Cup-seizing triumph since 1912, the front page banner headline in London's Daily Express read simply. FRED! The Brits ended France's six-year (11-victory) reign, 3-2, at Stade Roland Garros as Perry, dodging two set points in the second, overcame a spirited rookie, 19-year-old lefty Andre Merlin in the decisive fifth match, 4-6, 8-6, 6-2, 7-5. He stopped Cochet in five the first day, 8-10, 6-4, 8-6, 3-6, 6-1, blotting a set point in the third. Bunny Austin whipped Merlin fast, and it was 2-0. But Borotra and Brugnon raced through the doubles, and the third day crowd of 10,000 filling Stade Roland Garros was agog as Cochet tied it by outlasting Austin in five, 5-7, 6-4, 4-6, 6-4, 6-4, and then Merlin was a stroke from a two-set lead over Perry.

Austin had started something as a fashion plate, and only Perry, of the four single players, wore long trousers. But his season record was the longest of anyone to play with a Cup winner: working 13 of a possible 14 singles and six of seven doubles, he was 12-1 and 4-2. Austin was 13-1 in singles.

Bill Tilden's opponent on the professional tour was again Hans Nusslein of Germany. Tilden dominated, though gross receipts dropped from $86,000 the year before to $62,000. Henri Cochet also turned pro and was beaten by Tilden in his debut in Paris, 6-2, 6-4, 6-2.

1934

Fred Perry came into his own as the best, bringing his homeland its first Wimbledon championship since 1909 (Arthur Gore), the year he was born. Moreover he became the second man to hold three majors in one year, following up on Jack Crawford's splendid 1933. But just as Fred had dashed Crawford's bid for a Grand Slam at the U.S., his own were cancelled early, in the French quarters, by the forehands-only man, ambidextrous Italian racket-switcher Giorgio de Stefani. Perry's resistance was sapped by spraining his right ankle in the last set, the fourth.

Conversely, Crawford became the first to lose three majors in a year: Australian, French and his seventh straight major final, Wimbledon. He didn't enter the U.S. Fred shattered Jack's three-year grip on the Australian in Sydney, 6-3, 7-5, 6-1, and repeated in the U.S., over Texan Wilmer Allison, 6-4, 6-3, 1-6, 3-6, 8-6. In between he collaborated again with Bunny Austin to keep the Davis Cup in London, 4-1 over the U.S.

The only American Cup comeback ever from 0-2 put the quartet of Sidney Wood, Frank Shields, George Lott and Les Stoefen into the challenge round, 3-2, over Australia at Wimbledon. Lott and Stoefen won a holding action over Crawford and Adrian Quist, 6-4, 6-4, 2-6, 6-4, and then Wood and Shields reversed the first day's results: Sidney jolted Crawford, 6-3, 9-7, 4-6, 6-2, and Shields forcefully clinched over 18-year-old Viv McGrath, 6-4, 6-2, 6-4. However, Lott and Stoefen, the Wimbledon and U.S. champs, beating Harold Lee and George Hughes in four, weren't enough to divert the British tide. Austin and Perry beat up on Wood and Shields, although Perry had to rebound from 1-2 in sets to beat Wood, and then met tremendous resistance from Shields in clinching, 6-4, 4-6, 6-2, 15-13, after the tall American had served for the fourth set at 11-10, 15-0.

In his *History of Forest Hills,* Robert Minton wrote, "Perry combined speed with a wristy forehand developed from first playing table tennis, of which he became the world champion. He was an enormous crowd pleaser; handsome enough to be a movie star, and a cocky showman in a white blazer and an unlit pipe, as though he were a Lord, and not the son of a Labor Party member of Parliament. He never ruffled anyone with a display of temper, for he was phlegmatic and won his matches by outlasting his opponents. His physical condition was second to none."

Australia's Jack Crawford, No. 1 in the world rankings in 1933 after missing a Grand Slam, lost to Fred Perry in the 1934 Wimbledon final. (UPI)

Reporter Ferdinand Kuhn said of Perry's 6-3, 6-0, 7-5 Wimbledon triumph: "Perry was always the complete master. He didn't make a half-dozen bad shots in the whole match. He was lithe as a panther, always holding the opponent in check and beating Crawford at his own cool, cautious game. Once he performed the amazing feat of capturing 12 games in a row." Perry said, "If I live to be 100, I'll never play so well again."

At the end, with Crawford serving at match point, he hit what looked like an ace, but he was called for a foot fault. He was so shaken by the call, he then served into the net, the first time anybody could remember a Wimbledon final ending on a double fault.

Britain's joy was complete when Dorothy Round won the women's title, and afterward, to a tumultuous ovation, she and Perry were summoned to the Royal Box to be presented to King George V and Queen Mary.

The women's final had come to down to a meeting between Round, who had been beaten in the 1933 final by Helen Wills Moody, and Helen Jacobs, who had lost to Moody in the 1929 and 1932 finals. Playing before the King and Queen in a scene much like Virginia Wade's Wimbledon Centenary victory in 1977, Round won the first set, 6-2, lost, 7-5; then triumphed in the finale, 6-3.

Slick-stroking German nobleman, Baron Gottfried von Cramm, almost 25, made his first big move, taking the French title from Crawford, 6-4, 7-9, 3-6, 7-5, 6-3, by erasing a match point at 5-4 in the fourth with a brilliant overhead smash from the baseline. Repeaters were Joan Hartigan at the Australian and Peggy Scriven at the French. Scriven, the English southpaw who had won unseeded in 1933, registered probably her finest victory, 7-5, 4-6, 6-1, over U.S. champ Helen Jacobs. Hartigan, 21, fended off 40-year-old Mall Molesworth, the champ of 1922–23, 6-1, 6-4.

By now shorts and bare legs were much in evidence at Wimbledon. The Prince of Wales said, "I see no reason on earth why any woman should not wear shorts for lawn tennis. They are very comfortable and quite the most practical costume for the game; and I don't think the wearers lose anything in looks."

Elizabeth Ryan teamed with France's Simone Mathieu to win the women's doubles crown, her 19th at Wimbledon, a record that Billie Jean King later would tie and surpass in 1979. Ryan won 12 doubles and 7 mixed-doubles titles. Wimbledon official Duncan Macaulay discussed why Ryan, so strong in doubles, never won a major singles championship: "Firstly, her era coincided with that of two superlative singles champions, Suzanne Lenglen and Mrs. Moody; and secondly, Miss Ryan's only stroke on the forehead was a sizzling chop, very effective in doubles—particularly against women—but not so ef-

fective in singles as a good flat or topspin drive such as Lenglen or Moody played to perfection."

South African Vernon Kirby was the Forest Hills sensation, beating a 19-year-old future great, first-timer Don Budge, and first-seeded American Shields. But Perry cooled him in the semis, and steadied at the climax of the final to win, 8-6 in the fifth after a threatening Allison had volleyed away Fred's 5-2 lead. Several rainstorms caused the tourney to end four days late.

Sarah Palfrey Fabyan, almost 22 and playing her seventh U.S. Championships, got to her first final, but Jacobs—winning a third straight—was too tough, 6-1, 6-4, and Sarah would have to wait a long time to claim the title, until 1941. Lott and Stoefen, the team of the year, won the U.S. Doubles again, virtuoso George's fifth title, the 6-4 Stoefen his third partner.

The U.S. increased its Wightman Cup lead to 8-4 with a 5-2 triumph powered by Jacobs and Palfrey. Each won singles over Dorothy Round and Peggy Scriven, and they combined to win a doubles match.

The pro tour needed some new blood and got it with the arrival of Ellsworth Vines. With much fanfare before a Madison Square Garden crowd of 14,637, Vines, 23, made his debut against Bill Tilden, 41. The match grossed $30,125 and Tilden won, 8-6, 6-3, 6-2. They went on a tour of 72 cities, grossing $243,000, the most ever for the pros, and Vines beat Tilden, 47 matches to 26. Vines won a match in Los Angeles, 6-0, 21-23, 7-5, 3-6, 6-2. Another memorable match between old adversaries Tilden and Henri Cochet took place at the Garden before a crowd of 12,663, paying $20,000, and Tilden outlasted the 32-year-old Cochet, 7-9, 6-1, 4-6, 6-3, 6-3.

1935

Probably no player ever suffered as much frustration against an arch-rival as Helen Jacobs did against Helen Wills Moody. The only time Jacobs beat Moody, the victory was less than fully satisfying because it came as a result of a default when back trouble forced Moody to quit the 1933 final at Forest Hills while losing. All other times Jacobs lost to her, and among the toughest setbacks was the 1935 Wimbledon final.

Moody had played little the year before and was seeded only fourth in pursuit of her seventh Wimbledon title. Early in the season she had lost a set to Mary Hardwick, had lost a match to Kay Stammers, and in an early Wimbledon round against unknown Czech Slenca Cepkova she lost the first set and was within a point of trailing 4-1 in the second set before rallying.

In the final Jacobs, seeded third, fell behind, 4-0, almost tied at 4-4, then faltered and lost the first set 6-3. Of the second set British authority Max Robertson wrote, "Jacobs' length improved; her favorite forehand chop became as dangerous as a scimitar. Mrs. Moody tried to come to the net but she was never able to run up and down the court as well as she could cover it from side to side." Jacobs won the second set.

Jacobs took a 4-2 lead, knocking the racket from Moody's hand on one powerful serve. She then broke Moody to lead, 5-2, but Moody broke to 3-5, where she faced a match point at 30-40, and flicked a desperation lob with Jacobs at the net. It looked like a simple smash, but a gusty wind caused the ball to sink swiftly, so that Jacobs had to drop to her knees to hit it—into the net. That turned the match around. Jacobs went down fighting, serving two aces when trailing, 5-6, but lost the set and match, 6-3, 3-6, 7-5. It was her fourth loss to Moody at Wimbledon, the third time in a final. She also lost to her in the 1928 Forest Hills final.

Fred Perry was clearly the cream of the men's brew for the second straight year, even through an injury probably caused him to lose his U.S. title, and Jack Crawford rose up to deprive him of the Australian in a baselining rematch of the 1934 final, 2-6, 6-4, 6-4, 6-4. However, Fred would always chuckle over his triple-bageling (6-0, 6-0, 6-0) of Giorgio de Stefani in the quarters.

Wilmer Allison won his only U.S. Singles title in 1935. (USTA)

"I told Giorgio after he beat me in Paris '34 [possibly costing Fred a Grand Slam] that I wouldn't allow him a game next time, and I meant it." Illness kept Joan Hartigan from going for a third straight Aussie title, and instead two Englishwomen grappled for her crown, Dorothy Round beating Nancy Lyle, 1-6, 6-1, 6-3. However, a recovered Hartigan later toppled Round from her Wimbledon throne in the quarters.

In Paris, Perry had his revenge over Crawford, 6-3, 8-6, 6-3, in the semis, ending Jack's run of consecutive major final-round roles at eight (four in 1933, three in 1934). In the title round Perry bounced 1934 champ Gottfried von Cramm, 6-3, 3-6, 6-1, 6-3, thus adding the French to his stash and becoming the first to have won all four majors. His countrywoman, Peggy Scriven, didn't fare as well. After two straight titles and 14 match wins in a row on the clay, she delighted the locals by losing to Simone Mathieu in the semis, 8-6, 6-1. But their joy was short-lived as long-legged German-born Danish citizen Hilde Krahwinkel Sperling followed up on her semifinal elimination of favorite Jacobs (7-5, 6-3) to beat Mathieu for the title, 6-2, 6-1.

At Wimbledon, Perry beat Crawford in four sets, then trounced von Cramm, the first German male to make the final, 6-2, 6-4, 6-4. Von Cramm had eliminated Don Budge in a semi, and it was Budge, unseeded, who created the sensation of the tournament by beating third-seeded Bunny Austin in a quarterfinal. During that match there was an interruption for Queen Mary to take her seat in the Royal Box. It was written by one British reporter the next day that Budge had waved to the Queen. The story grew that Budge even said, "Hi, Queenie," and Budge took pains in his autobiography to point out that he did not wave, that he did wipe his brow, a reflex gesture with him. Two years later, though, when Budge was again at Wimbledon and met the Queen, she told him, he said, "You know, Mr. Budge, I did not see you a few years ago when you waved to me, but had I, I want you to know that I would have waved back."

The Wimbledon mixed final was marked by the appearance of Mr. and Mrs. Harry Hopman— she the former Nell Hall—of Australia. They were beaten by Perry and Dorothy Round, 7-5, 4-6, 6-2.

Budge appeared in the U.S. Davis Cup line-up for the first time and drove the team straight to the challenge round with five straight singles wins, the last two in four sets over Henner Henkel and von Cramm as the Yanks beat Germany, 4-1, at Wimbledon. Wilmer Allison and Johnny Van Ryn rescued five match points in winning the electrifying and pivotal doubles over von Cramm and Kay Lund, 3-6, 6-3, 5-7, 9-7, 8-6, to set up attack-minded Allison for the clincher over Henkel, 6-1, 7-5, 11-9. But the Americans' high spirits and hopes to seize the Cup from the Brits were splintered as Allison missed a huge opportunity in the tense five-set opener against Austin. Serving match game at 4-5, Austin double-faulted to 15-30 as the overflowing crowd of 16,000 in Centre Court groaned. Painful for the invaders was the next point: Allison, charging the net, netted a routine volley that would have placed him commandingly at double match point. Reprieved, Austin ran it out, 6-2, 2-6, 4-6, 6-3, 7-5, and the 5-0 British avalanche to a third straight Cup was underway. Perry sprang on Budge, 6-0, 6-8, 6-3, 6-4, and, startlingly, Allison and Van Ryn couldn't find their usual Cup touch in the clutch, falling to the newly paired Pat Hughes and Charles Tuckey, 6-2, 1-6, 6-8, 6-3, 6-3.

Thirty-year-old Allison would feel a lot better at Forest Hills in his eighth assault on the U.S. title. He had fallen short against Perry in the 1934 final, but this time Perry fell, literally and heavily, on damp grass in the seventh game of their semi. It was later learned that Perry, clutching his back throughout, had damaged a kidney. Fred was beaten, 7-5, 6-3, 6-2, losing the title he'd won the two previous years. Second-seeded Don Budge was felled, too, in unlikely fashion by tiny Bitsy Grant in the quarters. Thereupon Sidney Wood stepped over Grant to the final where he was a 40-minute lunch for Allison, 6-2, 6-2, 6-3. A quarter-finalist in 1929, semifinalist in 1932, Allison wasn't going to miss. His superb groundies and furious volleying made certain now, and Wilmer felt that the title was a suitable going-away gift to himself. He would not be seen at Forest Hills again.

For the first time the dolls were seen along with the guys in the merging of singles Championships, a togetherness continuing to this day. Relentless Jacobs, permitting 30 games and no sets in six starts, grasped the title a fourth consecutive year, equalling the 1915–18 surge of Molla Mallory. In a reprise of the 1934 final, Helen beat Sarah Palfrey Fabyan, 6-2, 6-4.

Both women played strong roles in a 4-3 Wightman Cup win. Though beaten by Kay Stammers the first day, as Britain jumped to a 2-1 lead, Jacobs rebounded to top Dorothy Round, 6-3, 6-2, and join Fabyan (a 6-0, 6-3 winner over

Phyllis King) in the decisive doubles triumph, 6-3, 6-2, over Stammers and Freda James.

George Lott and Les Stoefen turned pro, but Tilden, 42, let Lott know who was in charge. Before a record American crowd of 16,000 at Madison Square Garden the old master gave the 29-year-old rookie a 6-4, 7-5 paddling. Big Bill, though bageled twice, won his second U.S. Pro title, 0-6, 6-1, 6-4, 0-6, 6-4, over Karel Kozeluh.

1936

Fred Perry turned pro late in the year after dominating tennis for four years as few men have over such a span. He won three successive Wimbledon titles, three U.S. titles, a French and an Australian title, and nine out of 10 Davis Cup challenge round victories.

Perry had laid off for seven months after his kidney injury at Forest Hills in 1935, and when he was beaten in the French final by Gottfried von Cramm, 6-0, 6-2, 2-6, 6-2, 6-0—the last set in ten minutes—there was some question that he could retain his old form. At Wimbledon, however, he quickly established that he would be formidable by sailing through early-round opponents. He beat Bitsy Grant in straight sets, then had what would turn out to be his only difficult moments of the tournament, losing the first set to fifth-seeded Don Budge in the semifinals. Perry rallied to win in four sets, 5-7, 6-4, 6-3, 6-4. He then had an easy time in the final when von Cramm ruptured an Achilles tendon in the first set. Von Cramm continued, limping on a bad leg, and Perry won, 6-1, 6-1, 6-0, the widest margin of victory in a Wimbledon final.

It was the first time since the pre–World War I days that somebody had won three straight Wimbledons, and Perry was on hand in 1978 as a radio commentator when Bjorn Borg did the same.

It was the last Wimbledon in which the hosts fared so well, taking four of the five titles: Pat Hughes and Charles Tuckey, Freda James and

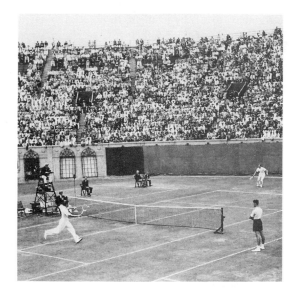

Fred Perry (far court) won his third U.S. Singles championship in 1936, defeating Don Budge. (UPI)

Kay Stammers prize winners in doubles, Perry and Dorothy Round in mixed. Only the women's singles was captured by an invader.

So many times Helen Jacobs had come agonizingly close to winning Wimbledon, as close as a 1935 title-round match point against her nemesis, the other Helen (Wills Moody) that was gone with the wind. But on her ninth visit she went all the way to goal-sweet-goal, in her fifth final, 6-2, 4-6, 7-5, over Hilde Krahwinkel Sperling, the French champ. Finishing jitters appeared to get her after leading 3-1 in the second and third sets. Serving for the championship at 6-5, 40-15, Helen missed out on two match points and then slumped to break point. Was it a sour echo of '35? Nope. She firmed up and took the last three points.

Kept out of the 1935 Australian by illness, Joan Hartigan was back to win her third straight, 6-4, 6-4, this over a fresh face, 18-year-old Nancye Wynne, presently a setter of records Down under. Nancye won the doubles with Thelma Coyne, a partnership that would account for ten homeland titles, the last in 1952. Jack Crawford's sixth straight final was his last, and it went the other way, to a rising shorty, Adrian Quist, only just, 6-2, 6-3, 4-6, 3-6, 9-7.

A repeat final at the French and a repeat champion. That was Sperling, who disappointed the home folks again by beating Simone Mathieu just about as soundly, 6-3, 6-4.

Crawford and Quist got together for Australia to astound the U.S. in merely the Americans' second Davis Cup series of the year, 3-2, at Germantown Cricket Club, despite Don Budge's beating both of them. It was, however, the last hurrah for U.S. champ Wilmer Allison—a hoarse one—as one of the more illustrious Cup careers, of eight years, ended in two defeats, the clincher by Crawford, 4-6, 6-3, 4-6, 6-2, 6-2. It had turned on the doubles, a debut together that went awry for Budge and Gene Mako, a great alliance in the making. Quist slithered out of two match points at 4-5, 15-40 in the fourth, initially as Mako bungled a short and simple smash, and the Aussies regrouped for a 4-6, 2-6, 6-4, 7-5, 6-4 victory that climaxed with their momentous running the last five games on a loss of seven points.

Not for a dozen years had a team from Down Under ascended to the challenge round. Australia had lost to the U.S. in 1924. Now the Aussies were back again, 3-2 victors over Germany in the penultimate series at Wimbledon. Von Cramm knocked out Quist altogether on the grim, blustery first day after Crawford had beaten a flu-ridden Henner Henkel (6-2, 6-2, default). Not only did the German ace save three match points at 7-8, 0-40 in the screamer that he won on a tenth match point of his own, 4-6, 6-4, 4-6, 6-4, 11-9, but it turned into a TKO because the scrappy Quist twisted an ankle and was finished for the series. From the bench came twenty-year-old Viv McGrath to stand forth as Cup hero. Siding with Crawford for a 6-4, 4-6, 6-4, 6-4 win over Henkel and von Cramm, Viv then clinched, 6-3, 5-7, 6-4, 6-4, over Henkel.

But the same good old impediments awaited the challenger: the one-two punches of Perry, the goodbye guy in the last four Cup successes, and

Austin. They did their first-day stuff for 2-0. Austin scored his first significant win over Crawford, 4-6, 6-3, 6-1, 6-1, before Perry sidestepped a set point while inflating from 5-1 down in the third to beat Quist, 6-1, 4-6, 7-5, 6-2. The Aussies stormed back to take the doubles from Hughes and Tuckey, 6-4, 2-6, 7-5, 10-8, and arrive at 2-2 as Quist stung Austin, 6-4, 3-6, 7-5, 6-2.

What a moment for Perry to stride onto the revered greensward for his Centre Court valedictory before 16,000 patriots. His 52nd and concluding Cup assignment on behalf of his country during six campaigns. He had broken a 2-2 deadlock three years before to wrest the Cup from France by beating Andre Merlin. Again he was in a similar cauldron with the Cup at stake. It was what he lived for, and Fred bolted from the starting gate, rushing his long-time foe and friend Crawford off the court, 6-2, 6-3, 6-3. During their four years on top, Britain's run of 10-0, Perry and Austin had been virtually untouchable in singles with respective marks of 18-1 and 17-3.

Perry and Budge, Wimbledon antagonists, met for a final time in a major setting, the U.S. title bout. It was a classic in five gripping sets, twice interrupted by downpours, a spiky encounter in which both wore spikes, and future Grand Slammer Budge, 21, clung to two match points on his serve at 5-3 in the fifth. But he lacked the resolve to cash one against fiercely resisting Fred, who won, 2-6, 6-2, 1-6, 8-6, 10-8. Point and counter-point they went as Budge, in his first major final, neared the championship again and again, serving for it also at 7-6 and 8-7, two points away, only to be blocked. Every point was a war, but Perry coolly won the last three games, the only man other than Bill Tilden to carry off three titles from Forest Hills. It was Fred's eighth major singles, good for second place all-time then behind Tilden's 10. They would be overtaken by Roy Emerson (12), Rod Laver and Bjorn Borg (11), Fred eventually tied by Ken Rosewall, Jimmy Connors, Ivan Lendl and Pete Sampras. Budge would play six more major finals winning them all.

Perry and Budge met again in a Forest Hills final that represented Budge's last chance to beat Perry in a major tournament before Perry turned pro. They played a classic five-set match twice interrupted by rain. Budge won the first set, 6-2, Perry the second by the same score. Budge won, 8-6, then Perry, 6-1.

Of the fifth set, Budge later wrote, "We held serve to 3-2, my favor, and then I got the break for 4-2. Promptly, I permitted Fred to break me back. My serve was a dishrag. However, tired as I was, I was able to break him back again, so I stood at 5-3, serving twice one point away for the Championship of my country against the No. 1 player in the world. All I had to do was hold my serve. I could not. I was so exhausted in reaching up to hit my serve that I felt as if I were leaning on the ball. There was no life in my shots. The stretching and reaching for the serve particularly wore on me. He broke me again—our fourth loss of service in a row—held his own serve at last, and tied the set at 5-all."

Probably the greatest recovery from physical and emotional trauma was Alice Marble's to win the U.S. Championship in 1936, at least until those of Thomas Muster in 1990 and Monica Seles in 1995 (Muster's left knee had been wrecked in an auto accident in 1989; Seles had been stabbed in 1993). Ranked No. 3 in the U.S. for 1933, she collapsed during a match in Paris the following spring and was hospitalized. Cut down by anemia and pleurisy, Alice didn't play competitively for almost two years. But she was rehabilitated by the American summer of '36, raring to go again. Even though she won the Southern California title on concrete in May, the doubting USTA didn't select her for the Wightman Cup team, even refused her entries to Eastern grass-circuit tourneys. Marble had to prove herself in practice matches at Forest Hills before she was allowed to play at the height of the season. But her fitness was clear as she won two grass-court events enroute to the Championships: Longwood and Seabright (N.J.).

Alice, in the month of her 23rd birthday, was ready to puncture the U.S. bubble of Helen Jacobs, who had won four straight years and took a 28-match Forest Hills streak into the final. Neither had lost a set in the tourney, Jacobs relinquishing but 14 games in five matches. But the striking advances made by the 5-foot-8 Marble, who'd become a net-seizing serve-and-volleyer, were obvious in her surge to a 4-6, 6-3, 6-2 triumph, winning 10 of 11 games from 0-2 down in the second. "The first set was a relief," recalled Marble, who would become an all-timer, the dominant female until she turned pro after winning her fourth U.S. title in 1940. "I was afraid Helen would whitewash me. But I came close, and knew I could beat her."

Without Marble the Wightman Cup thrilled Wimbledon with the closest finish ever, right down to 5-5 in the last set of the last doubles. Sarah Palfrey Fabyan was the heroine of the 4-3 U.S. victory, beating lefty Kay Stammers in a critical second-day singles after both Stammers and Dorothy Round had stopped Jacobs. Moreover, Sarah propped Jacobs in the decisive doubles revival, from 1-3 in the third to 1-6, 6-3, 7-5, to disappoint a crowd of 14,000.

It was a year of struggle and money-losing tours for the pros. Promoter Bill O'Brien's gimmick was signing on two American women of little appeal. Ethel Burkhardt Arnold beat Jane Sharp—they were Nos. 2 and 13 in the U.S. rankings of 1935—in the usual tour opening at Madison Square Garden. In the Wembley indoor tourney in London, at times the best of the pros' infrequent tournaments, Ellsworth Vines won for the third successive year, beating Hans Nusslein, 6-4, 6-4, 6-2.

1937

The line of dominant players, which started with Bill Tilden in the 1920s and continued through the French trio of René Lacoste, Henri Cochet and Jean Borotra, then Ellsworth Vines and Fred Perry, added the imposing red-headed

Princess Helena Victoria presents the Davis Cup to non-playing captain Walter Pate in 1937 as (left to right) Don Budge, Gene Mako, Frank Parker and Bitsy Grant look on. (Fischer Collection/SPS)

figure of Don Budge. Budge, 22, swept Wimbledon and Forest Hills and sailed through all Davis Cup competition, winning what many rate as the greatest Davis Cup match ever played.

Almost 29 and apparently subsiding, Jack Crawford, expected to grace a seventh straight Australian final, failed because a decidedly bizarre-stroking 18-year-old, John Bromwich, was in his way in the semis. Bromwich was also on his own way to the Hall of Fame, a loping left-hander who served rightie with a loosely strung racket and used a two-handed backhand on the right side. Viv McGrath, at 21, reached his zenith, barely beating Brom for the title, 6-3, 1-6, 6-0, 2-

6, 6-1, the first major final in which both competitors employed both-handed backhands. Nancye Wynne, 19, took the first of her six Aussie titles, 6-3, 5-7, 6-4, over Emily Hood Westacott.

With Franco-German tension expanding, the home folks didn't much care for the second straight Teutonic double at Roland Garros, especially Hilde Krahwinkel Sperling (German-born but a Danish citizen through marriage) beating Parisienne Simone Mathieu for a third year in a row, 6-2, 6-4. Sperling's three-straight duplicated Helen Wills' 1928–30 feat, the two of them overtaken by Monica Seles' French reign, 1990–92. Although Gottfried von Cramm didn't defend, his

22-year-old Davis Cup sidekick Henner Henkel came through for the Fatherland, 6-1, 6-4, 6-3, over Bunny Austin.

With Perry moving to the professional ranks, it was obvious that Great Britain would yield the Davis Cup to the strong challenger that emerged from the inter-zone final. Budge spearheaded United States victories over Japan and Australia, beating Aussies Jack Crawford and John Bromwich, to set up a showdown against Germany.

Before Davis Cup play came the Wimbledon in which Budge was seeded first and Gottfried von Cramm second. On his way to the final Budge lost only one set, to Frank Parker in the semifinals, while von Cramm was extended to five sets by Crawford. Budge then defeated von Cramm, 6-3, 6-4, 6-2. Budge also became the first man ever to score a Wimbledon triple, adding the men's doubles title with Gene Mako and the mixed doubles with Alice Marble.

On to the Davis Cup and a match that had implications beyond the tennis court. "War talk was everywhere," Budge recalled. "Hitler was doing everything he could to stir up Germany. The atmosphere was filled with tension although von Cramm was a known anti-Nazi and remained one of the finest gentlemen and most popular players on the circuit."

Two weeks after Budge won Wimbledon, he and teammates Gene Mako, Frank Parker and Bitsy Grant were back on Centre Court to clash with Germany, and stayed there, winning on a July Tuesday. They began stripping the Cup from Britain four days later. Von Cramm took about an hour to beat Bitsy Grant, 6-3, 6-4, 6-2, and Budge less than that to flatten Henkel, 6-2, 6-1, 6-3 and knot the teams at 1-1. Wimbledon doubles champs Budge and Mako held together in the crunch to win the vital, nip-and-tuck doubles over Henkel and von Cramm, 4-6, 7-5, 8-6, 6-4, even though Henkel served for the second set at 5-4, the Germans had a set point against Budge at 4-5 in the third and led 4-1 in the fourth. How vital it was became clear not long after the third

day commenced: Henkel, with stronger serve and better volley, ran up big leads in all but the second set and hung on to topple Grant, 7-5, 2-6, 6-3, 6-4. That set up the decisive match—tantamount to determining the fate of the Cup itself—with that dedicated Budge fan, Queen Mary, in the Royal Box.

Just before Budge and von Cramm went out to the court, von Cramm was called to the telephone. It was a long-distance call from Adolf Hitler exhorting von Cramm to win for the Fatherland. Budge recalls that "Gottfried came out pale and serious and played as if his life depended on every point." (Von Cramm would later be imprisoned for anti-Nazi views, and eventually sent to the Russian front as a soldier, seemingly a death sentence. Henkel was killed in that campaign. However, von Cramm performed valiantly and won an Iron Cross.)

Von Cramm won the first two sets. Budge rallied, took the next two, then fell behind, 1-4, in the fifth. At this point he decided to take desperate measures. Attacking von Cramm's service and going to the net behind it, he got the matching break in the seventh game, making the score, 3-4, and held service to tie, 4-all. The score went to 5-5, then 6-6. In the 13th game Budge achieved another break. He then reached match point five times on his own service only to see von Cramm fight back to attain the sanctuary of deuce. "The crowd was so quiet I am sure they could hear us breathing," Budge recalled.

"On the sixth match point, there was a prolonged rally," Will Grimsley wrote. "Von Cramm sent up a lob. Budge raced back and returned it. Von Cramm then hit a forehand crosscourt. Budge tore after the ball, got his racket on it and took a desperate swing, sprawling to the court. It was a placement—game, set, match and the Davis Cup series. The final score was 6-8, 5-7, 6-4, 6-2, 8-6. The 2-hour, 33-minute match ended at 8:45 p.m. in semi-darkness. The two players went to their dressing rooms, relaxed, dressed and returned more than an hour later to find most of the crowd still on hand, buzzing over the spectacular final."

Because von Cramm was the underdog and the British thought they might have a better chance in a Davis Cup final against the Germans, the crowd slightly favored von Cramm. An oddity of the competition was that the Germans were coached by Bill Tilden. It was not unusual for a pro in one country to coach another country's Davis Cup team, but it was uncommon for a coach to hold the post when it meant working against his own nation. At one point Tilden was so animated in his rooting he infuriated American show-business celebrities Jack Benny, Paul Lukas and columnist Ed Sullivan (a future TV host), who challenged Tilden to a fight. Tilden later told Budge this was the greatest tennis match ever played.

Strictly anticlimactic was the challenge round in which Britain, bereft of Perry, could win only the opening match, Bunny Austin's 6-3, 6-2, 7-5 decision over Parker, inserted for Grant. Rookie Charlie Hare, an attack-minded southpaw, kept 11,000 loyalists hopeful of a 2-0 lead for a long while, leading 3-1 and serving for the first set at 5-4. But Budge was unbudgeable, 15-13, 6-1, 6-2, and a 4-1 victory was in the works. Had the Brits, Frank Wilde and Charles Tuckey, cashed a set point against Mako at 9-10 in the fourth, they might have caused some panic in the go-ahead doubles, but it was won by Gene and Don, 6-3, 7-5, 7-9, 12-10. That left it to Parker to apply the finishing touches which he, too nimble and stingy, did smartly to Hare, 6-2, 6-4, 6-2. The Cup was headed home after 11 years abroad. As 10,000 applauded the transfer, who could guess that Parker 11 years later would win both his singles to help the U.S. defeat Australia in the challenge round, the lone man to play singles with Cup-winners before and after World War II.

The Americans returned with the trophy to a ticker-tape parade in New York, and Budge later was greeted with a parade in his hometown of Oakland, receiving a signet ring that featured the city seal flanked by diamonds. At Forest Hills

von Cramm was pushed hard on his way to the final: four sets by Don McNeill and Hal Surface, followed by three full-distance battles—9-7, 2-6, 2-6, 6-3, 6-3, with pesky Bitsy Grant in the quarters; 0-6, 8-6, 6-8, 6-3, 6-2, with another feisty wind up doll, Bobby Riggs, advanced to No. 6 in the U.S. rankings.

Von Cramm extended Budge to five sets, yet Budge said he felt none of the trauma he found at Wimbledon, which he had won in straight sets. The score this time: 6-1, 7-9, 6-1, 3-6, 6-1. The packed crowd of 14,000 (5,000 were turned away) roared all the way for Budge. He was voted athlete of the year and became the first tennis player to win the Sullivan Award, annually presented to the outstanding amateur athlete in the U.S.

Despite the victory by Alice Marble over Helen Jacobs at Forest Hills the year before, Jacobs was seeded first at Wimbledon and Marble fifth. Alice was first, Helen second at the U.S. But seedings and marquee names meant nothing in a curious year for the women's two biggies where the mischief-makers were a couple of hardly-knowns who'd been playing well in England: a chunky, unpronounceable and unrestrainedly hard-hitting Pole, Jadwiga Jedrzejowska, and a subtle mite of a Chilean, 5-footer Anita Lizana. Seventh-seeded at Wimbledon, Dorothy Round, the champ of 1934, deflated the defender, Jacobs, in the quarters, and Jedrzejowska brought down Marble in the semis, and led Round in their third set, 4-2. But championship experience kept Dorothy calm in her third final, and she took it, 6-2, 2-6, 7-5.

Lizana, a quarterfinal loser who had led champ Jacobs at the same stage in 1936 (4-2, 30-0 in the third), crossed the Atlantic for an incomprehensible tour de force: one visit only to Forest Hills, one title, no sets lost (in fact merely 28 games in six never-bothered matches). Around her tumbled: third-seeded ex-finalist Sarah Palfrey Fabyan in a first-round shaker to No. 13 American Dorothy Andrus; a too casual Marble in the quarters to eager 21-year-old Dodo Bundy; Jacobs in the semis to Jedrzejowska. Lizana cooled the blazing forehand of the Pole in winning, 6-4, 6-2, the first all-foreign U.S. final. That completed a shutout of American women at the four majors, making it their most poverty-stricken year since 1918 when Norwegian Molla Mallory won the U.S., the lone major available in that war year.

International success came in Wightman Cup play with a 6-1 victory over Great Britain, the United States' seventh straight for an 11-4 edge in the series. Marble and Jacobs won twice in singles from Kay Stammers and Mary Hardwick; Sarah Palfrey Fabyan defeated Margot Lumb; and Marble and Fabyan won a doubles point.

Interest in professional tennis revived with the debut of Fred Perry playing a cross-country tour against Ellsworth Vines, promoted by Frank Hunter, Bill Tilden's old doubles partner, and S. Howard Voshell. Perry opened at Madison Square Garden in fine fashion, defeating Vines, 7-5, 3-6, 6-3, 6-4, before a record crowd of 17,630, paying $58,120, a financial record for the tour. Perry won the first six matches, but Vines finished strong, winning the series, 32-29. The tour grossed $412,181. Perry, under his guarantee, received the bigger slice, $91,335, while Vines got $34,195.

Though Vines was regarded as the "official" pro champion at this time, Tilden scheduled himself against Perry in the Garden later in the year. Tilden was 44, Perry 28, and though the crowd of 15,132 cheered mightily for the old guy, he was outclassed. He lost in the Garden for the first time, 6-1, 6-3, 4-6, 6-0. Al Laney wrote in that period, "All they can do is beat him, they cannot ever be his equal." It was estimated that Tilden had netted $500,000 (in Depression dollars) since turning pro six years before.

The Europeans won the significant pro tournaments: German Hans Nusslein the French over Henri Cochet, 6-2, 8-6, 6-3, and Wembley over Tilden, 6-4, 3-6, 6-3, 2-6, 6-3; Czech Karel Kozeluh, his third U.S. over Texan Bruce Barnes, 6-2, 6-3, 4-6, 4-6, 6-1.

In October, a premature—31 years before its time—and rather plaintive event advertised as the "first open championship" was held in the West Virginia Hills at the posh Greenbrier resort. Prize money was offered, but no amateurs of note rushed in to test the waters, and the few unknowns who did were suspended by the USTA. Vines, Tilden and Perry stayed away, too. The event was dominated by the second-line pros, Karel Kozeluh beating Bruce Barnes, 6-2, 6-3, 4-6, 4-6, 6-1, for America's allegedly first open title.

1938

Don Budge at 23 had the single most successful year of any player in tennis history to that time. He won the four major championships—Australia, France, Wimbledon and the U.S.—a feat that came to be known as the Grand Slam after Budge accomplished it. He also won the triple crown at Wimbledon for the second straight year and helped the U.S. retain the Davis Cup.

Budge had received his first substantial offer to go professional in 1937. He turned it down because he felt he owed a debt to amateur tennis to the extent of helping defend the Davis Cup the U.S. had won in 1937 for the first time since 1926. "The Grand Slam then occurred to me as something of an afterthought," Budge said. He laid his plans carefully, telling only his pal/doubles partner Gene Mako, resolving not to extend himself at any time, so that he shouldn't tire along the way, as Jack Crawford had in 1933 when he won the first three titles, but lost in the final at Forest Hills.

Budge started in Australia, after losing frequently in leisurely tune-ups, and he swept through the championships, beating John Bromwich, 6-4, 6-1, 6-1. Shortly after the players' return to their home countries, Gottfried von Cramm of Germany, Budge's friend, was arrested and thrown into jail, charged with homosexuality, but probably imprisoned because of his opposition to Nazi rule. Budge led a committee of

It was the birth of the Grand Slam when Don Budge won the four majors in 1938. (UPI)

athletes appealing without success for von Cramm's release.

In the French Championships, though Budge suffered from diarrhea, he had a fairly easy time. Extended to five sets by a Yugoslav lefty, Franjo Kukuljevic, Budge was never behind and said later he didn't feel threatened. Where von Cramm might have been his opponent in the final, he faced 6-foot-4 Czech Roderich Menzel, an outstanding clay-court player. Budge romped, 6-3, 6-2, 6-4, in less than an hour. He recalled best about that feat the party afterward at which cellist Pablo Casals gave a concert in Budge's honor in Casals' apartment within view of the Eiffel Tower.

At Wimbledon, Budge won without losing a set, yet there was a time in the tournament when he said he was near panic because he had been having trouble with his backhand, his most celebrated weapon, considered by many to have been the greatest backhand of them all. He had been undercutting the stroke, and only while watching an older woman member of the All England Club on a side court, hitting with topspin on her backhand, did he realize his error. He won his second successive Wimbledon by sailing through

Britain's Bunny Austin in the final, 6-1, 6-0, 6-3, then completed another triple with Mako in the men's doubles and Alice Marble in the mixed.

Peppery Bobby Riggs, Davis Cup rookie starting to be noticed, on his way to No. 1 as Budge's successor—he won the U.S. Clay Court title for a third successive year—was just the singles collaborator Budge needed. Lobbing and passing cleverly, Riggs led off with a 4-6, 6-0, 8-6, 6-1 victory over net-charging Adrian Quist at the delight of 10,000 customers. Budge followed up, 6-2, 6-3, 4-6, 7-5, over John Bromwich, who today calls Budge, "the greatest player I've ever seen or played against." Quist and Bromwich kept it alive by beating Budge and Mako, 0-6, 6-3, 6-4, 6-2, giving Don the opportunity to close his Cup career with a clinching crushing of Quist, 8-6, 6-1, 6-2, ending with a 12-match streak.

Budge had been suffering from the flu and a loss of voice off and on during the year. But he proceeded to romp through the U.S. Championships, defeating Welby Van Horn, Bob Kamrath, Charlie Hare, Harry Hopman and Sidney Wood to reach the final against Mako, who had become the first unseeded player ever to reach the final at Forest Hills.

To some it looked like a setup for Budge, but he responded, "Gene was as likely to roll over and play dead for me as peace was to come in our time." Mako actually won the second set, only the fifth Budge lost in the four tournaments. Budge then had to explain that he did not intentionally throw a set to his friend, certainly not at Forest Hills with so much at stake. "And I had too much respect and affection for Gene to treat him as if he were an inferior player who could be given a set for his troubles, rather like a condescending pat on the head."

Bromwich and future king Riggs, who would be ranked Nos. 3-4 in the world for the year, were the only ones given a chance to jam the Slam. But second-seeded Bobby left early, removed in the fourth round by No. 19 American Gil Hunt, who paced himself with nolo-con-tendere sets to win, 6-2, 0-6, 9-7, 0-6, 6-4. The deposed Riggs may have muttered, "After me the deluge!" because soon it came with a vengeance: the Northeast-devastating 1938 hurricane shut down proceedings for six days, making it the longest (Sept. 8–24) of U.S. Championships prior to the open era. When the water receded, four semifinalists were left: No. 8 American Mako, who had removed third foreign seed Puncec, then pierced first foreigner Bromwich, 6-1, 7-5, 6-4; Budge got rid of Sidney Wood, 6-3, 6-3, 6-3. Mako didn't recede. He kept playing at this best, but nobody could deal with the tidal wave called Budge, rolling grandly to the Grand Slam, 6-3, 6-8, 6-2, 6-1, as 12,000 witnessed an historic first.

An undefeated season was not to be for Budge, who took a 1937–38 winning streak back home to California. The Aussies got him at last. Quist, in the semis of the Pacific Southwest at Los Angeles, 7-5, 6-2, 5-7, 6-3, ended the 92-match, 14-tournament string that dated from a January 1937 loss to Bitsy Grant at Tampa, FL. Then Harry Hopman made Budge's farewell to amateurism a downer, 6-2, 5-7, 6-1, in the quarters of the Pacific Coast. But for two years nobody beat Don when it really mattered. His summary for 1938: won six of eight tournaments, 43-2 in matches. While winning Prague he beat a 17-year-old named Jaroslav Drobny, who 45 years later would join him in the Hall of Fame.

Dodo Bundy shared some of the hurrahs with Budge in Adelaide as the first American woman to conquer the Australian, beating Dorothy Stevenson, 6-3, 6-2. Today, as Mrs. Dodo Cheney (81 in 1997), she has far outreached any of her contemporaries, continuing to add to her record number of U.S. senior championships. Simone Mathieu heartened her neighbors by winning the French, a title that eluded her in six other finals, including the immediately previous three to Hilda Krahwinkel Sperling, who didn't enter. Mathieu beat Nelly Adamson Landry, the only Belgian to reach a major final, 6-0, 6-3. Moreover, Simone won the doubles and mixed, an uncommon triple, a dis-

tinction she shares only with Suzanne Lenglen (1925–26) among French at the French.

Aside from Budge's heroics, Wimbledon was marked by one of the stronger women's fields, featuring the return after a two-year absence of 32-year-old Helen Wills Moody, seeking a record eighth title. Though she had been extended by Kay Stammers in Wightman Cup play and had lost in a minor tournament to Hilde Sperling, she was seeded first.

Although unseeded, Helen Jacobs, closing in on her 30th birthday, knew her way around to uproot the eighth and third seeds (Peggy Scriven, Jadwiga Jedrzejowska). She next beat the second, ex-U.S. champ Alice Marble, 6-4, 6-4, spoiling the final everyone wanted: the aging goddess, Moody, against the fresh phenom. Sperling, seeded fourth, tried to wreck it, too, bowing to Moody, 12-10, 6-4, in a tough semi. But the final, their fourth at Wimbledon and the last of 11 Helenic confrontations, was a bust. Unfortunately Jacobs, playing so well, had severely strained an achilles tendon. She came onto the court with it bandaged, struggled to 4-4, then was useless in a 6-4, 6-0, defeat.

Moody, with the edge, 10-1, in their celebrated rivalry, shut her major championships book at 19 singles titles, the record until Margaret Smith Court stepped ahead in 1970 on the way to 24. Steffi Graf also passed her by one in 1996, and in 1990 Martina Navratilova pushed ahead of her at Wimbledon with a ninth title. But can anybody possibly surpass Helen's match record of 55-1 at the Big W, the last 50 uninterrupted? During the tournament Suzanne Lenglen, the woman never beaten there (27-0), died from pernicious anemia. She was 39.

All the female favorites at Forest Hills were imperiled at one time or another. First-seeded Jacobs, four-time champ and never worse than a quarter-finalist since a 1927 debut, was bounced in the third round by a young British lefty, Margot Lumb, 7-5, 6-2. Marble, reinstating herself as champ, escaped by hairs—two match points—

from Sarah Palfrey Fabyan in a volley-rich roller-coaster semi, 5-7, 7-5, 7-5. Marble led 5-1, then trailed 0-4 and 2-5, 15-40, in the second, 1-3 in the third. Aussie Nancye Wynne, the other finalist, scraped through three consecutive three-setters, beating Bundy, 5-7, 6-4, 8-6, to reach the title round. There wasn't much left, however, and for 22 minutes Marble was Hurricane Alice, 6-0, 6-3.

Moody bade goodbye to Wightman Cupping as well as Wimbledon, having been absent since 1932 and scoring wins over Scriven and the clincher, 6-2, 3-6, 6-3, over Kay Stammers, her 18th win in 20 singles starts. Marble also beat Scriven, and Fabyan beat Lumb, enough to assure an eighth straight U.S. victory over the Brits, 5-2.

An eighth straight Wightman Cup success for the United States over Britain, this time 5-2, consisted of two singles triumphs by Moody in her first appearance since 1932, a split in singles by Marble, a singles triumph by Fabyan and a doubles victory by Marble and Fabyan. Moody lost with Bundy in doubles, Moody's seventh defeat in 10 Wightman Cup doubles matches. Moody's overall singles record: 18-2.

Fred Perry and Ellsworth Vines joined together as co-promoters and foes on the pro tour, won by Vines, 49 matches to 35. But Perry won the U.S. Pro title, 6-3, 6-2, 6-4, over Bruce Barnes while Hans Nusslein ruled the European roost, beating Bill Tilden in the Wembley and French Pro finals.

1939

Don Budge, the Grand Slammer, had gone to the pros, the world teetered in precarious shape and Wimbledon was on the brink of going dark for the six years of World War II. But a cocky and quick little Californian was ready to take over for Budge, showing up in three of the major finals and winning two: Wimbledon and the U.S.

Another Californian, Alice Marble, outdid him in her invincibility, winning those two majors—and everything else she went after to craft an undefeated season: nine for nine in tournaments, 45-0 in matches. Suzanne Lenglen and Helen Wills Moody had recorded unbeaten years, but not embracing so many tournaments.

Bobby Riggs's fresh attitude, his willingness to bet on anything, his entire shtick, may have clouded his greatness on court, his resourcefulness in all situations. But foes, especially the better ones, never doubted. He is singular as the only man to play Wimbledon once and win all three titles. He claimed he also won $108,000 wagering on himself to make a triple.

"I started with 500 bucks," he recalled. "A London bookmaker gave me 3-to-1 odds on the singles where I was seeded second behind Bunny Austin. I said if I win, let it ride on the doubles so he gave me 6-to-1 on that. I said let's keep going, so he gave me 12-to-1 on the mixed. I had to win the three or lose it all.

"Even though bookmaking was legal there, I was an amateur, and the USTA would have frowned on betting on tennis. I was afraid of what the USTA would do if they knew an amateur had all that money so I was hush-hush about it. I left the dough in a London bank, figuring I'd pick it up after I turned pro. But the war came, so it sat there gathering interest. A nice nest egg when I got out of the Navy."

Alice Marble also won the singles—6-2, 6-0, over Kay Stammers after double-bageling ex-French champ Heidi Krahwinkel Sperling in the semis—and, with Sarah Palfrey Fabyan, the doubles. But she had no idea how important the mixed was to Bobby. Her triple, hand in hand with a tripling man, was also unique. Sixth-seeded Stammers had knocked off ex-champ, second-seeded Helen Jacobs. When it got down to the last two days, even Riggs may have been a little edgy. He had a harder time than usual beating sixth-seeded Elwood Cooke for the title from 1-4 down in the second, 2-6, 8-6, 3-6, 6-3, 6-2. Partner Cooke had done him a big favor by removing Austin and fifth-seeded Henner Henkel.

Holcombe Ward, president of the USTA, presents the U.S. Singles trophy to Bobby Riggs, victor over Welby Van Horn in 1939. (UPI)

"When I was down 2-1 in sets I thought about my investment," Riggs said. "I think the parlay was a big incentive to my success. We had some close calls in the doubles, but I was too near to let it get away." Probably the toughest was his and Cooke's 6-3, 3-6, 6-8, 6-2, 11-9 quarterfinal over Brits Henry Billington and Pat Hughes. They beat two more Brits, Charlie Hare and Frank Wilde, in the final, 6-3, 3-6, 6-3, 9-7. In the mixed Bobby and Alice lost a couple of sets, but finished strong over Brits Nina Brown and Wilde, 9-7, 6-1. Bobby was rich.

No Americans followed the paths of Budge and Dodo Bundy to Australia, where John Bromwich, who sandwiched his two titles around the war, beat his doubles partner, Adrian Quist, 6-4, 6-1, 6-3. Emily Hood Westacott beat Nell Hall Hopman, 6-1, 6-2, for the other singles, but Nell won the mixed with her spouse, Harry Hopman, who would captain the Aussies to the most astounding of Davis Cup triumphs.

Just 21, a college boy from Kenyon, Don McNeill was a scholarly surprise at the French, beating Riggs for the first time while running 11 games in the final, 7-5, 6-0, 6-3. United with another American, Charlie Harris, he also took the doubles, 4-6, 6-4, 6-0, 2-6, 10-8, over the remaining Musketeers, Jacques Brugnon, 44, and Jean

Borotra, 40, even though Borotra had four match points on serve at 6-5. Love was blooming in the mixed, won by Cooke and Mrs. Fabyan, who would become Mrs. Cooke.

Minus Budge, the U.S. was nevertheless favored to retain the Davis Cup against the Aussies at Merion Cricket Club, and the singles lineup of holdovers of 1938 and 1937 victories, Riggs and Frank Parker respectively, looked solid the first day. Riggs crushed his conqueror of the 1938 challenge round, Bromwich, 6-4, 6-0, 7-5, rising from 0-4 in the third, and Parker hung on to take Quist, 6-3, 2-6, 6-4, 1-6, 7-5. The 0-2 deficit wasn't the worst of it for the Aussies. Gloom thickened the next day, Sept. 3: as part of the British Empire, they were at war against Germany.

Bromwich recalls, "We didn't know if we'd ever play tennis again. We reckoned we'd have to go into the service almost immediately." (They were permitted to remain for the completion of the U.S. summer season.) "But we also felt we still had a chance here. Quisty and I were sure we could win the doubles [they'd recently won the U.S. title], and that we'd play better singles on the third day. We badly wanted to be the first to win as Australia." The last Cup triumph for the Down Under guys had been in 1919 as Australasia.

But 0-2? No country had ever rebounded before (or since) to win the Cup from that far back. But that year, the Aussies did. Rookies Joe Hunt, 20, and Jack Kramer, 18 (the youngest American to play a challenge round), both future U.S. champs, were an untried team, and couldn't hold up against the canny Bromwich and dashing Quist, 5-7, 6-2, 7-5, 6-2, despite leading 3-0 in the third. Once they had a sniff of champagne from the Cup, the Aussies went all out to insure a swill. Riggs fought well after falling way behind, but Quist's passing shots brought him down, 6-1, 6-4, 3-6, 6-4. "I made up my mind to hit a thousand balls to Parker's forehand if that's what it took," says Bromwich, who unswervingly concentrated on Frank's right side in long rallies until it collapsed entirely to the dismay of the crowd of 9,000. Bromwich won the first seven

games and the Cup, 6-0, 6-3, 6-1, the most one-sided clinching singles until 1989 when Boris Becker of Germany beat Mats Wilander of Sweden, 6-2, 6-0, 6-2.

Despite victory the atmosphere was somber as it had been in 1914 when the Australasian side of Brookes and Wilding had lifted the Cup from the U.S. just after the outbreak of World War I. There would be a long hiatus in Davis Cup again, this time six years as the treasure sat out the war in the Bank of New South Wales at Melbourne.

The Wightman Cup would go into storage, too, after a 5-2 U.S. victory sparked by Marble's two singles wins and clinched in doubles, Bundy and Mary Arnold over Betty Nuthall and Nina Brown, 6-3, 6-1.

A mere footnote, but one boding immense implications for the future, was the initial televising of tennis in the U.S. (it had begun in 1937 at Wimbledon). Matches at the Rye, N.Y., tournament were covered by NBC primitively, including Riggs' 1-6, 6-4, 6-4, 7-5, victory in the final over Parker. Few sets (with 4-by-3 inch screens) were in use, and, according to *American Lawn Tennis* magazine; "When the entire court was shown the figures of the players were so small and far-away-looking that only general movements could be followed; the ball was seldom discernible."

At Forest Hills, Riggs ran into a bright young hope in 19-year-old Welby Van Horn, unseeded, who beat seeds Bromwich, Wayne Sabin and Cooke on his way into the final. Riggs eliminated Joe Hunt in the semis. Van Horn opened with two aces, and the supportive crowd roared with approval. Riggs then took charge. As Robert Minton wrote in *A History of Forest Hills*, "Serving a high twist ball to Van Horn's backhand, keeping the ball down the middle of his forehand, to increase the youngster's tendency to crowd his powerful drive, interspersing drop shots, throwing up lobs and constantly mixing his speed and length, Riggs won the match not so much on his ability to finish off the rallies as on his success in prodding Van Horn into mistakes." The score: 6-

4, 6-2, 6-4, and the U.S. had its first short-trousered champ.

In the women's championship, Marble, completing one of the most powerful seasons ever enjoyed by a woman, was threatened by Helen Jacobs, the 32-year-old four-time champion who reached the final by overcoming Stammers, her conqueror at Wimbledon. Bageled in the first set, 6-0, Jacobs won the second , 10-8, and took a 3-1 lead in the third set before Marble recovered to win, 6-0, 8-10, 6-4.

Allison Danzig wrote in *The New York Times:* "Here was one of the most dramatic battles that women's tennis had produced in years, fought out for an hour-and-a-half in gusty crosscurrents of wind that raised havoc with the strokes, while the gallery of 8,500 roared and screamed its encouragement at Miss Jacobs. The crescendo of the enthusiasm was reached in the final game, a furiously disputed 20-point session in which Miss Jacobs five times came within a stroke of 5-all and twice stood off match point, only to yield finally to Miss Marble's more powerful attacking weapons."

Thus, Marble completed her second straight U.S. triple, having won in Boston the women's doubles with Sarah Palfrey Fabyan for the third straight year and then the mixed doubles, not with Riggs, but with the 33-year-old Australian, Harry Hopman. Riggs' splendid season encompassed nine titles in 13 tournaments, 54 wins in 59 starts.

When Don Budge made his pro debut in Madison Square Garden in January, he was a slight underdog to Ellsworth Vines, the champion. A crowd of 16,725, paid $47,120, and many of them were USTA officials who showed their devotion to Budge for his loyalty in putting off his departure from the amateur ranks a year in order to defend the Davis Cup. Budge trounced Vines, 6-3, 6-4, 6-2, and it may have been because Vines had played only eight matches with Fred Perry in South America that summer.

Later, Budge made a second Garden appearance against Perry, who had been his master as an amateur. Budge won easily, 6-1, 6-3, 6-0. On the tour played mostly in big cities, Budge asserted his superiority, beating Vines, 21-18, and Perry, 18-11. Budge collected more than $100,000, including a $75,000 guarantee from the $204,503 gross. Vines got $23,000, then deserted tennis for a successful pro golf career. Budge, however, stayed out of the $2,000 U.S. Pro Championships, won in a brilliant three-hour struggle by Vines over Perry, 8-6, 6-8, 6-1, 20-18, at Beverly Hills. Elly collected the magnificent sum of $340.05.

1940

Bombs crashed down on Wimbledon during the Nazi blitzing of London, and international play virtually ceased, at least in the most important locations beyond the U.S. Wimbledon and the French were out of business until 1946. The curtain didn't fall as quickly on the Australian as had been feared. Adrian Quist won his second title, and Jack Crawford, in his seventh final, didn't win his fifth, 6-3, 6-1, 6-2. Nancye Wynne, on the road to six of them, got the second at the expense of her doubles partner, Thelma Coyne, 5-7, 6-4, 6-0.

Stade Roland Garros had a shameful wartime chapter as a concentration camp, first run by a frantically insecure French government to intern political dissidents, aliens and other suspect types. Later, with the German occupation, it housed Jews who would be shipped East to their doom. Probably the most famous inmate was the humanist author Arthur Koestler, an outspoken liberal whose book, *Darkness at Noon,* was a classic of political imprisonment life. He wrote later, "We called ourselves at Roland Garros the cave dwellers, about 600 of us who lived beneath the stairways of the stadium. We slept on straw, wet straw because the place leaked. A few of us had blankets, but they weren't provided. We were so crammed in sleeping we felt like sardines in a can. Few of us knew anything about tennis, but when we were allowed to take our walk in the

Don McNeill took the U.S. title in 1940. (Fischer Collection/SPS)

stadium we could see the names Borotra and Brugnon on the scoreboard." (Five months before, those two had lost the French doubles final to Americans Don McNeill and Charlie Harris.) "We would make jokes about mixed doubles." Fortunately for Koestler, a Jew, he escaped later Nazi detention and made his way to England. "Compared to our experiences in the past and the future," he wrote of himself and fellow cave dwellers, "Roland Garros was almost an amusement park."

Not up to Nazi standards, Roland Garros was returned to the French Federation in 1941. Regardless of an acute shortage of balls and rackets, national tournaments of sorts were held through 1945. Yvon Petra, recovered from his war wounds in the French army and stint as a POW, won the men's title in 1943, 1944 and 1945, staying fit for his successful shot at the first post-war Wimbledon title. In 1943 he beat a reappeared 41-year-old Musketeer, Henri Cochet, in the final. A friend, ex-French Davis Cupper Robert Abdesselam, says that Cochet, the champ in Paris four times between 1926 and 1932, as well as winner of Wimbledon and the U.S., "felt it im-

portant to play during the war, to show himself so that our dispirited youth would know that a Frenchman had been a world champion."

Wimbledon's courts languished untended. It was used as a civil defense center, the parking lots tilled and planted as victory gardens as well as a home for pigs and chickens. The first bombs struck on Oct. 11, blowing a hole in the Centre Court roof. The club would be damaged from the air three more times during the year.

But the American season went on normally—meaning Alice Marble was omnipotent for a second successive unbeaten year. Not so normal, though for No. 1 Bobby Riggs. Riggs' loss of his U.S. Championship (and No. 1 ranking) to Don McNeill, the newly crowned king of the Intercollegiates for Kenyon, took some of the luster off his record and he had to wait a year before turning pro. McNeill, a 22-year-old Oklahoman, fought one of the great come-from-behind battles against Riggs in a match marked by outstanding sportsmanship. McNeill won, 4-6, 6-8, 6-3, 6-3, 7-5.

McNeill had no fear of Riggs. He'd beaten Bobby a few weeks before in the final of the U.S. Clay, 6-1, 6-4, 7-9, 6-3, and in the French final the year before. But Bobby felt confident on the faster surface, having escaped from Don in the U.S. Indoor final, 3-6, 6-1, 6-4, 2-6, 6-2.

With the score tied at 4-all and deuce in the final set, McNeill hit a shot to Riggs' sideline that the linesman first called out. As Riggs turned his back and prepared to serve, the official reversed his call, declaring it good. Riggs did not know of the change until he heard the call, "Advantage McNeill." Allison Danzig wrote, "The defending champion, who rarely questions a decision, turned at the call and then walked back toward the linesman, asking him why he had changed his ruling. The official maintained that the ball was good and Riggs, without further quibbling, accepted the costly decision and lost the next point and the game."

Then, in the opening rally of the final game, Riggs had to hit a ball that was falling just over the net and he gingerly endeavored to keep from touching the tape as he made his volley. The umpire instantly announced his foot had touched the net and he lost the point. "At that critical state," Danzig wrote, "it was a bitter pill to swallow, but Riggs took it without arguing. McNeill, however, apparently did not like to win the point that way, even though the ruling was correct, and when he knocked Riggs' next service far out of court, the stadium rang with applause."

After losing the first set, McNeill rallied from 1-5 and 15-40 in the second set to tie, saved four set points, went on to take a 6-5 lead, but then dropped the set anyway. Down by two sets, he still came back, and with the crowd almost completely behind the valiant underdog, he pulled out the final set and the match.

Alice Marble, about to turn 27—and pro—was supreme-plus, charging to her fourth U.S. singles title, never endangered, on the loss of none of 12 sets and only 27 games. This put the puissant finishing touches on her amateur career that had purred uninterruptedly victorious since a Wimbledon semifinal defeat by Helen Jacobs in 1938. As in 1939, Alice won nine tournaments, 45 matches, moreover, she was 27-0 in doubles, 11-0 in mixed for a stupendous 83-0 campaign. She left intact a 22-tournament-111-match streak, second only to Helen Wills Moody's 27-158 up to the 1933 U.S.final.

Regal and self-assured in her jaunty white cap, tallest of U.S. champs at 5-foot-8 until Althea Gibson (5-11) came along, Alice was too strong in the final for the 32-year-old ex-champ, second-seeded Jacobs, 6-2, 6-3, a tame rematch of their 1939 championship encounter. England's Mary Hardwick, after ousting two seeds, fifth Sarah Palfrey and third Pauline Betz, harried Jacobs in the semis, 2-6, 6-1, 6-4. Having won in Boston the doubles, a third straight with Palfrey, and the mixed with Riggs, Marble became a triple-tripler. That put her on a peak with Hazel Hotchkiss Wightman (1909, 1910, 1911) and Mary K. Browne (1912, 1913, 1914) in U.S. annals. Other triple-triplers in the majors: Suzanne Lenglen at

Lt. (J.G.) Don McNeill (left) and Pvt. Frank Kovacs appeared at Forest Hills in a tennis benefit for the Red Cross Victory Fund in 1944. (New York Herald Tribune)

Wimbledon (1920, 1922, 1925), Margaret Smith Court at the Australian (1963, 1965, 1969), Nancye Wynne Bolton at the Australian (1940, 1947, 1948). Newlyweds Sarah Palfrey and Elwood Cooke, he a U.S. quarterfinalist, were nationally ranked Nos. 6 and 9 in singles, the second spousal pair in the upper echelon together.

Although there was no pro tour, Don Budge remained monarch, taking his first U.S. Pro title, 6-3, 5-7, 6-4, 6-3, over Fred Perry.

1941

Frustration ended at Forest Hills for Sarah Palfrey Cooke and Bobby Riggs. Hers was longer-term. Sarah, who had divorced Marshall Fabyan and married sometimes mixed-doubles partner, Elwood Cooke, arrived at the U.S. Championships for a 13th time, seeded second, after having done everything but win. A 15-year-old when she first appeared in 1928, a dark-haired good-looker and volleyer, she had been seeded every year since 1933, made the final twice (1934 and 1935 to Helen Jacobs), the semis (1938), the quarters (1933) flopped in the first round (1936 and 1937) when seeded second and third.

No woman had waited longer for the championship. But her hour at last had come, and Sarah, though the path was strewn with champs, past and future, remained in an offensive frame of mind all the way to win driving over her successor, Pauline Betz, 7-5, 6-2, in the final. She was days from her 29th birthday. Only Maud Barger Wallach, 38 in 1908, and Molla Mallory, 31 in 1915, were older first-time champs. U.S. junior champ Louise Brough, who would rule six years down the road, was a stubborn first-round obstacle (4-6, 6-1, 6-1), as was Sarah's long-time nemesis, Jacobs (6-3, 2-6, 6-1) in the semis. Since she'd delighted her hometown, Boston, by winning the doubles with Margaret Osborne and the mixed with Jack Kramer, Sarah had herself a triple, joining a select group of 15 U.S. female triplers. Jacobs' illustrious career at Forest Hills closed after 14 years, four titles, four other finals and 63 match wins, second at the time only to Molla Mallory's 65, although both would be surpassed by Chris Evert (101), Martina Navratilova (89), Steffi Graf (71).

Riggs, the happy-go-lucky hustler and shrewd strategist, mourned that by losing the 1940 final to Don McNeill he'd wasted a big income year (a $25,000 guaranteed offer to turn pro was withdrawn). Bobby made sure not to flunk Forest Hills this time, making 1941 the year he checked out of amateurism as No. 1. The coup de grace was his 5-7, 6-1, 6-3, 6-3 triumph over Frank Kovacs, his most difficult adversary of the year. Riggs' hardest task was beating Stanford collegian Ted Schroeder in the semis, 6-4, 6-4, 1-6, 9-11, 7-5. Kovacs, a handsome, tall-dark-and-highly-talented-entertaining 21-year-old who sometimes let his showboating get in the way of winning, would earn the No.2 ranking and turn

Sarah Palfrey Cooke displays the form that won her the U.S. crown over Pauline Betz in 1941. (UPI)

pro with Riggs. His semifinal victim was the defender, McNeill, 6-4, 6-2, 10-8.

Riggs won six tournaments, but was beaten in the final of the U.S. Clay, 6-3, 7-5, 6-8, 4-6, 6-3, by Frank Parker, who also took six titles. Kovacs won four, including a U.S. Indoor triumph over Wayne Sabin, 6-0, 6-4, 6-2. Betz won six, among them the U.S. Clay (over Mary Arnold, 6-3, 6-1) and U.S. Indoor (over Dodo Bundy, 6-1, 10-12, 6-2. Sarah Cooke's collection of six would be her last until 1945. Motherhood and life as a Navy wife were to intervene.

Marble joined the pros and beat Britain's Mary Hardwick, 8-6, 8-6, in their debut at Madison Square Garden. Bill Tilden, 48, came out of semi-retirement to face Don Budge and lost, 6-3, 6-4. The tour was a relative bust, Budge winning 51 of 58 matches. Budge wrote: "Tilden was still capable of some sustained great play that could occasionally even carry him all the way through a match. Most of the time he could, at his best, hang on for at least a set or two. Despite his age, he was no pushover. The people came out primarily for the show—to see me at my peak, and to see Tilden because they might never have the chance again. Bill could invariably manage to keep things close for a while. It was seldom, however, that he could extend me to the end."

Johnny Faunce did more than extend defending champ Budge in a shook-up U.S. Pro tourney, a show stolen by hardly known teaching pros. One of them, Faunce, shocked everyone by stopping Don in the second round, 6-4, 6-1, 6-3. Keith Gledhill ousted third-seeded Tilden. Another pedagogue, the unexpected finalist, Dick Skeen, who had eliminated ex-champ Joe Whalen, was beaten by Fred Perry, 6-4, 6-8, 6-2, 6-3.

1942

The U.S., stunned by Pearl Harbor, was at war, enveloped in all the uncertainties that entailed. But organized sports—prominently baseball and college athletics—were given the go-ahead to continue by the White House, as morale boosters for the home front and troops overseas, and the USTA voted cautiously at its annual meeting to hold the U.S. Championships at Forest Hills "as usual, unless. . . ." By that USTA President Holcombe Ward (an original Davis Cupper) meant, "We will gladly eliminate tennis if it interferes with winning the war. But our government doesn't want us to abandon tennis. On the contrary, the Physical Fitness Program, sponsored by the government, calls for expansion in sports. As long as the government releases moderate amounts of reclaimed rubber for the manufacture of balls, we'll carry on."

Still, numerous tournaments were cancelled for the duration—notably the oldest, Newport, unplayed 1943–45—or, like the U.S. at Forest Hills, reduced in time and entrants. It was decided that all five U.S. titles would be bunched in New York, removing the Doubles Championships tournament from Boston to cut down on travel, and permit servicemen on short furloughs to play. Men's matches were best-of-three sets until the semis.

Players were advised to use balls longer, that there would be a shortage. Men were being called up for service in the armed forces by their draft boards. The women's game was pretty much unaffected and maintained a high standard. "We got more attention at the tournaments with the top men gone," says Pauline Betz Addie. "Transportation could be difficult, but the Eastern grass tournaments were pretty close together, and we'd pool gas rationing coupons, share cars. We got around."

In London there were no balls to be purchased. Clubs such as Queen's rented them on a per-match basis to members to be used, re-used and overused until disintegrating.

The annual pro tour, Lex Thompson promoter, was launched December 26, 1941, at Madison Square Garden before 8,000 customers and introduced two headstrong individualists, Bobby Riggs and Frank Kovacs, as neophytes. According to USTA officials, Riggs and Kovacs, ranked Nos. 1-2, had deserted amateurism not a moment too soon. They were to be suspended for accepting too much expense money, hardly an uncommon practice. Seeming snakebitten, the tour didn't last long. Wartime travel difficulties and injuries to Kovacs and Fred Perry closed the show April 5, in Palm Springs, the 71st stop. On opening night of the round-robin barnstorming, Kovacs beat Don Budge and Riggs beat Perry, who fell damagingly on his right elbow, an injury that virtually finished Fred's career. At the end Budge had a 15-10 edge on Riggs, a rivalry they would take up again on the first post-war tour, and headed the pack with a 52-18 record. Riggs was 36-36, Kovacs 25-26, Perry 23-30. All would soon be in military uniforms, but they did reassemble a couple of months later for the U.S. Pro at Forest Hills, where Budge trimmed Riggs, 6-2, 6-2, 6-2.

The first prominent players to enter the service were No. 4 Don McNeill, the U.S. champ of 1940, into the Navy, and Hal Surface, No. 12 in 1940, and Frank Guernsey, National Intercollegiate champ for Rice in 1938–39, into the Army Air Force.

The U.S. Clay Court tourney in St. Louis was an amusing mess. Heavy rains, delaying the windup, necessitated using hard courts for several late-round matches. If that wasn't unconventional enough, the final between two collegians on mucky footing was defaulted in progress—then resumed against "orders" only to be lost by the supposed victor, through his good sportsmanship. Both finalists, Harris Everett of North Carolina and Seymour Greenberg of Northwestern, were expected immediately in New Orleans for the Intercollegiate Championships. The train that would get them there on time was leaving at 6 p.m. Locked at 6-6 in the fifth set, Greenberg was ordered by his coach, Paul Bennett, to default so they could catch the train, the college event deemed more important. On the way to the dressing room, Everett, apparently the champ, said to Greenberg, "Aw, to hell with New Orleans. I don't want to win it this way. Let's go back and finish." They did. Greenberg won the next two games and became the genuine champ, 5-7, 7-5, 7-9, 7-5, 8-6. They caught the train the next day, and were excused the tardy arrival.

Neither one got to the final. It was a unique Stanford *über alles* production as Ted Schroeder beat teammate Larry Dee, 6-2, 0-6, 6-2, 6-3, and they beat two other teammates, Emery Neale and Jim Wade, 6-3, 6-3, 6-1, to monopolize the title rounds. Moreover, Ted, 21, a volleying virtuoso, said so-long to civilian life on a very high note. He conquered Forest Hills on his fourth attempt, 8-6, 7-5, 3-6, 4-6, 6-2, over long-suffering Frank Parker, 26, on his 11th, a quarterfinalist as far back as 1934. It seemed only logical progression to Ted, loser in the third round in 1939, then the quarters and semis. It put him in a class with McNeill, the only men to win the Intercollegiate and U.S. title in the same year. Ted lost a set in the third round to Jimmy Evert, a Chicagoan whose future daughter, Chris, would carry off the title 33 years later. In the semis he beat one of eight servicemen in the 64 draw, Naval Lt. Gardnar Mulloy, presently to command a landing craft in African and European combat. Another Chicagoan in the third round, Robert Smidl, who earned No. 21 recognition, would be killed with the Army in Europe, the first player with a national ranking to perish.

Nineteen-year-old Louise Brough, winning the grass tests at Easthampton, N.Y., Boston and Manchester, Mass., came into Forest Hills as the top-seeded favorite. But swift-footed Pauline Betz, 23, the finalist 12 months before, proved a tough cookie under pressure, launching her three-year reign by snapping back to beat Brough in the title match, 4-6, 6-1, 6-4. It was tighter in the semis where Pauline quashed a match point with Margaret Osborne leading 5-3 in the third to win, 6-4, 4-6, 7-5. Only 5,148 attended the finals. Many of the usual customers had other things on their minds.

But tennis did go on here and there elsewhere, South America and India to name prominent locales, and Lt. McNeill, showing up in Buenos Aires as Naval attache, won the Argentine title over Andres Hammersley of Chile.

1943

Francisco "Pancho" Segura, a curious and ebullient character, arrived on the scene from Ecuador in 1941 with a big smile, little English, scrawny bowed legs and a deadly double-fisted forehand. He had the two-handed act all to himself now that Viv McGrath and John Bromwich were in the Australian army. By 1943 Pancho had the depleted tournament circuit practically all to himself, too. Shipped to the University of Miami for an education, he was definitely a tennis scholar, winning a record three straight U.S. Intercollegiate titles through 1945. In 1943 his victim, 6-2, 6-1, 6-3, was future Wimbledon finalist and U.S. Davis Cupper Tom Brown of California (Berkeley). Segura, 22, who had the year's most impressive slate, winning seven of 10 tournaments, 38 of 41 matches, scorched the grass courts. He took titles at Rye, N.Y., and Southampton, N.Y., and moved easily to the semis of the U.S., which had been compressed to six days and 32 entries, 12 of them servicemen on leave.

But two of those excused from duty for a few days were strapping blond Californians of serve-and-volley persuasion: second-seeded Coast Guard Seaman Jack Kramer, 22, and seventh-seeded Naval Lt. Joe Hunt, 24, a tragic figure who had won Intercollegiate titles for Southern California in doubles (1938) and the singles (1941) for the Naval Academy. As kids they were Davis Cup doubles partners in 1939, their defeat by Adrian Quist and Bromwich igniting the Australian revival to victory from 0-2. Another was Cpl. Frank Parker of the Army Air Force, who got the top seed ahead of Segura. Bill Talbert, kept out of the service by diabetes, was the lone civilian in the semis, losing to Hunt, 3-6, 6-4, 6-2, 6-4, after Hunt had bulldozed Parker, 8-6, 6-2, 6-3. Though weakened by food poisoning, Kramer hung on to beat Segura, 2-6, 6-4, 7-5, 6-3. However, Kramer spent three sets against Hunt, who became champion, 6-3, 6-8, 10-8, 6-0. Jack, who served for the third set at 5-4, remembers the bizarre ending, "I hit a forehand long on match point. If I'd kept that ball in court I think I would have been the champ by default." Because as the ball flew beyond him, Hunt crumpled onto the court with leg cramps, probably unable to play another point!

Hunt would not return to Forest Hills. Unable to get leave from sea duty in 1944, he was killed in a plane crash on a training mission in 1945. Joe, playing only four tournaments in 1943, and winning one other, LaJolla, was accorded the No. 1 ranking.

Pauline Betz, who won seven tournaments, completed a national surface triple at Forest Hills, after taking the U.S. Indoor (over Kay Winthrop, 6-4, 6-1) and the U.S. Clay (over Nancy Corbett, 6-0, 6-1). Beating Catherine Wolf, 6-0, 6-2, for the Tri-State title in Cincinnati, Pauline scored a golden bagel, winning all 24 points while stroking 18 winners. Gunning for her second title in New York, she got it in a re-match struggle of the first-second seeds, beating Louise Brough, 6-3, 5-7, 6-3. Doris Hart, 18, the U.S. junior champ—12 years short of winning the big one—took Betz to three sets in the quarters. A first-round loser to seventh-seeded Mary Arnold was Gloria Thompson, who had won St. Louis earlier in the summer. She would be back

years later with the son she reared to be a great champion: Jimmy Connors.

Keeping the pros alive was the Officers Club of Ft. Knox, Ky. As an entertainment treat—free admission—for the post, and the town, the Army played host to the U.S. Pro, building an 11,000-seat temporary stadium with floodlights, and putting up a $2,000 purse. The stands were filled, possibly the event's largest-ever crowd, as Navy Lt. Bruce Barnes beat teaching pro John Nogrady, 6-1, 7-9, 7-5, 4-6, 6-3, for the title.

1944

Civilians Bill Talbert and Pancho Segura had things pretty much their way during the American season—until Forest Hills, another six-day event with 32 entries in singles, 15 of them servicemen on leave. Dauntless Sgt. Frank Parker of the Army Air Force's Muroc (Cal.) Base reappeared to snatch the title he had sought for a dozen years. Seeded fourth, Frank had played only one prior tournament, but proved that the 13th time never fails. The longest male chase for the title was over as dark-haired 28-year-old Parker, in dark glasses, brought down third-seeded Talbert for the title, 6-4, 3-6, 6-3, 6-3, before a finals-day gathering of 8,000. Talbert wore himself down expelling top seed Segura, 3-6, 6-3, 6-0, 6-8, 6-3, while Parker won his semi over ex-champ, Navy Lt. Don McNeill, 6-4, 3-6, 6-2, 6-2. In the second round McNeill beat 46-year-old Gil Hall, who had been discharged from the Army earlier in the year, a veteran of tank warfare. Hall made a unique mark that week, not only winning a round in the Championship but capturing the concurrent Senior (over 45) title, becoming the only man to hold an unusual dual national ranking: No. 10 among the men and No. 1 among the seniors. He would hold the latter title through 1950. The junior champ was in the service, too. Air Cadet Bob Falkenburg won the 18s title on leave.

A third straight U.S. title for Pauline Betz was the outcome on the ladies' side as she sprinted through the tourney on the loss of one set (6-4,

6-8, 6-4, over Virginia Wolfenden Kovacs in the quarters), brushed aside 1943 finalist Louise Brough, 6-2, 6-3, in the semis and Margaret Osborne, 6-3, 8-6, in the final. The second set was troublesome, Pauline accelerating from 1-4, and dodging a set point at 4-5.

Busiest player Segura, again the Intercollegiate champ, beat Talbert, 9-11, 6-2, 7-5, 2-6, 7-5, to win the U.S. Clay, and altogether bagged six of 10 tournaments on 36-4 in matches. Talbert won two of nine on 32-7 while Parker, who won two of three tournaments on 13-1, got the No. 1 ranking. Betz won eight of 13 on 44-5, but didn't retain the U.S. Clay, beaten in the semis by Dodo Bundy, the champ on a 7-5, 6-4, decision over Mary Arnold. Osborne won three of 11 on 33-8 and Brough three of 12 on 30-9.

The U.S. Pro tourney became a wartime casualty, but ever energetic Bill Tilden, 51, kept on the go, playing exhibitions for the troops at military bases all over the country, or at benefits for such as the Red Cross and other charitable causes associated with war relief. Don Budge, in the Army Air Force, beat Coast Guardsman Jack Kramer, 7-5, 7-5, heading a midwinter fund-raiser at New York's 7th Regiment Armory that sold $2,706,000 in war bonds. Naval couple Elwood and Sarah Palfrey Cooke, out of sight since 1941, made a cameo at the LaJolla tourney, each winning the singles.

The uncle Chris Evert never knew, Jack Evert, 22, one of the four tennis-playing brothers from Chicago, was killed with the Army in France where a future champ, Art Larsen, was also fighting. Jacque Virgil Hunt, wife of the 1943 champion, Lt. Joe Hunt, won the Southern title. Refused leave from Naval flight training to compete at Forest Hills, Joe and 1942 champ Ted Schroeder had to settle for a weekend near their base, the Pensacola Labor Day tourney. Playing his last competitive tennis, Joe defeated Ted in the final, 6-3, 7-5.

1945

Peace was clearly on the way, and broke out only days before Forest Hills threw open its gates again for a joyful renewal of the U.S. Championships. Attendance was up: 35,506, compared to 26,999 for the 1944 tourney and 23,893 for 1943. Sixteen of the male entry list, enlarged to 48, were still in uniform, but wouldn't be for long. Wimbledon, closed six years, had invited the public in June 30 for a U.S. vs. British Empire match between allied armed forces teams. Centre Court had been too badly damaged by bombing to be available, but 5,000 witnesses, including Queen Mary, were happy to be back in Court 1. Army Sgts. George Lott and Charlie Hare spurred a 4-1 U.S. victory.

Out of the Navy and traveling the American circuit again were Elwood and Sarah Palfrey Cooke, to reclaim Top Ten national rankings last held in 1941, this time No. 1 for her, the champion at Forest Hills, No. 4 for him, a semifinalist, the highest finish ever for a married couple. An extreme illustration of the manpower shortage was the leniency of tourney officials at the Tri-State in Cincinnati, permitting the Cookes to enter the men's doubles as a team. A singular feat, they got to the final, losing to Bill Talbert and Hal Surface, 6-2, 6-2.

A somber note was the absence of 1943 champion Joe Hunt, Naval pilot killed February 2 in the never-explained plunge of his fighter plane into the Atlantic off Florida on a training exercise. Hunt, 26, was the highest regarded American player to die in the war, expected to shine brightly in the peacetime game.

Army Air Force Sgt. Frank Parker, the defender, was thought to be far out of the picture, stationed on Guam. But his commanding general, Curtis LeMay, had other ideas, ordering Frank to fly back to the U.S. in time to enter (and win) the Easterns at Rye, N.Y., as a tune-up for Forest Hills. Parker, who'd been playing exhibitions with such as Naval Seaman Bobby Riggs for the troops on Pacific Islands, was fit and ready. Top seeded, Frank cruised to his second U.S. title by

Sgt. Frank Parker was the U.S. champ in 1944 and 1945. (New York Herald Tribune)

winning all 13 sets he played, encountering real difficulty only at the outset of the rematch final against Bill Talbert, 14-12, 6-1, 6-2. Subsequently Frank won the Pacific Southwest and the Pan American. His four-for-four and 19-0 match mark assured him of keeping the No. 1 ranking.

As civilians, Talbert and Pancho Segura, winner of a third successive Intercollegiate title for the University of Miami, were again the dominant figures on the circuit. Bill won eight of 11 tournaments, on 48-3 in matches. He beat Segura for the U.S. Clay title, 6-4, 4-6, 6-2, 2-6, 6-2, and took three of four grass-court tests, losing only to Parker at Rye. Segura won two of 10 on 33-8.

But in defeating third-seeded Segura, 7-5, 6-3, 6-4, in the semis, second-seeded Talbert wrenched his left knee. Gamely, wearing trousers to hide the strapping, Bill endured an epic finals afternoon of four matches and 96 games, cheered by 11,556 onlookers, as he won two titles after bowing to Parker. He held a set point against Parker's serve at 9-10 in the 76-minute first set, 22 games, the longest to that time in a singles final. But that was Talbert's last thrust in the nearly two-hour struggle. Parker's consistency was too much.

Returning to the court to complete the doubles final, halted by darkness the previous evening at 10-10 in the third, Talbert and Naval Lt. Gardnar Mulloy finished their second title triumph together, 12-10, 8-10, 12-10, 6-2, over Army Sgt. Jack Tuero and Air Cadet Bob Falkenburg. Then it was time for mixed: a semifinal that Talbert and Margaret Osborne won over Louise Brough and Frank Shields, 6-3, 9-7. It was 6:45 p.m. and the final remained. Osborne, who had won the doubles with Brough, was in the third match of her two-title 65-game afternoon. She and Talbert had to play quickly and surely to beat darkness at 7:25 plus Doris Hart and Falkenburg, 6-4, 6-4, Talbert serving it out at love.

Sarah Cooke, a sharp volleyer who won 16 major doubles titles, had always wanted to win the U.S. singles, emulating her mentor, Hazel Hotchkiss Wightman, and finally came through in 1941, on a 13th attempt. Now Sarah wanted to follow Hazel again by winning as a mother, and so she did, joining an exclusive matronly club whose third member would be Margaret Smith Court in 1973. In a sensational comeback for her last season as an amateur, after almost four years away from the game, Sarah won seven of 13 tournaments on 43-6 in matches. Her chief rival, defending champion Pauline Betz—they were 1-2 in the rankings—won six of 12 on 42-6. Sarah beat Pauline for the U.S. Clay title, 8-6, 7-5, and at Forest Hills clipped Pauline's streak of three titles and 19 matches, 3-6, 8-6, 6-4.

"She was a good friend and a thorn in my side," says Pauline, who might well have won a record six straight U.S. crowns except for Sarah, her conqueror in the 1941 and 1945 finals. Sarah led 5-2 in the second, almost let it slip away, then stormed back in the third from a service break to

3-4 to take the last three games. Both women turned pro at the end of the season to tour against one another.

Brough and Osborne's 6-3, 6-3, victory over Betz and Hart was their fourth straight doubles title, breaking the three-straight record (1918–20) of Marion Zinderstein and Eleanor Goss, and there would be more to come.

The pros regrouped to reestablish their U.S. Championship after a one-year layoff, won by Welby Van Horn over John Nogrady, 6-4, 6-2, 6-2.

3

THE 25 GREATEST PLAYERS
1914-45

They changed a game played at moderate pace into one of thunder and lightning, fire and guts. They revolted against playing in long dresses or in long-sleeved shirts. One player used a flat-top racket, another played wearing a white cap, still another wore a white eyeshade. They had nicknames such as the Wizard, Big Bill, Little Miss Poker Face, the Crocodile. They all had one thing in common: They were champions, the best tennis players in the years 1914 to 1945.

To select the 25 top players from this period is a challenging task, for there was an unusually large number of performers of first class in the world. Tennis had its full share of all-time greats during the Golden Twenties and in the '30s, too.

There are no such things as computer points and professional earnings by which to rank these players. The professional game carried small weight and small money except for the top two or three touring pros. More prestigious was amateur competition in the major national tournaments and in the Davis and Wightman Cups. When a woman wins Wimbledon eight times, when a man becomes the first to complete the Grand Slam, there can be little doubt of his or her greatness. A champion who played the big game of serve-and-volley 25 years before it became the standard method of play certainly deserves recognition among the best.

It is much harder for me to draw the line and leave out so many of the following who deserve mention but who did not make the top 25, players like Mary K. Browne and Hazel Hotchkiss Wightman, both trailblazers in women's tennis, both national champions before World War I, and both prominent afterward . . . Elizabeth Ryan, one of the best volleyers in the 1920s . . . Lili de Alvarez of Spain, whose carefree style of playing in the late 1920s was so captivating . . . Cilly Aussem, the only German to capture the Wimbledon crown (prior to Steffi Graf), winning in 1931 . . . Simone Passemard Mathieu of France, twice French champion, six times a Wimbledon semifinalist . . . Anita Lizana of Chile, who won the 1937 U.S. title . . . Jadwiga Jedrzejowska, the hard-hitting Pole of the '30s and '40s.

Among the men left out were Wilmer Allison, the 1935 U.S. champion and a formidable doubles player with John Van Ryn . . . John Bromwich and Adrian Quist, the tough Australian duo of the late '30s and '40s . . . Vivian McGrath, the 1937 Australian champion and the first of the two-handed hitters to win renown . . . Bunny Austin, a Davis Cup mainstay for Great Britain in the 1930s . . . Frank Parker, a U.S. Davis Cupper in the late 1930s who blossomed into the U.S. singles champion in 1944 and 1945 . . . Sidney Wood and Frank Shields, native New Yorkers who both advanced to the 1931 Wimbledon final round . . . Vincent Richards, a great volleyer of the 1920s and one of the first pros . . . George Lott, a dynamic doubles player in the 1930s . . . Frank Hunter, a late bloomer born in 1894 who didn't make his big tennis moves until the late 1920s and the 1930s . . . and John Doeg, the smooth lefty who was 1930 U.S. champion.

—Allison Danzig

JEAN BOROTRA
France (1898–1994)

In many ways, Jean Robert Borotra fit the image of the cosmopolitan Frenchman: a spectacular, debonair personality, a gallant kissing ladies' fingertips, a host of elegant parties aboard the *Ile de France* or at his fashionable residence in Paris.

Borotra, a right-hander (6-foot-1, 160), was spectacular, too, on the tennis court in the 1920s and early '30s. He won Wimbledon in 1924 and 1926 and was runner-up in 1925 and 1927. He won the championship of France in 1924 and 1931 and the Australian title in 1928. And he was a demon in international play, one of the Four Musketeers who in 1927 broke the U.S. grip on the Davis Cup and brought it to France for the first time.

Born on Aug. 13, 1898, at Arbonne, Basque Pyrenees country near Biarritz, France, he first attracted wide attention when he played in the 1921 covered-court championship in Paris. Standing out with a dramatic, aggressive style of play—and with the blue beret he always wore—Borotra became known as the "Bounding Basque from Biarritz."

His energy on the court was limitless, marked by headlong assaults and dashes for the net, both on his service and return of service, then a stampede back to retrieve lobs. No player could start faster or dash so madly. His service was not a cannonball, but it was not to be trifled with. His backhand return of service and backhand volley were vividly individual, thrusts for the kill.

Borotra was named to France's Davis Cup team in 1922, and in 1923 he assembled with René Lacoste, Henri Cochet, and Jacques Brugnon, a great doubles player, to form the Four Musketeers. Not only did the French win their first Cup in 1927, but they also held it for five years thereafter.

In the 1932 Challenge Round, Borotra reached heights of inspiration against the U.S. He defeated Ellsworth Vines, the winner of Wimbledon and the U.S. Championship that year. On the final day, Borotra lost the first two sets to Wilmer Allison, and with the Texan holding a fourth match point in the fifth set, Borotra's second serve appeared to be out. Allison ran forward for the handshake, thinking he had won, but the linesman insisted the serve was good and play resumed. Borotra pulled out the victory and France retained the Cup.

With his dazzling performances, Borotra was popular everywhere. This included the Seventh Regiment Armory in New York, where he was in his element on the fast board courts and four

Jean Borotra: Bounding Basque in blue beret. (Fischer Collection/SPS)

times won the U.S. Indoor Championship. He was not rated quite the player that Cochet and Lacoste were, but Borotra's celebrity endured and the legs that ran like fury kept him active in tennis into his 70s as a competitor in the senior division at Wimbledon. He was among the champions honored at the 1977 Wimbledon Centenary a year after he was enshrined with the three other Musketeers in the Hall of Fame.

He was ranked in the World Top Ten nine straight years from 1924, No. 2 in 1926. He entered the Hall of Fame in 1976 and died July 17, 1994.

MAJOR TITLES *(16)—Australian singles, 1928; French singles, 1931; Wimbledon singles, 1924, '26; Australian dou-*
bles, 1928; French doubles, 1925, '28, '29, '34, '36; Wimbledon doubles, 1925, '32, '33; French mixed, 1927, '34; Wimbledon mixed, 1925; U.S. mixed, 1926. DAVIS CUP—*1922, '23, '24, '25, '26, '27, '28, '29, '30, '31, '32, '33, '34, '35, '36, '37, '47; record: 19-12 in singles, 17-6 in doubles.* SINGLES RECORD IN THE MAJORS—*Australian (5-0), French (30-6), Wimbledon (55-10), U.S. (13-6).*

NORMAN BROOKES
Australia (1877–1968)

They called him the Wizard. A figure of heroic stature, Sir Norman Everard Brookes was renowned both as a player—for many years Australia's best—and as an administrator. He stood 5-foot-11, weighed 150, had a sallow complexion and pale blue eyes, austere in bearing, rather taciturn, a man of strength and character to command respect and win honors.

And win honors he did. Born Nov. 14, 1877, in Melbourne, Australia, he became in 1907 the first male from overseas to win the championship at Wimbledon, having lost the 1905 final to Laurie Doherty. He won Wimbledon again in 1914 and was runner-up in 1919 after returning from World War I. Long ranked as the best of left-handed players, the first to win Wimbledon, he was a member of nine Australasian Davis Cup teams between 1905 and 1920 and played in eight challenge rounds.

World rankings were instituted after his best days, but he was in the Top Ten in 1914, 1919, and 1920, the last at 43.

He was an exponent of the serve and volley game, the "big game" that was supposed to have originated after World War II. Brookes played that type of game in 1914, but he had more than a serve and volley. He had ground strokes adequate to hold his own from the back of the court. Because his serve was so big an asset—flat, slice, twist, even reverse twist—and he volleyed so much, his methods were characterized as unorthodox when he was in his prime. He often used the same side of the racket for forehand and backhand.

In 1907 Brookes' decisive 6-2, 6-0, 6-3 win over Roper Barrett settled Australasia's 3-2 victory at Wimbledon to break Britain's four-year hold on the Davis Cup and take the prize Down Under for the first time. It stayed there until a British reprisal in 1912, Brookes going 5-1 in singles and 3-0 in doubles as his side beat the U.S. three times. Even though he, 36, lost the memorable first-day match to 24-year-old Maurice McLoughlin, 17-15, 6-3, 6-3, in 1914, the Aussies spirited the Cup away, 3-2, as he clinched, 6-1, 6-2, 8-10, 6-3, over Dick Williams. Five years later, at age 41, he won the doubles with Gerald Patterson as the Aussies beat Britain, 4-1, the oldest to play with a Cup winner. A year after that, his Cup swan song, he gave Big Bill

Norman Brookes: An unorthodox southpaw. (UPI)

Tilden a furious battle, 10-8, 6-4, 1-6, 6-4, as the Americans retrieved the sterling bowl.

Returning to Wimbledon in 1914, his first appearance since winning seven years before, Brookes again demonstrated his all-around strength in a severe all-comers final test (6-2, 6-1, 5-7, 4-6, 8-6, over German Otton Froitzheim) preparatory to wresting the title from his close friend and teammate, Tony Wilding, 6-4, 6-4, 7-5, with a display of faultless ground strokes. Brookes' durability was demonstrated again in 1924 at Wimbledon when, at 46, he ousted World No. 5 Frank Hunter, finalist in 1923 and 17 years his junior.

But five war years passed, and in his next go at Wimbledon, as the defending champ he couldn't hold off Patterson in the challenge round, 6-3, 7-5, 6-2. However, that summer the two of them went to America to win the U.S. Doubles over Tilden and Vinnie Richards, 8-6, 6-3, 4-6, 4-6, 6-

2, the first of many Aussies to cart off American titles. He gave incoming champ Tilden—who called him "the greatest tennis brain" —a fright in the singles quarters, 1-6, 6-4, 7-5, 6-3. Brookes, who had won his first major, Wimbledon, 1907, took his last in 1924, the Aussie doubles with James Anderson. He was in his 47th year, the elder of all major champions.

The honors didn't stop for the man who seemed to command them. In 1926, he was named president of the Lawn Tennis Association of Australia, a post he held until 1955. He was decorated with the French Legion of Honor for his services in World War I as a captain in the British Army and, in 1939, he was knighted.

He died Sept. 28, 1968, in Melbourne and entered the Hall of Fame in 1977.

MAJOR TITLES (7)—*Australian singles, 1911; Wimbledon singles, 1907, '14; Australian doubles, 1924; Wimbledon doubles, 1907, '14; U.S. doubles, 1919.* DAVIS CUP—*1905, '07, '08, '09, '11, '12, '14, '19, '20; record: 18-7 in singles, 10-4 in doubles.* SINGLES RECORD IN THE MAJORS—*Australian (5-0), Wimbledon (25-2), U.S. (4-2).*

DON BUDGE
United States (1915—)

In sheer achievement, John Donald Budge accomplished what nobody before 1938 had been able to do—he won the Grand Slam of tennis, capturing the championships of Australia, France, Wimbledon and the United States in the same year. People were suddenly speaking of Budge in the same breath with the already immortal Bill Tilden.

Born June 13, 1915, in Oakland, Calif., Budge had been less interested in tennis than in baseball, basketball and football while growing up in the California city, where his Scottish-born father, a former soccer player, had settled.

When the 6-foot-1, 160-pound right-hander turned to tennis, his strapping size enabled him to play a game of maximum power. His service was battering, his backhand considered perhaps the finest the game has known, his net play emphatic, his overhead drastic. Quick and rhythmic, he was truly the all-around player and, what is more, was temperamentally suited for the game. Affable and easygoing, he could not be shaken from the objective of winning with the utmost application of hitting power.

The red-haired young giant was a favorite wherever he played, and he moved quickly up the tennis ladder. At the age of 19, he was far enough advanced to be named to the Davis Cup team. The next year, 1936, he lost at Wimbledon and Forest Hills to Fred Perry, the world's No.1 amateur, but beat Perry in the Pacific Southwest tournament.

In 1937 Perry turned pro and Budge became the world's No. 1. He won at Wimbledon and Forest Hills and led the U.S. to its first Davis Cup in 11 years, 4-1 over Britain. The most brilliant act therein was his famous revival in the fifth set of the fifth match against Germany in the person of the stylish Baron Gottfried von Cramm to win the interzone final at neutral Wimbledon. He had already beaten Henner Henkel and won the doubles with Gene Mako over Henkel–von Cramm, so, with the score knotted, 2-2, up came the decisive test, another of his classic jousts with von Cramm. Not only was Budge far back, by two sets, but he had to rise from 1-4 in the fifth to win on a sixth match point, 6-8, 5-7, 6-4, 6-2, 8-6, and tip the series to the U.S., 3-2.

After that the Challenge Round against Britain, also at Wimbledon, was relatively easy, though Don had to beat lefty Charlie Hare in a rugged first set, and take him, 15-13, 6-1, 6-2, to offset Frank Parker's leadoff loss to Bunny Austin. Budge and Mako won the doubles, and Don beat Austin on the third day, his 18th successive singles win on his seeming home turf. Culminating a fantastic year, Budge received the Sullivan Award as America's top amateur athlete, the first tennis player to be so honored.

The high regard in which Budge was held by fellow players, spectators and officials was reflected by the loyalty he demonstrated in 1937.

Don Budge: The grandest slam of all. (UPI)

He was a big attraction for pro tennis but decided against leaving the amateur ranks for another year. The United States had the Davis Cup and he decided that, in return for all tennis had done for him, he must help in the defense of the Cup for at least another year.

So he turned down the professional offers, aware that poor fortunes in 1938 could hurt, if not end, his earning power as a pro. As it turned out, 1938 would be his most glorious year. He defeated John Bromwich, 6-4, 6-2, 6-1, in the Australian final, losing only one set in the entire tournament. In the French championship he beat Roderich Menzel of Czechoslovakia in the final, 6-3, 6-2, 6-4, and yielded three sets in the tourna-

ment. At Wimbledon he did not lose a single set, beating Bunny Austin of Britain, 6-1, 6-0, 6-3, for the title, and at Forest Hills he gave up but one set—to Gene Mako in the final—in winning the U.S. crown, 6-3, 6-8, 6-2, 6-1.

Budge had won the Grand Slam and was the toast of the tennis world. After helping the U.S. retain the Davis Cup over Australia, beating Adrian Quist and Bromwich, and after four years in the World Top Ten, No. 1 in 1937–38, and five years in the U.S. Top Ten, he left the amateur ranks. He did so with the blessing of the USTA president, Holcombe Ward, and the Davis Cup captain, Walter L. Pate, who wished him well in his pro career.

Budge's 1938 season was limited to eight tournaments, of which he won six on 43-2 in matches. His incredible 92-match, 14-tournament winning streak that began after a January 1937 loss to Bitsy Grant was ended by Quist in four sets at the Pacific Southwest. His farewell to amateurism was a defeat by Bromwich in his home territory, Berkeley, in the Pacific Coast tourney.

He made his professional debut at Madison Square Garden in New York early in 1939 and, before a crowd of 16,725, defeated Ellsworth Vines, 6-3, 6-4, 6-2. On tour, Budge defeated Vines, 21 matches to 18, and also defeated Perry, 18-11. On tour with the 47-year-old Tilden, Budge beat him, 51-7.

Budge won two U.S. Pro titles at Forest Hills before entering the Air Force in 1942: 1940 over Perry, 6-3, 5-7, 6-4, 6-3, and 1942 over Bobby Riggs, 6-2, 6-2, 6-2. A shoulder injury suffered in military training reduced his post-war effectiveness, and he lost the pro tour hegemony to challenger Riggs in a close journey of one-nighters, 24-22. Still, he battled to the U.S. Pro tourney finals of 1946, '47, '49, and '53, losing the first three to Riggs and the last to 25-year-old Pancho Gonzalez, 13 years his junior, and left little doubt as to his greatness. "I consider him," said Bill Tilden, "the finest player 365 days a year who ever lived."

He was elected to the Hall of Fame in 1964.

MAJOR TITLES *(14)—Australian singles, 1938; French singles, 1938; Wimbledon singles, 1937, '38; U.S. singles, 1937, '38; Wimbledon doubles, 1937, '38; U.S. doubles, 1936, '38; Wimbledon mixed, 1937, '38; U.S. mixed, 1937, '38.* OTHER U.S. TITLES—*Clay Court doubles, 1934, with Gene Mako; Pro singles, 1940, '42; Pro doubles, 1940, '41, with Fred Perry; 1942, '47, with Bobby Riggs; 1949, with Frank Kovacs; 1953, with Richard (Pancho) Gonzalez.* DAVIS CUP—*1935, '36, '37, '38; record: 19-2 in singles, 6-2 in doubles.* SINGLES RECORD IN THE MAJORS— *Australian (5-0), French (6-0), Wimbledon (24-2), U.S. (23-3).*

DOROTHEA CHAMBERS
Great Britain (1878–1960)

What a clash of eras and customs it was in the Wimbledon final of 1919 when the sturdily conformed, long-skirted 40-year-old matron, Dorothea Katherine Douglass Lambert Chambers, seven times champion between 1903 and 1914, faced the slim new kid half her age, audacious, skimpily dressed (for the time) Suzanne Lenglen. They battled through the longest final up to that time, 44 games, Mrs. Robert Lambert Chambers narrowly missing two match points in the third set of the 10-8, 4-6, 9-7 decision, the first of six titles for Lenglen, never beaten at Wimbledon.

With King George V, Queen Mary, and the Princess Royal in the committee box, one of the finest matches to be played at Wimbledon, by men or women, was enacted.

Against the all-court game of Lenglen, the right-handed Chambers delighted the gallery with superb resistance. She drove with such power and length from both forehand and backhand, passed so accurately, put up lobs so irretrievable, and had so much touch on her drop shot that her young opponent was showing signs of physical distress and found herself in danger of losing.

After two sets, the match was even and Lenglen was sipping brandy to ease her peril. In the third set, trailing, 4-1, Chambers put on a remarkable comeback and seemed to have the victory in hand at 6-5, 40-15, on her service at double match point. But, just as remarkably, Lenglen rallied and pulled out the match, 10-8, 4-6, 9-7. Both players were so exhausted that when asked to come to the Royal Box, they said they were physically unable to do so. It had been an epic struggle between the past and the future in tennis.

Despite the interruption of World War I, she was in 11 Wimbledon singles finals—third behind Blanche Hillyard's 13 and Martina Navratilova's 12—the last in 1920 when she lost again to Lenglen, and, at 41, was the oldest female finalist. Continuing to play the Big W through 1927, she played 115 matches in all there: 32-8 in singles, 29-11 in doubles, 24-11 in mixed. Dolly as some called her, won two of her

*Dorothea Douglass Chambers: Ageless champion.
(UPI)*

Wimbledons after the birth of her first child, two more after the birth of her second.

As Britain's Wightman Cup captain in 1925, at 46, she helped her side win, 4-3, at Forest Hills by beating 30-year-old Eleanor Goss, 7-5, 3-6, 6-1. She also captained the team in 1926. She was born Sept. 3, 1878, in Ealing, England and died in 1960. She entered the Hall of Fame in 1981.

MAJOR TITLES (7)—*Wimbledon singles, 1903, '04, '06, '10, '11, '13, '14.* WIGHTMAN CUP—*1925, '26; record: 1-1 in doubles.* SINGLES RECORD IN THE MAJORS— *Wimbledon (32-8), U.S. (3-1).*

HENRI COCHET
France (1901–87)

It could be said that Henri Jean Cochet had as pronounced a gift for playing tennis as anyone

who attained world supremacy. A racket in his hand became a wand of magic, doing the impossible, most often in a position on the court considered untenable, and doing it with nonchalant ease and fluency. He took the ball early, volleys and half-volleys rippling off the strings. His overheads invariably scored, though his service seemingly was innocuous.

He developed his skills early in Lyon, France, where he was born Dec. 14, 1901, and where his father was secretary of the tennis club. Henri worked at the club as a ball boy and practiced with his friends and sister when nobody was using the courts. In 1921 he went to Paris where he and Jean Borotra, both unknowns, reached the final of the covered-court championship. Cochet was the winner.

The next year, he and Borotra played on the Davis Cup team, and in 1923 they joined with René Lacoste and Jacques Brugnon in the origin of the Four Musketeers. Cochet won 10 successive Davis Cup challenge round matches from the time the Musketeers wrested the Cup from the U.S. in 1927.

A sensitivity of touch and timing, resulting in moderately hit strokes of genius, accounted for the success the little Frenchman (5-foot-6, 145) had in turning back the forceful hitters of the 1920s and early '30s. Following a stunning victory over Bill Tilden in the quarterfinals of the 1926 U.S. Championships, ending Tilden's six-year sway, and a triumph over William Johnston in the 1927 challenge round, the right-handed Cochet established himself in 1928 as the world's foremost player. Winner of the U.S. and French Championships that year, and runner-up at Wimbledon, he became more of a national hero than ever as he scored three victories in the Cup challenge round.

With Lacoste's retirement from international play in 1929, Cochet was France's indispensable man. He led his country to victory over the United States in the challenge round in 1929, 1930 and 1932, and over the British in 1931.

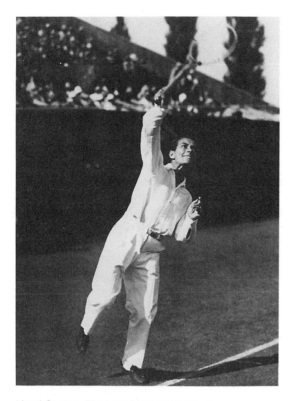

Henri Cochet: The Little Musketeer. (Fischer Collection/SPS)

"The Ballboy of Lyon," as he was called, was champion of France five times (four times after it was opened to non-French citizens in 1925), and won two Wimbledons (1927, 1929) and one U.S. (1928). Probably justifiably he felt unfairly treated in trying for a second U.S. in 1932. Darkness shut down his semifinal win over Wilmer Allison at 2-2 in sets. He had to complete that victory, 7-5, the following day, and then, after two hours rest, contest the final in which the weary Frenchman was no match for a fresh Ellsworth Vines, 6-4, 6-4, 6-4.

But for three matches as he closed out his 1927 Wimbledon championship, fourth seeded, he was a singular Henri Houdini. No one has concluded a major in such spectacular escapes, and all from Hall of Famers. Down two sets, he beat Frank Hunter in the quarters, 3-6, 3-6, 6-2, 6-2, 6-4. Trailing the great second-seeded Tilden, three

points from defeat at 1-5, 15-all in the third, he reeled off 17 straight points, also survived a service break to 3-2 in the fifth and won the last four games to seize their semi, 3-6, 4-6, 7-5, 6-4, 6-3. For an encore magnifique in the final, he lagged again and had to repel six match points to beat third-seeded Borotra, 4-6, 4-6, 6-3, 6-4, 7-5: hurdling a match point at 2-5, and five more with Borotra serving at 5-3!

He ranked No. 1 from 1928 through 1931 and was in the World Top Ten 10 times between 1922 and 1933. After France lost the Davis Cup to Great Britain in 1933, Cochet turned professional. He did not have much of a career as a pro, however, and after the war, in 1945, one of the most naturally gifted tennis players in history received reinstatement as an amateur, a role in which he had once ruled the tennis world, and continued playing well. Elected to the Hall of Fame in 1976, he died April 1, 1987, in St. Germain-en-Laye, France.

MAJOR TITLES (15)—*French singles, 1926, '28, '30, '32; Wimbledon singles, 1927, '29; U.S. singles, 1928; French doubles, 1927, '30, '32; Wimbledon doubles, 1926, '28; French mixed, 1928, '29; U.S. mixed, 1927.* DAVIS CUP—*1922, '23, '24, '26, '27, '28, '29, '30, '31, '32, '33; record: 34-8 in singles, 10-6 in doubles.* SINGLES RECORD IN THE MAJORS—*French (38-4), Wimbledon (43-8), U.S. (15-3).*

SARAH PALFREY COOKE
United States (1912–96)

If any player may be said to have been the sweetheart of tennis, as Mary Pickford was of the movies, her name was Sarah Palfrey.

Twice U.S. champion, Sarah Hammond Palfrey Fabyan Cooke Danzig was twice a runner-up for the title to Helen Jacobs, nine times U.S. Doubles champion, and twice doubles champion at Wimbledon, and she was an international attraction on both sides of the Atlantic and west to the Pacific.

Born Sept. 18, 1912, in Sharon, Mass., she was a carefully reared girl of upper-register Boston and a protégé of Hazel Hotchkiss Wight-

Sarah Palfrey Cooke: The sweetheart of tennis. (USTA)

man. The galleries loved her radiant smile and her unfailing graciousness in triumph and defeat alike, and they marveled at the cleverness and dispatch she used in the volleying position and at the execution of her sweeping backhand. She was one of the most accomplished performers around the net, thanks in part to the instruction of Wightman, a pioneer in introducing the volley as a major component of the women's game. A slip of a girl (5-foot-4, 116), Sarah was remarkable in the way she stood up to the more powerful hitters.

Sarah was so prized as a doubles partner in the 1930s and 1940s that she had the pick of the best. Seven times in Wightman Cup play she teamed with Jacobs, three times with Alice Marble, and once with Helen Wills Moody. But prestige comes from superiority in singles play, and in this the artful right-hander ranked no fewer than 13 times in the U.S. Top Ten. She was No. 1,

No. 2 or No. 3 seven times. She was in the World Top Ten six times between 1933 and 1939.

A 15-year-old Sarah made her Forest Hills debut in 1928, but not until her 13th campaign in 1941 did she go all the way. She joyfully remembered her initial trip abroad, so different from the casual jet-jaunting of today: "It was 1930, and I was 17. My mother and a sister went with me aboard the liner Scythia. We dressed for dinner and danced away every night."

Unable to defend her 1941 U.S. Singles title because of pregnancy and wartime family commitments to her husband, naval officer Elwood Cooke (1939 Wimbledon finalist to Bobby Riggs), Sarah made an extraordinary comeback to the Forest Hills scene in 1945 to win again, this time as a mother on the verge of her 33rd birthday. She mirrored her idol Wightman in this, too, becoming only the second to win the U.S. after bearing a child.

"She was a thorn for me," says four-time champ Pauline Betz Addie, recalling that but for Sarah she might well have run a record six straight championships. Pauline was in six successive finals, but Sarah won in 1941, 7-5, 6-2, and in a 1945 thriller, 3-6, 8-6, 6-4. "That 1945 final was the best I played, but still Sarah beat me with her volleying." She won the last three games from a service break behind.

An oddity was Sarah's appearance on a male championship honor roll. Because of the wartime manpower crisis, she and husband Elwood were permitted to enter the men's doubles of the Tri-State Championships in Cincinnati. They went to the final, losing to Hal Surface and Hall of Famer Bill Talbert.

A brood of tennis prodigies were the five Palfrey sisters, each of whom won at least one U.S. junior title, but Sarah was the one to achieve international renown. After her playing career, she was a successful business executive (as Mrs. Jerry Danzig in New York), and wrote on tennis in books and magazines.

Along with Alice Marble she lobbied the USTA to remove the color bar and allow future Hall of Famer Althea Gibson to play at the upper level amid whites in 1950. "She was calmly persuasive, had clout as an ex-champ, and got Althea into the U.S. Championships in 1950," says Gladys Heldman, founder of the women's pro tour. She was voted into the Hall of Fame in 1963, and died Feb. 27, 1996, in New York.

MAJOR TITLES *(18)—U.S. singles, 1941, '45; Wimbledon doubles, 1938, '39; U.S. doubles, 1930, '32, '34, '35, '37, '38, '39, '40, '41; French mixed, 1939; U.S. mixed, 1932, '35, '37, '41.* OTHER U.S. TITLES—*Clay Court singles, 1945; Indoor singles, 1940; Indoor doubles, 1928, '29, '30, '31, '33, with Hazel Hotchkiss Wightman; Indoor mixed, 1931, with Larry Rice; 1933, with G. Holmes Perkins; Clay Court mixed, 1945, with Elwood Cooke.* WIGHTMAN CUP—*1930, '31, '32, '33, '34, '35, '36, '37, '38, '39; record: 7-4 in singles, 7-2 in doubles.* SINGLES RECORD IN THE MAJORS—*French (2-2), Wimbledon (16-6), U.S. (41-14).*

JACK CRAWFORD
Australia (1908–91)

Few players so completely won the gallery as did John Herbert Crawford, called by one commentator the "most popular Wimbledon winner in history."

Indeed, Crawford, a right-hander, was an exemplary sportsman, as well as a handsome figure on the court (6-foot-1, 168) in his long, white flannels and long-sleeved shirt. And he moved easily, gracefully, over the turf with his flat-topped racket, a model of early vintage. He was in the World Top Ten six times, 1932–37, No. 1 in 1933.

Crawford, born March 22, 1908, in Albury, Australia, was a masterful player from the back of the court, driving the ball with length and pinpoint control with seemingly little strain. He played the classical game of solid, fluent strokes, and he played it so well that he came within one set of completing a Grand Slam five years before Don Budge accomplished the feat of winning the four major championships in one year.

Crawford's bid came in 1933, a year after he won 16 tournaments, starting with a victory over

Jack Crawford: Picture player. (UPI)

Keith Gledhill, 2-6, 7-5, 6-3, 6-2, in the Australian final. Next Crawford won the French Championship, beating Henri Cochet, 8-6, 6-1, 6-3, for the title. At Wimbledon came a legendary final against Ellsworth Vines that Crawford won, 4-6, 11-9, 6-2, 2-6, 6-4.

Crawford, a 5-to-1 short-ender with London bookies, twice held from 0-40 in the critical second set, and came to the wire breaking Vines at love with four winners, abruptly surging to the net in the last two games. Al Laney wrote: "For superlative play on both sides, the blending of stroke and strategy, the unrelenting speed of serve and considered counterstroke, I cannot remember another to place above it."

So a reluctant, fatigued Crawford moved on to Forest Hills and the U.S. Championships with an opportunity to complete the ultimate sweep. After defeating Frank Shields in the semifinals,

Crawford faced Fred Perry as the last obstacle in his path. Crawford lost the first set, but then won the next two and was one set away from a Slam. But his strength faded, owing in part to the asthma and insomnia he had at the time. Perry went on to victory in the next two sets, dashing Crawford's hopes, 6-3, 11-13, 4-6, 6-0, 6-1.

Still, the gallery loved this man— "Gentleman Jack," they called him—from Down Under. He won the championship of his country four times, and he did it all his way, seemingly never hurried, his every move appearing effortless, his serve belonging in a picture book. Jack Crawford was one of the greats of his time while playing tennis in the style of a gentleman of the old school.

Like most Aussies he got immense pleasure from Davis Cup, selected first in 1928, and was proud of being a member of the victorious 1939 team although he didn't play. In 1936 Jack led the team to a 3-2 upset of the U.S. in Philadelphia as he beat Wilmer Allison in the decider, 4-6, 6-3, 4-6, 6-2, 6-2. A victory over Germany, with him winning both singles, put the first Down Under entry into the Cup round since 1924, but Britain resisted, 3-2, as Jack was beaten by long-time rival, Perry, in the fifth match, 6-2, 6-3, 6-3.

When he beat Perry to win the 1935 Australian, Jack was taking part in an eighth straight major final (he didn't enter the U.S. in 1934), extraordinary consistency. Rod Laver would equal it when he got to the Wimbledon final in 1968 (Wimbledon, U.S. finalist, 1961, a Grand Slam in 1962, plus French of 1968, following his banishment as a pro). Bill Tilden was in 10 straight (1918–26), but his forays included only U.S. and Wimbledon. Crawford's seventh Aussie singles final, a record later tied by Roy Emerson, was lost in 1940 to Adrian Quist, but, at 32, he did knock off defending champ John Bromwich in the semis.

He took delight in winning three straight Aussie mixed titles with his wife, Marjorie Cox Crawford (1931–33). They were a unique wedded couple in appearing in major finals simultaneously in 1931, he winning, she losing the Australian.

He entered the Hall of Fame in 1979, and died Sept. 10, 1991, in Sydney.

MAJOR TITLES (17)—*Australian singles, 1931, '32, '33, '35; French singles, 1933; Wimbledon singles, 1933; Wimbledon doubles, 1935; Australian doubles, 1929, '30, '32, '35; French doubles, 1935; Australian mixed, 1931, '32, '33; French mixed, 1933; Wimbledon mixed, 1930.* DAVIS CUP—*1928, '30, '32, '33, '34, '35, '36, '37; record: 23-16 in singles, 13-5 in doubles.* SINGLES RECORD IN THE MAJORS— *Australian (52-15), French (19-4), Wimbledon (36-8), U.S. (10-4).*

KITTY GODFREE
Great Britain (1896–1992)

Kathleen McKane Godfree, a sturdy, good-natured competitor, may have been the best female player Britain has produced. In winning Wimbledon for the first time in 1924, she charged back from 1-4 in the second set to hand Helen Wills her lone defeat in nine visits to the Big W, 4-6, 6-4, 6-4. She also beat Wills in the British Wightman Cup victory that year at Wimbledon. Who else could boast of royal-flushing "Little Miss Poker Face" twice in a season?

Kitty won Wimbledon again two years later over Lili de Alvarez, who was within a stroke of a 4-1 lead in the decisive third, 6-2, 4-6, 6-3. Thus Kitty and Dorothy Round (1934, '37) were the only Brits to win twice since World War I. She was one of a select group to play more than 100 matches (146) at Wimbledon, 19th on the list: 38-11 in singles, 33-12 in doubles, 40-12 in mixed between 1919 and 1934.

In 1923 Kitty had reached her third Wimbledon final by beating Elizabeth Ryan, 1-6, 6-2, 6-4, but lost to Suzanne Lenglen, 6-2, 6-2. In the U.S. Championships that year, Kitty offered a dangerous quarterfinal challenge to Wills, coming from 2-5 to 5-all in the third set before losing, 2-6, 6-2, 7-5. In 1925 she pushed Wills in the final of the U.S. Championships, losing 3-6, 6-0, 6-2, after eliminating Molla Mallory and Ryan.

She was a member of the British team that played the United States for the Wightman Cup in

Kitty McKane Godfree: Dynamic Britisher. (UPI)

in singles. Four years later, a silver in doubles with Phyllis Covell and a bronze in singles. Active throughout her long life, she was a 92-year-old spectator at the 1988 Games in Seoul, and approved the entry of professionals, saying, "It's a sign of the times if you want the best in the Olympics."

Kitty and her husband, Leslie Godfree, were the only married couple to win the Wimbledon mixed, in 1926. In 1922 she and Margaret Mc-Kane Stocks were the only sisters to contest a Wimbledon doubles final, losing to Lenglen and Ryan. She was in the World Top Ten 1925, 1926, and 1927, No. 2 in 1926.

She was among the champions of the past who received Centenary medallions on Wimbledon's Centre Court in 1977 and was inducted into the Hall of Fame in 1978. Born May 7, 1896, in London, she died there at the age of 96, June 19, 1992.

MAJOR TITLES *(7)—Wimbledon singles, 1924, '26; U.S. doubles, 1923, '27; U.S. mixed, 1925; Wimbledon mixed, 1924, '26.* WIGHTMAN CUP—*1923, '24, '25, '26, '27, '30, '34; record: 5-5 in singles, 2-5 in doubles.* SINGLES RECORD IN THE MAJORS—*French (6-2), Wimbledon (38-11), U.S. (7-2).*

HELEN JACOBS
United States (1908—)

Helen Hull Jacobs had the misfortune to be a contemporary of Helen Wills Moody. Four times in the battle of Helens in the final round at Wimbledon, Jacobs lost. She also lost to her arch-rival at Forest Hills in the 1928 U.S. final.

On top of all those defeats to Helen the First, Jacobs was beaten in the 1934 Wimbledon final by Dorothy Round of Britain, and three times she was turned back in a U.S. final by Alice Marble (1936, 1939, 1940).

Particularly bitter for her to take was a defeat in the 1935 Wimbledon final. Moody that season was struggling, and in the final round Jacobs led at match point, 5-3. Victory seemed at hand when Wills threw up a lob that barely got to the net,

the inaugural matches in 1923 in the Forest Hills stadium. She lost to Wills and Mallory, both members of the host team. But the following year, in the first of these international team competitions held in Britain, Kitty beat Mallory as well as Wills, and the home team won by a surprising margin of 6-1. Then in 1925 the British won again, 4-3, with Kitty defeating Mallory and losing to Wills. In 1926 she beat both Mary K. Browne and Ryan, but the British lost, 4-3, at Wimbledon despite Kitty's heroics.

In 1925 she arrived in the French final but was beaten by Lenglen, 6-1, 6-2.

Speedy, smart and a fighter with an all-around game, she was her country's most successful Olympian, gathering five medals in the 1920 and 1924 Games. In 1920 she won a gold in the doubles with Winifred McNair, a silver in mixed doubles with Max Woosnam and a bronze

Helen Jacobs: Artist at the net. (New York Herald Tribune)

and Jacobs waited to smash it for the final point. But a wind current caught the ball and Jacobs, off balance, hit it into the net. Moody rallied and went on to her seventh Wimbledon title. At the time, Jacobs had none.

In spite of so much adversity, Jacobs, a 5-foot-6, 145-pound right-hander, born Aug. 6, 1908, in Globe, Ariz., was as stout of heart as any champion. A U.S. finalist eight times over a stretch of a dozen years (1928–40), Jacobs won four straight, 1932–35, ringing up a 28-match winning streak until dropping a hard-fought 1936 final, 4-6, 6-3, 6-2, to her Forest Hills nemesis, Alice Marble. Only Helen Wills (46) and Chris Evert (31) had longer U.S. streaks, but she and Evert were the only victors four straight years. In 1932 at Forest Hills she caused a sartorial furor, introducing shorts to the female tournament. At last in 1936 she took the victor's silver at Wim-

bledon, beating Hilda Krahwinkel Sperling, 6-2, 4-6, 7-5. Twice she made it to the French final, but fell to the other Helen, 6-2, 6-1, in 1930, and lefty Peggy Scriven, 7-5, 4-6, 6-1, in 1934.

Jacobs' unflagging courage, her iron will to win, was her biggest asset. She had little of the power that Moody applied, and Jacobs' forehand stroke was so unsatisfactory that she forsook it for a sliced cut at the ball, not too effective either to stand off a full-blooded drive or to repel a volleyer. Her backhand, while not severe, was steadfast, reliable against any amount of pressure, and she won heavily with it.

It was at the net where she was most effective. She was not as conclusive with her volley or her smash as Marble, but she was a determined, skilled foe at close quarters, and her fighting traits counted most, whatever her position on the court. Even when afflicted with injuries, she refused to be discouraged. Her admirable qualities, including sportsmanship and great self-reliance, had a strong appeal for tennis galleries.

A feud was built up in publications between the two Helens that Jacobs said never existed. Moody was pictured as resenting Jacobs following in her footsteps. Both played at the Berkeley (Calif.) Tennis Club, had the same coach, William "Pop" Fuller, won national junior championships two years in a row and attended the University of California. The Jacobs' family lived in the Wills' former home. The two Helens did not see each other except in connection with tennis.

Jacobs, after eight losses to Moody, finally got the victory she was after in the 1933 U.S. Championships, although even then it was not a complete one. She won the first set against Moody, 8-6, and lost the second, 6-3. When the score went to 3-0 in Jacobs' favor in the third set, Moody walked to the umpire's stand, informed the official that because of pain in her back she was unable to continue, and conceded the match. Jacobs had dealt Moody her first big defeat since 1926. It would be Jacobs' lone win in an 11-match rivalry.

She was ranked in the World Top Ten 12 straight times from 1928, No. 1 in 1936, and in the U.S. Top Ten 13 times between 1927 and 1941, No. 1 in 1932, 1933, 1934, and 1935, and served in the Navy in World War II.

She was elected to the Hall of Fame in 1962.

MAJOR TITLES *(10)—Wimbledon singles, 1936; U.S. singles, 1932, '33, '34, '35; U.S. doubles, 1932, '33, '34, '35; U.S. mixed, 1934.* WIGHTMAN CUP—*1927, '28, '29, '30, '31, '32, '33, '34, '35, '36, '37, '39; record: 14-7 in singles, 5-4 in doubles.* SINGLES RECORD IN THE MAJORS— *French (21-7), Wimbledon (55-11), U.S. (64-11).*

BILL JOHNSTON
United States (1894–1946)

William M. Johnston's name is inevitably associated with Bill Tilden's. Tilden was "Big Bill" (6-foot-2) and Johnston "Little Bill" (5-foot-8½) and they were the twin terrors who turned back the Australasians, French and Japanese in the Davis Cup challenge round from 1920 through 1926, a seven-year span of invincibility unequaled in those international team matches.

Big Bill and Little Bill were teammates and they were also rivals. It was Johnston's bad luck that his career was contemporaneous with the player many regard as the greatest ever. Otherwise Johnston might have won the U.S. Championships most of the years it fell to Tilden, from 1920 to 1925. As it was, Little Bill won it twice, in 1915 and in 1919, defeating Maurice McLoughlin the first time and Tilden in the 1919 final. Johnston was runner-up six times, and in five of those years it was Tilden who beat him in the final.

Until the French began to catch up to Big Bill and Little Bill in 1926, Johnston had been winning his Davis Cup matches with the loss of few sets. In seven challenge rounds, he won 11 of 14 matches in singles. He lost only once until 1927, when his age and his health began to tell. He ranked in the World Top Ten eight straight years from 1919 and in the U.S. Top Ten 12 times between 1913 and 1926, No. 1 in 1915 and in 1919.

Bill Johnston: Tops with topspin forehand. (Fischer Collection/SPS)

The topspin forehand drive he hammered with the western grip was one of the most famous and effective shots in tennis history. No other player executed it as well as he did, taking the ball shoulder high and leaping off the ground on his follow-through. He was also one of the best volleyers the game has known, despite meeting the ball near the service line, where he stationed himself because of his shortness. He used the same face of the racket for backhand and forehand.

A right-hander, Johnston was born Nov. 2, 1894, in San Francisco and developed many of his skills on public parks courts. His whole game was aggressive and he played to win on the merit of his strokes rather than on the opponent's errors. Though he did not have a big serve, overhead he was secure and angled his smash effectively. He had as much fight as anyone who was ever champion, and many times when he came off the court, dripping with perspiration after a prolonged struggle, he was five to eight pounds below his usual weight of 125.

Such was the case in his U.S. final with Tilden in 1922 at the Germantown Cricket Club in Philadelphia in which Johnston won the first two sets and led by 3-0 in the fourth. It seemed that every spectator in the stands was cheering for Johnston, the favorite of galleries virtually every time he went on the court. Both he and Tilden had two legs on the challenge trophy, and Little Bill had his heart set on retiring it for his permanent keeping in this match. It was a crushing disappointment when he lost in five sets.

Following the 1927 season, Johnston retired from competition. His health had not been robust from the time he served in the Navy in World War I. He died May 1, 1946, and 12 years later was enshrined in the Hall of Fame. Little Bill had made a big name in tennis.

MAJOR TITLES (7)—*Wimbledon singles, 1923; U.S. singles, 1915, '19; U.S. doubles, 1915, '16, '20; U.S. mixed, 1921.* OTHER U.S. TITLES—*Clay Court singles, 1919, '20; Clay Court doubles, 1919, with Sam Hardy.* DAVIS CUP— *1920, '21, '22, '23, '24, '25, '26, '27; record: 14-3 in singles, 4-0 in doubles.* SINGLES RECORD IN THE MAJORS— *Wimbledon (8-1), U.S. (59-11).*

RENÉ LACOSTE
France (1904–96)

He was not particularly athletic in build or in his movements, and as a reserved and rather shy youth he seemed to be more fitted for the world of education, law or medicine than for athletic achievement. But Jean René Lacoste, known as the Crocodile, would win Wimbledon and the U.S. twice, the French thrice and become a member of the Four Musketeers, the scourges of the tennis world in the 1920s. He was in the World Top Ten six straight years from 1924, No. 1 in 1926–27.

Lacoste was a self-made champion, a player who won world renown through sheer hard work and devoted application rather than through the benefit of natural talent. Born in Paris, July 2, 1904, he did not go onto a court until he was 15 years old, while on a trip with his father to England. His development after that was slow.

His father, a wealthy manufacturer of automobiles, agreed to his son's devoting himself to tennis, but with the understanding that he must set himself the task of becoming a world champion and achieve his goal within five years or drop it.

In his determination to excel, Lacoste trained faithfully and read and observed everything, even keeping a notebook on the strengths and weaknesses of his contemporaries. He became a master of the backcourt game, choosing to maintain a length of inexorable pressure to exact the error or the opening for the finishing shot, and repelling the volleyer with passing shots and lobs.

In recognition of his growing success, he was selected in 1923 as the fourth Musketeer to blend with Jean Borotra, Jacques Brugnon and Henri Cochet in the alliance that would bring France the Davis Cup, and the following year he was in his first major final, Wimbledon, only to lose to Borotra, 6-4 in the fifth. But in 1925 he came back to win the Big W in a four-set rematch, and took it for a second time in 1928 over Cochet. Also in 1925 Lacoste won the French, over Borotra, whom he also beat in a memorable rainy 1929 final, 6-3, 2-6, 6-0, 2-6, 8-6.

As the French drew closer to the Cup, losing the challenge round to the U.S., 4-1, in 1926, Lacoste made the breakthrough for team morale, beating Tilden, 4-6, 6-4, 8-6, 8-6, Big Bill's first Cup loss after 16 wins. The year 1927 was momentous, enclosing three victories over Tilden: the first a two-match-points-saving French final, 6-4, 4-6, 5-7, 6-3, 11-9; a challenge round-squaring (2-2), 6-3, 4-6, 6-3, 6-2 triumph as the French grabbed the Cup; the U.S. final.

Perhaps the U.S. was the most stirring, where the efficiency of his backcourt game thwarted the great one. The 34-year-old Tilden attacked for close to two hours and volleyed far more than was his custom, but despite efforts that brought him to

René Lacoste: Relentless as a crocodile. (Fischer Collection/SPS)

mark, a crocodile, on the breast, starting the flood of apparel logos. Lacoste also developed the split-shaft steel racket that appeared in 1967 as the Wilson T2000, used so successfully for years by Jimmy Connors.

His wife, Simone Thion de la Chaume, was a French amateur golf champion, and his daughter, Catherine Lacoste, won the U.S. Open golf title in 1967. He died Oct. 12, 1996, in St. Jean-de-Luz, France.

MAJOR TITLES *(10)—French singles, 1925, '27, '29; U.S. singles, 1926, '27; Wimbledon singles, 1925, '28; French doubles, 1925, '29; Wimbledon doubles, 1925.* DAVIS CUP— *1923, '24, '25, '26, '27, '28; record: 32-8 in singles, 8-3 in doubles.* SINGLES RECORD IN THE MAJORS— *French (29-3), Wimbledon (28-5), U.S. (19-3).*

SUZANNE LENGLEN
France (1899–1938)

In the days of ground-length tennis dresses, Suzanne Rachel Flore Lenglen played at Wimbledon with her dress cut just above the calf. She wept openly during matches, pouted, sipped brandy between sets. Some called her shocking and indecent, but she was merely ahead of her time, and she brought France the greatest global sports renown it had ever known.

Right-hander Lenglen was No. 1 in 1925–26, the first years of world rankings. She won Wimbledon every year but one from 1919 through 1925, the exception being 1924, when illness led to her withdrawal after the fourth round. Her 1919 title match, at the age of 20, with 40-year-old Dorothea Douglass Chambers is one of the hallmarks of tennis history.

Chambers, the seven-time champion, was swathed in stays, petticoats, high-necked shirt-waist, and a long skirt that swept the court. The young Lenglen was in her revealing dress that shocked the British at the sight of ankles and forearms. After the second set, Lenglen took some comfort from her brandy and won, 10-8, 4-6, 9-7, in a dramatic confrontation, rescuing two match points.

the point of exhaustion, he could not win a set. The sphinx-like Lacoste, 22, kept the ball going back the full length of the court with the inevitability of fate and hardly an inexcusable error. The score of the fabulous match was 11-9, 6-3, 11-9, enabling Lacoste to retain the U.S. title he had won the previous year against Borotra.

In 1928 Lacoste lost the opener in the Davis Cup to Tilden and it marked the Frenchman's last appearance in international team matches, owing to his health. After winning the French title in 1929, he withdrew from competition, having more than fulfilled the goal he once never seemed suited for—that of a tennis champion.

He captained the victorious French Davis Cup teams of 1931–32. Ever seeking to improve playing conditions, he designed the first shirts specifically for tennis, the short-sleeved cotton polo so common now, and put his familiar trade-

After her victory, Lenglen became easily the greatest drawing card tennis had known, and she was one of those who made it a major box-office attraction. Along with a magnetic personality, grace and style, she was the best woman player the world had seen.

Lenglen, born May 24, 1899, in Paris, played an all-court game such as few had excelled at. She moved with rare grace, unencumbered by the tight layers of garments others wore. She had extraordinary accuracy with her classical, rhythmic ground strokes. For hours daily her father, Charles Lenglen, had her direct the ball at a handkerchief he moved from spot to spot. Her control was so unfailing that she thought it shameful to hit the ball into the net or beyond the line. In addition, she had so keen a sense of anticipation that she invariably was in the right position to meet her opponent's shot.

Her 1926 match against Helen Wills in a tournament at Cannes, France, caused a sensation. Tickets brought unheard-of wealth to scalpers, and the roofs and windows of apartments and hotels overlooking the court were crowded with fans. Lenglen, on the verge of collapse during the tense match, but saved by smelling salts and brandy, defeated the 20-year-old Wills, 6-3, 8-6.

Lenglen's career was not free of setbacks, however. In the 1921 U.S. Championships, having lost the first set badly to Molla Mallory, Lenglen walked weeping and coughing to the umpire and said she could not continue, defaulting the match. She made up for it the next year at Wimbledon by defeating Mallory, 6-2, 6-0, in the final and did not lose another match for the remainder of her amateur career.

In the 1926 Wimbledon, Lenglen had a terrifying ordeal. She kept Queen Mary waiting in the Royal Box for her appearance when, owing to a misunderstanding or a failure of communications, Lenglen did not have the correct information about the time she was to be on court. The ghastly error was too much. She fainted and Wimbledon saw her no more as a competitor. She with-

Suzanne Lenglen: The magnificent swinger. (Fischer Collection/SPS)

drew from the tournament, and that year went on a tour for money in the United States under the management of C. C. Pyle, winning all 38 matches against Mary K. Browne. It marked the start of professional tennis as a playing career.

At the age of 39, Lenglen died of pernicious anemia, July 4, 1938, in Paris. She was elected to the Hall of Fame in 1978. There was speculation that her health had been undermined by her long hours of practice as a young girl. But she had brought the glamour of the stage and the ballet to the court, and queues formed at tennis clubs where before there had been indifference. She had emancipated the female player from layers of starched clothing and set the short-hair style as well. During her career she won 81 singles titles (seven without the loss of a game!), 73 doubles and 8 mixed. She had brought the game of tennis into a new era.

MAJOR TITLES (21)—*French singles, 1925, '26; Wimbledon singles, 1919, '20, '21, '22, '23, '25; French doubles, 1925, '26; Wimbledon doubles, 1919, '20, '21, '22, '23, '25; French mixed, 1925, '26; Wimbledon mixed, 1920, '22, '25.* SINGLES RECORD IN THE MAJORS— *French (10-0), Wimbledon (32-0), U.S. (0-1).*

MOLLA MALLORY
Norway/United States (1884–1959)

Anna Margarethe "Molla" Bjurstedt Mallory had less in the way of stroke equipment than most players who have become tennis champions. But the sturdy, Norwegian-born woman, the daughter of an army officer, had the heart and pride of a gladiator, could run with limitless endurance, and was a fierce competitor. She won the U.S. Championship a record eight times and she administered the only post-World War I defeat that Suzanne Lenglen suffered as an amateur.

It was her match with Lenglen in the second round of the U.S. Championship at Forest Hills in 1921 that won Mallory her greatest celebrity. She won the first set, 6-2, playing with a fury that took her opponent by surprise, running down balls interminably to wear out the French girl in long rallies, and hitting her mighty topspin forehand down the line for blazing winners. Lenglen, the Wimbledon queen, out of breath from running, coughing and weeping, walked to the umpire's stand after two points of the second set and informed the official that she was ill and could not continue. This was as sensational a reversal as ever recorded on the courts.

Mallory, a right-hander, whose game was developed in Oslo, Norway, where she was born March 6, 1884, came to the United States as Molla Bjurstedt in 1915 and won the U.S. Championship 1915, 1916, 1917, 1918, 1920, 1921, 1922 and in 1926 at age 42, as the elder among all major champions.

She was a player of the old school. She held that a woman could not sustain a volleying attack in a long match and she put her reliance on her

Molla Mallory: A striking force out of Norway. (UPI)

baseline game. That game amounted to a forehand attack and an omnivorous defense that wore down her opponents. She took the ball on the rise and drove it from corner to corner to keep her rival on the constant run and destroy her control. The quick return made her passing shots all the more effective.

In her first U.S. Championship final—in 1915, against Hazel Hotchkiss Wightman, who had won the title three times—Mallory yielded only the first set, after which Wightman began to tire and could not get to the volleying position, and won, 4-6, 6-2, 6-0.

Eleanor Goss in the 1918 final and Marion Zinderstein in the 1920 final were strong volleyers, like Mrs. Wightman, but neither could win a set against the Norwegian native.

Mallory yielded her title to Helen Wills in 1923, 6-2, 6-1, after defeating her in the 1922 final, and lost to her again in 1924. In 1926 Mallory hit one of the heights of her career when she came back from 0-4 in the third set of the final against Elizabeth Ryan and saved a match point in winning her eighth championship. Never had a gallery at Forest Hills in the years of her triumphs cheered her on as it did in this remarkable rally.

Mallory reached the final at Wimbledon in 1922 and lost to Lenglen, 6-2, 6-0. Mallory was twice a semifinalist at Wimbledon, and she played on the Wightman Cup team in 1923, 1924, 1925, 1927 and 1928.

Although she had won an Olympic bronze in singles for Norway in 1912 at Stockholm, and was the champion of her homeland, Molla was relatively unknown when she arrived in New York as Miss Bjurstedt to begin work as a masseuse in 1915. She entered the U.S. Indoor Championships that year unheralded and beat defending champ Marie Wagner, 6-4, 6-4, the first of five singles titles on the boards. Having thus made something of a name, she went outdoors to enlarge on it on Philadelphia turf by beginning her record collection of eight U.S. titles, winning the fifth as Mrs. Franklin Mallory in 1920. In 15 years at Forest Hills her worst finish was a quarterfinal in 1927 at age 43!

She was in the World Top Ten in 1925, 1926 and 1927, its first three years, and the U.S. Top Ten 13 times between 1915 and 1928, No. 1 in 1915, 1916, 1918 through 1922, and 1926. She bade farewell to the U.S. Champion-ships as a 45-year-old semifinalist in 1929. She entered the Hall of Fame in 1958 and died Nov. 22, 1959, in Stockholm.

MAJOR TITLES (13)—*U.S. singles, 1915, '16, '17, '18, '20, '21, '22, '26; U.S. doubles, 1916, '17; U.S. mixed, 1917, '22, '23.* OTHER U.S. TITLES—*Indoor singles; 1915, '16, '18, '21, '22; Indoor doubles, 1916, with Marie Wagner; Indoor mixed, 1921, '22, with Bill Tilden; Clay Court singles, 1915, '16; Clay Court mixed, 1916, with George Church.* WIGHTMAN CUP—*1923, '25, '27, '28; record: 5-5 in singles, 1-1 in doubles.* SINGLES RECORD IN THE MAJORS—*French (1-1), Wimbledon (19-9), U.S. (67-7).*

ALICE MARBLE

United States (1913–90)

One of the most attractive players to grace the courts, Alice Marble was deceptive. Her blonde loveliness and her trim athletic but feminine figure belied the fact that she played tennis in the late 1930s in a masculine manner that more closely approximated the game of Don Budge or Ellsworth Vines than it did the game of any woman.

There had been women before her who could volley and hit overheads—Suzanne Lenglen and Helen Wills Moody among them—but none played the "big game," the game of the big serve-and-volley, as it was to be called years later, as their standard method of attack the way Marble did regularly. No woman had a stronger service. Her first serve was as severe as any, and she delivered the taxing American twist serve as few women have been able to do. She followed it to the net for emphatic volleys or the strongest kind of overhead smash.

A right-hander pressing the attack without a letup, she could win from the back of the court as well as at the net. Her ground strokes, made with a short backswing and taking the ball on the rise, were not overpowering, and her forehand was not always steadfast against the many fine backcourt players of her day, in part because of her daring in playing for winners. But in the aggressive all-court game she played, with her speed and agility and with her skill in the use of the drop shot, they served to carry her to four U.S. titles and to the Wimbledon Championship. World War II brought about French, Wimbledon and Australian tournament suspension or she might have added appreciably to her major conquests.

Her dominance is evidenced by her record of invincibility in 1939 and 1940. She did not lose a match of consequence either year. In winning her fourth U.S. title in 1940, she did not yield a set. She was voted by sportswriters the Woman Athlete of the Year in 1939 and 1940.

She was in the World Top Ten 1933, 1936, 1937, 1938 and 1939, No. 1 the last year, and in the U.S. Top Ten those years, plus 1932 and 1940, No. 1 from 1936 through 1940.

Second-seeded at Wimbledon in 1938, but jolted in the semis by unseeded Helen Jacobs, 6-4, 6-4, Alice then embarked invulnerably on one of the greatest passages in the game's history. She won the remaining 18 tournaments and 111 matches of her amateur tenure, posting nine tourney titles and 45-0 match marks in 1939 and 1940. The streak was second only to Helen Wills Moody's 27 titles, 158-match procession to the 1933 U.S. final. Thus for her last three years of amateurism she won 23 of 24 tournaments, 120 of 122 matches.

Born Sept. 28, 1913, on a farm in Plumas County, Calif., she was a product of the public courts of San Francisco's Golden Gate Park, a natural athlete who worked out with the minor league baseball players of the local Seals (including Joe DiMaggio) when she was their 13-year-old mascot. Marble made perhaps the most remarkable recovery from illness and obscurity in the game's annals to become the very best of her time.

Her soaring career—in 1933 she was No. 10 in the world, a U.S. quarterfinalist—seemed over by her 20th birthday, and she vanished from the scene for almost two years. In a weekend tourney at Easthampton, N.Y., that year she had to play singles and doubles semifinals and finals on the last day (108 games!) in 100-degree heat. The result was sunstroke, keeping her from Wightman Cup singles, weakening her for the remainder of the season. The following spring, during team matches in Paris, Alice collapsed and was hospitalized. Cut down by anemia and pleurisy, frustrated and depressed by misdiagnosis of tuberculosis and the medical judgement that she must forget tennis, she didn't recover her health fully until 1936 when, startlingly, she won the first of her four U.S. titles, deposing Helen Jacobs, 4-6, 6-3, 6-2.

She began to play again in 1935 in California, and changed to the eastern grip. When in

Alice Marble: The lady was a tiger. (UPI)

1936 Marble returned to the East, officials of the USTA were fearful that she might jeopardize her health permanently if she resumed serious competition. But she was determined, and with the assistance of her coach, Eleanor Tennant, she undertook to re-establish herself and get back to the top.

At Forest Hills she came up against Jacobs in the U.S. final. Jacobs had held the title four years in a row, raising serious doubts about Marble's chances. But Marble won, attaining the No. 1 ranking. In 1937 she lost in the quarterfinals but again was ranked No. 1, and she held the top spot in 1938, 1939 and 1940, winning the U.S. crown all three years and winning all three titles at Wimbledon in 1939. In four years of Wightman Cup play she lost but one match in singles and one in doubles.

An aging Bill Tilden, 48, and Don Budge, 25, at the top of his game, headlined the 1941 pro tour that opened at Madison Square Garden, along with Alice Marble and Mary Hardwick. Budge won, 51-7, and Marble was 72-3 in the head-to-head series of matches.

In her 1991 autobiography, *Courting Danger,* Alice wrote that she decided to turn pro at the end of 1940 because, "What's left for me? I'm champion . . . and may as well make the most of it." She got a $75,000 guarantee from L. B. Icely, the president of Wilson, who bankrolled the tour. This, she said, despite a $100,000 offer from the wealthy tennis fan Will duPont (who later married Margaret Osborne) to not turn pro because he enjoyed watching her on the Eastern grass circuit. During World War II she played exhibitions at military installations across the U.S., and revealed in her book that she was sent as a government agent to Switzerland in 1945 to spy on Nazis before the war ended.

She entered the Hall of Fame in 1964, and died Dec. 13, 1990, in Palm Springs, California.

MAJOR TITLES (18)—*Wimbledon singles, 1939; U.S. singles, 1936, '38, '39, '40; Wimbledon doubles, 1938, '39; U.S. doubles, 1937, '38, '39, '40; Wimbledon mixed, 1937, '38, '39; U.S. mixed, 1936, '37, '38, '40.* OTHER U.S. TITLES— *Clay Court singles, 1940; Clay Court doubles, 1940, with Mary Arnold.* WIGHTMAN CUP—*1933, '37, '38, '39; record: 5-1 in singles, 3-1 in doubles.* SINGLES RECORD IN THE MAJORS— *Wimbledon (14-2), U.S. (31-4).*

MAURICE McLOUGHLIN
United States (1890–1957)

He came out of out the West with a cannonball service, spectacular volleys and overhead smashes. He created great excitement in the East and abroad at Wimbledon with the violence of his attack. And more than anything else, Maurice Evans "Red" McLoughlin, known as the California Comet, opened the eyes of the public to tennis as a demanding game of speed, endurance and skill.

Tennis at the turn of the century was a moderately paced game contested from the back of the court. But McLoughlin, a right-hander, carried this attack forward, projecting the cannonball serve and rushing in behind it to meet the return near the net with a cataclysmic overhead or a masterful volley. The volley was not new to the game (it had been used in the first Championship in 1881), but it had not nearly been the finishing stroke that Red Mac made it.

Born Jan. 7, 1890, in Carson City, Nev., McLoughlin polished his game on the public parks courts of northern California, and this in itself was a departure in the direction of democratizing the game. Most of the top-ranking players had developed their games on the turf of exclusive clubs in the East or their own private family courts.

At 19 he had developed sufficiently to be named to the Davis Cup team to play alongside another San Francisco teenager, Melville Long, 18, against Australasia in the 1909 Challenge Round. They were whitewashed but Red absorbed valuable international seasoning. He enlivened five straight U.S. finals, starting in 1911, winning 1912 and 1913 battles over Wallace Johnson and Dick Williams, losing his title to Williams in the Championships' farewell to Newport. At the Forest Hills inaugural, an all-San Francisco clash, he was beaten by the rising Bill Johnston, 1-6, 6-0, 7-5, 10-8.

His one venture to England, 1913, was an artistic success as the U.S. regained the Davis Cup, and he helped draw unprecedentedly large crowds to Wimbledon, where he won the all-comers over Aussie Stanley Doust, 6-3, 6-4, 7-5. In the Challenge Round he fought defending champ Tony Wilding all the way, but missed a set point at 5-4, 40-30, and was beaten, 8-6, 6-3, 10-8. Then came the Cup tests, shutouts of Germany and Canada, and a 1-1 first day split against Cup-holding Britain. That evolved to a 3-2 U.S. victory as McLoughlin partnered Harold Hackett to a five-set win over Roper Barrett and Charles Dixon. It set up Red for the finisher over Dixon, 8-6, 6-3, 6-2.

McLoughlin reached his peak the next year in the Davis Cup final, even though the Cup was

Maurice McLoughlin: California Comet. (USTA)

said he was burned out from his violent exertions on the court.

On Dec. 10, 1957—the year of his entry into the Hall of Fame—the Comet died. But in the short time that he had lighted the tennis firmament, as no one before him, he had started the sport on its way to becoming a popular game for Americans. He ranked No. 1 in 1914 and was in the U.S. Top Ten seven straight years from 1909, No. 1 in 1912, 1913 and 1914.

MAJOR TITLES (5)—*U.S. singles, 1912, '13; U.S. doubles, 1912, '13, '14.* DAVIS CUP—*1909, '11, '13, '14; record: 9-4 in singles, 3-4 in doubles.* SINGLES RECORD IN THE MAJORS—*Wimbledon (7-1), U.S. (49-9).*

HELEN WILLS MOODY

United States (1905—)

It scarcely seems possible that two players of the transcendent ability of Helen Newington Wills Moody Roark and Suzanne Lenglen could have been contemporaries. They were ranked for close to half a century as the two best female tennis players of all time. Their records are unmatched and hardly have been approached.

While indeed contemporaries, they were rivals in only one match, played in 1926 and won by Lenglen, 6-3, 8-6, at Cannes, France. Lenglen, not yet 27, was at the crest of her game, with six Wimbledon championships in her possession. Wills' game at 20 had not quite attained full maturity, though she had been in the Wimbledon final of 1924, and would win eight times. Their rivalry was limited to the single meeting, for later that same year Wills was stricken with appendicitis and Lenglen turned pro.

It would be difficult to imagine two players of more different personalities and types of game. Between 1919 and 1938 Wills won 52 of 92 tournaments on a 398-35-match record, a .919 average, and had a 158-match winning streak (27 tournaments to the 1933 U.S. final, the only time she lost to Helen Jacobs in 11 meetings).

lost. The matching of McLoughlin and Norman Brookes of Australasia brought forth tennis that was a revelation to the thousands who attended. The match was characterized as "never been equaled." McLoughlin won, 17-15, 6-3, 6-3. The matches attracted 14,000 people daily, and McLoughlin was given much of the credit for the large crowds.

After the Davis Cup success, the 1915 *Tennis Guide* said, "In McLoughlin America undoubtedly has the greatest tennis player of all time." Yet he never again attained that form. Absent from the East for several years, he returned after Army duty in World War I and was hardly recognizable. He had lost his cannonball and his punch. Gone was his whirlwind speed. After he was defeated by Dick Williams decisively in the 1919 quarters, he left the tennis scene for golf, where he soon was shooting in the low 70s. His tennis career had come to a premature end. Some

Quiet, reserved, and never changing expression, Wills, known as Little Miss Poker Face, played with unruffled poise and never exhibited the style, the flair or the emotional outbursts that Lenglen did. From her first appearance in the East in 1921, when she was national junior champion, Wills' typical garb on the court was a white sailor suit, white eyeshade and white shoes and stockings.

The game she played right-handed was one of sheer power, which she had developed in practice against men on the West Coast. From both forehand and backhand she hammered the ball almost the full length of the court regularly, and the speed, pace and depth of her drives, in conjunction with her tactical moves, sufficed to subdue her opponents. She could hit winners as spectacularly from the baseline on the backhand as on the forehand.

She went to the net occasionally, not nearly as often as Lenglen, and Wills was sound in her volleying and decisive overhead with her smash. Her slice service, breaking wide and pulling the receiver beyond the alley, was as good as any female player has commanded.

Her footwork was not so good. She did not move with the grace and quickness of Lenglen, and opponents fared best against her who could use the drop shot or changes of length to draw her forward and send her running back. Anchored to the baseline, she could run any opponent into the ground. Because of her exceptional sense of anticipation, she seemed to be in the right spot, and it was not often that she appeared to be hurried in her stroking.

She was born Oct. 6, 1905, in Centreville, Calif., and the facts of her invincibility are stark. She won the Wimbledon title a record eight times (surpassed by Martina Navratilova's nine in 1990) in nine tries, her only loss coming in her first appearance, in 1924. She won the U.S. championship seven times. From 1927 to 1932 she did not lose a set in singles anywhere. She won seven U.S., five Wimbledon and four French

Helen Wills Moody: Little Miss Poker Face. (USTA)

championships without loss of a set until Dorothy Round of Britain extended her to 6-4, 6-8, 6-3 in the 1933 Wimbledon final.

In Wightman Cup play from 1923 to 1938, she won 18 singles matches and lost two, both in 1924. She won the Olympic singles and doubles in Paris in 1924. When she scored her first Wimbledon victory, in 1927, she was the first American woman to be crowned there since May Sutton in 1905.

Two of her three most remarkable matches were her meeting with Lenglen in 1926 and her default because of back pain to rival Helen Jacobs when trailing 0-3 in the third set of the 1933 U.S. Championships. The third remarkable match was in the 1935 Wimbledon final in which Jacobs led, 5-2, in the third set and stood at match point, only to see the then Mrs. Moody rally and add one more victory to her astounding record.

In 1928 she became the first player to win three majors in the same year—French, Wimbledon and U.S.—and the first American to rule at Stade Roland Garros, where she was unbeaten while winning four titles. Her total of 19 major singles titles was the record for 32 years, until Margaret Smith Court (24) passed her in 1970. But her success was the most phenomenal ever, considering that she won 19 of 22 entered, winning 126 of 129 matches (.977), never worse than finalist.

She became Mrs. Aidan Roark in 1939 and was inducted into the Hall of Fame in 1969.

MAJOR TITLES *(31)—French singles, 1928, '29, '30, '32; Wimbledon singles, 1927, '28, '29, '30, '32, '33, '35, '38; U.S. singles, 1923, '24, '25, '27, '28, '29, '31; French doubles, 1930, '32; Wimbledon doubles, 1924, '27, '30; U.S. doubles, 1922, '24, '25, '28; Wimbledon mixed, 1929; U.S. mixed, 1924, '28* WIGHTMAN CUP—*1923, '24, '25, '27, '28, '29, '30, '31, '32, '38; record: 18-2 in singles, 3-7 in doubles.* SINGLES RECORD IN THE MAJORS— *French (20-0), Wimbledon (55-1), U.S. (51-2).*

BETTY NUTHALL

Great Britain (1911–83)

Until Betty Kay Nuthall came along from England, no one in the 20th century had taken the women's championship out of the U.S. It was a far less widespread and organized game when Irishwoman Mabel Cahill won at Philadelphia in 1891–92. In 1927, the 16-year-old Nuthall, a prodigy who had won the British Hard Court title in the spring (a quarterfinalist there at 14), was not only threatening a long-lived American monopoly at Forest Hills but a record of Bessie Moore, the 16-year-old finalist to Cahill in 1892.

Still serving underhanded, as she had all her life—a habit she would soon change—Betty might have been the youngest of all U.S. champs. But Helen Wills took care of that in the U.S. final, 6-1, 6-4. Nevertheless, Nuthall, exactly the same age, to the day, as Moore had been, shared the "youngest finalist" record with her

Betty Nuthall: Serving with distinction. (USTA)

until Pam Shriver, a younger 16, displaced both of them in 1978.

Three years later, 1930, and still a teenager, Nuthall did get the U.S. title, beating in succession the second-first seeds, Midge Morrill and Mrs. Anna McCune Harper, 6-1, 6-4. Defending the title, she reached the 1931 semis, losing, 6-2, 3-6, 6-4, to Wightman Cup teammate Eileen Bennett Whitingstall. Nuthall again was a semifinalist in 1933, startling onlookers by pushing the champ, Helen Wills Moody, 2-6, 6-3, 6-2. As the youngest to play for Britain when she joined the team in 1927, she was a Wightman Cupper eight years, beating the redoubtable Helen Jacobs in her debut.

She had a fine French in 1931, beating Jacobs before having to contend with the Germans who would clash for the Wimbledon title weeks later. Betty beat Hilde Krahwinkel in the semis to prevent a preview of Wimbledon's all-German final, but lost the title match to the tiny woman who ruled Paris and London, 5-footer Cilly Aussem, 8-6, 6-1. But she took the doubles with Whitingstall.

The main strength of Betty's game was her forehand. Holding the racket out with extended right arm, she used it as a flail, and hit with great power. Speed was the essence of her game; there was no temporizing. She hit with length and discernment, and was resourceful and wise in tactics.

Born May 23, 1911, in Surbiton, Surrey, she took up the game at seven with her father's guidance. She accomplished little in 1928 after her success the previous year, which included a beating of reigning U.S. champion Molla Mallory at Wimbledon to gain the quarters. It was not until she was bypassed for the Wightman Cup team in 1930 that she decided to take matters into her own hands and campaign alone. Packing her trunk, and accompanied by her brother, Jimmy (the English junior champ), she sailed for the U.S., and her perseverance, initiative and faith in herself were rewarded. This time, serving overhanded, she came through, the only Brit to rule Forest Hills until Virginia Wade in 1968, thus establishing herself as one of her country's most distinguished performers, ranking in the World Top Ten, 1927, 1929, 1930, 1931 and 1933.

Selected for the Hall of Fame in 1977, she died Nov. 8, 1983, in New York, where she had been a resident, as Mrs. Franklin Shoemaker.

MAJOR TITLES (9)—*U.S. singles, 1930; French doubles, 1931; U.S. doubles, 1930, '31, '33; French mixed, 1931, '32; U.S. mixed, 1929, '31* WIGHTMAN CUP—*1927, '28, '29, '31, '32, '33, '34, '39; record: 3-5 in singles, 3-2 in doubles.* SINGLES RECORD IN THE MAJORS— *French (13-5), Wimbledon (27-13), U.S. (24-6).*

FRED PERRY

Great Britain (1909–95)

It was the technique of one particular stroke that was the making of Fred Perry as a world

Fred Perry: Britain's finest. (UPI)

champion—and as a tennis player considered the best Great Britain has produced.

The knack of making the stroke baffled the promising Briton for so long that he was on the verge of giving up in despair. He had been advised that to get very far he would have to learn to take the ball early on his continental forehand, the racket making impact instantly as the ball rose from the court.

For months he could not master the timing. Then suddenly, like riding a bicycle, it came to him and he was on his way—on his way to the net on a running forehand, going forward with the swing of the racket to gain good volleying position if the drive did not win outright. And on his way to three Wimbledon Championships, three U.S. Championships, an Australian, a French and a lucrative pro career.

Born May 18, 1909, in Stockport, England, the right-handed Frederick John Perry did not take up tennis until he was 18 years old. But he had good coaching and took to the game quickly, for he had been playing table tennis for years and winning tournaments and international recognition.

Perry developed an undercut backhand that came off with surprising pace. He hit the ball smartly with good length and regularity on the service, was sharp and sound with his smash, perfect in his footwork and timing, and volleyed with dispatch. None of his strokes was overpowering, but his attack was impetuous and relentless, ever challenging, and he ran like a deer in retrieving.

He was the completely equipped and efficient adversary, jaunty, a bit cocky in his breezy self-assurance, with gallery appeal. He could be sarcastic and some thought him egotistical, but it was a pose and he had an ever-ready grin. He cut a handsome figure with his regular features, raven black hair, and physique that was perfection for the game. Once he developed the stroke that had eluded him, he was virtually unstoppable.

In 1933 Perry led the British Isles to a 4-1 victory over the United States in the inter-zone final and to the glorious 3-2 victory over France that brought the Davis Cup back to Britain after a wait of 21 years. As Stade Roland Garros boiled with patriotic fervor, a seventh straight Cup in the balance for the home side, Fred icily erased a set point in the second to take the last match from rookie Andre Merlin, 4-6, 8-6, 6-2, 7-5. It was the climax of the greatest individual season for a Cup winner: 12-1 in singles, 4-2 in doubles.

Britain retained the Cup through 1936 as Perry won every singles match he played in the four challenge rounds. England had not produced a Wimbledon singles champion for a quarter-century, but Perry took care of that, too. He won three straight Wimbledon finals without loss of a set, defeating Jack Crawford in 1934 and Gottfried von Cramm in 1935 and 1936.

At Forest Hills in 1933 he was the stopper as Crawford reached the U.S. final with an unprecedented Grand Slam within reach: 6-3, 11-13, 4-6, 6-0, 6-1. The next year Fred might have had the first Slam himself but for a quarterfinal defeat at the French by Giorgio de Stefani, 6-2, 1-6, 9-7, 6-2.

Perry was also impressive elsewhere, winning the U.S. Championship in 1933, 1934 and 1936, an assault interrupted only in 1935, when he suffered a painful kidney injury and lost in the semifinals to Wilmer Allison. In 1934 he won the Australian Championship and in 1935 the French Championship, the first and one of only four men to take all four majors. His total was eight, behind only Roy Emerson (12), Rod Laver and Bjorn Borg (11), Bill Tilden (10), and even with Ken Rosewall, Jimmy Connors and Pete Sampras among the men.

When Perry joined the professional tour, he drew huge crowds to see him play Ellsworth Vines and Bill Tilden. Perry won the U.S. Pro Championship in both 1938 and 1941.

After his playing career, he became associated with the manufacture of tennis clothes, was a tennis correspondent for a London newspaper and took part in radio and television coverage of tennis. He was elected to the Hall of Fame in 1975 and died Feb. 2, 1995, in Melbourne. He ranked in the World Top Ten from 1931 through 1936, No. 1 the last three years.

MAJOR TITLES (14)—*Australian singles, 1934; French singles, 1935; Wimbledon singles, 1934, '35, '36; U.S. singles, 1933, '34, '36; Australian doubles, 1934; French doubles, 1933; French mixed, 1932; Wimbledon mixed, 1935, '36; U.S. mixed, 1932.* DAVIS CUP—*1931, '32, '33, '34, '35, '36; record: 34-4 in singles, 11-3 in doubles.* SINGLES RECORD IN THE MAJORS—*Australian (7-1), French (22-5), Wimbledon (35-5), U.S. (34-4).*

BOBBY RIGGS
United States (1918–95)

Though he had little of the power of Don Budge and Jack Kramer, and though his physique was hardly comparable to that of these six-footers, right-hander Bobby Riggs was one of the smartest, most calculating and resourceful court strategists tennis has seen, particularly in his defensive circumventions. He had a temperament that was unruffled in all circumstances and he hung in the fight without showing a trace of discouragement other than a slight shake of the head. He won the championship at Wimbledon and twice at Forest Hills.

Budge, with his vast power, usually had to work his hardest to turn back the little Californian, whose forte was to subdue the fury of the big hitters. Riggs had both the brains and the shots to quell the cannonaders, particularly the drop shot from both forehand and backhand, and a lob matched by few in the way he masked it and his control of its length. Most often Budge required four sets, if not five, to win when they were amateurs. When they met as pros, Riggs won his full share.

Born Feb. 25, 1918, in Los Angeles, Robert Larimore Riggs first began to make tennis progress at the age of 12, when Dr. Esther Bartosh saw him hitting balls and took over his instruction. In 1934, at 16, he beat Frank Shields, a finalist at Wimbledon and Forest Hills. Two years later Riggs was ranked No. 4 in the country, and he was second to Budge in 1937 and 1938.

Riggs had his best record—the best in the world—in 1939, racking up a triple at Wimbledon the only time he played there, adding the U.S. while winning nine of 13 tournaments and 54-5 in matches. He said he "scraped up every dime I could find" to bet on himself with a London bookmaker to win the three Wimbledon titles, and came off with $108,000.

After yielding his U.S. title to Don McNeill in the 1940 final, he regained it in 1941, beating Frank Kovacs, a spectacular shotmaker. His career as an amateur soon ended. Riggs was in demand on the pro circuit.

In 1942 he competed in the U.S. Pro Championships and lost in the final to Budge. But the next time they met was after World War II, in 1946, and this time Riggs beat Budge in the U.S. Pro final at Forest Hills. They went on tour and Riggs won 24 matches to 22 for Budge. Again in 1947 they met in the final of the Pro Championships and Riggs won in five long sets. Late in the year Jack Kramer made his pro debut at Madison Square Garden in New York and Riggs

Bobby Riggs: The canny campaigner. (New York Herald Tribune)

beat him before a crowd of 15,114 who had plowed through 25 inches of snow in a blizzard. However, Kramer won the tour, 69-20.

After losing to Kramer in the final of the U.S. Pro at Forest Hills and regaining the title in 1949 against Budge, Riggs began to taper off as a player and tried his hand as a promoter when Gussy Moran and Pauline Betz made their debuts as pros in 1950. Years later, in 1973, after fading into virtual obscurity as a senior player who would make a bet on the drop of a hat, Riggs was back, taking on first Margaret Court and then Billie Jean King in mixed singles matches that gave tennis much publicity. He defeated Court, but King made him look like Humpty Dumpty, 6-4, 6-4, 6-3, before a record tennis crowd of 30,472, at Houston's Astrodome. Few things ever fazed Riggs, though, or made him unhappy. And nothing ever made him forget his good manners and sportsmanship in the years when he was playing serious tennis.

He made the World Top Ten, 1937, 1938 and 1939, No. 1 the last year, and the U.S. Top Ten, 1936 through 1941, and was named to the Hall of

Fame in 1967 and died Oct. 10, 1995, in Leucadia, Calif.

MAJOR TITLES *(6)—Wimbledon singles, 1939; U.S. singles, 1939, '41; Wimbledon doubles, 1939; Wimbledon mixed, 1939; U.S. mixed, 1940;* OTHER U.S. TITLES—*Indoor singles, 1940; Clay Court singles, 1936, '37, '38; Indoor doubles, 1940, with Elwood Cooke; Clay Court doubles, 1936, with Wayne Sabin; Indoor mixed, 1940, with Pauline Betz; Pro singles, 1946, '47, '49; Pro doubles, 1942, '47, with Don Budge.* DAVIS CUP—*1938, '39; record: 2-2 in singles.* SINGLES RECORD IN THE MAJORS— *French (5-1), Wimbledon (7-0), U.S. (27-4).*

DOROTHY ROUND

Great Britain (1909–82)

Dorothy Edith Round Little was the leading British female player at the time Helen Wills Moody ruled the courts in the 1930s. Round distinguished herself on several counts, among them that she was the only British player besides Kitty McKane Godfree to win Wimbledon twice since World War I, and she was in 1935 the only woman from overseas to win the Australian Championship.

Born July 13, 1908, in Dudley, Worcestershire, England, she developed a right-handed groundstroke game of power and precision and volleying ability equaled by few. She won the Wimbledon crown in 1934 and repeated in 1937. Her play at the net was a factor in her victory over Helen Jacobs in the 1934 final, 6-2, 5-7, 6-3. In the 1937 final, she defeated the strong Polish woman, Jadwiga Jedrzejowska, 6-2, 2-6, 7-5, overcoming a 1-4 deficit in the final set.

To get to the Wimbledon final of 1937, Round defeated Jacobs and Simone Mathieu, France's leading player. Round appeared to rise to her best form when confronted by Jacobs or Moody. In 1933 Round got to the final at Wimbledon and gave Moody one of the most challenging fights of her career, yielding at 6-4, 6-8, 6-3. That same year in the U.S. Championships, she lost to Jacobs, 6-4, 5-7, 6-2, in the semifinals.

Dorothy Round: All-round game. (UPI)

Round was not as successful, however, in Wightman Cup matches as in tournaments for the championship of England, U.S. and Australia.

She was a member of the British team from 1931 to 1936. She lost to Jacobs four times before defeating the American in 1936, in her final appearance in the international team matches, 6-3, 6-3. Round (Mrs. Douglas Little in 1937) probably relished that victory particularly, for it was the year Jacobs finally achieved her ambition of winning Wimbledon.

She was in the World Top Ten from 1933 through 1937, No. 1 in 1934, and was named to the Hall of Fame in 1986. She died Nov. 12, 1982, in Kidderminster, England.

MAJOR TITLES *(6)—Australian singles, 1935; Wimbledon singles, 1934, '37. Wimbledon mixed, 1934, '35, '36* WIGHTMAN CUP—*1931, '32, '33, '34, '35, '36; record: 4-7 in*

BILL TILDEN
United States (1893–1953)

If a player's value is measured by the dominance and influence he exercises over a sport, then William Tatem "Big Bill" Tilden II could be considered the greatest player in the history of tennis.

From 1920 through 1926, he dominated the game as has no player before or since. During those years he was invincible in the United States, won Wimbledon both times he competed there, and captured 13 successive singles matches in the Davis Cup challenge round against the best players from Australia, France and Japan.

As an amateur (1912–30) he won 138 of 192 tournaments, lost 28 finals and had a 907-62 match record—a phenomenal .936 average.

His last major triumph, the Wimbledon singles of 1930, gave him a total of 10 majors, standing as the male high until topped by Roy Emerson (12) in 1967, and later Rod Laver and Bjorn Borg (11). He missed another by two match points he held against René Lacoste in the 1927 French final. Bill won the U.S. Mixed with Mary K. Browne in 1913–14, but had been beaten in the first round of the 1912 Singles at Newport by fellow Philadelphian Wallace Johnson (whom he would defeat in the 1921 final). He didn't feel sure enough of his game to try again until 1916, in New York. He was 23, a first-round loser to a kid named Harold Throckmorton. Ignominious, tardy starts in an illustrious career that would contain seven U.S. titles and 69 match victories (a record 42 straight between 1920 and 1926).

By 1918, a war-riddled year, he got to the final, blown away by a bullet-serving Lindley Murray, 6-3, 6-1, 7-5. But he'd be back: seven more finals in a row. In 1918 Big Bill's electrifying rivalry with Little Bill Johnston began—six U.S. finals in seven years, more than any other two men skirmished for a major. After losing to Little Bill in 1919, Tilden, disgusted with his puny defensive backhand, hid out all winter at the indoor court of a friend, J. D. E. Jones, in Providence, retooling. He emerged with a brand new, fearsome, multifaceted backhand and complete game, and was ready to conquer the world. He did not lose to Little Bill again in a U.S. final, and held an 11-6 edge in their rivalry. His concentration could be awesome, as during a two-tournament stretch in 1925 when he won 57 straight games at Glen Cove, N.Y., and Providence. Trailing Alfred Chapin, one of few to hold a win over him, 3-4 in the final, he ran it out, 6-4, 6-0, 6-0. Staying in tune on the next stop he won three straight 6-0, 6-0, matches, then 6-0, 6-1. Another 6-1 set made it 75 of 77 games.

When he first won Wimbledon, in 1920, he was 27 years old, an advanced age for a champion. But he had a long and influential career, and at the age of 52, in 1945, he was still able to push the 27-year-old Bobby Riggs to the limit in a professional match.

Tilden, a right-hander, born Feb. 10, 1893, in Philadelphia, had the ideal tennis build, 6-foot-2, 155, with thin shanks and big shoulders. He had speed and nimbleness, coordination and perfect balance. He also had marked endurance, despite smoking cigarettes incessantly when not playing. In stroke equipment, he had the weapons to launch an overpowering assault and the resources to defend and confound through a variety of spins and pace when the opponent was impervious to sheer power.

Nobody had a more devastating service than Tilden's cannonball, or a more challenging second serve than his kicking American twist. No player had a stronger combination of forehand and backhand drives, supplemented by a forehand chop and backhand slice. Tilden's mixture of shots was a revelation in his first appearance at Wimbledon. Gerald Patterson of Australia, the defending champion, found his backcourt untenable and was passed over and over when he went to the net behind his powerful service. Tilden won, 2-6, 6-3, 6-2, 6-4.

Bill Tilden: Greatest of all? (UPI)

The backcourt was where Tilden played tennis. He was no advocate of the "big game," the big serve and rush for the net for the instant volley coup. He relished playing tennis as a game of chess, matching wits as well as physical powers. The drop shot, at which he was particularly adroit, and the lob were among his disconcerting weapons.

His knowledge and mastery of spin has hardly ever been exceeded, as evidenced not only on the court but also in his *Match Play and the Spin of the Ball,* a classic written more than half a century ago. Yes, Tilden was a writer, too, but he longed to be an actor above anything else. Unsuccessful in his efforts to the point of sinking most of his family wealth, his tennis earnings and his writing royalties into the theater, he was happiest when playing on the heartstrings of a tennis gallery.

Intelligent and opinionated, he was a man of strong likes and dislikes. He had highly successful friends, both men and women, who were devoted to him, and there were others who disliked him and considered him arrogant and inconsiderate of officials and ball boys who served at his matches. He was constantly wrangling with officers and committeemen of the USTA on Davis Cup policy and enforcement of the amateur rule, and in 1928 he was on the front pages of the American press when he was removed as captain and star player of the Davis Cup team, charged with violating the amateur rule with his press accounts of the Wimbledon Championships, in which he was competing. So angry were the French over the loss of the star member of the cast for the Davis Cup challenge round—the first ever held on French soil—that the American ambassador, Myron T. Herrick, interceded for the sake of good relations between the countries, and Tilden was restored to the team.

When Tilden, in the opening match, beat René Lacoste, the French gallery suffered agony and cursed themselves for insisting that "Teelden" be restored to the team. It all ended happily for them, however, as the French won the other four matches and kept the Davis Cup. On Tilden's return home, he was brought up on the charges of violating the rule at Wimbledon. He was found guilty and was suspended from playing in the U.S. Championships that year.

Eligible for the U.S. title again in 1929, after the lifting of his suspension, he won the crown for the seventh time, defeating his doubles partner, Frank Hunter. In 1930 he won Wimbledon for the third time, at the age of 37. After the U.S. Championships, in which he was beaten in the semifinals by John Doeg, he notified the tennis association of his intention to make a series of motion pictures for profit, thus disqualifying him for further play as an amateur. He was in the World Top Ten from 1919 through 1930, No. 1 a record six times (1920–25), and in the U.S. Top Ten 12 straight years from 1918, No. 1 a record 10 times (1920–29). He was named to the Hall of Fame in 1959.

In 1931 he entered upon a professional playing career, joining Vincent Richards, Hans Nusslein and Roman Najuch of Germany and Karel Kozeluh of Czechoslovakia. Tilden's name revived pro tennis, which had languished since its inception in 1926 when Suzanne Lenglen went on tour. His joining the pros paved the way for Ellsworth Vines, Fred Perry and Don Budge to leave the amateur ranks and play for big prize money. Tilden won his pro debut against Kozeluh, 6-4, 6-2, 6-4, before 13,000 fans in Madison Square Garden.

Joining promoter Bill O'Brien, Tilden toured the country in 1932 and 1933, but the Depression was on and new blood was needed. Vines furnished it. Tilden and O'Brien signed him on, and in 1934 Tilden defeated Vines in the younger man's pro debut, 8-6, 6-3, 6-2, before a turnaway crowd of 16,200 at Madison Square Garden. That year Tilden and Vines went on the first of the great tennis tours, won by Vines, 47-26.

The tours grew in the 1930s and '40s, and Tilden remained an attraction even though he was approaching the age of 50. For years he traveled across the country, driving by day and sometimes all night and then going on a court a few hours after arriving. At times, when he was managing his tour, he had to help set the stage for the matches.

Tragically, his activity and fortunes dwindled after his conviction on a morals charge and imprisonment in 1947, and again in 1949 for parole violation (both terms less than a year). He died of a heart attack under pitiful circumstances, alone and with few resources, on June 5, 1953, in Los Angeles. His bag was packed for a trip to Cleveland to play in the U.S. Pro Championships when perhaps the greatest tennis player of them all was found dead in his room.

MAJOR TITLES (21)—*Wimbledon singles, 1920, '21, '30; U.S. singles, 1920, '21, '22, '23, '24, '25, '29; Wimbledon doubles, 1927; U.S. doubles, 1918, '21, '22, '23, '27; French mixed, 1930; U.S. mixed, 1913, '14, '22, '23.* OTHER U.S. TITLES—*Indoor singles, 1920; Indoor doubles, 1919, '20, with Vincent Richards; 1926, with Frank Anderson; 1929, with Frank Hunter; Indoor mixed, 1921, '22, with Molla Mal-lory; 1924, with Hazel Hotchkiss Wightman; Clay Court singles, 1918, '22, '23, '24, '25, '26, '27; Pro singles, 1931, '35; Pro doubles, 1932, with Bruce Barnes; 1945, with Vincent Richards.* DAVIS CUP—*1920, '21, '22, '23, '24, '25, '26, '27, '28, '29, '30; record: 25-5 singles, 9-2 in doubles.* SINGLES RECORD IN THE MAJORS—*French (14-3), Wimbledon (30-3), U.S. (69-7).*

ELLSWORTH VINES
United States (1911–94)

One night in 1930, an 18-year-old lad sat in a rocking chair on the porch of the Peninsula Inn in Seabright, N.J., looking out to sea and thinking that his tennis dreams were shattered. "I guess I'm just a flash in the pan like they say," said Henry Ellsworth Vines, Jr.

Weeks earlier they had been calling him another California Comet. He had come out of the West, a lanky youth who had the kick of a mule in his cannonball service and who terrorized the Eastern grass court circuit.

Vines, a right-hander, born Sept. 29, 1911, in Los Angeles, ambled along mournfully like slow molasses when not in hot pursuit of a tennis ball. On the court he was devastating, wherefore came the comparisons to Maurice McLoughlin, the original California Comet.

Vines, the Southern California champ, a cornstalk at 6-foot-2, 143 pounds, had easily disposed of two of the better Americans, Frank Hunter and Frank Shields, at Seabright, but now he had lost the final to Sidney Wood, unable to cope with Wood's seemingly innocuous game of moderate strokes, and some were saying the new Comet had burned out already. It looked more that way at Forest Hills where George Lytleton Rogers beat him in the third round from two sets down. But Elly didn't settle for that. He went home, won the Pacific Southwest, practiced all winter and spring against slow-ball strategy and came back East in 1931 to win the U.S. title over George Lott, 7-9, 6-3, 9-7, 7-5, after trailing 5-3 in the third and 5-2 in the fourth.

His 1932 was a splendid campaign decorated with the Wimbledon title and another U.S. in 59 minutes over Henri Cochet, 6-4, 6-4, 6-4, after a semifinal recovery two points from defeat by the offspeed stuff of Cliff Sutter. As a Davis Cup rookie he was 9-1, driving the U.S. to the Challenge Round, a 3-2 loss to France. He won four of eight tournaments, 46-5 in matches, and was No. 1 in the world.

Vines played amateur tennis on the grass circuit only four years, 1930–33, making the World Top Ten the last three years, and the U.S. Top Ten in 1930–32, No. 1 the last two years. But in those four years he established at Forest Hills and Wimbledon that he had one of the best serves, if not the very fastest serve ever turned loose, with almost no spin. He also had as fast and as risky a forehand as ever seen, a murderous overhead, and a skill in the volleying position to compare with the best.

Moreover, his disposition and temperament were foolproof. Where others might explode in protest against a line call, Vines would slowly turn his head and grin under his white cap at the linesman.

He was a gambler on the court. He hit his forehand flat, with all his whizzing might, and closer to the net and the lines than anyone dared. At his best he was equal to beating any player, but his margin of safety was so thin that on days when he did not have the feel and touch, his errors could be ruinous.

Wimbledon crowds marveled at the devastating fury of his attack in beating Bunny Austin, 6-4, 6-2, 6-0 in the 1932 Wimbledon final, which ended with his 30th service ace. The ball catapulted by Austin so fast that the Briton said afterward he did not know whether it went by him to the left or to the right. Don Budge marvels, "Thirty aces in 12 serving games! Considering it was against one of the finest players of the era, and a Wimbledon final, it could be the greatest serving demonstration ever."

But 1933 was a comedown. In one of the magnificent Wimbledon finals Elly lost his title to Jack Crawford, failing to cash numerous second-set break points, 4-6, 11-9, 6-2, 2-6, 6-4.

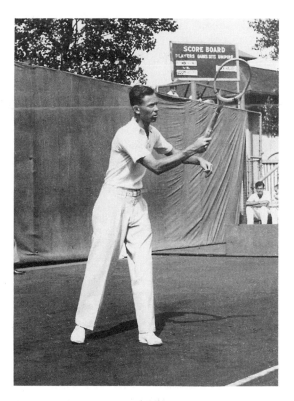

Ellsworth Vines: Master gambler. (UPI)

Both Austin and Fred Perry beat him as the U.S. lost the Davis Cup semifinal in Paris, a prelude to Britain seizing the Cup from France, and so did the mite, Bitsy Grant, in the fourth round at Forest Hills. Disgusted, Vines could not wait to cut the gut out of his rackets and leave for home, his tennis career as an amateur soon at an end.

He signed a professional contract to go on tour with Bill Tilden and lost their opening match, 8-6, 6-3, 6-2, before 16,200 fans at Madison Square Garden. But Vines ultimately beat the aging Tilden, 47 matches to 26. A match in the Garden between Vines and Perry drew 17,630. He was considered the No. 1 pro through 1937, winning the Wembley World Pro title over Tilden in 1935, Hans Nusslein in 1936 and 1937.

Near the end of the decade, Vines' interest in tennis waned. He turned to golf and became the best golfer who was ever a top tennis player. For years he prospered as a teaching pro, and he was good enough to reach the semifinals of the 1951 Professional Golf Association Championship.

He was enshrined in the Hall of Fame in 1962, and died March 17, 1994. In 1977 he attended the Wimbledon Centenary as one of the former champions receiving commemorative medals. He had turned out to be much, much more than a flash in the pan.

MAJOR TITLES *(6)—Wimbledon singles, 1932; U.S. singles, 1931, '32; Australian doubles, 1933; U.S. doubles, 1932; U.S. mixed, 1933.* OTHER U.S. TITLES—*Clay Court singles, 1931; Clay Court doubles, 1931, with Keith Gledhill; Pro singles, 1939.* DAVIS CUP—*1932, '33; record: 13-3 in singles.* SINGLES RECORD IN THE MAJORS—*Australian (2-1), Wimbledon (13-1), U.S. (16-2).*

BARON GOTTFRIED VON CRAMM

Germany (1909–76)

If any player was the prince charming of tennis, he was Gottfried von Cramm, a baron of the German nobility, six feet tall, with blond hair, green eyes, and a magnetism that, in the words of Don Budge, "made him dominate any scene he was part of."

The most accomplished tennis player Germany had known, von Cramm must be one of the finest players never to have won the Wimbledon Championship, for which he was runner-up three years in a row—to Fred Perry in 1935 and 1936, and to Budge in 1937.

Von Cramm, who was known as The Baron, was also runner-up to Budge for the U.S. Championship in 1937 and runner-up yet again to Budge in what has been termed the greatest Davis Cup match ever played, the fifth and deciding match in the 1937 semifinal between the United States and Germany. Budge came from 1-4 and had match point five times before he hit the final shot, racing across the court beyond the alley, and he lay sprawled on the ground as the umpire declared the United States to be winner. The score of the match: 6-8, 5-7, 6-4, 6-2, 8-6.

Gottfried von Cramm: The Baron. (Fischer Collection/SPS)

Said The Baron at the end, when he stood at the net waiting for Budge to pick himself up from the ground: "Don, this was absolutely the finest match I have ever played in my life. I'm very happy I could have played it against you, whom I like so much. Congratulations." The next moment, their arms were around each other.

Von Cramm, a right-hander, born July 7, 1909, at Nettlingen, Hanover, Germany, was noted on the court for his endurance and tenacity. In recalling their thrilling Cup match, Budge related how he put four successive first serves in play, his very best, and all four came back as winners for von Cramm.

Few have endured as he did in taking the first of his two French titles in 1934. Five set matches were the rule as he fought through four of them (of six), and snatched a match point away from Jack Crawford in the final, 6-4, 7-9, 3-6, 7-

5, 6-3. Two years later another five-setter was his ticket to victory over the World No. 1 Fred Perry, ending with an astounding shutout, 6-0, 2-6, 6-2, 2-6, 6-0. But Perry beat him in 1935 and 1936, and Budge bested him in 1937 as von Cramm lost three straight Wimbledon finals, a record for frustration he shares with Herbert Lawford (1884–86) and Fred Stolle (1963–65). He won six German titles, 1932–35, and remarkably, after the war, in 1948 and 1949, the last at age 40.

But that wasn't the last that aficionados heard of The Baron. He had always loved representing the Fatherland in Davis Cup, was saddened by the Nazi takeover, and elated at the welcoming back of a democratic Germany to the tennis community in 1951. He played three more years for the Cup, leading Germany in 1951 to four wins and the final of the European zone with a 9-1 singles record, beating men half his age such as Dane Kurt Nielsen, soon to be a Wimbledon runnerup. In 1953, at 44, he returned to Paris to say adieu in defeat by France, registering the last of his 58 Cup singles wins over Paul Remy, 30. He was a Cup centurion, one of the select 14 who played more than 100 matches (111). His most productive year was 1935: 11-1 in singles, 4-1 in doubles. In 1937, the year he came so close to winning the Cup, he was 7-2 in singles, 4-1 in doubles.

Popular everywhere he went, von Cramm delighted Americans in 1937 as a U.S. champ and runnerup, finalist to Budge at Forest Hills and victor with Henner Henkel over Budge and Gene Mako in Boston, and at the Australian in 1938 where the two Germans were doubles runners-up to John Bromwich and Adrian Quist.

Von Cramm, at the height of his career when Hitler was preparing for Germany to launch World War II, declined to speak for Nazism in his tennis travels and was imprisoned by the Gestapo in 1938. After the war, during which he was a hero on the Russian front, he had a successful business career and was an administrator in tennis, serving as president of Lawn Tennis Club Rot-Weiss in Berlin. The Baron died in an automobile crash near Cairo, Egypt, Nov. 8, 1976, and a year later was enshrined in the Hall of Fame.

MAJOR TITLES (5)—*French singles, 1934, '36; French doubles, 1937; U.S. doubles, 1937; Wimbledon mixed, 1933.* DAVIS CUP—*1932, '33, '34, '35, '36, '37, '51, '52, '53; record: 58-10 in singles, 24-11 in doubles.* SINGLES RECORD IN THE MAJORS— *Australian (3-1), French (18-1), Wimbledon (26-7), U.S. (5-1).*

TONY WILDING
New Zealand (1883–1915)

The British idolized Tony Wilding. He was a superb figure of a man, his sportsmanship was exemplary, and, besides, he learned his tennis at Cambridge University.

Anthony Frederick Wilding, born Oct. 31, 1883, in Christchurch, New Zealand, stood with Norman Brookes as two of the foremost players in tennis for nearly a decade. On his sixth try, 1910, Tony won Wimbledon, unseating Arthur Gore, 6-4, 7-5, 4-6, 6-2, in the Challenge Round, and kept the title through 1913. In the 1913 Challenge Round, with an 8-6, 6-3, 10-8 beating of Maurice McLoughlin, the formidable California Comet, Wilding was particularly impressive. "He was in prime physical condition," wrote distinguished British tennis authority A. Wallis Myers. "All his best fighting instincts were aroused, his tactics were as sound as his strokes and he won a great victory, the greatest of his career, in three sets."

Wilding, a 6-foot-2, 185-pound right-hander, lost his title to Brookes in 1914 and joined with the Australian "Wizard" to win the Davis Cup back from the United States that very year. Wilding's triumph over Dick Williams of the U.S. on the first day of the Cup was a shock. Williams was one of the most daring and brilliant shotmakers in history, but Wilding, playing almost unerringly, won quickly, 7-5, 6-2, 6-3.

Wilding played the classic game in vogue at the time. His drives were the strength of his attack and his defense was outstanding. He could hit with immense pace and overspin, but when

Tony Wilding: Wimbledon hero. (UPI)

prudence and judgment dictated security of stroke rather than speed, as against a player of Williams' daring, Wilding could temper his drives and play faultlessly from the baseline.

Wilding made his debut on the Australasian Davis Cup team at the age of 21 in 1905. After winning the second Australian Championship in 1906 over a fellow New Zealander, lefty Francis Fisher, 6-0, 6-4, 6-4, his Antipodean partnership with Brookes took off. They stripped the Davis Cup from Britain, 3-2, at Wimbledon in 1907, his win over Roper Barrett sandwiched between Brookes' two singles wins. They were hard-pressed to keep the trophy the next year at Melbourne, turning back the U.S., 3-2, as Wilding won the decisive point over Fred Alexander, 6-3, 6-4, 6-1. Then they blanked the U.S., 5-0, in 1909. Tony was absent as Australia lost the 1911–12 showdowns. His reappearance for the 1914 invasion of the U.S. marked his farewell to tennis. The stunning leadoff victory over Dick Williams, plus a hand in the winning doubles, helped accomplish the 3-2 triumph that practically coincided with the outbreak of World War I.

Following their victory at Forest Hills, he and Brookes went to war. Wilding never came back. At the age of 31, on May 9, 1915, he was killed in action at Neuve Chapelle, France. He had been No. 3 in the world ranking in 1914, and was named to the Hall of Fame in 1978.

MAJOR TITLES *(11)—Australian singles, 1906, '09; Wimbledon singles, 1910, '11, '12, '13; Australian doubles, 1906; Wimbledon doubles, 1907, '08, '10, '14.* DAVIS CUP— *1905, '06, '07, '08, '09, '14; record: 15-6 in singles, 6-3 in doubles.* SINGLES RECORD IN THE MAJORS—*Australian (10-0), Wimbledon (23-6).*

DICK WILLIAMS
United States (1891–1968)

Richard Norris Williams II survived the sinking of the *Titanic,* and after that harrowing experience, tennis must have seemed easy, for he became one of the outstanding players of his time, ever a risk-taking shotmaker. Born of American parents in Geneva, Switzerland, Jan. 29, 1891, he left for the United States in 1912 aboard the *S.S. Titanic,* which struck an iceberg and sank.

At the insistence of his father, who went down with the ship, Dick dived from the deck at the last possible moment, swam to a half-submerged lifeboat and clung there, in near-freezing water, for six hours. When rescued, a ship's doctor advised amputation of the frozen-stiff, seemingly useless legs, common treatment at the time. Fortunately, Williams refused, and only months later was in the quarters of the U.S. Championships, losing in four to the champ, Maurice McLoughlin.

He lived a long life, until age 77, and for that the tennis world was always grateful.

Williams, a right-hander, had learned to play in Switzerland, using the continental grip and hitting his ground strokes with underspin. He devel-

Dick Williams: Unsinkable. (UPI)

Dick captained six Cup winners, 1921–26, plus the team of 1934. He was a victorious doubles player four of those Cup-keeping years, a volleyer whose doubles titles were numerous, including Wimbledon in 1920 with Chuck Garland. He laughed about his 1924 Olympic gold medal in mixed alongside Hazel Wightman: "I had a sprained ankle and suggested to her that we default. Not on your life with her. She told me to stay at the net, and she'd do the running. It worked [6-2, 6-3, over compatriots Marion Jessup and Vinnie Richards] even though I was 34 and she 37." He continued playing the U.S. Championships (21 in all, the fifth-highest total) through 1935 when he won a round, at 44, and won 65 of 84 matches, tied for fifth with John McEnroe.

Williams had a daring style of play, taking every possible ball (when not in volleying position) on the rise with hair-trigger timing. Always he hit boldly, sharply for the winner, and that included serving for the winner on both the first and second ball. He did not know what it was to temporize.

On occasion, his errors caused by his gutsy tactics might bring defeat by opponents of inferior ability. But it was the commonly held opinion that Williams, on his best days, when he had the feel and touch and his breathtaking strokes were flashing on the lines, was unbeatable against any and all, and once he won a set over Bill Tilden in five minutes.

He made the World Top Ten in 1914, 1919, 1920, 1921, 1922, 1923 and 1925, was No. 4 in 1923, No. 5 in 1925, and was in the U.S. Top Ten 12 times between 1912 and 1925, No. 1 in 1916. In 1957 he was elevated to the Hall of Fame. He died June 2, 1968, in Bryn Mawr, Pa.

MAJOR TITLES (6)—*U.S. singles, 1914, '16; Wimbledon doubles, 1920; U.S. doubles, 1925, '26; U.S. mixed, 1912.* OTHER U.S. TITLES—*Clay Court singles, 1912, '15; Intercollegiate singles, 1913, '15; Intercollegiate doubles, 1914, '15 with Dick Harte.* DAVIS CUP—*1913, '14, '21, '23, '25, '26; record: 6-3 in singles, 4-0 in doubles.* SINGLES RECORD IN THE MAJORS— *Wimbledon (10-3), U.S. (65-19).*

oped his game further as a Harvard University undergraduate, winning the Intercollegiate championship in 1913 and 1915.

The next year, he was runner-up at Newport, but in 1914 he won, ousting McLoughlin, 6-3, 8-6, 10-8, in a stirring final before a large crowd on the new championship court at the Casino. Throughout the three sets Williams maintained a terrific pace and marvelous control, averting the loss of the final set several times with bursts of speed and master strokes that thwarted even so aggressive and courageous a foe as the Comet.

In 1916 he won the U.S. title again, this time over Little Bill Johnston, and attained the No. 1 ranking. Beginning in 1913, he played on five winning Davis Cup teams. After wartime combat service in France with the Army, a decorated hero (a French Croix de Guerre among his medals),

4

UNDER THE TABLE

1946-67

World War II was over and international tennis resumed much as before with some of the familiar pre-conflict faces, Frank Parker, Don McNeill and John Bromwich, factors again as civilians, and new champions such as Jack Kramer, Pancho Gonzalez and Dinny Pails bursting from uniform. Unfortunately, despite agitation for a broader outlook, the conservative officials who operated the largely amateur game could see no reason to integrate pros and amateurs into "open tennis," emulating golf.

Thus the division remained, until 1968, keeping the game separated and unequal. So-called amateurs held sway in the conventional tournament world, anchored by the four major name-value championships—Australian, French, Wimbledon, U.S.—plus the Davis Cup. On the other side, the professionals wandered almost anonymously, city to city, continent to continent, a gypsy band on a treadmill of one-nighters plus a few tournaments. They took their money in broad daylight, on the table.

Even when the pros were the best players, they reaped little attention, most of which was focused on the amateur side. Paid "expenses" under the table as gate-primers by tournaments or their national federations (keeping them eligible for team use such as Davis and Federation Cup), the leading amateurs, especially Europeans, could maintain themselves at the top level. Others of lesser quality came along for room and board or just plain fun. They were known as "shamateurs" or "tennis bums," in the U.S., sometimes national heroes elsewhere, particularly Australia, where a dynasty was forming, and the blossoming Down Undertakers—Frank Sedgman, Lew Hoad, Ken Rosewall, Rod Laver—were put on sporting goods firms' payroll.

Burgeoning air travel, eventually jets, was making the game more far flung than ever. Australia wasn't so inaccessible any more and the thought of playing all four majors within a year, for players other than Aussies, wasn't as fantastic as in Don Budge's 1938 odyssey to a Grand Slam.

1946

The year 1946 was one of reconstruction for international tennis. The French and Wimbledon championships and the Davis Cup had last been played in 1939, the Australian Championships in 1940. The U.S. Championships had continued uninterrupted.

Jack Kramer, who had entered the Coast Guard as a seaman and was discharged as a lieutenant after seeing action in the Pacific, returned at the age of 24 to claim the No. 1 U.S. ranking that had been predicted for him since 1942.

It was comparatively easy restarting championships in countries that had not been ravaged by the war. In Australia, John Bromwich re-established a thread with the prewar era. He had been the 1939 singles champion and regained the Australian title with a five-set victory over countryman Dinny Pails, 5-7, 6-3, 7-5, 3-6, 6-2. In doubles, it was as if the war had never occurred: Adrian Quist, the last prewar singles champion, who had won his national doubles title with Don Turnbull in 1936 and 1937 and with Bromwich in 1938, 1939 and 1940, successfully teamed with Bromwich once again, re-establishing a monopoly that lasted through 1950.

In Paris, French tennis fans crowned the first native champion since Henri Cochet in 1932: left-hander Marcel Bernard. Intending to play only doubles, Bernard was put in the draw when another player dropped out, and he upset the favorite, Czech Jaroslav Drobny, 3-6, 2-6, 6-1, 6-4, 6-3. Then he teamed with countryman Yvon Petra to win the doubles.

More startling was Petra's triumph in the singles at Wimbledon, the first Frenchman to win there since Cochet beat Jean Borotra in the all-French final of 1929. (Borotra was refused entry to Wimbledon in 1946 because he had been Minister of Sport in the Vichy government of France, though he was later a Nazi prisoner.)

Kramer, though seeded second, was the favorite, but he was done in by a nasty blister on his right hand that had caused him to default at the Queen's Club tune-up tournament the week

Ashore at last, Jack Kramer won the U.S. Singles, defeating Tom Brown in 1946. (UPI)

before. Drobny beat him in the round of 16, 2-6, 17-15, 6-3, 3-6, 6-3, after Kramer had lost only five games in the three previous rounds despite his handicap.

Pails, 25, was the top seed, but he got lost on the London Underground on his way to Wimbledon for his quarterfinal match and arrived late. Unsettled, he lost to fifth-seeded Petra in four sets. Petra—a lanky 6-foot-5 player with less than polished strokes—then reached the final by beating San Franciscan Tom Brown, 4-6, 4-6, 6-3, 7-5, 8-6. Petra did not figure to have a chance in the final against Australian Geoff Brown, a player of medium build with a devastating serve and great pace on the rest of his shots, the first to show a two-fisted backhand in a Wimbledon final. But Brown made the curious tactical miscalculation of trying to slow-ball during the first two sets. He did win the third and fourth, but by that time was psychologically exhausted, and when he dropped his serve in the opening game of the fifth set, Petra ran out the match, 6-2, 6-4, 7-9, 5-7, 6-4.

Kramer, playing with his damaged racket hand encased in bandages and a glove, dominated the doubles final, teaming with Tom Brown for a straight-set victory over Geoff Brown and Pails.

There had been some reluctance on the part of the All England Lawn Tennis & Croquet Club to stage the Championships at all in 1946. The club had been heavily damaged by German bombs, and a gaping hole in the Centre Court competitors' stand and adjacent seats had to be cordoned off. The organizing committee did not want to have a tournament if Wimbledon's prewar standards of preeminence could not be maintained. Colonel Duncan Macaulay, who returned as the club's full-time secretary after the war, summarized the obstacles in his book *Behind the Scenes at Wimbledon:*

"The groundsmen were not back from the war, the mowers wouldn't work, the rollers wouldn't roll, nothing would function. We were surrounded by bomb-shelters, improvised buildings and huts of every sort. The back part of the club was covered with broken glass as a result of flying bombs. Britain was under a tight wartime economy and nothing could be obtained without a license or a coupon. There was the difficulty of supplies of balls and rackets and the printing of tickets. Paper was very short. . . . Soap, too, was strictly rationed. Clothes were rationed and tennis flannels and costumes were almost non-existent. And of course, food was rationed, too—and there would be hungry thousands to be fed each day. The club's ration of whiskey was one bottle a month!"

Nevertheless, with customary efficiency and industry, the Championships was staged and again established as a showcase of the tennis world. There was considerable drama on court, both because of the early upsets of the favorites and the uncertainty of form that resulted from the wartime hiatus.

One fact amply demonstrated was the superiority of American women players, who put a stranglehold on the distaff game in the immediate postwar years and maintained it through the 1950s, until Australia, Latin America, and Europe again began producing champions in the early 1960s.

Macaulay explained the phenomenon quite logically. "Least upset by the war of all the lawn tennis-playing nations was the United States. Whereas lawn tennis in Britain and on the Continent closed down completely during the war and only started up again with many creaks and groans, with ruined courts and grave shortages of equipment, the American lawn tennis courts and clubs remained in being and the U.S. Championships continued all through the war. It was in the sphere of women's tennis that the United States gained such a tremendous advantage during these years."

Few non-Australian women ventured Down Under in those days, so the Australian Championships remained a native affair, but American women won just about every title of consequence, setting the pattern for ensuing years.

Margaret Osborne, saving a match point, defeated Pauline Betz, 1-6, 8-6, 7-5, in the French final, and the two of them teamed with Louise Brough and Doris Hart to rout Great Britain in the resumption of the Wightman Cup at Wimbledon. The Americans did not lose a set in romping, 7-0. None of the four had ever been to England before, but this was the strongest Wightman Cup team assembled to date, and they would all leave their mark.

Betz, an accomplished groundstroker, lost only 20 games in six matches in winning her first Wimbledon title, and overcame net-rusher Brough in the final, 6-2, 6-4. Betz had won the U.S. Championship in 1942, 1943 and 1944, beating Brough the first two years and Osborne the third, but had been runner-up to Sarah Palfrey Cooke in 1945. In her sixth straight year as finalist, a female record, Pauline took her fourth title,

11-9, 6-3, over Hart. Winning her last 27 matches, she etched a marvelous season embellished with eight titles in a dozen tournaments.

Brough and Osborne teamed to win the first of their three French and five Wimbledon doubles titles. The two of them continued their homeland streak as the U.S. Doubles Championships returned to Boston, winning a fifth straight time. But the sensation was the men's final, a third trophy for Bill Talbert and Gardnar Mulloy, who sidestepped seven match points in the fifth set of the longest title bout, beating Frank Guernsey and Don McNeill, 3-6, 6-4, 2-6, 6-3, 20-18.

Don Budge and Bobby Riggs, the best players in the world immediately before the war, were antagonists again on the pro circuit. Riggs, who had succeeded Budge as Wimbledon and Forest Hills champ in 1939 and won the U.S. crown again in 1941, was signed by promoter Jack Harris when he got out of the service. In an abbreviated tour against Budge, Bobby won, 18 matches to 16, lobbing incessantly to take full advantage of Budge's ailing shoulder. He trounced Budge, 6-3, 6-1, 6-1, in the final of the U.S. Professional Championship, which went virtually unnoticed at the West Side Tennis Club.

The tournament that did draw attention at Forest Hills, naturally, was the U.S. Nationals, as America's premier tennis event was called before it became the U.S. Open in 1968. It was here that Jack Kramer finally assumed the crown and top ranking that had been more or less reserved for him, as Hannibal Coons intimated in an article in Collier's in August 1946:

"Six-feet-one, powerfully built and a natural athlete, Jack Kramer has been the logical heir to the American tennis throne since he was fourteen. Successively U.S. Boys' and Interscholastic champion, a Davis Cupper at 18, and three times U.S. Doubles champion, twice with Schroeder and once with Parker, Kramer has for four years been shoved away from the singles title only by the whim of circumstance."

Gardnar Mulloy (left) and Billy Talbert took their third U.S. Doubles at Longwood in 1946. (UPI)

Kramer had re-established himself as a force in the game after his three-year military service by winning the singles, doubles (with Schroeder), and mixed doubles (with Helen Wills Moody Roark) without losing a set at the Southern California Championships at Los Angeles in May. His Wimbledon blisters had extended his reputation as "the hard-luck kid," but at Forest Hills there was no stopping him. Kramer had developed his aggressive, hard-hitting game on the concrete courts of the Los Angeles Tennis Club under the watchful eye of the longtime iron-handed developer of Southern California junior talent, Perry T. Jones, and his coach and onetime idol, Ellsworth Vines. Kramer always had a thunderous serve and forehand, and with the formidable backhand he developed on a South American exhibition tour in 1941 also in harness, he ravaged Tom Brown—who had beaten defending champ Frankie Parker and Gar Mulloy—in the Forest Hills final, 9-7, 6-3, 6-0.

There was one task left for Kramer in 1946: recovery of the Davis Cup. He had been an 18-year-old rookie for the U.S. in 1939, playing only

Jack Kramer holds the Challenge Cup presented to him by King George VI and Queen Elizabeth after he won Wimbledon in 1947. (UPI)

doubles with Joe Hunt in a four-set loss to Adrian Quist and John Bromwich as Australia won, 3-2. Now Kramer and his friend Schroeder, 12 days his senior, went to Kooyong Stadium (the name, in the aboriginal tongue, means "haunt of the wild water-fowl") in December and socked it to the Aussies, 5-0, inaugurating a four-year U.S. reign. Captain Walter Pate had tough choices to make with six hungry guys available. Talbert and Mulloy thought they should play the doubles. Parker, Mulloy, Schroeder and Brown each thought he should have the other singles job with Kramer. Pate gambled with Schroeder all the way, a two-man lineup, and when Ted delivered in the opener, 3-6, 6-1, 6-2, 0-6, 6-2, over

Bromwich, it was a parade that rained on 15,000 faithful jamming Melbourne's Kooyong.

Kramer and Schroeder were the first Davis Cuppers to fly to Australia—then a four-day trip in a propeller-driven aircraft, complete with sleeping berths. Prior to 1946, tennis players had gone to Australia by boat, making the journey in a leisurely month, stopping off and playing exhibitions at ports en route to stay sharp.

1947

The tennis world returned to normal in 1947. Of the nine countries (Germany, Italy, Japan, Bulgaria, Finland, Hungary, Romania, Thailand and Libya) that had been expelled from the ITF at its first postwar meeting in 1946, four (Italy, Hungary, Finland, and Romania) were readmitted, reflecting a cooling of hatreds that had been kindled by the war. This trend would continue.

If 1946 had marked Jack Kramer's emergence, 1947 verified his greatness. He dominated the amateur game, paving the way for the most significant pro-contract signing of the era. Kramer did not play the Australian or French Championships, but he won the singles and doubles titles of Wimbledon and the United States, and won both his singles (over Dinny Pails and John Bromwich) in straight sets as the U.S. defended the Davis Cup with a 4-1 victory over Australia at the West Side Tennis Club.

Pails and Bromwich were again the finalists in the Australian Championships, but this time Pails reversed the decision of the previous year in another five-setter, 4-6, 6-4, 3-6, 7-5, 8-6, for his only major singles title. Nancye Wynne Bolton beat Nell Hopman, wife of the Australian Davis Cup captain, 6-3, 6-2, for the fourth of her six Australian singles titles (1937, 1940, 1946, 1947, 1948 and 1951). She also teamed with Thelma Long for the sixth of their 11 doubles titles together, re-grasping the championships they had captured from 1936 through 1940 under their maiden names of Wynne and Coyne.

Readmission of Hungary to the ITF permitted Joszef Asboth, an artistic clay court specialist, back into the international fixtures, and he won the French over South African Eric Sturgess, 8-6, 7-5, 6-4, a slim but accomplished player with superbly accurate ground strokes. Pat Canning Todd, a statuesque and graceful Californian who was largely overshadowed by her American contemporaries, beat Doris Hart for the French women's title, 6-3, 3-6, 6-4.

Hart, a remarkable player who had been stricken with a serious knee infection at age 11 and took up tennis to strengthen her right leg, beat Louise Brough, 2-6, 8-6, 6-4, in the semifinals at Wimbledon, but had little left for Margaret Osborne in the final and was relegated to being runner-up, 6-2, 6-4. Brough and Osborne had successfully defended their French doubles title, but were dethroned in the Wimbledon final by Hart and Todd, despite holding three match points, 3-6, 6-4, 7-5.

The U.S. Wightman Cup team, a powerhouse—Brough, Osborne, Hart, Todd—gooseegged the Brits again, 7-0, but did concede a couple of sets in the process. No. 1 Pauline Betz had won her first three tournaments of the year, including the U.S. Indoor over Hart, 6-2, 7-5, and had a 39-match streak going when the USTA sternly suspended her indefinitely for merely discussing the possibility of turning pro. So she did, to barnstorm with Sarah Palfrey Cooke, with whom she'd split 18 matches as an amateur.

With Betz banished, Brough came through at the U.S. to the first of her six major singles titles, beating her championship doubles partner, Osborne, 8-6, 4-6, 6-1. But she was fortunate to escape Aussie Nancye Bolton in the semis, 4-6, 6-1, 7-5. Bolton held three match points, serving at 5-2, 40-0 in the third, but lost the game. At 5-3 the match was blacked out by nightfall. Unluckily for Bolton, still so close to victory, the two had agreed beforehand to utilize a rule available at the time: to replay any set halted by curfew, which they did the following day. Brough also won the mixed with John Bromwich, wrapping up a triple.

Kramer's domination of Wimbledon was so great that John Olliff, longtime tennis correspondent of London's *Daily Telegraph,* referred to him as "a presence of unutterable awe." In his book *The Romance of Wimbledon,* Olliff recalls: "It became almost boring to watch him mowing down his victims when it was so obvious that nothing short of a physical injury could possibly prevent him from winning. . . . He was an automaton of crushing consistency."

Kramer lost only 37 games in seven matches. In the quarterfinals he beat Geoff Brown, the 1946 runner-up, 6-0, 6-1, 6-3; in the semis, Dinny Pails, 6-1, 3-6, 6-1, 6-0, and in the final, Tom Brown, 6-1, 6-3, 6-2, in just 48 minutes. King George VI and

Queen Elizabeth were in the Royal Box, and His Majesty presented the champion's trophy to Kramer, the first titlist to have worn shorts instead of long white flannels. It was the King's first visit to Wimbledon since, as the Duke of York, he had played in the men's doubles in 1926.

Ted Schroeder did not play Wimbledon, but Kramer teamed with Bob Falkenburg—another tall American with a big serve—to win the doubles without losing a set. In the Davis Cup challenge round, Kramer and Schroeder won all four singles but lost the doubles to Bromwich and Colin Long. Jack and Ted then teamed to win the U.S. Doubles for the third time at Longwood.

And so on to Forest Hills, Kramer was again top-seeded and considered a cinch winner; in fact, he had already signed on Sept. 3, 1947, with promoter Jack Harris to play a tour against Bobby Riggs in 1948. Riggs had beaten Don Budge on a short tour for the second consecutive year, 24 matches to 22 this time, and had edged Budge for the U.S. Pro title, 3-6, 6-3, 10-8, 4-6, 6-3. Kramer was to be the new challenger for pro king Riggs, but the deal had to be hushed up until after the U.S., which ended Sept. 14.

Everything went according to plan until, as Kramer recalled in a *Sports Illustrated* article, "I almost blew the whole thing sky high. Here I was, signed and sealed for delivery to Riggs, and I lost the first two sets in the final to Frankie Parker. He was playing his best, but I did my best to help him. I can still remember looking up into the first row of the stadium seats and seeing the top of Jack Harris' bald head because he had it bowed forward in despair." But Kramer pulled himself together, starting the third set with two aces and the first of many winning drop shots. He purged the errors from his game and brought Harris back to life by winning the last three sets easily before a full house of 14,000.

Allison Danzig, the venerable tennis writer of *The New York Times,* reported on the final: "Not since Sidney Wood tamed the lethal strokes of Ellsworth Vines at Seabright in 1930 with his soft-ball strategy and reduced the Californian to a state of helplessness, has so cleverly designed and executed a plan of battle been in evidence on American turf as Parker employed in this match.

"In the end, the plan failed, as the challenger's strength ebbed and the champion, extricating himself from a morass of errors, loosed the full fury of his attack to win at 4-6, 2-6, 6-1, 6-0, 6-3. But the gallery would long remember the thrill and the chill of those first two sets and also the tense final chapter as the 31-year-old Parker gave his heavily favored and younger opponent the scare of his life."

Kramer exited amateurism on a 41-match streak. He had lost only once during the year, early to Talbert in the Bahamas, taking eight of nine tournaments on 48-1 in matches, including the U.S. Indoor over Bob Falkenburg, 6-1, 6-2, 6-2. Jack's match loss total after returning to civilian life in 1946: three.

1948

Perhaps the most unforgettable event of the tennis year 1948 actually took place on December 26, 1947: Jack Kramer's professional debut against Bobby Riggs at Madison Square Garden as a raging blizzard buffeted New York.

" . . . The city lay paralyzed by the heaviest snowfall in its history," esteemed columnist Red Smith recalled the night in *The New York Times* 30 years later. "Yet with taxis, buses, commuter trains and private cars stalled and the subways limping, 15,114 customers found their way into the big barn at Eighth Avenue and 50th Street."

Kramer, the top amateur of 1947, had been signed to face 1946–47 pro champ Riggs on a long tour. Francisco "Pancho" Segura of Ecuador and Australian Dinny Pails came along as the preliminary attraction—"the donkey act," in the vernacular of the tour. As was customary, the long and winding road of one-night stands began in the Garden, then the American Mecca of pro tennis.

Riggs won the opener, 6-2, 10-8, 4-6, 6-4, but Kramer gradually got accustomed to the grind

Jack Kramer (far right) joins Pancho Segura, Bobby Riggs and Dinny Pails on the pro circuit. (UPI)

of the tour and the style that playing night after night on a lightning-fast canvas court required. He learned to hit a high-kicking second serve to keep the quick and clever Riggs from scooting in behind his return, and to attack constantly, rushing the net on virtually every point and hammering away at Riggs' backhand.

"I began to really get comfortable with this new style around the time our tour reached San Francisco, when we were tied at 13 matches apiece," Kramer reminisced. "I won there, and then we flew to Denver, and Bobby got something started with the stewardess, and that gave me Denver, and then we went into Salt Lake City, where we played on a tremendously slick wood

surface. Bobby couldn't handle my serve there, and all of a sudden it was 16-13. And that was it. Now he had to gamble on my serve. He had to take chances or I could get to the net, and he was dead. He was thoroughly demoralized."

By the time the tour worked its way through the hinterlands, Riggs was "tanking" matches. Kramer won 56 of the last 63, finishing with a 69-20 record, the last amateur to overthrow the pro king. Kramer, whose cut of the opening-night receipts at the Garden had been $8,800, earned $89,000. Riggs made $50,000.

Kramer also won the U.S. Pro Championships at the West Side Tennis Club. He had a tough match against Welby Van Horn in the quar-

Twenty-year-old Pancho Gonzalez (right) was the victor, Eric Sturgess the vanquished, in the 1948 U.S. Singles. (UPI)

terfinals, then beat aging but still formidable Don Budge in the semifinals, 6-4, 8-10, 3-6, 6-4, 6-0. Al Laney, who covered tennis for 50 years, many of them for the New York *Herald Tribune,* made no secret of his low regard for the pros "because for so many years they have preferred exhibitions to real tournaments," but he begrudgingly put this one on his list of all time memorable matches. The next day Kramer put away Riggs, 14-12, 6-2, 3-6, 6-3, becoming the undisputed ruler of the pros as he had been of the amateurs.

With Kramer out of the amateur ranks, three other Americans took major titles. Frankie Parker won the French over Jaroslav Drobny, 6-4, 7-5, 5-7, 8-6. Bob Falkenburg startled Wimbledon by taking the men's singles over John Bromwich. Richard "Pancho" Gonzalez stormed to the first of his back-to-back U.S. titles, over Eric Sturgess, 6-2, 6-3, 14-12.

Adrian Quist, the last prewar champ, had regained the Australian singles title over doubles partner Bromwich, 6-4, 3-6, 6-3, 2-6, 6-3, but was able to win only one set in the Davis Cup challenge round as Australia fell to the United States 5-0, at Forest Hills. Parker—who had been denied a singles berth in 1946 and 1947—and Ted Schroeder beat Quist and Bill Sidwell to sweep the four singles matches. Bill Talbert-Gardnar Mulloy won the clinching doubles point over Sidwell and Colin Long, 8 6, 9 7, 2 6, 7-5.

Falkenburg, 23, was a tall and skinny Californian who dawdled between points sometimes apparently stalling to upset opponents; and threw games or whole sets to grab a breather and pace himself. He later moved to Rio de Janeiro and played in the Davis Cup for Brazil. Seeded seventh, he beat Frank Sedgman in the fourth round, Lennart Bergelin (conqueror of Parker in five sets) in the quarters, and Mulloy in an acrimonious semifinal. Then he met Bromwich, 29, in the final. Lance Tingay, in his book *100 Years of Wimbledon,* described the match-up:

"Bromwich was a much-loved player. Not only did he have a gentle personality but a persuasively gentle game. Craft and skill and guile were his all, never muscle and pace. His racket was lightweight, the grip small and could have been a girl's. With a lefty forehand, he was doubled-fisted on the right. His ability to tease pace-making opponents into defeat by the accuracy of his slow returns was entrancing to watch.

"Falkenburg, having won the first set, 7-5, palpably threw the second at 6-0. The tactics were legitimate but they hardly endeared him to the crowd. He took the third set, 6-2. Bromwich won the fourth, 6-3. By then the effectiveness of Falkenburg's big serve had declined. And he was missing much with his forehand volley. . . . Bromwich controlled the fifth set decisively, so much so that he led 5-2, 40-15, on his own service. On the two match points Falkenburg played shots that were pure gambles, screaming backhand returns of service. Bromwich had his third match point at advantage and Falkenburg repeated his performance. The Australian 'died' as an effective player from that stage. Falkenburg devoured the remaining games. If Bromwich was heart-broken he shared the sentiment with nearly every spectator round the court."

Louise Brough dominated women's play in 1948.
(New York Herald Tribune)

Bromwich never did win the Wimbledon singles, but he salvaged some consolation by taking the doubles title with the 20-year-old Sedgman, and successfully defended the mixed doubles title with Louise Brough.

After all the Wimbledon surprises, Forest Hills in 1948 was considered a wide-open affair. Ted Schroeder, generally regarded as Kramer's heir apparent, did not play. Frank Parker was the top-seeded American, ahead of Falkenburg. Virtually ignored, seeded eighth, was Gonzalez, 20, one of seven children of a poor Mexican American family from Los Angeles. His father wished he would give up tennis and get an education, but Pancho preferred to be a truant, going to movies or developing the blazing serve that was his hallmark.

Gonzalez—a lean 6-foot-3, 185-pounder whose theatricality, smoldering Latin temper, sex appeal, and combination of power and touch gave him a kind of animalistic magnetism—upset Parker in the quarterfinals, Drobny in the semis, 8-10, 11-9, 6-0, 6-3, and the South African Sturgess in the final. A friend had once described Gonzalez as "even-tempered—he's *always* mad."

The fact that his worthiness as champion was questioned because Schroeder had not played made him an even angrier young man.

U.S. women continued to rule internationally, though Nancye Bolton regained Australia. A Belgian-born French citizen, Nelly Adamson Landry won in Paris, beating Shirley Fry by the bizarre score of 6-2, 0-6, 6-0, the only non-American to win between 1946 and 1958. The U.S. clobbered Great Britain again in the Wightman Cup, 6-1, at Wimbledon. Louise Brough won her first major singles title overseas, starting a three-year Wimbledon reign by beating Doris Hart, 6-3, 8-6. Margaret Osborne, who had become Mrs. William duPont, beat Brough in a scintillating Forest Hills final, 4-6, 6-4, 15-13, the first of her three consecutive triumphs there, and she and Brough combined for an eighth successive U.S. title.

Hart and Pat Todd dethroned Brough-duPont at the French Championships, as they had at Wimbledon the year before, but Brough-duPont turned the tables at Wimbledon. When Brough left the Centre Court at 8:15 p.m. on the final Saturday of Wimbledon, after defending her title with Bromwich over Sedgman and Hart, she was the reigning singles, doubles, and mixed champion of both the United States and Great Britain, a feat previously achieved only by Alice Marble in 1939.

1949

Ted Schroeder won the Wimbledon singles on his first and only attempt, and Pancho Gonzalez proved that he was not the "cheese champion" some had called him. But 1949 will always be remembered as the year of "Gorgeous Gussy" Moran and the lace-trimmed panties that shocked Wimbledon.

Couturier Teddy Tinling, a tennis insider since he umpired matches for Suzanne Lenglen on the Riviera decades earlier, had waged a one-man battle against the unflattering white jersey and skirt that pretty much constituted women's

Gussy Moran's lace-trimmed panties stirred staid Wimbledon in 1949. (UPI)

tennis attire. He had experimented with touches of color on the dresses he made for English-woman Joy Gannon in 1947, without objection, but ran into problems in 1948 when Mrs. Hazel Wightman, captain of the U.S. team playing for the cup she had donated, objected to bits of color on the Tinling frock of British No. 1 Betty Hilton. This resulted in Wimbledon officials issuing an "all-white" rule.

In 1949, unable to use color as requested by the attractive and sexy Gertrude Moran of Santa Monica, Cal., Tinling put a half inch of lace trim around her panties, trying to satisfy Gussy's wish for some distinctive adornment. This was done innocently, but when the flamboyant Gussy posed for photographers at the pre-Wimbledon garden party at the Hurlingham Club, she caused a sensation. The first time she twirled on Centre Court a tremor went through the staid old arena. "Ten-

nis was then suddenly treated to the spectacle of photographers lying flat on the ground trying to shoot Gussy's panties," Tinling remembered. The "coquettish" undergarment became the subject of Parliamentary debate and photo-stories on front pages around the world.

"No one in their wildest dreams could have foreseen the furor, the outcry, the sensation. . . ." Tinling wrote. "Wimbledon interpreted the lace as an intentional device, a sinister plot by Gussy and myself for the sole purpose of guiding men's eyes to her bottom. At Wimbledon I was told that I had put 'vulgarity and sin' into tennis, and I re-signed the Master of Ceremonies job I had held there for 23 years." Fortunately, he continued de-signing for and dressing most postwar women champions.

The year had begun with Frank Sedgman, age 21, winning his first major title, beating John Bromwich, 6-3, 6-3, 6-2, in the final of the Aus-tralian Championships. Bromwich was thus run-ner-up for the third straight year after winning in 1946, but again captured the doubles with Adrian Quist—which seemed almost a formality by now. So it was as well for Nancye Bolton and Thelma Long in the women's doubles, but Doris Hart ended Bolton's quest for a fifth consecutive sin-gles title. Her 6-3, 6-4 triumph in the final made Hart the first overseas champion since Californ-ian Dodo Bundy in 1938.

Frank Parker defended his French singles title over the elegant Budge Patty, 6-3, 1-6, 6-1, 6-4, and teamed with Gonzalez to win the dou-bles. Margaret duPont recovered the singles title she had won in Paris in 1946, dethroning Nelly Landry, 7-5, 6-2, and teamed with Louise Brough to regain the doubles title they had won in 1946 and 1947.

At Wimbledon, spectators were anxious to see the man Americans called "Lucky" Schroed-er. Though almost 28, he had never played the world's premier championship, but was well-known worldwide for his Davis Cup exploits. "Rather stocky, he had a rolling gait which made him look as though he had just got off a horse," remembered Lance Tingay. "Except when he was actually playing he always seemed to have a pipe in his mouth, a corn cob as often as not." Britons found him an intriguing character.

Top-seeded Schroeder lost the first two sets of his first-round match to the dangerous Gardnar Mulloy, whom he had beaten in the final at Queen's Club just two days earlier. In the quarters, he was again down two sets to Frank Sedgman, trailed 0-3 in the fifth, and had a match point against him at 4-5. He was called for a foot fault, but coolly followed his second serve to the net and hit a winning volley off the wood. He saved another match point at 5-6, this time with a bold backhand passing shot, and finally pulled out the match at 9-7, never having led until the final minutes.

Schroeder continued to live precariously, coming back from two sets to one down against Eric Sturgess in the semifinals. In the final, he had his fourth five-setter in seven matches, edging the popular Jaroslav Drobny, 3-6, 6-0, 6-3, 4-6, 6-4, after being within a point of a 0-2 deficit in the final set. "Lucky" Schroeder, indeed; he was always living on the edge of the ledge.

The women's final came down to a memorable duel between the No. 1 seed, Louise Brough, and the No. 2, Margaret duPont. Brough won the first set, 10-8, duPont the second, 6-1, and at 8-all in the third the difference between them was no more than the breadth of a blade of Wimbledon's celebrated grass. Brough served out of a 0-40 predicament like a champion, and then broke for the match and successful defense of her title.

Gonzalez, beaten early by Geoff Brown, and Parker added the Wimbledon doubles to the French they had won earlier, while Brough and duPont joined forces to defend their title over Pat Todd and Gussy Moran. The scores were 8-6, 7-5—close enough to prevent anyone from quipping that the champs had beaten the lace panties off Gorgeous Gussy.

The American women continued their relentless domination of the Wightman Cup, drubbing Great Britain, 7-0, at Philadelphia. Schroeder and Gonzalez gave the U.S. all four singles points as the U.S. men made it four straight victories over Australia in the Davis Cup challenge round at Forest Hills. Schroeder was up to his usual five-set high-jinks in the opening match, beating Bill Sidwell, 6-1, 5-7, 4-6, 6-2, 6-3, but he put away Sedgman in straight sets, 6-4, 6-3, 6-3, to clinch. The Americans lost only the doubles. Sidwell and Bromwich, who also won the 1949 U.S. Doubles at Longwood, beat Bill Talbert and Gar Mulloy, 3-6, 4-6, 10-8, 9-7, 9-7.

There was keen interest in a Schroeder-Gonzalez showdown at Forest Hills. Because Gonzalez, seeded second at Wimbledon, had gone out to Geoff Brown in the round of 16, there was speculation that his 1948 U.S. victory had been a fluke. One writer flatly called him a "cheese champ"—which is how Gonzalez got his nickname of "Gorgo," short for "Gorgonzola."

Gonzalez was taken to five sets by Art Larsen and by Parker, who let him off the hook in the semis. Schroeder was pushed to the limit by Sedgman in the quarters and Bill Talbert in the semis. But finally the men people wanted to see arrived safely in the final.

The old 15,000-seat horseshoe stadium at the West Side Tennis Club was packed and tense as Schroeder and Gonzalez fought to 16-all in the first set. Gonzalez fell behind 0-40, but three big serves got him back to deuce. A net-cord winner gave Schroeder another break point, and Gonzalez lost his serve on a volley that he thought was good. A linesman called it wide. Schroeder served out the set, then donned spikes on the slippery turf and quickly ran out the second set, 6-2. Gonzalez seethed.

But "Gorgo" always had a knack of channeling his temper, and he turned the rage surging within him to his advantage. Serving and attacking furiously, he achieved one of the great Forest Hills comebacks, 16-18, 2-6, 6-1, 6-2, 6-4.

Ted Schroeder had his day at Wimbledon in 1949, but Forest Hills was spoiled for him by Pancho Gonzalez. (UPI)

Margaret duPont, meanwhile, won her second "Big Four" title of the year with an easy 6-4, 6-1 victory over Doris Hart in the women's final, and the sure-thing form of Brough-duPont rolled to their eighth U.S. Doubles in a row.

Jack Harris had quit the promotional game after the successful Kramer-Riggs tour. The new promoter was Riggs, who had won the U.S. Pro title at Forest Hills over Don Budge, 9-7, 3-6, 6-3, 7-5, while Kramer sat out, awaiting a new amateur king.

That was supposed to be Schroeder, who actually had signed after winning Wimbledon but then changed his mind, deciding that his intense constitution was not suited for the nightly grind of the tour. If he had won Forest Hills, Schroeder undoubtedly would have signed so as not to leave his old friend Kramer in the lurch; Kramer thought that in the back of his mind, Schroeder wanted to lose to Gonzalez for that reason.

But in any event, Gonzalez—as two-time Forest Hills champ—became the only viable alternative, and Riggs signed him for the longest

head-to-head tour yet. Frank Parker came along to play Pancho Segura in the prelims. The tour stretched from October 1949 to May 1950, and Kramer clobbered the talented but surly and immature Gonzalez, 96 matches to 27. Both players made $72,000, but the future seemed a dead end for Gonzalez, who was only 21 years old.

1950

The year 1950 was in many ways not only the start of a new decade, but also of a new era in tennis. With Kramer, Gonzalez, and Parker now pros, the American stranglehold on the international game was loosened. A new crop of Yanks was coming along—led by touch artists Art Larsen and Herbie Flam, the expatriate Californian Budge Patty and the forthright Tony Trabert and Vic Seixas. But Frank Sedgman, Ken McGregor and Mervyn Rose signaled a powerful new line of Australian resistance.

Germany and Japan were readmitted to the ITF, indicating that wartime wounds had healed. The Italian Championships was played for the first time since 1935, revived by the energetic promotion of Carlo della Vida, who was intent on building it into one of the international showcases. Despite rains that threatened to flood the sunken Campo Centrale (center court) at Rome's Il Foro Italico, the tournament was a success, won by the clay court artist, Jaroslav Drobny.

The self-exiled Czech, who traveled on an Egyptian passport until becoming a British citizen in 1959, also won the German championship, which had started to rebuild slowly as a Germans-only affair in 1948 and 1949. The elegant and sporting prewar star, Baron Gottfried von Cramm, had won both years. The Hamburg and Rome tournaments were destined to rise simultaneously to a stature just below the French Championships as the most important clay court events of Europe.

Sedgman, an athletic serve-and-volleyer with a crunching forehand, defeated McGregor for his second straight Australian singles title, 6-3, 6-4,

4-6, 6-1, while Adrian Quist and John Bromwich won their record eighth doubles title.

J. Edward "Budge" Patty, an urbane California native who lived in Paris, won the French over Drobny in a duel of enchanting shotmaking, 6-1, 6-2, 3-6, 5-7, 7-5. Patty then became the first player since Don Budge in 1938 to win the Paris-Wimbledon "double," beating Frank Sedgman on grass, 6-1, 8-10, 6-2, 6-3, as gracefully as he had overcome Drobny on clay.

Patty was a great stylist, fluent on all his strokes and mesmerizing with the effortlessness of his forehand volley. He was also a painter and patron of the arts—"I have a way to go to catch Rembrandt, but Renoir doesn't stand a chance," he commented once, upon the opening of an exhibition of his canvases in Paris. "He gave the impression," noted Tingay, "of being the most sophisticated champion of all time."

Unsophisticated, flaky, eccentric, and totally original was Art "Tappy" Larsen, so nicknamed because of his habit, one of many superstitions, of tapping objects from net posts to opponents in ritualistic "good luck" sequences. Patty was known as a suave playboy who only occasionally trained; Larsen was an eager if unpolished ladies' man who never trained. But he had a great gift for the game, and magnificent touch, as he amply demonstrated in winning the U.S. title over his pal Flam in a lovely match of wits and angles, 6-3, 4-6, 5-7, 6-4, 6-3.

In doubles, Bill Talbert partnered his athletic Cincinnati protégé, Tony Trabert, also a star University of Cincinnati basketball guard, to the French title. Quist and Bromwich won their only Wimbledon title together, outlasting Geoff Brown and Bill Sidwell, 7-5, 3-6, 6-3, 3-6, 6-2. Bromwich and Sedgman won the U.S. Doubles over four-time champs Bill Talbert and Gardnar Mulloy.

Australia ended the four-year American grip on the Davis Cup with a 4-1 victory in the challenge round at Forest Hills. Sedgman walloped Tom Brown, 6-0, 8-6, 9-7, and McGregor ambushed Ted Schroeder, 13-11, 6-3, 6-4, in the

Southpaw Art "Tappy" Larsen outplayed fellow Californian Herbie Flam for the U.S. Singles title in 1950. (UPI)

opening singles, and then Sedgman and Bromwich sealed the Aussie triumph by beating Schroeder and Mulloy in the doubles, 4-6, 6-4, 6-2, 4-6, 6-4.

America's women extended their monotonous superiority over Great Britain with another 7-0 Wightman Cup Wimbledon, and hoarded all the "Big Four" titles in singles and doubles. The Australian final was the first all-American affair, Brough succeeded Doris Hart as champion with a 6-4, 3-6, 6-4 victory over the defender. They then teamed to win the doubles, interrupting the long reign of eight-time champions Nancye Bolton and Thelma Long, 6-2, 2-6, 6-3.

Hart won her first French singles, over Pat Todd, 6-4, 4-6, 6-2. Brough won her third straight Wimbledon title, beating Margaret duPont, 6-1, 3-6, 6-1, while duPont took her third

In 1950 Althea Gibson became the first black to play in the U.S. Championships and came within one game of defeating Louise Brough in the second round. (UPI)

straight Forest Hills crown, dispatching Hart in the final, 6-3, 6-3.

A historic footnote at Forest Hills was the appearance of a future champion and Hall of Famer, 23-year-old Althea Gibson, the first black American to play in the U.S. Championships. It was a leap of the color bar in tennis as Jackie Robinson's debut with the Brooklyn Dodgers had been three years before, a breakthrough that was almost sensational since Gibson nearly toppled the Wimbledon champ, fourth-seeded Louise Brough, in the second round.

Starting off with a prophetic victory over Barbara Knapp, 6-2, 6-2, Gibson overcame nerves and a 1-6 opening set against Brough to seize the second, 6-3. As the sky darkened, Gibson battled to a 7-6 lead in the decisive set. At that moment Brough may have been reprieved: Forest Hills was struck by a thunderstorm so fierce that lightning knocked one of the brooding concrete eagles from the upper rim of the stadium. Resuming the following afternoon, Gibson may have had too much time to think about victory lying within her long reach—four points away. Brough held serve, and won the next two games to escape.

"When lightning put down that eagle," Gibson laughed, "maybe it was an omen times was changing. Brough was a little too experienced for me in that situation — but my day would come." So it did with titles in 1957 and 1958.

Brough had also teamed with Eric Sturgess for her fourth Wimbledon mixed doubles title in five years, with three different partners. Hart and Shirley Fry began a four-year rule in the French doubles, while duPont and Brough won their third consecutive Wimbledon and ninth consecutive U.S. doubles crowns, both over Fry-Hart.

A new order was brought to the U.S. Pro Championship as Pancho Segura knocked off Jack Kramer in the semis, where Frank Kovacs uprooted 1949 champ Bobby Riggs. Kovacs broke down with cramps in the final, a 6-4, 1-6, 8-6, 4-4 TKO for Segura. There was no amateur recruit to challenge Kramer for supremacy of the pro game, but Riggs put together a tour with Segura—the swarthy little Ecuadorian with bowed legs, a murderous two-fisted forehand and enormous competitive heart—as the challenger at $1,000 per week against 5 percent of the gate. Kramer got 25 percent. Unfortunately, the cunning "Segoo" simply could not handle Kramer's big serve on fast indoor courts, and the tour was not competitive. Riggs tried to spice it up by signing Gussy Moran to a lucrative contract— $35,000 guaranteed, against 25 percent of profits—to play Pauline Betz. Gussy got tremendous publicity as the glamour girl of the lace pants, but she was not in the same class with Betz, who was overwhelming even after Riggs suggested she try to "carry" her fashionable but outclassed opponent.

The tour was an artistic, competitive, and financial flop. Kramer was still the king, Segura went back to being a prelim boy, Moran tried to make it in showbiz, and Betz, who married noted *Washington Post* sportswriter Bob Addie, became a respected teaching pro in Washington.

1951

The new era continued to take shape on the world's tennis courts in 1951. American Dick Savitt surprisingly won the Australian and Wimbledon singles titles, but Frank Sedgman and Ken McGregor helped forge the foundation of a new Australian dynasty, holding onto the Davis Cup and fashioning the only male Grand Slam of doubles. Meanwhile, American women continued their postwar supremacy, but the dominance of Louise Brough, Margaret Osborne duPont, Doris Hart and Shirley Fry was challenged by a stirring new teen-age talent: Maureen Connolly.

Savitt, 24, a rawboned and hulking competitor from Orange, N.J., and Cornell University, sported a big serve, a solid ground game, and an impressive, hard-hit backhand. He was the first American to win the Australian singles—in fact, the first non-Australian finalist—since Don Budge in 1938, beating McGregor, 6-3, 2-6, 6-3, 6-1.

Like Ted Schroeder two years earlier, sixth-seeded Savitt won Wimbledon on his first attempt. He was aided by Herb Flam's defeat of top-seeded Sedgman from two sets down in the quarters, Englishman Tony Mottram's third-round upset of Jaroslav Drobny, and defending champion Budge Patty's demise in the second round, at the hands of former Tulane star Ham Richardson.

Savitt also had a narrow escape from Flam, whom the BBC's extraordinary radio commentator Max Robertson called "the Paul Newman of tennis players, with hunched and self-deprecating look." Savitt trailed 1-6, 1-5 in the semifinals before salvaging the second set, 15-13, to turn the match around. "A couple of points the other way and my whole life might have been different," Savitt mused on the occasion of Wimbledon's Centenary "parade of champions" in 1977. As it happened, he lost only five games in the third and fourth sets against Flam and then chastened McGregor in the final, 6-4, 6-4, 6-4.

Drobny—the crafty left-hander with the sad countenance, spectacles, and wonderful repertoire of touch and spin to go with his tricky serve—defeated Eric Sturgess, 6-3, 6-3, 6-3, to win the French singles for the first time after being runner-up in 1946, 1948 and 1950.

Sedgman, the personification of robust Australian fitness with an unerring forehand volley, atoned for his Wimbledon failure by winning the first of back-to-back U.S. titles.

He was the first Australian player to win the U.S., the first in the final since Jack Crawford in 1933. Sedgman got there in devastating form, ravaging defending champion Art Larsen in the semifinals, 6-1, 6-2, 6-0, in just 49 minutes, the worst beating ever inflicted on a titleholder. Wrote Allison Danzig in *The New York Times,* "The radiance of the performance turned in by the 23-year-old Sedgman has not often been equaled. With his easy, almost effortless production of stabbing strokes, he pierced the dazed champion's defenses to score at will with a regularity and dispatch that made Larsen's plight almost pitiable."

In the final against Philadelphian Vic Seixas, Sedgman was nearly as awesome, winning 6-4, 6-1, 6-1 Seixas had played superbly until then, beating McGregor, Flam, and then Savitt in the semifinals, 6-0, 3-6, 6-3, 6-2. Savitt was the top seed, but severely hobbled by an infected left leg, which had to be lanced the day before he faced Seixas.

Savitt had played zone matches against Japan (readmitted to the Davis Cup, along with Germany, for the first time since the war) and Canada. But Captain Frank Shields passed him over—angering him and many supporters—for the challenge round in Sydney. Seixas handled Mervyn Rose, and Sedgman beat Ted Schroeder to make it 1-1 after the opening singles, but the match hinged on the doubles. Schroeder had one of his worst days—"I wanted to cry for him, he was so bad," recalls old friend Jack Kramer—and he and Trabert were beaten by Sedgman and McGregor, 6-2, 9-7, 6-3. Schroeder did pull himself together after a nervous, sleepless night and beat Rose with a gritty performance, but Sedgman rolled over Seixas in the fifth match, 6-4, 6-2, 6-2, for a 3-2 Australian victory.

It was appropriate that Sedgman-McGregor won the pivotal doubles, for this was their Grand

Dick Savitt, Australian and Wimbledon champion in 1951, wore a bonnet to withstand the heat in a Davis Cup match against Japan's Jiro Kumamaru in Louisville. (UPI)

Slam year as a tandem. They swept the Australian, French, Wimbledon and U.S. doubles titles, the only male pair ever to do so. They ended the eight-year monopoly of Adrian Quist–John Bromwich in the Australian final, beating the champions, 11-9, 2-6, 6-3, 4-6, 6-3, then went on to capture the French over Savitt and Gardnar Mulloy, 6-2, 2-6, 9-7, 7-5, and Wimbledon over Drobny and Sturgess, 3-6, 6-2, 6-3, 3-6, 6-3. They completed the Slam by taking the U.S. title over countryman Don Candy and Merv Rose, 10-8, 4-6, 6-4, 7-5, the final having been moved to Forest Hills after heavy rains at Longwood.

U.S. women—Doris Hart, Shirley Fry, Maureen Connolly, Pat Todd, and Nancy Chaffee—cruised by Great Britain again, 6-1, in the Wightman Cup at Longwood.

Maureen Connolly, at 16 the youngest until 1979 to win the U.S. title, is shown in 1951 in Los Angeles (after capturing the Pacific Southwest crown) with former U.S. champions May Sutton, Helen Wills Moody and Marion Jones. (UPI)

In the absence of an overseas challenge, Nancye Bolton recaptured the Australian singles title over her partner Thelma Long, 6-1, 7-5, but Americans again won everything else. Fry, persistent as ever from the backcourt, beat Hart in the French final, 6-3, 3-6, 6-3, but got her come-uppance at Wimbledon, where Hart thrashed her, 6-1, 6-0. This was Hart's only singles title—she had been runner-up in 1947 and 1948—and she parlayed it into a triple, taking the women's doubles with Fry (starting a three-year rule) and the mixed doubles with Sedgman (first of her five successive triumphs, two with Sedgman and three with Vic Seixas).

In fact, Hart-Fry and Hart-Sedgman swept the women's and mixed doubles titles of France, Wimbledon, and the U.S. in 1951 as Brough-duPont were absent. Hart was the top seed at Forest Hills and thought she was the best woman player in the world, but she was given a rude jolt in the semifinals by 16-year-old Maureen Connolly of San Diego. Blasting her flawless ground strokes from both wings, Connolly overcame a 0-4 deficit to win the first set on a drizzly, miserable day, 6-4. Hart asked several times that the match be halted. It was, but Connolly won the second set the following afternoon. In the final, the tenacious and mentally uncompromising

Connolly beat Fry, 6-3, 1-6, 6-4, for the first of three straight championships, becoming the youngest ever U.S. champion until Tracy Austin in 1979. "I later kidded Maureen that she was lucky to beat me in '51," Hart has said. "But after that she became, unquestionably, the greatest woman player who ever lived."

A distasteful Forest Hills outburst by No. 7 American Earl Cochell brought swift retribution from the USTA, a demonstration of the arbitrary power national associations held over players prior to the open era and the forming of player unions. Clearly Cochell was out of line in the fourth-rounder, a four-set loss to Gar Mulloy. He argued many line calls, erupted in bursts of temper, argued with the umpire and spectators, tried to climb the umpire's chair and grab his microphone to lecture the crowd, and blatantly threw a number of games, batting balls into the stands or playing left-handed (he was right-handed). What really did him in was his abusive verbal attack on the referee, Dr. Ellsworth Davenport, who reprimanded him.

The upshot was that the USTA suspended Cochell for life. No agent, lawyer or union to protect him then. Some years later the sentence was lifted, but Cochell, unfairly unranked for 1951 (he was 29) lost perhaps his best years.

It was Little Pancho (Segura) against Big Pancho (Gonzalez) for the U.S. Pro crown, and Segura defended successfully at Forest Hills, 6-3, 6-4, 6-2.

1952

Another patch in the nearly complete postwar reconstruction of tennis was put in place in 1952 when the King's Cup, a European team competition for a trophy donated by Swedish monarch and tennis patron Gustav V in 1936, was resumed. But other than Jaroslav Drobny's second straight French title, Europe had little impact on the world tennis stage. Australian men and American women dominated the major championships.

Frank Sedgman prevailed at Wimbledon and here against Gardnar Mulloy (far court) in the U.S. final at Forest Hills in 1952. (UPI)

Among the men, it was Frank Sedgman's year. The aggressive, diligent Aussie was in all of the "Big Four" finals, singles and doubles, and led Australia's successful Davis Cup defense.

He was on the losing end of the first two singles finals, however, beaten by his partner McGregor in the Australian, 7-5, 12-10, 2-6, 6-2, and by the ever-dangerous Drobny on the salmon-colored clay of Paris, 6-2, 6-0, 3-6, 6-3.

Sedgman got his revenge on "Old Drob" in the final at Wimbledon, 4-6, 6-2, 6-3, 6-2, becoming the first Aussie champ there since Jack Crawford in 1933. Two other Aussies—Lew Hoad (who, with Ken Rosewall, was making his first overseas tour, the 17-year-olds reaching the semifinals in doubles) and McGregor—gave Drobny trouble en route. Hoad took him to four tough sets in the fourth round, and McGregor came within two points of beating him in the quarters. American Herbie Flam also pushed him to the five-set limit in the semis.

Drobny took the first set of the final, but Sedgman seized control of the match in a

Lew Hoad and Maureen Connolly reach for the ball in mixed doubles against Rex Hartwig and Julie Sampson at Forest Hills. The U.S. championship went to Frank Sedgman and Doris Hart in 1951 and 1952. (New York Herald Tribune)

swirling wind on Centre Court when he tuned in his crushing overhead smash. Sedgman, in fact, lost only two sets at Wimbledon, underscoring his superiority, and rolled impressively to his second straight Forest Hills title. He crunched countryman Merv Rose in the semis and made the final against surprising 37-year-old Gardnar Mulloy look as easy as one, two, three—6-1, 6-2, 6-3.

Sedgman, who also won the Italian Championship in his last year as an amateur, defended his Wimbledon doubles title with McGregor and the mixed with Doris Hart, becoming one of only three men to achieve such a triple. (The others were Don Budge in 1937 and 1938 and Bobby

Riggs in 1939.) Sedgman-McGregor again won the Australian and French doubles but were denied a second consecutive doubles Grand Slam when the unusual Australian-American alliance of Merv Rose and Vic Seixas barely beat them in the final of the U.S. Doubles at Longwood, 3-6, 10-8, 10-8, 6-8, 8-6. Since Sedgman had won the 1950 U.S. title with John Bromwich, his record run of eight straight doubles majors was ended.

Sedgman-Hart did defend their U.S. mixed title, however, as they had the French and Wimbledon.

Sedgman beat both Seixas and Tony Trabert in straight sets, and partnered McGregor to a four-set triumph in doubles, as Australia won the Davis Cup challenge round for the third year in a row, 4-1. Seixas salvaged the only point for the United States, beating McGregor in the meaningless fifth match.

American women again avoided the long journey to Australia, allowing Thelma Long to win her first singles title, 6-2, 6-3, over Helen Angwin and team with Nancye Bolton for their 10th doubles title together. (Long later won two more.)

But U.S. women were oppressive in the other major championships, as had become their custom. Doris Hart won her second French singles title, reversing the final-round result of a year earlier to beat Shirley Fry, 6-4, 6-4. Maureen Connolly ascended to the world No.1 ranking at age 17 by beating three-time champ Louise Brough, 7-5, 6-3, in the Wimbledon final, and Hart 6-3, 7-5, to defend her Forest Hills crown.

Connolly's first appearance at Wimbledon, seeded second behind Hart, was a celebrated event. "The pressures under which she played were enormous," noted Lance Tingay. "There was the basic pressure of being expected to win. There was a blaze of publicity because Miss Connolly, for reasons of her skill, her charm and achievement, was 'news' in everything she did. And her guidance went sour at this her first Wimbledon challenge. Her coach—the strong-willed, overly protective, and domineering Eleanor 'Teach' Tennant, who had also developed Alice Marble and imbued her with killer psychology— advised Connolly to withdraw because of a mild shoulder strain. Maureen refused and parted company with Tennant forever, removing a stifling weight from her personality."

Connolly lost sets to Englishwomen Susan Partridge, who slow-balled her, giving neither the pace nor angle on which Maureen thrived, and to Thelma Long in the quarterfinals. Partridge, the Italian champion, proved her toughest foe, taking her to 6-3, 5-7, 7-5. Hart was beaten in a long quarterfinal by Pat Todd, leaving Connolly to mow down Fry and Brough in straight sets in the final two rounds. Connolly's scythelike strokes were as deadly as the British had heard; in fact, in three years she never lost a single match in Great Britain.

Hart and Fry extended their doubles title streaks in the French (three years), Wimbledon and U.S. doubles (two years each), and the U.S. again rolled over Great Britain in the Wightman Cup, losing only one set in a 7-0 triumph at Wimbledon.

Bobby Riggs had tried to sign Sedgman and McGregor to tour as pros with himself, Pancho Gonzalez and Pancho Segura in 1952, dismissing Jack Kramer by saying he had retired. Riggs struck a deal, but later Gonzalez wanted to change the agreed-upon terms, and Riggs—who was about to re-marry—got disgusted and left the promoting business.

There was no pro tour in 1952, but Segura startled Gonzalez in the final of the U.S. Pro Championships, 3-6, 6-4, 3-6, 6-4, 6-0, from 3-0 down in the fourth, at Lakewood Park in Cleveland. Afterwards the victor chortled, "Here I am, 30, six years older, and I outlast him." Kramer, who had no intention of retiring, took over as player-promoter, signing Sedgman to a contract ($75,000 guarantee) that was announced right after the Davis Cup challenge round. McGregor also turned pro to face Segura in the prelims on the 1953 tour.

1953

The year 1953 provided the tennis world with lovely days of "Mo" and Rosewall.

The incomparable Maureen Connolly, nicknamed "Little Mo" because she was as invincible as the World War II battleship Missouri ("Big Mo"), swept the Australian, French, Wimbledon and U.S. singles, and won 10 of 12 tournaments, compiling a 61-2 record. This was the crowning year of an abbreviated career that was to end through injury, after three-and-a-half awesome seasons, in 1954.

Meanwhile, Kenneth Robert Rosewall, 21 days older than his fellow Australian "Whiz Kid" Lew Hoad, took the Australian and French singles titles, the first major accomplishments of a career matchless in its longevity. Rosewall would still be going strong a quarter of a century later, nine years after Connolly's death from cancer at age 34.

Connolly, at 18, was the first to emulate Don Budge, who took all the "Big Four" singles titles in 1938 and popularized the feat by calling it the Grand Slam. In doing it, she trampled 22 opponents, losing just one set and 82 games.

"Little Mo" started in Australia, demolishing her partner Julie Sampson, 6-3, 6-2, before they teamed up to win the doubles. In the quarterfinals at Paris, Connolly lost that lone set—to Susan Partridge, her toughest rival at Wimbledon the year before, who by this time had married France's Philippe Chatrier. She slow-balled again, but Connolly hit her way out of trouble, blasting her ground strokes even harder, deeper, and closer to the lines than usual, prevailing by 3-6, 6-2, 6-2. Then she drubbed Doris Hart in the final, 6-2, 6-4.

Hart was also her final-round opponent at Wimbledon and Forest Hills. "The Wimbledon final was the finest match of the Slam: 8-6, 7-5. The two great players called it the best of their life," noted a silver anniversary tribute to Little Mo's wondrous 1953 record. "In the homestretch at Forest Hills, Connolly won driving, as they say at the racetrack, 6-2, 6-3 over Althea Gibson in the quarters; 6-1, 6-1 over Shirley Fry; and 6-2, 6-4 over Hart."

In fact, Connolly lost only two matches during the year: to Hart in the final of the Italian, and to Fry in the Pacific Southwest at Los Angeles.

Connolly and Hart teamed for the French doubles title, but Little Mo—never a great doubles player because of her distaste for net play—was not destined for a doubles Slam. Hart and Fry won their third consecutive Wimbledon doubles, whitewashing Connolly and Sampson, 6-0, 6-0,

minutes after Maureen had gotten a telephone call from her fiancé, Olympic equestrian Norman Brinker, telling her he was being sent to Korea by the U.S. Navy. Hart and Fry also won the third of their four successive U.S. Doubles titles, but it was a titanic struggle to end at 41 matches and nine titles the record major doubles streak of Louise Brough and Margaret duPont, 6-2, 7-9, 9-7. Brough-duPont, abstainers from the 1951 and 1952 Championships, looked safe when they pinched Fry at 2-5 and two match points, but a skillful barrage of lobs undid the perennial champs.

Rosewall, 18, a 5-foot-7, 145-pounder with an angel face and neither a hair nor a footstep out of place, took the first of his four Australian singles titles, spanning 19 years, by beating left-hander Mervyn Rose, 6-0, 6-3, 6-4. Rosewall beat Vic Seixas, 6-3, 6-4, 1-6, 6-2, in the French final, the first tournament covered by a new magazine, *World Tennis,* which debuted in June 1953 and would become an influential force in the game. It was edited and published by New Yorker Gladys Heldman. The story under Gardnar Mulloy's by-line described Rosewall as "a young kid with stamina, hard-hitting groundstrokes and plenty of confidence."

The Wimbledon and U.S. titles came back into American possession, property of Vic Seixas and Tony Trabert.

Seixas, according to Lance Tingay's official history of Wimbledon, was "hardly the prettiest player in the world, for his strokes smacked more of expediency than fluency and polish, but he gave the impression of being prepared to go on attacking forever." He edged Hoad in the quarters and Rose in the semis, both in five long sets. In the final, he beat Dane Kurt Nielsen—whose chopped forehand down the middle of the court had upset top seed Rosewall in the quarters—9-7, 6-3, 6-4.

The match of the tournament was the third-round classic in which Jaroslav Drobny defeated his good friend and constant touring companion,

Jaroslav Drobny (left) and Budge Patty wearily leave the court at Wimbledon after their 93-game marathon match in 1953. (UPI)

Budge Patty, 8-6, 16-18, 3-6, 8-6, 12-10. The herculean epic began at 5:00 p.m. and ended at nightfall 4 hours, 23 minutes later, Drobny surviving three match points in the fourth set, three more in the fifth, winning the last two games after the referee's decision at 10-10 was conveyed to a groaning full-house crowd; only enough light remained to play two more games that evening. Its 93 games, played at a consistently high standard, were the most in any Wimbledon singles to that time. But Drobny had torn a muscle in his right leg, and after somehow limping through victories over Australian Rex Hartwig and Swede Sven Davidson, lost to the surprising Nielsen in the semis.

Trabert did in Rosewall, and Seixas beat Hoad in the U.S. semifinals at Forest Hills, and then Trabert—serving and volleying consistently

and returning superbly whether Seixas charged the net or stayed back—beat the Wimbledon champ in the final, 6-3, 6-2, 6-3, in just one hour. Trabert was less than three months out of the U.S. Navy, but he had trained hard to regain his speed and match fitness, and he leveled Seixas with a vicious onslaught from backcourt and net, off both wings—especially his topspin backhand.

Hoad and Rosewall captured the Australian, French, and Wimbledon doubles titles, but missed a Grand Slam on the last leg, the U.S. at Longwood, upset in the quarters by Americans Straight Clark and lefty Hal Burrows, 5-7, 14-12, 18-16, 9-7. Their countrymen, Hartwig and Rose, took the title over popular oldies Bill Talbert, 35, and Gar Mulloy, 38.

Australia was favored in the Davis Cup challenge round at Melbourne but nearly threw it away when the team selectors ordered Captain Harry Hopman to nominate Hartwig and Hoad, both right-court players, as his doubles team instead of either of the experienced pairs available: Rosewall-Hoad or Hartwig-Rose. The confused Aussie duo lost to Trabert-Seixas, 6-2, 6-4, 6-4.

Hoad had beaten Seixas, and Trabert had stomped Rosewall the first day. But Australia won from 1-2 down, Hoad beating Trabert, 13-11, 6-3, 2-6, 3-6, 7-5 in the pivotal fourth match—one of the greatest in Davis Cup history. As a crowd of 17,500 huddled under newspapers to protect themselves from rain, Trabert lost his serve at love at 5-6 in the desperate final set, double-faulting to 0-40 and then netting a half volley off a return to his shoetops. Next day Rosewall, recently turned 19, as had Hoad, finished the thriller over Seixas, 6-2, 2-6, 6-3, 6-4. Never before or since had a couple of teenagers been responsible for winning the Cup.

Meanwhile Frank Sedgman, the Davis Cup hero of a year earlier, lost a pro tour to Jack Kramer, 54 matches to 41, but earned $102,000, the highest total to date. The tally was closer than it might have been because Kramer was bothered by an arthritic back and was as interested in promoting as playing. Pancho Gonzalez won the U.S. Pro title over Don Budge, 4-6, 6-4, 7-5, 6-2, at Lakewood Park in Cleveland, the first of a record eight triumphs in nine years for Gonzalez in this shakily maintained event for the handful of outcast pros.

1954

The quotation that hangs above the competitors' entrance to the Centre Court at Wimbledon, and was also adopted for a similar exalted position in the marquee at the Forest Hills stadium, is from the poem "If" by Rudyard Kipling. It says, "If you can meet with triumph and disaster, and treat those two impostors just the same. . . ." The words seldom seemed more appropriate than in 1954, for it was a year of continued triumph and then sudden disaster for Maureen Connolly.

"Little Mo" did not go to Australia to try for another Grand Slam. Experienced Thelma Long, 35, filled the gap, winning her homeland's title a second time, 6-3, 6-4, over Jenny Staley, Lew Hoad's wife-to-be. But Maureen defended her French (6-4, 6-1, over Ginette Bucaille) and Wimbledon titles, and also beat Pat Ward, 6-3, 6-0, to take the Italian that had eluded her in 1953. At Wimbledon she defeated Louise Brough in the final, 6-2, 7-5. Lance Tingay wrote, "The whole event was accounted a trifle dull because of the inevitability of the eventual winner. Miss Connolly, without losing a set, won 73 games and lost but 19."

Little did anyone know that this would be Little Mo's last major title. Between Wimbledon and Forest Hills, she was riding her horse, Colonel Merryboy—a gift from a group of San Diegans after her 1952 Wimbledon triumph—and was struck by a truck. Most people thought she would return in 1955, but in her autobiography Maureen wrote that she knew she was finished: "My right leg was slashed to the bone. All the calf muscles were severed and the fibula broken. Eventually, I got on-court again, but I was aware that I could never play tournament tennis."

Vic Seixas, 31, in his 13th try, won his first U.S. Singles in 1954. (UPI)

It was the shortest of great careers, but few got more done in many more years. During those three-and-a-half years when she was undisputed No. 1, the youngest of five Grand Slammers won nine straight majors, a singular accomplishment: Australian, 1953; French, 1953 and 1954; Wimbledon, 1952, 1953 and 1954; U.S. 1951, 1952 and 1953, on a match record of 50-0. (Her complete record for the majors was 52-2, since she lost in the second round of the U.S. in 1949–50.) Moreover, there were the Italian, 1954; Irish, 1952 and 1953; the U.S. Clay, 1953 and 1954; plus 7-for-7 in Wightman Cup.

Mervyn Rose won his only Australian singles title in 1954, over countryman Rex Hartwig, 6-2, 0-6, 6-4, 6-2. Rugged Tony Trabert—firing like the big guns that adorned the aircraft carrier on which he had served the year before—blasted fellow American Art Larsen in the French final,

6-4, 7-5, 6-1. But the year ultimately belonged to three players who savored sentimental triumphs that came when they were seemingly a shade past their prime: Jaroslav Drobny, Vic Seixas, and Doris Hart.

Drobny, age 34, still had a punishing serve, though not as oppressive as it had been before a shoulder injury. He was seeded only 11th in his 11th appearance at Wimbledon, but upset Lew Hoad in the quarterfinals and beat old rival Budge Patty in the semifinals. In the final Drobny defeated Ken Rosewall, 13-11, 4-6, 6-2, 9-7, in 2 hours, 37 minutes, becoming only the second left-handed champion, following Norman Brookes, 1907. No one could have imagined that Rosewall, in the final for the first of four times at age 19, would never win the singles title he coveted most. The galleries loved Drobny, the expansive Czech refugee in dark prescription glasses. "No better final had been seen since Crawford and Vines 21 years before," judged Lance Tingay. "The warmth of Drobny's reception as champion could not have been greater had he been a genial Englishman. In a sense he was, for he had married an Englishwoman and lived in Sussex."

The U.S. triumphs of Vic Seixas and Doris Hart at Forest Hills were just as popular with the American audience. Seixas, age 31 and competing for the 13th time, finally won in his third appearance in the final. He stopped Rex Hartwig, who had upset defending champion Tony Trabert and Rosewall, 3-6, 6-2, 6-4, 6-4. Hart, runner-up five times in 13 appearances but never champion, at last triumphed, 6-8, 6-1, 8-6, vaulting three match points as Brough netted backhand returns, one at 4-5, two more at 5-6.

Seixas, according to Allison Danzig's report in *The New York Times,* "made the most of his equipment and he never lagged in carrying the attack to his opponent. His speed and quickness, the effectiveness of his service, his strong return of service and his staunch volleying all contributed to the victory. Too, he found a vulnerable point in his opponent's game and exploited it by directing his twist service to Hartwig's backhand."

Hart and Seixas teamed for the mixed doubles title of the U.S. as they had at Wimbledon. Both also won the doubles, Hart with Shirley Fry for the fourth consecutive year and Seixas with Trabert, whom he had also partnered to the French title. Elsewhere, Hartwig and Rose won the Australian and Wimbledon doubles; Connolly and Nell Hopman took the doubles at the French, while at Wimbledon, Brough and Margaret duPont recaptured the title they had won in 1948, 1949 and 1950.

Connolly, in her last Wightman Cup appearance, led the United States to a 6-0 frolic over Great Britain at Wimbledon. The U.S. also recovered the Davis Cup after four straight losses, Captain Bill Talbert's duo upsetting Australia, 3-2, in the challenge round at Sydney. Trabert and Seixas, who earned his spot because of his Forest Hills form, were the conquering heroes. In a flip-flop of 1953 Trabert outgunned Hoad, 6-4, 2-6, 12-10, 6-3, and Seixas, previously Rosewall's pigeon, came through for a 2-0 lead, 8-6, 6-8, 6-4, 6-3. Lew, serving a set point at 10-9 in the second, saw it whisked away by Tony's desperate two-handed reflex volley. They combined to beat Hoad-Rosewall, 6-2, 4-6, 6-2, 10-8, in the decisive doubles. The largest crowds ever to watch tennis at the time, 25,578, jammed White City Stadium each day.

Jack Kramer retired as undefeated pro champion and promoted a round-robin tour involving Pancho Gonzalez, Frank Sedgman, Pancho Segura and Don Budge. Gonzalez won it, narrowly defeating Sedgman, and thus gained a previously unheard-of second life in the head-to-head pro tour. He also won the U.S. Pro title over Sedgman, 6-3, 9-7, 3-6, 6-2, at the Cleveland Arena.

1955

At the midpoint of the postwar decade, 1955, American Tony Trabert established himself as the best player in the world, his Australian rivals snatched back the Davis Cup with a vengeance, and a couple of gallant American women who

Tony Trabert soared in 1955, winning the French, Wimbledon and U.S. (UPI)

had left a considerable legacy—Louise Brough and Doris Hart—took their final bows as soloists in the world tennis arena.

Ken Rosewall beat Lew Hoad, 9-7, 6-4, 6-4, for his second Australian singles title, but Trabert—the All-American boy from Cincinnati with his ginger crewcut, freckles, and uncompromisingly aggressive game—won the French, Wimbledon and U.S. singles.

In the Italian Championships, two of the most unorthodox but combative clay-court specialists of Europe—tall and gangly Fausto Gardini ("The Spider") and tiny, gentle Beppe Merlo ("The Little Bird")—met in an all-native final before a raucous Roman crowd. They had their customary epic battle—"We were always like a dog and a cat," Merlo recalls—with Gardini claiming victory as Merlo collapsed with cramps. To make sure his opponent could not recover and win, Gardini counted off one minute while Merlo writhed in pain, then rolled down the net and raised his arms triumphantly.

There were no such histrionics in Paris, where Trabert bulled his way to the French title over Swede Sven Davidson, 2-6, 6-1, 6-4, 6-2. At Wimbledon, Trabert eliminated defending champion Jaroslav Drobny in the quarters and Budge Patty (conqueror of Hoad) in the semis.

In the final Trabert expected to meet Rosewall, but instead came up against 1953 runner-up Kurt Nielsen, who beat the Australian champ in the semis. "Nielsen clearly remembered his success against the Little Master in 1953, when he hit his approach shots down the middle and came to the net, making it difficult for Rosewall to play his favorite passing shots decisively," wrote Max Robertson. "He pursued the same tactics and with the same result; for the second time he had reached the final unseeded—a record which could stand forever." Trabert denied him a more satisfying immortality, however, 6-3, 7-5, 6-1.

The only real stain on Trabert's record for the year in which he won 18 tournaments came in late August, in the Davis Cup challenge round at Forest Hills. After Rosewall had beaten Vic Seixas, 6-3, 10-8, 4-6, 6-2, Trabert went down, 4-6, 6-3, 6-3, 8-6, to Hoad in the critical second match; Hoad played with immense power and brilliance.

The next afternoon, Hoad and Rex Hartwig—who two years earlier had been thrown together as first-time doubles partners, with disastrous results—blended beautifully to clinch the Cup with a 12-14, 6-4, 6-3, 3-6, 7-5 victory over Seixas and Trabert that had 12,000 spectators howling with delight through five scintillating sets. The Aussies had their cake and put frosting on it too, running up a 5-0 final margin the next day.

Trabert had the last laugh, though, banishing Rosewall in the final of Forest Hills, 9-7, 6-3, 6-3. That set him up as the new amateur champ. Actually, promoter Jack Kramer had signed Hoad and Rosewall as well, to tour with him and Trabert playing a Davis Cup–style format, but the deal fell through. Slazenger, the racket company that Rosewall represented, gave him a bonus, and Jenny Hoad persuaded her husband to make one more grand tour as an amateur. So Trabert's indoctrination into the pros in 1956 wound up taking the more conventional form, a head-to-head tour against the champ, Pancho Gonzalez.

On the women's side, new singles champions were crowned in Australia, where Beryl Penrose defeated Thelma Long, 6-4, 6-3, and in France, where England's Angela Mortimer topped Dorothy Head Knode, 2-6, 7-5, 10-8.

At Wimbledon, 1948, 1949 and 1950 champion Louise Brough, seeded second, defeated demonstrative newcomer Darlene Hard in the semis, reaching the final for the seventh time. Her opponent was ambidextrous, a non-backhanded racket-switcher, Beverly Baker Fleitz, who upset top seed Doris Hart in the semis.

"Louise was always prone to tighten up at important points but had a greater breadth of stroke and experience at her command, which just saw her through a keenly fought struggle," reported Max Robertson. "In the sixth game of the second set, for example, it was only after nine deuces and five advantages to Fleitz that Louise wrong-footed her near exhausted opponent with a backhand slice down the line to lead 4-2. This was the turning point and Louise went on to win her fourth singles, 7-5, 8-6."

That was Brough's last major singles title. Doris Hart, also a majestic champion, won her last one at Forest Hills, site of her narrow and jubilant victory over Brough the year before. This time it was much easier. Doris routed Patricia Ward, the Italian titleholder, 6-4, 6-2. Hart also made her last appearance in the Wightman Cup in 1955 as the U.S. defeated Great Britain, 6-1, at Westchester Country Club in Rye, N.Y. She had been on the U.S. team since 1946, compiling a record of 14-0 in singles and 8-1 in doubles. She became a teaching pro at the end of the year.

As for doubles titles in 1955, Brough and Margaret duPont, who had reigned nine successive years between 1942 and 1950, took the U.S. title from Fry-Hart, 6-3, 1-6, 6-3, starting a new three-year run. Seixas and Trabert won the Aus-

tralian and French titles, but Hoad and Hartwig, presaging their Davis Cup heroics, won Wimbledon. The little-known team of Kosei Kamo and Atsushi Miyagi won the U.S. Doubles, primarily because they were willing to hang around Longwood Cricket Club through Hurricane Diane as most of the favored teams fled Boston. When the waters that turned the grass courts into ponds finally receded, the Japanese pair triumphed over Bill Quillian and Jerry Moss in five. World War II truly was a long time past.

1956

In 1956, the 21-year-old former "Whiz Kids" of Australia, Lew Hoad and Ken Rosewall, had clearly grown up into the best amateur tennis players in the world. They smothered the United States in the Davis Cup challenge round, 5-0, for the second straight year, and played each other in three of the "Big Four" singles finals. Ultimately, on the last day of Forest Hills, it was Rosewall who prevented his three-weeks-younger countryman from pulling off a Grand Slam.

This was the Diamond Jubilee year of the U.S. Championships, and Rosewall captivated a crowd of 12,000 at the Forest Hills stadium with his 4-6, 6-2, 6-3, 6-3 victory in the first all-foreign final since 1933, when Britain's Fred Perry thwarted Australian Jack Crawford's bid for a Grand Slam.

"If there were any doubts about the little Australian measuring up to the caliber of a truly great player they were dispelled by his play in the championship," wrote Allison Danzig in his vivid and authoritative story, "A Grand Slam Trumped," in The New York Times. "His performance in breaking down the powerful attack and then the will to win of the favored Hoad was even more convincing, considering the breezy conditions, than his wizardry in his unforgettable quarterfinal round match against Richard Savitt.

"Against the powerful, rangy Savitt, Rosewall's ground strokes were the chief instruments of victory in a crescendo of lethal driving ex-

Ken Rosewall lost to Lew Hoad in the Wimbledon and Australian finals, but Rosewall repulsed his countryman in 1956 at Forest Hills. (UPI)

changes seldom equaled on the Forest Hills turf. Yesterday's match between possibly the two most accomplished 21-year-old finalists in the tournament's history was a madcap, lightning-fast duel. The shots were taken out of the air with rapidity and radiance despite a strong wind that played tricks with the ball."

So it had been much of the year, the blond-haired, blue-eyed, muscular, and positively engaging Hoad rousing galleries around the world with his remarkable weight of shot and free-wheeling attack; the immaculate, compact, and quicksilver Rosewall challenging him but constantly rebuffed, until now.

Hoad had beaten Rosewall in the finals of the Australian, 6-4, 3-6, 6-4, 7-5, and Wimbledon, 6-2, 4-6, 7-5, 6-4. He had beaten Sven Davidson in

the French final, 6-4, 8-6, 6-3. He had won the Italian and German titles on clay as well. But finally Rosewall got him, and with Hoad changing his mind again about signing a pro contract with Kramer, it was Rosewall who signed on to face Pancho Gonzalez the following year.

Doris Hart, who had climaxed 15 appearances with back-to-back Forest Hills titles in 1954 and 1955, had, like Trabert, turned pro to give lessons at the end of the year. In her absence, her old doubles partner, Shirley Fry, took the Wimbledon and Forest Hills singles titles for the first and only time. At Wimbledon, Shirley beat Englishwoman Angela Buxton, 6-3, 6-1, and at Forest Hills, her final victim was Italian and French champion Althea Gibson of New York's Harlem. Gibson's 6-0, 12-10 victory in Paris over Angela Mortimer was the first major title for a black.

For Shirley Fry, it was a glorious journey's end. Begun as a 14-year-old with a first-round look-in at Forest Hills in 1941, the long trip, the quest, was over at destination championship: Shirley's 6-3, 6-4 victory over Althea Gibson completed the most drawn-out of all treks to a U.S. title. It was her 16th sortie, from youngest entrant ever (a record that stood until Kathleen Horvath, a younger 14 in 1979) to one of the oldest champs. She had beaten Althea at Wimbledon and to win the U.S. Clay, 7-5, 6-1. This time Fry maintained her mastery by attacking the net constantly in the first set, then staying back and thwarting Gibson's attack with deep, accurate ground strokes in the second.

The addition of Buxton, Shirley Bloomer and Mortimer (runner-up to Gibson in the French) made the British Wightman Cup team more competitive than it had been at any time since the war, but the U.S. still prevailed, 5-2, at Wimbledon.

Gibson teamed with Buxton to win the French and Wimbledon doubles titles, but Louise Brough and Margaret duPont continued their unmatched supremacy in the U.S. Doubles, winning their 11th.

Shirley Fry took over at Wimbledon and Forest Hills in 1956. (UPI)

Hoad and Rosewall won the Wimbledon and U.S. doubles titles, and single-handedly achieved the Davis Cup shutout of the United States in the challenge round at Adelaide. Hoad beat Herbie Flam easily, Rosewall kayoed Vic Seixas in four sets, and Hoad and Rosewall thumped Seixas and Texan Sammy Giammalva in a four-set doubles to make sure that the contest was decided before the third day, on a loss of two sets.

Pro promoter Jack Kramer would have liked to sign Hoad, who had won 15 tournaments, but Rosewall was a fine attraction to oppose Pancho Gonzalez in 1957. Kramer had started training to play 1955 amateur king Tony Trabert in 1956, but was persuaded by Gonzalez' wife, Henrietta, to let Pancho face Trabert on the head-to-head tour. Kramer, now badly afflicted with arthritis, was just as happy to do the promotion and let the strong and hungry Gonzalez play.

Gonzalez, very likely the best player in the world even though few realized it, crushed Trabert, 74 matches to 24. Gonzalez also won the U.S. Pro Championship over Pancho Segura at Cleveland, and beat Frank Sedgman, 4-6, 11-9, 11-9, 9-7, in a match remarkably of high quality at Wembley.

"Wembley, a London suburb of fast-fading respectability, is a shrine of English soccer. In those days its indoor arena was also a shrine of pro tennis," wrote Rex Bellamy in *World Tennis* more than two decades later. "That night, public transport ceased long before the match did. Stranded spectators did not much mind. They were unlikely to see such a match again."

1957

The order that had prevailed in international tennis in the early part of the 1950s was changing rapidly by 1957. A year that began with Lew Hoad and Shirley Fry on top of the world ended with Althea Gibson as the dominant woman and surprising Mal Anderson challenging Ashley Cooper for the top spot among the men.

Any designs Hoad may have on the Grand Slam he had come within one match of achieving in 1956 were shattered quickly. The "baby bull" was upset in the semifinals of the Australian singles by a promising young left-hander, Neale Fraser, son of a prominent Labor politician. Cooper—a rather mechanical but solid and determined player who, with Fraser and Anderson, represented the new products off Harry Hopman's Australian Davis Cup assembly line—then won his first major title by beating Fraser in the final, 6-3, 9-11, 6-4, 6-2. Hoad and Fraser took the doubles.

Shortly after the pro tour between Pancho Gonzalez and Ken Rosewall—which Gonzalez would win, 50-26—had begun in Australia at the New Year, Hoad had a friend contact promoter Jack Kramer and tell him that he was again interested in turning pro. Kramer was baffled, since Hoad had recently refused his entreaties. Later Kramer figured that Hoad was starting to encounter the back problems that eventually cut short his career, and decided he'd better get his payday while he still could.

Kramer signed Hoad—sending Ted Schroeder to the bank with him to make sure he cashed a $5,000 advance, which would provide proof of a contract if Hoad changed his mind again—but agreed to keep the pact secret until after Wimbledon.

Sven Davidson, the Swedish Davis Cup stalwart who was runner-up the previous two years, won the French singles over Herbie Flam, the last American man in the Paris final for 19 years, 6-3, 6-4, 6-4. Anderson and Cooper were the doubles titlists.

Hoad, whose season had been erratic, made his last amateur tournament a memorable one. At Wimbledon he lost only one set, to fellow Aussie Merv Rose in the quarters. Then he routed Davidson, the only non-Australian semifinalist, while Cooper won a tougher semifinal in the other half over Fraser. In the final, Hoad was brilliant, humbling Cooper, 6-2, 6-1, 6-2, in a mere 57 minutes. "It was a display of genius and it is to be doubted if such dynamic shotmaking was sustained with such accuracy before. If Cooper felt he had played badly, he had no chance to do anything else," wrote Lance Tingay. "Hoad was superhuman. It never began to be a contested match."

Gardnar Mulloy, age 43, and Budge Patty, 10 years younger, won their only Wimbledon doubles title—an exciting and sentimental occasion—over top-seeded Fraser and Hoad, 8-10, 6-4, 6-4, 6-4.

Hoad joined the pros, Kramer carefully trying to get him ready for a serious run at Gonzalez the following year. "I used him in a couple of round-robins in the States, and then I made myself into a sparring partner and, with Rosewall and [Pancho] Segura, we took off on an around-the-world tour to get Hoad in shape for Gonzalez," Kramer recalled. "If Hoad could beat Gonzalez, that was my chance to get rid of that tiger. Gonzalez knew what I was doing, too, and he was furious. We played a brutal death march, going to Europe, then across Africa, through India and Southeast Asia, all the way to Manila. I

was impressed by how strong Hoad was. He was personally as gentle as a lamb, but on the trip his body could tolerate almost anything."

With Hoad gone, the 20-year-old Cooper was the top seed and heavy favorite to win Forest Hills. But he was upset by Anderson, the first unseeded champion of the U.S.

Anderson, a country boy from a remote Queensland cattle station, had lost to Cooper in five of six previous meetings. But in the month before Forest Hills, the thin, quick, dark-haired lad of 22 had become an entirely different player. Early in the year he had suffered from nervous exhaustion and heat prostration. At Wimbledon he broke a toe. But at Newport, R.I., on the U.S. grass court circuit, he beat U.S. No. 1 Ham Richardson and got a confidence-boosting title under his belt.

At Forest Hills, he clobbered Dick Savitt, who had a cold, 6-4, 6-3, 6-1, then put on a dazzling display of piercing service returns and passing shots to crush Chilean Luis Ayala, 6-1, 6-3, 6-1. In the semifinals, he overcame Sven Davidson—conqueror of Vic Seixas at Wimbledon—from a 1-2 deficit in sets, 5-7, 6-2, 4-6, 6-3, 6-4.

In his 10-8, 7-5, 6-4 triumph over Cooper, Anderson was so good that he inspired rhapsodic prose and superlatives from Allison Danzig in the next day's *New York Times*: "Anderson's performance ranks with the finest displays of offensive tennis of recent years. His speed of stroke and foot, the inevitability of his volley, his hair-trigger reaction and facileness on the half-volley, the rapidity of his service and passing shots and the adroitness of his return of service, compelling Cooper to volley up, all bore the stamp of a master of the racket. It was offensive tennis all the way, sustained without a letup. The margin of safety on most shots was almost nil. The most difficult shots were taken in stride with the acme of timing, going in or swiftly moving to the side."

Less artistically satisfying, but just as dramatic, was Althea Gibson's 6-3, 6-2 victory in the women's final over Louise Brough. In 1950, when Gibson made history as the first black player admitted to the U.S. Championships, she had gained widespread attention by nearly beating Brough, then the Wimbledon champion, in the second round.

At the start of the year, Shirley Fry captured the Australian, the only one of the major singles titles she had not previously won, over Gibson, 6-3, 6-4. They teamed to win the doubles; these were Fry's last big titles before retiring to become a housewife and teaching pro in Connecticut.

Englishwoman Shirley Bloomer, whose victory in the Italian had been overshadowed by the first men's title of the stylish Nicki Pietrangeli, took the French over Dorothy Knode, 6-1, 6-3, and teamed with Darlene Hard for the doubles crown. But thereafter Gibson reigned supreme, clobbering Californian Hard, 6-3, 6-2, in the Wimbledon final, winning two singles and a doubles as the U.S. defeated Great Britain, 6-1, in the Wightman Cup, and then winning Forest Hills. Althea also won the Wimbledon doubles with Hard, but they lost in the U.S. Doubles final to Louise Brough and Margaret duPont, who took their last title—the third straight and 12th in all, a record, completing another record, their 20th major.

Fifteen years earlier, Gibson had been playing paddle tennis on the streets of Harlem. She had as difficult a path to the pinnacle of tennis as anyone ever did. She had to stare down bigotry as well as formidable opponents. Some tournaments had gone out of existence rather than admit her. But finally, at age 30, she was standing on the stadium court at Forest Hills, already the Wimbledon champion, accepting the trophy that symbolized supremacy in American women's tennis from Vice President Richard Nixon. The cup had white gladiolus and red roses in it, and "Big Al" had tears in her eyes.

There was one other important piece of silverware at stake in 1957. With Hoad and Rosewall gone, Australia was vulnerable to a U.S. raiding party invading Melbourne for the Davis

Althea Gibson made it to the top in 1957. (UPI)

Cup challenge round. But Anderson edged big-serving Barry MacKay, 6-3, 7-5, 3-6, 7-9, 6-3; Cooper bumped 34-year-old Vic Seixas in a similarly tortuous match, 3-6, 7-5, 6-1, 1-6, 6-3; and Anderson and Merv Rose—chosen even though Cooper and Fraser had won the U.S. Doubles—combined to demoralize MacKay and Seixas, 6-4, 6-4, 8-6, in the clincher.

The second-largest Davis Cup crowds—22,000 a day at Kooyong—witnessed. There were no flowers in the cup, but for the third straight year Aussies drank libations of victory beer from it.

1958

In 1958, Australians Ashley Cooper, Mal Anderson and Mervyn Rose were the top men in amateur tennis, and American Althea Gibson the

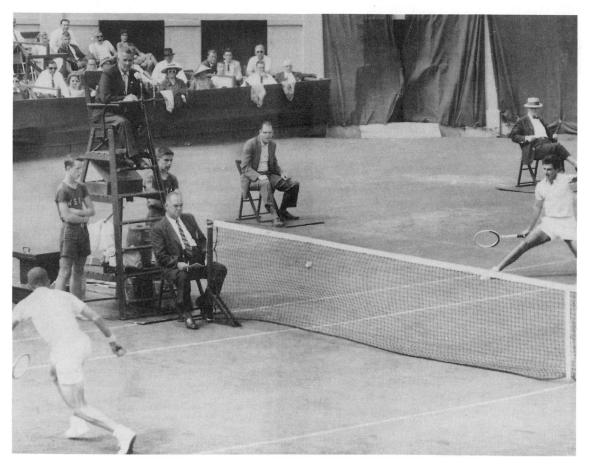

Ashley Cooper, netting the ball against Neale Fraser in the 1958 semifinals at Forest Hills, proceeded to win the championship in his finest year. (New York Herald Tribune)

outstanding woman. By the end of the year, they had all turned professional, underscoring the rapidly growing distance in quality between the small band of pros who wandered around the world playing one- and two-night stands as unsanctioned outcasts and the amateurs who basked in the limelight of the traditional fixtures.

The previous year the issue of "open competition" between amateurs and pros was raised formally within the councils of the USTA for the first time since the 1930s. A special committee report favored open tournaments. This document was promptly tabled since the leadership of the USTA was not nearly as progressive as the com-

mittee, but the ferment that ultimately led to the open game a decade later had started, and not only in America.

With Hoad and Rosewall touring professionally with Jack Kramer's World Tennis, Inc., Cooper took over the top amateur ranking by winning the three legs of the Grand Slam played on grass courts: the Australian, Wimbledon and Forest Hills.

He reversed the result of the 1957 Forest Hills final and took the Australian singles by beating Mal Anderson, 7-5, 6-3, 6-4, and then teamed with Neale Fraser for his only U.S. Doubles title.

At Wimbledon, Anderson injured himself in the quarterfinals, and Cooper very nearly stumbled in the same round, probably coming within one point of defeat against Bobby Wilson, the pudgy but talented Englishman who delighted British galleries with his deft touch. Wilson had a break point for 6-5 in the fifth set, but Cooper rifled a backhand crosscourt winner within an inch of the sideline, and thereafter fortune favored the bold. Cooper dominated Rose after losing the first set, and then beat Fraser—who had won a gallant semifinal over Kurt Nielsen—in the final, 3-6, 6-3, 6-4, 13-11.

Cooper and Fraser were beaten in the doubles final, however, as the title went to an unseeded pair for the second straight year, the strapping Sven Davidson and Ulf Schmidt becoming the first Swedes to have their names inscribed on a Wimbledon championship trophy, 6-4, 6-4, 8-6.

At Forest Hills, Cooper and Anderson advanced to the final for the second consecutive year, but this time Cooper prevailed in the longest final since Gonzalez-Schroeder in 1949, 6-2, 3-6, 4-6, 10-8, 8-6. Gardnar Mulloy, reporting the match for *World Tennis,* wrote that the final set had "all the drama of a First Night," and suggested that Cooper merited an Oscar for his theatrics. The even-tempered Anderson served for the match at 5-4, but lost his serve at love. At 6-6, 30-15, Cooper apparently twisted an ankle, writhed in pain, hobbled to the sideline, and finally went back out to play after several minutes, to tumultuous applause. He "ran like a deer and served as well or better than he had all afternoon," opined Mulloy, a bit skeptical about the "injury." Cooper promptly held serve and then broke Anderson for the match. "Cooper is strong, tenacious, smart, and merciless," wrote Mulloy. "And don't forget his famous one-act play, 'The Dying Swan,' a real tear-jerker which clinched the championship for him."

Ham Richardson and Alex Olmedo foreshadowed a U.S. revival in the Davis Cup by winning the U.S. Doubles at Longwood in their first tournament together, beating Sammy Giammalva and Barry MacKay in the final after bumping Cooper and Fraser in a four-set semi.

Merv Rose, with his tormenting left-handed serve, was the leading Aussie on clay, winning both the Italian and the French, ripping the Chilean Davis Cupper Luis Ayala in the Paris final, 6-3, 6-4, 6-4. The most astounding match of the tournament was Frenchman Robert Haillet's resurrection in the fourth round to beat ex-champ Budge Patty, 5-7, 7-5, 10-8, 4-6, 7-5, after Patty served at 5-0, 40-0 in the fifth, and had a fourth match point at 5-4. Cooper and Fraser won the doubles, as they had in Australia, but were to advance no farther toward a Grand Slam.

Australia was heavily favored to defend the Davis Cup at the end of the year, but the United States had a potent and somewhat controversial weapon—the sleek, bronze-skinned, outgoing Alejandro "Alex" Olmedo, 22, from Arequipa in the snowcapped Peruvian Andes. The nimble 6-foot, 160-pounder was a student at the University of Southern California, and a protégé of Perry Jones, czar of tennis in the Southern Cal section. Jones was also U.S. Davis Cup captain and he lobbied successfully for Olmedo's inclusion, permissible since Peru did not have a Davis Cup team. "The Chief," as he was called because of his regal Incan appearance, had lost a tough five-setter to Fraser at Forest Hills, but in the 3-2 Davis Cup victory Olmedo was magnificent.

In the opening singles, before a capacity crowd of 18,000 at the Milton Courts in Brisbane, Olmedo stunned Anderson, 8-6, 2-6, 9-7, 8-6. Cooper beat MacKay in four sets to make it 1-1, but on the second day Olmedo teamed with Richardson to outlast Fraser and Anderson, 10-12, 3-6, 16-14, 6-3, 7-5—82 games, a Cup record for final-round doubles.

Olmedo, the U.S. Intercollegiate champion, then capped his heroic performance by clinching the Cup with a 6-3, 4-6, 6-4, 8-6 victory over Cooper. Olmedo was rewarded with the No. 2 U.S. ranking behind Richardson.

No. 1 among the women, in the U.S. and the world, was clearly the 5-foot-11, 145-pound Gibson, who used her thunderous serve and overhead, long reach and touch on the volley, and hard, flat, deep ground strokes to defend the Wimbledon and U.S singles titles. At Wimbledon she beat Angela Mortimer—who had won the Australian title over Lorraine Coghlan—in the final, 8-6, 6-2. At Forest Hills, Gibson's final victim was Darlene Hard, 3-6, 6-1, 6-2. Gibson teamed with Maria Bueno—an enchanting Brazilian who, making her first overseas tour at age 18, had won the Italian title—for the Wimbledon doubles title. But they were beaten in the final of the U.S. Doubles by Jeanne Arth and Hard. This was the first of Hard's five successive U.S. women's titles; she won six in all, with four partners.

Gibson lost only four matches during the year, three in the early season (to Beverly Baker Fleitz and Janet Hopps twice), but the one that hurt was to tall Englishwoman Christine Truman in the pivotal match of the Wightman Cup. The British had a fine young team with Truman, Shirley Bloomer (runner-up to Hungarian Suzi Kormoczi in the French Championships), and left-hander Ann Haydon, even though Angela Mortimer didn't play. To the glee of the crowd at Wimbledon's Court 1, the British won the Cup for the first time since 1930, 4-3. Truman's 2-6, 6-3, 6-4 upset of Gibson paved the way, and the left-handed Haydon's scrambling 6-3, 5-7, 6-3 triumph over Mimi Arnold was the clincher.

After Forest Hills, Gibson announced her retirement "to pursue a musical career." She needed a source of income. The next year she accepted an offer to turn pro and play pregame exhibitions at Harlem Globetrotters' basketball games against Karol Fageros, a popular glamour girl noted for her gold lamé panties, but not a player of Gibson's standard. Gibson won the tour with a 114-4 record, and said she made $100,000.

Lew Hoad found pro tennis much more lucrative. Even though he lost his 1958 tour against Gonzalez, 51-36, Hoad made $148,000. Gonzalez, who rallied from a 9-18 deficit after Hoad developed a stiff back in Palm Springs, Cal., made over $100,000.

"That was the last tour to make any real money, though," promoter Kramer later said. It had been a doozy. In Australia at the start of the year, Hoad was awesome, winning eight of 13 matches against a stale and overweight Gonzalez. In San Francisco, on a canvas court indoors, Hoad won, 6-4, 20-18, to inaugurate the U.S. segment of the tour. The next night Gonzalez won in his hometown of Los Angeles, 3-6, 24-22, 6-1. Before a crowd of 15,237 at Madison Square Garden, Gonzalez won the only best-of-five-setter, 7-9, 6-0, 6-4, 6-4.

Then Hoad, strong as an ox and beating Gonzalez in every department—serve, overhead, volley, ground strokes—surged to an 18-9 lead. But the bad back got him, and he was never again the factor he had been. Gonzalez won the tour and beat Hoad in the U.S. Pro Championships at the Arena in Cleveland, 3-6, 4-6, 14-12, 6-1, 6-4. Gonzalez was the best in the world, and the next year—when Cooper, Anderson, and Rose came aboard for a round-robin—he proved it decisively.

1959

The folly of the uneasy arrangement between amateur officials and pro promoter Jack Kramer during the "shamateur" days of the late 1950s and early 1960s was apparent in this passage from a 1958 *Sports Illustrated* story on Kramer by Dick Phelan:

"'I look on the amateurs as my farm system' he [Kramer] says flatly, and this has been true particularly in Australia. There he is denounced as a public enemy because his money tempts the best Australian players to abandon their amateur status and thus their eligibility for Davis Cup play. Then when his troupe arrives in Australia the very public that reviled him flocks to his matches and profits mount. This leads the amateur tennis officials, whose own tournaments

Dick Savitt (left) congratulates Alex Olmedo after the transplanted Peruvian won the U.S. Indoor in 1959. (New York Herald Tribune)

Olmedo, still buoyed by his herculean accomplishment in the Davis Cup challenge round at the end of 1958, stayed and took the 1959 Australian singles title over southpaw Fraser, 6-1, 6-2, 3-6, 6-3. Rod Laver and Bob Mark took the first of their three straight Aussie doubles titles.

Olmedo then returned to the United States and won the U.S. Indoor at New York, 7-9, 6-3, 6-4, 5-7, 12-10, withstanding 28 aces, over Dick Savitt. Olmedo did not play the Italian Championship, where Luis Ayala prevailed over Fraser, or the French, where the great Italian artist Nicola Pietrangeli beat Fraser in the semis and then South African Ian Vermaak in the final, 3-6, 6-3, 6-4, 6-1. Pietrangeli and Italian Davis Cup teammate Orlando Sirola won the doubles over the champions of Italy, Fraser and Roy Emerson.

Olmedo's 1958 Davis Cup triumph for the United States made him a national hero in his native Peru, and he made a triumphant tour there along with teammates Butch Buchholz, Davis Cup captain Perry Jones—and the Cup itself. Olmedo added to his skyrocketing reputation by winning Wimbledon, beating Emerson in the semifinal, and Laver, a left-hander of enormous but as yet unconsolidated talent, in the final, 6-4, 6-3, 6-4. Emerson took the first of his eventual record 16 major men's doubles titles, alongside Fraser.

Wimbledon was the peak of Olmedo's year, however. Fraser beat him in the U.S. final at Forest Hills, 6-3, 5-7, 6-2, 6-4, the Chief's serve lacking its customary zip because of a shoulder strain he had suffered in a mixed doubles match the night before.

Australia regained the Davis Cup at Forest Hills, 3-2, Olmedo never finding the form to which he had risen in the previous December. Fraser beat him again in the opening match, 8-6, 6-8, 6-4, 8-6. Barry MacKay, the hulking "Bear" of Dayton, Ohio, served mightily in beating Laver, 7-5, 6-4, 6-1, but in the doubles Emerson and Fraser outclassed Olmedo and Butch Buchholz, 7-5, 7-5, 6-4. The Aussies had prevailed in

sometimes follow Kramer's and don't draw nearly so well, to lambaste him afresh. But they let him come back. Their share of his gate receipts helps support the Australian amateurs."

After the heady peak of the Pancho Gonzalez–Lew Hoad tour in 1958, the profits of Kramer's World Tennis, Inc., started to dwindle, despite his personal flair for promotion. Anderson and Cooper joined the vanquished Hoad and the victorious Gonzalez in a round-robin tour, but the thrill was gone. They did not draw well, nor did similar tours with other personnel. If they had, it might have hastened the willingness of the amateur officials to consider open tennis. With Cooper, Anderson, and Mervyn Rose gone, Alex Olmedo and Neale Fraser ruled the amateur roost, sharing the world stage with the fiery Latin grace of Maria Bueno.

Barry MacKay makes the return to Rod Laver in the course of winning their Davis Cup match in 1959, but Australia regained the Cup when Neale Fraser vanquished MacKay in the deciding duel. (UPI)

leying beautifully, playing with breathtaking boldness and panache, the lithe Brazilian became the first South American woman to win the Wimbledon singles, beating Darlene Hard in the final, 6-4, 6-3. Hard did team with Jeanne Arth to add the Wimbledon doubles to the U.S. crown they captured the previous year, and won the mixed with Laver.

Bueno then inspired the galleries at Forest Hills as she had at London, beating the tall and sporting Truman in the final, 6-4, 6-1. Hard and Arth repeated as U.S. Doubles champions at Longwood.

The United States regained the Wightman Cup from Great Britain with a 4-3 victory at the Edgeworth Club in Sewickley, Pa. The British won the final two matches, but only after Hard's 6-3, 6-8, 6-4 victory over Angela Mortimer and Beverly Baker Fleitz's 6-4, 6-4 conquest of Truman had given the Americans an unbeatable 4-1 lead.

Gonzalez remained the pro champion. He beat Hoad for the second straight year in the final of U.S. Pro Championships at Cleveland, 6-4, 6-2, 6-4, after romping in the round-robin tour against Hoad, Cooper, and Anderson.

1960

Once again, the start of a new decade was the dawn of a new era in tennis. As 1950 had been, so 1960 was an eventful year.

It began with an Australian Championships that heralded a man and woman who would be king and queen of tennis. Rod Laver skirted a match point at 4-5 in the fourth to beat fellow Aussie left-hander Neale Fraser in an epic final, 5-7, 3-6, 6-3, 8-6, 8-6, to take the first of his eventual 11 Big Four singles titles. Margaret Smith, who would later become Mrs. Barry Court, beat her countrywoman Jan Lehane, 7-5, 6-2, for the first of seven consecutive Australian titles and 24 major singles titles in all—both records. It was a teen-age final that Smith, 17, and Lehane, 18, would repeat in 1961, unique to

the U.S. Doubles by the breadth of their fingernails, 3-6, 6-3, 5-7, 6-4, 7-5, but this time the nails became claws.

Olmedo raised his game to beat Laver, 9-7, 4-6, 10-8, 12-10, to tie the series at 2-all, but Fraser clinched by beating MacKay in a match that was played over two days. They split sets before darkness forced a postponement, but after a long rain delay, Fraser, returning splendidly, won the last two sets easily for a soggy 8-6, 3-6, 6-2, 6-4 victory.

On the women's side, Mary Carter Reitano won the Australian singles, 6-2, 6-3, over South African Renée Schuurman, who teamed with her countrywoman Sandra Reynolds for the doubles crown. Englishwoman Christine Truman, 18, won both the Italian and French titles, dethroning clay-court specialist Suzi Kormoczi in the Paris final, 6-4, 7-5, to become the youngest champ until Steffi Graf, 17, in 1987. Reynolds and Schuurman won the doubles.

Thereafter the season belonged to the incomparably balletic and flamboyant Bueno. Volthe majors until Arantxa Sanchez Vicario, 17, beat Steffi Graf, 19, to win the 1989 French.

It would have been much more of a landmark year but for five votes at the annual general meeting of the ITF. By that slim margin, a proposal calling for sanction of between 8 and 13 "open" tournaments in which pros and amateurs would compete together failed to muster the two-thirds majority needed for passage. The proposal had the backing of the U.S., British, French and Australian associations, and the proponents of the "open" movement were bitterly disappointed when it failed.

Another proposal put forth by the French Federation calling for creation of a category of "registered" players who could capitalize on their skill by bargaining with tournaments for appearance fees higher than the expenses allowed amateurs, was tabled. The USTA had voted to oppose this resolution on the basis that "registered player" was just another name for a pro.

Maria Bueno did not reach the semifinals of the Australian singles, but she teamed with Christine Truman to win the doubles over Margaret Smith and Lorraine Coghlan Robinson, 6-2, 5-7, 6-2. That was the first leg of a doubles Grand Slam by Bueno. She went on to win the French, Wimbledon and U.S. titles with American Darlene Hard, losing only one more set along the way—to Karen Hantze and Janet Hopps in the semifinals at Wimbledon.

Hard won her first major singles title at Paris, struggling through three three-set matches in the early rounds and then whipping Bueno in the semis and the quick little Mexican Yola Ramirez in the final, 6-3, 6-4. Hard also won her first U.S. Singles at Forest Hills, beating Bueno, 6-4, 10-12, 6-4, after the final was postponed nearly a week by Hurricane Donna.

At Wimbledon, where American women had been so dominant for more than a decade after the war, not one of the 10 Americans who entered reached the semifinals. This had not happened since 1925. Hard, the best U.S. hope, lost in the quarterfinals to South African Sandra Reynolds, who reached the final but lost to Bueno, 8-6, 6-0. A year earlier, journalist Lance Tingay had pointed out that the difference between being very good or very bad was, for Bueno, a thin line based on her timing. "Mundane shots did not exist for her." he observed. "It was either caviar or starvation." For the second year in a row it was mostly caviar, and a feast for the spectators. Her Wimbledon performance was good enough to earn Bueno the No.1 world ranking by a shade over Hard.

Britain won the Wightman Cup for the second time in three years, snatching a 4-3 victory at Wimbledon by winning the final two matches. Hard had given the U.S. a 3-2 lead with a 5-7, 6-2, 6-1 triumph over Ann Haydon, but Angela Mortimer beat Janet Hopps, 6-8, 6-4, 6-1, and Christine Truman paired with Shirley Bloomer Brasher to beat Hopps and Dorothy Head Knode, 6-4, 9-7.

Nicki Pietrangeli defended his French singles title over Luis Ayala, runner-up for the second time in three years, 3-6, 6-3, 6-4, 4-6, 6-3. Ayala was also second best in Rome, where Barry MacKay served and volleyed on the slow clay, winning the final by a most peculiar score: 7-5, 7-5, 0-6, 0-6, 6-1. MacKay had won the U.S. Indoor on wood in February, 6-2, 2-6, 10-12, 6-1, 6-4, over Dick Savitt, so within four months he took titles on just about the fastest and slowest court surfaces in the world. Roy Emerson and Neale Fraser combined for the French doubles title, the first of six straight for Emerson, with five partners.

Fraser took over as the No.1 man in the amateur ranks by winning Wimbledon and the U.S. Championship.

As with the women, no American man got to the semis at Wimbledon. MacKay was beaten in the quarterfinals by Pietrangeli, and Butch Buchholz, 19, led Fraser by 6-4, 3-6, 6-4, 15-15, in the same round and had five match points in the fourth set before being seized with cramps that

Darlene Hard and Neale Fraser made off with the silverware at the 1960 U.S. Championships. (USTA)

left him unable to continue. Fraser, 26 and playing for the seventh time, was a sporting and popular champion. His left-handed serve had a wicked kick, and he was a daring and resourceful volleyer. He beat Laver, five years his junior, in the final, 6-4, 3-6, 9-7, 7-5.

A small measure of U.S. pride was saved when the unseeded team of Dennis Ralston, 17, and agile 21-year-old Mexican Rafael Osuna won the men's doubles, the second-youngest team to win Wimbledon. They beat Britons Humphrey Truman and Gerald Oakley in the first round, 6-3, 6-4, 9-11, 5-7, 16-14, and second-seeded Laver and Bob Mark, the Australian champions, 4-6, 10-8, 15-13, 4-6, 11-9, in the semifinal. After that pulsating contest, the final was comparatively easy: 7-5, 6-3, 10-8 over Welshman Mike Davies and Englishman Bobby Wilson.

Laver foreshadowed greatness to come by ripping up the U.S. Eastern grass court circuit, winning consecutive titles at Merion, Southampton, Orange and Newport. Laver and Mark got revenge on Ralston and Osuna in the semis of the U.S. Doubles at Longwood, but lost the final to Fraser and Emerson.

At Forest Hills, Laver got to the U.S. final by beating Buchholz, who had three match points before again suffering a debilitating attack of cramps and losing, 4-6, 5-7, 6-4, 6-2, 7-5. Fraser beat the precocious Ralston and then, after sitting around through a week of hurricane rain and wind, slogged to the title over Laver, 6-4, 6-4, 10-8.

For the first time since 1936, the United States failed to reach the challenge round of the Davis Cup, falling to Italy, 3-2 in the inter-zone semifinals at Perth, Australia, in December.

Buchholz beat the lanky Orlando Sirola in the opening match, and MacKay gave the U.S. a 2-0 lead in an all-time classic, saving eight match points in beating Pietrangeli, 8-6, 3-6, 8-10, 8-6, 13-11. But Sirola and Pietrangeli beat Buchholz and Chuck McKinley in a long four-set doubles, Pietrangeli beat Buchholz, 6-1, 6-2, 6-8, 3-6, 6-4, to even the series, and then Sirola—definite underdog on grass instead of his preferred clay—served and played like a dream to upset MacKay, 9-7, 6-3, 8-6.

Italy's first appearance in the challenge round a couple of weeks later was less auspicious, a 4-1 Aussie victory that was over in three matches as Fraser and Laver swept opening day in Sydney: Neale beat Sirola, 4-6, 6-3, 6-3, 6-3, and Rod went through Pietrangeli, 8-6, 6-4, 6-3. Fraser and Emerson mopped up the two Italians, 10-8, 5-7, 6-2, 6-4.

This time the Aussies suffered no defections to the pro tour immediately after the Davis Cup, but the Americans did. MacKay and Buchholz, undoubtedly thinking that open tennis was near and wanting a piece of Jack Kramer's checkbook before it arrived, signed to make a tour in 1961 with Lew Hoad, Frank Sedgman, Tony Trabert,

Ashley Cooper, Alex Olmedo and the Spaniard Andres Gimeno.

Meanwhile the 1960 tour won by Pancho Gonzalez over Olmedo, Pancho Segura and Ken Rosewall was not a financial success. Olmedo, the Wimbledon champ a year before, beat Trabert in the U.S. Pro final, 7-5, 6-4, at Cleveland.

1961

In 1961, the amateur tennis establishment was stunned and smarting from a wholesale raid on its ranks by pro promoter Jack Kramer, who in 1960 signed to contracts several middling players: Spaniard Andres Gimeno, Welshman Mike Davies, Frenchman Robert Haillet and Dane Kurt Nielsen, as well as young Americans Butch Buchholz and Barry MacKay. Kramer tried without success to lure into his fold Australian Neale Fraser, the Wimbledon and Forest Hills champion; Italian Nicki Pietrangeli, champion of France; and Chilean Luis Ayala, runner-up in the 1960 Italian and French Championships.

When a proposal for introducing "open tournaments" was unexpectedly stymied by just five votes at the 1960 ITF annual meeting, there was relatively little official grieving among the member national associations and their officials. However, Kramer's response of taking out his wallet and waving it in front of practically every player of moderate reputation—which the amateur powers-that-be thought both irresponsible and reprehensible—started alarm bells sounding. Suddenly the national associations saw their tournaments, and hence their revenues, in grave danger. Kramer became Public Enemy No. 1.

But if his motive was to force the ITF into open competition by his mass signings, as most suspected, he failed. Amateur officials did not like being bullied. A new "open tournament" proposal was rejected at the 1961 ITF annual meeting at Stockholm. Delegates approved a resolution agreeing "to the principle of an experiment of a limited number of open tournaments," but referred the matter to a committee for another year

of study to see how the experiment might be conducted. A U.S.-sponsored "home rule" resolution, which would have permitted national associations to stage open tournaments at their own discretion, was defeated. The ITF was able to stand up to Kramer because he had been able to sign only two of the previous year's top handful of players: No. 3, MacKay, and No. 5, Buchholz. The amateurs still had Fraser, Rod Laver, Pietrangeli, Roy Emerson and Ayala. But the battle lines had been drawn. Instead of the uneasy coexistence of the past, the amateur associations and Kramer were now at war.

Emerson—a magnificently fit and affable fellow with slick black hair that shone like patent leather and a smile that sparkled with gold fillings—served and volleyed relentlessly to defeat his fellow Queenslander Laver in the Australian final, 1-6, 6-3, 7-5, 6-4. This was the first of six Australian titles in seven years for "Emmo," the first of a men's record 12 major singles titles in all. Laver and Bob Mark annexed the doubles crown for the third straight year. On the women's side, "Mighty Margaret" Smith beat Jan Lehane again in the singles final, 6-1, 6-4, and teamed with Mary Carter Reitano for the first of Smith's eight Australian doubles titles.

In Paris, the two greatest European virtuosi of the '60s met in the final. English writer Rex Bellamy was there:

"Nicola Pietrangeli, the favorite to win for the third consecutive year, was beaten by the young Manuel 'Manolo' Santana, the first Spaniard to win a major title. The match lasted five sets. Santana and Pietrangeli were like artists at work in a studio exposed to a vast public in the heat of the afternoon. Each in turn played his finest tennis. The flame of Pietrangeli's inspiration eventually died, his brushstrokes overlaid by Santana's flickering finesse. But long before that, these two Latins had established a close rapport with a Latin crowd enjoying a rare blend of sport and aesthetics. At the end there was a tumult of noise. Santana, his nerves strung up to the breaking point, dropped his racket and cried. And

Pietrangeli, disappointed yet instantly responsive to the Spaniard's feelings, went around the net, took Santana in his arms, and patted him on the back like a father comforting a child."

The score was 4-6, 6-1, 3-6, 6-0, 6-2, but bald numbers could hardly convey the emotion of this long afternoon, especially for the toothy Santana, who got to the final by upsetting cannonball-serving Englishman Mike Sangster, Emerson and Laver (runner-up to Pietrangeli in Rome).

A vivid contrast in style to the gliding and caressing strokes of the singles finalists was provided by Laver and Emerson, who bore in on the net for murderous volleys in winning the doubles. Ann Haydon showed the legs, heart, and brain of a clay-court stalwart in beating agile volleyer Yola Ramirez, 6-2, 6-1, for the women's title. South Africans Renée Schuurman and Sandra Reynolds won the doubles.

Maria Bueno, who had beaten Australian Lesley Turner in the Italian final, lost to Suzi Kormoczi in the quarterfinals at Paris and then was bedridden with hepatitis. Lacking funds to pay for hospital care, she was confined to a tiny hotel chamber for a month, with the rest of the floor quarantined, until she was able to go home to Brazil.

Bueno was thus unable to defend her Wimbledon title. Darlene Hard, her doubles partner and the U.S. champ, also withdrew and stayed in Paris to care for her friend. Karen Hantze was the only American to reach the women's quarterfinals; Schuurman, who had beaten Haydon, did her in. This was the 75th-anniversary Wimbledon, and through the wreckage came seventh- and sixth-seeded Angela Mortimer and Christine Truman, opponents in the first all-British women's final since 1914.

The crowd adored Truman, 20, a tall and smiling lass with a big forehand and attacking game who epitomized all the best British sporting traits, and they moaned when she fell awkwardly on a rain-slicked court in the third set of the final.

Unseeded teenagers in 1961, Karen Hantze and Billie Jean Moffitt won the women's doubles at Wimbledon. (UPI)

That tumble cost her the momentum she had built up against the more defensive Mortimer, 29, who, on her 11th try, didn't hesitate to lob and drop-shot in a 4-6, 6-4, 7-5 victory.

Hantze, age 18, and bouncing, bubbly Billie Jean Moffitt, 17, won the doubles unseeded, the youngest pair ever to seize a Wimbledon crown. Eighteen years later, Billie Jean Moffitt King's 10th doubles title would give her the all-time record for career Wimbledon titles in all events: 20.

Laver, the red-haired Queenslander called "Rocket," won the men's title for the first time, over American Chuck McKinley, 6-3, 6-1, 6-4. This was the start of an unprecedented reign: Laver would win 31 singles matches without a defeat at Wimbledon in five appearances to the fourth round in 1970, winning four singles titles plus a BBC-sponsored pro tournament in 1967. Fraser, who had lost his title in the round of 16 to Englishman Bobby Wilson, captured the doubles with Emerson, but then returned home to Australia to tend an ailing knee.

Great Britain had both Wimbledon singles finalists and the French champion on its team, but was startlingly ambushed in the Wightman Cup by a "mod squad" of eager American juniors. Hantze beat Haydon and Truman, Moffitt beat Haydon, and 18-year-old St. Louis lefty Justina Bricka shocked Mortimer, the first British Wimbledon champ since 1937. Hantze-Moffitt clobbered Truman–Deidre Catt, and the U.S. won the final doubles when Mortimer defaulted with foot cramps. Truman's singles win over Moffitt was the only one the shell-shocked English could salvage in the 6-1 massacre at Chicago's Saddle and Cycle Club.

Texan Bernard "Tut" Bartzen won his fourth U.S. Clay Court singles since 1954, beating Donald Dell, 6-1, 2-6, 6-2, 6-0, who earlier in the year had gone with doubles partner Mike Franks on a State Department tour of South Africa, the Middle East and the Soviet Union, the first Americans to play in Russia since the 1917 Revolution.

McKinley and Dennis Ralston won the rain-delayed U.S. Doubles over Mexicans Rafe Osuna and Antonio Palafox. Hard teamed with Turner for her fourth successive women's doubles title, and was supposed to play with Ralston against Margaret Smith and Bob Mark in the mixed final, at Longwood. But rain postponed the match until Forest Hills, and Ralston, unfairly treated by the USTA, was unable to play because he was suspended for his behavior earlier, in a Davis Cup match against Mexico.

At Forest Hills, Whitney Reed—a spacy, unorthodox player who never trained, partied all night, but had such a wonderful touch that he earned the No. 1 U.S. ranking—upset McKinley in the third round. He fell to Osuna, and Dell to Laver, leaving no Americans in the men's semis. Emerson just got by the catlike and clever Osuna, 6-3, 6-2, 3-6, 5-7, 9-7, in a rousing semifinal. Emerson grabbed the first two sets in just 35 minutes, but Osuna kept scrambling for every ball, even making shots from flat on his back. He saved two match points in the fourth set and leveled after trailing 0-3 in the fifth. Finally three fine passing shots brought Emerson to match point again at 8-7, and this time he wouldn't let it get away. Then the speedy and powerful Emerson overwhelmed Laver in the final, 7-5, 6-3, 6-2, to lay claim to the No. 1 ranking among the amateurs.

Darlene Hard, the only American in the women's quarterfinals, battled past Ramirez, 6-3, 6-1; Smith, 6-4, 3-6, 6-3; and Haydon in the final, 6-3, 6-4, for her second straight U.S. title.

With MacKay and Buchholz professionals, U.S. Davis Cup Captain David Freed named a 14-man squad that accented youth. The U.S. beat British West Indies, Ecuador, Mexico (losing Ralston via suspension) and India, but again lost to Italy in the inter-zone semifinals, 4-1. Jon Douglas astonishingly upset Fausto Gardini on the clay at Rome's Il Foro Italico, 4-6, 3-6, 7-5, 10-8, 6-0, from 2-5 in the third, but Pietrangeli beat Whitney Reed—who trained for the occasion, and later said that spoiled his game—2-6, 6-8, 6-4, 6-4, 6-4. Orlando Sirola and Pietrangeli beat Reed and Dell in the doubles, and Pietrangeli spanked Douglas in straight sets to clinch. Gardini came from behind to beat Reed, 3-6, 7-5, 3-6, 8-6, 6-4, as a raucous Italian crowd exulted in his adding to the margin of victory.

Gardini refused to go to Australia for the challenge round unless he was assured of a singles berth. However, he wasn't, and Pietrangeli and Sirola never got a set on the grass at Melbourne until Emerson and Laver in singles and Emerson and Fraser in doubles had closed out the Aussie defense of the Cup. The final score was 5-0.

Kramer's expanded traveling circus—Pancho Gonzalez, Lew Hoad, Frank Sedgman, Tony Trabert, Ashley Cooper, Alex Olmedo, Gimeno, MacKay and Buchholz as principals, plus the others—did not make enough to cover his vastly increased overhead. Gonzalez beat Sedgman, 6-3, 7-5, in Cleveland for his record eighth and last U.S. Pro title, but the pros were in trouble, and Kramer's grandstanding of the previous autumn had not helped the cause of open competition.

1962

The Australian grip—both hands firmly around the throat of players of any other nationality—was in vogue in 1962, the season of Rod Laver's first Grand Slam and Margaret Smith's first near-Slam.

Laver duplicated Don Budge's supreme feat of 1938, sweeping the singles titles of Australia, France, Great Britain (Wimbledon) and U.S. He also won the Italian and German titles, not to mention the less prestigious Norwegian, Irish and Swiss, and led Australia to a 5-0 blitz of upstart Mexico in the Davis Cup challenge round. In all, Laver won 19 of 34 tournaments and 134 of 149 matches during his long and incomparably successful year.

Smith was staggered in the first round of Wimbledon by the pudgy chatterbox who would grow up to be her arch-rival—Billie Jean Moffitt—but otherwise won just about everything in sight. Smith's only other loss was to another young American, Carole Caldwell, but "Mighty Maggie" won 13 of 15 tournaments, including the Australian, French and U.S., and 67 of 69 matches.

Laver, the "Rockhampton Rocket" from that Queensland town, started his Slam at White City Stadium in Sydney, beating Roy Emerson, 8-6, 0-6, 6-4, 6-4. Emerson and Neale Fraser took the doubles.

Laver lived precariously in Paris, the only leg of the Slam on slow clay. He saved a match point in beating countryman Marty Mulligan in the quarterfinals, 6-4, 3-6, 2-6, 10-8, 6-2. He also went five sets with Fraser in the semis, 3-6, 6-3, 6-2, 3-6, 7-5, and with Emerson again in the final, 3-6, 2-6, 6-3, 9-7, 6-2. Emerson and Fraser racked up another doubles title.

At Wimbledon, Laver lost only one set to Manolo Santana in a 14-16, 9-7, 6-2, 6-2 victory. There were no Americans in the quarterfinals for the first time since 1922, and hardly room for anyone but Australians: six of them. There were only Aussies in the semis: Laver, Mulligan (advanced over Emerson, who had an injured toe),

Rod Laver: Grand Slam in 1962. (UPI)

Neale Fraser and his brother John Fraser, a physician by profession, who got an uncommonly lucky draw. Laver beat Neale Fraser, 10-8, 6-1, 7-5, and trampled Mulligan in the final, 6-2, 6-2, 6-1. With Emerson sidelined, Aussies Bob Hewitt and Fred Stolle won the doubles.

At Forest Hills, Laver lost only one set again en route to the U.S. final—to gangly American Frank Froehling in a 6-3, 13-11, 4-6, 6-3 quarterfinal victory. The athletic Emerson was back, but Laver repelled him as he had in Sydney, Rome and Paris. Laver hit four fearsome backhand returns to break serve in the first game and dominated the first two sets with his varied backhand, either bashed or chipped, a topspin forehand, and ruthless serving and net play. Emerson, always barreling forward and battling, aroused a crowd of 9,000 by winning the third set, but Laver closed out the match and the Slam, 6-2, 6-4, 5-7, 6-4, and was greeted by Budge in the marquee.

Astonishingly, there were again no Aussies in the U.S. Doubles final at Longwood, where the "Mexican Thumping Beans," collegians Rafe Osuna and Tony Palafox, out-hustled temperamental Americans Chuck McKinley and Dennis Ralston, reversing the previous year's final result, 6-4, 10-12, 1-6, 9-7, 6-3.

Osuna and Palafox had scored a victory of much greater import over Ralston-McKinley earlier in the year, in the pivotal match of Mexico's 3-2 upset of the U.S. in the Davis Cup. Palafox beat Jon Douglas in the rarefied atmosphere of Mexico City after McKinley had disposed of Osuna in three straight sets in the opener. The doubles point provided the impetus, and then Osuna was carried off on the shoulders of his jubilant countrymen when he outnerved Douglas, 9-7, 6-3, 6-8, 3-6, 6-1, for the clinching 3-1 point. This was the first time Mexico had won the American Zone, and Osuna and Palafox lugged their adoring nation past Yugoslavia, Sweden and India to the challenge round. But Laver and Neale Fraser in singles and Laver-Emerson in doubles had too much serve-and-volley power on the slick grass at Brisbane, winning 5-0.

Margaret Smith drubbed Jan Lehane, 6-0, 6-2, in the final of the Australian, but had a much closer final in Paris against another countrywoman, Lesley Turner. Smith had shown she could play on clay too, however—she had won the Italian title as a tune-up—and she prevailed, 6-3, 3-6, 7-5, rescuing a match point at 3-5 in the third. By that time Smith, just shy of 20, must have been entertaining thoughts of duplicating the Grand Slam accomplished by only one woman previously, Maureen Connolly in 1953. But 18-year-old Billie Jean Moffitt, who had a premonition weeks earlier that she would draw Smith in her opening match at Wimbledon, rudely wrecked the dream, 1-6, 6-3, 7-5. It was the first time that the No. 1 female seed had failed to survive one round (Steffi Graf would lose to Lori McNeil in 1994), and established "Little Miss Moffitt" as a force to be reckoned with on the Centre Court that already was her favorite stage.

It was eighth-seeded Karen Hantze Susman, with whom Moffitt repeated as doubles champion, who took the singles at age 19. An outstanding volleyer, Susman captured the title with a 6-4, 6-4 victory over unseeded Vera Sukova of Czechoslovakia, who had scored successive upsets over the defending champ sixth-seeded Angela Mortimer, second-seeded Darlene Hard and third-seeded Maria Bueno.

Smith was back in form at Forest Hills. With her enormous reach, athleticism, weight of shot and solid arsenal from the backcourt and net alike, she beat Hard in a nerve-wracking match, 9-7, 6-4 to become the first Australian woman to win the U.S. singles. She saved a set point in the 10th game of the first, and benefitted from 16 double faults by Hard, who was perplexed by numerous close line calls and burst into prolonged tears in the sixth game of the second set.

Hard beat Christine Truman, 6-2, 6-2, and Ann Haydon, 6-3, 6-8, 6-4, as the United States edged Britain, 4-3 in the Wightman Cup at Wimbledon. Captain Margaret Osborne duPont, age 44, teamed up with Margaret Varner to show that she could still win at doubles.

While the interest generated by Laver and Smith signaled a banner year for amateur tennis, the pros were struggling. Pancho Gonzalez had retired for the time being, leaving Butch Buchholz to win the U.S. Pro title over Pancho Segura, 6-4, 6-3, 6-4, in Cleveland.

Jack Kramer had also given up the ghost as promoter. "We had all the best players, but the public didn't want to see them," he recalled. " . . . There was no acceptance for our players. The conservative and powerful amateur officials were secure. Among other things, they had succeeded in making me the issue. If you were for pro tennis, you were in favor of handing over all of tennis to Jack Kramer. That was the argument."

That is vastly oversimplified, of course. Kramer in many ways had only himself to blame for antagonism. But name-calling aside, the pro game was in sorry shape.

Ken Rosewall was the top dog, but he had little flair for promotion, and the top amateurs no longer were tempted to turn pro and face an uncertain, anonymous future. Under-the-table payments afforded a comfortable if not lavish lifestyle for the top "amateurs." For the second time in the postwar era, there was no pro tour in the United States. Rosewall and Lew Hoad were contemplating retirement. Their only chance at reviving interest, they thought, was to induce Laver to join them, and they pooled resources and personally guaranteed him $125,000 to come aboard for 1963.

1963

With Rod Laver out of the amateur ranks, another Australian—the peerlessly fit and universally popular Roy Emerson of rural Blackbutt, Queensland—set his sights on the Grand Slam that Laver had achieved in 1962. Emerson won the first two legs, but was thwarted at Wimbledon as Australian supremacy waned. By the end of the year Latin America had scored a unique "double" at Forest Hills, and the United States had both recovered the Davis Cup and captured the inaugural Federation Cup, the women's equivalent.

Politically, it was not a progressive year. With Jack Kramer retired from promoting, amateur officials worldwide felt they had won a battle against some dark specter, and the movement for open competition lagged. In the United States, which had supported the principles of "self-determination" and experimentation with open tournaments, the Old Guard reasserted itself, repudiating USTA president Ed Turville, a supporter of open tennis. The USTA instructed its delegates to the ITF to oppose "opens" and "home rule."

Emerson, 26, romped to the Australian title over countryman Ken Fletcher, 6-3, 6-3, 6-1, while Bob Hewitt and Fred Stolle took the doubles. Margaret Smith ritually slaughtered two-fisted back-hander Jan Lehane, 6-2, 6-2, for the fourth straight year in the women's final and teamed with Fletcher to beat Lesley Turner and

Chuck McKinley returned the U.S. to Wimbledon supremacy in 1963 after a long drought. (UPI)

Stolle in the first leg of a mixed doubles Grand Slam. They took the French, Wimbledon and U.S. titles as well.

Emerson won the French over the first native to reach the men's final since 1964: the suave and sporting Pierre Darmon, who in the 1970s would return to Roland Garros as tournament director and preside over the greatest period of prosperity in the tournament's history. The score was 3-6, 6-1, 6-4, 6-4, and Emerson then teamed up with Spaniard Manolo Santana for the doubles title.

Smith's designs on a singles Slam were upset by the steadiness of Vera Sukova, the unseeded Wimbledon finalist of 1962, who was more at home on Parisian clay. The title did remain in Australian hands, however, Lesley Turner beating Ann Haydon Jones, 2-6, 6-3, 7-5. Jones teamed with Renée Schuurman for the doubles trophy.

Wimbledon, which had seen five all-Australian men's singles finals in seven years, got its first American male champion (discounting the Peruvian Alex Olmedo in 1959) since Tony Trabert in 1955: 22-year-old Chuck McKinley, a Missourian attending Trinity University in San Antonio, Tex. He was the first since Trabert to win the title without losing a set, but it was a peculiar year. No seeded players wound up playing each other in the men's singles.

Emerson, the favorite, ran into Germany's Wilhelm Bungert on a hot day and was beaten in the quarters, 8-6, 3-6, 6-3, 4-6, 6-3. McKinley, a small but athletic man who charged the net like a toy top gone wild, was too sure in his volleying for Bungert in the semis and Fred Stolle in the final, 9-7, 6-1, 6-4. This was the first of three straight years as runner-up for the tall, angular Stolle, who never did win the singles. Mexican Davis Cuppers Rafe Osuna and Antonio Palafox won the doubles.

Margaret Smith, who had already won four Australian, two Italian, one French and one U.S. title, became the first Australian woman to win the Wimbledon singles. In the final, she avenged her early defeat by Billie Jean Moffitt the year before, 6-3, 6-4. The title was not decided until the start of the third week because of rain, and thus Miss Smith did not get to dance the traditional champions' first foxtrot with McKinley at the Wimbledon Ball. He was perhaps relieved, since he was four inches shorter than Smith; instead, he guided his wife around the hardwood floor.

The Federation Cup was inaugurated to celebrate the 50th anniversary of the ITF. The U.S. blanked the Netherlands, Italy, and Great Britain, then upset Australia, 2-1, in the women's international team competition, which drew 16 nations. It was set up to be more compact than the Davis Cup—played in best-of-three (two singles, one doubles) series instead of best-of-five, with all participating countries together at one site for one week. Smith blitzed U.S. No. 1 Darlene Hard, 6-3, 6-0, in the opening match, but then Moffitt upended Turner, 5-7, 6-0, 6-3, and teamed with

Hard to take the excruciating doubles from Smith and Turner, 3-6, 13-11, 6-3, indoors because of inclement weather at London's Queen's Club.

The U.S. also beat Britain, 6-1, in the Wightman Cup at the Cleveland Skating Club. Ann Jones beat Hard in the opening match, 6-1, 0-6, 8-6, but Moffitt beat Christine Truman, 6-4, 19-17 (the second set a female record) to turn things around for teammates Hard, Nancy Richey and Donna Floyd Fales. Richey won the first of her six consecutive U.S. Clay Court titles, 6-1, 6-1, over Vicky Palmer.

For the first time, the U.S. did not have a woman in the semifinals at Forest Hills. Hard, a finalist the last three years and champion twice, was beaten by Jones in the quarters. Even more curious, Australia was shut out of the men's quarterfinals after having had both finalists in six of the previous seven years.

This was a south-of-the-border year, Mexican Rafe Osuna taking the men's singles, and Brazilian Maria Bueno recapturing the women's title she had won in 1959 with a breathtaking display of shotmaking.

Osuna, a gallery favorite because of his quickness of hand, foot, and smile, ousted Wimbledon champ McKinley in the semis and unseeded Floridian Frank Froehling III in the final, 7-5, 6-4, 6-2. Froehling had served devastatingly to upset top seed Emerson, but Osuna cleverly neutralized his power with wonderfully conceived and executed tactics, especially lobbed service returns from 10 to 12 feet behind the baseline. Occasionally Osuna would stand in and take Froehling's serve on the rise, chipping the backhand, but more often he lobbed returns to disrupt Froehling's serve-volley rhythm and break down his suspect overhead. In fact, Osuna climbed the wall of the stadium to retrieve smashes and float back perfect lobs, frustrating Froehling with his nimble speed around the court, touch and tactical variations.

Bueno was also brilliant, especially in the second set of her 7-5, 6-4 victory over Smith.

"With the score 1-4 and 0-30 against her, Miss Bueno set the gallery wild with the dazzling strokes that stemmed from her racket," wrote Allison Danzig in the next morning's *New York Times*. "Her service was never so strong. Her volleys and overhead smashes were the last word, and she hit blazing winners from the backhand and threw up lobs in an overwhelming assault."

At Longwood, Hard was not able to snag a sixth straight women's doubles title; she and Bueno fell in the final to Smith and Robyn Ebbern. McKinley and Dennis Ralston met Osuna and Palafox for the third straight year in the men's final, saving two match points in recapturing the title, 9-7, 4-6, 5-7, 6-3, 11-9, before a record crowd of 7,000.

That was immediately after they combined to beat Osuna and Palafox, 4-1, in a Davis Cup match at Los Angeles. Captained by Bob Kelleher and coached by Pancho Gonzalez, the Americans also conquered Iran, Venezuela, Britain and India to return to the challenge round for the first time in three years.

It had been a long campaign, taxing competitively and medically. Ralston nearly lost an eye in England, McKinley had dysentery in India, Froehling needed his abscessed backside lanced, and McKinley had back spasms. But the squad persevered and took the Cup back from Australia, which had held it in a Melbourne bank vault 11 of the last 13 years.

Ralston squandered three match points on serve, but pulled himself together to win the jittery opener over Cup rookie, 19-year-old John Newcombe, 6-4, 6-1, 3-6, 4-6, 7-5. The Americans had a 2-1 lead after a 6-3, 3-6, 11-9, 11-9 defeat of Emerson and Neale Fraser, 30, and bowing out. Emerson, who won both his singles, flattened Ralston to tie it again, and with a sellout Adelaide crowd of 7,500 roaring behind him, power-serving Newcombe built a 4-2, 30-0 third-set lead. But the iron-willed teddy bear McKinley—"this is where I want to be, everything riding on one match"—retaliated with backhand

passers and quickness to heist the Cup, 10-12, 6-2, 9-7, 6-2.

In the pro ranks, Laver was beaten regularly by both Ken Rosewall and Lew Hoad, who had staked him to a $125,000 bankroll to try to keep the fading pro game alive. They succeeded, but barely. Rosewall was supreme, beating Laver in the final of the U.S. Pro Championships at Forest Hills, 6-4, 6-2, 6-2, but the tournament went bust, and at presentation time Rosewall got only a handshake from Laver.

1964

As if any additional evidence were necessary to prove the depth of tennis talent in Australia, the Davis Cup went back Down Under for the 11th time in 14 years even though three members of the Aussies squad fled to other countries because of an altercation with the autocratic Lawn Tennis Association of Australia.

Roy Emerson, Fred Stolle, Marty Mulligan, Bob Hewitt and Ken Fletcher were all suspended by the LTAA for the grievous offense of leaving for the overseas tournament circuit earlier than permitted. Emerson and Stolle were reinstated after reaching the Wimbledon final—Emerson beat Stolle in the singles finals of the Australian, Wimbledon and U.S. Championships in 1964 but had his notions of a Slam punctured by Nicki Pietrangeli at the French semis. "Emmo" and Fred were the core of the raiding party that took the Cup back from the U.S. in Cleveland, the first time a challenge round in the U.S. was played out of the East and off grass. The battleground was clay.

The other three continued to have problems. Mulligan moved to Italy, where he married, became a successful businessman, and played in Davis Cup competition in 1968, nicknamed "Martino Mulligano." (He had been on the Australian squad but never played, so was eligible to play for Italy when he became a citizen.) Hewitt married a Johannesburg model and became a mainstay of the South African Davis Cup team, continuing to develop into one of the world's best doubles players. Fletcher took up residence in Hong Kong. It is a measure of the strength of Aussie captain Harry Hopman's production line that Australia won the Cup four years in a row, never missing this trio of talented players.

The affable Emerson—strong enough to quaff beer and sing choruses of "Waltzing Matilda" into the wee hours of the morning, then get up early to train and play magnificently athletic tennis—ruled the amateur world in 1964. He won 55 straight singles matches in one stretch, finishing the year with 17 tournament championships and a 109-6 record, including two singles victories in the Davis Cup challenge round.

Emmo thumped Stolle in the Australian final, 6-3, 6-4, 6-2; at Wimbledon, 6-4, 12-10, 4-6, 6-3; and at Forest Hills, 6-4, 6-1, 6-4. He also took the French doubles, practically an annual acquisition, with Fletcher. Hewitt and Stolle took the Australian and Wimbledon doubles, while Chuck McKinley and Dennis Ralston captured the U.S. title at Longwood for the third time in four years, the first three-timers since Bill Talbert and Gardnar Mulloy (1942, 1945, 1946 and 1948).

A preview of America's Davis Cup fate was offered in the most dramatic match of the U.S. Championships, a quarterfinal in which Ralston fought back from two sets down against Stolle, saved a match point at 3-5 in the fifth, and hauled himself back to 7-7 before the gripping encounter was halted by darkness. Ralston had two break points at 15-40 as Stolle served the first game of the resumption the next morning, but the lean Aussie with the pained gait and delightful wit held and broke Ralston in the next game for the match.

It was the 25-year-old Stolle's 7-5, 6-3, 3-6, 9-11, 6-4, triumph over Ralston on a clay court at newly built and jam-packed (7,000 a day, at top dollar) Harold T. Clark Stadium in Cleveland that broke America's back in the challenge round. As only nine months before, the Americans had a 2-1 lead on Chuck and Denny's squeaky win over

Roy Emerson led the Aussie raiding party in 1964. (UPI)

Roy and Fred, 6-4, 4-6, 4-6, 6-3, 6-4. On a gray day, after a long rain delay, they played a majestic match for a national television audience. Ralston saved one match point, serving at 4-5 in the fifth, but Stolle blasted a forehand crosscourt passing shot by him on the next. Emerson wrapped up a 3-2 Australian victory the next afternoon, running like a greyhound and whacking piercing ground strokes and volleys to sear McKinley, 3-6, 6-2, 6-4, 6-4, sending the Davis Cup back to Melbourne.

The French, Italian and German titles, the three biggest on continental clay, all went to Europeans. Manolo Santana beat Pietrangeli, 6-3, 6-1, 4-6, 7-5, in a rematch of their more memorable meeting in the Parisian final three years earlier; Jan-Erik Lundquist of Sweden won in Rome, and Wilhelm Bungert took his national title in Hamburg.

Among the worldly women of tennis, Margaret Smith had an awesome record, losing only two matches during the year, but those were at Wimbledon and Forest Hills. Maria Bueno won those titles, and thus took back the No.1 world ranking that illness and Smith had stripped from her.

Smith beat her countrywoman Lesley Turner 6-3, 6-2, in the Australian singles, and Bueno, 5-7, 6-1, 6-2, at Paris. Bueno beat Smith only once in three meetings, but it was the most important: the final at Wimbledon, 6-4, 7-9, 6-3. This was a match of almost unbearable tension, a patchwork of glorious shots and awful ones, and Bueno ultimately controlled her nerves better. Smith seemed more serene beforehand, but her anxiety showed in her usually oppressive serve. She was a little tentative, and double-faulted badly on several key points. "I guess I beat myself. I felt pressure all the way," she said afterward. "It was like beating my head against a wall."

Karen Hantze Susman, the 1962 Wimbledon champion who was back for a fling after temporary retirement for childbirth, troubled Smith in the first round at Wimbledon and beat her in the fourth round at Forest Hills, 4-6, 6-4, 6-4. That paved the way for Bueno, who raced through the championship without losing a set. In the final she met surprising ninth-seeded Carole Caldwell Graebner, who had resolutely upset Susman and Nancy Richey despite suffering from painful second-degree sunburns of the arms, face and hands. In the final, it was not the sun's rays but Bueno who blistered her, 6-1, 6-0, in just 25 minutes.

Bueno thus usurped Smith's throne as the No. 1 player, even though her record of 82-10 and seven titles was not quite as formidable as Smith's 67-2 and 13 championships. Smith had a 39-match winning streak at one point in the season.

Lesley Turner blended with Judy Tegart to win the Australian doubles and with Smith to win at Paris and Wimbledon, but, once more with Smith, was denied a Grand Slam in the final of the U.S. by Susman and Billie Jean Moffitt, 3-6, 6-2, 6-4.

With Darlene Hard, the U.S. No.1 of the past four years, retired to a teaching pro career, the U.S. relinquished the Federation Cup to Australia, 2-1, in the final of a 24-nation assemblage in Philadelphia. Smith beat Moffitt, 6-2, 6-3, and Turner did in No. 1 American Nancy Richey, 7-5, 6-1.

Richey and Moffitt won both their singles, over Deidre Catt and Ann Haydon Jones, and Carole Graebner added a victory over Elizabeth Starkie as the U.S. swept the singles and the Wightman Cup at Wimbledon, 5-2.

Most of the men pros were scattered around the globe, playing the odd exhibition here and there, badly disorganized. Ken Rosewall, the pro king, was observed playing Pancho Segura in a shopping-center parking lot exhibition in Los Angeles.

One who thought this was wrong was Ed Hickey of the New England Merchants National Bank in Boston, who convinced his boss to put up $10,000 in sponsorship money to revive the U.S. Pro Championships. John Bottomley, president of Longwood Cricket Club, threw his support to the project. Jack Kramer was enlisted to contact the far-flung gypsies and put together a short summer tournament circuit with $80,000 in prize money. A dozen pros were assembled and Rod Laver won the climactic event at Longwood over Pancho Gonzalez, 4-6, 6-3, 7-5, 6-4, in a rainstorm that turned the grass into a quagmire.

It was a humble renaissance with a $2,200 first prize, but the 37-year-old U.S. Pro, the longest-running pro tourney, somehow stayed in business and was to become a fixture at Longwood, as was Laver. He won there four more times. It wasn't strawberries-and-cream *à la* Wimbledon, but the pros were on the rocky road to a comeback.

1965

The gloom of a drizzly, gray September afternoon in Forest Hills was pierced by Spanish singing and dancing, and the unmistakable click of castanets filled the old concrete stadium of the West Side Tennis Club. There were loud choruses of *"Olé!"* and *"Bravo, Manolo!"* The discreet charm of the bourgeoisie that so long characterized tennis audiences gave way to unabashed Latin celebration as Manolo Santana beat South African Cliff Drysdale in four absorbing sets, 6-

2, 7-9, 7-5, 6-1, to become the first Spaniard to win the U.S. singles title.

The balletic and crowd-pleasing Santana, age 28, provided other occasions for rejoicing in 1965, but few places came alive as Forest Hills did when a troupe of entertainers from the Spanish Pavilion at the nearby World's Fair arrived to urge him on with an up-tempo Latin beat. Santana was arguably the No. 1 amateur in the world, winning 10 of 16 tournaments, compiling a 71-7 record, and a 25-match winning streak, longest of the season. He did not enter Wimbledon, devoting his summer instead to Davis Cup preparation and duty on clay. Such diligence paid off. Santana (singles wins over Frank Froehling and Denny Ralston) & Co. lit up the Barcelona sky by bumping off the U.S., 4-1, and were on their way to the Challenge Round. An unknown to the Americans, awkward-looking Juan Gisbert stayed steady from 1-4 in the second set to paralyze Ralston, 3-6, 8-6, 6-1, 6-3, at the outset. A momentous resurgence in the doubles by Santana and Lis Arilla over Ralston and Clark Graebner settled the outcome, 4-6, 3-6, 6-3, 6-4, 11-9, even though Ralston came within two points, serving for it at 9-8, deuce. That set off a bullring-style fiesta, pillows flying from the overjoyed crowd of 5,000, littering the court where the two Spaniards were carried round and round triumphantly by strong-shouldered aficionados.

Not that Spanish music replaced "Waltzing Matilda" as the anthem of the world tennis empire. Australia won the Cup again, for the 14th time since 1950, as Roy Emerson and Fred Stolle gunned down Santana & Co., 4-1, at Sydney. Australians also captured the Federation Cup and all the other Grand Slam singles titles, men's and women's. Most of the finals were all-Aussie affairs.

Emerson outslugged Stolle, who seemed capable of beating anybody else, from two sets down in the Australian final, 7-9, 2-6, 6-4, 7-5, 6-1. John Newcombe and Tony Roche, the latest in a long line of great Aussie pairs, took their first of a record 12 major doubles titles.

The Spanish reign: Manolo Santana defeats South Africa's Cliff Drysdale for the 1965 U.S. Singles crown. (UPI)

Roche, a ruggedly muscular left-hander with an unerring backhand volley, spoiled Emerson's latest vision of a Grand Slam in the French semifinals. With his chief nemesis out of the way, Stolle prevailed in Paris over Roche, 3-6, 6-0, 6-2, 6-3—winning his first major title after being runner-up in one Australian, two Wimbledons, and one U.S. Emerson and Stolle took the doubles, Emerson's sixth in a row in Paris with five partners.

Emerson powered his way through the Wimbledon draw again, a *tour de force* justifying his top seeding, and made Stolle the bridesmaid for the third consecutive year. This time it was easier than in 1964, 6-2, 6-4, 6-4. Newcombe and Roche won the first of their five Wimbledon doubles titles together.

At Forest Hills, where there had been all Aussie finals seven of the last nine years, none of the men from Down Under made the semis, however. Charlie Pasarell ambushed Stolle in the second round, and Arthur Ashe, who was to gain the No. 2 U.S. ranking behind Dennis Ralston, delivered big serves and fatal backhands in enough glorious clusters to topple Emerson.

Santana, shrewdly changing speeds and spins as he danced around the turf, erased Ashe in a four-set semifinal. Drysdale, who had beaten Ralston in a five-set quarterfinal, got by Mexican Rafe Osuna in the other half. Santana vs. Drysdale was thoughtful tennis, much of it from the backcourt, between two intelligent and stylish men. Two-fisted backhands would become common after Chris Evert arrived six years later, but Drysdale's was the first to be seen in a U.S. final. Rain interrupted the match and made the footing slick, but it couldn't dampen Santana's flashy shotmaking or the castanets.

Emerson and Stolle were unbeaten in doubles on the U.S. circuit, winning six tournaments and 31 matches, a run climaxed by a 6-4, 10-12, 7-5, 6-4 triumph over Pasarell and Frank Froehling in the U.S. final at Longwood.

Emerson won seven of 22 tournaments in singles for an 85-16 record. He was 0-2 against Santana, demolished on clay in the Swedish Championship final and edged, 2-6, 6-3, 6-3, 15-13, on grass at Sydney in the Davis Cup final. But it was decided by then. A lifelong dream to play for his country in his hometown was fulfilled by Stolle as leadoff man. Recovering his composure after falling way behind, Fred snapped Santana's 19-match Cup streak, 10-12, 3-6, 6-1, 6-4, 7-5, closing a tense struggle with his 19th ace to reward a cheering throng of 10,000 at White City. Emerson took care of Gisbert quickly for his 13th Cup singles win without defeat, and the rookies, Newcombe and Roche, put it away, 6-3, 4-6, 7-5, 6-2, over Arilla-Santana. Though meaningless to the result, Santana did hand Emerson his lone Cup defeat on the third day, 2-6, 6-3, 6-4, 15-13.

Australia beat the United States, 2-1, in the final of the Federation Cup at Kooyong in Melbourne. Lesley Turner beat Carole Graebner, 6-3, 2-6, 6-3, and Margaret Smith stopped Billie Jean Moffitt, 6-4, 8-6.

Smith, 23, won three of the major singles titles in one season for the second time in her still ascendant career. She beat Maria Bueno, who retired with an injury while trailing 2-5 in the final set in the Australian final; Bueno again at Wimbledon, 6-4, 7-5; and Moffitt at Forest Hills, 8-6, 7-5. The only match that prevented a Grand Slam was the final of the French, which she lost to Turner, 6-3, 6-4.

After that, Smith didn't lose another all year, piling up 58 consecutive victories for a season record of 103-7, including 18 titles in 25 tournaments.

Bueno, 25, won the Italian Championship and two other of the 11 tournaments she entered, finishing 40-8 in a year in which she was hampered by a knee injury that required surgery. She played Forest Hills against the advice of her doctor, losing to Moffitt in the semis.

Moffitt led Smith by 5-3 in both sets of the Forest Hills final, and had two set points in the second. Even though she lost, Moffitt later said this was a turning-point match in her career, adding a great deal to her self-awareness. She knew that the forehand she had gone to Australia to rebuild from scratch the previous year was coming around, complementing her exquisite backhand and volleying, and that she had the ability to rival Smith for No. 1. Billie Jean married Larry King shortly after Forest Hills, and she knew she was coming of age as a player.

She was co-ranked No. 1 in the U.S. with Nancy Richey, an unprecedented decision by the USTA ranking committee. Moffitt had shone on the grass court circuit, which Richey avoided after winning the U.S. Indoor and Clay Court. Both were 1-1 in singles in the 5-2 U.S. victory over Britain in the Wightman Cup.

Maria Bueno (left) and Billie Jean Moffitt won the Wimbledon doubles in 1965, marking the fourth time that the Brazilian beauty had been a winner in this event. (UPI)

Richey and Carole Graebner (whose husband, Clark, ranked No. 13 among the U.S. men and would return to the Top Ten the next year) earned the top U.S. ranking in doubles after winning at Longwood. They beat defending champs Moffitt and Karen Susman in the final, 6-4, 6-4.

Turner teamed with Judy Tegart to win the Australian doubles and with Smith to take the French. Moffitt captured her third title at Wimbledon with her second partner, Maria Bueno. Smith and Ken Fletcher won the French, Wimbledon and U.S. mixed doubles. They might well have repeated their 1963 Grand Slam, but the mixed final of the Australian was abandoned because of bad weather.

The itinerant pros of tennis were still trying to organize. Mike Davies, Butch Buchholz and Barry MacKay were among the driving forces behind the International Professional Tennis Players' Association (IPTPA) formed in 1965 to try to give some structure to the amorphous, struggling pro game. The U.S. Pro Championships returned to Longwood, Ken Rosewall regaining the title he had won in 1963—and getting paid, albeit modestly ($3,000) this time—by beating Rod Laver, 6-4, 6-3, 6-3.

Patrician scoring reformer Jimmy Van Alen of Newport, R.I., whose "Van Alen Streamlined Scoring System" (VASSS) became the basis for "sudden death" tie-breakers in 1970, hosted a pro tournament at famed Newport Casino, where the U.S. Championships had been played from their inauguration in 1881 until 1914. Van Alen put up $10,000 in prize money, on the condition that the pros use his radical VASSS round-robin, medal-play format, in which every point counted and each was worth $5. The players were happy to play any way as long as they were paid, though Pancho Segura spoke for most of his colleagues when he disparaged the Van Alen system, saying "It seems half-VASSS to me."

1966

If variety is indeed the spice of life, 1966 was a flavorful year for international tennis. There were no one-man or one-woman gangs, as the game's major titles got spread around. For the first time since 1948, no player, man or woman, captured more than one of the four major singles crowns.

Fred Stolle, thought to be past his prime at age 27, didn't win a single tournament until August, then came on like the old Australian Mafia. He won the German Championship on clay and took the U.S. title at Forest Hills unseeded. There he routed nemesis Roy Emerson in the semifinals, 6-4, 6-1, 6-1, with an astounding display of power and control, and withstood 21 aces served by the similarly unseeded John Newcombe to win the final, 4-6, 12-10, 6-3, 6-4. Thereafter Stolle won tournaments in California on concrete and

Australia on grass, and beat both Ramanathan Krishnan and Jaidip Mukerjea as Australia pummeled India, 4-1, in the Davis Cup challenge round. (The lone Aussie loss, delaying champagne celebrations in Melbourne until the third day, was the doubles upset of Newcombe and Tony Roche, 4-6, 7-5, 6-4, 6-4 by Mukerjea and Krishnan. The latter's son, Ramesh Krishnan, would follow in the old man's sneaker steps to a Cup final 20 years later in Sweden, a father-son feat that is theirs alone.) That was the climax of Stolle's amateur career as he turned pro at the end of the year.

Stolle's Davis Cup accomplice, Emerson, started the year by grabbing his national championship for the fourth consecutive time, a 6-4, 6-8, 6-2, 6-3 extinguishing of Arthur Ashe, who had burned up the Aussie circuit, winning four of seven tournaments. Emmo went right back on court, accompanied by Stolle, to complete the doubles final over Newcombe and Roche, an 87-game, three-match point-saving victory, 7-9, 3-6, 8-6, 14-12, 12-10, that had stopped for darkness at 7-7 in the fourth the previous evening. That meant Emerson played 128 games within 4 hours. He and Fred went on to post the year's best doubles record, adding the Italian, South African and U.S. Championships.

Emerson was perhaps never in better condition or form than at the start of Wimbledon, where he was keen to become the first man to win three successive singles titles since Fred Perry in 1934, 1935 and 1936. He looked as if he would until fate and his own eagerness intervened during his quarterfinal against fellow Aussie Owen Davidson. Richard Evans described what happened in *World Tennis:*

"The first set took Emerson precisely 14 minutes to win 6-1. His first service was going in, his volleys were crisp and accurate, his groundstrokes laden with power and spin. There was no danger in sight unless it lay in the greasy, rain-slicked turf and of this, surely, Emerson was aware. So it surprised many people when he raced for a Davidson drop-volley in the third

Australia's Fred Stolle, unseeded, defeated countryman Roy Emerson in the semis and John Newcombe in the final to win at Forest Hills in 1966. (UPI)

game of the second set. And it horrified us all when he skidded headlong into the umpire's chair and brought the BBC microphone crashing down on top of him. He was up in a moment, flexing his left shoulder and telling Davidson that he thought he had heard something snap. In fact he had torn the shoulder ligaments—an injury that, in a fatal second, had shattered a dream, ruined weeks of arduous preparation and deprived Wimbledon of its champion."

Manolo Santana, the clay-court artist who had proved himself a man for all surfaces by winning Forest Hills on grass the previous year, inherited the throne that Emerson abdicated, and he was a popular champion. Grinning and playing extraordinary shots when behind, he beat Ken Fletcher and then Davidson, both in deuced fifth sets, to get to the final. There he eliminated Dennis Ralston, who had more firepower but less control, 6-4, 11-9, 6-4.

But Santana had his own problems with injuries during the season—a bad shoulder that plagued him as Spain, the 1965 runner-up, went out to Brazil in the Davis Cup elimination rounds, and a bad ankle that reduced his Forest Hills' defense to a limp.

It was not Santana but Australian lefty Tony Roche who was the 1966 man of the year on clay. He won the Italian and French singles, beating Hungarian roadrunner Istvan Gulyas in the Paris final, 6-1, 6-4, 7-5. Thereafter ankle problems sapped his effectiveness as well.

So who was the world's No. 1 amateur? Take your pick. Stolle won four of 19 tournaments, 70 of 85 matches; Emerson won eight of 16 tournaments, including the rising South African Championships, and 67 of 78 singles; Santana was 52-16, winning only two of 17 tournaments, but one of those was the biggest: Wimbledon; Roche played the most ambitious schedule, winning 10 of 29 tournaments and 106 of 125 matches.

Ralston, generally considered No. 5 in the world, was top-ranked in the U.S. for the third year in a row, the first man so honored since Don Budge in 1936, 1937 and 1938, but frustrated by his failure to win a major singles title. He turned pro with Stolle at the end of the year, leaving Ashe—a lieutenant in the U.S. Army—as heir apparent.

Ralston did have one particularly satisfying doubles triumph, teaming with Clark Graebner to become the first American champions of France since 1955. Their final-round victims, little known until later, were the hulking Romanian Ion Tiriac and his wet-behind-the-ears but gifted protégé, Ilie Nastase. Ralston and Graebner were runners-up for the U.S. title at Longwood to Emerson-Stolle, 6-4, 6-4, 6-4. Newcombe, separated from regular partner Roche, won the Wimbledon doubles anyway, with Ken Fletcher.

It was a dark year for the U.S. in the Davis Cup as captain George MacCall's team was bush-whacked, 3-2, by unheralded Brazil at Porto Alegre. Cliff Richey was upset in singles by both Edison Mandarino and Tom Koch, and Mandarino took Ralston in the fifth match, 4-6, 6-4, 4-6, 6-4, 6-1.

The world's most successful player was the No. 1 woman, Billie Jean King, who won her first Wimbledon singles title at age 23 and spearheaded successful team efforts in the Federation and Wightman Cups. A virus infection diminished her effectiveness later, but Billie Jean won 10 of 16 tournaments and compiled a 57-8 record, the female best.

Nancy Richey, co-ranked No. 1 with Billie Jean in 1965, slipped to No. 2 despite reaching the finals of the Australian, French and U.S. singles, and winning six of 14 tournaments, with a 55-9 record. She also won her fourth straight U.S. Clay Court title, beating lefty Stephanie DeFina, 6-2, 6-2, while her brother, Cliff, 19, topped Frank Froehling, 13-11, 6-1, 6-3, to complete a singular family double. Nancy won three of the major doubles titles: the Australian with Carole Graebner, and Wimbledon and the U.S. with Maria Bueno.

Margaret Smith won her seventh consecutive Australian singles title, by default over Richey (injured knee in the semis), and her third consecutive French doubles (with Judy Tegart), but was increasingly burdened by the pressure and loneliness of big-time tennis competition. Shortly after being beaten by King, 6-3, 6-3, in the semifinals of Wimbledon, she announced her retirement at age 24 to open a clothing boutique in Perth—the first of several short-lived retirements, as it turned out.

Ann Haydon Jones won her second French singles over Richey, 6-3, 6-1, the American having been spent in a semifinal victory over Smith.

King, seeded fourth, was magnificently aggressive at Wimbledon. Grass staining her knees on the low volleys, she played better than anyone else, as her husband of less than a year sat nervously in the competitors' guest stand. Having dispatched one old rival, top-seeded Smith, 6-3, 6-3, in the semis, she did in another, second-seeded Bueno, in the final, 6-3, 3-6, 6-1, then tossed her racket high in the air and squealed with glee.

King, Julie Heldman and Carole Graebner carried the U.S. to a 3-0 victory over surprise finalist West Germany in the Federation Cup on clay at Turin, Italy. King, Richey, Mary Ann Eisel and Jane Albert were the Americans who played in a 4-3 Wightman Cup victory over Great Britain at Wimbledon. Richey and Eisel contributed the decisive point in doubles, over Elizabeth Starkie and Rita Bentley, 6-1, 6-2.

Maria Bueno captured her fourth U.S. title—the last of her seven major singles crowns—by beating Richey, 6-3, 6-1, with an all-court display of grace and shotmaking magic that completely thwarted Richey's backcourt game. They had teamed for the U.S. doubles title at Longwood, 6-3, 6-4, over the new but potent partnership of King and Rosemary Casals, but in the singles final Bueno treated Richey more like a stranger, winning in just 50 minutes. The best match of the tournament had been Bueno's 6-2, 10-12, 6-3 victory over the diminutive, 17-year-old Casals, a feast of dazzling footwork and shotmaking that captivated a crowd of 14,000.

Also noteworthy in 1966 were the longest matches on record in top-level competition: Roger Taylor of Britain defeated Wieslaw Gasiorek of Poland, 27-29, 31-29, 6-4, on a slick wood surface in a King's Cup match that stretched until the early hours of a bitterly cold Warsaw morning; and American Kathy Blake outlasted Elena Subirats of Mexico, 12-10, 6-8, 14-12 on grass at the Piping Rock Country Club.

The pros had decided to cast their fate to small tournament-format events rather than head-to-head tours, as in the past, but the going was still rough. The U.S. Pro at Longwood remained an encouraging beacon, lighting the future, and Rod Laver signaled his takeover from Ken Rosewall as the pro king, beating "Muscles," 6-4, 4-6, 6-2, 8-10, 6-3. He had also beaten Rosewall, 6-2,

6-2, 6-3, for his third straight World Pro title at Wembley, a crown that Ken wore in 1957 and 1960 through 1963. But Rosewall was Laver's master for a fourth year in a row at the French Pro, 6-3, 6-2, 14-12, his seventh straight triumph (a record eight altogether) in Paris.

1967

By sweeping the singles titles at Wimbledon and Forest Hills, Australian John Newcombe and Californian Billie Jean Moffitt King reigned as the king and queen of amateur tennis in 1967, the last year of the amateur era. By the end of the year two professional troupes—World Championship Tennis (WCT) and the National Tennis League (NTL)—had been formed, Newcombe and a half dozen other leading amateur men had turned pro. With the blessing of the All England Club and its forceful chairman, Herman David, pros appeared in late summer on Centre Court for an eight-man tourney sponsored and televised by the BBC. The brilliant final, Rod Laver over Ken Rosewall, 6-2, 6-2, 12-10, dwarfing the Newcombe-Bungert Wimbledon final the month before, was but another factor in whetting the public's appetite for "open" tennis, and taking the game to the brink of rebellion destined to change forever the old order in tennis.

The call to revolution was sounded in December by the Lawn Tennis Association of Britain, spurred by David, who had denounced shamateurism as "a living lie" and urged open competition for some time. When the ITF again voted against opens once more at its midyear annual meeting, David declared, "It seems that we have come to the end of the road constitutionally." He vowed that Wimbledon would continue to be the world's premier tournament, with a field commensurate with that reputation, even if it had to "go it alone" as a pioneer of open competition. Backing him, the LTA took an unconstitutional, revolutionary step by voting overwhelmingly at its December meeting to make British tournaments open in 1968.

The ITF threatened to expel the British from the international organization, but its hand had been forced. A number of compromises later, open tennis became a reality in 1968, though in a much more limited and qualified way than the British had envisioned.

Early in the year, such upheaval did not seem to be in prospect. The USTA hired Robert Malaga, a successful promoter of Wightman Cup and Davis Cup matches in his hometown of Cleveland, as its first full-time executive secretary and signed a product-endorsement agreement with Licensing Corporation of America.

The competitive year began the same way the previous four had, with Roy Emerson winning his native Australian singles title. Arthur Ashe was his victim in the final for the second straight year, this time in straight sets: 6-4, 6-1, 6-4. The triumph was Emerson's sixth in seven years, but he was unable to defend his doubles crown. Newcombe and Tony Roche, who would go on to win the French and U.S. doubles as well, beat Owen Davidson and Bill Bowrey in a rousing final, 3-6, 6-3, 7-5, 6-8, 8-6.

Nancy Richey, runner-up as Margaret Smith won her seventh consecutive singles title the year before, took advantage of Margaret's temporary retirement to capture the women's title with a 6-1, 6-4 triumph over Lesley Turner. Turner and Judy Tegart captured the doubles.

Turner upended Maria Bueno, 6-3, 6-3, in the Italian final and won the first set of the French final before losing it to Francoise Durr, whose 4-6, 6-3, 6-4 victory was the first by a native woman at Paris since Simone Mathieu in 1939. Durr teamed with Australian Gail Sherriff for the first of five consecutive doubles titles: two with Ann Jones, and two more with Gail, who had become a French citizen as Mme. Jean Baptiste Chanfreau. (Gail would win again in 1976 as Mme. Lovera, with Uruguayan Fiorella Bonicelli.)

Emerson, fit as ever, powered his way to the French men's singles title, dethroning fellow

Billie Jean King and John Newcombe display their trophies in 1967 after winning the U.S. Singles. (UPI)

Aussie Roche in the final, 6-1, 6-4, 2-6, 6-2. Roche had earlier lost his Italian title to Marty "Martino Mulligano" Mulligan.

Having cleared the troublesome hurdle of Parisian clay, Emerson set his sights again on the elusive Grand Slam, but his vision was shattered in the fourth round at Wimbledon by tall Yugoslav Nikki Pilic. Emerson was the favorite after the startling first-round ambush of Manolo Santana by American Charlie Pasarell in the curtain-raiser on Centre Court, the only time a defending male champion and top seed was ever beaten in the first round at Wimbledon.

That was the prelude to an upset-filled fortnight. By the quarterfinals, there were no seeded players left in the top half of the draw. The only meeting of seeds came in the quarterfinals, third Newcombe overpowering sixth Ken Fletcher. Pilic and rugged Yorkshireman Roger Taylor, both left-handers, were unseeded semifinalists, as was Germany's Wilhelm Bungert.

Bungert erased Taylor, but was spent by the final and offered only token, halfhearted resistance as Newcombe claimed the title, 6-3, 6-1, 6-

1, equaling the most lopsided postwar men's finals (Lew Hoad over Ashley Cooper in 1957 and Rod Laver over Mulligan in 1962).

In doubles, Newcombe and Roche—reunited and favored to regain the title—fell in the quarters to Englishmen Graham Stilwell and Peter Curtis. The title went to the newly minted South African Davis Cup team of Bob Hewitt (who, as an Australian, had won twice with Fred Stolle) and Frew McMillan. They drubbed Emerson and Fletcher, winner the previous year with Newcombe, 6-2, 6-3, 6-4.

Cumulative attendance for the last amateur Wimbledon exceeded 300,000 for the first time, as 301,896 spectators went through the turnstiles.

Newcombe took the No. 1 world ranking at age 23 by winning eight of 24 tournaments and 83 of 99 matches. A sciatic nerve condition nearly cost him the U.S. Doubles championship, which was decided for the 46th and last time at Longwood Cricket Club, but he and Roche pulled through over Bowrey and Davidson, 6-8, 9-7, 6-3, 6-3. His lower back was still worrying "Newk" going into the U.S. singles, but he experienced no ill effects in plowing to victory at Forest Hills with the loss of but four sets.

It was Emerson who was plagued first by back problems, then by torn thigh muscles suffered in his quarterfinal loss to Clark Graebner. Graebner, one of several players using the new steel T-2000 racket recently introduced by Wilson Sporting Goods, crunched 25 aces in his 8-6, 3-6, 19-17, 6-1 victory, and three in a row from 30-40 to end his scintillating 3-6, 3-6, 7-5, 6-4, 7-5 semifinal victory over Jan Leschly, the clever and sporting left-handed Dane. Newcombe outslugged Graebner, seeking to become the first native champ since 1955, in a serve-and-volley final, 6-4, 6-4, 8-6.

Sharing attention with the winners at Forest Hills were the much-publicized steel rackets used by women's champ Billie Jean King, Rosemary Casals, Graebner and Gene Scott, among others. Wilson's equipment innovation, adapted from a French design pioneered by clothier and ex-

champion René Lacoste, was the harbinger of a wave of new racket designs and materials that flooded the market in the next decade. Scott, then a 29-year-old Wall Street lawyer and part-time player who would later become the self-styled Renaissance Man of tennis in the '70s, fulfilled many a Walter Mitty fantasy by working mornings in his office and taking the train to Forest Hills, where he reached the semis before Newcombe jolted him back to reality, 6-4, 6-3, 6-3. Scott predicted that wood rackets would soon be obsolete, but his accurate prophecy did not come to pass immediately.

Woman of the Year in tennis in 1967 was Billie Jean Moffitt King, 24, who scored triples—victories in singles, doubles and mixed doubles—at both Wimbledon and the U.S. Only Don Budge in 1938 and Alice Marble in 1939 have also achieved this feat.

Billie Jean also won all her singles in leading the United States to victories in the Federation and Wightman Cups. She teamed with Rosie Casals to sweep past Rhodesia, South Africa, Germany and Great Britain without losing a match in the Federation Cup on clay at Berlin, and with Nancy Richey, Carole Graebner and Mary Ann Eisel for 6-1 triumph over Great Britain at Cleveland. Richey won the decisive fourth point with a gritty 3-6, 8-6, 6-2 victory over Virginia Wade despite a pulled muscle in her back that pained her through the last six games.

King compiled a 68-5 record during the ranking season and won 10 tournaments. In addition to seizing the Wimbledon and Forest Hills titles without losing a set, she won the U.S. Indoor, 6-1, 6-0, over Netherlander Trudy Groenman, and the South African Championship, and had the season's two longest winning streaks: 23 and 25 matches. In Johannesburg, beating Bueno, 7-5, 6-4, she scored another triple, teaming triumphantly with Casals (her partner in U.S. and Wimbledon doubles victories) and Aussie Owen Davidson (her partner in French, Wimbledon, and U.S. Mixed Doubles Championships). Davidson scored a Mixed Grand Slam, having first teamed with Lesley Turner to win the Australian title.

King beat Ann Jones, the tenacious British left-hander, in the Wimbledon final, 6-3, 6-4, and again in the Forest Hills title match, 11-9, 6-4. In the latter, Jones ignored a pulled hamstring and gallantly fought off nine match points before succumbing. Injuries had influenced the women's singles from the outset, four-time champion Maria Bueno pulling out with tendinitis in the right arm and Nancy Richey with the back ailment sustained in the Wightman Cup.

Richey had earlier won her fifth consecutive U.S. Clay Court title, gunning down Casals, 6-2, 6-3, after little Rosie conquered King in the semis. Arthur Ashe, whose duties as a lieutenant in the U.S. Army kept him out of Wimbledon and Forest Hills, won the men's title for the only time, beating Marty Riessen, 6-3, 6-1, 7-5. Ashe was ranked No. 2 in the U.S. behind Pasarell, who beat him twice in three meetings: in the finals of the U.S. Indoor, 13-11, 6-2, 2-6, 9-7, and in the Richmond Indoor, in Ashe's hometown.

The U.S. outdoor season survived the longest (147 games) tournament match of all time, in the doubles of the Newport (R.I.) Casino Invitational. Dick Leach and Dick Dell defeated Len Schloss and Tom Mozur, 3-6, 49-47, 22-20. The marathon consumed six hours and 10 minutes over two days, and undoubtedly provided impetus for the scoring reform championed by Newport's Jimmy Van Alen—whose "sudden death" tie-breaker, designed to terminate such monster matches, was finally adopted in 1970.

For the third consecutive year under hapless captain George MacCall, the U.S. Davis Cup team was upset on foreign soil—slow, red clay. The 1967 loss to Ecuador at Guayaquil was the most ignominious of all, undoubtedly the most startling upset in the long history of Davis Cup competition. Ecuador's two players, Pancho Guzman and Miguel Olvera, were barely known internationally.

Cliff Richey, the most comfortable of the Americans on clay, won the first and inconsequential fifth matches, but the middle three spelled disaster for the United States. Olvera, a 26-year-old who had been sidelined by tuberculosis, beat Ashe—who had not lost a set in his 10 previous Cup matches—4-6, 6-4, 6-4, 6-2. Ecuadorian captain Danny Carrera was so thrilled he attempted to leap the net to embrace Olvera, tripped and broke his leg. Still, the 1-1 score did not seem too worrisome for the U.S. until the scrambling Olvera and his 21-year-old sidekick Guzman overcame a 0-6, 2-5, deficit and stunned Americans Riessen and Graebner, 0-6, 9-7, 6-4, 4-6, 8-6, setting the stage for a raucous third day. The giddy crowd of 2,200 at the Guayaquil Tennis Club cheered wildly for their sudden heroes and unsettled the Americans with a shower of abuse. Panic set in on MacCall as the slow-balling Guzman withstood two rushes from Ashe and won the decisive match by a score as bizarre as the whole series: 0-6, 6-4, 6-2, 0-6, 6-3.

With the U.S. out, South Africa was expected to reach the challenge round against Australia with Bob Hewitt, Cliff Drysdale and young Ray Moore, three formidable singles players, and Hewitt-McMillan the doubles team of the year. (Their 53-1 record included victories in the Italian, Wimbledon and South African Championships, plus seven other tournaments. Newcombe-Roche won 12 of 19 tournaments, including the Australian, French and U.S.)

But Hewitt broke his ankle in the quarterfinal series against India and was unavailable for the semis, in which Spain eliminated South Africa, 3-2. In Australia for the challenge round for the second time in three years, Spain was outclassed again. Emerson took advantage of one of Santana's rare poor matches and won the opener in a rout, 6-4, 6-1, 6-1. Newcombe swamped 18-year-old Cup rookie lefty Manuel Orantes, 6-3, 6-3, 6-2, then teamed with Roche to scald Santana Orantes, 6-4, 6-4, 6-4, losing only 16 points in 15 service games. The 3-0 lead at Brisbane assured Australia's 15th Cup victory in 18 years.

Emerson, 31, blasted Orantes, ending a peerless Davis Cup career in which he won 11 of 12 singles matches plus six doubles matches in nine challenge rounds, eight of them won by Australia. Emmo, whose overall Cup record (including zone matches) was 10-2 in singles, 14-3 in doubles, guzzled champagne triumphantly from the sterling tub on eight occasions, more than any other player, and had played the clincher five times, thrice in doubles. Newcombe's last match as an amateur was not as successful. He lost to Santana, making the final score 4-1.

Immediately after the challenge round, Newcombe, Roche, Emerson and Davidson turned pro. Newcombe and Roche signed with New Orleans promoter Dave Dixon, who—bankrolled by Texas oilman Lamar Hunt and his nephew, Al Hill, Jr.—had founded World Championship Tennis, Inc. (WCT). Emerson signed with MacCall, who had corralled Rod Laver, Ken Rosewall, Pancho Gonzales, Andres Gimeno (runner-up to Laver in the U.S. Pro final), Fred Stolle and a few others for his National Tennis League (NTL). Davidson became the pro at the All England Club and Britain's national coach.

The formation of WCT's "Handsome Eight" barnstorming troupe had an enormous impact on the amateur tennis establishment. In one day, Dixon and his partner Bob Briner, a tennis neophyte who would later become executive director of the Association of Tennis Professionals, signed Newcombe, Roche, Nikki Pilic and Roger Taylor, accounting for three of the 1967 Wimbledon semifinalists. Dennis Ralston had been their first signee, and they soon added Cliff Drysdale, Butch Buchholz and Pierre Barthes.

"We had in one fell swoop taken all the stars out of the game. If anyone was ever going to see them again at Wimbledon and Forest Hills, the ITF had to make an accommodation," Briner remembers. "Open tennis came about so fast after that, it was pitiful."

5

THE OPEN ERA
1968-96

n the 1970s, tennis became truly the "in" sport of the great middle class, first in the United States, then abroad. In a single decade, the sport threw off and trampled its starched white flannel past and became a favored diversion of the modern leisure class—attired in pastels and playing tie-breaker sets in public parks and clubs. They were equipped with a bewildering variety of gear, from optic yellow, heavy-duty balls to double-strung graphite rackets.

All this was inspired by the advent of Open Tennis in 1968. If competition between amateur and professionals did not trigger the tennis boom outright, it unquestionably fueled it. By making tennis at the top level professional, honest, and unabashedly commercial, open competition ushered in an era of dramatic growth and development.

For an expanding group of pros, this was boomtime, a veritable bonanza of opportunities. They enjoyed and reaped the benefits of a Brave New World of televised matches and two-fisted backhands, evolution of technique and technology, full-blown tours for women and over-45s, exposure and prize money undreamed of even by Wimbledon champions in the pre-open era.

1968

The advent of "open competition" between amateurs and professionals, some 40 years after the issue was first raised, made 1968 truly a watershed year for tennis.

The British "revolt" of December 1967, reinforced by the USTA's vote in favor of Open Tennis at its annual meeting in February 1968, led to the emergency meeting of the ITF at Paris and approval of 12 open tournaments for 1968.

Unfortunately, the hypocrisy and confusion of the "shamateur" period was not done away with quickly and cleanly. Rather than accept the British proposal that all competitors would be referred to simply as "players," abolishing the distinction between amateur and professional, the ITF bowed to heavy pressure from Eastern European countries and their voting allies and effected a compromise that called for four classifications:

1. Amateurs, who would not accept prize money.

2. Teaching professionals, who could compete with amateurs only in open events.

3. "Contract professionals," who made their living playing tennis but did not accept the authority of their national associations affiliated to the ITF, signing guaranteed contracts instead with independent promoters.

4. "Registered players," who could accept prize money in open tournaments but still obeyed their national associations and retained eligibility for amateur events including the Davis, Federation, and Wightman Cups.

The prime example of this last strange and short-lived new breed was Dutchman Tom Okker, who won the Italian and South African Championships (not yet prize-money events) and was runner-up to Arthur Ashe in the first U.S. Open at Forest Hills. Okker pocketed $14,000 in first-prize money while Ashe, then a lieutenant in the U.S. Army and a member of the Davis Cup team, had to remain an amateur (the USTA had not yet adopted the "registered player" concept) and received only $28 per day expenses.

Other ludicrous examples abounded. Margaret Court, for instance, won and accepted nearly $10,000 in open tournaments in Britain, then came to America and played in the U.S. Amateur in Boston for expenses only, beating old rival Maria Bueno in the final, 6-2, 6-2.

But despite such anomalies of the transition period, great progress had undeniably been made toward a more honest and prosperous international game.

The first open tournament, a month after the concept was approved at the conference table,

It was a landmark year for tennis, and Army Lt. Arthur Ashe, winning the first U.S. Open in 1968, helped make it memorable. (UPI)

was the $14,000 British Hard Court Championships (in Europe, "hard court" refers to a clay surface, not concrete or similar hard surface as the term is used in the U.S.) at the coastal resort of Bournemouth. History was made on a drizzly, raw Monday, April 22. The "open era" began with an undistinguished young Briton, John Clifton, winning the first point but losing his match against Australian pro Owen Davidson— then the British national coach—on the red shale courts of the West Hants Lawn Tennis Club.

The field at Bournemouth was not as distinguished as the historic nature of the occasion warranted. The "Handsome Eight" of World Championship Tennis were off playing their own tour, leaving the professional portion of the field to come from George MacCall's National Tennis League, plus Davidson and former Chilean Davis Cupper Luis Ayala, then a coach in Puerto Rico, who paid his own way to take part. The top-line amateurs, wary of immediate confrontation with the pros, stayed away. None of the World Top Ten amateurs entered, and Englishman Bobby Wilson was the only amateur seeded. On the women's side, the only four pros at the time—Billie Jean King, Rosemary Casals, Françoise Durr and Ann Haydon Jones, who had just signed contracts with MacCall—were otherwise engaged.

The male pros were expected to dominate the amateur field of Englishmen and a few second-line Australians. But many of the pros were nervous; they knew their reputations were on the line, and the most discerning realized they were ill prepared, given long absence from best-of-five-set matches and exposure to new faces and playing styles.

Pancho Gonzalez particularly recognized the hazards posed by sudden emergence from a small circle of familiar opponents, with its well-established pecking order. It didn't take long for his apprehension to prove justified. In the second round, Mark Cox, a Cambridge-educated, 24-year-old English left-hander ranked only No. 3 in Britain, outlasted Gonzalez, 0-6, 6-2, 4-6, 6-3, 6-3, becoming the first amateur to topple a pro.

Gonzalez, only a month from his 40th birthday, hadn't played a five-set match in four years, but his defeat sent shock waves through the tennis world. Buoyed by his instant celebrity, Cox ousted first-year pro Roy Emerson the next day to reach the semifinals.

Obviously the pros were not invincible—a notion that would be reinforced convincingly throughout the year. But the best of their number, Rod Laver and Ken Rosewall, proved they still inhabited the top echelon. Laver canceled Cox's heroic run in the semis, 6-4, 6-1, 6-0, and Rosewall—a man for all seasons whose longevity at the top level of international competition is unsurpassed—beat Laver, 3-6, 6-2, 6-0, 6-3, in the title match that, because of rain, stretched over two days. Ken, ruling the 32-man draw, collected the initial "open" paycheck, $2,400, while the loser settled for half.

Attracting almost 30,000 customers during a damp and chilly week at the small club, pioneering Bournemouth was deemed a grand success. There was no going back. Virginia Wade, the British No. 1 (No. 8 in the world), would be going forward as a pro, but later in the year. However, as wary as Cox about abdicating amateur status at this mysterious time, she declined the female first prize ($720) for winning that title over Winnie Shaw, 6-4, 6-1. Virginia and kindred cautious amateurs—"Suppose it doesn't work, and we're banned as amateurs, out in the cold?" was the common plaint—got $120 for expenses. Luis Ayala, the pro half of the first integrated heterosexual open team, with Valerie Ziegenfuss as the amateur half, won all of $24 for their semifinal finish in the mixed. Since he got $96 as a second-round singles loser, Luis and Valerie came out even. But could they afford room and board? Welcome to the new land of milk and honey.

Rosewall beat Laver again in the final of the second open, the French Championships, also on clay. The first of the traditional "Big Four" tournaments to be open, its field still lacked most of the top American men and Okker, but was stronger than Bournemouth had been.

The French was also memorable because it was played during the general strike and student riots of 1968. Paris was a troubled, crippled city, without public transportation or essential services, but record crowds flocked to Stade Roland Garros on the western outskirts of the city—many by bicycle or on foot—because literally nothing else of a sporting nature was happening. Players, many of whom had harrowing true-life adventures getting to Paris, found accommodations within walking distance of the courts.

"Roland Garros was a port in a storm," recalled Rex Bellamy of the *London Times*. "One thought of Drake and his bowls, Nero and his fiddle. In a strife-torn city, the soaring center court blazed with color. People even perched on the scoreboards, which was as high as they could get without a ladder.

"So the fortnight's excitement was two-edged: a revolution on the courts, and a whiff of revolution in the streets. . . . The first major open was played in the sort of environment that nightmares are made of. But the tennis was often like a dream."

In the quarterfinals, Laver was taken to five sets by the lumbering Romanian Ion Tiriac, one of numerous protracted struggles that kept the packed galleries gasping appreciatively. Laver then easily handled Gonzalez, who had enchanted spectators earlier, but in the final Rosewall again asserted his clay-court mastery, 6-3, 6-1, 2-6, 6-2.

The women's singles was also full of surprises. Amateurs Gail Sherriff (later Gail Chanfreau Lovera) and Elena Subirats eliminated pros Françoise Durr and Rosie Casals in straight sets. Nancy Richey, a clay-court specialist playing as an amateur and regretting it, beat Billie Jean King, who always preferred faster and more sure-footed surfaces, in the semifinals and won the title over the last of the four women pros, Ann Jones, who had been considered the world's leading lady on clay, 5-7, 6-4, 6-1. In the first set, Jones led, 5-1, but lost 11 of the next 13 points. In the second she led, 4-2, then lost 15 of the ensuing 16 points. "A fortnight earlier," Bellamy recalled of Richey, "she had asked anxiously: 'How do we get out of here?' Like the rest of us, she was glad she stayed."

There was more upheaval on the courts, amid the giddy jubilation of a once-in-a-lifetime occasion, at the first open Wimbledon. This was a richly sentimental fortnight, as legendary champions who had been stripped of their All England Club membership upon turning pro were welcomed back to the shrine of the game and again permitted to wear its mauve-and-green colors. Even old-time champions no longer able to compete came back for the festivities surrounding the enactment of a long-held dream. The tournament began with five days of intermittent rain, which held down crowds, but even this couldn't dampen soaring spirits.

Wimbledon, offering a $63,000 pot, was also the first of the open tournaments that every player of consequence entered. The seeding list for the men's singles read like a Who's Who of the pre-sent and immediate past: top-seeded Laver, Rosewall, Andres Gimeno, defending champion John Newcombe, Emerson, Manolo Santana, Lew Hoad, Gonzalez, Dennis Ralston, Butch Buchholz, Fred Stolle, Okker, Ashe, Cliff Drysdale, Tony Roche and Nikki Pilic.

There were numerous surprises, none more unsettling to the pros than the third-round defeat of third-seeded Gimeno, the elegant Spaniard who was regarded as just a shade below Laver and Rosewall, by long-haired, unheralded, 21-year-old South African Ray Moore. Hoad was beaten by Bob Hewitt, and Gonzalez by Soviet Alex Metreveli in the same round, demonstrating again that the pros were unaccustomed to this Brave New World. Indeed, in the quarterfinals only two old pros—Laver and Buchholz—shared the stage with two relatively recent pros (Ralston and Roche), three amateurs (Clark Graebner, Ashe and Moore) and the lone "registered player," Okker.

Second-seeded Rosewall, who had won everything but Wimbledon as an amateur in the '50s, was upset in the fourth round by the tricky left-handed spins of Roche, who went on to beat Buchholz and unseeded Graebner (conqueror of Santana, Stolle, and Moore) to reach the final. Laver got there by beating Gene Scott, Stan Smith, Marty Riessen, Cox, Ralston, and Ashe, then clobbered Roche, 6-3, 6-4, 6-2, in 59 minutes to again command the stage he had made his in 1961 and 1962, and in the eight-man BBC pro event the summer before.

Having artistically made the pros' return to the premier championship of the game triumphant, Laver received $4,800, but said decisively that money had never entered his thoughts. "Wimbledon's first open tournament enabled this fine left-hander to prove his magnificent worth. Wimbledon endorsed his quality," wrote Lance Tingay of London's *Daily Telegraph*. "Equally, Laver endorsed Wimbledon's renewed status as the *de facto* world championship."

The cream also rose in the women's singles. Billie Jean King won her third consecutive singles title and $18,000, equaling a feat last achieved by Maureen Connolly in 1952–54, over a surprise finalist: seventh-seeded Judy Tegart. An accomplished doubles player, this affable Australian earned her day in the sun by beating second-seeded Margaret Court in the quarters and third-seeded Nancy Richey in the semis, but King was not to be denied her throne. The score of the final was 9-7, 7-5.

Billie Jean, weary and ill three weeks before the tournament, was pressed to three sets only in the semifinals. Ann Jones led her, 6-4, 5-4, 15-15, three points away from the match on her own serve. But BJK saved the next point with a lob and was off on a 13-point binge that carried her to 1-0 in the final set and out of trouble, 4-6, 7-5, 6-2, on a July 4 she could truly celebrate.

King also repeated her doubles triumph of 1967 with Casals, but was unable to defend the mixed doubles title with Owen Davidson for a second consecutive "triple." Australians Ken Fletcher (then playing out of Hong Kong) and Court ended their reign in the semis and went on to defeat Metreveli and Olga Morozova, the first Soviet players to reach a Wimbledon final, 6-1, 14-12. Newcombe and Roche beat Rosewall and Stolle in a doubles final made up entirely of Aussie pros.

There was one more great "first open" of 1968—the $100,000 U.S. Open at Forest Hills, richest of the year's events, which was lavishly promoted by Madison Square Garden in the first year of an ultimately uneasy five-year contract with the USTA.

By the end of the summer, observers were no longer startled when amateurs knocked off pros, as Ray Moore did in repeating his Wimbledon victory over Andres Gimeno, this time in the first round. The biggest upsets were the fourth-round knockouts of the Wimbledon men's singles finalists: a badly off-form top-seeded Laver by Cliff Drysdale, 4-6, 6-4, 3-6, 6-1, 6-1, and second-seeded Roche by the clever and rejuvenated Gonzalez, 8-6, 6-4, 6-2.

Gonzalez, 40, the graying but still glorious "Old Wolf," was the darling of the crowds in the stadium where he had prevailed as a hungry young rebel with a cause in 1948 and 1949, but the speedy "Flying Dutchman," Okker, was too fresh for him in the quarters. Gonzalez melted in a broiling sun, 14-16, 6-3, 10-8, 6-3.

Joining Okker in the semis were Rosewall (over Ralston), Ashe (over Drysdale), and Graebner (over defender John Newcombe). Okker was too quick for Rosewall, and Ashe was too powerful for Graebner in four-set semis. Ashe simply had too much flashing firepower—26 aces, a lightning backhand, and superior volleying—for Okker in a superb final, 14-12, 5-7, 6-3, 3-6, 6-3. That was the first five-set final since Ashley Cooper over Mal Anderson a decade earlier, and produced the first native champion since Tony Trabert in 1955.

Ashe and Gimeno, an unlikely duo, survived two match points and beat Graebner and Charlie Pasarell, 6-4, 3-6, 4-6, 20-18, 15-13, in the semifinals of the doubles, the longest match in Forest Hills history to that point. But they had little left for the final. Stan Smith and Bob Lutz, ascending 21-year-old Californians who had won the U.S. Amateur Doubles two weeks earlier without losing a set, took the title, 11-9, 6-1, 7-5. They won 11 of 19 tournaments, 57 of 66 matches on the season, to claim the No. 1 U.S. doubles ranking for the first time.

Billie Jean King was unable to defend her title as she had done at Wimbledon. Like Laver, she was far from peak form and struggled three sets with Maryna Godwin in the quarters and Maria Bueno in the semis. Sixth-seeded Virginia Wade, a 23-year-old Englishwoman of regal bearing recently graduated from Sussex University with a degree in math and physics, beat BJK in the final, 6-4, 6-2. Wade had won at Bournemouth, but this was infinitely more impressive, athletically and financially, as she beat in succession Casals, then the third, second, first seeds: Tegart, Jones, King, all in straight sets. She, who had worked Bournemouth for an expense check of $120, raked in the $6,000 first prize. Court and Bueno dislodged the defending champs, King and Casals, in the women's doubles finals.

There was only one other open tournament in the U.S., the Pacific Southwest at Los Angeles, and form held truer on concrete, Laver beating Rosewall in the final, 4-6, 6-0, 6-0. Casals beat Bueno for the women's title, 6-4, 6-1.

Despite Laver's Wimbledon triumph and No. 1 world ranking, Ashe was the Man of the Year in tennis, winner of 10 tournaments to earn the No. 1 U.S. ranking for the first time after three straight years at No. 2. The first black male to win one of the major titles, he triumphed at Forest Hills while commuting to his Army duties as a data processing instructor at West Point, N.Y. Ashe won 30 straight matches from the start of the Pennsylvania Grass Courts through the Inter-Service Championships (beating Air Force Pfc. Pasarell, who plunged from No. 1 to No. 7 in the U.S. rankings), the U.S. Amateur, U.S. Open and the Las Vegas Invitational, to the semis of the Pacific Southwest. Also included were singles victories over Juan Gisbert and Manolo Santana in the 4-1 U.S. victory over Spain in the Davis Cup.

As cautious about open tennis as some of the players, the USTA, closing down a 51-year-old tradition, the Doubles Championships in Boston, gave that pre-Forest Hills week at Longwood over to a U.S. Amateur Championships. The uncertain thought was that this event would be a continuation of the national tournament that dated to 1881. In case this two-headed newcomer—long-awaited and long-feared—called the U.S. Open turned out to be a monster, it could be laid away with a minimum of fuss, and the old structure would be in place. Of course the Open only got bigger, better and more profitable, transforming the creaky, penny-pinching USTA into what it is today: a wealthy bureaucracy.

But during the transitional year of 1968 the Amateur was a significant event, a useful vehicle especially for the U.S. Davis Cup team that a young new captain, Donald Dell, was grooming to take over for the Aussie dynasty that had been riddled by Newcombe, Roche and Emerson turning pro. Curiously, contract pros were ineligible for Davis Cup. Open tennis was still closed here and there.

It was at the Amateur, nationally televised on PBS, that Arthur Ashe really began to make his name. Top-seeded, he crashed 18 aces and came through an exciting five-set final over unseeded Bob Lutz, 4-6, 6-3, 8-10, 6-0, 6-4. He had launched a singular double, never possible before, that he would complete by winning the U.S. Open two Sundays later. Amateur and Open champ. Arthur alone. It will never happen again. Even though a U.S. Amateur Championships exists today, it is for honest-to-goodness amateurs, people who couldn't get near Flushing Meadow.

Ashe and Graebner were the singles players for the U.S. as it recaptured the Davis Cup for the first time since 1963 at Adelaide in December, recording a 4-1 victory over the Australian team. Imbued with great *esprit de corps* and dedication by 29-year-old Dell, a former player, the Americans (Ashe, Graebner, Smith, Lutz and Pasarell) trained hard and made winning back the Cup into, as Ashe called it, "a quest." They lost only three matches plowing through the West Indies, Mexico, Ecuador, Spain, India and Australia to end the three years of U.S. Cup disaster.

Australia had waited five years for a U.S. challenger to arrive. Challenge rounds against the Yanks had been continent-consuming events, but Adelaide was lukewarm about a defense by a second-rate home side. Bill Bowrey was their best. He had won a dull Australian—still an amateur affair before opens were approved—over Juan Gisbert, 7-5, 2-6, 9-7, 6-4, while Billie Jean King in a livelier women's field shocked Margaret Court, 6-1, 6-2. Bowrey had his moments in the shaky first match, but Graebner, who was in captain Dell's doghouse right up to post time, responded in the desired manner, 8-10, 6-4, 8-6, 3-6, 6-1. Ashe, nervous at first, followed with his 11th straight of the campaign (a U.S. record for singles wins in one year) over lefty Ray Ruffels,

6-8, 7-5, 6-3, 6-3. The "Boy Boppers," Smith and Lutz, got the Cup point quickly, 6-4, 6-4, 6-2, over the makeshift pair of Ruffels and 17-year-old John Alexander, youngest to play for his country. Though Ashe lost to Bowrey to make the score 4-1, it didn't matter. The U.S. had the Cup and would hang onto it until 1973 when the solid-gold Aussies were certified for inclusion.

There were a couple of other notable achievements during this landmark season.

Nancy Richey made one of the fantastic comebacks in tennis history to beat Billie Jean King, 4-6, 7-5, 6-0, in the semifinals of the Madison Square Garden International, the first tourney in the new building. BJK had a match point at 5-1 in the second set, and apparently had the match won with an angled overhead. Richey retrieved it and lobbed again, however, and this time King bungled the smash, then inexplicably collapsed. Richey ran 12 straight games thereafter, 39 of the last 51 points.

That was King's last match as an amateur. Within days she and Roy Emerson signed on with George MacCall's troupe. Richey beat Tegart in one Garden final, 7-5, 7-5, and Ashe won the other over Emerson, 6-4, 6-4, 7-5. Nancy won her sixth straight U.S. Clay, 6-3, 6-3, over Linda Tuero (Graebner beat Smith, 6-3, 7-5, 6-0, to share top billing). She equaled Bill Tilden's 1922–27 reign, and took over the No. 1 U.S. ranking, finishing 2-0 for the year over BJK, whom she also beat at the French.

With King and Casals unavailable for duty in the still amateur women's team competitions, the U.S. relinquished both the Federation Cup (Netherlands beat the U.S. in the semis at Paris, then lost the final to Australia, 3-0) and the Wightman Cup, 4-3. The Truman sisters, Nell and Christine Janes, were socko siblings in the decisive seventh match, beating Stephanie DeFina and Kathy Harter, 6-3, 2-6, 6-3, to leave a Wimbledon gathering delighted.

The longest match on national championship record, in terms of elapsed playing time and games, took place at Salisbury, Md., when Englishmen Bobby Wilson and Mark Cox defeated Pasarell and Graebner, 26-24, 17-19, 30-28, in a U.S. Indoor doubles quarterfinal: 6 hours, 20 minutes, 144 games.

1969

The second year of Open Tennis was one of continued progress but lingering confusion on the political front, and indisputably towering oncourt performances by Rod Laver and Margaret Court.

There were 30 open tournaments around the world and prize money escalated to about $1.3 million. Laver was the leading money-winner with $124,000, followed by Tony Roche ($75,045), Tom Okker ($65,451), Roy Emerson ($62,629) and John Newcombe ($52,610).

The Davis Cup and other international team competitions continued to be governed by reactionaries, however, and admitted only players under the jurisdiction of their national associations. This left "contract pros" —who were paid guarantees and committed by contract to play where scheduled by independent promoters—on the outs, while players who accepted prize money but remained under the aegis of their national associations were allowed to play. At the end of the year a proposal to end this silly double standard and allow "contract pros" back in was defeated by the Davis Cup nations on a 21-19 vote.

The "registered player" concept, borne of compromise a year earlier, persisted until finally being abolished by a newly elected and more forward-looking ITF Committee of Management in July. Still, the public found it difficult to understand who was and who was not a pro. In the United States, those who took prize money but remained under the authority of the USTA were officially called "players." Under the leadership of captain Donald Dell, the members of the U.S. Davis Cup team preferred to call themselves "independent pros," making it clear that they were competing for prize money.

Rod Laver, returning the ball to fellow Australian Tony Roche in the 1969 Open final, took home the most money. (UPI)

The USTA leadership would have preferred to keep the U.S. tournament circuit amateur, paying expenses only, except for five open events given ITF sanction (Philadelphia Indoor, Madison Square Garden, U.S. Open, Pacific Southwest, Howard Hughes Invitational). This would have kept down spiraling overhead costs, a threat to the exclusive clubs, which resisted sponsorship but did not want to lose their traditional events. Dell and the Davis Cup team refused to play in tournaments that offered expenses and guarantees instead of prize money, however, and thus effectively forced a full prize-money circuit into being in the U.S.

Dell led the way by organizing the $25,000 Washington *Star* International in his hometown. It was a prototype tournament in many ways: commercially sponsored and played in a public park for over-the-table prize money rather than under-the-table appearance fees. Other tournaments followed suit, and a new and successful U.S. Summer Circuit began to emerge. In all, 15 U.S. tournaments offered $440,000 in prize money, with the $137,000 U.S. Open again the world's richest event. In 1968, there had been only two prize-money open tournaments in the U.S., with combined purses of $130,000.

A few peculiar hybrid events—half amateur and half pro—remained. The most obviously unnecessary was the $25,000 National Singles and Doubles at Longwood Cricket Club, which welcomed amateurs and independent pros but excluded the "contract pros." Stan Smith beat Bob Lutz, 9-7, 6-3, 6-0, and Margaret Court prevailed over Virginia Wade, 4-6, 6-3, 6-0, for the singles titles, but the grandly named tournament was essentially meaningless and vanished from the scene the next year in a natural sorting-out process.

If the labels put on tournaments and players boggled the public mind, there was no doubt as to who the world's No. 1 players were: Australians Laver and Court were truly dominant.

Laver repeated his 1962 Grand Slam—something only he, Don Budge (1938) and Maureen Connolly (1953) had achieved—by sweeping the Australian, French, Wimbledon and U.S. titles the first year all four were open.

Laver also won the South African Open over Tom Okker, 6-3, 10-8, 6-3, and finished the season with a 106-16 record for 32 tournaments, 17 of which he won. He didn't lose a match from the start of Wimbledon in June until the second round of the Pacific Southwest Open in late September, when Ray Moore ended the winning streak at 31 matches. During that stretch, Laver won seven tournaments, including his fourth Wimbledon (where he had not lost since the 1960 final), his second Forest Hills and his fifth U.S. Pro Championship. By the time he got to Los Angeles, Rod just wanted to get 45 minutes farther south to his adopted home of Corona Del Mar, Calif., where his wife, Mary, had just given birth to his son, Rick Rodney.

The most difficult match for Laver of the 26 that comprised the Slam came early, in the semifinals of the Australian. He beat Tony Roche, 7-5, 22-20, 9-11, 1-6, 6-3, in a match that lasted more than four hours in the sweltering, 105-degree heat of a Brisbane afternoon. Both players got groggy in the brutal sun, even though they employed an old Aussie trick of putting wet cabbage leaves in their hats to help stay cool. It was so close that it could easily have gone either way, and a controversial line call helped Laver grasp the final set. Having survived, Laver beat Andres Gimeno in the final, 6-3, 6-4, 7-5.

His tall countryman, Dick Crealy, took the first two sets from Laver in a second-rounder at the French Championships, but the red-haired "Rocket" accelerated and ultimately played one of his best clay-court matches to beat Ken Rosewall in the final, 6-4, 6-3, 6-4.

An unheralded Indian named Premjit Lall similarly captured the first two sets in the second round at Wimbledon, but Laver awoke to dispose of him, 3-6, 4-6, 6-3, 6-0, 6-0. Stan Smith took Laver to five sets in the quarterfinals, and Arthur Ashe and John Newcombe to four in the semis and final, respectively. But despite Newcombe's thoughtful game plan of using lobs and changes of pace instead of the straightforward power for which he was known, Laver prevailed, 6-4, 5-7, 6-4, 6-4.

Then it was on to Forest Hills, where Philip Morris and its tennis-minded chairman of the board, Joe Cullman, had infused heavy promotional dollars into the U.S. Open and brought flamboyant South African promoter Owen Williams in from Johannesburg to run a jazzed-up show and foster corporate patronage. They drew record crowds until the weather turned surly. Rain inundated the already soft and uneven courts, played havoc with the schedule and pushed the tournament three days past its scheduled conclusion.

Despite the trying conditions and the imminent birth of his son on the West Coast, Laver remained intent on the task at hand. He was taken to five sets only by Dennis Ralston in the fourth round. After that Laver disposed of Roy Emerson in four sets, Arthur Ashe in three straight, and—after two days of rain—donned spikes in the sec-ond set to climb over Roche, 7-9, 6-1, 6-3, 6-2, on a gloomy Tuesday before a crowd of only 3,708 fans who sat through rain delays of 90 and 30 minutes.

The weather certainly dampened the occasion, but it was appropriate that Roche—clearly No. 2 in the world, and regarded as Laver's heir apparent until a series of arm injuries started to plague him the next year—provided the final hurdle. The ruggedly muscular Roche was the only player with a winning record (5-3) for the year over Laver, and Roche got to the final by beating his doubles partner, John Newcombe, in a splendid marathon, 3-6, 6-4, 4-6, 6-3, 8-6.

Laver shed a few tears as USTA President Alastair Martin presented him the champion's trophy and check for $16,000, saying, "You're the greatest in the world . . . perhaps the greatest we've ever seen."

"I never really think of myself in those terms, but I feel honored that people see fit to say such things about me," said Laver shyly. "Tennis-wise, this year was much tougher than '62. At the time the best players—Ken Rosewall, Lew Hoad, Pancho Gonzalez—were not in the amateur ranks. I didn't find out who were the best until I turned pro and had my brains beaten out for six months at the start of 1963."

Now, in the open era, there was no question who was best.

Margaret Court, who had returned to action following a brief retirement (the first of several in her long career), was almost as monopolistic as Laver. She lost only five matches the entire season, winning 19 of 24 tournaments and 98 of 103 matches.

She won the Australian over Billie Jean King, 6-4, 6-1, after trailing Kerry Melville, 3-5, in the final set in the semis. In the French, Court beat Pat Pretorius Walkden, Melville, defending champ Nancy Richey and Ann Jones, 6-1, 4-6, 6-3—all splendid clay-court players—in the last four rounds.

The aging Pancho Gonzalez, still a crowd favorite, provided excitement in a new era. (UPI)

Court's dream of a Grand Slam ended at Wimbledon, however, where Ann Jones beat her in the semifinals, 10-12, 6-3, 6-2. To the unbridled joy of her British countrymen, the left-handed, 30-year-old Mrs. Pip Jones then won her first Wimbledon title after 14 years of trying, squashing Billie Jean King's bid for a fourth consecutive crown, 3-6, 6-3, 6-2. Billie Jean was shaken by the noisy partisanship of the customarily proper British gallery and what she thought were some dubious line calls, but the British extolled the popular Jones as a conquering heroine.

Injury kept top-seeded Jones out of the U.S. Open, won by second-seeded Court on a loss of no sets. In fact, she lost more than two games in a set only twice in six matches, in beating fellow Aussie Karen Krantzcke in the quarters, 6-0, 9-7, and fifth-seeded Virginia Wade in the semis, 7-5, 6-0. Sixth-seeded Nancy Richey—eschew-ing her usual baseline game for net-rushing tactics quite foreign to her—helped out by eliminating third-seeded King in the quarters, 6-4, 8-6, but found herself passed repeatedly in the final by some of Court's finest groundstroking. The score was 6-2, 6-2.

But if Laver and Court clearly reigned supreme, there were other notable heroes and achievements in 1969.

Pancho Gonzalez, at 41, buried Peter Curtis, John Newcombe, Ken Rosewall, Stan Smith and Arthur Ashe, 6-0, 6-3, 6-4, in succession to win the $50,000 Howard Hughes Open at Las Vegas. Gonzalez also won the Pacific Southwest Open and had a 2-0 record over Smith, who was ranked No. 1 in the U.S. for the first time. Gonzalez was the top U.S. money-winner with $46,288, and might have returned to the No. 1 spot he occupied in 1948 and 1949 if the USTA had included "contract pros" in its rankings.

Gonzalez' most dramatic performance, however, came at Wimbledon, where he beat Charlie Pasarell in the first round in the longest match in the history of the oldest and most prestigious of championships. It consumed 5 hours and 12 minutes and 112 games over two days. Gonzalez lost a marathon first set and virtually threw the second, complaining bitterly that it was too dark to continue play. He was whistled and hooted by the normally genteel Centre Court crowd, but won back all his detractors the next day with a heroic display. Pasarell played well, but Gonzalez was magnificent. In the fifth set he staved off seven match points, twice serving out of 0-40 holes, and won, 22-24, 1-6, 16-14, 6-3, 11-9—112 games. Gonzalez lasted until the fourth round, when his protégé, Ashe, beat him in four sets.

Stan Smith won eight tournaments, including the U.S. Indoor over Egyptian lefty Ismail El Shafei, 6-3, 6-8, 6-4, 6-4, to replace Ashe atop the U.S. rankings. Ashe, bothered by a nagging elbow injury and numerous non-tennis distractions following his big year in 1968, won only two tournaments but had an 83-24 match record and more wins than any other American. He was

The U.S. Wightman Cup winners: (Standing, from left)—Coach Doris Hart; Mary Ann Curtis, Hazel Wightman, captain Betty Pratt, Nancy Richey and Julie Heldman. (Kneeling)—Valerie Ziegenfuss and Jane "Peaches" Bartkowicz. (UPI)

a semifinalist at Wimbledon and Forest Hills, losing to longtime nemesis Laver at both, and was ranked No. 2, ahead of Cliff Richey and Clark Graebner, even though they had more tournament victories—eight and seven, respectively.

The United States defeated long-shot Romania, 5-0, in the Davis Cup challenge round on a fast asphalt court at Cleveland, painted and polished to make it even slicker, to the home team's benefit. Ashe defeated Ilie Nastase in the opening singles, 6-2, 15-13, 7-5, and Smith escaped the hulking and wily Ion Tiriac, 6-8, 6-3, 5-7, 6-4, 6-4, in the pivotal second match. Smith and Lutz closed out the Romanians, 8-6, 6-1, 11-9.

President Richard M. Nixon, a bowler and golfer who secretly despised tennis, had both teams to a reception at the White House. This was a nice gesture, but the Chief Executive caused a few awkward stares when, as a memento of the occasion, he presented each player with a golf ball. Perhaps these were left over, some speculated, from the golf-happy Eisenhower administration.

Tiny Romania, with the lion-hearted Tiriac and the immensely talented Nastase its only players of international standard, was proud to have gotten past Egypt, Spain, the Soviet Union, India and Great Britain (which, with a heroic 10-2 singles run from unranked Graham Stilwell, reached the semifinals for the first time since relinquishing the Cup in 1937). Never before had Romania won more than two rounds.

Australia failed to reach the final for the first time since 1937—beaten in its first match by Mexico, 3-2, the first opening-round loss for the Aussies since falling to Italy in 1928. Rafael Osuna, Mexico's popular tennis hero, defeated Bill Bowrey in the fifth match, 6-2, 3-6, 8-6, 6-3, and was hailed triumphantly by his countrymen. This was the engaging Osuna's last hurrah, however; he died tragically shortly thereafter, at age 30, when a private plane carrying him on a business trip crashed into the mountains outside Monterrey.

In another significant development, the Davis Cup nations voted South Africa and Rhodesia out of the competition for 1970 and 1971 because demonstrations against their racial policies, and the refusal of some nations to play them, made their presence in the draw disruptive.

Nancy Richey was upset in the semifinals of the U.S. Clay by Gail Sherriff Chanfreau, ending her tournament record female winning streak at 33 straight matches over seven years. She was trying to become only the second player to win seven consecutive titles, matching the feat of Richard Sears in the first seven U.S. Men's Championships (1881–87). Chanfreau won that title over Linda Tuero, 6-2, 6-2, Yugoslav Zeijko Franulovic the other over Ashe, 8-6, 6-3, 6-4. Clark Graebner, uniting with Bill Bowrey in a 6-4, 4-6, 6-4 victory over Aussies Dick Crealy and Allan Stone, had his fifth Clay doubles title, passing Bill Talbert's record set in 1946.

Richey retained the No. 1 U.S. women's ranking, winning four of 13 tournaments for a 46-10 record and splitting four matches with old rival Billie Jean King, who as a "contract pro" was not ranked. Richey teamed with Julie Heldman and Jane "Peaches" Bartkowicz to regain the Federation Cup at Athens and the Wightman Cup at Cleveland.

Richey was undefeated in singles and Heldman lost only to Margaret Court as the U.S. defeated Bulgaria, Italy, Netherlands and Australia, 2-1, for the Federation Cup. Richey and Bartkowicz, an unlikely doubles team made up of two confirmed baseliners, upset the world's No. 1 team—Court and Judy Tegart—in the final match, 6-4, 6-4, Bartkowicz stayed in the backcourt throughout, even when Richey served, but the Americans astonishingly won the curious match with energetic retrieving and deft lobbing.

Heldman, a clever player who nicknamed herself "Junkball Julie," set the tone of the 5-2 Wightman Cup victory by upsetting Wade in the opening match. Ranked No. 2 nationally with eight victories in 20 tournaments and a 67-13 match record, Heldman also became the first American woman to win the Italian Championship since Althea Gibson in 1956, beating three outstanding clay-courters—Lesley Turner Bowrey (wife of Bill), Ann Jones and Kerry Melville, 7-5, 6-4.

One of the most remarkable and crowd-pleasing victories of the year was that of Darlene Hard and Françoise Durr in the U.S. Open women's doubles. They were a "pickup" team; Hard, by then a 33-year-old teaching pro, had entered as a lark. Out of tournament condition, she was an embarrassment in losing the first eight games of the final, but seemed suddenly to remember the skills and instincts that had made her the world's premier doubles player in her time, winner of five previous U.S. women's titles. As the crowd loudly cheered their revival, Hard and Durr stunned heavily favored Court and Wade, 0-6, 6-3, 6-4.

Forest Hills had begun with a match of record duration—F. D. Robbins defeated Dick Dell, younger brother of Donald, 22-20, 9-7, 6-8, 8-10, 6-4, the longest in number of games—100—in the history of the U.S. Championships. When the tournament ran three days over, the men's doubles finished in a disgraceful shambles, Ken Rosewall and Fred Stolle beating Denny Ralston and Charlie Pasarell, 2-6, 7-5, 13-11, 6-3, before a few hundred spectators on a soggy Wednesday. Pasarell-Ralston got defaults from

Wimbledon champs Newcombe and Roche in the quarters and Australian Open winners Laver and Emerson in the semis.

Newcombe-Roche were urged to leave waterlogged New York by their employers, WCT, in order to meet other commitments, a decision that rankled the ITF in its increasingly uneasy dealings with the new pro promoters. After all, it was unseemly for the No. 1 team—they had repeated at Wimbledon, over Tom Okker–Marty Riessen, and won four other tournaments, including the Italian and French—to walk out on one of the "Big Four" showcase championships.

1970

As in 1950 and 1960, the beginning of a new decade also was, in many ways, the start of a new era for tennis. In 1970, the professional game for both men and women fitfully began to assume the structure that would characterize the decade of its most rapid growth.

This was the first year of the men's Grand Prix—a point system, under the aegis of the ITF, that linked together tournaments, leading to year-end bonus awards for the top finishers in the standings and berths in a new tournament at the end of the year: the Grand Prix Masters.

The brainchild of Jack Kramer, the Grand Prix was announced late in 1969 and sponsored by Pepsico. Players earned points, round by round, in the Grand Prix tournaments they entered, and at season's end the top men received cash awards scaled according to their order of finish.

Cliff Richey, for example, collected $25,000 for topping the standings; Arthur Ashe earned $17,000 for placing second; Ken Rosewall $15,000 for coming in third, etc. There were 19 tournaments in the Grand Prix in 1970. The "bonus pool" totaled $150,000 and another $50,000 was at stake in the six-man Masters.

The underlying intent of the Grand Prix clearly, was to keep players from signing guaranteed contracts with the professional troupes,

World Championship Tennis (WCT) and the struggling National Tennis League (NTL). WCT, which loomed as an ever more formidable rival to the ITF and its 93-member national associations for control of the burgeoning pro game, responded by swiftly signing more players to contracts, then increasing its "stable" to 30 players by swallowing the NTL in May.

Mike Davies, executive director of WCT, became a member of the ITF scheduling committee, but wariness and distrust between the maneuvering giants continued. It became increasingly difficult for traditional tournaments to count on the participation of the WCT players because of the "management fees" demanded by WCT in order to cover their guarantees to the players.

In September, at the U.S. Open, WCT took the wraps off a Grand Prix-style competition of its own, announcing a "million-dollar circuit" for 1971. The first World Championship of Tennis, for 32 players to be selected by an international press panel, would consist of 20 tournaments with uniform prize money and point standings, leading to a rich, nationally televised playoff with a $50,000 first prize.

This was considered a declaration of war by WCT against the ITF, especially since Davies had never mentioned it to the ITF calendar committee. The battle intensified when, shortly thereafter, WCT announced that it had signed Arthur Ashe, Charlie Pasarell and Bob Lutz to five-year contracts in a package deal.

The ITF went ahead and announced an expanded Grand Prix, worth $1.5 million, in 1971, but the battle lines had already been drawn.

The beneficiaries of the infighting, of course, were the players, who found themselves the objects of a giddy bidding war between the ITF, which offered ever-bigger prize money tournaments but no guarantees, and WCT, with its long-term, guaranteed contracts.

Rod Laver did not retain any of the "Big Four" titles he monopolized in 1969, but still became the first tennis player to crack the $200,000 barrier in winnings.

He collected $201,453, compared to the $157,037 won by Lee Trevino, top earner on the professional golf circuit. This had heretofore been considered unimaginable. But prize money was escalating at a rate no one had foreseen—nearly $1 million was up for grabs in U.S. tournaments alone—and three players (Laver, U.S. Open champ Ken Rosewall and Arthur Ashe) won more than $100,000.

Growing along with the total purses, however, was the disparity in prize money for men and women. Despite Margaret Court's fulfillment of a long-held ambition—a singles Grand Slam of the Australian, French, Wimbledon and U.S. titles—1970 was for the majority of women players the autumn of their discontent. A group of pioneers, led by the strong-willed Gladys Heldman—a tough, shrewd businesswoman who had founded *World Tennis* magazine in 1953—decided that the women would have to split away from mixed tournaments and found their own tour if they were ever to corner a significant share of the sport's mushrooming riches and publicity. This was a bold step, but the women decided to take it in September, and from a little acorn—a $7,500 renegade tournament for nine women in Houston—there eventually grew a mighty oak: the women's pro tour in the U.S.

The political kettle was boiling, but 1970 was also a spectacularly eventful year on the court. It was made singularly exciting by the advent of the game's first major scoring innovation—tie-breakers—and towering performances by several players, notably Rosewall and Court.

"Mighty Margaret" had twice before won three of the "Big Four" singles titles in a season. In 1970, at age 28, she finally corralled the Grand Slam previously achieved by only one woman—Maureen Connolly in 1953. Court compiled a 104-6 record, winning 21 of 27 tournaments, and had the season's longest winning streak: 39 matches.

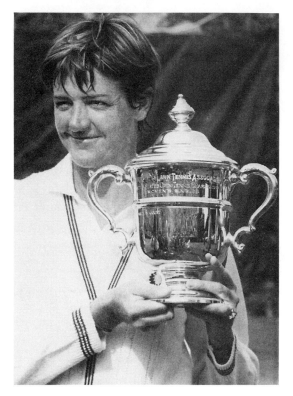

Margaret Smith Court, with her U.S. Open trophy, was the leading lady in 1970. (UPI)

But a glitch for Margaret was a small September post-Open tournament at Charlotte, N.C., where she was beaten in the semis by a pony-tailed adolescent whom she would presently face on major battlegrounds: 15-year-old Chris Evert defeated her, 7-6, 7-6. The kid, an amateur in her first final among pros, then lost the final to Richey, 6-4, 6-1.

Court lost only three sets during the Slam, none in winning her ninth Australian singles title. She defeated Kerry Melville—one of only four women to beat her during the season—in the final, 6-3, 6-1, and teamed with Judy Tegart Dalton to win the doubles by the same score over Melville and Karen Krantzcke.

In the French, only Russian Olga Morozova pushed Court to three sets, in the second round. Court's next four victories were all in straight sets, German Helga Niessen falling in the final, 6-2, 6-4. Françoise Durr won her fourth consecutive doubles title, alongside Gail Sherriff Chanfreau.

At Wimbledon, the tall, languid Niessen—not considered a threat on grass courts—took the first set from Court in the quarterfinals, but did not get another game. The final between Court and Billie Jean King was a masterpiece of drama and shot-making under duress. Both players were hurt. Court had a painfully strained and swollen ankle tightly strapped as she went on court; she had taken a pain-killing injection beforehand. King was hobbling on a deteriorated kneecap, which required surgery immediately after Wimbledon.

Nevertheless, BJK broke service in the first set three times. Each time Court broke back. Their injuries partially dictated the pattern of play, but both players produced magnificent shots under pressure. It was the longest women's final ever at Wimbledon—46 games—Court finally winning by 14-12, 11-9, in 2½ hours, after the anesthetic effects of her injection had worn off. King saved three match points with gutsy shots worthy of the contest. "It was a bit like one of those 990-page novels that Trollope and Arnold Bennett used to write," suggested British journalist David Gray, who in 1977 would become general secretary of the ITF. "It started a little slowly, but had so many fascinating twists of character and plot that in the end it became a matter of utter compulsion to see how it all ended."

King took her sixth doubles title, her third with Rosemary Casals (who teamed with Ilie Nastase to win the mixed). Billie Jean was the only player who truly challenged Court, splitting their four matches during the year, but King was still recuperating from her post-Wimbledon surgery. In her absence, Court completed the Slam, losing only 13 games in mowing down Pam Austin, Patti Hogan, Pat Faulkner, Helen Gourlay and Nancy Richey to reach the final. Casals, attacking furiously, won the middle set of the final, but it was a futile effort. "Her arms seemed a mile long," shrugged the diminutive "Rosebud," only 5-foot-2 to Court's 5-foot-11,

after her 6-2, 2-6, 6-1 beating. Court also took the doubles, in tandem with Judy Dalton, and the mixed doubles with Marty Riessen, her first U.S., fifth major triple.

Court won approximately $50,000 in prize money on the year, about one quarter of what Laver earned for a far less productive season. In most tournaments, the women's share of the prize money was one quarter or less that of the men's. In the Italian Open, for example, Billie Jean King received a mere $600 for beating Julie Heldman, 6-1, 6-3, in the final, while Ilie Nastase earned $3,500 for whipping Jan Kodes, 6-3, 1-6, 6-3, 8-6, in the men's final.

Court, never a crusader or champion of causes, wanted no part of a "women's lib" movement in tennis, but King and several others resented the growing inequity in prize-money ratio between men and women. They enlisted fiery activist Gladys Heldman as their negotiator and spokeswoman, and focused on the Pacific Southwest Open at Los Angeles—which favored men by an 8-to-1 ratio—as an example of their plight.

Heldman tried to get tournament chairman Jack Kramer to raise the women's purse. He would not. At a highly publicized Forest Hills press conference, a group of nine women declared they would boycott the Los Angeles tournament and play in a $7,500 event in Houston, sponsored by Virginia Slims cigarettes. The USTA said it would not sanction this rebel event. The women said they would play anyway—and did. After signing token one-dollar contracts with Heldman, the Houston Nine (King, Casals, Kristy Pigeon, Peaches Bartkowicz, Judy Dalton, Valerie Ziegenfuss, Kerry Melville, Julie Heldman and Nancy Richey) competed in an event that was unexpectedly successful, paving the way for the first Virginia Slims circuit the next year. Casals won over Dalton, 5-7, 6-1, 7-5.

Meanwhile, in men's tennis, the Grand Slam singles titles monopolized by Laver in 1969 went to four different players:

- Arthur Ashe, the runner-up in 1966 and 1967, became the fourth American to win the Australian singles, the first since Dick Savitt 19 years earlier. Laver did not defend, and Dennis Ralston eliminated Newcombe in a marathon quarterfinal, 19-17, 20-18, 4-6, 6-4—94 games, the sixth-longest in history. Ashe took out Dick Crealy in the final, 6-4, 9-7, 6-2, while Stan Smith and Bob Lutz captured the doubles, the first American men to do so since Vic Seixas and Tony Trabert 17 years earlier.

- With Laver, Rosewall, and their fellow "contract pros" out of the French Championships because their bosses could not come to a financial accommodation with the French Tennis Federation for their appearance, Czech Jan Kodes, Yugoslav Zeljko Franulovic, American Cliff Richey, and Frenchman Georges Goven reached the semifinals of the richest ($100,000) tournament outside America. Kodes beat Franulovic, 6-2, 6-4, 6-0, for the $10,000 top prize. Romanians Ilie Nastase and Ion Tiriac took the doubles.

- At Wimbledon, Laver's 31-match winning streak (dating back to 1961) in the world's most important tournament was snapped when he came up badly off-form against English lefty Roger Taylor in the fourth round and tumbled, 4-6, 6-4, 6-2, 6-1. John Newcombe withstood five break points in the fifth set of an excruciating three-hour quarterfinal against fellow Aussie Roy Emerson, won it by 6-1, 5-7, 3-6, 6-2, 11-9, then crushed Spaniard Andres Gimeno (conqueror of Ashe) and beat Rosewall, 5-7, 6-3, 6-2, 3-6, 6-1. This was the first five-set final in 21 years, and the 10th all-Aussie men's final in 15 years.

Rosewall had beaten left-handers Tony Roche and Taylor to reach the final for the third time, 14 years after losing to fellow Aussie "Whiz Kid" Lew Hoad, but again failed at the last hurdle. Newcombe and Roche teamed for their third consecutive doubles triumph, the first to achieve this since Reg and Laurie Doherty, the English brothers in 1903–5.

- Rosewall, two months shy of his 36th birthday, reigned at Forest Hills, where 14 years earlier he had halted Hoad's Grand Slam bid. It was a wild tournament, the richest in the world with a $176,000 pot. Pastel clothing was permitted in lieu of the traditional "all white," and red flags flew every time a set reached 6-6 and went into the "sudden death" best-of-nine-points tie-breaker. Suddenly strange-looking 7-6 scores (typographical errors) were blossoming.

Record crowds totaling 122,996 came out to see all the revolutionary happenings, but Rosewall interjected a reactionary note. After Dennis Ralston had achieved one of his career high points, knocking off defending champ and top-seeded Laver in the fourth round, 7-6 (5-3), 7-5, 5-7, 4-6, 6-3, to lead a charge of four Americans into the last eight, third-seeded Rosewall took over. He blasted Stan Smith and second-seeded Newcombe in straight sets, then relegated fourth-seeded Roche to the runner-up spot for the second consecutive year, 2-6, 6-4, 7-6 (5-2), 6-3. Rosewall was the oldest champ at Forest Hills since Bill Tilden, who was 36 when he won for the seventh and last time in 1929.

The men's doubles event was notable for several reasons. Pancho Gonzalez, the oldest man in the tournament at 42, entered with a then unknown protégé, Jimmy Connors, who at 18 was the youngest man. They reached the quarters. Nikki Pilic of Yugoslavia and Pierre Barthes of France slew Emerson and Laver in the final, 6-3, 7-6 (5-2), 4-6, 7-6 (5-4), to become the second European team to win the U.S. Doubles, 34 years after Germany's Gottfried von Cramm and Henner Henkel. The victors won eight of their 15 sets in tie-breakers, the scoring innovation by Jimmy Van Alen that was given its first widespread exposure in the U.S. Pro Championships and U.S. Open.

Players were skeptical— "It's like rolling dice," said Newcombe—but spectators, schedule-makers and television producers loved them, so tie-breakers were here to stay—although the more conservative 12-point, win-by-two method gradually won favor over nine-point sudden death in professional tournaments.

- Laver, at 32, did win five significant tournaments on four continents, but in addition to losing his Grand Slam titles, he gave up his four-year stranglehold on the U.S. Pro title. Roche beat him in the final at Long-wood, 3-6, 6-4, 1-6, 6-2, 6-2. Laver also won the "Tennis Champions Classic," a series of head-to-head, winner-take-all challenge matches played in seven cities. He beat Rosewall for the $35,000 top prize at Madison Square Garden, 6-4, 6-3, 6-3.

- Nastase underscored his emerging brilliance by winning titles on one of the world's fastest courts—the canvas of the U.S. Indoor at Salisbury, Md., where he escaped a two-set deficit and two match points in the fourth set to beat Cliff Richey, 6-8, 3-6, 6-4, 9-7, 6-0—as well as on one of the slowest, the red clay of Foro Italico in Rome.

Richey, a scrappy Texan with more tenacity than natural talent, earned the No. 1 U.S. ranking, thereby establishing a unique family achievement. His sister, Nancy, had been the top-ranked U.S woman in 1964, 1965, 1968 and 1969.

Richey won eight of 27 tournaments he played during the season, was runner-up in five more and went farther than any other American man at Forest Hills—to the semifinals. His match record for the year was 93-19.

Even so, he did not clinch the top ranking until the Pacific Coast Championships at Berkeley in late September, when he played Stan Smith—who had beaten him in two of three previous 1970 meetings—in the semifinals. Both men knew the No. 1 ranking hinged on his match, and what an extraordinary battle it turned out to be! After a long afternoon of furious scrambling and shotmaking, it all came down to 4-points-all in the sudden-death tie-breaker: simultaneous match point for both players. Richey served to Smith's backhand and charged the net. Smith cracked a backhand return crosscourt that Richey could barely get his racket on. He nudged the ball crosscourt, and Smith lashed what appeared to be a winning passing shot down the line. Richey dived for the ball, throwing everything into a desperate last lunge and astonishingly volleyed a winner to seize the breaker, 5-4, and the match, 7-6 (5-2), 6-7 (2-5), 6-4, 4-6, 7-6 (5-4).

Richey also was the unlikely hero of the lackluster 1970 Davis Cup challenge round. U.S. captain Ed Turville agonized over the selection, but finally chose Richey over Smith to face upstart Germany on a fast asphalt court at Cleveland. Richey, who felt he had been slighted by not being chosen in 1969, responded by clobbering Christian Kuhnke, 6-3, 6-4, 6-2, and Wilhelm Bungert, 6-4, 6-4, 7-5, to spearhead a 5-0 U.S. victory. Arthur Ashe beat Bungert, 6-2, 10-8, 6-2, in the opener and erased Kuhnke, 6-8, 10-12, 9-7, 13-11, 6-4, in the meaningless fifth match, the longest singles—86 games—ever in a Davis Cup final. Smith and Bob Lutz beat Bungert and Kuhnke, 6-3, 7-5, 6-5, becoming the only doubles team to clinch the Cup three straight years.

It was a disappointing final, concluding a tarnished Davis Cup campaign. The exclusion of contract pros, even though all major tournaments were now "open," left the Davis Cup a second-rate event. Australia, denied the services of perhaps its 10 best players, fell pathetically to India. Other countries suffered a similar fate. Kuhnke and Bungert, moonlighting from their full-time occupations as lawyer and sporting-goods merchant respectively, were hailed as "the last of the great amateurs" as they surged through six matches, then played like halfhearted amateurs in the finale. Future political turmoil within the Cup was also foreshadowed as South Africa was expelled for two years because the apartheid racial policy of its government was considered disruptive to the competition, and Rhodesia withdrew to avoid political problems.

Largely because contract pros were excluded from the Davis Cup, a new competition—grandly misnamed the World Cup—was organized as a charity event in Boston. It put a two-man team of Australian pros—Newcombe and Fred Stolle—against U.S. Davis Cuppers Richey, Smith, Ashe and Clark Graebner for $20,000 in prize money. The Aussies won, 5-2, at Harvard University's indoor clay courts and, even though the ITF opposed the event, a new Australian-U.S. pro team rivalry had begun.

Australia won the Federation Cup at Freiburg, West Germany, even though Margaret Court opted not to play. Judy Dalton and Karen Krantzcke swept through the competition without losing a match, whitewashing West Germany—2-1 victors over Americans Peaches Bartkowicz, Julie Heldman and Mary Ann Eisel Curtis—in the final.

With Billie Jean King winning two singles and collaborating with Bartkowicz for the first time to win the decisive doubles, the U.S. scored a 4-3 Wightman Cup victory over Great Britain at Wimbledon. King beat Virginia Wade in the opening singles, but had to stop Ann Jones and then team with Bartkowicz for a 7-5, 3-6, 6-2 triumph over Wade and Winnie Shaw to salvage victory after Wade's singles win over Nancy Richey gave the British a 3-2 lead.

The season ended with the first Grand Prix Masters tournament, a six-man round-robin in Tokyo. Cliff Richey, who topped the Grand Prix point standings, was ill and could not participate. Stan Smith and Rod Laver both had 4-1 records in the round-robin, but Smith took the $15,000 first prize because of his head-to-head win over Laver, 4-6, 6-3, 6-4.

The next year, because of the growing strain of the tug-of-war between WCT and the ITF, Smith and Laver would not be playing in the same season-ending playoff tournament. There were negotiations throughout the fall of 1970, trying to develop an accord, and in December WCT and the ITF issued a joint communique pledging that they would "work together toward the development and spectator appeal of the game throughout the world." An agreement in principle for the appearance of WCT contract pros in the 1971 French, Wimbledon, and U.S. Open Championships also was announced, but the cautious harmony turned out to be short-lived.

1971

In 1971, both men's and women's professional tennis were split into rival camps. It was an uneasy, acrimonious year politically, but the game prospered.

On court, there were many highlights: John Newcombe's second consecutive Wimbledon triumph, after he trailed U.S. Army Cpl. Stan Smith by two sets to one in the final; Smith's impressive triumph at Forest Hills; the first "World Championship of Tennis," in which Ken Rosewall upset Rod Laver in the final; a new women's pro tour, dominated by the indefatigable Billie Jean King; and the emergence of Evonne Goolagong, who won the French Open and Wimbledon at age 19, and Chris Evert, who reached the semifinals of the U.S. Open at 16.

Rosewall, who in 1970 had captured his second U.S. Championship 14 years after the first, continued to perform geriatric marvels. He dethroned Arthur Ashe in the Australian Open final, 6-1, 7-5, 6-3, regaining a title he first held in 1953. Newcombe and Tony Roche won the third of their four Australian doubles titles.

Unfortunately, for much of the season the 34 men under contract to World Championship Tennis and the "independent pros" who remained under the authority of their national associations played separate tournaments.

WCT's new "World Championship of Tennis" —a million-dollar series of 20 tournaments in nine countries on four continents—got off to a promising start with the Philadelphia Indoor, where Newcombe beat Laver, 7-6, 7-6, 6-4, for only the second time in a dozen career meetings.

Evonne Goolagong, French and Wimbledon victor, ranked No. 2 in the World Top Ten in 1971. (UPI)

Meanwhile, the independent pros were playing on an expanding indoor circuit promoted by Bill Riordan under the aegis of the USTA. The highlight was the U.S. Indoor at Riordan's hometown of Salisbury, Md., where Clark Graebner came from two sets down to upend Romanian Ilie Nastase in the semifinals, then saved two match points in beating Cliff Richey for the title, 2-6, 7-6, 1-6, 7-6, 6-0.

The Italian Open at Rome was one of several strange hybrid events—co-promoted by WCT as part of its 20-tournament series, but also open to noncontract pros. This made for a week of exceptional matches and excitement on the red clay of Il Foro Italico. Record crowds and profits were recorded before Laver defeated Czech Jan Kodes in the final, 7-5, 6-3, 6-3.

Only a few of the WCT players entered the French Open. After five months of a grueling travel and playing schedule, Ashe—never a factor on European clay—was the only one of WCT's top "names" who opted to go to Paris for two weeks of physically demanding best-of-five-set matches. The mass nonappearance of the "contract pros" infuriated the ITF and was a major

factor in polarizing opposition to WCT. Meanwhile, the dour but energetically industrious Kodes won his second straight French title, beating the more gifted but less persistent Nastase, 8-6, 6-2, 2-6, 7-5, in an absorbing final. Ashe and Marty Riessen, the top two WCT players entered, won the doubles. (Both had been beaten in singles by surprising Frank Froehling, who survived a match point against Ashe in the quarterfinals.)

At Wimbledon, No. 1 seed Laver was ambushed by the inspired serving and volleying of American Tom Gorman, who didn't lose a serve, 9-7, 8-6, 6-3, in the quarterfinals. The best match was an enchanting four-hour quarterfinal in which Rosewall finally outstroked Richey, 6-8, 5-7, 6-4, 9-7, 7-5. The final between Newcombe and Smith had fewer breathtaking rallies and was dominated by slam-bang points accentuating each's serve-volley power, but it also became gripping in the end. Smith seemed in control after a seven-game run that took him to 1-0 in the fourth set, but this was his first major final and he got "a little tired mentally." Newcombe was tougher and seized control, ending his 6-3, 5-7, 2-6, 6-4, 6-4 triumph with an ace. Roy Emerson, twice a winner with Neale Fraser (1959 and 1961), partnered Laver to the latter's first Wimbledon doubles title over Ashe and Dennis Ralston, 4-6, 9-7, 6-8, 6-4, 6-4.

The U.S. Open—minus Laver, defending champ Rosewall, and Emerson, who opted to rest—was less than three hours old when Wimbledon champ Newcombe was rudely dismissed by Kodes—who was unhappy about being unseeded, even though he said tennis on grass courts was "a joke" that he found totally unfunny. This was the first time in 41 years that a top seed failed to survive his opening match—top foreign seed Jean Borotra lost in the 1930 opening round to Berkeley Bell. In 1928 George King beat top American seed John Hennessey in the first round, but Borotra hadn't come in as Wimbledon champ, and Hennessey was no Newcombe.

But Kodes proved it was no fluke. He came back from two sets down against Pierre Barthes, and from two sets to one and a service break down in the fourth to beat Arthur Ashe in the semifinals. Kodes also won the first set of the final against Smith, but the 6-foot-4 Californian had learned from his near miss at Wimbledon. Unflinching on the crucial points, he erased the "bouncing Czech," 3-6, 6-3, 6-2, 7-6 (5-3).

Smith and Erik van Dillen were even at two sets apiece against Newcombe and Englishman Roger Taylor in the doubles final when darkness forced a halt. Rather than resume the next day, it was agreed questionably and with no precedent to improvise: a nine-point sudden-death tie-breaker would decide the championship in a cheap abbreviation unique to the majors. Newcombe-Taylor won it, 5-3.

It was indeed a curious year for men's tennis, climaxed by separate playoffs for the leading "contract" and independent pros.

Laver, Tom Okker, Rosewall, Cliff Drysdale, Ashe, Newcombe, Riessen and Bob Lutz were the top eight men in the WCT standings. They had their playoffs in Houston and Dallas, Rosewall won two magnificent tie-breakers to seize the $50,000 top prize at Dallas Memorial Auditorium over Laver, 6-4, 1-6, 7-6, 7-6.

Smith, Nastase, Zeljko Franulovic, Kodes, Richey, Barthes and Gorman were the seven men who made the round-robin Grand Prix Masters at Paris. Smith collected the $25,000 top bonus prize from the season-long point standings, but Nastase went 6-0 in the Masters, whipping Smith, 5-7, 7-6, 6-3, and collected the tournament's $15,000 top prize. It was the first of Nastase's four victories in the Masters.

At year's end Newcombe and Smith shared Player of the Year honors, but there was no clear-cut No. 1.

The Italian was Laver's biggest title, but he won 7 of 26 tournaments, 82 of 100 matches, and was far and away the leading money winner with $292,717, which made him tennis's first career millionaire. His nine-year pro winnings: $1,006,974.

Despite Army duty, Stan Smith managed to cop the U.S. Open and winnings of more than $100,000 in 1971. (UPI)

His most astounding string came in the second and last Tennis Champions Classic, a series of head-to-head, winner-take-all matches in various cities, leading to a four-man playoff in Madison Square Garden. Laver incredibly swept all 13 of his matches, against top opponents, to win $160,000 in this one event, beating Tom Okker in the final, 6-5, 6-2, 6-1.

Rosewall won 7 of 23 tournaments, including the Australian and South African Opens and his third U.S. Pro Championship, and 70 of 86 matches. He earned $138,371 and would have been unchallenged as "Old Man of the Year" had not Pancho Gonzalez—43, and already a grandfather—beaten Roscoe Tanner, Richey and Jimmy Connors (conqueror of Smith in the semis), 3-6, 6-3, 6-3, in succession to win the $10,000 top prize in the Pacific Southwest Open at Los Angeles.

Newcombe captured five of 19 tournaments, 53 of 67 matches, and amassed $101,514. Smith, who missed the early season because he was in basic training with the U.S. Army, won 6 of 19 tournaments and compiled a 70-13 record that included beating Nastase in the opening match and Ion Tiriac in the decisive singles of the 3-2 U.S. Davis Cup challenge round victory over Romania. Smith earned $100,086. Nastase, who finished the season spectacularly, was the top "independent" earner with $114,000 in winnings.

Relations between the ITF and WCT, strained at the start of the year and aggravated by the French Open, broke down completely at Wimbledon. In a bitter, turbulent press conference, fueled by misunderstanding over several WCT "points of negotiation" that were falsely interpreted by ITF as "demands," both sides admitted that talks aimed at establishing a unified circuit for 1972 had failed miserably.

Two weeks later, at its annual meeting in the northern Italian resort town of Stresa, the ITF voted to ban WCT's "contract pros" from all tournaments and facilities controlled by the ITF and its 93 member national associations, effective at the start of 1972. After 3½ years of "open" tournaments, the contract pros were to be made outcasts again.

In November, new ITF president Allan Heyman announced that Commercial Union Assurance, a London-based worldwide insurance group, was taking over sponsorship of the Grand Prix from Pepsico, and expanding the financial commitment to more than $250,000. WCT, meanwhile, said that it would focus its attention on strengthening its own tournament series, which it shifted to a May windup in 1972 for maximum TV exposure in the U.S. In the first week of 1972, Ken Rosewall won his second consecutive Australian Open; ironically, the man who had won the first Open tournament in 1968 also won the last of the now interrupted Open era, setting a longevity record for the majors: 18 years between his first and last titles, both Australia, 1953 and 1971.

Meanwhile, women's tennis—which a year earlier seemed to be overshadowed by the men's game and suffering from a dearth of refreshing young talent—took a dramatically vibrant upturn.

From the renegade Virginia Slims of Houston tournament the previous September sprang a new women's tour with $309,000 in prize money. Billie Jean King, who energetically promoted the Virginia Slims Circuit—one observer suggested that she "single-handedly talked it into prominence" —won the lioness' share of the rewards: $117,000. She became the first woman athlete to break the $100,000-in-a-year milestone.

Publisher Gladys Heldman was the behind-the-scenes driving force, arranging 14 tournaments with combined prize money of $189,100 for the first four months in 1971, while King was the oncourt dynamo and chief drumbeater. Trumpeting that she had her "wheels back" after knee surgery in July 1970, Billie Jean won the first five tournaments on the new tour, at San Francisco, her native Long Beach, Milwaukee, Oklahoma City and Chattanooga. She beat Rosemary Casals in the first four finals, then Ann Jones, and teamed with Casals to win the doubles at the first seven Slims tournaments.

At Philadelphia—where word came that the USTA had lifted its suspension of the "rebel" women—Françoise Durr snapped King's singles streak in the semifinals, and Casals won the tournament. King, who had been ineligible as a "contract pro" for two years, then recovered the U.S. Indoor title she had held from 1966 through 1968, beating Casals again in the final, 4-6, 6-2, 6-3. Rosie, so long the whipping girl, got revenge in the tour's disappointing New York stop at the dingy old 34th Street Armory. In all, King won eight of the inaugural 14 tournaments. Ann Jones won the biggest prize ($9,000) at Las Vegas, and amateur Chris Evert was the most surprising winner, striking down Durr, Judy Alvarez, an ailing King, and Julie Heldman, 6-1, 6-2, to capture her first of 157 pro tourney titles, at St. Petersburg, Fla.

The winter/spring tour—which captured a great deal of media attention, thanks to the clever and energetic promotion of Heldman and King and the emerging fascination with "women's liberation" —was so successful that the women's tour added five summer tournaments, starting with a $40,000 Virginia Slims International at Houston. King captured the $10,000 first prize there, beating Australian Kerry Melville in the final, and went on to take the $10,000 top bonus in the first women's Grand Prix. King's total of $117,000 in prize money was the highest sum for any American, male or female.

While King & Co. were pioneering under the banner of "Women's Lob," Margaret Court and Evonne Goolagong dominated the traditional early season. Court beat Ann Jones in three tough sets, Goolagong walloped Virginia Wade, and Court teamed with hometown girl Lesley Hunt to beat Wade and Winnie Shaw as Australia won the 1971 Federation Cup at Perth (actually played the last week in 1970) with a 3-0 victory over Great Britain in the final. With most of the top U.S. players suspended as punishment for taking part in the new women's pro group, the USTA sent a young team of Patti Hogan and Sharon Walsh, who lost to Britain in the semis.

The Australian Open was played in March, three months later than usual, and Court beat Goolagong, 2-6, 7-6, 7-5, to take her sixth consecutive major singles title (1969 Forest Hills, 1970 Australian, French, Wimbledon, and U.S., 1971 Australian). Margaret beat Evonne again, 6-3, 6-1, in the final of the South African Open (Goolagong, of one-eighth aboriginal descent, was the first "nonwhite" woman to compete in Johannesburg). They teamed to win the doubles.

Virginia Wade won the Italian Open and Billie Jean King the German, both over Helga Niessen Masthoff in the finals, and then Court's major winning streak of 35 matches was surprisingly terminated in the third round of the French by Gail Sherriff Chanfreau, who played the match of her life to win, 6-3, 6-4. She lost in the next round to Helen Gourlay, who went on to beat 1968 titlist Nancy Richey in the semis. Goolagong came through the other half easily and beat Gourlay in the final, 6-3, 7-5, the first player since Althea Gibson in 1956 to win the

tournament the first time she played. Durr, alongside Chanfreau, won her fifth consecutive doubles title.

Having won the most prestigious clay-court title, third-seeded Goolagong cemented the No. 1 women's ranking for the year by winning Wimbledon in her second appearance on the grass of the All England Club. The most ethereal of tennis players, graceful, smiling, and free-spirited, she captivated the galleries in dismissing Nancy Richey Gunter in the quarters, 6-3, 6-2; second-seeded Billie Jean King in the semis, 6-4, 6-4; and first-seeded Court in the final, 6-4, 6-1. Couturier Teddy Tinling made Goolagong a special dress for the final, white with a scalloped hem and lilac lining and adornments; his staff worked through the night to get it ready, and sent it to Wimbledon with a "good luck" message sewn in, and a silver horseshoe. Such was the spirit of the occasion as Evonne became the youngest champion since Karen Susman, 19, in 1962. King and Casals collaborated on their fourth Wimbledon doubles title, and King–Owen Davidson took the mixed over Court–Marty Riessen, 3-6, 6-2, 15-13, the final set being the longest in any Wimbledon mixed final.

Despite her triumphs in Paris and London, Goolagong's coach, Vic Edwards, adhered to his long-range plan of not having Evonne play the U.S. circuit until 1972. Therefore, she did not enter the U.S. Open. Neither did Margaret Court nor Ann Jones, both of whom were pregnant. But just when it appeared that Billie Jean King would have the stage to herself, another appealing young rival emerged: Chris Evert.

A 16-year-old high-school student from Fort Lauderdale, Fla., she had beaten Court on clay in Charlotte, N.C., the previous fall and won the Virginia Slims tournament at St. Petersberg on the same surface. But she gained national attention for the first time as the heroine of the 4-3 U.S. Wightman Cup victory over Great Britain on an ultra-slow rubberized court in Cleveland in August. Three months younger than Maureen Connolly had been in her debut 20 years earlier, Chris crunched Winnie Shaw, 6-0, 6-4, in the opener and a nervous and off-form Virginia Wade, 6-1, 6-1, in the decisive sixth match, which clinched victory for the injury-riddled U.S. team.

Evert then moved on to the Eastern Grass Court Championships at South Orange, N. J., and won there, even though her only previous tournament on grass had been the National Girls 18 singles. At Forest Hills, she immediately became the darling of the crowds, the star of the show since three prominent men were missing. Playing every match in the old concrete stadium, she beat Edda Buding, 6-1, 6-0; Mary Ann Eisel, 4-6, 7-6, 6-1, after Eisel had six match points; Françoise Durr, 2-6, 6-2, 6-3; and Lesley Hunt, 4-6, 6-2, 6-3, to supplant Little Mo Connolly as the youngest American semifinalist since 1951—16 years, 9 months, to 16 years, 11 months. Betty Nuthall of England had been 16 years, 3½ months in 1927. Eisel, Durr and Hunt all departed in tears, intimidated by Chrissie's nerveless backcourt stroking and the wildly partisan crowds cheering for "Cinderella in Sneakers."

King had too much of a fast-court arsenal for Evert and ended her fairy tale in the semis, 6-3, 6-2. BJK wrapped up her second Forest Hills title by beating Casals, 6-4, 7-6, sealing the No. 1 U.S. ranking for the fifth time. Her record for the season was 112-13, including victories in 17 out of 31 tournaments.

King's persistent drive to the $100,000 landmark was slowed when she and Casals walked off the court because of a line call dispute at 6-6 in the first set of the final of the Pacific Southwest Open, which they had boycotted the year before. It was one of the strangest episodes in U.S. tournament history and both players were later fined for their "double default." BJK finally went over the 100-grand mark at Phoenix, where she again beat Casals, 7-5, 6-1, in the final. King celebrated with champagne in the dressing room, and at a news conference in New York the following week received a congratulatory phone call from President Richard Nixon.

Preparing for the last challenge round, a 71-year-old format through which the Cup-holding country was required to play only the challenging country, U.S. captain Ed Turville infuriated his singles ace of 1970, Cliff Richey, by sportingly deciding that the 1971 windup would be contested on clay, at Charlotte, N.C. Romania, on the backs of Ilie Nastase and Ion Tiriac, had come through six matches to reach the ultimate round for a second time. Two years earlier in Cleveland they had been blasted off a lickety-split asphalt court, and Turville felt it would be more entertaining and fairer to stage this one on clay. Richey felt it was treason, giving it away to the dirt-bred Romanians—and quit the team.

Turville contended it would be more exciting, and it certainly was, 3-2. Searching for a singles replacement for Richey to accompany Smith, he came up with a surprise, 28-year-old Frank Froehling, III, who hadn't been on the team for six years. After Smith beat Nastase to give the U.S. a 1-0 lead, long-legged Froehling (called "Spider Man") had his own surprise for Tiriac: the greatest Cup-round comeback for an American in more than a half-century, 3-6, 1-6, 6-1, 6-3, 8-6. That was the critical point for the U.S. since Nastase and Tiriac snuffed Smith and Erik van Dillen in doubles, and Nastase beat Froehling, though after Smith clinched over Tiriac, 8-6, 6-3, 6-0. With little more than a forehand, and heart, Froehling survived seven break points, three in the opening game, to take the third set and begin turning it his way. Tiriac fought back from a break down, saved a match point in the fifth to 5-5; and darkness, at 6-6, pushed them to the next day, which was all the American's. He broke Tiriac on a second match point with a buzzing forehand, and the U.S. was on its way to a fourth straight Cup.

Tiriac's straight-set win over Edison Mandarino in the decisive fifth match at São Paulo had clinched a 3-2 victory over Brazil and landed the Romanians in Charlotte.

1972

In 1972, a peace agreement was reached between the International Tennis Federation and

World Championship Tennis, reintegrating a men's game that had briefly and regrettably regressed into segregated "contract pro" and "independent pro" circuits, but not in time for the 32 WCT contractees to participate in the French Open or Wimbledon. Stan Smith's triumphs over Ilie Nastase in the Wimbledon final and the Davis Cup gave him the edge over the mercurial Romanian, who won the U.S. Open, for the No. 1 men's ranking. Meanwhile, Billie Jean King swept the French, Wimbledon and U.S. Open titles—she didn't enter the Australian—and again dominated the ascending Virginia Slims circuit, emphatically ruling women's tennis and giving the U.S. dual supremacy in men's and women's tennis for the first time since 1955.

Despite the unsatisfactory separate circuits for men most of the year, prize money kept spiraling, to more than $5 million worldwide. Nastase was the top earner at $176,000, with Smith second at $142,300, even though he was in the U.S. Army. Four other men (WCT employees Ken Rosewall, Arthur Ashe, John Newcombe and Rod Laver) and one woman, King, collected more than $100,000.

It also was a year of outstanding matches, none finer than the three-hour, 34-minute classic between Rosewall and Laver in the final of the WCT Championships at Dallas in May. Laver was favored to grab the $50,000 plum that had eluded him the previous November, but Rosewall—an enduring marvel at age 38—again stole it. Laver revived himself from 1-4 in the final set, saved a match point with an ace, and had the match on his racket at 5-4 in the "lingering death" tie-breaker, with two serves to come. He pounded both deep to Rosewall's backhand corner, but tennis' most splendid antique reached for vintage return winners. Laver failed to return the exhausted Rosewall's last serve and it was over, 4-6, 6-0, 6-3, 6-7, 7-6. This had been a duel of torrid, exquisite shotmaking on a 90-degree Mother's Day afternoon, and the sell-out crowd of 9,500 at Moody Coliseum and a national television audience of 21 million were enthralled. Many old hands said it might have been the greatest match

of all time, and it was certainly the one that put tennis over as a TV sport in America. It was the closest finish of an important tourney until 1988, when Boris Becker won the Masters final over Ivan Lendl, also a 7-5 fifth-set tie-breaker.

In order to restructure its season for a spring windup, the most advantageous time for U.S. television, WCT counted the last 10 tournaments of 1971 and 10 between January and April 1972 in its point standings. Laver won the Philadelphia opener, rechristened the U.S. Pro Indoor, and four more tournaments to top the point standings heading into the Dallas playoffs. Behind him were Rosewall, Tom Okker, Cliff Drysdale, Marty Riessen, Arthur Ashe, Bob Lutz and John Newcombe.

Meanwhile, the "independent pros" were playing the USTA Indoor Circuit organized by Bill Riordan. Smith played only five of 13 events, but won four in a row, starting with the U.S. Indoor over Nastase, 5-7, 6-2, 6-3, 6-4. Also prominent were rookie pro Jimmy Connors—he dropped out of UCLA after becoming the first freshman to win the Intercollegiate singles in 1971—and "Old Wolf" Pancho Gonzalez, who, at 43, beat Frenchman Georges Goven from two sets down, 7-6, 6-3, 7-5, to win the Des Moines Indoor. He was the oldest title winner of the open era.

Rosewall had begun the New Year by beating 37-year-old fellow Aussie Mal Anderson in the final of the Australian Open, the last ITF tournament open to WCT pros before the ban voted the previous July went into effect. Rosewall's last Australian championship came 19 years after his first, a unique span between major championships.

Another veteran Aussie, 35-year-old Roy Emerson, saved a match point and beat Lutz, 4-6, 7-6, 6-3, to give Australia the pivotal point in a 6-1 victory over the U.S. in a World Cup marked by Laver's first appearance.

A contemporary of Laver and Emerson, the elegant Spaniard Andres Gimeno, nearly 35, who had left WCT to return to "independent pro" status, won his only major singles title, taking the French Open, over surprising ninth-seeded Frenchman Patrick Proisy, 4-6, 6-3, 6-1, 6-1. Gimeno became the event's oldest champ. Proisy had ended top-seeded Jan Kodes' 17-match French winning streak and bid for a third successive title in the quarters, and had eliminated Italian and fourth-seeded German champ Manuel Orantes in the semis. Bob Hewitt and Frew McMillan captured their first French doubles title, and within a month would add the Wimbledon crown.

Smith, 1971 runner-up to the now disenfranchised Newcombe (who went to court to try to break the ITF ban and get a crack at a third straight title), was an overwhelming favorite at Wimbledon. The men's singles was dull until the final—the first ever played on Sunday, after a rain delay—when Smith and Nastase went after each other for five absorbing sets. It was Smith's serve-volley power and forthright resolve against Nastase's incomparable speed, agility and eccentric artistry. The fifth set was electrifying. Smith escaped two break points in the fifth game, which went to seven agonizing deuces, the first with a lunging volley off the frame of his wood racket. Nastase brushed aside two match points on his serve at 4-5, saved another after having 40-0 at 5-6, then netted an easy, high backhand volley on match point No. 4. The scores of Smith's scintillating triumph: 3-6, 6-3, 6-3, 4-6, 7-5.

Back in America, Lutz won the U.S. Pro Championship at Longwood, over Tom Okker, 6-4, 2-6, 6-1, 6-4, ending a nine-year Australian rule to become the first American champ since Butch Buchholz in 1962. But it was the U.S. Open that commanded the most attention.

Lamar Hunt, the Texas millionaire who bankrolled WCT, and Allan Heyman, the Danish-born English lawyer who was president of the ITF, had been meeting secretly throughout the winter and spring, prompted by Americans Donald Dell and Jack Kramer to find a solution to re-unify the men's game. In April, they reached an accord to divide the season into two segments, starting in 1973. WCT would have free reign the

first four months of the year, expanding to two groups of 32 players each that would play an 11-tournament series to qualify four men from each group for the May WCT finals in Dallas. During that period, no other tournaments with more than $20,000 would be sanctioned. The last eight months of the year would belong to the ITF for its Grand Prix and Masters.

With this agreement—later modified considerably, under pressure of an antitrust suit by Bill Riordan, who felt he had been sold down the river—the ban of WCT players from the traditional circuit was removed in July, making Forest Hills the year's only big event open to everybody.

It turned out to be a wild tournament. Second-seeded Rosewall was beaten by Mark Cox in the second round; third-seeded Laver by Cliff Richey in the fourth; first-seeded Smith by Ashe in the quarters; fifth-seeded Newcombe by Fred Stolle; seventh-seeded Tom Okker by Roscoe Tanner; and eighth-seeded Kodes by Alex "Sandy" Mayer, all in the third round. Three Americans (Ashe, Richey and Tom Gorman) made the semis for the first time in 21 years, but the lone foreigner, fourth-seeded Nastase, won the tournament.

"Nasty" incurred the enmity of 14,690 spectators with temper tantrums early in the final but gradually won them over with his shot-making genius. He trailed by two sets to one, 1-3 and 2-4 in the fourth set, and had a break point against him for 1-4. Ashe failed to get a backhand return in play, and faded thereafter, Nastase running five straight games for the set and recovering quickly after losing his serve in the first game of the fifth. Nasty became the first European since Manolo Santana in 1965, and the first ever from Eastern Europe to triumph on the soft grass at Forest Hills, 3-6, 6-3, 6-7 (1-5), 6-4, 6-3. Roger Taylor, champ with Newcombe the year before, teamed up with Cliff Drysdale to whip Newcombe and Owen Davidson in the doubles final.

Smith sealed his No. 1 ranking in the fall, winning the Pacific Southwest Open, Stockholm and Paris Indoor and giving a towering performance in the Davis Cup final at Bucharest.

The Davis Cup nations had voted in 1971 to do away with the challenge round in which the defending nation sat out and waited for a challenger to plow through zonal competitions. Thus the U.S. had to follow an unprecedented road for a defending champion, five matches, all in the foes' backyards, the last four on dreaded red clay. The U.S. lost but one singles match in sprinting past Commonwealth Caribbean, Mexico and Chile to the 3-2 semifinal in Spain. Gritty little 19-year-old rookie Harold Solomon was an essential on the baseline, winning both singles at Santiago, and getting everything back to get back into his opening test against the man captain Dennis Ralston remembered as his own tormentor the last time the U.S. visited Barcelona for a 4-1 defeat in 1965: Juan Gisbert. After Smith lost to Gimeno, just turned 35 and back on the team after 11 years as a banned pro, it was a must-win situation for Solly. Reprieved by nightfall after the third set, he was rejuvenated the next day to win, 9-7, 7-5, 0-6, 1-6, 6-4.

Unbeaten for the campaign, Smith and Erik van Dillen got the doubles point and a 2-1 lead. When Gimeno beat Solomon, 6-3, 6-1, 2-6, 6-1, it was up to Smith. The Cup stalwart, for whom clinching was a specialty, started feeling more comfortable on European soil in patiently beating Gisbert, 11-9, 10-8, 6-4, ordering the tickets for the final destination. Surprisingly it turned out to be Bucharest.

Although the draw for the new Cup format gave the U.S. choice of ground for the final against Romania, the shrewd Ion Tiriac convinced USTA President Robert Colwell that the Romanians were being treated unfairly and should have that privilege since they'd played the 1969 and 1971 challenge rounds in the U.S. The U.S. team, startled and hurt that Colwell would give away the home-court edge, threatened mutiny. Ralston, ever calm, sold them on being underdogs, beating the other guys at their place.

Romania, with the brilliant Nastase and the menacing Tiriac at home on the red clay of the

Romania's Ilie Nastase led the run to the bank in 1972, winning at Forest Hills, the first European to do so since Spain's Manolo Santana in 1965. (UPI)

Progresul Sports Club, was a heavy favorite. Nastase boasted, "We cannot lose at home" —and his record of 19 straight Cup singles victories and 13 consecutive Romanian triumphs in Bucharest seemed to support his braggadocio. Slow clay, an adoring and vocal home crowd and notoriously patriotic linesmen all favored Nastase and Tiriac.

This was the first Davis Cup final in Europe in 39 years, and perhaps the greatest international sporting occasion ever in Bucharest, where likenesses of Nastase and Tiriac were everywhere. But the pressure of great expectations worked in reverse. Smith played undoubtedly his finest match on clay, while Nastase was high-strung and erratic as the American took the critical opener, 11-9, 6-2, 6-3, though Nastase served for the first set at 9-8. Tiriac, the brooding former ice hockey international who claims kinship with Dracula, used every ploy of gamesmanship, orchestrating the crowd and the linesmen, to come from two sets down and beat Tom Gorman, 4-6, 2-6, 6-4, 6-3, 6-2, in the second match. The doubles, however, was a Romanian disaster.

Once one of the world's premier teams, Nastase and Tiriac had fallen out as friends, and their incompatibility showed as Smith and van Dillen, playing with skill and élan, humiliated the home team, 6-2, 6-0, 6-3. Tiriac summoned all his wiles and battled heroically in the fourth match, but Smith was too good for him and clinched the Cup, 4-6, 6-2, 6-4, 2-6, 6-0. Nastase beat Gorman in the meaningless fifth match.

It had been a wild weekend in Bucharest, made unforgettable by the fervor of the fans, the thievery of the linesmen, the machinations of Tiriac, and extraordinarily heavy security in the aftermath of the Olympic massacre at Munich. (There had been rumors of threats against two Jewish members of the U.S. squad, Solomon and Brian Gottfried.) But in the end, captain Dennis Ralston's brigade could savor the finest victory ever by a U.S. team away from home.

Once again there were separate playoffs for "contract pros" and "independents" at the end of the year. WCT scheduled a makeshift "winter championship" in Rome for the top eight men in a summer-fall circuit that filled the gap before a new two-group format started in 1973. Ashe won the $25,000 first prize, beating Nikki Pilic, Okker and Lutz, 6-2, 3-6, 6-3, 3-6, 7-6.

The Commercial Union Masters was played in Barcelona with the new format—two four-man round-robin groups, with the two players with the best records in each advancing to "knockout" semis and final. Gorman had Smith beaten in one semi, but hurt his back and defaulted so as not to wreck the final. Nastase repeated as champion, beating Smith in a rousing final, 6-3, 6-2, 3-6, 2-6, 6-3, but it was his only victory in five meetings on the year with the tall Californian.

One of the most significant developments of 1972 was the formation, at the U.S. Open, of a new players' guild—the Association of Tennis Professionals. Some 50 players paid $400 initial dues, and Washington attorney Donald Dell—former U.S. Davis Cup captain, then personal manager for a number of top players—enlisted Jack Kramer as executive director. The urbane Cliff Drysdale was elected president and Dell became the Association's legal counsel. Other players' associations had come and gone in the past, but the ATP was carefully constituted and loomed as a major new force in the pro game's politics and administration.

The politics of women's tennis in 1972 began with conciliation and ended with a new rift.

Early in the year Gladys Heldman, organizer of the rebel women's pro tour the year before, was appointed by the USTA as coordinator of women's tennis and director of the women's tour in a peace effort. Thus empowered, she expanded the winter tour to $302,000 in prize money. But by September the honeymoon was over. Heldman resigned her USTA post amid mutual mistrust and formed the Women's International Tennis Federation. She took the USTA to court for alleged antitrust violations. Meanwhile, the USTA appointed U.S. Wightman Cup captain Edy McGoldrick to form a women's tour in opposition to Heldman's in the winter-spring of 1973.

On the tennis court, there was no question who was boss in 1972. King did not play the Australian Open, but swept the rest of the major singles titles with the loss of only one set, to Virginia Wade in the quarterfinals at Wimbledon. Billie Jean won 10 of 24 tournaments, compiled an 87-13 record, ran away with the women's Grand Prix top prize, and exceeded her prize money landmark of 1971, earning $119,000. Against her greatest career rivals, she was 3-2 over Margaret Court (back on the circuit after the birth of her first child, Daniel) and 4-3 over Nancy Richey Gunter for the year.

Wade won her first Australian Open title, over Goolagong, 6-4, 6-4. King won her first French Open title—joining Doris Hart, Maureen Connolly, Shirley Fry and Court as the only women to have won all four major singles titles—with a 6-3, 6-3 triumph over Goolagong. (They would be joined by Chris Evert in 1982, Martina Navratilova in 1983 and Steffi Graf in

1988.) BJK also dethroned Goolagong, 6-3, 6-3, at Wimbledon after Evonne had thrillingly won her first meeting with Chris Evert in the semis.

At the U.S. Open, King beat Wade in the quarters, 6-2, 7-5; Court in the semis, 6-4, 6-4; and Kerry Melville—who ripped Evert in the semis by skidding clever slices short, low and wide to Chrissie's two-fisted backhand—for the $10,000 first prize, 6-3, 7-5.

Dutchwoman Betty Stove was the Woman of the Year in doubles, teaming with King to win the French and Wimbledon and with Françoise Durr to take the U.S. Open. She was the first woman to win all three in a season since Darlene Hard and Maria Bueno did so in 1960.

Evert, still an amateur at age 17, was the only player with a winning record over King for the year: 3-1, including a 6-1, 6-0 victory in the final of the Virginia Slims tournament in her hometown of Fort Lauderdale. She also won the richest women's tournament, the inaugural season-climaxing $100,000 Virginia Slims Championship at Boca Raton, Fla.—beating King and Melville, 7-5, 6-4, in the final two rounds after her 15-year-old sister, Jeanne, erased Court in the third round—but could not accept the $25,000 first prize.

Evert ranked No. 3 in the U.S. behind King and Gunter (who beat her all three times they played), compiling a 47-7 record, winning four tournaments. She spearheaded the 5-2 U.S. Wightman Cup victory over Great Britain at Wimbledon, beating Wade and Joyce Williams in singles; then beat Court and Goolagong for the only two U.S. victories in a 5-2 loss to Australia in the inaugural Bonne Bell Cup at Cleveland. Evert also won her first adult national title—the first of four consecutive U.S. Clay Court singles at Indianapolis—by beating Court in the semis and Goolagong in the final, 7-6, 6-1.

The Maureen Connolly Brinker Indoor at Dallas was the first tournament in which both Goolagong and Evert competed, but King delayed their first meeting. She fought off a 1-3, 15-40 deficit and later cramps in the final set to beat Evert in the quarters, and came from behind again to beat Goolagong in the semis. Exhausted, she fell easily to Gunter in the final, 7-6, 6-1.

The magical first encounter between the two radiant new princesses of women's tennis came, appropriately, in the semis at Wimbledon. It was a majestic match worthy of the occasion, Goolagong winning, 4-6, 6-3, 6-4, after trailing 0-3 in the second and 2-3 (down a break) in the third. Evert promptly won the next two meetings, however, setting the tone for their career rivalry.

The Virginia Slims circuit continued to grow, offering $525,775 in prize purses for 21 tournaments, but the appeal of Evert and Goolagong—who could not be enticed by Heldman to side with her in a war against the ITF establishment—made them the cornerstones of the rival USTA circuit in 1973.

1973

A questionable Centennial was celebrated throughout tennis in 1973. It commemorated the then-accepted, but subsequently disproved, theory of origin of the modern sport at a shooting party in Wales. Supposedly Major Walter Clopton Wingfield introduced the game he later patented in 1874. Perhaps it was fitting, considering that 1973 was the game's most peculiar year.

The landmark match of the year did not come in any of the traditional major tournaments. There was nothing traditional at all about the celebrated "Battle of the Sexes" between 29-year-old Billie Jean King and 55-year-old Bobby Riggs, the self-proclaimed "king of male chauvinist pigs," at Houston's Astrodome the night of September 20. But this spectacle—roughly equal parts tennis, carnival, and sociological phenomenon—captured the fancy of America as no pure tennis match ever had. The crowd of 30,472, paying as much as $100 a seat, was the largest ever to witness a tennis match. Some 50 million more watched on prime-time television. The

In the "Battle of the Sexes" in 1973, Bobby Riggs cleared the net, and Billie Jean King cleared $100,000. (UPI)

whole gaudy promotion was worth supposedly $3 million, and King collected a $100,000 winner-take-all purse, plus ancillary revenues, for squashing Riggs, 6-4, 6-3, 6-3. He got a big chunk of cash, too.

Riggs, the outspoken hustler who had won Wimbledon and the U.S. Championship in 1939, created the bonanza by a challenge proclaiming that women's lib was a farce and that the best of the female tennis pros couldn't even beat him, "an old man with one foot in the grave." He challenged Margaret Court to a winner-take-all challenge match on Mother's Day at a California resort he was plugging in Ramona. She was the ideal victim for his well-perfected "psych job" and assortment of junk shots. Margaret choked and Riggs won, 6-2, 6-1. That set the stage for the challenge against Billie Jean, the leading voice of women's lib in sports.

The whole ballyhooed extravaganza was just right for the times, and it became a national media event, front-page news in papers and magazines across the country. King exulted in her victory, not as a great competitive triumph but as "a culmination" of her years of striving to demonstrate that tennis could be big-league entertainment for the masses, and that women could play.

Tennis was clearly the "in" sport of the mid-'70s. Sales of tennis equipment, clothing and vacations were burgeoning, and though the pro game remained plagued with disputes—notably an antitrust suit in women's tennis and a boycott of Wimbledon by the men's Association of Tennis Professionals—it continued to grow quickly. Prize money in 1973 rose to nearly $6 million.

World Championship Tennis introduced the new format agreed to in its 1972 accord with the International Lawn Tennis Federation: a January-through-May series with a field of 64 players split into two groups of 32, playing parallel tours of 11 $50,000 tournaments. The top four men of each group (Stan Smith, Rod Laver, Roy Emerson and John Alexander of "A" ; Ken Rosewall, Arthur Ashe, Marty Riessen and Roger Taylor of "B") went to Dallas for the $100,000 final.

Smith, who had won four consecutive tournaments and 6 of 11 to top Laver (three victories) in his group, took the $50,000 top prize by beating Ashe, 6-3, 6-3, 4-6, 6-4. Ashe had ended Rosewall's bid for a third straight Dallas title in a five-set semi, and Smith waylaid Laver.

For the first time, WCT also conducted a doubles competition, using the same format as singles. Smith and Lutz won the $40,000 first prize in the playoffs at Montreal, beating Riessen and Tom Okker, 6-2, 7-6, 6-0.

Running concurrently with the WCT tour for three months was the USTA Indoor Circuit of Bill Riordan, who refused to be dealt out by the WCT-ITF deal dividing the season, and threat-

John Newcombe made the winner's circle at the 1973 Open and helped bring the Davis Cup back to Australia. (UPI)

ened restraint-of-trade proceedings if forced to limit the prize money in his tournaments. His headliners were Jimmy Connors and Ilie Nastase, both of whom he managed at the time. Connors won six of the eight events he played, including the U.S. Indoor over Germany's Karl Meiler, 3-6, 7-6, 7-6, 6-3.

John Newcombe started the year by winning his first Australian Open title over New Zealander Onny Parun, 6-3, 6-7, 7-5, 6-1, and sharing the doubles with countryman Mal Anderson. Newcombe also won the French doubles with Okker, but slumped badly until rededicating himself late in the year, winning the U.S. Open and teaming with Laver to return the Davis Cup to Australia in the first year it was open to "contract pros."

On balance, the No. 1 ranking had to go to Nastase, the volatile Romanian (he accumulated fines totaling $11,000) who won 15 of 31 tournaments, 118 of 135 matches, and led the money earning list with $228,750, including a $55,000 bonus for topping the Grand Prix standings. He clobbered Manuel Orantes in the Italian Open final, 6-1, 6-1, 6-1; swept through the French

Open without losing a set (Nikki Pilic was his final victim, 6-3, 6-3, 6-0), topped the Grand Prix standings and won the Masters for the third straight year, beating Newcombe in the round-robin and personal nemesis Okker in the final, 6-3, 7-5, 4-6, 6-3, at Boston.

Nastase played indifferently at Wimbledon, where he was considered a shoo-in because of the boycott, but was beaten in the fourth round by Intercollegiate champ Sandy Mayer, and he was defeated at Forest Hills, where Andrew Pattison ambushed him in the second round. But his overall record was the best.

The No. 1 U.S. men's ranking was shared for the only time in history. The ranking committee could not choose between Smith, who won eight of 19 tournaments and 81 of 103 matches but lost his world-beating form after peaking in May, and Connors, who won 10 of 21 tournaments and 81 of 97 matches, capturing the U.S. Pro and South African Open titles.

Connors, just 20, was the brightest of several ascending youngsters, including Bjorn Borg and Brian Gottfried (winner of the $30,000 first prize at the ATP's Alan King Classic in Las Vegas, over Ashe). Connors was the youngest man atop the American rankings since one of his mentors, Pancho Gonzalez, ruled at 20 in 1948, and Smith was the first to be No. 1 four times since Bill Tilden gained the top spot for the 10th time in 1929.

Connors, brimming with confidence after his fine showing on the less-strenuous-than-WCT U.S. Indoor circuit, knocked off top-seeded Smith in the first round of the U.S. Pro Championships and went on to whip Ray Moore, Dick Stockton, Cliff Richey and Arthur Ashe, 6-4, 4-6, 6-4, 6-2, for the title. He saved a match point in beating Smith again at the Pacific Southwest and escaped another match point in beating out Smith, 6-0, 3-6, 7-6, for a semifinal berth in the Grand Prix Masters, giving him a 3-0 record against Stan for the calendar year. (Smith was the only player to reach both the WCT and Masters playoffs.)

The already turbulent political waters in tennis were muddied further by formation of a league called World Team Tennis, which planned to start intercity team competition using a unique, Americanized format in 1974. Dennis Murphy, who had helped found the American Basketball Association and the World Hockey Association, envisioned 16 teams with six players apiece under contract competing in a May-through-August season.

Jack Kramer and the ATP board came out staunchly opposed to WTT, saying it would harm the long-range players' interest in a healthy worldwide tournament circuit, but even as discussions between the ITF and ATP about team tennis were scheduled, a more immediate problem arose.

When ATP member Nikki Pilic was suspended by the Yugoslav Tennis Federation for failing to participate in a Davis Cup series to which he had allegedly committed himself, ATP members objected, claiming that this was precisely the sort of arbitrary disciplinary power by a national association that the players' association had been formed to counteract. An ATP threat to withdraw all its 70 members from the French Open if Pilic was barred from the tournament was averted by a delaying tactic: an appeal hearing before the ITF Emergency Committee, which reduced Pilic's suspension from three months to one month.

This did not satisfy the ATP board, which contended that only their own association should have disciplinary authority over players. Many also felt that the one-month suspension, which included Wimbledon, was devised by the ITF to demonstrate its muscle because it believed the players would never support a boycott of the world's premier tournament. Thus "the Pilic Affair" became a test of the will and organization of the new association. Many ATP leaders felt that if they gave in on this first showdown, they would never be strong, whereas if they held firm and proved to the ITF that even Wimbledon was not sacred, the ATP's unity and power would never be doubted in the future.

After days of tortuous meetings and attempts to find compromises, including the ATP's seeking an injunction in Britain's High Court forcing Wimbledon to accept Pilic's entry, ATP members voted to withdraw en masse if Pilic were barred from Wimbledon. Seventy-nine men did withdraw their entries, including 13 of the original 16 seeds; Ilie Nastase, Englishman Roger Taylor and Australian Ray Keldie were the only members who did not withdraw. (They were later fined by the ATP.)

Amid ferocious press criticism and bitterness, the tournament was played with a second-rate men's field. The British public, taking up the press crusade that "Wimbledon is bigger than a few spoiled players," turned out in near-record numbers. They made heroes of Nastase, Taylor and such bright newcomers as Connors and Swedish teenager Borg, who became the immediate heartthrob of squealing British schoolgirls.

Nastase, an overwhelming favorite, was beaten at the end of the first week by Mayer, who went on to reach the semifinals. Jan Kodes won the championship, the first Czech to do so since expatriate Jaroslav Drobny in 1954, beating Soviet No. 1 Alex Metreveli, 6-1, 9-8, 6-3, in a predictably uninspiring final. Nastase and Connors clowned their way to a five-set victory over Australians John Cooper and Neale Fraser in the doubles final.

In one sense, the success of the boycotted Wimbledon was a triumph for the tournament, proving again what an unshakable institution it is, an important part of British summer life. But in the long run, the boycott made the ATP. The players' message to the ITF was clear. They were finally united in an organization to influence their own destiny. If they could stand up to Wimbledon, they could stand up to any authority. The ATP was established as a political force to be reckoned with in the future.

Meanwhile, with Wimbledon sacrificed for one year, the U.S. Open became the men's most important competitive test of 1973. Nastase, co-seeded No.1 with Smith, squandered a two-set lead and lost to Rhodesian journeyman Pattison. Kodes, who resented being downgraded as a "cheese champion" at Wimbledon, returned serve spectacularly in going all the way to the final, saving a match point at nightfall to outstroke Smith, 7-5, 6-7, 1-6, 6-1, 7-5, in the semifinals. Kodes almost repeated his 1971 upset over Newcombe, this time in the final instead of the first round, but the rugged Australian ultimately had too much firepower and won a spectacular finale, 6-4, 1-6, 4-6, 6-2, 6-3. Newcombe and Davidson beat countrymen Laver and Rosewall in the doubles final.

Even though they'd been away from Davis Cup for a long time in the wilderness of professionalism, each artifact in Capt. Neale Fraser's "Antique Show"—Ken Rosewall, 38, Mal Anderson, 38, Laver, 35, Newcombe, 27—made solid contributions in victories over Japan, India, Czechoslovakia and the U.S. that restored the silver tub to Australia. They may have been the greatest quartet assembled for such a purpose, Laver absent for 10 campaigns, Rosewall 16, Anderson 14, Newcombe 5. Laver decided late in autumn to be part of it, and played his way into the lineup by winning the Australian Indoor, beating Rosewall, then Newcombe, 3-6, 7-5, 6-3, 3-6, 6-4, just prior to the semi against the Czechs on Melbourne grass. He won all four of his singles in that engagement (6-3, 6-3, 7-5, over Wimbledon champ Kodes) and a 5-0 whitewash of the U.S. in the final, ending the Americans' five-year reign. In the Cup's first indoor final, before disappointing crowds totaling about 10,000 for three days at Cleveland's Public Auditorium, Newcombe set the tone by beating Smith in the opener, 6-1, 3-6, 6-3, 3-6, 6-4. Artistically, this might well have been the match of the year, Newcombe—an enforced absentee from Davis Cup compensation since 1967—coming back from 1-3 and a break point in the fifth set with some sublime play. Laver beat Tom Gorman, 8-10, 8-6, 6-8, 6-3, 6-1, in the second match, then surprisingly teamed with Newcombe to pummel Smith and Erik van Dillen in the decisive doubles, 6-1, 6-2,

6-4. (Earlier in the year, in the American Zone final, Smith and van Dillen had beaten Chileans Jaime Fillol and Patricio Cornejo, 7-9, 37-39, 8-6, 6-1, 6-3—122 games, the longest Davis Cup match on record.)

The Aussies were so strong that neither Anderson nor Rosewall—whose brilliant singles victories over Marty Riessen and Smith and inspired doubles alongside John Alexander had spurred Australia to a 5-2 World Cup triumph over the U.S. at Hartford in March—couldn't crack the final-round lineup. Newcombe and Laver handled the stunned Gorman and Smith in the final singles for the 5-0 sweep, concluding the record U.S. streak of 17 wins, dating to 1968.

At year's end, the ATP board remained opposed to World Team Tennis and to guaranteed contracts for players—a stance it was forced to reverse the next year, under growing pressure from members who wanted to accept guarantees. WTT named former U.S. Davis Cup captain George MacCall as its commissioner, announced that it would begin operations in May 1974, and signed such prominent players as Newcombe, Rosewall, Billie Jean King and Evonne Goolagong to lucrative contracts.

In women's pro tennis, two separate tours were played in the winter and spring of 1973. The Virginia Slims Circuit consisted of 14 events, starring Billie Jean King and Margaret Court, conducted under the auspices of the Women's International Tennis Federation (WITF), incorporated as an autonomous body by Gladys Heldman. The USTA—claiming that it had been hoodwinked and double-crossed by Heldman—hastily arranged a circuit of eight tournaments featuring Chris Evert, Evonne Goolagong and Virginia Wade.

Noticed by no one but the two players themselves was a first-round match at Akron, a 7-6 (5-4), 6-3 win by Evert (the tournament victor) over a chubby Czech named Martina Navratilova. That initial meeting was merely the first step in the lustrous rivalry that was to run for 80 encounters over 16 years.

In Heldman's suit against the USTA in Federal District Court in New York, Judge Milton Pollack ruled against her, rendering the WITF short-lived. The players who signed with WITF were declared ineligible for the 1973 Commercial Union Grand Prix (won by Chris Evert), but by June an agreement was reached between the USTA and Philip Morris, Inc., parent company of Virginia Slims, for a single women's tour under USTA/ITF auspices starting in September 1973. Part of the compromise was that Heldman would not be involved.

Out of the wreckage of the WITF, a new women players' guild—the Women's Tennis Association—was formed at Wimbledon. With Billie Jean King as its first president, the WTA worked closely with the USTA's Edy McGoldrick in organizing a strong women's circuit for 1974 and beyond.

It is ironic that, because of Bobby Riggs, 1973 will be remembered as the year of Court's humiliation and King's triumph. In fact, Court was the dominant women's player of the season—winner of the Australian, French, and U.S. Opens, 18 of 25 tournaments, and $204,000 in prize money, the female high. Dating from her loss to Jeanne Evert in Boca Raton the previous fall, Court won 59 consecutive matches. For the calendar year her record was 102-6, and she beat King in three of four meetings.

Court started the year by beating Evonne Goolagong in the final of the Australian Open for the third consecutive year, 6-4, 7-5. She then teamed with Virginia Wade to win the doubles for the eighth time in 13 years, with her sixth different partner.

Court was down 3-5, second set, in the final of the French, but recovered to beat Evert, 6-7 (5-7), 7-6 (8-6), 6-4, and became the only woman other than Suzanne Lenglen to win five singles titles in Paris. (Only two of Lenglen's six, 1925 and 1926, count in the standings of all-time

champs since non-French citizens couldn't enter prior to 1925.) This was a battle of torrid groundstroking, the most memorable women's match of the year. Court also won her fourth French doubles title, with Wade. Loser Evert would later pass Court with seven French titles.

Only Wimbledon prevented Court from recording a second Grand Slam. All eight seeds advanced to the quarterfinals, and the only reversal of form was fourth-seeded Evert's 6-1, 1-6, 6-1 defeat of top-seeded Court in the semis—as unexpected a result on the grass that Margaret liked so much as was her comeback in the French final on Chrissie's beloved clay. King, superbly conditioned physically and mentally and operating at a high emotional pitch, beat Goolagong in the semifinals, 6-3, 5-7, 6-3, and blasted Evert in the final, 6-0, 7-5. BJK became the first five-time singles winner since Helen Wills Moody four decades earlier and also teamed with Rosemary Casals to win the doubles and with Owen Davidson to capture the mixed, her second Wimbledon "triple." The women's doubles triumph was King's ninth, with four partners, and fifth with Casals.

At the U.S. Open, 1971–72 champion King walked off court while trailing Julie Heldman, 1-4, in the final set of a fourth-round match played in exhausting heat and humidity. Heldman complained, as was her right under the rules, that King was taking far more than the one minute allowed at changeovers. "If you want the match that badly, you can have it," seethed King, who later said she was suffering from a virus that had sapped her strength. King's defeat—3-6, 6-4, 4-1, ret.—recalled two other celebrated U.S. surrenders by champions: Suzanne Lenglen to Molla Bjurstedt Mallory in 1921, and Helen Wills Moody to Helen Jacobs in 1933.

Court beat Wade in two tie-breakers in the quarterfinals, avenged her Wimbledon defeat by Evert, 7-5, 2-6, 6-2, in the semis, and made Goolagong a bridesmaid again in the final, 7-6, 5-7, 6-2. For her victory Margaret received $25,000, the same as Newcombe, as the women achieved prize money parity with men in a major championship for the first time. The singles triumph was her record 24th major and last in a Big Four event. Court teamed with Wade for Court's 18th major doubles title.

King, despite being hampered by injuries in the early season, won eight of 19 tournaments and 58 of 68 matches. Including her $100,000 triumph over Riggs, she earned $197,000 for the year. In taking the No. 1 U.S. ranking for the seventh time, she equaled a feat previously achieved only by Mallory (between 1915 and 1926) and Moody (between 1923 and 1931).

Evert—who turned pro on her 18th birthday, December 21, 1972—earned $151,352 in her rookie season. She virtually monopolized the USTA winter tour, winning six of seven tournaments, beating Goolagong in the final of the last three. Evert went on to win 12 of 21 tournaments, 88 of 98 matches, including the Virginia Slims Championship at Boca Raton over her personal nemesis, Nancy Richey Gunter, 6-3, 6-3. Evert was disappointed to lose three big finals in a row at midseason—the Italian Open to Goolagong, the French to Court, and Wimbledon to King— but she took her first significant international title in the autumn, the South African Open over Goolagong, 6-3, 6-3. During this tournament she also announced her engagement to Jimmy Connors, later called off.

Evert also led the U.S. to a 5-2 victory over a young and, except for Virginia Wade, inexperienced British team in the Wightman Cup. This was the 50th anniversary of the competition, and was therefore played at Longwood Cricket Club, only yards from the home of Cup donor Hazel Hotchkiss Wightman, who was present and active in the celebrations at age 86.

Australia, led by Evonne Goolagong, defeated South Africa, 3-0, in the final of the Federation Cup at Bad Homburg, Germany, and Goolagong's 6-2, 6-3 victory over Evert and Kerry Melville's triumph over Julie Heldman spearheaded an Australian comeback and 6-3 victory over the U.S. in the second Bonne Bell Cup, at Sydney.

Other notable happenings during the year: Rosie Casals took the biggest check, $30,000, for beating King in the semis and Gunter, 3-6, 6-1, 7-5, in the final of the new Family Circle Cup at Hilton Head, S.C., the first tourney to offer a purse of $100,000 to the women. Goolagong beat Evert in the final of the Western Championships at Cincinnati, 6-2, 7-5, Chris's last defeat on clay for nearly six years. Evert won her second U.S. Clay Court title the next week over Veronica Burto, 6-4, 6-3, beginning an astounding streak on her favorite surface that had stretched to 25 tournaments and 125 matches (including the only three U.S. Opens played on clay) until her defeat by Tracy Austin in the Italian Open semifinals in May 1979.

Kathy Kuykendall turned pro at age 16, and then Californian Robin Tenney did her one better, becoming the youngest pro to date at age 15—though three years later, having been unsuccessful on the tour, she applied for and was granted a return to amateur status in order to play college tennis.

Previously denied a visa to South Africa because of his anti-apartheid views and statements, Arthur Ashe made an emotional pilgrimage to that country in 1973, becoming the only "nonwhite" male to win a South African title. That was the doubles with Tom Okker over Lew Hoad and Rob Maud, 6-2, 4-6, 6-2, 6-4. Connors was too strong for him in the singles final, 6-4, 7-6, (7-3), 6-3. Evert, beating Goolagong, 6-3, 6-3, made it a lovebird sweep. Goolagong had hurdled the color bar on entrants in 1971, followed in 1972 by minor players Wanaro n'Godrella, a black Frenchwoman from New Caledonia, and Bonnie Logan, a black American. Logan was a first-round loser. But Ashe, playing an exhibition in Soweto, and meeting with political leaders, white and black, was widely covered, making a distinct impact.

1974

Two young Americans—21-year-old Jimmy Connors and 19-year-old Chris Evert, who had an-

The king and queen of Wimbledon: Jimmy Connors and Chris Evert in 1974. (UPI)

Almost as surprising as the rate of the participation boom was a Louis Harris survey that indicated a substantial rise in tennis' popularity as a spectator sport. "The number [of sports fans] who say they 'follow' tennis has risen from 17 to 26 percent just in the last year, by far the most dramatic change in American sports preferences," the Harris organization said. This growth was reflected in the tennis industry, as new companies rushed in to offer a dizzying variety of equipment to the burgeoning market, and in the professional game, where prize money continued to skyrocket. Four men and one woman exceeded the $200,000 prize money barrier, which had seemed unattainable just a few years earlier. Connors ($281,309) and Evert ($261,460) led the parade of six-figure earners.

Connors rampaged to the most successful season of any American man since Tony Trabert in 1955, and also became the center of a new political storm in men's tennis.

Connors won 99 out of 103 matches during the year, 15 of 21 tournaments, including the Australian Open, Wimbledon, U.S. Open, U.S. Indoor, U.S. Clay Court and South African Open. He was denied a chance at the Grand Slam when the French Tennis Federation, then led by the strong-willed Philippe Chatrier, barred any player who had signed a contract to compete in the new World Team Tennis league in the U.S., which Europeans viewed as a threat to their summer tournaments.

Thus Connors, who had signed to play some matches with the WTT Baltimore Banners, and Evonne Goolagong, contracted to the Pittsburgh Triangles, were kept out of the world's premier clay court championship after having won the Australian at the start of the year. Bill Riordan, the maverick Connors' maverick manager, knew there was no way he could sue the French Federation directly, but filed a $40 million antitrust suit against Association of Tennis Professionals officers Jack Kramer and Donald Dell (who had been anti-WTT activists) and Commercial Union Assurance, sponsor of the ITF Grand Prix, alleging

nounced their engagement late in 1973 but called it off before getting to the altar the next fall—reigned as the king and queen of tennis in 1974. And as the American game celebrated its Centennial, two startling surveys revealed just how popular the game had become in the United States.

The respected A. C. Nielsen Company made its first survey of tennis in 1970, estimating that 10.3 million Americans played occasionally and projecting that the number would increase to 15 million by 1980. A second survey in 1973 indicated that the growth rate was much faster, and fixed the number of players at 20.2 million. A third study, released in September 1974, indicated a staggering 68 percent increase to 33.9 million Americans who said they played tennis "from time to time," and a more significant estimate that 23.4 million played at least three times a month.

a conspiracy to monopolize professional tennis and keep Connors (and other WTT players) out of the French.

Few envisioned what a world-beating year it would be for the brash left-hander Connors when he beat Australian Phil Dent, 7-6, 6-4, 4-6, 6-3, for the Australian title. Aussies Geoff Masters and Ross Case took the doubles at Kooyong in Melbourne, their first major title.

Connors dominated Riordan's USTA Indoor Circuit—which was played at the same time as an expanded, three-group World Championship Tennis circuit—winning seven of the nine tournaments he played, including the U.S. Indoor, his second of a record seven such titles, over Frew McMillan, 6-4, 7-5, 6-3.

At Wimbledon, Connors came within two points of defeat at the hands of Dent in the second round, but pulled away to win from 5-6, 0-30 in the fifth set. He beat Jan Kodes in five rugged sets in the quarterfinals, Dick Stockton (conqueror of Ilie Nastase) in a four-set semi, and then ravaged 39-year-old Ken Rosewall, 6-1, 6-1, 6-4, in the final.

Rosewall, 39, had masterfully beaten 1970–71 champ and top seed John Newcombe in the quarters and come from two sets and a match point in the third-set tie-breaker to beat 1972 champ Stan Smith, 6-8, 4-6, 9-8 (8-6), 6-1, 6-3, in one of Wimbledon's most memorable comebacks.

But Connors' ferocious returns of Rosewall's unintimidating serves kept the old man constantly on the defensive, the young lion always on the attack. Consequently, Connors became the youngest champion since Lew Hoad beat Rosewall at age 22 in the 1956 final, and Rosewall—the sentimental choice who had been runner-up in 1954, 1956 and 1970—remained, along with Pancho Gonzalez, Gottfried von Cramm and Fred Stolle, "the greatest players who never won Wimbledon."

Meanwhile, Newcombe captured his sixth doubles title, the fifth with fellow Aussie Tony Roche.

Connors had a virus that left him doubtful for the last U.S. Open played on grass courts. He lost a great deal of weight, but turned out to be lean and mean as he barreled through the tournament without serious danger, beating Alex Metreveli in the quarters, Roscoe Tanner (who had stopped Nastase and Smith) in the semis and Rosewall again in the final.

Rosewall, two months shy of his 40th birthday, trimmed Newcombe (who had beaten Arthur Ashe in a marvelous five-set quarterfinal) in the semis, but was humiliated by Connors, 6-1, 6-0, 6-1, the worst final-round flogging in the history of the U.S. Championships. Connors became the youngest Forest Hills champion since, ironically, Rosewall in 1956. The doubles title also stayed in America, Smith and Bob Lutz regaining the prize they first won in 1968.

Connors was the main man, but there were other outstanding performers during the year. Bjorn Borg, the ascending "Teen Angel" from Sweden, became the youngest player to win the Italian and French Opens and the U.S. Pro Championship. He celebrated his 18th birthday during the French, where he lost the first two sets of the final and then stomped Manuel Orantes, 2-6, 6-7, 6-0, 6-1, 6-1. He had been 17 when he won the Italian, dethroning Nastase in the final, 6-3, 6-4, 6-2. At the U.S. Pro, Borg beat Tom Okker, 7-6, 6-1, 6-1, after resurrecting himself from 1-5 in the fifth set to beat Jan Kodes in an astonishing semifinal, 7-6, 6-0, 1-6, 2-6, 7-6.

Borg won nine tournaments and was runner-up in five more, including the WCT finals at Dallas. There he coolly beat Ashe and Kodes before running up against Newcombe, 30, who won this one for the older generation, 4-6, 6-3, 6-3, 6-2.

Borg was also runner-up to Connors in the U.S. Clay Court, 5-7, 6-3, 6-4, their only meeting of the year. Borg had won their first meeting in the quarterfinals of the 1973 Stockholm Open, but now Connors was off on a seven-match run in what would develop into the rivalry of the '70s in men's tennis.

Roscoe Tanner ousted Ilie Nastase and Stan Smith before losing to Jimmy Connors in the 1974 U.S. Open semifinals. (Jack Mecca)

Newcombe was the dominant player of the WCT season, winning five of the 11 tournaments in his group (Nastase and Laver won four each in theirs). But the new format of tricolor groups (Red, Blue, Green), each playing 11 tournaments to qualify their two point leaders plus two "wild cards" for the eight-man Dallas final, was not very successful. The product was too diluted, difficult to follow, and the zigzagging global travel schedule taxed the players. WCT, which two years before had the inside track in the men's pro game, had overexpanded and suffered in prestige in the process.

Bob Hewitt and Frew McMillan won the WCT doubles final at Montreal, sharing $40,000 for beating Newcombe and Owen Davidson in the final, 6-2, 6-7, 6-1, 6-2. A makeshift young doubles team of Brian Gottfried and Mexican

Raul Ramirez was formed in the spring and immediately proved to be a successful partnership, winning the first of four consecutive Italian doubles titles.

After Wimbledon, another 22-year-old left-hander arose and edged out Connors for the $100,000 top prize in the Commercial Union Grand Prix. Guillermo Vilas of Argentina, who had shown promise of things to come by knocking out defending champ Andres Gimeno at the French Open in 1973, ruled the U.S. Summer Circuit and won six of his last 15 tournaments.

The attractive and sensitive young Latin, a former law student and part-time poet, also won the Grand Prix Masters at Melbourne, which Connors boycotted. (He claimed a dental problem, but most blamed his suit against sponsor Commercial Union for his absence.) Even though Vilas did not like grass courts, which were not well suited to his heavy topspin game, he beat Newcombe, Borg and Onny Parun to win his round-robin group, then Ramirez in the semis and Nastase in a brilliant final, 7-6, 6-2, 3-6, 3-6, 6-4, to claim his biggest title to date.

At season's end, Vilas was not far behind Connors on the money list, having earned $274,327. Newcombe was third with $273,299, Borg fourth with $215,229. Laver won six tournaments, including the U.S. Pro Indoor over Ashe (his 15th consecutive victory over Arthur in 15 years), 6-1, 6-4, 3-6, 6-4, and the rich Alan King Classic, and temporarily remained the all-time money winner with a career total of $1,379,454. Connors would catch him soon enough.

Meanwhile, World Team Tennis made its raucous debut in May, offering players a lucrative alternative to tournaments during the summer. Sixteen teams embarked on a schedule of 44 contests each, the format being five one-set matches (men's and women's singles and doubles, plus mixed doubles), with the cumulative games won in all five deciding the outcome.

The Philadelphia Freedoms, with Billie Jean King as player-coach, defeated Ken Rosewall's Pittsburgh Triangles in the ballyhooed opener at Philadelphia's Spectrum, 31-25. Philadelphia had the best season record, 39-5, but lost the playoffs in two straight to the Denver Racquets, who promptly moved to Phoenix. No team made money, and the average loss per franchise was estimated to be $300,000. The league was cut down to 12 teams in 1975, and only one came back for the second season with the original owners.

A more traditional team competition, the Davis Cup, continued to be tarnished by political problems and cumbersome scheduling that often left countries playing matches without their best players, who had conflicting commitments elsewhere. Such was the case with both the U.S., which was ambushed by Colombia, 4-1, at Bogota in January, and Australia, which traveled to India undermanned and was beaten by the same score.

It was another of those ignominious—though glorious for the home side—defeats on alien clay as slightly-knowns Jairo Velasco and lefty Ivan Molina left the Americans for dead the first day. Velasco took Harold Solomon, usually reliable in such straits, 6-1, 3-6, 4-6, 6-3, 7-5, and would clinch the third day, 6-0, 7-5, 4-6, 6-3, over Erik van Dillen, whom Molina had beaten, 6-4, 7-5, 6-2.

For the first time in the history of the competition, the 74-year-old Cup was decided by default. South Africa became the fifth nation to hold the sterling silver punchbowl when the Indian Government refused to let its team play the final, in protest of South Africa's apartheid racial policies.

Connors declined to play for the U.S. in either the Davis Cup or the World Cup—won by Australia at Hartford, 5-2, with Newcombe spearheading the attack, beating both Ashe and Smith in singles and teaming with Roche to beat them in doubles.

Evert became the youngest woman to gain the No. 1 U.S. ranking since Maureen Connolly

reigned supreme in 1951–52. Chrissie won 16 tournaments—including Wimbledon, the French, Italian and U.S. Clay Court—and was never beaten before the semifinals in compiling a 100-7 record in 23 tournaments. Her $261,460 in prize money far outdistanced Margaret Court's record of the previous year. In winning her third straight U.S. Clay, Chrissie savaged the 1969 champ Gail Chanfreau, 6-0, 6-0, rationing five opponents to a total of eight games.

Evert did not have things entirely her own way, even though she did compile a 55-match winning streak in midseason. Evonne Goolagong beat her in four of six meetings, including the finals of the Australian Open and the Virginia Slims Championship at Los Angeles, and the semifinals of the U.S. Open. Billie Jean King won the Open and took two of three from Evert, including the final of the U.S. Indoor, which BJK captured for the fifth time, 6-3, 3-6, 6-2.

Goolagong played inspired tennis in celebrating the New Year with a 7-6, 4-6, 6-0 triumph over Evert at Melbourne, winning her native title for the first time after being runner-up the previous three years. Evonne also paired with American Peggy Michel, her Pittsburgh Triangles teammate and partner in WTT, to win the Australian and Wimbledon doubles.

With Goolagong, King, Kerry Melville (who would marry her Boston Lobsters teammate Raz Reid), and most of the other leading women playing WTT during the summer, Evert had the European clay-court season pretty much to herself. She beat Martina Navratilova, the promising young Czech left-hander who had played the USTA women's circuit at age 16 in 1973, in the Italian final, 6-3, 6-3, and Soviet No. 1 Olga Morozova in the French final, 6-1, 6-2. Evert and Morozova won both doubles titles.

Evert barely survived her opening match at Wimbledon—she squeezed by Lesley Hunt, 8-6, 5-7, 11-9, in a thrilling match that was delayed for several hours by rain, breathtakingly played despite a slippery court, and suspended overnight by darkness at 9-9 in the third set—but went on to complete her European hat trick by crunching eighth-seeded Morozova in the final, 6-0, 6-4.

Evert did not have to play her two greatest rivals, top-seeded King and Goolagong, because they both came up flat and were stunned in the quarterfinals—King by Morozova, 7-5, 6-2, and Goolagong by Melville, 9-7, 1-6, 6-2. Evert beat Melville, and Morozova erased Virginia Wade in the semis, and Evert got to dance the champions' traditional first foxtrot at the Wimbledon Ball with her fiancé, Connors. The "lovebird double," a Connors-Evert parlay, paid bettors 33-1 in England's legalized gambling shops.

Evert won 10 consecutive tournaments after losing the U.S. Indoor to King, but her streak ended at 55 matches in the semifinals at Forest Hills. Goolagong raced to a 6-0, 4-3 lead before rain suspended their match. The next day, Evert pulled level after Goolagong served for the match at 5-4 in the second set, four times reaching deuce, and came within two points of victory twice more when she served at 6-5. Evert broke again, won the tie-breaker by 5 points to 3, but could not contend with Goolagong's outstanding volleying in relinquishing the excruciating final set, 6-3.

King avenged her bitter loss of the year before by beating Julie Heldman, 2-6, 6-3, 6-1, in the other semifinal, and toppled Goolagong, 3-6, 6-3, 7-5, in a final of thrilling shotmaking that delighted a Monday sellout crowd of 15,303. Vastly more entertaining than the massacre of a men's final, this one was alive until the very end; Goolagong broke at love when King served for the match at 5-4, but BJK won eight of the last nine points to seal her fourth singles title. She also collaborated with Rosemary Casals for their second U.S. doubles crown. Bulldozers moved into the stadium at the West Side Tennis Club the next day to dig up the grass courts, which were to be replaced with synthetic clay.

Goolagong beat Evert, 7-5, 3-6, 6-4, in the final of the Virginia Slims tournament at Denver

and again in the Slims playoff, where she took the richest women's prize to date—$32,000—with a 6-3, 6-4 victory over the 1972–73 champ. That evened their career rivalry at 8-8 over three years.

Melville, who had been runner-up, 6-1, 6-3, to Evert for the $30,000 top prize in the Family Circle Cup in the spring, won the South African Open, her biggest international title, over Australian 17-year-old Dianne Fromholtz, 6-3, 7-5. Fromholtz had eliminated Margaret Court, making a comeback after the birth of her second child.

America's top two players, Evert and King, sat out the Federation, Wightman and Bonne Bell Cups. Player-captain Heldman beat both Goolagong and Hunt in leading the U.S. to a shocking 5-4 victory over Australia in the third Bell Cup, at Cleveland, after which the competition was unfortunately abandoned.

Great Britain, psyched by player-captain Virginia Wade's 5-7, 9-7, 6-4 victory over Heldman, sprinted to a 6-1 victory in the Wightman Cup, only their eighth in 46 meetings with the U.S., at Deeside, Wales. Cup donor Hazel Wightman died at age 87 in December, shortly after the series.

Heldman and Jeanne Evert—Chrissie's younger sister, who ranked No. 9, making the first time since Ethel and Florence Sutton in 1913 that sisters were among the U.S. Top Ten simultaneously—got to the final of the Federation Cup at Naples, Italy, before falling to Australia, 2-1. Goolagong beat Heldman for her 13th straight Fed Cup singles without a loss and teamed with Janet Young for the clincher after Jeanne beat Fromholtz, 2-6, 7-5, 6-4.

Chris Evert was elected to succeed the more activist King as president of the Women's Tennis Association at Wimbledon, where the women threatened to boycott in 1975 unless they received "equal parity" with the men in prize money, as Evert put it. That was about the only political story in the women's game, however, and it turned out to be no more than a mild tempest in a teapot, solved by teatime.

1975

Jimmy Connors joined world leaders as a cover subject for *Time* magazine in 1975, as he beat first Rod Laver and then John Newcombe (avenging a loss in the Australian Open final) in ballyhooed "Heavyweight Championship of Tennis" challenge matches in Las Vegas.

These extravaganzas—the focal point of a TV sports scandal two years later because of the CBS network's misleading "winner-take-all" hype—gained high ratings and massive exposure. Connors and his clever, prizefight-style manager Bill Riordan—who were to split bitterly before the end of the year as Connors dropped the controversial antitrust suit he filed in 1974—were the kings of hype. But the ruler of men's tennis was King Arthur Ashe.

At age 32, after nearly 15 years in the big time, Ashe finally fulfilled the promise that had been acclaimed for him in 1968 and gradually abandoned. Seemingly a perennial bridesmaid, loser of 14 of his last 19 final-round matches coming into the year, Ashe became the best by dedicating himself to training and positive thinking as never before.

In 29 tournaments he got to 14 finals, winning nine of them, including the two he really set out to win: the WCT final at Dallas (over Bjorn Borg, 3-6, 6-4, 6-4, 6-0) and Wimbledon (over Connors in a stunner, 6-1, 6-1, 5-7, 6-4). Ashe's $338,337 earnings for the year boosted his total in seven years as a pro to $1,052,202, making him the sport's third million-dollar winner.

Meanwhile, despite Billie Jean King's dramatic sixth Wimbledon singles title, a postwar record, Chris Evert was the indisputable sovereign of women's tennis.

Before celebrating her 21st birthday on December 20, Chrissie defended her Italian and French Open titles, won the first U.S. Open on clay by outgritting archrival Evonne Goolagong, dethroned Goolagong to recapture the Virginia Slims throne, won 16 of 22 tournaments for the year and set an all-time single-season winnings

record of $350,977. She didn't lose a match the last six months of the season after succumbing to King in the Wimbledon semis, and was never beaten before the quarterfinals of a tournament.

Ashe was the Man of the Year, but the season began with another self-reclamation project. John Newcombe, who was slowed by injuries after winning the WCT title in May 1974, and who was to miss Wimbledon and the U.S. Open with new ailments, flogged himself into shape for the Australian Open by doing miles of roadwork and charging countless times up the hill behind his attractive split-level home in the Sydney suburb of Pymble. He struggled to the final, but was ready for Connors, serving ferociously to win, 7-5, 3-6, 6-4, 7-5.

Already set before the loss to Newcombe was the first of Connors' challenge matches at Caesar's Palace, the Las Vegas hotel-casino. The opponent was Laver, the Grand Slammer of 1962 and 1969—a "natural" pairing since they had never played each other. Connors won, 6-4, 6-2, 3-6, 7-5, seizing what was said to be a $100,000 "winner-take-all" purse, but it was widely reported that both players took home big checks from "ancillary" revenues.

The success of the venture of CBS-TV made a second "Heavyweight Championship" inevitable, Newcombe being the logical challenger after his popular victory at Melbourne on New Year's Day. Connors won again, 6-3, 4-6, 6-2, 6-2. Connors was said to receive a $250,000 "winner-take-all" purse, but it was later revealed that the match had been structured like a championship prize fight, each player receiving a pre-agreed percentage, win or lose. Connors made $480,000; Newcombe, $280,000.

Although he won these indoor bouts amid the heavyweight hoopla on which he thrives, Connors lost in the finals of the three major championships he had swept the previous year. Newcombe set the tone in Australia. Ashe, considered a prohibitive underdog (10-to-1 on the day), came up with a tactical masterpiece at

Wimbledon. He changed speed and spin smartly, fed junk to Connors' forehand, exposing the vulnerability of that wing to paceless shots, and sliced his serves wide to Connors' backhand, exploiting the slightly limited reach of his two-handed shot.

This was an extraordinary final, the first ever between litigants in a lawsuit since President Ashe, along with other officers of the Association of Tennis Professionals, were named in the $40-million antitrust suit Connors and Riordan had filed against attorney Donald Dell, Jack Kramer and Grand Prix sponsor Commercial Union. There were several other suits and counterclaims associated with this one, but all were quietly settled, out of court and without payment of damages, not long after Ashe's emotion-charged and enormously popular victory.

Ashe was not considered a serious threat at the U.S. Open after the grass courts at the West Side Tennis Club in Forest Hills were dug up immediately after the 1974 tournament, replaced with a synthetic pea-green clay called Har-Tru, which became the predominent surface of the U.S. Summer Circuit. Sure enough, clay specialist Eddie Dibbs—one of a group of scrappy young Americans coming up to succeed Ashe's generation—beat fourth-seeded Arthur in the fourth round, 6-4, 6-2, 6-3.

Forest Hills, previously dominated by grass-loving Americans and Australians, suddenly became a happy hunting ground for clay-reared Europeans and South Americans. The most successful was third-seeded Manuel Orantes, the elegant left-hander from Barcelona. In the semifinals, he revived himself from two sets and 0-2 down, and from 0-5 in the fourth set, saving five match points to beat second-seeded Argentinian left-hander Guillermo Vilas, 4-6, 1-6, 6-2, 7-5, 6-4. That three-hour, 44-minute marathon did not end until 10:40 p.m. on Saturday—the installation of all-weather courts permitted floodlighting and night play for the first time—and Orantes did not get to bed until 3:00 a.m. because of a plumbing failure in his hotel room. He was assumed to be a

Spain's Manuel Orantes overcame every obstacle in 1975, including Jimmy Connors at Forest Hills. (Peter Mecca)

lamb going to slaughter in the final against top-seeded Connors, who had hammered Borg in the other semifinal, 7-5, 7-5, 7-5, early the previous afternoon.

But taking his cue from Ashe's strategy at Wimbledon, Orantes slow-balled Connors and cleverly mixed up his game. He drop-shotted and lobbed, chipped and passed, traded ground strokes and sometimes dashed in to take away the forecourt, snaring Connors in his butterfly net.

It was 10 years to the day since Manuel Santana had become the first Spaniard to win at Forest Hills, and again the old concrete stadium was filled with Latin chants and shouts of *"Bravo!"* as 15,669 spectators roared Orantes to an astonishing 6-4, 6-3, 6-3 victory. At the end, he fell to his knees, jubilantly, his toothy face the definitive portrait of ecstasy. Why not? His last 24 hours had constituted the most remarkable feat of any player in a major championship since Wimbledon in 1927, when Frenchman Henri Cochet elevated himself from two sets and 1-5 down to beat Bill Tilden in the semifinals, then from two sets down to overhaul Jean Borotra in the final.

Connors lost his stranglehold on men's tennis, but did not have a bad year by anyone's standards except his own. He entered 19 tournaments and won nine—five of them on Riordan's USLTA Indoor circuit, including the U.S. Indoor over Vitas Gerulaitis, 5-7, 7-5, 6-1, 3-6, 6-0. Connors was runner-up in six others, including the Australian, Wimbledon, and U.S. Open. Connors compiled an 83-10 record and made well over a half-million dollars with all his "special" matches, but Ashe was the prize-money leader with $306,712.

Connors also split with Riordan in the fall. He had prospered, financially and competitively, under Riordan's tutelage, but also had become the isolated man of the locker room, despised and openly cold-shouldered by his colleagues. With the divorce from his manager, Connors gradually came in from the cold, re-establishing cordial if never close relations with his fellow players. "I think Jimmy just decided that it wasn't worth going through life hated," said his contemporary, Roscoe Tanner.

Ashe, who had been one of the first to recognize that a deep freeze by his peers would be the most effective way of ending the divisive lawsuits Connors fronted for Riordan, won four of eight tournaments in his group during the WCT season, while Connors was playing the smaller Riordan-organized tour. Laver won four consecutive WCT tournaments and 23 straight matches, but Ashe earned a solid gold tennis ball, valued at $33,333, as the top point-winner on the tour, which was divided into three groups (Red, Blue and Green) playing a total of 25 tournaments. He won the $50,000 top prize in the eight-man WCT final at Dallas by beating Mark Cox, John Alexander and Bjorn Borg.

Ashe also played a substantial number of events in the $4-million dollar Commercial Union Grand Prix, which embraced 42 tournaments in 19 countries during its May-through-December calendar, boosting the total prize money available in men's tennis to more than $8 million dollars. Ashe compiled a 16-match winning streak in the fall, winning tournaments at Los Angeles and San Francisco, and qualified for the eight-man Grand Prix Masters playoff at Stockholm. He had visions of a unique WCT-Masters "double," but was upended in the semis of the Masters by Borg, 6-4, 3-6, 6-2, 6-2, and concluded, "I don't think anybody is strong enough, mentally and physically, to win WCT and the Masters in the same year."

Borg was runner-up in both—to Ashe in Dallas and to Ilie Nastase (who came back from a disqualification against Ashe in his opening round-robin match of the Masters) in Stockholm. "Teen Angel" was in the waning days of his 18th year when he beat Laver in a magnificent four-hour semifinal at Dallas, perhaps the year's finest match, 7-6, 3-6, 5-7, 7-6, 6-2. He had turned 19 by the time he clobbered Guillermo Vilas, 6-2, 6-3, 6-4, for his second consecutive French Open title. Later he steamrolled Vilas again, 6-3, 6-4, 6-2, to defend his U.S. Pro crown. Borg won five of 23 tournaments on the year, amassed a 78-19 record, and carried Sweden to its first possession of the Davis Cup, winning all 12 of his singles matches against Poland, West Germany, the Soviet Union, Spain, Chile and Czechoslovakia. His record of 16 consecutive Davis Cup singles victories over three years tied the all-time Cup record set by Bill Tilden between 1920 and 1926, and would stretch to 33 by his retirement.

Vilas didn't win any of the big international titles, but won six of 23 tournaments—including Washington and Louisville during a 16-match winning streak early in the U.S. summer circuit—and reached at least the quarterfinals of 21 to seize the $100,000 top prize in the Commercial Union Grand Prix for the second straight year. Orantes, who counted the German, Swedish,

Canadian, British Hard Court, U.S. Clay Court (6-2, 6-2, over Ashe) and U.S. Open titles among the seven tournaments he won, finished second in the Grand Prix standings.

Nastase won the Masters for the fourth time in five years, coming back from his opening disqualification. (Ashe, disgruntled by Nastase's behavior and stalling, uncharacteristically stormed off the court, but was declared the winner the following day.) "Nasty" beat Orantes and Adriano Panatta in his remaining round-robin matches, Vilas in the semifinals, and a badly off-form Borg in the final, 6-2, 6-2, 6-1. This was by far the biggest of Nastase's seven tournament victories for the year, but he set a dubious achievement record by being defaulted three times, quitting his semifinal match in the Italian Open to ultimate champion Raul Ramirez, and "tanking" the Canadian Open final to Orantes after getting upset by a line call in the first-set tie-breaker.

For this unprofessional conduct, Nastase was fined $8,000 by the newly formed Men's International Professional Tennis Council, a tripartite body made up of three representatives each of the male players, the ITF, and worldwide tournament directors. Nastase's lawyers appealed, and the fine was reduced, but the "Pro Council" had established itself as an important new administrative and judicial force in the men's game. It was designed to be legislative as well, and became the autonomous governing body of the Grand Prix circuit.

It was a peculiar year in men's doubles. Australians John Alexander and Phil Dent won their national title for the first time, but Brian Gottfried and Raul Ramirez were the Team of the Year. They began their reign in the U.S. Pro Indoor at Philadelphia, and won the WCT doubles title at Mexico City over Mark Cox and Cliff Drysdale, 7-6, 6-7, 6-2, 7-6. Gottfried-Ramirez also won a special "Challenge Match" during the WCT singles finals at Dallas, 7-5, 6-3, 4-6, 2-6, 7-5, over South African Davis Cuppers Bob Hewitt and Frew McMillan, who had been rudely kicked out of Mexico shortly after their arrival for the dou-

bles playoff—a clumsy power play by the Mexican government to protest the apartheid racial policies of South Africa.

Gottfried-Ramirez also won the French title, over Alexander-Dent, and the U.S. Pro, but they came up flat at the end of the year, failing to win a match in the Masters as a four-man doubles playoff was inaugurated alongside the singles. The doubles was a round-robin affair, which proved to be an unsatisfactory format when three teams tied with identical 2-1 records. Spanish Davis Cuppers Orantes and Juan Gisbert were declared champions on the basis of having the best percentage of games won for their three matches, even though they were beaten head-to-head by the spirited new American tandem of Sherwood Stewart and Freddie McNair. (The Masters doubles was changed to a knock-out format in succeeding years.)

The Wimbledon doubles turned into a wildly unpredictable scramble as only one seeded team reached the quarterfinals. Sandy Mayer and Vitas Gerulaitis, who had not blended well earlier in the year, became the first American champions in 18 years with a 7-5, 8-6, 6-4 victory in the final over similarly unseeded Allan Stone of Australia and Colin Dowdeswell of Rhodesia, who had never even met each other until introduced in the tea room the first day of the tournament. Their regular partners were injured, so they formed a patchwork alliance and filled a late vacancy in the draw.

Connors got his only major title of the year by teaming with Nastase to win the U.S. Open doubles over Marty Riessen and Tom Okker. Connors seldom played doubles thereafter, a trend soon followed by Borg and Vilas as top players began to concentrate singularly on singles.

Connors also ended—only temporarily, as it turned out—his one-man boycott of the U.S. Davis Cup team. Former French, Wimbledon and U.S. champion Tony Trabert replaced Dennis Ralston as the American captain after Raul Ramirez led a 3-2 Mexican ambush of the U.S. at

Palm Springs in February 1975, ironically the same weekend that Connors was beating Laver in the first Las Vegas Challenge Match. Ramirez, the best Mexican to play the game other than Rafe Osuna, a quick, resourceful, strong volleyer, was peskier for the U.S. than Pancho Villa. He led two raiding parties within 10 months that chased the *norteamericanos* out of two years in the space of one. In the first he beat Stan Smith, 3-6, 6-4, 6-1, 8-6, and clinched over Tanner, 7-5, 7-9, 6-4, 6-2.

Trabert coaxed Connors, who had long feuded with Ralston (this was really a proxy fight between Riordan and Ralston's agent, former Cup captain Donald Dell), onto the American squad for a first-round conquest of undermanned Venezuela at Tucson. But the notion that Connors' presence alone assured victory in the American Zone was dispelled as Ramirez, an inspired Davis Cup player, teamed with Marcelo Lara in doubles and led his nation to another 3-2 upset in the second round of the 1976 competition, which was actually played December 19–21, 1975. It all came down to the No. 1 players of the two countries in the decisive fifth match, and Ramirez, who had beaten Gottfried, 6-1, 6-4, 6-2, was as high as the 6,000-foot altitude of Mexico City as he beat Connors, 2-6, 6-3, 6-3, 6-4, in a match suspended overnight by darkness.

The 1975 final was played the same weekend at Stockholm's Kungliga Tennishallen. Borg was virtually a one-man gang, on court for nine sets, a trio of straight-set victories over Jiri Hrebec and Jan Kodes, and a doubles collaboration with losing singles player Ove Bengtson over Kodes and Vladimir Zednik as Sweden defeated Czechoslovakia, 3-2, to become the sixth nation to hold the Davis Cup. Both teams were first-time finalists.

The Davis Cup continued to be plagued by political turmoil. Mexico, after eliminating the U.S., refused to play South Africa. Colombia similarly defaulted, putting South Africa—winner of the Cup by default the previous year—into the American Zone final without playing a match. But the South Africans were eliminated by Chile at Santiago.

Chilean No. 1 Jaime Fillol, who had won both his singles, received a death threat from opponents of the military junta in his homeland, and it was only with massive security precautions that Chile was able to play the semifinal in Sweden. The stadium at Baastad was kept almost empty except for thousands of police and troops; boats patrolled the harbor, aircraft hovered overhead, and huge nets around the stadium protected the players from projectiles hurled by anti-Chile demonstrators, who chanted and set off firecrackers a block away. In this unnerving atmosphere, Borg and Birger Anderssen—who helped win four of Sweden's matches along the way, but sat down in favor of Bengtson in the final—whipped the Chileans, 4-1, and set up the final in Stockholm just before Christmas. Considering the tension, Fillol had done well the first day to beat Anderssen, 6-3, 6-2, 6-3.

The ATP, in a rather clumsy effort to force a consolidation of the Davis Cup into a one- or two-week showdown at one site, staged a new competition with just such a Federation Cup–style format, calling it the Nations Cup. The American team of Ashe and Tanner defeated Great Britain's Roger Taylor and Buster Mottram, 2-1, in Jamaica, but the competition was not a success. Meanwhile, Laver and 40-year-old Ken Rosewall helped Australia to a 4-3 victory over the U.S. in the World Cup at Hartford, showing that the Aussie dynasty was not entirely dead—though a group of younger Aussies was beaten by Czechoslovakia in the semifinals of the Davis Cup at Prague.

World Team Tennis, despite the huge financial losses of its inaugural season and a ludicrous player draft (numerous showbiz personalities were named by teams in a publicity stunt that made a mockery of the league), surprised many by coming out for a second season. There were 12 teams, four fewer than in 1974, and only one returned with the original ownership, but the league staggered along. Pittsburgh, led by Vitas Gerulaitis and Evonne Goolagong, beat the San Francisco Bay Area's Golden Gaters in the championship series.

Goolagong started the season by repeating as Australian Open champion, beating Martina Navratilova, 6-3, 6-2, in an emotional final. (Evonne's father had been killed in an auto accident, and Evonne cried on the shoulder of her coach and guardian, Vic Edwards, at the presentation ceremonies.) Goolagong also successfully defended her doubles title with WTT teammate Peggy Michel.

Evert won the biggest check for women in "special events" —$50,000 for winning the four-woman L'Eggs World Series over King at Lakeway, Tex., 4-6, 6-3, 7-6. She also won $40,000 for adding her third triumph in the Virginia Slims Championship at Los Angeles, over Navratilova, 6-4, 6-2. Navratilova won the U.S. Indoor at Boston, beating Virginia Wade, Margaret Court and Goolagong, 6-3, 6-4, but she lost again to Evert, 7-5, 6-4, in the final of the rich Family Circle Cup at Amelia Island, Fla.

With most of the top women committed to World Team Tennis, Evert and Navratilova were the class of the women's field in the Italian and French Opens. They reached the singles finals of both, Evert winning in Rome by 6-1, 6-0 and in Paris by 2-6, 6-2, 6-1. Chris and Martina then teamed up to win both the doubles titles.

King always considered the Centre Court at Wimbledon her favorite stage, and she never performed more majestically there than in coming from 0-3 down in the third set to beat Evert in the semifinals, 2-6, 6-2, 6-3, and burying Goolagong, 6-0, 6-1, in the most lopsided women's final since 1911. BJK's sixth singles title was her 19th in all at Wimbledon, tying the career record of Elizabeth Ryan, who never won the singles but captured 12 doubles and seven mixed crowns between 1914 and 1934. King said this was her last appearance in singles because of a deteriorating knee— "I want to quit on top," she said, "and I can't get much higher than this" —but she eventually returned, in 1977.

The women's doubles champions turned out to be as unlikely as the men's, Kazuko Sawamatsu of Japan and Ann Kiyomura, an American of Japanese ancestry, teaming to upset Françoise Durr and Betty Stove in the final. Margaret Court teamed with Marty Riessen for the mixed doubles title over Stove and Allan Stone.

Evert won the U.S. Open, dropping only one set. That was in the final, where her 5-7, 6-4, 6-2 victory over Goolagong relegated Evonne to the record books as the only woman to lose three consecutive U.S. singles finals. Chris was just too formidable on the clay she loved so well, as she demonstrated by grinding out the last four games of the match in a baseline duel. Court and Wade took the doubles title over King and Casals; this was the 19th doubles and the last of Court's record 62 Big Four titles in singles and doubles.

More important than tennis was Navratilova's decision, announced at Forest Hills, to defect from her native Czechoslovakia and seek U.S. citizenship. She made the decision after the Czech tennis federation, chiding her for becoming "too Americanized," initially refused her a visa to compete in the U.S. Open. Navratilova felt she had to follow the lead of the great Czech player Jaroslav Drobny, who defected in 1949, if she were to develop as a tennis player and as a person, but the decision was painful. She knew that her action meant that it would be years before she would see her parents and younger sister Jana again.

Navratilova and Renata Tomanova had led Czechoslovakia past Ireland, Netherlands, West Germany, France and Australia to win the 30-nation Federation Cup at Aix-en-Provence in southern France. Australia beat the United States in the semifinals, Goolagong and Helen Gourlay stopping U.S. captain Julie Heldman and Janet Newberry, 11-9, 6-1, in the doubles that swung a 2-1 decision. That put the Aussies in the final for the 10th time, but Navratilova ended Goolagong's 16-match unbeaten streak in Fed Cup singles, 6-3, 6-4, and Tomanova ambushed Gourlay, 6-4, 6-2. The Czechs then teamed to beat Gourlay and Dianne Fromholtz for a 3-0 verdict, clinching the Cup for the first time.

Great Britain also humbled the U.S. in the Wightman Cup for the second straight year, its first back-to-back wins since 1924–25. Evert won both her singles, over Wade and Glynis Coles, in straight sets, but with Heldman sidelined with a sore shoulder, the U.S. did not have the depth it needed to contend with Wade, Coles and Ann Jones, who returned to the battle at age 37. Coles' 6-3, 7-6 victory over Mona Schallau was the clincher in a 5-2 British victory at Cleveland's Public Auditorium.

The most spectacular comeback of the year belonged to Evert, who trailed Nancy Richey Gunter, 6-7, 0-5, 15-40—double match point—in the semifinals of the U.S. Clay Court at Indianapolis. After that, Chrissie didn't make a mistake in roaring back to win, 6-7, 7-5, 4-2 ret. Gunter finally had to quit with cramps. Evert went on to thrash Fromholtz in the final, 6-3, 6-4, for her fourth consecutive U.S. Clay Court crown.

A couple of administrative happenings during 1975 are worthy of note. Over the protests of tournament chairman and director Bill Talbert, the U.S. Open adopted a 12-point tie-breaker (win by two) instead of the nine-point "sudden death" that had been in use since 1970. This was a victory for the ATP, whose members preferred the less nerve-wracking "lingering death." The change of the surface at Forest Hills permitted night play there for the first time, and a resultant dramatic increase in total attendance, to 216,683. This was also the year the U.S. Lawn Tennis Association voted to drop the "Lawn" from its name, becoming simply the USTA. It was the beginning of a fashion that would, in 1977, see the International Lawn Tennis Federation become the ITF.

1976

Jimmy Connors returned to the pinnacle of men's tennis in 1976 and Chris Evert consolidated her stranglehold on the women's game. But the most bizarre and compelling story of the year was the emergence of professional sport's first transsexual.

Martina Navratilova made a big decision in 1975—she defected from Czechoslovakia. (UPI)

Richard Raskind, a 41-year-old ophthalmologist, was enough player to captain the Yale University varsity in 1954, play at Wimbledon and Forest Hills, and later reach the semifinals of the National 35-and-over championships in 1972. In August 1975, he had sex reassignment surgery and moved west to Newport Beach, Calif., to start a new life and practice as Dr. Renée Richards.

In July 1976, Dr. Richards—a 6-foot-2 left-hander—entered and won a local women's tournament in La Jolla, Calif. A former acquaintance noticed her resemblance in playing style to Richard Raskind, verified her identity and tipped off a San Diego television sportscaster, who broke the story.

Dr. Richards, who had sought a clean start in California, far from her former wife and four-year-old son in New York, decided to "go public" and put aside her brilliant career as an eye surgeon in order to play professional tennis.

"I started getting letters, poignant letters from other transsexuals who were considering suicide, whose friends and families won't see them," she explained to *Newsday* reporter Jane Gross. "I realized that this was more than just a tennis thing, my hobby; I could easily give that up. But, if I can do anything for those people, I will. I am in a position to try and make people see that such individuals should be allowed to hold up their heads. I realize this is important from a social standpoint."

The Richards case caused an extraordinary, highly publicized stir in women's tennis. The Women's Tennis Association opposed her eligibility for tournaments, and sided with the USTA in its hasty ruling that women would have to pass an Olympic-style chromosome test before being accepted for women's national championships, including the U.S. Open. Dr. Richards refused to take the test, claiming that it was an unsatisfactory means of determining gender, given the advances of modern medicine.

Many women felt that Dr. Richards would have an unfair competitive advantage because of her size, strength and past experience in competition against men. Others feared that her acceptance would set a bad precedent, paving the way for a younger, stronger transsexual to dominate women's tennis in the future. Many WTA members liked Richards personally, admired her courage, but still opposed her acceptance in tournaments.

Dr. Richards was denied admission to the U.S. Open—she took her case to court, and was admitted in 1977 by court order—but did play in a pre-Forest Hills tournament at South Orange, N.J. Most WTA members withdrew in protest, but the tournament attracted national television coverage and massive publicity. Richards was beaten in the semifinals by 17-year-old Lea Antonoplis, early evidence that fears Dr. Richards would upset the competitive balance of

Dr. Richard Raskind, an ophthalmologist, switched to a career in tennis as Renée Richards. (Peter Mecca)

the women's game were unfounded. Richards played several other tournaments, winning one at Kauai, Hawaii, at the end of the year over Kathy Kuykendall, ranked No. 10 in the U.S.

Along more conventional lines, Jimmy Connors recaptured the No. 1 world ranking even though he won only one major championship, the U.S. Open, in which he edged his major rival, Bjorn Borg, in a superlative final, 6-4, 3-6, 7-6 (11-9), 6-4.

Connors compiled a 100-12 record, winning 13 of 23 tournaments he played. He won the only two WCT events he entered, the two big prize-money events put on by the Association of Tennis Professionals (American Airlines Games at Palm Springs, Alan King Classic at Las Vegas), and six of the 10 Commercial Union Grand Prix events he played. He collected $303,335 in tournament prize money, plus more than double that amount in exhibitions—including $500,000 for beating up on Spaniard Manuel Orantes in another "Heavyweight Championship of Tennis" Challenge Match at Las Vegas. (Orantes, guaranteed more than $250,000 just for showing up, did little more than that, winning three games in three pathetic sets.)

More important in deciding the global game of king-of-the-hill, Connors was 3-0 in head-to-head clashes with Borg. Connors vanquished the young Swede in the U.S. Pro Indoor final at Philadelphia, 7-6, 6-4, 6-0, the American Airlines Games and the Forest Hills final.

Otherwise, Borg had an outstanding season, winning seven of 19 tournaments and 63 of 77 matches. He continued his domination of his good friend and sometimes doubles partner, Guillermo Vilas, to win the WCT Final at Dallas, 1-6, 6-1, 7-5, 6-1, in May, 27 days before his 20th birthday. He failed in his bid for a third consecutive French Open title, but prepared diligently on grass courts and became the third youngest champion in the history of Wimbledon, the first man to sweep through the most prestigious of championships without losing a set since Chuck McKinley in 1963. Borg pulled a muscle in his abdomen in a doubles match the first week, but deadened the pain in his last four singles matches by taking pre-match cortisone injections and spraying his abdomen at changeovers with an aerosol freeze spray. Despite the injury, he never served or smashed more authoritatively than in routing Brian Gottfried, Vilas, Roscoe Tanner (quarterfinal conqueror of Connors) and Ilie Nastase in the final, 6-4, 6-2, 9-7.

After a seven-week layoff to recuperate—a period during which Sweden relinquished the Davis Cup—Borg extended his winning streak to 19 matches, winning a third consecutive U.S. Pro title (over Harold Solomon, 6-7 [3-7], 6-4, 6-1, 6-2) and reaching the final of the U.S. Open. That match hinged on a tingling third-set tie-breaker in which Connors escaped four set points and finally prevailed, 11-9, tilting an epic his way.

Defending champ Orantes, seeded sixth and plagued by a sore arm, made a game effort to keep his crown. Two points from defeat, he slipped past ex-champ Stan Smith, 3-6, 1-6, 6-2, 7-6 (7-5), 6-1, and into the quarters, where he battled gallantly against second-seeded Borg—survivor of a harrowing fourth-rounder with Gottfried, 6-7 (3-7), 3-6, 6-4, 6-4, 6-2—to the wire, 4-6, 6-0, 6-2, 5-7, 6-4. Into the final confidently went Connors, who'd lost no sets (6-4, 6-2, 6-1, over third-seeded Vilas), and Borg (over fifth-seeded Nastase, 6-3, 6-3, 6-4).

The year began with perhaps the most startling result ever in one of the major championships: 21-year-old Australian Mark Edmondson—an anonymous serve-and-volleyer recently removed from employment as a janitor and odd-jobs man—won the Australian Open. Lowest ranked to win a major, No. 212, he beat two former champions, 42-year-old Ken Rosewall in the semifinals and defender John Newcombe, 6-7, 6-3, 7-6, 6-1, in a final played in fierce winds and the eerie weather of a gathering storm.

Edmondson was hardly a Grand Slam threat. He quickly found his level again, losing in the first round of the French Open to Paraguayan Victor Pecci. Adriano Panatta, the handsome and dashing Italian No. 1, won the French during a dazzling 16-match winning streak that established him as the king of European clay for the year.

Panatta withstood 11 match points against Aussie Kim Warwick in the first round of the Italian Open, then went on to win the title before his adoring hometown fans in Rome, beating Vilas in the final, 2-6, 7-6 (7-5), 6-2, 7-6 (7-1). Panatta was nearly a goner in the first round in Paris, too, saving a match point against an unorthodox and virtually unknown Czech, Pavel Hutka, with a desperate, lunging volley winner. After that narrow escape, however, Panatta was superb, dispatching Borg in the quarterfinals, Eddie Dibbs in the semis, and gritty Harold Solomon, 6-1, 6-4, 4-6, 7-6 (7-3), in the final. Solomon, who roared from behind in five of his seven matches, was the first American finalist at Paris since Herbie Flam in 1957.

Arthur Ashe, No. 1 in the world in 1975, got off to the best start of his career, winning five of his first six tournaments and 29 of 30 matches. He again topped the WCT point standings, earning a $50,000 bonus, but lost his crown in the first round of the WCT playoffs at Dallas, beaten by Solomon, 7-5, 3-6, 6-1, 6-3, and did little thereafter. His fade was in part attributed to inflammation of a chronic heel injury that required surgery in February 1977.

A pinched nerve in his elbow slowed another of the 1975 heroes, Orantes, much of the season, but therapy and a switch to a lighter aluminum racket revived him in the autumn. The smooth left-hander won five of his last eight tournaments (including the year's longest winning streak: 23 matches), reached two other finals and resurrected himself from 1-4 down in the fourth to win a stirring Grand Prix Masters final at Houston over Poland's Wojtek Fibak, the most improved pro of the year, 5-7, 6-2, 0-6, 7-6, 6-1.

The Houston Masters concluded five years of Grand Prix sponsorship by the Commercial Union Assurance group, which withdrew because of flagging profits in the insurance business and was replaced by Colgate-Palmolive, which already had undertaken sponsorship of the women's Grand Prix, known as the Colgate International Series. Commercial Union's swan song was soured when Connors decided to pass up the Masters for a third consecutive year (thereby forfeiting the $60,000 he already had earned from the Grand Prix bonus pool for finishing third in the season-long standings), and Borg and Nastase chose to play exhibitions in the fall instead of Grand Prix tournaments that could have qualified them for the eight-man Masters.

Mexican Raul Ramirez won only four of 32 tournaments, but he was a tireless and consistent campaigner. His diligence paid off as he earned both the $150,000 prize for topping the Grand Prix singles standings and the $40,000 award for

Harold Solomon ousted Arthur Ashe in the 1976 WCT playoffs and reached the French final against Adriano Panatta. (Wide World)

heading the doubles standings, a unique accomplishment. In all, the Grand Prix encompassed 48 tournaments (and produced 23 different winners) in 22 countries, with more than $5 million in prize purses. With the WCT (24 16-man tournaments) and U.S. Indoor circuits added in, more than $9 million was available in men's tournaments worldwide.

The riches available were demonstrated graphically when Ilie Nastase collected $180,000 in a single tournament: the WCT-run Avis Challenge Cup, a series of winner-take-all round-robin matches played throughout the winter and spring in Hawaii. Nastase beat Ashe in a five-set final on asphalt, 6-3, 1-6, 6-7, 6-3, 6-1. On the year, Nastase won five of 23 tournaments, compiled a 76-17 record, reached the final at Wimbledon and the semifinals at Forest Hills, and was the only player with a winning record over Connors (4-1), shutting off Jimmy's four-year hold on the U.S. Indoor, 6-2, 6-3, 7-6. But Connors won the U.S. Clay for a second time, 6-2, 6-4, over Fibak.

In doubles, John Newcombe and Tony Roche won their fourth Australian championship, but team-of-the-year honors were shared by Ramirez–Brian Gottfried and Sherwood Stewart–Freddie McNair, who underscored the old axiom that the ordinary singles players can blend extraordinarily in doubles.

Stewart-McNair won the French Open, dethroning Gottfried-Ramirez, 7-6, 6-3, 6-1, and came back from 1-4 in the fourth set to stun the same team in the Masters doubles final, 6-3, 5-7, 5-7, 6-4, 6-4. Those triumphs earned Stewart-McNair the No. 1 U.S. ranking in doubles. (Connors was No. 1 in singles, regaining the spot he occupied in 1973 and 1974.)

Fibak and Karl Meiler won the WCT doubles at Kansas City, after beating Gottfried-Ramirez in a five-set semifinal. Gottfried-Ramirez won their third straight Italian title, over Newcombe–Geoff Masters, even though completion of the final was delayed by darkness and continued four months later indoors at the Woodlands, outside Houston. They also won Wimbledon, knocking off curiously unseeded Newcombe-Roche (five-time champions) in the first round and Masters–Ross Case in a rousing final, 3-6, 6-3, 8-6, 2-6, 7-5, as well as the $100,000 ATP Doubles at the Woodlands. Tom Okker and Marty Riessen took the U.S. Open over surprising Aussies Paul Kronk and Cliff Letcher, 6-4, 6-4.

It was a quiet year politically in men's tennis, aside from the Davis Cup and storms arising from Nastase's tempestuous behavior. The rambunctious Romanian was at his worst in an ugly second-round victory over Germany's Hans Pohmann at Forest Hills. Nastase's gamesmanship and outbursts of obscene language, gestures and spitting, along with delays when Pohmann suffered cramps that should have disqualified him, caused this match to get out of control. Nastase

was eventually fined $1,000, which increased his aggregate disciplinary fines for a 12-month period to more than $3,000 and triggered an automatic 21-day suspension, under provisions of a new Code of Conduct enacted by the Men's International Professional Tennis Council. The suspension was a joke, however, since it applied only to Grand Prix tournaments; Nastase played exhibition tournaments and earned more than $50,000 during the time he was supposed to be disciplined.

In the Davis Cup, Mexico—after upsetting the U.S. in the American Zone—refused to play South Africa for the second consecutive year, and defaulted. When the Davis Cup nations refused to take action against Mexico at its annual meeting, the U.S. led a walkout of the major Cup nations, including France and Great Britain, for 1977. A compromise was worked out within two weeks, however, and these nations returned. The Soviet Union defaulted its semifinal series to Chile in protest of the military junta that had overthrown the Marxist regime of Salvador Allende in Santiago in 1973. This was precisely the sort of political disruption that the U.S. was opposing, and a reconstituted Davis Cup Committee of Management threw the USSR out of the 1977 competition.

Italy, runner-up in 1960 and 1961, won the Davis Cup for the first time, beating Chile in Santiago, 4-1, in a final distinguished more by the enthusiasm and sportsmanship of the sellout crowds at Santiago than by the quality of play. Corrado Barazzutti upset Chilean No. 1 Jaime Fillol at the start, 7-5, 4-6, 7-5, 6-1, and Panatta beat game but overmatched Patricio Cornejo, then teamed with Paolo Bertolucci to down Cornejo-Fillol for an unbeatable 3-0 lead as captain Nicola Pietrangeli, the star of the 1960 and 1961 Italian teams, exulted at courtside. The political situation had been tense, Italian leftists opposing the matches, but the Italians' joy at winning was unrestrained.

Earlier in the year Connors had made his first appearance for the U.S. in the World Cup.

Both he and Ashe thrashed Newcombe and Roche in singles, leading captain Dennis Ralston's American squad to a 6-1 victory over declining Australia before sellout crowds of 10,000 in Hartford.

World Team Tennis was more stable in its third season, but even with Chris Evert as a shining new attraction and the respected Butch Buchholz aboard as commissioner, all of the 10 franchises continued to operate in the red. The New York Sets—led by league most valuable player Sandy Mayer, Billie Jean King, Virginia Wade and Phil Dent—captured the league title with a 3-0 sweep of the Golden Gaters (San Francisco Bay Area) in the playoff final series. Evert, of the Phoenix Racquets, was the female MVP, her singles winning percentage (.700) the best of any player in WTT.

Evert was unquestionably the queen of tournament tennis as well. She won 75 of 80 matches, 12 of 17 tournaments, including Wimbledon, the U.S. Open and the rich Colgate Inaugural (over Françoise Durr, 6-1, 6-2) at Palm Springs in October, which launched the new Colgate International Series, and was to serve thereafter as its climactic playoff. Its $45,000 top prize was the biggest of the year in women's tennis. It boosted Evert's season winnings to $289,165 and her career winnings to $1,026,604, making her the first woman to earn more than $1 million in prize money.

Only four players—Evonne Goolagong (twice), Wade, Martina Navratilova and Dianne Fromholtz—were able to beat Evert during the year.

Goolagong (newly married to Roger Cawley) started the year by winning her third straight Australian Open title, a 6-2, 6-2 rout of Czechoslovakia's Renata Tomanova, and teaming with Helen Gourlay to defend the doubles title she had won the previous two years with Californian Peggy Michel.

The lithe Australian was at her best during the January through April Virginia Slims circuit,

Captain Tony Trabert talks strategy with doubles players Bob Lutz (center) and Stan Smith, winners over Mexico in 1976 Davis Cup competition. Italy won the Cup for the first time. (UPI)

winning 38 of 40 matches, dropping only 10 sets, and at one point running off 16 consecutive victories without loss of a set. She climaxed her record $133,675 Slims season (en route to a $195,452 year) by beating Evert, 6-3, 5-7, 6-3, in a magnificent match at the Los Angeles Sports Arena, the final of the Virginia Slims championship. That was the high point of Goolagong's year.

On the season, Evonne won eight of 14 tournaments, 58 of 64 matches. She reached the final of every tournament she played, was 7-0 vs. Virginia Wade, 6-0 vs. Rosemary Casals, 4-0 over Navratilova and 4-0 over Sue Barker. Evonne had the second-best winning percentage in singles among WTT players, and aside from one-set WTT matches lost to only two players: Evert five times, and Billie Jean King in the Federation Cup at Philadelphia. This was Evonne's most consistent season but still, as she announced at season's end that she was taking maternity leave, she was overshadowed by Evert.

After losing the Virginia Slims final, Chrissie won her next six tournaments in a dazzling 36-

match winning streak, and lost only one more match the rest of the year.

Her streak began with her third consecutive triumph in the Family Circle Cup, over Australian Kerry Melville Reid, 6-2, 6-2, at Amelia Island, Fla.

At Wimbledon, where all eight seeds reached the quarterfinals, Evert beat Olga Morozova in the quarterfinals, Martina Navratilova in the semis, and Goolagong, 6-3, 4-6, 8-6, in a thrilling final that ended Evonne's 25-match streak. This was Evert's first triumph ever over Goolagong on grass. Then Evert and Navratilova took the doubles title over Betty Stove and Billie Jean King—who did not play singles, and was thwarted in her attempt to seize a record 20th career Wimbledon title—6-1, 3-6, 7-5. (King and her New York Sets teammate Sandy Mayer were upset in the second round of the mixed doubles by South Africans Bob Hewitt and Greer Stevens, leaving BJK tied with Elizabeth Ryan, who never won the singles but captured 19 Wimbledon doubles and mixed titles between 1914 and 1934.)

Evert was at her dominating best on the clay at Forest Hills, winning her second consecutive U.S. Open title with the loss of only 12 games in six matches. (The only more devastating run through the field was accomplished by Helen Wills, who gave up eight games in six matches in 1929.) Evert stomped Goolagong, 6-3, 6-0, in the most lopsided final since 1964, running the last 10 games. This extended Evert's astounding clay-court winning streak to 21 tournaments and 101 matches, dating to August 1973.

A shocker was the first-round dumping of third-seeded Navratilova by No. 8 American Janet Newberry, 1-6, 6-4, 6-3, a low point in Martina's career that left her sobbing beside the court. She wouldn't lose an opening-rounder again in a major until her farewell French in 1994 (Miriam Oremans). But it was a tough early-going year for names: fourth, fifth and seventh-seeded Virginia Wade, Nancy Richey and Kerry Melville were all bounced in the second round, respectively, by Mimi Jausovec, Virginia Ruziei and Zenda Liess.

Delina "Linky" Boshoff and Ilana Kloss startlingly won the doubles title over Wade and Morozova, 6-1, 6-4, becoming the first South African women to win a U.S. title. King and another WTT teammate, Phil Dent, won the mixed doubles over Stove and Frew McMillan.

King came out of her self-imposed singles retirement in the Federation Cup at Philadelphia in August. Colgate assumed sponsorship of this women's team competition, and infused it with prize money for the first time: $130,000 for teams representing 32 nations, $40,000 to the winners. Unfortunately, a political hassle developed when the Soviet Union reneged on a previous promise and led a four-nation walkout (1975 champion Czechoslovakia, Hungary and the Philippines joined the USSR in refusing to play) to protest the inclusion of South African and Rhodesia in the draw. The defaulting nations were subsequently fined by the ITF, but they had succeeded in making the draw a shambles.

Billie Jean filled in unexpectedly in singles for Evert, who withdrew with a sore wrist. Playing for the U.S. for the first time since 1967, she teamed with old doubles partner Rosie Casals in a two-woman *tour de force*. They sprinted through four 3-0 victories to a meeting with favored Australia in the final. Kerry Reid beat Casals, but King found a wellspring of her old inspiration to beat Goolagong, 7-6, 6-4, in a match of exceptionally high standard. King-Casals then toppled Reid-Goolagong, 7-5, 6-3, for the championship.

After rare back-to-back losses in 1974 and 1975, the U.S. regained the Wightman Cup with a 5-2 victory over Great Britain, indoors at London's Crystal Palace. Evert led the way, beating Wade and then Sue Barker in the decisive match, 2-6, 6-2, 6-2. In the absence of the leading women, who were contracted to WTT, Barker had won the German and French (over Renata Tomanova, 6-2, 0-6, 6-2), sharing with Italian Open champ Mima Jausovec preeminence on European clay for the year. Evert put her U.S. Clay title on hold after four victorious years, and tall

Kathy May, 20, swung into the void to beat South African Brigitte Cuypers, 6-4, 4-6, 6-2.

Evert was ranked No. 1 in the U.S., of course, but Nancy Richey achieved a milestone in earning the No. 3 ranking. It was the 16th time she figured in the U.S. Top Ten, a record for consistency at the top previously held only by Louise Brough.

A major innovation in equipment was introduced in 1976. New rackets in a dizzying variety of designs and materials—wood, metal, fiberglass, alloys, composites—had been marketed over the previous decade, but the biggest stir since the introduction of Wilson's steel T-2000 in 1967 was created by the Prince racket, with its oversized head. Howard Head, founder of Head Ski and architect of that company's headlong plunge into tennis equipment, joined forces with the manufacturer of Prince ball machines to produce the revolutionary and subsequently imitated new racket, which had much the same balance as conventional rackets but twice the hitting area.

One hundred years after it began, Bjorn Borg won Wimbledon in 1977. (Jack Mecca)

1977

By any standard, 1977 was a landmark year for tennis. Wimbledon, the oldest of tournaments, celebrated its Centenary. The U.S. Open was played at Forest Hills for the last time. And a technological innovation, the "double strung" or "spaghetti" racket, caused such a stir that it was banned from tournament play several months after gaining notoriety, and led to the definition of a racket for the first time in the official rules of the game.

Three men—Bjorn Borg, Guillermo Vilas and Jimmy Connors—waged their own version of the year's hit movie, the science-fiction classic *Star Wars*. They were in a stratospheric super class, a galaxy above anyone else in tennis.

Borg won Wimbledon and had the most solid record, including winning margins against both his rivals. Vilas won the French and U.S. Opens and fashioned the longest winning streak of the

10-year-old Open era. Connors won the World Championship of Tennis in Dallas and the Grand Prix Masters, and was runner-up at Wimbledon and Forest Hills. The debate as to who was No. 1 continued right through the Masters which, because of U.S. television considerations, was moved back by new Grand Prix sponsor Colgate-Palmolive to the first week of January 1978.

There was no similar disagreement as to who was the ruler of women's tennis. Chris Evert remained the indisputable No. 1, despite Virginia Wade's coronation—after 15 years as the lady-in-waiting—as the queen of Wimbledon.

The celebrations of Wimbledon's Centenary fortnight began with the All England Lawn Tennis and Croquet Club honoring 41 of the 52 living singles champions at a luncheon. Afterward, a crowd of 14,000 in the packed Centre Court rose, and their applause swelled. As the Band of the Welsh Guards, resplendent in scarlet uniforms and polished brass, played "The March of the Kings" from the opera *Aida,* a wonderfully nostalgic "Parade of Champions" began, the former winners striding out onto the most famous lawn in the tennis world to receive commemorative medals from the Duke of Kent in a brief, dignified ceremony.

In a touching final gesture, medals were presented to Elizabeth "Bunny" Ryan, 85, and Jacques "Toto" Brugnon, 82, "representing all the doubles champions." Ryan—winner of 12 women's doubles and seven mixed titles between 1914 and 1934—moved slowly, on walking sticks, but cast them aside to wave to the crowd. Brugnon—who won Wimbledon doubles titles twice each with fellow French "Musketeers" Henri Cochet and Jean Borotra—used a cane and later held the arm of the fourth "Musketeer," René Lacoste. Toto died the next winter, but for this moment he was ebullient. When the presentations were over, the band started to play again, softly. The champions posed for photos, then joined arms and sang "Auld Lang Syne."

The tournament was also richly memorable. Left-hander John McEnroe, 18, of Douglaston, N.Y., became the youngest semifinalist in Wimbledon's 100 years, the first player ever to come through the qualifying rounds and get that far. He won eight matches in all before Connors brought him back to reality, 6-3, 6-3, 4-6, 6-4. In the other semifinal, Borg defeated the swift and flashy Vitas Gerulaitis, 6-4, 3-6, 6-3, 3-6, 8-6, in a breathtaking match. The sustained quality of the shotmaking and drama made this, in the opinion of longtime observers, one of the all-time Centre Court classics.

The final also lived up to a majestic standard, Borg and Connors—destined to be remembered as the archrivals of the '70s in tennis—battling each other from the baseline in torrid rallies seldom seen on grass courts. Connors seemed out of it at 0-4 in the fifth set, but roused himself for one last challenge and came back to 4-4 before a cru-

cial double fault in the ninth game cost him his momentum, his serve and the match, 3-6, 6-2, 6-1, 5-7, 6-4.

In the women's singles, 14-year-old Californian Tracy Austin became one of the youngest players to compete at Wimbledon. She defeated Ellie Vessies Appel, then showed tremendous poise and groundstrokes in losing a Centre Court match to defending champion Evert, 6-1, 6-1. That match, and her first victory ever over Billie Jean King on grass—6-1, 6-2 in the quarterfinals—took an enormous emotional toll on Evert, and left her curiously flat for her semifinal against Wade.

"Our Ginny," as the British affectionately called Wade, had never prepared better for a tournament, nor felt more self-confident. She had never gone beyond the semifinals in 15 previous Wimbledons, but she kept the pressure on with bold approach shots and magnificent net play to beat Evert, 6-2, 4-6, 6-1. Wade was much more passive in the final against 6-foot, 160-pound Betty Stove—the first Dutch finalist at Wimbledon—but settled down and let her erratic opponent make the mistakes. Wade won nine of the last 10 games and the match, 4-6, 6-3, 6-1.

The tennis was commonplace, but the occasion unforgettable. Wade, the first Englishwoman to win her national title since Ann Jones in 1969, accepted the gold championship plate from Queen Elizabeth II, who was making her first appearance at Wimbledon since 1962 in honor of the Centenary and her own Silver Jubilee celebration. British reserve gave way to an unbridled outpouring of patriotic sentiment. The Duchess of Kent waved excitedly to Wade from the Royal Box, and thousands of delighted Britons broke into a spontaneous, moving chorus of "For She's a Jolly Good Fellow."

Stove wound up a triple loser, runner-up with Martina Navratilova in the women's doubles to unseeded JoAnne Russell and Helen Gourlay Cawley, 6-3, 6-3, and with Frew McMillan in the mixed doubles to Bob Hewitt and

Only 14, Tracy Austin became a crowd favorite from Wimbledon to Forest Hills. (Peter Mecca)

Greer Stevens, 3-6, 7-5, 6-4. In the men's doubles, defending champions Brian Gottfried and Raul Ramirez fell to Jim Delaney and Sashi Menon in the first round, paving the way for an all-Australian final. Ross Case and Geoff Masters, runners-up in five sets the previous year, beat John Alexander and Phil Dent in another thriller, 6-3, 6-4, 3-6, 8-9, 6-4.

Wimbledon was the highlight of the year, but the most impressive achievement was the winning streak Vilas compiled the last six months of the year, after losing listlessly to Billy Martin in the third round at Wimbledon.

Vilas started the year as runner-up to Roscoe Tanner, the hard-serving left-hander, in the Australian Open, 6-3, 6-3, 6-3. By winning the French Open in the absence of Borg and Connors—Vilas lost only one set in seven matches

and his 6-0, 6-3, 6-0 victory over Brian Gottfried in the final was the most decisive since the tournament went international in 1925—Vilas shed his image as "The Eternal Second" and removed an enormous psychological burden.

Driven by his coach-manager, the hirsute and menacing Romanian Ion Tiriac, Vilas became the fittest and most iron-willed player on the professional circuit. His last six months of 1977 were a tour de force. He won 13 of 14 tournaments, 80 of 81 matches, including the U.S. Open. His 50-match, July-through-September winning streak was by far the longest since the advent of open tennis, eclipsing Rod Laver's 31 straight matches of 1969, previously the male record. And he immediately launched another streak of 30.

The record streak ended controversially the first week in October in the final of a tournament at Aix-en-Provence, France, Vilas defaulting angrily after losing the first two sets to Ilie Nastase, who was using the "spaghetti" racket that had just been barred, effective the following week.

The crowning glory of Vilas' streak was winning the U.S. Open, which was played at the West Side Tennis Club in the Forest Hills section of New York's borough of Queens for the last time, after 68 years there as the Championships site. Clumsy last-ditch efforts by the club's officials to retain the Open could not compensate for their years of foot-dragging on making physical improvements. W. E. "Slew" Hester of Jackson, Miss., president of the USTA, decided that the West Side Tennis Club was too congested, its management too stubbornly old-fashioned, to accommodate America's premier tournament, which was given 28 hours of television coverage by CBS-TV under a new five-year, $10-million rights contract. Hester set in motion ambitious plans for building a new USTA National Tennis Center in nearby Flushing Meadow Park, site of the 1939–40 and 1964–65 New York World's Fairs.

Vilas helped make "the last Forest Hills" memorable. He lost only 16 games in five match-

Argentina's Guillermo Vilas made money, and Jimmy Connors furious, in 1977. (Peter Mecca)

cial Union Assurance as the Grand Prix sponsor. On the year, Vilas won a record 17 tournaments and $800,642 in prize money—more than he had earned in five previous pro seasons. He played the most ambitious tournament schedule of any of the top men and finished with a 145-14 record, including Davis Cup matches. (With Vilas and Ricardo Cano playing singles, Argentina upset the United States in the American Zone final to reach the Cup semifinals for the first time.) During his 50-match streak, Vilas won an astonishing 109 of 125 sets. Starting with the French Open, he won 57 consecutive matches on clay.

But even though *World Tennis* magazine declared him No. 1 for the year, most other authorities disagreed and bestowed that mythical honor on Borg, who, top-seeded, defaulted to Dick Stockton, 3-6, 6-4, 1-0, in the fourth round of the U.S. Open with a shoulder injury. The 21-year-old Swede had the best winning percentage for the season—.920, on a record of 81-7. He won 13 of the 20 tournaments he played. Including the Masters—played in 1978, but considered the climax of the 1977 season—Borg was 3-0 over Vilas (two victories in the spring, the third in the semis of the Masters) and 2-1 over Connors, who beat him in the Masters final, 6-4, 1-6, 6-4, before a crowd of 17,150 at Madison Square Garden.

Connors may have had the season-ending last laugh, but he finished No. 3 after having been the best player in the world in 1974 and 1976 and No. 2 to Arthur Ashe in 1975. Connors won seven of 21 tournaments, 70 of 81 matches, and was in four big finals (winning the WCT playoffs over Dick Stockton, 6-7, 6-1, 6-3, 6-3, and the Masters, losing to Borg at Wimbledon and to Vilas at Forest Hills). But Connors was 1-2 head-to-head against Borg and 0-2 against Vilas, including a gripping match in the round-robin portion of the Masters, won by Vilas, 6-4, 3-6, 7-5. This spellbinder kept a record tournament crowd of 18,590 riveted to their seats in the Garden until 12:42 a.m. on a Friday morning.

While Borg, Vilas, and Connors constituted the ruling triumvirate of men's tennis, there were

es up to the semifinals, in which he beat Harold Solomon in straight sets. In the final, Vilas displayed great physical and mental stamina and a new technical weapon—a fine sliced backhand approach shot—to beat Connors in a match of brutish grace, 2-6, 6-3, 7-6 (7-4), 6-0. The sellout crowd of more than 16,000 cheered for the popular Argentinian left-hander against "the ugly American." After the last point, many Latins in the crowd hoisted Vilas to their shoulders and carried him around the old horseshoe stadium like a conquering hero. Connors, furious at both the outcome and the reception given the victor, left in a huff, not bothering to wait for the trophy presentation ceremonies.

Vilas dominated the Grand Prix point standings, winning the $300,000 prize ear-marked as the top share of the $1.5-million bonus pool put up by Colgate, which took over from Commer-

other noteworthy performers. Spaniard Manuel Orantes underwent surgery to repair a pinched nerve in his left elbow in the spring, but came back splendidly to bedazzle Connors, 6-1, 6-3, in the U.S. Clay Court final at Indianapolis and to topple Eddie Dibbs, 7-6 (7-3), 7-5, 6-4, in the 50th U.S. Pro Championships. Vitas Gerulaitis became the first American since 1960 to win the Italian Open, on slow clay, beating Tonino Zugarelli, and later demonstrated his versatility by winning the second Australian Open of the calendar year—the tournament was moved up to mid-December so that it could be included in the Grand Prix—on grass at Melbourne. Floridian Brian Gottfried won four tournaments in a six-week span early in the year and reached 15 finals during the season, winning five of them and compiling a 108-23 record.

In doubles, South Africans Bob Hewitt, 37, and Frew McMillan, 35, won 13 tournaments, even though separated for four months during the summer because McMillan played World Team Tennis. Their biggest victory came at Forest Hills, where they captured their first U.S. Open doubles title over Gottfried and Raul Ramirez, 6-4, 6-0. Hewitt and McMillan also won the Masters over Stan Smith and Bob Lutz, 7-5, 7-6, 6-3.

Gottfried and Ramirez won the Italian Open doubles for a record fourth consecutive year and recaptured the French Open title. Arthur Ashe and Tony Roche won the Australian Open title in January, and Aussies Allan Stone and Ray Ruffels took it in December. Vijay Amritraj and Dick Stockton made their only doubles victory together count, collecting $40,000 apiece for beating the makeshift pair of Adriano Panatta and Gerulaitis in the WCT doubles finals at Kansas City, 7-6, 7-6, 4-6, 6-3.

The Colgate Grand Prix embraced 76 tournaments, with total prize money of approximately $9 million. Worldwide, men's tournaments offered about $12 million, excluding World Team Tennis and exhibition matches. Fifteen players made more than $200,000 in prize money, including Hewitt ($234,184), whose earnings came mostly in doubles. Five players (Vilas, Borg, Ramirez, Smith, and Orantes) crossed the once unimaginable $1-million career earnings mark, increasing the number of tennis millionaires to 13 since Laver first passed the milestone in 1971.

In team competitions, Australia recovered the Davis Cup for the first time since 1973 and tied the U.S. for the most possessions (24). Vilas was a rock (8-0 for the campaign) and beat both Phil Dent and John Alexander in the semis, but they got around him, 3-2, by winning their singles over Ricardo Cano and the heated, vital doubles, edging out Guillermo and Cano, before an avid drum-beating Buenos Aires crowd, 6-2, 4-6, 9-7, 4-6, 6-2.

Italy, arriving in Sydney to defend, got a left-handed surprise. Tony Roche—at 32, seemingly well past his prime—had last played for the Cup 10 years before, then only in the clinching doubles with John Newcombe over Spain. But he was Captain Neale Fraser's ace from deep in the hole for the showdown on grass, and justified the long-shot gamble with serve-and-volleying flair to astound Adriano Panatta, 6-3, 6-4, 6-4. Alexander took care of Barazzutti, combative though never having won a match on the green, 6-2, 8-6, 4-6, 6-2, and it looked like a romp. However Panatta and the "Pasta Kid," rotund Paolo Bertolucci, jarred Alexander and Dent, 6-4, 6-4, 7-5. It was 2-1. With a goodly number of Italian immigrants in the crowd screaming for him—"Dai [come on], Adriano!"—an aroused Panatta drove Alexander to the brink of defeat in a difficult swirling wind, serving for the match at 6-5, 30-all in the fourth. A double fault hurt him, and there J. A. shoved harder when pushed to wrap up the Cup in five, cleverly using lobs at the tense conclusion, 6-4, 4-6, 2-6, 8-6, 11-9.

There was no beating Vilas in Buenos Aires, and when the overlooked Cano led off over Dick Stockton, 3-6, 6-4, 8-6, 6-4, another ambush of the *Yanquis* on a Latin dirt road was assured. This was the third consecutive year that the U.S. failed to survive the American Zone, eclipsing 1965–67 as the dimmest period in U.S. Davis Cup history.

World Team Tennis completed its fourth season, with the Boston Lobsters topping the East Division, and the Phoenix Racquets the West Division. Ten teams played 44 matches each, and again all operated in the red. The New York Apples, led by Billie Jean King and Sandy Mayer, won the league championship, defeating Phoenix in the final round of the playoffs.

Chris Evert won three of the four biggest tournaments in women's tennis: her fourth Virginia Slims Championship, played at Madison Square Garden, over Englishwoman Sue Barker, 2-6, 6-1, 6-1; her third consecutive U.S. Open, matching a feat last accomplished by Maureen Connolly in 1951–53, over Australian Wendy Turnbull, 7-6 (7-3), 6-2; and the Colgate Series Championship—eight-woman finale of the Colgate International Series, the women's equivalent of the men's Grand Prix—over Billie Jean King, 6-2, 6-2, at Rancho Mirage, Calif.

Evert represented the United States for the first time in the Federation Cup, which attracted 42 nations to the grass courts of Devonshire Park in Eastbourne, England, the week before Wimbledon. Chrissie did not lose a set in singles as the United States romped past Austria, Switzerland, France, South Africa and Australia. Evert defeated Kerry Reid, 7-5, 6-3, and King disposed of Dianne Fromholtz, 6-1, 2-6, 6-2, to clinch the championship.

Evert also led America's 39th victory in the 54-year-old Wightman Cup rivalry against Great Britain, played on the West Coast for the first time, at Oakland Coliseum. Chrissie opened with a 7-5, 7-6 victory over Wade, King blistered Barker, 6-1, 6-4, and a 7-0 rout was on. Even though the outcome was already decided, a record Wightman Cup crowd of 11,317 turned up on the final evening of the three-day event to see King beat Wade in a glorious match, 6-4, 3-6, 8-6.

In all, Evert at age 22 won 11 of 14 tournaments, 70 of 74 matches, and $453,134 in prize money. She was ranked No. 1 in the U.S. for the fourth consecutive year and No. 1 in doubles for the first time, with Rosemary Casals. Evert won the U.S. Open without losing a set for the second straight year and stretched her remarkable clay-court winning streak to 23 tournaments and 113 matches, dating back to August 1973. Even though Fromholtz surprised her in the round-robin portion of the Colgate Series Championships, Evert reached the final with a bitterly fought 1-6, 6-4, 6-4 victory over Wade, and went on to claim the richest prize in women's tennis: $75,000.

Although Evert was the dominant force, and Wade the sentimental success story, there were other notable achievements in women's tennis in 1977:

- Tracy Austin, five feet tall and weighing 90 pounds, reached the quarterfinals of the U.S. Open, beating fourth seed Barker en route. The 14-year-old took enough time off from her eighth- and ninth-grade classes in Rolling Hills, Calif., to play 10 professional tournaments and wound up ranked No. 12 in the world on the computer of the Women's Tennis Association and No. 4 in the United States—the youngest ever to crack the Top Ten until Jennifer Capriati, a younger 14 in 1990.

- Martina Navratilova, starting the season slimmed down and determined to make up for a disappointing 1976, won four of 11 tournaments on the Virginia Slims circuit, beating Evert in the final of the season opener at Washington, D.C.

- Sue Barker, with an improved backhand to go with her already devastating forehand, won two Slims tournaments and lost three finals to Navratilova. Barker finished third on the circuit, but beat Navratilova, seeded twelfth, to get to the final of the Slims Championships.

- Wendy Turnbull, so swift afoot she was nicknamed "Rabbit," emerged as a player to be reckoned with by upsetting sixth-seeded Casals, third-seeded Wade and second-seeded Navratilova, 2-6, 7-5, 6-4, to reach the U.S. Open final, the lowest seed to do so.

- Transsexual Renée Richards won her year-long legal struggle for acceptance in women's tournaments when a New York judge ruled that she could not be barred from the U.S. Open for failing the Olympic chromosome test. The court ruled that medical evidence proved Richards was "female," and the USTA and WTA dropped efforts to bar her. She lost in the first round of the Open singles to Wade, but reached the doubles final with Californian Bettyann Grubb Stuart before losing to Navratilova and Stove, 6-1, 7-6. (Stove also won the mixed doubles, with Frew McMillan, over King and Gerulaitis, 6-2, 3-6, 6-3.) Thereafter, Richards became a regular competitor on the women's circuit, though several players defaulted against her to protest her inclusion in their tournaments.

- King, recovered from knee surgery the previous November, worked her way back into shape and won three consecutive tournaments and 18 straight matches in the autumn to reach the playoff finale of the $2-million Colgate Series, which carried a $600,000 bonus pool. She was 0-4 on the year against Evert, but 2-0 against WTT teammate Wade, 3-0 against Navratilova, 1-0 against Barker and 4-0 against Stove. King, winning six titles, finished the year with a 53-6 record, ranked No. 2 in the U.S. and again a major factor in the women's game. While the topcats were away, employed in WTT, lesser ladies were at play in Europe: Janet Newberry won the Italian, Mima Jausovec became the first Yugoslav to win the French, beating Romanian Florenta Mihai, 6-2, 6-7, 6-1.

- Kerry Reid, at 29, won the Australian Open for the first time, over fellow Aussie Dianne Fromholtz, 7-5, 6-2. Fromholtz and Helen Gourlay Cawley captured the doubles.

- Evonne Goolagong Cawley, kept out of the January version of the Australian Open because she was pregnant, gave birth to her first child—daughter Kelly—in May, and launched a comeback in the fall. She won the December version of the Australian Open over Gourlay. Formally it was Mrs. Roger Cawley defeating Mrs. Robert Cawley, 6-3, 6-0, the respective English and Australian husbands unrelated. This was Evonne's fourth Australian title and she extended her unbeaten streak in the tournament to 20 matches.

The hottest political controversy of the year concerned the rise and fall of the "double strung" or "spaghetti" racket, which was actually a radical stringing technique that could be applied to any standard racket frame. There were several versions, but they all used two sets of vertical strings, supported by five or six cross strings threaded through them, and braced with fish line, adhesive tape, rope or other protuberances, including a plastic tubing called "spaghetti." While rackets thus strung generally had a very low tension—between 35 and 55 pounds—they were able to generate tremendous power because of a "trampoline effect," the ball sinking deep in the double layer of strings and being propelled out. Because the dual layer of strings also moved, they were able to "brush" the ball, artificially imitating a heavy topspin stroke. Thus, some players were able to hit the ball extremely hard from the backcourt and still keep it in play. The "spaghetti" racket was all the more maddening to play against because the ball came off it with a dull thud that made it difficult to judge.

The "double strung" racket was invented in West Germany by a former horticulturist named Werner Fisher, and it created a major scandal in club and national tournaments there as second- and third-line players became champions with it. An adaptation of the racket was first used in a

The controversial spaghetti racket, subsequently banned, was used by France's Christophe Roger-Vasselin in the 1977 Poree Cup finals in which he lost to Guillermo Vilas. (UPI)

major tournament by Australian lefty Barry Phillips-Moore in the French Open. A number of professional players used it in Europe during the summer and it gained further notoriety at the U.S. Open when an obscure American player named Mike Fishbach used his homemade version to trounce Billy Martin and 16th-seeded Stan Smith in the first two rounds.

A couple of weeks later, Ilie Nastase was beaten by a player using a "spaghetti" racket in Paris and swore he would never play against it again. The following week he turned up with one and used it to win a tournament at Aix-en-Provence, ending Guillermo Vilas' long winning streak in the final. Vilas quit after two sets, claiming that playing against the exaggerated spin injured his elbow.

The ITF had already acted by that time, however, putting a "temporary freeze" on use of the double-strung rackets in tournaments, effective Oct. 2. The ITF based its decision on a report by the University of Brunswick in West Germany, which indicated that every hit with the racket was in fact a "double hit," in violation of the rules.

The ITF made its "ban" permanent the following June by adopting a definition of a racket for the first time: "A racket shall consist of a frame, which may be of any material, weight, size of shape and stringing. The stringing must be uniform and smooth and may be of any material. The strings must be alternately interlaced or bonded where they cross. The distance between the main and/or cross strings shall not be less than one quarter of an inch nor more than one-half inch. If there are attachments they must be used only to prevent wear and tear and must not alter the flight of the ball. They must be uniform with a maximum protrusion of .04 of an inch."

1978

In 1978, as Wimbledon began its second century, Stade Roland Garros in Paris—home of the French Championships—celebrated its 50th anniversary, and the U.S. Open moved to the new USTA National Tennis Center in Flushing Meadow, Queens, N.Y., the most important new arena for international tennis in half a century.

Bjorn Borg and Jimmy Connors continued their spirited battle of king-of-the-hill in men's tennis, Martina Navratilova and Chris Evert waged a similarly lovely little war for the No. 1 ranking among the women, and several precocious young talents blossomed—19-year-old John McEnroe starting to challenge the top men, and high-school girls Tracy Austin and Pam Shriver asserting themselves in women's tournaments.

Perhaps nothing better symbolized what happened to the once-elitist, white-flanneled sport of tennis in the 1970s than the fact that the U.S. Open, America's premier tournament, moved to a public park. The National Tennis Center was built, remarkably, in one year on 16 acres of city-owned land in Flushing Meadow Park, adjacent to Shea Stadium.

Conducted to Flushing by drawling, cigar-chomping W. E. "Slew" Hester, a 66-year-old wildcat oilman from Jackson, Miss., the U.S. Championships was retreating from 97 years in patrician clubs—first for the men at high society bastion Newport (R.I.) Casino, then (for the women) the Philadelphia Cricket Club and subsequently for both the West Side Tennis Club at Forest Hills, not to mention a three-year visit (1921–23) to Philadelphia's Germantown Cricket Club by the men.

Hester talked like a Southern conservative, but proved in a memorable two-year term to be perhaps the most progressive president in the history of the USTA.

Many people second-guessed Hester in September 1977 when, fed up with the reactionary board of governors of the West Side Tennis Club, he announced that the Open would not be played again at Forest Hills. Few thought the new complex Hester envisioned a couple of miles away could be completed in 12 months, and many considered the project "Hester's Folly." But Hester's perseverance and leadership, despite arthritis so severe it was difficult for him to walk, enabled the USTA to cut through bureaucratic red tape, union disputes and cost overruns and get the splendid complex built in time for the 1978 Open.

The National Tennis Center was dedicated on Aug. 30, 1978. Its main arena—Louis Armstrong Stadium, site of the Singer Bowl for the 1964–65 World's Fair and named for the late jazz great who lived nearby—accommodated nearly 20,000 spectators, with barely a bad seat in the house. In addition to the steeply banked, red, white and blue stadium, the complex included a 6,000-seat grandstand, 25 additional lighted outdoor courts, and nine indoor courts, all with the same acrylic asphalt surface that approximates the hard courts most Americans play on. Under a 15-year lease agreement between the USTA and

The new home of the U.S. Open—The National Tennis Center in Flushing, N.Y. (Jack Mecca)

the city of New York, the facility is open to the public year-round and is available to the USTA for tournaments and special events 60 days a year, at a modest fee. The USTA, in turn, spent $10 million to renovate and enlarge a stadium that was intended for concerts but that had fallen into terrible disrepair.

The result was the most significant new venue for world tennis since the modern All England Club was opened in the London suburb of Wimbledon in 1922 and Stade Roland Garros was dedicated as a civic monument in Paris for the 1928 Davis Cup challenge round.

Roland Garros celebrated its golden anniversary during the 1978 French Open Championships. On balance, this was a dull tournament, but on a day when 32 past champions were honored in gala center court ceremonies, Bjorn Borg asserted himself as one of the greatest by winning the most important clay-court test of Europe for the third time, five days past his 20th birthday.

Two weeks after winning the Italian Open in five sets over Roman matinee idol Adriano Panatta, 1-6, 6-3, 4-6, 6-3, Borg repeated the arduous clay-court "double" he had first achieved in 1974. He swept through seven matches in Paris in 21 straight sets, dropping only 32 games. In the final, he trounced defending champion Guillermo Vilas, 6-1, 6-1, 6-3.

Borg went on to become the first man since Rod Laver in 1962 to sweep the Italian, French and Wimbledon singles titles in one season. In dominating the grass of Wimbledon as he had the clay in Rome and Paris, Borg also equaled a more important milestone. He became the first man since Englishman Fred Perry in 1934–36 to win the Wimbledon singles three successive years.

Borg's dream of duplicating Perry's feat nearly ended in the first round. Victor Amaya, a 6-foot-7, 220-pound left-hander with a thunderous serve, led him by two sets to one, 3-1, in the fourth, 30-40 on Borg's serve. Borg escaped a second service break only by the margin of a bold second serve, then broke Amaya and came back to win, 8-9 (8-10), 6-1, 1-6, 6-3, 6-3.

Thereafter, Borg grew increasingly sharper and stronger. He routed a rejuvenated Tom Okker in the semifinals and thrashed archrival Connors, 6-2, 6-2, 6-3, in the final. Never before had Borg served, volleyed and smashed with such authority, and he also displayed a new weapon—a sliced backhand approach shot to Connors' vulnerable forehand, which stayed low on the fast grass. "The way Borg played today," marveled Perry, who hustled down from behind his microphone in the BBC radio commentary booth to congratulate the young Swede on Centre Court, "if he had fallen out of a 45th-story window of a skyscraper, he would have gone straight up."

At the midpoint of the season, it seemed that Borg, with his beefed-up serve, had begun to dominate his grand rivalry with Connors. Despite

Bjorn Borg wins in 1978 for the third straight year at Wimbledon as Jimmy Connors, his victim, stonily departs the scene. (UPI)

a loss in the 1977 Grand Prix Masters the first week of the new year, Borg had won five of their last six meetings, giving up only 11 games in the last six sets, through Wimbledon.

But Connors immediately began to train for another showdown, vowing to "follow that sonofabitch to the ends of the earth" for revenge. He worked on adding oomph to his serve—which had deserted him in the Wimbledon final—and shoring up his forehand. Having won 18 straight matches going into the Wimbledon final, he didn't lose another the rest of the summer, winning Grand Prix tournaments at Washington, Indianapolis (the U.S. Clay Court over Jose Higueras, 7-5, 6-1) and Stowe, Vt., as he groomed his game to peak at the U.S. Open.

Connors' moment of truth at the Open came in a fourth-round victory over Panatta, the dash-

Slew Hester, whose dream of a USTA National Tennis Center became a reality in 1978, beams as Jimmy Connors displays the U.S. Open trophy he won at the facility's inaugural. (Jack Mecca)

ing and talented Italian. Panatta served for the match at 5-4 in the fifth set of this 3-hour, 36-minute epic, came within two points of victory at 30-30, and later fended off four match points. Connors got to the fifth with an astounding shot: a backhand down the line on the dead run from 10 feet wide of the court, which he somehow reached and drilled one-handed around the net post for a winner.

Moments later, Connors had the match, 4-6, 6-4, 6-1, 1-6, 7-5, and that, he said later, gave him the impetus to steamroll through the final three rounds without losing a set to Brian Gottfried, John McEnroe and Borg. Never before were Con-

nors' skill, will and churning internal aggression better shown than in the final. He annihilated Borg, who had a blister on the thumb of his racket hand, almost as badly as he had been ravaged at Wimbledon, 6-4, 6-2, 6-2, ending the Swede's 39-match streak.

Connors, the first man since Bill Tilden in the 1920s to reach the singles final five consecutive years, thus became the first man since Perry in 1933, 1934 and 1936 to win three U.S. singles titles, and the first American to do so since Tilden. By quirk of history, Connors also gained the singular distinction of having won on grass (1974), clay (1976), and hard court (1978).

The U.S. Open final was the last meeting of the year between Borg and Connors. The last four months of the season belonged to McEnroe, the brash left-hander from Douglaston, N.Y., who was the only man other than Ken Rosewall, 19 in 1954, to have reached the semifinals at both Wimbledon and the U.S. Championships while still a teenager.

After losing to Connors in the Open, McEnroe won four Grand Prix tournaments (Hartford, over Johan Kriek, 6-2, 6-4, San Francisco, Stockholm, London) in singles, seven in doubles, led the U.S. to its first possession of the Davis Cup since 1972 with a spectacular singles debut, and won both the singles and doubles titles at the Colgate Grand Prix Masters at Madison Square Garden the second week in January 1979. His singles record over that stretch was 49-7. In the six months since turning pro in June after winning the National Intercollegiate singles title as a Stanford University freshman, McEnroe collected $463,866.

At Stockholm, on a fast tile court, he won his first meeting with Borg, 6-3, 6-4. His left-handed serve, sliced low and wide so that it skidded away from Borg's two-fisted backhand, was so effective that McEnroe lost only seven points in 10 service games. It was the first time that Borg, 22, had lost to a player younger than he.

McEnroe made his Davis Cup debut in doubles in September, partnering Brian Gottfried to the decisive point in America's 3-2 victory over Chile in the American Zone Final at Santiago. McEnroe made his singles debut in the Final at Rancho Mirage, Calif., and lost his serve only once in demoralizing John Lloyd, 6-1, 6-2, 6-2, in the opening match and Buster Mottram, 6-2, 6-2, 6-1, in the clincher of the 4-1 U.S. victory over Great Britain. This ended a five-year drought for the U.S. and gave it possession of the trophy symbolizing international team supremacy in tennis for a record 25th time. As for McEnroe's dominance, it should be noted that never before in 67 Davis Cup finals had a player lost as few as 10 games in two singles matches. Bill Tilden in 1924, Jack Kramer in 1946 and Borg in 1975

"The best player in the world the last four months of 1978," Arthur Ashe said of young John McEnroe. (Peter Mecca)

gave up 12. Mac was the only teenager to spearhead a U.S. Cup triumph with two singles wins, although Michael Chang, at age 18 in 1990, would win one.

McEnroe went into the season-ending Masters playoff eager for a showdown with Connors, who had beaten him in all four of their career meetings. The Masters, designed to bring together the top eight finishers in the previous year's Grand Prix standings for a $400,000 shootout, had lost much of its luster because Borg and Guillermo Vilas declined invitations. They had not played the minimum 20 Grand Prix tournaments required to qualify for shares of the $2-million Grand Prix bonus pool, and so turned their backs on the showcase finale. Connors did not qualify for his bonus either, but was coaxed at the 11th hour into defending his title.

The Connors-McEnroe duel was seen as the savior of a disappointing tournament, but it also fizzled because Connors aggravated a blood blister on his foot in the first set of their meeting in the round-robin portion of the tournament, and defaulted while trailing, 5-7, 0-3. McEnroe went on to beat Eddie Dibbs in the semifinals and comebacking Arthur Ashe, 6-7, 6-3, 7-5, in a scintillating final, McEnroe reviving himself from 1-4 down and two match points in the final set.

But even if McEnroe was, as Ashe called him, "the best player in the world the last four months of 1978," he was not in the running for Player of the Year honors based on his full-season record of 75-20. The run for the No. 1 ranking was strictly a match race between Borg and Connors.

Tennis magazine's ranking panel voted for Connors, but *World Tennis* and the International Federation—which instituted a "world champion" award—went for Borg.

The "World Champion" title was a new honor to be awarded annually by the ITF for men and women, intended to establish an official No. 1 player for each calendar year, eliminating the confusion caused by diverse and often contradictory sets of unofficial rankings.

Borg was the unanimous choice of the selection committee of three former champions: Fred Perry, Australian Lew Hoad and Californian Don Budge. Their decision was based primarily on his superior record in traditional major events, although Borg also held a 3-2 edge over Connors in head-to-head meetings, including three four-man "special events."

Borg's record for the entire season was 88-8, including a 10-0 singles record in spurring Sweden to the semifinals of the Davis Cup. He won 12 titles.

Connors, who won 14, was 84-7 overall. He monopolized the U.S., winning: Indoor, 7-6, 6-3, over Tim Gullikson, Clay Court and Open titles. Following the Wimbledon final, he compiled a 30-match winning streak.

Other notable achievements in 1978:

- "Broadway" Vitas Gerulaitis, the flamboyant 23-year-old New Yorker, got a default over Borg in the semifinals and captured the $100,000 top prize in the eight-man World Championship of Tennis finals at Dallas with an impressive 6-3, 6-2, 6-1 victory over Eddie Dibbs. Gerulaitis also collected the $100,000 top prize in WCT's 12-man, $300,000 invitational tournament at Forest Hills in July, beating Ilie Nastase in the final, 6-2, 6-0.

- Dibbs won four Grand Prix tournaments (Tulsa, Cincinnati, North Conway, Toronto), 84 of 111 matches in 30 tournaments, and finished third in the Grand Prix standings. Because Connors and Borg did not qualify, Dibbs received the top prize of $300,000 from the bonus pool and headed the Association of Tennis Professionals' "official money" list (tournament winnings and bonuses only) with $575,273. Borg ($469,441), Raul Ramirez ($463,866) and McEnroe were also over the $400,000 mark. Connors ($392,153) led a parade of six more players who won in excess of $300,000. Fourteen players were over $200,000 and a total of 34 collected over $100,000. In all, more than $12 million was at stake in 93 Grand Prix tournaments around the world.

- Guillermo Vilas won eight tournaments, including the German Open and the Australian Open, which ended Jan. 3, 1979. His 6-4, 6-4, 3-6, 6-3 triumph over unseeded John Marks was his third Big Four singles title, to go along with his French and U.S. Open crowns of 1977.

- Ashe, the Wimbledon champion and World No. 1 of 1975, started the year ranked only No. 257 because he had missed almost the entire 1977 season after surgery on a chronic heel ailment. He won three Grand Prix tournaments (San Jose, Columbus,

Los Angeles), reached the Masters final and finished the season ranked No. 11.

- Bob Hewitt and Frew McMillan won seven doubles titles, including their third at Wimbledon. Tom Okker and Wojtek Fibak also won seven tournaments, including the WCT finals at Kansas City, for which they split an $80,000 prize. Stan Smith and Bob Lutz captured their third U.S. Open doubles and won crucial Davis Cup matches in America's 3-2 victory over Sweden in the semifinals at Goteborg and the 4-1 victory over Great Britain. John McEnroe and Peter Fleming were the hottest team the second half of the season, winning six tournaments together between August and December, plus the 1978 Masters early in January. Brian Gottfried and Raul Ramirez, a standout team the previous four years, won only the U.S. Indoor at Memphis together in 1978 and split up their partnership after the French Open.

On the women's side, the first half of the year belonged to Martina Navratilova, the second half to Chris Evert.

With Evert taking the first three months of the year as a vacation, Navratilova, at age 21, began to fulfill her rich promise. She dominated the Virginia Slims winter circuit—the last under the cigarette company's sponsorship—winning the first seven tournaments and the $150,000 final playoff at Oakland, Calif., over Evonne Goolagong, 7-6, 6-4. That was Navratilova's most important victory to date, an important psychological break-through for the expatriate Czech left-hander.

Evert returned to competition in the spring, but Navratilova, supremely fit and confident, beat her in the final of a pre-Wimbledon grass court tournament at Eastbourne, England, coming back from 1-4 in the final set and saving a match point, 6-4, 4-6, 9-7.

They met again in the Wimbledon final, and this time Navratilova came back from 2-4 in the final set, serving magnificently and outsteadying as well as overpowering Evert to win, 2-6, 6-4, 7-5. Navratilova, whose emotions had regularly overwhelmed her abundant talent, won 12 of the last 13 points. She held at love the last two times she served, missing only one first serve, while Evert made three uncharacteristic unforced errors to lose her serve to 5-6 in the most crucial game of an absorbing match.

When it was over, Navratilova looked ecstatically toward her friend and manager, Hall of Fame golfer Sandra Haynie, an important stabilizing influence in her life who sat beaming in the competitors' guest box. Then Martina shed a flood of tears into a towel and was puffy-eyed when she received the championship trophy from the Duchess of Kent.

"I don't know if I should cry or scream or laugh. I feel very happy that I won, but at the same time I'm very sad that I can't share this with my family," said Navratilova, who had not seen her parents or her 15-year-old sister since defecting to the United States during the 1975 U.S. Open. Her victory, predictably, was all but neglected in the government-controlled media of Czechoslovakia, but her parents watched it on German television by driving to a town near the German border.

Navratilova and Billie Jean King—again foiled in her attempt to win a record-setting 20th career Wimbledon title—were upset in the quarterfinals of the Wimbledon women's doubles by Mona Schallau Guerrant and Sue Barker, but they did win the U.S. Open title, over Wimbledon champs Kerry Reid and Wendy Turnbull, 7-6, 6-4. Australians Reid and Turnbull saved two match points in the tie-breaker to take the Wimbledon crown, a 4-6, 9-8 (12-10), 6-3 thriller over French Open champs Mima Jausovec and Virginia Ruzici. Betty Stove and Frew McMillan won the mixed doubles at both Wimbledon and Flushing Meadow.

Navratilova won her first 37 matches of the year, but the winning streak finally came to an

Sixteen-year-old Pam Shriver had to settle for roses after a noble try against Chris Evert in the 1978 U.S. Open final. (UPI)

end in the quarterfinals of the Virginia Slims in Dallas. She was beaten by 15-year-old Californian Tracy Austin, 6-3, 2-6, 7-6 (5-4). The tingling match before 10,000 enthralled spectators went down to the final point of a best-of-nine-point tiebreaker, simultaneous match point for both.

The Dallas tournament produced several startling upsets and three teenaged semifinalists—Austin, 15-year-old Pam Shriver of Lutherville, Md., and 18-year-old Anne Smith of Dallas. Goolagong, 26, eventually beat Austin in the final, 4-6, 6-0, 6-2. "Someday, that tournament may be looked upon as a landmark, the beginning of a new order," predicted women's tennis pioneer Billie Jean King.

Those words appeared prophetic as Austin, Shriver and Smith all landed in the U.S. Top Ten rankings for 1978—Austin at No. 3, Shriver at No. 5, and Smith at No. 8. They appeared to be the vanguard of a wave of promising young women players, a notion fortified by the victory of 13-year-old Andrea Jaeger in the 18-and-under division of the prestigious Orange Bowl junior tournament at the end of the year.

Austin rose to No. 6 in the world before turning 16 on Dec. 12, 1978. She beat Shriver in the finals of the U.S. Girls' 16 and 18 Championships, increasing her record total of U.S. junior titles to 27. She turned pro in October, won her first tournament as a professional at Stuttgart,

Germany, over Betty Stove, 6-3, 6-3, and collected $70,000 in prize money within three months.

Shriver, while 0-9 against Austin in their junior careers, one-upped her at the U.S. Open, becoming the youngest finalist in the tournament's history. Shriver upset Kerry Reid, an injured Lesley Hunt, and Navratilova, 7-6, 7-6, in a rain-interrupted semifinal. That was arguably the greatest upset in women's major tournament history. Playing nervelessly and aggressively with her Prince (oversized head) racket, Shriver used her serve-and-volley game to extend Evert to 7-5, 6-4 before losing an exciting final.

Both Austin and Shriver, who remained an amateur, were named to the U.S. Wightman Cup team, which was upset by Great Britain, 4-3, at London's Royal Albert Hall. Evert routed Sue Barker, 6-2, 6-1, and Virginia Wade, 6-0, 6-1, but the British preyed on the inexperience of the American teenagers. Michele Tyler upset Shriver, Wade and Barker each beat Austin, and Wade and Barker teamed up to beat Shriver and Evert, 6-0, 5-7, 6-4, in the decisive doubles match.

Austin also joined Evert and captain Billie Jean King as the U.S. won the Federation Cup for the third straight year, at Melbourne, Australia. The U.S. nipped Australia, 2-1, in the final, Evert and King teaming for the decisive point over Reid and Turnbull, 4-6, 6-1, 6-4.

Evert did not lose a tournament match after the Wimbledon final, winning her last 34 of the year, including three over Navratilova. Evert finished with a 56-3 record, six victories in 10 tournaments, and $443,540 in prize money. She became only the third woman to win the U.S. singles four consecutive years, the first since Helen Jacobs in 1932–35. Evert won the U.S. Open without losing a set for the third consecutive year, an astonishing feat, especially since the surface was changed from clay (on which she had not lost since August 1973) to the medium-fast hard courts that were not ideally suited to her backcourt game.

Evert finished the year with a 3-2 record against Navratilova and was voted the ITF "World Champion" by a panel of three former women champions: Ann Jones, Margaret Court and Margaret Osborne duPont.

Again devalued in the female precinct by the absence of the strength working in WTT, the Italian went to Czechoslovak Regina Marsikova, the French to Romanian Virginia Ruzici, the first women of their countries to win those titles.

Evert also was voted the Most Valuable Player in World Team Tennis, leading her Los Angeles Strings to their first championship of the intercity league. The Strings beat the Boston Lobsters in the playoff finale.

But after five years of financial losses, WTT was on shaky ground as the year ended. Half of the league's 10 teams announced that they were ceasing operations in the fall, and despite some optimistic noises from the commissioner's office in St. Louis, the chances of finding replacements appeared slim. Plans for a seven-week, $1-million women's tournament circuit in Europe in the spring gave Evert, Navratilova and the other women stars of WTT a lucrative alternative. The failure of the league to sign top players for 1979 caused several influential owners to give up the ghost, and the league seemed to unravel quickly after the Boston Lobsters and the New York Apples folded.

Virginia Slims, which had pioneered the promotion of women's tennis since 1971, startlingly departed from the sponsorship scene in April when the WTA board of directors voted not to renew its contract for the winter circuit. The WTA cited "differences in philosophy on the structure of the circuit" for the divorce from the company, which had poured more than $8 million into women's pro tennis over eight years.

Some women players thought the termination of the contract was a grave mistake and that no comparable patron of the women's game could be found. But in June it was announced that Avon—the huge cosmetic and costume jewelry firm that had for two years sponsored the "Futures" satellite circuit—had signed a two-year contract, with additional renewal options, to take over sponsorship of the major circuit as well as the "Futures." Avon's $2.2-million annual commitment was to fund 11 "Championship" tournaments with purses between $125,000 and $200,000, leading to a $325,000 singles and doubles championship playoff, and an expanded circuit of $25,000 "Futures" tournaments.

Despite growing pains, sometimes acute, it was obvious that professional tennis was still on the rise as the 1980s approached.

1979

The United Nations designated 1979 as the "International Year of the Child," and in tennis, youth was well served. This was most evident at the U.S. Open, where 16-year-old Tracy Austin became the youngest women's singles champion in the history of America's premier championships, and 20-year-old John McEnroe reigned as the youngest men's champion since Pancho Gonzalez in 1948.

But while firmly establishing themselves as contenders for the No. 1 world rankings, the "kids" were not ready to ascend the throne quite yet. The positions of honor in the last year of tennis' remarkable "growth decade" belonged to "old-timers" Martina Navratilova, 22, who won the Avon Championships climaxing the women's indoor circuit and her second consecutive Wimbledon title, and the irrepressible Bjorn Borg, 23, who captured his fourth French Open title and his fourth in a row at Wimbledon, a feat no man had accomplished since before World War I.

Still, it was an exceptional season for those young overachievers, Austin and McEnroe. In addition to her triumph in the Open, Tracy was runner-up to Navratilova in the Avon Championships and snapped Chris Evert Lloyd's six-year, 125-match clay-court winning streak en route to victory in the Italian Open, her first big international title. McEnroe, who had started the year by win-

Martina Navratilova won Wimbledon in 1979 for the second year in a row. (UPI)

ning the 1978 Grand Prix Masters, added the World Championship of Tennis title, beating Jimmy Connors and Borg back-to-back, and teamed with Peter Fleming to win the Wimbledon and U.S. Open doubles. Prodigious in their successes, they were clearly the best doubles pair in the world.

The rapid ascendance of Austin and McEnroe did symbolize a significant change in the old order that had ruled much of the latter part of the decade.

Chris Evert and Jimmy Connors—who had reached the pinnacle of the game in 1974 as "the lovebird double," young champions engaged to wed—finally did get married. But not to each other. Evert became the bride of British Davis Cup player John Lloyd. A few weeks earlier, Connors revealed that he had secretly married former *Playboy* magazine Playmate-of-the-Year Patti McGuire in Japan the previous autumn. The couple's first child, Brett David, was born in August.

Meanwhile, though still formidable players, neither Evert Lloyd nor Connors was quite the force of before. Their marriages and apparent off-court happiness seemed to coincide with a slight but noticeable decline in their competitive fires.

Evert Lloyd said she was no longer obsessed with the ambition to be the No. 1 player in the world. She did recapture the French Open title in the absence of Navratilova and Austin, but never really resembled her dominant and awesomely consistent form of the prior five years. She failed to reach the semifinals of the Avon Championships, was runner-up to Navratilova at Wimbledon for the second straight year and succumbed to Austin one hurdle short of an unprecedented fifth consecutive U.S. Open title.

Connors, after being in the finals at Wimbledon four of the five previous years and at the U.S. Open five straight times, fell in the semis of each and at the same stage in the WCT playoffs and French Open as well. Moreover, Borg established indisputable superiority in their long-running and splendid rivalry—crushing Connors in straight sets in four meetings on four different surfaces (clay at Boca Raton, Fla., concrete at Las Vegas, grass at Wimbledon, indoors in Tokyo), never losing more than three games in a set.

Connors did defend his titles in both the U.S. Pro Indoor at Philadelphia and the U.S. Indoor at Memphis, beating Arthur Ashe—who had made an impressive comeback from heel surgery, but shockingly suffered a mild heart attack at age 36 in August—in both finals. Connors romped in Philly, 6-3, 6-4, 6-1. Memphis was closer, Ashe fighting valiantly for the only U.S. National singles title he had never won, before losing, 2-6, 6-4, 6-4, Jimmy's fifth.

It was at Moody Coliseum in Dallas, at the end of the winter-spring men's indoor season, that McEnroe gave a convincing glimpse of great things ahead. Playing in the WCT final for the first time, he beat Australian John Alexander, 6-4, 6-0, 6-2; Connors, 6-1, 6-4, 6-4; and Borg, 7-5, 4-6, 6-2, 7-6, to win the $100,000 first prize with the kind of left-handed serve-and-volley attack—rich in variations of speed and spin, touch and

Tracy Austin is a study in concentration during her straight-set victory over Chris Evert Lloyd in the U.S. Open final in 1979. (UPI)

improvisation—not seen since the salad days of Rod Laver.

Navratilova was the prevailing figure on the 12-week, $2.2-million Avon Championship Series, winning four of seven tournaments she played plus the showcase $275,000 finale at Madison Square Garden. In the climactic match, Martina clinched the $100,000 top prize by overcoming her own shaky backhand and Austin's persistent backcourt game, 6-3, 3-6, 6-2. Veterans Betty Stove and Françoise Durr won the doubles over Sue Barker and Ann Kiyomura, 7-6 (7-1), 7-6 (7-3).

The most startling development of the Avon Championships, which climaxed a successful first year for the cosmetics firm as heir to Virginia Slims in sponsoring the women's indoor circuit, was the failure of Evert to get through the round-robin portion of the playoffs to the semifinals. Until 1979, Chrissie had never lost two matches in a row in her professional career. That astounding landmark of consistency was broken when she was beaten by Navratilova in the final of an Avon tournament at Oakland and then by Greer Stevens in the first round at Hollywood, Fla. In the playoffs at New York, Evert—whose mind was obviously more on her upcoming wedding than on her tennis—lost listlessly on successive nights to Austin, 6-3, 6-1, and Australian Dianne Fromholtz, 6-2, 6-3.

Evert did regroup to win her last tournament before her April 17 nuptials, coming from behind to beat Fromholtz (conqueror of Navratilova), 3-6, 6-3, 6-1, for the $100,000 first prize in the four-woman Clairol Crown special event at Carlsbad, Calif.

After a two-week honeymoon, Evert Lloyd teamed with Austin, Billie Jean King, and Rosemary Casals to give the U.S. its fourth consecutive triumph in the Federation Cup, on clay at Madrid. In the final, the American juggernaut overwhelmed Australia (Fromholtz, Wendy Turnbull, Kerry Reid), 3-0. Later in the year, an expanded U.S. squad also whitewashed Great Britain, 7-0, in the Wightman Cup at Palm Beach, Fla.

This was the year the Women's Tennis Association embarked on a bold experiment of breaking away from joint events with the men in the leading championships of Europe and playing their own separate tournaments, except in Paris. After years of secondary billing and proportionally low prize money, the women concluded they were ready to go it on their own in the European clay-court tournaments, even though interest in women's tennis was traditionally lacking.

Attendance at the new women's-only events was generally disappointing. This was especially true in Rome, where the paid attendance was only about 5,000 for the week, despite the glorious semifinal in which Austin defeated Evert Lloyd, 6-4, 2-6, 7-6, 7 points to 4 in the final-set tie-breaker. This was on May 12 and it marked the first time Evert Lloyd had lost a match on a clay court since Aug. 12, 1973, when Evonne Goolagong beat her in the final of the Western Championships at Cincinnati. Evert Lloyd's incredible streak had covered 25 tournaments and 125 matches over nearly six years, only eight of which went to three sets. Evert Lloyd said she was more relieved than stunned when the streak finally ended. Austin was thrilled, and celebrated the next day by beating West German left-hander Sylvia Hanika—voted the most improved player of the year by the WTA—in the final, 6-4, 1-6, 6-3.

It was a shame that the streak ended before such a sparse and seemingly disinterested audience, however. There were only about 1,500 spectators at Il Foro Italico, compared with a howling sell-out throng of more than 9,000 for the final of the men's Italian Open two weeks later. That was a glorious match, too. Vitas Gerulaitis, the flamboyant New Yorker, defeated Guillermo Vilas, 6-7 (4-7), 7-6 (7-0), 6-7 (5-7), 6-4, 6-2, in an enthralling battle of wit and grit begun in the mid-afternoon sunshine and ended in the cool of the evening. In terms of playing time, this is the longest final ever in big tournament history: 5 hours and 8 minutes.

Interest in the women's matches was also clearly secondary in the French Open at Stade Roland Garros, where the center court was enlarged to 17,000 seats as part of a major renovation targeted at producing a second "show" arena in 1980. Twelve of the tournament's 14 days were sold out, the French Open having become almost as much of an "in thing" in Paris as Wimbledon is in London, but only 10,000 spectators turned out on the final Saturday to view the women's singles final. This was a terribly tedious match in which Evert Lloyd monotonously ground down erring Wendy Turnbull, 6-2, 6-0. Evert Lloyd, the champion of 1974 and 1975, lost only one set in regaining the title she had abdicated in order to play in World Team Tennis, the American intercity league which was gasping for

Vitas Gerulaitis won his second Italian Open in 1979. (Jack Mecca)

breath at the end of 1978 and was pronounced officially dead early in 1979.

The men's singles in Paris was expected to produce another duel between Borg and Connors. Jimmy entered the premier clay-court championship of the world for the first time since 1973, ending his personal boycott, a reaction to the tourney barring him in 1974 for his WTT affiliation. Instead, it was exciting primarily because of Victor Pecci, a 6-foot-3 Paraguayan with a diamond in his right ear who entered the tournament ranked No. 30 in the world and unseeded. He knocked off four seeds in succession—15, 6, 3, 2: 1978 semifinalist Corrado Barazzutti, 1976 runner-up Harold Solomon and 1977 champion Guillermo Vilas in straight sets, and Connors in four. In the final, Pecci stirred a capacity crowd on a drizzly day by coming back from two sets and 2-5 down to push Borg before bowing, 6-3,

6-1, 6-7 (6-8), 6-4. Gene and Sandy Mayer won the men's doubles over Australians Ross Case and Phil Dent. The Americans were the first brothers to win a major since U.S. champs Bob and Howard Kinsey in 1924. Betty Stove and Wendy Turnbull won the women's doubles over Virginia Wade and Françoise Durr, 2-6, 7-5, 6-4.

McEnroe, who had missed Rome and Paris because of a pulled groin muscle, returned to action and won a Wimbledon tune-up tournament on grass at London's Queen's Club over Pecci—and was simultaneously grilled in the British press for his surly deportment. Dubbed "Superbrat," he dominated pre-Wimbledon publicity and was seeded second to Borg, largely because Connors did not reveal until after the draw was made whether he would play or remain at home with his expectant wife.

McEnroe, still bothered by the groin pull, was upset in the fourth round by Tim Gullikson, culminating a first week that was tumultuous for the men (10 of the 16 seeds were beaten in the first five days) and formful for the women. Most observers thought the semifinal between Borg and Connors, who had met in the previous two finals, would be the *de facto* title match, but Borg was in his most devastating form and annihilated his longtime arch-rival, 6-2, 6-3, 6-2.

Left-hander Roscoe Tanner, seeded fifth, had been a semifinalist twice before, and this time came through the wreckage in the other half of the draw to reach the final for the first time. Attacking at every opportunity, playing thoughtfully and well, he pushed Borg to the limit in an absorbing final that kept 15,000 spectators and a live television audience in 28 countries spellbound for 2 hours, 49 minutes. Half an hour after his 6-7 (7-4), 6-1, 3-6, 6-3, 6-4 triumph, which made him the first man since New Zealander Tony Wilding in 1910–13 to win the Wimbledon singles four years running, Borg said: "I feel much, much older than when I went on the court. Especially at the end of the match, I have never been so nervous in my whole life . . . I almost couldn't hold my racket."

That was a revealing admission from the astonishing Swede who, after a narrow second-round escape against Vijay Amritraj, 2-6, 6-4, 4-6, 7-6 (7-2), 6-2, the only man in four years to have a match game against Borg at Wimbledon, had said he gets more relaxed when matches are at their tightest.

Coupled with Navratilova's 6-4, 6-4 victory over Evert Lloyd in the women's final the previous day, Borg's victory marked the first time that both the men's and women's singles champions had successfully defended their titles since Bill Tilden and Suzanne Lenglen won in 1920 and 1921.

Navratilova was entitled to a first-round bye, but chose instead to play a match in order to enjoy the champion's traditional honor of playing the opening contest on Centre Court. She had good reason for making this decision: watching her from the competitors' guest box was her mother, whom she had not seen in nearly four years, since defecting from Czechoslovakia during the 1975 U.S. Open. Mrs. Jana Navratilova was granted a two-week tourist visa to visit her daughter in London with the personal approval of Czechoslovakian Prime Minister Dr. Lubomir Strougal. "Winning here last year was the greatest moment of my career," a tearful Navratilova said after an unexpectedly tense 4-6, 6-2, 6-1 victory over qualifier Tanya Harford, "but yesterday [her airport reunion with her mother] was one of the greatest moments of my life."

Fighting a cold, Navratilova struggled into the semifinals, losing sets to Greer Stevens and Dianne Fromholtz. But she did not lose a set in the last two rounds, beating Austin and Evert Lloyd. Her stepfather and 16-year-old sister, who were not granted visas, watched the match, live on West German television in the border town of Pilsen, as they had the year before. But this time, instead of ignoring the expatriate's victory, the government-controlled Czech media gave it prominent attention in newspapers and on television.

Navratilova had another thrill in partnering Billie Jean King to the women's doubles title, 5-7, 6-3, 6-2, over Turnbull and Stove. This was King's record 20th Wimbledon title, a 10th doubles to go with six singles and four mixed in the world's most prestigious tournament.

But the occasion was saddened by the death the previous day of 87-year-old Elizabeth Ryan, with whom King had shared the record since 1975.

Miss Ryan, a native Californian who lived in London, was stricken with a heart attack while watching the women's singles final, collapsed in a ladies room at the All England Club and died on the way to a hospital. Winner of 12 doubles and seven mixed doubles titles between 1914 and 1934, but never the singles, Ryan had told friends of a premonition that this would be the year King broke her cherished record. She dreaded the moment, but never saw it. She died less than 24 hours before being erased from the record book.

Back in the United States, Connors won the U.S. Clay Court singles for the fourth time, beating Vilas in the final, 6-1, 2-6, 6-4. Evert Lloyd—returning after a three-year absence—won her fifth title, over Evonne Goolagong, 6-4, 6-3, extending her personal winning streak in the tournament to 26 straight matches. Both joined 16 other former champs in ceremonies dedicating a superb new 10,000-seat stadium at the Indianapolis Sports Center.

The U.S. Open was played for the second time at the National Tennis Center in Flushing Meadow, N.Y., and amid the cacophony of planes roaring overhead and spectators moving about during play, the youngsters came to the fore.

McEnroe's toughest battle came in the second round against Ilie Nastase, no longer the exquisite shotmaker he once was, but still a tempestuous personality. McEnroe won, 6-4, 4-6, 6-3, 6-2, in a stormy match that could be completed only with great difficulty after the raucous pro-Nastase crowd of 10,000 at a session that ran past midnight—many of them heavily into their cups—became a negative influence. Veteran umpire Frank Hammond, growing flustered, had already hit Nastase earlier in the match with a warning, presently a point penalty for conspicuous stalling. When Hammond justifiably awarded McEnroe a penalty game, raising his lead to 3-1 in the fourth, the customers reacted furiously. They showered the court with beer cans and other refuse in protest. Nastase's refusal to play brought referee Mike Blanchard onto the court. Amid the clamor he appealed to the audience, via the PA system, for a restoration of order, and urged the players to resume. But the noise worsened. As Nastase refused to comply, Blanchard instructed Hammond to "put the clock on him." Hammond had no choice but to invoke correctly the fourth step in the penalty route: default. That nearly brought the house down. Tourney director Bill Talbert, fearful of a riot, reinstated Nastase and removed Hammond from the chair, replacing him with Blanchard. With that bone thrown to the assemblage, the second-round match was completed in four more games.

McEnroe—at home on the asphalt-based courts less than 15 minutes from his front door in Douglastown, N.Y., but never a favorite with the home crowds because of his incessant pouting and grousing—won two matches by default, including his quarterfinal over Eddie Dibbs. But he stayed sharp playing doubles, and in the semifinals routed Connors, who was inhibited by back spasms, 6-3, 6-3, 7-5. He won the final with similar ease over Long Island neighbor Gerulaitis, 7-5, 6-3, 6-3.

Gerulaitis had made a magnificent comeback from two sets and a service break down in the semifinals to beat Tanner, who had served magnificently in upsetting No. 1 seed Borg in the quarterfinals, 6-2, 4-6, 6-2, 7-6. Borg—who hated playing at night, especially against a big server like Tanner—was thus foiled for the second straight year in his attempt to nail down the third leg of a possible French-Wimbledon-U.S.-Australian Grand Slam. Borg seemed to see the handwriting on the tape when late in the fourth set one of Tanner's rocket serves actually knocked the net down, snapping the cable. Bjorn shivered mournfully in the cool of night during a

The U.S. Open trophy was John McEnroe's after his straight-set conquest of Vitas Gerulaitis in 1979. (UPI)

six-minute delay of the inevitable while a replacement net was found and cranked into place.

In the women's singles, Pam Shriver—who a year earlier had become the youngest finalist in the tournament's history at 16 years, 2 months—lost in the first round to qualifier Julie Harrington. Shriver had played only 24 matches in the year between Opens because of school commitments and then a persistent shoulder ailment that robbed her of her oppressive serve. Seven of the top eight seeds reached the quarterfinals, but third-seeded Austin stopped second-seeded Navratilova in the semis, 7-5, 7-5, and Evert Lloyd in the final, 6-4, 6-3. At 16 years, 9 months, the cool Californian became the youngest U.S. champion ever, three days younger than May Sutton in 1904 and several months younger than Maureen Connolly in 1951.

"I thought the title might intimidate her," said Evert Lloyd, who until a three-set victory over Sherry Acker in the fourth round had not lost a set in the U.S. Open since the 1975 final and took a 31-match Open streak into the final. "But she was out there like it was just another tennis match."

McEnroe and Fleming won the men's doubles over fellow Americans Stan Smith and Bob Lutz, 6-2, 6-4. The sentimental story, however, was the reunion of Australians Roy Emerson, 42, and Fred Stolle, 40, who had last played together in the U.S. Doubles when it was held in Boston. They were the champions of 1965 and 1966, and added four more victories to reach 15 in a row before Smith and Lutz toppled them in the semifinals, 7-5, 3-6, 7-5. Stove-Turnbull reversed the result of the Wimbledon final, beating King-Navratilova for the women's doubles title, while Greer Stevens and Bob Hewitt repeated their Wimbledon victory over Stove and Frew McMillan in the mixed doubles final.

In the Davis Cup final, McEnroe and Gerulaitis with two singles wins apiece led the 5-0 blitz of Italy, a totally straight-set affair in 15 sets. McEnroe was 8-0 in singles for the campaign. Smith and Lutz, with a 6-4, 12-10, 6-2 decision over Adriano Panatta and Paolo Bertolucci, registered their fourth (1968, 1969, 1970 and 1979) Cup-clinching performance, a record eclipsing the 1904, 1905 and 1906 wins of the British Doherty brothers, Laurie and Reggie. Smith set an individual Cup-clinching record of six, having won the decisive singles in 1971 and 1972. Staged at San Francisco's Civic Auditorium, it was the first final won indoors by the U.S., which would not play another in fresh air.

But to get to the final the Americans had to overcome quick scene and time-zone changes in a tough semi at Sydney to beat the Aussies, 4-1. Having flown non-stop from the San Francisco indoor tourney won by McEnroe, John and Vitas had only two days grass practice. It might have all come apart (since Smith and Lutz suffered their lone Cup defeat, 9-7, 6-4, 6-4, by John

Alexander and Phil Dent) if Gerulaitis hadn't made one of the all-time recoveries from three match points down to win the leadoff singles. Though Vitas looked gone at 7-8, 0-40, third set, he mightily volleyed his way from that trap, 6-8, 14-16, 10-8, 6-3, 6-3, and snuffed the hosts two days later, beating Alexander, 5-7, 6-4, 8-6, 6-2.

McEnroe was nearing the end of an open-era season record for dual labor and production: 27 titles overall, surpassing Nastase's 23 (15 singles, 8 doubles) in 1973. Mac won 10 of 22 singles tournaments on 91-13 in matches, 17 of 21 doubles on 84-5.

Not long after the U.S. Open, Volvo, the Swedish auto manufacturer, announced that it would assume and expand sponsorship of the men's Grand Prix of tennis, following Colgate-Palmolive's decision to drop out of the men's game after three years of Grand Prix sponsorship. The advent of the fourth Grand Prix sponsor in 11 years (following Pepsico, Commercial Union, and Colgate), Volvo promised continued growth of the $12-million men's major tournament circuit in the 1980s, despite the persistence of troubling political problems and battles for control of the men's game.

1980

For such a moment is the grass maintained with tender loving care. For such a moment are the vines trimmed and the roses tended. For such a moment are the stands of the All England Lawn Tennis & Croquet Club retouched every year in a somber shade of green.

The moment is everything. It is at the root of all this, beneath the ivy and the proper manners and even the hallowed lawns. Scratch deep enough at Wimbledon and a hundred matches of high drama rise from the earth. They are the foundation of the most significant tennis tournament in the world, the source of the tradition which sets the event apart from all others.

Wimbledon exists for Borg vs. McEnroe, Centre Court, July 5, 1980. The defending champion reeling. His opponent seeking to score the most memorable of upsets. And a huge crowd engrossed in great theatre.

That's Wimbledon at its best, the most marvelous of backdrops for a haunting match, perhaps the most gripping in the history of what club officials call simply The Championships. Bjorn Borg survived the loss of seven match points in the fourth set of the men's final and, finally, the set itself. Then he survived the loss of seven break points in the deciding set before defeating the American upstart, 1-6, 7-5, 6-3, 6-7 (16-18), 8-6, in a three-hour, 53-minute epic.

At the instant he fell to his knees in that signature ritual of triumph, the man was at the top of his game and at the peak of a career that challenged history for an equal. It marked his fifth consecutive Wimbledon title, following on the heels of a fifth French Open championship, all achieved at the tender age of 24. He would close out the year by winning the Volvo Masters for a second successive year and stand unchallenged as the leading figure in the sport.

But even in his most satisfying season, there were intimations that Borg's grip on tennis was loosening. He had won his last 13 five-set matches when he looked across the net at McEnroe at the start of yet another life-and-death encounter in the final of the U.S. Open. This time he couldn't summon the will to outlast the upstart American on his home turf.

McEnroe's 7-6 (7-4), 6-1, 6-7 (5-7), 5-7, 6-4 victory, which enabled him to claim a second consecutive U.S. title, canceled plans for a tennis migration to Australia for what would have been the concluding act of a quest for a men's Grand Slam, last achieved by Rod Laver in 1969. Without that added incentive, Borg and most of his major adversaries bypassed the Christmas season in Melbourne, leaving the Australian Open to lesser mortals. American Brian Teacher won the men's title by defeating Aussie Kim Warwick, 7-5, 7-6, 6-3.

Although overshadowed by the duel of titans on the male side, Chris Evert Lloyd starred in a

On the ropes, Bjorn Borg came back to win Wimbledon for the fifth time in a row in 1980. (Russ Adams)

drama of her own making by dominating the spotlight on the women's tour. Suffering from fatigue, burnout or mid-life crisis—take your pick—she emerged from a three-month sabbatical to capture clay titles at Rome and Paris, reach the final of a Wimbledon which belonged, unexpectedly, to a blithe spirit from the past, Evonne Goolagong Cawley, and reclaim her U.S. Open birthright by overcoming, among others, Tracy Austin, her most recent nemesis.

Austin failed to add a major title to her collection, yet she won a dozen others—including the Avon championship and the Colgate Series championship—and banked more than $600,000 in prize money, not bad for a high-school student. She also teamed with an older sibling, John, to become the only sister-brother team to capture the mixed doubles title at Wimbledon.

Another fast-rising teenager, the graceful Hana Mandlikova of Czechoslovakia, advanced to the final of the U.S. Open and climaxed an outstanding season by defeating Wendy Turnbull for the Australian title at age 18, 6-0, 6-5. Precocious Andrea Jaeger, 15, was a quarterfinalist at Wimbledon and a semifinalist at Flushing Meadow. Martina Navratilova, suddenly caught in a time warp, had no majors to call her own. She compensated by leading all women in prize money with earnings of $749,250.

Still, it was the men who held the attention of the world, particularly in those instances when Borg and McEnroe shared a major stage. If the Swede added to his legend on the English grass, then the Yank confirmed his mettle by holding his ground on American asphalt. Their two matches formed an exquisite set of mantelpieces that bracketed the summer of 1980.

As the Wimbledon Championships got underway, Borg was in a class of his own. In the French Open, he had ripped through a field that featured 17 of the top 20 players in the world, with consummate ease. The man dropped no sets and never more than the seven games he yielded to Vitas Gerulaitis in his 6-4, 6-1, 6-2 dismissal in the final. With that victory, he became the only man to win the tournament three years in a row and five times in all.

"For most of us, Paris is a great tournament because of the city, the food, the Continental experience . . . ," said Victor Amaya, who won the doubles in the company of Hank Pfister. "But some people don't realize this is the Borg Invitational. They think they can actually win the thing. What a joke!"

At Wimbledon, the Swede was busy establishing the Borg Invitational II. Unlike his experience in previous years, he needed no escape hatches in advancing to the men's final, losing only two sets along the way. Centre Court belonged to him as it did to no other.

Only McEnroe, jeered at the start of the tournament for intemperate outbursts, stood between

Nine years after she'd earned the crown at Wimbledon, Evonne Goolagong Cawley won a second time in 1980. (Russ Adams)

Borg and a measure of immortality. Earlier in the week, when he was questioned about his motivation after having won so easily, the Swede said he would like the final "to be 12-10 in the fifth, but only if I know I win." McEnroe came perilously close to meeting that challenge, so much so that Borg actually doubted he would win.

It was in the 34-point fourth set tie-breaker that a battle for the ages was joined. At 5-4, Borg had only to serve it out for his 35th consecutive triumph on Wimbledon grass. He promptly rolled to a 40-15 advantage, double match point. But McEnroe saved both points and then broke service.

At 6-6, the combatants began a tie-breaker that lasted 22 minutes. It featured five championship points for Borg, seven set points for his opponent. Finally, on the 34th point, with the crowd exhausted from the emotion of the moment, the champion failed to execute a difficult drop volley and the match was tied at two sets apiece.

"I thought mentally he'd get down after that," McEnroe said. "It would've gotten me a little down, but it didn't seem to get to him. He's won it four times. You'd think he might let down and say forget it."

Indeed, Borg did admit to being discouraged at the start of the fifth set. "When I lost those match points, I couldn't believe it," the man conceded. "I was thinking then maybe I will end up losing the match. It is a terrible feeling."

The disappointment lasted two points into the fifth set. Borg fell behind 0-30 on his serve, then dipped deeply into his vast reserve of spirit. He won the next four points to take a 1-0 advantage. From that instant, McEnroe was waging an uphill fight.

Borg would serve 25 more times in the match and win 24 points, losing at 40-0 in the ninth game. He gained his break in the 14th game when, at 15-15, the Swede won the last three points with a return down the line, a volley McEnroe couldn't retrieve and a backhand passing shot. Then he fell to his knees in supplication, as ever, and added an impromptu collapse on the well-worn grass.

"At this rate," McEnroe said, "I don't know when he's ever going to lose here. He hits harder than when I first saw him. He volleys better."

And it was not out of the question then to consider him in the context of Tilden, Budge, Laver. Not with 10 major championships, not with the U.S. Open and a Grand Slam within his sights. "I want to be remembered as the greatest ever," Borg said.

In the afterglow of that triumph, Borg took a bride, the fair Mariana Simionescu, a Romanian player of modest accomplishment. His warmup for the U.S. Open was jeopardized by a knee injury which caused him to retire in the midst of the Canadian Open final against an ascending star, 20-year-old Ivan Lendl of Czechoslovakia. Earlier in the same tournament, McEnroe twisted an ankle and defaulted in the second round, then was beaten in the first round at Atlanta the following week.

Despite hysterical headlines suggesting that neither man might be able to walk—let alone run—on the court at Louis Armstrong Stadium, there was no stopping the two from an appointment in the Open finale. Their journeys, however, were not without obstacles. Borg's were psychological as well as physical.

Only the previous year, serving so hard that one of his missiles collapsed the net, Roscoe Tanner had ousted Borg from the Open in a quarterfinal match staged at night. When they met again, in the same round, it appeared that the only difference was the presence of daylight. Tanner continued to blast away—he was credited with 19 aces and 26 service winners—in building a lead of 2-1 in sets, 4-2 in games.

But Borg, displaying the same resilience that had been the hallmark of his Wimbledon success, rallied to salvage the fourth set, 7-5, and closed out the match, 6-4, 3-6, 4-6, 7-5, 6-3. Nor was that his last scare. He yielded the first two sets to Johan Kriek in the semifinals before overwhelming the expatriate South African, 4-6, 4-6, 6-1, 6-1, 6-1.

Kriek became the fifth player to take the first two sets of a best-of-five match against Borg. Not one of them—not Guillermo Vilas at the Italian in '74, not Manuel Orantes at the French in the same year, not Brian Gottfried at the Open in '76, not Mark Edmondson at Wimbledon in '77, not Kriek at the Open in '80—had been able to put away the Swede. The challenge of facing Borg was enough to make a man believe his heart rather than the scoreboard. And, in his heart, Borg usually held the advantage.

Meanwhile, McEnroe was having a devil of a time himself. He had some shaky moments against Lendl in the quarterfinals before rallying for a 4-6, 6-3, 6-2, 7-5 victory. That qualified him for a semifinal berth against three-time champion Jimmy Connors.

They produced an amazing match that stretched more than four hours. Connors appeared to be in control when he took a 2-1 lead in sets, 2-0 in games. Instead, McEnroe rallied to win the fourth set and served for the match at 5-4 in the fifth, only to be broken. Mac finally prevailed in a tie-breaker, 6-4, 5-7, 0-6, 6-3, 7-6 (7-3), not the ideal preparation for a final against Borg scheduled to start less than 24 hours later.

This was the pairing everyone hoped to see, even McEnroe. "I just want to win the tournament," the defender said on the first day of the two-week event, "but if I knew beforehand that I'd win, I'd rather play Borg in the final. Say 22-20 in the fifth set." When a man noted they play fifth-set tie-breakers at the Open, Mac altered the score. "Okay," he said, "make it 7-0 in the tie-breaker."

As it developed, a decisive tie-breaker wasn't necessary. But that was about all the match lacked. Such was the pressure in what became a battle of survival that McEnroe felt like wilting after Borg squared the score at two sets apiece. "When I lost the fourth set," the 21-year-old American said, "I thought my body was going to fall off."

Neither man played with the artistry that marked the historic match at Wimbledon two months earlier. The record Open crowd of 21,072 appeared not to notice. If it wasn't a classic, it still left people breathless with excitement.

McEnroe jousted with the umpires and with a linesman. He slammed a racket against his chair and at one stage he felt so strongly about his game that he handed his weapon to Jack Kramer, seated in a courtside box. Borg served with all the assurance of a waiter in an earthquake. He was reported missing in action during the second set. He kicked one ball over the net after breaking his racket on a serve and it was his best-looking shot in several games.

"I was trying my best," he said, "but I was not playing well. I had no feel for the ball."

And yet somehow the two staggered into an excruciatingly dramatic final scene, stumbling into a cliffhanger finish. Call it destiny. The tension was suffocating.

The fatal break occurred in the seventh game of the fifth set after Borg had committed two of his uncharacteristic nine double faults. McEnroe laid claim to the title with a sharp volley at 40-15 of the 10th game, four hours and 13 minutes after the initial serve. He became the first repeat champion since Australian Neale Fraser in 1959 and 1960 and the first Yank to win national honors in consecutive years since Pancho Gonzalez in 1948 and 1949.

"I think our Wimbledon match was much better," Borg said. "I think I can play much better and John can play much better. The two tie-breakers, that's why it was so exciting. In the future, I think John and I have some great matches. For as long as we play."

It wouldn't be as long as the public surmised. They met only twice more during the 1980 season, Borg triumphing, 6-3, 6-4, at the Stockholm Open in November and in three tight sets, 6-4, 6-7 (3-7), 7-6 (7-2), in the preliminary round of the Masters.

McEnroe enjoyed a superb year, leading the men in earnings ($972,369) and tournament victories (10). Despite his losses to Borg at Wimbledon and to Connors, 2-6, 7-6, 6-1, 6-2, in the WCT Finals played at the brand new Reunion Arena in Dallas, he was a legitimate candidate for the top spot in the world when the leading players converged on Madison Square Garden for the Masters. There, he inexplicably lost all three preliminary round-robin matches, to Gene Mayer and Jose-Luis Clerc as well as Borg.

The latter overcame Connors in the semifinal and then whipped Lendl, 6-4, 6-2, 6-2, for the $100,000 top prize and the clear designation as No. 1. Lendl, who scored a season-high 113 victories in a gruelling 142 tournament matches, had his greatest satisfaction in team competition, leading Czechoslovakia to a 4-1 victory over Italy in Prague for its first Davis Cup.

Ivan was unbeaten (7-0 in singles, 3-0 in doubles), but it was Tom Smid who sent the home team off to a bright start by bringing down favored Adriano Panatta, 3-6, 3-6, 6-3, 6-4, before a howling crowd. Lendl followed, 4-6, 6-1, 6-1, 6-2, over Corrado Barazzutti, and he and Smid persisted to settle it over Panatta and Paolo Bertolucci, 3-6, 6-3, 3-6, 6-3, 6-4. The Czechoslovakians took a 3-2 semifinal over Argentina, the 4-1 conqueror of Cup-holding U.S. in the American Zone final. In Buenos Aires Guillermo Vilas and Jose-Luis Clerc let the U.S. know that whatever its status, Latin clay was still quicksand. Both beat Brian Gottfried and, in grinders, McEnroe: Jose-Luis, 6-3, 6-2, 4-6, 14-12, Guillermo in the clincher, 6-2, 4-6, 6-3, 2-6, 6-4. Prague was the end of the contending line for the Panatta-backboned Italians. The 1976 victors were appearing in their fourth final in five years, but would not place so high again.

Comebacks marked women's play, the most remarkable being Goolagong's at Wimbledon. Her previous victory on the lawns had occurred nine years earlier as an ethereal teenager. "I just happened to win," she recalled. "I didn't think much of it at the time."

And the thought remained buried as she went on to lose her next seven appearances in a Wimbledon or U.S. final. But neither age, nor her marriage to Roger Cawley nor motherhood had dimmed the luster of her strokes and the effortless grace of her movement. She rose to the occasion one last time at 28.

Her career had been interrupted several times by injuries and illness but 1980 had been particularly trying. Before she returned to action in June, she had not hit a ball for seven weeks. Goolagong considered that a positive. "I get stale if I play too much," she said.

Goolagong played herself into shape at Wimbledon. She was down a set (Betty Stove) in her third-round match and trailed by a set and a break (Hana Mandlikova) in the fourth. That experience served her well in the semifinals when she faced Austin, who had won 35 of her previous 36 matches.

Despite the loss of seven consecutive games, Goolagong eliminated the young American, 6-3, 0-6, 6-4. Then she upset Evert Lloyd, 6-1, 7-6 (7-1), marking the only time in the tournament's history that a singles championship had been decided by a tie-breaker. She was the first mother to claim a Wimbledon singles title since Dorothea Lambert Chambers in 1914.

That represented one of the few setbacks suffered by Evert Lloyd after her return to competitive tennis in time for the European clay circuit. After being beaten by Austin in the opener of the Avon series at Cincinnati and losing to Navratilova at Chicago, Evert Lloyd had departed the tour in Seattle for what she later called a "leave of absence."

Apparently refreshed, she seized her third Italian title in Rome, 5-7, 6-2, 6-2, over Virginia Ruzici, and then, in the absence of Austin, Navratilova and Goolagong, won her fourth French championship, thrashing 1978 champ Ruzici, 6-0, 6-3, in the final. Evert Lloyd increased her winning streak to 25 matches by dispatching Navratilova, 4-6, 6-4, 6-2, in a Wimbledon semifinal before falling to Goolagong.

She stepped up the pace back in the States, winning a U.S. Clay Court title for the sixth time, over Jaeger, 6-4, 6-3, tying Nancy Richey's record (1963–68), and taking a second Canadian title. Evert Lloyd was primed to regain her Open crown and to defeat Austin, the clone who had whipped her five consecutive times. She got her opportunity in the semifinal round at Flushing Meadow.

On the eve of the match, she described herself as a nervous wreck. And she told her husband, "I've never wanted a match more." It showed at the start, when she dropped the first four games and the set, 4-6. But the slimmed-down, quicker, hungrier version of the former champion emerged in magnificent fashion thereafter. Forcing Austin into 54 errors in the match, she swept into the final by winning the last two sets convincingly, 6-1, 6-1.

What she called her "most emotional victory" preceded her most satisfying moment of the year. Evert Lloyd had invited her father and first teacher from Florida to witness the final. Jim Evert, preferring to stay far in the background and not engage his nervous system, had never seen his daughter win a major championship in person.

So Evert Lloyd's 5-7, 6-1, 6-1 conquest of Mandlikova represented a first of sorts even as it reestablished an old pattern. The Czech, who had upset her idol, Navratilova, and overcome Jaeger in a 6-1, 3-6, 7-6 (7-4) battle of prodigies, began strongly against Evert Lloyd but didn't have the concentration or will to withstand the relentless American. After claiming her fifth Open championship, Evert Lloyd had a 53-5 match record in the tournament.

Nor did she stop there. A month later, she annexed her 100th professional tournament title at Deerfield Beach, Fla., over Jaeger, 6-4, 6-1.

Evert Lloyd also enjoyed remarkable success in team play. She captained the U.S. team in the Wightman Cup. In the Federation Cup, she (5-0) and teammates won all 15 of their matches, including a 3-0 sweep of Australia in the championship round at West Berlin. Chris concluded a remarkable campaign by leading the U.S. over Britain in the Wightman Cup, 5-2.

The captain won both singles and teamed with Rosie Casals to win her doubles match in the event staged at Albert Hall in London. Furthermore, she recovered from double match point (at 15-40, 1-5 in the third) to defeat Virginia Wade, 7-5, 3-6, 7-5, in the deciding match. It was her 23rd overall victory in Wightman play, surpassing Louise Brough's record.

Another Brough standard, one she shared with Nancy Richey for most years ranked among the Top Ten in the U.S. (16), was eclipsed by Billie Jean King. The latter celebrated her 17th year

A revived Chris Evert Lloyd captured all the majors except Wimbledon in 1980. (Russ Adams)

among the elite with a fifth-place finish. King, who turned 37 in November, won three singles titles and 11 doubles titles, including the U.S. championship in partnership with Navratilova. It was her 39th—and last—Big Four title, second then only to Margaret Smith Court's 62. But it was Navratilova's ninth, and she was on her way to eclipsing King with 54 in 1990.

1981

In a land rich in ceremony, men's tennis staged a changing of the guard. Not only did John McEnroe topple Bjorn Borg from his Wimbledon throne in 1981 but he usurped the man's place as the ruler of his sport. By year's end, the former monarch relinquished all claims to the territories he once commanded.

Borg's decision to reduce his schedule was so drastic that it resulted in virtual retirement from competitive tennis following humbling four-set losses to McEnroe in the finals of both the Wimbledon and U.S. Open championships. It represented a stunning development in the wake of the Swede's victory at Paris, his sixth French Open title and his 11th major. There would be no others. At 25, the man decided to remove his headband and let down his hair after a decade of single-minded devotion.

He may have been suffering from burnout or come to the realization that he was never going to achieve a U.S. title, let alone the Grand Slam that seemed so close and yet so far. Clearly, the brash McEnroe, three years his junior, had gained sufficient composure and mental toughness to suggest he wasn't going to be easily dislodged.

At Wimbledon, the American had battled with linesmen, umpires, tournament officials and the tabloid press and still exhibited the poise to deprive Borg of a sixth successive title on his own personal lawn. Two months later, McEnroe completed his coup on the hard courts at Flushing Meadow. The defeat was the Swede's fourth in a U.S. Open final and marked him as the most accomplished player never to claim the U.S. championship: zero for 10 years.

There was no such seismographic activity in the women's ranks. Each of the four major titles was claimed by a different player. Hana Mandlikova won her first French Open, Chris Evert Lloyd excelled at Wimbledon for the third time, Tracy Austin added a second U.S. Open and Martina Navratilova triumphed over a complete women's field in Australia.

Yet, there wasn't much doubt that Navratilova enjoyed the finest year of the four, and not only for the quality of her tennis. She won 10 tournaments playing singles, a circuit best, and she also combined with Pam Shriver to claim 11 doubles titles, including Wimbledon. Additionally, she was granted U.S. citizenship in midsummer and then bathed in the sustained applause of the crowd at the National Tennis Center, her National Tennis Center, following a loss to Austin in a brilliant Open final. She received the affection she craved with tears in her eyes.

If Borg cried following his loss to McEnroe the following day, it was on the inside. For the first time in memory, the well-mannered Swede ignored the protocol of the trophy presentation, spoke not a word to the fans or the media assembled at Flushing Meadow and left the grounds in a huff or, as one timekeeper noted, a minute and a huff. Only the previous day, while blasting Jimmy Connors in a men's semifinal, he had been the subject of a telephoned death threat. But for the man who had purchased a luxurious house on Long Island for the express purpose of establishing a home-court advantage at the previously inhospitable playground, it seemed the disappointment of the moment simply overwhelmed him.

That it would be the final picture of Borg at a championship event was perhaps the cruelest twist of fate. His season had started with such promise at Paris where his 6-1, 4-6, 6-2, 3-6, 6-1 triumph over Ivan Lendl left him tied with the great Rod Laver at 11 major singles titles, one behind all-time male leader Roy Emerson. At the time, it appeared inevitable that the Swede would establish a standard of his own for men's tennis, perhaps before the year was out.

His performance in the French Open temporarily silenced questions about the man's future. Borg had reported to Paris following an absence from competition that extended nearly two months, the result of a tender right shoulder. Since he had played in only three tournaments since January and failed to advance past the second round in two of them, even he was uncertain of his form.

Still, two weeks of serious practice had left him fit. "I feel strong," he said. "I can be out on the court for a long time if I have to."

It wasn't necessary, at least not until the final. The man mowed down his half of the draw until he came to Lendl, who had overcome Italian

Martina Navratilova became a U.S. citizen in 1981 and had an outstanding campaign that soared even in her U.S. Open defeat at the hands of Tracy Austin. (Russ Adams)

Open champ Jose-Luis Clerc in a five-set semifinal. The ascendant Czech answered back twice after Borg took the first and third sets but, in the end, he was worn down by the champion's sheer inexhaustibility.

"In the fifth, anyone can win," Borg said. "But I was ready to give everything, to stay out and rally and not take chances."

With a fourth straight French title added to his résumé, he turned his attention to Wimbledon. A sixth consecutive championship in the London suburb would tie him with Willie Renshaw, who competed before the turn of the century (1881-86) when defenders were treated to a bye into the final, the challenge round. Borg prepared in his usual fashion, shunning warmup tournaments in favor of long practice hours on

the grass with coach-adviser Lennart Bergelin and sparring partner Vitas Gerulaitis. There was no reason to believe the outcome would be any different this time.

While McEnroe did receive a greater share of attention at Wimbledon from the outset, it was for all the wrong reasons. On the occasion of his first match, versus Tom Gullikson, the man launched a verbal assault on umpire Ted James ("the pits of the world") and tournament referee Fred Hoyles, whose presence at courtside he demanded. The tournament committee actually considered showing him the gate before settling on $1,500 in fines.

The hornet's nest he stirred quickly spread to the demon barbers of Fleet Street, ever alert to scandal. They reached for their sharpest blades and headlines of a size normally reserved for world wars and the royal family. "Superbrat" was among the fondest of compliments they could muster.

McEnroe grumbled his way into the semifinals where he again dressed down Hoyles during an interminable victory over unseeded Australian Rod Frawley that was fraught with objections and unprintables. But the real brouhaha began in the interview room after the Yank had vented his spleen on the British tabloid press in the wake of some baiting by a gossip columnist. There followed a dialogue on the nature of journalism among emissaries from various countries and soon an Englishman, Nigel Clark, and an American, Charlie Steiner, were rolling on the floor.

Through all the tumult, Borg kept rolling toward his appointment with destiny. He overcame a major challenge from Connors in the semifinals, rallying from yet another two-set deficit to oust his old adversary, 0-6, 4-6, 6-3, 6-0, 6-4, in a match that rivaled any the two had produced for quality and tension, the last Bjorn would win there. "He had to play his best stuff to beat me," Connors said. And it was true.

But even a sharp and determined Borg wasn't enough to hold off a McEnroe who had

It was goodbye Bjorn Borg as John McEnroe (forecourt) hastened the Swedish master's abrupt exit following Wimbledon and U.S. Open setbacks in 1981. (Russ Adams)

learned to orchestrate his talents, if not his temper. Uncharacteristically, the defender started fast. Shockingly, he finished second. The American triumphed, 4-6, 7-6 (7-1), 7-6 (7-4), 6-4. The king was dead.

For all practical purposes, Borg lost his title in game 10 of the third set, where he enjoyed four set points for a 2-1 lead. First, McEnroe served out of a 15-40 hole, then overcame two Borg ads in the six-deuce game. He took control of the tie-breaker with two sensational passing shots after Borg served at 3-4.

In the fourth set, the one that terminated Borg's Wimbledon male-record winning streak at 41, McEnroe attacked at every opportunity. He also continued to dominate with his big first serve, winning 79 percent of the points when he was on target. In the critical tie-breakers, he missed only one of 10 first serves.

"I was surprised that I served so well," McEnroe said. "I wanted to show that Bjorn's not the only one who can come from behind and win."

The denouement occurred on the Fourth of July in a country not disposed to celebrating revolutions. Attired in blue and white tennis togs and sporting a jaunty red headband— "Stick a feather in his cap and call him McEnroney," telecaster Bud Collins observed—Superbrat closed out an era with a forehand volley winner on his second championship point.

Horrified officials of the All England Club had their revenge. They declined to tender McEnroe an honorary membership, a traditional spoil of victory. Not that the man had any desire to join.

If anything, the loss seemed to spur Borg to new heights of resolve. He settled into his mansion fronting Long Island Sound during the summer and stepped up his practice routine for the Flushing hothouse. "We don't have a tennis court," Bergelin noted, "but the house is on the water. Very nice. Very nice." And it wasn't far from the home of Gerulaitis, who did have a hard court in his backyard.

As usual, McEnroe practiced while playing, whipping Chris Lewis in the final of the ATP championship in Cincinnati in advance of the Open. The American circuit had been otherwise dominated by Clerc, who walked off with four clay-court titles, including the U.S. Clay Court championship in Indianapolis, where he defeated Lendl, 4-6, 6-4, 6-2. But the lean Argentine would be no factor on the Open surface.

The field was reduced to the usual suspects in time for the semifinals. McEnroe, who had lost opening sets to the likes of Juan Nunez and Ramesh Krishnan earlier in the tournament, waved goodbye to his concentration on several occasions against Gerulaitis before breaking a racket string against the intrusive CBS courtside microphone. Relieved, he then completed a 5-7, 6-3, 6-2, 4-6, 6-3 triumph.

For the third consecutive year, Borg was matched against Roscoe Tanner in the quarterfinals. For the second straight Open, he survived, 7-6 (7-4), 6-3, 6-7 (4-7), 7-6 (9-7). "Could you have him win the tournament this year?" Tanner said to Bergelin afterward. "Then they'll stop writing that he's won everything but this and maybe I won't have to play him in the quarterfinals again."

It seemed a genuine possibility after Borg, serving as well as he ever had, demolished Connors in their semifinal meeting, 6-2, 7-5, 6-4,. He had 14 aces plus many unreturnable serves and all of them appeared to occur on the big points. "It seemed like every first serve was going in," he said. "I was a little surprised."

The victory extended Borg's streak over Connors to 10 matches. Shortly before the match, which began at dinnertime, the switchboard operator at the National Tennis Center received a call from a man threatening Borg's life. Additional security guards ringed the stadium court as a precaution but Borg was not informed until after he had vanquished Connors.

As he had at Wimbledon, Borg jumped out in front of McEnroe in the final. But the Yank swept the last three sets to post a 4-6, 6-2, 6-4, 6-3 victory, stamping him as the first man to capture a third successive U.S. singles title since the legendary Bill Tilden strung together six during the Roaring '20s.

Borg's best chance evaporated in the third set when, leading 4-3, he was broken in stunning fashion as McEnroe unleashed four winners, including a pair of spectacular running topspin lobs, to draw even. "I felt I could do anything," the American said. He won eight of the last 11 games as Borg's future flashed before his eyes. It did not include competitive tennis.

One month later, the former No. 1 player in the world said he was taking his first extended vacation from tennis until the following April. He also said he would participate in only seven tournaments, a number insufficient for placement in the main draw under the rules of the Men's International Professional Tennis Council. He would have to quality for every Grand Prix tournament he entered, a course he would pursue with apparent disinterest.

Suddenly, the stage was all McEnroe's. Although Johan Kriek—whom Mac had defeated in the WCT final at Dallas, 6-1, 6-2, 6-4—would emerge from a depleted field to take the Australian title by virtue of a 6-2, 7-6 (7-1), 6-7 (1-7), 6-4 victory over Steve Denton and despite Lendl's first-place finish in the Grand Prix standings and his subsequent 6-7 (5-7), 7-6 (8-6), 6-2, 6-4 triumph over Gerulaitis in the Masters final, McEnroe was the unchallenged leader of the pack.

Not only did the left-hander from the New York borough of Queens win 9 of 17 singles tournaments, but he also teamed with Peter Fleming to win an equal number of doubles titles, including both the Wimbledon and U.S. championships. Additionally, he guided the U.S. to a third Davis Cup during his tenure, winning seven of eight singles and two doubles, sparkling as a three-way stretcher in the tight windup against Argentina, 3-1 at Cincinnati's Riverfront Coliseum in the newly remodeled competition. Henceforth a World Group of 16 countries embraces the only eligibles for the Cup, with the remainder consigned to zonal warfare below, striving for acceptance on high the following year. Connors played a helpful cameo for Captain Arthur Ashe in the quarterfinal defeat of Czechoslovakia, an unlucky draw for Cup-gripping Czechoslovakia, falling 4-1 at Flushing Meadow the weekend after Wimbledon. Only six days after dethroning Borg, Mac was beaten by Lendl, 6-4, 14-12, 7-5. However, Connors got a first-day tie, by beating Tom Smid, 6-3, 6-1, 6-2, against whom Mac applied the finisher, 6-3, 6-4, 6-1, after Stan Smith and Bob Lutz's 9-7, 6-3, 6-2 win over the two Czechs. Connors thereafter vanished from the Cup scene for three years.

Jose-Luis Clerc, with his deadly, rolling top-spin backhand, was primed for Cincy, even though the footing was carpet rather than the clay of Argentina's triumph the year before. Clerc whipped Roscoe Tanner, 7-5, 6-3, 8-6, after McEnroe quickly bashed Guillermo Vilas, 6-3, 6-3, 6-2. Although the Argentines seemed no threat combined (4-4 in cup jobs), they played the doubles of their lives against Peter Fleming and McEnroe, constantly changing tactics in the wild and acrimonious battle—the teams came close to a fistfight at one point—and actually moved into winning position late in the fifth set: match game, Vilas serving at 7-6. Four points away, and with a 2-1 lead, the Argentines could envision taking the Cup home.

They came no closer as McEnroe took over, swinging through a virtuoso game, cracking three winners and an awesome backhand return to capsize Vilas. Mac held brilliantly through four deuces and two break points to 8-7, and Vilas averted a match point to 9-9. But McEnroe's net-skimming backhand return tipped Clerc at match point and the 4-hour, 11-minute wowser ended, 6-3, 4-6, 6-4, 4-6, 11-9. It was up to the raging Mac. To the roars of 13,327 filling the building, he fulfilled their pleas, again in a boiling fifth set, 7-5, 5-7, 6-3, 3-6, 6-3. His serves (15 aces) and volleys overcame the tall Latin's groundies. Clerc had served for the first set, 5-4, deuce, and led 3-1 in the third during the long ordeal. No man had swept the singles at Wimbledon, the U.S. and in the Cup final since Don Budge in 1938, the year of his Grand Slam.

Furthermore, his facility in doubles marked him as the most complete champion since John Newcombe was lending his mustache to a line of tennis gear. Fittingly, the representatives of two generations held an improbable meeting on the stadium court at Flushing Meadow in the doubles semifinals. Newk, 37, and partner Fred Stolle, 42, both singles titlists at the Open in their salad days, had a merry romp through the first four rounds of the draw, in contrast to the grim attitude of Mac and Fleming.

Stolle and Newcombe darned near won the title, squeezing Mac and Fleming into a fifth set tie-breaker, losing by a measly four points. Their semi was tantamount to a final since Heinz Gunthardt fell ill after he and Peter McNamara won the other semi, and the championship was defaulted to the young Americans who beat the devil-may-care Aussie geezers, 6-2, 6-2, 5-7, 6-7 (2-7), 7-6 (7-3). They won the match but not the crowd, which cheered and laughed as the old Aussies reprised a few vaudeville routines, sometimes sending one man to the other side of the net to help the grim Americans. "We always had a fair bit of fun playing doubles in my day," Stolle said.

To Newcombe, who chose not to live his life between the white lines, the current attitude was unfortunate. "I feel sorry for them," he said. "It's a sport. It's a living, too, yes, but they take it over the fringe."

The fine schedule for the year indicated just how much court conduct had deteriorated. McEnroe, Gerulaitis and Ilie Nastase all drew 21-day suspensions for exceeding $5,000 in fines. Of the three, Gerulaitis created the biggest stir, walking out of the Melbourne indoor final in a protest against officiating, an offense which earned him a record $10,000 penalty.

Tim Mayotte, the 21-year-old Intercollegiate champion from Stanford, made an auspicious professional debut and was honored as Rookie of the Year. He reached the quarterfinal round at Wimbledon in only his second pro tournament, won 28 of 43 matches in 15 events and finished the year at No. 31 on the computer.

The march of children into the women's ranks continued with the presence of Kathy Rinaldi at the French Open. In becoming the youngest player to compete in that tournament, the 14-year-old skipped her graduation exercises at St. Joseph's School in Stuart, Fla., and journeyed to Paris where she upset eighth-seeded Dianne Fromholtz and 11th-seeded Anne Smith before bowing to Hana Mandlikova, 6-1, 6-3, in the quarters.

Having disposed of the latest princess, Mandlikova went after the queen. Now 19, she sent Evert Lloyd to her second defeat on clay in the last 191 matches, 7-5, 6-4, in the semifinals. Mandlikova closed out her first major title by stopping Sylvia Hanika, a semifinal winner over Andrea Jaeger, 6-2, 6-4.

She carried her form onto the grass at Wimbledon, a tournament which lost its defending champion when Evonne Goolagong Cawley interrupted her career to give birth to a second child. That absence was offset by the return of Austin, who missed the first five months of the season with a sciatic nerve condition. In the pres-

A second championship for Tracy Austin in the U.S. Open in 1981. (Wide World)

ence of Rinaldi and Jaeger, Austin, 18, was perceived as a veteran. "I can't believe this is my fifth Wimbledon," she said.

Rinaldi became the youngest player to win a match at Wimbledon, beating South African Sue Rollinson, 6-2, 3-6, 9-7, in a two-and-a-half hour struggle. But she advanced no farther. Jaeger, 16, was upset by Mima Jausovec and an unsteady Austin was stunned in the quarters by Pam Shriver, whom she had dispatched in all 11 previous encounters.

The semifinals matched Mandlikova against Navratilova, and the younger woman—seeded second despite her ranking of No. 5 on the computer—justified her placement by tournament officials with a 7-5, 4-6, 6-1 victory, winning 11 of the last 13 points in the process. Now all she had to do to claim her third consecutive major title was beat Evert Lloyd, who had moved into a flat just down the road with her husband, John.

No small feat that. Evert Lloyd, who had practiced hard in preparation, was peerless once the tournament began. Her 6-3, 6-1 rout of Shriver in the semifinal was typical of her fortnight. So was the final.

After three consecutive defeats in the championship round, she took apart a nervous Mandlikova, 6-2, 6-2. "I told myself that if I played Hana at Wimbledon," she said, "I would beat her." And so she did, with relative ease.

Youth was served on the summer circuit. Most notably at Indianapolis, where Jaeger became the youngest winner of the U.S. Clay Court championship, thrashing the seasoned Romanian, Virginia Ruzici, in the final, 6-1, 6-0. Austin demonstrated she had regained her fitness by outlasting Shriver at San Diego, 6-2, 5-7, 6-2, and then dethroning Evert Lloyd at the Canadian Open, 6-1, 6-4.

It was ideal preparation for the U.S. Open, where she breezed through 12 effortless sets to reach the final. The path for the third-seeded Austin was smoothed by Jaeger's second-round collapse against Andrea Leand. One of those rare birds, an amateur, sturdy, dark-haired 17-year-old Leand from Brooklandville, Md., moreover was in her first pro tourney, having no ranking. A powerful groundstroking wild card who was about to enter Princeton, Andrea did have reporters clustered around her after pulling one of the largest upsets in U.S. annals over second-seeded Jaeger, 1-6, 7-5, 6-3, in the second round. She pushed ahead to within two points of the quarters, losing to 11th seeded Barbara Potter, 6-7 (5-7), 7-6 (7-5), 6-3. Two unseeded Americans who did gain the last eight were Anne Smith of Dallas, who got there by outvolleying eighth-seeded Shriver, 6-4, 1-6, 7-5, and another amateur, tiny 17-year-old Barbara Gerken from Thousand Oaks, Calif., who beat Brit Jo Durie, 7-6, 6-1.

Form prevailed in the other half of the draw where Evert Lloyd advanced to her 11th consecutive Open semifinal. Her opponent was Navratilova, who had been frustrated in the tournament since that September day in 1975 when she announced her defection to the U.S. at Forest Hills. After years of complaining about the noise, the constant movement of the crowds and all the other distractions that threw her off her game, she triumphed over all and dispatched Evert Lloyd, 7-5, 4-6, 6-4, in a marvelous and emotional match.

That qualified Navratilova for her first U.S final, where she seized the initiative in the first set, 6-1. But the gritty Austin fought back to win the last two sets in tie-breakers, 7-6 (7-4) and 7-6 (7-1), and claim the first major championship decided by an ultimate set tie-breaker. The fans' reaction to the loser's efforts thrilled Navratilova as much as anything in her career.

Their warm applause interrupted her concession speech on several occasions. She cried from happiness as she turned to all four sides of the court and made a little bow, the kind expected at Wimbledon but seen so rarely in the New World. "I want to thank each and every one of you who was pulling for me today," she said. "I really didn't think that would happen." At long last love.

One month later, Navratilova snapped Austin's 28-match winning streak with a 6-0, 6-2 victory in the U.S. Indoor final at Minneapolis. Gene Mayer won the male version over Tanner, 6-2, 6-4, in Memphis where Trey Waltke sabotaged top-seeded McEnroe in the first round, 6-3, 6-4. Navratilova also annexed the Avon championship and won the final major event of the year, overcoming Evert Lloyd, 6-7 (4-7), 6-4, 7-5, in the Australian final. That boosted her singles titles in 1981 to 10 which, combined with the 11 doubles titles she shared with Shriver, enabled her to set a one-season earnings record of $865,437.

Austin rebounded to win the Toyota Series championship that closed out the year. Evert Lloyd, who ran her singles records in the Wight-

For Chris Evert Lloyd and Jimmy Connors, 1982 would mark the last time they would share the winner's circle at a major tournament. (Russ Adams, Mitchell Reibel)

man Cup and Federation Cup to 20-0 and 23-0, respectively, as the U.S. won all its matches in both competitions, raised her total of tournament singles titles to 110 with nine more and regained the top spot in the USTA rankings.

1982

It would have been out of place in such a proletarian celebration as the U.S. Open, staged in a municipally-owned complex in a public park. After all, people at the National Tennis Center consider a sweater looped over the shoulders as evening wear. But just this once the tournament of the people, by the people and for the people deserved a formal conclusion.

Something on the order of the Wimbledon Ball would have been appropriate. And for one reason. So Jimmy Connors, men's champion,

could have the first dance with Chris Evert Lloyd, the women's champion.

What a picture that would have made. And what a fitting commentary on the state of the sport eight years after they reigned as the sweethearts of Centre Court. They had taken divergent paths since 1974 and yet, before the eyes of enthralled spectators and in front of a worldwide television audience, they wound up in the same spot. Champions of the New World, Connors at 30 and Evert Lloyd at 27.

They grew up before our eyes. The girl who was Chrissie, a beribboned semifinalist at the event at sweet 16, did so with considerably more grace, but Connors got there nonetheless, maturing after his marriage to Patti McGuire and the birth of a son. They had first appeared in the tournament when it was staged at Forest Hills, when the surface was grass, when tennis players dressed only in white.

So Connors' 6-3, 6-2, 4-6, 6-4 victory over Ivan Lendl, which followed by a day Evert Lloyd's 6-3, 6-1 conquest of Hana Mandlikova, was—as much as anything—a triumph of the familiar. And it continued an all-American winning tradition in the singles since the tournament was shifted to the former World's Fair ground five years earlier. Czech-mate. Czech-mate.

It was at the U.S. where Martina Navratilova's quest for a Grand Slam ended prematurely in a quarterfinal loss to her doubles partner, Pam Shriver. Evert Lloyd made the most of that opportunity, then defeated Navratilova in the Australian final, 6-3, 2-6, 6-3, to even the score in Big Four tournaments at two apiece. But the naturalized American still reigned as the foremost figure in women's tennis, winning 29 tournaments (15 in singles), earning a record of $1,475,055 and securing the season-closing Toyota Series playoffs, climaxed by a 4-6, 6-1, 6-1 triumph over Evert. Her match record: a phenomenal 90-3 in singles, 70-4 in doubles.

Among the men, Connors stood alone after completing a double that appeared beyond his reach at the age of 30. The irrepressible left-hander prevailed over John McEnroe in the first Wimbledon final of the post-Borg era, then turned back Lendl at Flushing Meadow, while climbing back to the pinnacle from which he had been ousted by Borg and McEnroe.

Mats Wilander, from the first class of Swedish youngsters inspired by Borg, ascended to the French Open title at the tender age of 17 years, 10 months. In becoming the youngest man to annex a major title—Borg was two months older when he won at Paris for the first time in 1974—Wilander outlasted 1977 champion Guillermo Vilas, 1-6, 7-6 (8-6), 6-0, 6-4, in his very first tournament on the Roland Garros clay. Before the year was over, he would finish first in four of 20 tournaments, compile a match record of 60-18 and walk off with rookie honors.

Johan Kriek made headlines in 1982, winning the Australian championship and topping John McEnroe in the U.S. Indoor and in fines. (Wide World)

In what was a replay of the 1981 Australian Open final, Johan Kriek, a native South African resettled in Florida, routed hard-serving Texan Steve Denton, 6-3, 6-3, 6-2, at Melbourne. Earlier in the year, the man had stripped McEnroe of yet another prize, the U.S. Indoor championship, 6-3, 3-6, 6-4. Mac wasn't nearly as upset by Kriek's other coup, replacing the feisty left-hander atop the punitive standings: $11,500 to $2,060 in fines.

Lendl continued to outwork—and outearn—everyone else on the men's tour. Balancing his schedule between the Grand Prix and the more lucrative rival circuit, World Championship Tennis, the lean Czech captured 15 of the 23 tournaments he entered, won 107 of 116 matches and overpowered Yannick Noah, Connors and McEnroe to claim a second consecutive Masters title. He also threatened Vilas' Open-era record of 50 before Noah terminated his match-winning streak at 44 in February, the LaQuinta, Calif. final, 6-4, 3-6, 6-2.

For all of that, and despite a record one-season haul of $2,028,850 that almost doubled Connors' payoff of $1,173,850, Lendl was denied the No. 1 position by his failure to win a major event. He didn't even bother to enter Wimbledon, claiming an allergy to grass while he worked on his golf game back in the States. Nor was he the only defector from the world's most prestigious tournament. No fewer than five of the top 10 males on the ATP computer skipped the event, including the mysterious Borg, and Vilas, whose country was at war with Great Britain over the status of the Falkland Islands.

By then, Borg had become a figure of intrigue. Deciding to play again in the spring but refusing to commit to 10 Grand Prix events, he petitioned the Men's International Professional Tennis Council for a rule change. The nine members, including three player representatives, met in Monaco in conjunction with the Monte Carlo Open, which happened to mark the Swede's debut as a qualifier.

Sir Brian Burnett, chairman of the Wimbledon Championships, joined the discussions. He was eager for a compromise that would make it unnecessary for Borg to qualify at Wimbledon. The council was willing. "But," said Arthur Ashe, a council member, "Borg wasn't. For him, it was a matter of principle."

Standing on principle, Borg won his three qualifying matches in Monte Carlo, where he made his home. But he performed strangely in the main draw. He prepared to serve from the wrong side of the court in one match. In another, he served underhanded after two double faults. And he whistled during a loss to Noah in the quarterfinals. This certainly was not the man of steely concentration who had exhausted the will of so many opponents.

Burnett announced the compromise proposal the following week in London. Borg would be accepted for the main draw at Wimbledon if he agreed to play in 10 Grand Prix tournaments before March 31, 1983. Borg, who had taken his principle to Tokyo for a couple of lucrative exhibition matches, declined. He would play according to the dictates of his own schedule, and he would not play qualifying matches at Wimbledon. So much for tradition.

While officials were digesting that news, Borg made a surprise appearance in the qualifying round of the glitzy Alan King–Caesars Palace Tennis Classic at Las Vegas in April. He played like it was a death sentence, squeaking past Victor Amaya before his elimination at the hands of Dick Stockton. In the course of the latter match, the former champion missed a lob and served with an extra ball in his left hand. Borg, observers recalled clearly, hits his backhand with two hands on the racket. "I don't think he had his heart in the qualifying," Stockton reported.

Following that experience, Borg stated he would play only exhibitions for the remainder of the year but return to the circuit in 1983. Months later, during the Masters, he amended that decision with the announcement he was retiring from competitive tennis.

No wonder it was so much easier to follow the fortunes of the women, especially given the dominant manner in which Navratilova started the season. She was unbeaten in five tournaments on the Avon circuit before the cosmetics company withdrew as winter sponsor, to be replaced by year-round angel Virginia Slims. No sooner had her 27-match winning streak been interrupted by Sylvia Hanika, 1-6, 6-3, 6-4, in the Avon finale at Madison Square Garden then she began a 41-match run that wouldn't be stopped until defeat by Shriver at the U.S. Open in September. Her loss at Flushing Meadow marked the first time all year she had failed to reach a tournament final.

To her immense satisfaction, Navratilova proved as formidable on the clay as she had been on the grass by sweeping both the Family Circle Cup at Hilton Head, S.C., and the French Open.

On both occasions, Andrea Jaeger had done the dirty work, eliminating perennial champion Chris Evert Lloyd in the semifinals.

Prior to her meeting with the Illinois high-school student, Evert Lloyd not only had won all six previous Family Circle Cups but all 64 sets in which she had participated. Jaeger showed her disrespect with a 6-1, 1-6, 6-2 triumph. A few weeks later, she gave herself a 17th-birthday present by stunning Evert Lloyd, favored to win a fifth French title, 6-3, 6-1.

In both cases, however, Jaeger received her comeuppance from Navratilova. She followed a 6-4, 6-2 victory at Hilton Head with a 7-6 (8-6), 6-1 decision at Paris, saving a set point in the tie-breaker. Thus ended the run of the youngest French finalist.

Although Navratilova carried her form onto grass, winning at Eastbourne, the major news of the pre-Wimbledon circuit was provided by Billie Jean King. After playing only a few matches in 1981, when she was buffeted by the agonizing, highly publicized palimony lawsuit filed by ex-lover Marilyn Barnett, the 38-year-old Founding Mother of the women's tour returned with a vengeance. In the Edgbaston Cup at Birmingham, she defeated Rosalyn Fairbank, 6-2, 6-1, for her first tournament singles title in two years and her 66th as a pro. It was a most favorable omen for a Wimbledon desperately in need of an electric charge.

Wimbledon was inundated by so much rain during the first week that the vice chairman of the tournament was summoned to the interview room to discuss the weather. "Somebody once asked us," said Richard Holt, "why we didn't play the tournament in summer, and I thought that was pretty accurate." Of course, Wimbledon '82 had begun on the first day of the summer solstice. The only dry thing about the British on this occasion was their humor.

A subway strike only added to the gloom, flooding streets around the club with traffic. Into this dreary setting stepped a revitalized B. J. King

and the old tennis shrine fairly glowed with her reflection. On the occasion of her first match, her 100th singles battle at Wimbledon, the club planned to present her with a centennial plate.

Officials didn't announce the ceremony in advance because they feared she would lose to 19-year-old Claudia Pasquale of Switzerland. They also sent her to Court 14, "out in the boondocks" according to King, because her seeding of 12th was based as much on sentiment as recent results. The gift appeared to be the British equivalent of a gold watch: Thanks for your contributions to the game and enjoy your retirement.

But the self-styled Old Lady had other plans. She hammered Pasquale, 6-3, 6-2, saved triple match point against South African Tanya Harford in a remarkable 5-7, 7-6 (7-2), 6-2 third-round triumph and then announced she was a genuine title contender by overcoming third-seeded Tracy Austin, 3-6, 6-4, 6-2 in the quarterfinals. She hadn't come back to Wimbledon, her favorite tennis haunt, just for a testimonial.

King knew what she wanted when she took a look in the mirror the previous fall. She lifted weights and she ran and she took the first steps back up the ladder, occasionally falling but getting back on her feet and climbing higher. Wimbledon was her goal and she had more than a trinket in mind when she walked onto the grounds.

She wanted the Duke and Duchess of Kent and everyone else who occupied the Royal Box to empty their pockets on the table. This was a holdup. "Unless you win the whole *woiks*" she said, flavoring the All England Club with a dollop of Brooklynese, "it doesn't mean anything."

Three years earlier, she had played Austin for the first time. It was on Centre Court, in the quarters, and Austin triumphed in three sets. At the time, it appeared she was ready for the waxworks at Madame Tussaud's.

But, in 1982, she was in superior physical condition. Despite five operations on her knees and one on her foot, King was the stronger of the two. Troubled by sciatica, Austin would win only one of the 11 tournaments she entered.

Still, the reigning U.S. Open champ had no excuses for her Wimbledon exit, only praise for her conqueror. She recalled a fifth-grade assignment that required a composition about a famous person. Austin chose King. "I was mad because I only got an A-minus," she said, "and I had pictures and everything."

King's victory catapulted her into a semifinal match against Evert Lloyd, one that was all anyone could have anticipated and more. They presented the tournament with a blast from the past. The younger woman prevailed, but not before King fought off four match points and performed a medley of her greatest shots, perfected over two decades. So small was the edge in Evert Lloyd's 7-6 (7-4), 2-6, 6-3 triumph that the two women split the 30 games and King achieved one more service break.

Meanwhile, Navratilova was cruising through an upset-strewn half of the draw, without the loss of a set. "I really can't believe I've won as easily as I have," she said. "I haven't been tested."

Her test came in the final when she found herself down a break in the third set. A finalist for the sixth consecutive year, Evert Lloyd won the last four games of the second set and broke Navratilova's service in the third game of the third set, stirring uneasy memories of the 1981 U.S. final when the latter unraveled in two tiebreakers against Austin.

"Martina kind of choked that match," Evert Lloyd said. "When she's been in a tough situation in the past, Tracy or I have come out better. But she won this match. She played well under pressure."

Indeed, Navratilova needed mental strength commensurate with her physical talents to beat Evert Lloyd, 6-2, 3-6, 6-2, for her third successive Big Four title, including the Australian Open championship she had claimed in December.

All went well until the second week of the U.S. Open where, top-seeded Navratilova claimed, her condition was weakened by a case of toxoplasmosis, a viral condition transmitted by her cat. Ironically, she was victimized by Shriver who, at 16, had upset Navratilova to reach her only Open final in 1978. In this instance, Shriver rallied from a 1-6, 4-5, 15-30 predicament to oust her doubles partner, 7-6 (7-5) and 6-2 in the third. The two women then hugged at the net and both left the court in tears.

Shriver failed to survive the semifinals, beaten by Hana Mandlikova, 6-4, 4-6, 6-2, who earlier had eliminated defending champ Austin, 4-6, 6-4, 6-4, competing in only her second tournament since Wimbledon. Second-seeded Evert Lloyd received her only real challenge in the quarters from an unlikely source, a 19-year-old former gymnast from Florida who had reached the final at Monte Carlo against Virginia Ruzici. On her way to women's rookie honors, Bonnie Gadusek not only took the first set from Evert Lloyd but broke serve to begin the second.

Thereafter, it was no contest, Evert Lloyd sweeping the last 12 games for a 4-6, 6-1, 6-0 triumph. It was a harbinger of what was to come. The queen of Flushing overwhelmed Jaeger, 6-1, 6-2, in the semis and then dispatched Mandlikova, 6-3, 6-1, to clinch her sixth Open singles title.

Like circled wagoneers, two collegians, 18-year-old freshman Gretchen Rush of Trinity (Tex.) and 21-year-old senior Rodney Harmon of Southern Methodist—lonely amateurs in an overwhelming crowd of pros—held their own right down to the last eight. Gretchen, a sharp-volleyer from Pittsburgh, toppled sixth-seeded Wendy Turnbull, 6-3, 4-6, 6-2, but wore down in a rush toward the semis against fourth-seeded Jaeger, 3-6, 6-1, 6-0. Arthur Ashe, the lone amateur to win the Open (1968), watched with pride the progress of a guy from his Richmond, Va., neighborhood, wild-card Harmon, as Rodney, a big-serving 6-foot-3, got past Scott Davis and Swedish Davis Cupper Henrik Sundstrom. Then he served 15 aces, the last on match point, to bag a seasoned pro, eighth-seeded Eliot Teltscher, 6-4, 4-6, 6-3, 3-6, 7-1 (7-1). Connors was too much for him, however, 6-1, 6-3, 6-4. As the most successful amateurs since McEnroe's fourth-round venture in 1977 and Barbara Gerken's to the quarters in 1981, they were also the last to do so well.

Evert Lloyd continued winning until Navratilova stopped her streak at 31 matches in the final at Brighton, England, in late October, 6-1, 6-4. Five weeks later, she reversed the outcome, defeating Navratilova, 6-3, 2-6, 6-3, for her first Australian title. In that instant she became the 10th player of either sex to win all four major singles championships.

The two rivals also teamed for the first time in Federation Cup play as the U.S. stretched its unbeaten streak to 34 rounds en route to its seventh consecutive team championship, 3-0 over Germany. Evert Lloyd also captained the American squad to its fourth consecutive Wightman Cup victory over Great Britain, 6-1, winning both her singles and surpassing Helen Wills Moody's U.S. record for most matches entered with 32.

Connors' resurrection salvaged what had been a lackluster Wimbledon among the men. With so many top players absent and with the rain pelting down, the primary topic of conversation was McEnroe's relationship with the All England Club. He complimented officials for their attitude following his opening match but he was not entirely pleased, noting that he had not yet received his trophies from the previous year.

Ted Tinling, the liaison between players and the club, explained that McEnroe had not picked up the silver replicas of the President's Cup, the Challenge Cup and the Renshaw Cup on his way out the door in 1981. Nor had he attended the champion's dinner that night. Tinling said the club considered shipping the silverware to New York but found the insurance prohibitive.

So there they sat until the player's father claimed the prizes later that day. As for membership in the club, which Mac also sought, Tinling said that was another matter entirely. "I explained to Mr. McEnroe," he said, "that it's not an automatic to become a member if you win. It's an elected privilege."

Unlike the previous year, his advance to the final was virtually free of controversy. He was warned once, for ball abuse, in a second-round victory over Eddie Edwards and drew a $500 fine for verbal abuse in his 6-3, 6-1, 6-2 semifinal thrashing of Tim Mayotte, the unseeded second-year pro who improved one round on his Wimbledon debut in 1981. His title defense would be against Connors, who easily turned aside another surprise semifinalist, 12th-seeded Mark Edmondson, 6-4, 6-3, 6-1.

It had been eight years since Connors reigned as men's singles champion. He was a whiz kid of 21 when he demolished Ken Rosewall in the '74 final. Only Big Bill Tilden (1921–30) and Evonne Goolagong (1971–80) had gone a longer time between Wimbledon titles.

Brandishing a redesigned serve and hungry for another major championship, Connors outlasted McEnroe, 3-6, 6-3, 6-7 (2-7), 7-6 (7-5), 6-4, in a match that was distinguished more by its length (four hours, 15 minutes) than its brilliance. Despite 13 double faults, Connors grabbed hold of his sixth major tournament victory, charging back when it seemed he must lose. McEnroe, with a 2-1 lead in sets, was merely points from victory at 3-2 in the tie-breaker with two serves to come, then 4-3—three points away—after his 17th ace, but Jimmy allowed him no closer. "I'm not a one-timer," he announced, "someone to be forgotten. I've had chances [in finals] three times since then. And I was going to do anything not to let the chance slip by today."

As a special consolation prize, McEnroe was granted the honorary membership denied the previous year. He was so advised between the singles final and doubles final, which he and Peter Fleming lost to Peter McNamara and Paul McNamee of Australia, relinquishing the title they won in 1981. "I guess I'm happy," Mac said after being welcomed to the club.

Two months later, in New York, he was separated from his other major singles title. The culprit this time was Lendl, whose serves backed McEnroe almost to the wall in a 6-4, 6-4, 7-6 (8-6) semifinal victory. Connors had a better idea. After dismissing Vilas in the semifinals, he dared Lendl to drive the ball past him. Standing almost contemptuously just behind the baseline, he startled and demoralized the Czech with his returns in a 6-3, 6-2, 4-6, 6-4 triumph that returned the man to the top of the tennis world just when his career appeared to be in eclipse.

"When I won before," Connors said, "everybody thought I would. When I won now, everybody thought I wouldn't. And that's very satisfying." So he was joining the likes of Tilden, Fred Perry, Don Budge, Rod Laver and McEnroe as the only men twice to win Wimbledon and the U.S. in the same year.

Although winning no major individual titles for the first time in four years, McEnroe did lead the U.S. to a second consecutive Davis Cup. The 4-1 final over France in Grenoble was notable mainly for the man's 12-10, 1-6, 3-6, 6-2, 6-3 victory over Yannick Noah on a clay court built to stop him inside the former Olympic ice rink. But even that superb 4-hour, 21-minute battle paled in comparison to Mac's extraordinary 9-7, 6-2, 15-17, 3-6, 8-6 triumph over Mats Wilander in a decisive fifth match of the U.S.-Sweden quarterfinal at St. Louis. Time of play: a Cup singles record of 6 hours, 32 minutes.

1983

Considering their backgrounds, their forehands and their achievements, one would not expect to mention them in the same sentence. But on May 28, Martina Navratilova and Kathy Horvath shared a court in Paris. In retrospect, it may have been the most significant match of the year.

Even at the time, it was something special. Navratilova had won her first 36 matches of 1983 before meeting the teenager in the fourth round of the French Open. A former child prodigy, Erika

Kathleen Horvath had won a satellite tournament and had been runner-up to Chris Evert Lloyd in the German Open the previous week. But nothing prepared her or the tennis world for what happened at Stade Roland Garros.

The unseeded American, a pupil of Harry Hopman, posted a stunning 6-4, 0-6, 6-3 victory. The ramifications of that upset wouldn't be felt for months. Following the defeat, Navratilova won her next 50 matches and swept the field of Wimbledon, the U.S. Open and Australian Open championships. Not only had Horvath denied her the opportunity of achieving a Grand Slam but spoiled what might have been the first perfect campaign in the open era.

Navratilova's domination among the women, marred only by that single loss, and Chris Evert Lloyd's subsequent march to a record-tying fifth French title, was the story of the year in tennis. It overshadowed a mad scramble on the men's circuit as the major championships were divided four ways for the first time in seven years and the race for No. 1 wasn't decided until the Masters in the 13th month of an exhausting season. At the end, the distinction belonged once again to John McEnroe, who boasted a second Wimbledon crown among his seven singles titles.

For breadth of accomplishment, however, Mats Wilander emerged as male Player of the Year. Not only did he win the most matches (82) and singles tournaments (9) but he went 8-0 in Davis Cup play while leading Sweden to second place behind Australia and he compiled the best record in the major tournaments. He captured the Australian title, was runner-up at the French, reached the quarterfinals at the U.S. and the third round at Wimbledon. He also finished atop the Volvo Grand Prix standings, pocketing a $600,000 bonus which enabled him to finish third in prize money behind Ivan Lendl and McEnroe.

In terms of shock value and fan satisfaction, however, perhaps nothing compared to Yannick Noah's victory in Paris. By turning back defending champ Wilander in the final, the acrobatic athlete from Cameroon became the first French citizen in 37 years to hold the French title. He also became such a celebrity that he found it necessary to flee to little old New York for privacy.

On another national front, Jimmy Connors continued his mastery of the Flushing Meadow hard courts, claiming his fifth U.S. crown while denying Lendl a first Big Four title. The angular Czech also stumbled in the Masters final. He was consoled by checks totaling $1,747,128.

Lendl's earnings exceeded even those of Navratilova but the $1,456,030 she collected, more than triple the take of Evert Lloyd, was only one indicator of the success she enjoyed. At the very least, it was the most stellar female performance since Margaret Smith Court completed her Grand Slam in 1970. Suzanne Lenglen of France and Americans Helen Wills Moody and Alice Marble had posted unbeaten seasons earlier in the century, but they didn't play in all the major championships or endure the same demanding schedule.

Consider that Navratilova won 16 of the 17 singles events she entered and added 13 doubles championships, including 11 in the company of Pam Shriver. Her greatest satisfaction occurred in New York, where she annexed her first U.S. Open title. That brought to 11 the number of players, male and female, to have won all four of the major championships.

But for the intervention of Horvath, it might have been a season unlike any other. Horvath at 17 was almost four years removed from her greatest moment of fame. She had advanced through the qualifying rounds to reach the main draw of the 1979 U.S. Open less than a week after her 14th birthday, the youngest ever entered, and received a first-round bye before being ousted, not without a struggle, by sixth-seeded Dianne Fromholtz, 7-6, 6-2.

After two years of consistent progress, Horvath received a setback in 1982 when she was sidelined for four months by a back injury. But she worked her way up to No. 33 on the computer by the spring of 1983, winning an event on the

Viva le Frenchman Yannick Noah, winner of the French championship in 1983. (Russ Adams)

satellite circuit, reaching the semifinals of the Italian Open and then defeating Bonnie Gadusek, Andrea Leand, Bettina Bunge and Andrea Jaeger en route to the final of the German Open, where she succumbed in straight sets to Evert Lloyd, 6-4, 7-6 (7-1).

Understandably, these achievements paled alongside those of Navratilova, who stormed through four tournaments on the Virginia Slims circuit, then overpowered Evert Lloyd, 6-2, 6-0, in the championship finale at New York. Adapting quickly to clay, she won a second consecutive Family Circle Cup at Hilton Head, overcoming Tracy Austin, 5-7, 6-1, 6-0. Limited by injuries to eight tournaments, the luckless Austin appeared in only the one final.

Entering the French, Navratilova appeared unbeatable. She was backstopped by a trainer and motivator (Nancy Lieberman), a regular coach (Mike Estep), a strategist (Renée Richards) and even a nutritionist. "Team Navratilova" the entourage was called, and it made her appear even more formidable than she already was.

Against the biggest arsenal in the game, Horvath marshalled her resolve and an attack strategy that contrasted with her earlier years as a baseline mechanic. "To be in the rankings these days," she said, "you have to be really steady from the baseline but you also have to be able to finish up the point. Against a serve-and-volleyer, when it's close, it's important to get to the net first. They're used to being there, and if you take that away from them, they get shaky."

She did exactly as planned against Navratilova, and the defending champion was as bothered as Horvath had hoped. The youngster kept hitting to Navratilova's backhand and volleying her increasingly weak returns.

"I was trying to outsteady her at the beginning instead of going for shots," Navratilova said. "Tactically, if I had to play the match over, I'd start off by going for broke. I think I played it too conservative, and that's not my game. Once it gets close, it's hard to go for it."

Evert Lloyd didn't appear any more pleased than her rival when she heard the score. "All I thought was, 'Damn, I wish I'd been the one to beat her,'" she said.

In six meetings that year, Evert Lloyd failed to do just that but she never got the chance on her best surface. She had to be satisfied with beating Hana Mandlikova, Jaeger and Mima Jausovec in the last three rounds to clinch her fifth French title, tying Court's record. Jausovec, the 1977 champion who ended Horvath's dream in the quarterfinals with the loss of two games, succumbed in the final, 6-1, 6-2. It didn't take Navratilova long to start on a new streak. She prepared for Wimbledon by routing Wendy Turnbull in the final at Eastbourne and was at her devastating best at Wimbledon, where her average match lasted 47 minutes. Only Sherry Acker,

Only one loss—to Kathy Horvath in the French—kept Martina Navratilova from a perfect 1983. (Russ Adams)

holding two set points in the second round, provided a semblance of a struggle, 7-6 (7-5), 6-3.

The field was weakened notably by Evert Lloyd's dismissal in the third round. Suffering from the after-effects of flu, the three-time champion was eliminated by Kathy Jordan, 6-1, 7-6 (7-2). It marked the first time in 35 major tournaments, dating back to 1971, that she had failed to reach the semifinals.

In her absence, Billie Jean King made another run at the championship at the age of 39. For the second consecutive year, she won the warmup at Birmingham and then advanced to the round of four with a 7-5, 6-4 triumph over Jordan in the quarterfinals.

The Old Lady, however, was no match for Jaeger in the semis. The 18-year-old, less than half King's age, passed and lobbed her opponent into submission, 6-1, 6-1, to become the youngest women's finalist at Wimbledon since Mo Connolly in 1952. She had little time or reason to savor the honor.

Navratilova, who had crushed unseeded Yvonne Vermaak, 6-1, 6-1, in the semifinals, overwhelmed third-seeded Jaeger, 6-0, 6-3, and proudly accepted the mantle of No. 1 player in the world. "Is there any doubt in anybody's mind?" she said. Anything else would have been false modesty.

Not that she thought she had played to her full potential. "Today I didn't serve really well," she said. "I can still adjust better during the matches. I can improve my concentration. My thinking could be better. My backhand can be stronger."

Although no other female player on earth possessed her combination of strength and agility, there remained the faintest of doubts about her composure as she prepared for her final frontier, the U.S. Open. It was the mental edge to which Evert Lloyd clung, even after she fell in the finals to Navratilova at the Virginia Slims of Los Angeles, 6-1, 6-3, and the Canadian Open, 6-4, 4-6, 6-1, in consecutive weeks. The defending champ seemed to be counting upon her rival to fall apart at Flushing Meadow once again. "Nerves might enter in," she decided.

Certainly, no other threat materialized in the course of the tournament. Navratilova waded through the field with almost as much dispatch as she displayed at Wimbledon. She failed to drop more than four games in any of her first five matches and she continued to limit her court time to under one hour through the semis, where she avenged her 1982 loss to Shriver in businesslike fashion, 6-2, 6-1.

Nor did Evert Lloyd struggle unduly. Her run of straight-set victories included a 6-3, 7-6 (8-6) triumph over Jordan in the fourth round. In turning back Jo Durie of Great Britain, 6-4, 6-4, in the semifinals, she qualified to defend the title she had regained the previous year. If there was

any stopping Navratilova, this was the time and, particularly, the place.

But Navratilova had come too far, had worked too hard to trip over her own anxieties. She took charge of the match at the outset, en route to a decisive 6-1, 6-3 victory, the most satisfying of her career on her 11th try after one final and four semifinals. "If I don't win another tournament in my life," she said, "I can still say I've done it all."

With the last jewel in her crown, she silenced criticism of her emotional fortitude. In the second set, Evert Lloyd had rallied briefly for her lone break and then held serve at love for a 3-2 lead. It was as if she had read the writing in the sky— Good Luck Chrissie—fashioned by a squadron of planes hired by a sponsor, Lipton Tea, although she said she barely noticed. Instead of cracking, however, Navratilova tightened the screws, holding her own serve and then breaking Evert Lloyd at love before running out the set.

Evert Lloyd's only consolation, and it was minimal, was pushing Navratilova three minutes beyond an hour. Still, the first-time U.S. champion set a record for fewest games lost in a seven-match tournament (19 of 103). It was the decisive triumph she had longed for in the national championship of her adopted country and it pleased her so much she said the first prize money of $120,000 (and a $500,000 bonus from Playtex for winning at Hilton Head, Wimbledon and Flushing Meadow) was incidental.

"If I had been guaranteed a title," Navratilova said, "I would have been happy not to win a dime. You can't buy a U.S. Open championship."

Not that she was content to rest on it. Navratilova continued to cut a swath through the women's tour all the way to Melbourne. There, in the absence of Evert Lloyd, she was almost undone by a soggy lawn and the eighth seed, Durie. The Englishwoman captured the first set before rain postponed the match but Navratilova rallied the following day to win, 4-6, 6-3, 6-4, taking five of the last six games.

She then turned back Shriver, 6-4, 6-3, and Jordan, 6-2, 7-6 (7-5), completing the campaign with her 50th consecutive victory in her ninth successive tournament final. Remarkably, Navratilova also teamed with Shriver to retain the doubles title, defeating Turnbull and Anne Hobbs, 6-4, 6-7 (5-7), 6-2. It gave the pair a sweep of the Wimbledon, U.S. and Australian Open championships. (They had scratched from the French due to a Shriver injury).

No female doubles team had won three majors in a season since Court and Virginia Wade 10 years earlier. Their lone defeat, to King and Anne Smith at the Tournament of Champions final in April, ended a 40-match streak, so they started another that reached 31 by season's end.

Navratilova also assumed Evert Lloyd's former role as captain and chief assassin of the Wightman Cup team, leading the U.S. to a 6-1 victory over Great Britain. But neither was available for the Federation Cup in Zurich. Czechoslovakia, behind Hana Mandlikova and Helena Sukova, triumphed for the first time since 1975 when Navratilova was rising to prominence in her native country.

Only two women other than Navratilova won more than two tournaments all year. Evert Lloyd captured six titles and, aside from her six losses to Navratilova, slipped only twice—to Jordan at Wimbledon and to Lisa Bonder in the first round at Tokyo. Andrea Temesvari, a 17-year-old Hungarian, won three events, including the Italian Open over Bonnie Gadusek, 6-1, 6-0, and the U.S. Clay Court over Zina Garrison, 6-2, 6-2. And Kathy Horvath, the obstacle to perfection at Paris, won the Ginny championships at Honolulu in November over Carling Bassett, 4-6, 6-2, 7-6, and finished the year No. 9 in the U.S., the only time she would ever be ranked among the Top Ten of the USTA.

Although the men offered no transcendent figure, they were a lot more competitive from the start of the European season to the finish of a dandy Masters in January, 1984. In a year of new faces, the youngest and freshest belonged to Jimmy Arias, who became the dirt-kicking King of Italy, waving his huge forehand as a scepter in sweeping the country's soil: first Florence over Francesco Cancellotti, 6-4, 6-3; then the Open in Rome over Jose Higueras, 6-2, 6-7 (3-7), 6-1, 6-4, at age 18; finally Palermo as a new 19-year-old over Jose-Luis Clerc, 6-2, 2-6, 6-0. A three-year pro who was in the first wave of coach Nick Bollettieri's baseline prodigies, Arias would go on to capture the U.S. Clay Court over Andres Gomez, 6-4, 2-6, 6-4, skyrocket to No. 6 on the ATP computer and, besieged by injuries, fail to win another tournament in the decade.

Emotionally, no one made a more spectacular jump than Yannick Noah, even though he was 23 and had been a steady winner on the tour for five seasons. Until this year, however, he hadn't advanced beyond the quarterfinal of a major event. But on the occasion of the 1983 French Open, he was more than a gifted entertainer. He was a champion.

With a running start provided by his victory at the German Open, where he deposed Jose Higueras, 3-6, 7-5, 6-2, 6-0, Noah tore through Paris, dropping only one set, that to Lendl in the quarterfinals. The fans at Roland Garros were treated to the extraordinary sight of two Frenchmen in the semifinals after Christophe Roger-Vasselin, No. 230 on the computer, shocked top-seeded Connors in straight sets, 6-4, 6-4, 7-6 (7-5), the upset of the year and one of the most stunning in French history. Noah easily disposed of his countryman, 6-3, 6-0, 6-0, and then ground down the defending champ, resourceful Mats Wilander, 6-2, 7-5, 7-6 (7-3).

It marked the culmination of a long journey by Noah, who left behind his family in the modest capital of Yaounde, Cameroon, at the age of 11 to study tennis in Paris. Afterward, he cried with joy, as did his father. The trophy was presented by Marcel Bernard, the last native to hold the title in 1946.

The aftermath wasn't nearly so inspirational. Noah was idled by a 42-day suspension for failing to represent France at the World Team Cup in Dusseldorf and by a knee injury. He played in only four more tournaments, including the U.S. Open where he lost to Arias in a splendid quarter-final match.

But before Flushing Meadow, there was Wimbledon and a new cast of up-and-comers. These included Nduka "Duke" Odizor of Nigeria and the University of Houston, who bounced fourth seed Guillermo Vilas in the first round and reached the round of 16; hard-serving Kevin Curren of South Africa and the University of Texas, who dismantled top-seeded Connors, 4-6, 7-6 (7-4), 6-2, 7-6 (8-6), in the fourth round with the help of 33 aces and smashed his way to the semifinals; and, finally, Chris Lewis, a dashing Kiwi who didn't seem to know his place on the lawns of the All England Club.

Lewis was ranked No. 91 in the world at the start of the event. Although he won the Wimbledon junior title in 1975, he had advanced beyond the semifinals of only three pro tournaments. But, once inside the gates on Church Road, he wouldn't leave. He scooted through the top half of the draw with amazing grace and grit, outlasting Curren in a brilliant five-set semifinal that left the participants applauding each other, 6-7 (3-7), 6-4, 7-6 (7-4), 6-7 (3-7), 8-6.

As a result, he became the first unseeded player to reach a Wimbledon final since Willy Bungert in 1967 and the first New Zealander in the championship match since matinee idol, Tony Wilding, won four consecutive titles, 1910–1913. There, however, reality struck in the form of McEnroe's impenetrable service and superb court sense. In three immaculate sets of serve-and-volley tennis, the American won easily, 6-2, 6-2, 6-2, in 85 minutes, to regain the honor he last held in 1981.

Two surprise packages at the U.S. Open were a stocky double-hander all the way, Greg Holmes, the Intercollegiate (Utah) and Pan American Games champ, and skinny 16-year-old Aaron Krickstein from Grosse Pointe, Mich., the coun-

try's youngest junior champ. Both made the last 16. Holmes, ranked No. 450, knocked off an ex-champ, sixth-seeded Guillermo Vilas, 6-2, 6-2, 6-3. Amateur Krickstein, with no ranking, was—like Arias—a product of Bollettieri's Florida finishing school of two-fisted backhands. In his first major he attracted attention by waylaying a big name, 15th-seeded Vitas Gerulaitis from way behind, 3-6, 3-6, 6-4, 6-3, 6-4.

He then fell to Noah, who in turn was eliminated by Aaron's stablemate, Arias, in a match of very good feeling and trick shots, 7-6 (7-4), 4-6, 6-3, 1-6, 7-5. Arias, who had celebrated his 19th birthday three weeks earlier, became the youngest U.S. semifinalist since 17-year-old Oliver Campbell in 1888. This impressed Lendl not a bit, and he sent the King of Italy home to Bradenton, Fla., 6-4, 6-4, 7-6 (7-4).

Awaiting him in the final was the defending champion. To reach the championship round for a seventh time, third-seeded Connors gave a 6-2, 6-3, 6-2, brushoff to slick-volleying Texan Billy Scanlon, who had outnerved and outserved McEnroe in the fourth round, 7-6 (7-2), 7-6 (7-3), 4-6, 6-3. Scanlon labored hour after hour well into the following morning to defeat, in a 7-4 fifth-set tie-breaker, the tourney's overachiever, No. 96 Mark Dickson, a Floridian dawdler who routinely bounced the ball 30-or-so times before serving. That inspired a plaintive wall message in red paint in a men's room: I SURVIVED SCANLON-DICKSON—4:14. Since Connors had just turned 31, was playing with a bone spur on his right little toe, was suffering from diarrhea (he rushed to the men's room late in the second set) and was combating court temperatures in excess of 100 degrees, the time appeared ripe for Lendl.

After splitting the first two sets, the Czech expatriate served for the third set at 5-4. The title appeared within his reach. Then, inexplicably, he double-faulted at set point. After that, he said, "I could never recover." In a mysterious meltdown, the man who hadn't lost a set until the final never won another game. Connors whipped through the last nine games to win his fifth U.S. title, 6-3, 6-7

(2-7), 7-5, 6-0. Since an international statistical panel recently had ruled that some of his early achievements were of an exhibition nature and revised his total of career tournament victories to 99, Connors recelebrated his centennial in his favorite setting.

One of those was on the carpet at Memphis, where Jimmy broke a tie with a forgotten rival while winning the U.S. Indoor for a record sixth time. In beating Gene Mayer, 7-5, 6-0, he renewed a title he first won at Salisbury, Md., a decade before. That sent him ahead of long-departed Wylie Grant from deep in the long-trousered era, a player who had won five times, too (1903, 1904, 1906, 1908, 1912).

As the season waned, young Krickstein found his way into the record book, too, by winning his first tournament as a pro. He was 16 years, 2 months, the youngest to take a professional title, Israel. It was a long-shot special: Aaron, No. 489, beating No. 189, German Christopher Zipf at Tel Aviv, 7-6, 6-3. Krickstein had been, at age 15 earlier in the year, the youngest to play in a pro event, Philadelphia, losing in the first round to Fritz Buehning, 6-2, 6-3.

At the Australian Open, which Connors bypassed but which attracted the rest of the elite, the 19-year-old Wilander knocked off defending champion Johan Kriek, McEnroe and, finally, Lendl, 6-1, 6-4, 6-4, to become the youngest champion Down Under since Ken Rosewall won at 18 in 1953. It was his ninth victory of a season in which 10 players won three or more tour events and 46 men earned at least $100,000 in prize money.

Parity was in the air, and a handful of players had a chance to claim the No. 1 ranking when the Masters got underway at Madison Square Garden. There was only one notable absentee, 1974 champion Vilas, who had been hit with a one-year suspension by the MIPTC for allegedly accepting $60,000 illicit appearance money at Rotterdam. He subsequently lost an appeal and was fined $20,000. Although the suspension was

For Mats Wilander, 1983 was a year to remember. (Russ Adams)

waived in January 1984, he already had been sidelined for six months.

After reversing his fortune against Wilander, 6-2, 6-4, in the semifinal, McEnroe decisively whipped Lendl, 6-3, 6-4, 6-4, for the title and the top ranking. "John deserves to be No. 1," Lendl said. "He had the most consistent year."

For good measure, McEnroe and Peter Fleming, the best doubles team in the world, reprised their Wimbledon and U.S. championship performances by beating the second-best team of Pavel Slozil and Tom Smid, 6-2, 6-2. It was their sixth Masters doubles crown in as many years.

1984

Rare as it may be for any athlete to be identified as a genius, it's more unlikely still to be branded a tormented genius. But John McEnroe fit the billing, never more than in 1984. En route to the greatest season of his career, he jousted with the furies and toyed with his peers.

But for an occasional slip, it might have been said that the only man capable of beating McEnroe this year was McEnroe himself. Certainly, he had to be credited at least with an assist when he allowed himself to be distracted while holding a two-set lead over Ivan Lendl in the final of the French Open. Lendl went on to win the match for his first major triumph.

Thereafter, McEnroe was magnificent in duplicating his 1981 feat of sweeping Wimbledon and the U.S. Open. He also counted the U.S. Pro Indoor, the WCT championship, the Canadian Open and the season-ending Masters among his 13 tournament victories. In addition to the loss in Paris, he suffered only two more singles defeats, to Vijay Amritraj in the first round at Cincinnati and to Henrik Sundstrom in the Davis Cup final at Goteborg.

McEnroe's 82-3 record produced a .965 winning percentage, highest of the Open era among men. In finishing at the top of the computer rankings for the fourth consecutive year, he enjoyed the most dominant season since Jimmy Connors won the only three major events he entered and compiled a 99-4 mark in 1974. The latter still was going strong 10 years after his big year, claiming five titles, reaching the final at Wimbledon and pushing McEnroe to five sets in a brilliant semifinal showdown at Flushing Meadow.

Andres Gomez, the finest player from Ecuador since Pancho Segura, ascended to the Top Ten by winning five tournaments, including the Italian Open over Aaron Krickstein, 2-6, 6-1, 6-2, 6-2, and the U.S. Clay Court over Balazs Taroczy, 6-0, 7-6 (7-5). But the biggest breakthrough occurred among the Swedes. Bjorn Borg's legacy was a nation of nine million swarming with tennis talent. Mats Wilander and four compatriots—Sundstrom, Anders Jarryd, Joakim Nystrom and Stefan Edberg—not only seized the Davis Cup for the first time in nine years but they accounted for 14 tournament victories.

Yet, the only individual to challenge McEnroe for supremacy and attention was Martina Navratilova, who continued her mastery of the

Until the French in 1984, Ivan Lendl had never won a major crown. (Russ Adams)

women's tour. She won three of the Big Four tournaments and 78 of 80 singles matches, a phenomenal season by any standard but the one she established the previous year. This time Navratilova fell two victories short of a Grand Slam when she was upset by Helena Sukova in the semifinals of the Australian Open in December. She had suffered her only other loss of the year to Hana Mandlikova 11 months earlier in Oakland. Ironically, both women once had served as ballgirls at Navratilova's matches in Czechoslovakia.

Beyond her 13 tournament victories, the world's top female player posted the longest (74 matches) and third-longest (54) winning streaks of the Open era. And she also surpassed her great rival, Chris Evert Lloyd, in head-to-head competition by winning all six meetings, with the loss of only one set.

Evert Lloyd did claim the Australian Open title by beating Sukova, thereby extending to 11 years her streak of having won at least one major championship. She also amassed her 132nd professional tournament victory, a record for either sex, and increased her total of matches won to 1,003, having nailed her 1,000th over Pascale Paradis, 6-1, 6-7 (5-7), 6-2.

Manuela Maleeva, a 17-year-old Bulgarian, made the biggest jump among the women. She vaulted from No. 31 to No. 6 in the world rankings by winning four tournaments, among them the rain-plagued Italian Open, where she stunned five-time champion Evert Lloyd, 6-3, 6-3, Manuela's third victory of a strenuous last day. Headed in the opposite direction were Tracy Austin, who played in only one tournament before being sidelined again with a chronic back ailment, and Andrea Jaeger, who withdrew from the tour to enter college after lackluster efforts in six events.

But the year will belong forever to McEnroe and Navratilova, who never again would stand unchallenged. (Although only 25, McEnroe would not win another major.) The two shared a physical characteristic, left-handedness, and a love for doubles.

McEnroe won seven doubles titles. In six of those tournaments, including Wimbledon and the Masters, he was joined by his steady partner, Peter Fleming. Together, they raised their victory total to 52.

According to Fleming, "The best doubles team in the world is John McEnroe and whoever he plays with." As if to prove it, Mac took his 17-year-old brother Patrick, a top junior, to a WCT tournament in Richmond and they routed Kevin Curren and Steve Denton, the 1982 U.S. Open champions, in the final, 7-6 (7-3), 6-2.

Navratilova enjoyed even greater success in doubles, losing one of 61 matches. But with Pam Shriver she was perfection. She and Pam completed the open era's first undefeated season by a team: 11 titles, 53 matches. Pam's personal dou-

Helena Sukova upset Martina Navratilova and went on to take the Australian title in 1984. (Russ Adams)

bles match record was 59-2. The pair also registered the only Grand Slam by a female doubles team, equaling the 1951 feat of Aussies Frank Sedgman and Ken McGregor. Martina and Pam were 22-0 over that four-way stretch, losing two sets. By beating Sukova and Claudia Kohde Kilsch, 6-3, 6-4, they added the Australian title to the French, Wimbledon and U.S. championships. It was their 52nd career triumph.

Despite the parallel success of the two champions, however, there was a significant distinction in their approach to the sport. Having reshuffled her entourage midway through the 1983 season, Navratilova continued to improve her conditioning under coach Mike Estep and to digest only the proper foods. She was a disciple of Robert Haas, the nutritionist whose "Eat to Win" diet found favor among a number of tennis players, including Ivan Lendl.

That led a reporter to inquire of McEnroe, who played doubles in order to avoid tedious practice sessions and whose appetite was ruled by his taste buds, whether he had tried the Haas diet. "No," he smirked, "I prefer the Haagen-Dazs diet."

Yet, when the man was in tune with himself, his dedication and his fitness seemed not to matter. McEnroe had such astonishing touch and such finely honed instincts for the game that the points just flowed off his racket. To Robert Green, a bright candidate for a masters degree in Soviet studies and a first-time opponent at the U.S. Open, "He almost anticipates the shot before you think of it. He gets to places you don't think he should be."

And McEnroe was never better than in 1984, which he began in spectacular fashion. Following his Masters victory, he thrashed Lendl at the U.S. Pro Indoor in Philadelphia, 6-3, 3-6, 6-3, 7-6 (7-3), the Belgian Indoor in Brussels, 6-1, 6-3, the WCT Tournament of Champions at Forest Hills, 6-4, 6-2, and the World Team Cup at Dusseldorf, 6-3, 6-2. He also dismissed Tomas Smid at the Grand Prix de Madrid and overwhelmed Connors, 6-1, 6-2, 6-3, at the WCT finals in Dallas. In reaching the championship round of the French Open for the first time, he extended his winning streak to 42 matches, an open-era high for an American man.

Not that his form left him serene. Paris was a struggle from the outset. There, in addition to opponents, Mac battled the usual suspects—courtside photographers, groundskeepers, linespersons—as well as the ambience of the tournament and city itself, of which he had once declared in full voice, "I hate this place."

McEnroe demanded court repairs during a third-round victory over Mel Purcell, drilled two balls into the photographers' pit while beating Jose Higueras in the next match and complained so much about calls in a semifinal rout of Connors that the latter offered some free advice while

Wimbledon and the U.S. Open were among John McEnroe's many titles in 1984. (Mitchell Reibel)

approaching the net. "Shut up," the onetime bad boy yelled. "Grow up. You're a baby."

While the top seed battled his personal demons, Lendl tore through his half of the draw virtually unscathed. After an undistinguished spring that included only one victory (at Luxembourg) and an abandoned final at Rotterdam when a one-set lead over Connors was erased by a bomb threat, he appeared in Paris with a stronger serve and greater patience. He dropped only one set in reaching the final and blasted the steady Wilander, 6-2, 6-3, 7-5, who had eliminated defending champion Yannick Noah, in the semifinals, 7-6 (7-4), 2-6, 3-6, 6-3, 6-3.

For the first two sets of their showdown on clay, McEnroe was completely in charge, granting only 10 points on his serve. He appeared certain to become the first American male since

Tony Trabert (1954 and 1955) to win at Roland Garros and given his form and past performances at Wimbledon and the U.S. Open, a Grand Slam was not out of the question. At that critical juncture of history, however, McEnroe snapped.

With Lendl preparing to serve at 1-1 in the third set, the American objected to a television cameraman's headset that was emitting a director's instructions and cast it aside. Once Lendl fell behind, 0-30, Mac began grousing at photographers, allowing his opponent to collect himself. Lendl held serve there but fell behind, 0-40, two games later.

By then, the crowd was hooting and whistling at the leader. McEnroe blew the triple-break point as well as another ad point and Lendl recovered, broke serve in the following game and ran out the set.

The result was what McEnroe later called "a snowball effect. I had gotten to such a high level early, when I went down I couldn't come back. Then the crowd got into it. It's frustrating."

Although the man held two service breaks in the fourth set, to 1-2, 2-3, McEnroe could convert neither. And, as his first serve continued to wane, he became more and more vulnerable. Lendl earned the set with a superb lob in the 12th game.

His reputation for gagging in the majors did not hold up on this day, Lendl's fifth major final, when he finally hit the jackpot. He was the stronger down the fifth-set stretch, although they were neck-and-neck. Ivan had to clamber out of 15-40, two break points (McEnroe missed forehands), to get to 4-3, en-route to a 3-6, 2-6, 6-4, 7-5, 7-5 triumph achieved in four hours, eight minutes. McEnroe saved one match point at 15-40 in the 12th game but then mis-hit a shoulder-high forehand volley. "It feels great to finally answer some different questions," the new champion said after becoming only the 14th man in 107 years to overcome a two-set deficit in the final of a Big Four event. An alleged choker no more, Lendl had the first of his eight majors that decorated a great career, after failing in his title bids

on this court in 1981, the U.S. in 1982 and 1983 and the Australian in 1983.

McEnroe appeared to have learned his lessons from Paris and a subsequent squall at the Queen's Club in time for Wimbledon. Either that or the uncharacteristically benign weather left him mellow. The defending champ behaved impeccably at the All England Club and he performed brilliantly. Whether the one had anything to do with the other was pure conjecture.

He ceded only one set in the tournament—to Paul McNamee in the first round—and was mesmerizing in dismissing Connors, 6-1, 6-1, 6-2, in the final. Even McEnroe, the perfectionist, allowed that it was "maybe the best match of my life."

It had been 46 years since a Wimbledon championship was concluded in such decisive fashion (Don Budge over Bunny Austin, 6-1, 6-0, 6-3). Incredibly, McEnroe didn't commit the first of his two unforced errors until the 62-minute mark of Connors' hour-and-a-half ordeal. The champion served 75 percent, with 11 aces, and never permitted Connors a break point in becoming the second American male to win Wimbledon for a third time, following the lead of Bill Tilden, and the first to hold consecutive titles since Budge in 1937 and 1938.

Seven years after, another Long Islander, 21-year-old Paul Annacone, a big server from Bridgehampton, followed the original McEnroe path through the Big W. As a No. 238-ranked qualifier, Paul, an All-American out of Tennessee (who would become Pete Sampras's coach in 1995), took his professional bow with a flourish, traveling to the last eight. Defying superstition, Paul won his 13th match on grass, at Court 13 over No. 13 Johan Kriek, 6-3, 6-2, 6-4. But he ran into the proverbial black cat on Centre Court: the clawing Connors, who stopped him a round short of emulating Mac, 6-2, 6-4, 6-2.

Although this would be the last of 15 major finals for 31-year-old Connors, he had more bullets in his gun, some of them fired at Memphis, where he extended his U.S. Indoor record to seven titles, beating Henri Leconte, 6-3, 4-6, 7-5. Only three American men had won that many U.S. prizes on a particular surface: Dick Sears, Bill Larned and Bill Tilden ruled the foremost U.S. Championship, then played on grass, seven times. Jimmy joined them with his hothouse variety. There were bullets, too, for the U.S. Open, where he fed on the energy of the crowds.

En route to the next duel of American titans, McEnroe suffered his second loss of the year. He was defeated by Vijay Amritraj, a budding film star, at Cincinnati on the day after he wrapped up his first Canadian Open championship with a straight-set conquest of Vitas Gerulaitis, 6-0, 6-3. Amritraj, who had slipped to 104th in the rankings, had won his first Grand Prix tournament in four years only a month earlier, overcoming Tim Mayotte on the grass at Newport, 3-6, 6-4, 6-4.

Still, there wasn't any question but that McEnroe was poised to dethrone Connors at the U.S. Open. Not only was his form comparable to the level he displayed at Wimbledon but so was his approach.

"I understand how people get turned off by seeing a guy jumping around and screaming at the chair," he explained. "Of course, they don't understand that's a result of pressure. But I'm finding out life isn't fun when you're banging your head against a wall."

On the Flushing hard courts, McEnroe raced through his first five opponents, including the young Swede who had won an unofficial gold medal (demonstration class) at the Los Angeles Olympics. The 6-1, 6-0, 6-2 rout of Stefan Edberg was a barometer of how well he was playing. Meanwhile, Connors, back home on his favorite surface, also won all 15 sets in advancing to the semifinal, including a victory over surprising quarterfinalist, John (Mr. Chris Evert) Lloyd.

Those who couldn't wait for the showdown of the perennial bad boys had a very long afternoon on Super Saturday at the National Tennis Center. They went on last following a men's 35 match between legends John Newcombe and

Stan Smith, the first men's semifinal between Lendl and brash Pat Cash and the women's final between those rivals for the ages, Navratilova and Lloyd. All four matches were carried to the ultimate set and the tennis, which began at 11 a.m., didn't conclude until 11:14 p.m.

Even McEnroe, annoyed that he didn't strike his first ball until 7:28, allowed that "It had to be the best day (for fans) at the Open . . . ever." Certainly, the day's finale qualified as the match of the tournament, if not the year.

After 37 minutes, Connors had equalled the four games he won in the Wimbledon final. Within 90 minutes, he had won a set and broken McEnroe's serve for the fourth time for a 3-1 lead in the third set. In the end only a scant few shots separated the pair, perhaps none more important than a missed forehand by Connors on break point in the seventh game of the final set.

Connors finished with 45 winners, to 20 for the winner. But McEnroe's 19 aces pushed him over the top in a magnificent 6-4, 4-6, 7-5, 4-6, 6-3 victory. Both agreed the match was superior to their epic 1980 semifinal.

"We're both better players now," Connors said. "Four years ago, the match had great emotion. This had all that and better tennis."

Remarkably, the best server in the game had been broken seven times by the best service returner. Yet, McEnroe had produced the final break to emerge in a match devoid of animosity or histrionics. "I just don't see how either of us could play much better," he said.

Fortunately for him, he didn't have to the following afternoon. Lendl, who barely survived his semifinal over Cash, 3-6, 6-3, 6-4, 6-7 (5-7), 7-6 (7-4), with the help—at match point—of a running topspin lob that fell on the baseline, was no match for a McEnroe at his peak. Eighteen hours after vanquishing Connors, he routed Lendl, 6-4, 6-3, 6-1, to claim his fourth U.S. title.

The rest of the year wasn't nearly so satisfying for Mac, whose dark side returned while winning the Stockholm Open. In the course of a semifinal victory over Jarryd, he was fined for ball abuse, abuse of an official and unsportsmanlike behavior. The total pushed him over the $7,500 limit, triggering a 21-day suspension.

During his stay on the sidelines, he injured his left wrist in practice. That caused him to withdraw from the Australian Open, where Wilander had a clear path to his second consecutive title, bashing two-time champ Johan Kriek, 6-1, 6-0, 6-2, in the semifinals with the loss of three games and overcoming Curren in the final, 6-7 (5-7), 6-4, 7-6 (7-3), 6-2.

McEnroe was healed in time for the Davis Cup final in Goteborg, where he was joined by Connors. On paper captain Arthur Ashe's side was perhaps the strongest of all U.S. Cup lineups, containing the world Nos. 1 and 2 in singles and No. 1 in doubles. But it was played not on paper but clay, a surface on which 8 of 10 previous U.S. defeats over the last 20 years had occurred. Priced at $30,000, a specially-laid American-swallowing red bog was installed within the Scandinavium. A court made of 42 tons of crushed bricks—something like throwing the originals through John and Jimmy's looking glasses—was surrounded by a building-bulging throng of 11,500 unbelieving but jubilant Swedes. Connors had committed himself to the full year of Cup play for the first time but was distracted by the impending birth of his second child and was as unprepared as McEnroe for the tough Swedes on clay. He hadn't competed in six weeks.

In what was a dark first day for American tennis, both Connors and McEnroe were drubbed and Connors embarrassed himself and his team by incurring a game penalty and adding a $2,000 fine for profane language. Wilander handled Connors easily, 6-1, 6-3, 6-3, but the real surprise occurred in the next match when McEnroe was upset by lanky 20-year-old Henrik Sundstrom, 13-11, 6-4, 6-3. The first set, in which McEnroe held four set points, consumed two hours. Sundstrom, after smiting a backhand passer on match

point, seemed dazed: "I didn't have a thought of even having a chance."

One day later, Jarryd and Edberg applied the finishing touch against the seasoned doubles team of McEnroe and Fleming. The pair had won 14 Cup matches without defeat but weren't up to the task against the Swedes. The 18-year-old Edberg was particularly effective in the right court and with his kicking serve in the 7-5, 5-7, 6-2, 7-5 triumph and became the youngest winning player in a Cup title round.

Although McEnroe's 6-3, 5-7, 6-3 third-day victory over Wilander was mostly cosmetic, it did spare the U.S. the ignominy of a 5-0 shutout and helped to prepare him for the season-ending Masters. Back in New York, McEnroe defeated both Jarryd and Wilander en route to the final, where he crushed Lendl, 7-5, 6-0, 6-4, raising his earnings to $2,026,109. For good measure, he then combined with Fleming to turn back Mark Edmondson and Sherwood Stewart, 6-3, 6-1, for their seventh consecutive Masters doubles title.

In the scarcely shared opinion of the International Tennis Federation, which ruled in 1982 that a player need only win four consecutive majors to claim a Grand Slam, Navratilova completed the quartet in early June at the French Open. In recognition, it awarded a $1-million bonus. Still, few were prepared to grant her admission to the select group of those who had won the Big Four in the course of a calendar year—Don Budge, Maureen Connolly, Rod Laver (twice) and Margaret Court.

After Navratilova routed Evert Lloyd, 6-3, 6-1, in Paris, however, few doubted that this would be the year for such a feat. She hadn't lost a match since her first tournament in January, the Virginia Slims of Oakland, where Mandlikova prevailed, 7-6 (8-6), 3-6, 6-4. And only Mandlikova, in the semifinals, took a set off her at Stade Roland Garros.

At Wimbledon, she was even more formidable. Her only persistent opposition in England came from the tabloid press, which outdid itself in pursuing Navratilova's relationship with her newest traveling companion, former Texas beauty queen Judy Nelson. On the court, she was tested only in the championship match when Evert Lloyd began with two service breaks for a 3-0 lead.

Not to worry. Navratilova stormed back for a 7-6 (7-5), 6-2 victory, handing Evert Lloyd her sixth final-round defeat. It marked the second consecutive Wimbledon in which she had failed to drop a set and her third successive title was the first for a female since Billie Jean King's 1966–68 run.

The pattern continued at Flushing Meadow, which produced one notable sidelight. Gabriela Sabatini, a 14-year, 4-month-old Argentine, introduced herself to the world. She became the youngest player ever to win a U.S. Open match, 6-3, 3-6, 6-2, over Paula Smith. Dissatisfied with one, she actually won two matches before losing in straight sets to Sukova.

The latter reached the quarterfinals, where she was beaten by Navratilova, whom her mother, 1962 Wimbledon finalist Vera Sukova, once had coached back in Czechoslovakia. The top-ranked player in the world marched into the final without the loss of a set. Ditto her great rival, Evert Lloyd.

When they collided in Louis Armstrong Stadium on Sept. 8, their series stood at 30 victories apiece. Additionally, Navratilova had won 54 consecutive matches, one shy of her opponent's open-era record. With all that and an Open title at stake, Evert Lloyd played superb tennis, perhaps the best of any of her nine U.S. finals.

Still, it was insufficient. Navratilova rallied for a 4-6, 6-4, 6-4 victory. "It's just not enough to play a good match against her anymore," Evert Lloyd lamented.

The pair added to their friendship by sharing bagels while awaiting the outcome of the first men's semifinal and the delayed start of their match. Afterward, Navratilova gave a gracious acceptance speech in which she said, of their rivalry, "I wish we could have stopped at 30 [wins] all. She's a great champion and I'm sorry one of us had to lose."

With six majors in a row to her credit, the Australian Open appeared a formality. Navratilova had prepared herself for the grass at Kooyong Stadium by winning a doubles tournament at Brisbane and the singles at Sydney the following week. She dropped only one set (to Kathy Rinaldi) in advancing to the semifinals at Melbourne and raced through a 6-1 first set against Sukova.

But the 6-foot-2 19-year-old who had just notched her first important singles title at Brisbane was not discouraged. She broke for 4-2 in the second set and, at 5-5 in the third set, achieved the deciding break. Navratilova did not go down without a fight, saving five match points with a series of admirable forehands before her backhand return sailed over the baseline.

"It hurts but I'm sure I'll get over it," she said after the 1-6, 6-3, 7-5 defeat that terminated her streak at 74 matches and ended the dream of a genuine Grand Slam. Sukova, the ninth seed, carried the momentum into the final but couldn't sustain it as the steady Evert Lloyd rallied for a 6-7 (4-7), 6-1, 6-3 triumph, her 16th major singles championship.

Earlier, Evert Lloyd, with two singles wins, had led the U.S. to its sixth successive Wightman Cup triumph over Britain, 5-2. In the absence of both Evert Lloyd and Navratilova, the American team was upended by Australia in a Federation Cup semifinal, 2-1, as Liz Sayers and Wendy Turnbull took the decisive doubles over Kathy Jordan and Anne Smith, 7-6, 6-4, after Jordan beat Turnbull, 6-3, 7-6, and Kathy Horvath fell to Anne Minter, 6-3, 6-4. Minter made it a perfect five-for-five in singles, beating Sukova, 7-5, 7-5, but the Czechs rebounded to their second successive Cup as Mandlikova floored Sayers, 6-1, 6-0, and combined with Sukova, 6-2, 6-2, over Sayers-Turnbull. The latter was beaten in the final by the Czech team of Mandlikova and Sukova, 2-1, marking that country's second consecutive championship.

1985

Attention, please. Or, in the native tongue of Boris Becker, *achtung!* Not only did a new champion appear on the tennis scene in 1985; he also ushered in a new era. The baby boomers turned over several aces.

In a year that sparkled with fresh faces, the brightest and most engaging belonged to a 17-year-old son of a West German architect, a teenager either too cool or too naive to know he had no business playing with grown men. At Wimbledon, a tournament that prizes tradition above all else, Becker challenged the past and won.

Never had anyone so young claimed a men's title at The Lawn Tennis Championships. Never had an unseeded player been fitted for a singles crown. Never had a German male ascended to the throne of tennis. Becker changed all of the above in the span of three hours, 18 minutes on one sun-lit, summer afternoon. Game, set and match.

The youngster, who had won only one previous event on the men's tour (three weeks earlier at Queen's Club in London), climaxed a breath-taking rise to prominence by wearing down eighth-seeded Kevin Curren, 6-3, 6-7 (4-7), 7-6 (7-3), 6-4, in the Wimbledon final. By the end of the season, he had made a spectacular jump in the rankings from No. 65 to No. 6 and become the symbol of change sweeping over the sport.

When Stefan Edberg of Sweden, 22 months older than Becker, dethroned countryman Mats Wilander at the Australian Open, this represented the first time two teenaged males reigned as champions of Big Four tournaments in the same year. Following Wilander's victory in the French Open and Ivan Lendl's breakthrough in the U.S. Open, this also completed a Continental sweep of the major events. Never before had European males held all four major championships.

Starting with Boris Becker at Wimbledon, youth took over in 1985. (Russ Adams)

Although Lendl's presence was a familiar one and although he was a relatively old 25, he made a significant contribution to the new order by completing his long and arduous climb to the top of the ATP computer rankings. He posted the biggest triumph of his career by overwhelming John McEnroe, who hadn't lost in four previous U.S. finals, at Flushing Meadow, 7-6 (7-1), 6-3, 6-4. And he solidified his position at the season-ending Masters in January, 1986, where he didn't lose a set en route to his third title in five years.

Newcomers also made an impact on the women's circuits although none came away with major prizes. In what were portents of the future, 15-year-old Gabriela Sabatini reached the semifinals of her first French Open and 16-year-old Steffi Graf of West Germany advanced to the final four of the U.S. Open. Additionally, Katerina Maleeva, at 16, two years younger than older sister Manuela, won two tournaments, and Floridian Mary Joe Fernandez became the most callow winner of a U.S. Open match (14 years, eight days), over Laura Garrone, 3-6, 6-1, 6-3.

While Martina Navratilova remained queen of the sport, she yielded two of her dominions. Chris Evert Lloyd unseated her at the French Open and Hana Mandlikova did the honors at the U.S. Open. Navratilova even was separated from her No. 1 ranking by Evert Lloyd after 156 consecutive weeks at the top but she regained her place by the end of the season in which she added the Australian championship to her sixth Wimbledon singles title.

The stranglehold Navratilova and Pam Shriver had on women's doubles competition also was loosened. Their monumental 26-month winning streak, comprising 109 matches and 23 tournaments, ended on Centre Court in the Wimbledon final where they were beaten by the Aussie-American alliance of Liz Sayers Smylie and Kathy Jordan, 5-7, 6-3, 6-4, despite leading 3-0 in the third. They later surrendered their U.S. title to the twin towers, 6-foot-1 Claudia Kohde Kilsch of Germany and 6-foot-2 Helena Sukova of Czechoslovakia.

Coincidentally, McEnroe and Peter Fleming abdicated after the better part of a decade atop men's doubles. Mac decided to put doubles aside after three tournaments, among them Wimbledon, where they faltered before Aussies Pat Cash and John Fitzgerald two rounds short of defending their title. Their lone victory, at Houston, raised their career total to 53.

The vacuum quickly was filled by a pair of young Americans. Ken Flach and Robert Seguso, both 22, inherited the U.S. Davis Cup role from the perennial team, compiled a match record of 62-22 and won eight tournaments, including the U.S. Open and U.S. Clay Court.

But the French pair, Yannick Noah and Henri Leconte, hotly disputed the title outcome of Flushing Meadow, during and after the final they lost to the home side, 6-7 (5-7), 7-6 (7-1), 7-6 (8-

6), 6-0. Did the French lose by a hair? They thought so: Flach's hair. And they accused the Americans of cheating. The play in question came with Seguso serving at 4-6 in the third-set tie-breaker, set point (the Americans had saved six of them). In a furious exchange Leconte swatted a ball that bounded off the net cord and appeared to touch Flach's abundant afghan houndly mane on its way out of court. The French claimed a clear touch, thus the point and set. Seguso indicated agreement by starting to change courts. But Flach said, "It could have, but I'm not sure, so I couldn't make the call. We're pros—it's up to the umpire."

Umpire Zeno Pfau said he didn't see it, so couldn't rule. The French chafed and moaned as though wearing hairshirts, saying their foes had violated the sporting code by not calling the point against themselves. The Americans accused the French of the professional sin of giving up after losing the set, as seemed true. It was a $65,000 question (first prize). The result stood. Noah and Leconte went home feeling they'd been clipped.

But there was no arguing that Americans Steve "Bull" Denton and Richard Matuszewski served like a couple of unshorn Samsons in a hardly noticed first-rounder. It went to No. 482 Matuszewski, a qualifier who hummed 19 aces, 6-7 (8-10), 7-6 (7-4), 6-7 (8-10), 6-4, 6-3. But not before they'd bashed away 4 hours, 11 minutes, and Denton had set a U.S. record with 39 aces (not to mention 24 double faults). It was a record, too, as the most ace-ridden match (58), a mark that would last a decade.

However, nowhere were the changing times better illustrated than at Wimbledon. None of the usual suspects even made it to the last day. Second-seeded Lendl, whose bid for a second successive French title was ended in the final by Wilander, 3-6, 6-4, 6-2, 6-2, was wiped out in the round of 16 by Leconte, 3-6, 6-4, 6-3, 6-1. Curren, who became a U.S. citizen in March, demolished top-seeded McEnroe, 6-2, 6-2, 6-4, in the quarterfinals and third-seeded Jimmy Connors, 6-

Ivan Lendl broke John McEnroe's finals streak at the U.S. Open in 1985. (Wide World)

2, 6-2, 6-1, in the semifinals with an arsenal of powerful serves.

Bellyflopping Boris, who threw himself all over the place with teenage abandon, had been carried off Wimbledon's "Graveyard" (Court 2) on a stretcher, and out of the tournament the previous year with a severe ankle injury. He injured the left ankle again in the fourth round on a far-out court against Tim Mayotte, and wanted to quit after the fourth set. His manager, Ion Tiriac, dissuaded him. Becker probably should have been defaulted because of the overly long delay in being treated. He resumed thanks only to the sporting forbearance of Mayotte. It was soon obvious that this was a charmed fortnight for the husky redhead. In the third round Joakim Nystrom twice served to beat him in the fifth set, at 5-4 and 6-5, but Boris wasn't letting go, 3-6, 7-6 (7-5), 6-1, 4-6, 9-7. Five sets with Mayotte: 6-3,

4-6, 6-7 (7-9), 7-6 (7-5), 6-2. Boris, an 18-to-1 shot with London bookies at the outset, could easily have been down two sets to Leconte, but wriggled out of their tie-breaker, 7-6 (9-7), 3-6, 6-3, 6-4. In the semis fifth-seeded Anders Jarryd had two set points to lead by two, but Becker bashed his way out with an ace and service winner. He had to brood overnight when rain stopped him at 1-1 in the third, but just kept breezing with a kid's exuberance, 2-6, 7-6 (7-3), 6-3, 6-3. Three of his first six matches were suspended and held over for another day, a circumstance that would unnerve even veteran players.

Not Becker. He responded to every challenge like a man, yet still reacted with the infectious enthusiasm of a boy. After completing his semifinal victory over Jarryd on Saturday morning, he hung around to watch the Duke and Duchess of Kent present Navratilova with the women's singles plate after beating Evert Lloyd.

If his play belied his years, Becker acted his age as he peered around the backdrop separating Centre Court from the players' entrance after the women's match. He hurriedly removed a set of headphones from his ears and practically snapped to attention as the royal couple walked by, oblivious to his presence. Then he returned to his vantage point, looking for all the world like the tallest member of the knothole gang.

A day later, he appeared on the other side of the screen and walked off with the men's trophy. Before a capacity crowd that included a few assorted princes and princesses, the 6-foot-3 man-child answered Curren's serve with a bludgeon of his own 21 aces to Kevin's 19, outvolleyed and outsteadied his 27-year-old opponent from the baseline.

"I should have had the advantage," Curren said. "Being older, being to the semifinals [in 1983], being on Centre Court. Maybe he was too young to know about all that stuff."

Or at least too young to rattle. He became such a sensation in the early stages of the tournament with his reckless dives— "Usually, he comes off the court with blood on him," observed his manager, Ion Tiriac, the former Romanian star—that the bookmaking chain, Ladbrokes, installed Becker as a 7-4 favorite after the quarterfinals at a time when two-time champion Connors still was on the premises.

His popularity with the fans was not echoed in the British press, which did not let anyone forget he was a German. Even the respectable broadsheets relentlessly used war analogies in describing the player. In *The Times,* the respected Rex Bellamy duly noted that scheduled television programming in Becker's homeland was interrupted to carry his quarterfinal victory over Leconte and added, "How odd it was that Germany should have such a personal interest in a court on which, in 1940, they dropped a bomb."

It's true a bomb did land on the roof of Centre Court in October 1940, destroying 1,200 seats. And no German was permitted to enter the tournament for four years after it was resumed in 1946. That represented a concession on the part of officials who had banned Germans for nine years after World War I.

Ironically, Becker's shining moment occurred on July 7, the birthdate of Baron Gottfried von Cramm. The latter, long acknowledged as Germany's greatest player, would have been 76 had he lived. For more than half of the century, he was regarded as one of the finest tennis players never to have won Wimbledon. It had been 50 years since he reached the final for the first of three consecutive years, 50 years since he was victimized by Fred Perry.

"He was a very good player," recalled Perry, the three-time champion who was an analyst for the BBC radio network. "He walked like an aristocrat. And he had a long, elegant swing. When he played Bunny Austin in the semifinals, it was like a picture book. You could turn the page and see one classical shot after another."

Perry, the finest British player of the modern era, was taken with Becker. "What impresses me," he said, "is that he's got no fear. I saw him in the juniors at Paris a few years ago and he'd hit four in and nine out. But he'll consolidate."

Already, he had combined with other teenagers to energize the oldest of the Grand Slam events. "As far as the game itself is concerned," tournament chairman Buzzer Hadingham said, "it is most exciting to see the emergence of a new generation of talented, young players."

The new generation of males wasn't as successful in the cauldron that was Flushing Meadow. Becker made 64 unforced errors in bowing to Nystrom in four sets in the round of 16, which was where Edberg came to grief against Connors. Wilander, an old man of 21, did push McEnroe to five sets in the semifinals but couldn't put the 26-year-old codger away. The American survived, 3-6, 6-4, 4-6, 6-3, 6-3.

"That was a legitimate five-setter," McEnroe observed. "I was scrounging. And it was just so hot [115 degrees at courtside] that you couldn't keep your concentration all the time. In that kind of heat, you've got to go through cycles."

Two other familiar faces turned up in the other semifinal, where Lendl romped over Connors, 6-2, 6-3, 7-5. It had been a frustrating season for the 33-year-old campaigner. For the first time in his professional career, Connors failed to win a tournament all year. Yet, he reached the semis of the French, Wimbledon and the U.S., the latter for the 12th successive year.

For Lendl, the victory also was the continuation of a streak. This was his fourth consecutive final at Flushing Meadow. Alas, he had lost in all three previous trips. After their Saturday night match, Connors said he didn't expect the man to play well on Sunday. "Because he never has," the gracious loser said.

Certainly, there was little in the early going to indicate otherwise. Lendl was broken in his first service game and failed to get a single point off McEnroe's serve through seven games, creating a 2-5 deficit. But, at set point, the Czech who had moved into a comfortable estate in nearby

Greenwich, Conn., hit a crosscourt backhand winner for deuce, held service and then broke McEnroe for the first time. He eventually won a tie-breaker by a stunning 7-1 margin and raced through the next two sets, 6-3, 6-4, for the most satisfying triumph of his career.

"It's the biggest tournament in the world," the first-time titleholder said dryly. "And it is the championship of the country where I enjoy living so much. I have won the Czechoslovakian Open three times, in my native country, but I don't think that is the same."

McEnroe said that his energy was sapped from the five-setter in the previous day's heat and complained about the schedule of matches on consecutive days for the benefit of network television. But he also gave credit to Lendl. "He put a lot of pressure on me," the former No. 1 said. "It was one of the best matches he's ever played against me."

It was the climax of a superb year for the winner. He annexed the first of 11 titles by beating Tim Mayotte at the WCT finals in Dallas, 7-6, 6-4, 6-1, after McEnroe, the defender and four-time champ, had been bounced by Nystrom, 6-4, 7-6, 6-3. In the Tournament of Champions, Lendl prevailed over Mac, 6-3, 6-3, and he also stopped the lefty at Dusseldorf although a singles victory by Connors and a doubles triumph by Flach and Seguso over Lendl and Tom Smid lifted the U.S. to a 2-1 victory over Czechoslovakia and the World Team Cup.

Top-seeded in the Australian Open, Lendl appeared to have a clear path to another major title when Becker was bounced in the first round by No. 188, Dutchman Michiel Schapers, and McEnroe was eliminated by Bobo Zivojinovic of Yugoslavia, 2-6, 6-3, 1-6, 6-4, 6-0. But that's when Edberg asserted himself.

After routing Schapers in the quarters, the teenager from Vastervik snapped Lendl's 31-match winning streak, 6-7 (3-7), 7-5, 6-1, 4-6, 9-7 and then overpowered defending champ Wilander, 6-4, 6-3, 6-3, in a rain-delayed final. It marked the first time two Swedes met for a Big Four championship.

Both McEnroe and Lendl argued so incessantly about the slippery condition of the courts and other distractions that they surpassed the fine limit, earning 21-day suspensions. Not that either was inclined to play any more in December. For the first time in a while, McEnroe didn't even have Davis Cup commitments.

He had declined to sign a so-called "behavior guideline" instigated by the U.S. team's sponsor, Louisiana Pacific, to guarantee there would be no repetition of the ruckus at Goteborg the previous year. Since Connors—the prime instigator—had no intention of returning, the U.S. squad was led by Eliot Teltscher and Aaron Krickstein, who turned 18 just in time for a second-round encounter against West Germany.

That was as far as the Americans went, Germany winning, 3-2, as Becker bashed Krickstein in the decisive fifth match, 6-2, 6-2, 6-1.

Becker carried the fatherland all the way to the final and nearly upset the Swedes as he defeated both Edberg, 6-3, 3-6, 7-5, 8-6, and Wilander, 6-3, 2-6, 6-2, 6-2, to tie it, 2-2. Not for 21 years, when Roy Emerson beat Chuck McKinley to lift the Cup from the U.S. to Australia, had the fate of the Cup hung on the fifth match. As the sellout crowd of 11,000 rocked Munich's Olympiahalle with their stomping and chanting of "Mee-Kile! MEE-KILE!," hulking, powerful 20-year-old Michael Westphal, ranked No. 51, served ace after ace (15) past 19-year-old Edberg to win the first set. In the semifinal victory over Czechoslovakia (5-0), Westphal had exploded for 36 aces in winning one of the longest of all Cup matches (6 hours, 1 minute) over Tom Smid, 6-8, 1-6, 7-5, 11-9, 17-15. But Edberg, No. 5, blunted the German's fury with his own serve-and-volley rhythms, overcame the aces (28) and silenced the home crowd, 3-6, 7-5, 6-4, 6-3, enabling Sweden to become the first European nation to retain the Cup in five decades.

Remarkably, that nation qualified four men for the season-ending Grand Prix Masters, whose field was raised to 16 under the first-time sponsorship of Nabisco. But none of the Swedes was a major factor. Edberg lost in the first round to Johan Kriek, Wilander was beaten by Becker in the quarters and Jarryd, who had defeated Nystrom in a first-round match and later would team with Edberg to win the doubles, was stopped by Becker in the semifinals. The most resounding loss of all, however, involved McEnroe who, tired and out of sorts, went down in the first round to Brad Gilbert, 5-7, 6-4, 6-1.

In the end, Lendl reverting to the form he had displayed in the U.S. Open, turned back Becker in commanding fashion, 6-2, 7-6 (7-1), 6-3, and raised his earnings to $1,971,074. At last, he was clearly the top male player in the world.

For the first time in what seemed like ages, there actually was some doubt about the identity of the leading woman. The competition wasn't settled until Navratilova beat Mandlikova, her U.S. Open conqueror, in the semifinals of the Australian Open and then wore down French Open queen Evert Lloyd, 6-2, 4-6, 6-2 in the final at Melbourne. She concluded her season with 12 tournament victories and an 80-5 match record, slightly ahead of Evert Lloyd's 10 titles and an 81-8 mark. The latter also led the U.S. to its seventh consecutive victory over Great Britain in Wightman Cup play.

By defeating Navratilova in their thrilling French final, 6-3, 6-7 (4-7), 7-5, Evert Lloyd won the tournament for an unprecedented sixth time and extended to a dozen years her standard for winning at least one of the major titles. It also marked the second time in five months she had overcome her nemesis, the first being at Key Biscayne in late January.

Following that loss and one to Mandlikova in the U.S. Indoor semis, Navratilova went to an eye doctor. She emerged with spectacles and promptly won 23 consecutive matches (and 46 sets), including the Virginia Slims Championship over Mandlikova and Sukova after Evert Lloyd was ambushed by Kathy Jordan. That string was interrupted at Paris, where her old rival held

serve after falling behind 0-40 at 5-5 in the third set and then closed out the match in extraordinary fashion.

"I just hope she stays around a little bit longer," Navratilova said, "because, quite honestly, she's playing better tennis now than she ever did. It must be nice to know that you can still improve at 30."

Defeat cost Navratilova the honor of being the first player since Margaret Court in 1964 to hold three French titles simultaneously. She combined with Shriver to win the women's doubles, their eighth consecutive major championship, and with Heinz Gunthardt to win the mixed.

Sabatini had created a sensation at Hilton Head in April by beating three Top 10 players (Garrison, Shriver, Manuela Maleeva) en-route to the final. She had a tall order Sunday morning, 35 games prior to a meeting with Evert Lloyd, finishing a rain-delayed quarter with Shriver and defeating Maleeva, 6-1, 7-6 (11-9). The rules said she could put off the final until the following day, but Gaby, the youngest to reach a pro final at that time (14-11), insisted on being part of the televised title match, and competed well for a set, losing to Chrissie, 6-4, 6-0. In Paris, now 15, she topspun her way into the semifinals. Her victims there included Ros Fairbank, Anne White and fourth-seeded Manuela Maleeva. Once again, it took a woman twice her age to stop her. Evert Lloyd prevailed, 6-4, 6-1.

Sabatini's showing convinced her coach, Pato Apey, with whom she resided in Florida, that she should enter Wimbledon, where she became the youngest player ever to be seeded (15th at 15 in a masterstroke of British symmetry). Her presence caused an immediate stir. The tabloids dubbed her "Gorgeous Gaby" and the special eligibility Commission of the International Tennis Federation called for a "gradual, carefully monitored entry" into pro tennis, restricting the number of events in which a player can enter before reaching 16.

She won two matches on the grass, one fewer than another kid wonder, Germany's Steffi Graf, 16 and 11th seeded, who was denied a berth in the quarterfinals by Shriver, 3-6, 6-2, 6-4. The most surprising of the final eight was No. 154 Molly Van Nostrand, a 20-year-old qualifier from New York who defeated fourth-seeded Manuela Maleeva and was only three games from a semifinal meeting with Navratilova before faltering against Zina Garrison, 2-6, 6-3, 6-0. And Kathy Rinaldi, still only 18, made her deepest penetration in a Grand Slam event when she advanced to the semifinals.

Not that there was ever any doubt but that the women's competition was a two-horse race. In a most unusual move, the tournament committee jointly seeded Evert Lloyd and Navratilova No. 1. And their final was almost as close, with Navratilova rallying for a 4-6, 6-3, 6-2 victory.

She became only the third woman in history to win four singles titles in a row and the first since Helen Wills Moody in 1930. "This court," Evert decided, "is her court." It also marked Navratilova's sixth triumph in as many Wimbledon finals, equalling the feat of Suzanne Lenglen, the legendary French star of the Roaring '20s.

One of the most affecting moments of the tournament was Virginia Wade's 205th Wimbledon match, her last in the singles draw. "Our Ginny," England's last great champion, was beaten by the fifth-seeded Shriver, 6-2, 5-7, 6-2, in an enthralling third-round match one week shy of her 40th birthday. She left to a standing ovation. "How can I feel sad?" Wade said. "I've had more out of tennis, more fun out of playing Wimbledon, than anybody. . . ."

Youth once again was served at the start of the U.S. Open when Mary Joe Fernandez, who had just turned 14, beat towering Sarah Gomer, a 6-foot-3 Brit, 6-1, 6-4, in the first round, undercutting by four months the Sabatini of 1984 as the greenest to win a match here. But the teenager who wowed the crowds at Flushing Meadow was Graf. In reaching the semifinals, she not only knocked off Manuela Maleeva but overcame Pam

Hana Mandlikova made history as a European in winning the 1985 U.S. Open. (Russ Adams)

Shriver, 7-6 (7-4), 6-7 (4-7), 7-6 (7-4), in the match of the tournament. It marked the only major match composed entirely of tie-breakers and the longest women's struggle (39 games) since the advent of such overtimes in 1970.

Still, it was a brilliantly attacking Mandlikova who took home the prize. And she did it in remarkable fashion, beating two ex-champs—Evert Lloyd, 4-6, 6-2, 6-3, and Navratilova, 7-6 (7-3), 1-6, 7-6 (7-2)—the first time that had happened since 1962 when Margaret Smith (Court) won over 1959 champ Maria Bueno and defender Darlene Hard. Her victory was the first by a European citizen in the U.S. championship.

"I've been working on myself, my game, my head, everything," said Mandlikova, finally harnessing her immense talent. "I'm 23 now and I'm maturing slowly. I've been working very hard."

The Open title was one of two great rewards in 1985. The second occurred a month later in Nagoya, Japan, where she won all five of her singles and two deciding doubles in Czechoslovakia's third successive victory in Federation Cup play. She beat Kathy Jordan, 7-5, 6-1, in the 2-1 Cup-round defeat of the U.S. and Sukova beat Elsie Burgin, 6-3, 6-7 (6-8), 6-4.

It was at the Australian Open that order was restored. Navratilova dispensed with Mandlikova, 6-7 (5-7), 6-1, 6-4, en route to another final showdown with Evert Lloyd. It was their 67th meeting and Navratilova's all-out attack won the day, 6-2, 4-6, 6-2, increasing her margin in the rivalry of the age to 35-32.

"Martina and I have pushed each other to get better and better," Evert Lloyd said. And they weren't planning to stop anytime soon.

1986

They got together on a Sunday in September at a public park. Two men and two women raised in Czechoslovakia met for an afternoon of tennis. Twenty years earlier, when the iron curtain and the sport both were closed, they might have been limited to a game of mixed doubles in Prague but now they gathered as professionals in New York to contest the most important singles championships in the New World.

What an extraordinary development not only for the U.S. Open but for the sport. When Ivan Lendl and Miloslav Mecir followed Martina Navratilova and Helena Sukova onto the stadium court of the National Tennis Center, they raised the profile of a nation whose government was young but whose culture was old. Theirs was an unprecedented achievement.

The presence of four finalists born in the same distant land had occurred only four times previously in the history of the major tournaments, twice at Wimbledon and twice at the French Open. Never before had it happened at the U.S. Open and never before had the delegation hailed from Czechoslovakia. Suddenly, the country of 15-million inhabitants ranked as the first nation of tennis.

That Navratilova had received her citizenship papers in the U.S. and that Lendl was an aspiring Connecticut Yankee didn't diminish the impact. All had learned the game, had taken their first steps to prosperity on Czech clay. And, by virtue of their victories in the final major tournament of the year, the expatriates solidified their places at the top of the women's and men's rankings.

Better yet for the land of their youth, Prague welcomed the first significant international tennis event in Eastern Europe. The Federation Cup attracted teams from 40 nations to brand new Stvanice Stadium where the Czech defenders were denied a fourth successive triumph by the U.S. It so happened that Navratilova won her singles match and paired with Pam Shriver to win the doubles in a 3-0 victory that completed an emotional homecoming for the woman who had defected 11 years earlier.

"The whole experience," she said through tears after a heartwarming reception, "was beyond my wildest dreams."

Aside from the success of its foreign imports, the U.S. endured a desultory year. Chris Evert Lloyd, who won yet another French Open, was the only American-born player to reach the final of a major event, whose number temporarily was reduced to three when the Australian Open was pushed to the front end of the calendar in time for the 1987 season. She also was the only native of either gender to be ranked among the top five players in the game.

Of course, as Navratilova pointed out at Flushing Meadow, if you stress only the country of origin, ". . . then John McEnroe was born in Germany but he's as red-blooded American as you can get." It's true that McEnroe was born in Wiesbaden, where his father was serving as an officer of the U.S. Air Force. But then McEnroe was not relevant to the discussion, having decided to take a sabbatical for the first six months of the year and having been bounced out of the Open in the very first round by Paul Annacone.

In his absence, Jimmy Connors was the highest-ranked American male, No. 8 on the computer at year's end. But, for a second consecutive season, he failed to win a tournament. Connors didn't even survive the first round at Wimbledon and was a third-round victim at Flushing Meadow.

Once again, the men's tour was dominated by Europeans. Lendl won both the French Open, defeating Mikael Pernfors of Sweden in the final, and the U.S., as well as capturing the Masters. He also reached the final at Wimbledon, only to be stopped one step short of his goal by defending champion Boris Becker. The latter also pressed Lendl at the Masters and rose to No. 2 in the world at the age of 18.

On the women's side, Navratilova continued her reign over Wimbledon by defeating another Czech, Hana Mandlikova. Her only major defeat of the year occurred in Paris, where Evert Lloyd prevailed in a bid for a record seventh singles championship. By the end of 1986, however, it was clear that Steffi Graf was prepared to challenge both women.

Fraulein Forehand, as the teenaged German was known, won eight tournaments, two more than Evert, and almost denied Navratilova the U.S. Open title. Graf held three match points, the last in a sensational third-set tie-breaker, in the semifinals. "I was lucky," Navratilova said. "I was lucky and I was gutsy, too. But anyone could have won."

Two months later, Navratilova again held off Graf at the second Virginia Slims Championships in Madison Square Garden. This represented one of several schedule adjustments that finally brought tennis into line with the calendar. Back in March, Martina had won the first Virginia Slims, the one that purported to be the season-ending event of the 1985 circuit, a 6-2, 6-0, 3-6, 6-1 triumph over Mandlikova. With a 7-6 (8-6), 6-3, 6-2 victory over Graf, she clinched the designation of No. 1 for 1986.

The men also managed to cram their play into a 12-month season. For the first time since 1976, the Masters was given December dates. Lendl certainly didn't appear rushed. After reaching the final for the seventh consecutive year, he blasted an eager Becker, 6-4, 6-4, 6-4, forestalling the future a while longer.

Perhaps the most far-reaching development of the year occurred at the start. In the wake of a disappointing loss to Brad Gilbert, 5-7, 6-4, 6-1, in the first round of the (1985) Masters in January, McEnroe decided to drop off the tour for at least 60 days. His long-standing relationship with actress Tatum O'Neal and impending fatherhood had become more important than his career.

"My attitude is very bad, very negative," he said. "I'm not happy with my movement . . . I shouldn't be playing tennis now . . . I'm letting things affect me and I'm embarrassed. As a person I'll learn and grow from what is happening. I hope others do, too. They didn't seem to learn from Borg. Now they see it happening to me."

McEnroe was 26, one year older than Bjorn Borg when the latter walked away from competitive tennis. Like Borg, McEnroe was No. 2 in the world. Unlike the Swede, the American would be back, although not with the same fire.

Meanwhile, Connors sabotaged his own season by walking out of a semifinal match against Lendl in the Lipton International Players championship at Boca Raton, Fla. Lendl was leading, 5-2, in the fifth set when Connors began arguing a linesman's call. He insisted that umpire Jeremy Shales overrule the call and, when that failed, demanded that Shales be removed from the chair.

Eventually, Connors was defaulted. Not only did he lose the match but he was suspended for 70 days, a period that carried through the French Open, where he had been a semifinalist in each of the two previous years. He was also fined a record $20,000.

With the field at Paris thinned by the abstention of the two top Yanks, Sweden was in position to take over the men's competition. Not only had a Swede won the 1985 edition and six of the previous eight, but representatives of that nation were granted four of the top eight seeds. Ironically, the only Swede to make it to the quarterfinals and beyond was a total outsider.

Pernfors, a 22-year-old who had gone the American collegiate route, made his French Open debut a memorable one. The two-time Intercollegiate champion from the University of Georgia upset fifth, third and eighth-seeded Stefan Edberg, Becker and local favorite Henri Leconte en route to the final. Wilander, the defending champ. was stunned in the second round by Andrei Chesnokov of the Soviet Union, ranked No. 81 in the world.

Meanwhile, Lendl thundered through the top half of the draw with the loss of only one set, a tie-breaker against Andres Gomez of Ecuador which he repaid by winning the next two sets of their quarterfinal at love. With the same championship form he had displayed in winning his first Italian Open three weeks earlier, Lendl dispatched the scrappy Pernfors, 6-3, 6-2, 6-4.

Some uncertainty was injected into the women's competition by Mary Joe Fernandez. The Florida teenager, who had become the youngest player ever to win a match at the U.S. Open eight months earlier, overcame two seeds, 14th Andrea Temesvari and 4th Claudia Kohde Kilsch, in advancing to the quarterfinals. There the 14-year-old was stopped by Sukova, 6-2, 6-4.

It was also in the quarters that Graf's 23-match winning streak—which included tournament victories at the WTA championships over Kohde Kilsch, 6-4, 5-7, 7-6, the U.S. Clay Court over Sabatini, 2-6, 7-6, 6-4, and the German Open—came to an abrupt end. After holding a match point on Mandlikova, the German succumbed 2-6, 7-6 (7-3), 6-1. The final was one more reprise of the familiar, Navratilova vs. Evert Lloyd, who had beaten Mandlikova, 6-1, 6-1.

The world would never see its like again. Although no one realized it at the moment, it was the last time the two would meet in the championship round of a major event. Evert Lloyd, in her last Big Four final, made the most of it with a commanding 2-6, 6-3, 6-3 victory, closing the second set from 0-40, four break points. That raised her total of major singles titles to 18 and extended to 13 years her record of at least one major conquest.

The cosmetic changes at the 100th edition of Wimbledon included the introduction of yellow tennis balls, the unavailability of McEnroe, who was back in the States changing diapers, and the earliest departure on Connors' record. The two-time champion and five-time finalist was shown the gate by young Robert Seguso, ranked No. 31 and known as a doubles specialist, in the first round.

"You don't know what you have until you lose it," said Connors, indicating Wimbledon would miss him more than he would Wimbledon, "and that's what you're feeling toward McEnroe right now." Connors, third-seeded, was beaten, 6-3, 3-6, 7-6 (7-5), 7-6 (10-8), 14 years after his only other opening-round eviction from a major, that by Tom Gorman at the U.S. Open. The first-round failures also included 11th-seeded Kevin Curren to No. 32 Eric Jelen, 6-4, 6-7 (4-7), 2-6, 6-4, 12-10. Never had the previous year's runner-up lost in the first round, but Curren wasted four match points. John Lloyd also lost, in five to Christo Steyn, and immediately retired.

Meanwhile, Lloyd's wife experienced unaccustomed difficulty of her own. A finalist in seven of the previous eight years, Evert Lloyd struggled through a difficult draw, dropping sets to Pam Casale and Sukova. She got no farther than the semifinals, where she was eliminated by Mandlikova, 7-6 (7-5), 7-5.

The latter said she was much better prepared for her second Wimbledon final than her first, five years earlier against Evert Lloyd. On the night before the showdown against Navratilova, she said, "I slept very well. Maybe, as it turned out, too well," she decided afterward.

By contrast, Navratilova was particularly eager for the meeting after rolling unopposed through her first six matches. "I've never, ever been so excited about being in a final," she said. "I couldn't wait to go to sleep so I could get up and play."

Not since the reign of Suzanne Lenglen six decades earlier had a woman won five consecutive singles championships at Wimbledon. And history was no more prepared to stop her than was Mandlikova, although the latter served for the first set at 5-3. She got no closer to a title.

Beginning in the eighth game of that set, through the tie-breaker and into the third game of the second set, Navratilova put 22 consecutive first serves in play and won 14 points on those serves, including three aces. She finished off the challenger, 7-6 (7-1), 6-3, in 72 minutes. In five years of supremacy, she had dropped only two sets.

"Unbelievable," Mandlikova said. "It's like Bjorn Borg." But he, like Lenglen, no longer was around. Navratilova stood alone.

Lendl, the top-seeded male, worked harder than any player in the tournament in his effort to secure a Wimbledon title. He struggled past Matt Anger, who had four set points in their hectic closing tie-breaker, 6-7 (7-9), 7-6 (7-2), 6-4, 7-6 (12-10). Then he overcame Tim Mayotte in their quarter, 6-4, 4-6, 6-4, 3-6, 9-7. He was pushed to the limit again by 6-foot-6 Slobodan Zivojinovic, 6-2, 6-7 (5-7), 6-3, 6-7 (1-7), 6-4 in the semifinal.

His opponent in the final was the defending champ, as comfortable on the grass as Lendl was wary. Seeded fourth, Becker marched through a bottom half of the draw that was pockmarked by upsets, most notably Mecir's dismissal of second-seeded Edberg, 6-4, 6-4, 6-4, and fifth-seeded Wilander's 4-6, 7-5, 6-4, 6-3 beating by Pat Cash, who entered the tournament as a wild card one month following an appendectomy and would almost singlehandedly drive Australia to victory in Davis Cup competition later in the year. Becker's semifinal victim was Leconte.

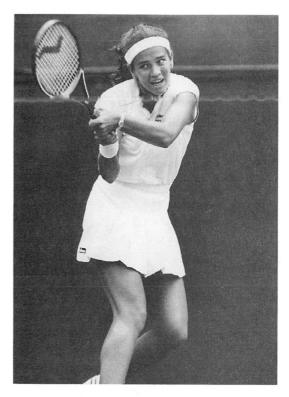

Fourteen-year-old Mary Joe Fernandez returns a shot from Chris Evert Lloyd in the first round at Wimbledon in 1986. (Wide World)

One point illustrated the distinction in the opponents' approach to the grass. In the final game of the third set, with Becker serving for the match, Lendl hit what appeared to be a forehand winner down the line. The German knifed through the air to intercept with a backhand stop volley but the ball caught the net cord and crawled over after Becker had landed on his stomach. Without a moment's hesitation, he sprang to his feet and spontaneously chipped a backhand winner crosscourt.

He then pounded two more service winners at Lendl to formalize the 6-4, 6-3, 7-5 victory. No wonder Becker said Wimbledon "feels like my tournament." Lendl, fighting the grass and his allergies and the fans who rallied behind more graceful and flamboyant players, had never felt that.

Two weeks after completion of Wimbledon, the top female players in the world assembled in Czechoslovakia for the most eagerly anticipated Federation Cup in the 24-year history of the event. From start to finish, it was Navratilova's show. Certainly, there was supreme irony in the idea of her leading an American team into Prague. It was shortly after she had contributed to Czechoslovakia's first Cup victory, in 1975, that she made the decision to seek political asylum in the U.S.

For the longest time, her success was not publicized in her native land. Her name did not appear in the Czech press, her matches were not seen on television. Yet, she was welcomed home as a returning heroine. She set out to demonstrate to her long-lost fans what they had missed.

"They may know about me," she said, "but they haven't actually seen me—not for a very long time, anyway. I want to show them what I can do."

Nor did she disappoint. Navratilova played brilliantly, winning every set in the course of carrying an unblemished record into her anxiously awaited final-round confrontation with Mandlikova, who made news of her own by marrying a Sydney restaurant owner in Prague's town hall.

The tournament produced one freak accident when an umbrella stand fell on Graf's foot, breaking her big toe, and one monumental upset, Evert Lloyd's loss to Anna Maria Cecchini of Italy in the quarterfinal round, 3-6, 6-4, 6-3, after 30 consecutive singles victories in Cup competition. Evert Lloyd was wearing a brace on a balky knee at the start of the event but, following the loss, she removed the brace and won her last two matches, against Bettina Bunge of Germany, 6-3, 6-4, and Sukova, 7-5, 7-6 (7-5).

Evert Lloyd scored the first point in the final round, leaving Navratilova in position to regain the Cup for the U.S., which she did by beating Mandlikova, 7-5, 6-1. Then she combined with Shriver, a pairing that won all three major events contested in 1986, to defeat Mandlikova and

Sukova in doubles, 6-4, 6-2. Martina was cheered loudly. Afterward, she cried tears of happiness.

The journey to her old neighborhood only intensified Navratilova's desire to win another U.S. Open which she now considered her national tournament. "I'll always be a Czech," she said at Flushing Meadow. "I'm not trying to deny it. I think I appreciate living here a lot more than people who have been born here and sort of take it for granted. I had to earn it. I had to learn and take a test."

The biggest test she would face in New York was administered by Graf after she breezed through the first five rounds. It happened in an epic semifinal match that required two hours and 16 minutes stretched over two days. Navratilova held a 4-1 lead in the first set when rain interrupted play on Friday night and she quickly closed out the set upon its resumption on Saturday.

Thereafter, however, it was a struggle, with both the second and third sets decided by tie-breakers. Graf had two match points in the 10th game of the third set and then a third at 8-7 in the tie-breaker. The champion weathered them all, with the help of the tape that barely denied Graf's attempted backhand pass for the upset.

"The last time I saved three match points [and won]," Navratilova said after the 6-1, 6-7 (3-7), 7-6 (10-8) victory, "I think I was 10 years old. I know I faced 15 match points once and I lost. Whenever it happened last, I know I was little."

Her great rival, Evert Lloyd, wasn't able to dig so deep against Sukova in their semifinal. The tall Czech hadn't beaten the American in 14 previous meetings but it took her only 70 minutes to dispose of the six-time Open champion, 6-2, 6-4. "Helena, Hana, Steffi, they're not intimidated by Martina or me anymore," said Evert Lloyd, who rested her ailing knee for the remainder of the season, passing up another 7-0 Wightman Cup romp by the U.S.

Still, Navratilova held the hammer over Sukova, once a ballgirl for Martina back in

Prague. In the final that was pushed back until Sunday and staged just before the men's championship, the No. 1 player in the world scored a 6-3, 6-2 victory in 60 minutes. She was presented with her third Open trophy and a check for $210,000, as much as any player had ever won at a single tournament.

The men's competition, even as it wound to a predictable conclusion, was much less orderly. McEnroe and Connors, responsible for seven of the eight previous singles titles, failed to last the first week. In fact, McEnroe, ninth-seeded, didn't make it past sundown on the first day, drilled by Annacone's 25 aces in four sets, 1-6, 6-1, 6-3, 6-3.

To make matters worse, the former king of Queens and partner Peter Fleming arrived six minutes late for their first doubles start and were defaulted. McEnroe's subsequent profane tirade resulted in a $1,000 fine. Weeks later, after winning three fall tournaments, the man's intemperate outburst at the Paris Indoor Championships led to a $3,000 fine, pushing him beyond the $7,500 limit and triggering a 42-day suspension that removed whatever slim possibility existed of his qualifying for the Masters.

Those expecting sixth-seeded Connors to ride to the rescue at Flushing Meadow were sadly disappointed. The five-time champion saved six match points but finally bowed to third-year pro, No. 95 Todd Witsken, 6-2, 6-4, 7-5, in the third round. It was his earliest exit from his national since 1972.

Remarkably, no native reached the semifinals for the first time in two decades. The last of the Mohicans was the unlikely Tim Wilkison, ranked No. 32, who was dusted by Edberg in the quarterfinals, 6-3, 6-3, 6-3.

Fittingly, the mystery man of the Open was a Slovak. The 6-foot-3 Mecir, forever disinterested in appearance but astonishingly quick to the ball, knocked off the second-seeded Wilander, 6-7 (3-7), 6-3, 6-4, the seventh-seeded Joakim Nystrom, 6-4, 6-2, 3-6, 6-2, and the third-seeded Becker, 4-6, 6-3, 6-4, 3-6, 6-3, in succession to arrive at the

One of the four Czechs in the U.S. Open finals in 1986, Helena Sukova fell before the onslaught of Martina Navratilova. (Wide World)

final. He had presented his credentials at Wimbledon, where he reached the quarterfinals, but at Flushing Meadow his performance stunned observers, especially considering how much he professed to dislike New York ("too big") and how much he missed his favorite form of entertainment ("fishing").

"He is maybe the fastest player I've ever played against," Becker said. Indeed, the 22-year-old was called "Gattone" (Big Cat) by Italians. And his assortment of junkballs and deceptive strokes befuddled some of the best players in the world, especially Swedes, against whom he was 18-3.

But in Lendl he met his match. Lendl, who had dropped only one set, was not mesmerized by the sight of his former countryman. And Mecir, so fluid earlier in the tournament, seemed rooted to the ground, content merely to trade groundies with the steady Lendl. The match produced a lot of yawns in the crowd, which shrank steadily in size over the course of the 6-4, 6-2, 6-0 rout by the two-time champion.

Lendl finished the year with a match record of 74-6 and nine titles, second in the world only to Navratilova's 90-3 mark and 14 championships. In the race to the bank between the two practicing capitalists from Czechoslovakia, Lendl won by a nose—$1,987,537 to $1,905,841.

Cash flow settled the Davis Cup account in Australia's favor for a 26th time as Patrick Cash flowed through a 6-0 singles and 3-1 doubles campaign. He capped it with a tremendous triple on turf, illuminated by a bounce-back singles victory in his hometown, Melbourne, to strip Sweden of the old silver crock, 3-2. Slow starts and brilliant finishes characterized vicious volleyer Cash's singles wins. From 1-5, he accelerated to overtake and beat the king of Kooyong, Stefan Edberg, Aussie Open title-holder, 13-11, 13-11, 6-4. But Mikael Pernfors, the French Open finalist, deadlocked the first day, 6-3, 6-1, 6-3, over Paul McNamee. Cash was inescapable in doubles, yoked to John Fitzgerald in an upset, 6-3, 6-4, 4-6, 6-1, of Edberg and Anders Jarryd, the guys who splotched McEnroe and Fleming's perfect Cup record two years before. But No. 24 Patrick seemed to have cashed his chips as Pernfors, No. 12, stacked up a two-set lead.

Only once before with the Cup at stake had the decisive match been won from two sets down: Jean Borotra of France over American Wilmer Allison in 1932. Cash seconded that comeback motion, charging relentlessly and eventually irresistibly to what captain Neale Fraser called "Australia's greatest Davis Cup performance"—2-6, 4-6, 6-3, 6-4, 6-3, as 12,000 townsfolk whooped it up. That statement covers an awful lot of ground, but so did 21-year-old Cash.

Patrick was the clincher, too, in the 4-1 semifinal victory over the U.S., beating Tim Mayotte on opening day, 4-6, 6-1, 6-2, 6-2, and Brad Gilbert, 3-6, 6-2, 6-3, 6-4, on Brisbane sod. The chief American problem was the absence of John McEnroe, whose accumulated churlish behavior got him ruled off by USTA President Randy Gregson.

Oddly enough, the U.S. won two series on historically troublesome Latin clay, at Guayaquil and Mexico City. Despite Andres Gomez' two wins, Aaron Krickstein and Jimmy Arias beat up on the second banana, Raul Viver. Arias' bit, 6-3, 6-1, 6-4, sealed the 3-2 decision over Ecuador. Captain Tom Gorman got two wins from Gilbert in the 4-1 decision over Mexico, but it was Mayotte as the unlikely clincher after he'd double-faulted (23) his way to an opening defeat by Pancho Maciel, 2-6, 13-11, 6-4, 6-4. Nevertheless, Tim, who'd never won a pro match on clay, lurched and lambasted his way grittily, weirdly past Leo Lavalle in claw-choke-and-claw-some-more manner for four hours, 7-5, 4-6, 0-6, 6-4, 9-7. He double-faulted plenty again (16), lagged at 1-3 in the fifth, then 3-5, 15-40: double match point. Yet he just kept serving-and-volleying—and hoping—to rescue himself there, broke serve, bungled three match points for himself at 5-6, and got home with a ripping backhand return. Here was a gringo who felt like doing a Mexican hat dance.

1987

In a year of mixed blessings for the most relentless campaigners on the world stage, Martina Navratilova and Ivan Lendl added to their collections of major tournament titles by two apiece. But there was a down side for both in 1987. She lost one of her most treasured possessions and he failed once again to win the prize that mattered most.

Navratilova's reign as the No. 1 female practitioner of tennis ended despite victories at Wimbledon and the U.S. Open. The queen was far from dead but, nonetheless, someone else was seated on her throne at the conclusion of the season. Her successor was Steffi Graf, who not only won her first major title at Paris but 75 of the 77 matches in which she participated.

Fortified by triumphs at the French Open and at Flushing Meadow, Lendl continued to hold the top spot in the men's rankings. But he would have traded all his trophies and perhaps thrown in a generous share of his $2,003,656 earnings for the great honor that eluded him for a second successive year. Once more, he lost in the final at Wimbledon. His nemesis was Pat Cash, who had beaten Lendl six months earlier in the last Australian Open played on grass.

But for those two flaws, the Czech native might have joined the list of Grand Slam immortals. As it was, Lendl forged the most victories (25) in Big Four tournaments by a male since Rod Laver went 26-0 in his 1969 sweep. Yet he had to stand by and watch forlornly as Cash joyously celebrated the first Wimbledon championship by an Aussie mate in 16 years with an unprecedented climb through the stands at Centre Court. "It's a miserable feeling," the losing finalist decided.

Before the year was out, Lendl would win eight tournaments, including a third consecutive Masters, for a total of 70. He tied John McEnroe for second place behind Jimmy Connors (105) in the all-time standings. Remarkably, neither American won an event in 1987 although the 35-year-old Connors did reach the semifinal round at both Wimbledon and the U.S. Open and rose to No. 4 on the ATP computer.

The shutout was the first in McEnroe's professional career. Not only was he afflicted by lapses in concentration and an aching back but he contributed to his demise with temper tantrums at the World Team Cup in May and at Flushing Meadow. For walking off the court in Dusseldorf, he defaulted the match to Miloslav Mecir and was fined $10,000. For a profane tirade during a third-round victory over Slobodan Zivojinovic at the U.S. Open he received point and game penalties, fines totaling $17,500 and a two-month suspension.

It was a measure of McEnroe's season that his most courageous and impressive performance came in defeat. In a Davis Cup relegation playoff to determine which nation would be banished to the boondocks (zonal competition) the following year, he played an historic five-set match on behalf of the U.S. against Boris Becker, representing West Germany, in late July. Becker's 4-6, 15-13, 8-10, 6-2, 6-2 victory consumed six hours and 20 minutes, 12 minutes shy of the Cup singles record set by McEnroe and Mats Wilander in a 1982 quarterfinal round match at St. Louis. McEnroe might have won in straight sets had he been able to penetrate Becker in the critical 22nd game of the two-hour, 35-minute second set. There Boris muscled his way out of 0-40, a total of five break points to 11-11.

Tim Mayotte, whose five tournament victories topped U.S. players, teamed with McEnroe for America's last stand at the Hartford Civic Center. However, the 3-2 defeat seemed sealed when the 26-year-old right-hander lost the opening match in five sets to No. 68 Eric Jelen, 6-8, 6-2, 1-6, 6-3, 6-2, and the deciding contest, also in five sets, to Becker, 6-2, 6-3, 5-7, 4-6, 6-2. As a result of the 3-2 defeat by Paraguay in the relegation round, the U.S. dropped from the 16-entry World Group while Germany, a first-round loser to Mexico, stayed in. The trouble began for the U.S. in Asuncion, where an intimidating crowd and a revved-up Victor Pecci took the decision and forced the Yanks into the relegation round. Pecci, who beat both Jimmy Arias, 6-3, 4-6, 6-4, 7-5, and, in the clincher, Aaron Krickstein, 6-2, 8-6, 9-7, wasn't quite enough. The difference was made by the unlikely Hugo Chapacu, another of those anonymous king-for-a-day gringo-grillers who stand out as roadblocks throughout U.S. Cup annals. With his side behind, 2-1, Chapacu, ranked No. 285 and heard of neither before nor after, was out of it after a good start. He trailed Arias, 1-5, in the final set, but dodging three match points, somehow pulled out perhaps the

Wimbledon in 1987 belonged to the colorful Aussie, Pat Cash. (Russ Adams)

most astounding victory ever against the U.S., 6-4, 6-1, 5-7, 3-6, 9-7. Pecci wrapped it up for Paraguay, and though there was a chance to avoid demotion against Germany, the U.S. plunged to the American Zone for 1988, ineligible to compete for the Cup for the first time.

Mats Wilander was the strength as the Swedes won a third Davis Cup in four years. He and Anders Jarryd handled the singles in the 5-0 final-round bogging down of upstart India on indoor clay in Goteborg. But the Indians made a nice story, the peerless sportsmen from the sub-continent seeming to be players from another, earlier era. It was a splendid career closer for the Flying Amritraj Brothers—Vijay and Anand—to play a final.

Thirteen years before, they'd lifted India to the same position where they were forced to de-fault to South America, their government's anti-apartheid gesture. But in their 16th year of Davis Cup they'd made it again, along with another name in their country's sporting history: Krishnan. This was Ramesh, son of the man—Ramanathan Krishnan—who had carried India to the Cup round in 1966, a gallant loss to Australia.

Never before had a father and son played in Cup finals. Incredibly they beat Australia in the semis, 3-2, on Sydney greensward. Vijay, nearly 34, stopped Wally Masur, 1-6, 6-3, 12-10, 6-4, and Krishnan beat John Fitzgerald, 6-1, 6-2, 3-6, 8-6, on the first day, and Ramesh enmeshed Masur in the deciding fifth match with delicate touch, 8-6, 6-4, 6-4. The Brothers Amritraj were the third such pair to grace a final, following the British Reg and Laurie Doherty of 1902–06 and Robert and George Wrenn of the U.S. in 1903.

American females weren't treated so badly, not with Navratilova still near the top of her form, but there was one jarring note. Chris Evert not only jettisoned her married name following a divorce from John Lloyd but she also relinquished her hold on the majors. For the first time since 1974, she failed to win any of the Big Four tournaments. In fact, she wasn't even a finalist.

Furthermore, her performance at Flushing Meadow signalled the beginning of the end of a remarkable career. For the first time since her debut at Forest Hills in the era of grass, she failed to reach the semifinals of the U.S. Open. At least her conqueror was an American, 23-year-old Lori McNeil, up from the public parks of Houston.

By taking Evert's accustomed spot in the final four, McNeil provided "a shot in the arm" for minorities. Not since Arthur Ashe, in 1972, had a black player advanced to a singles semifinal at the Open. Not since Althea Gibson won the tournament in 1958 had a black woman had such an impact. And McNeil did herself proud by pushing Graf to a third set before succumbing, 4-6, 6-2, 6-4.

In the end, of course, it was Navratilova's tournament. Not only did she defeat Graf for the singles title but she also won the women's doubles with Pam Shriver over Kathy Jordan and Liz Sayers Smylie, 5-7, 6-4, 6-2, from 4-2 down in the second and, after a lunch break, a thrilling mixed with Emilio Sanchez over Betsy Nagelsen and Paul Annacone, 6-4, 6-7 (6-8), 7-6, (14-12). In the wildest finish of a major final, Martina won it herself with a seventh match-point volley after she and Emilio had squelched two match points. It took Martina 40 fewer minutes to win those two absorbing finals on Monday than Wilander and Lendl tediously devoted to their own. Billie Jean King had scored the last triple, at Wimbledon, in 1973. No one had tripled at the U.S. Championships since Margaret Court in 1970.

Still, despite her brilliant Open, the fact she was a finalist in all four majors and the 36-1 record she and Shriver compiled in doubles (losing only in the quarters at Wimbledon to Russians Larisa Savchenko and Svetlana Parkhomenko, 6-2, 6-4), it was a disappointing season for Navratilova. She won only four of the 12 tournaments she entered, fell short of the $1-million mark ($932,102) for the first time since 1981 and faltered in the season-ending Virginia Slims Championships. She never got to contest Graf's claim to No. 1, her 21-match winning streak in the event terminated in straight sets by Gabriela Sabatini.

Graf, whose only two defeats were inflicted by Navratilova in major finals, overcame Sabatini, 4-6, 6-4, 6-0, 6-4, to win her first Slims title and confirm her place at the top of women's tennis. She also raised her earnings for the year to $1,063,785. "Steffi's No. 1, no doubt about that," Navratilova said.

The woman's slip began showing early. While Evert and Graf bypassed the resurrected Australian Open, staged for the last time on the grass at Kooyong Stadium, Navratilova journeyed Down Under and came away empty, beaten in the final by Hana Mandlikova, 7-5, 7-6 (7-2). That curtailed a 58-match winning streak dating back to the 1986 French Open and sent her into a downward spiral.

Forced to contend with a persistent foot injury and a breakup with coach Mike Estep, she was beaten, 6-3, 6-2, by Graf in the semis at the International Players Championship (Lipton). "Today," Navratilova said, "she was the best player in the world and she will be until I play her again."

While she waited for the next meeting, Navratilova was overcome by Evert, 3-6, 6-1, 7-6 (7-4), at the Virginia Slims of Houston and routed by Sabatini, 7-6 (7-2), 6-1, in the semifinals of the Italian Open in Rome, where the ladies at long last returned after being relegated to the hinterlands for six years, five at Perugia, 1986 at Taranto. Graf beat Gaby for the title, 7-5, 4-6, 6-0, but was not amused by journalists' satirical references to her nose and didn't return until 1996.

It was in Paris where Navratilova appeared to regain her form, smashing Evert, 6-2, 6-2, in the semifinal and earning another shot at Graf, who had come from 3-5 in the third set against Sabatini to reach the championship round, 6-4, 4-6, 7-5. Again, in a magnificent final, the German lass trailed 3-5 in the third. Again, Graf escaped with a 6-4, 4-6, 8-6 triumph for her second French crown. It ran her string of victories to seven tournaments comprising 39 matches.

Navratilova had to take solace in extending her record for most consecutive final appearances in major tournaments (9). "Don't try to dethrone me," she instructed the press. Nonetheless, it was Graf she had to worry about.

Even the return to blessed English grass didn't reverse her fortunes, at least not instantly. At Eastbourne, where she had tuned her game for Wimbledon by winning in each of the five preceding years, she was denied by Helena Sukova, 7-6 (7-5), 6-3. Only the previous day, Sukova had outlasted Evert, 4-6, 6-4, 8-6, and she fell behind Navratilova 0-5 in the first set of their final before rallying.

Just when it seemed that her fall was complete, Navratilova dug in her heels at the All England Club. She defeated Evert, 6-2, 5-7, 6-4, in a

Steffi Graf won Paris and lost only two matches in 1987.
(Russ Adams)

match worthy of the great rivalry. Yet, it was a sign of the times that the 73rd meeting of the pair occurred in the semifinal. Theirs had become a warmup act.

In the other half of the draw, Graf bludgeoned Shriver, 6-0, 6-2, in 51 minutes. "I can't believe Steffi is only 18 and is so strong," the loser said. "There is something there that is special. The ball comes off her racket with unbelievable force."

That force finally was blunted, at least temporarily, in the final when Navratilova needed all her athleticism and her experience to emerge with a 7-5, 6-3 victory. Not only did it stop Graf's 45-match streak but it elevated the winner to another plateau in the history of the sport. It was an unprecedented sixth consecutive Wimbledon singles championship and her eighth overall, tying the

record established by Helen Wills Moody 49 years earlier.

"How many more Wimbledons do you want?" Graf asked as the players waited for the Duchess of Kent to present the trophies.

Replied Navratilova, "Nine is my lucky number."

She was invigorated by the outcome after 229 days without a tournament triumph and began mapping plans for another successful defense at Flushing Meadow. Meanwhile, Graf plunged on. She led West Germany into the final of the Federation Cup at Vancouver, where the U.S. was poised to defend.

Her 6-2, 6-1 rout of Evert offset Shriver's 6-0, 7-6 victory over Claudia Kohde Kilsch and the two German ladies then rallied from a 1-6, 0-4 deficit to defeat Evert and Shriver, 1-6, 7-5, 6-4, in the decisive doubles. Thus did the Fatherland become the fifth nation to own a piece of the Cup. Two weeks later, after Evert posted a semifinal victory over Navratilova, 6-2, 6-1, in Los Angeles, Graf dismissed her elder, 6-3, 6-4, in the final and ascended to No. 1.

So shaky was the game of the former Ice Maiden that she even lost to Shriver, in the semifinal round of the Canadian Open. After nine years and 18 unsuccessful attempts, Shriver defeated Evert, 6-4, 6-1, then followed with a 6-4, 6-1 triumph over Zina Garrison for her most significant singles title. She would finish a splendid season with four tournament victories, a match record of 67-13 and the honor of captaining the U.S. Wightman Cup team, which beat a British squad for the ninth straight year, by the score of 5-2.

The most touching moment of the U.S. Open didn't occur in the final or even during Evert's quarterfinal loss to McNeil. It took place in the round of 16, where McNeil was matched against Garrison, her friend since childhood. The two were protégés of John Wilkerson, a public parks coach in Houston who was teaching McNeil's mother, Dorothy, when the woman decided to entrust her 10-year-old to his care.

Garrison and McNeil, whose father, Charlie, once played defensive back for the San Diego Chargers, were doubles partners and virtually inseparable on the tour. One month older, Garrison had enjoyed the more successful career and had won two of her first three tournaments in 1987, at Sydney and Oakland. But this was McNeil's moment, her tournament, and she survived two match points and defeated Garrison in a third-set tie-breaker, 7-6 (7-0), 3-6, 7-6 (8-6).

That boosted her into the quarterfinals, where her attacking game wore down Evert, 3-6, 6-2, 6-4, before an agonizing crowd. Needing to hold serve to hang on, the former champion lost the last four points from 15-0. She called it a bad day. "And that happens," she said, "when you get older."

Evert started, stopped and interrupted herself as she tried to place the premature exit in perspective. "I think that anybody who plays . . . I don't want to say over 30 . . . but when you get to a point at the end of your career . . . I've had some terrible days this year," she said. "I'm just not as consistent as I was when I was 17, 18 years old."

Without a clothing company to dress her or endorsements decorating her outfit, McNeil proved she belonged in such surroundings when she jumped on Graf to take the first set of their semifinal. She charged the net at every opportunity and defied the top seed, who was suffering from a cold and fever, to pass her. The definitive moment came in the seventh game of the third set, when McNeil held a break point for a 4-3 lead.

However, she netted a relatively easy volley and a relieved Graf took control. Navratilova, who'd won all 12 sets, awaited the German in the final. The defending champ was prepared to use the same tactics, but with the benefit of experience and a fierce determination to retain what she had.

The match turned in the tie-breaker when, at 3-3, Graf missed two backhands. Navratilova assumed command and closed out the challenger, 7-6 (7-4), 6-1, in one hour, 17 minutes. "She was the champion," Graf said. "I knew it was going to be difficult to beat her."

As Navratilova held up the trophy, her fourth U.S. singles prize, both she and Graf were aware that the result wouldn't alter the computer ratings. "I'm not going to say anything against that," Graf said.

After convincing victories in the world's two biggest tournaments, Navratilova said, "I'd have to think I have the edge right now." She paused. "Nothing is worse than when people say you're washed up."

She was a long way from that but still she needed to outlast Graf at the Slims Championships if she hoped to reclaim her eminence for the year. Instead, she faltered in the quarterfinal, bowing to Sabatini, 6-4, 7-5. Her old rival had an even worse experience as pudgy lefty Sylvia Hanika spanked Evert, 6-4, 6-4, in the opening round. A new generation made its mark as Graf closed out the season with her 11th title and the designation as best in the game.

There would be no change at the top of the men's computer but that didn't mean the circuit suffered from tired blood. The man who put a charge into the season was Cash, the Australian with the checkered headband, a diamond stud in his ear, a chip on his shoulder and an American temper. He regarded himself as a "yobbo," one of the boys.

In his hometown of Melbourne, he became one of the finalists. Starting as the 11th seed, Cash advanced to the title match of the Australian Open by beating third-seeded Yannick Noah and then Lendl, 7-6, 5-7, 7-6, 6-4, in the semifinal round. In the championship match, Edberg prevailed, 6-3, 6-4, 5-7, 6-3, the first of six tournament victories that would boost him into second place in the rankings.

Lori McNeil ousted Chris Evert and reached the U.S. Open semis in 1987. (Russ Adams)

He followed with a victory at the U.S. Indoor in Philadelphia where Connors, a seven-time champion, suffered a knee injury and had to retire at 3-6, 1-2. Edberg's countryman, Mats Wilander, warmed up for Paris by beating McEnroe and Martin Jaite, 6-3, 6-4, 6-4, in the last two rounds of the Italian Open.

For McEnroe, his form on the clay was encouraging after a frustrating early season where he reached the finals of the U.S. Pro Indoor and the WCT finals, only to lose to Mayotte, 3-6, 6-1, 6-3, 6-1, and Mecir, 6-0, 3-6, 6-2, 6-2, respectively. But it proved to be an illusion as he staggered in the very first round of the French Open, falling, 4-6, 6-2, 6-4, 6-2, to No. 49 Horacio de la Pena. He flew home with a sore back, not to be seen again until the Davis Cup match, with West Germany.

So depressed was the state of American men's tennis that Connors, 34, was the only Yank to reach the quarters, where he was blown away by Becker, 6-3, 6-3, 7-5. The final, between Lendl and Wilander, was an excruciatingly tedious exchange of groundstrokes that consumed 4 hours, 30 minutes. The first set alone took 100 minutes. Lendl emerged with a 7-5, 6-2, 3-6, 7-6 (7-3) victory.

But it was Wimbledon—one of the wettest—for which Lendl hungered. This looked like it might be the year after Peter Doohan, an Aussie ranked No. 70, stunned Becker, the two-time defending champ, in the second round, 7-6 (7-4), 4-6, 6-2, 6-4. Lendl almost stubbed his toe in the same round, surviving a stiff five-set challenge from No. 45, Italian Paolo Cane, who volleyed his way to a 2-1 lead in sets, and served with two points for a 5-3 lead in the fourth. Stupendous passing shots got Ivan out of trouble there. The slim, volatile Cane double-faulted away his chances and the set-closing 12th game, cursing the sun which appeared at the wrong time for him; he surrendered the fifth, 6-1. Ivan had smoother sailing thereafter. His semifinal defeat of Edberg, 3-6, 6-4, 7-6 (12-10), 6-4, dodging two set points in the tie-breaker, was impressive.

If his passage was relatively quiet, that was the result of some pyrotechnics in the other half of the draw, most of it caused by that old rabble-rouser, Connors. In the round of 16, the man staged one of the great rallies in the history of tennis by rising from a 1-6, 1-6, 1-4 deficit against Mikeal Pernfors to win the last three sets 7-5, 6-4, 6-2. "Phenomenal," Connors decided, "right?" Right.

Then the codger dodged the thunderbolt serves of Zivojinovic in a 7-6 (7-5), 7-5, 6-3 quarterfinal triumph. It appeared he might really have a chance to win a third title but he was no match for Cash in the semifinal, 6-4, 6-4, 6-1.

That wasn't the only indication the 11th-seeded Aussie was ready to take the biggest step of his career. But grass was his best surface. He was fit after an injury-plagued season and he was a battler. Cash didn't grow up worshipping Laver, Lew Hoad, Ken Rosewall or John Newcombe, the last Digger to win Wimbledon in 1971. He favored the rough-and-tumble proponents of Australian rules football.

"We have footballers who'll go in all the time," said his coach, Ian Barclay. "We have players who hang back on the fringes. When we're cruel, we call them gutless. Patrick doesn't know how to hang back."

What he did know was how to play on grass. It was instinctive, the way he covered the net, the way he volleyed. For all his countless hours of practice, Lendl wasn't a natural. He was mechanical. And it showed as the 22-year-old Cash crushed his opponent's spirit, 7-6 (7-5), 6-2, 7-5.

There followed perhaps the most amazing victory celebration in the annals of the proper All England Club. Cash didn't wait to accept the congratulations of the Duke and Duchess of Kent. Instead, he clambered through the crowd massed at one corner of Centre Court and over the ledge to the second level of stands where were gathered his coach, psychologist, sister, father and girlfriend as well as the couple's 14-month-old son, not to mention his London pubmate. And Lendl, so formal, had to watch this riotous scene and force a smile. "I believe the second player shouldn't be there," said the man, who wanted to be anywhere else. "He should be allowed to leave."

Lendl tuned up for the green slabs of Flushing Meadow by winning at Washington, reaching the rained-out final at Stratton Mountain against McEnroe and beating Edberg in the Canadian Open, 6-4, 7-6 (7-2). Cash continued to celebrate, which helped to explain his first-round loss to No. 47 Peter Lundgren at the U.S. Open. (Later, a knee injury limited him to doubles duty as Australia was upended in Davis Cup competition by India.)

The home team received a nice surprise when Michael Chang, the new junior champion

at 15½, and the youngest male to compete in the U.S. Championships since Vinnic Richards, 15 years, 5 months in 1918, defeated ex–Aussie Davis Cupper, 32-year-old Paul McNamee, 6-3, 6-7 (5-7), 6-4, 6-4, in his first match. Duke Odizor sent him packing in the second round and it wasn't long before the American presence was reduced, once again, to McEnroe and Connors.

Mac caused a commotion not with his play but his behavior. He went ballistic, spewing curses at chair umpire Richard Ings and a courtside cameraman while beating Zivojinovic in the third round. Awaiting sentencing, he got to the quarters, where he was overpowered by Lendl, 6-3, 6-3, 6-4. The suspension he received ended his season.

Once again, Connors was the lone American survivor in the final four but he, too, was no match for Lendl, 6-4, 6-4, 6-2. The final, against Wilander, delayed one day by rain, was a replay of the French. Although the quality of tennis was higher, so was the quantity. Lendl's 6-7 (7-9), 6-0, 7-6 (7-4), 6-4 victory lasted a U.S. final record 4 hours, 47 minutes, a record these two players would break in 1988.

Neither Lendl nor his new Connecticut neighbor was prepared to attack, resulting in a war of attrition. That was fine with the champ. "Probably because of not having as much talent as other players and working harder because of that," Lendl said, " I am steadier than others. But I'm not as flashy. It's tougher to be flashy all the time."

Three weeks after the Open, he was shocked by Lundgren at San Francisco, ending a 25-match winning streak. But he steadied himself for the Masters, where he dropped only a set in the round-robin and pounded Wilander, 6-2, 6-3, in the final for a record fifth title, topping Ilie Nastase (1971, 1972, 1973 and 1975). Once again, Ivan was No. 1, with an asterisk that noted "except for Wimbledon."

1988

The trophy was not his to give but at least Don Budge had a hand in the presentation. That made the man who first realized the achievement more than a bystander to history. Standing under the flags of four nations, he reached across a gulf of 50 years and offered his congratulations.

Steffi Graf made the Grand Slam a permanent part of her résumé in 1988, adding the U.S. Open title to the championships of Australia, France and Wimbledon. And Budge, who had swept all four of the world's major tournaments a half-century earlier, witnessed each of the woman's conquests. While the West German prodigy expressed mostly relief, the courtly American seemed enormously pleased with her 6-3, 3-6, 6-1 victory over Gabriela Sabatini.

In welcoming Graf to the most exclusive club in tennis, Budge whispered into her ear during the award ceremonies at Flushing Meadow. "He said he knew it all the way," she recalled later. "He said he thinks I'm going to do it a couple more times."

That would make Graf unique. Of the five persons who have claimed the four major titles in the same year, only Rod Laver did so twice. "She doesn't look behind," said Papa Peter Graf, her coach throughout her formative years. "She always looks forward. She wants to play in two-three years her best tennis."

But people would look back at 1988 from the perspective of the future and recognize the accomplishment. If Graf herself failed to comprehend the enormousness of what she had done, perhaps it was because, as her father said, "She doesn't know so many things from the history of tennis." What she knew about the Grand Slam was what other people had told her.

Graf lost but two sets in her triumphant march, the first to Martina Navratilova in the Wimbledon final and the second to Sabatini. Budge said he expected Graf to capture the Slam after watching her in Australia. At the Wimbledon Ball, he told her, "Steffi, when you win the Grand Slam, I hope they let me present the trophy."

The USTA was too conscious of tradition to allow such a radical departure. But Budge was included in the ceremony on the golden anniversary of his achievement. He held one handle of the silver jug while Gordon Jorgensen, the USTA president, held the other. They were surrounded by the Stars and Stripes, the Union Jack, the Tricolor and the Southern Cross.

"I'm glad she did it," Budge said. "It's going to give the game a shot in the arm. There aren't any men now who I think are Grand Slam material. Sooner or later, a man will come along."

A man like Budge or Laver, who completed a Slam as an amateur in 1962 and repeated as a professional in 1969. Clearly, however, the sport's dominant player in 1988 was a teenaged female who followed in the steps of Maureen Connolly and Margaret Smith Court. In fact, she took a few steps beyond when she added the Olympic title to her collection.

This marked the first time since 1924 that tennis had been included as a medal sport in the Olympic Games and Graf took full advantage of the opportunity to establish a new standard of excellence. Not only was she queen of the Big Four but, by Zeus, an Olympic champion in the same year. "There's nothing quite as special as winning a gold medal for your country," she exulted after earning the last of her Fab Five titles on a hard court in Seoul, Korea. The acceptance of tennis as a full-fledged medal sport marked a breakthrough—or official breakdown of amateurism—hardly noticed at the time. The ITF got permission from the IOC (International Olympic Committee) to approve the best players available for the Games if nominated by their countries. That meant out-and-out pros. It changed the complexion of the next Games in 1992 at Barcelona, where the NBA "Dream Team" appeared to take basketball gold, and numerous other declared pros took part. Tennis had led the way, for better or worse.

A slam of sorts was registered in men's competition as well. But this was national and

Mats Wilander racked up all the majors except for Wimbledon in 1988. (Russ Adams)

Eighteen-year-old Andre Agassi burst on the scene in 1988, soaring to No. 3 in the World Top Ten. (Russ Adams)

not individual. As the result of Mats Wilander's victories at the Australian, French and U.S. championships and Stefan Edberg's ascendancy at Wimbledon, each of the major events was captured by a Swede. There hadn't been a male sweep by citizens of one country since Laver ran the table in 1969.

In the course of his season that would have been lionized if not for Graf's transcendent performance, Wilander also bumped Ivan Lendl from the top spot on the computer. In slipping from the No. 1 position for the first time in 156 weeks, Lendl reached only one Big Four final, at Flushing Meadow. He also surrendered his Masters title, which he had held for three years, to Boris Becker.

The latter, who was beaten by Edberg in the Wimbledon final, won seven tournaments and also

led West Germany to its first Davis Cup title, dethroning Sweden, 4-1, at Goteborg. Miloslav Mecir, the enigmatic Czech, took home the Olympic gold medal. He also denied Wilander any chance of a Grand Slam by defeating the Swede in the Wimbledon quarterfinals, 6-3, 6-1, 6-3.

It was another empty year for America's two controversial stars. Neither John McEnroe nor Jimmy Connors advanced beyond the quarters of a major event and both sagged in the rankings, Mac to No. 11 and Connors to No. 7. Each won two tournaments, the first for Connors in four years.

Suddenly, however, the future appeared bright for men's tennis in the U.S. Andre Agassi, an 18-year-old graduate of Nick Bollettieri's groundstroke academy who had won his first Grand Prix tournament only the previous November at Itaparica, Brazil, captured six titles, reached the semifinals at the French and U.S. Opens and shot from No. 25 to No. 3 in the world standings. Andre also led the "back from the boonies" march (included was a McEnroe cameo) to the American zone title with victories over Peru, 3-0, and Argentina, 4-1. That won the U.S. a return ticket into the Davis Cup World Group for 1989, deliverance from the purgatory of relegation, a descent on 1987 losses to Paraguay and Germany. Nervous and demanding were the first two days for two rookies in Lima—also for captain Tom Gorman, considering that the U.S. was 9-9 since 1962 on Latin loam. But Jay Berger held together at the important junctures of his 5-hour, 35-minute baptismal to beat Pablo Arraya, 7-5, 6-1, 5-7, 1-6, 7-5, at dusk. Only enough daytime remained for 10 games.

Next day Agassi, starting sluggishly from 5-5, took Jaime Yzaga, 6-8, 7-5, 6-1, 6-2, and Ken Flach and Robert Seguso wrapped, 6-2, 4-6, 6-4, 6-3, over Yzaga and Carlos DiLaura. Amid McEnroe's awesome Cup record were four (of his seven) singles defeats that particularly rankled: 1980 and 1983 shutouts in Buenos Aires. At last, at 29, saying humbly, "I hope to win one," he got it, as the starter, overhauling Guillermo Perez-Roldan from a break down, 3-2 in the fifth, 6-2, 5-7, 6-2, 3-6, 6-3. Agassi whipped through Martin Jaite, 6-2, 6-2, 6-1, and Flach and Seguso did likewise, 6-2, 6-3, 6-4, over Javier Frana and Christian Miniussi. The year in the wilderness was over.

Two years younger than Agassi, Michael Chang also made great strides. By defeating Johan Kriek, 6-3, 6-3, at San Francisco in early October, he became the second-youngest winner of a men's professional tournament at 16 years, 7 months (Aaron Krickstein had been 16 years, 2 months when he triumphed at Israel five years earlier). Chang rose 133 places in the rankings, from No. 163 to No. 30, in his first full season on the circuit.

Graf's monumental accomplishment guaranteed that U.S. women would be denied a major title for the first time since Court's Grand Slam

Neither foot-faults nor rain could keep Stefan Edberg from his destiny at Wimbledon in 1988. (Russ Adams)

18 years earlier. Additionally, Navratilova hadn't been blanked in the Big Four since 1980. The latter still was a solid No. 2, winning nine tournaments (two fewer than Graf) and amassing a 70-7 record.

But Navratilova reached the final of only one major tournament, Wimbledon. In the first Australian Open played on hard courts in the sparkling new complex at Flinders Park, she was a straight-set, semifinal loser to Chris Evert. At the French, she was stunned by 17-year-old Russian Natalia Zvereva in the fourth round, 6-3, 7-6 (7-5). Zina Garrison did the honors in a quarterfinal match at Flushing Meadow.

In doubles, Navratilova and Pam Shriver continued their successful pairing, winning 28 of 30 matches and five championships, including a sixth Australian and record-tying fourth French.

Shriver later teamed with Garrison to win an Olympic gold medal for doubles, equalling the feat of the more experienced Ken Flach and Robert Seguso. Garrison had defeated Shriver in the quarterfinal round of the singles tournament and earned a bronze medal.

The first Olympic women's singles champion since Helen Wills in 1924, Graf lost but three matches all year. Sabatini triumphed twice, beating her for the first time after 11 consecutive losses to win Boca Raton, 2-6, 6-3, 6-1, in March and again at Amelia Island one month later, a semi, 6-3, 4-6, 7-5. Shriver applied the final blemish to Graf's record in the semifinals of the Virginia Slims Championship, which the 18-year-old Sabatini won for her fourth title of the season.

Graf zipped through the Australian without the loss of a set but she was pressed in the final by Evert, who had been sharp in a 6-2, 7-5 semifinal victory over Navratilova. For Evert, it was the 34th and last major final of her career but for tennis the match was unprecedented, a schizophrenic outdoor-indoor title bout made possible by the new stadium's sliding roof. It was, according to Evert, "the weirdest [final] I ever played."

Rain suspended the match with Graf ahead, 2-1 in the first. Officials decided to close the roof and, after a 91-minute delay, the outdoor tournament resumed indoors. Graf adapted better to the change, racing to a 6-1, 5-1 lead before Evert steadied herself. She won four of the next five games and came within two points of squaring the match before the German prevailed, 6-1, 7-6 (7-1).

Navratilova won five consecutive tournaments and 29 matches in the U.S. before she was again stopped by Evert at Houston in their 77th meeting, 6-0, 6-4. But Navratilova would win their final three matches, raising her record in the enduring rivalry to a concluded 43-37.

Any semblance of competition at the French vanished when third-seeded Evert was dismissed in the third round by 16-year-old Arantxa Sanchez of Spain, 6-3, 7-6 (7-4), and Navratilova

It was a Grand Slam for Steffi Graf in 1988. (Russ Adams)

was surprised by 13th-seeded Zvereva in the round of 16. Zvereva then upset Helena Sukova, 6-2, 6-3, and outlasted unseeded Nicole Provis of Australia, 6-3, 6-7 (3-7), 7-5, landing in her first major final.

Graf, who had beaten Sabatini in the semifinals, 6-3, 7-6 (7-3), was brutally efficient against her powerless opponent. Her 6-0, 6-0 rout lasted only 32 minutes, the most exciting feature of which was an hour rain delay. There hadn't been such a one-sided major tournament championship match since 1911 when Dorothea Chambers rang up two goose eggs over Dora Boothby in an all-English Wimbledon final.

It was Wimbledon, of course, that loomed as the biggest obstacle to a Slam. Wimbledon was the seat of Navratilova's power. "Wimbledon is the last thing she's holding onto, the last thing she dominates in women's tennis," Shriver said.

The naturalized American was in position to surpass the record for most singles championships at the All England Club and she prepared in her usual fashion, winning at Eastbourne, where she had the satisfaction of victimizing Zvereva, 6-2, 6-2. But Navratilova was less than commanding once the tournament got underway on Church Road. She struggled both in the quarterfinals and semifinals, edging both Ros Fairbank, 4-6, 6-4, 7-5, and Evert.

Indeed, after holding out through three match points in their 78th meeting, (6-1, 4-6, 7-5), Evert suggested Navratilova was "beatable" and picked Graf to win. The German, despite a 6-1, 6-2 rout of Shriver in the other semifinal, was more respectful. "This is her surface," Graf said of her opponent. "She can play so much better, so you've got to watch out."

Graf did more watching than playing in first set of the final. She appeared jumpy, served below her standard and committed a bundle of unforced errors. Before long, Navratilova had raced to a 7-5, 2-0 lead and appeared well on her way to another glorious moment. That's when Graf drew the line.

She broke Navratilova's second service of the second set. Remarkably, the defending champion would not hold service again in the match. Graf allowed Navratilova only one more game and the only delay in a 5-7, 6-2, 6-1 triumph was caused by rain after four games of the third set.

"I hit good volleys," Navratilova reasoned. "I hit good balls that other people wouldn't get to, and then she hits winners. I didn't succumb to pressure today. I succumbed to a better player . . . I still played pretty damn well, but she was hitting winners all over the place." And so ended forever one segment of Martina's hounding of Helen Wills Moody, who won eight Wimbledons on a record 50 consecutive matches. Graf snipped her match streak at 47, but Martina would get the ninth title two years down the road.

So the torch, or at least the Ladies' Challenge Plate, was passed to a new generation. And Graf

was only one tournament away from an achievement that had eluded Navratilova in her prime. She even teamed with Sabatini to win the Wimbledon doubles championship, defeating the Soviet pairing of Zvereva and Larisa Savchenko, 6-3, 1-6, 12-10, who had stopped Navratilova and Shriver in the third round.

Fittingly, the only genuine competition Graf faced at the U.S. Open was contemporary in nature. Having failed to derail her at Wimbledon, Navratilova lost any opportunity at Flushing Meadow when she was ousted in an exciting quarterfinal by Garrison, 6-4, 6-7 (3-7), 7-5. Zingin' Zina choked a few times in the match of the fortnight but always rebounded. She blew a 5-0 lead and four match points in the second, failed to serve it out at 5-4 in the third, broke serve and wasted another match point before firming up for two closing strokes, an ace and drop volley. An upset all right, considering that Zina had been 0-21 against Martina, but not an all-timer like stubby 30-year-old qualifier Kim Steinmetz, No. 183, beating the eighth-seeded French finalist, Zvereva, in the opening round, 4-6, 6-3, 6-4. Evert, recently married to former Olympic skier Andy Mill, earned a chance to thwart the Grand Slam in the semifinal round but had to withdraw on the day of the match with a stomach virus that left her so weak she could barely get out of bed.

That left Sabatini, Graf's doubles partner and the person responsible for the "2" in Graf's 61-2 record at that point. Sabatini became the first Argentine to qualify for a major women's final with a 6-4, 7-5 victory over Garrison but she wasn't prepared to go further. In the end, although Sabatini did extend the fraulein to a third set, Graf's principal opponent may have been her nerves.

Playing conservatively, even tentatively, Graf nonetheless added the U.S. title to her necklace of jewels with a 6-3, 3-6, 6-1 victory. "Steffi wasn't herself," her father insisted. "Normally, she's not nervous. She has the best nerves of the whole tennis scene."

His daughter seemed more relieved than thrilled. She didn't jump for joy or kneel in supplication. Graf merely jogged to the stands to embrace her family and she barely smiled during the award ceremony. "Now I've done it," she said. "There's no more pressure. There's nothing else you can tell me I have to do."

She didn't have much time to savor the moment. By that evening, she was on a flight to her home in Bruhl. The Olympic tournament was scheduled to begin in a week.

Naturally, Graf was seeded first. Naturally, she won. In the final, she again bested Sabatini, this time by the definitive score of 6-3, 6-3. A sign of the times: Of the seven Americans representing the U.S. in tennis at Seoul, the only player not to medal was Evert, a third-round victim of Italy's Raffaella Reggi, 2-6, 6-4, 6-1.

Neither Evert nor Navratilova survived the quarters at the season-ending Slims Championships in New York. Martina lost to Sukova, 2-6, 7-5, 6-3. Shriver, who had knocked off Evert, 7-5, 6-4, terminated Graf's 46-match winning streak with a 6-3, 7-6 (7-5) decision in the semifinals. But Sabatini upheld the new order with a 7-5, 6-2, 6-2 victory.

Garrison, the captain, and her pal, Lori McNeil, starred in a 7-0 Wightman Cup victory over a woefully weak British squad that won only one set. But McNeil, beaten by Catarina Lindqvist, 6-4, 7-5, and Patty Fendick, defeated by Maria Strandlund, 6-3, 7-6 (7-5), were a second-round Federation Cup flop for the U.S., 2-1 to Sweden. Sukova was the anchor for a fifth Czechoslovak triumph, 2-1 over the Soviet Union. Both she, beating Zvereva, 6-3, 6-4, and Radka Zrubakova, beating Larisa Savchenko, 6-1, 7-6 (7-2), went unbeaten in five singles, but the date and place of the Federation Cup—December in Melbourne—weakened the level of competition.

Eleven months earlier in Melbourne, the baptism of Flinders Park (named for Capt. Matthew Flinders of the British Navy, an explorer of these parts near the end of the 18th century)

drew 20,836 customers. Two separate crowds (13,798 in the afternoon, the very first session; 7,038 as floodlights came to the Open) turned out to inspect the complex that sent Australia well ahead of the rest of the tennis world, a very long jump from 61-year-old grass-carpeted Kooyong Stadium. The focal point was the asphalt-floored $70-million techno-wonder, the 15,000-seat stadium with air-cooled private boxes, a mint green open-and-shut case whose sliding ceiling put an end to rainouts.

It was a lively, controversial debut. Curiously, in this he-man land, a "sheila" (woman) was selected to do the opening honors, 14th-seeded left-hander Dianne Fromholtz Ballestrat. Curiouser, Ballestrat, 31 and well past her world No. 7 ranking of 1979, was beaten by a totally unknown 23-year-old American qualifier, No. 304 Wendy Wood from Lexington, Mass., 6-2, 4-6, 8-6, in two hours. In her singular moment in the sun, Wood skipped past a match point in taking her first (and last) victory in a major. By the time that was over, Todd Woodbridge, on an outside court, had scored the initial victory for a native, 6-2, 6-0, 6-1, over American John Letts.

The crowd within was restive, anxious for Wood and Ballestrat to move on so they could watch the hometown hero, fourth-seeded 1987 runner-up Patrick Cash, beat Thomas Muster, 7-5, 6-1, 6-4. Well, not heroic to all. Cash had attracted some barbs for playing in South Africa—winning that country's Open over Brad Gilbert, 7-6 (9-7), 4-6, 2-6, 6-0, 6-1, a few weeks before, near the end of the 1987 season. On entering the court he was greeted by anti-apartheid banners and shouting protesters. On the changeover after the seventh game, the young activists pitched two-dozen black tennis balls at Patrick before they were ushered out by security officers. After he left, Cash learned that he'd been fined $500 for calling Muster a nasty name. Apparently out to absorb as much opening-day atmosphere as possible, fifth-seeded Yannick Noah and Bahamian Roger Smith, No. 147, stayed on court for four hours, 51 minutes, an Aussie record that held for three years. Ignoring two match points in the 16th game of the last set, Noah sprang back to win the 73-game joust, 6-7 (7-9), 5-7, 6-4, 6-2, 16-14.

Ironically, the only outsider was the native, Pat Cash. For the second consecutive year, he qualified for the final by beating Ivan Lendl, 6-4, 2-6, 6-2, 4-6, 6-2, and for the second consecutive year he lost his national championship in five sets to a Swede.

In 1987, Cash slipped on the grass against Edberg. This time, on hard courts, he was beaten by Wilander, 6-3, 6-7 (3-7), 3-6, 6-1, 8-6, in what would be remembered as the year's most captivating major final, an all-around battle of extraordinary offense and defense as Wilander's retrieving and lobs finally broke down Cash's volleying. Cash fell behind, 2-0, in the decisive set, rose to 5-4 and in the next game was twice two points from the title against the Swede's serve. By defeating Edberg, 6-0, 6-7 (5-7), 6-3, 3-6, 6-1, and Cash back-to-back, Wilander not only eliminated the two previous champions but became only the second man to win major titles on three different surfaces-grass, clay, now hard—matching the achievement of Connors.

Memphis was the launch pad for Agassi, ranked No. 18 after winning his second career tournament, the U.S. Indoor Championships, over Mikael Pernfors, 6-4, 6-4, 7-5. At 17 years, 10 months, he was the youngest player to win the second oldest of U.S. titles. He followed with victories over Jimmy Arias in the U.S. Clay Court, 6-2, 6-2, and Slobodan Zivojinovic in the Tournament of Champions at Forest Hills, 7-5, 7-6 (7-2), 7-5. As a result, he was seeded ninth in the French Open.

Agassi reached the semifinals, the best American finish in three years, before he was worn down by Wilander, 4-6, 6-2, 7-5, 5-7, 6-0. But the Yank who received the best reception was, of all people, McEnroe. The man, who returned from a seven-month hiatus (and a plunge to No. 25 in world rankings) to defeat Edberg in the final of the Japan Open, 6-2, 6-2, wowed the

crowd in Paris with a reasonable facsimile of his championship form and three straight-set victories, the last over Chang, 6-0, 6-3, 6-1.

He even won a first-set tie-breaker over Lendl before falling, 6-7 (3-7), 7-6 (7-3), 6-4, 6-4. Lendl, the defending champ, then was eliminated, 7-6 (7-5), 7-5, 6-2, by unseeded Swede Jonas Svensson, who in turn was beaten by Frenchman Henri Leconte, 7-6 (7-3), 6-2, 6-3. Wilander breezed in the final, missing only two of 74 first serves and committing only nine unforced errors in a 7-5, 6-2, 6-1 rout of the local hero, who had served for the first set at 5-4.

Wimbledon was an American wasteland other than in doubles, where Flach and Seguso earned a second consecutive title. Agassi, no fan of grass, went home to Las Vegas after the French. McEnroe should have followed his lead. The man, seeded an unrealistic eighth, won only one match at the All England Club before being flattened by an Aussie, No. 64 Wally Masur, 7-5, 7-6 (7-5), 6-3. Connors, the fifth seed, lasted until the fourth round where he was bounced by hefty-serving German Patrik Kuhnen, 5-7, 7-6 (9-7), 7-6 (7-2), 6-7 (4-7), 6-3, over two rainy afternoons in the sodden "Graveyard" (Court 2), where the ball hardly bounced.

Connors, twice champion, winner of more singles here than any other man (81), was understandably peeved to be assigned for interment in that plot at that stage of the tournament and his career. He said he wouldn't return (but of course he did). Tim Mayotte, seeded 10th, was the last American. He was beaten in the quarters by his nemesis, Lendl, 7-6 (7-2), 7-6 (7-1), 6-3, against whom Tim was 0-12, 0-10 in tie-breakers. Lendl was having his usual harrowing lawn party: 6-1 in the fifth over Michiel Schapers (on haunted Court 2), then escaping a fifth-set match point—with a serve-and-volley no less!—and Mark Woodforde, 7-5, 6-7 (6-8), 6-7 (4-7), 7-5, 10-8.

Any dreams Wilander had of a Grand Slam ended in the quarters, where he was tormented by Mecir, 6-3, 6-1, 6-3. "My style is not suited to this surface," Wilander said. "If we played three of the four majors on clay, maybe I'd have a chance for the Slam."

One Swede whose style was suited to grass was Edberg. He was down two sets to love and 0-3, 0-40 in the third against the crafty Mecir before staging the comeback of his young career, 4-6, 2-6, 6-4, 6-3, 6-4. "It makes you feel really strong," he said, "that you should never give up."

That boosted him into the championship match against Becker. The two-time champion had slugged the incumbent, Cash, 6-4, 6-3, 6-4, and Lendl, 6-4, 6-3, 6-7 (8-10), 6-4, en route to another final and decided that, in his mind, he already had won a third title. Two weeks earlier, Edberg had double-faulted away the final of the Queen's Club tournament to Becker.

But this time, Edberg was mentally prepared for the challenge, even after London's dismal weather interrupted play in the first set and delayed completion of the match until Monday. He served well and volleyed impeccably in scoring a 4-6, 7-6 (7-2), 6-4, 6-2 victory that fulfilled the Swede's immense promise. Edberg fell to his knees and then onto his back on match point. "I couldn't think of anything else to do," he said.

Connors bounded back into the picture by beating Andres Gomez, 6-1, 6-4, in 102-degree heat in Washington, his first tournament victory in 45 months, and rolled into the U.S. Open quarterfinals without much opposition. But there the past was no match for the future as Agassi blasted him, 6-2, 7-6 (8-6), 6-1, securing the No. 1 U.S. ranking for the year, before bowing to Lendl, 7-6 (7-4), 6-1, 3-6, 6-1, the hardy perennial.

McEnroe, seeded a lowly 16th, stumbled in the other half of the draw, falling to Mark Woodforde in the second round, 7-5, 4-6, 6-7 (3-7), 6-3, 6-1. Wilander, the second seed, defeated two more unseeded players, Emilio Sanchez and No. 33 Darren Cahill of Australia, who had knocked off Becker, 6-3, 6-3, 6-2, in the second round, to earn the other berth in the final.

Seeking to become the first man to win four consecutive U.S. championships since the era of Bill Tilden and closing in on Connors' record of 159 weeks at the top of the rankings, Lendl fell one set and three weeks short against his Connecticut neighbor. In the longest Open final on record (four hours, 54 minutes), Wilander soared to his third major title of the year and to the top of the ATP ladder, 6-4, 4-6, 6-3, 5-7, 6-4. "I don't think I've ever felt better," he said.

Earlier in the tournament, he had served as a spokesman for the ATP, the players' association, which announced it was assuming control of the men's tour starting in the 1990 season. Nothing that happened in the final three months of 1988 altered the final standings. Not Mecir's 3-6, 6-2, 6-4, 6-2 victory over Mayotte in the Olympic gold-medal match, nor Becker's gutsy 5-7, 7-6 (7-5), 3-6, 6-2, 7-6 (7-5) conquest of Lendl in the Masters final. That ended with a whimper, a netcord dribbler off Boris' racket, equaling the closest finish—two points—of an important final: Ken Rosewall's 7-5 fifth set tie-breaker win over Rod Laver in the 1972 WCT final.

Ironically, neither Wilander nor Edberg, the major champions of the season, could stop Becker and West Germany from wresting away the Davis Cup, 4-1, at Goteborg in the waning days of the year. No fan of clay, Becker nevertheless beat Edberg, 6-3, 6-1, 6-4, opening day on the formerly good earth within the Scandinavium, where Sweden had mired the U.S. in 1984 and India 12 months before. But it was No. 79-ranked Charlie Steeb who truly stunned the home folks by ducking a match point while leading off with a resurgent 8-10, 1-6, 6-2, 6-4, 8-6, triumph over Wilander. That was no left-handed compliment Steeb paid Wilander, whose No. 1 ranking (made with three majors and three other titles on a 53-11 mark in 15 tourneys) quickly vanished, like the Cup.

1989

At the end of a memorable decade, the world said hello to Michael Chang and goodbye to

Chris Evert. If further proof were needed that a new era was at hand, it was to be found in the disposition of the Grand Slam events. Only one of the eight singles championships was awarded to a player older than 21.

That individual was Ivan Lendl, the fit Czech expatriate who captured his first Australian Open title at the outset of the season, regained his No. 1 ranking and, at the advanced age of 29, held off a late charge by Boris Becker. The latter added a first U.S. Open crown to his third Wimbledon title and capped an outstanding year by leading West Germany to its second consecutive Davis Cup. However, it was Chang, the 17-year-old American, who provided the most distinctive victory on the men's tour with an improbable triumph at the French Open.

Chang was born in 1972, one year after Evert, then 16, made her sensational debut in the U.S. Open. At 34, Evert decided to make her final tournament appearance in the same event where she first rose to prominence. The last of her major matches was a quarterfinal loss to Zina Garrison, 7-6 (7-2), 6-1, at Flushing Meadow. She concluded her career one month later by teaming with Martina Navratilova in the U.S. drive to a Federation Cup title in Tokyo.

As she had the previous year, Steffi Graf dominated the women's tour. At 20, the German lass even surpassed her 1988 record by winning 86 of 88 matches and 14 of 16 tournaments. But she was denied an unprecedented second successive Grand Slam when she was upset by Arantxa Sanchez Vicario, 7-6 (8-6), 3-6, 7-5, in the French final.

Sanchez Vicario thus became the first Spanish woman to win at Paris as well as the youngest of any nationality, at 17 years, 6 months. At least, she had a reputation as a dogged competitor on clay, had risen to No. 10 on the computer before the start of the tournament and was seeded seventh in the event. By comparison, Chang was a nobody.

Well, that's not completely true. He also demonstrated the patience to play forever, a re-

Seventeen-year-old Michael Chang was the toast of Paris—and his American followers—when he won the French Open in 1989. (Russ Adams)

quirement on dirt, had climbed to No. 19 in the rankings and was seeded 15th. Still, who was he to beat the likes of Lendl and Stefan Edberg? Well, he was the youngest male (17 years, 3 months) to win any of the four major events and he was the first U.S. man to succeed at Roland Garros in 34 years.

Not since Tony Trabert defeated Sven Davidson for his second consecutive title in 1955 had an American reigned in Paris. It was a drought that defied such U.S. champions as Arthur Ashe, Jimmy Connors and John McEnroe, as well as a legion of lesser players better suited to clay, among them Harold Solomon and Vitas Gerulaitis. And Chang's breakthrough heralded a reversal in the direction of U.S. tennis fortunes.

By the end of the season, no fewer than six Americans held places in the Top Ten, topped by

Arantxa Sanchez Vicario took the French from Steffi Graf in 1989, spoiling the German wunderkind's quest for consecutive Grand Slams. (Russ Adams)

McEnroe's climb to No. 4. For the first time since the advent of the computer in 1973, however, the elite group did not include Connors. The 37-year-old campaigner slipped to No. 11 despite increasing to 109 his record for tournament victories with triumphs at Toulouse (over McEnroe, 6-3, 6-3) and Tel Aviv (over Gilad Bloom, 6-1, 4-6, 6-1).

Connors won his first major tournament in 1974 (Australia), the same year Evert made her breakthrough at the French. They were more than contemporaries. Once upon a time, they were engaged to be married. But whereas Evert formally bade farewell to the crowd at Flushing Meadow, Connors vowed to press on even after being eliminated in the same round.

Of course, there was a major difference in the amount of fight left in the player. The 37-year-old Connors forced 19-year-old Andre Agassi, the top-ranked American, to a fifth set before yielding in a men's quarterfinal. He never surrendered. "The people were excited," Connors decided. "You know what? I was excited, too."

Damn right, he was planning to continue. But Evert knew she had had enough after her first season without a single tournament victory, let alone a major. She lost three consecutive finals in the spring, to Graf at Boca Raton 4-6, 6-2, 6-3, to Gabriela Sabatini at Key Biscayne (Lipton), 6-1, 4-6, 6-2 and, finally—did this convince her?—to 15-year-old Monica Seles of Yugoslavia (the female tour's newest sensation) at Houston, 3-6, 6-1, 6-4. Evert did manage to reach the semifinals at Wimbledon for the 17th time in 18 appearances and she bashed Seles, 6-0, 6-2, in her penultimate match at Flushing Meadow.

The symbol of athletic consistency finished on a high note, winning all five of her matches in Federation Cup play. Navratilova also was 5-0 as the U.S. won the team championship for the first time since the great rivals last pooled their talents in 1986 at Prague. They beat Spain, 3-0, Chris' valedictory: 6-3, 6-2, over Conchita Martinez. Sadly, Evert and Navratilova did not oppose each other at all in 1989 and the record of their meetings remained fixed in history at 43-37 in favor of Navratilova.

Although the latter retained her No. 2 ranking and won eight of 15 tournaments, Navratilova was frustrated by Graf in the two most significant tournaments she entered. The fraulein needed three sets on both occasions but nonetheless defeated Navratilova in the final at Wimbledon, 6-2, 6-7 (1-7), 6-1, and Flushing Meadow, 3-6, 7-5, 6-1. Graf also turned back the naturalized American in the final of the Virginia Slims Championships, 6-4, 7-5, 2-6, 6-2.

Sanchez Vicario's victory at Paris upset the rankings as well as Graf. By the end of the year, Arantxa had scrambled from No. 18 to No. 5, one place ahead of Seles. The 15-year-old Yugoslav, operating out of her new home base in Florida, made a stunning professional debut at Washington. She beat Larisa Savchenko, Robin White and Manuela Maleeva to reach the semifinals where an ankle injury forced her to default to Zina Garrison. Then she defeated Evert in the Houston final before pushing Graf in the French Open semifinals, 6-3, 3-6, 6-3.

Another teenager, Spain's Conchita Martinez, also made inroads, zooming to No. 7 on the WTA computer as a result of three tour victories. And, in a brief promo of coming attractions, 13-year-old Floridian Jennifer Capriati blitzed Clare Wood, 6-0, 6-0, in the course of another 7-0 Wightman Cup wipeout of the Brits by the U.S. Still an amateur, Capriati was the youngest participant ever in the event by a full two years.

While Graf remained atop the women's rankings, Mats Wilander began a precipitous drop from No. 1 to No. 13 at the Australian Open, one of three major titles he had claimed the previous year. The Swede, a three-time champion in the event, stumbled in the second round against No. 51 Ramesh Krishnan of India and never regained his equilibrium. Complaining of shin splints and a loss of motivation, Wilander failed to win a single tournament. He lost his only final, at the U.S. Pro in Boston, to Andres Gomez, 6-1, 6-4.

The other Swede with a major title to his credit in 1988 also was shut out. But Edberg was a finalist both at Paris and Wimbledon and he actually climbed the ladder to No. 3 with a strong finish, culminating in a 4-6, 7-6 (8-6), 6-3, 6-1 victory over Becker in the 20th and final edition of the season-ending Grand Prix Masters. He, too, had his problems in Melbourne when he suffered a back injury in the course of a 6-4, 6-0, 6-2 fourth-round victory over Pat Cash and had to withdraw.

With the field thinned, Lendl had a clear shot to one of the two Big Four titles that had eluded him and he made the most of the opportunity. He blasted 7th-seeded John McEnroe in a 7-6 (7-0), 6-2, 7-6 (7-2) quarterfinal, overcame 11th-seeded Thomas Muster of Austria in the semis, 6-2, 6-4,

5-7, 7-5, and then overpowered 9th-seeded Miloslav Mecir in the final much as he had at the 1986 U.S. Open, 6-2, 6-2, 6-2.

The women weren't much more competitive after Helena Sukova handed Navratilova a 6-2, 3-6, 9-7 quarterfinal defeat, recalling the 1984 semifinal upset that cost Martina a Grand Slam. Sukova outlasted unseeded Belinda Cordwell of New Zealand in the semis, 7-6 (7-2), 4-6, 6-2, but received a 6-4, 6-4 spanking in the final from Graf, who had crushed Sabatini in the semis with the loss of three games.

It was at Paris that the season took an abrupt turn. After both Evert and Navratilova declined to enter—preferring to devote extra time on preparations for Wimbledon—and Sabatini was upset in the fourth round by Mary Joe Fernandez, 6-4, 6-4, a third French title for Graf appeared a mere formality. She ceded a set to Seles in the semifinal, but it seemed unthinkable Steffi would lose to a 17-year-old appearing in her first major final.

Not since the 1962 Wimbledon final (Karen Hantze Susman over Vera Sukova) had a woman seeded as low as seventh won a major against a world-class field. But Sanchez Vicario had the spunk, the shots and the determination to stay in a gruelling match against a woman primed for her sixth consecutive Big Four title. Their match consumed 2 hours, 58 minutes, and it was a riveting demonstration of championship tennis.

Sanchez Vicario, unwilling to err in the clutch, achieved her upset with an extraordinary comeback from 3-5 in the third set, winning the last four games and 16 of the last 19 points. "This is a great day for me," she said. "This is the tournament I wanted to win all my life. This is the one I've been dreaming about."

She had grown up the smallest at 5-foot-5 in a tennis family. Two older brothers, Emilio and Javier, were on the men's tour and an older sister, Marisa, had played for Pepperdine University in California. She was the most competitive of the group.

"Off the court, she is sweet and charming," said her coach, Juan Nunez. "But when she gets on the court, she turns into a lion. What you saw out there was the lion."

Graf appeared pale and sad-eyed after failing to equal Navratilova's streak of six consecutive major titles. "Arantxa is a wonderful girl and she played unbelievable to win," said the German, who suffered cramps in the third set. "But I did nothing at all. It wasn't me out there. It was another person hitting those balls."

It was the second and final loss of the year for Graf (following a three-set defeat by Sabatini at Amelia Island, 3-6, 6-3, 7-5) but, for Sanchez Vicario, it was a peerless achievement. At the end of the match, she tossed her racket into the air and collapsed on the red clay. "It is the most joyous moment of my life," she said. "I cannot believe this. I have never been so happy."

No less remarkable was Chang's feat. If anything, it may have been more improbable. The 5-8, 135-pounder would have been unseeded if not for the absence of McEnroe and Muster, who suffered a serious knee injury when hit by a drunken driver on the eve of the Lipton final. The son of research chemists who had emigrated from Taiwan, the 17-year-old youngster seemed too small and too inexperienced for such a herculean task.

But he proved his stamina and his mettle in a fourth-round battle against the top-ranked Lendl, whom he trailed two sets to love. Instead of capitulating, he fought through debilitating cramps to oust the No. 1 player, 4-6, 4-6, 6-3, 6-3, 6-3. He was in such distress late in the fourth set and early in the fifth that he stood at changeovers, munched on bananas, staggered about the court between points and even served underhanded on one occasion, and psyched Lendl into a double fault, ending the 4-hour, 39-minute struggle by standing directly behind the service line to receive.

"I've never seen a player show such courage on a tennis court," said Trabert. Chang's coach, Jose Higueras, called it "the most incredible match I've ever seen."

But that only earned him a berth in the quarterfinals, where he beat Ronald Agenor in four sets. There was much more grinding ahead, including five lost sets in perhaps the hardest won of French titles: Agenor, the Haitian, 6-4, 2-6, 6-4 (from 1-4), 7-6 (8-6), saving a set point, in 3 hours, 12 minutes; tenacious Russian Andrei Chesnokov, 6-1, 5-7, 7-6 (7-4), 7-5, in 4 hours, 5 minutes; then 3 hours, 41 minutes for the title with third-seeded Edberg. Stefan had beaten Italian Open champ Alberto Mancini, 6-1, 6-3, 7-6 (7-5), and second-seeded Becker, 6-3, 6-4, 5-7, 3-6, 6-2.

Realistically, that should have been the end of the road for Chang. But the youngster stretched the imagination once more, rallying from one set down and saving 13 straight break points over one stretch. He emerged with a shocking 6-2, 3-6, 4-6, 6-4, 6-2 victory from 0-2 in the fifth. "Whatever happens from now on, good or bad," he said, "this will stay with me for the rest of my life."

Edberg, with three major titles to his credit as well as a superior serve and volley, appeared rattled by his opponent's bottomless reserve. He had 26 break points in the match and converted only six.

"He just keeps coming back," the Swede said. "I have to admire him for it. But you know these young guys. They just hit. They don't have to think."

With his victory, Chang surpassed Wilander (17 years, 9 months) as the youngest male winner in Paris and supplanted Becker (17 years, 7 months) as the youngest male winner of a major event. One of the people who was happiest for him was Trabert, the last previous American to win the French title.

"Chang is a little bit different from other young players," said Trabert, now a television analyst. "Too many of them aren't patient and willing to play long points. I think it should be a personal point of pride to be a well-rounded player." Michael's patience had lasted through 21 hours,

18 minutes on court in burying the U.S. jinx at Roland Garros, where 532 American guys had been laid to rest in the amber soil between Trabert's and his victory.

If that event offered an unlikely duo of titlists, the next major produced a seemingly inevitable pairing. Becker and Graf had been raised in nearby towns in the southeastern corner of West Germany and had known each other since they were children. "I used to be the worst in the boys and she was the best in the girls," Becker recalled with good humor. "So, when I was maybe nine and she was eight, I would have to hit with her."

Each had grown up to be a Wimbledon champion but not in the same year. In 1989, on the grass of the All England Club, they became the Teutonic Twosome. Even the weather cooperated, in a fashion. Rain pushed back the women's final one day so that Graf and Becker might receive their awards at Centre Court on the same afternoon.

Graf, the defender, had the tougher final. She dropped the first set of the tournament before subduing Navratilova, 6-2, 6-7 (1-7), 6-1. But she finished in championship form, firing an ace past the eight-time titleholder. Graf won 17 of 22 points on her serve in the final set and said she was playing so well. ". . . I was starting to laugh . . . I was so loose out there and it showed in my tennis."

Earlier in the tournament, she had toyed with the opposition, including Evert. The latter struggled from 2-5 in the third set to defeat Laura Golarsa of Italy, 6-3, 2-6, 7-5, and earn the satisfaction of one last trip to the Wimbledon semifinals, her 17th. At least, that gave her an opportunity to wave goodbye from Centre Court after her thrashing by Graf, 6-2, 6-1.

"A lot of things were going through my mind," Evert said. "You know, Centre Court is the greatest court in the whole world and I'll always remember it."

In contrast to Graf, Becker had a difficult semifinal and smooth sailing in the final. He was thankful for the 76-minute rain delay in the midst of the third set against Lendl, wherein he regained his composure and posted a 7-5, 6-7 (2-7), 2-6, 6-4, 6-3 victory. Taking the first set in 22 minutes, he then overpowered Edberg, 6-0, 7-6 (7-1), 6-4, to reverse the result of the previous year's final.

It was Becker's third Wimbledon title but, after two years of disappointment, he seemed to appreciate this one more than the others. "Then it was like a fairy tale," he said of the consecutive championships he won as a teenager. "It wasn't true. I didn't know what I was doing."

This was real. And the two champions from a country with no previous championship there shared the first dance at the Wimbledon Ball.

The U.S. Open lacks such a formal conclusion. Otherwise, the pair could have continued their dance in New York. Graf and Becker each left Flushing Meadow with another major title. They had to work harder than they had at Wimbledon and they had to share the spotlight with a departing champion.

Graf was severely tested twice, by Sabatini in the semifinals, 3-6, 6-4, 6-2, and, once again, by Navratilova in the ultimate match. Against the Argentine, she lost the first set and overcame leg cramps in the stifling heat to triumph. Afterward, she had to be treated with liquids and an ice massage.

Navratilova appeared to have the final won on at least a couple of occasions. She was only two games from victory in the second set before double-faulting away a service game. Then she had a break point for a 5-4 lead and squandered that. Seeing the opening, Graf mobilized her gifts and won, 3-6, 7-5, 6-1. "I thought I had lost," the champion said, "but I kept fighting. I think I made her do more."

"I was close," said Navratilova, her face streaked with tears. "I was as close as you get."

Close but no trophy. Graf got that, for the seventh time in her last eight major finals.

Becker almost didn't make it out of the second round, where he faced two match points against vagabond Derrick Rostagno in a fourth set tie-breaker. On the second, his running forehand ticked the net and hopped over the Californian's waiting racket. Becker took that bit of good luck and won the next two points for the set, and the arduous match that had looked lost long before, 1-6, 6-7 (1-7), 6-3, 7-6 (8-6), 6-3. "I've thought about that shot every day for 10 days," he said on the day he won his first U.S. Open Championship.

Connors' 16th trip to the quarters was unrewarded as Agassi made a surprising charge to score his own first victory in a five-set trial, 6-1, 4-6, 0-6, 6-3, 6-4. Jimmy, straining with the crowd behind him, gave them hope as Andre served for it at 5-2. Flashing the old moxie, the champ seized nine of 10 points to 5-4, 0-15—but had nothing more to give. McEnroe, seeded fourth, didn't get that far, upended in the second round by a qualifier, No. 110 Paul Haarhuis, 6-4, 4-6, 6-3, 7-5, an astonishing reversal.

"Where are you from?" a reporter asked the anonymous Dutchman. "Mars," was the smiling reply, and Mac may have believed it. Defending champ Wilander, fifth-seeded, undoubtedly wondered about the provenance of his kid conqueror, also in the second round, 5-7, 6-3, 1-6, 6-1, 6-4. The 18-year-old's name was Pete Sampras, who in 12 months would illuminate the Meadow, and continue to do so, passing Mac and Wilander, catching up with Connors in the matter of majors.

Cruising past Aaron Krickstein in the semis, 6-4, 6-3, 6-4, Becker needed 3 hours and 51 minutes to defeat Lendl, 7-6 (7-2), 1-6, 6-3, 7-6 (7-4). The latter was appearing in his eighth consecutive final, a Tilden-tying achievement. But once Becker got a full head of steam, neither Ivan nor the ghost of Big Bill could stop him. "He just has more power in his game than I do." Lendl said.

For Becker, the victory proved that the man was more than splendor in the grass, that he was able to beat a world-class field somewhere other than Wimbledon. He had filled in the gaps in his game since the summer of '85, had firmed his groundstrokes along with his tenacity. Now he was a worthy challenger for the honor of top-ranked men's player on the planet. "If I'm not No. 1," he said, "then I'm quite close to it."

But he couldn't close the narrow gap before year's end, despite his two majors and a 64-8 match record on winning six of 13 tournaments. Boris' magnificent year had included possibly the most remarkable win—6-7 (4-7), 6-7 (5-7), 7-6 (7-3), 6-3, 6-4, over Agassi in the Cup semis. They had stopped at midnight, returning the next day for the fifth. From a break behind in the last set, 4-3, Boris swooped to take the last three games, and launch the 3-2 victory over the U.S. at Munich. After the always willing Brad Gilbert, called up to sub for sore-shouldered McEnroe, beat Charlie Steeb, 6-2, 2-6, 2-6, 6-4, 6-4, Agassi served for a brisk victory over Becker at 6-5, 30-15, in the third. Andre appeared a lock, assuring his country a place in the final: merely two points away—but two points Boris refused to relinquish as he began to turn the splendid match his way on the slick, fast carpet.

Enspirited by finishing off Agassi, Boris took a brief rest, then kept going in the doubles. His flame ignited Eric Jelen, and together they stunned Ken Flach and Robert Seguso, 3-6, 7-6 (7-5), 6-4, 7-6 (7-3), for a 2-1 lead. But then Agassi, who started out as if to stomp Steeb (3-2 in the second, 2-0, 40-0 in the third), strangely, simply melted away uncompetitively, 4-6, 6-4, 6-4, 6-2.

If anything, Boris was even more brutally Beckerian in the final (3-2 over Sweden at Stuttgart for a second straight Cup). He ripped up No. 3 Edberg and the previous year's No. 1 Wilander on a loss of 12 games: respective 6-2, 6-2, 6-4, and 6-2, 6-0, 6-2 triumphs, probably the worst thrashings dealt such elite men in Cup history. Boris wrapped those around his and Jelen's rock-ribbed, tense victory over Jan Gunnarson and Anders Jarryd, 7-6 (8-6), 6-4, 3-6, 6-7 (4-7), 6-4.

With all his heroics, Becker was still second to Lendl, who won 10 of 17 starts on a 79-7 record and won record earnings of $2,334,367. Ivan lost the Masters semifinal to Edberg, 7-6 (7-5), 7-5, who then cut down Becker the following day, 4-6, 7-6 (8-6), 6-3, 6-1.

Still, the Open was as notable for a dignified exit as for Becker's grand entrance into the circle of champions. Evert made her last stand on the stadium court in the quarterfinals against Garrison, an opponent who had lined up for her autograph 10 years earlier in Houston. In the end, her nerves betrayed her. Twice she served for the first set and was broken both times, 7-6 (7-1), 6-2.

Afterward, Garrison was as spent as Evert. "It was the hardest match I've ever played," the winner said, "because it was so emotional." At the end, Evert's eyes were red but her voice was unshaken.

"This place is special to me," she said. "I knew my last match here would be sad, win or lose."

Evert departed with records for most Open victories (101) and most career singles titles (157). Her 5-0 record in subsequent Federation Cup brought her lifetime record to 1,309-146, an astonishing percentage of .900.

"I really can't fathom it [her retirement] because we have been at it since 1973," Navratilova had said at Wimbledon. "So a piece of me will be gone with her." And a piece of tennis as well.

Also fading away was the men's Grand Prix format, a victim of the ATP revolt. For the record, the last GP event in history was the Masters Doubles at the Royal Albert Hall in London on Dec. 10. McEnroe's younger brother, Patrick, teamed with Jim Grabb to beat Wimbledon champions Anders Jarryd and John Fitzgerald in the match that brought down the curtain on two decades of play, Jack Kramer's brainchild, the Grand Prix, 7-5, 7-6 (7-4), 5-7, 6-3.

The Davis Cup, Wimbledon and the U.S. Open made Boris Becker's hit list in 1989. (Mitchell Reibel)

1990

For the first time in the Open era, tennis was just that. The four major singles titles for men and women were divided eight ways. The champions represented seven different nations on three continents and at least two generations.

While Martina Navratilova set a record for the ages, Monica Seles established another for the underaged. Although the gap wasn't quite so large among their male counterparts, Andres Gomez scored a stunning triumph for the 30-and-over crowd in Paris and Pete Sampras became a U.S. Open champion 28 days after celebrating his 19th birthday. Ironically, each defeated Andre Agassi for his first major title.

This also was the year in which Stefan Edberg, the Wimbledon champion for a second time, dislodged from No. 1 Ivan Lendl, who successfully defended his Australian title. Graf continued at the top of the women's charts but, after losing the French and U.S. finals to Seles and Gabriela Sabatini, respectively, her reign was seriously threatened. And John McEnroe paid for his years of sins against the tennis establishment when he was defaulted in the midst of a major tournament, the Australian.

Astonishing, and then some, was Thomas Muster. Not only was he back in uniform—he was winning, and more impressively than ever, rising to his highest ranking, No. 7! This only months after his career seemed to have been left in a Miami parking lot where his left knee was wrecked in a collision with a drunken driver. It was the evening before he was to play the 1989 Lipton final against Ivan Lendl. Severed ligaments required immediate surgery, and the prognosis for resuming tennis wasn't good. But the bellowing Moo Man was as steel-willed off court as on. He went at rehab as though it were a major final, and he showed up at the Italian Open, in a wheel chair, vowing he would play at Il Foro Italiano in 1990. True to his word, he returned to take the Italian title, beating Andrei Chesnokov, 6-1, 6-3, 6-1, after eluding three match points in the semi over Andres Gomez, 5-7, 6-4, 7-6 (7-2). He had actually returned to competition in autumn of 1989, reaching the quarters at Barcelona, semis at Vienna. Eight months after the accident, in January, he won Adelaide over Jimmy Arias, 3-6, 6-2, 7-5, and never looked back.

Perhaps the most encouraging development at the start of a new decade was the emergence of Florida teenager Jennifer Capriati, who received $5 million in endorsement contracts before striking her first pulverizing groundstrokes for pay. Making the most widely ballyhooed professional debut in tennis history, 23 days before her 14th birthday at Boca Raton, Fla., she declared perceptively, "The press is out of control!" True enough as reporters and cameras appeared from across the world to record the carnival and the child's initial pro steps, a 7-6 (7-1), 6-1, win over seasoned Mary Lou Piatek Daniels.

Fourteen-year-old Jennifer Capriati wasted no time in fulfilling her $5-million endorsement contracts. (Mitchell Reibel)

True, too, she demonstrated what the fuss was all about, mowing down four more foes before losing a close final to Sabatini, 6-4, 7-5. She even had an odd-couple doubles win (first and last pro appearances) with 46-year-old Billie Jean King (6-2, 6-3, over Laura Golarsa and Claudia Porwik) in a tournament that quickly became known as the Virginia Slims of Capriati. Then she became the youngest ever semifinalist at any major, the French. A fourth-rounder at Wimbledon and the U.S., she plucked her first title at Puerto Rico (over Zina Garrison, 5-7, 6-4, 6-1), had a 42-11 match record and a No. 8 world ranking at season's close.

Another prosperous rookie was the men's tour, managed for the first time by the players themselves. The ATP conducted 75 tournaments on six continents, culminating in season-ending singles and doubles championships. Agassi won the former, defeating Edberg in the final at Frankfurt, 5-7, 7-6, 7-5, 6-2, and the team of Guy Forget and Jakob Hlasek triumphed over Sergio Casal and Emilio Sanchez in the latter, 6-4, 7-6, 5-7, 6-4, staged at Sanctuary Cove, Australia.

Less successful was the Grand Slam Cup, inaugurated by the International Tennis Federation in conjunction with officials of the four majors. Although the December event carried a staggering purse of $6 million, many elite pros—including German star Boris Becker—boycotted the competition in Munich because it detracted from the ATP Tour playoffs. Sampras defeated fellow American Brad Gilbert in straight sets for the $2-million first prize, 6-3, 6-4, 6-2.

There were no melancholy retirement scenes such as that provided the previous year by Chris Evert but an historic event passed from the tennis calendar with the suspension of the Wightman Cup between U.S. and British women. The competition, first staged in 1923, had grown too one-sided to attract attention on either side of the Atlantic. The U.S. had won the last 11 contests for a 51-10 lead.

The U.S. claimed each of the other major team championships. Capriati, the rookie, won all five of her singles matches without the loss of a set, beating Leila Meskhi, 7-6, 6-2, in the final. But it took a Gigi Fernandez–Zina Garrison doubles operation as the clincher, 6-4, 6-3, over Larisa Savchenko and Natasha Zvereva, as the U.S. retained the Federation Cup by defeating the Soviet Union, 2-1, in Atlanta. Agassi and Michael Chang were the stalwarts as the host country took possession of the Davis Cup for the first time in eight years by beating Australia, 3-2.

Agassi led off, struggling to beat young unknown giant, 6-foot-4 Richard Fromberg, 4-6, 6-2, 4-6, 6-2, and Chang crushed Darren Cahill, 6-2, 7-6 (7-4), 6-0, for a 2-0 lead, setting up Jim Pugh and Rick Leach for the clincher, 6-4, 6-2, 3-6, 7-6 (7-2) over Pat Cash and John Fitzgerald. It was a bizarre windup to the 29th Cup for the

U.S., played indoors in Florida while sun baked the roof of St. Petersburg's Suncoast Dome. And on clay, so often the burial ground for U.S. teams. But the dirt, specially trucked in at a cost of $50,000, was what the doctor—captain Tom Gorman—ordered to bog down the best Aussie, Cash, who thus wasn't even selected to oppose the American baseliners.

Aussie captain Neale Fraser thought it was a dirty trick, the Yanks souping-down the court for the 42nd renewal in the 85-year-old rivalry between the Cup's most competitive—yet closest—adversaries. But the USTA had learned in 1984 from the Swedes, who mired their American visitors with a hastily spread earthen rectangle indoors at Gotenborg. The engagement drew American record Cup crowds, a 50,962 total of which the middle day 18,156 was high, topping 17,994 on the first day as well as 17,445 at Flushing Meadow for the 1981 opener against Czechoslovakia.

Czechoslovakia was the quarterfinal problem in Prague solved largely by life-saver Aaron Krickstein, 4-1, a last-minute stand-in for pouting Agassi. The Kricker stopped towering Milan Srejber, 4-6, 7-6 (7-5), 7-6 (7-5), 6-7 (4-7), 6-3, and got the decider over hot lefty Petr Korda, 6-2, 6-3, 1-6, 6-3, after Leach and Pugh beat the two Czechs, 6-4, 6-4, 6-4. But it was 18-year-old Chang, youngest American to play for a Cup winner, who gave the key push to the final in a 3-2 screamer at Vienna. In the decisive fifth match, he lost the first two sets to Horst Skoff, then won the third before they were halted by darkness. On the following gloomy, soggy afternoon, gritty Michael wrapped up the semifinal, 3-6, 6-7 (4-7), 6-4, 6-4, 6-3.

Thomas Muster, improving his clay-court Cup record to 24-0, had busted both American starters, Chang, 4-6, 6-2, 6-2, 6-4, and the returned prodigal, Agassi, 6-2, 6-2, 7-6 (7-2), but couldn't quite make it in doubles as he and Alex Antonitsch were blocked by an almost airtight, drizzle-disregarding performance by Leach and Pugh, 7-6 (7-4), 3-6, 6-0, 7-5. That left it all to

Chang and Skoff as 18,000 in a chilly soccer stadium kept warm by blowing horns and roaring themselves hoarse for "Horstie."

No American had been in quite such a predicament since Don Budge 53 years before in the semifinal against Germany that would assure the end of the only Cup drought longer than this one: 10 years. With everything riding on the fifth set of the fifth match in 1937, both Budge (over Gottfried von Cramm) and Chang revived from two sets down. Such dissimilar characters and settings: these two Californians—tall, stylish Budge, a big server comfortable in his forays to the net, and stumpy Chang, the relentless baseline retriever. Budge was on the sunny lawn of neutral Wimbledon. Chang, in the *Sturm und Drang* of the bleak enemy camp, had to go to bed as the loser, behind 2-1 in sets. But Budge and he had fighting hearts in common. Budge surged from 1-4 in the fifth; Chang and Skoff kept breaking each other in the tipsy fourth and fifth (11 breaks in 19 games), but the teenager's nerve and legs were stronger.

For a topsy-turvy year, 1990 began in conventional fashion. Graf won an eighth major championship in her last nine attempts by bashing Mary Joe Fernandez, 6-3, 3-6, 6-4, at the Australian Open. The latter had upset third-seeded Zina Garrison, 1-6, 6-2, 8-6, en route to her first major final in a field that did not include Navratilova and Seles.

The top men turned out in greater numbers at Finders Park but the final ended in disappointment. Edberg, who played brilliantly in routing Mats Wilander in the semifinals, 6-1, 6-1, 6-2, suffered a torn abdominal muscle in the midst of the third set of his showdown with Lendl and could not continue. Lendl was awarded a 4-6, 7-6 (7-3), 5-2 (ret.) victory and his second consecutive Australian title.

At Melbourne, the first of the major tournaments was spiced by the spectacle of McEnroe's banishment. After the testy one received two code violations for racket abuse and intimidation of a linesman during his fourth-round match against Mikael Pernfors, he cursed umpire Gerry Armstrong and referee Ken Farrar. Under the new three-step code of conduct introduced at the start of the season, Mac was automatically disqualified, though ahead, 1-6, 6-4, 5-7, 4-2.

Despite his history of misbehavior, it marked the man's only default in a major, in fact the only such disqualification from a major event during the open era. McEnroe, who had disqualified himself in 1987 by walking away from a World Team Cup final, defaulting to Miloslav Mecir, was fined $6,500 and the setback was the first of many in an erratic year that saw him, fourth-seeded, bounced in the first round at Wimbledon by No. 129 Derrick Rostagno, 7-5, 6-4, 6-4, reach the semifinals of the U.S. Open, post a lone tournament victory and drop from No. 4 to No. 13 in the ATP rankings.

As it had been the previous year, Paris was the site of two startling results. Considering the form she displayed in routing Navratilova, 6-1, 6-1, at the Italian Open and in terminating Graf's 66-match winning steak (second longest of the modern era) in the final of the German Open, 6-4, 6-3. Seles' triumph in the French was not a stunning upset on a par with Sanchez Vicario's victory in 1989. Still, the two-fisted teenager's 7-6 (8-6), 6-4 conquest of Graf suggested a new order in women's tennis.

Before taking on the top-ranked German, Seles eliminated Capriati, 6-2, 6-2, in a match that was a preview of the future. For Capriati, who had dropped only 20 games in her five previous matches, the 62-minute rout was an educational experience, not unlike her first visit to Notre Dame. And her opponent was sure she would be back. "I have the feeling we're going to be playing many, many more times," Seles said.

Her current rivalry, however, was with Graf and, suddenly, they appeared to be equals. Although the German still had that booming forehand, her slice backhand left her vulnerable to Seles, who powers the ball from both sides. "She hits like she means it," Graf said.

Additionally, the favorite was bothered by allergies that plague her every spring in Paris and press reports from back home that charged her father with impregnating a German model only slightly older than Steffi. There was a vulnerability about her that no one had sensed since she ascended to the top.

Graf rallied from a 1-4 deficit to force a tie-breaker, where she won the first five points and led, 6-2. One point from the set, however, she dropped the next six, double-faulting on her fourth and final set point. "That's when I knew I had her," Seles said.

In her first major final, the latter saved two break points in the ninth game of the second set and then broke Graf in the following game for the biggest victory of her burgeoning career. Then Seles tossed her racket to the clouds and hugged her father, Karolj, the cartoonist who took his daughter from Yugoslavia to Florida with the intention of making her a champion. He used to draw pictures of comic-strip characters on the balls and have Seles slug them.

At the very least, the victory at Roland Garros made her famous for something other than her grunting on court, her cackle during press interviews and her unruly mane. "I didn't want to go into the history books 20 years from now," she said, and have people read, 'She was a great grunter, a great giggler and had a lot of hair.' "

Now she had one for the books, a major championship. Graf appeared wasted after the defeat, only the second in her last 74 matches. "I'm lacking a little bit right now," she said. "I'm not hitting the ball like I used to. There's something missing."

Among the missing in Paris were Navratilova and Lendl. Both were consumed with preparations for Wimbledon, a tournament where the woman would be seeking a record ninth title and the man a fulfilling first. Inadvertently, Lendl's decision not to enter the French had a major impact on the results.

Gomez, the man who would become king on the clay, was weighing an offer to serve as a commentator on Ecuadorian television at Paris until he learned that Lendl was bypassing the tournament to practice on grass. The Czech star had eliminated him in four previous French Opens. Gomez had taken a vacation from the tour in 1988 after the birth of his first son and even considered a permanent leave after his ranking plunged to No. 43.

At 30, he seemed an unlikely semifinalist, let alone champion. But, given his first chance at a final four in a major event, he bulldozed Thomas Muster of Austria, 7-5, 6-1, 7-5. That earned him a berth opposite the outrageous Agassi, who appeared finally to be living up to his advertising image as the hottest thing on tour.

The youngster from Las Vegas, seeded third, emerged as the favorite in the draw after the Tuesday Massacre, the unprecedented first-round removals of the first and second seeds, and by teenagers: Edberg, the finalist of 1989, tumbling to the consistency of No. 46, Sergi Bruguera (a future champ), 6-4, 6-2, 6-2, and Becker, riddled by a missile-serving lefty (19 aces), No. 51 Goran Ivanisevic, 5-7, 6-4, 7-5, 6-2. Agassi also gained attention by engaging in a verbal battle with Philippe Chatrier, president of the ITF and the reigning potentate of the tournament, after the official took one look at Agassi's hot lava (pink) and black tennis ensemble and issued a statement that the French Open would consider requiring predominantly white clothing the following year. Agassi responded by calling the man a "bozo," an insult even in a country that reveres Jerry Lewis.

But the man brought more than bicycle shorts and a matching bandana to the event. He had the talent to whip his 1989 Paris conqueror, Jim Courier, 6-7 (8-10), 6-1, 6-4, 6-0, defending champion Michael Chang, 6-2, 6-1, 4-6, 6-2, and Jonas Svensson, 6-1, 6-4, 3-6, 6-3, en route to what appeared to be a coronation. Gomez was one of the most popular players in the world among his peers but, Agassi pledged, "He's going to be in for a long afternoon because I want it bad."

Surprise. Gomez made relatively short work of the American, 10 years his junior. In the match of his career, he dismissed Agassi, 6-3, 2-6, 6-4, 6-4, claiming the first Big Four title for Ecuador. "I've been coming here for many years," he said, "and I've been dreaming about this day."

The South American served 10 aces to his opponent's one and he demonstrated more bounce despite the age differential. Although Gomez had 72 unforced errors, he also hit 58 winners in becoming the oldest French singles champ in 18 years. "I don't think of this as a sunset," he said. "I think of it as a sunrise."

At 33, Navratilova was seeking a final sunrise of her own at Wimbledon. Three years without a major victory, she trained diligently under Craig Kardon and her latest coach/motivator, Billie Jean King, for the triumph that would distance her from Helen Wills Moody, the eight-time champion of an earlier era. As it developed, she was virtually unchallenged.

Despite her problems in Paris, Graf still was favored. But from the moment she set foot in London, the German was under siege. If it wasn't the sinus problem that caused her to fly home for treatment during a weekend break, then it was the tabloid press which had a field day with the story of her father and the suddenly nefarious Nicole Meissner, whose provocative photos appeared almost daily in the sensational journals. Tournament officials limited questions to tennis at interview sessions although that failed to stop the gossip.

When they weren't harassing Graf, the arbiters of England's morals were going after the new generation of grunters, Seles in particular. *The Sun* unveiled a Grunt-o-meter, with which it allegedly measured the chief offender at 82 decibels— "between a pneumatic drill and a diesel train." As silly as this appeared, the new chairman of the tournament, John Curry, said he would "readily relax the all-white clothes rule if I could just get rid of the grunts."

"Gaby [Sabatini], [Anke] Huber and Jennifer grunt," Seles said. "But probably I'm the loudest. I don't know. I don't even realize I do it until I watch tape of myself on television. I think it's better than it was last year or in the French Open but I can't get rid of it."

Zina Garrison saved officials the trouble of silencing the teenager. Overcoming a match point with a forehand blast, the U.S. veteran rallied to defeat Seles in the quarterfinals, 3-6, 6-3, 9-7. Not only did it halt her opponent's winning streak at six tournaments and 36 matches but it prevented a semifinal showdown between Seles and Graf.

"Playing within my older self," Garrison called her more relaxed approach. And she laughed. "I'm 26," she explained. "Old person on the tour now."

From one standpoint, at least, she had been bypassed. Garrison spent years trying unsuccessfully to crack the ranks of the elite when Chris Evert and Navratilova ruled the sport. Then Graf had zoomed past, followed by Seles. Only last fall, after her loss to Navratilova at Flushing Meadow and her marriage to Willard Jackson, she said, "Since I was 16, I felt I would win Wimbledon and the U.S. Open. I still do."

It didn't seem to faze her that her next opponent would be Graf, who had ended Capriati's summer vacation with a 6-2, 6-4 decision in the fourth round. Although Garrison had beaten Graf only once in six matches—in their first meeting when the German was 16—the American was confident. "I've always wanted to play her on the grass," she said.

She made the most of the opportunity in what the normally understated Dan Maskell, who had been telecasting the championships for the BBC since the dawn of time, called an "epic match."

In denying Graf entry to a major final after a record 13 consecutive appearances, Garrison overcame not only the German but her own nerves in a 6-3, 3-6, 6-4 triumph. She served out the match by winning the last four points in succession, capped by a glorious ace.

"My first thought was to hit it to the forehand," she said, "and right at the last moment, for some reason, my racket went to the backhand court, and it worked. I mean, it was just meant to be, I think."

To her credit, Graf declined to blame her third loss of the year on either physical or emotional problems, although the ever-vigilant club committee shielded her from elaboration. "I was eager, I was ready," she said. "It was not my day. She didn't make mistakes. She used to make much more errors, unforced errors especially, but she didn't do that today at all." Nevertheless, Graf decided, her conqueror had no chance in the final. "Zina doesn't have the game to beat Martina," she said.

Certainly, there was little in the head-to-head record that suggested a titanic struggle. Of the 28 matches between the two friends, Navratilova had won 27. Moreover, in her 6-3, 6-4 semifinal victory over Sabatini, she had demonstrated she was still near the top of her form.

Garrison, who didn't have a clothing deal and was wearing Navratilova's signature line, was compensated on the eve of the championship by a six-figure contract with Reebok, one of several the player landed for her attention-getting run. Additionally, her presence in the title match stirred Althea Gibson, the last black woman to win a major event in 1958, to fly in from New York. "She came out and watched me practice," Garrison said. "She's a very nice lady."

But no amount of personal or financial support for her opponent was going to stop Navratilova when she was this close to an historic accomplishment. In the match and the tournament that defined her career, Navratilova was more than triumphant. She was regal in a 6-4, 6-1 victory.

Her virtually flawless performance at Centre Court, where nerves can be stretched as taut as racket strings, was one to be preserved in a time capsule. "It was my match to win," Navratilova decided, "and I wasn't afraid of it."

Thus did she surpass Helen Wills Moody, who lost only one of 56 singles matches at Wimbledon in nine tournaments from 1924 through 1933.

"Little Miss Poker Face," as she was known, won her last Wimbledon final at the age of 32 years, 270 days, making her the oldest female champion since 1914. The 33-year-old Navratilova, 99-9 on the most famous lawns in the world, also took that distinction from Wills. Charlotte Cooper Sterry was 37 as the 1908 champ.

Navratilova was rewarded for her decision to train harder, to bypass Paris for additional practice on the grass. Lendl, who made a greater commitment, who journeyed to Australia during the winter for seven weeks of training under coach Tony Roche and who (after attending the birth of his first child, Marika) spent six weeks on the grass in England, did not. After playing brilliantly in the traditional warmup tournament at Queen's Club, blasting McEnroe and Becker among others, he wilted at Wimbledon.

Lendl, top-seeded, used a Czech term to describe his obsession for the only major title he lacked. "Zazrany," he called it. "It means very much into it, almost stubborn." Alas, after weaving fitfully into the semifinals, he staggered out of the tournament following a crushing 6-1, 7-6 (7-2), 6-3 loss to Edberg. He promised to return.

Edberg, third-seeded, earned his third trip to the final, all against second-seeded Becker, who received a scare from 18-year-old hotshot Ivanisevic—his conqueror at the French Open—before advancing, 4-6, 7-6 (7-4), 6-0, 7-6 (7-5). Not since 1894, when Wilfred Baddeley challenged Joshua Pim in their fourth consecutive championship match, had the title contest been an object of such familiarity.

Pete Sampras aced Andre Agassi to death in the U.S. Open final in 1990 and capped the year by banking $2 million in Munich from the Grand Slam Cup. (Russ Adams)

This time they produced the longest men's final since Jimmy Connors—sidelined almost the entire 1990 season by a wrist injury that would require surgery—defeated McEnroe in 1982. However, the five-setter wasn't nearly as strained, partly because their similar serve-and-volley styles allowed for no rallies, partly because they were unable to play their best tennis at the same time. Edberg won, 6-2, 6-2, 3-6, 3-6, 6-4.

It was a match full of British civility, one in which each player attempted to hand the championship to the other. Becker made the final gesture when he blew a routine volley and lost his serve from 3-1, 30-0 in the fifth set. The two hugged at the conclusion.

Inspired by the victory, Edberg won his next three tournaments, at Los Angeles, Cincinnati and Long Island, displacing Lendl at the top of the rankings on Aug. 13. Inexplicably, the No. 1 player in the world then lost his first-round match at the U.S. Open to No. 52, lefty Alexander Volkov of the Soviet Union, 6-3, 7-6 (7-1), 6-2, an all-time opening upset, considering Edberg's top seeding and Wimbledon title.

Lendl also was disappointed, failing to reach the final at Flushing Meadow for the first time since 1981. In fact, he didn't survive the quarter-finals, beaten in five sets by the eager Sampras, who was credited with 24 aces and 27 service winners, 6-4, 7-6 (7-4), 3-6, 4-6, 6-2.

Much of the crowd's attention at the Open was diverted by the restoration of the McEnroe legend. Unseeded for the first time since his Open debut 13 years earlier, the former champion went back to his old coach, Tony Palafox, prepared diligently and then won over the fans by beating 10th-seeded Andrei Chesnokov, 6-3, 7-5, 6-4, seventh-seeded Emilio Sanchez with much of the old delicate touch, cancelling a set point in the tie-breaker, 7-6 (8-6), 3-6, 4-6, 6-4, 6-3, and David Wheaton, 6-1, 6-4, 6-4. But he couldn't cope with Sampras' power, the youngster finishing him off, 6-2, 6-4, 3-6, 6-3, with his 17th ace. "It's been a great run," McEnroe decided.

It was an even more remarkable tournament for Sampras, the lanky and laid-back Californian who was ranked No. 81 as recently as January, who hadn't won his first pro tournament until February in Philadelphia, over Gomez, 7-6 (7-4), 7-5, 6-2. But the best was yet to come—against Agassi, who had overcome Becker, 6-7 (10-12), 6-3, 6-2, 6-3, setting the stage for the first all-American men's final since 1979.

Agassi, who had changed to "electric lime" for this tournament, was nearly undressed in the championship match. Sampras fired 13 more aces, raising his tournament total to 100, added 12 service winners and never was broken in demolishing his opponent, 6-4, 6-3, 6-2, in one hour, 42 minutes. "It was a good old-fashioned street mugging," Agassi said.

Gabriela Sabatini dethroned Steffi Graf in the U.S. Open in 1990. (Russ Adams)

Sampras was the youngest male player to win America's national championship, supplanting Oliver Campbell, an older 19 one century earlier. Sampras shrugged. "I'm just a normal 19-year-old with an unusual job, doing unusual things," he said.

At 20, Sabatini had been doing unusual things for five years, since her breakthrough season of 1985. But she had reached only one major final (U.S., 1988) until 1990 when, attacking boldly, she applied the finishing touch to Graf's unhappy post-Australian campaign in the majors. Gaby hadn't been too happy herself, feeling she hit a low point in her career only two weeks before, a third-round loss in Los Angeles to Stephanie Rehe. But at the urging of new coach Carlos Kirmayr, she abruptly began to implement a bold new offensive game plan. Displaying a propensity for chip-and-charging, she yanked a

seemingly lost semifinal away from Mary Joe Fernandez, 7-5, 5-7, 6-3, from 4-1 down in the first and closing the steaming two-hour, 43-minute duel on a four-game spurt festooned with touch volleys.

In the final (Graf had mashed Sanchez Vicario, 6-1, 6-2), Gaby bounded off to 4-0, and would win, 6-2, 7-6 (7-5). But not before a torrid back-and-forth windup as Graf nearly pulled herself off the ledge, and Sabatini was clearly fading. Gaby, with partisans crying, "Vamos!," broke to 5-4, but got no closer than 15-30. Steffi went to 6-5 from 0-30, had two set points in the next game, but a missed backhand and Gaby's volley opened the way for overtime in which the German jumped to 3-1. But the sagging Argentine kept pressing to the net to win six of the last eight points, closing with a last-gasp all-or-nothing rolling forehand that nicked the sideline. "I had to win in two," she confessed wearily. Thirteen years after her childhood hero, Guillermo Vilas, ruled Forest Hills, fifth-seeded Sabatini gave Argentina another U.S. champ, the first Latin woman to embrace a major since Brazilian Maria Bueno's 1966 U.S. conquest.

Nevertheless, Steffi retained No. 1 because her pursuer, Seles, was bumped in the third round by No. 82 Linda Ferrando, marvelous volleyer-for-a-day, 1-6, 6-1, 7-6 (7-3). That was one of two huge first-week upsets. Second-seeded Navratilova was burned by Manuela Maleeva Fragniere in the fourth round, 7-5, 3-6, 6-3.

Graf recovered to win four tournaments in the fall, including two at Sabatini's expense, but Seles served notice of future intentions when she became the youngest to win a Virginia Slims championship in November at Madison Square Garden. In the final, she defeated Sabatini, 6-4, 5-7, 3-6, 6-4, 6-2, wowing 17,290 witnesses for 3 hours, 47 minutes. It was the first five-set women's match since flowing skirts and corsets were de rigueur and Bessie Moore beat Myrtle McAteer, 6-4, 3-6, 7-5, 2-6, 6-2, for the 1901 U.S. title before a handful of patrons at Philadelphia Cricket Club. A new day was at hand.

Her talent was undeniable. After she won the three major events she chose to enter, her credentials were impeccable. By the end of the year, only Monica Seles' *judgment* was considered suspect.

In her third season as a professional, Seles dislodged Steffi Graf as the No. 1 woman in the world and won more money ($2,457,758) than any previous practitioner of tennis, male or female. Not until she had wrapped a ribbon around 1991 by earning a second consecutive Virginia Slims Championship did she turn 18. The teenager pursued and embraced both fame and fortune.

It was the source of the former that the tennis establishment found distasteful, if not embarrassing. A professed admirer of pop singer Madonna and the glamour associated with movie stars, Seles gained a greater share of attention not for her victories at the Australian, French and U.S. Opens but for her mysterious withdrawal from Wimbledon without a suitable explanation. Her subsequent self-imposed exile created a rash of rumors popular in supermarket tabloids.

If her disappearance from public view revealed a fascination for Garbo, her return to tennis at an exhibition event for which she reportedly received a $300,000 appearance fee indicated she also had studied Gabor. On the day of her arrival at the Pathmark Tennis Classic in New Jersey, she posed for photographers with her dog tucked under her arm. Zsa Zsa would have been proud, darling.

In Seles' absence, Graf did manage to regain self-respect by claiming a third Wimbledon title. But the top ranking she had held for an unprecedented 186 weeks slipped away on March 10. The German did regain the No. 1 position for two brief periods during the summer but Seles zoomed back in front after her victory over Martina Navratilova at Flushing Meadow and opened a comfortable margin by winning three late-season tournaments and the Slims Championship,

Her opponents grumbled while Monica Seles grunted her way to women's supremacy in 1991. (Russ Adams)

where Graf was upset by Jana Novotna in the quarterfinals, 6-3, 3-6, 6-1.

Graf, in fact, failed to reach a final in any major outside of Wimbledon. She barely held off Gabriela Sabatini for second place. Although Navratilova fell to fourth and endured a drawn-out palimony suit brought by former companion Judy Nelson, she surpassed Chris Evert's record of 1,309 tour-match victories and equalled her standard of 157 career singles titles by defeating Seles, 6-3, 3-6, 6-3, at Oakland in November. She also advanced to the finals of the Slims in New York before falling to the transplanted Yugoslav, 6-4, 3-6, 7-5, 6-0.

As was the case the previous year, no man won more than one major. Boris Becker won the Australian Open for the first time but was a losing finalist at Wimbledon for the second consecutive year, bowing to countryman Michael Stich in the first all-German title match at the world's most prestigious tournament. Jim Courier became the third young American in three years to win a major event when he defeated Andre Agassi at the French but he was overwhelmed by Stefan Edberg in the final of the U.S. Open.

The last of the Big Four tournaments was energized by the spectacular comeback of Jimmy Connors. After losing all three of his matches the previous year before undergoing surgery on his left wrist, the man was reborn in 1991 when he celebrated his 39th birthday at Flushing Meadow with a sentimental journey to the semifinals. Over the course of a season in which he also earned standing ovations in Paris and London, Connors rose from No. 936 on the ATP computer to No. 48, a gain of 888 positions.

Courier, a Floridian who turned 21 in mid-August, had the most significant jump of all. With his first major title, the baseline basher with the baseball cap vaulted from No. 25 to No. 3 in the men's rankings, the highest achievement by an American since John McEnroe in 1985. The latter fell from No. 13 to 28, his lowest finish as a pro, despite gaining his 77th career title. It occurred in Chicago at the expense of his younger brother, 24-year-old Patrick, 3-6, 6-2, 6-4, who rose to No. 36 after he reached the Australian Open semifinals and achieved his first singles tournament final.

Edberg, who spent much of the year dueling Becker for the top spot, took command at the U.S. Open and became only the fifth player in the era to finish No. 1 for consecutive seasons, joining Connors, Borg, McEnroe and Ivan Lendl. He won six of eight finals, compiled a tour-best 76-17 match record and earned a men's record $2,363,575.

Tendinitis in the knee, however, caused the Swede to withdraw from the ATP championships at Frankfurt. Pete Sampras, whose hangover from his remarkable 1990 success lasted until August, added the season-ending title to three other tour

Jim Courier catapulted to No. 3 in the world in 1991 as he won the French and reached the finals of the U.S. and ATP championships. (Russ Adams)

victories in the second half of the season. But the Californian finished the year on a down note when he lost both his singles matches in an emotional Davis Cup final won by France at Lyon.

In a bizarre sideshow, Bjorn Borg attempted a comeback at Monte Carlo 10 years after his last major event. He played with a wooden racket, and lost in the opening round to Jordi Arrese, 6-2, 6-3. After saying he would make an appearance at the French Open, he decided not to ask for a wild card into the main draw, and did not appear again for a year.

Seles, born six months before Borg won his first major tournament, emerged as the youngest world champion in history. She began her climb to the top at the Australian Open, where she dropped only 12 games in the first five rounds.

She qualified for the final by struggling past Mary Joe Fernandez, escaping a match point, 6-3, 0-6, 9-7, and then overcame the loss of the first set to beat Novotna, 5-7, 6-3, 6-1.

The Czech had upset Zina Garrison, Graf and Arantxa Sanchez Vicario to reach her first major final. Her 5-7, 6-4, 8-6 victory over Graf marked the only time in the last 17 Big Four appearances that the German had failed to advance as far as the semifinals.

Graf's 1,310-day reign as No. 1 ended with her loss to Sabatini in the final at Boca Raton, 6-4, 7-6 (8-6). She did have the satisfaction of defeating Seles, 6-4, 6-3, at the U.S. Hard Court Championships in San Antonio three weeks later and at Hamburg five weeks after that, 7-5, 6-7 (4-7), 6-3. But Seles entered the French Open as the top-ranked player and emerged as the clearcut leader.

Both Graf and Sabatini had the opportunity to move to the top of the ladder with a victory in Paris. But Seles defeated Sabatini, 6-4, 6-1, in the semifinals shortly after Graf (with 44 errors) was humbled by Sanchez Vicario, 6-0, 6-2. The two games were the fewest won by Graf in a complete match since turning pro in October 1982, at the age of 13.

"That hasn't happened in a long, long time," Graf said. "And I hope it's going to be a long, long time until it happens again. I can't remember the last time I played that bad," she said.

Seles, who had dropped only one set in the tournament, defeated Sanchez Vicario in routine fashion, 6-3, 6-4, for her second consecutive French title. It was somewhere between Paris and London, at least in terms of the WTA schedule, that the season took a strange twist.

With the public considering the possibility of a second female Grand Slam in three years, Wimbledon officials were startled to receive a message that Seles had withdrawn from the event "due to an injury caused by a minor accident." There was no additional explanation, no contact with the player herself and the tournament was due to start in three days. Her whereabouts became the hottest topic in tennis.

She was undergoing treatment for a knee injury in Vail, Colo. Or she was having her legs checked in New York. Or she was in hiding at entrepreneur Donald Trump's vast estate in Florida.

Maybe it wasn't an injury at all, some tabloids speculated, coming to the conclusion that she was pregnant. Another report had her skipping the grass-court event to preserve her ranking and a $1-million bonus from the company that manufactures her racket. About the only possibility overlooked was that she had been spirited away by a UFO. Meanwhile, she could not be reached by reporters, her agents nor the WTA, which levied a $6,000 fine for a late withdrawal.

While she was away, Jennifer Capriati had the time of her life at Wimbledon. The 15-year-old not only became the youngest semifinalist in tournament history but she did so at the expense of Navratilova. Capriati stunned the most honored singles champion in the annals of the All England Club in the quarterfinals, 6-4, 7-5.

Against the person she called in her schoolgirl shorthand "the lege," as in legend, the youngster won the first set but was down a break at 2-3 when the match was postponed by rain to the following day. After holding her own serve from 0-40, she then broke Navratilova in the eighth game and went on to victory. "I can't believe it," Capriati said. "I'm really happy but I can't believe it."

For the loser, it was her earliest exit from Wimbledon in 14 years and ended a record streak of nine consecutive finals. Capriati scored her first triumph over a player ranked in the top four and qualified for the semifinals against Sabatini. She got no further, losing to the Argentine, 6-4, 6-4.

Meanwhile, Graf took the opportunity to emerge from her personal cloud cover, whipping Zina Garrison, 6-1, 6-3, and Mary Joe Fernandez, 6-2, 6-4, en route to the final. The championship match was anything but stellar and the

German was sufficiently shaky to double-fault away the ninth game of the third set, presenting Sabatini the chance to serve for the trophy at 5-4, again at 6-5, 30-15. Gaby failed to get the last two points and Graf went on to a 6-4, 3-6, 8-6 victory, the first extended women's final at Wimbledon since 1976.

Sabatini, coming so close, hesitated at the critical moments. She relented in the attacking that brought her to the U.S. Open 10 months before, and shoved Graf almost to defeat here. She would attain such a height never again.

"In many ways, it means a lot to me," Graf said. "It gave me so much pleasure to see myself getting through, winning a tough match, a close match, not letting up. I needed to win again. I needed it for myself."

The Seles media circus was called to order one week later at Mahwah, New Jersey. Underneath a hot tent on the campus of Ramapo College, Monica made her first public appearance since her withdrawal from Wimbledon. Sixteen microphones and 13 television cameras were in place as she met the press.

The truth, she said, was that she had skipped the most prestigious tournament because of "shin splints and the beginning of a stress fracture [left leg]. People were looking for more exciting answers. It's so simple, but they were expecting me to say, 'Yes, I'm pregnant.' Or, 'Yes, it's the Yonex contract.' Or, 'Yes, it's some other reason.' I mean, why would I miss Wimbledon? It's the biggest tournament."

Her representative explained that she had hit herself in the leg with the racket during the French Open, aggravating her shin splints. She agreed that "maybe the wording [of her withdrawal] could have been better," but chose not to make any public statements. "I wasn't ready to talk to anyone," she said.

The site of her return certainly didn't mollify WTA officials. She chose an exhibition tournament, offering a huge guarantee, over an official

tour event the following week in nearby Westchester County, N.Y. For that offense, she was fined $20,000, a penalty assumed by the local promoter, John Korff. He also paid the $2,500 fine assessed to Capriati, who defeated Seles in the final of the 16-woman event.

From there, Capriati flew to Nottingham, England, where the U.S. team qualified for the final of the Federation Cup. Despite her singles victory over Conchita Martinez, 4-6, 7-6 (7-3), 6-1, the Americans lost, 2-1, to Spain as Sanchez Vicario defeated Mary Joe Fernandez, 6-3, 6-4, and the team of Garrison and Gigi Fernandez was thwarted by the two in the doubles, 3-6, 6-1, 6-1.

Seles offered three reasons why she was not representing Yugoslavia in the international team competition. She said she didn't think it was good for her leg. She didn't think she was ready to play at that level of competition. And, she said, "Nobody asked me."

Returning to the tour at the end of July, Seles was upset by Capriati, 4-6, 6-1, 7-6 (7-2), at San Diego in a match that boasted a pairing of the two youngest finalists in the open era. Two weeks later, Seles beat Kimiko Date, 6-3, 6-3, to win in Los Angeles. Twice in August, however, Graf supplanted Seles at the top of the rankings and the German entered the U.S. Open in the familiar role of No. 1.

It was not to last at this Open, which became the Garden of the Golden Oldies: 39-year-old semifinalist James Scott Connors and 34-year-old finalist Martina Navratilova. Never had two players in one tournament given so much joy to the geriatric set. Playing her classic serve-and-volley stuff, the oldest woman in the place ousted Graf, 7-6 (7-2), 6-7 (6-8), 6-4, advancing to her eighth U.S. and a date with Seles.

There was nothing subtle about the other semi, a slugfest of nakedly ferocious, thundering groundies that absorbed the crowd for almost two hours. Mysterious Monica won by the skin of the last four points, stopping Capriati, 6-3, 3-6, 7-6 (7-4). Capriati, a singular saboteur, had beaten defending champ Sabatini, 6-3, 7-6 (7-1) in the quarters, following up on her removal of Queen Martina at Wimbledon. She nearly had the French champ, too, led 3-1 in the third, twice served for Seles's scalp, at 5-4, and (two points away), 6-5, 30-all. No go. Monica held on with both hands on both sides. In a frantic stretch run of seven service breaks to the tie-breaker, thence seven straight points against serve, Seles got out on an error plus her massive backhand and forehand winners, bringing tears to Jenny's eyes.

On the following afternoon, Seles demolished Navratilova, 7-6 (7-1), 6-1, passing her elder at will from either end of the baseline. Navratilova won only 34 points on 76 approaches to the net and committed 26 unforced errors to the champion's five. Seles thus won her third major title of the season in as many attempts. She did not win many new fans, especially after publicly thanking the controversial Trump in post-match ceremonies.

The victory restored her to the top spot on the computer, which she held for the remainder of the year. Seles said she didn't regret the decision to withdraw from Wimbledon. "I can't erase it," she said. "But if I were to play Wimbledon, I don't think I could have played the Open [because of the time for recuperation]. . . . There will always be that little emptiness."

Seles finished the season in style, defeating Navratilova, 6-4, 3-6, 7-5, 6-0, at Madison Square Garden in the final of the Slims Championships. Navratilova teamed with her old partner, Pam Shriver, to win the doubles title for the first time in three years, their 10th in this event, over Jana Novotna and Gigi Fernandez, 4-6, 7-5, 6-4.

The men's tour offered surprises as early as the first major tournament, where one of the semifinalists advised the press, "It's just like you all expected—Edberg, Lendl, Becker and McEnroe." Except that the speaker was Patrick McEnroe and it was the doubles specialist who had advanced to the final four, rather than older brother John. The latter hadn't even made the trip following his disqualification the previous year.

McEnroe, who had defeated Jay Berger, Mark Woodforde and Cristiano Caratti in his best major showing, battled Becker for four sets before the German prevailed, 6-7 (2-7), 6-4, 6-1, 6-4. Becker went on to a 1-6, 6-4, 6-4, 6-4 victory over Lendl, who had survived two match points against Edberg, 6-4, 5-7, 3-6, 7-6 (7-3), 6-4.

Paris belonged to the Americans. For the first time since 1954, a pair of Yanks qualified for the final. But long before Courier and Agassi walked into Roland Garros to contest the championship, Connors stole the show. A wild-card entry in the only major championship he never won, the 38-year-old Connors eliminated Todd Witsken, outlasted No. 28 Haitian Ronald Agenor, 6-4, 6-2, 3-6, 0-6, 6-4, in 3 hours, 39 minutes, winning three of the last four games, recording his last of 40 victories in Paris. In another crowd-tugging drainer of 3:32 Jimmy won the last point—but ex-champ Michael Chang got the win, 4-6, 7-5, 6-2, 4-6, 0-15. After belting a backhand return winner for the first point of the fifth—"I was ahead, wasn't I?"—Connors surrendered to a man half his age, giving in to a gimpy back and exhaustion.

"I'm sorry," he said to umpire Bruno Rebeuh. "I did all I could. I just can't play anymore. Believe me, if I could . . . , I would."

Certainly, that's what the public believed. The fans accorded him several standing ovations. "To be honest, I felt awful," Connors said after getting an ice massage and an intravenous solution. "I've been run ragged and my back's stiff. But, boy, was it fun. To get a stadium rocking like that is a kick you can't believe."

Agassi, wearing a purple, gray and white outfit that was subdued in comparison to the hot pink ensemble of 1990, advanced to his second consecutive French final by blasting Becker in the semis, 7-5, 6-3, 3-6, 6-1. Courier, four months younger than Agassi, had a more adventurous trip to his first major title match, ousting top-seeded Edberg in the quarterfinals, 6-4, 2-6, 6-3, 6-4, before beating Stich, 6-2, 6-7 (8-10), 6-2, 6-4. It marked only the fourth all-American men's final in Paris and the first since Tony Trabert defeated Art Larsen 37 years earlier.

"I'd like to slap around the people who asked where American tennis was about five years ago," said Courier, a frustrated baseball player whose style was to swing for the fences. "This says, 'Here we are.'"

Both players had trained at the Nick Bollettieri Tennis Academy, but Courier left when he decided Agassi was receiving most of the coach's attention. And Agassi had taken a faster track to the spotlight. But it was Courier who was the more poised in the end, ignoring a couple of rain delays and strong winds in a 3-6, 6-4, 2-6, 6-1, 6-4 victory.

An infant's wail on Court 1 may have changed Courier's luck in the trying fourth-round win over a big-hitting big Swede (6-foot-5), No. 46 Magnus Larsson, 6-3, 4-6, 4-6, 7-5, 6-2. As a Larsson drop shot pushed Jim to 0-40 at 1-2 in the fourth set, a cranky baby's voice was heard. Courier laughed, "Guess that kid didn't like the shot any better than I did." He loosened up, held serve, and wasn't to be stopped.

It was Courier's fourth career triumph in as many finals and the $451,660 he pocketed exceeded his total prize money from 1990. He closed with an ace, then flopped backward onto the clay. "There have been lots of happy moments in my life and there will be lots more," the champion said, "but at the moment this is the happiest."

Agassi received greater attention just for showing up at Wimbledon than he did for any of his 1991 results. He hadn't made an appearance at the All England Club since a first-round loss to Henri Leconte in 1987, 6-2, 6-1, 6-2, in under an hour. He said he wasn't ready for the grass and it wasn't clear if officials were ready for a peacock.

And then Agassi removed the white warmup suit in which he practiced, teasing photographers and spectators alike, to reveal all-white attire without a stripe of color. His only concession to the '90s and his image was the pair of lycra tights that peeked from beneath his white denim shorts. More significantly, he played reasonably well on the lawns, winning four matches before he was shot down by David Wheaton, a 22-year-old American with a big serve, 6-2, 0-6, 3-6, 7-6 (7-3), 6-2.

The unseeded Wheaton, who would cap his season with the $2-million first-place check for beating Chang, 7-5, 6-2, 6-4, at the Grand Slam Cup in December, was the only outsider in the semifinals of a tournament that, in an unprecedented move, opened the gates on the middle Sunday in order to clear a backlog of matches postponed by massive amounts of rain. Tickets were hastily printed after the announcement on Friday and all seats were unreserved, causing a mad dash from the turnstiles. So enthusiastic and unfamiliar with tradition were the fans at Centre Court that they even performed a wave.

Order was restored in time for the final between Becker, who had turned back Wheaton, 6-4, 7-6 (7-4), 7-5. His 6-foot-4 countryman, stick-figure-thin Stich, uprooted defender Edberg, 4-6, 7-6 (7-5), 7-6 (7-5), 7-6 (7-2), the loser having lost serve not once, a unique semifinal curiosity. Tiebreaker maven Stich—"I can say my name but you can't spell it or say it," he joshed reporters—prevented a fourth straight Becker-Edberg title bout. Strikingly, on this most tie-breakerish day at the Big W, the man who concocted the set-terminating method in 1965 died at Newport, R.I. Jimmy Van Alen was 88. "If he hadn't lived," Edberg said afterwards, not disrespectfully, "Michael and I might still be out there playing."

By winning his match after Edberg lost, Becker climbed to No. 1 in the rankings for the second time in the season. But the added stature did not intimidate Stich. Eleven months younger than Becker, the relatively anonymous German had only one tournament title (Memphis in 1990) to his name when he broke his more celebrated compatriot in the first game, slugged 16 aces (for a tournament total of 97) and overwhelmed the three-time champion, 6-4, 7-6 (7-4), 6-4. He would be remembered as the man who beat No. 1 twice in the same tournament.

"It's an incredible feeling," Stich said. To which Becker nodded in agreement. "I know the feeling," the loser said. "He was a nobody, but today he is a star."

Becker held onto the top spot in the rankings until the U.S. Open, where he was upset in the third round, 6-3, 6-4, 6-2, by No. 45, spoiler Paul Haarhuis. Edberg, who had never reached the final at Flushing Meadow in the major tournament he liked least, made the most of the opportunity. He beat Chang, 7-6 (7-2), 7-5, 6-3, Javier Sanchez, 6-3, 6-2, 6-3, and Lendl, 6-3, 6-3, 6-4, and finally Courier, 6-2, 6-4, 6-0. Chang stayed up past everybody's bedtime to eliminate John McEnroe at 1:30 a.m. after 4½ hours, 6-4, 4-6, 7-6 (7-1), 2-6, 6-3. Courier, who had terminated the 361-day reign of Sampras in the quarters, 6-2, 7-6 (7-4), 7-6 (7-5), wasn't off against Edberg. But Jim was off the court in 2 hours, 2 minutes because Stefan, climaxing his eighth Open, was in such an oppressive serve-and-volleying state, erasing the loser's only two break points with onerous serves. Edberg would often refer to this as "the best match I ever played."

Still, the star of the tournament was none of the above. It was Connors, the wild card with a No. 174 ranking, who owned the crowds in winning five matches against Patrick McEnroe, Michiel Schapers, 10th-seeded Karel Novacek, Aaron Krickstein and Haarhuis. Jimmy, whose memorable battles with big brother John had aroused the Meadow, went from one day to the next to subdue little brother Patrick in the opening round, signalling his incredible rejuvenation. It took 4 hours, 18 minutes, so far back was Connors, two sets and 0-3, but by 1:35 a.m. he had it, 4-6, 6-7 (4-7), 6-4, 6-2, 6-4. Schapers was easy, 6-3, 6-2, 6-3, and so was a bewildered Novacek, 6-1, 6-4, 6-3. Next it was "Happy Birthday to me!" time, Sept. 2, as Jimmy, now 39, lit candles beneath himself and scorched Krickstein, who had rudely sent fourth-seeded Agassi home on the first day, 7-5, 7-6 (7-4), 6-2.

Connors had always been a bright birthday boy at the Open, but never pulled such a melodrama as this to win, 3-6, 7-6 (10-8), 1-6, 6-3, 7-6 (7-4), even though Krickstein had two set points in the second. When Aaron held to 5-2 in the fifth, through eight deuces and three break points, Jimmy looked stuck in the mud for good, especially being two points from defeat twice as Krickstein served at 5-3. But Jimmy was putting everything he knew together with his eternal legs—lobs, sneak volleys, line drives and heart—and came out of it after 4 hours, 41 minutes with everybody singing, "Happy Birthday!"

It was Haarhuis' turn in the turn-back-time machine, and he, too, looked the winner, serving for a two-set lead at 5-4. Some customers for the nocturnal quarterfinal had paid scalpers $500 to get in, and felt they got off cheaply. Getting into the match was Jimmy with a sweet backhand return to break point, followed by the point of the tourney: intercepting four smashes with his legs and lobs, he ended it with a ripping backhand passer that made 20,000 shrieking loyalists practically leap onto the court to hug him. It was 5-5 and Jimmy was prancing to the final four, 4-6, 7-6 (7-3), 6-4, 6-2. He was the second oldest semifinalist in U.S. history, behind Ken Rosewall, whom he drubbed in the 1974 final on grass at Forest Hills. He was also the first wild card to advance that far. Even competitors were caught up in the excitement he generated.

But he ran out of miracles against Courier. The latter scored a 6-3, 6-3, 6-2 victory that was coldly efficient and brutally quick. To that point, Courier hadn't dropped a set in the tournament, yet he proved unable to handle Edberg.

The new champion devoted part of his post-match interview to honoring Connors. "I think what happened here is great for tennis," Edberg said. "Jimmy Connors' performance here has created a lot of publicity. It has given the U.S. Open a boost. I thank him."

Courier also reached the final of the ATP World Championship, which Sampras won 3-6, 7-6 (7-5), 6-3, 6-4. In the doubles event, which reopened South Africa to the men's tour, John

Michael Stich prevailed over Boris Becker in Wimbledon's all-German final in 1991. (Russ Adams)

only four months before, had broken in as a 19-year-old in 1982, alongside Noah, losing both his singles to John McEnroe and Gene Mayer in a final-round defeat by the U.S. in Grenoble. But Noah had convinced him the Cup could yet be his—"our dream for France"—and Henri demonstrated his extraordinary recovery by handling the novitiate, 20-year-old Sampras, constantly attacking as Forget would, 6-4, 7-5, 6-4. This after Agassi had posted a 1-0 U.S. lead, 6-7 (7-9), 6-2, 6-1, 6-2, over Forget.

Leconte awakened the wall-to-wall crowd of 8,000 in the cozy, smoke-filled Palais des Sports, and it was bedlam the rest of the way, a Niagara of noise that swept the French to victory. Agassi, who had propped the 3-2 semifinal victory over Germany in Kansas City by beating Michael Stich, 6-3, 6-1, 6-4, and, in the decisive match, Charlie Steeb, 6-2, 6-2, 6-3, wouldn't get another chance. Forget and Leconte, their volleying in tune, shoved aside Ken Flach and Robert Seguso in their Cup farewell, 6-1, 6-4, 4-6, 6-2, leaving it to Forget. Guy, 26, was ready to be France's guy, cancelling a set point in the first-set tie-breaker with one of his 17 aces, and saving 10 of 11 break points. Davis Cup debuts have been rough on the nerves of other greats. Pete joined the club. When Forget pumped four aces while serving out of three deuces and four break points to win the third set, the 3-hour, 33-minute ordeal was virtually over.

Presently an hour-long celebration would break out with Noah and his latter-day Musketeers hoisted on jubilant shoulders, a conga line formed to snake around the court and everybody tearfully singing "La Marseillaise." One of the celebrants, sharing champagne from the Cup, said he "couldn't wait much longer" for this reprise. He was 93-year-old Jean Borotra, an original of the "Four Musketeers," who pried the Cup from the U.S. in 1927 and kept it six years.

Fitzgerald and Anders Jarryd culminated an outstanding year in which they claimed the French, Wimbledon and U.S. Open titles by beating Ken Flach and Robert Seguso, 6-4, 6-4, 2-6, 6-4, at Johannesburg.

Still, the historic highlight of the season occurred at Lyon when a French team of "Two Musketeers," Guy Forget and Leconte—the only pair of lefties to win the Cup—and motivated by captain Yannick Noah, posted an inspirational victory over the U.S., returning the Davis Cup to France for the first time since 1932. Forget, who enjoyed his finest year as a pro with six singles titles and his first Top Ten ranking, defeated Sampras in the clinching match, 7-6 (8-6), 3-6, 6-3, 6-4, after he had combined with Leconte to upset Flach and Seguso in doubles, 6-1, 6-4, 4-6, 6-2. Leconte, descended to No. 159 and thought to be finished because of a gimpy back, operated on

1992

In a year in which the U.S. regained the summit of men's tennis, Americans accounted for all but one of the major singles titles. Ironically, the championship that eluded them was the one they prized most, the U.S. Open. Stefan Edberg, the Swede who discovered New York can be a nice place to visit, triumphed at Flushing Meadow for the second consecutive year.

Elsewhere, however, the U.S. reigned supreme. Jim Courier added a second French title to the Australian crown he won five months earlier and finished the season as the No. 1 player in the world, the first Yank to claim that honor since John McEnroe in 1984. Andre Agassi finally annexed his first major at Wimbledon, of all places. And Pete Sampras, a beaten finalist at the U.S. Open, compiled the best match record, 70-18, while gaining No. 3 in the final ATP rankings.

Then, in a classic melding of generations, Courier, Agassi and Sampras combined with McEnroe to reclaim the Davis Cup for the U.S. Courier was a loser on opening day to Olympic champ Marc Rosset, 6-3, 6-7 (9-11), 3-6, 6-4, 6-4. But Jim won the clinching singles in an uproarious 3-1 U.S. triumph at Ft. Worth, Tex., a former cow town where hundreds of cowbells clanged incessantly in the crowds of 12,000, wielded by a good-natured contingent of 1,500 Swiss supporters, justly proud of their astonishing two-man gang.

Switzerland, never before a factor in the Cup, rode Nos. 35 and 36 Rosset and Jakob Hlasek all the way to the small country's lone final, through defending champ France, 3-2, and very close to total victory. Had Rosset, the 6-foot-7 flame-thrower who buzzed 27 aces against Courier, held serve to 6-6 in the third set of the doubles, he and Hlasek, winner of two previous tie-breakers, might have captured a third for a 2-1 lead. But the going-and-coming alignment— Daddy and the Disciple?—McEnroe, 33, and Sampras, 21, delivered forehand returns to grab the middle set, and won, 6-7 (5-7), 6-7 (7-9), 7-5, 6-1, 6-2, the first such final-round doubles comeback since Ham Richardson and Alex Olmedo won the 1958 Cup in Australia. Agassi, who completed a perfect season (7-0), led off by beating

Stefan Edberg made it back-to-back titles at the U.S. Open in 1992. (Russ Adams)

Hlasek, 6-1, 6-2, 6-2, and Courier finished over Hlasek, 6-3, 3-6, 6-3, 6-4.

Sampras, devastated by his two singles losses in the French victory of 1991, felt a lot better after lending McEnroe a hot hand in winning both doubles they played, the other over Edberg and Anders Jarryd, 6-1, 6-7 (2-7), 4-6, 6-3, 6-3, clinching the 4-1 semifinal against Sweden in Minneapolis. The first day belonged to Agassi, beating Edberg, 5-7, 6-3, 7-6 (7-4), 6-3, and Courier, 4-6, 7-6 (7-1), 6-3, 7-5, responding sternly to stiff opposition from surprise starter, No. 71 Niklas Kulti, who served for the second and fourth sets at 5-4.

The American influence was apparent throughout the entire tour as players from the States accounted for 24 of the 82 singles titles, triple the total of runners-up Spain and Germany.

Five U.S. citizens ranked among the Top Ten men, including No. 8 Ivan Lendl, who ended a 14-month drought by winning the Seiko championships in Tokyo three months after receiving his naturalization papers. In all, 43 individuals from 18 countries captured at least one tournament and no player won more than five.

Of the three who shared that distinction—Courier and Sampras were the other two—Boris Becker finished the year on the highest note. The German, shut out of a major final for only the second time in eight years, won the ATP World Championship by defeating Courier, 6-4, 6-3, 7-5, in Frankfurt on his 25th birthday. It marked his third victory in the final eight weeks of the season and raised his ranking to No. 5.

A somber note was Arthur Ashe's revelation in April that he had contracted AIDS through a blood transfusion while undergoing surgery in 1988. Characteristically, he asked not for sympathy, but continued a heavy schedule of obligations in charitable work and TV commentary. He also became active in the fight against AIDS, raising funds for education, research and treatment.

Competition among the women was more one-sided. For the second successive year, Monica Seles captured the Australian French and U.S. Open titles, won the Virginia Slims Championship, finished atop the WTA rankings and established a record for tennis earnings ($2,622,352). But, in 1992, she was not denied a Grand Slam by an error of omission.

This time she entered Wimbledon and took her case to the final, where she was overwhelmed by Steffi Graf. The German, whose eight victories included a four-tournament winning streak in the fall, demolished Seles, 6-2, 6-1, equalling Martina Navratilova's 6-0, 6-3 conquest of Andrea Jaeger in 1983 as the second most lopsided Wimbledon of the Open era. Graf's singles title was her fourth in five years at Wimbledon and her 11th in a major event.

Although Navratilova slipped to No. 5 and failed to reach a Big Four final, she won Chicago

For Andre Agassi, it was sweet strawberries at Wimbledon in 1992. (Russ Adams)

over Jana Novotna to break the record for most tournament victories she had shared with Chris Evert at 157. After saving two match points in beating Novotna, 7-6 (7-4), 4-6, 7-5, Martina concluded the season with three more titles for a total of 161, the last achieved in Filderstadt, Germany, over Gabriela Sabatini, 7-6 (7-1), 6-3, on the occasion of her 36th birthday. And the grande dame did reach the last round of the Virginia Slims Championship in New York, where she was drubbed by Seles, 7-5, 6-3, 6-1.

Two months earlier, in a gimmick-ridden sendup of the Battle of the Sexes waged by Billie Jean King and Bobby Riggs 19 years earlier, Navratilova had unraveled in a match against Jimmy Connors at Caesars Palace. She double-faulted on set point in the first set and lost, 7-5, 6-2, despite getting two serves to her opponent's one and hitting into a court four feet wider. Each

It didn't have the hoopla of Bobby Riggs vs. Billie Jean King and it wasn't ladies' day for Martina Navratilova, humbled by Jimmy Connors in their made-for-Caesars-Palace exhibition at Las Vegas in 1992. (Wide World)

player received $500,000 in appearance money and Connors, who had won his first-round match over Jaime Oncins in the U.S. Open on his 40th birthday, earned an extra half-million for his tame victory.

Of greater consequence, 16-year-old Jennifer Capriati picked up a gold medal in the Olympic Games at Barcelona. She did so in dream-like fashion, defeating the defending champion in the final. Her 3-6, 6-3, 6-4 victory over Graf, the first of her career, lifted her out of the doldrums in a season in which she reportedly balked at the heavy schedule arranged by her father and appeared to lose her zest for tennis.

Three months later, when they next met in the semifinals at Philadelphia, Graf drubbed the American teenager, 6-0, 6-1, en route to her fourth consecutive tournament victory, over Arantxa Sanchez Vicario, 6-3, 3-6, 6-1. The German, upset by Lori McNeil in the first round of the Slims showdown, 7-6 (7-1), 6-4, hadn't lost prior to the quarterfinals since 1985. She finished the season ranked No. 2 behind Seles.

Graf was not on hand when Seles took her first major step of the year toward continued domination of women's tennis. She was recuperating from—no kidding—German measles during the Australian Open, where Seles was not taxed. The champion won her second Aussie, 6-2, 6-3, over Mary Joe Fernandez, who had upset Sabatini in the semis, 6-1, 6-4.

In contrast, the French Open provided some of the finest moments and tightest matches of the year. Merely to qualify for an epic final against Graf, Seles twice had to rally from third-set deficits. The first of her comebacks occurred in the fourth round when she trailed No. 150-ranked Akiko Kijimuta of Japan, 1-4, before running off five consecutive games for a 6-1, 3-6, 6-4 victory. Then, in the semifinals, she was down 2-4 against the eminently more formidable Sabatini before putting her away, 6-3, 4-6, 6-4.

When it was over, the loser was dumbfounded. "She seemed tired and then suddenly she started hitting the ball very hard," Sabatini said. "I don't know where she got the power."

Graf also passed a critical test in the semifinals by overcoming Arantxa Sanchez Vicario, who had demolished the German, 6-0, 6-2, in similar circumstances a year earlier. When Graf lost the first set at love, she couldn't help but recall the scenario of 1991. Yet, she rallied for a 0-6, 6-2, 6-2 triumph with the help of her opponent, who committed 29 unforced errors in the last two sets. The result was a final for which the Paris fans were clamoring.

Their match, the first between the two in more than a year, disappointed no one save the loser and her family. And even Graf conceded it was a remarkable experience after saving five championship points in Seles' 6-2, 3-6, 10-8 victory that consumed two hours and 43 minutes. "It definitely was a special match, no doubt about it," Graf said.

For Seles, who became the first woman to win three consecutive French singles titles since Hilde Krahwinkel Sperling in 1935–37, the match culminated an exhausting tournament that merely confirmed what the world already suspected. Namely, that she was the most tenacious as well as most successful tennis player on the planet. "That's the hardest I've ever had to work

Olympic gold was Jennifer Capriati's harvest in the 1992 Olympics at Barcelona. (Russ Adams)

for a Grand Slam title," she decided after amassing her sixth major (and fifth in the last five she had entered.)

Four times Graf was confronted with a match point on her own serve at 3-5 in the third set. Four times she withstood the pressure. Fraulein Forehand then broke Seles in the 10th game when her opponent, suddenly impatient, committed four unforced errors. They exchanged service breaks in the 15th and 16th games before Graf, after saving a fifth match point in the 18th game, netted a forehand.

On the following day, Courier joined Seles, a fellow Florida resident, halfway to a Grand Slam. In the Australian Open final, he avenged the blowout by Edberg in the 1991 U.S. Open four months earlier by beating the Swede, 6-3, 3-6, 6-4, 6-2. He celebrated the victory, which enabled him to leapfrog Edberg in the rankings, by jumping into the nearby polluted Yarra River.

His ascent to the top, the first of five changes at the top in 1992, ended nearly a seven-year drought for Americans since McEnroe was toppled from No. 1 in mid-1985 by Lendl. At 21 years, five months, Courier was the third-youngest male to hold the No. 1 spot, after McEnroe (21 and 15 days) and Bjorn Borg (21 and two months). Yet, his elevation apparently failed to impress Agassi, with whom he had split matches in the two previous French Opens.

Once more, the pairings in Paris pitted the longtime rivals, this time in the semifinals. Agassi carried the pre-match buildup by claiming that Courier's game was built on hard work and mental strength because "I don't think he has a lot of natural ability to fall back on." Courier saved his talk for after the match, which he won most convincingly, 6-3, 6-2, 6-2.

"I've been reading about how I don't have much talent," Courier said. "There are many different talents besides hitting a tennis ball. Having guts on the court is a talent; having desire is a talent; having courage to go for a shot when you are love-40 down is a talent. I may not hit the ball as cleanly as anybody out there, but I have got a few talents that are just as good as anybody else's."

That triumph pushed his winning streak to 22 matches, which he extended in the final by blasting seventh-seeded Petr Korda of Czechoslovakia, 7-5, 6-2, 6-1. Unlike the women's final, the men's match offered little drama. Courier finished off his nervous opponent in one hour, 59 minutes. The normally free-swinging lefty Korda, who had never previously advanced beyond the third round of a Big Four event, had 49 unforced errors and nine double faults.

"I think I played big feet today," he said. "I tell you I was very nervous. My hand is still tight. I couldn't play my game. My body didn't work too much today."

So routine was the decision that the two-time champion received greater attention for his post-match behavior. He flavored his acceptance speech with French, charming the crowd at Roland Garros.

Wimbledon, of course, represented a huge hurdle to the singles leaders, hard-hitting baseliners not at home on grass. Neither had advanced beyond the quarterfinals in previous appearances.

Courier's quest and a 25-match streak came to an abrupt end in the third round when he stumbled against an obscure Russian, the No. 193-ranked Andrei Olhovskiy, a qualifier, 6-4, 4-6, 6-4, 6-4. That defeat opened the door for McEnroe, a first-round washout at the French who had gained impetus in what he said would be his last Wimbledon. In an engaging 4-hour, 9-minute clash of aging ex-champs, No. 30 Mac beat No. 191 Patrick Cash, 6-7 (3-7), 6-4, 6-7 (1-7), 6-3, 6-2. Another old-boy champ saying goodbye, Connors, did it fast in his 20th Big W, a first-round loss to a Mexican lefty, No. 86 Luis Herrera, 6-2, 1-6, 7-5, 6-3. But Jimmy left behind the male wins record, 84 of 102 matches. After beating David Wheaton, 6-3, 6-4, 6-4, and Olhovskiy, 7-5, 6-3, 7-6 (12-10), McEnroe stepped up to his eighth semi, over ninth-seeded Guy Forget, 6-2, 7-6 (11-9), 6-3, prestidigitating his way out of six set points in the tie-breaker. He had become the talk of tennis and a crowd favorite at the tournament where so often he had played the boor.

Awaiting him was another surprise. In the midst of a sour season, Agassi had managed to overcome his fear of grass to win five matches, most notably over three-time Wimbledon champ Becker in the quarters, 4-6, 6-2, 6-2, 4-6, 6-3. The meeting of the old rebel and the young anarchist was a stunning development, enriched by their growing friendship. After being thrust together on the Davis Cup team, they played doubles in the French Open, became occasional dinner companions and frequently practiced against each other.

Indeed, Agassi asked McEnroe for his advice on coping with the Wimbledon grass and the flattered former champion readily agreed. "We hit it off well," McEnroe said. "He's young, he's really inquisitive and he's very, very smart. He asks good questions."

Agassi learned his lessons well. The only help he needed from McEnroe on, fittingly, the Fourth of July was a reminder to bow to the Duke and Duchess of Kent as he was departing the court. Then again, he had played with such command he didn't want to leave.

The shaggy-haired American required only one hour, 51 minutes to cut down McEnroe, 6-4, 6-2, 6-3. Agassi, returning brilliantly, converted all seven break points he held, lost his serve only twice and was in control from the very first game, which McEnroe double-faulted away. At 12th, Andre was not only the lowest seed to advance to the Wimbledon final since the unseeded Becker in 1985 but he found himself as the senior member of the pairing. McEnroe departed Wimbledon as he greeted it in 1977, a semifinalist, compiling a 59-11 record for 14 visits.

On the other side of the draw the Incendiary I, Goran Ivanisevic, was a skinny 6-foot-4 conflagration, the most prolific firer of aces the place had known. Seeded eighth, he had 34 against Mark Woodforde, 23 against Lendl, 33 in beating Edberg, 6-7 (10-12), 7-5, 6-1, 3-6, 6-3, and 36 in a semifinal over Pete Sampras, 6-7 (4-7), 7-6 (7-5), 6-4, 6-2, a battle of 20-year-old prodigies with fearsome serves.

Ironically, maturity may have been Agassi's greatest advantage in the final. He failed to wither when confronted by Ivanisevic's serve, which produced 37 more aces for a stunning tournament record total of 206, failed to lose serve until the second game of the fourth set and appeared much more calm than the easily-distracted Croat. The 22-year-old Yank persevered 6-7 (8-10), 6-4, 6-4, 1-6, 6-4 for his first major title.

At the moment of triumph, Andre, whose past displays had seemed as calculated as his television commercials ("Image is everything"), fell to his knees, sprawled face-first on the turf and appeared genuinely moved. "I've realized my dream of winning a Grand Slam tournament," he said. "To do it here is more than I could ever ask for. If my career was over tomorrow, I got a lot more than I deserved, than I could ever ask for."

Nor did McEnroe leave the All England Club empty-handed. Fitter and sharper than he had been in years working with new coach Larry Stefanki, he teamed with Michael Stich, the grass-court whiz of 1991, to claim the men's doubles prize. The unseeded pair defeated fourth-seeded Americans Jim Grabb and Richie Reneberg in a match that consumed a final-round record five hours and one minute, was decided by a 36-game fifth set—Wimbledon's longest ultimate set—and had to be completed on the day following the singles championship because of rain delays, 5-7, 7-6 (7-5), 3-6, 7-6 (7-5), 19-17.

Seles was a lot more successful than Courier in her assault on the grass but she also endured greater frustration. The complaints about her grunting actually grew in volume and opponents joined in the controversy fueled by the tabloid press. Nathalie Tauziat of France raised the issue before her straight-set dismissal, 6-1, 6-3, in the quarterfinals and Navratilova did her one better, reporting Seles to umpire Fran McDowell, who called her to the chair for an admonition in the midst of the ladies' semifinal. Seles still prevailed, 6-2, 6-7 (3-7), 6-4.

"It just gets loud and louder," Navratilova said. "You cannot hear the ball being hit . . . I am not saying I lost because of her grunting. I would have said this if I won . . . I know she is not doing it on purpose, but she can stop it on purpose."

That's exactly what Seles did in the final. She barely uttered a peep against Graf. Was she psyched out? Whether that was a cause or an effect of her listless performance was a matter for conjecture. The German woman was crisp and dominating from the outset and Seles appeared as limp as the weather, which forced three delays. Although the match lasted 5½ hours, only 58 minutes were devoted to tennis, 6-2, 6-1.

"I didn't want to think about it," the loser said of her sudden silence. "I just thought hopefully I can start [not grunting] somewhere, so I started here." Call it bad timing. Monica was stopped after winning five major titles and 41 matches in a row, her only loss in seven major finals.

Because she failed to participate in the 1991 Federation Cup, Seles was not eligible for the Olympic tournament. Neither was Navratilova nor Sabatini. But Graf, who had helped Germany to the 1992 Federation Cup title over Spain, 2-1, the previous month (she beat Sanchez Vicario, 6-4, 6-2, and Anke Huber beat Conchita Martinez, 6-3, 6-7 [1-7], 6-1), arrived for Barcelona clay in pursuit of a second consecutive gold medal.

She was one match away from a repeat of Seoul. Capriati, who had terminated Seles' streak of 21 consecutive final-round appearances in the Lipton quarterfinals, 6-2, 7-6 (7-5)—Sanchez Vicario won the title over Sabatini, 6-1, 6-4—but hadn't won a tournament herself, was ready to interfere with Graf, too. Jenny emerged from her growing pains to stun Fraulein Forehand, 6-3, 3-6, 6-4. She bubbled with delight on the medal stand. "I had chills the whole time," the youngster said. "Right now this means more to me than any of the Grand Slams."

The men's competition in intense heat on turgid courts produced bigger surprises. Five of the first six seeds were dispersed fast: first Courier, bombed in the third round, 6-4, 6-2, 6-1, by the man of destiny, the Swiss Rosset; second Edberg, booted immediately by Russian Andrei Chesnokov, 6-0, 6-4, 6-4; third Sampras, eroded by another Russian, Andre Cherkasov, in the third round, 6-7 (7-9), 1-6, 7-5, 6-0, 6-3; fifth Becker, worn out in the third round by France's Fabrice Santoro, 6-1, 3-6, 6-1, 6-3; sixth Chang, startled in the second round by Brazilian Jaime Oncins, 6-2, 3-6, 6-3, 6-3. Rosset, who didn't let the clay hamper his serving, drove the Spanish crowds to anguish by beating the homeboys, Emilio Sanchez in the quarters, 6-4, 7-6 (7-2), 3-6, 7-6 (11-9), and, for the gold medal, the just-as-unexpected 16th seed, Jordi Arrese. Surviving a mid-match attack of cramps, and winning the last two games from the dogged little Spaniard, No. 44-

ranked Rosset claimed a rare medal for Switzerland, in a dehydrating slog of 5 hours, 3 minutes, 7-6 (7-2), 6-3, 3-6, 4-6, 8-6, sprinkling 38 aces along the way for a total of 93. The seed who did hold up, fourth, Croat Ivanisevic, was beaten by Rosset in the semis, 6-3, 7-5, 6-2, and got a bronze along with Cherkasov in singles and another with countryman Goran Prpic in doubles.

Becker and Stich combined to win the men's doubles for a unified German team over South Africa's Wayne Ferreira and Piet Norval, 7-6 (7-5), 4-6, 7-6 (7-5), 6-3. Ferreira-Norval were their nation's first medalists since 1960 in Rome, when South Africa took a silver in track and field, and two bronze in boxing. The unrelated Fernandez women, Gigi and Mary Joe, captured the gold medal in doubles for the U.S., beating home-towners Sanchez Vicario and Conchita Martinez, 7-5, 2-6, 6-2.

In retrospect, Gigi Fernandez may have enjoyed the best season of any American woman. In addition to her Olympic honor, she teamed with Natalia Zvereva of Minsk to win doubles championships at the French Open, Wimbledon and the U.S. Open. They had no Grand Slam opportunity since each had another partner at the Australian. Joining forces at the French, to win over Martinez and Sanchez Vicario, 6-3, 6-2, they would become one of the finest teams in history, amassing 12 majors by 1996.

At Flushing Meadow, Navratilova suffered a shocking second-round defeat administered by No. 17 Magdalena, the third of the three Maleeva sisters on the circuit. One year after she became the oldest woman's finalist in open tournament history, she was ousted by a 17-year-old precisely half her age, 6-4, 0-6, 6-3. It marked her earliest exit from the Open since 1976 when she departed in tears following a first-round knockout by Janet Newberry at Forest Hills.

Maggie advanced to the quarterfinals, where she fell, 6-2, 5-3 (ret.), to the oldest of her sisters, ninth-seeded Manuela Maleeva Fragniere. In the same round Sanchez Vicario eliminated Graf, 7-6

(7-5), 6-3, and Mary Joe Fernandez toppled Sabatini, 6-2, 1-6, 6-4. The wave of upsets cleared any major obstacles from Seles' path and she cakewalked to the title without the loss of a set, turning back Fernandez in a semifinal, 6-3, 6-2, and Sanchez Vicario in the final, 6-3, 6-3. Seles was slowed only by a nasty cold and a sore throat.

The men had much greater difficulty settling their differences. They played from here to "Infiniti," which happened to be the corporate sponsor of the men's singles. Although all four top seeds reached the semis, it was not without a struggle.

Seldom, if ever, had a champion labored longer for his silver and gold than Edberg. Of the 21 five-set matches recorded, he played three—in a row—that were among the six matches that consumed over four hours. Stefan's last four steps to his second title took 19 sets, one under the maximum, a journey such as taken by only one other U.S. champ, Bob Wrenn, almost a century before, 1896. Edberg played 203 games from the fourth round on, Wrenn 201. There was no breathing room until Stefan reached the final, a steadfast performance of only 2 hours, 52 minutes, as Sampras came apart, 6-3, 4-6, 7-6 (7-5), 6-2.

But before that came ordeals to the limit: Richard Krajicek, 6-4, 6-7 (6-8), 6-3, 3-6, 6-4, the Dutchman up a break in the fifth, 1-0; Lendl's last significant appearance, 6-3, 6-3, 3-6, 5-7, 7-6 (7-3), spread over two days by rain, Ivan ahead by a break, 4-3 in the fifth; the epic with Chang, 6-7 (3-7), 7-5, 7-6 (7-3), 5-7, 6-4, that grew and grew until it was the longest of either's life, 5 hours, 26 minutes. In fact it was the longest of all major matches, outdoing the 5:12 two-day Wimbledon siege that Pancho Gonzalez won over Charlie Pasarelli in 1969.

Moreover it roamed across one blazing afternoon, taking so many twistings and turnings that it seemed neither could win as Edberg bore in constantly and Chang counter-punched. Edberg trailed 1-4 in the first set, blotted six set points and still lost it. Chang rebounded similarly from 1-4 to 5-5, but couldn't win the second. Chang, again down 1-4 in the third, lost the first six

points of the tie-breaker. Michael jumped ahead again, 5-3, couldn't serve it out, but broke Edberg in the final game to prevent another overtime. One set for everything. Chang spurted halfway home to 3-0. Somehow Edberg slipped out of two break points, punched through Chang to 2-3—then lost serve again. But from 2-4, he swept forward in a four-game Swedish gale.

In the other semi Sampras gunned down top-seeded Courier, 6-1, 3-6, 6-2, 6-2, then went down himself, racing to the bathroom with stomach problems. Had Pete beaten Edberg, Americans would have possessed all four major championships for the first time since Don Budge did it singlehandedly in 1938. Their last triple was accomplished by Connors (Australian, Wimbledon, U.S.) in 1974.

Edberg lost his place at the top of the computer in the fall and failed a final opportunity at the ATP World Championship when he was eliminated in preliminary round-robin play by losses to Sampras, 6-3, 3-6, 7-5, and Becker, 6-4, 6-0. Nevertheless, Edberg finished the season as the leader in official earnings, with $2,341,804.

Of course, Stich almost equalled that total in one December weekend. Although he plummeted from the Top 10, the German managed to regain his singles form in time for the Grand Slam Cup in Munich, where he won the first-place prize of $2 million by defeating Chang in the final, 6-2, 6-3, 6-2. Semifinalist Ivanesevic belted 25 aces while losing to Chang, 6-7 (3-7), 6-2, 6-4, 3-6, 6-3, ending the year with a record 1,017.

The men's season was notable for two other developments. Lendl posted his 1,000th tour victory, second only to Connors, by beating Brett Steven of New Zealand, 7-5, 7-5, at the Sydney indoor championships in October, and Borg, 36, failed to capture a set in eight matches of a murky comeback attempt. He would play three more tourneys in 1993, when the closest Bjorn came to winning a match was his definite farewell to the big league in a town he was visiting for the first time, Moscow. A match point was yanked away

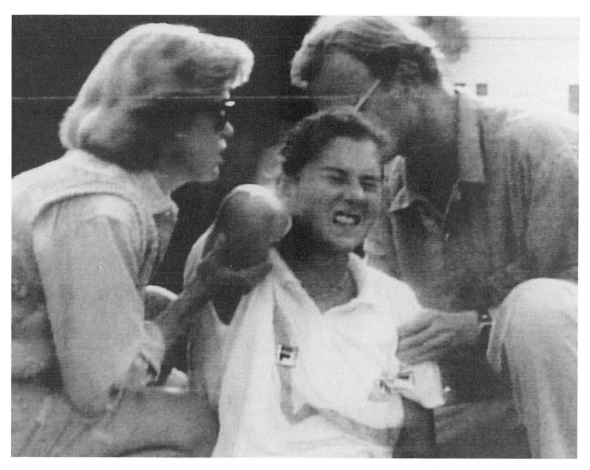

Monica Seles grimaces in pain after being stabbed by a spectator in Hamburg, Germany, in 1993. (Wide World)

by Aleksandr Volkov, who beat him, 4-6, 6-3, 7-6 (9-7), in the Kremlin Cup. The legend did, however, win his first tournament of any kind since 1981 when he handled Roscoe Tanner, 6-4, 6-1, at the Advanta Tour of Chicago for players 35 and older. The Australian duo of Todd Woodbridge and Mark Woodforde won eight doubles titles, including the ATP World Championship in Johannesburg.

Among the women, Navratilova pledged to continue playing a full schedule through 1993 but she ended the 12-year doubles partnership with Pam Shriver in order to concentrate on singles. After 79 titles, 20 majors—all four in 1984 for a Grand Slam—plus 10 trips to the winner's circle at the Virginia Slims Championship, they went their separate ways following the season-ending event at Madison Square Garden. The defending champions lost in the Slims semifinals, 6-4, 7-5, to the champs, Sanchez Vicario and Helena Sukova.

1993

Seemingly it was just another April afternoon in Hamburg, Germany. Monica Seles found herself engaged in a Citizen Cup quarterfinal on the slow red clay against the Bulgarian Magdalena Maleeva. The 19-year-old left-hander was sitting at a changeover, holding a 6-4, 4-3 lead, hoping to use this tournament to propel her toward a fourth consecutive French Open championship beginning the following month.

But then, suddenly, a deranged German named Guenther Parche emerged from the stands and stabbed Seles in the back with a nine-inch boning knife. The world No. 1 was carried off the court and rushed to the hospital. The physical harm from this tragic moment was not terribly damaging, but the psychological scars would stay with her for some time to come. She wouldn't return to competition until nearly 28 months later.

The Seles Saga was without question the most significant story of 1993, transcending the sport, reminding everyone that even in the relatively tranquil world of tennis, random acts of violence could take place. The game triumphed on a number of other levels, with a surging Pete Sampras and a stalwart Steffi Graf setting the pace, establishing themselves as the top-ranked players for the year.

Sampras captured the two most prestigious titles, collecting his first major crown in nearly three years when he won Wimbledon, then concluding a remarkable summer with a second U.S. Open triumph. Graf secured three of the four biggest crowns, sweeping her third French Open, her fifth Wimbledon, and her third U.S. Open. Beyond that, the 22-year-old American and the 24-year-old German were prolific winners across the board on the men's and women's tours.

Sampras was victorious in 8 of 23 tournaments, finishing with an impressive 85-16 (.841) match record, posting a 19-match winning streak in the spring. Graf won 10 of 15 tournaments and 76 of 82 matches for an astounding .927 winning percentage. Only once in her last nine tournament appearances was Graf beaten, suffering one other loss in Federation Cup competition. Graf garnered the season-ending Virginia Slims Championship at New York's Madison Square Garden while Sampras got to the final of the ATP Tour Championships in Frankfurt.

But neither Sampras nor Graf came through in the first of the season's premier events. Jim Courier, the No. 1-ranked player in the world for 1992, successfully defended in the Australian Open final, defeating Stefan Edberg, 6-2, 6-1, 2-6, 7-5. Courier's crackling backhand returns off Edberg's renowned kick serve were too much for the stylish Swede. Edberg had eliminated Sampras, 7-6 (7-5), 6-3, 7-6 (7-3), in the semifinals, recouping from 0-4 in the opening set and 2-5 in the third on his way to a second straight major triumph over the American.

When Seles collided with Graf in the women's final at Melbourne, it marked the third time in the last four major events that the two superstars had battled in the final. Seles had somehow held back her chief adversary, 6-2, 3-6, 10-8, in the French Open in 1992 but then had been battered, 6-2, 6-1, in the Wimbledon final a month later. Now they had another bruising skirmish under a broiling sun.

Although Seles prevailed, 4-6, 6-3, 6-2, to extend her winning streak to three titles and 21 matches in a row at Flinders Park, the match was much closer than the score reflects. They produced one glorious rally after another, driving their groundstrokes with astonishing pace and precision, exploring every inch of the court, pushing each other to the hilt. It took a top-of-the-line Seles to get through this arduous struggle against an almost defiant Graf. On this occasion, the superior shotmaker beat the better athlete.

When all of the leading players assembled again at the world's premier clay-court championship, Courier narrowly failed in his spirited bid to become the first American man ever to capture the French three years in a row. The 22-year-old Floridian played with immense pride and professionalism on a day when his primary weapon— the inside-out forehand—was often betraying him, and in the end the wily and unwavering Spaniard Sergi Bruguera was too solid in a 6-4, 2-6, 6-2, 3-6, 6-3 victory. In the process, Bruguera picked up his first major tournament title. Not since Manolo Orantes was the victor at

The French Open was captured by Spain's Sergi Bruguera in straight sets over Ukraine's Andrei Medvedev in 1993. (Wide World)

Forest Hills on clay in 1975 had a Spanish male taken a major.

Bruguera, 22, had thus closed the curtain on a superb fortnight on his favorite red clay courts, ousting Sampras in the quarterfinals, 6-3, 4-6, 6-1, 6-4, before dismissing the gifted Russian Andrei Medvedev, 6-0, 6-4, 6-2, in a semifinal.

Graf, meanwhile, was far from the upper level of her game on her worst surface. In turn, the German was bothered by a nagging foot injury and may have suffered in a strange way from the absence of Seles.

Graf was challenged in the final by none other than Mary Joe Fernandez, the popular American whom she had beaten in the final of the 1990 Australian Open. That had been a relatively uneventful straight-set skirmish with the issue

seldom if ever in doubt; this one was a suspenseful showdown from beginning to end, a match Graf won much more on willpower than talent.

The 21-year-old from Miami had never beaten Graf in 10 previous meetings, but had given the German a serious 4-6, 6-4, 6-3 semis test when they had last clashed a few weeks earlier in Berlin. Here at Roland Garros, Fernandez seized the first set by virtue of her backcourt play, then lost her edge in the second as Graf gained control of the baseline exchanges. But Fernandez had some big chances in the third. She was ahead, 2-0, with two break points for 3-0. She broke for 4-3 on a double fault from Graf, and reached 30-15 when she served for 5-3. Graf simply would not surrender, sweeping the last three games for a 4-6, 6-2, 6-4 triumph, winning at Roland Garros for the first time since 1988.

Nevertheless, the fifth-seeded Fernandez distinguished herself in defeat as she had in her wins on her way to the title match. In the quarterfinals, she had staged one of the most extraordinary comebacks ever. Facing her friendly rival Gabriela Sabatini, Fernandez fell behind, 6-1, 5-1, 40-30, with the popular Argentine at match point. Sabatini gave that one away with a double fault. A resolute Fernandez proceeded to save three more match points in (5-3, 40-15 and ad in) turning the second set around. What started as an easy one-hour victory for Sabatini expanded into a 3-hour, 34-minute nightmare, a French epic. Fernandez won the set in a 7-4 tie-breaker, but had to resist again as Sabatini served for victory a last time at 7-6 in the third. Understandably dismayed when she couldn't close it there, Gabriela then fought off four match points herself before Mary Joe concluded the screamer with a backhand winner, 1-6, 7-6, 10-8. It was the fourth time in five major tournament confrontations that Fernandez had cut down Sabatini. Buoyant after that astounding escape, Fernandez routed the 1989 French Open titlist, second-seeded Arantxa Sanchez Vicario, 6-2, 6-2.

On to Wimbledon. Sampras had taken over the No. 1 ranking on the ATP computer back in

April, but was still searching for his first major prize since the 1990 U.S. Open. A shoulder injury nearly kept him out of the tournament. But, ultimately, Sampras was ready to make his move.

In an all-American final held appropriately on the fourth of July, Sampras stopped a tenacious Courier, 7-6 (7-3), 7-6 (8-6), 3-6, 6-3. Sampras lost his serve only once in four sets. He was clearly the better grass-court player, but was also fortunate. Down set point in the second-set tiebreak, he poked a forehand volley into Courier's vacant backhand corner which appeared to be floating long. That volley fell inches inside the baseline, and soon Sampras had the set.

The end, however, was not easy for Sampras. When he served for the match and reached 40-15, he crouched over in obvious pain with stomach cramps. Courier saved the first match point, but Sampras sealed his title on the second. "I was more nervous for this match than for any match I have ever played. I wanted that Wimbledon title, and I couldn't sleep the night before," Sampras said.

In the quarterfinals, he had ousted defending champion Andre Agassi in a captivating Centre Court skirmish witnessed by Agassi's renowned friend Barbra Streisand, who caused a considerable commotion when she walked into the celebrated cathedral of the sport. At the outset, Sampras seemed to have borrowed his tactics from Arthur Ashe, confounding Agassi just as Ashe had done against Jimmy Connors on the same court 18 years earlier in a triumphant final.

Feeding the Las Vegas native a barrage of soft sliced backhands and moderately paced forehands, robbing Agassi completely of his rhythm, Sampras stormed to a two-sets-to-love lead. But then Agassi blasted his way into the contest with some spectacular returns and stellar passing shots. It took stupendous serving and a cool head to pull Sampras through, 6-2, 6-2, 3-6, 3-6, 6-4. Serving for the match at 5-4 in the fifth, he delivered three consecutive aces for 40-0 to firmly settle the issue.

Coming off that emotionally draining victory, Sampras had to deal with three-time former titlist Boris Becker in a semifinal. But Sampras did not lose his serve in a convincing 7-6 (7-5), 6-4, 6-4 win.

The women's final featured Jana Novotna at the peak of her powers right up until the absolute crunch of her contest against the top-seeded Graf. After losing the first set, the 24-year-old Czech demonstrated why she is the most complete player in the women's game. She attacked persistently and intelligently to win 10 of the next 12 games, building a 4-1 third-set lead. It seemed certain that Novotna was going to secure her first major title.

The eighth seed reached game point for 5-1, only to double-fault and let that crucial game slip from her grasp. Then Novotna wasted two break points in the following game. To make matters even worse, Novotna served three more double faults in losing her serve at 4-3. Amazed to still be in the match, Graf lost only one more point in the last two games. Graf's 7-6 (8-6), 1-6, 6-4 victory was surely a fortunate escape as Novotna flagrantly choked.

"The worst part for Novotna is not so much that she lost the final but that she gave it away, and that will be very hard to live with," said Ann Jones, the 1969 Wimbledon champion who called the match for BBC.

It was a lost opportunity of spectacular proportions for Novotna, her 17th defeat in 20 career showdowns with Graf. But she had performed with poise in her semifinal victory over second-seeded Martina Navratilova. For the 16th time in 21 Wimbledon appearances, Navratilova had reached the semifinal round, but she seemed ill at ease and out of sorts throughout her 6-4, 6-4 loss. Novotna was much crisper on the volley, served with more power and accuracy, and returned far more skillfully than a sluggish Navratilova, who had raised the expectations of her brigade of supporters by winning an 11th singles title at Eastbourne the week before Wimbledon, over Miriam Oremans, 2-6, 6-2, 6-3.

Pete Sampras (right) won his first Wimbledon crown in 1993, defeating Jim Courier. (Wide World)

When the last major championship of the season, the U.S. Open, took place at Flushing Meadow, the No. 1 world ranking was on the line. It seemed likely that Courier and Sampras would meet in the final to settle the issue. Courier had appeared in the last three major finals, while Sampras had plainly picked up steam with his Wimbledon success. But that scenario was spoiled when Courier gave a desultory performance on a dark afternoon against the gifted yet erratic Frenchman Cedric Pioline.

The 15th seed had never beaten Courier before. Only three weeks earlier in Indianapolis, Courier had dispatched Pioline in straight sets. But here in the round of 16, Courier lost his in-

tensity and couldn't find his range off the ground. He went down somewhat tamely, 7-5, 6-7 (4-7), 6-4, 6-4, only moments before rain arrived in the stadium. In every conceivable way, Courier had lost his timing.

Not so Sampras. He was stable and confident despite a wave of upsets surrounding him all through the tournament. In the final, Sampras overwhelmed Pioline, 6-4, 6-4, 6-3, for his second Open crown. He was a class above the 24-year-old Frenchman, serving too severely, returning with more authority and consistency.

Courier was not the only leading player who did not deliver. Joining the top-seeded Courier in the land of upsets was third-seeded Stefan Edberg, the two-time defending champion who fell in a second-round, 7-6 (7-3), 6-4, 4-6, 6-4, to the Czech Karel Novacek. Fourth seed Becker was taken apart by Sweden's Magnus Larsson, No. 60, in the third round, 6-2, 6-3, 3-6, 7-5. There were so many surprises that former Wimbledon semifinalist Tim Mayotte could only conclude early in the second week of the event, "I have never, ever, ever seen anything like this here. Never." Probably because there hadn't been such a shakeup "here," meaning the Meadow: three semifinalists of such lowly station—unseeded Wally Masur and 14th and 15th seeds Aleksandr Volkov of Russia and Pioline high-lifting it—to share the final four with second-seeded Sampras.

You had to search back to 1967 at Forest Hills to uncover a more common crowd: two un-seeded semifinalists, Gene Scott and a Dane, Jan Leschly, keeping company with first-third seeds John Newcombe and Clark Graebner. Masur, 30, the heady old boy Aussie, No. 24, was having the tournament of his life (he'd been a semifinalist at the Australian in 1987). Serving and volleying cleverly, he'd puzzled baselining foes. Wally made an all-time Open spring-back against coun-tryman Jaimie Morgan in the fourth round. Revving up from two sets, then 0-5 down in the fifth, he cancelled a match point in the seventh game, winning, 3-6, 4-6, 6-3, 6-4, 7-5, on a rush of 25 of 28 points after Morgan missed a fore-hand that would have ended it. Reprieved, Masur had Larsson going in many directions, all of them wrong, 6-2, 7-5, 7-5. But Pioline got him, 6-1, 6-7 (3-7), 7-6 (7-2), 6-1. Volkov, after denying two match points at 4-5 in the fifth to beat Thomas Muster, 7-6 (8-6), 6-3, 3-6, 2-6, 7-5, went pacifist against Sampras, 6-4, 6-3, 6-2.

The women had some surprises of their own, but nothing to compare with the men. Graf won her third Open and her first since 1989, a 6-3, 6-3 triumph over 13th seed Helena Sukova, the 28-year-old Czech who had lost the 1986 final to Martina Navratilova. Graf was too quick, confi-dent and relaxed. She exploited her topspin back-hand passing shot with inordinate success. It was hardly a contest.

Sukova had come from behind to startle her doubles partner, Sanchez Vicario, 6-7 (7-9), 7-5, 6-2, in the semifinals, toppling the second seed with her shrewd, attacking game plan. Sukova also knocked out the third-seeded Navratilova 7-5, 6-4 in the round of 16 with first rate serving-and-volleying, calling to mind her upset of Marti-na in the 1984 Australian Open, preventing her rival from winning a Grand Slam that year and also ending Martina's Open Era record 74 match-winning streak.

Despite the absence of Becker, Germany captured the Davis Cup with a 4-1 victory over Australia in Dusseldorf. The 1991 Wimbledon champion, Michael Stich, led the charge with vic-tories over Jason Stoltenberg from 0-2 in the fifth, 6-7 (2-7), 6-3, 6-1, 4-6, 6-3, and the icer over Richard Fromberg, 6-4, 6-2, 6-2. A superior accomplishment probably was the least expected, Stich joining Patrik Kuhnen to jar the world's foremost pair, Mark Woodforde and Todd Wood-bridge, 7-6 (7-4), 4-6, 6-3, 7-6 (7-4). That offset Fromberg's incredible first-day snap-back to top Marc Goellner, 3-6, 5-7, 7-6 (10-8), 6-2, 9-7, res-cuing three match points in the tie-breaker and two more at the end, 6-7, 15-40.

Disappointingly, the U.S. had bowed out in the opening round, 4-1 to Australia on grass in Melbourne, this only shortly after regaining the Cup against Switzerland at the close of 1992 with a team of Andre Agassi, Courier, Sampras and John McEnroe. None of those cared to make the trip Down Under, and the hosts virtually wrapped it up the first day before slight gatherings at Kooyong, a crowded bastion during the Aussies' glory days. Masur beat Brad Gilbert, 6-3, 6-7 (6-8), 6-4, 6-2, and Woodforde stopped David Wheaton, 3-6, 7-6 (7-1), 6-4, 6-4.

But Agassi reappeared as the U.S. avoided a free-fall to the nether regions (as in 1987) in the September relegation match, a 5-0 win over the Bahamas at Charlotte, N.C., the last of captain Tom Gorman's U.S. record 16 victories. Andre led off over Roger Smith, 6-2, 6-2, 6-2. Then MaliVai Washington, the first black rookie to start for the U.S. in 30 years, since Arthur Ashe broke in against Venezuela in 1963, was aided by foe Mark Knowles' heat exhaustion in winning, 6-7 (5-7), 6-4, 4-6, 15-all, default. Another McEnroe, rookie Patrick, the kid brother, took part in the decisive doubles, with Richey Reneberg, over Knowles and Smith, 7-5, 6-4, 6-2. Patrick and John were the second pair of brothers to play for the U.S., following Bob and George Wrenn of the 1903 team.

Spain's accomplished duo of Sanchez Vicario and Conchita Martinez took apart the Australians in the Fed Cup final at Frankfurt, winning, 3-0. But Aussie Nicole Provis produced an astonishing upset in the opening round, a 2-1 win over Germany. Nicole—a semifinalist at the French Open back in 1988—startled Steffi Graf, 6-4, 1-6, 6-1, in the upset of the year among the women.

Meanwhile, the Germans Graf and Stich came through to claim the singles crowns at the season-ending events in New York and Frankfurt. Graf got off to a good start and resisted a challenge from Sanchez Vicario in the Virginia Slims final, prevailing 6-1, 6-4, 3-6, 6-1. Sanchez Vicario had won a compelling semifinal showdown from a calmer and more composed Mary Pierce, but Pierce had picked up more than a small measure of confidence from her wins over Sabatini and Navratilova on the indoor carpet.

Stich had his most impressive win of the year when he upended Sampras in the final of the ATP Tour Championships at Frankfurt. Serving seven consecutive aces over two service games in the fourth set, Stich surprised the American, 7-6 (7-3), 2-6, 7-6 (9-7), 6-2, to conclude a terrific late-season surge and move past Courier to No. 2 in the year-end ATP computer rankings.

All in all, it was a captivating year. In 88 ATP Tour events, 45 different champions surfaced. Americans accounted for 27 of those titles, with no other nation coming close to that total.

On another statistical note, Sampras' superiority as a server was reflected emphatically in his tour-leading numbers. He served no fewer than 1,011 aces in 94 charted matches, more than 200 beyond the total of anyone else. He held serve 90 percent of the time and won 82 percent of his first serve points.

Meanwhile, the exuberant combination of Gigi Fernandez and Natasha Zvereva came within two matches of a Grand Slam in doubles, a feat last realized by Navratilova and Pam Shriver in 1984. Fernandez-Zvereva reached the penultimate round of the U.S. Open but their bid for a sweep of the four major championships was halted by Sukova-Sanchez Vicario, 1-6, 6-3, 6-4. The fact remained that the year was a celebration for the top-ranked partnership in the women's game.

Ultimately, beyond all of the positive developments in 1993, looking past the traumatic experience of Seles, the tennis world mourned the loss of one of its most remarkable leaders. On February 6, Arthur Ashe died of AIDS complications at 49. A singularly revered statesman and spokesman, unofficial worldwide ambassador for the sport, always a voice of reason and integrity, Ashe left behind a shining legacy.

The winner of the first U.S. Open in 1968, Australian Open titlist two years later, and a dignified Davis Cup player and captain for his country, Ashe had enjoyed the crowning moment of his career in 1975 when he toppled the mighty Jimmy Connors, 6-1, 6-1, 5-7, 6-4, with a strategic masterpiece in the Wimbledon final.

1994

As the curtain closed on 1994, two of the greatest players in the history of the game retired simultaneously, taking unparalleled accomplishments with them and leaving with few regrets. Martina Navratilova had planned her departure from singles events nearly a year earlier and realized this would be her final campaign. Ivan Lendl had no intention of quitting, but a nagging back injury forced him to step permanently away from the sport he had dominated with pride and professionalism.

Lendl had little to show for his last year on the ATP Tour. He finished with a mediocre 28-18 match record, reaching only one final in Sydney, sinking to No. 54 in the year-end rankings. In his last match as a professional, he walked off the court at the U.S. Open, his back causing him too much pain to continue in his second-round meeting with Germany's Bernd Karbacher. Lendl left the stadium that afternoon a 6-4, 7-6 (7-5), 1-0 loser, and no one had a clue he wouldn't return.

But he was 34, his best days clearly behind him. When the year came to an end, he acknowledged that he would no longer compete. He had amassed a career-record prize-money total of $21,624,417. He had been ranked No. 1 in the world on the ATP computer for a record 270 weeks in all, including 157 weeks in a row during one stretch. He had appeared in a Tilden-tying record eight consecutive U.S. finals (1982–89), winning the tournament three times in that span. He had captured three French Opens, two Australian Opens and had twice been a Wimbledon finalist.

He finished four years at No. 1 in the world on the computer (1985, 1986, 1987 and 1989), and from 1981 through 1992 was never out of the Top Five. Altogether, he won 94 tournament singles titles across his powerfully productive career, second to Jimmy Connors' 109 for the open era.

Navratilova lived along the same lines of achievement, but was more of a force in her final year. Three months before she turned 38, she reached her 11th Wimbledon singles final, only to fall narrowly short of a 10th title. Nevertheless, she concluded the year at No. 8 in the world, celebrating her 20th consecutive season among the Top Ten. Remarkably, 1994 was the only time in that span that Navratilova failed to finish a year in the Top Five.

She was nine times the Wimbledon singles champion, collecting four U.S. Open titles, three Australian, and two French. She won an open-era record 167 singles titles, was ranked No. 1 in the world for a total of 332 weeks, concluding seven seasons on top of the charts. And in one nearly impeccable stretch, she enjoyed five years on the edge of invincibility, winning 44 of 50 tournaments from 1982 through 1986, taking 254 of 260 matches, and setting a modern record with her 74-match winning streak in 1984. Her career match record was 1,438-212 (.872).

And yet, while the departures of Lendl and Navratilova—she would continue to play top-flight doubles and mixed doubles over the next couple of years—were of significance, there were other prominent themes developing during the year.

In the women's game, the effervescent Arantxa Sanchez Vicario came of age at 23. Heading into the 1994 campaign, she had secured only one of the major championships, coming through at Roland Garros five years earlier. This time around, the cunning baseliner was the only woman to win two of the major tournaments, capturing a second French Open crown in June and sealing a first U.S. Open championship three months later.

Although Steffi Graf would remain at No. 1 on the year-end WTA computer, most experts accorded the less talented but incomparably tenacious Spaniard the top ranking, including the ITF. The game's venerable governing body named Sanchez Vicario as their official "World Champion" for 1994 over Graf, an assessment based on Sanchez Vicario's greater accumulation of Virginia Slims points for the year.

But both the ITF and keen analysts among the media based their belief in Sanchez Vicario's preeminence primarily on her outstanding showing in the majors. Meanwhile, Steffi did seize a fourth consecutive major singles title at the start of the season in Melbourne, gaining a fourth Australian Open Championship. But it became a year of unexpected diversity after that, with Sanchez Vicario posting her two big triumphs and her country-woman Conchita Martinez breaking through at Wimbledon for her initial major success.

As was the case with the women, three different men took the prizes of highest prestige. Pete Sampras was victorious at the Australian Open for the first time and won Wimbledon again. Sergi Bruguera held on stubbornly to his French Open title. And then a resurgent André Agassi captured the championship of his country at long last, sweeping the U.S. Open at the end of summer.

The season started with the favorites flowing Down Under. Sampras had missed two of the previous three Australian Opens with injuries, and was appearing at Flinders Park for only the fourth time. But the deeply driven American proceeded to register a third major championship in a row, becoming the first man since Rod Laver in the Australian's Grand Slam campaign of 1969 to pull off this hat trick of sorts. Sampras stopped his countryman and golfing buddy Todd Martin in the final, overcoming a tentative start to win comfortably, 7-6 (7-4), 6-4, 6-4.

Sampras had peaked for his semifinal confrontation with Jim Courier, who was hoping to take this tournament for the third year in a row. But sparring successfully with his big-hitting countryman from the backcourt and serving well, Sampras rolled without the loss of a single service game to win, 6-3, 6-4, 6-4. Martin came from behind to oust ex-champ Stefan Edberg, 3-6, 7-6 (9-7), 7-6 (9-7), 7-6 (7-4), for his only place in a major final.

Sampras had survived a second-round showdown with the ascending Russian Yevgeny Kafelnikov, prevailing 6-3, 2-6, 6-3, 1-6, 9-7, coming within two points of defeat in the fifth set.

Graf was close to letter perfect in her 6-0, 6-2 dismantling of Sanchez Vicario in the Australian final: driving her formidable forehand with depth and accuracy, serving with overwhelming power and precision, keeping her mind completely on her business. Both the top-seeded German and the second seed from Spain were clearcut semifinal victors, Graf upending 10th seed Kimiko Date of Japan, 6-3, 6-3, and Sanchez Vicario dismissing Gabriela Sabatini, 6-1, 6-2.

Her reaction says it all for Spain's Arantxa Sanchez Vicario, who subdued Steffi Graf in the 1994 U.S. Open final. (Wide World)

When the best players in the business came to Roland Garros for the French Open, there were many pieces of intrigue spread out across the clay-court capital of the world. But above and beyond anyone else, it was Mary Pierce's tournament. The 19-year-old citizen of France who had been born in Montreal and grew up in Florida was flourishing in Paris, hitting her lethal groundstrokes with a velocity seldom if ever seen in the women's game, blitzing through the draw with awesome ease.

On her way to a first appearance in a major final, Pierce conceded a mere ten games in six matches. The 12th seed was picking everyone apart meticulously. Even the great Graf couldn't contain her. In a dazzling display in the penultimate round, Pierce toppled the top seed incredibly, 6-2, 6-2. In eight service games, Graf was broken a staggering six times, seldom looking so helpless. It was arguably the single most potent performance by a woman all year long, reminiscent in some ways of Monica Seles.

Pierce's remarkable run was suitably noticed by her rivals. As American Lindsay Davenport said, "Even Monica Seles could not destroy Steffi Graf the way Mary did. It's amazing what Mary had done, great for our game. This is just what we needed, not another Steffi French Open."

But then reality set in for the final. Facing 1989 champion Sanchez Vicario, Pierce was forced to sit around all afternoon, waiting for the rain to stop. They finally started at 6:22 p.m., but had to stop when it rained again with Sanchez Vicario serving at 1-2 and a break point down in the first set.

Pierce had been given too much time to think about what might be in store for her. When they returned at noon the next day to complete the title match, the pendulum swung decidedly, 6-4, 6-4 for the Spaniard.

Sanchez Vicario revived from 1-3 to take five of the next six games and took three of the last four games from 3-3 in the second as Pierce self-destructed, overhitting wildly at times, breaking down badly against a top-notch percentage player.

As for the men, Sampras saw his 25-match winning streak in majors come to an end at the hands of Courier in the quarterfinals. The week before Roland Garros, Sampras' career-high 29 match-winning streak had come to an end in the World Team Cup against Michael Stich, 3-6, 7-6 (9-7), 6-2. Despite winning the Italian Open, Pete didn't seem to believe it was his time to rule on the red clay of Paris. Courier was close to the top of his game in a 6-4, 5-7, 6-4, 6-4 win over his old rival, defeating Sampras for only the third time in 13 career meetings.

But for the second year in a row, Courier couldn't cope with an imperturbable Bruguera. With the wind blowing fiercely all over Roland Garros, the defending champion simply used the adverse conditions to his advantage while Courier sprayed his groundstrokes dismally out of court. Bruguera won, 6-3, 5-7, 6-3, 6-3, and then handled his unorthodox countryman Alberto Berasategui, 6-3, 7-5, 2-6, 6-1, to keep his French crown.

At Wimbledon, Sampras reaffirmed his status as the best player in the world, losing only a single set in seven matches, setting the record straight with his troublesome adversary Goran Ivanisevic. In 1992, Ivanisevic had stopped Sampras in a four-set semifinal, but this time the American prevailed, 7-6 (7-2), 7-6 (7-5), 6-0, in the final.

Ivanisevic had demoralized Sampras in their 1992 meeting when he released 36 aces over four sets. The towering left-handed Croat came at Sampras with full force again in this battle, releasing 16 aces in the first set alone, holding from 4-5, 0-40 with four aces in the next five points. But Sampras came through in the two tie-breaks and then glided through the third as his opponent surrendered.

In the semifinals, Sampras had removed Martin, 6-4, 6-4, 3-6, 6-3, avenging a loss to his countryman at Queen's Club a few weeks earlier. Ivanisevic overpowered Boris Becker 6-2, 7-6 (7-6), 6-4, to settle a score in his semifinal. Four years earlier, Becker had ousted Ivanisevic in the same round.

The women's Wimbledon was turned upside down on a dark and rainy Tuesday afternoon. Graf was a firm favorite to win her fourth crown in a row, a sixth overall. But she drew the dangerous Lori McNeil in the first round and didn't survive. The 30-year-old from Houston—a U.S. Open semifinalist seven years earlier and a first-rate grass-court player—produced one of the most significant upsets in the history of the tournament, holding her nerve admirably through two rain delays, and saving a set point at 3-5 down in the second set with an audacious ace on her way to a 7-5, 7-6 (7-5) triumph.

Never before in the history of the world's most prestigious tournament had the women's No. 1 seed fallen in the first round. Not since the 1984 U.S. Open—when she lost to her country-woman Sylvia Hanika—had Graf made a first-round exit from a major tournament. The No. 22–ranked McNeil was unswerving on this occasion, sticking sensibly to her attacking tactics even when Graf rallied from 2-4 back to 5-5 in the first set, and maintaining her poise after Graf appeared to have the second set in hand.

That startling turn of events opened up windows everywhere on that half of the draw, and ultimately third seed Conchita Martinez was best positioned to exploit the opportunity. She engineered an unprecedented run of four consecutive three-set wins to take the title, halting Navratilova with a flock of backhand passers, 6-4, 3-6, 6-3, in the final. It was Martina's 22nd and last appearance as a singles competitor.

Their showdown on a sweltering afternoon was easily the most compelling major final of the year for the women. In the end, Navratilova harmed herself irreparably when she double-faulted at break point in both the first and fifth games. When Martinez held from 15-40 at 4-3 in that fascinating final set, she had handled her last crisis.

When it was over, Navratilova took some blades of Centre Court grass with her, and then paid proper tribute to the magnificent counter-attacking of her rival. "No one has ever passed me better off the backhand than Conchita did today," she asserted.

In the semifinal, Navratilova had stopped the surprising Gigi Fernandez, the No. 99–ranked player in singles, arguably the best doubles player in the world. Navratilova won, 6-4, 7-6 (8-6), but not before the 30-year-old had two set points in the second set. Martinez edged McNeil, 3-6, 6-2, 10-8. McNeil came within two points of the final with Martinez serving at 5-6, 30-30.

Through the end of Wimbledon, Sampras had won 8 of his 12 tournaments and was thoroughly dominating the game. But over the summer he hardly competed as tendinitis in his ankle kept him off the ATP Tour after a Davis Cup loss to Richard Krajicek in Holland. Sampras didn't play a single hard-court tournament on the way to the Open as he tried to heal.

That set the stage for an unpredictable U.S. Open. Sampras came in cold and lost gamely on a scorching afternoon, 3-6, 6-3, 4-6, 7-6 (7-4), 7-5, to the Peruvian Jaime Yzaga. His fourth-round defeat made many men believe in their chances, but it was an unseeded American who sensed better than anyone else what was entirely possible. The 1992 Wimbledon champion, Andre Agassi, was ranked a deceptively low No. 20 in the world because he had started his season in March after wrist surgery the previous December. But, like the last unseeded U.S. victor, Fred Stolle, way back in 1966, Andre, the third to pull it off, had too outstanding a dossier to be considered an upstart. The true outsider was Aussie Mal Anderson, champ in 1957. In a record run, Andre knocked out five seeds on his way to the Open crown that eluded him in the 1990 final. Vic Seixas, the champ of 1954, also beat five seeds but he was seeded second himself. Most notable was Andre's removal of sixth-seeded Michael Chang, 6-1, 6-7 (3-7), 6-3, 3-6, 6-1, a round-of-16 collision, surely the match of the tournament. From there, Agassi erased 13th seed Thomas Muster, 7-6 (7-5), 6-3, 6-0, and 9th seed Todd Martin, 6-3, 4-6, 6-2, 6-3, the only man in 1994 to appear in three major semifinals.

In the final, Agassi had the perfect foil in the 1991 Wimbledon champion, fourth-seeded Michael Stich. Stich was appearing in his first major final since his stunning run through Wimbledon three years earlier, but on the Flushing hard courts he couldn't stay with Agassi off the ground. Stich's first serve and agility around the net were more than neutralized by Agassi's incomparable return of serve and phenomenal passing shots, 6-1, 7-6 (7-5), 7-5.

Cheered on at courtside by his actress companion, Brooke Shields, Agassi didn't lose serve, allowing the gifted German 13 points in

Andre Agassi rolled to the U.S. Open title in straight sets over Germany's Michael Stich in 1994. (Wide World)

14 service games. Agassi won 69 of 89 points on serve not because he was hurting Stich severely with his serve; the damage was done in the baseline exchanges. Agassi was utterly in control of the rallies.

His triumph propelled Agassi forward among the elite once again. Pushed in a positive way by his new coach Brad Gilbert—they had been working together since the spring—Agassi was more motivated than ever before, more determined to explore his full potential. And Gilbert was not about to let his pupil become complacent, telling Agassi at courtside immediately after the U.S. Open final, "That was great, but now we start getting ready for the Australian Open. That's next."

The women's final at Flushing meadow was a stirring clash between Graf and Sanchez Vic-

ario. The two leading players had won one major apiece in 1994. Furthermore, Sanchez Vicario had already stopped Graf twice during the year from the most precarious of positions, saving two match points in the final of Hamburg, 4-6, 7-6 (7-3), 7-6 (8-6), and four more in the final of the Canadian Open, 7-5, 1-6, 7-6 (7-4). Both were big wins for different reasons. Graf was riding the wave of a 32-match winning streak when she lost to the Spaniard in Hamburg and it cut deeply into her confidence coming into the French Open. Same for the loss in Canada prior to the U.S. Open.

Now they were at it again on a hard court and Sanchez Vicario's opportunistic ways continued, 1-6, 7-6 (7-3), 6-4, in 2 hours, 7 minutes. Graf, winning 20 of the last 24 points, raced through a 22-minute first set. She was up a break, 2-1 in the second. She had a break point for 5-4, and might have served for the title if she hadn't missed a backhand return. But Steffi looked apprehensive—a trainer had come on court to treat her painful back after the ninth game—and Arantxa was accelerating. Even though Graf saved three set points to 5-5, and had a 3-2 lead in the tie-breaker with two serves to come, the bouncy Spaniard closed in a five-point rush. They kept breaking each other in the tumultuous third, cheered by 21,045 witnesses. But, holding to 4-3, Steffi couldn't resist the scrambling Arantxa, who hung on in match game through four deuces and two break points.

Although the German remained safely ahead of Sanchez Vicario in the race for No. 1 on the computer, this enormously important match convinced the cognoscenti that Sanchez Vicario was now the best player in the world. She had come through in the clutch against her greatest rival and had been the better player in the tight corners.

In the semifinals, Graf rescued herself from 2-5 in the second set of a 6-3, 7-5 triumph over Novotna while Sanchez Vicario saved a set point in the second set of a 6-1, 7-6 (8-6) win over 1990 champion Sabatini.

In the autumn, the long-awaited debut of 14-year-old Venus Williams captivated the public. Having been away from even junior tournaments for three years, the tall and talented black Californian made her first professional appearance in Oakland. She upended the American Shaun Stafford in her first-round match and then bolted to a stunning 6-2, 3-1 lead against Sanchez Vicario. The Spaniard needed all of her renowned guile and match-playing experience to pull her through, 2-6, 6-3, 6-0. But the fact remained that Williams had demonstrated her athleticism and shotmaking prowess. It was readily apparent that she could be a serious force in the years ahead.

Sanchez Vicario won the tournament over Navratilova, 1-6, 7-6 (7-5), 7-6 (7-3), the end of the singles finals line for Martina, her record 239th title bout.

At the end of the season, it was time for Sampras to step forward again and underline his greatness. Having been hobbled by injuries too often in the second half of the year, he won the ATP Tour Championship in Frankfurt to remain No. 1 in the world for the second straight year. After overcoming a surging Agassi, 4-6, 7-6 (7-5), 6-3, in a hotly contested semifinal, Sampras reversed the result of a match he had played against Boris Becker in the round robin by besting the German, 4-6, 6-3, 7-5, 6-4. The key to it all was Sampras' critical ace at 4-5, 30-40 in the third. Climbing out of that corner, Sampras didn't look back. He had won his 10th tournament of the year, a feat last realized by Lendl in 1989. That same November week at New York's Madison Square Garden, Gabriela Sabatini came out of a long slump to capture the Virginia Slims Championship. The 24-year-old Argentine stylist had opened the week with an emotional 6-4, 6-2 victory over Navratilova in Martina's last singles appearance. It was "Martina Navratilova Night" in the Garden as a banner bearing her name was hoisted to the rafters.

Nevertheless, Martina was not bathing herself in self pity. She told Sabatini, "If you play like that, you can beat anybody." Sabatini took that comment to heart and went all the way, crushing Lindsay Davenport, 6-3, 6-2, 6-4, in the final for her first tournament triumph since the 1992 Italian Open. It broke an agonizing 43-tournament losing streak and lifted Sabatini's spirits decidedly.

Meanwhile, there was one more big prize-money event left for the men, the Grand Slam Cup in Munich, and Sweden's Magnus Larsson took it. The multi-faceted 24-year-old ousted Agassi in the quarterfinals, Martin in the semifinals, and then upended Sampras, 7-6 (8-6), 4-6, 7-6 (7-5), 6-4.

Larsson, an intimidating 6-foot-5 blond basher, collected $1,500,000, but his role as Davis Cup hero while Sweden seized the grand prize for a fifth time meant more to him. Rookie U.S. Davis Cup captain Tom Gullikson put too much faith in Sampras, and Pete wanted too hard to help out in the semifinal against Sweden at Goteborg in September. Even though he barely got through the first day against serve-crashing Larsson, 6-7 (3-7), 6-4, 6-2, 7-6 (7-3), Sampras shouldn't have been there. Pete's lack of fitness, so apparent at the Open, caught up with him. He was finished, defaulting to Edberg with a calf injury after losing the first set. Since Martin had opened strongly, 6-2, 2-6, 6-4, 6-3, over Edberg, the 2-0 U.S. lead looked safe. But for the third time in U.S. Cup history, it wasn't. Jan Apell and Jonas Bjorkman, the ATP world doubles champs, and 4-0 in Cup play, kept it alive with a 6-4, 6-4, 3-6, 6-2 win over Jared Palmer and Jonathan Stark. After a nervous start, Larsson rose up to club Martin, 5-7, 6-2, 6-2, 6-4, for the 3-2 triumph. The U.S. had suffered similar deflatings from 2-0 at the hand of Australia in 1939 with the Cup at stake, and 1960 in the semifinal against Italy.

Moscow was a brand new stopover for the peripatetic 94-year-old Cup, and the Russians were brand new finalists, having astonishingly sabotaged Germany in Hamburg. The home side, led by the brilliant 22-year-old Kafelnikov, had a wonderful chance, but the Swedes were more composed in the crunch, winning the first three matches over the five-set distance in a 4-1 decision. Local hopes were pumped up and punctured again and again.

It all may have turned when lefty Volkov, No. 25, roared back from an indifferent beginning to serve a match point against No. 7 Edberg at 5-4 advantage, in the fifth set of the opener. Olympic Stadium boiled as 14,000 raised the roof for Volkov, "I never saved a match point in Davis Cup before," exulted Stefan after his see-sawing success that unmade the day of a spectator called Boris Yeltsin, the first hacker of the country. His backhand winner ended a tense rally and got Edberg to deuce. He then swatted two winning backhand returns to break serve. Thereupon President Yeltsin and entourage arrived, delaying play for about 10 minutes and apparently unnerving Volkov, who won only one more game as victory receded on Edberg's racket, 6-4, 6-2, 6-7 (2-7), 0-6, 8-6. Larsson was heartened, Kafelnikov the opposite, but Magnus had to hold off a belated charge, 6-0, 6-2, 3-6, 2-6, 6-3. Apell and Bjorkman, fending off three break points against lefty Apell's serve to 3-2 in the fifth, stayed cool to take the exciting doubles and the Cup over Kafelnikov and Andrei Olhovskiy, 6-7 (4-7), 6-2, 6-3, 1-6, 8-6.

Spain, in the persons of Sanchez Vicario and Martinez, ruled the women's world again, beating the U.S. 3-0 in the Federation Cup finale. Neither singles starter came close in the worst of all American beatings (14 games): Davenport lost to Arantxa, 6-2, 6-1; Mary Joe Fernandez to Conchita, 6-2, 6-2.

A total of 37 different champions from 19 countries were victorious on the ATP Tour while 29 women were winners in 55 official WTA Tour events. Goran Ivanisevic set a record with 1,169 aces in 85 official matches.

But nothing seemed to matter more when the year was over than the exits of Lendl and Navratilova, two towering Czechs who became U.S. citizens and changed the world of tennis immeasurably just by showing up.

1995

All year long, they went at it in a genuine battle for supremacy. They met in the first major final of the season and again in the last. Their contrasting playing styles and personalities gave the game a spark that had been missing. To be sure, this was a rivalry between two great players devoid of animosity toward each other. But the fact remained that both Pete Sampras and Andre Agassi shared the same goals and knew that more often than not they would need to go through each other to get what they wanted. That meant competing on a very lofty level, which the two Americans emphatically did over and over again.

In the end, it was Sampras who demonstrated beyond a doubt that he was the better big-match player despite losing three of his five skirmishes with his countryman. Agassi had come out of the blocks in style at the Australian Open, overcoming the defending champion Sampras in a hard-fought, four-set final. Sampras retaliated at Indian Wells, Agassi struck back at the Lipton Championships in Florida, and then he subdued Sampras again to take the Canadian Open title.

By the time the two best players in the world reached the final of the U.S. Open in September, they were not deceiving themselves in the least; they knew precisely what was at stake, fully recognized the magnitude of the moment. With Sampras having won Wimbledon two months earlier and Agassi boasting a record of decidedly more consistency, this was the closest tennis could come to a heavyweight championship of the world. And when it was over, only Sampras was still standing, a four-set winner over his worthiest rival, and now the holder of the two most prestigious prizes in tennis.

And yet, the year provided drama on other levels. At Wimbledon, the volatile left-handed American Jeff Tarango confronted Germany's Alex Mronz in a third-round match on an outside court. Mronz had won the first set in a tie-break, then fell behind early in the second. Umpire Bruno Rebeuh overruled on a service call which was questioned by Tarango. The crowd came

Jeff Tarango of the U.S. walks off the court at Wimbledon after receiving two code violations in his 1995 match with Germany's Alex Mronz, the winner by forfeit. (Wide World)

On to the interview room. Here, Tarango disgraced himself even more with a rambling press conference, elaborating on his ludicrous charge of "corruption" against Rebeuh. He was fined $5,000 for walking off the court, $10,000 for his insulting remarks about Rebeuh, and another $500 for his "shut up" stance against the courtside crowd.

But the largely self-inflicted damage was not done. He was suspended from ATP Tour events for two weeks later in the year, and fined $20,000, a figure upheld by the ATP. Furthermore, Tarango was banned from Wimbledon the following year for his actions.

Beyond the Tarango happening and the Sampras-Agassi rivalry, the game welcomed back a superstar, a player of inimitable shotmaking skills, a champion who realized that the time had come for her to put the past behind her and get on with her future. Monica Seles did just that, did it as only she can, and made a remarkable return to tennis.

Still trying to sort out that horrific moment in April 1993 when she had been stabbed in Hamburg, she had taken a long time to recover emotionally. Now she was ready at last, and the 21-year-old made a spectacular return in Toronto. She had been gone almost 28 months but there was scant evidence of that as she resumed her winning ways immediately.

Cracking groundstrokes with her customary old authority, moving opponents around at will, competing with unabashed joy, she rolled through the field at the Canadian Open, dropping only 14 games in 5 matches, routing Gabriela Sabatini, 6-1, 6-1, in the semifinals, crushing Amanda Coetzer in a lopsided final, 6-0, 6-1. She was nearly as impressive at the U.S. Open and despite losing a rousing final to Steffi Graf, she remained on top of her game. But tendinitis in her knee and an ankle injury kept her out of action for the rest of the year.

It was a year which began with Mary Pierce delivering on the promise she had made the pre-

down on Tarango, with some of the fans yelling at him, prompting Tarango to respond, "Shut up!"

Rebeuh then gave Tarango a code violation for "audible obscenity," a very questionable decision in light of Tarango's relatively tame comment. Tarango was losing control now, and called Rebeuh "corrupt." The umpire then assessed a point penalty against Tarango, which cost Tarango a game. Tarango asked for a supervisor, who stuck by Rebeuh's decisions. Tarango then walked off the court.

As if that was not extraordinary theater in itself, Tarango's wife, Benedicte, went after Rebeuh, catching up to the umpire near the referee's office and slapping him a couple of times according to an eyewitness.

vious year as runner-up at the French Open. Having trained with dedication in the month leading up to the Australian Open, she was rewarded with her first major title. In seven nearly flawless matches, she did not drop a set; not once was she pushed beyond 6-4.

In turn, she cut down a cluster of players who had given her serious problems in the past. Fourth-seeded, she halted Germany's Anke Huber, 6-2, 6-4, in the round of 16, Natasha Zvereva, 6-1, 6-4, in the quarters, second seed Conchita Martinez, 6-3, 6-1, in the semifinals, and then avenged her Roland Garros defeat to Sanchez Vicario, toppling the top seed, 6-3, 6-2, in the final.

Mary had come a long way in a few years, enduring the pain of an abusive father, Jim Pierce, who was banned from all tournaments for his unruly behavior. But while she paid tribute to her then coach Nick Bollettieri for her breakthrough triumph in Melbourne, she also gave her father the credit she felt he deserved for the work ethic he established for Mary in the early years. As Pierce said after her Australian Open success, "I used to train all day long until the sun went down. My father pushed me very hard. In eight years, I probably did the equivalent of 15 years work. But I don't regret it. I have the discipline now, and I am a perfectionist."

Andre Agassi could have spoken almost identical words after the Australian, his second straight major title. He, too, had a father, Mike Agassi, who pushed him to the hilt, and now he was reaping the rewards of his tennis upbringing, not to mention his hard work and strong strategic guidance alongside the brainy Brad Gilbert. Agassi beat Sampras, 4-6, 6-1, 7-6 (8-6), 6-4, in a remarkable final which was settled in the third-set tie-break. As Gilbert would say later, "I felt whoever won that tie-breaker would take control of the match."

That assessment was on the money. With Sampras serving at 6-4, double-set point, Agassi nailed a forehand return down the line for a win-

Mary Pierce won her first Grand Slam crown at the Australian Open in 1995, downing top seed Arantxa Sanchez Vicario of Spain in the final. (Wide World)

ner off a wide slice. Agassi saved another when Sampras missed a running forehand down the line, and that was essentially that. Sampras battled gamely in the fourth set and produced 13 of his 28 aces in that stretch, but lost his serve at 4-4 and soon the match.

For Agassi, who was in his first Australian Open, it was a landmark achievement. For Sampras, it was a stressful time. His coach and close friend Tim Gullikson had collapsed early in the tournament during a practice session, was sent to the hospital for tests, and had to fly home for treatment of a brain tumor before Sampras met Courier in the quarterfinals.

Sampras bested Courier from two sets to love down, 6-7 (4-7), 6-7 (3-7), 6-3, 6-4, 6-3, in a classic, but not before a fan yelled out early in the final set, "Do it for your coach." That jarred the normally imperturbable Sampras, who broke down in tears at a changeover and continued to cry when he went to the opposite side of the court to serve the next game. But he somehow kept serving aces through his tears and got the job done. Already—before Gullikson had gone back to Chicago—Sampras had recouped from two sets to love down against Magnus Larsson, 4-6, 6-7 (4-7), 7-5, 6-4, 6-4. After Courier, he came from a set down to stop Michael Chang to reach the final, 6-7 (6-8), 6-3, 6-4, 6-4.

All in all, it had been an exhausting two weeks and a time of self discovery. As Sampras reflected, "This taught me a lot about myself and how important Tim is. It put everything into perspective. Tennis is a great game and I want to win every match I play, but it is not the most important thing in your life. Your health is the most important thing. This just shows me how vulnerable we all are."

By the time the French Open had begun, Sampras himself was more vulnerable on the court than he had been for a long while. He had suffered a crisis of confidence on the European clay-court circuit, losing early at the Italian to France's Fabrice Santoro, and this culminated in a first-round loss spread over two days to an Austrian, persistent No. 24 Gilbert Schaller, 7-6 (7-3), 4-6, 6-7 (4-7), 6-2, 6-4, even though Sampras led 3-1 in the third at nightfall.

Agassi, who had moved past Sampras to No. 1 on the weekly ATP computer in April, was a bigger threat to win on the slow red clay of Roland Garros. He stormed into the semifinals without the loss of a set but then was ushered out of the tournament abruptly by the Russian Yevgeny Kafelnikov, 6-4, 6-3, 7-5.

Kafelnikov was no match for the relentlessly consistent Austrian, left-hander Thomas Muster, who moved into his first major final with full conviction. Muster's self-assurance was more than justifiable; he would win 65 of 67 matches on clay over the season, and secure no fewer than

11 titles on that surface. Muster was simply not to be stopped, and the 27-year-old defeated 1989 French Open victor Michael Chang, 7-5, 6-2, 6-4. From 2-5 down in the opening set, Muster took nine games in a row to break the contest wide open. Chang had eliminated defender Sergi Bruguera.

"My dream since I was a kid came true today," said a surprisingly emotional Muster when it was over. "This was the one big thing missing for me."

Steffi Graf had been missing at the Australian Open, unable to compete because of a calf injury. Coming into Roland Garros, she was skeptical about her chances of playing there as perennial problems with her back persisted. But Graf came to play, and played to win, and emerged with an immensely satisfying 16th major title.

In securing a fourth French Open crown, Graf renewed her rivalry with Sanchez Vicario. The defending champion looked likely to hold on to her title when she split the first two sets of the final with Steffi, but Graf produced perhaps the best set of clay-court tennis in her career to prevail, 7-5, 4-6, 6-0. In the final set, a devastating Graf won 24 of 30 points, overwhelming Sanchez Vicario with her piercing shot combinations.

"There were some very difficult weeks for me before I came to this tournament," reflected Graf. "I never really thought I could get to the final. I only had eight or nine days of practice before the tournament and I had been sick. I wasn't sure if that would be enough to get me through."

In the semifinals, Graf held off Martinez, 6-3, 6-7 (5-7), 6-3. Martinez had won four consecutive clay-court tournaments en route to Paris and had a 24-match winning streak going for her. She began slowly, and Graf had four game points for a 5-1 second-set lead. The Spaniard willed her way back into the match, took the tie-break, then reached 0-40 with Graf serving at 3-3 in the third. But here Martinez collapsed under pressure.

Sanchez Vicario beat the guileful Kimiko Date, 7-5, 6-3, in her semifinal after Date defeated the promising Croatian Iva Majoli, 7-5, 6-1. Majoli had crushed an error-prone third seed Pierce, 6-2, 6-3, in the round of 16.

At Wimbledon, Sampras took another substantial step up the historical ladder of the sport, becoming the first American man ever to win the world's most prestigious tournament three years in a row. A morale-boosting tournament triumph at Queen's Club in London eight days before Wimbledon—only the second tournament win for Sampras all year—gave the big-serving American just the lift he needed, and he closed in on his target.

In a battle of Wimbledon heroes for the title, Sampras was too good for the three-time titlist Boris Becker. In four sets, he did not lose his serve and never even faced a single break point. Thus, in three Wimbledon finals encompassing eleven sets and a trio of different opponents—Sampras had lost only one service game.

Becker gave himself a considerable boost by taking the first set, 7-5, in the tie-break, but was soundly beaten, 6-7, 6-2, 6-4, 6-2, as Sampras broke him five times over the next three sets. "In the 1980s," said a sporting Becker after his loss, "Centre Court was my court. But now it belongs to Pete Sampras."

Nevertheless, Becker had brought back those glory days of the '80s in a rousing semifinal comeback over top seed Andre Agassi. Agassi was almost beyond belief at the outset, sprinkling the Centre Court with brilliant service returns and passing shots, making the game look impossibly easy in building a 6-2, 4-1, two-service-break lead.

But then Becker found his form. When the burly German got back on even terms by seizing the second set, 7-1, in the tie-break, Agassi's despondency was almost tangible. The American was permanently wounded, and Becker completed a 2-6, 7-6 (7-1), 6-4, 7-6 (7-1) triumph, finish-

ing off one of the most celebrated comebacks at the shrine of the sport in the modern era.

Sampras was given a demanding test by Ivanisevic in his semifinal as the Croatian left-hander released 34 aces across the first four sets, winning 20 straight points on serve in the fourth. But Sampras' greater stability pulled him through in the fifth and Ivanisevic served only four more aces. Sampras was the victor, 7-6 (9-7), 4-6, 6-3, 4-6, 6-3. The closeness of the contest was reflected in this: Sampras won 146 points, Ivanisevic 145.

The men surely had a very good Wimbledon, but in many ways the women upstaged them at the end. Graf and Sanchez Vicario contested a final which will be placed up there among the five best Open Era title matches.

It had already been a bruising and alluring battle when the two towering competitors reached 5-5 in the third. But the 11th game of the final set took the match into another category altogether. They fought ferociously for 20 minutes, through 13 deuces and 32 points. Sanchez Vicario had eight game points before Graf broke through on her sixth break point. It was perhaps the single greatest game in the history of women's tennis at Wimbledon.

Sanchez Vicario had never been beyond the quarterfinals at Wimbledon, and she seemed likely to lose decisively against Graf on grass. But it was apparent from the outset that she was ready to test the favorite. She set a strong tone with a pair of effective serve-and-volley combinations early on. And in taking the first set, she gave up only five points in five service games. But ultimately, Sanchez Vicario lost a third straight major tournament final, 4-6, 6-1, 7-5. Nonetheless, she had gained a wave of new admirers with her tactical range and her inexhaustible fighting spirit.

That was a fitting conclusion for the tournament, with the two top seeds engaging in an outstanding final. But the semifinals had been extraordinary in their way as well. Graf ousted fourth seed Jana Novotna in a repeat of the 1993 final,

Celebration at the Savoy Hotel in London: Steffi Graf and Pete Sampras share the spotlight after winning Wimbledon in 1995. (Wide World)

5-7, 6-4, 6-2, but there was one striking difference this time around: Novotna clearly did not choke. This match was worthy of a final with Novotna pushing the champion close to her limits. Sanchez Vicario dethroned 1994 titlist Martinez, 6-3, 6-7 (5-7), 6-1, after Martinez surged back from 2-5 down to take the second set.

And so the players moved into the heart of summer, and no one sizzled more than Agassi. Along the way to Flushing Meadow, Agassi played too well for his own good, capturing four tournament titles in a row—Washington, Montreal, Cincinnati, and New Haven—and winning 20 matches in a row over that span. He thrived in the oppressive heat as few players can, and made himself the clear favorite to win the U.S. Open.

But Sampras was not unduly worried by Agassi's string of successes, even after losing to

his chief rival in the final of the Canadian Open, 3-6, 6-2, 6-3. In that confrontation, Sampras had fallen into the same pattern that had plagued him all year long, losing the lead. Sampras had captured the opening set in all four of their meetings, but had succeeded in only one of those contests

He broke that pattern when it counted at Flushing. This pivotal showdown of the year, this final that everyone had been hoping for, was settled to a very large extent by the final point of the opening set. Agassi was serving at 4-5, advantage out, when the two players produced a rally they might not replicate for the rest of their careers, driving each other from corner to corner, going for their shots boldly but not recklessly, playing out each point as if their lives depended on it, hitting the ball as crisply and cleanly as they conceivably could.

Finally, Sampras concluded this suspenseful 22-stroke sequence with a perfectly controlled, high-trajectory topspin backhand crosscourt into an empty space. His arms triumphantly raised, fists clenched, and his spirits soaring, Sampras had the set and it carried him swiftly through the second set. Although Agassi came from a break down to take the third, he could not hold Sampras back in the fourth. Sampras was serving prodigiously and he delivered 11 of his 24 aces in that set, winning 24 of his 29 service points, serving four in a single game at 2-3. Sampras closed out the account, 6-4, 6-3, 4-6, 7-5, and the enormous significance of his success was not lost on him.

"That was the biggest match of the year for me," he commented, "and one of the biggest in my career. Everything kind of built up to that match the whole year. When I woke up in the morning I thought if I lost, how crushed I would have felt, how great it would be to win. I realized how important it all was to me."

Sampras and Agassi had both won top-notch, four-set semifinals. Sampras defeated a resurgent Courier, 6-4, 5-7, 6-4, 7-5, with breaks in the final games of the first, third and fourth sets, losing his serve only once. Courier had beaten

French Open champion Muster with crushing efficiency off the forehand. As for Agassi, he avenged his loss to Becker at Wimbledon with a 7-6 (7-4), 7-6 (7-2), 4-6, 6-4 triumph.

The women, meanwhile, were celebrating a similar conclusion to their Open. Not since January of 1993—when Seles beat Graf at the Australian Open—had Monica and Steffi met head-to-head. This was a particularly emotional reunion for the two superstars, both vividly recalling that a deranged Guenther Parche, allegedly a fan of Graf's, had interrupted Seles' career for more than two years with a knife stroke.

The two great champions were ready for this confrontation, plainly delighted to be bringing out the best in each other. The first set was as good as the women's game can get, featuring one remarkable baseline rally after another. Graf lost only six points in six service games on her way to a first-set tie-break which Seles led, 6-5, serving at set point. Monica was convinced she had served an ace on the center line at this critical point, but it was called fault, a fraction of an inch wide.

Seles was rattled. Then Graf rifled a forehand return winner off a second serve. Steffi took that sequence 8 points to 6, but let her guard down, and Seles struck all of her targets in a 6-0 second set. Graf was down, 0-30, in the first game of the third and break point in the third game, but held on both times. It was her match now as her serve regained velocity and accuracy, and her conviction came back. Seles seemed weary, and her forehand return deteriorated. And so for the seventh time in 11 career meetings—and the fourth time in seven at major events—Graf had won, 7-6 (8-6), 0-6, 6-3. But Seles had unmistakably triumphed by even returning to that elite level of the game.

In November, the men's and women's season-ending championships needlessly competed against each other again. In Frankfurt, Becker was at his best in a 7-6 (7-3), 6-0, 7-6 (7-5) final-round win over Chang. Chang had ousted Sampras, 6-4, 6-4, in the semifinals, but Sampras was

aware by then that the No. 1 computer ranking for the year already belonged to him though he was nowhere near the top of his game. Becker won a close three-set skirmish with Sweden's Thomas Enqvist in his semifinal.

Meanwhile, at Madison Square Garden in New York the same week, Graf managed to conduct one last piece of productive business. She survived an entertaining and fast-paced five sets with countrywoman Anke Huber to win the WTA Tour Championships, 6-1, 4-6, 6-1, 4-6, 6-3. With this triumph, she concluded what she acknowledged was her most satisfying year. She waged a more selective campaign, playing fewer matches than any of her other big years, but won the three most important tournaments and four of the top five events.

Furthermore, Graf won 47 of 49 matches, losing only opening-round upsets to Amanda Coetzer at the Canadian Open and Mariaan de Swardt at Brighton. She won 32 matches in a row and 6 consecutive tournaments before Coetzer. It was indeed a very good year.

Sampras, whose Davis Cup singles experiences hadn't been positive, turned that part of his life around by winning all six starts—the last two spectacular—as the U.S. took the Cup in a Cold War–revisited drama over Russia, 3-2, at Moscow. Pete illuminated his greatness within Olympic Stadium, on a clay court that had been trucked in especially to thwart him, by belting his way to the rarest of triples: having a hand in all the points in a 3-2 (or 3-1) victory. He is only the tenth member of that club, launched by Henri Cochet of France in 1931, including three other U.S. stalwarts (Alex Olmedo against Australia, 1958; Stan Smith against Romania, 1972; John McEnroe against Argentina, 1981), and most recently Boris Becker against Sweden, 1989.

But it all may have come down to one stroke, the last one Pete hit in his opening salvo, a 3-6, 6-4, 6-3, 6-7 (5-7), 6-4, squeaker over ceaseless retriever Andrei Chesnokov. Chessie, the hero of Russia's 3-2 semifinal (from 0-2) jolting of Germany, had scored the decisive point in a totally unbelievable 4-hour, 18-minute triumph over Michael Stich, 6-4, 1-6, 1-6, 6-3, 14-12. That boiled down to the wild 20-minute 14th game of the last set, Stich serving for victory at 7-6. The spindly German came so close he could sniff it, but somehow Chessie fought off his charges through nine deuces and nine match points! It ended more than an hour later with a drained Stich double-faulting.

The Russians had set a speed trap for Germany's Becker and Stich by importing clay footing from Sweden at a cost of $70,000. The expenditure was repeated, the seating enlarged to 16,000 for the American visitors, but there was no dirty trick permitted this time. To further slow the Germans, the hosts had watered the court down to a morass. For that bit of liquid refreshing of the home-court advantage, the Russian federation was fined $25,000 by the ITF.

Sampras, however, needed water. He was dehydrated and cramping as he and Chesnokov neared the climax. Pete was inwardly cursing himself for allowing a 4-2, 40-15 lead to get away from him in the fourth set. Now, at 5-4, 40-15 in the fifth, he missed a volley, blowing a first match point. Then came a desperate all-court exchange. Pete going to the net, being pushed back. Stroke after stroke. Pete approached again on a net-skinning forehand, the 22nd stroke, and Chesnokov ran feverishly, overtaking the ball—but couldn't flick it within the court. As he raised his arms in victory, Sampras abruptly collapsed. He was lugged to the dressing room by teammates to be revitalized.

"If my ball is good I don't think Pete can hit another shot . . . I win," said Chesnokov. Sampras tended to agree. "I don't know if I could have gone on."

But he did go on the next day, as a surprise. "If you need me I'll play doubles," he told captain Tom Gullikson. Gullikson needed, since Kafelnikov had beaten Courier, 7-6 (7-1), 7-5, 6-3, to make it 1-1. Pete and Todd Martin (returning superbly from the left court) were dynamite in demoralizing Kafelnikov and Andrei Olhovskiy, 7-5, 6-4, 6-3. "It was the match we had to win. We didn't expect to see Pete," said Kafelnikov.

He didn't expect to see the Pete who beat him in the clincher either. His was a bravura Cup-embracing performance that quickly dampened and muted the crowd of 16,000, 6-2, 6-4, 7-6 (7-4). Determined yet loose and flowing, Sampras powed the last of 16 aces on match point, blasted 19 winning forehands and felt like czar-for-a-day-on-clay.

Davis Cup–like alterations came to the Federation Cup, the name of which was pointlessly shaved to Fed Cup. A World Group was formed for eight countries to compete for the Cup itself in a Davis Cup-style best-of-five match series, either home or away, over a period of seven months. This replaced the best-of-three match format used since 1963, with all entrants gathering in one location for a week of competition.

The results didn't change in 1995. Those sensational senoritas, Sanchez Vicario and Martinez, won a third straight Cup for Spain, 3-2, over the U.S. in Valencia. Martinez (6-0 for the season) had led off over Chanda Rubin, 7-5, 7-6 (7-3), and clinched the next day in the third match, over Mary Joe Fernandez, 6-3, 6-4.

In the final analysis, this was a campaign to remember in many different ways. On the ATP Tour, there were 18 first-time tournament winners, the largest number since 1981. An impressive 41 champions were produced in 85 tournaments, and they came from 23 countries. Only 14 Americans could be found in the year-end computer rankings—the least since the computer was introduced in 1973—although Sampras and Agassi were No. 1 and No. 2 for the second year in a row with Chang at No. 5 and Courier at No. 8.

The women created their own brand of excitement. Croat Iva Majoli was the year's youngest tournament winner at 18 years, 50 days when she took Filderstadt indoors. Zina Garrison Jackson was the oldest to garner a singles title, coming through at Birmingham on English grass at age 31. A total of 29 different champions were honored at 51 official WTA Tour events, with 17 countries represented among the winners.

But, in the end it was the year of Sampras and Graf.

1996

Many a performer has felt naked on Centre Court, stripped bare and defenseless by an overpowering opponent. Tony Roche, after losing the 1968 Wimbledon final in under an hour to Rod Laver, lamented, "I just wanted to dig a hole and disappear."

But 23-year-old Englishwoman Melissa Johnson took it a few steps further in a distinctive Centre Court debut. She was a winner, judging from public reaction to her truly letting it all hang out as no champion before. In a final-day dash across the greensward as the Championships' singular streaker, she was perhaps Britain's most notable unclothed athlete since the jockey Godiva.

As she entered unannounced, there were the two finalists ready to play for the most important title. Dutchman Richard Krajicek and American MaliVai Washington stood side by side, posing for the photographers, celebrating a moment they had dreamed about. The tension surrounding them was almost palpable, but then huge grins broke across their faces as they witnessed an event unlike any other in the history of the tournament.

To their astonishment and everyone else's, a striking Melissa raced onto the court. She ran past the players and continued, flashing her small white apron and body at a stunned Duke and Duchess of Kent in the Royal Box. Moments later, a pair of policemen escorted her off the court, arrested her and took her to the police station, where she was identified as a part-time Wimbledon waitress.

The final proved anticlimactic. Washington lost in straight sets. Asked what role the streaker had played in his performance, the American

Richard Krajicek of the Netherlands smiles as a surprise entry, Melissa Johnson, interrupts the start of the 1996 Wimbledon final against America's MalaVai Washington. (Wide World)

replied: "I saw these things wobbling around and, jeez, she smiled at me. I was flustered. Three sets later, I was gone: If she'd come back, I might have had more luck."

Seldom has the interview room been filled with such unabashed laughter.

While that was a rare time of irreverence for a sport sometimes lacking lighter moments, this was a year of serious business for the best players. With the Olympic Games slated for summer in Atlanta, schedules were more crowded than ever, goals hard to achieve, priorities difficult to set.

Boris Becker knew precisely what he wanted to achieve when he commenced his campaign Down Under at Melbourne. Now 28, he was coming off an enviable 1995 and searching for his first major singles title in five years. He realized that considerable goal when he took apart the tenacious Michael Chang in the final of the year's first major. Becker sparred successfully with Chang from the backcourt, served him off the court and attacked whenever that avenue was available. With his 6-2, 6-4, 2-6, 6-2 triumph over fifth seed Chang, the fourth seed garnered a sixth major crown over an 11-year span.

Becker's wife Barbara had never witnessed him winning a major tournament. She told him, "Please do it for me because I have never seen you win one." He would say later, "Now finally I have won one for Barbara and tomorrow, when I have read the papers it will probably sink in and I will scream all day."

Aside from Becker's showing, and Chang's strong surge into the final, culminating with a 6-1, 6-4, 7-6 (7-1) win over 1995 titlist Agassi, the tournament was somewhat devoid of drama. Only the 19-year-old Australian Mark Philippoussis, a 6-foot-4, 202-pounder, had provided the early rounds with a surprise, and what a big surprise it was!

In this battle of Greek descendants, Philippoussis caught the world No. 1 completely off guard, serving 29 aces in three sets, closing out 10 of his 17 service games with untouchable serves, and refusing to allow Pete Sampras to break him a single time in the course of a 6-4, 7-6 (11-9), 7-6 (7-3) third-round victory.

It was a practically perfect performance, and even when "Scud" was twice down set point on his serve in the critical second-set tie-break, he came through with extraordinary poise under pressure.

After that striking display against the man who had captured the last two major tournaments, it seemed entirely possible that Philippoussis could make a serious bid to become the first Australian to reach the final at Flinders Park since Pat Cash in 1988, or possibly the first to take the title since Mark Edmondson in 1976. But the big win over Sampras was more than Philippoussis could handle. He was picked apart skillfully, 6-2, 6-2, 6-2, in the round of 16 by a countryman who knew his game much too well, left-handed Mark Woodforde, who went all the way to the penultimate round himself before losing to a blazing Becker, 6-4, 6-2, 6-0.

Germany's Boris Becker made the winner's circle for the first time in five years, vanquishing Michael Chang of the U.S. in the Australian Open in 1996. (Wide World)

With Graf unable to appear at Flinders Park for the second year in a row—she was coming off foot surgery the previous month—Monica Seles was left as the class of the field. But she was battling a variety of injuries and hurt her shoulder prior to a semifinal showdown with the talented and athletic Chanda Rubin, a 19-year-old black American with an explosive all-court game.

Rubin was coming off a 6-4, 2-6, 16-14 quarterfinal upset of third-seeded Arantxa Sanchez Vicario, prevailing in 3 hours, 33 minutes, a tournament record for women. Now she was ready to take on Seles without a shade of trepidation. Rubin was decisive in the first set tie-breaker (7-1). But Seles recovered to even the match, only to slip way behind as Chanda attacked and moved within sight of a gigantic upset, thrice within two points of victory while serving at 5-3. However, a bold double fault at 30-15 impeded her progress and Seles pounced to win 15 of the last 18 points, and the match, 6-7, 6-1, 7-5, saying, "I was lucky to win."

But there was no luck involved in the hard-hitting final, a 6-4, 6-1 victory over German Anke Huber, debuting in a major final. Unbeaten in Australia (32-0), Monica had her fourth Open title, ninth major crown, and felt, "I've had to go through so much, the pain, the setbacks, the therapy, the training. And I am still back playing. Sometimes I can't believe I'm here."

She could have said something similar when she arrived in Paris for the French Open four months later. Seles had made a questionable professional judgment by moving on from Melbourne to Tokyo the week after the Australian Open, losing in the quarterfinals to the steadily improving Iva Majoli. Having won in Sydney the week before Melbourne, she had scheduled herself for a fourth consecutive week in Tokyo. That must have exacerbated her shoulder injury, and she didn't return to tournaments until the week before Roland Garros. She played one match in Madrid, then pulled out to protect her shoulder.

Seles struggled on and off until the quarterfinals of the French and then was halted, 7-6 (9-7), 6-3, by Jana Novotna. Her 25-match winning streak in the world's most prestigious clay-court event came to an end, and she simply was not the same player who had dominated the tournament as the champion from 1990 to 1992. Her ground game lacked all severity, her serve wasn't penetrating, her court coverage not nearly what it was.

With Seles gone, and Novotna losing in the semifinals to her doubles partner Sanchez Vicario, 6-3, 7-5, it was time for another Graf–Sanchez Vicario final. This one was even better than the 1995 Wimbledon title match.

It lasted 3 hours and 4 minutes—a female French Open final record—and it was hard fought from beginning to end. Graf took the first set and seemed headed for a straight-set win when she got to 4-1 in the second-set tie-break.

Only three points from a fifth French Open championship, Graf was right where she wanted to be. But then the Spaniard snapped a forehand winner to make it 4-2 and Graf sunk into a nervous patch. Four straight unforced errors and a double fault later, she had lost the tie-break, 7 points to 4, and she found herself in a third set she could hardly have relished.

Graf fell behind 2-4 in the third set and Sanchez Vicario twice reached break point for 5-2. Graf held on. But the unwavering Sanchez Vicario served for the match twice at 5-4 and 7-6, only to be denied again. In those two memorable games, Graf did not make a single unforced error. In the end, Graf came through, 6-3, 6-7 (4-7), 10-8. It was a final so stupendous that only Chris Evert's 6-3, 6-7 (4-7), 7-5 triumph over Martina Navratilova in the 1985 final and Seles' 6-2, 3-6, 10-8 title win over Graf in 1992 could be rated above it.

The heart of the men's event at Roland Garros took place long before the final, and the one who took over the spotlight was none other than Sampras. On his way to a first French Open semifinal—he had been in the quarterfinals, 1992 through 1994—the world No. 1 survived three bruising five-set skirmishes as he was confronted with a demanding draw. He beat 1993–94 titlist Sergi Bruguera in a gruelling second-round contest, 6-3, 6-4, 6-7 (2-7), 2-6, 6-3, then subdued his countryman, 29-ace serving Todd Martin, in the third round, 3-6, 6-4, 7-5, 4-6, 6-2.

There was more. In the quarterfinals, Sampras dropped the first two sets to Courier, his omnipresent adversary, but fought back to win his third five-set confrontation of the tournament with a 6-7 (4-7), 4-6, 6-4, 6-4, 6-4 triumph, replicating the same gritty climb he had made from two sets to love down against the same man in Melbourne 17 months earlier. This one was settled with Sampras serving at 3-4, 15-40 in the fourth set. He saved the first break point with an ace, then broke a string on his first serve at 30-40. Changing rackets, he picked up a new frame and came up with a magnificent second-serve ace and went on to hold. Right then and there, Courier's spirit was essentially broken, his confidence sorely shaken, even though he'd served 29 aces (to Pete's 28). Jim couldn't stay with a man who seemingly knew no bounds.

But even with two days off to rest, the bounds—Pete's physical and emotional limits—had been reached. His coach, Tim Gullikson, was lost to brain cancer three-and-a-half weeks before, and a mourning Sampras hadn't prepared for Roland Garros as he would have wanted. He had played his way through to the penultimate round with Gullikson at the center of his mind, wanting to win this one for a friend he had cherished and for a coach he knew had turned him into a true champion. But with the thermometer soaring to 93 degrees, Sampras wilted in the heat and surrendered to Yevgeny Kafelnikov, 7-6 (7-4), 6-0, 6-2, conceding that "the balloon had burst."

Defending champion Thomas Muster had seemed a safe bet to retain his title. He had won 16 of his last 20 tournaments, 97 of his last 100 matches on clay when he took the court against 1991 Wimbledon champion Michael Stich in the round of 16. When he moved ahead by a set and a break against the 27-year-old German, Thomas seemed well on his way to another victory. But a rejuvenated Stich upended Muster, 4-6, 6-4, 6-1, 7-6 (7-1).

Having endured ankle surgery three months before, Stich had come to Paris hoping only to get a few matches in before Wimbledon. He had considered bypassing the event but was persuaded by his coach Sven Groenveld to play. With a routine straight-set semifinal win over Switzerland's Marc Rosset, Stich found himself in his third major final. He was so free of inhibition as he approached his final with Kafelnikov that many believed he would come through.

But the adroit 22-year-old Russian had told locker-room colleagues that the winner of the match between himself and Sampras was going to take the tournament, and his prognosis was correct. Kafelnikov stopped Stich 7-6 (7-4), 7-5,

7-6 (7-4), even though Stich led 5-2 in the second, 3-1 in the third. Kafelnikov, the lone Russian to rule a major, doubled his good fortune by taking the other title with Czech Daniel Vacek, the first to win both men's titles in Paris since Ken Rosewall at the first Open in 1968. Stefan Edberg, a startling resident in the fourth round on a brilliant 4-6, 7-5, 6-0, 7-6 (7-1) defeat of fourth-seeded Michael Chang (revenge for their 1989 final?), had been the last to make the singles-doubles at a major, Australia 1987.

It was not a vintage Wimbledon. The weather during the second week was miserable, rain constantly causing delays during big matches, and the atmosphere dampened for everyone. Nevertheless, the towering Krajicek produced the brightest brand of tennis in his career and thoroughly deserved his major title. The 6-foot-5, 24-year-old Netherlander became the only man from his nation to win one in singles.

He was ranked No. 13 but overlooked by the Wimbledon seeding committee. But when the seventh-seeded Muster withdrew with an injury, Krajicek was placed in the draw as the next in line, and, after the fact, considered the unorthodox 17th seed by the All England Club. This was way after the world press had correctly anointed Krajicek as the only unseeded winner other than Becker in 1985.

He had a terrific run. He upset 1991 titlist Stich, 6-4, 7-6 (7-5), 6-4, in a quarterfinal and then brought down the mighty Sampras, 7-5, 7-6 (7-3), 6-4, in the quarters, a rain-delayed match contested over two days. Sampras had won 24 straight matches at Wimbledon but he could not break his unwavering opponent once in three sets or cope with Krajicek's razor-sharp backhand. Pete seemed down on himself throughout the battle. Krajicek then ousted Jason Stoltenberg, 7-5, 6-2, 6-1, after the Australian upset fourth seed Goran Ivanisevic in the quarters, 6-3, 7-6 (7-3), 6-7 (3-7), 7-6 (7-3).

On the opposite half of the draw, Washington was having the time of his life. The 27-year-old

American upset ninth-seeded Thomas Enqvist, 6-4, 7-6 (7-5), 6-3, in the second round, saved two match points in a five-set quarterfinal win over Germany's Alex Radulescu, 6-7 (5-7), 7-6 (7-1), 5-7, 7-6 (7-3), 6-4. Then he stunned countryman and close friend Todd Martin by reviving from 1-5 down in the fifth to win their semifinal, 5-7, 6-4, 6-7 (5-7), 6-3, 10-8. But he was overwhelmed by Krajicek, 6-3, 6-4, 6-3, in the final as the Dutchman released 14 aces to raise his tournament-high total to 147.

Seeded second and in excellent shape to follow up on his Aussie title, Becker fell out in the third round, a fluke accident and default to qualifier Neville Godwin at 6-6. Boris suffered a severe wrist injury in mis-hitting a return, and would miss the U.S. Open, too. Agassi, seeded third, flopped even harder than at the French, where No. 73 Chris Woodruff took him out in the second round. In an all-time opening round reversal, No. 281 Doug Flach, a qualifier from Atlanta (younger brother of former Davis Cupper Ken Flach), interred Agassi in the Graveyard (Court 2), 2-6, 7-6 (7-1), 6-4, 7-6 (8-6).

The women couldn't reproduce their dazzling moments of 1995. Graf was just too good. In a rematch of the 1995 final, she confronted Sanchez Vicario, but the German was too sharp and concentrated this time around. She moved rapidly to a 6-3, 4-0 lead. Sanchez Vicario was typically combative in fighting her way back to 5-5, taking advantage of two damaging double faults from Graf, serving for the match at 5-4. Had it gone into a third set, Graf could well have been vulnerable, but she raised her game markedly in the next two games, conceding only one more point to close out a 6-3, 7-5 victory for her seventh singles title on Centre Court.

Many believed the champion, Graf, was protected, perhaps unfairly saved in the semis by the referee's decision to halt her struggle with enterprising slow starter Kimiko Date at 8:56 P.M., following the second set. Date, beaten the next day in what amounted to a best-of-one-set windup, 6-2, 2-6, 6-3, had been coming on strong with her tough groundies, and felt there was sufficient light to keep going. Sanchez Vicario accounted for the unseeded American Meredith McGrath, 6-2, 6-1, in the same round. Seles' first appearance at Wimbledon since her final-round loss in 1992 was deeply disappointing for her. Monica fell in the second round to a Slovak, No. 59 Katarina Studenikova, 7-5, 5-7, 6-4. It was the earliest exit for Monica from a major since her 1990 third-round loss at the U.S. Open against Linda Ferrando.

Agassi crashed from his dismal slump by winning the prize he had proclaimed was utmost on his 1996 wish list: the Olympic gold medal on the hard courts of Atlanta's Stone Mountain complex. He did it after numerous escapes, particularly from South African Wayne Ferreira (7-5, 4-6, 7-5), who served for their quarter-final at 5-4 in the third, and, previously, Italian Andrea Gaudenzi (2-6, 6-4, 6-2), who led him 3-0 in the second. Finally in tune, Andre got the gold by assaulting Spaniard Sergi Bruguera (6-2, 6-3, 6-1), the semifinal conqueror of MaliVai Washington.

Even more impressively, another American won in women's singles. Californian Lindsay Davenport was seeded only ninth but she toppled fifth seed Anke Huber, fourth seed Iva Majoli, seventh seed Mary Joe Fernandez, and third seed Arantxa Sanchez Vicario, 7-6 (8-6), 6-2, to garner her gold.

Despite his proud achievement, Agassi was fortunate not to have been thrown out of the Olympics for untoward behavior that included incredibly abusive language directed at complaisant umpires. But he wasn't so proud a couple of weeks later at encountering ATP officials at Indianapolis who wouldn't stand for that sort of treatment, and disqualified him. Andre was the first prominent player since John McEnroe, at the Australian of 1990, to be ejected. While winning easily against Canadian Daniel Nestor in the second round, he was tossed out after a warning for ball abuse and then a four-letter-word tirade against umpire Dana Loconto. Supervisor Mark Darby, told by Loconto precisely what Agassi had said, had the gumption to evict one of the game's greatest drawing cards.

Controversy surrounded the U.S. Open before a single ball was struck. The USTA has almost always used the current ATP computer rankings to determine seedings for the last major championship of the season. But this time around, tourney officials chose to make a number of significant departures from the rankings in their projection. They moved Michael Chang past Thomas Muster to second in the seedings (reversing their rankings), elevated Agassi from his No. 8 ranking to 6th in the seedings to take into account his recent record, and made a few other suspect changes as well without telling the ATP beforehand.

French Open champion Yevgeny Kafelnikov was furious. He had talked about possibly pulling out of the Open the week before because of an injury. Then he became petulant about the seedings and elected to withdraw. The Russian claimed that his pride had been wounded irreparably by being seeded seventh instead of where he stood in the rankings at No. 4. On top of all of this, the USTA did have to remake the draw after breaking procedure the first time around—and untraditionally in secret—although they defiantly stuck by their seedings.

In the end, order was restored as the unquestionable world No. 1 Sampras secured his only major crown of the season, seventh over the last four years, and eighth altogether, tying him with Jimmy Connors, Ken Rosewall, Ivan Lendl and Fred Perry in the all-time chase, not too far behind Roy Emerson (12), Rod Laver and Bjorn Borg (11), and Bill Tilden (10).

Sampras was blazing at the start of his final with Chang, revealing the full range of his fluid talent, breaking down his adversary from the baseline, applying pressure when he needed to, serving with striking assurance. Before Chang knew what had hit him, he was down two sets to love. Sampras fought off a set point, serving at 5-6 in the third and then calmly and confidently completed his mission, 6-1, 6-4, 7-6 (7-3), for a fourth Open crown and an eighth major title.

Pete Sampras wrapped up the 1996 season with his U.S. Open triumph over Michael Chang in a fitting tribute to his departed mentor, Tim Gullikson. (Wide World)

The seedings had held up well. In the semifinals, the top-seeded Sampras had defeated fourth seed Goran Ivanisevic, 6-3, 6-4, 6-7 (9-11), 6-3, after letting a 6-3, triple-match-point lead slip from his grasp in the tiebreaker. Sampras broke the big left-hander at 3-4 in the fourth, and went unbroken in four sets. Chang obliterated Agassi, 6-3, 6-2, 6-2, cracking 16 aces and not losing his serve. It was his third win in five 1996 meetings with Agassi and his second in a major event.

But none of those matches could compare to Sampras' monumental struggle with 22-year-old Spaniard Alex Corretja in the quarterfinals. In a 4-hour, 9-minute confrontation, Sampras trailed two sets to one, struck back to win the fourth. But burdened by extreme dehydration, he vomited near the back of the court at 1-1 in the fifth-set tie-breaker, and was given a code violation warning for taking too much time between points.

As the tie-breaker progressed, it was increasingly apparent that Sampras was in agony. At 6-5, Sampras had a match point but missed a running forehand. He then went down match point at 6-7 and somehow came up with a stunning forehand stretch volley into an open court. Exhausted now, wanting the ordeal to be over, Sampras sent the stadium crowd into a complete frenzy when he hooked an audacious 90 m.p.h. second-serve ace wide to Corretja's forehand in the right court. "How could he do that?" sighed Corretja later. Pete said, "I don't know where it came from, but I knew I didn't want to hit another ball. I don't know if I could have." He didn't have to. Until then No. 31 Corretja had played the match of his life, giving away nothing, in fact outplaying Sampras—even out-acing him with 25. But Pete's second-ball ace seemed to unnerve Alex. The only way the Spaniard could lose was to not put the ball into play—a double fault. As Alex's second serve landed beyond the service line, Sampras was the winner, 7-6 (7-5), 5-7, 5-7, 6-4, 7-6 (9-7). It was the match of the '90s at Flushing Meadow, and easily among the five best in the Open Era.

For the second year in a row, Graf completed a sweep of the three majors she entered when she repeated her 1994 final-round triumph over Seles, 7-5, 6-4, but this was more thorough. Fraulein Forehand's blasts kept the less fit Seles running from corner to corner, and in vain. Graf, 27, banged 10 aces, lost serve but once, was too unrelentingly skillful in securing her 21st major title, fifth U.S. She had broken from the pack in Paris, leaving Chris Evert and Martina Navratilova behind with 18 majors apiece. At Wimbledon she cruised past Helen Wills Moody's 19, and now Margaret Smith Court's mighty record 24—once seeming Everest—appeared within reach.

But she nearly tripped in the semis over the latest Martina, Childe Hingis, 15. Cunning Martina II was having a good time, playing and winning more (19 hours, 44 minutes, 12 victories)

Monica Seles (left) grimly accepts defeat at the hands of Steffi Graf in the U.S. Open final in 1996. (Wide World)

than anyone else in reaching the semis of singles, doubles and mixed, the first such accomplishment since Martina I tripled in 1987. Her doubles title at Wimbledon (in the company of 31-year-old Helena Sukova, 5-7, 7-5, 6-1, over Larisa Neiland and Meredith McGrath), made Hingis, 15 years, 10 months, the youngest by three days to win a major female title, undercutting Lottie Dod, the 1887 Wimbledon singles champ, also 15-10. After eliminating third-seeded 1994 champ Sanchez Vicario, 6-1, 3-6, 6-4, and seventh-seeded Jana Novotna, 7-6 (7-1), 6-4, she had her sights on Graf. Only Steffi's stonewalling of five set points in the first set (one at 5-3, four more at 4-5 from 0-40 and ad out) rescued her, 7-5, 6-3.

Captain Billie Jean King's U.S. team, with a rookie, Seles, on board, pried the Fed Cup away from Spain (a.k.a. Sanchez Vicario and Martinez), 5-0 at Atlantic City. But Mary Joe Fernandez, with a triple, was the life-saver at the sticky start, 3-2 over Austria at Salzburg. Her wins over Judith Wiesner, 6-3, 7-6 (7-5), and Barbara Paulus, 6-3, 7-6 (7-4), backboned the victory that went down to the last match: Gigi Fernandez and Mary Joe over Wiesner and Petra Schwarz, 6-0, 6-4. Then a lineup of Seles and Davenport overpowered Japan, 5-0, at Nagoya, both beating up the home ace, Date: Lindsay, 6-2, 6-1; Monica, 6-0, 6-2. The Spaniards' streak of three years (10 straight victories) was doomed the first day as Monica popped Martinez, 6-3, 6-4, and Davenport repeated her Olympic put-down of Sanchez Vicario, 7-5, 6-1. Seles finished them, 3-6, 6-3, 6-1, over Sanchez Vicario.

Befitting the year's number ones, Sampras and Graf won the climactic playoffs, the ATP World Championship at Hanover, Germany, and WTA (Chase Championships) at New York's Madison Square Garden respectively, though each was pushed to the five-set limit. Beaten by Becker in the round-robin phase, Sampras rebounded to tip Boris in a gripping 4-hour final, 3-6, 7-6 (7-5), 7-6 (7-4), 6-7 (11-13), 6-4, breaking serve only once. Muting a Boris chorus of 15,000, Pete had his third ATP, and eighth title for the year (a career 44th), during which he won 65 of 76 matches, and $3,702,919. Graf seemed in trouble as 16-year-old Hingis, the youngest finalist since Andrea Jaeger, 15, in 1981, led her 5-1 in the fourth set. But leg cramps shortly seized the kid, and Steffi came through in the year-ender for a fifth time, 6-3, 4-6, 0-6, 6-4, 6-0, her seventh title of a season in which she won 54 of 58 matches and a female record $2,665,706.

As in 1993, indifference at the top scuttled U.S. hopes of keeping the Davis Cup. Sampras, Agassi and Courier declined invitations to go for another Davis Cup, saying the team event interrupted their schedules. Martin, the only holdover from Moscow '95 willing to show for a quarterfinal in Prague was admirable in the 3-2 defeat by the Czech Republic, securing both points. Todd beat Petr Korda, 6-2, 6-4, 7-5, and Daniel Vacek, 7-6 (7-1), 6-3, 6-1. But in the decisive fifth encounter, Washington, who had lost a tense struggle to Vacek (4-6, 6-3, 6-4, 5-7, 6-4), couldn't hold off Korda, 7-6 (7-1), 6-3, 6-1, and the U.S. was sidelined in the quarters, 3-2, by the Czech Republic in Prague.

But perhaps it was poetic that the year of the passing of 92-year-old René Lacoste, the last of France's magnificent Four Musketeers, was capped by an unexpected, nerve-jingling French triumph, 3-2, in the Davis Cup final at Malmo, Sweden. It featured the longest (9 hours, 12 minutes), and possibly the wildest last day in Cup annals. Full-house crowds of 5,600, prepared to hail the farewell appearances of No. 14 Stefan Edberg, were saddened instead by his injury, a twisted right ankle, in losing the opener to No. 21 Cedric Pioline. Further grief was theirs two days later as No. 31 Arnaud Boetsch battled uphill to win the closest of all Cup finale fifth matches, the decider, over Edberg's stand-in, No. 64 Nicklas Kulti, 7-6 (7-2), 2-6, 4-6, 7-6 (7-5), 10-8. Boetsch revived from triple-Cup point, 6-7, 0-40 in 4 hours, 47 minutes. Swede Thomas Enqvist, No. 9, came from way back, too, to tie it, 2-2, by beating Pioline from 2-5 in the fifth, 3-6, 6-7 (8-10), 6-4, 6-4, 9-7, in 4 hours, 25 minutes. But it turned out that wasn't enough to keep the Cup from the French.

Crowed inspirational captain Yannick Noah, who had led France's 1991 victory over the U.S., "Davis Cup's not about rankings, reputations, or schedules. It's about team, and who will give up things for others, for the team."

6

THE 40 GREATEST PLAYERS
1946-96

A thletes in all sports are getting better all the time, measurably in some, apparently in others. Obviously more exceptional tennis players abound today than ever before. With a few exceptions, I believe the best tennis players have appeared since World War II, and probably even better ones are coming. Thus a selection of the foremost 40 (24 men, 16 women) inevitably neglects some standouts.

I also feel that greats in one era would be greats if transposed to another. Big Bill Tilden and Helen Wills, benefitting from startling improvements in equipment, coaching and training methods, immersed in a highly professionalized environment, would be champions today. So would Jack Kramer and Maureen Connolly, Rod Laver and Billie Jean King. Nobody has played the game any better.

But they would find themselves surrounded by a deeper, more imposing cast, hitting the ball harder, battling for fantastic financial awards, ever monitored and classified by the cold-hearted computer.

Because my faith in the current unprecedented crop—hundreds of quality pros—is high, I've chosen five yet active at the top level among the all-timers: Andre Agassi, Steffi Graf, Pete Sampras, Arantxa Sanchez Vicario, Monica Seles.

While narrowing the field, with difficulty, to 40, I want to salute others who have made outstanding marks, notably the following whose tributes will be found in the Hall of Fame chapter: Rosie Casals, Ashley Cooper, Neale Fraser, Darlene Hard, Jan Kodes, Chuck McKinley, Frank Parker, Nicola Pietrangeli, Tony Roche, Vic Seixas, Fred Stolle, Bill Talbert, Guillermo Vilas, Virginia Wade. Plus Michael Chang, Jim Courier, Françoise Durr, Nancy Richey and Lesley Turner, who will be found in the chapter entitled They Also Serve.

—Bud Collins

ANDRE AGASSI
United States (1970—)

A player of tremendous flair and appeal since appearing on the professional landscape as a 16-year-old in 1986, Andre Kirk Agassi, the first Nevadan to make an impact on the game, took longer than expected to make the leap predicted for him: to a major championship.

This occurred at the least likely location, Wimbledon, in 1992, after failures, as the favorite, to beat Pete Sampras for the U.S. Open title in 1990, Andres Gomez and Jim Courier for the French in 1990 and 1991. After a quick and unhappy thrashing by Henri Leconte 6-2, 6-1, 6-2, at Wimbledon in 1987, Agassi assiduously avoided the grass until 1991, a successful reappearance ending in a quarterfinal loss to David Wheaton, 6-2, 0-6, 3-6, 7-6 (7-4), 7-5.

Realizing the greensward wasn't that forbidding, he returned a year later, to take it all, his 12th seeding making him the lowest regarded champion at the starting gate other than 11th Jaroslav Drobny, 1954, 11th Pat Cash, 1987, non-seeds Boris Becker, 1985, and Richard Krajicek, 1996. "This was not the one people looked for me to win," he said correctly, after his buzzing groundies outdid the missile attack of 36 ace-serving Goran Ivanisevic in the final, 6-7 (8-10), 6-4, 6-4, 1-6, 6-4.

Now only the lack of a French denies 5-foot-11, right-handed Andre a full-house of majors. Ranked low again in 1994, No. 20, he became only the third non-seed to win the U.S., taking it on his ninth shot, over Michael Stich, 6-1, 7-6 (7-5), 7-5, joining Mal Anderson (1957) and Fred Stolle (1966) in the exclusive unseeded club. He had also made excuses for skipping the long trip to Australia, yet won it on his first try, 1995, sensationally over Sampras, 4-6, 6-1, 7-6 (8-6), 6-4.

A brilliant shotmaker from the beginning, an attacker from the baseline, Agassi needed time to sort out whether being a commercial success was enough. As the most widely-marketed player of all-time— "image is everything" was one of his sales pitches—he made more millions than available on court. Fortunately he decided to utilize his gifts to attract as much attention by winning. Never has there been such a controversial figure so broadly associated with the game, thanks to TV commercials. His ever-changing hairstyle, brightly hued attire, and such items as black shoes, and denim shorts, considered garish by traditionalists, lured countless buyers as hip or avant-garde. His engagement to actress Brooke Shields (granddaughter of Hall of Famer Frank Shields), whom he married on April 19, 1997, didn't hurt Andre's visibility that transcends the sports page.

But beneath the peacock and the pop idol is a tennis player whose timing, anticipation, coordination and determination (when it's turned on) enable him to deliver withering, topspinning barrages with flicks of the wrist. "When Andre's on, forget it," says Sampras. "He does practically everything better than anybody else."

Agassi was born April 29, 1970, in Las Vegas, and lives there, although he was farmed out to Nick Bollettieri's Tennis Academy at Brandenton, Fla., at age 13, and has been on his own since. His father, Iranian immigrant and naturalized U.S. citizen Mike Agassi, a strict taskmaster, was determined that Andre would make his way to the top in tennis. Papa pushed the kid from cradle onward, then gave the prodigy over to surrogate father Bollettieri. An Olympic boxer for Iran in 1952, Mike fell for tennis and taught Andre "the new game, based on the way a fighter throws punches, plus a two-handed backhand for added power."

It all worked, and led Andre to his own Olympics, 1996 in Atlanta, where he made off with the gold medal by thumping Spaniard Sergi Bruguera, 6-2, 6-3, 6-1, in 78 minutes. Again it had taken him an inordinate amount of time to put his act together. He had declined taking part in 1988 and 1992.

By lifting the Australian crown from Sampras in '95, Agassi also took Pete's No. 1 jersey, and they dueled throughout the year for the top. But Pete ended Andre's excellent summer streak of four tournaments and 26 matches with a four-set final-round defeat to regain his U.S. Open title and top ranking. That loss seemed to deflate Agassi, and 1996—other than the Olympics—was a downer, his worst in the majors: ghastly first- and second-round losses at Wimbledon (No. 186 Doug Flach) and the French (No. 73 Chris Woodruff), and desultory semifinal losses to Michael Chang at the Australian and the U.S.

His has been an uneven course through an 11-year career, up one year, down another (four first-round losses at the U.S. Open for instance), but the sheer firepower within makes him a threat to blast anybody off any court at any time. He has been a Top Ten entry eight times between 1988 and 1996, No. 2 in 1994–95. Bollettieri, feeling he didn't work hard enough, severed their decade-long relationship in 1993, but he won his next two majors with Brad Gilbert as coach. Plunging to No. 24, his lowest adult ranking, after losing the first round of the 1993 U.S. Open to No. 61 Thomas Enqvist, he required surgery to repair a damaged wrist—"I thought my career was over." But he came back strong.

In 1988, as one of the youngest U.S. Davis Cup rookies, he won all his singles on Latin clay (historic trouble ground for gringos) at Peru and Argentina, to spearhead his fallen nation's recovery from the perdition of relegation. He became a valuable hand in the Cup triumphs of 1990, 1992 and 1995 with a 22-4 record. He declined to play Davis Cup in 1996, keeping intact a 13-match winning streak. At the close of 1996, he had won 34 of 113 singles tournaments. He was 457-145 (.759) in singles.

Andre made his first splash at Stratton Mountain, Vt., in 1987, beating the Wimbledon champion, Pat Cash, 7-6 (10-8), 7-6 (8-6), on the way to the semis, where No. 1 Ivan Lendl had all he could do to win, 6-2, 5-7, 6-3. He shortly took his first title, Itaparica (Brazil), over Luiz Mattar, 7-6 (8-6), 6-2, and wound up in the U.S. Top Ten (No. 10) for the first of 10 successive years, No. 1 in 1988, 1990 and 1996. In 1988 he made marvelous efforts in the French, a five-set joust with

Andre Agassi: Best bet from Las Vegas. (Wide World)

the champ, Mats Wilander, and the U.S., a five-set win over Jimmy Connors before losing the semis to Lendl. His most productive season was 1995: seven titles on 73-9 in matches. His career earnings through 1996 were $12,901,331.

MAJOR TITLES (3)—Australian singles, 1995; Wimbledon singles, 1992; U.S. singles, 1994. OTHER U.S. TITLES (2)—Indoor singles, 1988; Clay Court singles, 1988. DAVIS CUP—1988–93, 1995; record: 22-4 in singles. SINGLES RECORD IN THE MAJORS: Australian (12-1), French (31-9), Wimbledon (23-6), U.S. (38-10).

ARTHUR ASHE
United States (1943–1993)

A singular figure in the game's history as the only black male to win a major singles titles—three of them in fact—Arthur Robert Ashe, Jr., also set a record in 1968 that is most unlikely to be equaled: he won both the U.S. Amateur and Open

Arthur Ashe: More than tennis. (UPI)

championships, the first time such a double was possible. No one has come remotely close since.

That first season of the open era was a whirlwind year for him, then 1st Lt. Ashe of the U.S. Army. In order to maintain Davis Cup eligibility and gain time away from duty for important tournaments, Ashe was required to maintain his amateur status. Determining that the traditional (and previously amateur) U.S. Singles Championships at Forest Hills would become the inaugural U.S. Open in 1968, the USTA designated Longwood Cricket Club in Boston as the site for a U.S. Amateur tournament. Seeded first in Boston, Ashe came through to the title by surging past teammate Bob Lutz in the exciting final, 4-6, 6-3, 8-10, 6-0, 6-4.

However, with pros introduced to Forest Hills, Ashe was a lightly regarded fifth seed. Nevertheless, at 25, he came of age as an internationalist. Unflappable over the New York fortnight, he served-and-volleyed splendidly. In the final he clocked 26 aces, returned with precision, and held his cool in a five-set final-round victory over pro Tom Okker, 14-12, 5-7, 6-3, 3-6, 6-3.

An amateur would never do so well again. As the last remaining pro, Okker got the $14,000 first prize while Ashe was happy to settle for $28 daily expenses for his historic triumph, the first major for a black since Althea Gibson's Forest Hills triumph a decade before. Ashe's victory also boosted American morale by ending the U.S.

male championship drought that dated back 13 years to Tony Trabert's 1955 win.

That year Ashe was also a Davis Cup drought-buster, spearheading the U.S. drive to the sterling tub last won five years before. He won 11 straight singles (the most in one campaign for an American) in the drive to retrieve the Cup from Australia in Adelaide. In the finale he beat Ray Ruffels easily on opening day, and, after the Cup was clinched by Bob Lutz and Stan Smith in doubles, finally gave way, losing to Bill Bowrey in a meaningless third-day match. The season closed with Ashe winner of 10 of 22 tournaments on a 72-10 match record.

He would win both his singles in 1969 and 1970 as the U.S. successfully defended the Cup against Romania, then West Germany, at Cleveland. In the latter his third-day defeat of Christian Kuhnke, 6-8, 10-12, 9-7, 13-11, 6-4, was the longest match (86 games) in a Cup-deciding round. Eight years later he reappeared for a vital cameo that led to another Cup for the U.S.; his 6-2, 6-0, 7-5 singles victory over Kjell Johansson was the clincher over Sweden, 3-2, in the semifinal at Goteborg.

Ashe put in 10 years of Davis Cup, topped for the U.S. only by John McEnroe's 12 and Bill Tilden and Stan Smith's 11 each, and won 27 singles, second only to McEnroe's 41.

He returned in 1981 as captain for five years, piloting the victors of 1981 and 1982.

Ashe was born July 10, 1943, in Richmond, Va., where he grew up. Since racial segregation was the law there during his childhood and early youth, Ashe could not play in the usual junior tournaments. With the aid of the concerned Lynchburg, Va., physician, Dr. Walter Johnson (who had also befriended and helped Althea Gibson), Ashe finished high school in St. Louis, where he could get the necessary tennis competition.

In 1961, after Dr. Johnson's lobbying got him into the previously segregated U.S. Interscholastic tourney, Ashe won it for Sumner High.

Four years later, leading man of his alma mater's varsity (University of California at Los Angeles), he won the U.S. Intercollegiate singles.

Although Ashe was ever a winner, a man of strong character, poised and able to overcome racial blocks, it took him a while to harness his power, groove his groundstrokes and become a thoughtful player, comfortable on all surfaces. As one whose career overflowed the amateur and open eras, he followed the 1968 breakthrough with 11 sterling years as a professional that netted 33 singles titles including the 1970 Australian and the gloriously unexpected Wimbledon '75. He won 35 amateur singles tournaments.

In 1975, days before his 32nd birthday, seeded sixth, he was a longer shot than he had been seven years earlier at Forest Hills. Defending champ Jimmy Connors, seemingly inviolable, was a 10-to-1 favorite in the final, but Ashe was too slick and cerebral in one of the momentous upsets, 6-1, 6-1, 5-7, 6-4. Changing pace and spin cleverly, startling Connors with a sliced serve wide to the two-fisted backhand, Ashe foxed the man a decade his junior.

This was the centerpiece of Ashe's preeminent year, a heavy-duty season when he won 9 of 29 tourneys on a 108-23 match record and wound up No. 1 in the U.S., No. 4 in the world. He reached No. 2 in 1976. Improving with age, he unfortunately was grounded prematurely, and permanently, by a heart attack in July 1979. In 1992 he revealed that he'd contracted AIDS through a 1988 blood transfusion.

For 12 years he was in the World Top Ten, and for 14 years, through 1979, in the U.S. Top Ten, No. 1 in 1968 and 1975. He was one of the founders of the ATP in 1972, served as president and had been a reasoned, intelligent spokesman for the game, served on numerous corporate boards and received several honorary degrees.

A long-time protester of apartheid in South Africa, he was, after several refusals, granted a visa to visit that country in 1973, and became the first black to win a title there, the doubles (with

Okker) in the South African Open. "You have shown our black youth that they can compete with whites and win," poet Don Mattera lauded him.

He was gratified to return again after the overturning of apartheid and meet with president Nelson Mandela (who identified himself as "an Ashe fan.") Ashe lent himself, his name and his money to various enlightened causes. He was arrested not long before his death in a protest against what he regarded as cruel U.S. policies toward Haitian refugees. His principal cause was fostering and furthering education for needy kids, and he was the guiding light in the Safe Passage Foundation for that purpose. He was also a warrior in the fight against AIDS. A tennis player who went well beyond the game, Arthur upheld the qualities that distinguished him as a champion: he showed that it was possible to compete ferociously while maintaining personal honor and sportsmanship. Having entered the Hall of Fame in 1985, he died Feb. 6, 1993, leaving his wife, Jeanne, and six-year-old daughter, Camera.

MAJOR TITLES (5)—*Australian singles, 1970; Wimbledon singles, 1975; U.S. singles, 1968; Australian doubles, 1977; French doubles, 1971.* OTHER U.S. TITLES (8)—*Amateur singles, 1968; Clay Court singles, 1967; Hard Court singles, 1963; Intercollegiate singles, 1965; Indoor doubles, 1967, with Charles Pasarell; 1970, with Stan Smith; Clay Court doubles, 1970, with Clark Graebner; Intercollegiate doubles, 1965, with Ian Crookenden.* DAVIS CUP (As player)—*1963, 1965, 1966, 1967, 1968, 1969, 1970, 1975, 1977, 1978; record: 27-5 in singles, 1-1 in doubles; (As captain)— 1981, 1982, 1983, 1984, 1985; record: 13-3, 2 Cups.* SINGLES RECORD IN THE MAJORS: *Australian (25-5), French (25-8), Wimbledon (35-11), U.S. (53-17).*

BORIS BECKER
Germany (1968—)

A redheaded phenomenon, Boris Becker illuminated 1985 and 1986 with his Wimbledon triumphs at the improbable ages of 17 and 18.

The records came tumbling down in 1985 when the unseeded German teenager beat eighth-seeded Kevin Curren, 6-3, 6-7 (4-7), 7-6 (7-3), 6-4, in the final. He was the first German champ, first non-seed to win—Boris was ranked No.

20—and the youngest male ever to win a major at 17 years, 7 months. (Michael Chang, at 17 years, 3 months, lowered that four years later in winning the French).

A big man (6-foot-3, 180) playing a big, carefree game of booming serves, heavy forehand, penetrating volleys and diving saves, he was an immediate crowd favorite. Despite his youth, he showed sensitivity in rejecting an early, obvious nickname, " Boom Boom," considering it "too warlike."

For Germany, never better than a 1970 finalist in the quest for the Davis Cup, Becker was an instant hero. Almost alone he carried his country to the 1985 final in Munich and beat both Stefan Edberg and Mats Wilander in the 3-2 loss to Sweden.

Three years after that he lifted the Fatherland to the Cup in a 4-1 victory over the Swedes in Goteborg. Boris beat Edberg, then paired with Eric Jelen for the clinching doubles win over Edberg and Anders Jarryd. In 1989 he won both his singles, the doubles again with Jelen at Stuttgart as Germany kept the Cup, 3-2, over Sweden. His third-day beating of Wilander, 6-2, 6-0, 6-2, was the clincher.

By the close of the 1992 season he had won 21 straight Cup singles, and had lost only two of 34 starts, both to Sergio Casal of Spain. He didn't play in 1993–94, but in 1995 extended the streak to 22, second longest in Cup history (to Bjorn Borg's 33), before losing to Paul Haarhuis in a victory over the Netherlands.

Becker beat Ivan Lendl in straight sets in 1986 for his second Wimbledon title, and Edberg just as swiftly in 1989 for a third, developing the feeling that Centre Court was his special haunt. He and Edberg also contested the 1988 and 1990 finals, Edberg winning. They were the first men in almost a century, since Wilfred Baddeley and Joshua Pim split the finals in 1891–94, to monopolize the final for at least three successive years. In the only all-German final on Centre Court, Michael Stich upset him in 1991.

It took him four years to work his way back to a seventh Wimbledon final, but then he gave one of his more brilliant Centre Court performances, beating favored Andre Agassi from a set and 1-4 (two breaks) down, 2-6, 7-6 (7-1), 6-4, 7-6 (7-1). But he couldn't solve Pete Sampras' serve in the title match, 6-7 (5-7), 6-2, 6-4, 6-2. After Becker had to default to Neville Godwin with a freak wrist injury (mishitting a return) in the 1996 tourney's third round, his Wimbledon match record was 64-10.

By 1996 it seemed that his days of winning majors were past. He was 28, had a wife, Barbara, and a young son. But he arrived in Melbourne fit and eager, (inspired by Barbara's plea, "I never saw you win a big one,") and captured his sixth, the Australian, with a blistering attack on the perpetual motion machine, Chang, 6-2, 6-4, 2-6, 6-2. He appeared ready to contend for another Wimbledon only to break down. It wasn't until late in the year that he was sound again, winning Stuttgart in five hard sets over No. 1 Sampras, who called him "the best man I've ever played indoors. He's the Michael Jordan of Germany, King Boris."

Boris Franz Becker, a right-hander, was born Nov. 22, 1967, in the small town of Leiman, Germany, and grew up there, not far from Bruhl, where the other German wunderkind, Steffi Graf, was raised. A promising junior, he dropped out of high school to become a pro. An atypical European player, he prefers faster surfaces to his native clay. His best finishes at the French have been semifinals in 1989 and 1991.

At the conclusion of 1988 he squashed Ivan Lendl's bid for a sixth Masters title by the narrowest possible of final-round margins—two points—on a net-cord dribbler that won the fifth-set tie-breaker, 7-5. It stands as one of the two closest significant tournament finishes, along with Ken Rosewall's 1972 WCT (World Championship Tennis) victory over Rod Laver, also a fifth-set tie-breaker, 7-5. Boris won the tourney (which became the ATP Championship) twice

Boris Becker: A boomer. (Mitchell Reibel)

more, in 1992 over Jim Courier, and 1995 over Chang, both in straight sets.

His marvelous 1989 season, during which he won 6 of 13 tournaments on a 64-8 match record, included his fourth major, the U.S. Open in a 7-6 (7-2), 1-6, 6-3, 7-6 (7-4) victory over No. 1-ranked Ivan Lendl. It was the lone major male final to conclude in a tie-breaker.

His fifth major (the third he won over Lendl) was the Australian at the outset of 1991, giving him the No. 1 ranking momentarily. During his 13 years as a pro he has been in the World Top Ten 11 times and won 48 singles titles, standing ninth on the all-time roll.

In 1992 he won an Olympic gold in doubles, alongside Stich, in a 7-6 (7-5), 4-6, 7-6 (7-5), 6-3 triumph over South Africa's Wayne Ferreira and Piet Norval.

By the close of 1996, which he capped by winning the Grand Slam Cup over Goran Ivanisevic, Boris had won 49 singles, 14 doubles pro titles and $23,841,402 in prize money. In singles he was 669-187 (.781).

MAJOR TITLES (6)—*Australian singles, 1991, 1996; Wimbledon singles, 1985, 1986, 1989; U.S. singles, 1989. DAVIS CUP—1985, 1986, 1987, 1988, 1989, 1991, 1992, 1995; record: 35-3 in singles, 14-7 in doubles.* SINGLES RECORD IN THE MAJORS: *Australian (29-8), French (26-9), Wimbledon (64-10), U.S. (37-10).*

PAULINE BETZ

United States (1919—)

Many believe Pauline May Betz Addie was the finest of the post-World War II players of the U.S., even though her career was cut short in her prime by a controversial ruling by the USTA. In 1947 she was declared a professional for merely exploring the possibilities of making a pro tour.

There was no pro tennis as such for women at the time, but she did make two tours of one-night stands against Sarah Palfrey Cooke in 1947, and Gussy Moran in 1951, dominating both opponents. Then she became a teaching professional and married sportswriter Bob Addie.

Born Aug. 6, 1919, in Dayton, Ohio, she grew up in Los Angeles, and became noted for her extreme speed and mobility. Although she could get to the net quickly and volley with sureness, she preferred to run down balls and pass the net-rushers, particularly with a penetrating backhand.

World War II deprived her of the chance for much international play, but she won Wimbledon the only time she entered, in 1946, without losing a set. Her closest start was the 6-2, 6-4 final with Louise Brough. In Betz's only Wightman Cup series against Britain, in 1946, she helped the U.S. win by taking both her singles matches and her doubles.

Betz was first ranked in the U.S. Top Ten, at No. 8 in 1939, and stayed in that select group for seven more years, standing at No. 1 in 1942,

Pauline Betz: Speediest afoot. (New York Herald Tribune)

1943, 1944 and 1946, the years she won the U.S. Championship in singles at Forest Hills. She held the No. 1 world ranking in 1946.

She closed out her amateur career in 1946 by winning 8 of 12 tournaments, and her last 27 matches. That was the fourth of her most productive campaigns that netted seven titles in 1943, eight in 1944, six in 1945. In 1943 she emphasized her superbly rounded game by making a U.S. triple, with Indoor and Clay Court singles titles preceding Forest Hills success. Beating Catherine Wolf, 6-0, 6-2, to win the Tri-State of 1943, Pauline relinquished no points in the first set. Top-seeded Louise Brough was the 4-6, 6-1, 6-4, victim in her first triumph at Forest Hills, but the semi was tougher, 6-4, 4-6, 7-5, over Margaret Osborne (duPont), from match point down at 3-5.

Two other years, 1941 and 1945, she was runner-up to Sarah Palfrey Cooke, thus setting a

Forest Hills record of six straight years in the final. In playing Forest Hills eight times, she won 33 of 37 matches.

She captured 19 U.S. titles on various surfaces, including the Clay Court singles in 1941 and 1943 and the Indoor singles in 1939, 1941, 1943 and 1947. Twice she scored triples at the Indoor Championships, winning the singles, doubles and mixed doubles in 1941 and 1943, a feat equaled only by Billie Jean King in 1966 and 1968.

Tennis historian Jerome Scheuer called her "the fastest woman on foot ever to play the game." A charming grandmother, she continues to play in a club league, "trying to keep up with the kids."

She was selected for the Hall of Fame in 1965.

MAJOR TITLES (6)—*Wimbledon singles, 1946; U.S. singles, 1942, 1943, 1944, 1946; French mixed, 1946.* OTHER U.S. TITLES (15)—*Indoor singles, 1939, 1941, 1943, 1947; Indoor doubles, 1941, with Dorothy Bundy; 1943, with Hazel Hotchkiss Wightman; Indoor mixed, 1939, with Wayne Sabin; 1940, with Bobby Riggs; 1941, 1943, with Al Stitt; Clay Court singles, 1941, 1943; Clay Court doubles, 1943, with Nancy Corbett; 1944, 1945, with Doris Hart.* WIGHTMAN CUP— *1946; record: 2-0 in singles, 1-0 in doubles.* SINGLES RECORD IN THE MAJORS: *French (4-1), Wimbledon (6-0), U.S. (33-4).*

BJORN BORG
Sweden (1956—)

Before he was 21, Bjorn Rune Borg had registered feats that would set him apart as one of the game's greats—and before he was 26, the headbanded, golden-locked Swede was through. No male career of the modern era has been so brief and bright.

Tennis is filled with instances of precocious achievements and championships, but none is quite as impressive as those of the seemingly emotionless Borg. Just before his 18th birthday he was the youngest winner of the Italian Championship, and two weeks later he was the youngest winner of the French Championship (a record lowered by Mats Wilander, 17, in 1982, and subsequently by Michael Chang, a younger

Bjorn Borg: Power without passion. (Mitchell Reibel)

17 in 1989). Eighteen months later, at 19, he climaxed a Davis Cup record winning streak of 19 singles by lifting Sweden to the 1975 Cup for the first time in a 3-2 final-round victory over Czechoslovakia. His Cup singles streak of 33 was intact at his retirement, still a record.

Although Lew Hoad and Ken Rosewall were a few months younger in 1953 when they won the Davis Cup for Australia, both were beaten during the final round. But Borg won both his singles over Jan Kodes and Jiri Hrebec and teamed with Ove Bengtson for the doubles win. Borg's Davis Cup debut at 16 in 1972 as one of the youngest ever in that competition was phenomenal: a five-set win over seasoned pro Onny Parun of New Zealand. Borg was also the youngest winner of the oldest professional championship, the U.S. Pro, whose singles he took in 1974 at 18 (and, subsequently, 1975 and 1976). Aaron Krickstein, 16, lowered that record in 1984.

A player of great strength and endurance, he had a distinctive and unorthodox style and appearance, bowlegged, yet very fast. His muscular shoulders and well-developed torso gave him the strength to lash at the ball with heavy topspin on both forehand and backhand. He used a two-handed backhand, adapted from the slap shot in hockey, a game he favored as a child. By the time he was 13 he was beating the best of Sweden's under-18 players and Davis Cup captain Lennart Bergelin cautioned against anyone trying to change Borg's rough-looking, jerky strokes. They were effective. Through 1977 he had never lost to a player younger than himself.

Born June 6, 1956, in Sodertalje, Sweden, where he grew up, Bjorn was fascinated by a tennis racket his father had won as a prize in a ping-pong tournament. His father gave him the racket and that was the start.

Borg preferred to battle from the baseline, trading groundstrokes tirelessly in long rallies, retrieving and waiting patiently to outlast his opponent. Volleying, with his Western grip forehand and two-fisted backhand, was troublesome, and his serve was not impressive at first. He didn't do much on grass until 1976, when he was determined to win Wimbledon, and did so after devoting himself to two weeks of solid practice on serve-and-volley tactics. He won the most important tournament without loss of a set, beating favored Ilie Nastase in the final, 6-4, 6-2, 9-7. Borg was the youngest champion of the modern era at 20 years, one month, until Boris Becker, 17, won in 1985. Borg repeated in 1977, although the tournament was more demanding. His thrilling five-set victories over Americans Vitas Gerulaitis in the semifinals, 6-4, 3-6, 6-3, 3-6, 8-6, and Jimmy Connors, 3-6, 6-2, 6-1, 5-7, 6-4, in the final were considered two of the best ever played at Wimbledon. By that time Borg had more confidence and proficiency in his volleying. Borg repeated over Connors in 1978, becoming the first to win three successive years since Fred Perry (1934–36). He made it four in a row with a five-set triumph over American Roscoe Tanner in the 1979 final, thus becoming the first player since Tony Wilding (1910–13) to win four straight years.

His fifth straight Wimbledon championship, in 1980, climaxed with an all-time great final, a 1-6, 7-5, 6-3, 6-7 (16-18), 8-6 triumph over John McEnroe. During one of the most electrifying passages in tennis history, the 34-point tie-breaker, Borg was stymied on five match points and saved six set points before giving way. But his famous resolve brought him through in the brilliantly battled fifth.

Borg, a right-hander, was now flirting with the ancient Wimbledon record of six straight titles. That was the much less demanding feat of Willie Renshaw (1881–86) since in that day of the challenge round format, Renshaw needed to play only one match each to win the last five titles. Thus his match winning streak was only 13, up to an 1888 defeat by Willoughby Hamilton.

While winning 1980, Borg also surpassed Rod Laver's Wimbledon male match winning-streak record of 31. Bjorn built that to his own record 41 (Helen Wills Moody won 50 straight between 1927 and 1938) by reaching the 1981 final. There he was finally dethroned by McEnroe, 4-6, 7-6 (7-1), 7-6 (7-4), 6-4.

When he won his male record sixth French title in 1981, with another record, his 28th straight match win, it seemed that Borg, then 25, would surely surpass Roy Emerson's male record of 12 major singles titles. Borg had 11. But he would not win another, remaining tied with Laver.

His left-handed nemesis, McEnroe, followed up on Wimbledon by beating Borg in a second successive U.S. Open final to take over the No. 1 ranking that the Swede had held in 1979 and 1980. That defeat, 4-6, 6-2, 6-4, 6-3, effectively ended Borg's career. He won only two more matches, reaching the quarters of Monte Carlo in 1982. Shortly after that he retired, having won 62 singles titles, including the Masters of 1979 and 1980, and was inducted into the Hall of Fame in 1987. Nevertheless, he did try comebacks in 1991,

1992 and 1993, all unsuccessful, losing his reappearance match at Monte Carlo to Jordi Arrese.

The balletic footwork and marvelous anticipation couldn't be coaxed to return with him, even though others had stayed afloat and earning at 35. He lost eight first-rounders in 1992, three in 1993. Bjorn's parting shot, in Moscow's Kremlin Cup, was as close as he got, holding a match point in a farewell tie-breaker while losing to Aleksandr Volkov, 4-6, 6-3, 7-6 (9-7). Thereafter he confined himself to senior events, renewing his rivalry with Connors, against whom he had been 10-7. He was 7-7 lifetime against McEnroe.

The U.S. Open was his particular jinx. He failed to win in 10 tries, losing four finals, 1976 and 1978 to Jimmy Connors, and 1980 and 1981 to McEnroe. Thrice (1978, 1979 and 1980) he was halfway to a Grand Slam after victories at the French and Wimbledon only to falter at the three-quarter pole at Flushing Meadow, lefty Tanner his conqueror in 1979.

Borg's career prize money was $3,609,896.

MAJOR TITLES *(11)—French singles, 1974, 1975, 1978, 1979, 1980, 1981; Wimbledon singles, 1976, 1977, 1978, 1979, 1980.* DAVIS CUP—*1972, 1973, 1974, 1975, 1978, 1979, 1980; record: 37-3 in singles, 8-8 in doubles.* SINGLES RECORD IN THE MAJORS: *Australian (1-1), French (49-2), Wimbledon (51-4), U.S. (40-10).*

LOUISE BROUGH

United States (1923—)

One of the great volleyers in history was Althea Louise Brough, whose handiwork at the net earned her 13 titles at Wimbledon alone, in singles, doubles and mixed, including a rare triple—championships in each—in 1950. Of the foremost U.S. females only Chris Evert (19 times) and Billie Jean King (18) lasted longer in the American Top Ten. Brough was there 16 times between 1941 and 1957, No. 1 in 1947. She was in the World Top Ten 12 times, 1946 through 1957, No. 1 in 1955.

Louise Brough: The art of volley. (New York Herald Tribune)

Louise Brough was born March 11, 1923, in Oklahoma City, Okla., but grew up in Southern California, where she came to prominence as a junior, winning the U.S. 18-and-under title in 1940 and 1941.

Wimbledon was not held during World War II, but when the tournament reopened in 1946 Brough was ready to play a dominant role for a decade in the leading tournament, and is recalled as one of the most overwhelming players to compete there. In the first postwar visit she appeared in every final and just missed out on a triple, losing the singles to Pauline Betz. But the right-handed Brough won the doubles with Margaret duPont and the mixed doubles with Tom Brown. During the Brough decade a Wimbledon final without her was unusual. Between 1946 and 1955, she won her way into 21 of the 30 finals, taking the singles in 1948, 1949, 1950, and 1955, the doubles also in 1946, 1948, 1949, 1950 and 1954 with duPont, and the mixed doubles in 1946 with Tom Brown, in 1947 and 1948 with John Bromwich and in 1950 with Eric Sturgess.

Although she won the U.S. Singles Championship at Forest Hills only in 1947, she was a finalist on five other occasions. Doubles was the stage for her utmost success in the U.S., allied with duPont in possibly the finest female team ever, certainly the most victorious in major events. They won 20 Big Four titles together (12 U.S., five Wimbledon, three French), a mark equaled by Martina Navratilova and Pam Shriver in 1989.

Included in their record dozen U.S. titles was the longest championship run in any of the Big Four Events: nine straight doubles between 1942 and 1950. (Max Decugis and Maurice Germot won the French doubles 10 straight times between 1906 and 1920, but competition then was restricted to French citizens.) Brough and duPont did not enter the U.S. doubles in 1951 and 1952, but they returned to increase their record match winning streak to 41 before narrowly losing the 1953 final to Doris Hart and Shirley Fry, 6-2, 7-9, 9-7, despite holding two match points. As a team in the U.S. doubles they won 12 of 14 times entered and 58 of 60 matches, losing but five sets.

Altogether, Brough won 35 of the major titles in singles, doubles and mixed doubles to rank fifth on the all-time list behind Margaret Court (62), Martina Navratilova (56), Billie Jean King (39) and Margaret duPont (37). Brough won the Australian singles in 1950. Her various U.S. titles amounted to 18, and she was inducted into the Hall of Fame in 1967.

A willowy blonde, 5-foot-7½, she was quiet and diffident but the killer in the left court when at play alongside duPont. Despite their close friendship and partnership, they were keen rivals in singles, and Brough's most difficult Wimbledon triumphs were the three-set wins over duPont in 1949 and 1950, the most stirring the 10-8, 1-6, 10-8 decision in 1949.

After retiring from the amateur circuit she married Dr. A. T. Clapp, and later occasionally played in senior (over 40) tournaments, winning the U.S. Hard Court Doubles in that category in 1971 and 1975 with Barbara Green Weigandt.

MAJOR TITLES (35)—*Australian singles; 1950; Wimbledon singles, 1948, 1949, 1950, 1955; U.S. singles, 1947; Australian doubles, 1950; French doubles, 1946, 1947, 1949; Wimbledon doubles, 1946, 1948, 1949, 1950, 1954; U.S. doubles, 1942, 1943, 1944, 1945, 1946, 1947, 1948, 1949, 1950, 1955, 1956, 1957; Wimbledon mixed, 1946, 1947, 1948, 1950; U.S. mixed, 1942, 1947, 1948, 1949. Other U.S. title—Hard Court doubles; 1948, with duPont.* WIGHTMAN CUP—*1946, 1947, 1948, 1949, 1950, 1952, 1953, 1954, 1955, 1956, 1957; record: 12-0 in singles, 10-0 in doubles.* SINGLES RECORD IN THE MAJORS: *Australian (5-0), French (10-4), Wimbledon (56-7), U.S. (57-17).*

MARIA BUENO
Brazil (1939—)

Maria Esther Andion Bueno came swirling out of Brazil as a teenager to quickly establish herself as one of the world's most graceful and proficient athletes, a delight to watch and dangerous to deal with since she had a wide repertoire of shots and the skill and grace to deliver them constantly.

As the São Paulo Swallow, she was slim, tall (5-foot-7) and quick, swooping to the net to conquer with piercing volleys. She was a blend of power and touch, a woman of superb movement and rhythms. Stylishly gowned by the tennis couturier, Ted Tinling, she was the frilly treasure of Wimbledon's Centre Court, where she was at her best and won eight titles: three in singles (1959, 1960, 1964), and five in doubles.

Grass was her favorite surface, suiting her attacking nature. Born Oct. 11, 1939, in São Paulo, she was clearly the best female player to come from Latin America, and was rated No. 1 in the world in 1959, 1960, 1964 and 1966, a member of the Top Ten 10 times between 1958 and 1968. In her regal choreography, the versatile right-hander was one of a triumvirate of women—including Frenchwoman Suzanne Lenglen and Australian Evonne Goolagong—whose fluidity and artistry set them apart.

She was agreeable, but reserved, a private person who underwent a number of physical career-harming agonies, without complaint. Her best days were as an amateur. By the time open tennis and prize money dawned in 1968 she was hobbled by a variety of arm and leg injuries. After a long retirement, she felt sufficiently well to try the pro tour in 1975, and returned to Wimbledon for a spiritual triumph in 1976 after a hiatus of seven years. There were glimpses of the wondrous Maria as she won three rounds, and most spectators were gratified to see her again. "In her day she was so marvelous to watch," said Billie Jean King, an old rival and doubles accomplice, after defeating Maria at Wimbledon in 1977. "But it was painful to play her today. I wanted to remember her as she was."

Bueno seemed undismayed to be a loser. "I have always loved tennis, and still enjoy playing. I've had my glory," she said. She crashed through to a first major singles triumph by defeating another aggressor, Darlene Hard, 6-4, 6-3, in the 1959 Wimbledon final. Two months later, in a rare teenage final at Forest Hills, Maria, 18, beat the British 6-footer Christine Truman, 19, for the U.S. title, 6-1, 6-4. That was her first of four U.S. singles prizes. She winged to the heights in the finals of 1963 and 1964, taking a shot-making feast from Margaret Smith (Court), 7-5, 6-4, to wow the gallery, and the following year stunning the spectators by destroying Carole Caldwell Graebner, 6-1, 6-0. At Wimbledon in 1964 she and Margaret staged another rouser of volleying violence for the title that went to Maria, 6-4, 7-9, 6-3. She won her last major singles final, the U.S. of 1966, over Nancy Richey, 6-3, 6-1, but was beaten in her last important final, the U.S. Amateur of 1968, by Margaret, 6-2, 6-2.

At 18, in the company of Althea Gibson, Maria won her first Wimbledon prize, the doubles of 1958. In all she won 19 Big Four titles in singles, doubles and mixed, including the U.S. Singles at Forest Hills in 1959, 1963, 1964 and 1966. She and American Darlene Hard were one of the best teams, taking the Wimbledon title twice and the U.S. twice. Maria's skill at doubles was such that she won her 12 majors with six partners and in 1960 scored one of three doubles Grand Slams, with two partners: Christine Truman in the Australian, Hard in the French, Wim-

Maria Bueno: Fluidity and artistry. (Peter Mecca)

bledon and U.S. She won the Japan Open in 1974, her lone pro title in singles, to complement 62 as an amateur, making her an unusual champ who won titles in three decades.

MAJOR TITLES (18)—*Wimbledon singles, 1959, 1960, 1964; U.S. singles, 1959, 1963, 1964, 1966; Australian doubles, 1960; French doubles, 1960; Wimbledon doubles, 1958, 1960, 1963, 1965; U.S. doubles, 1960, 1962, 1966, 1968; French mixed, 1960.* FEDERATION CUP—*1965; record: 1-0 in singles, 0-1 in doubles.* SINGLES RECORD IN THE MAJORS: *Australian (6-2), French (33-10), Wimbledon (50-9), U.S. (48-7).*

MAUREEN CONNOLLY

United States (1934–1969)

A too-brief flash on the tennis scene was that of Maureen Catherine Connolly, but it was of brilliant incandescence; she may have been the finest of all female players.

Nicknamed "Little Mo" for her big-gunning, unerring ground strokes (it was an allusion to "Big Mo," the U.S. battleship Missouri), she was devastating from the baseline, and seldom needed to go to the net. A small and compact right-hander (5-foot-4, 120 pounds), she won her major singles championships as a teenager: three successive Wimbledons, 1952–54, and U.S. Championships at Forest Hills, 1951–53. At 16 years, 11 months, she was the youngest U.S. champ ever until Tracy Austin won in 1979 at 16 years, 9 months. In addition, Connolly won three other American titles and held the No. 1 U.S. rankings, 1951–53. She was undisputed world leader, 1952–1954. Connolly was born Sept. 17, 1934, in San Diego, Cal., and grew up there. She was a pupil of Eleanor "Teach" Tennant, an instructor who had guided a previous world champ, Alice Marble. Connolly first came East in 1949 to win the U.S. junior title and repeated in 1950. She entered Forest Hills both years, losing in the second round. But she would soon have the world under her right thumb while still technically a junior, not yet 19, an obstreperous intruder overthrowing the established order of older women. Her third time around at the U.S. biggie, seeded fourth, she ran six games from 1-4 down in the first set while beating top-seeded 26-year-old Hart, 6-4, 6-4, in a semi halted by rain after the first game of the second, and resumed the following day. A day after that completion, Maureen was given a harder time by second-seeded 24-year-old Shirley Fry, but her long-range shelling was decisive, 6-3, 1-6, 6-4.

A cheerful and sporting competitor, she crushed the opposition, never losing an important match, only occasionally losing a set. She helped the U.S. beat Britain in the Wightman Cup matches of 1951–54, winning all seven of her singles.

Fifteen years after Don Budge scored the first Grand Slam, Connolly traveled the same route in 1953, winning all the major singles championships (Australian, French, Wimbledon, U.S.) within a calendar year to achieve the first female Slam. She lost only one set in doing so.

Maureen Connolly: The force of a battleship. (UPI)

Following the Aussie triumph over doubles partner and fellow Californian, Julie Sampson, 6-3, 6-2, Maureen had to get past Hart: 6-2, 6-4, at the French, 8-6, 7-5, at Wimbledon, 6-2, 6-4, in the home stretch. That season she won 10 of 12 tournaments on a 61-2 match record. By winning the three French titles in 1954 she became the fourth of five players to score a triple in Paris.

Nobody has measured up to her perfect record in the majors after early U.S. defeats in 1949–50. She sailed through nine successive majors (three U.S., three Wimbledons, two French, one Australian), unbeaten in 50 matches. The closest to that were four other greats who won six straight: Budge, 1937–38; Margaret Court, 1969–70, Martina Navratilova, 1983–84; Steffi Graf, 1995–96. Helen Wills Moody, who played irregularly, won 15 straight majors between 1924 and 1933.

In 1954 her playing carer ended with heart-breaking suddenness, aborted by an unusual traffic accident, not long after she won her last titles, the U.S. Clay singles and doubles. While riding horseback, she was struck by a truck, severely injuring a leg. "I knew immediately I'd never play again," she said. By then she was Mrs. Norman Brinker. She recovered sufficiently to give tennis instruction, and helped a number of players with their games, but she died at 34 in 1969 of cancer.

She was inducted into the Hall of Fame in 1968 and is memorialized by the Maureen Connolly Brinker Cup, an international team competition between the U.S. and Britain for girls under 21.

"Whenever a great player comes along you have to ask, 'could she have beaten Maureen?'" That was the standard of Lance Tingay, the Hall of Fame tennis correspondent of the *Daily Telegraph* of London. "In every case the answer is, I think not."

MAJOR TITLES *(12)—Australian singles, 1953; French singles, 1953, 1954; Wimbledon singles, 1952, 1953, 1954; U.S. singles, 1951, 1952, 1953; Australian doubles, 1953; French doubles, 1954; French mixed, 1954.* OTHER U.S. TITLES *(3)—Clay Court singles, 1953, 1954; Clay Court doubles, 1954, with Doris Hart.* WIGHTMAN CUP—*1951, 1952, 1953, 1954; record: 7-0 in singles, 2-0 in doubles.* SINGLES RECORD IN THE MAJORS: *Australian (5-0), French (10-0), Wimbledon (18-0), U.S. (19-2).*

JIMMY CONNORS

United States (1952—)

A marvel of longevity and self-motivation, he is (as one-time agent Bill Riordan boasted) "the one and only James Scott Connors."

Fiery of temperament and shotmaking, this lefty with a two-fisted backhand has pounded foes for more than two professional decades in rip-roaring baseline style, a ragdoll throwing himself into his groundies with utter gusto. Often controversial, he fought verbally with opponents, officials and the crowd.

Considered a feisty wiseguy in his earlier days, he eventually became a respected elder. The championships, honors and prize money piled up, but not as high as his zeal as he continued to compete forcefully against much younger men into his 41st year and through the 1992 season when he roused galleries in Paris, London and New York and compiled a 17-15 match record, ending the season with a remarkable No. 83 ranking.

Turning pro in 1972, Jimmy won his first title that year at Jacksonville, Fla., and continued at a prodigious pace, arriving at his 109th—a male record—in 1989 by winning in Israel. He attained 54 other finals, and has played more tournaments (401) and won more matches than any other male pro, 1,337-285 (.824), and, in fact, has never really retired. Having lost a first-rounder at Atlanta in 1996, he is the only player who has been on the ATP computer since its inception in 1973, latest ranking a not-too-shabby No. 1,304 at age 44.

He also won Wimbledon twice (1974 and 1982) and the Australian (1974) for a total of 8 singles majors, second only to Bill Tilden's 10 among American men, and tied with Fred Perry, Ken Rosewall, Ivan Lendl and Pete Sampras for fourth on the all-time roll.

His specialty has been the U.S. Open (five championships), where he was singular in winning on all three surfaces: grass (1974) and clay (1976) at Forest Hills, and hard (1978, 1982 and 1983) at Flushing Meadow.

Perhaps the most extraordinary year of his certain progression toward the Hall of Fame was 1991. His career had seemed ended. Troubled by a deteriorated left wrist, he had played (and lost) only three matches in 1990, dropping to No. 936 in the rankings. However, surgery restored him, and he came back smoking, playing 14 tournaments and climaxing with a phenomenal semifinal finish (his 14th) at the U.S. Open.

His first- and second-round victories as a Wimbledon wild card raised his tournament male record to 84 match wins. Wild-carded again at

Flushing, because of a No. 174 ranking, Jimmy exploded by beating Patrick McEnroe from two sets down as well as Michael Schapers and 10th-seeded Karel Novacek, then celebrated his 39th birthday in a tumultuous victory over Aaron Krickstein, soaring from 2-5 in the fifth set to win in a stirring tie-breaker, 3-6, 7-5 (10-8), 1-6, 6-3, 7-6 (7-4). Then he beat Paul Haarhuis from a set and a break down, outgunned at last against Jim Courier, 6-3, 6-3, 6-2. He was the oldest semifinalist since 39-year-old Rosewall lost the title match to none other than James himself 17 years before. Although Stefan Edberg won the title, it was Connors' Open in the public eye.

Ever a sensational celebrator of his own birthday (he has won 10 of 11 matches on that day at the U.S. Open), Jimmy took the cake in 1992 on his 40th by beating Jaime Oncins, 6-1, 6-2, 6-3, notching a tournament-record 98th match win.

He was raised to be a tennis player by his mother, a teaching pro named Gloria Thompson Connors, and "Two Mom," grandmother Bertha Thompson. Connors grew up in Belleville, Ill., across the Mississippi from St. Louis. Although he was always smaller than his contemporaries on his way up the ladder, he made up for that through determination and grit. He played in his first U.S. Championship, the U.S. boys' 11-and-under of 1961, when he was only eight. He was born Sept. 2, 1952, in East St. Louis, Ill., and claimed to have begun playing when he was two. "My mother rolled balls to me, and I swung at them. I held the racket with both hands because that was the only way I could lift it."

Connors, who grew to 5-foot-10, 155 pounds, became known as a maverick when he refused to join the ATP (Association of Tennis Pros) in 1972, the then-new union embracing most male professionals, and avoided the mainstream of pro tennis to play in and dominate a series of smaller tournaments organized by Bill Riordan, his manager, a clever promoter.

In 1974 he and Riordan began bringing lawsuits, eventually amounting to $10 million, against the ATP and its president, Arthur Ashe,

Jimmy Connors: Ageless, two-fisted backhander. (Wide World)

for allegedly restricting his freedom in the game. It stemmed from Connors' banning by the French Open in 1974 after he had signed a contract to play WTT (World Team Tennis) for Baltimore. Connors had sought to enter the French, the only major championship he did not win that year, but because the ATP and the French administration opposed WTT—it conflicted with their tournament—the entries of WTT players were refused. The 1975 Wimbledon final, then, was unique, a duel between opponents in a lawsuit. Ashe won, and shortly thereafter Connors dropped the suits, and parted with Riordan.

Deprived unfairly by the French of a second leg on what might have been a Grand Slam, Connors nevertheless enjoyed in 1974 one of the finest seasons ever, the best by an American since Tony Trabert's 1955. Connors lost only four matches in 20 tournaments, while winning 99.

Among the 14 tournaments he won—a record for American male pros—were the Australian, Wimbledon, South African, U.S. at Forest Hills, U.S. Clay Court and U.S. Indoor. He was clearly the No. 1 player in the world, a status he also held from 1975-78, an open era record for continuous hegemony. He took over No. 1 in July 1974, held it 159 straight weeks and was there a total of 263 weeks, second only to Ivan Lendl's 269.

Although he trailed his foremost rivals head-to-head—Bjorn Borg, 7-10; John McEnroe, 13-20; Lendl, 13-22—he had great moments at their expense. He saved four set points to win a thrilling and vital 11-9 third-set tie-breaker while beating Borg in the 1976 Forest Hills final, 6-4, 3-6, 7-6 (11-9), 6-4, and stunned the Swede (his conqueror at Wimbledon) to take the inaugural Flushing Meadow final in 1978, 6-4, 6-2, 6-2. Three points from defeat in the fourth-set tie-breaker, he startled McEnroe to win Wimbledon in five sets in 1982, bridging a gap of eight years between titles there. Jimmy's incredible service returning jolted Lendl in the 1982 and 1983 U.S. Open finals.

By winning the U.S. Indoor singles three straight years (1973–75) he tied a record set by Gus Touchard (1913–15). He made this his most successful tourney, adding wins in 1978, 1979, 1983 and 1984 for a record total of seven. At the U.S. Clay Court in 1974, 1976, 1978 and 1979, his four titles were the most since Frank Parker's five between 1933 and 1947.

Connors seemed to delight in keeping the public off-balance. He annoyed numerous tennis fans in the U.S. with his sometimes vulgar on-court behavior, and his refusal to play Davis Cup (except briefly in the 1976, 1981 and 1984 seasons). He was booed at Wimbledon—a rare show of disapproval there—for snubbing the Parade of Champions on the first day of the Centenary in 1977.

After irritating sponsors and tennis officials by shunning the climactic Masters for three years,

Connors entered and won the 1977 event over Bjorn Borg, having qualified by finishing among the top eight in the worldwide Grand Prix series.

His two crushing final-round victories over Ken Rosewall in 1974 (6-1, 6-1, 6-4 at Wimbledon, and 6-1, 6-0, 6-1, at Forest Hills) made Connors seem invincible. His manager, Riordan, proclaimed Jimmy "heavyweight champion of tennis," and arranged a series of challenges over three years at Las Vegas and Puerto Rico in which Connors retained his "title" by defeating Rod Laver, John Newcombe, Manolo Orantes and Ilie Nastase. Connors grossed over a million dollars from television rights for those four matches.

Beginning in 1974, Connors played in five successive U.S. finals, the first man to do so since Bill Tilden between 1918 and 1925. He was the first since Fred Perry (1933, 1934 and 1936) to win the U.S. title three years. Connors was beaten in the finals by Manolo Orantes in 1975 and by Guillermo Vilas in 1977, striking the last ball, an error, in championship play in Forest Hills Stadium.

Jimmy went to college one year at the University of California at Los Angeles, where he won the U.S. Intercollegiate Singles in 1971 and attained All-American status.

It was in 1973 that he made his first big splash by winning the U.S. Pro Singles, his first significant title, at 20, toppling Ashe, the favorite, in a five-set final. Ashe said, "I've played them all, and I never saw anybody hit the ball so hard for so long as Jimmy did." That year Connors was ranked co-No. 1 in the U.S. with Stan Smith, but was No. 1 alone seven other years, and in the U.S. Top Ten a record 20 times. During his 21-year pro career he was in the World Top Ten 16 times. His prize money amounted to $8,641,040. Jimmy, married with two children, lives on profitably as the mainstay of an "over 35" senior tour; the tour has various sponsors, but it's generally known as the "Connors Circuit."

MAJOR TITLES (10)—*Australian singles, 1974; Wimbledon singles, 1974, 1982; U.S. singles, 1974, 1976, 1978, 1982,*

1983; French doubles, 1973; U.S. doubles, 1975. OTHER U.S. TITLES (15)—*Indoor singles, 1973, 1974, 1975, 1978, 1979, 1983, 1984; Clay Court singles, 1974, 1976, 1978, 1979; Indoor doubles, 1974, with Frew McMillan; 1975, with Ilie Nastase; Clay Court doubles, 1974, with Nastase; Pro singles, 1973.* DAVIS CUP—*1976, 1981, 1984; record: 10-3 in singles.* SINGLES RECORD IN THE MAJORS: *Australian (11-1), French (40-13), Wimbledon (84-18), U.S. (98-17).*

MARGARET SMITH COURT
Australia (1942—)

For sheer strength of performance and accomplishment there has never been a tennis player to match Margaret Smith Court. As the most prolific winner of major championships, she rolled up 62 titles in singles, doubles and mixed doubles between 1960 and 1975, and took the Australian, French, Wimbledon and U.S. singles all within 1970 for the second female Grand Slam. She is the only player to achieve a Slam in doubles as well as in singles; Margaret and fellow Aussie Ken Fletcher won the four titles in mixed in 1963.

Her closest rivals statistically are not close: Martina Navratilova with 56 majors, and Roy Emerson heading the men with 28. Court has 24 alone in singles, three ahead of Steffi Graf.

From the country town of Albury in New South Wales, where she was born July 16, 1942, Margaret was one of the first Australian notables to be developed outside of the principal cities. Tall and gangling, nearly six feet, she worked hard in the gym and on the road, as well as on-court, to attain coordination and to marshal her prodigious strength. She was self-made through determination and training. Her power and incredible reach ("I call her the Arm," said rival Billie Jean King) first paid off and called international attention to her when she won the Australian singles at 18 in 1960. It was the first of her record 11 conquests of her homeland, the first seven in a row.

In 1961 she traveled abroad for the first time and played in her first Wimbledon final, the doubles that she and countrywoman Jan Lehane lost to Karen Hantze and a budding star, Billie Jean Moffitt (King).

Margaret was to win three Wimbledon, five French, and seven U.S. singles championships, and the greatest of those victories was probably the 1970 Wimbledon final. In considerable pain with a sprained ankle, she held off Billie Jean, 14-12, 11-9, in possibly the finest of female finals there, and certainly the longest in point of games, 46 (two more than the Suzanne Lenglen–Dorothea Chambers record in 1919).

She retired briefly upon marrying Barry Court in 1967, but was soon back on the trail of championships. Margaret was remarkable in that she continued to win major titles, such as the U.S. in 1973, after the birth of her first of three children, and was still competing at age 34 in 1977. She was shy, soft-spoken, and, late in her career, she became a lay minister.

Court was primarily an attacker, basing her game on a heavy serve and volley, and relying on athleticism and endurance. She could conquer with ground strokes, though, as she demonstrated in stopping clay-court terror Chris Evert in the splendid French final of 1973, 6-7 (5-7), 7-6 (8-6), 6-4. Sometimes Court fell prey to nerves, as in her 1971 Wimbledon final defeat by the crowd's favorite, Evonne Goolagong; or the bizarre televised challenge by 55-year-old Bobby Riggs in 1973, which she lost implausibly and badly. She couldn't reach the inspirational heights of her chief foe, King, but held a lifetime edge over Billie Jean, 22-10.

Her Grand Slam year, 1970, makes those of Maureen Connolly, 1953 (12 tournaments), and Steffi Graf, 1988 (14 tournaments), seem almost leisurely. Court won 21 of 27 tournaments on a 104-6 match record, earning $14,800 for the four titles while Graf's prize money take for the four was $877,724. Connolly was an amateur, and certainly several of Court's best years were as such during an 18-year career. As an amateur she had such years as 1962 (winning 13 of 15 tournaments on a 67-2 match record) and 1964 (13 of 16 on 67-2, including a 39-match winning streak).

Margaret Smith Court: "The Arm" and the attack. (UPI)

She won 79 pro singles titles, had her last sensational season in 1973, winning 18 of 25 tourneys on 102-6, among them the Australian, French and U.S. Representing Australia six times in the worldwide Federation Cup team competition, she played in the first in 1963 (a final-round defeat by the U.S.) and spearheaded Cup victories in 1964, 1965, 1968 and 1971, and was undefeated in 22 singles.

Tapped for the Hall of Fame in 1979, Court was born a left-hander. She was transformed to a right-handed player (like two other Famers, Maureen Connolly and Ken Rosewall), as frequently happened in that era. She had the best two-season run in history, 1969–70, with seven majors, missing out only at Wimbledon, 1969, where she lost in the semis to champion Ann Jones, 10-12, 6-3, 6-2. That defeat, as well as a first-round loss at Wimbledon to King in 1962, a final-round loss to Lesley Turner at the French in 1965, and a semi-

final loss at Wimbledon to Evert in 1973—her only major losses those years—may have cost her four additional Grand Slams.

She scored triples (singles, doubles, mixed titles) at the Australian in 1963, Wimbledon and the U.S. in 1970. She won her first major, Australian singles, in 1960 and last, U.S. doubles, in 1975, and between 1961 and 1975 was ranked in the World Top Ten 13 times—No. 1 seven times (1962, 1963, 1964, 1965, 1969, 1970, 1973), two behind Helen Wills Moody's record. Her career, overlapping the amateur and open eras, yielded $550,000 in prize money.

MAJOR TITLES (62)—*Australian singles, 1960, 1961, 1962, 1963, 1964, 1965, 1966, 1969, 1970, 1971, 1973; French singles, 1962, 1964, 1969, 1970, 1973; Wimbledon singles, 1963, 1965, 1970; U.S. singles, 1962, 1965, 1969, 1970, 1973; Australian doubles, 1961, 1962, 1963, 1965, 1969, 1970, 1971, 1973; French doubles, 1964, 1965, 1966, 1973; Wimbledon doubles, 1964, 1969; U.S. doubles, 1963, 1968, 1970, 1973, 1975; Australian mixed, 1963, 1964; French mixed, 1963, 1964, 1965, 1969; Wimbledon mixed, 1963, 1965, 1966, 1968, 1975; U.S. mixed, 1961, 1962, 1963, 1964, 1965, 1969, 1970, 1972.* FEDERATION CUP—*1963, 1964, 1965, 1968, 1969, 1971; record: 22-0 in singles, 15-5 in doubles.* SINGLES RECORD IN THE MAJORS: *Australian (60-3), French (20-1), Wimbledon (51-9), U.S. (51-6).*

JAROSLAV DROBNY
Czechoslovakia/Egypt (1921—)

Nobody at Wimbledon paid any attention to a 16-year old left-hander from Czechoslovakia who lost a lively first-rounder to an Argentine, Alejo Russell, 10-8, 6-4, 7-9, 6-3. His country was in the news, threatened by the Nazi dictator, Adolf Hitler. It was 1938, war was imminent. Jaroslav Drobny would get one more crack at the Big W, winning a couple of rounds in 1939, briefly noticed because he played two tough sets against top-seeded Bunny Austin before defaulting with an arm injury. Then he vanished into the cloud of World War II in his conquered homeland, wondering if he would ever play a big tournament again.

"We were just trying to stay alive. The torch of freedom with the Allies gave us hope," he says. Luckily he avoided deportation to Germany as a forced laborer, and was able to play hockey throughout the war, his best sport then. "Food was short, but we got along."

But he did take up tennis seriously again, seven years later, fashioning a magnificent 15-year amateur career that contained, despite so much time lost to the war, an amazing 133 singles titles—from Algeria to Knokke-le-Zoute—and membership in the world Top Ten for 10 successive years from 1946, No. 1 in 1954. In 1946 Drobny was permitted by the new Communist government to play Wimbledon again, the postwar reopening in 1946. Rusty from little play during the war, expecting nothing from himself, he beat the world's best, Jack Kramer, 2-6, 17-15, 6-3, 3-6, 6-3, in the fourth round, got to the semis and was hailed as a national hero at home, suddenly a name in the game in which he would become an all-timer.

At the time he was a remarkable two-sport world-class athlete: hockey in winter, tennis the rest of the time. So good was Drob as a forward on the ice that he played a leading role in Czechoslovakia's winning the world amateur championship in 1947 (he scored three goals in the final game against the U.S.), and gaining silver at the 1948 Olympics. By 1949, though, tennis had become his life. It was the year Drobny made the decision to leave his police-state homeland for good, defecting with Davis Cup teammate Vladimir Cernik during a Swiss tournament at Gstaad. Twice the two of them had carried their country to the cup semis, losses to Australia in 1947 and 3-2 in 1948. Drob won one of the exceptional matches in the latter, beating (fellow Hall of Famer-to-be) Adrian Quist on grass in Boston from match point down, 6-8, 3-6, 18-16, 6-3, 7-5.

A hockey injury gravely affected his eyesight, and he wore prescription dark glasses on court for the remainder of a long tennis career that included 17 Wimbledons, where his deft touch and agreeable nature made him a great favorite.

Drobny was born Oct. 12, 1921, in Prague and resided there until 1949, son of the Prague Lawn Tennis Club groundskeeper. "It was fortunate for me," he says, "because we lived at the club and I grew up in the game, ballboying, watching good players, starting out myself at age five." He won the Czechoslovak title 10 straight times before defecting, and solidified his 1946 Wimbledon reputation by reaching the final of the first postwar French (played after Wimbledon that year), losing to Marcel Bernard in five sets.

Paris was a happy hunting ground for portly Drob, a clever court manager and user of a full arsenal of varied speeds, spins, angles, lobs and drop shots. Good stuff on continental clay, but his fast and sliced serve and penetrating volleys made him a menace on fast courts as well. Five times he graced the French final, losing again in 1948 to Frank Parker and in 1950 to Budge Patty before crashing the winner's circle resoundingly. He beat Eric Sturgess, 6-3, 6-3, 6-3, in 1951 and, in 1952, disarmed the world No. 1, Frank Sedgman, 6-2, 6-0, 3-6, 6-4. Rome, too, was his territory as he won the Italian over Bill Talbert in 1950, Gianni Cucelli in 1951 and Lew Hoad in 1953, losing the 1952 final to Sedgman.

His fortune in the U.S. wasn't as good, though it took the champs to beat him, Kramer in 1947 and Pancho Gonzalez in 1948, both semis, Art Larsen in the 1950 third round.

In 1949, with a stunning three-set win over John Bromwich, he attained the Wimbledon final. But that was the year of Ted Schroeder's five-set acrobatics, and he got by Drob, too, 6-4 in the fifth. He was getting closer, but Sedgman got even for Paris in the four-set final of 1952. His most renowned match was a third-rounder that grew to epic proportions in 1953. For 4 hours, 20 minutes, until nightfall, he and Patty waged an engrossing war during which Drob circumvented six match points to win in 93 games, 8-6, 16-18, 3-6, 8-6, 12-10, the longest of Wimbledon singles before the 112-game, 5-hours-and-

Jaroslav Drobny: Citizen of the world. (UPI)

12-minutes saga of Pancho Gonzalez and Charlie Pasarell in 1969.

Though Drob, 32, was written off by 1954, 11 was his lucky number. Seeded 11th, on his 11th try, he came through, escaping Patty again, 6-2, 6-4, 4-6, 9-7, in a semi, and outmaneuvering a 19-year-old named Ken Rosewall for the title he most wanted, 13-11, 4-6, 6-2, 9-7, in 2 hours, 37 minutes, the longest final at that time. Drob was the Big W's remotest-chance success, although non-seeds Boris Becker (1995) and Richard Krajicek (1996), 11th-seeded Pat Cash (1987) and 12th-seeded Andre Agassi (1992) were to join his long-shot club. He was dethroned by the next champ, Tony Trabert, in the 1955 quarters, 8-6, 6-1, 6-4. Traveling on Egyptian papers then, he became a British citizen in 1959, and lives in London with his wife, the former Rita Anderson, one-time English tournament player. Drobny was tapped for the Hall of Fame in 1983.

MAJOR TITLES (5)—*French singles, 1951, 1952; Wimbledon singles 1954; French doubles, 1948, French mixed, 1948.* DAVIS CUP—*1946, 1947, 1948, 1949; record: 24-4 in singles, 13-2 in doubles.* SINGLES RECORD IN THE MAJORS: *Australian (0-1), French (47-13), Wimbledon (50-16), U.S. (15-5).*

MARGARET OSBORNE DUPONT
United States (1918—)

One of the most cerebral players, Margaret Evelyn Osborne duPont was a collector of major championships topped only by Margaret Court (62), Martina Navratilova (56) and Billie Jean King (39). In two decades duPont accumulated 37 championships in singles, doubles and mixed, although never entering the Australian.

Peerless at doubles, she was the canny 5-foot-5½, 145-pound, right-court player, superbly complementing Louise Brough in the most successful team prior to Navratilova and Pam Shriver. Together they won a record 20 major titles: 12 U.S., 5 Wimbledon, 3 French, a mark tied by Navratilova and Shriver in 1989. She won the U.S. doubles first with Sarah Palfrey Fabyan (later Cooke) in 1941, and the next time with Brough in a record streak that ran from 1942 through 1950. Their record match-win streak of 41 ended in the 1951 final, a 6-2, 7-9, 9-7 defeat by Shirley Fry and Doris Hart. As a team in the U.S. Championships, Brough and duPont won 12 of the 14 times they entered and 58 of 60 matches. DuPont, a right-hander, was the playmaker, utilizing a devilish forehand chop and a variety of other spins that kept the ball low. She lobbed and volleyed excellently, and set up her volley with an effective serve.

Although 31 of her major titles were doubles and mixed doubles, she was just as tough in singles, winning the U.S. thrice in five visits to the final, Wimbledon one-for-three and the French two-for-two. Her rivalry with Brough was as close as their friendship and partnership. They split two of the more spectacular finals at the two top championships. Brough won the 1949 Wimbledon final, 10-8, 1-6, 10-8, and duPont the 1948 Forest Hills, ducking a match point, 4-6, 6-

Margaret Osborne duPont: Wise playmaker. (UPI)

4, 15-13—48 games, the longest female final played there.

She won Forest Hills also in 1949 and 1950, Wimbledon in 1947 and the French in 1946 over Pauline Betz, 1-6, 8-6, 7-5, despite two match points, and in 1949. In the U.S. Mixed Doubles Championship she set a record by winning nine times: 1943 through 1946 with Bill Talbert; 1950 with Ken McGregor; 1956 with Ken Rosewall; and 1958 through 1960 with Neale Fraser. In the 1948 semifinal she and Talbert won the longest mixed doubles played until 1991, 71 games, over Gussy Moran and Bob Falkenburg, 27-25, 5-7, 6-1. Forty-three years later, Brenda Schultz and Michael Schapers exceeded that in a 77-game Wimbledon win over Andrea Temesvari and Tom Nijssen.

Born March 4, 1918, in Joseph, Ore., Margaret grew up in San Francisco. She made her ini-tial appearance in the U.S. Top Ten in 1938 at No. 7 and set a longevity record for U.S. females, ranking No. 5 two decades later at the age of 40 in 1958. Over the 20 years, she was ranked in the Top Ten 14 times, No. 1 1948–50. Between 1946 and 1957 she was in the World Top Ten nine times, No. 1 in 1947, 1948, 1949 and 1950.

She married William duPont in 1947 and later interrupted her career to give birth to a son. She was one of the few women to win a major title after childbirth.

Hers was one of the finest Wightman Cup records. In nine years of the British-U.S. series, she was unbeaten in 10 singles and nine doubles, and did not play on a losing side between 1946 and 1962. She also captained the U.S. team nine times, presiding over eight victories.

In 1967 she was inducted into the Hall of Fame.

MAJOR TITLES (37)—*French singles, 1946, 1949; Wimbledon singles, 1947; U.S. singles, 1948, 1949, 1950; French doubles, 1946, 1947, 1949; Wimbledon doubles, 1946, 1948, 1949, 1950, 1954; U.S. doubles, 1941, 1942, 1943, 1944, 1945, 1946, 1947, 1948, 1949, 1950, 1955, 1956, 1957; Wimbledon mixed, 1962; U.S. mixed, 1943, 1944, 1945, 1946, 1950, 1956, 1958, 1959, 1960.* **OTHER U.S. TITLES** (2)—*Hard Court doubles, 1948, with Louise Brough, Hard Court mixed, 1948 with Tom Brown.* **WIGHTMAN CUP**—*1946, 1947, 1948, 1949, 1950, 1954, 1955, 1957, 1961, 1962; record: 10-0 in singles, 9-0 in doubles.* **SINGLES RECORD IN THE MAJORS:** *French (5-0), Wimbledon (34-8), U.S. (54-14).*

STEFAN EDBERG

Sweden (1966—)

A stylistic misfit among the Swedish legion that rose in Bjorn Borg's sneakersteps and image, Stefan Edberg has ever been an extraordinarily graceful attacker. A serve-and-volleyer, he has done superbly with only one hand propelling his backhand.

Clay, on which he was reared, hasn't been his favorite surface, although he nearly beat Michael Chang in a five-set French final in 1989.

A splendid junior career led to great expectations, which he has fulfilled with six major singles—two each, Australian (1985 and 1987), Wimbledon (1988 and 1990), U.S. (1991 and 1992). In 1983 he became the lone achiever of a junior Grand Slam, winning the Australian, French, Wimbledon and U.S. 18-and-under singles.

Making his Davis Cup bow in 1984, at 18, he was the youngest to play for a Cup winner (until Chang, a slightly younger 18 in 1990). Edberg performed a consequential one-day role in Sweden's startling upending of the U.S. in the final at Goteborg. He and Anders Jarryd clinched the 4-1 victory by stunning Peter Fleming and John McEnroe, unbeaten in 14 previous Cup starts, 7-5, 5-7, 6-2, 7-5.

In successfully defending the Cup the following year in Munich, a 3-2 victory over Germany, Edberg won it at the wire, a thrilling, rebounding fifth-match decision over Michael Westphal, 3-6, 7-5, 6-4, 6-3. Though he didn't play in the final, he had an earlier hand in winning the 1987 Cup.

A brilliant end-of-the-line backhand seized victory from Aleksandr Volkov at match point down in the fifth set as the 1994 Cup final began in Moscow. Turning that upside down for a 6-4, 6-2, 6-7 (2-7), 0-6, 8-6 win, Stefan set the tone in a 4-1 triumph, Sweden's fifth Cup. Having slipped below the standard he set for himself, he announced that the 1996 season would be his valedictory. Stefan had a good year, beating Chang at the French, playing all four to stretch his participation record to 54 straight appearances in majors at the U.S. Open, where he knocked off Wimbledon champ Richard Krajicek, 6-3, 6-3, 6-3, and made the quarters (a 25th time at that stage). Fittingly his career concluded in Sweden with one more Davis Cup finale.

Edberg, a slim 6-foot-2 blond right hander, was born in the seaside town of Vastervik, Sweden, Jan. 19, 1966, and was reared there. He lives in London with his Swedish wife, Annette. He has a hammering serve, as well as a difficult

kicker and a raking backhand, and he is one of the finest of all volleyers. His groundstrokes improved continuously throughout his career. Outwardly unemotional, he dispelled doubts about his competitiveness by winning Wimbledon in 1988. He charged from two sets down to beat Miloslav Mecir in the semis, 4-6, 2-6, 6-4, 6-3, 6-4, and a set down to overcome favored Boris Becker, 4-6, 7-6 (7-2), 6-4, 6-2, for the title.

His rivalry with Becker was a highlight of the '80s and '90s. At the close of 1996, Becker was in the lead, 20-10.

Beating the 1983–84 champ, countryman Mats Wilander, in the final, 6-4, 6-4, 6-3, Stefan took the Australian in 1985, his first major. He repeated two years later, the last man to win it on grass, 6-3 in the fifth set over Patrick Cash.

Flushing Meadow was almost the mystery to him that it had been for Borg (no titles in 10 tries). But on his ninth, Edberg came through for the U.S. title in one of the most devastating final-round performances, 6-2, 6-4, 6-0, over Jim Courier, holding serve throughout. Edberg, a first-round loser the year before (to Aleksandr Volkov) was the second in the tournament's history to spring from such ignominy to the title. Mal Anderson did so in 1957. Edberg refused to relinquish the title, beating Pete Sampras, 4-6, 6-4, 7-6 (7-5), 6-2 in the 1992 final. In the semis he overcame Chang, 6-7 (3-7), 7-5, 7-6 (7-3), 5-7, 6-4, the longest-lasting major match—5 hours, 26 minutes. Edberg's last major final (his 10th) was the Australian of 1993, when he lost to Courier, 6-2, 6-1, 2-6, 7-5. During 14 professional seasons he was in the World Top Ten 10 times, No. 1 in 1990 and 1991.

Edberg represented Sweden in the 1988 and 1992 Olympics, winning a bronze in singles in the former.

Fittingly, he closed his career in Sweden, the 1996 Davis Cup final against France, to the cheering of countrymen at Malmo. However, he went out in defeat, slowed by ankle injury while losing to Cedric Pioline, and couldn't play the

Stefan Edberg: Super server-and-volleyer. (Russ Adams)

third day of the 3-2 loss. Stefan's career achievements: won 41 singles, 18 doubles pro titles and $20,630,941 in prize money through 1996. He had an 806-270 (.749) singles mark.

MAJOR TITLES *(8)—Australian singles, 1985, 1987; Wimbledon singles, 1988, 1990; U.S. singles, 1991, 1992, Australian doubles, 1987; U.S. doubles, 1987.* DAVIS CUP— *1984, 1985, 1986, 1987, 1988, 1989, 1990, 1991, 1992, 1993, 1994, 1995, 1996; record: 34-14 in singles, 12-8 in doubles.* SINGLES RECORD IN THE MAJORS: *Australian (56-11), French (30-13), Wimbledon (49-12), U.S. (39-11).*

ROY EMERSON

Australia (1936—)

In the grand days for Australia of domination of the tennis world, nobody played as large a role as the country boy out of Black Butt in Queensland, Roy Stanley Emerson.

Emerson, a slim, quick, athletic farm kid who strengthened his wrists for tennis by milking innumerable cows on his father's property, played on eight winning Davis Cup teams between 1959 and 1967, a record. He won 28 of the major singles and doubles championships—a record for men—including two Wimbledon singles in 1964 and 1965 and two U.S. singles at Forest Hills in 1961 and 1964. His accomplishments as a right-court doubles player who could make anybody look good amounted to 16 Big Four titles with five different partners, the last in 1971 at Wimbledon with his old Queensland pal, Rod Laver. His best-known alliance was with Aussie left-hander Neale Fraser, with whom he won Wimbledon in 1959 and 1961, the U.S. title in 1959 and 1960 and the doubles of the Davis Cup triumphs of 1959, 1960 and 1961.

Known as "Emmo" to his wide circle of friends on the circuit, he was a rollicking, gregarious six-foot right-hander who could lead the partying and singing without jeopardizing his high standards of play. Fitness was his hallmark. He trained hard and was always ready for strenuous matches and tournaments. Although primarily a serve-and-volleyer, he could adapt to the rigors of slow courts, winning the French singles in 1963 and 1967, and leading the Davis Cup victory over the U.S. on clay in Cleveland in 1964. That year he was unbeaten in eight Davis Cup singles as the Aussies regained the Cup. Emmo had a singles winning streak of 55 matches during the summer and autumn while establishing himself as No. 1 in the amateur game by winning 17 tournaments and 109 of 115 matches. The only prize to elude him in that majestic year of triumphs on three of the majors was a Grand Slam. Nicola Pietrangeli made that an impossibility on the second leg, winning their quarter-final at the French, 6-1, 6-3, 6-3.

Fate may have intervened to cost him a third straight Wimbledon in 1966 when he was heavily favored. Winning a fourth-rounder against Owen Davidson, he skidded chasing a short ball, crashed into the umpire's stand, damaging a shoulder, and was unable to do much but finish the match. Between 1961 and 1967, he won a male record six Australian singles titles, the last five in a row.

An outstanding team player who could fire up his teammates, Emerson also took part in two Australian victories in the World Cup, a since disbanded annual competition against the U.S.

He exemplified the Aussie code of sportsmanship and competitiveness, stating it as, "You should never complain about an injury. We believe that if you play, then you aren't injured, and that's that."

Emerson was born Nov. 3, 1936, in Black Butt, a crossroads, and his family moved to Brisbane, where he could get better competition and coaching, when his tennis talent became evident.

After resisting several offers, he turned pro in 1968 just before open tennis began, and was still competing in 1978 as player-coach of the Boston Lobsters in World Team Tennis, directing them to the semifinals of the league playoffs. Of all Australia's Davis Cup luminaries under captain Harry Hopman, Emerson made the best record. While helping win the eight Cups, he won 22 of 24 singles and 13 of 15 doubles. When the Cup was on the line, the score tied 2-2 with one match to be played in 1964, he beat American Chuck McKinley, 3-6, 6-2, 6-4, 6-4, to ice the 3-2 decision.

Beginning in 1959, he was ranked in the World Top Ten nine straight times, No. 1 in 1964 and 1965.

Emerson was elevated to the Hall of Fame in 1982 after a career that bridged the amateur and open eras and was credited with three pro titles in singles and 30 in doubles, and $400,000 in prize money. His son, Antony, was All-American in tennis at the University of Southern California and played the pro tour briefly. They won the U.S. Hard Court Father-and-Son title in 1978.

Emmo and Laver were often in each other's way on the grand occasions. He messed up whatever designs Rod had on a Grand Slam in 1961

Roy Emerson: Fittest of the fit. (UPI)

by winning their final round meetings at the Australian and U.S. When Laver did go all the way in 1962, he had to battle past Emmo in the Australian, French (five sets) finals, and the Slam gate-closing U.S., 6-2, 6-4, 5-7, 6-4. Seven years later, Laver's second Slam, Emmo was a thorn again, in a second rounder at the Australian, and a prickly quarter-final of the U.S., 4-6, 8-6, 13-11, 6-4. Laver said, "My old friend and rival has plagued me every step of the way because he never considers losing."

MAJOR TITLES (28)—Australian singles, 1961, 1963, 1964, 1965, 1966, 1967; French singles, 1963, 1967; Wimbledon singles, 1964, 1965; U.S. singles, 1961, 1964; Australian doubles, 1962, 1966, 1969; French doubles, 1960, 1961, 1962, 1963, 1964, 1965; Wimbledon doubles, 1959, 1961, 1971; U.S. doubles, 1959, 1960, 1965, 1966. DAVIS CUP— 1959, 1960, 1961, 1962, 1963, 1964, 1965, 1966, 1967; record: 21-2 in singles, 13-2 in doubles. SINGLES RECORD IN THE MAJORS: Australian (47-8), French (43-10), Wimbledon (60-14), U.S. (59-14).

CHRIS EVERT
United States (1954—)

In 1970, at a small, insignificant tournament in North Carolina, 15-year-old Christine Marie Evert gave notice to the world that a dynamo was on the way up. Chrissie defeated Margaret Court, 7-6, 7-6, who had recently completed her singles Grand Slam and was the No. 1 player of the world.

A year later in the U.S. Open at Forest Hills, Evert reconfirmed by marching resolutely to the semifinals—at 16 years, 8 months, 20 days, the youngest at that time to reach that stage. Before losing to Billie Jean King, 6-3, 6-2, the eventual champion, schoolgirl Evert bowled over a succession of seasoned pros, mostly in come-from-behind thrillers that raised tears on the defeated older players and cheers in the Forest Hills stadium that Chrissie filled day after day. They went down in a row: Edna Buding, 6-1, 6-0; Mary Ann Eisel, 4-6, 7-6 (5-1), 6-1; fifth-seeded Françoise Durr, 2-6, 6-2, 6-3; Lesley Hunt, 4-6, 6-2, 6-3. Against Eisel, the No. 4 American, Evert wowed the first national TV audience to behold her by stonewalling when Eisel served for the match at 6-5, 40-0. Undaunted, the kid made six match points melt with bold shotmaking.

Although essentially a slow-court baseline specialist, raised on clay in Fort Lauderdale, Fla., where she was born Dec. 21, 1954, the right-handed Evert showed that booming groundstrokes could succeed on the fast Forest Hills, Wimbledon and Australian grass. She was the Little Ice Maiden, a pony-tailed kid, deadpan, with metronomic strokes that seldom missed. Her two-handed backhand, a powerful drive, stimulated a generation of newcomers to copy her, even though her father, teaching pro Jimmy Evert, advised against it. "I didn't teach the two-hander to her," said her father, who had won the Canadian singles in 1947. "She started that way because she was too small and weak to swing the backhand with one hand. I hoped she'd change—but how can I argue with this success?"

It was such a success that by the time she completed a 20-year career in 1989 she had won $8,896,195 in prize money and a record 157 pro singles titles on a 1,309-146 won-lost record. That's an .8996 winning average, highest in pro history.

Martina Navratilova would overtake her in singles titles in 1992. Evert also was runner-up for 72 singles titles, which meant she made it to 76 percent of the finals of 303 tournaments entered.

An amateur until 1973, she was the first to reach $1 million in career prize money, in 1976.

Her major titles numbered 21—18 of them of 34 finals in singles—six behind Margaret Court, three behind Steffi Graf, one behind Helen Wills Moody, tied with Navratilova. Phenomenally, Chris won at least one major singles for 13 consecutive years, a record. She started in 1974 and ended in 1986 at the French where she was the all-time champ with seven championships on a 72-6 match record.

By winning the U.S. title a fourth consecutive time in 1978 she was the first to do so since Helen Jacobs' run of 1932–35. Between 1973 and 1979 she won 125 consecutive matches on clay, including 24 tournaments. The streak came to an end in the semifinals of the Italian Open in Rome when she lost, 6-4, 2-6, 7-6 (7-4), to Tracy Austin.

Her introduction to Goolagong was the 1972 Wimbledon semifinal, an exciting three-set struggle won by Goolagong, 4-6, 6-3, 6-4, the defending champion. That was the start of one of the two most compelling female rivalries of the open era, one in which Evert held a 21-12 edge. The other, perhaps the most renowned in the game's history, was Chris' friendly feud with Martina Navratilova. From 1973 through 1988 it stretched, 80 matches. Evert won the first meeting in Akron, Ohio, 7-6 (5-4), 6-3, and took a big early lead, but Navratilova overtook her, and came out ahead, 43-37, winning nine of 13 of their major final engagements.

During the open era, the Virginia Slims circuit and its championship became prominent in women's tennis. Evert won the first of her four

Chris Evert: The peerless baseliner. (Mitchell Reibel)

Slims championships in 1972 at 17. In choosing to preserve her amateur status until her 18th birthday that year, she disdained more than $50,000 in prize money, including the $25,000 Slims award for beating Kerry Reid, 7-5, 6-4.

Once she entered tennis for a living, she was a thorough exemplary professional in her relations with colleagues, press and public, and perennially a hard but sporting competitor. Fairly soon she lost her status as the darling little girl. Her style was based on flawless barrages from the backcourt, and her constant winning seemed monotonous to many. Nevertheless she was a smart player, able to maneuver a foe cleverly, scoring decisively with a well-disguised drop shot. She was also a better volleyer than given credit for, after overcoming an early distaste for the net. "I realize that a lot of fans think my game is boring, and they want to see me lose, or at least for somebody to give me a good fight all the time. But this is the game I played to win," she said. "Losing hurts me. I was always determined to be the best."

A lithe 5-foot-6, 125 pounds, she was No. 1 in the world 1975, 1976, 1977, 1980 and 1981, and in the World Top Ten 17 years, a paragon of consistency in that she entered 57 of the major tourneys, won 18, and was at least a semifinalist 53 times. Her worst efforts were two quarterfinal (U.S.) and two third-round losses (French and Wimbledon).

Ranking No. 1 in the U.S. 1974, 1975, 1976, 1977, 1978 and 1981, she was the first since Alice Marble (1936–40) to be on top five straight years. Her 19 years in the U.S. Top Ten were one better than Billie Jean King, although Navratilova subsequently held onto No. 1 for 11 straight years, through 1992.

As one of five tennis-playing Evert children, she was clearly the star, but her sister, Jeanne, three years younger, was also a pro.

In 1974 Jeanne ranked No. 9 in the U.S. and they were the first sisters to be ranked in the Top Ten since Florence (No. 3) and Ethel Sutton (No. 2) in 1913. Chris and Jeanne were teammates on the victorious U.S. Wightman Cup team of 1973, the only sisters to play together in the series against Britain.

Her final-round surges past Goolagong for a first U.S. Open crown in 1975 (5-7, 6-4, 6-2) and to the Wimbledon title of 1976 (6-3, 4-6, 8-6) are well remembered. But her most satisfying victories were probably the last majors, the French final upsets of Navratilova in 1985, 6-3, 6-7 (4-7), 7-5, and—at age 33—in 1986, 2-6, 6-3, 6-3.

Her farewell to Flushing Meadow was a quarterfinal defeat by Zina Garrison, leaving her with a record 101 match wins in that event. She closed her career by winning all five singles matches as the U.S. won the Federation Cup in 1989. It was her ninth year and eighth Cup-winning team. She was undefeated in Wightman Cup singles (26-0), helping the U.S. win 11 Cups in the 13 years she played.

Evert was the first player to win more than 1,000 singles matches as well as 150 tournaments, the only one other than Court and King to win more than 100 matches in a season, which she did during a mammoth 1974 when she won 16 of 24 tournaments on a 103-7 record. Her 55-match winning streak in 1974 (ended at the U.S. Open by Goolagong) was an open-era record until eclipsed by Navratilova's 74 in 1984.

Three seasons of World Team Tennis included 1976 and 1977 with Phoenix and 1978 with champion Los Angeles.

She played in the 1988 Olympics, but did not win a medal. Her eight-year marriage to English player John Lloyd ended in divorce. She then married ex-Olympic skier Andy Mill, with whom she has three sons.

MAJOR TITLES *(21)—Australian singles, 1982, 1984; French singles, 1974, 1975, 1979, 1980, 1983, 1985, 1986; Wimbledon singles, 1974, 1976, 1981; U.S. singles, 1975, 1976, 1977, 1978, 1980, 1982; French doubles, 1974, 1975; Wimbledon doubles, 1976.* OTHER U.S. TITLES *(6)—Clay Court singles, 1972, 1973, 1974, 1975, 1979, 1980.* FEDERATION CUP—*1977, 1978, 1979, 1980, 1981, 1982, 1986, 1987, 1989; record: 40-2 in singles, 17-2 in doubles.* WIGHTMAN CUP *(As player)—1971, 1972, 1973, 1975, 1976, 1977, 1978, 1979, 1980, 1981, 1982, 1984, 1985; record: 26-0 in singles, 8-4 in doubles; (As captain)—1980, 1981, 1982, 1985, 1986; record: 5-0, 5 Cups.* SINGLES RECORD IN THE MAJORS: *Australian (30-4), French (72-6), Wimbledon (96-15), U.S. (101-12).*

SHIRLEY FRY
United States (1927—)

One of the elite dozen men and women to win each of the major championships in singles, Shirley June Fry Irvin is also one of only five to win them all in doubles as well. The French was the first to fall to her, in 1951, the Australian the last, in 1957, after which she retired to become Mrs. Karl Irvin and live in Hartford, Conn.

She won Wimbledon and—on the 16th and last try—the U.S. in 1956, beating, respectively, Shirley Bloomer, 6-4, 6-4, and Althea Gibson. A

Shirley Fry: Ultimate in doubles. (UPI)

right-hander, born on June 30, 1927, and raised in Akron, Ohio, she was in 1941 the youngest ever to play in the U.S. Championships until slightly younger fourteen-year-olds Kathy Horvath (1979) and Mary Joe Fernandez (1985).

As a 15-year-old, she became, unseeded, the Championships' youngest quarterfinalist. She lost the 1951 final to Maureen Connolly, 6-3, 1-6, 6-4, but came through five years later, outsteadying Gibson, 6-3, 6-4. She had a solid groundstroking game, but showed her volleying skills in doubles alongside Doris Hart. They were the only team to win four straight French (1950–53). They won three straight Wimbledons (1951–53) and four straight U.S. (1951–54).

In their hard-fought 1953 final-round victory, 6-2, 7-9, 9-7, despite two match points, over Louise Brough and Margaret Osborne duPont, they ended the Brough-duPont record streaks of nine straight titles (1942–50) and 41 matches. Their own streak, until losing the 1955 final to Brough-duPont, was 20 matches.

Shirley, 5-foot-5, 125 pounds, ranked in the U.S. Top Ten 13 straight years (1944–56), No. 1 in 1956, and in the World Top Ten nine times between 1946 and 1956, No. 1 the last year. She played Wightman Cup for the U.S. six times, never on a loser, winning 10 of her 12 matches. She entered the Hall of Fame in 1970.

MAJOR TITLES *(17)—Australian singles, 1957; French singles, 1951; Wimbledon singles, 1956; U.S. singles, 1956; Australian doubles, 1957; French doubles, 1950, 1951, 1952, 1953; U.S. doubles, 1951, 1952, 1953, 1954; Wimbledon doubles, 1951, 1952, 1953; Wimbledon mixed, 1957.* OTHER U.S. TITLES *(4)—Clay Court singles, 1956; Clay Court doubles, 1946, with Mary Arnold Prentiss; 1950, with Doris Hart; 1956, with Dorothy Head Knode.* WIGHTMAN CUP—*1949, 1951, 1952, 1953, 1955, 1956; record: 4-2 in singles, 6-0 in doubles.* SINGLES RECORD IN THE MAJORS: *Australian (5-0), French (23-4), Wimbledon (34-7), U.S. (38-14).*

ALTHEA GIBSON
United States (1927–)

No player overcame more obstacles to become a champion than Althea Gibson, the first black to win at Wimbledon and Forest Hills.

Her entry in the U.S. Championships of 1950 at Forest Hills was historic: the first appearance of an American black in that event. It took seven more years for Gibson to work her way to the championship there, in 1957. Tennis was pretty much a segregated sport in the U.S. until the American Tennis Association, the governing body for black tournaments, prevailed on the U.S. Tennis Association to permit the ATA female champion, Gibson, to enter Forest Hills. Two years earlier, in 1948, Dr. Reginald Weir, a New York physician, was the first black permitted in a USTA championship, playing in the U.S. Indoor event.

Althea's first appearance at Forest Hills was not only a notable occasion, it was nearly a moment of staggering triumph. Making her historic debut in a 6-2, 6-2 win over Barbara Knapp, she encountered in the second round third-seeded Louise Brough, the reigning Wimbledon champion, and came within one game of winning. Recovering from nerves, Althea led, 1-6, 6-3, 7-6, when providence intervened: a thunderstorm struck Forest Hills, curtailing the match until the following day, when Brough reaffirmed her eminence by winning three straight games.

During the violent storm, a bolt of lightning had toppled one of the concrete guardian eagles from the upper reaches of the stadium. "It may have been an omen that times were changing," Althea recalled.

Born Aug. 25, 1927, in Silver, S.C., Gibson, a right-hander, grew up in Harlem. Her family was poor, but she was fortunate in coming to the attention of Dr. Walter Johnson, a Lynchburg, Va., physician who was active in the black tennis community. He became her patron, as he would later be for Arthur Ashe, the black champion at Forest Hills (1968) and Wimbledon (1975). Through Dr. Johnson, Gibson received better instruction and competition, and contacts were set up with the USTA to inject her into the recognized tennis scene.

Tall (5-foot-11), strong, and extremely athletic, she would have come to prominence earlier but for segregation. She was 23 when she first played at Forest Hills, 30 when she won her first of two successive U.S. Championships, in 1957. During the two years she won Wimbledon, 1957 and 1958, she was ranked No. 1 in the U.S. and the world, but she was never completely at ease in amateur tennis for she realized that, despite her success, she was still unwelcome at some clubs where important tournaments were played. She was ranked No. 9 in 1952, her first of six inclusions in the U.S. Top Ten.

A mark of general acceptance, however, was her 1957 selection to represent the U.S. on the Wightman Cup team against Britain. She played two years, winning three of four singles, and two of two doubles.

Gibson was a big hitter with an awesome serve. She liked to attack, but developed consis-

Althea Gibson: Breakthrough for a big hitter. (UPI)

head-to-head matches in 1960 against Karol Fageros, who had been ranked No. 8 in the U.S. Their tour was played in conjunction with the Harlem Globetrotters, the matches staged on basketball courts prior to Trotter games. Gibson won 114 of 118 matches. She said she earned over $100,000 in one year as her share of the gate, but there was no professional game in tennis for women then, and she turned to the pro golf tour for a few years. She showed an aptitude for that game, but was too late in starting.

Althea tried to play a few pro tennis events after open tennis began in 1968, but by then she was too old. She was married briefly to W. A. Darben, and worked as a tennis teaching pro after ceasing competition. She was inducted into the Hall of Fame in 1971.

MAJOR TITLES *(11)—French singles, 1956; Wimbledon singles, 1957, 1958; U.S. singles, 1957, 1958; Australian doubles, 1957; French doubles, 1956; Wimbledon doubles, 1956, 1957, 1958; U.S. mixed, 1957.* OTHER U.S. TITLES *(2)— Clay court singles, 1957; Clay Court doubles, 1957, with Hard.* WIGHTMAN CUP—*1957, 1958; record: 3-1 in singles, 2-0 in doubles.* SINGLES RECORD IN THE MAJORS: *Australian (4-1), French (6-0), Wimbledon (16-1), U.S. (27-7).*

tency at the baseline eventually, and won the French—the first major for a black (over Angela Mortimer, 6-0, 12-10)—and Italian Singles Championships on slow clay in 1956.

In all, Gibson won 11 major titles in singles and doubles. After six years of trying at Forest Hills, she seemed ready to win in 1956, when she reached the final. But she appeared overanxious and lost to the steadier Shirley Fry, 6-3, 6-4. A year later Gibson was solidly in control, beating Darlene Hard, 6-3, 6-2, to take Wimbledon and following up with a 6-3, 6-2 triumph over Louise Brough in the Forest Hills final to at last rule her own country.

It was in doubles that Gibson accomplished the first Wimbledon championship by a black, in 1956 alongside Englishwoman Angela Buxton.

After winning Forest Hills for a second time in 1958, Althea turned pro. She played a series of

PANCHO GONZALEZ
United States (1928–95)

Very much his own man, a loner and an acerbic competitor, Ricardo Alonso "Pancho" Gonzalez was probably as good as anyone who ever played the game, if not better. Most of his great tennis was played beyond wide public attention, on the nearly secret pro tour amid a small band of gypsies of whom he was the ticket-selling mainstay.

His rages against opponents, officials, photographers, newsmen and even spectators were frequently spectacular—but they only served to intensify his own play, and didn't disturb his concentration, as fits of temper do most others. Pancho got mad and played better. "We hoped he wouldn't get upset; it just made him tougher," said Rod Laver. "Later when he got older, he would get into arguments to stall for time and rest, and we had to be careful that it didn't put us off our games."

Gonzalez, a right-hander, born May 9, 1928, in Los Angeles, was always out of the tennis mainstream, a fact that seemed to goad him to play harder. Because he came from a Chicano family, he was never acceptable in the supposedly proper upper circles of his city's tennis establishment. And because he was a truant he wasn't permitted to play in Southern California junior tournaments. Once he got out of the Navy in 1946 there was no preventing him from mixing in the game, and beating everyone. He had a marvelously pure and effortless service action that delivered thunderbolts, and he grew up as an attacker on fast West Coast concrete.

Although not regarded as anything more than promising on his second trip East in 1948, he was at age 20 ready to win the big one, the U.S. Championship at Forest Hills. Ranked 17th nationally at the time, and seeded 8th, he served and volleyed his way to the final, where he beat South African Eric Sturgess with ease, 6-2, 6-3, 14-12. The following year Gonzalez met the favorite, a Southern California antagonist, top-seeded Ted Schroeder. It was one of the gripping finals. Schroeder won the first two sets as expected, but they were demanding and exhausting, 18-16, 6-2, and after that Gonzalez rolled up the next three, 6-1, 6-2, 6-4, for the title. In 1949 Pancho also helped the U.S. hold the Davis Cup against Australia, then went for the money, turning pro to tour against the monarch, Jack Kramer. Gonzalez was too green for Kramer, losing, 96-27, and he faded from view for several agonizing years.

When Kramer retired, Gonzalez won a tour over Don Budge, Pancho Segura and Frank Sedgman in 1954 to determine Jack's successor, and stood himself as Emperor Pancho, proud and imperious, for a long while, through the challenges of Tony Trabert, Ken Rosewall, Lew Hoad, Ashley Cooper, Mal Anderson, Alex Olmedo and Segura. For a decade Gonzalez and pro tennis were synonymous. A promoter couldn't hope to rally

Pancho Gonzalez: Thunderbolt server. (UPI)

crowds unless Pancho was on the bill. The other names meant little. During his reign Pancho won the U.S. Pro singles a record eight times.

By the time Rosewall and Laver were reaching their zeniths during the mid- and late-1960s, the aging Gonzalez hung on as a dangerous foe, still capable of defeating all. In 1964, his last serious bid for his ninth U.S. Pro title, he lost the final to Laver in four hard sets. Yet there was still much more glory ahead. In 1968, at 40, he beat second-seeded Tony Roche (Wimbledon finalist) to reach the quarters of the initial U.S. Open. A year later, this grandfather (literally) electrified Wimbledon by overcoming Charlie Pasarell in the tournament's longest match, 112 games, a first-rounder that consumed 5 hours, 12 minutes, a major tourney record that stood until 1992, eclipsed by 14 minutes by Michael Chang and Stefan Edberg at the U.S. Open.

The marathon with Pasarell began one afternoon and concluded on the next after darkness intervened. In winning, 22-24, 1-6, 16-14, 6-3, 11-9, Gonzalez saved seven match points in the fifth set.

Later that year, he beat John Newcombe, Rosewall, Stan Smith and Arthur Ashe, 6-0, 6-2, 6-4, in succession to win $12,500, second-highest prize of the year, and the title at a rich tournament at Las Vegas. Early in 1970, in the opener of a series of $10,000 winner-take-all challenge matches leading to a grand final, he toppled Laver. The Aussie, just off his second Grand Slam year (and the eventual winner of this tournament), was clearly No. 1 in the world, but Pancho warmed a crowd of 14,761 at New York's Madison Square Garden with a 7-5, 3-6, 2-6, 6-3, 6-2 victory.

Three months before his 44th birthday, in 1972, he was the oldest to record a tournament title in the open era, winning Des Moines (Iowa) over 24-year-old Georges Goven, 3-6, 4-6, 6-3, 6-4, 6-2. That year he was No. 9 in the U.S., the oldest to rank so high, and equaled Vic Seixas' Top Ten longevity span of 24 years. Seixas was No. 9 in 1942 and, at 43, No. 9 in 1966. Gonzalez had been No. 1 in 1948. As for the World Top Ten, he is alone in that he was a member in 1948 and 1949 and again in 1968 and 1969, ranking No. 1 in 1949, No. 6 in 1969.

In 1968, though still active, he was named to the Hall of Fame and he was a consistent winner on the Grand Masters tour for the over-45 champs beginning in 1973. Although his high-speed serve, so effortlessly delivered, was a trademark, Gonzalez, a 6-foot-2, 180-pounder, was a splendid athlete and tactician who excelled at defense, too. "My legs, retrieving, lobs and change-of-pace service returns meant as much or more to me than my power," he once said, "but people overlooked that because of the reputation of my serve." He won $911,078 between 1950 and 1972, and crossed the million mark as a Grand Master. He was married six times, the last to a good player, Rita Agassi, sister of another all-timer, Andre Agassi, by whom he had a son.

Not a bad tennis bloodline for the young man, Skylar Gonzalez. Gonzalez died July 3, 1995, of cancer in Las Vegas, where he had been a teaching pro for some time.

MAJOR TITLES (4)—*U.S. singles, 1948, 1949; French doubles, 1949; Wimbledon doubles, 1949.* OTHER U.S. TITLES *(17)—Indoor singles, 1949; Clay Court singles, 1948, 1949; Indoor mixed, 1949, with Gertrude Moran; Pro singles, 1953, 1954, 1955, 1956, 1957, 1958, 1959, 1961; Pro doubles, 1953, with Don Budge; 1954, 1958, with Pancho Segura; 1957, with Ken Rosewall; 1969, with Rod Laver.* DAVIS CUP—*1949; record: 2-0 in singles.* SINGLES RECORD IN THE MAJORS: *Australian (2-1), French (9-2), Wimbledon (10-5), U.S. (23-7).*

EVONNE GOOLAGONG
Australia (1951—)

The most improbable of a long line of champions from Down Under, Evonne Fay Goolagong Cawley is the only native Australian, an Aborigine, to become a tennis internationalist. Born July 31, 1951, in Griffith, New South Wales, she grew up to a lissome 5-foot-6, in near poverty. As one of eight children of an itinerant sheep-shearer, Ken Goolagong, and his wife, Melinda, she spent her formative years in the small country town of Barellan in wheat and sheep territory west of Sydney. Her father, long-armed and limber, knew nothing of tennis. It's unlikely that she would have left Barellan if a kindly resident, Bill Kurtzman, hadn't seen her peering through the fence at the local courts and encouraged her to play.

She was a natural, a free-flowing right-hander blessed with speed, lightning reflexes and a carefree temperament. Tipped off to this by two of his assistants, Vic Edwards, proprietor of a tennis school in Sydney, journeyed upcountry to take a look. He immediately spotted the talent that would eventually result in two Wimbledon, one French and four Australian championships and a 1988 posting to the Hall of Fame.

Edwards, knowing that she couldn't develop in the bush, convinced her parents to allow Evonne to move to Sydney and live in his household, where he could coach her. This she did in

Evonne Goolagong: Lightning on the loose. (UPI)

1967 at age 13, becoming one of the family and an early doubles partner of Edwards' daughter, Patricia.

Her rise was swift. On her second world tour, in 1971, Goolagong, just before turning 20, beat countrywoman Helen Gourlay to win the French. A month later, in her last act as a teenager, seeded third, she stunned defending champion and her girlhood idol, Margaret Court, in the Wimbledon final, 6-4, 6-1.

Called Sunshine Supergirl in London, she captivated crowds wherever she played with her graceful movement and gracious manner. Three more times she got to the final, losing to Billie Jean King in 1972 and 1975 and Chris Evert in 1976, and it appeared that her Wimbledon title days were over. However, a unique success was to be hers: victory again at the end of a nine-year gap, in 1980—her last tournament triumph. Seeded fourth, Evonne made a spirited run through 1977 runner-up Betty Stove, ninth-seeded Hana Mandlikova, Wendy Turnbull (sixth), Tracy Austin (second), 6-3, 0-6, 6-4, and Evert (third), 6-1, 7-6 (7-1), the only Wimbledon singles championship to end in a tie-breaker.

By then she had married Englishman Roger Cawley and had the first of their two children. Thus she was the first mother to win since Dorothea Douglass Chambers 66 years before. At

Wimbledon, Evonne was 49-9 in singles, 21-7 in doubles, 19-8 in mixed.

Her exciting rivalry with Evert—the volleyer against the baseliner—began at the top, the 1972 Wimbledon semis, which Evonne pulled out with a third-set rally, 4-6, 6-3, 6-4. Overall Evert led 21-12, but in the majors her edge was only 5-4, Chris winning three of their five finals. Goolagong took their initial championship encounter, the 1974 Australian, 7-6 (7-5), 4-6, 6-0. She beat Martina Navratilova to repeat in the Australian in 1975.

For a decade, Evonne, refreshing as a zephyr, illuminated the World Top Ten, retiring after the 1983 season. She won the season-climaxing Virginia Slims championship in 1974 and 1976, both over Evert, and had career totals of 43 singles and nine doubles titles, and $1,399,431 in prize money.

Although she won the U.S. Indoor in 1973 over Virginia Wade, 6-4, 6-4, she couldn't quite make it at the Open, the only woman to lose the final four successive years, 1973 through 1976, at Forest Hills, falling to Court, King, then twice to Evert. Her most winning seasons: 1973 with nine titles, including wins over Evert in the Italian and Cincinnati finals; 1976, eight titles.

A seven-year mainstay of Australia's Federation Cup team, she led the way to Cups in 1971, 1973 and 1974 and finals in 1975 and 1976.

MAJOR TITLES (13)—*Australian singles, 1974, 1975, 1976, 1977; French singles, 1971; Wimbledon singles, 1971, 1980; Australian doubles, 1971, 1974, 1975, 1976; Wimbledon doubles, 1974; French mixed, 1972.* FEDERATION CUP— *1971, 1972, 1973, 1974, 1975, 1976, 1982; record: 21-3 in singles, 11-2 in doubles.* SINGLES RECORD IN THE MAJORS: *Australian (39-9), French (16-3), Wimbledon (49-9), U.S. (26-6).*

STEFFI GRAF
Germany (1969—)

It was a grand moment for 16-year-old Stephanie Maria Graf: her first pro tournament victory victimized an all-timer, Chris Evert, in the final of the 1986 Family Circle Cup at Hilton Head, S.C.

A trim blonde, 5-foot-9, she was precocious and powerfully athletic, out of the small German town of Bruhl, and she would attain heights unimaginable before 1988. That year she registered the sixth Grand Slam (third female) and topped it off with a gold medal at Seoul as tennis returned to the Olympics after a 64-year absence. It was a quintessential quintuple for "Fraulein Forehand," a right-handed proprietor of that feared weapon.

Born June 14, 1969, in Neckarau, Germany, she became one of the fastest of all female players, a nimble retriever who prefers the baseline but volleys ably. She runs and plays speedily, hardly pausing, impatient to win the next point. She and Martina Navratilova are the greatest players produced in Europe since the 1920s heyday of Suzanne Lenglen.

But it's not over, and Steffi has her sights on being the greatest ever anywhere. Despite a variety of injuries and family crises, she continues to pile up major triumphs, passing Martina Navratilova and Chris Evert (18 singles each) and even Helen Wills Moody (19). Winning her fifth French, seventh Wimbledon and fifth U.S. titles in 1996 (matching her 1995 collection), she has 21 and approaches what was presumed to be the unassailable Himalayan peak of Margaret Court's 24 majors. Moreover, she had all these at age 27. Court finished collecting at 31, Moody at 32, Navratilova at 33, Evert at 31. Altogether, Steffi had 101 singles championships at the close of 1996.

Once she'd stunned Evert (the eight-time champ) at Hilton Head, 6-4, 7-5, Steffi began to roll up titles at an incredible pace: 11 in 1987 and 1988, 14 in 1989, 10 in 1990.

Days before her 18th birthday she grabbed her first major, the 1987 French, over Navratilova, 6-4, 4-6, 8-6. But it was in Paris three years later that she stumbled while strongly bidding for Navratilova's open-era record (74) for consecutive match victories. Steffi was stopped at 66 in the final by Monica Seles, 7-6 (8-6), 6-4.

As a pro she has won matches at an .868 clip. Evert was .899, Navratilova .878. By mid-1987 she deposed Navratilova at No. 1, and hung on to the top spot for four years (a record 186 weeks) until displaced in 1991 by Seles. She took over the penthouse again in 1993, traded it on and off with Sanchez Vicario in 1995, shared it with the returned Seles until having it all alone again at the close of 1996.

Steel-willed and industrious, she displays full-speed-ahead-damn-the-slings-and-arrows character in the face of daunting physical injuries and emotional trials. Probably no great champion has played hurt so often. She was kept from the Australian in 1995 by a calf injury, and in 1996 by foot surgery. Might she have had two more Grand Slams otherwise? Back and knee problems are constant, the left knee sidelining her during the 1996 Olympics. When would-be assassin Guenther Parche removed Monica Seles from the picture (and the No. 1 spot) with his knife in 1993, Steffi bore the anguish of his saying he did it to restore her to the top.

Peter Graf, who raised her specifically for tennis, turning her pro at 13 (October 1982) to support the family, has been a prized target of the tabloids for his waywardness. The father's most recent, and serious, scandal was his arrest and imprisonment in 1995 on the charge of income tax evasion of millions of dollars in managing her fortune. He was convicted and sentenced to a jail term in January 1997.

Nevertheless, she remained loyal to him, and steadfast in her pursuit of victory, though cutting down her schedule to 11 tournaments in 1995 and 1996. "These two years have meant more to me than anything in tennis. Many times I was surprised I could play at all," she said. "I couldn't imagine winning two more Wimbledon, French and U.S."

Court's aren't the only monumental records in danger. Suddenly Navratilova's towering nine-story Wimbledon no longer looks secure since Graf is playing far better in her late 20s than she did as the teen Grand Slammer. She stands alone in winning the four majors a minimum of four times each.

She said she missed the challenge of Seles, who beat her in a 4-6, 6-3, 6-2 battle for the Australian title in 1993, shortly before the assault by Parche, and welcomed Monica's return to the U.S. Open of 1995. In a highly-charged final, Steffi won, 7-6 (8-6), 0-6, 6-3, and one year later won the rematch even more impressively with quickness and battering forehands, 7-5, 6-4.

But the gems of those two years were Wimbledon '95 and the French '96 because of what it took to throttle the passionate opposition of Arantxa Sanchez Vicario in the finals. Perhaps the greatest single game ever was the 11th of their third set on Centre Court: a spellbinding 20-minute passage of 32 points—13 deuces—until Steffi punched through Arantxa's serve to 6-5, and won, 4-6, 6-1, 7-5. Twice the Spaniard served for victory at Roland Garros, at 5-4 and 7-6 in the third. Again, Steffi just wouldn't let her have it, 6-3, 6-7 (4-7), 10-8, in 3 hours, 3 minutes.

Centre has become her rumpus room as much as Martina's. In fact, it was she who literally ran off with the 1988 and 1989 finals at Martina's expense, 5-7, 6-2, 6-1, then 6-2, 6-7 (1-7), 6-1. Overtaking Navratilova's seeming winning shots again and again, Steffi either hit winners or prolonged points until she could win them. She thus halted Navratilova's run of six straight years on top and 47 consecutive match wins, three short of Moody's Wimbledon record.

In the 1993 Wimbledon final, Steffi kept her poise when it appeared she must lose to Jana Novotna. Jana, playing gloriously over a fiery 12-game stretch, built a 4-1, 40-30 lead in the third. However, her nerve wasn't as firm, and Steffi combined her own resolve with Jana's generosity to take the last five games and her fifth title, 7-6 (8-6), 1-6, 6-4.

On the other side of the coin the following year, Steffi added to Wimbledon history through defeat, the only first-seeded woman to fall in the

Steffi Graf: "Fraulein Forehand." (Mitchell Reibel)

first round: to Lori McNeil, 7-5, 7-6 (7-5). It was her lone failure to attain at least the quarters in 38 majors since making the semis of the U.S. in 1985 (29 of which she was in the final, and, of course, won 21).

Her Grand Slam year amounted to 11 singles titles in 14 tournaments on a 73-3 match record. In navigating the Australian, French, Wimbledon and U.S. finals, she beat Evert, 6-1, 7-6 (7-3); Natalia Zvereva, 6-0, 6-0; Navratilova, 5-7, 6-2, 6-1, and Gabriela Sabatini, 6-3, 3-6, 6-1, to close it out at Flushing Meadow. Then she beat Sabatini, 6-3, 6-3, for the 1988 Olympic crown, but relinquished it to Jennifer Capriati, 3-6, 6-3, 6-4, in 1992 at Barcelona.

Almost as impressive was 1989 with 14 wins in 16 tournaments on a 86-2 match record, and 1993, winning 10 of 15 tournaments on 76-6. Four times she won the season-closing WTA (née

Virginia Slims) Championship at Madison Square Garden, 1987, 1989, 1993 and 1995. Her swath of reaching 20 consecutive finals through the German Open of 1994 was second in that consistency to Navratilova's 23, 1983–84.

She led Germany to the 1987 and 1992 Federation Cups in which Singles record is 19-2. The ITF named her World Champion seven times, 1987, 1988, 1989, 1990, 1993, 1995 and 1996. Her 66-match winning streak (11 tournaments, 1989–90, second only to Navratilova's 74 of 1984 in the open era) was scissored by Seles in the Berlin final. After losing her first pro match to Tracy Austin (the only one she played in 1982), she became a winner (21-15) in 1983, registering at No. 98 on the computer.

Numbers, numbers, numbers. . . .

Long after most of them are filed away somewhere, the memory will remain luminous in our neural mush of this flaxen-haired goddess gamboling and gazelling across a white-lined plain to bash a forehand.

After 11 years as a pro, she has only been surpassed in career earnings by Martina Navratilova, $20,344,061 to her $19,846,316.

MAJOR TITLES (22)—*Australian singles, 1988, 1989, 1990, 1994; French singles, 1987, 1988, 1993, 1995, 1996; Wimbledon, 1988, 1989, 1991, 1992, 1993, 1995, 1996; U.S. singles, 1988, 1989, 1993, 1995, 1996; Wimbledon doubles, 1988.* FEDERATION CUP—*1986, 1987, 1989, 1991, 1992, 1993, 1996; record: 19-2 in singles, 8-1 in doubles.* SINGLES RECORD IN THE MAJORS: *Australian (40-4), French (73-9), Wimbledon (66-5), U.S. (70-8).*

DORIS HART
United States (1925—)

As a child Doris Jane Hart was certainly not a candidate for sports immortality. She was stricken by a serious knee infection later erroneously publicized as polio, and faced the prospect of being crippled for life. She began to play tennis at age six as therapy, and recovered so successfully that, despite bowed and uncertain-appearing legs, she became one of the all-time champions.

"One of the first newspaper stories on me described me as having recovered from polio," she once said. "It was a good story that just caught on. But it wasn't so."

Her total of 35 major (Australian, French, Wimbledon and U.S.) championships in singles, doubles and mixed ties her with Louise Brough, behind only Margaret Court (62), Martina Navratilova (56), Billie Jean King (39) and Margaret duPont (37). Hart and Court are the only players in history, male or female, to win all 12 of the major titles at least once, and she is one of 12 to win all four singles within her career.

For 14 successive years between 1942 and 1955 she was ranked in the U.S. Top Ten, standing at No. 1 in 1954 and 1955.

Possibly her finest tournament was Wimbledon of 1951, when she scored a triple—championships in singles, doubles, and mixed—and lost only one set, that in the mixed. After handing her good friend and partner, Shirley Fry, one of the worst beatings in the tournament's history (6-1, 6-0), Doris united with Shirley for the doubles title, then annexed the mixed with Frank Sedgman. Doris won the mixed the following year with Sedgman, and the next three years with Vic Seixas, a Wimbledon record of five straight years.

After being a runner-up at Forest Hills for the U.S. Singles Championship four times, including 1952 and 1953 to Maureen Connolly, Hart finally was rewarded on her 15th try at the title, beating Brough in a thriller, 6-8, 6-1, 8-6, in the 1954 title match, averting three match points. She retained that title, 6-4, 6-2, over Pat Ward, then retired to become a teaching pro.

Born June 20, 1925, in St. Louis, Hart, a right-hander, grew up in Coral Gables, Fla. She was an intelligent and solid all-around player whose strokes were crisp and stylish. She moved very well, despite the early handicap of her legs, and had an excellent disposition. She was effective at the net, or in the backcourt, as attested by her championships in the French singles of 1950 and 1952, and the U.S. Clay Court singles in 1950 over Fry, 6-1, 6-3.

Doris Hart: The complete performer. (UPI)

She and Shirley were one of the outstanding pairs in history, winning the French a record four straight from 1950, losing only one set in the finals while deposing long-time rivals Louise Brough and Margaret Osborne duPont in '50, 1-6, 7-5, 6-2. Gigi Fernandez and Natasha Zvereva tied the four-straight record four decades later as champs, 1992–95. Hart and Fry also won three Wimbledons in a row, beginning in 1951. In the 1953 U.S. final they ended the record streak of Brough and duPont at nine championships and 41 matches in a furious 6-2, 7-9, 9-7 struggle during which they avoided two match points at 2-5 in the third. In turn their own streak of four championships and 20 matches was stopped in the 1955 final by Brough and duPont.

During a decade of U.S. supremacy over Britain (1946–55) in the Wightman Cup, Hart won all 14 of her singles and eight of nine doubles. She captained the winning U.S. team in 1970.

Her U.S. championships on various surfaces amounted to 22 singles and doubles. In 1969 she was enshrined in the Hall of Fame.

Beginning in 1946 she was in the World Top Ten 10 successive years, No. 1 in 1951.

MAJOR TITLES (35)—*Australian singles, 1949; French singles, 1950, 1952; Wimbledon singles, 1951; U.S. singles, 1954, 1955; Australian doubles, 1950; French doubles, 1948, 1950, 1951, 1952, 1953; Wimbledon doubles, 1947, 1951, 1952, 1953; U.S. doubles, 1951, 1952, 1953, 1954; Australian mixed, 1949, 1950; French mixed, 1951, 1952, 1953; Wimbledon mixed, 1951, 1952, 1953, 1954, 1955; U.S. mixed, 1951, 1952, 1953, 1954, 1955.* OTHER U.S. TITLES (11)—*Clay Court singles, 1950; Hard Court singles, 1949; Indoor doubles, 1947, 1948, with Barbara Schofield; Hard Court Mixed, 1949, with Eric Sturgess; Clay Court doubles, 1944, 1945, with Pauline Betz; 1950, with Shirley Fry; 1954, with Maureen Connolly; Indoor mixed, 1947, 1948, with Bill Talbert.* WIGHTMAN CUP—*1946, 1947, 1948, 1949, 1950, 1951, 1952, 1953, 1954, 1955; record: 14-0 in singles, 8-1 in doubles.* SINGLES RECORD IN THE MAJORS: *Australian (8-1), French (28-5), Wimbledon (43-8), U.S. (57-13).*

LEW HOAD
Australia (1934–94)

During his quarter-century career as a professional, Pancho Gonzalez faced a vast array of first-rate players, and the one he considered the most devastating was Lewis Alan Hoad.

"When Lew's game was at its peak nobody could touch him," said Gonzalez, who cited Hoad as his toughest foe during his years of head-to-head one-night-stand pro tours.

Hoad, who turned pro in 1957, after winning his second successive Wimbledon singles, was one rookie who seemed able to dethrone Gonzalez as the pro king. They were just about even when Hoad's troublesome back gave way during the winter of 1958. Gonzalez won the tour, 51-36, but felt threatened all the way. It was Pancho's closest brush with defeat after taking over leadership in 1954.

Hoad, a strapping 5-foot-8, 175-pounder with a gorilla chest and iron wrists, may have been the strongest man to play tennis in the world

class. He blistered the ball and became impatient with rallying, preferring to hit for winners. It was a flamboyant style, and made for some bad errors when he wasn't in tune. But when his power was focused along with his concentration, Hoad came on like a tidal wave. He was strong enough to use topspin as an offensive drive. He was assault-minded, but had enough control to win the French title on slow clay in 1956.

Born Nov. 23, 1934, 21 days after Ken Rosewall, in the same city, Sydney, the right-handed Hoad was bracketed with Rosewall throughout his amateur days. Although entirely different in stature, style, and personality, the two were called Australia's tennis twins, the prodigies who drew attention as teenagers and were rivals and teammates through 1956. Hoad was stronger, but less patient and consistent, more easygoing. His back problems cut his career short in the mid-1960s while Rosewall, whose style was less taxing, kept on going into the next decade.

His countrymen fondly remember Hoad's Davis Cup triumph of 1953 over Tony Trabert on a rainy Melbourne afternoon. At 19, he and Rosewall had been selected to defend the Cup. The U.S. led, 2-1, in the finale and seemed about to clinch the Cup when the more experienced Trabert, already the U.S. champion, caught up at two sets all. Hoad hung on to win, however, 13-11, 6-3, 3-6, 2-6, 7-5, and Rosewall beat Vic Seixas the following day to save the Cup, 3-2.

Although they lost it to the Americans the next year, Hoad and Rosewall were awesome in 1955, retaking the prize, 5-0, and defended the Davis Cup for the last time together in 1956.

Their first major titles came in 1953, when Lew and Ken were allied to win the Australian, French, and Wimbledon doubles. They missed out on a Grand Slam on the last leg, the U.S. at Longwood, in a quarter-final upset by unseeded Americans Straight Clark and Hal Burrows, 5-7, 14-12, 18-16, 9-7. But, taking 19 of 20 matches, he (in the left court) and Ken were the only male team other than countrymen Frank Sedgman–

Lew Hoad: His strength lifted many a cup. (UPI)

Ken McGregor (1951–52) and John Newcombe–Tony Roche (1967) to win three of the four in one year. Lew won 13 major titles in singles and doubles, and in 1956 appeared on his way to win all four (Australian, French, Wimbledon and U.S.) singles within one year and thus achieve a rare Grand Slam. His Wimbledon final-round victory over the omnipresent Rosewall meant he was three quarters of the way to a Slam. Yet it was Rosewall who stood as the immovable obstacle in the final at Forest Hills, spoiling a Slam with a 4-6, 6-2, 6-2, 6-3, triumph. In his last significant tournament appearance in 1973, Lew reached the final of the South African doubles with Rob Maud, losing to Arthur Ashe and Tom Okker, 6-2, 4-6, 6-2, 6-4. He lost the final of the U.S. Pro singles to Gonzalez in 1958 and 1959.

Despite losing out on a Grand Slam, his 1956 season was a luminous hard-working campaign that netted 32 titles: 15 victories in 26 singles tourneys on a 95-11 match record, 17 victories in 23 doubles starts on 79-5. He had planned to turn pro after that but decided to go for the Slam again. That dream was drilled almost immediately in the semis of the Australian by Neale Fraser, 7-5, 3-6, 6-1, 6-4. Then a lesser Aussie, Neil Gibson, lulled him to defeat in the third round of the French, 2-6, 3-6, 6-4, 6-4, 6-4. Though Lew resolutely and smashingly did repeat at Wimbledon on the loss of one set, blasting Ashley Cooper in the final, 6-2, 6-1, 6-2, he felt it was time to cash in. He accepted an offer from promoter Jack Kramer and began preparing for Gonzalez. For five straight years, beginning in 1952, he was in the World Top Ten, No. 1 in 1956.

Hoad (5 attempts) and Bjorn Borg (10) are probably the two greatest players not to win the U.S. Open. Lew married another player, countrywoman Jenny Staley (finalist in the 1954 Australian singles). He died July 3, 1994, in Fuengirola, Spain, where he and Jenny operated a tennis resort.

MAJOR TITLES *(13)—Australian singles, 1956; French singles, 1956; Wimbledon singles, 1956, 1957; Australian doubles, 1953, 1956, 1957; French doubles, 1953; Wimbledon doubles, 1953, 1955, 1956; U.S. doubles, 1956; French mixed, 1954.* DAVIS CUP—*1953, 1954, 1955, 1956; record: 10-2 in singles, 7-2 in doubles.* SINGLES RECORD IN THE MAJORS: *Australian (15-5), French (17-5), Wimbledon (32-7), U.S. (21-5).*

BILLIE JEAN KING
United States (1943—)

The fireman's daughter, Billie Jean Moffitt King, began blazing through the tennis world in 1960 when she first appeared in the U.S. women's rankings at No. 4. She was 17. For more than two decades she continued as a glowing force in the game as the all-time Wimbledon champion, frequently the foremost player, a crusader in building the female professional game, and a million-dollar-plus winner on the tour.

Born Nov. 22, 1943, in Long Beach, Cal., Billie Jean, a 5-foot-4½, 130-pound right-hander, was named for her father, Bill Moffitt, a Long

Beach fireman and an enthusiastic athlete, though not a tennis player. Her brother, Randy Moffitt, became a pitcher for the San Francisco Giants. She developed on the public courts of Long Beach and first gained international recognition in 1961 by joining 18-year-old Karen Hantze for a surprising triumph in the Wimbledon women's doubles. They were the youngest team to win it. That was the first of 20 Wimbledon championships, making King the record winner of the most prestigious tourney.

In 1979 she got the 20th in her 19th Wimbledon, the doubles, in the company of Martina Navratilova, with whom she won her last major, the U.S. doubles, in 1980.

Elizabeth Ryan's 19 Wimbledon titles (between 1914 and 1934) were all in doubles and mixed doubles. King won 6 singles, 10 doubles, and 4 mixed doubles between 1961 and 1979, and in 1979 lengthened another Wimbledon record by appearing in her 27th final, the doubles. Ryan was in 24 finals. Of all the men and women to compete at Wimbledon only Navratilova played more matches (279) than King's 265, of which B.J. was 95-15 in singles, 74-12 in doubles, 55-14 in mixed.

Billie Jean's has been a career of firsts. In 1968 she was the first woman of the open era to sign a pro contract to tour in a female tournament group, with Rosie Casals, Françoise Durr and Ann Haydon Jones as the women's auxiliary of the National Tennis League, which also included six men (Rod Laver, Ken Rosewall, Pancho Gonzalez, Andres Gimeno, Fred Stolle, and Roy Emerson). A few women before King had turned pro to make head-to-head barnstorming tours, notably Suzanne Lenglen and Mary K. Browne, 1926–27; Alice Marble and Mary Hardwick, 1941; Pauline Betz and Sarah Palfrey Fabyan Cooke, 1947; Althea Gibson and Karol Fageros, 1960.

In 1971 B.J. was the first woman athlete over the 100-grand hurdle, winning $117,000. During that memorably monster season when she was toiling mightily to establish the women's tour,

she played 31 tournaments in singles, winning 17, and 26 in doubles, winning a record 21. She had a match mark of 112-13 in singles, a record number of wins, and 80-5 in doubles. Overall it added up to 38 titles on 192 match wins, both records. Imagine how many millions such a campaign would be worth today.

In 1973 Billie Jean engaged in a "Battle of the Sexes" challenge match, defeating 55-year-old ex-Wimbledon champ Bobby Riggs, 6-4, 6-3, 6-3, in a heavily publicized and nationally televised extravaganza that captured the nation's fancy and drew a record tennis crowd, 30,472, to Houston's Astrodome.

In 1974 she became the first woman to coach a professional team containing men when she served as player-coach of the Philadelphia Freedoms of World Team Tennis, a league she and her husband, Larry King, helped establish. Traded to the New York Apples, she led that team to WTT titles in 1976 and 1977 as a player.

Ten years after Riggs, B.J. was to establish a geriatric mark herself, winning Birmingham (England) over Alycia Moulton, 6-0, 7-5. At 39½ she was the oldest woman to take a pro title.

An aggressive, emotional player who has often said, "You have to love to guts it out to win," Billie Jean specialized in serve-and-volley tactics, aided by quickness and a highly competitive nature. She overcame several knee operations to continue as a winner into her 40th year. As a big-match player she was unsurpassed, excelling in team situations when she represented the U.S. In nine years on the Federation Cup team, she helped the U.S. gain the final each time, and win seven by winning 51 of her 55 singles and doubles. In the Wightman Cup against Britain she played on only one losing side in 10 years, winning 21 of her 26 singles and doubles.

Outspoken on behalf of women's rights, in and out of sports—and the game of tennis in particular—she was possibly the most influential player in popularizing professional tennis in the United States. She worked tirelessly to promote the Virginia Slims tour during the early 1970s when the women realized they must separate from the men to achieve recognition and significant prize money on their own. With the financial backing of Virginia Slims, the organizational acumen of Gladys Heldman and the salesmanship and winning verve of King, the women pros built an extremely profitable circuit.

Only two women, Margaret Smith Court (62) and Navratilova (56) won more majors than King's 39 in singles, doubles and mixed. In regard to U.S. titles on all surfaces (grass, clay, hard court, indoor), King is second at 31 behind Hazel Hotchkiss Wightman's 34. But Billie Jean is the only woman to win on all four, equalling Tony Trabert, the lone man. King and Rosie Casals were the only doubles team to win U.S. titles on all four surfaces. She won seven of her major doubles with Casals, her most frequent and successful partner.

King's most important titles were the Wimbledon singles, 1966, 1967, 1968, 1972, 1973 and 1975, and the U.S. singles at Forest Hills, 1967, 1971, 1972, and 1974. She also won the French singles in 1972 and the Australian in 1968 and 1971, becoming the fifth woman to win all four major singles titles. Ranked No. 1 in the U.S. seven times, she tied Molla Bjurstedt Mallory for most years at the top.

However, Navratilova would pass them both with 12. Between 1960 and 1982 Billie Jean was ranked in the U.S. Top Ten 18 times, topped only by Chris Evert's 19. Between 1963 and 1980 she was in the World Top Ten 18 times, at No. 1 in 1966, 1967, 1968, 1971 and 1974, and held her last ranking, No. 13, at age 40 in 1983.

She greatly aided Owen Davidson in making his mixed doubles Grand Slam in 1967 with two partners. King and Davidson won the French, Wimbledon and U.S. after he took the Australian with Lesley Turner. She scored three major triples, winning the singles, doubles and mixed at Wimbledon in 1967 and 1973, and at the U.S. in 1967. She won the longest singles set played by

Billie Jean King: Volleying trailblazer. (Russ Adams)

women (36 games) in a 1963 Wightman Cup win over Christine Truman, 6-4, 19-17.

Billie Jean's grand swan song occurred at 39 in 1983 at Wimbledon, a semifinal finish (her 14th), losing to 18-year-old Andrea Jaeger, 6-1, 6-1. Seven years later she played a cameo role in the Boca Raton, Fla., tourney, winning a doubles match with 13-year-old pro rookie Jennifer Capriati.

In a career encompassing the amateur and open eras, she won 67 pro and 37 amateur singles titles. She reached 38 other pro finals and had 677-149 singles match record as a pro. Her prize money: $1,966,487.

Divorce ended her marriage. A founder and ex-president of the WTA, B.J. remains active in World Team Tennis as commissioner. She returned to her USTA roots in 1995 as captain of the Federation Cup team, having been player-captain in 1965 (a loss) and 1976 (a win). In 1996 she guided the U.S. team to the Cup over Spain, and, as U.S. women's Olympic coach, Lindsay Davenport, Gigi Fernandez and Mary Joe Fernandez to gold medals.

MAJOR TITLES *(39)—Australian singles, 1968; French singles, 1972; Wimbledon singles, 1966, 1967, 1968, 1972, 1973, 1975; U.S. singles, 1967, 1971, 1972, 1974; French doubles, 1972; Wimbledon doubles, 1961, 1962, 1965, 1967, 1968, 1970, 1971, 1972, 1973, 1979; U.S. doubles, 1964, 1967, 1974, 1977, 1980; Australian mixed, 1968; French mixed, 1967, 1970; Wimbledon mixed, 1967, 1971, 1973, 1974; U.S. mixed, 1967, 1971, 1973, 1976.* OTHER U.S. TITLES *(18)—Indoor singles, 1966, 1967, 1968, 1971, 1974; Clay Court singles, 1971; Hard Court singles, 1966; Indoor doubles, 1966, 1968, 1971, 1975, with Rosie Casals; 1979, with Martina Navratilova; 1983, with Sharon Walsh; Clay Court doubles, 1960, with Darlene Hard; 1971, with Judy Tegart Dalton; Hard Court doubles, 1966, with Casals; Indoor mixed, 1966, 1967, with Paul Sullivan.* FEDERATION CUP *(As player)—1963, 1964, 1965, 1966, 1967, 1976, 1977, 1978, 1979; record 25-4 in singles, 27-0 in doubles; (As captain)—1965, 1976, 1995, 1996; record: 12-2, 2 Cups.* WIGHTMAN CUP—*1961, 1962, 1963, 1964, 1965, 1966, 1967, 1970, 1977, 1978; record: 14-2 in singles, 7-3 in doubles.* SINGLES RECORD IN THE MAJORS: *Australian (17-4), French (21-6), Wimbledon (95-15), U.S. (58-14).*

JACK KRAMER
United States (1921—)

The impact of John Albert "Jake" Kramer on tennis has been fourfold: as great player, exceptional promoter, thoughtful innovator and astute television commentator.

Kramer, born Aug. 1, 1921, in Las Vegas, Nev., grew up in the Los Angeles area. He achieved international notice in 1939 as a teenager when he was selected to play doubles, alongside Joe Hunt, for the U.S. in the Davis Cup finale against Australia. At 18, Kramer was the youngest to play in the Cup title round, although John Alexander of Australia lowered the record to 17 by playing in 1968.

Kramer and Hunt were the golden boys out of Southern California, their careers intertwined. Joe beat Jake, at Forest Hills in 1939, where they were both losing semifinalists the following year. (Kramer, 19, had a startling win over fourth-seed-

ed Frank Parker in the quarters, and pushed the champ, Don McNeill, to four sets in the semi). Both were to go to sea during World War II, Jake in the Coast Guard, Joe in the Navy, and to receive leaves to play again in the U.S. Championships of 1943, where they collided in the final. Hunt won, barely, sprawling on the court with cramps as Kramer's last shot flew long (6-3, 6-8, 10-8, 6-0). Kramer, who'd had a bout with food poisoning, laughed later, "If I could've kept that ball in play I might have been a champ on a default." Hunt was killed 17 months afterwards in a military plane crash.

Because of the war Jake had to wait three years to return to Forest Hills, to come into prominence as a splendid champion, no breaks from opponents needed, so dominant that he was voted fifth on a list of all-time greats selected by a panel of expert tennis journalists in 1969. The powerful right-hander was the leading practitioner of the "big game," rushing to the net constantly behind his serve, and frequently attacking on return of serve. His serve took opponents off the court, setting them up for the volley, as did his crushing forehand.

A blistered racket hand probably decided his gruelling fourth-round defeat (2-6, 17-15, 6-3, 3-6, 6-3) by cunning lefty Jaroslav Drobny, and prevented Jake from winning the first post-war Wimbledon. But he came back awesomely in 1947, the first to win in shorts, making short work of everybody. Whipping doubles partner Tom Brown in 48 minutes, 6-1, 6-3, 6-2, he lost merely 37 games in seven matches, the most lopsided run to the championship.

Brown had been his 1946 U.S. final-round victim, 9-7, 6-3, 6-0, another one-sided excursion for Jake, a crew-cut blond whose goal was to reclaim the Davis Cup that he and Hunt failed to clinch in 1939. In December he and good buddy Ted Schroeder—the U.S. doubles champs of 1940—were members of a highly talented team that captain Walter Pate took to Australia for the challenge round. Every man—those two plus Brown, Frank Parker, Gardnar Mulloy, Bill Talbert—thought he should play. Pate picked Ted and Jake to do it all, controversial until the pals paralyzed the favored Aussies on opening day. Schroeder won in five over John Bromwich and Kramer nailed Dinny Pails, 8-6, 6-2, 9-7. Together they grabbed the Cup by flattening the team that had beaten Hunt and Kramer in '39: Bromwich and Adrian Quist, 6-2, 7-5, 6-4.

The following summer, Jake and Ted repelled the Australian challenge for the Cup at Forest Hills, and then Kramer closed out his amateur career memorably by overhauling Parker in the U.S. final. Kramer lost the first two sets, and was in danger of losing out on a lucrative professional contract as well as his championship. Counterpunching, Kramer won, 4-6, 2-6, 6-1, 6-0, 6-3, and set off in pursuit of Bobby Riggs, the reigning pro champ. Kramer, who had lost only two matches in 1946, dropped but one (to Talbert) in 1947, winning eight of nine tournaments on 48-1, closing his amateur life with a 41-match rush.

Kramer knocked Riggs off the summit by winning their odyssey of one-nighters throughout the U.S., which was the test of professional supremacy of that day. Their opener was a phenomenon: New York was buried by a blizzard that brought the city to a stop, yet 15,114 customers made it on foot to the old Madison Square Garden on Dec. 27, 1947, to watch Riggs win. Bobby couldn't keep it up. Kramer won the tour, 69-20, and stayed in action while Riggs took over as the promoter and signed Pancho Gonzalez to challenge Kramer. Nobody was up to Kramer then. He bruised the rookie Gonzalez 96-27 on the longest of the tours. Kramer made $85,000 against Riggs as his percentage, and $72,000 against Gonzalez.

In 1952 Kramer assumed the position of promoter himself, the boss of pro tennis, a role he would hold for over a decade, well past his playing days. Kramer's last tour as a principal was against the first man he recruited, Frank Sedgman, the Aussie who was tops among amateurs. Kramer won, 54-41. An arthritic back led to Kramer's retirement as a player, but he kept the tour going, resurrecting one of his victims, Gonzalez, who became the strongman.

Jack Kramer: Power player and promoter. (UPI)

One of the shrewdest operators in tennis, Kramer was looked to for advice when the open era began in 1968. He devised the Grand Prix for the men's game, a series of tournaments leading to a Masters Championship for the top eight finishers, and a bonus pool to be shared by more than a score of the leading players. The Grand Prix, incorporating the most attractive tournaments around the world, functioned from 1970 until 1990, when the ATP Tour took over the structure. In 1972 he was instrumental in forming the Association of Tennis Pros, the male players' union, and was its first executive director. His role as leader of the ATP's principled boycott of Wimbledon in 1973 made him unpopular in Britain for a time. Nevertheless, it was a landmark act, assuring the players of the right to control their own destiny after being in thrall to national associations until then. Later he served on the Men's International Professional Tennis Council, the worldwide governing board.

For more than 20 years Kramer served as an analyst on tennis telecasts in many countries, notably for the British Broadcasting Corporation at Wimbledon and for all the American networks at Forest Hills, and at other events. He ranked in the

U.S. Top Ten five times between 1940 and 1947, No. 1 in the U.S. and the world in 1946 and 1947.

Kramer, winner of 13 U.S. singles and doubles titles, was named to the Hall of Fame in 1968. His son, Bob Kramer, continues the family's tennis interests as director of the Los Angeles ATP tourney.

MAJOR TITLES *(10)—Wimbledon singles, 1947; U.S. Singles, 1946, 1947; Wimbledon doubles, 1946, 1947; U.S. doubles, 1940, 1941, 1943, 1947; U.S. mixed, 1941.* OTHER U.S. TITLES *(6)—Indoor singles, 1947; Pro singles, 1948; Pro doubles, 1948, 1955, with Pancho Segura; Indoor doubles, 1947, with Bob Falkenburg; Clay Court doubles, 1941, with Ted Schroeder.* DAVIS CUP—*1939, 1946, 1947; record: 6-0 in singles, 1-2 in doubles.* SINGLES RECORD IN THE MAJORS: *Wimbledon (10-1), U.S. (24-5).*

ROD LAVER
Australia (1938—)

Rod Laver was so scrawny and sickly as a child in the Australian bush that no one could guess he would become a left-handed whirlwind who would conquer the tennis world and be known as possibly the greatest player ever.

A little more than a month before Don Budge completed the first Grand Slam, Rodney George "Rocket" Laver was born Aug. 9, 1938, at Rockhampton, Queensland, Australia. Despite lack of size and early infirmities, Laver grew strong and tough on his father's cattle property and emulated Budge by making the second male Grand Slam in 1962 as an amateur—then became the only double Grand Slammer seven years later by taking the major singles (Australian, French, Wimbledon, U.S.) as a pro.

Few champions have been as devastating and dominant as Laver was as amateur and pro during the 1960s. An incessant attacker, he was nevertheless a complete player who glowed in backcourt and at the net. Laver's 5-foot-8½, 145-pound body seemed to dangle from a massive left arm that belonged to a gorilla, an arm with which he bludgeoned the ball and was able to impart ferocious topspin. Although others had used topspin, Laver may have inspired a wave of heavy-hitting topspin practitioners of the 1970s such as Bjorn Borg and Guillermo Vilas. The stroke became basic after Laver.

As a teenager he was sarcastically nicknamed "Rocket" by Australian Davis Cup captain Harry Hopman. "He was anything but a Rocket," Hopman recalled. "But Rod was willing to work harder than the rest, and it was soon apparent to me that he had more talent than any other of our fine Australian players."

His initial international triumph came during his first trip abroad in 1956, when he won the U.S. Junior Championship at 17. Three years later he was ready to take his place among the world's best when he won the Australian singles and, with Bob Mark, the doubles, and was runner-up to Alex Olmedo for the Wimbledon championship. The Australian victories were the first of Laver's 20 major titles in singles, doubles and mixed, placing him fifth among all-time male winners behind Roy Emerson (28), John Newcombe (25), Frank Sedgman (22), Bill Tilden (21). Jean Borotra also won 20. His 11 singles (equaled by Bjorn Borg) were second to Emerson's 12.

The losing Wimbledon final of 1959 was the beginning of an incredible run of success in that tournament. He was a finalist six straight times he entered, losing in 1960 to Neale Fraser, winning in 1961 and 1962, and—after a five-year absence because professionals were barred until 1968—winning again in 1968 and 1969. Only two others had played in six successive finals, back before the turn of the century: Willie Renshaw, 1881 through 1886 and Wilfred Baddely, 1891 through 1896. Borg played in six straight, 1976 through 1981. While winning Wimbledon four straight times (the only man since World War I to win four prior to Borg) and proceeding to the fourth round in 1970, Laver set a male tournament record of 31 consecutive match wins, ended by his loss to Roger Taylor, and eclipsed by Borg in 1980.

The year 1969 was Laver's finest, perhaps the best experienced by any player, as he won an open-era record 17 singles tournaments (tied by

Guillermo Vilas in 1977) of 32 played on a 106-16 match record. In 1962 he won 19 of 34 on 134-15.

Unlike his Grand Slam year of 1962 as an amateur, he was playing in tournaments that were open to all, amateur and pro, and this Slam was all the more impressive. It was endangered only a few times—Tony Roche forcing him to a fifth set in an exhausting 90-game semifinal in the Australian championships 7-5, 22-20, 9-11, 1-6, 6-3; Dick Crealy winning the first two sets of a second-rounder in the French; Premjit Lall winning the first two sets of a second-rounder at Wimbledon; Stan Smith threatening in the fifth set of a fourth-rounder at Wimbledon; Arthur Ashe and John Newcombe pushing him to four sets in the Wimbledon semifinal and final (6-4, 5-7, 6-4, 6-4), respectively; Dennis Ralston leading 2 sets to 1 in the fourth round of the U.S.; Roche winning the opening set of the mucky U.S. final, 7-9, 6-1, 6-2, 6-2 (which Laver played in spikes).

But that year Laver could always accelerate to a much higher gear and bang his way out of trouble. The closest anyone came to puncturing either Slam was Marty Mulligan, who held a match point in the fourth set of their French quarterfinal in 1962, 6-4, 3-6, 2-6, 10-8, 6-2.

After his second year running as the No. 1 amateur, 1962, and helping Australia win a fourth successive Davis Cup, Laver turned pro. It was a life of one-nighters, but Pancho Gonzalez was no longer supreme. Kenny Rosewall was at the top and gave Laver numerous beatings as their long, illustrious rivalry began. Rosewall beat Laver to win the U.S. Pro singles in 1963, but the next year Laver defeated Rosewall and Gonzalez to win the first of his five crowns, four of them in a row beginning in 1966. He had a streak of 19 wins in the U.S. Pro until losing the 1970 final to Roche.

Gonzalez, pointing for a ninth crown in the 1964 final, was a formidable foe on a formidable afternoon. Astonishingly the show went on—the pros were that way in that day—in a raging nor'easter that swept Boston with a blustery downpour, turning Longwood's grassy stadium to a bog. They slipped and fell, but both proud men were up to it, somehow producing fabulous shots. In the rain Laver signaled the end of Pancho's reign, 4-6, 6-3, 7-5, 6-4.

When open tennis dawned in 1968, Laver was ready to resume where he'd left off at the traditional tournaments, whipping Roche in less than an hour, 6-3, 6-4, 6-2, to take the first open Wimbledon.

In 1971 Laver won $292,717 in tournament prize money (a season record that stood until Arthur Ashe won $338,337 in 1975), the figure enabling him to become the first tennis player to make a million dollars on the court. Until the last days of 1978, when he was playing few tournaments, Laver was still the all-time leading money-winner with $1,564,213. Jimmy Connors then surpassed him.

In 1973 all professionals were permitted to play Davis Cup, and Laver honed himself for one last effort, after 11 years away. He was brilliant, teaming with John Newcombe to end a five-year U.S. reign, 5-0. Laver beat Tom Gorman in five sets on the first day and paired with Newcombe for a crushing straight-set doubles victory over Stan Smith and Erik van Dillen that clinched the Cup, Laver's fifth. Of all the marvelous Aussie Davis Cup performers he was the only one never to play in a losing series.

He was also a factor in winning three World Cups (1972, 1974–75) for Australia in the since disbanded team competition against the U.S. In 1976, as his tournament career was winding down, Laver signed with San Diego in World Team Tennis and was named the league's Rookie of the Year at age 38!

During a 23-year career that spanned the amateur and open eras, he won 47 pro titles in singles and was runner-up 21 times. Laver was elevated to the Hall of Fame in 1981.

His 13 years in the World Top Ten ranged from 1959 to 1975, No. 1 in 1961, 1962, 1968 and 1969. His last year there he was No. 10 at age 37.

MAJOR TITLES (20)—*Australian singles, 1960, 1962, 1969; French singles, 1962, 1969; Wimbledon singles, 1961,*

Rod Laver: Ferocious attacker. (UPI)

1962, 1968, 1969; U.S. singles, 1962, 1969; Australian doubles, 1959, 1960, 1961, 1969; French doubles, 1961; Wimbledon doubles, 1971; French mixed, 1961; Wimbledon mixed, 1959, 1960. DAVIS CUP—*1959, 1960, 1961, 1962, 1973; record: 16-4 in singles, 4-0 in doubles.* SINGLES RECORD IN THE MAJORS: *Australian (21-6), French (25-6), Wimbledon (50-7), U.S. (44-10).*

IVAN LENDL

Czechoslovakia/United States (1960—)

Although he'd been a prodigious winner for four years, it was not until the French final of 1984 that Ivan Lendl began to really stake his claim to greatness. Then, from two sets down to the year's leading player, John McEnroe, Lendl battled back to win in five sets, 3-6, 2-6, 6-4, 7-5, 7-5, seizing the first of his eight major singles. He won two other French (1986 and 1987) and two Australian (1989 and 1990).

Until 1984, at 24, his competitive zeal in big finals had been questioned, particularly after his U.S. Open finals losses to Jimmy Connors in 1982 and 1983. But Lendl dispelled all that, and had the first of his three U.S. titles (also over McEnroe) in 1985, the second and third over Miloslav Mecir and Mats Wilander in 1986 and 1987.

His U.S. Open conquest of McEnroe hoisted him past the New Yorker to No. 1 in the world, a position he held until losing the Open in 1988 to Wilander—156 straight weeks, three short of Jimmy Connors's open era record. He returned to No. 1 for 1989 and has spent a record total 269 weeks at the peak during 13 seasons in the Top Ten.

His Flushing Meadow time has been spectacular: appearing in eight successive finals (from 1982), he equalled the record of Big Bill Tilden (1918–25). His loss of the 1988 final to Wilander halted a 27-match winning streak in the U.S. championship, second only to Tilden's string of 42 between 1920 and the quarters of 1926.

Born March 7, 1960, in Ostrava, Czechoslovakia, and reared there, he has an excellent tennis bloodline. His mother, Olga Lendlova, was a Top Ten player in their homeland, ranking as high as No. 2. His father, Jiri Lendl, also was a fine player, ranking as high as No. 15, and who, in 1990, became president of the Czechoslovak Tennis Federation.

Unlike countrywoman Martina Navratilova, he did not announce his defection, but left no doubt when he settled in the U.S. in 1984, and declined to play further Davis Cup after 1985. He became a U.S. citizen in 1992.

In 1980 Lendl, unbeaten in seven singles and three doubles, led Czechoslovakia to its lone Davis Cup. Before an uproarious final round crowd in Prague, he anchored the 4-1 triumph over Italy. He won both his singles, beating Corrado Barazzutti, 3-6, 6-1, 6-1, 6-2, on the first day. Then he and Tom Smid clinched with a stirring 3-6, 6-3, 3-6, 6-3, 6-4, doubles decision over Adriano Panatta and Paolo Bertolucci.

A 6-foot-2, 175-pound, right-handed paragon of hard work and fitness, he amassed stunning numbers campaigning tirelessly between 1980 and 1983, when he won 36 of 101 tournaments. He played 32 in 1980, winning three on a 113-29 match record, and won 15 of 23 in 1982 on 107-9. He won 11 of 17 in 1985 on 84-7. His last big production year was 1989: 10 of 17 on 79-7. His 92nd pro singles title in 1992 leaves him second only to Connors' 109 in the open era. In 1982 he put together the third longest winning streak of the open era, 44 straight matches, six shy of Guillermo Vilas's 1977 record, ending in a Palm Springs final defeat by Yannick Noah, 6-4, 3-6, 6-2. A basher from the baseline, relying on strength and heavy topspin, Lendl wasn't particularly stylish but got the job done with an intimidating will and appetite for victory. His anticipation and speed afoot were often overlooked.

Ivan's pursuit of the one prize beyond him, Wimbledon, was Jobian. But each time, 14 of them, he was afflicted by defeat. Strain and try as he did to become a serve-and-volleyer, and close as he came—final-round loses to Boris Becker, 1986, and Pat Cash, 1987—grass was his no-no. That may be unfair to say about a man who batted .774 there, was also thrice a semifinalist, but he joined Ken Rosewall and Pancho Gonzalez as the greatest never to win the Big W.

An aching back didn't help as, seeded seventh, he lost his last attempt, in 1993, to Arnaud Boetsch in the second round. The damaged back caused him to default in the third set of his second-rounder against Bernd Karbacher at the 1994 U.S. Open. He would not play again, and announced his retirement shortly after that at age 34, ranked No. 30. His last title, Tokyo (indoor) in 1993, was a 6-4, 6-4 win over Todd Martin, and his last final, Sydney 1994, was a loss to Pete Sampras, 7-6 (7-5), 6-4.

Lendl's was a hefty pro career of 17 years: 94 singles titles (second to Connors's open-era high by 15), six doubles titles, and a 1,279-274 match record (.805), topped only by Connors. He was the all-time prize money champ with $21,282,417 when he quit.

Regardless of the impressive numbers, he'll undoubtedly think back to that hot June afternoon in 1984 when he just said no to McEnroe with the French title at stake . . . even though he was

Ivan Lendl: Relentless baseline basher. (Mitchell Reibel)

so far behind, by two sets, twice a break down in the fourth, and down two critical break points in the fifth. Nor will he mind the memory of the U.S. Open semi that year when he deftly stole a match point from Pat Cash with a racing, stretching topspin lob that kissed the Aussie's baseline in the fifth set of a 3-6, 6-3, 6-4, 6-7 (5-7), 7-6 (7-4) victory.

MAJOR TITLES *(8)—Australian singles, 1989, 1990; French singles, 1984, 1986, 1987; U.S. singles, 1985, 1986, 1987.* OTHER U.S. TITLES—*Clay Court singles, 1985; Pro singles, 1992, 1993, 1994.* DAVIS CUP—*1978, 1979, 1980, 1981, 1982, 1983, 1984, 1985; record: 18-11 in singles, 4-4 in doubles.* SINGLES RECORD IN THE MAJORS: *Australian (48-10), French (53-12), Wimbledon (48-14), U.S. (73-13).*

JOHN McENROE
United States (1959—)

Right from the start, in his 1977 introduction to pro tennis, John Patrick McEnroe, Jr., was a hit.

An 18-year-old amateur (he would not turn pro until winning the U.S. Intercollegiate singles as a Stanford freshman in 1978), McEnroe made his first splash in Paris, a boy edging into man's territory. He won his first of 17 major titles there, the French mixed with childhood pal, Mary Carillo, as well as the French junior singles.

Soon after, electrifying Wimbledon, he went through the qualifying tourney and all the way to the semis, losing to Jimmy Connors, 6-3, 6-3, 4-6, 6-4. It was a major tourney record for a qualifier. It was also a record for an amateur in the open era. Immediately he was a player to reckon with.

Born on Feb. 16, 1959, in Wiesbaden, Germany, where his father was stationed with the U.S. Air Force, he grew up in the Long Island suburb of Douglaston, N.Y.

A 5-foot-11, 170-pound left-hander, McEnroe stands as perhaps the most skilled—and controversial—of all players. Brilliant in doubles and singles, he was distinguished by shotmaking artistry, competitive fire and a volatile temper. The last led to heavy fines, suspensions and, at the 1990 Australian Open, an extraordinary disqualification for showering abusive language on court officials while leading Mikael Pernfors.

A magnificent volleyer with a feathery touch, he was an attacker whose fast court style netted four U.S. Open and three Wimbledon singles. But he had the baselining strength to have done well on clay at the French, a title he might have won at his zenith in 1984. In the final he led Ivan Lendl, 2-0 in sets only to be distracted by temperamental outbursts, and was beaten, 3-6, 2-6, 6-4, 7-5, 7-5.

He revived American interest in the Davis Cup that had been shunned by Connors and other leading countrymen, saying, "My mother made me promise her I'd always play for my country if I was asked." Right from the start, as a 19-year-old rookie in 1978, he gave captain Tony Trabert's team a lift, and gave the U.S. the Cup that had belonged to other countries since 1973. In the championship round against Britain at Rancho Mirage, Cal., he evinced none of the jitters so common to many other greats making debuts in the nationalistic setting. Mac was a miser, rationing John Lloyd (6-1, 6-2, 6-2) and Buster Mottram (6-2, 6-2, 6-1) to 10 games. Nobody had been stingier in a final. He was the most callow American to do so well in the Cup round, although Lew Hoad, a younger 19 by eight months for victorious Australia, also took both his singles in 1953, and Michael Chang, 18, won one singles in the 1990 final.

McEnroe continued as a mainstay in helping the U.S. win four more Cups through 1992, and set numerous of his country's records: years played (12), ties (30), singles wins (41), singles and doubles wins altogether (59). A workhorse, he played both singles and doubles in 13 series, and he and Peter Fleming won 14 of 15 Cup doubles together.

An epic performance was his 6-hour-32 minute, five-set victory over Mats Wilander in St. Louis (9-7, 6-2, 15-17, 3-6, 8-6), clinching a 1982 quarterfinal 3-2 win over Sweden. Another thriller was his five-set win over Jose-Luis Clerc of Argentina (7-5, 5-7, 6-3, 3-6, 6-3) to send the Cup to the U.S. in the 1981 final at Cincinnati. In 1982 France built a home-court advantage for the final, especially to counter McEnroe, installing clay indoors at Grenoble. But Mac beat Yannick Noah, 12-10, 1-6, 3-6, 6-3, 6-2, at the outset to launch a 4-1 victory. He beat Henri Leconte, in singles, and paired with Fleming for the doubles win. A decade later he was on another Cup winner as doubles partner of Pete Sampras in the triumph over Switzerland at Ft. Worth, Tex.

At 20 he won the U.S. title for the first time over fellow New Yorker Vitas Gerulaitis, the youngest winner since Pancho Gonzalez, also 20, 31 years before. He repeated in dramatic battles with Bjorn Borg in 1980, 7-6 (7-4), 6-1, 6-7 (5-7), 5-7, 6-4, and 1981, 4-6, 6-2, 6-4, 6-3, the latter seeming the straw that broke the Swede's sensational career. Borg retired shortly thereafter. McEnroe won for the last time in 1984, over Lendl, 6-3, 6-4, 6-1. But he was defeated in the Flushing Meadow rematch 12 months later, relinquishing to Lendl the No. 1 ranking McEnroe had held for four years.

His most celebrated result may have been a loss, the 1980 Wimbledon final called by many the greatest of all. Beaten, 1-6, 7-5, 6-3, 6-7 (16-18), 8-6, McEnroe nervelessly staved off five match points during the monumental fourth-set tie-breaker to fight Borg to the fifth-set wire. A year later he cut down Borg on Centre Court, 4-6, 7-6 (7-1), 7-6 (7-4), 6-4, ending Bjorn's incredible five-year, 41-match Wimbledon run.

McEnroe won again in 1983 and 1984, reaching the pinnacle of his virtuosity in the latter, a virtually flawless wipeout of Connors, 6-1, 6-2, 6-2. There were so many ups and downs at Wimbledon, where he came close to being tossed out prior to his initial championship, 1981, for a second-round flareup while beating Tom Gullikson. It was the infamous scene of labeling the umpire, Ted James, "pits of the world," and calling the referee every name but Fred Hoyles (which was his name). He went out in grand manner in 1992. Unseeded at No. 30, 33-year-old Mac wound up where he'd begun 15 years before: the semis, on a stirring knockout of ninth-seeded Guy Forget, 6-2, 7-6 (11-9), 6-3, wiggling out of six set points from 3-6 in the tiebreaker. He'd already beaten 16th-seeded David Wheaton in three, and won a rousing 4-hour, 9-minute "battle of champions" over Pat Cash, 6-7 (3-7), 6-4, 6-7 (1-7), 6-3, 6-2. But champ-to-be Andre Agassi was too much in the goodbye singles, 6-4, 6-2, 6-3.

Yet there was more, and Mac's fading presence would be stretched triumphantly over two days and Wimbledon's longest closing act on the third Monday: his fifth doubles title, this time without old collaborator Peter Fleming, but with a stranger who did just fine: Michael Stich. Two points from defeat in the fourth-set tie-breaker, tied at darkness, 13-13, the German-American combine came through over Richey Renbeberg and Jim Grabb, 5-7, 7-6 (7-5), 3-6, 7-6 (7-5), 19-17, a record-length final, 5 hours, 1 minute. Eight years had passed since his last title. "It

John McEnroe: Playing with fire. (Russ Adams)

was a great atmosphere [Court 1 was packed with 6,500 Mac fans], a great way to go out," Mac said.

Three intense rivalries stand out during his career. He had the edge on Connors (31-20), but not Lendl (15-21), and was even with Borg (7-7).

Except for the French Open lapse against Lendl, he was virtually unbeatable in 1984, winning 13 of 15 singles tournaments on an 82-3 record. Other big seasons were 1979 (10 titles on a 94-12 record), 1980 (10 titles on 88-18). In 1979 he set an open-era record with 27 overall tournament victories, 17 in doubles, winning a record total of 177 matches. He won the season-climaxing Masters singles thrice, 1978, 1983 and 1984, and is the all-time overall professional leader with 154 tournament victories: a 77-77 singles-doubles split. He is third in singles titles behind Connors's 109 and Lendl's 92, second in doubles behind Tom Okker's 78. His career singles match record is 849-184.

Ten years he ranked in the World Top Ten, and 16 in the U.S. (No. 1 there seven times), and went out with a No. 20 world ranking.

His brother, Patrick McEnroe, younger by seven years, followed him as a standout pro, winning the French doubles (with Grabb) in 1989. In 1991 they met in the Chicago final, the second such clash of brothers (Emilio Sanchez defeated Javier Sanchez, 6-3, 3-6, 6-2, in the 1987 Madrid final). John won, 3-6, 6-2, 6-4. John's prize money for 15 years as a pro was $12,539,827. He has three children by ex-wife Tatum O'Neal.

MAJOR TITLES (17)—*Wimbledon singles, 1981, 1983, 1984; U.S. singles, 1979, 1980, 1981, 1984; Wimbledon doubles, 1979, 1981, 1983, 1984, 1992; U.S. doubles, 1979, 1981, 1983, 1984; French mixed, 1977.* OTHER U.S. TITLES (4)—*Indoor singles, 1980; Hard Court singles, 1989; Indoor doubles, 1980, with Brian Gottfried; Clay Court doubles, 1979, with Gene Mayer.* DAVIS CUP—*1978, 1979, 1980, 1981, 1982, 1983, 1984, 1987, 1988, 1989, 1991, 1992; record: 41-8 in singles, in 18-2 in doubles.* SINGLES RECORD IN THE MAJORS: *Australian (18-5), French (25-10), Wimbledon (59-11), U.S. (65-12).*

ILIE NASTASE
Romania (1946—)

No player in history has been more gifted or mystifying than the Bucharest Buffoon, Ilie Nastase, noted both for his sorcery with the racket and his bizarre, even objectionable behavior. He was an entertainer second to none, amusing spectators with his antics and mimicry, also infuriating them with gaucheries and walkouts.

Despite a fragile nervous system and erratic temperament, Nastase—a slender 6-footer, quick, leggy and athletic—could do everything, and when his concentration held together he was an artist creating with great originality and panache. His record in the season-closing Masters was spectacular. He won four times, 1971 through 1973 and 1975, and was finalist to Guillermo Vilas in five sets in 1974.

Born July 19, 1946, in Bucharest, he was the first Romanian of international prominence, and largely through his play that small country rose to the Davis Cup final on three occasions, 1969, 1971, and 1972, losing each time to the U.S. At the end of 1985 after playing Davis Cup since 1966, 18 years, Nastase ranked second among the most active players in Cup history, having won 109 of 146 singles and doubles engagements in 52 ties.

Romania was favored to lift the Cup from the U.S. in the 1972 finale on the friendly slow clay of Nastase's hometown. However, his nervousness combined with an inspired performance by Stan Smith added up to an 11-9, 6-2, 6-3 victory for the American in the crucial opening singles, and the U.S. kept the Cup, 3-2. Nastase's foremost disappointment occurred three months prior, when Smith narrowly defeated him in the Wimbledon final, 4-6, 6-3, 6-3, 4-6, 7-5, one of the most exciting championship matches there. Nastase was in another Wimbledon singles final in 1976, but was beaten easily by Bjorn Borg.

Nastase, a right-hander, first came to attention in 1966 when he and his first mentor, countryman Ion Tiriac, reached the final of the French doubles, losing to Clark Graebner and Dennis Ralston.

Romania was a nowhere nation in Davis Cup until Nastase came along to link with the hulking, Draculan ice hockey luminary, Tiriac, playing sporadically since first entering in 1922, winning only one tie before 1959. That year Tiriac, from Count Dracula's Transylvanian neighborhood, spurred a couple of wins. Still, Romania had won but nine prior to the 1969 Ilie-Ion splurge of five victories that carried them to the semis against Britain at Wimbledon. There the irrepressible duo, then unknown, flabbergasted everybody, themselves included—"we can't play on this grass," said Tiriac after beating Mark Cox on opening day—by winning 3-2.

It took a fifth match victory by Nastase over Cox, 3-6, 6-1, 6-4, 6-4, to propel them into the final against the U.S. in Cleveland. Another foreign surface, asphalt, plus Arthur Ashe and Stan Smith ended the unfamiliar joyride, 5-0. But they became very familiar figures, getting to the final in the U.S. again, and getting closer, 3-2. However, it was Ilie's failure against Smith in the opening match (7-5, 6-3, 6-1) that made the difference, as it was a year later in Bucharest, 11-9, 6-2, 6-3.

By 1970 Nastase began to assert himself as a champion. He won the Italian singles and jolted Cliff Richey in the final of the U.S. Indoor, 6-8, 3-6, 6-4, 9-7, 6-0, the only instance of a victor making up so big a deficit including two match points, in the title match.

Despite his Davis Cup and Wimbledon heartaches of 1972, Nastase had the immeasurable consolation of winning the U.S. Open at Forest Hills from a seeming losing position, down 2-4 in the fourth set and a service break to open the fifth against Arthur Ashe. The score: 3-6, 6-3, 6-7 (1-5), 6-4, 6-3. It was his only major grass-court singles prize.

His finest season was 1973, when he was regarded as No. 1 in the world after winning the Italian, French, and 13 other tournaments, and downing Tom Okker in the Masters final, 6-3, 7-5, 4-6, 6-3. That season he won 15 of 31 tourneys on a 118-17 match record, also eight doubles for an overall total of 23, tying Rod Laver's open-era record (17 singles, 6 doubles), broken in 1979 by John McEnroe's 27.

Though he provoked controversy, and his career was marred by fines, disqualifications, and suspensions, Nastase was good-natured and friendly off-court. He had a sense of humor in his oncourt shenanigans, but frequently did not know when to stop and lost control of himself. "I am a little crazy," he said, "but I try to be a good boy."

He was expert at putting the ball just beyond an opponent's reach, and applying discomfiting spin. He lobbed and retrieved splendidly, in his prime possibly the fastest player of all, and he could play either baseline or serve-and-volley. In 1976 he was the first European to exceed $1 million in career prize money, and had a career total of $2,076,761. Nastase played World Team Tennis for Hawaii in 1976 and Los Angeles in 1977 and 1978, leading the latter to the league title in 1978 as player-coach.

Ilie Nastase: The sorcerer's apprentice. (Jack Mecca)

Eight times between 1970 and 1977 he was ranked in the World Top Ten, No. 1, in 1973, the year he won the French and Italian back-to-back, an unusual coupling.

In a career begun in the amateur era and continued in the open era, he was one of five players to win more than 100 pro titles in singles (57) and doubles (51). He was inducted into the Hall of Fame in 1991. Ilie, who lives in New York with his American wife, Alexandra, reaped considerable international attention again by running for mayor of Bucharest in 1996, but he was defeated. "Probably a very good thing for him and Bucharest," chuckled Tiriac.

MAJOR TITLES (7)—*French singles, 1973; U.S. singles, 1972; French doubles, 1970; Wimbledon doubles, 1973; U.S. doubles, 1975; Wimbledon mixed, 1970, 1972.* DAVIS CUP— *1966, 1967, 1968, 1969, 1970, 1971, 1972, 1973, 1974, 1975, 1976, 1977, 1979, 1980, 1982, 1983, 1984, 1985; record: 74-22 in singles, 35-15 in doubles.* SINGLES RECORD IN THE MA-

MARTINA NAVRATILOVA
Czechoslovakia/United States (1956—)

As the game's most prolific winner of the open era—probably ever—Martina Navratilova, the puissant left-hander, continues to add to her record totals. Yet dabbling in doubles—she won the Wimbledon mixed in 1995 with Jonathan Stark—Marvelous Martina retired from singles at the 1994 year-end WTA Championships at Madison Square Garden in an opening-round defeat by Gabriela Sabatini, 6-4, 6-2. Thousands cheered and wept, saying goodbye and thanks for the memories. She had done so much in New York, winning that prime championship eight times in singles (five times runnerup), 10 times in doubles, plus four singles and 11 doubles titles across the East River at the U.S. Open.

Nobody, ever, has such a glittering trove of numbers. As a pro since 1973, she played the most singles tournaments (380) and matches (1,650), and won the most titles (167) and matches (1,438) with a won-lost mark of 1,438-212. She won more prize money, $20,344,061, than all but Ivan Lendl and Pete Sampras.

Her doubles feats, attesting to a grandeur of completeness, were as sparkling: played the second most tournaments (286) and the most matches (1,111), and won the most titles (162) and matches (989) with a won-lost mark of 989-122. Throw in infrequent but very positive mixed doubles: played 27 tournaments, won 8 with a won-lost of 94-19. Overall for this three-way stretcher: played the most tournaments (693) and matches (2,874); won the most titles (337) and matches (2,521) with a 2,521-353 won-lost. Thus she batted .872 in singles, .890 in doubles, .832 in mixed—.877 for everything. It means she won 48.6 percent of all the tournaments she entered. Whew!

In the matter of major titles, her starburst of 56 (18 singles, 31 doubles, 7 mixed) didn't quite reach Margaret Court's stratospheric 62 (24-19-

19). Despite her record nine Wimbledons in singles she's still a step behind Billie Jean King's overall record of 20, Martina holding 9-7-3.

A sure shot for the Hall of Fame, arguably the greatest player of all time, Martina was born on Oct. 18, 1956, in Prague, Czechoslovakia, and became a U.S. citizen in 1981, after defecting six years earlier. She was raised by her mother, Jana, and stepfather, Mirek Navratil, whose name she took.

Despite her upbringing on slow clay in the small town of Revnice, outside of Prague, she has always been a tornado-like attacker, a net-rusher. She attracted notice at 16 in Paris, the French Open of 1973, by serving-and-volleying a clay specialist and former champ, Nancy Richey, to defeat, and reaching the quarters unseeded.

Her lustrous 16-year rivalry with Chris Evert was launched that year in Akron, Ohio, an indoor defeat. "She was overweight, but eager and gifted," Evert remembered. "It was a close match (7-6, 6-3). Even though I'd never heard of her, and couldn't pronounce or spell her name, I could tell she'd be trouble. Especially if she got in shape."

She was trouble, and eventually the 5-foot-7½, 140-pound Navratilova made extreme fitness her trademark in chasing and overcoming Evert, who became her good friend. Although Evert led in the rivalry, 21-4, at the high point of her dominance, Navratilova won their last encounter, Chicago, in 1988, 6-2, 6-2, to wind up with a 43-37 edge. Three years later, also in Chicago, Martina scaled Evert's seemingly unattainable record of 157 pro singles tournament victories. By beating Jana Novotna from two match points down, 7-6 (7-4), 4-6, 7-5, she nailed victory No. 158, and kept going. She had unknowingly begun to stalk Evert at home with her initial title, Pilsen, in 1973.

Her proudest times were spent in the game's temple, Centre Court, Wimbledon, where she became the all-time singles champ by defeating Zina Garrison, 6-4, 6-1, in 1990—her ninth championship. The record of eight had been achieved more than a half-century before when Helen Wills Moody beat Helen Jacobs in 1938.

Navratilova, yet pudgy, began her run at Moody by coming from behind in the third set to beat top-seeded Evert, 2-6, 6-4, 7-5, in the 1978 final. She repeated over Evert, but was deterred, momentarily, in the 1980 and 1981 semis by Evert, 1-6, 6-1, 6-2, and Hana Mandlikova, 7-5, 4-6, 6-1.

Rebounding, she reeled off championships in six successive years, snapping Suzanne Lenglen's mark of five (1919–23). Driving to the 1988 final, she had rolled up 47 straight match wins, three short of Moody's Wimbledon record streak (Moody, who didn't enter annually, won her eight titles between 1927 and 1938). But Martina was stopped by the Grand Slammer of that year, Steffi Graf, 5-7, 6-2, 6-1.

Graf beat her for the title in 1989, too, but lost to Garrison in the 1990 semis. Thus Martina triumphed again in her 11th final. There would be one last Centre Court singles final, the 12th (a 31st major), in 1994—a no-lose situation since just getting there at 37 was a triumph itself. Martina was brilliant in a quarterfinal revival against 1993 finalist Jana Novotna, 5-7, 6-0, 6-1 (reversing their 1993 semi result), and sharp enough to get past unseeded Gigi Fernandez, 6-4, 7-6 (8-6). Whatever the sentiment of the occasion and the crowd, the record book says she did lose the final—valiantly, to Conchita Martinez's backhand passers, 6-4, 3-6, 6-3. The Big M left some lofty records at the Big W for her 22 years besides the titles: most consecutive finals (9), most matches (279), singles wins (119), doubles wins (80), overall wins (243). She was 119-13 in singles, 80-14 in doubles, 44-9 in mixed.

That, of course, has been her masterpiece, but Navratilova also won four U.S., three Australian and two French singles.

Winning the U.S. was her most frustrating trial. Not until her 11th try, in 1983 (having lost the 1981 final in a tie-breaker to Tracy Austin) did Navratilova make it: 6-1, 6-3, over Evert. In 1991, almost 35, she was the tourney's oldest losing finalist since 40-year-old Molla Mallory in 1924.

Only one prize, a singles Grand Slam, eluded her—barely in 1983 and 1984. Although 1983 was her most overpowering season (16 victories in 17 tournaments on an 86-1 match record), it was 1984 (13 victories in 15 tourneys on 78-2) when the Slam seemed certain. With three of the titles in her satchel, she reached the semis of the last that year, the Australian, on a pro record 74-match winning streak, eclipsing Evert's 55 of 1974. However, Helena Sukova intervened, 1-6, 6-3, 7-5. After that Martina took off on a 54-match streak, severed by Hana Mandlikova. Mandlikova also snipped her second longest streak, 56, in the Australian final of 1987.

In 1983 a Slam never got started. Kathy Horvath, ranked 33rd, upset Navratilova in the fourth round of the first major, the French. Thereafter Martina won the next three, and so Sukova ended her string of six major titles.

Navratilova did, however, register a doubles Grand Slam with Pam Shriver in 1984. Perhaps the greatest of all teams, Navratilova-Shriver won 20 majors (equaling the record total of Louise Brough and Margaret duPont, 1942–57). The Navratilova-Shriver combine produced 79 tournament victories, including 10 season-climaxing Virginia Slims titles, and a record 109-match winning streak between 1983 and a 1985 loss in the Wimbledon final to Liz Smylie and Kathy Jordan.

As a tireless all-round campaigner, Martina piled up awesome singles and doubles totals. She won more than 20 titles in singles and doubles six years: 29 in 1982 (15 singles) and 1983 (16 singles). Twelve years she won more than 100 matches overall, singles and doubles, a high of 160 (against seven losses) in 1982.

During 1985, 1986 and 1987, she was in the final of all 11 majors (Australian not held in 1986), winning six, a singular feat until Steffi Graf played in 12 straight between 1987 and 1990, winning 10.

In 1987 she made a rare triple at the U.S. Open (singles, doubles, mixed), the third of the open era.

Martina Navratilova: Greatest of all? (Russ Adams)

From 1973 through 1982 Navratilova was no worse than No. 4 in the world rankings, attaining No. 1 in 1978, keeping it in 1979. She returned for a record run of 150 weeks, 1982 into 1987, until supplanted by Graf in 1987, who broke the record with 186 straight weeks. She ranked in the U.S. Top Ten 14 years, no worse than No. 3 (1980 and 1981), and at No. 1 a record 12 years, 11 straight since 1982, also a record.

Disapproving of what was termed Navratilova's increasing "Americanization," sports federation authorities in the communist Czechoslovak government reportedly planned to curtail her travel. "Learning this," she said, "I knew I had to defect." She announced her intention of becoming a U.S. citizen at the U.S. Open of 1975. For years after she was considered a "non-person," her results never printed or announced in Czechoslovakia.

Returning to her homeland in triumph (and to the government's discomfort) as a U.S. citizen in 1986, she led her adopted country's team to a Federation Cup victory, as she had Czechoslovakia 11 years before. Playing for the U.S., she was peerless, unbeaten, and helped win two other Federation as well as one Wightman Cup.

Oakland was her last tour stop prior to the Garden in 1994, and Martina's last final on her own. She lost narrowly and gamely to Arantxa Sanchez Vicario, 1-6, 7-6 (7-5), 7-6 (7-3), despite leading 4-1 in the second, and serving for it at 5-3 in the third. "It would have been nice to have said goodbye to the tour with a win," she sighed after the 2-hour, 23-minute test.

But it had been a pleasure to watch Martina dominate for more than two decades.

MAJOR TITLES *(56)—Australian singles, 1981, 1983, 1985; French singles, 1982, 1984; Wimbledon singles, 1978, 1979, 1982, 1983, 1984, 1985, 1986, 1987, 1990; U.S. singles, 1983, 1984, 1986, 1987; Australian doubles, 1980, 1982, 1983, 1984, 1985, 1987, 1988, 1989; French doubles, 1975, 1982, 1984, 1985, 1986, 1987, 1988; Wimbledon doubles, 1976, 1979, 1981, 1982, 1983, 1984, 1986; U.S. doubles, 1977, 1978, 1980, 1983, 1984, 1986, 1987, 1989, 1990; French mixed, 1974, 1985; Wimbledon mixed; 1985, 1993, 1995; U.S. mixed, 1985, 1987.* OTHER U.S. TITLES *(8)—Indoor singles, 1975, 1981, 1984, 1986; Indoor doubles, 1979, with Billie Jean King; 1981, 1984, 1985, with Pam Shriver.* FEDERATION CUP— *1975, 1982, 1986, 1989; record: 20-0 in singles, 16-0 in doubles.* WIGHTMAN CUP—*1983; record: 2-0 in singles, 1-0 in doubles.* SINGLES RECORD IN THE MAJORS: *Australian (46-7), French (52-10), Wimbledon (119-13), U.S. (89-17).*

JOHN NEWCOMBE
Australia (1944—)

When John Newcombe and Tony Roche, an Australian pair, won the Wimbledon doubles of 1965, it was the start not only of an extraordinary string of major titles for Newcombe but also for the two of them as a unit.

Two years earlier, though, Newcombe, at 19, attracted international attention as one of the youngest Aussies ever to play Davis Cup. He was selected for the finale to play singles against the U.S. Though beaten by both Dennis Ralston and Chuck McKinley during a 3-2 U.S. victory, Newcombe served notice that he was a player to reckon with when he pushed Wimbledon champion McKinley to four hard sets in the decisive fifth match.

Newcombe and the left-handed Roche, one of the great doubles teams in history, won five Wimbledons together, a modern record (topped only by the English Doherty brothers, who won eight between 1897 and 1905, and the English Renshaw brothers, who won seven between 1880 and 1889). Newcombe and Roche also won the U.S. in 1967, the French in 1967 and 1969, and the Australian in 1965, 1967, 1971 and 1976, standing as one of only four teams to win all the Big Four titles during a career and leading all teams with 12 majors. Their three successive Wimbledons, 1968, 1969 and 1970, topped by countrymen Mark Woodforde and Todd Woodbridge's four straight from 1993 through 1996, enabled them to set a tourney record of 18 straight doubles match wins, eclipsed by the Woodies' 24.

It was in singles, though, that Newcombe made his name. He and Rod Laver are the only players to win the men's singles at Forest Hills and Wimbledon as amateurs and pros. Newcombe was the last amateur champion at Wimbledon in 1967, and repeated in 1970 and 1971 during the open era.

In all Newcombe, a 6-foot, 170-pound right-hander, won 25 major titles in singles, doubles, and mixed doubles to stand second behind Roy Emerson (28) in the list of all-time male championships.

John David Newcombe was born May 23, 1944, in Sydney, and was more interested in other sports as a youngster. Not until he was 17 did a career in tennis appeal to him. But he was powerful, athletic and extremely competitive, and Australian Davis Cup captain Harry Hopman was glad when Newcombe turned his full attention to tennis. Newcombe helped Hopman win four Cups, 1964–67, and then returned to Cup play in 1973, when all pros were reinstated, to be part of

perhaps the strongest team ever, alongside Laver, Ken Rosewall and Mal Anderson. In the finale that year Newcombe and Laver were overpowering. Both beat Stan Smith and Tom Gorman in singles, and teamed in crushing Smith and Erik van Dillen in the doubles during a 5-0 Australian victory that ended five-year possession of the Cup by the U.S.

Newcombe also played in the World Cup in 1970, the inaugural of the since disbanded team match between the Aussies and the U.S., and helped win five of those Cups for his country.

Newcombe's serve, forehand and volleying were the backbone of his attacking game, which was at its best on grass. His heavy serve was possibly the best of his era. Grass was the setting for his foremost singles wins, the three Wimbledons plus two U.S. Championships at Forest Hills in 1967 and 1973. "You're only as good as your second serve and first volley," was the motto of this intelligent, fun-loving Aussie, and he lived up to it.

Newcombe regretted missing successive Wimbledons of 1972 and 1973 when he felt he might have added to his string. In 1972 he was a member of the World Championship Tennis pro troupe that was banned because of the quarrels between its leader, Lamar Hunt, and the International Tennis Federation. In 1973 Newcombe was a member of the players union, Association of Tennis Pros, which boycotted Wimbledon in another dispute with the ITF. The following year he stretched his Wimbledon match win streak to 18 before losing to Rosewall in the quarter-finals. That year Newcombe won the World Championship Tennis singles over an adolescent Bjorn Borg, 17.

Newcombe felt, "I'm at my best in a five-set match, especially if I get behind. My adrenaline starts pumping." This was evident in two of his outstanding triumphs, both over Stan Smith, a strong rival for world supremacy in the early 1970s. Newcombe beat Smith, 6-3, 5-7, 2-6, 6-4, 6-4, in the 1971 Wimbledon title match, and 6-1,

John Newcombe: Best server of his time. (Peter Mecca)

3-6, 6-3, 3-6, 6-4, during the 1973 Davis Cup finale, rating the latter as his finest performance.

In 1967 he was the No. 1 amateur in the world, and in 1970 and 1971 No. 1 of all. He was one of the first to sign a contract to play World Team Tennis (with Houston) in 1974, his presence helping give the new league credibility, although he played just that one season. His best pro season was 1971, when he won five of 19 singles tourneys on a 53-14 match record.

He totaled 73 pro titles, 32 in singles, 41 in doubles, and won $1,062,408. Newcombe was named to the Hall of Fame, along with Roche, in 1986. He is married to former German player Angelika Pfannenburg and was appointed Australian Davis Cup captain in 1995.

MAJOR TITLES *(25)—Australian singles, 1973, 1975; Wimbledon singles, 1967, 1970, 1971; U.S. singles, 1967, 1973; Australian doubles, 1965, 1967, 1971, 1973, 1976;* *French doubles, 1967, 1969, 1973; Wimbledon doubles, 1965, 1966, 1968, 1969, 1970, 1974; U.S. doubles, 1967, 1971, 1973; U.S. mixed, 1964.* DAVIS CUP—*1963, 1964, 1965, 1966, 1967, 1973, 1975, 1976; record: 16-7 in singles, 9-2 in doubles.* SINGLES RECORD IN THE MAJORS: *Australian (45-14), French (17-9), Wimbledon (45-11), U.S. (45-9).*

KEN ROSEWALL
Australia (1934—)

As the Doomsday Stroking Machine, the remarkable Kenneth Robert "Muscles" Rosewall was a factor in three decades of tennis, winning his first major titles, the Australian and French singles in 1953, and continuing as a tournament winner past his 43rd birthday.

He was yet a tough foe into 1978. At the close of the 1977 season, he was still ranked as one of the top 15 players in the game on the ATP computer, having won two of 24 tournaments on a 44-23 match record.

"It's something I enjoy and find I still do well," was his simple explanation of his prowess in 1977, "but I never imagined myself playing so long when I turned pro in 1957."

The son of a Sydney, Australia, grocer, Rosewall was born in that city Nov. 2, 1934, and grew up there. A natural left-hander, he was taught to play right-handed by his father, Robert Rosewall, and developed a peerless backhand. Some felt his size (5-foot-7, 135 pounds) would impede him, but it was never a problem. He moved quickly, with magnificent anticipation and perfect balance, and never suffered a serious injury. Though his serve wasn't formidable, he placed it well, and backed it up with superb volleying. Rosewall was at home on any surface, and at the baseline or the net. He had an even temperament, was shy and reticent, but good-natured.

Although Rosewall, the little guy, always seemed overshadowed by a rival, first Lew Hoad, then Pancho Gonzalez and Rod Laver, he outlasted them all, and had the last competitive word. Even when Laver was acknowledged as the best in the world, Rosewall could bother him, and twice shocked Rod in the rich World Championship Tennis finals in Dallas (1971 and 1972), snatching the $50,000 first prize from the favorite's grasp. The latter match, thought by many to be the greatest ever played—a 3½-hour struggle watched by millions on TV—went to Rosewall, 4-6, 6-0, 6-3, 6-7 (3-7), 7-6, (7-5), when he stroked two magnificent backhand returns to escape a seemingly untenable position in the decisive tie-breaker and win by two points, the closest finish of an important championship until Boris Becker beat Ivan Lendl, also 7-5, in a fifth-set tie-breaker, for the 1988 Masters title.

Rosewall and Hoad, born only 21 days apart, Ken the elder, were linked as teammates and rivals almost from their first days on court. In 1952 as 17-year-olds they made an immediate impact on their first overseas tour, both reaching the quarterfinals of the U.S. Championships at Forest Hills, Ken beating the No. 1 American, Vic Seixas, 3-6, 6-2, 7-5, 5-7, 6-3. Late the following year (having won the Wimbledon doubles together), shortly after their 19th birthdays, they became the youngest Davis Cup defenders, joining for Australia to repel the U.S. challenge in the finale. Rosewall beat Seixas in the decisive last match, 6-2, 2-6, 6-3, 6-4, to ensure a 3-2 victory.

Though Hoad was considerably stronger physically than Rosewall, who had been given the sardonic nickname "Muscles" by his countrymen, Ken always managed to keep up with (and often surpass) him in the early days. Hoad beat Rosewall in the 1956 Wimbledon final, but his bid for a Grand Slam was spoiled when Rosewall knocked him off in the U.S. final at Forest Hills, 4-6, 6-2, 6-2, 6-3.

Linked in doubles as well as the public mind, Ken and Lew might well have made a Grand Slam together in 1953, but came up three wins short. After taking the Australian, French and Wimbledon, they had a bad day in Boston, dropping a close U.S. quarter-final decision to unseeded Americans Hal Burrows and Straight Clark, 5-7, 14-12, 18-16, 9-7. But they (Kenny

Ken Rosewall: The Iron Man with his backhand. (UPI)

unerring of return from the right court) grabbed that title in 1956, standing as one of four teams to win all four, apparently an Aussie specialty. Frank Sedgman and Ken McGregor preceded them, followed by Roy Emerson and Neale Fraser, and John Newcombe and Tony Roche.

After helping Australia win the Davis Cup over the U.S. in 1956, Rosewall turned pro to take on the professional king, Pancho Gonzalez. Gonzalez stayed on top, winning their head-to-head tour, 50-26, but it was apparent that Rosewall belonged at the uppermost level. Thus began one of the longest professional careers, certainly the most distinguished in regard to significant victories over so long a span. Rosewall won the first of his three U.S. Pro singles titles over Laver in 1963, the second by beating Gonzalez and Laver in succession in 1965 and the third over Cliff Drysdale in 1971.

He holds several longevity records. Fourteen years after his 1956 Forest Hills triumph over Hoad he beat the favored Tony Roche, 10 years his junior, 2-6, 6-4, 7-6 (5-2), 6-3, to win the U.S. Championship again. Eighteen years after, he was the finalist (having beaten favored John Newcombe, 6-7 (3-5), 7-6 (5-1), 6-3) but was crushed in 1974 by Jimmy Connors. Twenty years after appearing in the first of four Wimbledon finals, he lost the 1974 final to Connors. The only big one Rosewall missed out on was Wimbledon singles, but he won the doubles twice. Nineteen years after his first major title, the Australian, he won it again, in 1972. Twenty years after his first Davis Cup appearance he returned to help Australia win once again in 1973, and played his last cup match in 1975. He played on four Australian Davis Cup winners and three World Cup winners in the since disbanded team match against the U.S.

Altogether, Rosewall won 18 major titles in singles, doubles and mixed, the sixth-highest male total. In 1974 he tried World Team Tennis for a season, serving as player-coach of the Pittsburgh Triangles. He was the second tennis player to cross one million dollars in prize money, following Laver, and had a career total of $1,600,300.

Like Laver, Gonzalez and Hoad, and a few others, he had one of those rare careers spanning the amateur era, pro one-night stand years and the open era. His victories were innumerable, but in the last section, begun at age 33, he won 50 titles, 32 in singles, 18 in doubles. The first of those was the baptismal "Open," the British Hard Court singles at Bournemouth in April 1968; the second, the initial major open, the French, a month later—both over Laver. His last pro triumph, Hong Kong in 1977 over Tom Gorman, was recorded two weeks after his 43rd birthday, making him the second oldest (just shy of Gonzalez) to win an open-era title.

Still going, like some super battery, gray but the same in frame and slick of backhand, Ken is just warming up for the super senior wars ahead in the 85-and-over league.

Rosewall was named to the Hall of Fame in 1980, along with Hoad.

MAJOR TITLES *(18)—Australian singles, 1953, 1955, 1971, 1972; French singles, 1953, 1968; U.S. singles, 1956, 1970; Australian doubles, 1953, 1956, 1972; French doubles, 1953, 1968; Wimbledon doubles, 1953, 1956; U.S. doubles, 1956, 1969; U.S. mixed, 1956.* DAVIS CUP—*1953, 1954, 1955, 1956, 1973, 1975; record: 17-2 in singles, 2-1 in doubles.* SINGLES RECORD IN THE MAJORS: *Australian (45-10), French (24-3), Wimbledon (47-11), U.S. (57-10).*

PETE SAMPRAS
United States (1971—)

It just happened. He couldn't explain it or understand it. "I didn't know what I was doing. I was just a new kid. Everything I did worked," Pete Sampras would say later, discussing his Flushing Meadow triumph of 1990 that anointed him as the youngest of all U.S. champions at 19 years, 1 month.

He knows what he's doing now, doing it as Silky Sampras, smoothly gliding along a path of greatness in an outwardly unconcerned and effortless manner while he mounts a planned and concerted assault on the citadels of the past. Pete knows his tennis history, knows that he's edging closer to the spire man of major championships, Aussie Roy Emerson, who seized 12 singles between 1961 and 1967 (6 Australian, 2 each French, Wimbledon, U.S.). Squelching the perpetual motion of Michael Chang in the 1996 all-Californian U.S. Open final, 6-1, 6-4, 7-6 (7-3), Pete was the winner for a fourth time (the record is seven), and boosted his major total to eight. He had passed John McEnroe, Mats Wilander, John Newcombe, René Lacoste, Henri Cochet, and Willie Renshaw; stood even with Ivan Lendl, Jimmy Connors, Ken Rosewall, Fred Perry; was within sight of Emerson, Bjorn Borg and Rod Laver's 11, Bill Tilden's 10. Moreover, except for Borg, he was younger than any of them had been at the eighth, and Borg was finished at 25. At that age Pete felt he was just flexing his muscles.

Impressive flexing, although he had an off Wimbledon in 1996, losing in the quarters to the new champ Richard Krajicek, 7-5, 7-6 (7-3), 6-4. Pete was, after all, shooting for his fourth in a row, and had won 25 straight where only Borg (41) and Laver (31) had longer streaks. He would still close out his ninth professional campaign as No. 1 a fourth consecutive year. At 6-foot-1, 175 pounds, with a full head of dark hair, the lanky Greek high school drop-out from Palos Verdes (residing in Tampa, Fla.) was handling his affluence and standing modestly and well. "It's not a good year unless I win two majors. They're what count," he said.

But he was happy to salvage 1996 with one, considering the year's heartaches with the death of his coach and best friend Tim Gullikson of a brain tumor, which had been discovered at the Australian Open of 1995. Though unprepared for the French, which followed Gullikson's funeral, he made his finest showing in Paris, the one major that has befuddled him, falling in the semis to the champ Yevgeny Kafelnikov, 7-6 (7-4), 6-0, 6-2, after exciting, draining five-set wins over ex-champs Jim Courier and Sergi Bruguera as well as Todd Martin.

Born Aug. 1, 1971, in Washington, D.C., the right-hander grew up in Southern California. His older sister, Stella Sampras, played professionally and now coaches the women's varsity of her alma mater, UCLA. Pete's tennis life was changed at 14 by a pediatrician (and moonlighting tennis pedagogue), Dr. Pete Fisher. Fisher, feeling that Pete's two-handed backhand and baselining were childish, preached volleying, a free-flowing traditional backhand and reverence for the greats of yesteryear in performance and behavior, Rod Laver and Ken Rosewall. As Pete grew, so did his vaunted serve, and everything fell into place. Later it was Tim Gullikson, Pete says, "who helped me to grow up, compete, focus, learn to play on grass. I owe so much to him."

Pete was out of his first U.S. Open, 1988, almost before it opened. But he got a footnote in 1989, deposing the champ, Mats Wilander, in the second round, 5-7, 6-3, 1-6, 6-1, 6-4, and reached the fourth. The next year he was golden, if "un-conscious," a long-shot seeded 12th, ranked No. 81 when the season commenced, who went through in a spray of aces (100) on a loss of four sets. He showed his mettle by taking out ex-champs Lendl and McEnroe back-to-back. Pete demonstrated authenticity, the fact that he was unstoppable, by coolly sealing off canny third-seeded Lendl's counterattack in the quarters, 6-4, 7-6 (7-3), 3-6, 4-6, 6-2, embellishing with 26 aces. "He just kicked my ass," was Andre Agassi's terse summation of unbreakable Pete's 106-minute final-round caper, 6-4, 6-3, 6-2. Up jumped the name of Oliver Campbell, dead man dispossessed. He had held the record as youngest champ (19½) for one century. Pete was 19 years, 1 month.

A few months later Pete made a bigger financial splash, collecting a record $2 million for winning the inaugural Grand Slam Cup in Munich over Brad Gilbert, 6-3, 6-4, 6-2. Uncomfortable with all the attention brought by these deeds, and a rocketing No. 5 in the rankings, he actually seemed relieved to have the U.S. title lifted from him in the 1991 quarters by Courier. But he matured, accepted the responsibilities and challenges of life at the top, and became a solid No. 1. Though Agassi took it away momentarily by beating Pete in the 1995 Australian Open, Sampras struck back in the U.S. final eight months later, dispiriting Andre in a comprehensive four-set win. Their hot rivalry stood at 12-8 for Pete at the close of 1996.

Davis Cup was not altogether happy for Pete, especially his jitters-wracked debut in the 1991 final. A raucous, nationalistic French crowd in Lyon unnerved him, and Henri Leconte and Guy Forget pummeled him to defeats that gave the French an unexpected Cup. He played a winning right-court doubles part (alongside McEnroe) in the 3-1 Cup victory over Switzerland in 1992. In the 1995 final at Moscow, on a clay court spread especially to spread-eagle him within Olympic Stadium, Pete responded by taking charge in the 3-2 victory over Russia in as glorious a weekend triple as performed by any American abroad: a

Pete Sampras: Ever ready for the kill. (Wide World)

five-set out-grinding of dirt maven Andrei Chesnokov, and a nifty duet with Todd Martin in the straight-set doubles and a curtain-lowering riddling of Kafelnikov in a straight-set shower of aces (16) and forehand winners (19).

All his extraordinary qualities were on display: the grit and stubbornness underlying fluid groundies, thundering serves, casual yet deadly volleys and racing forehands.

It all appears so relaxed and glissando, although his head can still slump in adverse moments. Beneath the calm facade lurk certain physical and emotional frailties. This was evident when he collapsed the instant the Chesnokov ordeal ended, and the memorable 1996 evening at Flushing when he lost his lunch but not his title. Ill and vomiting in the conclusive fifth-set tie-breaker of his defining quarter-final win over Alex Corretja, Pete wormed his way out

of a match point with a lunging volley. Staggering, he hashed a second-serve ace—"I don't know where it came from . . . I was out of it"—to give himself match point at 8-7. Whereupon, "not wanting to hit another ball," he didn't have to as Corretja lost the only way Pete could win—a double fault. Kismet.

"Ah, but that's sweet Pete," says longtime friend and rival, Courier. "Just when you think he's dying, that's when he kills you."

At the close of 1996, he had won 44 of 142 singles tournaments on 502-139 (.796) in matches, 117-22 in the majors, and more prize money than anyone else, $25,562,347. In the majors he had won 18 of 21 five-set matches. His most productive season was 1994: he won 10 of 18 singles tournaments on 77-12; it was also productive financially, setting the single season record, $5,415,066. In the 1992 Olympics he was beaten in the third round by Russian Andrei Cherkasov, 6-7 (7-9), 1-6, 7-5, 6-0, 6-3.

MAJOR TITLES (8)—*Australian singles, 1994; Wimbledon singles, 1993, 1994, 1995; U.S. singles, 1990, 1993, 1995, 1996.* OTHER U.S. TITLES (2)—*Hard Court singles, 1991, 1992.* DAVIS CUP—*1991, 1992, 1994, 1995; record, 11-5 in singles, 3-0 in doubles.* SINGLES RECORD IN THE MAJORS: *Australian (23-5), French (19-7), Wimbledon (31-5), U.S. (44-5).*

ARANTXA SANCHEZ VICARIO
Spain (1971—)

Buzzing and flitting the width and breadth of arenas across the planet, the Barcelona Bumblebee—Arantxa Sanchez Vicario—is unceasing in determined pursuit of tennis balls, none seeming too distant to be retrieved in some manner and returned again and again to demoralize opponents. This has been going on most of her life, almost half of it as a professional, with no reduction in her zest or desire to win.

Long after the glamorous Lili de Alvarez of Madrid enhanced the 1926, 1927 and 1928 Wimbledon finals, industrious little Sanchez Vicario, a 5-foot-6, 130-pound right-hander, revived female tennis in their country. It happened on a June afternoon in Paris, 1989, as 17-year-old Arantxa faced defeat in the French final. Seventh-seeded, she had done very well to get that far on her third try. She had come to attention the year before by chasing the all-time champ out of town: Chris Evert's last stand, 6-3, 7-6 (7-4). But now Steffi Graf, winner of five consecutive majors, was across the net and serving for the title at 5-4 in the third. Whereupon the intransigent Barcelonan went into overdrive, punching topspin forehands and two-fisted backhand drives relentlessly, relinquishing only two points and winning, 7-6 (8-6), 3-6, 7-5. Not only the first Spanish woman to take a major, she was the youngest French champ—until Monica Seles weighed in at 16 the following year.

She would become one of 12 women to appear in the finals of all four majors, winning the French again over Mary Pierce in 1994 and the U.S. over Graf that year to be named the ITF's World Champion. She lost Wimbledon and French finals to Graf in 1995 and 1996, the Australian to Pierce in 1995.

Perhaps her finest matches were heart-stopping defeats by Graf as they goaded each other to the heights at Wimbledon '95 and French '96. Arantxa served for victory at 5-4 and 7-6 in a shot-making extravaganza in Paris, losing, 6-3, 6-7 (4-7), 10-8 in 3 hours, 3 minutes. On Centre Court they waged a game of games, the 11th of the third set. On it went for 20 minutes and 13 deuces. Serving, Arantxa had eight game points, but couldn't make it, 4-6, 6-1, 7-5, losing the last six points.

Aranzazu Isabel Maria "Arantxa" Sanchez was born Dec. 18, 1971, in Barcelona. The last of a historic tennis-playing Sanchez brood of four, she was a surprise to her non-tennis parents, Emilio and the former Marisa Vicario, whose name Arantxa attached as a tribute. Arantxa is also the subject of a family tale. After the births of Marisa (a varsity player at Pepperdine in Santa Monica, Cal.) and Emilio and Javier (both successful pros on the ATP circuit), Marisa (senior) was told she could have no more children. However, three years later, not long after taking the children on a roller-coaster ride, she became

Arantxa Sanchez Vicario: Two-fisted powerhouse. (Wide World)

pregnant. Now she has a special place in her heart for that shake-and-rolling rattler at the Tibidabo amusement park overlooking the city. The babe's given name, Aranzazu, is that of a Basque saint.

A woman of sunny nature, Arantxa presents a rather severe look at play, her flowing black hair tightly headbanded above a contentious countenance that conveys her outlook: surrender never. Ever a hustler on short, spirited legs, she never gets enough tennis. Strictly a baseliner at first, she has constantly improved her volleying to become one of the finer doubles players. She likes the dual load of singles and doubles, carrying it better than anyone else, usually leading women in matches played and won.

Arantxa has represented Spain handsomely in three Olympics and 11 years of Federation Cup. In 1992 she won a bronze in singles, silver in doubles with Conchita Martinez; in 1996, silver in singles, losing the final to Lindsay Davenport, 7-6 (8-6), 6-2, and bronze again with Martinez in doubles. She and Conchita wrapped up the Fed Cup four times, 1991 and 1993–95. As a pro for 11 campaigns she has been in the Top Ten every year between 1989 and 1996.

Manolo Santana: Magician on clay. (UPI)

At the close of 1996, amazing two-way Arantxa had won 24 of 182 singles tournaments on 534-166 (.762) in matches, 49 of 168 doubles tournaments on 423-119 (.780) in matches. That gave her 73 titles and a total of 957-285 in all matches (.771) plus $11,632,976 in prize money.

MAJOR TITLES *(11)—French singles, 1989, 1994; U.S. singles, 1994; Australian doubles, 1992, 1995, 1996; Wimbledon doubles, 1995; U.S. doubles, 1993, 1994. French mixed, 1990, 1992.* FEDERATION CUP—*1986, 1987, 1988, 1989, 1990, 1991, 1992, 1993, 1994, 1995, 1996; record: 35-13 in singles, 17-6 in doubles.* SINGLES RECORD IN THE MAJORS: *Australian (31-6), French (52-8), Wimbledon (27-10), U.S. (40-9).*

MANOLO SANTANA

Spain (1938—)

One of the masters of legerdemain, Manuel Martinez "Manolo" Santana was the first post–World War II European to gain universal respect because he not only won the most difficult clay-court event, the French singles in 1961 and 1964, but also the grass-court gems, Wimbledon of 1966 and the U.S. Championship of 1965 at Forest Hills. In doing so, the engaging Spaniard was the first European champ at Forest Hills since Frenchman Henri Cochet in 1928.

"He was a magician on clay," said Rod Laver. "Manolo could hit the most incredible angles, drive you crazy with topspin lobs or drop shots. And he improved his volleying so that he was dangerous on grass, too."

In 1965 Santana became a national hero in Spain and was decorated by the country's leader, Francisco Franco, with the coveted Medal of Isabella, qualifying for the title *Ilustrissimo.* That year Santana spearheaded the 4-1 upset of the U.S. at Barcelona during the Davis Cup campaign and led Spain all the way to the finale for the first time. Although the Spaniards were turned back, 4-1, Santana gave Roy Emerson his only defeat in 12 title-round singles. Two years later he drove Spain to the finale again, salvaging the only point in a 4-1 defeat by beating John Newcombe.

Only Italian Nicola Pietrangeli (164 singles and doubles in 46 ties) and Romanian Ilie Nastase played more Davis Cup than Santana, who played 120 singles (69-17) and doubles (23-11) in 46 matches between 1958 and 1973. He set Cup records by winning 13 singles matches in 1967 (equalled by Nastase in 1971), and also by winning 17 singles and doubles in 1965 and 1967 (topped by Nastase's 18 in 1971).

Born May 10, 1938, in Madrid, he worked as a ball boy at a local club and picked up the game. He was a very appealing player, a slender 5-foot-11 right-hander, who frequently smiled at play and was an admirable sportsman. His racket control was phenomenal, enabling him to hit with touch and power. He had great flair, the ability to improvise and to inspire himself and his partners and teammates. Never losing heart in the doubles of the 1965 Davis Cup against the U.S., he rallied partner Luis Arilla as they stormed back to beat Dennis Ralston and Clark Graebner, 4-6, 3-6, 6-3, 6-4, 11-9, in an emotional battle that clinched the decision. Cushions showered down on the two Spaniards as they were carried about the stadium court of the Real Club de Tennis in the manner of bullfighters. Santana and Arilla wept with joy at the most tremendous victory in Spanish tennis annals.

Less than a month later a similarly jubilant celebration was staged at Forest Hills after Santana jolted Cliff Drysdale in the U.S. final, 6-2, 7-9, 7-5, 6-1. A troupe of dancers from the World's Fair's Spanish Pavilion toted him from stadium to clubhouse, whereupon they serenaded him.

The following year was Santana's at Wimbledon, where he beat Ralston in the final, 6-4, 11-9, 6-4, and enthralled the gallery with his point and counterpoint thrusts.

His successes spurred the rapid development of tennis in Spain, where the sport was not much noticed prior to 1965. His protégé was Manuel Orantes, called Manolito (Little Manolo), who won the U.S. Championship at Forest Hills a decade after his own, though the surface had by then been transformed to clay.

Beginning in 1961, Santana was in the World Top Ten seven years, No. 1 in 1966. His career was virtually over when the open era arrived, but he did elate his countrymen by winning Barcelona in 1970, his last singles victory, plus three pro doubles titles.

Santana came out of retirement briefly in 1973 to play his last season of Davis Cup, and again in 1974 to act as player-coach for New York in the new World Team Tennis League. He was named to the Hall of Fame in 1984, the second Spaniard, following Manuel Alonso.

MAJOR TITLES (5)—*French singles, 1961, 1964; Wimbledon singles, 1966; U.S. singles, 1965; French doubles, 1963.* DAVIS CUP—*1958, 1959, 1960, 1961, 1962, 1963, 1964, 1965, 1966, 1967, 1968, 1969, 1970, 1973; record: 69-17 in singles, 23-11 in doubles.* SINGLES RECORD IN THE MAJORS: *French (33-6), Wimbledon (22-9), U.S. (25-7).*

Frank Sedgman: The first $100,000-a-year man. (New York Herald Tribune)

FRANK SEDGMAN

Australia (1927—)

The beginning of the most powerful dynasty in tennis history was in the strokes of Frank Allan Sedgman, the Australian savior of 1950.

Australia was sagging in the Davis Cup after World War II, losing four successive finales to the U.S. Then, in 1950, 22-year-old Sedgman—loser of both his singles the previous year—startled crowds at Forest Hills by beating Tom Brown and Ted Schroeder in singles, joining John Bromwich for the doubles win to spearhead a 4-1 victory for the Aussies.

Not since 1911—Norman Brookes—had an Aussie won three matches in a Cup triumph. In the company of Ken McGregor that year, Mervyn Rose and McGregor the next, and McGregor again in 1952, Sedgman led the way to three straight

Cups. In 1951 Sedgman became the first of nine Aussie men to win U.S. championships, 15 in all, at Forest Hills, and he repeated the following year.

Those Cup successes were the start of captain Harry Hopman's second stewardship under which Australia won the Davis trophy 15 times between 1950 and 1967. And also the start of Sedgman's nearly three years as the premier amateur.

Sedgman, an extremely athletic 5-foot-11, 170-pound right-hander, was born Oct. 29, 1927, in Mount Albert, Victoria, Australia, and was such an acquisitive winner of major titles during the briefest of stretches, 1949–53, that he stands third among all-time male champions with 22 major victories in singles, doubles and mixed doubles, three behind John Newcombe and six behind Roy Emerson.

In 1951 Sedgman and McGregor scored the only Grand Slam in men's doubles by winning all the majors (Australian, Wimbledon, French and U.S.) within a calendar year. They came oh-so-close to Slamming again the following year, going all the way to the U.S. final, where it took another Aussie, Merv Rose, allied with Yank Vic Seixas, to barely beat them, 3-6, 10-8, 10-8, 6-8, 8-6. As it was, Frank and Ken won seven straight major doubles, a male record, and Sedg had eight in a row, having taken the U.S. with John Bromwich in 1950. In 1952, his last season as an amateur, Sedgman was the last man to make a rare Wimbledon triple, adding the doubles (with McGregor) and mixed (with Doris Hart) to his singles conquest.

Speed, brilliant volleying and a heavy forehand were his chief assets, plus a fighting—yet good-natured—spirit.

Jack Kramer, proprietor of the professional tour and its foremost player, enticed Sedgman to become his challenger in 1953, and they played the customary head-to-head tour between the amateur-king-turned-pro-rookie and the incumbent, Kramer, who stayed on top, 54-41. However, Sedgman's share of the gate was $102,000, and he was the first male player to earn more than 100 grand in a season.

Sedgman continued to barnstorm with the pros into the 1960s. He was finalist to Pancho Gonzalez for the U.S. Pro singles championship in 1954 and won the U.S. Pro doubles with Andres Gimeno in 1961. Keeping himself unusually fit, he was able to launch a second professional career in 1974 when promoter Al Bunis formed the Grand Masters tour for ex-champs over 45. Sedgman won the Grand Masters championship in a season's-end playoff among the top eight players in 1975, 1977 and 1978, and in this second phase of professionalism won more than $250,000 over six seasons.

His fleeting residency in the World Top Ten covered 1949 through 1952, No. 1 the last two years. Sedgman was named to the Hall of Fame in 1979.

MAJOR TITLES (22)—*Australian singles, 1949, 1950; Wimbledon singles, 1952; U.S. singles, 1951, 1952; Australian doubles, 1951, 1952; French doubles, 1951, 1952; Wimbledon doubles, 1948, 1951, 1952; U.S. doubles, 1950, 1951; Australian mixed, 1949, 1950; French mixed, 1951, 1952; Wimbledon mixed, 1951, 1952; U.S. mixed, 1951, 1952.* DAVIS CUP—*1949, 1950, 1951, 1952; record: 16-3 in singles, 9-0 in doubles.* SINGLES RECORD IN THE MAJORS: *Australian (19-5), French (13-4), Wimbledon (26-6), U.S. (20-3).*

PANCHO SEGURA
Ecuador (1921—)

A curious sight was Francisco Olegario "Pancho" Segura when he appeared on the North American scene in 1941, a mite who began to make a big impression with jarring strokes and jovial personality despite seeming physical limitations. He had won his native Ecuadorian title at 17 in 1938 along with various other Latin American titles, and presently was on his way to big-time tennis in the U.S., riding a tennis scholarship at University of Miami.

A big smile and a yen for the battle offset what appeared, at first appraisal, to be disadvantages: an unorthodox two-fisted forehand, flimsy-looking bowed legs and a 5-foot-6 frame. Yet his footwork was admirable. He was quick, nimble, extremely effective. By 1942 he had a No. 4 U.S.

ranking, and would be the ever welcome center-piece at depleted homefront tournaments during World War II, his status as an alien keeping him out of uniform. Over the 1943–45 period he was the big winner, grabbing 15 of 30 tournaments (7 of 10 in 1943) and 107 of 122 matches. He could never realize his dream of conquering Forest Hills, coming as close as the semis, 1942–45, and the quarters in 1946 and 1947.

Segura was born June 20, 1921, in Guayaquil, Ecuador, and was raised there. A childhood attack of rickets deformed his legs but his will was strong, and he drove himself to play tennis well, even though he was so weak at first that he had to grip the racket with both hands. A right-hander, he was likely the first to utilize a two-fisted forehand.

At Miami he won the U.S. Intercollegiate singles in 1943, 1944 and 1945, the only man in this century to take three straight. He won the U.S. Indoor title of 1946 and the U.S. Clay Court of 1944, was a member of the U.S. Top Ten six times, No. 3 in 1943, 1944 and 1945. But his best days were ahead of him, as a professional. After settling in the U.S., he left the amateurs in 1947, signing on to play mostly the secondary matches on the tour of one-nighters. Unfortunately for Segura, he was out of the limelight once he became a professional, but while he beat Dinny Pails, Frank Parker, and Ken McGregor in their series, sharpening his strokes and tactics and becoming one of the great players, he received little recognition. Jack Kramer and Pancho Gonzalez were the stars, but Segura was making his mark in a small circle as a shrewd strategist, a cunning lobber, and a killer with a forehand.

He toured for nearly two decades and stands as one of the prominent figures in the history of the U.S. Pro Championships. Segura won the singles title three times in a row, first in 1950 over Frank Kovacs, then in 1951 and 1952 over Gonzalez. Segura lost the title to Gonzalez on three occasions, 1955, 1956 and 1957, and a fourth time, at age 41, to Butch Buchholz in 1962. Segura also won the doubles with Jack Kramer in 1948 and 1955, and with Gonzalez in 1954 and 1958.

Pancho Segura: First with two-fisted forehand. (Russ Adams)

Hardy and good-natured, Segura was a favorite with crowds. He could always smile and crack a joke, yet was thoroughly professional and a constant competitor. He never made big money. Open tennis arrived too late for him, but he entered the doubles of the first open Wimbledon in 1968 with Alex Olmedo, and in the second round they won the longest doubles match of Wimbledon's open era, 94 games, over Abe Segal and Gordon Forbes, 32-30, 5-7, 6-4, 6-4. The 62-game set was the longest ever at Wimbledon.

When his playing career ended he became a teaching pro, settling in Southern California, and making his mark as one of the sharpest minds in the game. He was instrumental in the development of Jimmy Connors. He was elected to the Hall of Fame in 1984.

U.S. TITLES (14)—*Intercollegiate singles, 1943, 1944, 1945; Indoor singles, 1946; Clay Court singles, 1944; Pro singles, 1950, 1951, 1952; Clay Court doubles, 1944, 1945*

Monica Seles: Elan with a slam. (Wide World)

with Bill Talbert; Pro doubles, 1948, 1955 with Jack Kramer; 1954, 1958 with Pancho Gonzalez. SINGLES RECORD IN THE MAJORS: *French (2-1), Wimbledon (2-2), U.S. (21-7).*

MONICA SELES

Yugoslavia/United States (1973—)

How could anybody stop her? An all-time prodigy, a unique No. 1 with her double-barrelled fusillades—both hands on both sides—Monica Seles was a 19-year-old tearing up tennis until that fateful day in Hamburg, April 30, 1993. An allegedly demented German spectator, Guenther Parche, stopped her, struck her down with a knife in the back as she sat beside the court on a changeover.

The quarter-final match against Maggie Maleeva ended at that abrupt moment, and so did tennis for a kid who seemed destined to be the greatest of all. She had won eight majors (three French, three Australian, two U.S.). After taking the U.S. of 1992 over Arantxa Sanchez Vicario, 6-3, 6-3, she was the youngest ever to hold seven of them (18 years, 8 months), undercutting Maureen Connolly by three months. (Curiously, Connolly, who wound up with nine, had been cut off, too, as a teenager, in a traffic accident.) Breaking Steffi Graf's four-year hold on the No. 1 ranking in 1991, Seles had held off Steffi in her last major appearance, the Australian, 4-6, 6-3, 6-2.

But putative assassin Parche intervened, claiming he knifed Seles to restore Graf to preeminence, a story the Seles family doubted. Twenty-eight months passed before Monica was seen on court again. The psychological damage had been more severe than the physical. She, like everybody else—except, apparently, the judge in Parche's trial and re-trial—wondered why he was not incarcerated. "He's still out there walking the streets," she worried.

Attempting to put it behind her, Monica emerged from trauma in August 1995, beating Martina Navratilova in an exhibition at Atlantic City, content with the co-No. 1 ranking granted her by the WTA. Then acting as though nothing had changed, she was back in business. Electrifyingly so. Opponents at the Canadian Open in Toronto acted as though they were seeing a ghost. They were—the ghost of championships past as she marched to the title on a loss of no sets, 12 games in five matches, ripping Amanda Coetzer in the final, 6-0, 6-1.

On to Flushing Meadow, where she'd won 14 straight matches. The opposition continued to melt until the final, where Graf ended the streak at 20, fitter in the third set, 7-6 (8-6), 0-6, 6-3. At 6-5 in the tie-breaker Monica groused at a call of fault on her bid—a fraction wide—for a set-point ace. She lost her composure momentarily, and may have missed the title by a smidgen of an inch.

Her return to Australia, where she'd never been beaten, was triumphant. She won Sydney from match point down over Lindsay Davenport,

4-6, 7-6 (9-7), 6-3, then the Open—Graf was absent—over Anke Huber, 6-4, 6-1, a ninth major. However, after that the 1996 season didn't go as well as she and her fans had hoped. Knee and shoulder injuries were bothersome. Her conditioning was suspect; she pulled out of several tourneys. Though she did win three more tournaments and help the U.S. regain the Federation Cup (victories over Kimiko Date, Sanchez Vicario and Conchita Martinez in wins over Japan and Spain), there was disappointment at the French and Wimbledon. Jana Novotna clipped her Paris streak of 25 in the quarters, 7-6 (9-7), 6-3. More painful perhaps was losing the last four games and a second-rounder at the Big W to an unknown Slovak, No. 59 Katerina Studenikova, 7-5, 5-7, 6-4. "I'm playing too defensively, not attacking the ball the way I used to," Monica said accurately. She was a finalist again at the U.S. Open but was pushed around by a charged-up Graf whose superior quickness showed, 7-5, 6-4.

Seles, a left-hander who has grown to nearly six feet, was born Dec. 2, 1973, of Serbo-Hungarian parentage, at Novy Sad in what was then Yugoslavia. Her father, Karolj Seles, a keen student of the game who got his daughter started, and her mother, Esther, felt her future lay in the U.S. They moved to Nick Bollettieri's Tennis Academy at Brandenton, Fla., in 1986 when Monica was 12, and headmaster Nick oversaw her early development. Papa has taken over the coaching again, at their Sarasota residence, and Monica became a U.S. citizen in 1995.

Monica sounded the alarm in 1989 as a 15-year-old by spoiling the last final of Chris Evert's illustrious career in Houston, 3-6, 6-1, 6-4. "She's the next," exulted an overwhelmed witness, historian Ted Tinling. Soon after, Moanin' Monica took her bubbly grimacing-and-grunting act to Roland Garros to show Parisians noisy tennis nouvelle: rip-roaring groundies, bludgeoned from anywhere in a baseball switch-hitting style (the backhand cross-handed). She constantly went for winners, seemingly off-balance and out-of-position but buoyed by excellent footwork and anticipation. Graf barely escaped in the semis, 6-3, 3-6,

6-3. But she wouldn't a year later, in the final, 7-6 (8-6), 6-4, though clutching four set points at 6-2 in the tie-breaker. Seles became a major player. Graf wasn't taken by surprise there—just before that Seles had dammed her longest winning streak, 66 matches, in the Berlin final, 6-4, 6-3. She bounded into the Top Ten that year, No. 6, and has been there ever since (except for non-ranked 1994).

For two-and-a-half years Monica was nearly invincible as the titles piled up and her ball-impacting shriek—"Uhh-eee!"—was heard across the globe. She charmed the public with girlish élan and mystified people by vanishing before Wimbledon in 1991 and then resurfacing to win the U.S. Open, despite coming within two points of defeat in a semifinal engagement of broadsides with another teen, Jennifer Capriati. She may have been psyched out of a 1992 Grand Slam when complaints about the grunting from Wimbledon victims Nathalie Tauziat and Martina Navratilova (leading to a warning from the referee) muted her in the final, where she was destroyed by Graf. Still, she was the first to win three majors in successive years since Margaret Court (three and four, 1969–70), a feat equaled by Graf, 1995–96. Among her souvenirs was the 1991 U.S. final, she, 17, over Navratilova, 34, a singular generation gapper.

At the close of 1996, after seven professional seasons, she had played 79 tournaments and won 38 singles titles with a 312-39 (.889) record, 101-10 in the majors. She had also won 4 doubles titles and $8,960,490 in prize money. She is young and may regain her wondrous form of better days as Alice Marble did after losing 1934 and 1935 to illness. It is to be hoped. Regardless, Monica has put an indelible signature on the game with her style, persona and championships, a woman doubtless traveling to the Hall of Fame.

MAJOR TITLES *(9)—Australian singles, 1991, 1992, 1993, 96; French singles, 1990, 1991, 1992; U.S. singles, 1991, 1992.* OTHER U.S. TITLES *(1)—Hard Court singles, 1990.* FEDERATION CUP—*1996; record: 4-0 in singles.* SINGLES RECORD IN THE MAJORS: *Australian (28-0), French (30-2), Wimbledon (14-4), U.S. (29-4).*

STAN SMITH

United States (1946—)

One of the great Davis Cup competitors, Stan Smith added the U.S. (1971) and Wimbledon (1972) titles to his laurels, and, with Bob Lutz, was part of one of the preeminent doubles teams. Smith, who overcame teenage awkwardness to become a feared 6-foot-3 foe with crashing serves and volleys, may have hit his zenith on alien clay. That was in Bucharest in 1972 as the U.S. won a fifth consecutive Cup, and he supplied the clinching victory—the insuperable third point—for a fifth time. That's a Davis Cup record to which he added in 1979, with Bob Lutz, in the 5-0 victory over Italy at San Francisco.

Stan was in at the finish of seven Cup victories, tying him with Bill Tilden for a U.S. high. And he had a smaller share of an eighth Cup, in 1981, when he and Lutz took a doubles over Ivan Lendl and Tom Smid, 9-7, 6-3, 6-2—the Cup adieu for Stan and Bob, at Flushing Meadow—in the win over Czechoslovakia en route to the final.

A notable sportsman, he had to "concentrate so hard I got a headache," he said after the three-day ordeal at the hands of a loud partisan crowd and overly patriotic line judges in Bucharest. It was an extended, rocky campaign during which Smith won seven of eight singles and, with Erik van Dillen, all five doubles. Stan scored the clinching point in each of five matches and nailed down two of the most dramatic singles victories ever by an American in the finale. Romania, loser to the U.S. in the 1969 and 1971 showdowns, appeared the favorite on home earth, but Smith shocked Ilie Nastase on the slow court, 11-9, 6-2, 6-3, to lead off, and then out-battled the sly, combative Ion Tiriac in a tense five-set struggle, 4-6, 6-2, 6-4, 2-6, 6-0.

Knowing that he had to hit outright winners well away from the lines to make sure of the points, Smith did just that to storm through a last-set bagel and send the U.S. safely ahead, 3-1, in the 3-2 victory.

Stan Smith: His Cup runneth over. (UPI)

Born Dec. 14, 1946, in Pasadena, Cal., he grew up there and was an All-American at the University of Southern California, where he won the U.S. Intercollegiate singles (1968) and, with Lutz, doubles in 1967 and 1968.

During a remarkable 11-year Davis Cup career that began in 1968, embracing 24 engagements, he was on the winning side 22 times, and 16 times provided the clinching point: three times in singles, 13 times in doubles (nine with Lutz, four with van Dillen). He and Lutz won 13 of 14 Cup matches together. As the U.S. ran up a record Cup streak of 17 victories from 1968 to the finale of 1973, Smith was involved in 14, the clincher in 12.

His 1972 Wimbledon triumph over Nastase, 4-6, 6-3, 6-3, 4-6, 7-5 was one of the outstanding finals, and his 1971 defeat of Jan Kodes at Forest Hills, 3-6, 6-3, 6-2, 7-6 (5-3), was the first U.S.

final to conclude in a tie-breaker. Smith and Lutz won the U.S. doubles four times, the Australian once. In a career spanning the amateur and open eras, he was one of five centurions, winning at least 100 pro titles overall in singles and doubles. Stan hit the century with 39 singles, 61 doubles, and made $1,774,881 in career prize money. Eleven times between 1967 and 1980 he was in the U.S. Top Ten, No. 1 four years, 1969, 1971, 1972 and 1973. Six straight times from 1970 he was in the World Top Ten, No. 1 in 1972.

Stan entered the Hall of Fame in 1987. He served in the U.S. Army.

MAJOR TITLES (7)—Wimbledon singles, 1972; U.S. singles, 1971; Australian doubles, 1970; U.S. doubles, 1968, 1974, 1978, 1980. OTHER U.S. TITLES (15)—Indoor singles, 1972; Indoor doubles, 1966, 1969 with Bob Lutz; 1970, with Arthur Ashe; Clay Court doubles, 1968, with Lutz; Hard Court singles, 1966, 1967, 1968; Hard Court doubles, 1966, with Lutz; Pro doubles, 1973, with Erik van Dillen; 1974, 1977, with Bob Lutz; Intercollegiate singles, 1968; Intercollegiate doubles, 1967, 1968 with Lutz. DAVIS CUP—1968, 1969, 1970, 1971, 1972, 1973, 1975, 1977, 1979, 1981; record; 15-5 in singles, 20-3 in doubles. SINGLES RECORD IN THE MAJORS: Australian (5-3), French (23-9), Wimbledon (45-17), U.S. (39-19).

Tony Trabert: A champ for all surfaces. (UPI)

TONY TRABERT
United States (1930—)

One of the finest seasons ever achieved was the 1955 of Tony Trabert, who won three of the Big Four singles titles—Wimbledon, French, and U.S.—to earn acclaim as the No. 1 amateur of that year. Only two other men, Don Budge (1938) and Rod Laver (1962 and 1969), en route to their Grand Slams, have won those three uppermost championships within a calendar year.

Moreover, Trabert also won the U.S. Indoor and U.S. Clay Court titles, adding them to the pre-eminent American championships on grass at Forest Hills.

For that year, probably the most productive ever by an American man—30 titles—he won 18 of 23 singles tourneys on a 106-7 match record. Included was a winning streak of 36 matches. He also won 12 doubles titles (with Vic Seixas).

An exceptional athlete, Marion Anthony Trabert was born Aug. 16, 1930, in Cincinnati, where he grew up. He was a standout basketball player at the University of Cincinnati, for which he also won the U.S. Intercollegiate singles title in 1951.

The French Championships has traditionally been the most difficult battleground for American men. Trabert won five titles in Paris, the singles in 1954 and 1955. Thirty-four years passed before another American, Michael Chang, won in 1989. Trabert also won the doubles in 1950 (with Bill Talbert) and in 1954 and 1955 (with Vic Seixas). Only a defeat by Ken Rosewall (the eventual champ) in the semifinals of the Australian Championships, 8-6, 6-3, 6-3, ruined Trabert's chance at a Grand Slam in 1955.

For five years Trabert was a mainstay of the U.S. Davis Cup team, along with Seixas. In each of those years the U.S. reached the challenge round finale, and Trabert's best-remembered match may have been a defeat, a tremendous struggle against Lew Hoad on a rainy afternoon in 1953 at Melbourne. Hoad won out, 7-5, in the fifth, and Australia kept the Cup. However, Trabert and Seixas returned to Australia a year later, where Trabert beat Hoad on the opening day in singles and he and Seixas won the doubles over Hoad and Rex Hartwig in a 3-2 triumph, the only U.S. seizure of the Cup from the Aussies during an eight-year stretch.

Though an attacker with a powerful backhand and strong volley, the competitive right-hander also had exceptional groundstrokes. In winning the U.S. Singles at Forest Hills twice, 1953 and 1955, and Wimbledon, 1955, he did not lose a set, a rare feat.

Amassing 13 U.S. titles in singles and doubles, he was one of two Americans (the other was Art Larsen) to win singles championships on all four surfaces: grass at Forest Hills, indoor, clay court and hard court.

Following the custom of the time, Trabert, as the top amateur, signed on with the professionals to challenge the ruler, Pancho Gonzalez, on a head-to-head tour in 1956. Gonzalez won, 74-27. Trabert was runner-up to Alex Olmedo for the U.S. Pro singles title in 1960, having won the doubles with Hartwig in 1956.

When his playing career ended, Trabert worked as a teaching pro and as a television commentator on tennis. In 1976 he returned to the Davis Cup scene as the U.S. captain, leading the Cup-winning teams of 1978 and 1979.

He had four years in the U.S. and World Top Ten, 1951, 1953, 1954 and 1955, No. 1 in each in 1953 and 1955, before turning pro. His amateur career was interrupted by service in the U.S. Navy. He was named to the Hall of Fame in 1978.

MAJOR TITLES (10)—*French singles, 1954, 1955; Wimbledon singles, 1955; U.S. singles, 1953, 1955; Australian doubles, 1955; French doubles, 1950, 1954, 1955; U.S. doubles, 1954.* OTHER U.S. TITLES (13)—*Intercollegiate singles, 1951; Indoor singles, 1955; Clay Court singles, 1951, 1955;*

Hard Court singles, 1953; Indoor doubles, 1954, with Bill Talbert; 1955, with Vic Seixas; Clay Court doubles, 1951, 1955, with Hamilton Richardson; 1954, with Seixas; Hard Court doubles, 1950, 1953, with Tom Brown; Pro doubles, 1956, with Rex Hartwig. DAVIS CUP *(As player)—1951, 1952, 1953, 1954, 1955; record: 16-5 in singles, 11-3 in doubles; (As captain)—1953, 1976, 1977, 1978, 1979, 1980; Record: 14-3, 2 Cups.* SINGLES RECORD IN THE MAJORS: *Australian (4-2), French (18-2), Wimbledon (13-2), U.S. (23-5).*

MATS WILANDER
Sweden (1964—)

No sooner had Swedes grieved the retirement of Bjorn Borg, and wistfully thought of his sixth French title in 1981, than an unheralded kid countryman conquered Paris the following year. That was unseeded 17-year-old Mats Arne Olof Wilander, a rugged 6-footer, who beat the powerful one-time champ, Guillermo Vilas, at his own baseline game to become the youngest of French champs, 1-6, 7-6, (8-6), 6-0, 6-4. It was the first of seven singles majors for Wilander over a seven-year stretch when he competed at the top of the game, reaching No. 1 in 1988.

Although Michael Chang, a younger 17 in 1989, usurped his male precocity record for the majors, Wilander won the French again in 1985 (dethroning Ivan Lendl, 6-2 in the fourth) and 1988, and the Australian, on grass, in 1983 and 1984.

But it was 1988, an all-time season, that stands as his masterwork. He won three of the majors, starting with a magnificent Australian final-round victory over home-towner Patrick Cash in Melbourne's newly opened Flinders Park, 6-3, 6-7 (3-7), 2-6, 6-1, 8-6. It was the Aussie Open's first year on hard courts, and victory meant that Mats was only the second man (emulating Jimmy Connors) to win majors on grass, clay and hard.

He won the French without too much trouble, but whatever dreams he had of a Grand Slam were pierced by Miloslav Mecir in the Wimbledon quarters, 6-3, 6-1, 6-3. An arduous U.S. backcourt duel with Lendl (who'd beaten him for the title the year before) lasted more than four hours. At last Wilander showed more offensive initiative to win, 6-4, 4-6, 6-3, 5-7, 6-4. As the first winner of three majors in a year since Connors in 1974, he completed 1988 with six victories in 15 tournament on a 53 11 match record, and with a personal prize-money high, $1,726,731.

But after that, having attained the No. 1 ranking, he seemed to lose motivation. He was through as a factor, and by 1991 he retired. His last of 33 career titles was at Itaparica (Brazil) in 1990. But, in some ways, Wilander outdid Borg. Bjorn never won three majors in a year, and led Sweden to but one Davis Cup to Mats' three. Stunning Connors, 6-1, 6-3, 6-3, on opening day in Goteborg in 1984, Wilander launched Sweden to a 4-1 upset of the U.S. He backboned a 3-2 win over Germany in 1985 in Munich, and a 5-0 win over India in 1987 in Goteborg.

In 1991 he had descended to No. 157 and retired. However, he felt the urge to play again in 1993, and came back to do moderately well, getting up to No. 45 in 1995, earning about $500,000. He was even selected as a starter for the Davis Cup semifinal against the U.S. in 1995, losing to Andre Agassi and Pete Sampras.

Speedy afoot and an unrelenting competitor through 1988, he was at first a pure topspinning grind-it-out baseliner, a right-hander with a two-fisted backhand. But Mats developed attacking skills and a good volley, winning the Wimbledon doubles in 1986 with Joakim Nystrom.

Two memorable matches were Davis Cup losses, the longest and third-longest played: 6:32 against John McEnroe (9-7, 6-2, 15-17, 3-6, 8-6) in 1982; 6:04 against Horst Skoff of Austria (6-7,

Mats Wilander: All but a Grand Slam. (Mitchell Reibell)

7-6, 1-6, 6-4, 9-7) in 1989. His career figures: 33 wins in 220 tournaments on a 524-164 match record. His earnings were $7,976,256.

He was born Aug. 22, 1964, in Vaxjo, Sweden, grew up there, and lives with his wife, Sonya, in Greenwich, Conn.

MAJOR TITLES (8)—*Australian singles, 1983, 1984, 1988; French singles, 1982, 1985, 1988; U.S. singles, 1988; Wimbledon doubles, 1986.* DAVIS CUP—*1981, 1982, 1983, 1984, 1985, 1986, 1987, 1988, 1989, 1990; record: 36-14 in singles, 7-2 in doubles.* SINGLES RECORD IN THE MAJORS: *Australian (36-7), French (47-9), Wimbledon (25-10), U.S. (36-11).*

Classic confrontation: John McEnroe arguing a call with the umpire at Wimbledon in 1980. (Wide World)

7

LAW AND DISORDER

Law and order? Every sport needs some, if only to keep the games moving according to the rules, assure that they begin and end properly and a winner and loser is determined correctly. This usually means some form of officiating, which isn't always easy in the heat of competition, when nerves twitch and tempers boil over.

Nowadays, with heavy money and computer points at stake (as well as reputations), the person in charge on court—the umpire—may feel like a cop/magistrate in restraining players with penalties from the Code of Conduct. The Code provides three steps to disqualification. But, as Andre Agassi learned at Indianapolis in 1996, one violation can warrant eviction if flagrant enough. His unacceptable profanity directed at umpire Dana Locanto got him tossed out by supervisor Mark Darby and fined $12,000 by the ATP. Later in the year Andre set an unwanted record for the weightiest fine ever: $50,000 for skipping the mandatory press conference after losing to Pete Sampras in the ATP Championship. Petty cash for him.

Considering that no more than four players are involved in a tennis match, the game may

seem top-heavy in officials. As many as 14 can oversee one match: umpire and net judge, plus the people who determine whether balls have landed in or out of court: two baseline judges, two serviceline judges, four sideline judges (one at each end on either side), two centerline judges (one at each end) and two foot-fault judges, one at each baseline.

Or as few as one: an umpire who keeps score and calls all lines from the high chair. There are variations in decreasing the crew size. Seldom are foot fault judges used; baseline judges can handle that duty. Usually one service line judge travels between lines. Sometimes sideline and center line judges are stationed only at one end, calling their line on the other side of the net as well. Frequently the net judge is dispensed with, and the umpire calls nets. In 1996 an electronic gadget was called on for that duty at the U.S. Open.

Recently, several inventors have developed electronic line-calling devices, dispensing with judges altogether. The Hopman Cup tournament at Perth, Australia, uses one such device, called the TEL system. In 1980, Wimbledon introduced an electric eye, called Cyclops, to judge the service lines, and "Cy" has appeared at numerous tournaments since, though not always successfully. The objective is to eliminate human error, but machines also remove the human element. With the TEL system, the umpire seems very lonely. Players have to address all their frustrations at him, because who wants to yell at a machine? Since players have always made more mistakes than the judges, do they really want to compete in a vacuum where all shadow of doubt is removed? Is automated line-calling a gimmick, or do tournament promoters hope to reduce officiating payrolls?

Apparently, the human job of umpiring is safe. Professionals handle that role and the positions of referee and supervisor on the ATP and WTA circuits as well as the majors. The umpire rules on court. His or her judgment, often questioned by a player (at times vitriolically), stands unchangeable. But, the umpire may summon the referee to adjudicate or interpret in the matter of the rules or behavior. The supervisor oversees all and has the last word in disputes.

One of the great disputers was Romanian Ilie Nastase. The introduction of the Code of Conduct in 1980, with its provisions for disqualifications for on-court misbehavior, was largely a reaction to his antics, such as the curious Masters match with two losers in 1975 at Stockholm. Nastase's stalling and baiting of his opponent, Arthur Ashe, finally was too much even for Ashe's celebrated cool. Arthur walked out, even though leading, thus disqualifying himself. Dismayed referee Horst Klosterkemper, unable to persuade Arthur to return, declared, "it was in my mind to disqualify Nastase at the moment Ashe departed. So I now disqualify Nastase." That left him with a double defeat, rectified the next day by the reinstatement of Ashe with the win in the round-robin phase of the tourney eventually won by—who else?—Nastase.

But, a no-winner dual default did occur in 1971, during the final of the Pacific Southwest at Los Angeles. At 6-6, Billie Jean King and Rosie Casals refused to continue, allegedly disapproving of the work of a line judge. However, their walkout seemed aimed at tournament promoter Jack Kramer. Kramer's unwillingness to increase the insignificant prize money for his 1970 women's event had planted the seeds of revolt. It caused Billie Jean, Rosie and others to boycott. They instead played their historic breakaway tournament, the hastily organized original Virginia Slims of Houston. Apparently it was payback time for Kramer, though it cost Casals and King their prize money plus a fine by the USTA.

King was later involved in one of the three most publicized and controversial walkouts, with each incident occurring during the U.S. Championships at Forest Hills, and each involving all-timers. In 1921, the seemingly invincible Suzanne Lenglen, trailing Molla Mallory, 2-6, 0-30, in the second round—her only American appearance as an amateur—quit, claiming illness. In 1933, defending champ Helen Wills Moody ended her record U.S. winning streak of 46 matches by quitting in the final at 0-3 in the third against Helen Jacobs, saying she couldn't go on. In 1973, defending champ King ended her 14-match streak by quitting an acrimonious third-rounder at 1-4 in the third against Julie Heldman.

But, with the widespread influence of TV by 1995, the unprominent Jeff Tarango's blow-up and walkout from a Wimbledon third-rounder against Alex Mronz may have achieved greater notoriety. He was fined a record $63,576 by the ITF and ATP and banned from Wimbledon in 1996. The fine was later reduced on appeal to $28,256, the amount of his prize money. It didn't hurt No. 80 Tarango's exposure that his wife, Benedicte, slapped umpire Bruno Rebeuh after the match.

Officiating can be dangerous. In Rome, referee Sergio Baruti was punched out by Norman Holmes, whom he had disqualified for showing up late for a match in the Italian Open of 1975. Second-seeded Jan Kodes was disqualified at the Italian of 1974 during a second-rounder against Tonino Zugarelli for grabbing and roughing up referee Michele Brunetti. Margaret Stancin, a net judge, was knocked cold by a speedy, errant forehand drive from Sherwood Stewart's racket at

San Francisco in 1976. In 1995 at the French Open, service line judge Pascal Maria was sent to the hospital after being nailed by a racket thrown in anger by Carsten Arriens, who was immediately disqualified.

All recovered quickly. But tragedy befell Dick Wertheim, a top official from Lexington, Mass., in the form of a Stefan Edberg serve at the U.S. Open in 1983. Wertheim, 61, working as a center line judge in the junior final, was hit in the groin by 17-year-old Edberg's swift serve. He toppled, striking his head on the asphalt, and passed out, suffering heart failure and a brain hemorrhage. Wertheim never regained consciousness. He died at nearby Flushing Hospital.

Nastase was a player who exploded easily and walked out of numerous tournaments, defaulting, notably, from the Italian semis against Raul Ramirez in 1975 and in 1972 against Clark Graebner during an indoor tournament in London, pleading intimidation. Graebner, wearying of Nastase's gamesmanship, crossed over the net and offered to flatten Ilie if he didn't behave. Nastase fled the court. Sometimes, after leaving in a huff in the pre-Code days, Ilie was convinced by tourney officials to return and play some more. That happened at the Masters of 1973 at Boston. After the calm and distinguished referee, Mike Blanchard, soothed him, Nastase reappeared on court to finish a win over Jan Kodes, and went on to take the title.

Referee Charles Hare threw him out of a Palm Springs tournament in 1976 for an on-court "mooning" of Hare. He was disqualified here and there by exasperated umpires or referees, twice in 1975 besides the Masters: British Hard Court against Pat Proisy, and Washington against Cliff Richey. But the most famous disqualification didn't stick: 1979 at the U.S. Open. Frank Hammond, one of the leading umpires, followed the Code to the letter, as instructed by referee Blanchard, during Nastase's stormy second-rounder against champ-to-be John McEnroe. Finally defaulting Nastase for stalling—his fourth violation—Hammond then found himself overruled.

Fearing the noisy crowd's hostile reaction to the default might turn into a very ugly scene, tournament director Bill Talbert countered by removing Hammond and reinstating Nastase. Blanchard umpired the rest of the match.

In a similar situation in 1976, transgressor Raul Ramirez was tossed out of the Masters at Houston, ostensibly a loser to Brian Gottfried, only to be sent back into action by the sponsor, Commercial Union, to appease ticket buyers. British umpire Bertie Bowron removed himself, and honorably so, during a tempestuous 1978 Italian semi involving the local god, Adriano Panatta, and Spaniard Jose Higueras. The crowd and the crew of line judges were so outrageously pro-Panatta that Bowron gave up. Shortly, so did Higueras. Two years before—same cauldron, same Panatta—a distraught Harold Solomon couldn't take the abuse of the crowd and bias of the officials any longer. Solly may have given the title to Panatta by exiting their quarter final even though serving for victory at 2-6, 7-5, 5-4, 0-30. The advent of neutral, professional supervisors and umpires has practically eliminated the officiating "home court advantage" of local sons and daughters.

Although monetary records haven't been fully kept, McEnroe and Nastase were obviously the most frequent recipients of fines, with Mac the record holder in amounts forfeited (it would run close to $200,000) and suspensions served. However, No. 7 American Earl Cochell was hit in 1951 with the harshest penalty, and that in the pre-fines amateur era. It was a lifetime suspension by the USTA for quixotic behavior during a U.S. fourth-round loss to Gardnar Mulloy and a profane tirade against referee Ellsworth Davenport. It was later rescinded, but Cochell lost the remainder of his best years.

Nastase was tagged with the first significant, and well deserved, fine, $6,000 in 1975 for clearly not trying in the Canadian Open final against Manolo Orantes. It cost more for "failing to give best efforts" in 1990. Thomas Muster was tagged $25,000 by the ATP in Prague for listlessly playing one game against Claudio Pistoles, then walking out. His walk from a contentious Davis Cup match in Brazil in 1996 earned Thomas an $8,000 fine from the ITF. Vitas Gerulaitis' stroll out of the 1981 Melbourne Indoor final left the title to Peter McNamara, and set him back $10,000.

McEnroe disqualified himself by quitting during the World Team Cup final against Miloslav Mecir in 1987. He became the first of the open era to be disqualified from a major, the Australian of 1990, for obscenities directed at umpire Gerry Armstrong and supervisor Ken Farrar during a fourth-rounder he led against Mikael Pernfors. Three years earlier Mac had said, "Oh, I'm an old pro. I was within one word of a default, but I always know what I'm doing." Those were his blithe words at the U.S. Open when he came close to default with three Code violations when the limit was four (and was fined $17,500 for misdeeds while beating Bobo Zivojinovic). But he didn't know the rules (amended for 1990) as he took his third misstep at Melbourne, and was chagrined to be waved off.

Presumably only Wimbledon umpire Ted James' feelings were hurt when McEnroe called him "pits of the world" in a first-round win over Tom Gullikson in 1981. The statement was hardly profane, but was among various insults of officials costing him $14,750 in that, his first championship year. He paid $10,000 at Wimbledon for profanely sassing a line judge in 1991. The fines for screaming obscenities at an umpire and kicking a photographer's camera at the French in 1983—$3,350—were hardly up to his standard. But it qualified McEnroe as the Grand Slurrer of officials, collecting fines for abusive language at all the majors.

A banner year for major disqualifications was 1995. Other than Tarango, who outdid himself, Wimbledon referee Alan Mills ruled off two others: Tim Henman, when a ball he smote in anger struck a ballgirl during a doubles match against Henrik Holm and, of all people, Tarango; and Murph Jensen, for failure to show up for a mixed doubles. Carsten Arriens had been pitched that same year for his racket pitch at the French.

For a long while, the record for the highest fine, $20,000, was held by Guillermo Vilas, convicted of accepting $50,000 up front to play Rotterdam in 1983, a breach of the MIPTC's unenforceable rule against guarantees exclusive of prize money. In 1986, fellow left-hander Jimmy Connors topped it, with $25,000, the result of a spat with umpire Jeremy Shales during a Lipton semi against Ivan Lendl. Though Jimmy didn't walk, the effect was the same. He went on a sit-down strike, refusing to play. Imprudent remarks by Boris Becker relieved him of $25,000 in 1995 after losing the Monte Carlo final to Muster, implying that Thomas had been using drugs.

The women have been tamer in their relationships with officials, and the WTA more coy in revealing fines. An irritated fourth-seeded Hana Mandlikova tried to demolish a scoreboard while losing to Claudia Kohde Kilsch at the U.S. Open in 1987, and was nicked for $500. In 1991 Monica Seles was fined $6,000 for an unexplained Wimbledon no-show. Not long after, she was slapped with a $20,000 penalty for playing an exhibition tournament at Mahwah, N.J., in opposition to a WTA event. Mahwah promoter John Korff reportedly picked up her tab.

Interestingly enough, another Romanian, Irina Spirlea, set the female on-court naughtiness record of $10,000 in 1996 at Palermo, assessed for her Nastase-style remarks to an umpire. Said she later, "It was worth it."

8

INTERNATIONAL TENNIS HALL OF FAME

Appropriately, the International Tennis Hall of Fame is located at the world's oldest active tournament tennis ground, the Newport (R.I.) Casino, dating back to 1880.

Design and construction of the Casino as an exclusive men's club was commissioned by James Gordon Bennett, Jr., publisher of the *New York Herald*. In this case "casino" was to adhere to one of its definitions as a place of entertainment, and not the more familiar gambling emporium.

Renowned New York architect Stanford White was the designer of the handsome wooden complex (now a historic landmark). It includes the two-story building with clock tower and horseshoe piazza that housed the club and is now devoted to the Hall of Fame and its museum. An additional building contains a theater, court tennis court and dressing rooms. The landscaped grounds include a 5,000-seat lawn tennis stadium, a dozen grass courts, and indoor courts.

As the cradle of American tennis, the Casino was the scene of the first U.S. Championships, for men, in 1881, and continued as the site of that tournament through 1914. Thereafter, the Casino Invitational for men was played until the end of the amateur era. Professional tournaments, introduced by the Casino's moving force, James H. "Jimmy" Van Alen, in 1965, continue annually. Davis Cup matches were played at the Casino in 1921 (Japan over Australia) and 1991 (U.S. over Spain.)

It was here that innovator Van Alen developed and put into play VASSS (Van Alen Streamlined Scoring System) that included the tie-breaker.

At the suggestion of his wife, Candy, Van Alen, as president of the Casino, proposed in 1952 the formation of a National Tennis Hall of Fame to the USTA, which sanctioned its establishment in 1954. The first class of tennis immortals was posthumously inducted in 1955.

Their entry has been followed almost annually by the installment of great players as well as such prominent off-court contributors to the game as administrators, organizers and journalists.

In 1975 the concept broadened, and the name changed to the International Tennis Hall of Fame. Fred Perry of Britain was, that year, the first non-U.S. inductee.

PLAYERS

FRED ALEXANDER

United States (1880–1969)

As the first foreigner to win the Australian titles, Frederick Beasley Alexander beat Alf Dunlop in 1908 and joined with native Dunlop to take the doubles, too. That year he and Beals Wright were the U.S. Davis Cup team in an unsuccessful attempt to pry the Cup away from Australasia (Norman Brookes and Tony Wilding), 3-2 in Melbourne. He lost a tough opener to Brookes, 6-3 in the fifth, and the decisive match to Wilding in three. Right-handed, a New Yorker and Princeton man, he won the U.S. Intercollegiate singles (1901) and doubles (1900).

He ranked six times in the U.S. Top Ten between 1904 and 1918, the last, at 38, his highest, No. 3 in 1908. He was Harold Hackett's partner in a standout doubles team, U.S. finalists a record seven straight times, beginning in 1905, winning in 1907, 1908, 1909 and 1910. In 1917, at 37, he won a fifth U.S. title, shepherding 19-year-old Harold Throckmorton to the doubles championship. Lean and lanky, a smooth stroker, he was born in New York Aug. 14, 1880, and died in Beverly Hills, Cal., March 3, 1969. Inducted into the Hall of Fame in 1961.

MAJOR TITLES (7)—*Australian singles, 1908; Australian doubles, 1908; U.S. doubles, 1907, 1908, 1909, 1910, 1917.* OTHER U.S. TITLES (8)—*Indoor doubles, 1906, 1907, 1908, with Harold Hackett; 1911, 1912, with Theodore Pell; 1917, with William Rosenbaum; Intercollegiate singles, 1901; Intercollegiate doubles, 1900, with Raymond Little.* DAVIS CUP—*1908; record: 0-2 in singles, 1-1 in doubles.* SINGLES RECORD IN THE MAJORS: *Australian (4-0), U.S. (27-12).*

WILMER ALLISON

United States (1904–77)

Although the firm of Allison & Van Ryn was synonymous with doubles excellence, Texan Wilmer Lawson Allison, who played the left court, had several singles triumphs at the top of the game. Foremost, he won the U.S. Championship in 1935 when, at age 30, he shot through not only 23-year-old ex-Wimbledon champ Sidney Wood, 6-2, 6-2, 6-3, in one of the most lopsided finals, but 1933, 1934 and 1936 champ Fred Perry in the semis, 7-5, 6-3, 6-3. That ended a Forest Hills streak of 18 matches for Perry, and eased some of Allison's pain of losing the 1934 final to Fred, 8-6 in the fifth.

As a Davis Cupper, primarily in doubles, he and Johnny Van Ryn—U.S. champs in 1931 and 1935 and Wimbledon champs in 1929 and 1930—won 14 of 16 doubles between 1929 and 1936, the best record by a U.S. team until Peter Fleming and John McEnroe's 14-1. Their 24 team matches (tied with Stan Smith and Vic Seixas) are second only to McEnroe's 30 in U.S. annals. They beat the topnotch French teams in Cup finals in Paris (Jean Borotra–Henri Cochet in 1929, Cochet–Jacques Brugnon in 1932) but could do no more than prolong successful French defenses.

A 5-foot-11, 155-pound right-hander, Allison experienced two extraordinary Cup singles matches in Paris in 1931 and 1932. Opening the 4-1 semifinal victory over Italy he made an all-time comeback to beat ambidextrous Giorgio de Stefani, 4-6, 7-9, 6-4, 8-6, 10-8. Allison squandered four set points of his own in the second, but the most exciting was to come; from 2-5 down in the fourth he saved two match points, and in the last set, from 1-5 down, 16 more.

Newport, R.I., 1891, site of the National Championships in which Oliver Campbell successfully defended his title against Clarence Hobart in five sets. (Fischer Collection/SPS)

The following year, with France ahead, 2-1, and the Cup at stake, he lost a controversial match to Borotra, 1-6, 3-6, 6-4, 6-2, 7-5, after the Frenchman saved four match points in the fifth set. On the fourth, at 4-5 advantage out, Borotra apparently double-faulted by a considerable margin. But the local linesman made no call, and it was a point against Allison, who was on his way to the net to shake hands.

Objective Al Laney wrote for the consumption of U.S. readers: "The U.S. has won the Cup, but the trophy remains in France. A linesman [Gerard de Ferrier] kept Allison from his just victory." Ellsworth Vines beat Cochet in the fifth

match, to make the score 3-2, France, but nobody can know how that match would have gone had it been decisive.

Allison played 44 singles and doubles Cup matches, third for the U.S. behind McEnroe (69) and Seixas (55), and won 32. Allison, who had also been a U.S. semifinalist in 1932, did not defend his title, withdrawing from the scene after losing a 1936 quarterfinal to Bunny Austin, 6-1, 6-4, 7-5, at Wimbledon, where he'd lost the 1930 final to Bill Tilden, Big Bill's last major title. He had been in the U.S. Top Ten from 1928, eight straight years, No. 1 in 1934 and 1935, and the World Top Ten five times between 1930 and

1935, No. 4 in 1932 and 1935. He was born Dec. 8, 1904, in San Antonio, and won the U.S. Intercollegiate title for his alma mater, Texas, in 1927.

During World War II he was a colonel in the U.S. Army Air Force. He entered the Hall of Fame in 1963, and died April 20, 1977, in Austin, Tex.

MAJOR TITLES (6)—*U.S. singles, 1935; Wimbledon doubles, 1929, 1930; U.S. doubles, 1931, 35; U.S. mixed, 1930. Other U.S. title—Intercollegiate singles, 1927.* DAVIS CUP— *1928, 1929, 1930, 1931, 1932, 1933, 1935, 1936; record: 18-10 in singles, 14-2 in doubles.* SINGLES RECORD IN THE MAJORS: *Wimbledon (16-5), U.S. (27-8).*

MANUEL ALONSO
Spain (1895–1984)

As the first Spanish male of international stature, Manolo Alonso de Areyzaga made his country's best showing at Wimbledon and the U.S. Championships before Manolo Santana won them in 1966 and 1965, respectively. He beat Zenzo Shimidzu in a terrific battle, 3-6, 7-5, 3-6, 6-4, 8-6, to reach the Wimbledon all-comers final of 1921, where he lost to Babe Norton in another tense struggle, 5-7, 4-6, 7-5, 6-3, 6-3. A U.S. resident for several years during the 1920s, he was a U.S. Championships quarterfinalist in 1922, 1923, 1925 and 1927 and was ranked in the U.S. Top Ten in 1925, 1926 and 1927, No. 2 in 1926. He was also in the World Top Ten three years, 1925, 1926 and 1927, No. 5 the last year.

A dark-haired 5-foot-9, 145-pound right-hander, he played Davis Cup for Spain. He was born Nov. 12, 1895, in San Sebastian and died Oct. 11, 1984, in Madrid. He entered the Hall of Fame in 1977.

DAVIS CUP—*1921, 1922, 1924, 1925, 1931, 1936; record: 11-7 in singles, 3-4 in doubles.* SINGLES RECORD IN THE MAJORS: *Wimbledon (8-3), U.S. (20-10).*

ARTHUR ASHE
United States (1943–93)

See page 377.

JULIETTE ATKINSON
United States (1873–1944)

Juliette Paxton Atkinson, a right-handed 5-footer who lived in Brooklyn, N.Y., was prominent in singles for four years at the U.S. Championships, a finalist, 1895–98, winning the title thrice: 1895, 1897 and 1898. She did not defend in 1899, defaulting the challenge round to Californian Marion Jones, who gave her a terrific struggle for the '98 title, 6-3, 5-7, 6-4, 2-6, 7-5—one of the longest matches in terms of games (51) ever played by women. But she did continue to compete through 1902.

She won the U.S. doubles seven times with five different partners between 1894 and 1902. She had five in a row with three partners (1894–98), the last two with her younger sister, Kathleen. Other than the Roosevelts, Ellen and Grace in 1900, they were the only sisters to win the title. They were the first sisters to face one another in the Championships, Juliette winning semifinals in 1895, 6-1, 6-4, and 1897, 6-1, 6-3. She was born April 15, 1873, in Rahway, N.J., died Jan. 12, 1944, in Lawrenceville, Ill., and entered the Hall of Fame in 1974.

MAJOR TITLES (13)—*U.S. singles, 1895, 1897, 1898; U.S. doubles, 1894, 1895, 1896, 1897, 1898, 1901, 1902; U.S. mixed, 1894, 1895, 1896.* SINGLES RECORD IN THE MAJORS: *U.S. (14-4).*

TRACY AUSTIN
United States (1962—)

One of the game's prodigies, Tracy Ann Austin was meteoric, an iron-willed girl whose blaze was glorious though fleeting. A variety of injuries cut short what had promised to be one of the great careers. At 14 her junior career was practically a memory.

She had won the U.S. 12s title at 10 in 1972, and added 21 more age-group titles. Arriving at Forest Hills in 1977, an unseeded amateur, she was already the youngest winner of a pro tournament, Portland (Ore.), earlier in the year. Sensationally, she made her way to the last eight of the U.S. Open by beating fourth-seeded 1976 French champ Sue Barker, 6-1, 6-4, and Virginia Ruzici, who would win the French in 1978, 6-3, 7-5. Wimbledon finalist Betty Stove stopped her there, 6-2, 6-2, but the 5-foot, 90-pound Tracy, in ponytail and pinafore, was the youngest of all major quarterfinalists—until Jennifer Capriati, a younger 14, was a French semifinalist in 1990.

Her performance earned no dollars, but she did get a congratulatory phone call from the First Hacker, President Jimmy Carter.

Two years later, 1979, at 16 years, 9 months, Tracy not only dethroned four-time champ Chris Evert, 6-4, 6-3, at Flushing Meadow but undercut Maureen Connolly (1951) as the youngest U.S. champ by a couple of months. Earlier that year she severed Evert's 125-match clay-court winning streak in the semis of the Italian, 6-4, 2-6, 7-6 (7-4), then won the title, her first important prize, over lefty Sylvia Hanika, 6-4, 1-6, 6-3.

She won the U.S. again in 1981 in a thrilling tie-breaker finish over Martina Navratilova, 1-6, 7-6 (7-4), 7-6 (7-1). That year she won seven other tourneys and had a 58-7 match record, and in 1980 12 titles on 68-7. Having made her Wimbledon debut in 1977 (a third-round loss to Evert, 6-1, 6-0), she was a semifinalist in 1979 and 1980, losing to the champs, Navratilova, 6-4, 6-7 (5-7), 6-2, and Evonne Goolagong, 6-3, 0-6, 6-4.

But back maladies began to impair her effectiveness and sideline her for long stretches. San Diego, 1982, was the last of Austin's 29 pro titles. By 1983, before her 21st birthday, she was virtually finished. She has tried comebacks, as recently as 1994, in two tournaments, the Australian and French Opens, but that was it. In Melbourne, however, she became the only post-induction Hall of Famer to win a major match, beating Elna Reinach, 6-1, 7-5, then losing to Sabine Hack, 6-1, 5-7, 6-2. In Paris, ranked No. 78, she lost to Marketa Kochta, 6-0, 6-1, and called it quits, posting a career record of 29 sin-

gles wins and 13 other finals of 122 tournaments on 348-87 (.800) in matches. She won four doubles titles. A near-fatal auto accident in 1989 was another discouraging factor. A resolute 5-foot-4 groundstroker, right-handed with a two-fisted backhand, she had immense patience and fortitude, and deadly passing shots. Few errors marred her performances.

Evert, who reclaimed her U.S. title in the 1980 final at Flushing, recalls, "Tracy's mental strength was scary. She had no weaknesses, she was obsessive about winning." By 1977 Austin was No. 4 in the U.S. rankings, the greenest to stand so high until Capriati's No. 3 in 1990. She continued in that elite group through 1983, No. 1 in 1980. Five straight years, from 1978, she was in the World Top Ten, No. 2 in 1980 and 1981. Briefly in 1980 she was No. 1 on the WTA computer, breaking the Evert/Navratilova stranglehold of nearly six years. She had tremendous battles with those two whose world she invaded. At the close of 1981 she won the Toyota Championship at East Rutherford, N.J., by beating Chris (6-1, 6-2) and Martina (2-6, 6-4, 6-2) in succession, the first of only three to accomplish that back-to-back double, preceding Hana Mandlikova and Steffi Graf.

Turning pro in October 1978, she won $1,966,487 in career prize money. She played on three winning Federation Cup teams (1978, 1979 and 1980) for the U.S., and two Wightman Cup winners (1979, 1981). Tracy was born into a tennis family Dec. 12, 1962, in Palos Verdes, Cal., and grew up in Rolling Hills. Her older sister and brothers—Pam, Jeff and John—played the pro circuit, and she and John won the Wimbledon mixed in 1980, the only brother-sister pairing to do so. She entered the Hall of Fame in 1992, married Scott Holt in 1994, has a child, and works frequently as a TV tennis commentator.

MAJOR TITLES (3)—*U.S. singles, 1979, 81; Wimbledon mixed, 1980.* FEDERATION CUP—*1978, 1979, 1980; record: 13-1 in singles.* WIGHTMAN CUP—*1978, 1979, 1981; record: 4-2 in singles, 2-0 in doubles.* SINGLES RECORD IN THE MAJORS: *Australian (3-2), French (7-3), Wimbledon (21-6), U.S. (31-4).*

KARL BEHR

United States (1885–1949)

A Yale man, Karl Howell Behr won the U.S. Intercollegiate doubles in 1904, and played on the 1907 U.S. Davis Cup team. Behr, a 5-foot-9½-inch, 155-pound survivor of the Titanic sinking in 1912, forever considered himself a lucky man. But he didn't have much good fortune in his lone Cup assignment, with Beals Wright, against Australasia, a 3-2 defeat at Wimbledon in 1907. He lost a toughie to Tony Wilding the first day, 1-6, 6-3, 3-6, 7-5, 6-3, dropping the last four games, and the clincher to Norman Brookes, 4-6, 6-4, 6-1, 6-2. But he and Wright did prolong it to the third day with a stirring doubles victory over Wimbledon champs Brookes-Wilding, 3-6, 12-10, 4-6, 6-2, 6-3. Brookes and Wilding proceeded to take the Cup from Britain, 3-2. Playing Wimbledon that year, Behr made one of the better American showings of that early time, reaching the fourth round where he gave the champ, Brooks, a stiff fight, 6-4, 6-2, 2-6, 3-6, 6-1.

He ranked in the U.S. Top Ten seven times between 1906 and 1915, No. 3 in 1907, and again in 1914 when he beat future champ Lindley Murray, 3-6, 6-2, 7-5, 3-6, 8-6, to reach the quarters in the U.S Championships at Newport. There he lost to the champion-to-be, Dick Williams, 6-2, 6-2, 7-5, in a battle of Titanic alumni. In 1906, ranked No. 11, Behr had jolted an all-time champ, No. 3 Bill Larned, in the second round, 6-4, 6-4, 7-5, and fought past No. 9 Raymond Little, 2-6, 6-2, 6-8, 11-9, 6-4, to the final of the all-comers, where Bill Clothier, en route to the championship, stopped him, 6-2, 6-4, 6-2. He was a semifinalist in 1912, losing to Wallace Johnson, 4-6, 6-0, 6-3, 6-2.

Behr, a right-hander, was born May 30, 1885, in Brooklyn, N.Y., and died Oct. 15, 1949, in New York. He entered the Hall of Fame in 1969.

U.S. TITLE—*Intercollegiate doubles, 1904, with George Bodman.* DAVIS CUP—*1907; record: 0-2 in singles, 1-0 in doubles.* SINGLES RECORD IN THE MAJORS: *Wimbledon (3-1), U.S. (31-13).*

PAULINE BETZ

United States (1919—)

See page 382.

BJORN BORG

Sweden (1956—)

See page 383.

JEAN BOROTRA

France (1898—)

See page 82.

JOHN BROMWICH

Australia (1918—)

Elected to the Hall of Fame in 1984 as one-half of the great Australian doubles team of Bromwich and Quist, John Edward Bromwich missed winning Wimbledon by the narrowest of margins. In the 1948 final Bob Falkenburg escaped him at three match-point junctures, from 3-5, 15-40, then advantage out, in the fifth set, won by the Californian, 7-5. But Bromwich did win two major singles, the Australian in 1939 and 1946, and was a three-time U.S. semifinalist, 1938, 1939, 1947. He lost the last one to the only other U.S. semifinalist playing before and after World War II, Frank Parker.

A loping, big-jawed man, 5-foot-10½, 152 pounds, with an unruly shock of blond hair, Bromwich was one of the most curious stylists in the game's history. A natural left-hander, he nevertheless served right-handed, stroked with two hands on his right side and one, the left, on his left side. Using an extremely loosely-strung racket, he had superb touch and chipped his returns maddeningly on his foes' shoetops. "People called my racket an onion bag," he laughs, "and complained they couldn't hear me hit the ball. But at least they didn't see me serve with both hands, which I did as a young player, sort of like chopping wood." He was an attacker, his volleys well placed, and his competitive fire ever burning high.

World War II interrupted the strong partnership of himself—the right court player—and Adrian Quist, but they won their native Australian title eight straight times, a team record for majors, and gave up the title only after a tremendous final-round struggle, 6-3 in the fifth against youngsters Frank Sedgman and Ken McGregor in 1951. Bromwich was 33, Quist 38. The two of them scored a singular triumph as the Australian Davis Cup team in 1939, rebounding from 0-2 down against the Cup-holding U.S. in Philadelphia to win. They began turning it around with a 5-7, 6-2, 7-5, 6-2 doubles victory over Joe Hunt and Jack Kramer, and Bromwich clinched in the decisive fifth match, 6-0, 6-3, 6-1, over Parker.

Ted Schroeder recalls, "Jack and Joe were up a set and a break, but after that Brom played the most phenomenal 2½ sets of doubles I've ever seen." Bromwich was described by journalist friend Jim Russell as "so tightfisted with a point he made Scrooge seem a philanthropist," and Schroeder seconds it: "You had to win the point from Brom; he never gave one away."

Bromwich smiles at that cordially, and remembers, "in '39 our tennis association was too poor to send us to the French and Wimbledon. But there was no doubt we'd get to the U.S. to challenge for the Cup. We were sure we'd win because we'd only lost 3-2 the year before, and their great Don Budge had turned pro. Three weeks by boat to California, then train to Philadelphia. War had been declared just before the matches began so everything was up in the air. We were surprised to be down 0-2, and didn't have much confidence, even after the doubles. But Quisty was back again at his best to beat Bobby Riggs in five, and it was up to me against Parker. Our coach, Fred Perry, told me if I hit one ball to Frankie's forehand to hit 5,000. That's all I did. They tell me the first point lasted two minutes, the first game 13, and his forehand came apart. Very satisfying because we wanted to be the first to win the Cup as Australia after the Australasia years.

"But more thrilling to me was to come back 11 years later, to Forest Hills, and be part of our next winner, at 32. The Yanks had been thrashing us after the war, and I wasn't surprised when Hop [captain Harry Hopman] went with the youngsters, Sedgman and McGregor, in the singles. I thought he'd play them all the way, but he said he wanted my experience with Sedg in the doubles, and we took the Cup by beating Schroeder and Gar Mulloy in five. A nice way for me to go out"—winning his 20th of 21 Cup doubles. Ranked in the world Top Ten on both sides of the war—he, Quist and Parker were the only ones of such longevity—Brom made the list in 1938, 1939, 1946, 1947 and 1948, coming back splendidly after army service in which he was wounded and contracted malaria in the New Guinea campaign.

Born Nov. 14, 1918, in Kogarah, New South Wales, he lives with his charming wife of 54 years, Zenda, at Point Lonsdale, outside of Melbourne.

MAJOR TITLES *(19)—Australian singles, 1939, 1946; Australian doubles, 1938, 1939, 1940, 1946, 1947, 1948, 1949, 1950; Wimbledon doubles, 1948, 1950; U.S. doubles, 1939, 1949, 1950; Australian mixed, 1938; Wimbledon mixed, 1947, 1948; U.S. mixed, 1947.* DAVIS CUP—*1937, 1938, 1939, 1946, 1947, 1949, 1950; record: 19-11 in singles, 20-1 in doubles.* SINGLES RECORD IN THE MAJORS: *Australian (39-9), French (4-1), Wimbledon (19-5), U.S. (16-5).*

MAJOR TITLES WITH QUIST *(10)—Australian doubles, 1938, 1939, 1940, 1946, 1947, 1948, 1949, 1950; Wimbledon doubles, 1950; U.S. doubles, 1939.* DAVIS CUP—*1938, 1939, 1946; record: 9-1 in doubles.*

NORMAN BROOKES
Australia (1877–1968)

See page 83.

LOUIS BROUGH
United States (1923—)

See page 385.

MARY K. BROWNE
United States (1891–1971)

As the first American female professional, Mary Kendall Browne left a splendid amateur record behind in 1926 to join promoter C. C. Pyle's original troupe of touring pros (France's great Suzanne Lenglen was the centerpiece. Others: Vinnie Richards, Howard Kinsey, Harvey Snodgrass and Paul Feret). During the winter of 1926–27, well past her prime, 35, she played one-night stands across North America as "the opponent" against the invincible Lenglen, losing all 38 matches.

A 5-foot-2 right-hander and staunch volleyer, Browne was born June 3, 1891, in Ventura County, Cal., and came East to dominate the U.S. Championships at Philadelphia, scoring triples—singles, doubles, mixed titles—in 1912, 1913 and 1914. Only Hazel Hotchkiss Wightman, the previous three years, and Alice Marble (1938, 1939 and 1940) swept the field as thoroughly.

She was unique for an American woman in transferring her talent to golf, spectacularly in 1924. Shortly after making the U.S. semis at Forest Hills, losing to Helen Wills in three sets, she entered the U.S. Women's Golf Championships and beat the legendary Glenna Collett Vare to reach the final. There she lost the title to Dorothy Campbell Hurd.

In one of the most demanding days in tennis annals, Mary played 82 games while winning the 1912 singles, doubles and mixed finals all in the same afternoon, much of it in a downpour. "The rain was coming down in torrents, and still we went on," she later recalled, "our rackets mushy and our clothes soaked." She beat Eleo Sears, 6-4, 6-2, in the all-comers singles to become champion since Wightman didn't defend the title. With Dorothy Green she won the doubles, 6-2, 5-7, 6-0, over Maud Barger Wallach and Mrs. Frederick Schmitz. And, with Dick Williams, she won the soggy mixed, 6-4, 2-6, 11-9, over Evelyn Sears and Bill Clothier.

Mary ranked No. 1 in the U.S. in 1913 and 1914, the first two years of the Top Ten, returning to the select group at No. 2 in 1921 and 1924, and No. 6 in 1925. In 1926 she had a world ranking of No. 6, the USTA declining to give her a high ranking that she'd earned because she turned pro. She was later married to Kenneth Kenneth-Smith. Browne, remaining a fine golfer in her 70s, capable of shooting close to her age, died Aug. 19, 1971, in Laguna Hills, Cal. She was elected to the Hall of Fame in 1957.

MAJOR TITLES *(13)—U.S. singles, 1912, 1913, 1914; Wimbledon doubles, 1926; U.S. doubles, 1912, 1913, 1914, 1921, 1925; U.S. mixed, 1912, 1913, 1914, 1921.* OTHER U.S. TITLES *(3)—Indoor doubles, 1926, with Elizabeth Ryan; Clay Court singles, 1914; Clay Court doubles, 1914, with Louise Riddell Williams.* WIGHTMAN CUP—*1925, 1926; record: 0-2 in singles, 1-1 in doubles.* SINGLES RECORD IN THE MAJORS: *French (4-1), Wimbledon (0-1), U.S. (22-4).*

JACQUES BRUGNON
France (1895–1978)

Jacques "Toto" Brugnon was the elder of France's celebrated Four Musketeers who won the Davis Cup in 1927 from the U.S., and kept it six years. He preceded the other three—Jean Borotra, Henri Cochet, René Lacoste—as an internationalist, playing first on the Cup team in 1921. A master at doubles, he won Wimbledon four times, 1926 and 1928 with Cochet and 1932 and 1933 with Borotra, and appeared in three other finals. He won the French five times, three with Cochet, two with Borotra, and the Australian with Borotra, plus two French mixed for a dozen major titles.

Although doubles expertise overshadowed his singles, the small (5-foot-6½, 139 pounds), neatly mustachioed and courtly Toto had many fine moments alone. He was ranked world Nos. 10 and 9 in 1926 and 1927, golden years for the French: they were 40 percent of the Top Ten, his fellow Musketeers occupying places in the first four, Lacoste at No. 1. In his greatest singles moment, his clever volleying took him to the Wimbledon semis of 1926 and five times a match point away from joining Borotra in the championship round. American Bob Kinsey got away from him, though, 6-4, 4-6, 6-3, 3-6,,9-7, slipping from 4-5, 15-40, and 5-6, 15-40 and ad out in the last set. Wallis Myers, the connoisseur, wrote: "Brugnon is a player of rare stroke variety and delicacy of touch." He was a quarterfinalist in 1927, and stands fourth among all male Wimbledonians in wins with 129: 37-19 in singles, 69-16 in doubles, 23-16 in mixed.

His Davis Cup career ran 11 years, and he had a hand in four of the Cup triumphs as a right-handed left-court player. For a time he was a teaching professional in California. He was born May 11, 1895, in Paris, and died there March 20, 1978. He entered the Hall of Fame in 1976.

MAJOR TITLES (12)—*Australian doubles, 1928; French doubles, 1927, 1928, 1930, 1932, 1934; Wimbledon doubles, 1926, 1928, 1932, 1933; French mixed, 1925, 1926.* DAVIS CUP—*1921, 1923, 1924, 1925, 1926, 1927, 1930, 1931, 1932, 1933, 1934; record: 4-2 in singles, 22-9 in doubles.* SINGLES RECORD IN THE MAJORS: *Australian (1-1), French (21-13), Wimbledon (37-19), U.S. (12-11)*

DON BUDGE
United States (1916—)

See page 85.

MARIA BUENO
Brazil (1939—)

See page 386.

MAY SUTTON BUNDY
United States (1886–1975)

Although May Godfray Sutton was, as a U.S. citizen, the first outsider from beyond the British Isles—and first American—to win Wimbledon, she had a distinct English connection. Born in Plymouth Sept. 25, 1886, daughter of a British Naval captain, Adolphus Sutton, she moved with the family at age six to a ranch outside of Pasadena, Cal. There her father built a concrete tennis court, the starting point for herself and three of her four sisters to become outstanding players.

Capt. Sutton was one of the greatest tennis sires: May won Wimbledon; grandchildren Dorothy Bundy (Cheney, daughter of May) won the Australian in 1938, John Doeg (son of Violet) won the U.S. in 1930; great grandson Brian Cheney had a U.S. national ranking and played the U.S. and Wimbledon. The saying in Southern California was "It takes a Sutton to beat a Sutton" because four of them—May, Violet, Florence, Ethel—dominated that section for almost a generation through 1915.

May, a husky 5-foot-4½, 140-pound, highly competitive right-hander with a powerful topspin forehand, was the best known of them, with her U.S. title of 1904, 6-1, 6-2, over defending Bessie Moore, and her two Wimbledon titles over Dorothea Douglass, in 1905 and 1907. She took the title from the Englishwoman, 6-3, 6-4, lost in the following year, and subdued Dorothea (who'd become Mrs. Lambert Chambers), 6-1, 6-4, as the two contested three successive finals. She shocked English crowds at first by rolling up her sleeves to bare her elbows, and wearing a shorter skirt than most, showing ankles.

In 1912 she married Tom Bundy, a top player who won three U.S. doubles titles (1912, 1913, 1914) with Maurice McLoughlin. Their daughter, Australian champ Dorothy Cheney, ranked as high as No. 6 in the world in 1946. Now in her 80s, she continues to win a record number of U.S. senior titles. May had her best days before U.S. rankings for women were established in 1913. But her groundstrokes were formidable enough when she made a comeback in 1921 to earn her the No. 4 ranking at age 35. That made her the third of the sisters to rank in the U.S. Top Ten—a record. Ethel was No. 2 in 1913; Florence 3, 2 and 4 in 1913, 1914 and 1915, respectively. Moreover May played Wightman Cup for the U.S. four years later and ranked No. 5 in 1928 at 42. She entered the Hall of Fame in 1956, and died Oct. 4, 1975, in Santa Monica, Cal.

MAJOR TITLES (4)—*Wimbledon singles, 1905, 1907; U.S. singles, 1904; U.S. doubles, 1904.* OTHER U.S. TITLES (2)—*Clay Court singles, 1912; Clay Court mixed, 1912, with Fred Harris.* WIGHTMAN CUP—*1925; record: 0-1 in doubles.* SINGLES RECORD IN THE MAJORS: *Wimbledon (14-1), U.S. (10-2).*

MABEL CAHILL
Ireland (1863–?)

Little is known of Mabel Esmonde Cahill except that, as an Irish citizen, she was the first foreigner to win one of the major championships. That was the U.S. singles of 1891 when she got even with Ellen Roosevelt, who had defeated her in the all-comers final of 1890 and gone on to win the title. In 1891, Cahill, a right-hander, decimated the Roosevelts, beating Ellen's sister, Grace, in the all-comers final, 6-3, 7-5, and then Ellen in the challenge round, 6-4, 6-1, 4-6, 6-3. She retained the title by defeating Bessie Moore in the 1892 challenge round, 5-7, 6-3, 6-4, 4-6, 6-2. That year she also won the mixed doubles with Clarence Hobart.

But she declined to return to Philadelphia for the 1893 Championships, defaulting her title to Aline Terry in the challenge round. During her residence in the U.S. she belonged to the New York Tennis Club. She was born April 2, 1863, in Ballyragget, County Kilkenny, Ireland. No details of her death, believed to have occurred in Ireland in 1904 or 1905, have been found. She was named to the Hall of Fame in 1976.

MAJOR TITLES (5)—*U.S. singles, 1891, 1892; U.S. doubles, 1891, 1892; U.S. mixed, 1892.* SINGLES RECORD IN THE MAJORS: *U.S. (6-1).*

OLIVER CAMPBELL
United States (1871–1953)

For a century Oliver Samuel Campbell had the distinction of being the youngest to win the U.S. singles title. He did it as a 19-year-old Columbia student in 1890. (Pete Sampras, a younger 19, became the youngest when he won the title in 1990.)

Four years earlier, Campbell, at 15 years, 5 months, had lost in the opening round at Newport to the man he would dethrone four years later,

Henry Slocum. Oliver was the youngest entry until 1918 when Vinnie Richards undercut him by a month.

After his first exposure to Newport, Campbell determined to transform himself from a baseliner into a net-storming volleyer. "I ran to the net behind every service until the day I retired," he later recalled. It paid off in a U.S. doubles title (his first of three) in the company of Valentine Hall in 1888, with whom he'd won the Intercollegiate doubles that year for Columbia.

Campbell, a 5-foot-11½ right-hander, lost to Slocum again in the 1888 semis, and to lefty Quincy Shaw in the 1889 all-comers final. But in 1890 he outbattled Bob Huntington, 3-6, 6-2, 5-7, 6-2, 6-1, in the semis, and Percy Knapp, 8-6, 0-6, 6-2, 6-3, in the all-comers final. Stronger physically, he kept rushing the net, and at last beat Slocum, deposing the champ, 6-2 4-6, 6-3, 6-1.

Campbell endured another struggle in the challenge round of 1891, 2-6, 7-5, 7-9, 6-1, 6-2, over Clarence Hobart. He made it three straight, 7-5, 3-6, 6-3, 7-5, over Fred Hovey in 1892, and retired, leaving the 1893 title to Bob Wrenn by default. In 1888 he made the U.S. Top Ten for the first of five straight years, No. 1 in 1890, 1891 and 1892. He was born Feb. 25, 1871, in New York, and died July 11, 1953, in Campellton, Canada. He entered the Hall of Fame in 1955.

MAJOR TITLES (6)—*U.S. single's, 1890, 1891, 1892; U.S. doubles, 1888, 1891, 1892. Other U.S. titles (2)—Intercollegiate doubles, 1888, with Valentine Hall; 1889, with Empie Wright.* SINGLES RECORD IN THE MAJORS: *U.S. (16-3).*

ROSIE CASALS
United States (1948—)

Citizen Kane, who wasn't much fun, had his mysterious "Rosebud." There was, however, no mystery about the Rosebud of tennis, Citizen Casals. She just wanted to be the best ever. Inch-for-inch she was—and the fun flowed in all directions from this diminutive dynamo who took such joy from playing, and passed it along to grateful witnesses.

Tiny package, explosive contents. Tennis was no waiting game at the baseline for 62-inch Rosemary "Rosie/Rosebud" Casals. She went for the jugular fast, a serve-and-volleying acrobat whose incredible arsenal of strokes and tankful of competitive verve were necessities merely to stay alive among the sisterhood that established female professional tennis during the 1970s.

"I'm out there with (5-foot-11 Margaret 'The Arm') Court" recalls San Franciscan Casals, "with those arms and legs that stretch forever, and I had to make my shots count right away."

They counted and counted and counted during a 15-year career in the stratosphere, 12 times in the World Top Ten (1966–77), No. 3 in 1970. So much so that she was elevated to the Hall in 1996.

Billie Jean King and protégé Rosie Casals . . . names that went together like wine and roses. No finer female combo illuminated doubles. But all the while their influence as pioneering pros ran deeper than the five Wimbledon and two U.S. titles together. Although Rosie, the riveting volleyer, is the smallest modern in the tennis valhalla, she and Billie Jean were giants in launching the long march of the "Long Way Babies" as the Virginia Slims circuit began to take shape in 1970.

With another Hall of Famer, Gladys Heldman, publisher of *World Tennis* magazine, as behind-the-scenes organizer and encourager, B.J. and Rosie were the ringleaders on court, close friends, doubles partners, frequent final-round foes, super saleswomen for the emerging tour. They were perfect role players, feisty but good-humored kids off the public courts who believed women had a destiny in professional sport. A born (Sept. 16, 1948) and bred San Franciscan, right-handed Rosie started at Golden Gate Park.

"Those early Slims days were an exciting time, and a little scary, too, although I laugh looking back at 1970," Rosie says. "Even though open tennis came in in 1968, the men got most of the money and publicity. The tournaments were still like the amateur days, men and women together. We knew we had to break away, go on our own. That first Slims tournament, '70 in Houston, the USTA didn't like our rebel ways and threatened to suspend us Americans if we played. They did, and for a while we wondered if that was the end of tennis for us. Of course it wasn't."

A full Slims tour commenced in 1971 and King and Casals "played our little bahoolas off"—Billie Jean's words. That year Rosie played a record 32 tournaments in singles, 31 in doubles, amounting to 205 matches while Billie Jean was in the same neighborhood with 36-21-210. More than 200 matches in a season? Steffi Graf has played as many as 117 only once.

Different times. "We had to play much more than they do today because the money was slight." Rosie offers her soulful gamine's smile, and shrugs when you mention her unapproachable record of playing 685 singles and doubles tournaments. "If you won both the singles and doubles it was worth only a couple of thousand bucks. You couldn't afford to default with an injury. And we were paying all our own expenses, not getting free hotel and per diem like the stars now. But I'm glad for them. We were trying to pave the way.

"I got $3,750 when I lost the U.S. Open final to Court, the last victim in her Grand Slam. Not even close to what a first-round loser got in '96. [$10,000]. But it didn't matter. We thought we were rich, and there was a great feeling of family, of being together to make the tour work, provide the future for the game."

A distant relative of the cello virtuoso, Pablo Casals, the Rosebud improvised brilliant cadenzas on her strings. For sheer shotmaking sorcery, plus merrymaking on one side of the net, the amalgam of Casals and Ilie Nastase, winning the Wimbledon mixed in 1970 and 1972, may never be equalled. "I had to take care of him, mother him a little when he went crazy," she says.

Doubles was her shtick, 56 of the titles with King. But Rosie was a singles contender at all the majors, and beat King and clay maven Nancy Richey in succession to win the first big bucks tourney, the Family Circle Cup, worth $30,000 to her, in 1973. She won 11 singles, 112 pro doubles titles, the latter second only to Martina Navratilova's 162, collecting the last as a 41-year-old, "for old times' sake," in Oakland in 1988 alongside Martina. Her prize money, $1,364,955. Casals was a quarterfinalist or better in all the majors: Australian semifinal, 1967; French quarterfinal, 1969 and 1970; Wimbledon semifinal, 1967, 1969, 1970, 1972; U.S. final, 1970, 1971, semifinal, 1969.

Dashing dressmaker, Hall of Famer Ted Tinling, adored her, gowning Rosie in spangles, sequins, a variety of color combinations. At Wimbledon '72 they caused a stir when his purple-squiggled dress—with Casals in it—was evicted. "It was predominantly white, complying with the rules," she says, "but the purple designs upset the referee. He ordered me off the court to change. I loved to get their goat and enjoyed the whole scene.

"It became a famous dress and beat me to the Hall of Fame to be displayed some time ago." But Citizen Casals has caught up with her notorious frock, and a Rosebud now blooms in Newport.

MAJOR TITLES *(12) (all doubles)—Wimbledon, 1967, 1968, 1970, 1971, 1973; U.S. 1967, 1971, 1974, 1982; Wimbledon mixed, 1970, 1972; U.S. mixed, 1975. OTHER U.S. TITLES (8)—Hard Court singles, 1965. Indoor doubles, 1966, 1968, 1975 (with King), 1976 (with Françoise Durr); Hard Court doubles, 1966 (with King); Clay Court doubles, 1970 (with Gail Chanfreau); Hard Court mixed, 1966 (with Ian Crookenden). Federation Cup, 1967, 1976, 1977, 1978, 1979, 1980, 1981, helped U.S. win all seven (8-1 in singles, 27-1 in doubles). Wightman Cup, 1967, 1976, 1977, 1978, 1979, 1980, 1981, helped U.S. win all seven (1-3 in singles, 6-1 in doubles). SINGLES RECORD IN THE MAJORS: Australian (9-5), French (10-7), Wimbledon (48-18), U.S. (47-21).*

MALCOLM CHACE
United States (1875–1955)

A Rhode Islander born in Valley Falls on March 12, 1875, beanpole Malcolm Greene Chace, 6-foot-1, 150 pounds, made his first mark in the game by winning the U.S. Interscholastic title in 1892 for University Grammar in Providence. In 1893 (for Brown) and 1894 and 1895 (for Yale), he became the only three-straight winner of both the U.S. Intercollegiate singles and doubles titles, the only man to win both for two different colleges. He was a semifinalist at the U.S. Championships in 1894, losing to Bill Larned and won the doubles title in 1895 with Robert Wrenn. Right-handed, he ranked in the U.S. Top Ten four times, beginning in 1892, No. 3 in 1895. He died July 16, 1955 in Yarmouth, Mass., and was named to the Hall of Fame in 1961.

MAJOR TITLE *(1)—U.S. doubles, 1895.* OTHER U.S. TITLES *(6)—Intercollegiate singles, 1893, 1894, 1895; Intercollegiate doubles, 1893, with Clarence Budlong; 1894, 1895, with Arthur Foote. SINGLES RECORD IN THE MAJORS: U.S. (16-9).*

DOROTHEA CHAMBERS
Great Britain (1878–1960)

See page 87.

CLARENCE CLARK
United States (1859–1937)

A member of a distinguished Philadelphia family, Clarence Monroe Clark had the distinction of winning the first U.S. doubles title at Newport in 1881. He and Fred Taylor beat Alexander van Rensselaer and Arthur Newbold, 6-5, 6-4, 6-5. Earlier they eliminated the favorites, Dick Sears and James Dwight. The next year at Newport he made it to the singles final, losing to Sears, the original champ, 6-1, 6-4, 6-0. His brother, Joe Clark (named to the Hall of Fame in 1955), won the first Intercollegiate title for Harvard in 1883.

Joe and Clarence tested foreign waters for America, journeying to England in 1883, playing and losing two doubles matches against the dominant Renshaw twins, Willie and Ernest. Clarence was the first secretary of the newly formed USTA in 1881 and was, along with Dwight and Eugenius Outerbridge, a guiding light in the organization's establishment. He was born Aug. 27, 1859, in Germantown, Pa., died there June 29, 1937, and was named to the Hall of Fame in 1983.

MAJOR TITLE *(1)—U.S. doubles, 1881.* SINGLES RECORD IN THE MAJORS: U.S. (7-2).

JOE CLARK
United States (1861–1956)

Two years after the first U.S. Championships at Newport, the Intercollegiate Championships was established in 1883 and won by Joseph Bill Clark of Harvard in both singles and doubles. Clark, a senior, was the Harvard champ that year, feeling justifiably proud of himself because he won the title over classmate Dick Sears, who happened to be the U.S. champion.

The first Intercollegiates, which Sears did not enter, was played on the grounds of a mental hospital in Hartford, and Clark recalled that some of the patients served as ball boys. Clark, a right-hander, was a Philadelphian, brother of Clarence Clark, who won the first U.S. doubles title with Fred Taylor. Together he and his brother were a formidable doubles team. They played in England in 1883 after beating the reigning U.S. champs, Sears and Dr. James Dwight, in matches in Boston and New York. They represented the U.S. against the foremost English pair, the Renshaw brothers, Ernest and Willie, in a series for the world championship. The Renshaws won the two matches played, losing one set in the first.

In 1885 Joe Clark joined Sears to win the U.S. doubles, 6-3, 6-0, 6-2, over Henry Slocum and Percy Knapp. Joe was a singles semifinalist in 1885, 1886 and 1887, and brother Clarence lost the 1882 final to Sears. Joe ranked in the U.S. Top Ten five straight years from 1885, No. 4 in 1888. He was born Nov. 30, 1861, in Germantown, Pa., entered the Hall of Fame in 1955, and died April 14, 1956. He was president of the USTA, 1889–91.

MAJOR TITLE *(1)—U.S. doubles, 1885*. OTHER U.S. TITLES *(2)—Intercollegiate singles, 1883; Intercollegiate doubles, 1883, with Howard Taylor.* SINGLES RECORD IN THE MAJORS: *U.S. (18-11).*

BILL CLOTHIER
United States (1881–1962)

Another Harvard man to win the Intercollegiate championship (1902) in the early days, William Jackson Clothier was the U.S. champ four years later, ranking No. 1 in the U.S. A right-handed net rusher, Clothier said that "he never played better" than in the 1906 Championships, gaining confidence from his quarterfinal victory over Fred Alexander, 8-6, 6-2, 4-6, 1-6, 7-5, in which he came from triple match point (2-5, 0-40) to race through the last five games. He took the title from Beals Wright in the challenge round, 6-3, 6-0, 6-4.

He lost the U.S. final to Holcombe Ward in 1904 and, in a five-set battle, to Bill Larned in 1909. He held a Top Ten ranking for 11 years between 1901 and 1914. In 1905 he beat two French champions, Max Decugis, 6-3, 6-4, 6-4, and Maurice Germot, 6-3, 5-7, 6-1, 6-3, in the first U.S. Davis Cup engagement abroad, a 5-0 victory over France at Queen's Club in London. Although he wasn't chosen for the next tie against Australasia or the final against Britain, Clothier, a powerful, aggressive 6-foot-2, 170-pounder, caught the attention of scribe Wallace Myers in a good Wimbledon showing. It was a fourth-rounder lost to future champ Tony Wilding, 5-7, 1-6, 8-6, 7-5, 10-8, in 3½ hours on Centre Court. Bill led 5-2, 40-15 with two match points in the third. "Both men were such splendid specimens of youth and vigor, such hard hitters, such gallant fighters," Myers wrote. He and his son, William Clothier II, won two U.S. Father and Son doubles titles in 1935 and 1936.

He was born in Philadelphia Sept. 27, 1881, and died there Sept. 4, 1962. He was inducted into the Hall of Fame in 1956.

MAJOR TITLE *(1)—U.S. singles, 1906*. OTHER U.S. TITLES *(2)—Intercollegiate singles, 1902; Intercollegiate doubles, 1902, with Edward Leonard.* DAVIS CUP—*1905 and 1909; record: 4-1 in singles.* SINGLES RECORD IN THE MAJORS: *Wimbledon (2-1), U.S. (57-18).*

HENRI COCHET
France (1901–87)

See page 88.

MAUREEN CONNOLLY
United States (1934–69)

See page 387.

SARAH PALFREY COOKE
United States (1912—)

See page 89.

ASHLEY COOPER
Australia (1936—)

Among the seemingly endless platoon of Aussies who were to dominate the world after Frank Sedgman showed them how, handsome, dark-haired Ashley John Cooper was the third of their number to win Wimbledon (1958) and the fourth to capture the U.S. the same year. Because he turned pro shortly after those successes, the right-handed Ash's career in the public eye was brief though very productive. His last two amateur years, 1957 and 1958, could compare well to anyone's: six finals and four championship out of eight major starts, and two semis at the French, the only ones he didn't win.

An athletic 5-foot-10, he was of an attacking mindset, like the others of his tribe, a thorough, smooth, if not spectacular, stroker in attaining his goals at the net. He also won the Australian championship in 1958, one of only 10 men to grab three majors in one year. But whatever hopes he had for a Grand Slam were dashed in Paris by Luis Ayala, 9-11, 4-6, 6-4, 6-2, 7-5. Still, he had one of the finest years with a 25-1 match record in the majors.

Cooper, who had lost the 1957 Wimbledon final to Lew Hoad, was upset in the U.S. final by unseeded Mal Anderson, but they got together three months later to successfully defend the Davis Cup against the U.S., 3-2. Despite an ankle injury incurred during their final at Forest Hills in 1958, Cooper regrouped and came from behind to beat Anderson, 6-2, 3-6, 4-6, 10-8, 8-6. Cooper spent three years, 1956–58, in the World Top Ten, No. 1

the last two years. He was born Sept. 15, 1936, in Melbourne, and entered the Hall of Fame in 1991.

MAJOR TITLES *(8)—Australian singles, 1957, 1958; Wimbledon singles, 1958; U.S. singles, 1958; Australian doubles, 1958; French doubles, 1957, 1958; U.S. doubles, 1957.* DAVIS CUP—*1957, 1958; record: 2-2 in singles.* SINGLES RECORD IN THE MAJORS: *Australian (16-3), French (13-3), Wimbledon (19-4), U.S. (20-4).*

MARGARET SMITH COURT
Australia (1942—)

See page 392.

JACK CRAWFORD
Australia (1908–91)

See page 91.

DWIGHT DAVIS
United States (1879–1945)

A left-handed, big-serving Harvardian who won the Intercollegiate title in 1899, 6-foot, 190-pound Dwight Filley Davis ranked in the U.S. Top Ten four times between 1898 and 1901, No. 2 in 1899 and 1900. But he is best known for launching in 1900 the great worldwide team competition that bears his name: Davis Cup. He intended for it to be called the International Lawn Tennis Challenge Trophy when he purchased the silver bowl at the Boston jeweler, Shreve, Crump & Low. His fellow members at Longwood Cricket Club, where the inaugural was staged in 1900, jocularly referred to it as "Dwight's pot." Soon, just-plain "Davis Cup" was the accepted handle.

The original U.S. team was a Harvard production, Davis captaining, he and schoolmates Malcolm Whitman and Holcombe Ward playing a 3-0 victory over the British Isle. Davis was a member of President Coolidge's cabinet as Secretary of War, and also served his country as governor-general of the Philippines. He was born in St. Louis July 5, 1879, and died Nov. 28, 1945, in Washington, D.C. He was inducted into the Hall of Fame in 1956.

MAJOR TITLES *(3)—U.S. doubles, 1899, 1900, 1901.* OTHER U.S. TITLES *(2)—Intercollegiate single, 1899; Intercollegiate doubles, 1899, with Holcombe Ward.* DAVIS CUP— *1900, 1902; record: 1-0 in singles, 1-1 in doubles.* SINGLES RECORD IN THE MAJORS: *U.S. (16-7).*

LOTTIE DOD
Great Britain (1871–1960)

Tall and athletic, Charlotte "Lottie" Dod became the youngest of major champions at 15 years, 10 months by winning Wimbledon in 1887, knocking off the defending champion, Blanche Bingley, 6-2, 6-0, in the challenge round. She played four other years, never lost—in 10 matches she dropped one set—though her championship foe, each time, now Mrs. Hillyard, did give her a tough match, 6-8, 6-1, 6-4, in the 1893 final. She also won the Irish title in 1887, was exceptional at ice skating, archery (an Olympic silver medalist in 1908), field hockey and golf. She represented Britain in international hockey in 1889 and 1890 and won the British Ladies Golf Championship in 1904 at Troon, defeating May Hezlet in the final, 1-up. She won 10 of 12 matches at Wimbledon. Born Sept. 24, 1871, in Lower Bebington, England, she died June 27, 1960, in Sway, England. She entered the Hall of Fame in 1983.

MAJOR TITLES *(5)—Wimbledon singles, 1887, 1888, 1891, 1892, 1893.* SINGLES RECORD IN THE MAJORS: *Wimbledon (10-2).*

JOHNNY DOEG
United States (1908–78)

As the fourth left-handed U.S. champ (following Bob Wrenn, Beals Wright, Lindley Murray), sixth-seeded John Thomas Godfray Hope Doeg hit the title jackpot in 1930. As a collateral exploit, he exploded 28 aces in the semis to thwart top-seeded Bill Tilden's fervent bid for a record eighth title, 10-8, 6-3, 3-6, 12-10. That was Big Bill's Forest Hills farewell. But there was more to Doeg's championship than that. His was a strenuous serve-and-volleying rush to the prize, a determination to keep pressure on foes with in-

cessant in-your-face forays to the net. Quite different from his baselining Aunt May (Sutton), who'd won the women's title 26 years before.

But at 6-foot-1, 170 pounds, 21-year-old blond Doeg could keep the pounding going. He lost seven sets in six matches, two to ex-Harvard football All-American Barry Wood at the outset, and two more in the quarters to Frank Hunter, 11-13, 6-4, 3-6, 6-2, 6-4. He got past the last-hurrahing 37-year-old Tilden, the Wimbledon champ (Doeg had lost there in the semis to Wilmer Allison), and was fiercely opposed by 11th-seeded 19-year-old Frank Shields. Refusing to bend in the record-length closing set of a major singles final, Doeg won, 10-8, 1-6, 6-4, 16-14. An ace cancelled Shields' set point at 13-14. The title won him the No. 1 U.S. ranking, No. 4 in the world, up from No. 7 in 1929. His brilliant serving, speed and spin, made him a feared foe for five years as he ranked in the U.S. Top Ten between 1927 and 1931.

Doeg and George Lott were Wimbledon doubles finalists in 1930 and won the U.S. titles of 1929 and 1930. He was the U.S. junior champ in 1926, the first of eight males to make the transition from the 18s to the adult championship. Johnny was born in Guayamas, Sonora, Mexico, Dec. 7, 1908, and grew up in California. He was a son of a Southern California champ, the former Violet Sutton.

He entered the Hall of Fame in 1962 and died April 27, 1978, in Redding, Cal.

MAJOR TITLES *(3)—U.S. singles, 1930; U.S. doubles, 1929, 1930.* DAVIS CUP—*1930; record: 1-0 in singles.* SINGLES RECORD IN THE MAJORS: *Wimbledon (5-1), U.S. (19-5).*

LAURIE DOHERTY
Great Britain (1875–1919)

Laurie, or "Little Do," born Hugh Laurence Doherty, was the shorter, at 5-foot-10, younger, and probably better, of the Cambridge (Trinity College)-educated Doherty brothers who illuminated the tennis skies in their native England and at Wimbledon at the turn of the century. Although

Laurie lost the 1898 Wimbledon final to Reggie, 6-1, in the fifth, he won the title five straight times, beginning in 1902.

The brothers carried Britain to its first four Davis Cups, beginning in 1903, by taking it from the U.S., 4-1, in Boston after falling short, 3-2, the previous year in Brooklyn. He never lost a Cup match, winning seven singles and five doubles.

The Dohertys, who parted their dark wavy hair in the middle, also devised the more aggressive doubles formation of parting the pair, with the receiver's partner at the net, to be joined by the receiver.

As the first serious foreign contenders for the U.S. singles crown, the brothers failed in 1902 at Newport. Laurie sportingly defaulted to Reggie rather than face him in the semis, whereupon Reggie beat Malcolm Whitman in the allcomers final, 6-1, 3-6, 6-3, 6-0, but lost the challenge round to the defender, Bill Larned, 4-6, 6-2, 6-4, 8-6.

But in 1903, after Reggie returned the default courtesy to his brother in the quarters, Laurie became the initial alien male champ of the U.S., beating Bill Clothier in the all-comers, 6-3, 6-2, 6-3, and unseating Larned, 6-0, 6-3, 10-8. The Brothers D took the U.S. doubles both years, and had been gold medalists in the 1900 Olympics, winning the doubles, and Laurie taking the singles as well. Laurie was born in London Oct. 8, 1875, and died Aug. 21, 1919, in Broadstairs, England. He accompanied his brother into the Hall of Fame in 1980.

MAJOR TITLES *(16)—Wimbledon singles, 1902, 1903, 1904, 1905, 1906; U.S. singles, 1903; Wimbledon doubles, 1897, 1898, 1899, 1900, 1901, 1903, 1904, 1905; U.S. doubles, 1902, 1903.* DAVIS CUP—*1902, 1903, 1904, 1905, 1906; record: 7-0 in singles, 5-0 in doubles.* SINGLES RECORD IN THE MAJORS: *Wimbledon (21-6), U.S. (12-0).*

REGGIE DOHERTY
Great Britain (1872–1910)

The appealing and dominant Doherty brothers, Reggie and Laurie, Cambridge (Trinity College) men, enhanced the popularity of tennis and Wimbledon in their homeland, England, at the turn of the century, and were the backbone of Britain's first four Davis Cup triumphs, 1903–06. Reginald Frank Doherty, the older and known as "Big Do," at 6-foot-1, only 140 pounds, was frequently ill with digestive problems, and wasn't considered as good as Laurie, but did win four straight Wimbledons (1897–1900), beating his sibling in the 1898 final, 6-1 in the fifth.

Contesting a record 10 straight doubles finals together (1897–1906), they won a record eight, losing only in 1896 to the Baddeley brothers, Herbert and Wilfred, and in 1902 and 1906 to Syd Smith and Frank Riseley. Reggie, who played the left court with his brother, was in 11 straight, losing with Harold Nesbit in 1897. They won all five Davis Cup doubles together, clinching the 1904, 1905 and 1906 Cups. Reggie was born Oct. 14, 1872, in London and died Dec. 29, 1910. They entered the Hall of Fame together in 1980.

MAJOR TITLES *(14)—Wimbledon singles, 1897, 1898, 1899, 1900; U.S. doubles, 1902, 1903; Wimbledon doubles, 1897, 1898, 1899, 1900, 1901, 1903, 1904, 1905.* DAVIS CUP—*1902, 1903, 1904, 1905, 1906; record: 2-1 in singles, 5-0 in doubles.* SINGLES RECORD IN THE MAJORS: *Wimbledon (9-5), U.S. (7-1).*

JAROSLAV DROBNY
Czechoslovakia/Egypt/Great Britain (1921—)

See page 393.

MARGARET OSBORNE DUPONT
United States (1918—)

See page 395.

JAMES DWIGHT
United States (1852–1917)

Hailed deservedly as the "Father of American Tennis," Doc Dwight, a Bostonian and graduate of Harvard and Harvard Medical, may have introduced the game to the U.S., playing with his cousin, Fred Sears, at Nahant, Mass., in 1874. It arrived from England at several locations that year. He did organize and win the initial tournament, a sociable competition at Nahant in 1876.

More importantly he was a driving force behind the organization of the USTA (then the U.S. National Lawn Tennis Association) in 1881, and its first National Championship that year at the Newport Casino, as well as the first Davis Cup match (1900) between the U.S. and the British Isles at his Boston club, Longwood Cricket Club.

As a player, right-handed and short (about 5-foot-5), he was more adept at doubles, sharing five U.S. titles with his protégé, Dick Sears, who defeated him in the 1883 singles final. He was No. 2 in 1885 and 1886, the first years of U.S. rankings, and No. 3 in 1888. He, Sears and A. L. Rives were the American pioneers at Wimbledon in 1884, Dwight the only one to win a round. He beat F. J. Ridgeway, 6-2, 6-1, 6-1, the first U.S. victory, a small one at the Big W. Doc fought gamely against ambidextrous Herbert Chipp, who had removed Rives, but fell to nothing but forehands, 6-1, 2-6, 6-3, 2-6, 7-5. Though Dwight and Sears reached the doubles semis, the U.S. champs were no match for the dynamic, ruling Renshaw twins, Willie and Ernest, 6-0, 6-1, 6-2. Dwight returned the following year, making greater strides, to the semis where future champ Herbert Lawford topspun him out, 6-2, 6-2, 6-3.

Shepherding the USTA through its formative years, he was president 21 years, 1882–84 and 1894–1911. He entered the Hall of Fame in 1955. Born in Paris July 14, 1852, he died July 13, 1917 in Mattapoisett, Mass. His son, Dr. Richard Dwight, a retired Paris physician, continues to compete, in super-senior events for the over-85s.

MAJOR TITLES (5)—*U.S. doubles, 1882, 1883, 1884, 1886, 1887.* SINGLES RECORD IN THE MAJORS: *Wimbledon (4-2), U.S. (8-3).*

ROY EMERSON
Australia (1936—)

See page 398.

CHRIS EVERT
United States (1954—)

See page 400.

BOB FALKENBURG
United States (1926—)

A gangling, dark-haired 6-foot-3 right-hander, Robert Falkenburg came from a tennis family. He and brother Tom won the U.S. Interscholastic title for Los Angeles Fairfax High in 1942, the same year Bob won the singles. Both played in the U.S. Championships at Forest Hills, as did sister Jinx. But Bob, seventh-seeded, made the family's name with a sensational Wimbledon triumph in 1948, eluding three match points while defeating second-seeded John Bromwich, 7-5, 0-6, 6-2, 3-6, 7-5. Bromwich served at 5-3, 40-15 and advantage. Falkenburg responded boldly with backhand passing returns. The last appeared futile. Brom made no attempt to play it, and the crowd gasped as the ball unexpectedly landed just inside the baseline.

He and Jack Kramer won the doubles the year before, and in 1944, at 18, he won the U.S. doubles with Don McNeill, one of the youngest to hold that title.

A slam-bang, big-serving net-charger, he attended the University of Southern California, winning the U.S. Intercollegiate title in 1946. He was an early success, his career short. He won the U.S. junior title in 1942 and 1943, the second year while in the U.S. Army Air Force. He was one of the youngest to make his entry into the U.S. Top Ten, 17 in 1943 at No. 7. He was there four more times through 1948, No. 5 the last year. He was No. 7 in the world rankings that year.

A semifinalist at the U.S. Championships in 1946 and a quarterfinalist in 1947, he lost both times to the champ, Kramer. He was also a quarterfinalist in 1948.

Bromwich had his revenge as Falkenburg defended the Wimbledon title in 1949, taking their quarterfinal, 3-6, 9-11, 6-0, 6-0, 6-4. Falkenburg did not endear himself to customers by his practice of tanking sets to rest.

Marrying a Brazilian and becoming a resident, Bob played Davis Cup for Brazil. He was born Jan. 29, 1926, in Brooklyn, N.Y., and entered the Hall of Fame in 1974.

MAJOR TITLES (3)—*Wimbledon singles, 1948; Wimbledon doubles, 1947; U.S. doubles, 1944.* OTHER U.S. TITLE—*Indoor doubles, 1947, with Jack Kramer.* DAVIS CUP—*Brazil 1954, 1955; record: 2-4 in singles, 1-3 in doubles.* SINGLES RECORD IN THE MAJORS: *Wimbledon (17-3), U.S. (18-8).*

NEALE FRASER
Australia (1933—)

A serve-bombing lefty whose onerous delivery was flat, sliced and kicked, Neale Fraser backed it up with tough volleying and was a marvelous competitor. Solidly built and athletic at 6-foot-1, he was especially overpowering on fast surfaces. Although he won Wimbledon in 1960 and the U.S. title in 1959 and 1960, Fraser found team play—doubles and Davis Cup—nearest his heart. As one of eight men to win all four majors in doubles, Fraser took three each Australian, French and U.S. and two Wimbledon with three different partners: Ashley Cooper, Lew Hoad, Roy Emerson.

His toughest match of the 1960 Wimbledon championship was won literally over the dead-weary body of Butch Buchholz. But before the frustrated American keeled over with cramps in their quarterfinal, Fraser had to dodge five match points in the 30-game fourth set. It ended with winner Fraser on the short end in games, 4-6, 6-3, 4-6, 15-15.

His most successful alliance was with Emerson for eight majors. Losing only one singles, he was a mainstay for four Cup-winning Australia sides, starting in 1959 at Forest Hills. Then he won both his singles, and, with Emerson, the doubles in heisting the punchbowl from the U.S., 3-2. On opening day he beat Wimbledon champ Alex Olmedo. In the decisive fifth match, he beat Barry MacKay, 8-3, 3-6, 6-2, 6-4, in a tense duel interrupted by rain and carried over to the following afternoon.

His love for Davis Cup showed when he succeeded legendary Harry Hopman as non-playing captain in 1970, and held the job for a record 23 years, piloting four winners: 1973, 1977, 1983 and 1986, and a record 49 series victories. He lost the 1990 final to the U.S. He was No. 1 in the world in 1959 and 1960 and in the Top Ten every year between 1956 and 1962. Although he retired in 1963, he played a cameo at Wimbledon 10 years later as doubles finalist (to Jimmy Connors and Ilie Nastase) with John Cooper, younger brother of Ashley Cooper, with whom he'd won the U.S. doubles in 1957. A brother, Dr. John Fraser, a physician, was also a fine doubles player, a Wimbledon semifinalist with Rod Laver, as was Neale with Emerson in 1962. Neale was born Oct. 3, 1933, in Melbourne, where he lives, and entered the Hall of Fame in 1984.

MAJOR TITLES (19)—*Wimbledon singles, 1960; U.S. singles, 1959, 1960; Australian doubles, 1957, 1958, 1962; French doubles, 1958, 1960, 1962; Wimbledon doubles, 1959, 1961; U.S. doubles, 1957, 1959, 1960; Australian mixed, 1956; Wimbledon mixed, 1962; U.S. mixed, 1958, 1959, 1960. Davis Cup (As player)—1958, 1959, 1960, 1961, 1962, 1963; record: 11-1 in singles, 7-2 in doubles; (As captain)—1970–92; record: 49-19; 4 Cups, 1973, 1977, 1983, 1986.* SINGLES RECORD IN THE MAJORS: *Australian (25-10), French (18-5), Wimbledon (38-13), U.S. (32-5).*

SHIRLEY FRY
United States (1927—)

See page 402.

CHUCK GARLAND
United States (1898–1971)

A Yale man who won the U.S. Intercollegiate doubles in 1919, Charles Stedman Garland joined a Harvardian, Dick Williams, the following year to beat Algernon Kingscote and James Parke, 4-6, 6-4, 7-5, 6-2, and become the first Americans to win the doubles at Wimbledon.

Ranked three times in the U.S. Top Ten, 1918, 1919 and 1920 (No. 8 each time), he was selected for the Hall of Fame in 1969 as much for his service to the USTA as committeeman as player. One of his duties was captaining the 1927 Davis Cup team. Garland, a 5-foot-7½ right-hander, was born Oct. 29, 1898, in Pittsburgh. He later lived in Baltimore and died there Jan. 28, 1971.

MAJOR TITLE *(1)—Wimbledon doubles, 1920.* OTHER U.S. TITLES *(4)—Intercollegiate singles, 1919; Intercollegiate doubles, 1919, with Ken Hawkes; Clay Court doubles, 1917, 1918, with Sam Hardy.* SINGLES RECORD IN THE MAJORS: *Wimbledon (12-3), U.S. (10-7).*

ALTHEA GIBSON
United States (1927—)

See page 403.

KITTY GODFREE
Great Britain (1896–1992)

See page 92.

PANCHO GONZALEZ
United States (1928—)

See page 404.

EVONNE GOOLAGONG
Australia (1951—)

See page 406.

BITSY GRANT
United States (1910–86)

A scrappy little guy, 5-foot-4, 120-pound Bryan Morel "Bitsy" Grant was the smallest American man to attain championship stature. A right-handed retriever supreme, he was able to beat such heavy-hitting greats as Don Budge and Ellsworth Vines even on grass. Between 1930

and 1941 he was ranked nine times in the U.S. Top Ten, No. 3 in 1935 and 1936. In 1936 and 1937 he was in the World Top Ten, Nos. 8 and 6, respectively.

Reared on the clay of his native Georgia, he won the U.S. title on that surface thrice (1930, 1934, 1935) but he had his moments on the grass at Forest Hills, reaching the U.S. semis in 1935 by beating second-seeded Budge, 6-4, 6-4, 5-7, 6-3, and in 1936, losing to eventual champion, Fred Perry, 6-4, 3-6, 7-5, 6-2. He was a quarterfinalist in 1937, losing to Gottfried von Cramm, 9-7, 2-6, 2-6, 6-3, 6-3, and reached the same round a year later.

He played Davis Cup 1935, 1936 and 1937, helping the U.S. regain the prize in 1937 after a 10-year slump. He continued to compete as a senior, winning 19 U.S. singles titles on the four surfaces: Grass Court—45s (1956 and 1957), 55s (1965, 1966, 1967 and 1968); Indoor—55s (1966); Clay Court—45s (1959, 1960, 1961 and 1963), 55s (1965, 1966, 1967, 1968 and 1969), 65s (1976 and 1977); Hard Court—65s (1976).

He was born in Atlanta, Dec. 25, 1910, and died there June 5, 1986. Named for him, the Bitsy Grant Tennis Center in his hometown is one of the finest public court complexes. He entered the Hall of Fame in 1972.

U.S. TITLES *(4)—Clay Court singles, 1930, 1934, 1935; Clay Court doubles, 1932, with George Lott.* DAVIS CUP— *1935, 1936, 1937; record: 8-2 in singles.* SINGLES RECORD IN THE MAJORS: *Wimbledon (8-2), U.S. (35-15).*

CLARENCE GRIFFIN
United States (1888–1973)

Clarence James "Peck" Griffin ranked in the U.S. Top Ten three times (1915, 1916, 1920), No. 6 the last two, but made his mark in doubles alongside fellow Californian Bill Johnston. They won the U.S. title thrice, 1915, 1916 and 1920. He was also in the 1913 final with John Strachan. He and Strachan won the U.S. Clay Court title that year, and in 1914 Griffin reached his singles apogee in a comeback beating of Elia Fottrell, 3-

6, 6-8, 8-6, 6-0, 6-2, for the Clay Court singles crown. That was the all-comers final.

Defender Strachan, unable to be in Cincinnati, defaulted the challenge round to Griffin. He was a 5-foot-7 right-hander, born Jan. 19, 1888, in San Francisco, and died March 28, 1973, in Santa Barbara Cal. He entered the Hall of Fame in 1970. His nephew is the well-known entertainer Merv Griffin.

MAJOR TITLES (3)—*U.S. doubles, 1915, 1916, 1920.* OTHER U.S. TITLES (2)—*Clay Court singles, 1914; Clay Court doubles, 1913, with John Strachan.* SINGLES RECORD IN THE MAJORS: *U.S. (18-9).*

HAROLD HACKETT
United States (1878–1937)

A New Yorker, Harold Humphrey Hackett was best known as the partner of Fred Alexander in one of the most successful doubles teams. The 5-foot-9 Hackett was the softer, more deceptive stroker of the two. Beginning in 1905 they were U.S. finalists a record seven successive years, winning in 1907, 1908, 1909 and 1910. A Yale man, and right-handed, he was born July 12, 1878, in Hingham, Mass. He and Alexander won the U.S. Indoor doubles thrice (1906–08), and he completed a sweep of the surface titles available then by taking the Clay doubles in 1912 with Walter Hall.

The following year, 1913, he was player-captain of the U.S. Davis Cup team that broke a decade drought by seizing the Cup in a 3-2 beating of Britain. He and Maurice McLoughlin won the vital go-ahead point over H. Roper Barrett and Charles Dixon, 6-4 in the fifth. He was ranked in the U.S. Top Ten twice, 1902 and 1906, No. 7 in 1906 when he was a U.S. quarterfinalist. He was inducted into the Hall of Fame in 1961. He died in New York Nov. 20, 1937.

MAJOR TITLES (4)—*U.S. doubles, 1907, 1908, 1909, 1910.* OTHER U.S. TITLES (5)—*Indoor doubles, 1906, 1907, 1908, 1909, with Fred Alexander; Clay Court doubles, 1912, with Walter Hall.* DAVIS CUP—*1908, 1909, 1913; record: 5-1 in doubles.* SINGLES RECORD IN THE MAJORS: *U.S. (3-2).*

ELLEN HANSELL
United States (1869–1937)

The original U.S. female champion, Ellen Forde Hansell Allerdice was a Philadelphian who won the title in 1887, in her hometown, not long before her 18th birthday. She beat Laura Knight, 6-1, 6-0, at the Philadelphia Cricket Club, but lost the title the following year to Bertha Townsend, and wasn't a factor again. A right-hander, she served sidearm, as, she said, did most of the women in that inaugural.

Forty-four years later, she recalled that she had been an anemic child, who showed some "enthusiasm and aptitude" for tennis. Her mother was advised by the family doctor to take Ellen out of school and put her on a court daily to build herself up. She remembered her mother making her tennis dresses of red plaid gingham: "A red felt hat topped the tight-collared and be-corseted body. I also wore a blazer of red and blue stripes . . . we did now and then grip our overdraped, voluminous skirts with our left hand to give us a bit more limb freedom when dashing to make a swift, snappy stroke, every bit as well placed as today, but lacking the force and great physical strength of the modern girl. Is it possible for you to envision the gallery? A loving, but openly prejudiced crowd standing within two feet of the court lines, calling out hurrahs of applause plus groans of disappointment, and some suggestive criticism, such as: 'Run to the net.' 'Place it to her left.' 'Don't dare lose this game.'"

She was born Sept, 18, 1869, in Philadelphia, and died, Mrs. Taylor Allderdice, May 11, 1937, in Pittsburgh. Induction into the Hall of Fame came in 1965.

MAJOR TITLE (1)—*U.S. singles, 1887.* SINGLES RECORD IN THE MAJORS: *U.S. (3-1).*

DARLENE HARD
United States (1936—)

An all-out attacking Californian with a splendid serve, volley and overhead, Darlene

Ruth Hard nevertheless won the French singles on slow clay (1960) as well as the U.S. title on grass at Forest Hills (1960, 1961), and was a Wimbledon finalist twice (1957, 1959). A stocky blonde right-hander, 5-foot-5½, 140 pounds, she was born Jan. 6, 1936, in Los Angeles and attended Pomona, for whom she won the U.S. Intercollegiate title in 1958.

She played with considerable zest, inspiring a variety of doubles partners, winning the U.S. title five straight years (1958–62) and again in 1969 with four different accomplices, the French twice with different partners and four Wimbledons with three different partners. The 1969 triumph with Françoise Durr—a last-minute, one-time amalgamation—may have been her most sensational in that Darlene, no longer competing, looked so out of place in the final. But after a disastrous start, losing the first eight games, she recalled the old moves as they beat Margaret Court and Virginia Wade, 0-6, 6-3, 6-4.

Between 1954 and 1963 she ranked in the U.S. Top Ten 10 times, No. 1 four straight years (1960–63), and in the World Top Ten nine times, No. 2 in 1960 and 1961. She was a standout Wightman and Federation Cup player.

As the grande dame of the original U.S. Fed Cup team, squiring 19-year-olds Billie Jean Moffitt (King) and Carole Caldwell (Graebner), Darlene, 27, led the way to 1963 victory. A blend of all-time doubles champs, present and future, she and B. J. won the Cup decider over Aussies Smith (Court) and Lesley Turner, 3-6, 13-11, 6-3, on a fast, slick, wooden court inside Queen's Club, London. She totaled 21 major titles in singles, doubles and mixed (3-13-5).

Inducted into the Hall of Fame in 1973, she married Richard Waggoner in 1977.

MAJOR TITLES (21)—*French singles, 1960; U.S. singles, 1960, 1961; French doubles, 1955, 1957, 1960; Wimbledon doubles, 1957, 1959, 1960, 1963; U.S. doubles, 1958, 1959, 1960, 1961, 1962, 1969; French mixed, 1955, 1961; Wimbledon mixed, 1957, 1959, 1960. Other U.S. titles (7)—Clay Court doubles, 1957, with Althea Gibson; 1960, with Billie Jean Moffitt King; 1962, with Sue Behlmar; 1963, with Maria*

Bueno; Hard Court singles, 1963; Hard Court doubles, 1963, with Paulette Verzin; Intercollegiate singles, 1958. FEDERATION CUP—*1963; record: 3-1 in singles, 3-0 in doubles.* WIGHTMAN CUP—*1957, 1959, 1960, 1962, 1963; record: 6-3 in singles, 4-1 in doubles.* SINGLES RECORD IN THE MAJORS: *French (14-4), Wimbledon (29-7), U.S. (43-9).*

DORIS HART
United States (1925—)

See page 410.

BOB HEWITT
Australia/South Africa (1940—)

Tapped for the Hall of Fame in 1992 in harness with his partner, Frew McMillan, Robert Anthony John Hewitt was the right-court player in the alignment of Hewitt and McMillan. They combined for five major championships and were one of the shrewdest, strongest of all teams, men whose prowess spanned the amateur and open eras. In 1974 they were central to South Africa's winning the Davis Cup, the fifth member of the exclusive club, and first newcomer since France in 1927.

Hewitt was a born and bred Aussie, beginning life Jan. 12, 1940, in Dubbo, New South Wales. He became one of a tribe that terrorized the tennis world, and first came to attention winning the Wimbledon doubles in 1962 and 1964 with compatriot Fred Stolle. But love broke up that potent alliance. Hewitt fell for a South African lass named Dalaille, and moved to Johannesburg to wed. Since he hadn't played Davis Cup for Australia, Hewitt was eligible, as a resident, to compete for South Africa.

In 1966 he and McMillan were put together as teammates, and they stayed together for much of the next 15 years to win Wimbledon thrice (1967, 1972, 1978), the French (1972), the U.S. (1977) plus 60 other titles. Hewitt, bald, bearded and sometimes volatile on court, was a blocky 6-footer with surprisingly delicate touch, an accurate and seldom failing returner.

He was the better singles player, taking seven pro titles in singles, along with 65 in doubles, the latter total placing him sixth on the all-time winners' list. He was a Wimbledon quarterfinalist in 1964 and 1966, won the U.S. Clay Court singles, and three other singles tourneys in 1972 and was ranked No. 6 in the world in 1967. Hewitt had six major mixed titles, too, one of five to win all four. He won three (Wimbledon, 1977–79, U.S., 1979) with Greer Stevens. His career prize money amounted to more than $1 million.

MAJOR TITLES *(15)—Australian doubles, 1963, 1964; French doubles, 1972; Wimbledon doubles, 1962, 1964, 1967, 1972, 1978; U.S. doubles, 1977; Australian mixed, 1961; French mixed, 1970, 1979; Wimbledon mixed, 1977, 1979; U.S. mixed, 1979.* DAVIS CUP—*1967, 1968, 1969, 1974, 1978; record: 22-3 in singles, 16-1 in doubles.* SINGLES RECORD IN THE MAJORS: *Australian (12-7), French (21-14), Wimbledon (34-19), U.S. (13-9).*

MAJOR TITLES WITH MCMILLAN *(5)—French doubles, 1972; Wimbledon doubles, 1967, 1972, 1978; U.S. doubles, 1977.* DAVIS CUP—*1967, 1968, 1969, 1974, 1978; record: 16-1 in doubles.*

LEW HOAD
Australia (1934—)

See page 412.

HARRY HOPMAN
Australia (1906–85)

A fine player, particularly in doubles, at which he won seven major titles, Henry Christian Hopman made his name as the most successful of all Davis Cup captains, piloting Australia to 16 Cups between 1939 and 1967. His was the era of perhaps the greatest Cup players of all, the Hall of Fame Aussies from Frank Sedgman through Lew Hoad, Ken Rosewall, Ashley Cooper, Mervyn Rose, Rex Hartwig, Mal Anderson, Neale Fraser, Roy Emerson, Rod Laver, John Newcombe, Fred Stolle, Tony Roche.

Emphasizing super fitness, he drove and inspired them, and built pride in their underpopulated country's beating up on the rest of the world. The first of his 22 teams, 1938, reached the challenge round final, losing to the U.S. But he was back with the same pair, Adrian Quist and Jack Bromwich, to win a singular victory over the U.S. in 1939, from 0-2 down after the first day in Philadelphia.

Hop concentrated on his job as a newspaperman after World War II. But after the Aussies lost the Cup to the U.S. in 1946, and three more finales through 1949, there was a clamor for him to return to the captain's chair. With two youngsters, Sedgman and Ken McGregor, he won the Cup in New York in 1950, and the Down Under-takers were in business for a glorious near-quarter-century. His teams compiled a 38-6 record.

As a player—a trim 5-foot-7, 133 pounds—he won the Australian doubles with Jack Crawford in 1929 and 1930 and four mixed titles with his first wife, the former Nell Hall, a record for married couples. In singles his high point was the U.S. Championships of 1938 when he beat fifth-seeded Elwood Cooke, 6-2, 4-6, 6-4, 10-8, and future U.S. and French champ Don McNeill, 6-4, 6-3, 7-5, to reach the quarters, where he was an historic footnote in Don Budge's original Grand Slam, 6-3, 6-1, 6-3.

Following his last Davis Cup match as captain, a loss to Mexico at Mexico City in 1969, he emigrated to the U.S. to become a highly successful teaching pro, counseling such champions-to-be as Vitas Gerulaitis and John McEnroe at the Port Washington (N.Y.) Tennis Academy. He later opened his own Hopman Tennis Academy with his wife, Lucy, at Largo, Fla. Hop was born Aug. 12, 1906, in Sydney and died Dec. 27, 1985, in Largo, Fla. He entered the Hall of Fame in 1978.

MAJOR TITLES *(7)—Australian doubles, 1929, 1930; U.S. mixed, 1939; Australian mixed, 1930, 1936, 1937, 1939. Davis Cup (As player)—1928, 1930, 1932; record: 4-5 in singles, 4-3 in doubles. (As captain)—1938, 1939, 1950, 1951, 1952, 1953, 1954, 1955, 1956, 1957, 1958, 1959, 1960, 1961, 1962, 1963, 1964, 1965, 1966, 1967, 1968, 1969; record: 38-6, 16 Cups.* SINGLES RECORD IN THE MAJORS: *Australian (34-16), French (8-6), Wimbledon (15-9), U.S. (9-6).*

FRED HOVEY

United States (1868–1945)

Frederick Howard Hovey, a Bostonian and Harvardian, won the U.S. Intercollegiate singles in 1890 and 1891 as well as the doubles with Bob Wrenn the second year. Four years later he, a 5-foot-8, 170-pound right-hander, beat lefty Wrenn, 6-3, 6-2, 6-4, to end his fellow Bostonian's two-year reign at the U.S. Championships. Wrenn returned the favor the next year, 1896, 6-1 in the fifth set of the challenge round.

Between 1890 and 1896 he was in the U.S. Top Ten seven times, No. 1 in 1895. In 1893 he and Clarence Hobart, twice U.S. champs in doubles, won the championship of the World Columbian Exposition at Chicago. He was born Oct. 7, 1868, in Newton Centre, Mass., and died Oct. 18, 1945, in Miami Beach. He entered the Hall of Fame in 1974.

MAJOR TITLES (3)—*U.S. singles, 1895; U.S. doubles, 1893, 1894.* OTHER U.S. TITLES (3)—*Intercollegiate singles, 1890, 1891; Intercollegiate doubles, 1891, with Robert Wrenn.* SINGLES RECORD IN THE MAJORS: *U.S. (25-5).*

JOE HUNT

United States (1919–45)

Nobody knows for certain what went wrong when Lt. Joe Hunt sent his Navy fighter plane into its last dive. Pilot error? Mechanical failure? There were rumors of both, but the Atlantic swallowed forever all evidence of the Grumman Hellcat—along with the 1943 U.S. champion.

Fifteen days short of his 26th birthday, Joseph Raphael Hunt of the U.S. Navy was a victim of World War II, killed Feb. 2, 1944, during a routine training mission off Daytona Beach, Fla. The accident, with his training nearly complete, was never explained. Thus Hunt was the shortest-lived of Hall of Famers, ranked No. 1 for his U.S. title-winning performance, but unable the following year, 1944, to get leave from duty to defend the title.

A sturdy, handsome blond Los Angeleno, 6-feet, 165 pounds, he came from a wealthy tennis family. His father, Reuben, won the Southern championship in 1906, and his older sister Marianne in 1934, and brother Charles in 1945, ranked No. 20 nationally. His wife, Jacque Virgil, had been the No. 1 Southern California junior and played Forest Hills in 1943, too.

"He was a strong guy, big serve and volley, and took to grass, coming from the Southern California concrete," says fellow Hall of Famer, Pancho Segura. "Everybody though he'd be the big man, along with Jack Kramer, after the war."

Joe was alone in his progression to the top, the only man to win the U.S. junior 15s and 18s, the Intercollegiate singles (for the Naval Academy) and then the U.S. Championship. In a bizarre finish to his title triumph over Southern California buddy and rival, Kramer (6-3, 6-8, 10-8, 6-0), Hunt, on leave from the Atlantic fleet, won the title, so to speak, lying down. He collapsed to the turf with leg cramps as Kramer's last shot flew out of court, and might not have been able to play another point. The humid 90-degree afternoon got to him in the unique all-military final. Seaman Kramer was also on leave, from the Coast Guard. It was the last important tennis tournament for Joe, who had to report back to his destroyer. However, a year later, at Pensacola, Fla., he did win a local Labor Day event over a fellow flight trainee, 1942 U.S. champ Ted Schroeder.

In 1938 at Southern Cal (doubles) and 1941 at the Naval Academy (singles), Hunt was the only player other than Malcolm Chace (Brown and Yale, 1893, 1894, 1895), to win U.S. Intercollegiate titles for two different schools. Husky and athletic, Hunt also played football at Navy. He, 20, and Kramer, 18, were the second youngest Davis Cup doubles pair for the U.S., losing in 1939 at Philadelphia to Australians John Bromwich and Adrian Quist, the first domino in the only final-round 3-2 loss from a 2-0 lead.

One of the youngest to make the U.S. Top Ten at 17 in 1936, he was a Forest Hills quarterfinalist in 1937 and 1938, semifinalist in 1939 and 1940, losing both times to Bobby Riggs. Born Feb. 17, 1919 in San Francisco, he was inducted into the Hall of Fame in 1966.

MAJOR TITLE *(1)—U.S. singles, 1943.* OTHER U.S. TITLES *(3)—Intercollegiate singles, 1941; Clay Court doubles, 1938, with Lew Wetherell; Intercollegiate doubles, 1938, with Wetherell.* DAVIS CUP*—1939; record: 0-1 in doubles.* SINGLES RECORD IN THE MAJORS: *U.S. (21-4).*

FRANK HUNTER
United States (1894–1981)

As one of the earlier touring pros, Francis Townsend Hunter joined the nomad ranks in 1931 after a distinguished amateur career. A right-handed New Yorker, he was born there June 28, 1894. He played extremely well for his country, taking a 1924 Olympic gold medal in doubles alongside Vinnie Richards, and helping build a 2-1 lead in the losing Davis Cup 1927 finale, yoked to Bill Tilden in a five-set win over France's Jacques Brugnon and Jean Borotra.

He came close, as finalist, to the U.S. title twice in succession: 1928 final, 6-3 in the fifth to Henri Cochet, and 1929, 6-4 in the fifth to Tilden. He also lost the 1923 Wimbledon final to Bill Johnston. And he was one of those unlucky three victims in a row who built two-set leads over 1927 champ Cochet, Hunter in the quarterfinals, preceding Tilden and Borotra. But he won the Wimbledon doubles twice, 1924 with Olympic sidekick Richards and 1927 with Tilden.

His greatest singles success was under cover at New York's Seventh Regiment Armory, winning the U.S. Indoor titles of 1922 over Frank Anderson, 6-4,1-6, 7-5, 6-2, and 1930 over Julius Seligson, 6-3, 6-2, 6-3. He lost the finals of 1923 and 1924 to Richards, and 1929 to Jean Borotra, and won the doubles in 1923 and 1924 with Richards and 1929 with Tilden. Hunter, a fine volleyer, stressed power in forehand and serve, putting his 5-11, 180-pound frame into those strokes. He ranked in the U.S. Top Ten five times between 1922 and 1929, No. 2 in 1927, 1928,

1929, and in the World Top Ten, 1923, 1927, 1928, No. 4 in 1928. He was named to the Hall of Fame in 1961 and died Dec. 2, 1981, in Palm Beach, Fla.

MAJOR TITLES *(5)—U.S. doubles, 1927; Wimbledon doubles, 1924, 1927; Wimbledon mixed, 1927, 1928, 1929.* OTHER U.S. TITLES *(5)—Indoor singles, 1922, 1930; Indoor doubles, 1923, 1924, with Vincent Richards; 1929, with Bill Tilden.* DAVIS CUP*—1927, 1928, 1929; record: 3-1 in singles, 1-1 in doubles.* SINGLES RECORD IN THE MAJORS: *French (7-3), Wimbledon (18-6), U.S. (38-13).*

HELEN JACOBS
United States (1908—)

See page 93.

BILL JOHNSTON
United States (1894–1946)

See page 95.

ANN HAYDON JONES
Great Britain (1938—)

The first left-handed woman to win Wimbledon, Adrianne Shirley Haydon Jones had to cool a rampaging Billie Jean King to do it in the 1969 final, 3-6, 6-3, 6-2. King had won three straight times and 24 straight matches. Before that, Ann had shown her all-around value and steadiness by winning the French in 1961 and 1966. She could attack or stay back, and had a compact service motion with little windup. In 1967, despite a leg injury that hobbled her, she pushed King hard (11-9, 6-4) in the U.S. final, gamely extricating herself from nine set points before losing the first, and two match points at the end.

A buxom blonde, 5-foot-7, 135 pounds, Ann was always a stalwart in playing for her country in Federation and Wightman Cups. In 1975, at 37, after she'd stopped touring, she set aside motherhood for a weekend to play a small but important doubles role in Britain's 5-2 Wightman triumph at Cleveland's Public Auditorium. She and Virginia Wade beat Julie Anthony and Janet

Newberry, 6-2, 3-6, 7-6. Deciding to go for dollars, she, King, Françoise Durr and Rosie Casals became the first professional female touring troupe, signing with George MacCall, promoter of the National Tennis League, in 1968.

Jones was born Oct. 7, 1938, in Birmingham, England, to parents who were outstanding table tennis players. She followed in their paddling steps as a five-time finalist for various world championship titles. But she was to make her name in tennis after winning the British junior championships of 1954 and 1955, moving on to place in the World Top Ten every year between 1957 and 1970 (except for 1964), No. 2 in 1967 and 1969.

Her Wimbledon triumph was a gem of persistence—Ann won on her 14th try—and, fourth-seeded, beat the 5th, 1st and 2nd seeds in the stretch to do so: Nancy Richey, 6-2, 7-5; Margaret Court, 10-12, 6-3, 6-2; and King. Jones played 157 matches at Wimbledon: 57-13 in singles, 33-15 in doubles, 29-10 in mixed. She married P. F. Jones in 1962 and entered the Hall of Fame in 1985.

MAJOR TITLES (7)—*French singles, 1961, 1966; Wimbledon singles, 1969; French doubles, 1963, 1968, 1969; Wimbledon mixed, 1969.* FEDERATION CUP—*1963, 1964, 1965, 1966, 1967, 1971; record: 11-8 in singles, 15-7 in doubles.* WIGHTMAN CUP—*1957, 1958, 1959, 1960, 1961, 1962, 1963, 1964, 1965, 1966, 1967, 1970, 1975; record: 10-11 in singles, 6-5 in doubles.* SINGLES RECORD IN THE MAJORS: *Australian (3-3), French (46-9), Wimbledon (57-13), U.S. (36-10).*

BILLIE JEAN KING
United States (1943—)

See page 413.

JAN KODES
Czechoslovakia (1945—)

Determination marked the grim-faced Jan Kodes, who clawed and battled to many a victory, though seemingly exhausted. As a sportsman he was even more a hero to many of his countrymen

for his refusal to leave the repressed country as Jaroslav Drobny, Martina Navratilova and Ivan Lendl had done. Thus they shared more fully in his major triumphs: Wimbledon of 1973, and the French of 1970 and 1971.

A compact, muscular 5-foot-9 right-hander, Kodes was a standout and dogged groundstroker. He volleyed well, too, but was disdainful of grass even though he signalled his ability there in 1971 by knocking top-seeded John Newcombe out of the U.S. Open in the first round, 2-6, 7-6 (5-1), 7-6 (5-1), 6-3. Nothing like that had happened since 1930 when Berkeley Bell grounded top foreign seed Jean Borotra in the opening round.

Pushing upward and onward, all the while moaning about "this joke tennis, this grass," Jan, beaten in the first round at Wimbledon, next escaped Pierre Barthes, (2-6, 5-7, 6-4, 6-4, 6-4), who served at 4-3, 40-30 in the fifth. In the semis he startled third-seeded Arthur Ashe, 7-6 (5-3), 3-6, 4-6, 6-3, 6-4, to become an unseeded U.S. finalist. He didn't break in tie-breakers (four-for-four) until the last one finished his astonishing journey: Stan Smith beat him in the final, 3-6, 6-3, 6-2, 7-6 (5-3). Two years later he was the Wimbledon champ, defeating Alex Metreveli in straight sets, and fought Newcombe through a brilliant five-set U.S. final, losing the last set, 6-3.

Kodes, seventh-seeded, easily beat Zeljko Franulovic, 6-2, 6-4, 6-0, to win the French in 1970, countered the artistry of Ilie Nastase, 8-6, 6-2, 2-6, 7-5, the following year, but fell to Patrick Proisy, 6-4, 6-2, 6-4, in the 1972 quarters, ending a 17-match run at Roland Garros.

As a devoted Davis Cupper, he played 15 years and 39 series for Czechoslovakia beginning in 1966, and was among the top 20 players in matches played (95) and won (60): 39-20 in singles, 21-15 in doubles. He led the team to the 1975 Cup round, a 3-2 defeat by Sweden at Stockholm, and played a cameo doubles role along the way in 1980 as he realized a dream—the Cup for Czechoslovakia, Lendl-powered.

Besides his three majors he won six pro titles in singles, 17 in doubles, and accumulated

$693,197 in career prize money. Jan was in the World Top Ten in 1971 and 1973, No. 5 in the former. Born March 1, 1945, in Prague, he has served as his country's national coach and Davis Cup captain, and entered the Hall of Fame in 1990.

MAJOR TITLES *(3)—French singles, 1970, 1971; Wimbledon singles, 1973.* DAVIS CUP—*1966, 1967, 1968, 1969, 1970, 1971, 1972, 1973, 1974, 1975, 1976, 1977, 1978, 1979, 1980; record: 39-20 in singles, 21-15 in doubles.* SINGLES RECORD IN THE MAJORS: *French (43-13), Wimbledon (19-14), U.S. (27-9).*

JACK KRAMER
United States (1921—)

See page 416.

RENÉ LACOSTE
France (1904–96)

See page 96.

BILL LARNED
United States (1872–1926)

One of the Big Three of the U.S. men's championship, William Augustus Larned won seven times, as did Dick Sears before him and Bill Tilden after. Like Tilden, he was a late achiever, 28 years old when, after failing in the final before Malcolm Whitman the previous year, he won the title in 1901 for a first time, over Beals Wright. His last, ending a five-year run, in 1911, made him the oldest male singles champ, 38.

He began playing the Championships in 1891 and in 19 years, through 1911, fell short of the semis only twice, making a 61-12 match record. He was ranked in the U.S. Top Ten 19 times, starting with No. 6 in 1892, and probably would have been there 20 straight years if he hadn't missed the 1898 season serving with the Rough Riders in the Spanish-American War. Nineteen years was a record for eight decades until topped by Jimmy Connors.

Bill, a strong-armed 5-foot-11, 170-pounder, was No. 1 eight times, tied by Connors, topped by Tilden's 10. Three of those years his younger brother, Edward Larned, was also in the Top Ten, No. 6 in 1903. He was a member of five Davis Cup teams, in 1902 a Cup winner. He was a powerful groundstroker with an oppressive topspinning right-handed forehand.

Bill was born Dec. 30, 1872, in Summit, N.J., and attended Cornell, for whom he won the Intercollegiate title in 1892. He committed suicide on Dec. 16, 1926, in New York. He was inducted into the Hall of Fame in 1956.

MAJOR TITLES *(7)—U.S. singles, 1901, 1902, 1907, 1908, 1909, 1910, 1911. Other U.S. title—Intercollegiate singles, 1892.* DAVIS CUP—*1902, 1903, 1905, 1908, 1909, 1911; record: 9-5 in singles.* SINGLES RECORD IN THE MAJORS: *Wimbledon (5-2), U.S. (61-12).*

ART LARSEN
United States (1925—)

A sleek left-hander with splendid touch, Arthur David "Tappy" Larsen in 1950 was the first southpaw champion of the U.S. in the post-World War II era, the first since Johnny Doeg two decades before. He battled fellow Californian, Herbie Flam, in a long-shot final—they were seeded fifth and second, respectively—to win at Forest Hills, 6-3, 4-6, 5-7, 6-4, 6-3.

A European-combat veteran of the U.S. Army in World War II, the 5-foot-10, 150-pound Larsen was delayed in his start in big-time tennis, making the U.S. Top Ten the first of eight successive times at No. 6 in 1949, at age 24. He was No. 1 in 1950, and ranked in the World Top Ten thrice, 1950, 1951, 1954, No. 3 the first year.

By adding the U.S. Clay and Hard Court (1952) and Indoor (1953) titles to this Forest Hills prize he became the first man to take the championships on the four surfaces. Only he and Tony Trabert have done so. Losing the French to Trabert in 1954, he was only the ninth of 15 American men to attain that final. Larsen was born April 17, 1925, in Hayward, Cal., and entered the Hall of Fame in 1969.

MAJOR TITLE (1)—*U.S. singles, 1950.* OTHER U.S. TITLES (8)—*Indoor singles, 1953; Clay Court singles, 1952; Hard Court singles, 1950, 1952; Indoor doubles, 1953, with Kurt Nielsen; Clay Court doubles, 1950, with Herb Flam; 1952, with Grant Golden; Hard Court doubles, 1952, with Tom Brown.* DAVIS CUP—*1951, 1952; record: 4-0 in singles.* SINGLES RECORD IN THE MAJORS: *French (16-4), Wimbledon (20-7), U.S. (31-8).*

ROD LAVER
Australia (1938—)

See page 418.

SUZANNE LENGLEN
France (1899–1938)

See page 97.

GEORGE LOTT
United States (1906–91)

A good baseball player at the University of Chicago, George Martin Lott, Jr., made his name principally in doubles, where, a slick tactician and volleyer, he could make any partner look good. He won the U.S. title five times with three different accomplices: John Hennessey, 1928; Johnny Doeg, 1929 and 1930; Les Stoefen, 1933 and 1934. He joined the touring pros in 1934.

He was a U.S. Davis Cup stalwart between 1928 and 1934, going undefeated in 11 doubles matches. He ranked in the U.S. Top Ten nine times between 1924 and 1934, No. 2 in 1931 when he lost the final at Forest Hills to Ellie Vines, keeping it close with his clever use of spin, 7-9, 6-3, 9-7, 7-5. George, a right-hander, came from way back to disappoint Johnny Van Ryn—his Wimbledon-winning comrade that year—in the quarters, 5-7, 0-6, 6-1, 7-5, 6-1, then unseat the defender, Johnny Doeg, 7-5, 6-3, 6-0. He also won the Wimbledon doubles with Stoefen in 1934. A 160-pound 6-footer, George beat dashing

dirt-kicker Bitsy Grant in a five-set struggle for the 1932 U.S. Clay Court title, 3-6, 6-2, 3-6, 6-3, 6-3, and had his ultimate clay opportunities in Paris as a singles starter for the U.S. in the Davis Cup finales of 1929 and 1930. The Frenchmen were just too tough at home. Henri Cochet beat him in the decisive fifth match in 1929, 6-1, 3-6, 6-0, 6-3, and Jean Borotra scored the painful clincher in 1930, 5-7, 6-3, 2-6, 6-2, 8-6.

He was born Oct. 16, 1906, in Springfield Ill., and died Dec. 2, 1991, in Chicago, where he was still active as varsity coach of Loyola University. He was inducted into the Hall of Fame in 1964.

MAJOR TITLES (12)—*French doubles, 1931; Wimbledon doubles, 1931, 1934; U.S. doubles, 1928, 1929, 1930, 1933, 1934; Wimbledon mixed, 1931; U.S. mixed, 1929, 1931, 1934. Other U.S. titles—Clay Court singles, 1932; Indoor doubles, 1932, with John Van Ryn; 1934, with Lester Stoefen; Clay Court doubles, 1932, with Bryan "Bitsy" Grant; Pro doubles, 1935, with Stoefen; 1937, with Vincent Richards.* DAVIS CUP—*1928, 1929, 1930, 1931, 1933, 1934; record: 7-4 in singles, 11-0 in doubles.* SINGLES RECORD IN THE MAJORS: *French (4-1), Wimbledon (16-5), U.S. (24-10).*

GENE MAKO
United States (1916—)

Though brief, the career of Hungarian-born Constantine Gene Mako was one of the most remarkable in that he achieved his foremost results after sustaining a devastating and painful right-shoulder injury that would have finished most men as competitors. As a teenager he had one of the most powerful serves, but he injured himself by overdoing it. This was compounded by a 1936 tumble in London that finished the job of wrecking his right (playing) shoulder, and kept him out of Wimbledon that year.

"I continued only because my friend and doubles partner, Don Budge, asked me to do so," Mako says. "I told him I'd be serving like a little old lady and would have to shovel the ball around, but it was okay with him."

Despite the sometimes puny appearance of his strokes, 6-foot, 170-pound Mako, in the right court alongside Budge, was a canny playmaker, a man who knew the angles and where to put the ball—and competed fiercely—as they became one of the greatest teams. They won Wimbledon in 1937 and 1938, and were in four successive U.S. finals from 1935, triumphing in 1936 and 1938.

A formidable singles player as well, he performed on four Davis Cup teams (two winners), seizing the go-ahead point with Budge in the 1937 lifting of the Cup from Britain, 4-1, to end a 10-year U.S. dry spell. They beat Charles Tuckey and Frank Wilde, 6-3, 7-5, 7-9, 12-10. Just as vital was their go-ahead win in the previous round, a 3-2 thriller over Germany—a 4-6, 7-5, 8-6, 6-4 squeeze past Henner Henkel and Gottfried von Cramm.

Mako was in the U.S. Top Ten in 1937 and 1938, No. 3 the second year, and No. 9 in the world ranking of 1938. That year he was the last obstacle between Budge and the original Grand Slam in the U.S. final at Forest Hills. Unseeded, Mako dashed to his only major singles final on victories over sixth-seed Frank Kovacs and the third and first foreign seeds, Franjo Puncec and John Bromwich. He resisted Budge well, holding off the inevitable for four sets, 6-3, 6-8, 6-2, 6-1. Mako had one of the four sets Budge lost during the Slam.

Gene had a brief fling at pro tennis while serving in the Navy during World War II, winning the U.S. pro doubles in 1943 with Bruce Barnes. Upon discharge, he made another sort of sporting name on the West Coast as a semipro basketball player. Born in Budapest Jan. 24, 1916, he moved with his family to Buenos Aires, then to Los Angeles when he was seven. There he remained, winning the intercollegiate singles and doubles for Southern California in 1934. Today he's a gregarious art dealer. He entered the Hall of Fame in 1973.

MAJOR TITLES (5)—*Wimbledon doubles, 1937, 1938; U.S. doubles, 1936, 1938; U.S. mixed, 1936.* OTHER U.S. TITLES (6)—*Clay Court doubles, 1933, with Jack Tidball; 1934, with Don Budge; 1939, with Frank Parker; Pro doubles, 1943, with Bruce Barnes; Intercollegiate singles, 1934; Intercollegiate doubles, 1934, with Philip Castlen.* DAVIS CUP—*1935, 1936, 1937, 1938; record: 0-1 in singles, 6-2 in dou-*

bles. SINGLES RECORD IN THE MAJORS: *Australian (2-1), French (0-1), Wimbledon (7-2), U.S. (18-8).*

MOLLA MALLORY
Norway/United States (1884–1959)

See page 99.

HANA MANDLIKOVA
Czechoslovakia (1962—)

Just possibly there are more appealing places to flop on your back than a grimy, steaming strip of asphalt in New York. But you won't convince Hana Mandlikova. It was her place in the furtive sun, and the bumpy landing she made, after whirling to bat a last spectacular volley, was a splendidly happy one. Hana gazed at the smoggy sky, and it seemed heaven as a deluge of applause and cheers from 21,169 captivated witnesses burst on her. The pavement of Flushing Meadow "didn't feel too bad. It felt nice," laughs Mandlikova, who arose from the floor as champion.

That was 1985. Seldom has the U.S. Open been illuminated by such a display of shotmaking fireworks. Hana's victim was Martina Navratilova at her zenith, 7-6 (7-3), 1-6, 7-6 (7-2). Like Martina, whom she'd admired while growing up in Prague (where she was born Feb. 19, 1962), Hana was a magnificent athlete who felt the only thing better than attacking was attacking more.

As the star of the 40th Hall of Fame class, 1994, Hana is the third Czech, following Jaroslav Drobny and Jan Kodes. Her relatively early retirement at 28 concluded a professional career that commenced in 1978 and closed in 1990 after she had accumulated 27 singles, 15 pro doubles titles and $3,340,959 in prize money. At singles Hana was 567-195 in matches (.783); at doubles 253-104. She left ranked No. 14, having graced the World Top Ten seven times, 1980–82, 1984–87, No. 3 in 1984 and 1985. Her time was emblazoned by the irresistible crescendos of winning four majors: two Australian (1980, 1987), a French (1981) and her crown jewel U.S. Open.

She had four other shots, finals of Wimbledon, 1981, 1986 and the U.S., 1980, 1982.

Her speed and jock genes came from her papa. Willem Mandlik, an Olympic 100-meter finalist for Czechoslovakia in 1956 and 1960, uttered a profound one-sentence summary of his nervous kid's one-sided defeat by Evert, 6-2, 6-2, in the 1981 Wimbledon final: "Boom-boom-boom . . . miss-miss-miss . . . quick-quick-quick!"

Leggy and limber, a 5-foot-8 right-hander coltish in her movement, she was as high-strung as a thoroughbred, living for flamboyant cavalry charges: "too impatient to stay on the baseline, on clay—even though I was raised on it—or anything," Hana smiles. "Jan Kodes was my first hero. I grew up watching him. I was a ballgirl for Martina [Navratilova] when I was 12, and she was a motivation for me. We played the same way—and I wanted to be good enough to beat her some day."

And she did, spoiling several big occasions for Martina. Even though she was 7-30 in their rivalry, Hana won four of 10 major meetings, beating her elder at Wimbledon, twice at the U.S., once at the Australian. The last, the 1987 final, 7-5, 7-6 (7-2), ended Navratilova's 58-match winning streak. Three years earlier, winning Oakland, Hana snipped another of Martina's strings at 54. They got together to win the U.S. doubles in 1989. "Nice memories," she says, balancing them with the terror, the "terrible memory of the Soviet tanks coming into Prague [1968]. I was only 6, but I understood. It was not nice to see my country invaded. But the political conditions proved a motivation for me and others—to improve, to be so good we could get out to travel abroad."

Billie Jean King says, "Hana could reach highs beyond any of us—inexplicable lows, too. She had incredibly broad shotmaking ability, but trouble sustaining her best. Maybe because she couldn't resist going for the most spectacular shots." She came at foes in a red-bandana'd rush like Geronimo in sneakers. So it was that September afternoon of '85 when she knocked off Chris Evert and Navratilova in succession for the U.S. title, a singular twin-killing of those two all-timers, only time in a major, although Tracy Austin and Steffi Graf did it on lesser occasions. Like her father, Hana represented her country proudly, backboning three successive Czechoslovak Federation Cup triumphs, 1983–85.

MAJOR TITLES (5)—*Australian singles, 1980, 1987; French singles, 1981; U.S. singles, 1985; U.S. doubles, 1989. Federation Cup, 1978, 1979, 1980, 1981, 1982, 1983, 1984, 1985, 1986, 1987; record: 34-6 singles, 15-6 doubles.* SINGLES RECORD IN THE MAJORS: *Australian (29-8), French (39-11), Wimbledon (34-11), U.S. (41-10).*

ALICE MARBLE

United States (1913–90)

See page 100.

CHUCK McKINLEY

United States (1941–86)

Bubbling with energy and grit, Charles Robert McKinley, Jr., was a tough little guy who hustled every minute and died tragically of a brain tumor shortly after learning, in 1986, that he had been named to the Hall of Fame. But he had achieved his utmost tennis goals, both in 1963—winning Wimbledon, and leading the U.S. to the Davis Cup with a 3-2 victory over the holder, Australia, at Adelaide.

A stubby, chesty, 5-foot-9 Missourian, he learned to play at a St. Louis YMCA, where he was already proficient at table tennis. He was a crowd-wowing player, hurling himself about the court, leaping for smashes at which he was expert since so many opponents tried to lob him. Although favored to win the U.S. Intercollegiate title in 1963 for Trinity in San Antonio, Chuck obtained permission from the college president to go for the larger prize, Wimbledon, and, seeded fourth, came through without losing a set or—luck of the draw—without facing a seeded opponent. He beat Fred Stolle in the final, 9-7, 6-1, 6-

4, showing that despite limited stature he could serve and volley with anyone.

Curiously, seeded eighth, he had opposed no other seeds in making his first Wimbledon splash in 1961, until losing the final to second-seeded Rod Laver in straight sets. As the defender in 1964, he was paid back by Stolle in a four-set semi, 4-6, 10-8, 9-7, 6-4. As the left-court player, he blended splendidly with Dennis Ralston in three U.S. doubles championships, 1961, 1963 and 1964. They beat Mexico's Rafe Osuna and Tonio Palafox the first two times, McKinley serving out of two match points in the exciting 11-9 fifth set in 1963.

During the long Cup campaign of 1963 he won six of eight singles, all four doubles matches with Ralston. The Cup round was McKinley's tour de force although he lost to Roy Emerson the first day. He and Ralston got the go-ahead point over Emerson and Neale Fraser, but after Ralston lost to Emerson on the third day it "was up to me. That's the way I wanted it, the Cup riding on one match."

It was a rare position for an American. None had (or has since) come through in the Cup-deciding fifth match. McKinley did, despite being down a service break in the fourth to the thunder-serving Aussie rookie John Newcombe, 10-12, 6-2, 9-7, 6-2, as the Memorial Drive stadium rocked with patriotic fervor for Newc. The following year, however, in Cleveland, McKinley couldn't repeat, losing the decisive fifth to Emerson, 3-6, 6-2, 6-4, 6-4, as Australia regained the Cup, 3-2.

More intent on getting a college degree and establishing himself in business, McKinley resisted professional offers, and his career was relatively brief without a great deal of international play. He was ranked seven successive years in the U.S. Top Ten from 1960, No. 1 in 1962 and 1963, and four times in the World Top Ten from 1961, No. 2 in 1963. The U.S. title eluded him, although he was a semifinalist three straight years, 1962–64, losing to champs Osuna in 1963,

6-4, 6-4, 10-8, and Emerson in 1962, 4-6, 6-4, 6-3, 6-2, and in 1964, 6-4, 11-9, 6-4. He was born Jan. 5, 1941, in St. Louis, and died Aug. 10, 1986, in Dallas.

MAJOR TITLES (4)—*Wimbledon singles, 1963; U.S. doubles, 1961, 1963, 1964. Other U.S. titles (9)—Indoor singles, 1962, 1964; Clay Court singles, 1962, 1963; Indoor doubles, 1962, with Rod Laver; 1963, 1965, with Dennis Ralston; Clay Court doubles, 1961, 1964, with Ralston.* DAVIS CUP—*1960, 1961, 1962, 1963, 1964, 1965; record: 16-6 in singles, 13-3 in doubles.* SINGLES RECORD IN THE MAJORS: *Wimbledon (20-4), U.S. (34-13).*

MAURICE McLOUGHLIN
United States (1890–1957)

See page 102.

FREW McMILLAN
South Africa (1942–)

Side by side again entering the Hall of Fame in 1992, Frew Donald McMillan was reunited with his one-time collaborator on the team of Hewitt and McMillan. The unorthodox McMillan—stroking with two hands on both sides in the left court—and Bob Hewitt were a dynamite blend, winning five major titles (three Wimbledons) and driving South Africa to the 1974 Davis Cup.

Love was the prime ingredient in bringing them together in 1966. It was Hewitt's romance with his South African wife-to-be that moved the Australian westward to Johannesburg. When he became eligible to play for his new land, Hewitt was yoked to McMillan in 1966, and they were an immediate hit. They won their first start together late that year, and didn't lose until the quarters of the French the following year, a 45-match streak.

In 1967 they won Wimbledon, and repeated in 1972 and 1978. A springy 6-foot-1, the slim McMillan was born in Springs, South Africa, May 20, 1942, and grew up there.

"We were touch and thrust," he says of the combination that was so winning over a 15-year period. "Right from the start each of us knew what the other would do. Bob had wonderful returning touch from the first court." McMillan, a right-hander, handled the racket like a cricket bat and could slug or chip. Distinctive beneath a tiny white cap that partially covered his shining dark hair, Frew was the first player of international prominence of two-way two-fisted swinging.

A straight-set Wimbledon quarterfinal win over five-time champs John Newcombe and Tony Roche en route to the 1978 title showed them at their very best. They continued lethally through the final, 6-1, 6-4, 6-2, over Peter Fleming and John McEnroe. Spanning the amateur and open eras, they added 60 titles to their five majors. McMillan's individual total of pro doubles titles was 74, third on the all-time list behind Tom Okker (78) and McEnroe (77). Frew won two pro singles titles. He also had five major mixed titles, two Wimbledons and two U.S. with Betty Stove, for a career total of 10 majors.

MAJOR TITLES (10)—*French doubles, 1972; Wimbledon doubles, 1967, 1972, 1978; U.S. doubles, 1977; French mixed, 1966; Wimbledon mixed, 1979, 1981; U.S. mixed, 1977, 1978.* DAVIS CUP—*1965, 1966, 1967, 1968, 1969, 1973, 1974, 1975, 1976, 1977, 1978; record: 2-0 in singles, 23-5 in doubles.* SINGLES RECORD IN THE MAJORS: *Australian (0-1), French (8-10), Wimbledon (9-17), U.S. (12-10).*

MAJOR TITLES WITH HEWITT (5)—*French doubles, 1972; Wimbledon doubles, 1967, 1972, 1978; U.S. doubles, 1977.* DAVIS CUP—*1967, 1968, 1969, 1974, 1978; record: 16-1 in doubles.*

DON McNEILL

United States (1918–96)

It was a long way to Paris from Oklahoma, but a tennis court in one place was the same as one in another to a college boy named William Donald McNeill, who became the second American man to win the French title. Doing so in 1939 by beating favorite Bobby Riggs—the year's No. 1—7-5, 6-0, 6-3, Don served notice that he would be a thorn in the little hustler's side and intentions.

Though McNeill may have lost his best years to World War II, in which he served as an officer in U.S. Naval intelligence, he stands as one of only four Americans to win on the grass at Forest Hills, the U.S. title (1940), and on the clay at Roland Garros, succeeding Don Budge, and preceding Frank Parker and Tony Trabert.

McNeill, a nimble 5-foot-10, 155, out of Oklahoma City, with a very sharp backhand, had gone to Europe on a lark. He returned to move unseeded to the U.S. quarterfinals, and give sixth-seeded Joe Hunt a scare, 6-4, 15-13, 8-10, 4-6, 6-2, in three-plus hours spread over two days. Don felt he could win it one day, and that day wasn't far off. Back to college he went, to graduate and win the Intercollegiate title for tiny Kenyon (Ohio) in 1940, then sting Riggs twice. If beating him in the U.S. Clay final, 6-1, 6-4, 7-9, 6-3, wasn't enough, he then completely wrecked defender Bobby's pro plans at Forest Hills. After taking Jack Kramer in the semis, Don staged a counterattack to seize the U.S. final, 4-6, 6-8, 6-3, 6-3, 7-5. McNeill was the third of five players in the championship round to rebound from two sets down. The victory completed an unusual coupling of headgear: wearing the college and national crowns in the same year, he would have only one such equal, Ted Schroeder in 1942.

His versatility shows in a record that includes the U.S. Clay Court title of 1940, and as the only man to win the U.S. Indoor before and after the war: as a 19-year-old collegian in 1938 over Frank Bowden, 9-7, 3-6, 6-4, 7-5, and in 1950 over Fred Kovaleskie, 11-9, 4-6, 6-2, 6-2. Not to mention numerous doubles prizes. Especially the French of '39 when he and Charlie Harris flinched not at two of the grand old Musketeers, and beat Jacques Brugnon and Jean Borotra for the title, 4-6, 6-4, 6-0, 2-6, 10-8, even though Borotra had four match points on serve at 6-5. McNeill was the first of only two American men to ring up a double in Paris. Tony Trabert emulated by winning both titles in 1964 and 1965.

He ranked in the U.S. Top Ten six times between 1937 and 1946, No. 1 in 1940, World No. 7

in 1939. On leave from the Navy, he won the U.S. doubles in 1944 with Bob Falkenburg.

"I thought I won it again," he laughed. "Several times that afternoon in Boston." He means the titanic U.S. doubles final of 1946 at Longwood. Don and Frank Guernsey had seven match points in the fifth set, but couldn't sway the champs, Bill Talbert and Gardnar Mulloy, 3-6, 6-4, 2-6, 6-3, 20-18. McNeill, born April 30, 1918, at Chickasha, Okla., spent most of his post-college life in New York as an advertising executive, and died Nov. 28, 1996, at Vero Beach, Fla. He was named to the Hall of Fame in 1965.

MAJOR TITLES (4)—*French singles, 1939; U.S. singles, 1940; French doubles, 1939; U.S. doubles, 1944.* OTHER U.S. TITLES (9)—*Indoor singles, 1938, 1950; Clay Court singles, 1940; Intercollegiate singles, 1940; Indoor doubles, 1941, 1946, with Frank Guernsey; 1949, 1950, 1951, with Bill Talbert.* SINGLES RECORD IN THE MAJORS: *French (6-0), Wimbledon (1-1), U.S. (27-9).*

HELEN WILLS MOODY

United States (1905—)

See page 103.

BESSIE MOORE

United States (1876–1959)

Elisabeth Holmes Moore, a New Yorker, was a young champ, winning the first of her U.S. titles at 20 in 1896. But four years before, she was in the final, losing the first five-set match played by women, 5-7, 6-3, 6-4, 4-6, 6-2, to Ireland's Mabel Cahill. She was the youngest U.S. finalist at 16 until Pam Shriver, a younger 16 in 1978.

Winning four singles titles (1896, 1901, 1903, 1905), she was in four other finals, and though she was eligible for a fifth in 1906 (as the 1905 champ), did not choose to play in the challenge round, defaulting the title to Helen Homans, the all-comers victor. Her U.S. total of eight finals was later surpassed by Molla Mallory's 10 and Helen Wills Moody and Chris Evert's

nine. Her longevity spread between the finals of 1892 and 1905 is also a U.S. record.

In 1901, she beat Marion Jones in the all-comers final, 4-6, 1-6, 9-7, 9-7, 6-3 (58 games, the longest of all major women's finals), then ousted defender Myrtle McAteer in the challenge round, 6-4, 3-6, 7-5, 2-6, 6-2, to become the lone woman to play five-set matches on successive days.

The 105 games alarmed the men who ran the USTA. They decreed best-of-three-set finals thereafter. Moore and the other women hadn't complained about five-set matches and she said they felt "dissatisfied" by the decision and patronized by the male establishment. Moore, a right-hander, was born March 5, 1876, in Brooklyn, N.Y., and died Jan. 22, 1959, in Starke, Fla. She was elected to the Hall of Fame in 1971.

MAJOR TITLES (8)—*U.S. singles, 1896, 1901, 1903, 1905; U.S. doubles, 1896, 1903; U.S. mixed, 1902, 1904.* OTHER U.S. TITLES (3)—*Indoor singles, 1907; Indoor doubles, 1908, with Helen Pouch; 1909, with Erna Marcus.* SINGLES RECORD IN THE MAJORS: *U.S. (25-6).*

ANGELA MORTIMER

Great Britain (1932—)

Turning a physical impairment to her advantage, Florence Angela Margaret Mortimer Barrett capped an excellent career with a rebounding, unexpected Wimbledon triumph in 1961. She was 29 and partially deaf.

"I could hear the applause of the crowd, but not much else," she recalled. "I think it helped me concentrate, shutting out distractions. When I hear players say they have to hear the ball, I smile. I couldn't."

Much applause stirred Centre Court the afternoon the 5-foot-6 Mortimer, seventh seed, overcame the crowd favorite, 6-foot and sixth-seeded 20-year-old Christine Truman, 4-6, 6-4, 7-5. It was the first all-English finale in 47 years.

Born April 21, 1932, at Plymouth, Mortimer didn't start playing tennis until she was 15. But her resolve, speed and intelligence combined to produce a strong all-around game, with emphasis on groundstrokes, particularly a battering forehand.

Mortimer lost the Wimbledon final to Althea Gibson in 1958 and was a quarterfinalist in 1953, 1954, 1956, 1959 and 1960. She won the French in 1955 and Australian in 1958. And the Wimbledon doubles in 1955.

She played Wightman Cup six years, helping Britain win, 4-3, in 1960 with a critical victory over Janet Hopps, 6-8, 6-4, 6-1, and captained the team seven years (1964–70), piloting the 1968 victory. She was in the World Top Ten, 1953–62, Nos. 1, 4 and 4 in 1961, 1955 and 1956, respectively. Following the 1961 season, in which she was a U.S. semifinalist, losing to Ann Hayden (Jones), 6-4, 6-2, she underwent a stapedectomy, improving her hearing significantly. But she was never again the player of her Wimbledon glory. Angela was a Wimbledon centurion, playing more than 100 matches, 35-18 in doubles, 5-6 in mixed.

She is married to John Edward Barrett, former British Davis Cup player and captain. They live in London.

MAJOR TITLES *(4)—Australian singles, 1958; French singles, 1955; Wimbledon singles, 1961; Wimbledon doubles, 1955.* WIGHTMAN CUP—*1953, 1955, 1956, 1959, 1960, 1961; record: 3-7 in singles, 1-4 in doubles.* SINGLES RECORD IN THE MAJORS: *Australian (5-0), French (9-2), Wimbledon (36-11), U.S. (10-5).*

GARDNAR MULLOY

United States (1913—)

An eternal beacon in the game, Gardnar Putnam Mulloy held his first U.S. national ranking in 1936 (No. 11 in men's doubles) and his most recent merely 60 years later, in 1996: No. 1 in 80s singles and doubles as a slim 6-footer with all his hair and wiles, bereft of maybe a step or two, seemingly fit as ever, he continues to play effortlessly. He is a man with a complete game, whose volleys and smashes lit up the left court as he and Bill Talbert became one of the finest teams.

They won the U.S. title four times (1942, 1945, 1946, 1948), and were finalists in 1950 and 1953. Probably the one they remember best almost got away seven times. That was the overblown 1946 final of 74 games as the tourney returned to Longwood after a wartime stay at Forest Hills, where Bill and Gar won their first two. In the record fifth set for any major, they just said no to seven match points while beating Don McNeill and Frank Guernsey, 3-6, 6-4, 2-6, 6-3, 20-18. Their six final-round appearances are one short of Fred Alexander and Harold Hackett's team record. He and Talbert won the clinching point in the 1948 Davis Cup victory over Australia at Forest Hills, beating Billy Sidwell and Colin Long. Gar was on the team six other years, helping also to win the Cups of 1946 and 1949, and was a winning player-captain in two zone matches, 1952 and 1953. Playing on the 1957 team at 43, he was the oldest U.S. Cupper.

Ranking in the U.S. Top Ten 14 times between 1939 and 1954, he was No. 1 in 1952, when he was U.S. finalist at Forest Hills, losing to 24-year-old Frank Sedgman. At 38, Mulloy was the oldest to attain that eminence, five weeks older than 38-year-old Bill Larned in 1911. He ranked in the World Top Ten thrice: 1946, 1949 and 1952, No. 7 the last year. His most startling triumph may have been the Wimbledon doubles in 1957, at 43, joined with Budge Patty, 33. Unseeded, they became the oldest championship team of the post-World War I era by stunning the top-seeded Lew Hoad, 22, and Neale Fraser, 23, 8-10, 6-4, 6-4, 6-4.

A right-hander, he was born Nov. 22, 1913, in Washington, D.C., but has been a lifelong Miamian, a graduate of the University of Miami and its law school, organizer-coach-leading player of its first tennis team. His first U.S. Championships were the Father and Son doubles with his father, Robin Mulloy, in 1939, 1941 and 1942, but they have continued to flow from his rackets unceasingly for more than a half-century. Campaigning among the seniors since he won the singles at the Grass Court 45s in 1960, he has racked up 52 U.S. titles in singles through the age groups and 47 in doubles including the Grass 45s of 1963, 1964, 1965 and 1967 with his old sidekick, Talbert. In 1995 and 1996, he won four 80s singles, two grass, one indoor and one hard court.

Serving in the U.S. Navy in World War II, he commanded a landing craft in North African and European invasions. He entered the Hall of Fame in 1972.

MAJOR TITLES (5)—*Wimbledon doubles, 1957; U.S. doubles, 1942, 1945, 1946, 1948.* OTHER U.S. TITLE—*Clay Court doubles, 1946, with Bill Talbert.* DAVIS CUP—*1946, 1948, 1949, 1950, 1952, 1953, 1957; record: 3-0 in singles, 8-3 in doubles.* SINGLES RECORD IN THE MAJORS: *Australian (3-1), French (13-4), Wimbledon (31-18), U.S. (51-20).*

LINDLEY MURRAY

United States (1892–1970)

A big-serving 6-foot-2 lefty out of California, Robert Lindley Murray was born Nov. 3, 1892, in San Francisco. He had a brief, bright run in the U.S. Championships, losing in the 1916 semis to Bill Johnston, 6-2, 6-3, 6-1, and taking the title in 1917 (over Nat Niles) and 1918 (over Bill Tilden).

He was ranked No. 1 in the U.S. in 1918, No. 4 in 1916 and 1919. A chemical engineer who graduated from Stanford, he was working on explosives production during World War I and had no intention of entering the 1917 Championships, billed as a "patriotic" tournament to raise money for the Red Cross. His employer, Elon Hooker of Hooker Chemical, talked Murray into it and he had an explosive tourney—the only one he played that summer.

"My strong points were a vicious serve, a quick dash to the net and the ability to volley decisively anything that came near me," he said.

His serve was lightning on the boards of the Seventh Regiment Armory in New York as Lindley won the 1916 U.S. Indoor over Alrick Man, 6-2, 6-2, 9-7.

He settled in the Buffalo area and died Jan. 17, 1970, in Lewiston Heights, N.Y. He was named to the Hall of Fame in 1958.

MAJOR TITLES (2)—*U.S. singles, 1917, 1918.* OTHER U.S. TITLE—*Indoor singles, 1916.* SINGLES RECORD IN THE MAJORS: *U.S. (21-3).*

ILIE NASTASE

Romania (1946—)

See page 424.

JOHN NEWCOMBE

Australia (1944—)

See page 428.

BETTY NUTHALL

Great Britain (1911–83)

See page 105.

ALEX OLMEDO

Peru (1936—)

Alejandro Olmedo, called "Chief" at the University of Southern California because of his regal bearing at 6-foot-1 and his Incan features, was an aggressive volleyer who constantly sought the net. He fared best on the quickest terrain: concrete (U.S. Intercollegiate titles in singles and doubles for USC in 1956 and 1958); boards (U.S. Indoor titlist in 1959 over Dick Savitt, 7-9, 6-3, 6-4, 5-7, 12-10) and grass (Wimbledon and Australian chieftain in 1959). His was a quick but huge splash that covered two years.

Born March 24, 1936, in Arequipa, Peru, he picked up the game in his homeland as an extremely agile athlete. But it was refined when he came to USC where he was thrust into the limelight—and controversy—by one of his patrons,

Southern California tennis czar Perry Jones. Jones, the U.S. Davis Cup captain in 1958 and 1959, saw in Olmedo the chance for victory after three lean years.

Lobbying successfully for Olmedo's inclusion on the basis that the Peruvian was a U.S. resident whose own country had no team, Jones installed him for the semifinal victory over Italy on grass at Perth. Alex won his debut over Nicola Pietrangeli, 5-7, 10-8, 6-0, 6-1. This launched a storm of press criticism over the U.S. using a non-citizen for the only time. Another hassle developed at the Cup round when the No. 1 American, Ham Richardson, was benched in singles in favor of Olmedo. But Jones' policy worked. Olmedo anchored the 3-2 victory over the Aussies at Brisbane with two singles victories and by joining his U.S. championship partner, Richardson, in an epic 82-game doubles win over Mal Anderson and Neale Fraser, 10-12, 3-6, 16-14, 6-3, 7-5. Alex led off by beating Anderson, 8-6, 2-6, 9-7, 8-6, and clinched over Wimbledon champ Ashley Cooper, 6-3, 4-6, 6-4, 8-6.

A half-year later Wimbledon belonged to Olmedo, 6-4, 3-6, 9-7, 7-5, over Rod Laver. Although he beat Laver again in the Cup round the following month, the U.S. lost the Cup to Australia, 3-2, at Forest Hills. Fraser, his conqueror in that series, also beat him for the U.S. title, 6-3, 5-7, 6-2, 6-4. In 1960 Olmedo turned pro and joined the nomads on their odyssey of one-night stands. His brief mention in the rankings were in 1958, No. 2 in the U.S.; 1959, No. 1 in the U.S., No. 2 in the world. His daughter, Amy Olmedo, won the U.S. Public Parks Championship for 12s in 1975. He entered the Hall of Fame in 1987.

MAJOR TITLES (2)—*Wimbledon singles, 1959; Australian singles, 1959.* OTHER U.S. TITLES (11)—*Indoor singles, 1959; Pro singles, 1960; Pro doubles, 1960, with Ashley Cooper; Indoor doubles, 1959, with Barry MacKay; Clay Court doubles, 1956, with Francisco Contreras; Hard Court singles, 1956; Hard Court doubles, 1957, with Mike Franks; Intercollegiate singles, 1956, 1958; Intercollegiate doubles, 1956, with Contreras; 1958, with Ed Atkinson.* DAVIS CUP— *1958, 1959; record: 5-1 in singles, 2-1 in doubles.* SINGLES RECORD IN THE MAJORS: *Australian (5-0), French (0-2), Wimbledon (10-3), U.S. (15-9).*

RAFE OSUNA
Mexico (1938–69)

Mexico's greatest player, Rafael Herrera Osuna, died tragically in an air crash near Monterey, June 6, 1969—shortly after one of his brightest performances. He had spearheaded Mexico's lone Davis Cup triumph over Australia, 3-2, in Mexico City by winning both his singles (the exciting fifth-match clincher over Bill Bowrey, 6-2, 3-6, 8-6, 6-3) as well as the doubles with Vicente Zarazua over John Alexander and Phil Dent. Ironically it was not only his last match, but the last appearance in the Australian captain's chair of the man whose side he defeated, legendary Harry Hopman.

Long the anchor of Mexico's team, the super-quick and clever 5-foot-10 Osuna, was the better known half of an extraordinary combine. He and Antonio Palafox showed what two good men could do for their country in 1962, taking Mexico past the U.S. for the first time, 3-2; Yugoslavia, 4-1; Sweden, 3-2; India, 5-0, all the way to the finale at Brisbane, where they lost to Cup-holding Australia, 5-0.

During that campaign en route to Australia, Osuna was 5-1 in singles, and with Palafox, 4-0 in doubles. Twice he came through in emotional and decisive fifth sets of fifth matches, beating Jack Douglas of the U.S. at the wire, 9-7, 6-3, 6-8, 3-6, 6-1, and Jan-Erik Lundquist of Sweden, likewise, 3-6, 6-4, 6-3, 1-6, 6-3, both at Mexico City.

Twice he won the doubles at Wimbledon, his country's only triumphs there, 1960 and 1963. The first time, at 21, with his University of Southern California pal and partner, Dennis Ralston, 17, they were unseeded, and the second-youngest champs, beating Mike Davies and Bobby Wilson, 7-5, 6-3, 10-8. In 1963 he and Palafox beat Pierre Darmon and Jean Claude Barclay. The two of them had a terrific series with Ralston and Chuck McKinley in three straight U.S. finals, 1961–63, the Mexicans winning in 1962 and holding fifth-set match points in 1963.

Ubiquitous on court, confusing to foes, ever seeking the net, he reached a zenith in singles by winning the U.S. title at Forest Hills in 1963, bewildering huge-serving Frank Froehling III, 7-5, 6-4, 6-2, with lobs, chips, angles, flying volleys and footspeed. Slouching, unimposing until his feet and hands whirred in action, he had a beguiling smile and a court manner that endeared him to galleries. At Southern Cal, where he was an All-American, he won the U.S. Intercollegiate singles in 1962 and was the first player since World War I to take the doubles three times: 1961 and 1962 with Ramsey Earnhart, 1963 with Ralston. Osuna was in the World Top Ten thrice, 1962–64, No. 1 in 1963. He was born Sept. 15, 1938, in Mexico City and he made it into the Hall of Fame in 1979.

MAJOR TITLES (4)—*U.S. singles, 1963; U.S. doubles, 1962; Wimbledon doubles, 1960, 1963.* DAVIS CUP—*1958, 1960, 1961, 1962, 1963, 1964, 1965, 1966, 1967, 1968, 1969; record: 23-13 in singles, 14-8 in doubles.* SINGLES RECORD IN THE MAJORS: *French (2-2), Wimbledon (17-6), U.S. (34-7).*

FRANK PARKER
United States (1916—)

Frank Andrew Parker, a marvelous groundstroker, particularly on the backhand side, was a paragon of durability, ranking in the U.S. Top Ten 17 straight years (1933–49), a male record until Jimmy Connors surpassed it in 1988. One of the youngest to rank with the elite, 17 in 1933, he was No. 1 in 1944 and 1945, and the oldest ever to play in the U.S. Championships, 52 in 1968.

He entered in 1968 for fun, this man who had teamed with Don Budge and Gene Mako to win the Davis Cup for the U.S. in 1937, saying he wanted to be part of yet another era, the "open." He lost his first match to eventual champion, Arthur Ashe, 6-3, 6-2, 6-2, thus completing a championship career that began with a third-round defeat by fourth-seeded George Lott, 6-1, 6-4, 4-6, 6-2, at Forest Hills in 1932. In between, as Sgt. Parker, Frankie won the U.S. title on his 13th try in 1944, again in 1945, both while on leave from the U.S. Army Air Force during World War II. He beat civilian Bill Talbert both times. A 6-3, 6-4, 6-8, 3-6, 6-1 quarterfinal defeat in 1946

by Tom Brown busted his dream of winning three straight. But he nearly jolted Jack Kramer by winning the first two sets of their 1947 final. After the 1949 Forest Hills, his 19th, ending in a semis loss, 3-6, 9-7, 6-3, 6-2, to champ Pancho Gonzalez, Frankie turned pro to tour with Kramer, Gonzalez and Pancho Segura.

Grass or clay? Didn't matter to 5-foot-8½, 145-pound Frank, at home anywhere, the third of only four American men able to win on the greensward of Forest Hills and the heavy salmon-toned soil of Roland Garros. In 1948 and 1949 at the French he followed Don Budge and Don McNeill, and preceded Tony Trabert. But his surefire groundies looked especially good in the U.S. Clay Court championship that he won five times between 1933 and 1947. His 24-match streak was ended in the 1949 final by Gonzalez, 6-1, 3-6, 8-6, 6-3. Parker built the streak on titles in 1941 (over Bobby Riggs, 6-3, 7-5, 6-8, 4-6, 6-3), 1946 (over Talbert, 6-4, 6-4, 6-2), 1947 (over Ted Schroeder, 8-6, 6-2, 6-4). Although he and Gonzalez were known primarily for singles, they played a brief but forceful duet on both sides of the English Channel in '49, winning the French and Wimbledon doubles.

Frank won 12 of 14 Davis Cup matches. In 1948 he won both singles in the successful defense against Australia. Coupled with his singles win while the U.S. heisted the Cup from Britain in 1937, this made him the only man to help win the Cup with singles victories at either end of World War II. He was ranked in the World Top Ten six times between 1937 and 1949, No. 1 in 1948. Born in Milwaukee Jan. 31, 1916, he was christened Franciszek Andrzej Paikowski. He entered the Hall of Fame in 1966.

MAJOR TITLES (6)—*French singles, 1948, 1949; U.S. singles, 1944, 1945; Wimbledon doubles, 1949; French doubles, 1949.* OTHER U.S. TITLES (7)—*Clay Court singles, 1933, 1939, 1941, 1946, 1947; Clay Court doubles, 1939, with Gene Mako; Indoor doubles, 1937, with Greg Mangin.* DAVIS CUP—*1937, 1939, 1946, 1948; record: 12-2 in singles.* SINGLES RECORD IN THE MAJORS: *French (12-1), Wimbledon (12-3), U.S. (60-18).*

GERALD PATTERSON
Australia (1895–1967)

A strapping 6-footer, Gerald Leighton Patterson followed Norman Brookes as Australia's second international tennis star. A heroic Military Cross winner with the Australian army in World War I, he played the game with daring, too, charging the net behind an explosive serve, both flat and twisting. His exemplary smash, stiff volleying and good forehand rewarded him with two Wimbledon championships.

An all-or-nothing outlook never was displayed more glaringly than in his Australian championship victory in 1927. Beating lefty Jack Hawkes, 6-3 in the fifth, he blasted 29 aces and 29 doubles faults. In 1919 Patterson took the Wimbledon title from Brookes, who had to wait five years, through World War I, to defend in the challenge round. Patterson lost it to Bill Tilden in 1920, but with Tilden failing to defend in 1922, he helped christen the "new" (present) site by defeating Randolph Lycett easily. It was over so fast (6-3, 6-4, 6-2) that no fat lady had a chance to sing. But the world's most famous singer was in the debuting Centre Court, beaming, if not screaming, for her Gerald. That was Dame Nellie Melba, the great Australian diva, Patterson's aunt and No. 1 fan. Patterson was known as the "Human Catapult" at home for his brutal serve, and there were tales that some of his aces were so forceful they bounded into the grandstand.

He spurred Australia to the Davis Cup finales of 1922 and 1924, and helped win the only point against the U.S. at Forest Hills, joining Pat O'Hara Wood for a doubles victory over Tilden and Vinnie Richards in 1922. In 1925 he was considerably ahead of his time, using for a while a steel racket strung with wire. His best U.S. showings were semifinal finishes at Forest Hills, losing to Tilden in 1922, 4-6, 6-4, 6-3, 6-1, and Bill Johnston, 6-2, 6-0. 6-0, in 1924. He did better against Johnston when Bill won the 1919 title, losing 7-5 in the fifth, a fourth-rounder. But that summer in Boston, Patterson and Norman Brookes made the first dent in the U.S. that would become a canyon: Aussies taking one of the Yanks' championships, the doubles, as they beat Tilden and Richards in five.

Five Aussie doubles titles were his between 1914 and 1927, three with Hawkes. He was among the World Top Ten six times between 1919 and 1925, No. 1 in 1919. Patterson was born Dec. 17, 1895, in Melbourne, and died there June 13, 1967. He was voted into the Hall of Fame in 1989.

MAJOR TITLES *(9)—Australian singles, 1927; Wimbledon singles, 1919, 1922; Australian doubles, 1922, 1925, 1926, 1927; U.S. doubles, 1919; Wimbledon mixed, 1920.* DAVIS CUP—*1919, 1920, 1922, 1924, 1925, 1928; record: 21-10 in singles, 11-4 in doubles.* SINGLES RECORD IN THE MAJORS: *Australian (19-4), French (2-1), Wimbledon (17-2), U.S. (10-3).*

BUDGE PATTY
United States (1924—)

A rare combination for an American male was "Budge" Patty's French-Wimbledon double of 1950. Only Don Budge in 1938 and Tony Trabert in 1955 achieved such a double.

John Edward Patty was born Feb. 11, 1924, at Ft. Smith, Ark., and grew up in Los Angeles, the tennis vineyard of his youth. He says a brother gave him the nickname "Budge" because "I was so lazy he said I wouldn't budge." It stuck, but he budged gracefully on a tennis court, and graciously in his bearing otherwise, a trim cosmopolitan fellow of 6-foot-1 who preferred to live in Europe after serving there with the U.S. Army in World War II. His smooth groundstroking game played well on the Continent's clay. He won the Italian in 1954. But he was a sharp volleyer, too, a fine doubles player. Seeded fifth, Patty beat second-seeded Bill Talbert in the quarters and top-seeded Frank Sedgman for his 1950 Wimbledon title, 6-1, 8-10, 6-2, 6-3.

At Paris the same year he overcame lefty Jaroslav Drobny for the title, 6-1, 6-2, 3-6, 5-7, 7-5. Defending in 1951, he was upset by Ham Richardson in the second round at Wimbledon, and by Lennart Bergelin in the fourth round at Paris. Probably his two most renowned matches, both at Wimbledon, were a singles defeat and a doubles victory. In the third round of 1953, despite six match points, he fell to Drobny at dusk in a 93-game, 4-hour-20-minute classic, 8-6, 16-18, 3-6, 8-6, 12-10. Four years later, he, 33, and Gar Mulloy, 43—unseeded—were the oldest team of the post-World War I era to win at the Big W, beating top-seeded Lew Hoad, 22, and Neale Fraser, 23, 8-10, 6-4, 6-4, 6-4.

They reached the title round of the U.S. Championships that year, the oldest finalists there, losing to Fraser and Ashley Cooper. Patty is also remembered in Paris for an incredible defeat, a 1958 fourth-rounder in which Robert Haillet revived from 5-0, 40-0 down, Patty serving, in the fifth set, to win, 5-7, 7-5, 10-8, 4-6, 7-5, saving four match points. Seldom appearing in the U.S., Patty was a quarterfinalist in the 1951 Championships, losing to Dick Savitt, 6-4 in the fifth, and played Davis Cup briefly, to get his only U.S. Top Ten ranking, No. 10. But he was ranked seven times in the World Top Ten between 1947 and 1957, No. 1 in 1950. He entered the Hall of Fame in 1977.

Over his 15-year amateur career, Patty won 76 singles titles.

MAJOR TITLES (4)—*French singles, 1950; Wimbledon singles, 1950; Wimbledon doubles, 1957; French mixed, 1946.* U.S. TITLES (2)—*Indoor doubles, 1952, with Bill Talbert; Indoor mixed, 1950, with Nancy Chaffee.* DAVIS CUP—*1951; record: 1-0 in singles, 1-0 in doubles.* SINGLES RECORD IN THE MAJORS: *French (44-14), Wimbledon (44-14), U.S. (16-6).*

TEDDY PELL
United States (1879–1967)

Theodore Roosevelt Pell made his mark inside, winning the U.S. Indoor singles in 1907, 1909 and 1911, and the doubles four times between 1905 and 1912. A right-hander, he had a particularly strong backhand, and was ranked in the U.S. Top Ten five times between 1910 and 1918, No. 5 in 1913 and 1915. Pell, a slender 6-foot New Yorker, did have a good time outdoors in 1915, though, in a run to the U.S. semis at Newport, beating two fellow Hall-of-Famers-to-be in straight sets, Watson Washburn and Beals Wright, on the way. But the "Comet" fell on him, Maurice McLoughlin, 6-2, 6-0, 7-5.

Born in New York, May 12, 1879, he died Aug. 18, 1967, in Sands Point, N.Y. He was elected to the Hall of Fame in 1966.

U.S. TITLES (7)—*Indoor singles, 1907, 1909, 1911; Indoor doubles, 1905, with H.F. Allen; 1909, with Wylie Grant; 1911, 1912, with Fred Alexander.* SINGLES RECORD IN THE MAJORS: *U.S. (21-13).*

FRED PERRY
Great Britain (1909–95)

See page 106.

NICKY PIETRANGELI
Italy (1933–)

Nicola "Nicky" Pietrangeli was Signor Davis Cup. That team competition seemed Nicky's private preserve, although he won his only Cup from the sidelines as Italy's non-playing captain in 1976. Before that, as a smooth touch operator, winner of the French (1957 over Beppe Merlo, 1961 over Rod Laver), he had made his name synonymous with Italy. He did it in Davis Cup by playing (164) and winning (120) more matches than anyone before or since during a Cup career that reached from 1954 through 1972. In 66 ties for his country he was 78-32 in singles, 42-12 in doubles.

Twice he carried Italy all the way to the Cup round, 1960 and 1961, but on alien grass in Australia, and during the reign of Aussie powerhouses, he and 6-foot-7 accomplice Orlando Sirola were unable to come closer to the Cup than a good look. Still, to get there in 1960 they pulled off one of Italy's greatest victories, 3-2 from 0-2, over the U.S. in the semifinal at Perth. Despite their discomfort on grass, Pietrangeli—he had squandered eight match points in losing to Barry

MacKay, 8-6, 3-6, 8-10, 8-6, 13-11—and Sirola, perhaps the finest doubles team developed in post-World War II Europe, struck back to beat Chuck McKinley and Butch Buchholz, 3-6, 10-8, 6-4, 13-11, seemingly only to prolong their distress. But Pietrangeli stopped Buchholz, 6-1, 6-2, 6-8, 3-6, 6-4, and Sirola clinched, 9-7, 6-3, 8-6, over MacKay.

Pietrangeli was too much for the U.S. to overcome in the following year's semi at Rome as he beat both Whitney Reed and Jack Douglas, teamed with Sirola again triumphantly in a 4-1 victory. But in the two finales, only Pietrangeli's third-day win over Neale Fraser could be salvaged as Australia won, 5-0 and 4-1.

Solidly built, possessing exceptional instincts for the game and anticipation, 5-foot-11 Nicky was an all-around performer who moved with grace and purpose. He was in four French finals, losing to Manolo Santana in 1961 and 1964, and four Italian. His best showing away from compatible clay was a 1960 Wimbledon semifinal which he lost to Laver, 6-4 in the fifth. His was a career of the amateur era during which he won 53 singles titles and was in the World Top Ten five times between 1957 and 1964, No. 3 in 1959 and 1960. Retired from the court, he captained Italy to the Cup round twice, defeating Chile in 1976 but losing to Australia in 1977. A right-hander, born Sept. 11, 1933, in Tunis, he is a bon vivant, ever popular with fans and colleagues. He and Sirola were the biggest winners of Cup doubles teams, 34-8.

He entered the Hall of Fame in 1986.

MAJOR TITLES (4)—*French singles, 1959, 1960 French doubles, 1959; French mixed, 1958.* DAVIS CUP—*1954, 1955, 1956, 1957, 1958, 1959, 1960, 1961, 1962, 1963, 1964, 1965, 1966, 1967, 1968, 1969, 1971, 1972; record 78-32 in singles, 42-12 in doubles.* SINGLES RECORD IN THE MAJORS: *Australian (2-1), French (46-12), Wimbledon (29-18), U.S. (5-3).*

ADRIAN QUIST
Australia (1913–91)

Elected to the Hall of Fame in 1984 as the left-court half of the great Australian doubles team of Bromwich and Quist, Adrian Karl Quist also won three major singles, the Australian, 1936, 1940 and 1948. Quist was the only man to win a major before and after World War II, in which he served in the Australian army.

He was also the only man to win a Wimbledon title before and after, doubles with Jack Crawford in 1935, and with Brom in 1950. It seemed fitting that the two old comrades who wreaked so much damage together should meet in the last Aussie singles final with a pre-war flavor, 1948, before the kids led by Frank Sedgman took over. And that it should go to the wire on a sweltering afternoon at Kooyong. Quisty scraped and scraped to hold onto serve to 3-3 in the fifth, then won the last three games from Brom.

His 13 Australian titles are high for that tournament, and he holds major doubles records: most titles, 10, and most with one partner, eight, alongside Jack Bromwich. They won those eight successively, also a record, between 1938 and 1950. Quist also won in 1936 and 1937 with Don Turnbull for a personal 10-straight, also a record.

He and Brom registered a unique triumph in lifting the Davis Cup from the U.S. in 1939. Losing their singles the first day in Philadelphia (Quist to Frank Parker, 7-5 in the fifth), they began the unparalleled comeback by beating Jack Kramer and Joe Hunt in a four-set doubles, even though they lost the first set and trailed 1-3 in the third. Hunt led 3-2, 30-15 on serve in the third when the turnabout began. Quist, a short (5-foot-6½), bouncy right-hander with an all-court game and telling volleys, then hung on after losing the third and fourth sets to beat Wimbledon champ Bobby Riggs, 6-1, 6-4, 3-6, 3-6, 6-4, even though Riggs saved a match point at 5-2 and reached 4-5. Bromwich beat Frank Parker in a groundstroking duel to ice it in the fifth match.

Quist and Bromwich won the U.S. doubles, too, in 1939, and, well beyond expectations, took their lone Wimbledon crown together in 1950, beating Billy Sidwell and Geoff Brown, 6-2 in the fifth. Quisty was within a month of his 37th birthday, Brom 31. Having won the French title with Jack Crawford in 1935, Quist—holder of 17 majors altogether—was one of 11 to win all four in doubles. Quist first appeared in the World Top Ten in 1936 at No. 4, No. 6 in 1938 and No. 3 in 1939. He was born Aug. 4, 1913, in Medindia, South Australia, and died Nov. 17, 1991, in Sydney.

MAJOR TITLES *(17)—Australian singles, 1936, 1940, 1948; Australian doubles, 1936, 1937, 1938, 1939, 1940, 1946, 1947, 1948, 1949, 1950; French doubles, 1935; Wimbledon doubles, 1935, 1950; U.S. doubles, 1939.* DAVIS CUP—*1933, 1934, 1935, 1936, 1937, 1938, 1939, 1946, 1948; record: 24-10 in singles, 19-3 in doubles.* SINGLES RECORD IN THE MAJORS: *Australian (42-12), French (8-4), Wimbledon (15-6), U.S. (11-4).*

MAJOR TITLES WITH BROMWICH *(10)—Australian doubles, 1938, 1939, 1940, 1946, 1947, 1948, 1949, 1950; Wimbledon doubles, 1950; U.S. doubles, 1939.* DAVIS CUP—*1938, 1939, 1946; record: 9-1 in doubles.*

DENNY RALSTON
United States (1942—)

Robert Dennis Ralston was one of those rare men who was a Davis Cup winner both as player and captain. He was considered a stormy figure early in his career although his actions seem tame in comparison with numerous who came after, and he has made a name as an outstanding educator and influence while varsity tennis coach at Southern Methodist University.

It was as a doubles player, in the right court alongside Chuck McKinley, that he made his strongest showing. They won the U.S. title thrice (1961, 1963, 1964) and were in the final in 1962.

Wimbledon and the tennis public first heard from him in 1960. As a 17-year-old joined with his University of Southern California teammate, 21-year-old Rafe Osuna, he took the doubles prize. Unseeded, they were the second-youngest to win at the Big W, 7-5, 6-3, 10-8, over Mike Davies and Bobby Wilson. He suffered many frustrations as a Davis Cup player, but it all came together for him and McKinley as they pried the punchbowl away from Australia, 3-2, at Adelaide in 1963.

During an arduous campaign he won six of seven singles and all five doubles, four with McKinley. He led off in a difficult win over rookie John Newcombe, firming up when all seemed lost, 6-4, 6-1, 3-6, 4-6, 7-5, and teamed with McKinley for the go-ahead doubles point. After he lost to Roy Emerson, McKinley clinched against Newcombe. They lost the Cup to the Aussies the following year, 3-2, though winning the doubles—he and McKinley were 8-2 in Cup doubles.

Between 1968 and 1971 he served as coach of winning U.S. teams, and in 1972 he became captain for a four-year term. His coolness and calming manner in the face of an uproarious crowd and patriotic local line judges in Bucharest was a highlight of the 1972 Cup victory over Romania.

A slim 6-footer, Ralston was a stylish stroker with a piercing backhand, a fine server and excellent volleyer who was in the U.S. Top Ten for seven straight years from 1960. He was, the first to be No. 1 three straight years (1963–65) since Don Budge (1936–38). His career spanned the amateur and open eras and he made the World Top Ten in both: 1963, 1964, 1965, 1966 and 1968, No. 5 in 1966 when he lost the Wimbledon final to Manolo Santana.

He had one pro singles title, five in doubles. Denny was an unseeded U.S. semifinalist in 1960, losing to the champ, Neale Fraser. But his best Forest Hills moment was a 7-6 (5-3), 7-5, 5-7, 4-6, 6-3 triumph in 1970 over No. 1 Rod Laver, the defender, to reach the quarters, where he lost to Cliff Richey. He and his dad, Bob Ralston, won the U.S. Father and Son title in 1964. He was born July 27, 1942, in Bakersfield, Cal. He entered the Hall of Fame in 1987 and now is tennis director at the Broadmoor resort at Colorado Springs, Colo. He was the first of three men to have won U.S. doubles titles on the four surfaces (grass, clay, indoor, hard), followed by Stan Smith and Bob Lutz.

MAJOR TITLES *(5)—French doubles, 1966; U.S. doubles, 1961, 1963, 1964; Wimbledon doubles, 1960.* OTHER

U.S. TITLES *(13)—Indoor singles, 1963; Clay Court singles, 1964, 1965; Hard Court singles, 1964, 1965; Indoor doubles, 1963, 1965, with Chuck McKinley; Clay Court doubles, 1961, 1964, with McKinley; 1966, with Clark Graebner; Hard Court doubles, 1964, with Bill Bond; 1965, with Tom Edlefsen; Pro Doubles, 1967, with Ken Rosewall. Davis Cup (As player)— 1960, 1961, 1962, 1963, 1964, 1965, 1966; record: 14-5 in singles, 11-4 in doubles; (As captain)—1972, 1973, 1974, 1975; record: 9-3, 1 Cup.* SINGLES RECORD IN THE MAJORS: *Australian (4-2), French (5-2), Wimbledon (29-13), U.S. (31-13).*

ERNEST RENSHAW
Great Britain (1861–99)

James Ernest Renshaw was the older of the fabled English Renshaw twins by 15 minutes, and he was a half-inch taller at 5-foot-10½. He wasn't, however, as successful in amassing singles titles as brother Willie. The two of them ushered in an attacking era and together were an a awesome pair at doubles, winning Wimbledon seven times between 1880 and 1889, a record surpassed by one by the Doherty brothers, Laurie and Reggie.

Ernest, who made the singles title round five times, won in 1888, and might have done better if brother hadn't been in the way, losing the prize to Willie thrice, 1882, 1883 and 1889, and to Herbert Lawford in 1887. Like the Dohertys, the Renshaws were miserable playing against one another. A right-hander, Ernest was born Jan. 3, 1861, in Leamington, England, and died Sept. 2, 1899, in Twyford, England. He entered the Hall of Fame in 1983.

MAJOR TITLES *(8)—Wimbledon singles, 1888; Wimbledon doubles, 1880, 1881, 1884, 1885, 1886, 1888, 1889.* SINGLES RECORD IN THE MAJORS: *Wimbledon (32-10).*

WILLIE RENSHAW
Great Britain (1861–1904)

Bjorn Borg said in 1981, "Yes, I know who Mr. Willie Renshaw was." Few others did. Borg, who had won five straight Wimbledons, was trying to overtake that bygone luminary, but couldn't make it. Nobody has. Not only did William

Charles Renshaw, a forceful right-handed aggressor, win an unequaled six straight Wimbledons from 1881, wresting the title from John Hartley, 6-0, 6-2, 6-1, but he added a record seventh title in 1889, defeating older (by 15 minutes) brother, Ernest Renshaw, in the title round, 6-4, 6-1, 3-6, 6-0.

In the all-comers final against Harry Barlow, Willie made an all-time recovery. He ducked six match points in the fourth set, trailing 5-2, and came back from 0-5 in the fifth to win, 3-6, 5-7, 8-6, 10-8, 8-6.

England's Renshaw twins (Ernest was also right-handed) were rivals and accomplices. Thrice Willie stopped Ernest for the Wimbledon title, but seven times between 1880 and 1889 they combined for the doubles championship, a record later topped by one by the Doherty brothers, Laurie and Reggie. Willie's 14 titles at the Big W are the male record. The offense-minded Renshaws played doubles as never before, rushing the net and volleying more frequently and effectively than their predecessors, helped by the lowering of the net to its present three feet in 1882.

Willie, noted particularly for his serve and overhead smash, was a third-round loser to O. E. Woodhouse in his Wimbledon debut, 1880. He lost only twice after that, to nemesis Willoughby Hamilton in the 1888 quarters, and again in the 1890 challenge round, 6-8, 6-2, 3-6, 6-1, 6-1. He won 22 of 25 Wimbledon matches in singles, and had a 14-match streak from 1881 to the 1888 defeat by Hamilton, having declined to defend in 1887 because of an elbow injury. That mark wasn't broken until after the challenge round system was abandoned and Fred Perry recorded a 15th straight match win in the first round of his 1936 title.

The Renshaws seemed to be the first to take the game really seriously, playing a full English summer schedule, and then competing on the Riviera during the winter, building a court at Cannes in 1880. Willie was born Jan. 3, 1861, in Leamington, England, and died Aug. 12, 1904, in Swanage, England. He entered the Hall of Fame in 1983.

MAJOR TITLES (14)—*Wimbledon singles, 1881, 1882, 1883, 1884, 1885, 1886, 1889; Wimbledon doubles, 1880, 1881, 1884, 1885, 1886, 1888, 1889.* SINGLES RECORD IN THE MAJORS: *Wimbledon (22-3).*

VINNIE RICHARDS
United States (1903–59)

Vincent Richards was the boy wonder of his day, and hasn't lost that luster: the youngest male to win any of the major championships. A volleying master all his life, he was 15 when Big Bill Tilden, on the verge of greatness, selected the kid as partner in the U.S. doubles championships of 1918 at Longwood Cricket Club in Boston. They marched through the field, and Vinnie must have felt as though he were in the geriatric ward.

He and Tilden, 25, beat a couple of 38-year-old ex-champs, Fred Alexander and Beals Wright, for the title, 6-3, 6-4, 3-6, 2-6, 6-2. They won twice more in 1921 and 1922, beating Davis Cup teammates Dick Williams and Watty Washburn, then the Australian Cup pair, Gerald Patterson and Pat O'Hara Wood. Fittingly, the last national title Richards and Tilden won was a valedictory together, the U.S. Pro doubles 27 years after, in 1945, over Welby Van Horn and Dick Skeen, 7-5, 6-4, 6-2.

Richards was a pro pioneer, signing on with promoter C. C. Pyle as leading man of the original professional touring troupe in 1926. His mates barnstorming North America during the winter of 1926–27 were the star attraction, Suzanne Lenglen and Paul Feret of France, and fellow Americans Mary K. Browne, Howard Kinsey and Harvey Snodgrass.

It was tough to break into the Davis Cup lineup in singles with Bill Johnston and Tilden around. But Vinnie got his chance in 1924, and beat both Patterson and O'Hara Wood in straight sets during the 5-0 victory over Australia. That year he won two Olympic golds (singles, doubles) and a silver (mixed). He was on four Cup-

winning teams, losing only a doubles with Tilden in 1922. In 1918 Richards was also the youngest ever to play or win a match in the U.S. singles, and he steadily advanced toward the top, a 19-year-old semifinalist in 1922, losing to Johnston, 8-6, 6-2, 6-1. He was back in the semis in 1924, battling the champ, Tilden, 4-6, 6-2, 8-6, 4-6, 6-4, repeating the next year but losing to Big Bill, 6-8, 6-4, 6-4, 6-1. In 1926 he was generally acknowledged as the best American, losing to Jean Borotra in the semis, 3-6, 6-4, 4-6, 8-6, 6-2, while Tilden lost in the quarters to Henri Cochet.

Many felt that 5-foot-10 Richards, who had refined his game well beyond his teenage volleying skills, deserved the No. 1 U.S. ranking. Instead, because he turned pro, the USTA unfairly awarded him no ranking for that year when he was No. 6 in the world rankings. He had been in the U.S. and World Top Ten five straight years from 1921, No. 2 in both in 1924.

Once the initial Pyle tour was disbanded, he was active in trying to find other opportunities for the fledgling professionals, no longer welcome at the traditional events. Vinnie, who championed the pros during those difficult years, even after his playing days were over, helped organize the first U.S. Pro Championships in New York in 1927, an event that continues as the longest-running pro tournament. The purse was $2,000. Richards beat Kinsey, 11-9, 6-4, 6-3, for that title and a first prize of $1,000, and was its singles victor three more times. Born March 20, 1903, and raised in Yonkers, N.Y., he died Sept. 28, 1959, in New York, shortly after entering the Hall of Fame.

MAJOR TITLES (9)—*French doubles, 1926; Wimbledon doubles, 1924; U.S. doubles, 1918, 1921, 1922, 1925, 1926; U.S mixed, 1919, 1924. Other U.S titles (20)—Indoor singles, 1919, 1923, 1924; Indoor doubles, 1919, 1920, with Bill Tilden; 1921, with Howard Voshell; 1923, 1924, with Frank Hunter; Clay Court doubles, 1920, with Roland Roberts; Pro singles, 1927, 1928, 1930, 1933; Pro doubles, 1929, with Karel Kozeluh; 1930, 1931, with Howard Kinsey; 1933, with Charles Wood; 1937, with George Lott; 1938, with Fred Perry, 1945, with Bill Tilden.* DAVIS CUP—*1922, 1924, 1925, 1926; record: 2-0 in singles, 2-1 in doubles.* SINGLES RECORD IN THE MAJORS: *Wimbledon (8-3), U.S. (26-9).*

BOBBY RIGGS
United States (1918—95)

See page 107.

TONY ROCHE
Australia (1945—)

With most of a glorious career behind him, it was extremely satisfying for the rugged, self-effacing Anthony Dalton Roche to make his biggest hit for Australia at 31 as a Davis Cup retread in 1977. In 1965 and 1967, alongside John Newcombe, he'd won the Cup-clinching doubles, both years against Spain. Ten years later he was recalled for singles duty before his friends and neighbors in Sydney, and came through.

In a stunning opening-day victory, he turned back Adriano Panatta (6-3, 6-4, 6-4), who had led Italy to the 1976 Cup. That set the tone for a 3-1 Australian victory. His yoking with Newcombe (Roche in the left court) was one of the all-time teams. They won Wimbledon five times (1965, 1968, 1969, 1970, 1974), the best showing of any 20th century male pair. Roche, with his wicked left-handed serve and magnificent volleying, took 12 major doubles, all in the company of Newcombe, setting a team record. They were among only four male teams to win all four majors.

But Tony, broad-shouldered and barrel-chested, had the groundstrokes to succeed on clay, winning the difficult Continental double in 1966, the Italian and French singles. Paradoxically he lost three major finals on his best surface, grass, and to older countrymen whom he'd idolized: Wimbledon, 1968, and the U.S., 1969, to Rod Laver; U.S., 1970, to Ken Rosewall.

Shoulder and elbow trouble curtailed a career that spanned the amateur and open eras, but he was in the World Top Ten in both, six straight years from 1965. No. 2 in 1969, and won 12 pro titles in singles, 27 in doubles. In 1968 he turned pro, signing with World Championship Tennis as one of the so-called "Handsome Eight" along with other rookies Newcombe, Cliff Drysdale,

Nikki Pilic and Roger Taylor. His prize money amounted to $529,199. He was a player-coach for Phoenix and Boston in World Team Tennis, and has tutored several pros including Ivan Lendl. Roche was a country boy, born in the New South Wales hamlet of Tarcutta on May 17, 1945, a son of the local butcher. He entered the Hall of Fame, along with Newcombe, appropriately, in 1986.

MAJOR TITLES (14)—*French singles, 1966; Australian doubles, 1965, 1967, 1971, 1976; French doubles, 1967, 1969; Wimbledon doubles, 1965, 1968, 1969, 1970, 1974; U.S. doubles, 1967; Australian mixed, 1966.* DAVIS CUP— *1964, 1965, 1966, 1967, 1974, 1975, 1976, 1977, 1978; record; 7-3 in singles, 7-2 in doubles.* SINGLES RECORD IN THE MAJORS: *Australian (33-13), French (23-5), Wimbledon (32-13), U.S. (25-8).*

ELLEN ROOSEVELT
United States (1868–1954)

The Roosevelt sisters, Ellen, 20, and Grace, 21, first played in the U.S. Championships in 1888, and two years later both were champions. Ellen Crosby Roosevelt won the 1890 singles over defending champ Bertha Townsend in the challenge round, 6-2, 6-2, and joined with Grace for the doubles championship, 6-1, 6-2, over Townsend and Margarette Ballard.

The Roosevelts, who were born and raised in Hyde Park N.Y., and were first cousins of U.S. President Franklin D. Roosevelt, were the first sisters to win a major title. They were emulated only by Juliette and Kathleen Atkinson at the U.S. of 1897 and 1898. In 1891, however, the Roosevelts were done in by an Irishwoman, Mabel Cahill. Cahill beat Grace, 6-3, 7-5, in the final of the all-comers, then deposed Ellen, 6-4, 6-1, 4-6, 6-3, in the challenge round. In the doubles Cahill and Mrs. Emma Leavitt Morgan unseated the sisters, 2-6, 8-6, 6-4.

The only Roosevelt reappearance in the Championships was Ellen's mixed-doubles title with Clarence Hobart in 1893. The Roosevelts, reared on a private court at home, may have been the first to be prodded by a tennis parent. Recalled original champ Ellen Hansell: "Their father [John Roosevelt] coached and treated them as if they were a pair of show ponies. We silly, non-serious-minded players giggled at their early-to-bed and careful food habits."

Ellen, a right-hander, was born in August 1868 and died in Hyde Park, Sept. 26, 1954. She entered the Hall of Fame in 1975. Also a right-hander, Grace Walton Roosevelt, who became Mrs. Appleton Clark, was born June 3, 1867, in Hyde Park and died there Nov. 29, 1945.

MAJOR TITLES *(3)—U.S. singles, 1890; U.S. doubles, 1890; U.S. mixed, 1893.* SINGLES RECORD IN THE MAJORS: *U.S. (5-2).*

KEN ROSEWALL
Australia (1934—)

See page 430.

DOROTHY ROUND
Great Britain (1909–82)

See page 109.

ELIZABETH RYAN
United States (1892–1979)

Elizabeth Montague "Bunny" Ryan, a magnificent doubles player who long held the major tournament record for total championships—19 at Wimbledon between 1914 and 1934—dearly wished to win a major in singles. But she missed out in three finals, losing to Suzanne Lenglen (1921) and Helen Mills Moody (1930) at Wimbledon, and coming closest in 1926, a heartbreaker at the U.S.

In the most elderly of major finals, Ryan, 34, led Molla Mallory, 42, 4-0 in the third, and had a match point in the 13th game only to fall, 4-6, 6-4, 9-7, at Forest Hills.

It may be that she was a bit too stout (at 5-foot-5½, 145 pounds) and slow of foot to equal her doubles success on the singles court. Still, with superb anticipation and tactics, she won numerous singles titles, including the last played in Imperial Russia in 1914. "I got the last train out as the war [World War I] descended," she later recalled.

Her 12 Wimbledon doubles titles (and 13 finals) are the tourney records, as are five straight with Lenglen (1919–23), plus 1925, and six straight doubles titles (1914–23; no play World War I, 1915–18). She won a record seven mixed (of a record 10 finals) with five different partners, three with Randolph Lycett. She and Lenglen never lost (31-0) at the Big W.

Yet standing is Ryan's Wimbledon doubles record of 50 straight match victories from 1914 to the 1928 final. She first played Wimbledon in 1912, reaching the quarters in singles, and was to set a championship longevity record: 20 years between first and last titles (1914–34). Only Billie Jean King (224) and Martina Navratilova (229) won more matches at Wimbledon, where Ryan was 189-29: 61-15 in singles, 77-4 in doubles, 80-10 in mixed.

Ryan, a right-hander with a severe chop, volley and drop shot, was born Feb. 5, 1892, in Anaheim, Cal., and while she played for her native land in the 1926 Wightman Cup, she spent most of her life as a London resident. She did work as a teaching pro for a time in the U.S. Intensely protective of her Wimbledon record of 19 titles (of 25 finals), she was uncomfortable sharing it with King when Billie Jean tied her by winning the singles in 1975. She was undoubtedly pleased not to see herself eclipsed.

Ryan collapsed and died July 8, 1979, at her beloved Wimbledon, the day before King got No. 20 by winning the doubles with Navratilova. Twice she played enough in the U.S. to make the Top Ten rankings, No. 2 in 1925 and 1926. She was in the World Top Ten five times between 1924 and 1930, No. 3 in 1927. She entered the Hall of Fame in 1972.

MAJOR TITLES *(26)—French doubles, 1930, 1932, 1933, 1934; Wimbledon doubles, 1914, 1919, 1920, 1921, 1922, 1923, 1925, 1926, 1927, 1930, 1933, 1934; U.S. doubles, 1926; Wimbledon mixed, 1919, 1921, 1923, 1927, 1928, 1930, 1932; U.S. mixed, 1926, 1933.* WIGHTMAN CUP—*1926; record: 1-1 in singles, 1-0 in doubles.* SINGLES RECORD IN THE MAJORS: *French (8-3), Wimbledon (47-15), U.S. (10-3).*

MANOLO SANTANA

Spain (1938—   )

See page 436.

DICK SAVITT

United States (1927—   )

Only three American men have won the Australian and Wimbledon titles in one year. Richard "Dick" Savitt was the second in 1951 (following Don Budge, 1938, and preceding Jimmy Connors, 1974). He beat Ken McGregor in both, four sets in the Aussie's lair and straight sets at Wimbledon.

Any hopes he had of a Grand Slam were squelched by champ Jaroslav Drobny, 1-6, 6-8, 6-4, 8-6, 6-3, in a quarterfinal of the French. Defending his Aussie title, Savitt was beaten in the 1952 semis by McGregor, 6-4, 6-4, 3-6, 6-4, and at Wimbledon by Mervyn Rose in a quarterfinal, 6-4, 3-6, 6-4, 4-6, 6-2. In the U.S. Championships he was a semifinalist in 1950, losing to the champ, Art Larsen, 6-2, 10-8, 7-9, 6-2; a semifinalist in 1951, losing to Vic Seixas, 6-0, 3-6, 6-3, 6-2; and a quarterfinalist in 1952, 1956 and 1958. In 1956 he lost a stirring baseline slugfest to the champ, Ken Rosewall, 6-4, 7-5, 4-6, 8-10, 6-1.

A large, broad-shouldered, dark-haired right-hander, 6-foot-3, 180 pounds, he was a powerful groundstroker and stubborn competitor. Sav was a king of the Seventh Regiment Armory, a boards runner, in his Manhattan neighborhood, winning the U.S. Indoor thrice. He deposed Bill Talbert in 1952, 6-2, 6-3, 6-4, beat Budge Patty in 1958, 6-1, 6-2, 3-6, 12-10, and, at 34 (no longer ranked), knocked off No. 1 American Whitney Reed, 6-2, 11-9, 6-3, in 1961. But the best remembered of his five finals was a rousing joust lost to world No. 1 Alex Olmedo, 7-9, 6-3, 6-4, 5-7, 12-10, in 1959. He ranked six times in the U.S. Top Ten between 1950 and 1959, No. 2 in 1951, and four times in the World Top Ten between 1951 and 1957, No. 2 in 1951.

A Cornell graduate, Dick was born March 4, 1927, in Bayonne, N.J. In 1981 he and his son, Robert, won the U.S. Father and Son doubles title. He was elected to the Hall of Fame in 1976.

MAJOR TITLES (?)—*Australian singles, 1951; Wimbledon singles, 1951.* OTHER U.S. TITLES (3)—*Indoor singles, 1952, 1958, 1961.* DAVIS CUP—*1951; record: 3-0 in singles.* SINGLES RECORD IN THE MAJORS: *Australian (8-1), French (8-2), Wimbledon (11-1), U.S. (29-12).*

TED SCHROEDER

United States (1921—   )

Emulating Don McNeill in 1940, Frederick Rudolph "Ted" Schroeder of Stanford became in 1942 only the second player to win the U.S. Intercollegiate and the U.S. singles in the same year. A standout big-situation competitor—especially in Davis Cup—volleying wizard Schroeder, along with his pal, John Kramer, recovered the Cup for the U.S. in 1946 after it had spent seven years in Australia during World War II.

Their teammates, Gar Mulloy and Frank Parker, weren't happy when captain Walter Pate selected attack-minded Kramer and Schroeder to play all the way against the favored Aussies in Melbourne. But Schroeder led off by stopping John Bromwich, 3-6, 6-1, 6-2, 0-6, 6-3, and the 5-0 sweep was on. A daring right-hander, Ted helped the U.S. keep the Cup in 1947-48-49 by winning both his singles against Australia each year.

But he was beaten by both Frank Sedgman and Ken McGregor as the Aussies lifted the Cup in 1950, and though he tied the 1951 finale at Sydney at 2-2 by beating Mervyn Rose, the U.S. was tipped, 3-2, and he retired. A part-time player, taking vacations from business to compete, Ted rose to his peak in 1949 when he won Wimbledon the only time he entered. That year Ted not only captured the title with his daring volleying, but he also captivated London with his personality as an outgoing, straightforward Yank smoking a corn-cob pipe. He was known admiringly as "Lucky Ted" for his five-set escapes, four of them, starting with an old antagonist, Gar

Mulloy in the first round, 3-6, 9-11, 6-1, 6-0, 7-5, and ending with Jaroslav Drobny in the final, 3-6, 6-0, 6-3, 4-6, 6-4. The last three went the distance—the only such run other than Henri Cochet's in 1927—and he appeared truly lost in the quarters against Sedgman, 3-6, 6-8, 6-3, 6-2, 9-7. Sedg held two match points against serve, one each at 4-5 and 5-6. Ted wriggled free with serve-and-volley—but on a second serve (having foot-faulted on the first), the volley off the frame! The second was a backhand passer. He was also behind Eric Sturgess in the semis, 3-6, 7-5, 5-7, 6-1, 6-2. Ted's 29 sets and four five-set matches outdid any other champ in that respect.

Seven years after winning Forest Hills, he reappeared in the U.S. final and seemed the winner after taking the first two sets from Pancho Gonzalez, but faded, 16-18, 2-6, 6-1, 6-2, 6-4. He and Kramer formed one of the great doubles teams, winning the U.S. title thrice, 1940, 1941 and 1947. He refused several offers to join Kramer as a pro. A Californian, he was born July 20, 1921, in Newark, N.J., and was ranked in the U.S. Top Ten nine times between 1940 and 1951, No. 1 in 1942. He was in the World Top Ten six straight times from 1946, No. 2 the first four years. He served in the U.S. Naval Air Force in World War II and entered the Hall of Fame in 1966. His son, John Schroeder, was an accomplished professional golfer.

MAJOR TITLES (6)—*Wimbledon singles, 1949; U.S. singles, 1942; U.S. doubles, 1940, 1941, 1947; U.S. mixed, 1942.* OTHER U.S. TITLES (9)—*Intercollegiate singles, 1942; Intercollegiate doubles, 1942, with Larry Dee; Hard Court singles, 1948, 1949, 1951; Clay Court doubles, 1941, with Jack Kramer; 1947, with Jack Tuero; Hard Court doubles, 1948, with Vic Seixas; 1949, with Eric Sturgess.* DAVIS CUP—*1946, 1947, 1948, 1949, 1950, 1951; record: 11-3 in singles, 2-3 in doubles.* SINGLES RECORD IN THE MAJORS: *Wimbledon (7-0), U.S. (20-4).*

ELEO SEARS

United States (1881–1968)

Eleonora Randolph Sears, though of a proper Bostonian background, was noted for her athleticism and vigor. She was an equestrian, golfer and determined walker (frequently striding the 40 miles between her Boston home and Providence, R.I.), and maintained a trim, healthful figure into old age.

The right-handed Eleo was from a tennis-playing family. Her father, Fred Sears, was one of the first (if not the first) to play tennis in the U.S., with Dr. James Dwight in 1874. Her uncle, Dick Sears, was the original U.S. champion.

Eleo made it to the U.S. singles final in 1912, losing to Mary K. Browne, and won four U.S. doubles, two with Hazel Hotchkiss Wightman (1911 and 1915) and Molla Bjurstedt Mallory (1916 and 1917), as well as the mixed with Willis Davis (1916). She ranked in the U.S. Top Ten twice, 1914 and 1916, No. 6 in the first year. She was born Sept. 28, 1881, in Boston, died March 16, 1968, in Palm Beach, Fla., and entered the Hall of Fame in 1968.

MAJOR TITLES (5)—*U.S. doubles, 1911, 1915, 1916, 1917; U.S. mixed, 1916.* SINGLES RECORD IN THE MAJORS: *Wimbledon (0-2), U.S. (27-14).*

DICK SEARS

United States (1861–1943)

Never beaten in the U.S. Championships, the original singles champ, Richard Dudley Sears, won his first of seven titles in 1881 while still a Harvard ('83) student. As one of 24 entries he, a Bostonian, ventured onto the lawn of the Newport (R.I.) Casino in knickerbockers, long wool socks, a necktie and cap, and wielding a slightly lopsided racket (similar to those for court tennis) that weighed 16 ounces.

Beating first-round opponent Powell, 6-0, 6-2, Dick was off on an 18-match streak that would carry him through the Championships of 1887, after which he retired from the game. Not until the challenge round format was abandoned and 1920–21 champion Bill Tilden beat Zenzo Shimidzu, 6-2, 6-3, 6-1, to reach the 1922 semis (and register a 19th successive win in the Championships), was Sears' record eclipsed.

Sears, 5-foot-9 and 150 pounds, later recalled the Championships' launching in '81: " . . . the nets were four-feet at the posts and three-feet at center. This led to a scheme of attack by playing, whenever possible, across court to avoid lifting drives over the highest part of the net at the sidelines. This method just suited me. I had taken up a mild form of volleying, and all I had to do was to tap the balls, as they came over, first to one side and then to the other, running my opponent all over the court."

A few of the players served underhand, though not the right-handed Sears. In the final, his fifth match, he beat William Glyn, an Englishman who regularly summered at Newport, 6-0, 6-3, 6-2. During his first three championships Sears lost no sets, concluding the 1883 tournament with a 6-2, 6-0, 9-7 victory over his mentor, James Dwight.

In that year he began to hit a topspin forehand that he'd seen used in England by the originator, Herbert Lawford. Since the challenge round was instituted in 1884 he had to play but one match, against the victor in the all-comers tournament, to retain the title the last four years. Then he lost one set each to Howard Taylor in '84, Godfrey Brinley in '85 and Livingston Beeckman in '86.

Those last four years he used a prized racket given to him in England by the all-time Wimbledon champ, Willie Renshaw, and won four singles and doubles titles with it. He and Dwight won the doubles five times together, and he won once with Joseph Clark, 1885. Sears was the first of the 19-year-olds to conquer the U.S., slightly older than Oliver Campbell in 1890, and the very youngest, Pete Sampras, in 1990. He was No. 1 in the U.S. 1885, 1886 and 1887, the first years of national rankings. Scion of a prominent Boston family, he was born there Oct. 16, 1861, and died there April 8, 1943. His older brother, Fred, played with Dwight, possibly the first tennis in the U.S., in 1874, and a younger brother, Philip, was in the U.S. Top Ten five years. A cousin, Eleo Sears, is also in the Hall of Fame. After giv-

ing up lawn tennis, Sears won the U.S. Court Tennis singles title in 1892. He served as USTA president in 1887 and 1888 and was elected to the Hall of Fame in 1955.

MAJOR TITLES (13)—*U.S. singles, 1881, 1882, 1883, 1884, 1885, 1886, 1887; U.S. doubles, 1882, 1883, 1884, 1885, 1886, 1887.* SINGLES RECORD IN THE MAJORS: *U.S. (18-0).*

FRANK SEDGMAN
Australia (1927—)

See page 437.

PANCHO SEGURA
Ecuador (1921—)

See page 438.

VIC SEIXAS
United States (1923—)

When Vic Seixas played—and won—the fifth-longest singles match in tennis history, he was 42. That was in 1966, when Vic went 94 games to beat a 22-year-old Australian Davis Cup player, Bill Bowrey, 32-34, 6-4, 10-8, during the Pennsylvania Grass Championships at Philadelphia. It took nearly four hours.

Elias Victor Seixas, Jr., born Aug 30, 1923, in Philadelphia, played the U.S. Championships at Forest Hills a record 28 times between 1940 and 1969, winning the singles in 1954 over Rex Hartwig, 3-6, 6-4, 6-4, 6-4. He played more Davis Cup matches than any other American, until John McEnroe, winning 38 of 55 singles and doubles encounters during his seven years on the team between 1951 and 1957. Thirteen times he was ranked in the Top Ten in the U.S. between 1942 and 1966, setting an American longevity record of a 24-year span between his first and last entries (later equaled by Pancho Gonzalez, 1948–72).

In 1953, when Seixas won the Wimbledon singles over Kurt Nielsen, 9-7, 6-3, 6-4, and led the U.S. to the Davis Cup Final, he was considered No. 3 in the amateur world, his high point.

Although he helped the U.S. attain the finale every year he played Davis Cup, the team could win only once, the high spot of 1954 when he and Tony Trabert were victorious. After Trabert opened with a win over Lew Hoad, Seixas followed with a stunning 8-6, 6-8, 6-4, 6-3 triumph over his nemesis, Ken Rosewall. That put the U.S. ahead, 2-0, on the first day, and Seixas and Trabert clinched the Cup the following day with a doubles victory over Hoad and Rex Hartwig, 6-2, 4-6, 6-2, 10-8, before a record outdoor crowd of 25,578 at Sydney.

Seixas won 15 major titles in singles, doubles and mixed, setting a Wimbledon record by winning the mixed four successive years, 1953, 1954, 1955 with Doris Hart, and 1956 with Shirley Fry.

Among his 13 U.S. titles were the Clay Court singles in 1953 and 1957, the Hard Court doubles (with Ted Schroeder) in 1948, and the Indoor doubles (with Trabert) in 1955, making Seixas one of the few to win national titles on all four surfaces. In 1971 he was named to the Hall of Fame.

The 6-foot-1, 180-pound right-handed Seixas was an attacker who won more on determination and conditioning than on outstanding form. His volleying was exceptional, and he had an excellent match temperament, but a thrashing topspin forehand and sliced backhand were utilitarian. His career was interrupted for three years by World War II, during which he served as a pilot in the U.S. Army Air Force. He graduated from the University of North Carolina. Seixas was one of the few extraordinary amateurs who did not join the pro tour, winning 56 singles titles. Eventually, though, after the age of 50, he did become a pro to compete on the Grand Masters circuit.

MAJOR TITLES (15)—*Wimbledon singles, 1953; U.S. singles, 1954; French doubles, 1954, 1955; U.S. doubles, 1952, 1954; Australian doubles, 1955; French mixed, 1953; Wimbledon mixed, 1953, 1954, 1955, 1956; U.S. mixed, 1953, 1954, 1955.* OTHER U.S. TITLES (7)—*Clay Court singles, 1953, 1957; Clay Court doubles, 1949, with Sam Match;*

1954, with Tony Trabert; Hard Court doubles, 1948, with Ted Schroeder; Indoor doubles, 1955, with Trabert; 1956 with Sam Giammalva. Davis Cup (As player)—*1951, 1952, 1953, 1954, 1955, 1956, 1957; record: 24-12 in singles, 14-5 in doubles; (As captain)—1952, 1957, 1964; record: 3-2.* SINGLES RECORD IN THE MAJORS: *Australian (4-2), French (17-4), Wimbledon (31-8), U.S. (74-26).*

FRANK SHIELDS

United States (1909–75)

A dashing, handsome performer who spent some time in Hollywood in bit movie roles, unseeded Francis Xavier Shields was the only Wimbledon finalist to lose without going onto the court. Frank defaulted the 1931 final to Sidney Wood beforehand, sidelined by an ankle injury suffered in the semis when he beat Jean Borotra, the 1924 and 1926 champ, 7-5, 3-6, 6-4, 6-4.

The 6-foot-3 right-hander was a came-close guy. Eleventh-seeded, in his first major final, the U.S. of 1930, he had a shot at Johnny Doeg, but couldn't connect on a set point against Doeg's rugged lefty serve at 13-14 in the deciding set and lost, 10-8, 1-6, 6-4, 16-14. In 1928, an 18-year-old seventh seed, he got to the U.S. semis, losing to the champ, Henri Cochet, 6-2, 8-6, 6-4, and again, second-seeded in 1933, falling to the foreign seeded Wimbledon champ Jack Crawford, 7-5, 6-4, 6-3. A year later at Wimbledon, he came closer but couldn't hold Crawford down, 2-6, 4-6, 6-4, 6-3, 6-4. Between 1928 and 1945 he was ranked eight times in the U.S. Top Ten, No. 1 in 1933, No. 2 in 1930. He was a U.S. Davis Cupper in 1931, 1932 and 1934, winning 19 of 25 matches, and was non-playing captain in 1951 when the team won four matches, then lost the finale in Australia, 3-2. In 1934 he sent the U.S. into the finale (a 4-1 loss to Britain) by winning the decisive fifth match, 6-4, 6-2, 6-4, over Viv McGrath to clinch a 3-2 victory over Australia at Wimbledon. It was the only time the U.S. came back from 0-2 to win a Cup tie.

Shields was born in New York Nov. 18, 1909, and died there Aug. 19, 1975. Movie and television actress Brooke Shields is his granddaughter. He was inducted into the Hall of Fame in 1964.

DAVIS CUP—*1931, 1932, 1934; record: 16-6 in singles, 3-0 in doubles.* SINGLES RECORD IN THE MAJORS: *French (2-1), Wimbledon (14-3), U.S. (37-23).*

HENRY SLOCUM
United States (1862–1949)

A football and tennis player at Yale, Henry Warner Slocum played in the first Intercollegiate Championships, in 1883, as partner of the great footballer, Walter Camp. He took time out from his New York law practice to refine his tennis (to the disapproval of his father), and on his fourth try at the U.S. title in Newport, 1887, he beat Howard Taylor, 12-10, 7-5, 6-4, in the all-comers final, only to become Dick Sears's last championship victim in the challenge round, 6-1, 6-3, 6-2.

But in 1888 he trained harder, and the players showed, he said, "more than the usual keenness" because Sears had announced he wouldn't defend. In the all-comers final, to decide the championship, Slocum, a 5-foot-10, 150-pound right-hander, was sharper against the quick 5-foot-4 Taylor, and became the second champion of the U.S., 6-4, 6-1, 6-0. He successfully defended in 1889 over lefty Quincy Shaw, 6-3, 6-1, 4-6, 6-2.

That year he and Taylor beat Valentine Hall and Oliver Campbell for the doubles crown, 6-1, 6-3, 6-2. It was Slocum's third time in the doubles final. He lost in 1885 with Percy Knapp and 1887 with Ollie Taylor. But Slocum, 28, was overtaken by 19-year-old collegian, Campbell, in the 1890 challenge round, 6-2, 4-6, 6-3, 6-1.

Slocum had realized his tennis ambitions, and immersed himself in law. But he returned to Newport for an 1892 cameo, registering one of the Championships' rare triple bagels—6-0, 6-0, 6-0, over W. N. Ryerson. He was back again 11 years later to play nine times between 1903 and 1913 when he made his last appearance, at 51, beating future World War I flying hero and Massachusetts Congressman Larry Curtis, 6-3, 6-2, 6-

3, and losing to future finalist (1921), 24-year-old Wallace Johnson, 6-1, 6-3, 6-3. For his U.S. career, covering 29 years (1884–1913), the remarkably durable Slocum had a 26-14 singles record. In the 1888 quarters, he gave the godfather, James Dwight, 36, his last singles defeat, 4-6, 6-3, 6-0, 6-2. Five straight years, from 1886, he was in the U.S. Top Ten, No. 1 in 1888 and 1889. Slocum was born May 28, 1862, died Jan. 22, 1949, and entered the Hall of Fame in 1955. He was president of the USTA, 1892–93.

MAJOR TITLES (3)—*U.S. singles, 1888, 1889; U.S. doubles, 1889.* SINGLES RECORD IN THE MAJORS: *U.S. (26-14).*

STAN SMITH
United States (1946—)

See page 442.

FRED STOLLE
Australia (1938—)

A loose-limbed, slender 6-foot-3 blond, Frederick Sydney Stolle had his Wimbledon singles frustrations, but overflowed with success everywhere else as one of the overpowering phalanx of Aussies in the 1960s and '70s. Known as "Fiery Fred" or "Fiery" to his teammates for his outspoken competitiveness, he became also known as the "Old Hacker" at the U.S. Championships of 1966. A proven grass-court player for some time, member of winning Australian Davis Cup teams, and thrice Wimbledon runner-up (1963, 1964, 1965), he was outraged on arriving at Forest Hills, fresh from winning the German title, to find himself unseeded.

"I guess they think I'm just an old hacker," said he, almost 28. Then he proceeded to win the title, the second unseeded man to do so, over unseeded John Newcombe, chortling, "Well, I guess the Old Hacker can still play a bit."

He had won the French in 1965, showing that he could be patient at the baseline, too, although his strengths were a high-velocity serve, stinging volleys and a splendid backhand. These paid off in his 16 major doubles titles. He is one of 11 men to win all four majors, and had his greatest success with Bob Hewitt (two Wimbledons, two Australian), Roy Emerson (two U.S. and an Australian), Ken Rosewall (a U.S. and French).

As a member of three victorious Australian Davis Cup teams, 1964, 1965 and 1966, he scored his most memorable win the first year in the Cup round at Cleveland, 7-5, 6-3, 3-6, 9-11, 6-4, over Dennis Ralston. Down a break in the fifth, with his side trailing the U.S. 2-1, Stolle pulled it out so that Emerson could win the Cup-lifting clincher over Chuck McKinley. Perhaps his lead-off win in the following year's Cup finale meant more since it came in his hometown, Sydney, and he had to dig himself from a very deep hole to beat the Spanish ace, Manolo Santana, 10-12, 3-6, 6-1, 6-4, 7-5, to send the Aussies on their way.

His career spanned the amateur and open eras, and he was in the World Top Ten four years, starting with 1963, No. 2 in 1964 and 1966. He turned pro in 1967, and as a pro won two singles and 13 doubles titles, and about $500,000 in career prize money. He had a last U.S. fling in 1972, at 33, beating 5th and 11th seeds Newcombe and Cliff Drysdale to gain the quarters, where he lost to the champ, Ilie Nastase, 6-4, 3-6, 6-3, 6-2.

Born Oct. 8, 1938, in Hornsby, New South Wales, Fred has worked as a teaching pro, was player-coach of the title-winning New York Apples of World Team Tennis in 1976 and 1977, and of Australia 10 times (5-5) in the since disbanded World Cup against the U.S., 1970–79. His son, Sandon, is a touring pro, and has played the major championships. For some time Fred has been a successful television commentator on tennis. He entered the Hall of Fame in 1985.

Fred won 31 amateur singles titles.

MAJOR TITLES (18)—*French singles, 1965; U.S. singles, 1966; French doubles, 1965, 1968; U.S. doubles, 1965, 1966, 1969; Australian doubles, 1963, 1964, 1966; Wimbledon doubles, 1962, 1964; Australian mixed, 1962; U.S. mixed, 1962,* *1965; Wimbledon mixed, 1961, 1964, 1969.* DAVIS CUP— *1964, 1965, 1966; record: 10-2 in singles, 3-1 in doubles.* SINGLES RECORD IN THE MAJORS: *Australian (21-9), French (25-8), Wimbledon (31-12), U.S. (25-9).*

BILL TALBERT
United States (1918—)

Adapting intelligently and inspiringly to life as a diabetic at a time when a quiet, unstrenuous regimen was prescribed, William Franklin Talbert became a champion. Urbane, immaculately groomed, he represented the game handsomely not only as a winning player but a thorough Davis Cup captain and thoughtful administrator as director of the U.S. Open. Thwarted twice in U.S. singles finals, 1944 and 1945, by Frank Parker, the 5-foot-11 right-handed Talbert made his strongest showing in doubles in the right court alongside Gardnar Mulloy.

They were in the U.S. final six times, one short of Fred Alexander and Harold Hackett's team record, winning four, 1942, 1945, 1946 and 1948. The 1946 title was the prickliest and most noteworthy, a 74-game drama with Frank Guernsey and Don McNeill, 3-6, 6-4, 2-6, 6-3, 20-18, the longest windup set for any major final. It seemed ended numerous times, but Talbert and Mulloy kept shunning match points. Five of them came and went against Mulloy's serve (6-7, 0-40 and 10-11, 15-40). But the sixth at 13-14, 30-40 caused a great furor. Talbert, serving, sent back Guersey's return crosscourt with an angled backhand volley that looked wide to many. Guernsey and McNeill rejoiced, shaking hands. "It didn't look good for us," Talbert remembers. "But there was no call. The sidelinesman was signaling my shot was good. Barely touched the line, I guess." Play resumed. After losing a point, Talbert saved match point seven with a good serve that Guernsey netted. The next match point, 10 games later, settled it for the comebackers, and the closest of all U.S. finals was over. "There'll never be another one like that because of tie-breakers," says Talbert. He was the most instrumental in the acceptance of the elongated-set-dooming innovation at the Open in 1970, the first of his 10 years in charge. The other majors followed his lead.

Bill himself was in the U.S. doubles final nine times.

He and Mulloy won the clinching point in the Davis Cup victory over Australia in 1948 at Forest Hills, defeating Billy Sidwell and Colin Long. He was on the team six years, winning nine of 10 matches, and captained it to the victory over Australia in 1954, as well as the full seasons of 1955, 1956 and 1957 and portions of 1952 and 1953, compiling a 13-4 record.

A stylish groundstroker and excellent volleyer and tactician, he ranked in the U.S. Top Ten 13 times between 1941 and 1954, No. 2 in 1944 and 1945. He was in the World Top Ten in 1949 and 1950, No. 3 the first year. An Ohioan, born Sept. 4, 1918, in Cincinnati, he grew up there, moving to New York during his playing career. He and Margaret Osborne duPont won the U.S. mixed a record four straight years, 1943–46.

With Bruce Old, Talbert wrote definitive books, *The Game of Singles in Tennis* and *The Game of Doubles in Tennis*. He also wrote an autobiography, *Playing for Life* and a history of the U.S. men's singles championships, *Tennis Observed*. He has been involved in the financial printing business for many years, and entered the Hall of Fame in 1967.

MAJOR TITLES *(9)—French doubles, 1950; U.S. doubles, 1942, 1945, 1946, 1948; U.S. mixed, 1943, 1944, 1945, 1946:* OTHER U.S. TITLES *(14)—Indoor singles, 1948, 1951; Clay Court singles, 1945; Indoor doubles, 1949, 1950, 1951, with Don McNeill; 1952, with Budge Patty; 1954, with Tony Trabert; Clay Court doubles, 1942, with Bill Reedy; 1944, 1945, with Pancho Segura; 1946, with Gardnar Mulloy; Indoor mixed, 1947, 1948, with Doris Hart. Davis Cup (As player)— 1946, 1948, 1949, 1951, 1952, 1953; record: 2-0 in singles, 7-1 in doubles. (As captain)—1952, 1953, 1954, 1955, 1956, 1957; record: 13-4.* SINGLES RECORD IN THE MAJORS: *Australian (1-1), French (5-1), Wimbledon (4-1), U.S. (46-17).*

BILL TILDEN
United States (1893–1953)

See page 110.

BERTHA TOWNSEND
United States (1869–1909)

A Philadelphia-born right-hander, Bertha Louise Townsend appeared in the Championships in her hometown five times. She won in 1888, unseating original champ, Ellen Hansell, in the challenge round, 6-3, 6-5. She fought off the challenge of Lida Vorhees, 7-5, 6-3, to become the first repeating female champ, but then fell to Ellen Roosevelt, 6-2, 6-2, in the 1890 challenge round.

She reappeared, married, in 1894, to reach the final of the all-comers, losing 6-2, 7-5 to Helen Hellwig, who became champion. The following year she was a semifinalist, and that ended her career with an 8-3 U.S. singles record.

She was born March 7, 1869, died May 12, 1909, in Haverford, Pa. as Mrs. Harry Toulmin, and was inducted into the Hall of Fame in 1974.

MAJOR TITLES *(2)—U.S. singles, 1888, 1889.* SINGLES RECORD IN THE MAJORS: *U.S. (8-3).*

TONY TRABERT
United States (1930—)

See page 443.

JOHNNY VAN RYN
United States (1905—)

Allison and Van Ryn were a headline combination during their bright career between 1929 and 1936 as one of the most formidable U.S. Davis Cup partnerships. Wilmer Allison and John William Van Ryn, Jr. won 14 of 16 Cup matches together, the best for Americans until Peter Fleming and John McEnroe's 14-1.

Their 24 team ties (tied with Stan Smith and Vic Seixas) are second only to McEnroe's 30 in U.S. annals. Van Ryn's 24 doubles matches and 22 wins are highs for the U.S. They beat the splendid French teams in Parisian Cup finals (Henri Cochet–Jean Borotra in 1929, Cochet–Jacques Brugnon in 1932), but could do no more than stave off France's successful defenses. A Princeton man (class of '28), Van Ryn, right-handed, superb at the net, and returning from the right court, won the U.S. Intercollegiate doubles in 1927.

Allison and Van Ryn were in the U.S. final six times, one behind Fred Alexander and Harold Hackett's record, winning in 1931 and 1935. They also won Wimbledon in 1929, 1930 and "should've won again in '35," says the engaging Van Ryn, recalling the splendid mixture of himself and Allison, as choice as gin and vermouth. "We had a match point in the fifth set of the final against Jack Crawford and Adrian Quist. They put up a fluky little lob. My ball. Easy. But for some reason I hesitated in starting for it. Wilmer noticed, and decided he'd better take it—and missed the shot. My fault. All those years together," he smiles, "and we mess up a simple play." Van Ryn, 5-foot-10½, 155 pounds, a fluid, well-rounded strokesman, remembers, "My best Wimbledon in singles was '31. I beat (fourth-seeded) Christian Boussus, got to the quarters."

In 1931 Van Ryn teamed with George Lott to win the French and Wimbledon, the only American to win the latter three successive times. He ranked in the U.S. Top Ten six times between 1927 and 1932, No. 4 in 1931 when he was a five-set quarterfinal loser at Forest Hills to George Lott. He was also a quarterfinalist in 1929 and 1930, losing to Bill Tilden each time in four sets, and 1936 and 1937. In 1929 and 1931 he was in the World Top Ten. He was born June 30, 1905, in Newport News, Va., grew up in Orange, N.J., and resides in Palm Beach, Fla., with his wife of 50 years, Cornelia. He was previously married to Marjorie Gladman, also an excellent doubles player, and in 1930 and 1931 they were the first of four married couples to be ranked together in the U.S. singles Top Ten, he Nos. 9 and 4, she 7 and 8. Van Ryn was taken into the Hall of Fame in 1963.

MAJOR TITLES (6)—*French doubles, 1931; Wimbledon doubles, 1929, 1930, 1931; U.S. doubles, 1931, 1935.* OTHER U.S. TITLES (2)—*Indoor doubles, 1932, with George Lott; Intercollegiate doubles, 1927, with Kenneth Appel.* DAVIS CUP—*1929, 1930, 1931, 1932, 1933, 1934, 1935, 1936; record: 7-1 in singles, 22-2 in doubles.* SINGLES RECORD IN THE MAJORS: *Australian (1-1), French (4-1), Wimbledon (13-6), U.S. (29-15).*

GUILLERMO VILAS
Argentina (1952—)

Seldom has a player found such empathy beyond his own borders as did Guillermo Vilas, the "Young Bull of the Pampas," during his pro career. As the foremost Latin American male, he is the only Argentine to be tapped for the Hall of Fame (1991), and the first to win major titles (four of them).

The burly 5-foot-11, 175-pound left-hander captivated audiences everywhere with his sportsmanship and sensitivity of a poet—which he is. An appealing headbanded figure of the 1970s and early 1980s, his chestnut hair flowing below his shoulders, Vilas was the epitome of strength and fitness, endurance and patience on court, outlasting opponents from the baseline with his high-rolling topspinning strokes—hour after hour, a destructive metronome.

His 1977 was a monumental year in the game's history: he won 17 of 33 tournaments (tying Rod Laver's record) on a record of 145 match wins against 14 losses. Among his souvenirs were an open-era winning streak record of 50 matches and the French and U.S. titles. His streak, begun after Wimbledon, was stopped at Aix-en-Provence in September by Ilie Nastase, who used one of the controversial "spaghetti" rackets that produced weird strokes and bounces. Vilas quit in disgust; such rackets were shortly banned.

Although he reveled in the backcourt, Vilas startled Jimmy Connors with volleying forays that turned the U.S. Open his way, and set off a wild celebration after he'd won the last championship match in the 54-year-old Forest Hills Stadium, 2-6, 6-3, 7-6 (7-4), 6-0. Joyous fans carried him on victory laps within the concrete arena, as though he were a triumphant bullfighter.

Though grass seemed anathema to the clay-loving Villas, he did win the Australian twice (1978 and 1979) and the Masters of 1974 at the same place, Melbourne's Kooyong. Perhaps he wasn't a serve-volley smoothy, but his Australian Open record is excellent: two titles plus a final-round loss to Roscoe Tanner in 1977, and a 16-match streak to a semis loss to Kim Warwick in 1980, 6-7, 6-4, 6-2, 2-6, 6-4.

As Argentina's foremost Davis Cupper he took great satisfaction in bulwarking three American Zone wins over the U.S. (1977, 1980, 1983). Vilas won all six of his singles on the Buenos Aires loam, including victories over John McEnroe the last two years. In 1981 he led Argentina to the Cup round, a narrow 3-1 defeat by the U.S. in Cincinnati where, in the fifth set, Guillermo actually served for an improbable doubles victory at 7-6, and an unrealized 2-1 lead (with Jose-Luis Clerc) against McEnroe and Peter Fleming. Vilas and Clerc were hardly a team, or doubles players; McEnroe and Fleming were the best. But the match, lost 6-3, 4-6, 6-4, 4-6, 11-9, showed Guillermo's heart and desire on behalf of his homeland.

He was in four French finals, but couldn't get past the Swedes, losing to Bjorn Borg in 1975 and 1978 and, wearing down before 17-year-old Mats Wilander in 1982. It was his last major final in a career that landed him in fifth place among the all-time pro winners headed by Connors: 62 singles titles, even with Borg. His career prize money amounted to $4,904,922. It was in Paris, 1973, that he first gained notice, removing defending champ Andres Gimeno from the French in the second round, 6-2, 5-7, 8-6.

Beginning in 1974 he graced the World Top Ten for nine straight years, No. 2 in 1977. He was born Aug. 17, 1952, in Mar del Plata, Argentina, where he grew up.

MAJOR TITLES (4)—*Australian singles, 1978, 1979; French singles, 1977; U.S. singles, 1977.* DAVIS CUP—*1970, 1971, 1972, 1973, 1975, 1976, 1977, 1978, 1979, 1980, 1981, 1982, 1983, 1984; record: 45-10 in singles, 12-14 in doubles.* SINGLES RECORD IN THE MAJORS: *Australian (23-3), French (56-17), Wimbledon (15-11), U.S. (43-14).*

ELLSWORTH VINES
United States (1911–94)

See page 112.

GOTTFRIED VON CRAMM
Germany (1909–76)

See page 114.

VIRGINIA WADE
Great Britain (1945—)

If ever a player achieved high drama by winning Wimbledon, it was "Our Ginny," as her compatriots throughout the United Kingdom called her. It was 1977, Sarah Virginia Wade's 17th try, and the year of the magnificent Wimbledon Centenary. Moreover Queen Elizabeth appeared for the first time in a quarter-century to present the women's prize. Ginny had set the stage by deposing 1976 champ Chris Evert in the semis, 6-2, 4-6, 6-1.

Attacking incessantly, heedless of whatever mistakes she made, Wade finished strongly to beat Betty Stove for the title, 4-6, 6-3, 6-1, nine days short of her 32nd birthday. An extraordinary jubilant Centre Court crowd of more than 14,000, unaccustomed to homegrown success, became a chorus in singing "For She's a Jolly Good Fellow!" A tennis queen was saluted by her Queen.

Dark-haired Wade was slender (5-foot-8) and nimble, of elegant bearing. She had the longest and, considering the highly competitive age in which she sparkled, the most fruitful career of any Englishwoman. Her career spanned the amateur and open eras, and in 1968 she scored two notable firsts. As an amateur she won the inaugural open, the British Hard Court at Bournemouth, turning down the $720 first prize, and five months later, as a pro, she captured the initial U.S. Open (and $6,000), upending the favored defender and Wimbledon champ, Billie Jean King, 6-4, 6-2.

As a pro she won 55 singles titles, seventh among the all-time leaders, and amassed $1,542,278 in career prize money. She won the Australian title in 1972, only the third Brit to do so, following Dorothy Round (1935) and Angela Mortimer (1958). With her severely sliced backhand approach and splendid volleying, right-handed Ginny was a natural on grass. But she showed her clay mettle in winning the Italian in 1971. She added doubles majors at the Australian, French and U.S., all with Margaret Court.

She continued to play Wimbledon through 1987—a record 26 years in all—getting as far as a semifinal defeat by Evert, 8-6, 6-2, in her 1978 defense, and the quarters in 1979 and 1983, when ranked No. 63. She is fifth among all players in matches played there (212): 64-23 in singles, 53-24 in doubles, 24-24 in mixed. She entered the World Top Ten in 1967 and was there 13 straight years, No. 2 in 1968. She set records for participation in Federation Cup (18 years) and ties (57). She has played (99) and won (66) the most matches. She is tied for third in most singles won (36), and, for Britain, years of Wightman Cup play (21 years) and total wins (12-23 in singles, 7-13 in doubles).

She was born July 10, 1945 in Bournemouth, England, learned to play tennis in South Africa, where she lived, and was inducted into the Hall of Fame in 1989.

MAJOR TITLES (7)—*Australian singles, 1972; Wimbledon singles, 1977; U.S. singles. 1967; Australian doubles, 1973; French doubles, 1973; U.S. doubles, 1973, 1975.* FEDERATION CUP—*1967, 1968, 1969, 1970, 1971, 1972, 1973, 1974, 1975, 1976, 1977, 1978, 1979, 1980, 1981, 1982, 1983; record: 36-20 in singles, 30-13 in doubles.* WIGHTMAN CUP—*1965, 1966, 1967, 1968, 1969, 1970, 1971, 1972, 1973, 1974, 1975, 1976, 1977, 1978, 1979, 1980, 1981, 1982, 1983, 1984, 1985; record: 12-23 in singles, 7-14 in doubles.* SINGLES RECORD IN MAJORS: *Australian (10-4), French (16-13), Wimbledon (64-23), U.S. (49-19).*

MARIE WAGNER
United States (1883–1975)

Queen of the boards, Marie Wagner, a New Yorker, was the scourge of Manhattan's Seventh Regiment Armory where she won the U.S. Indoor singles a record six times (1908, 1909, 1911, 1913, 1914, 1917), and the doubles four times. She was also singles finalist in 1915 to Molla Mallory. Her best outdoor showing was as the 1914 U.S. finalist to Mary K. Browne, losing, 6-2, 1-6, 6-1.

She ranked No. 6 in 1913 when the U.S. Top Ten was established, and was in that select group every year through 1920—No. 3 in 1914—as well as 1922 when she was No. 9 at age 39. A right-hander, she was born Feb. 2, 1883, in Freeport, N.Y., and died April 1, 1975. She entered the Hall of Fame in 1969.

U.S. TITLES (10)—*Indoor singles, 1908, 1909, 1911, 1913, 1914, 1917; Indoor doubles, 1910, 1913 with Clara Kutroff; 1916, with Molla Bjurstedt; 1917, with Margaret Taylor.* SINGLES RECORD IN THE MAJORS: *U.S. (17-7).*

MAUD BARGER WALLACH
United States (1870–1954)

A late-in-life tennis success, Maud Barger Wallach—"I started to play at about 30"—became the oldest major champion in 1908. She was 38 when she toppled the defending U.S. champ, lefty Evelyn Sears, 6-3, 1-6, 6-3, in the challenge round, after having beaten Marie Wagner, 4-6, 6-1, 6-3, in the all-comers. Molla Mallory, winning in 1926 at 42, took away her old-age record.

In her first shot at the title, 1906, Maud lost the final to Helen Homans, 6-4, 6-3. Hazel Hotchkiss Wightman, who took the crown from her in the 1909 challenge round, recalled that Mrs. Richard Wallach had a good forehand "but not much of backhand. I concentrated on it until I was well ahead"—winning, 6-1, 6-0.

Maud was a New Yorker, a right-hander, born there June 15, 1870. She was a familiar summer figure at Newport, R.I., generally playing beneath a distinctive wide-brimmed straw hat. "Mine was not a great career," she recalled, "but a long and happy one."

At 46 she made the U.S. quarterfinals of 1916 (losing to runner-up Louise Raymond, 6-1, 6-3) and ranked No. 10, the oldest to do so well in the tournament and the rankings. National rankings for women weren't instituted until 1913, then largely because of her lobbying. But she was No. 5 in 1915. After dying in Baltimore, April 2, 1954, she was buried at Newport, not far from her beloved Casino, and was placed there eternally on her 1958 induction into the Hall of Fame.

MAJOR TITLE—*U.S. singles, 1908.* SINGLES RECORD IN THE MAJORS: *U.S. (16-6).*

HOLCOMBE WARD
United States (1878–1967)

One of the originals, the Harvard Three forming the first U.S. Davis Cup team, Holcombe Ward is also credited with originating the American twist serve which bedeviled the British invaders as the Cup was put into play in 1900. He accompanied donor Dwight Davis—his partner in two subsequent U.S. doubles championships— to the clinching doubles win in the 3-0 victory over the British Isles.

The 5-foot-9, 135-pound right-hander played for the Cup-winners again in 1902, and the losers, to the Brits in 1905 and 1906. At Harvard, Ward partnered Davis to the Intercollegiate doubles title in 1899, and broke through as U.S. singles champ in 1904, over Bill Clothier, 10-8, 6-4, 9-7. That year he was ranked No. 1, the acme of his seven years in his country's Top Ten. In 1922 Ward and Davis reunited to win the U.S. Seniors 45s doubles title. He served as president of the USTA between 1937 and 1947.

A New Yorker, he was born there Nov. 23, 1878, and died Jan. 23, 1967, in Red Bank, N.J. He was inducted into the Hall of Fame in 1956.

MAJOR TITLES (7)—*U.S. singles, 1904; U.S. doubles, 1899, 1900, 1901, 1904, 1905, 1906.* OTHER U.S. TITLES (2)— *Indoor singles, 1901; Intercollegiate doubles, 1899, with Dwight Davis.* DAVIS CUP—*1900, 1902, 1905, 1906; record: 3-4 in singles, 4-3 in doubles.* SINGLES RECORD IN THE MAJORS: *Wimbledon (0-1), U.S. (19-8).*

WATTY WASHBURN
United States (1894–1973)

A New Yorker and a Harvard man, Watson McLean Washburn had a hand early on in the U.S. record run of seven Davis Cups that began in 1920. Watty played in the first defense, at Forest Hills in 1921, where he and Dick Williams won the Cup-clinching match over Japan's Zenzo Shimidzu and Ichiya Kumagae, 6-2, 7-5, 4-6, 7-5.

A 6-foot right-hander who won the U.S. Intercollegiate doubles while at Harvard in 1913, Washburn served in the U.S. Army in World War I. He ranked seven times in the U.S. Top Ten between 1914 and 1922, No. 5 in 1921, and continued to play extremely well into his 50s, winning the U.S. 45s singles in 1940 and the doubles in that category thrice, 1940, 1942, 1944.

He was born June 13, 1894, in New York, was a committeeman for the USTA, and died in New York, Dec. 2, 1973. He was inducted into the Hall of Fame in 1965.

U.S. TITLES (2)—*Indoor doubles, 1915, with Gus Touchard; Intercollegiate doubles, 1913, with Joe Armstrong.* DAVIS CUP—*1921; record: 1-0 in doubles.* SINGLES RECORD IN THE MAJORS: *Wimbledon (7-4), U.S. (38-24).*

MAL WHITMAN
United States (1877–1932)

One of the Harvard Three, the original U.S. Davis Cup team, Malcolm Douglass Whitman led off in the initial clash—U.S. vs. British Isles—in 1900 by beating Arthur Gore, 6-1, 6-3, 6-2. Classmate Dwight Davis, the Cup donor, won a singles and joined Holcombe Ward for the doubles clincher for the 3-0 triumph at Boston's Longwood Cricket Club.

A quarterfinalist in the 1896 and 1897 U.S. Championships, Whitman came through at Newport in 1898 with the first of his three straight championships. In the all-comers title match he beat Davis, 3-6, 6-3, 6-2, 6-1, and was crowned champion because 1897 victor Bob Wrenn, off to the Spanish-American War, didn't defend in the challenge round.

After another successful defense in 1899, Whitman had to first win a fight with his father, who wanted him to concentrate on law school (Harvard) and put away his racket. The son won, and that enabled him to put down challenger Bill Larned, 6-4, 1-6, 6-2, 6-2, for his third crown. Whitman had a weirdly bounding reverse twist serve (a stroke no longer seen) and was a sharp volleyer.

He didn't defend in 1901 but returned for a 1902 cameo "to represent my country," helping turn back the British invaders once more, and he reached the U.S. all-comers final, only to be stung by Reggie Doherty, 6-1, 3-6, 6-3, 6-0.

In the Davis Cup showdown he won both his matches (over Joshua Pim, 6-1, 6-1, 1-6, 6-0, and over Reggie Doherty, 6-1, 7-5, 6-4) and the U.S. kept the Cup, 3-2.

Whitman, a handsome 6-foot-2 right-hander, was through, after posting an unbeaten Cup record and a 19-3 U.S. match record at Newport. He was in the U.S. Top Ten six times from 1896, No. 1 1898, 1899, 1900, and No. 2 in 1902. Ever absorbed by the game's history, he wrote *Tennis Origins and Mysteries,* published in 1931. Born March 15, 1877, in New York, he committed suicide there Dec. 28, 1932. He was named to the Hall of Fame in 1955.

MAJOR TITLES (3)—*U.S. singles, 1898, 1899, 1900.* OTHER U.S. TITLES (3)—*Intercollegiate singles, 1896; Intercollegiate doubles, 1897, 1898 with Leo Ware.* DAVIS CUP—*1900, 1902; record: 3-0 in singles.* SINGLES RECORD IN THE MAJORS: *U.S. (19-3).*

HAZEL HOTCHKISS WIGHTMAN
United States (1886–1974)

"Lady Tennis," as she came to be known, remembered herself as a shy, somewhat awed and fascinated college girl when she arrived at the Philadelphia Cricket Club in 1909 for the U.S. Championships. A Californian, Hazel Virginia Hotchkiss hadn't played on grass, but with her attacking style and rock-ribbed volleying—she was the first woman to rely so heavily on the volley—22-year-old Hazel, a right-hander, scythed through the field to lift the title effortlessly (6-0, 6-1) from 39-year-old Maud Barger Wallach in the challenge round.

She lost only one set, in the all-comers final over Louise Hammond, 6-8, 6-1, 6-4. That triple was the start of the first of the three U.S. triples (singles, doubles, mixed titles for three straight years) registered by American women. Hazel repeated in 1910 and 1911, and was emulated by Mary K. Browne (1912, 1913, 1914) and Alice Marble (1938, 1939, 1940). Hazel had no trouble with Hammond in the 1910 challenge round, but an old West Coast rival, May Sutton—champion in 1904—pushed her hard in 1911, 8-10, 6-4, 9-7.

Marrying Bostonian George Wightman in 1912, she didn't defend. But, responding to a challenge from her father—to win after becoming a mother, a U.S. first—she reappeared in 1915 to lose the singles final to Molla Mallory, and win the doubles and mixed. But papa's wish came true for the spunky 125-pound 5-footer in another comeback, 1919. At 32, she won her fourth singles title. She lost only one set, beating Marion Zinderstein, 6-1, 6-2, in the final, and reaching the doubles final. Thereafter her long-lived and unapproached success (U.S. adult titles between 1909 and 1943) was confined to doubles, at which she was one of the supremes.

Hazel, devoted to the game in all aspects, generously instructed innumerable players, at no charge, throughout her life, and was able to win important titles with two of her protégés who would join her in the Hall of Fame: Wimbledon, U.S. and Olympic doubles with Helen Wills in 1924; U.S. Indoor doubles with Sarah Palfrey 1928 through 1931. Her second Olympic gold in 1924 came in the mixed with Dick Williams.

She envisioned a team tournament for women similar to the Davis Cup, and offered a silver vase as prize. In 1923 British women were the strongest apart from Americans, and Julian Myrick of the USTA decided that a U.S.-Britain competition would be in order for the Wightman Cup. The event, with Hazel captaining and playing for a winning U.S. side, opened the newly constructed stadium at Forest Hills. A treasured series, it lasted through 1989, disbanded unfortunately with the Brits no longer able to offer competition.

The last of Hazel's record 34 U.S. adult titles was recorded in 1943 as she, 56, and Pauline Betz, 24, won the Indoor doubles over Lillian Lopaus and Judy Atterbury, 7-5, 6-1. Though short, she anticipated and moved extremely well and competed fiercely though undemonstrably. She perfected her volleying early, hitting the ball against the family home in Berkeley, where she grew up and graduated from the University of California. She refused to let the ball bounce because the yard was so uneven. She used to play against her four brothers and then the proud and spiky Sutton sisters.

As the Bostonian Mrs. Wightman, she was in the U.S. Top Ten in 1915, 1918 and 1919, No. 1 the last. She was born Dec. 20, 1886, in Healdsburg, Cal., and died Dec. 5, 1974, in Chestnut Hill, Mass. She entered the Hall of Fame in 1956.

MAJOR TITLES (17)—*U.S. singles, 1909, 1910, 1911, 1919; Wimbledon doubles, 1924; U.S. doubles, 1909, 1910, 1911, 1915, 1924, 1928; U.S. mixed, 1909, 1910, 1911, 1915, 1918, 1920.* OTHER U.S. TITLES (18)—*Indoor singles, 1919, 1927; Indoor doubles, 1919, 1921, 1924, 1927, with Marion Zinderstein Jessup; 1928, 1929, 1930, 1931, 1933, with Sarah Palfrey; 1943, with Pauline Betz; Indoor mixed, 1923, with Burnham Dell; 1924, with Bill Tilden; 1926, 1927, with G. Peabody Gardner, Jr.; 1928, with Henry Johnson; Clay mixed, 1915, with Harry Johnson.* SINGLES RECORD IN THE MAJORS: *Wimbledon (2-1), U.S. (22-4).*

TONY WILDING
New Zealand (1883–1915)

See page 115.

DICK WILLIAMS
United States (1891–1968)

See page 116.

SIDNEY WOOD
United States (1911—)

Playing in knickerbockers against the great Frenchman, René Lacoste, 15-year-old Sidney Burr Beardsley Wood was the youngest Wimbledon entrant ever in 1927. Four years later he became the second-youngest champion of Centre Court, and without stepping onto the hallowed sod. Frank Shields, with an injured ankle, withdrew, marking the only time Wimbledon has had a defaulted final.

Born Nov. 1, 1911, in Black Rock, Conn., Wood, a 5-foot-9½ right-hander, never reached that 1931 eminence again, although he did get to play a major final, losing the U.S. to Wilmer Allison in 1935, 6-2, 6-2, 6-3. A slim, nimble blond, he ranked in the U.S. Top Ten 10 times between 1930 and 1945, No. 2 in 1934, and was in the World Top Ten five times between 1931 and 1938, No. 5 in 1938, No. 6 in 1931.

He was a Davis Cupper in 1931 and 1934, and in the latter year was part of the most astounding U.S. comeback, from 0-2 against Australia in London. Having lost the first day to Viv McGraw, Wood was heartened by George Lott and Les Stoefen's holding action doubles victory over Adrian Quist and Jack Crawford, and he knocked off Jack Crawford, 6-3, 9-7, 4-6, 4-6, 6-2, to open the third day and tie the score at 2-2. Then Shields beat McGrath, and the U.S. entered the finals, losing, 4-1, to Britain. There, on opening day, Wood battled the Cup-holder's main man, Fred Perry, losing 6-1, 4-6, 5-7, 6-0, 6-3, and also lost to Bunny Austin on the third day. An inventive man, he was a developer of Supreme Court, the synthetic carpet on which most indoor events are played. He was inducted into the Hall of Fame in 1964.

MAJOR TITLE—*Wimbledon singles, 1931.* DAVIS CUP—*1931, 1934; record: 5-6 in singles, 3-0 in doubles.* SINGLES RECORD IN THE MAJORS: *French (2-1), Wimbledon (21-5), U.S. (42-25).*

BOB WRENN
United States (1873–1925)

A four-time U.S. singles champ, Robert Duffield Wrenn won the last of those titles in 1897 before serving in Cuba with Teddy Roosevelt's Rough Riders in the Spanish-American War. One of Bob's comrades in arms was future champion Bill Larned. Unfortunately Wrenn contracted yellow fever during that campaign and never regained pre-war form.

He came from a prominent Chicago family of several fine athletes, and became a topflight football, baseball and tennis player at Harvard. Noted for swiftness and court coverage, a defensive star featuring devilish lobs, he was the first left-hander to win the U.S. singles. He beat Fred Hovey for the 1893 title, 7-5, 3-6, 6-3, 7-5, and kept it by repelling Manliffe Goodbody in the 1894 challenge round.

Hovey took it from him easily in 1895. But Bob wrested it back, 7-5, 3-6, 6-0, 1-6, 6-1, in the 1896 challenge round, and fended off the first Aussie to chase a U.S. title, Wilberforce Eaves, 4-6, 8-6, 6-3, 2-6, 6-2, in the 1897 challenge round. War service prevented him from defending in 1898. He did team with his right-handed younger brother, George Wrenn, as the U.S. Davis Cup doubles pair in 1903 when they lost to the British Dohertys, Laurie and Reggie, 7-5, 9-7, 2-6, 6-3, the only instance of brothers clashing for the Cup.

They were the only brothers to play together for the U.S., and to rank concurrently in the U.S. Top Ten: Bob was No. 1 in 1893, 1894, 1896 and 1897, No. 8 in 1892 and 1900; George four times No. 6 during his five years up there between 1896 and 1900. Another brother, Everts, ranked No. 18 in 1896. In Bob's last thrust for the U.S. singles title he was beaten by George in a 1900 quarterfinal, 6-4, 6-1, 6-4, the only such brotherly battle in the Championships. George then lost the all-comers, 6-3, 6-2, 6-2, to Larned.

After leaving Harvard, Bob became a stockbroker in New York, and was president of the USTA from 1912 through 1915. Born Sept. 20, 1873, in Highland Park, Ill., he died in New York Nov. 12, 1925, and was named to the Hall of Fame in 1955.

MAJOR TITLES (5)—*U.S. singles, 1893, 1894, 1896, 1897; U.S. doubles, 1895.* OTHER U.S. TITLES (1)—*Intercollegiate doubles, 1892, with F. B. Winslow.* DAVIS CUP—*1903; record: 0-2 in singles, 0-1 in doubles.* SINGLES RECORD IN THE MAJORS: *U.S. (20-3).*

BEALS WRIGHT
United States (1879–1961)

Before the turn of the century, Beals Coleman Wright was a national champion, winning the Interscholastic singles for Boston's Hopkinson School in 1898 at 18, and repeating the following year when he made his first of 11 entries in the U.S. Top Ten at No. 8. In 1900 his brother, Irving, won the Interscholastic for the same school.

In 1905, dethroning Holcombe Ward, he was the second lefty to win the U.S. singles, following Bob Wrenn. He had to beat the future champ, Bill Clothier, 9-7, 6-2, 6-2, and an ex-champ, Bill Larned, 4-6, 6-3, 6-2, 6-2, plus Clarence Hobart, to reach the challenge round to topple Ward, 6-2, 6-1, 11-9.

Extremely aggressive, Wright received inside the baseline and approached with his returns and serves. Few liked to play against his fiendish chop and wide-spinning serve.

His biggest year was 1905. It included one of his three U.S. doubles titles (with Ward), and Davis Cup victories over Australian greats Tony Wilding, 6-3, 6-2, 6-4, and Norman Brookes, 12-10, 5-7, 12-10, 6-4, that sent the U.S. into a losing Cup round against Britain. In 1908 he beat those two again, even more stunning victories since it was the Davis Cup finale at Melbourne, their home turf. But it wasn't enough in a 3-2 defeat. He was born Dec. 19, 1879, in Boston, lived in Brookline, Mass., and died Aug. 23, 1961, in Alton, Ill. He was inducted into the Hall of Fame in 1956.

Wright won the Canadian singles thrice, 1902–04, and brother Irving won it in 1906.

MAJOR TITLES *(4)—U.S. singles, 1905; U.S. doubles, 1904, 1905, 1906.* DAVIS CUP—*1905, 1907, 1908, 1911; record: 6-4 in singles, 3-3 in doubles.* SINGLES RECORD IN THE MAJORS: *Wimbledon (6-2), U.S. (47-11).*

COURT TENNIS

PIERRE ETCHEBASTER
France (1893–1980)

A Basque maestro of the racket in the complex game of court tennis, the short, trim, elegant Pierre Etchebaster, a professional, was probably the greatest to roam the arcane concrete cubicle. Migrating to New York from his French homeland, he became the resident paragon at the Racquet & Tennis Club on Park Avenue, as player and instructor. Traveling to London to challenge for the world title in 1927, he lost to the champion G. F. Covey, 7-sets-to-5 in Prince's Club.

However, a year later on the same court he dethroned Covey, 7-5. Thereafter, he repelled seven challenges himself, the first at Prince's, the remainder on his home paving, Racquet & Tennis: 1930, Walter Kinsella, 7-1; 1937, Ogden Phipps, 3-1, injured; 1948, Phipps, 7-2; 1948; James Deal, 7-4; 1949, Phipps, 7-1; 1950, Alastair Martin, 7-0; 1952, Martin, 7-2.

He retired as unbeaten champion in 1954 at age 60. A right-hander, he was born Dec. 8, 1893, in St. Jean de Luz, France, and died there March 24, 1980. He entered the Hall Fame in 1978.

TOM PETTITT
Great Britain (1859–1946)

As a youngster, 17, English-born Tom Pettitt emigrated to Boston. He became a wizard at racket sports, and was immensely popular as teaching professional of court tennis at Boston's Tennis & Racquet Club, and that game as well as lawn tennis at the Newport (R.I.) Casino, where he was a familiar walrus-mustachioed figure for 65 years until his death in 1946. He was one of the very first lawn tennis players and instructors, having learned the game in 1876, shortly after its inception. He stopped teaching in 1929, remaining at the Casino as its supervisor. A nimble 5-foot-9, 176 pounder, he could beat any of the members at either lawn or court tennis in his heyday. An old pal, Jimmy Van Alen, liked to tell about Tom using a taped champagne bottle as a bat and winning friendly lawn tennis games. Tom entered the Hall of Fame in 1982 on the basis of his world championship court tennis prowess.

He won the title in a successful 1885 challenge to George Lambert, 7-sets-to-5, at King Henry VIII's old playpen, Hampton Court, outside of London. In an 1890 defense he turned back Charles Saunders, 7-5, at St. Stephens Green, Ireland, resigning the title later unbeaten. In the earliest pro lawn tennis tour, he and Irish pro champ George Kerr played a series of three well-attended matches in New England in 1889. Kerr, won at Boston, Springfield (Mass.), and Newport. Pettitt was born Dec. 19, 1859, in Beckenham, England, and died Oct. 17, 1946, in Newport, R.I.

JOURNALISTS

BUD COLLINS
United States (1929—)

Ubiquitous Arthur Worth "Bud" Collins, Jr. is the most visible and versatile U.S. tennis journalist. An estimable writer, broadcaster, editor, he is a man about the game whose wit, understanding and flamboyance make him more recognizable than many star players. His memory and knowledge of tennis, its history and characters, is encyclopedic.

From printed page to broadcast booth, he is identified with the sport he has done much to popularize, yet to protect for the purists. "He is to tennis what pasta is to Italy," was a line in a *Sports Illustrated* profile. Born June 17, 1929, in Lima, Ohio, he grew up in Berea (outside of Cleveland) about 50 yards from the dirt tennis courts of Baldwin-Wallace College, from which he graduated in 1951, and where his father had been head coach of football, basketball, baseball and track, as well as athletic director. He moved east after U.S. Army service in 1954 to attend Boston University graduate school, then joined the *Boston Herald* as a sportswriter. In 1963, the year he shifted to the *Boston Globe,* Collins first did television commentary (covering the U.S. Doubles at Longwood Cricket Club) for Boston's PBS outlet, WGBH, a station that for the next 20 years, with Greg Harney as producer, would pioneer American coverage of the sport.

He worked the U.S. Open for CBS (1968–72), signed on with NBC in 1972 (thereafter closely identified with that network's presentation of Wimbledon and the French), becoming the point man for all the dualists—print–television journalists—to follow. At the *Globe* his columns on sport, travel, and a variety of other subjects, including coverage of the Vietnam War, are a continuing delight. His prose and commentary style are as multi-hued as Joseph's Amazing Technicolor Dream Coat. Seldom one to take himself or sports too seriously, he brightens reports with nicknames as colorful as his rainbow neckties and trousers, occasionally with flights of fancy. However, he can be absolutely authentic, a meticulous curator of the game's annals, passionate keeper of the flame.

He also writes for magazines and newspapers across the world such as the *Independent* in London, and the *Age* in Melbourne. His books include *The Education of a Tennis Player* (with Rod Laver, 1971), *Evonne! On the Move* (with Evonne Goolagong, 1974), a memoir, *My Life with the Pros* (1989) and three editions of this encyclopedia.

Although he refers to himself—and everyone else who plays below the level of the pros—as a "hacker," Collins is an accomplished now-and-again player, known for his touch, tactical cunning and preference for playing barefoot on grass courts. He won the U.S. Indoor mixed doubles (with Top Tenner Janet Hopps) in 1961, and was a finalist in the French Senior doubles (with Jack Crawford) in 1975. Engaging and irrepressible, he has even coached tennis, the Brandeis University varsity, 1959–63, whose "name" player was future hippie icon Abbie Hoffman.

Befriending generations of journalists and tennis fans, Bud has been, in the words of that *Sports Illustrated* piece: "the hackers' delegate in the Chambers of Aces." He entered the Hall in 1994.

—*Barry S. Lorge*

ALLISON DANZIG
United States (1898–1987)

The familiar and authoritative identification that topped *New York Times* stories for 45 years—By Allison Danzig—was reassuring to readers until his retirement in 1967. Before that he was a sportswriter for the *Brooklyn Eagle,* developing an incisive, perceptive style that made him the widest regarded literary voice of the game in the U.S. Al Danzig, the first journalist to enter the Hall of Fame (1968), was a thoroughgoing gentleman respected throughout the game and his profession. He covered the game from its first great impact during the Tilden, Wills and Lenglen days of the 1920s to the dawn of the open era, and also was a nationally known chronicler of college football, rowing and the Olympic Games.

He was one of the few who could write knowledgeably about court tennis, ancestor of lawn tennis. Born in Waco, Tex., Feb. 27, 1898, he graduated from Cornell, where he played football despite a diminutive stature, and served in the U.S. Army during World War I. He became a New Yorker following college, but kept Texas in his speech, and in the kitchen. This softspoken man was celebrated for his torrid chili. Always immaculately turned out—coat and tie whatever the summer temperature on the Eastern grass circuit—he was generous in helping young reporters and had the respect of generations of players. He wrote books on tennis, football, the Olympics and court tennis. Danzig died Jan. 27, 1987, in Ridgewood, N.J. The Danzig Award, established by Longwood Cricket Club in Boston—he was the first recipient in 1963—honors leading tennis writers, and is presented periodically during the U.S. Pro Championships.

DAVID GRAY
Great Britain (1927–83)

David Gray was such a fine chronicler of the game for two decades with an exceptional English newspaper, *The Guardian,* that many regretted his departure from journalism in 1976 to become an official of the ITF. A well-educated and witty man, he showed his grasp of tennis, its figures, matches, history and politics in his literate daily reports from across the world. But he served the game well, even without byline, as the ITF's diplomatic general secretary from 1976 until his untimely death of cancer in 1983. He was also secretary of the Men's International Professional Tennis Council.

As a journalist he strongly advocated the abolition of phony amateurism and the adoption of open tennis in 1968. Gray was influential in reorganizing the Davis Cup, returning tennis to the Olympics in 1988 and broadening the game's base, especially by encouraging its development on the African continent. Among the large and competitive British press contingent he was a standout, and he brought to the game's administration a keen overall view and perception, much wider than that of most tennis officials.

A graduate of Birmingham University, he worked his way up to the *Guardian* through the *Wolverhampton Express and Star,* the *Northern Daily Telegraph* and the *News Chronicle.* He could, and did, write anything and everything well, a political reporter and theater critic before getting the tennis assignment. Hall of Famer Ted Tinling wrote of him: "David's political experiences gave him a ready taste for the personal in-

trigues and machinations that form the perennial backdrop to our ballet of forehands and backhands out front." A collection of his writings, *Shades of Gray,* was published in 1988 by Willow Books (William Collins & Sons).

He was born Dec. 31, 1927, in Kingswinford, England, and died Sept 6, 1983, in London. He was named to the Hall of Fame in 1985.

GLADYS HELDMAN
United States (1922—)

For more than two decades, brilliant Gladys Medalie Heldman was the game's anchor, first as founder-owner-publisher-editor-chief-writer of *World Tennis* magazine (launched in 1953), later as the instigator and housemother of a separate professional circuit for women, begun in 1970. Under her guidance, *WT* became the international literary voice of tennis. A slim, petite dynamo, who often seemed shy, she came to tennis through marriage to a first-flight player, left-handed Julius Heldman, who was the U.S. junior champ in 1936.

She, a previously non-athletic New Yorker, quickly absorbed his enthusiasm for the game, becoming a maven. Their two daughters, Trixie and Julie, held national junior rankings, and Julie went on to win the Italian Open in 1969, and rank No. 5 in the world that year and in 1974. In 1970, Gladys and her magazine became the allies of disgruntled female players—Billie Jean King and Rosie Casals foremost—who felt, justifiably, that they were being demeaned, financially and attitudinally, by the game's male establishment. They believed it was necessary to break away from the traditional dual-sex tournament format and go it alone.

Heldman encouraged them, and urged a friend, Joe Cullman, head of Philip Morris, to provide an initial bankroll. Joined by the "Houston Nine" (King, Casals, daughter Julie, Peaches Bartkowicz, Kerry Melville, Valerie Ziegenfuss, Nancy Richey, Kristy Pigeon, Judy Tegart Dalton), Heldman staged the first Virginia Slims tournament in that city late in 1970. Although the Americans among the Nine risked (and received brief) suspensions from the USTA, that tourney, and another in Richmond, Va., succeeded.

They prompted Virginia Slims to underwrite a 1971 tour, and the stunning progress of the "Long Way Babies" commenced. Heldman counseled and editorially backed the circuit which she first dubbed "Women's Lob" featuring "The Little Broads."

Heldman, who became a better-than-average player herself, sold the magazine and withdrew from tennis politics in the mid-1970s, and now lives with her husband in Santa Fe, N.M. She was born May 13, 1922, in New York, and entered the Hall of Fame in 1979.

AL LANEY

United States (1895–1988)

A fine writer who made his name covering sports, Albert Gillis Laney was usually associated with tennis and golf, but he covered everything on the menu, from big league baseball to football to championship fights, with his usual understanding of what was at foot, and a keen reportorial touch. Laconic, mustachioed, usually beneath a gray fedora, he settled in Paris for a time after World War I, worked for James Joyce as secretary, and joined the staff of the renowned *Paris Herald* (now the *International Herald Tribune*).

He had an eye for compelling features, and his coverage of the epic 1926 showdown of Suzanne Lenglen and Helen Wills at Cannes graces several anthologies. He spanned the generations, having observed another epic, the Maurice McLoughlin–Norman Brookes Davis Cup duel at Forest Hills in 1914, and worked as a reporter until his last newspaper, the *New York Herald Tribune,* folded in 1966. That paper had a legendary sports staff headed by Stanley Woodward, who felt Laney's story on blind, down-and-out

Sam Langford, onetime great boxer, was an American masterpiece.

His *Courting the Game,* a tennis memoir, remains one of the splendid tennis books. Laney was born Jan. 11, 1895, in Pensacola, Fla., retained a Southern lilt in his speech, and died Jan. 31, 1988, in Spring Valley, N.Y. He entered the Hall of Fame in 1979.

DAN MASKELL

Great Britain (1908–92)

To his legion of admirers Dan Maskell was the voice of Wimbledon from his first broadcast for BBC-TV in 1951 to his last in 1991. Dan's mellow and mellifluous tones, always thoughtful, always reverent, never wasteful, would illuminate the matches he covered with masterly understatement. Dan's reflections—perhaps a subtle change of tactics or a revealing grimace that told a story—added to the enjoyment of his viewers without being intrusive. "Oh, I say!" was a trademark, a meaningful exclamation that told much in three words.

Before his television career began, Dan spent two years with BBC-radio at Wimbledon, working as the summarizer with Max Rolbertson. He was the ideal choice because his whole life had been spent in the game. He didn't miss a single day of play at Wimbledon from 1929 to 1991, and had seen every final from 1924.

Maskell was born April 11, 1908, in the London neighborhood of Fulham, just a pitch-and-putt from Queen's Club. He was the seventh of eight children, the fourth boy. As he grew up Dan was captivated by the glamor of the famous club with its affluent members, many of them prominent in the worlds of entertainment, politics and sport.

First as a ballboy, then as a coach—never having a chance to play as an amateur—Dan was on the Queen's staff from 1923 to 1929 when he moved to the All England Lawn Tennis and Croquet Club at Wimbledon to become their first-ever teaching professional. For 16 years Maskell, an excellent player, was the professional champion of Britain. In 1931 he competed in the U.S. Pro Championships at Forest Hills, losing in the quarters to fourth-seeded Howard Kinsey, the 1926 Wimbledon finalist.

In 1933 Dan was surprised to be selected to accompany the British Davis Cup team to Paris for the semifinal against the U.S. This was unprecedented in those amateur days. Professionals never aided teams, which seems curious today when most leading players have personal coaches. Victories over the U.S. and then Cup-holding France began a four-year British reign, with Maskell a fundamental part of that success: practicing with the players, advising, helping keep morale high.

It was partly this team experience that prepared Dan to make an important contribution to his country during World War II. As the Royal Air Force's first rehabilitation officer, charged with the task of helping wounded airmen recover full health and fitness, he revealed qualities of devotion and innovation that were recognized by the Crown with the award of an OBE (Order of the British Empire) in 1945.

Following the war Dan resumed his duties at the All England Club for nine years. In 1955 he ended his coaching duties there to become the Lawn Tennis Association's training manager. He was in charge of the training of coaches and promoting the game nationwide. He also coached Prince Charles and Princess Anne. In 1982 he received his second award from the Crown, a CBE (Commander of the British Empire) for services to tennis, including broadcasting, and also an honorary MA degree from Loughborough University, where he was based during the war.

He died Dec. 10, 1992, at 82, leaving warm memories of one of the most recognizable and respected voices to come over British airwaves.

—*John Barrett*

LANCE TINGAY
Great Britain (1915–90)

As the dean of a sizeable platoon of British tennis writers of his time, Lance Tingay, friendly, erudite, helpful to colleagues, covered the game for a half-century, present as it evolved from the amateur into the open and highly professional era. He covered his first Wimbledon in 1932 and was the thorough, informed and informative tennis correspondent for *The Daily Telegraph* of London from 1950 to 1980, writing his dispatches from across the world.

Ever good humored, even while pounding his typewriter on deadline, he was a leading historian of the game, the author of *History of Lawn Tennis in Pictures, One Hundred Years of Wimbledon,* and *Royalty and Lawn Tennis,* and he wrote for numerous tennis publications and yearbooks. Tingay was born in London July 15, 1915, and died there March 10, 1990. He was named to the Hall of Fame in 1982.

INNOVATORS

TED TINLING
Great Britain (1910–90)

The Leaning Tower of Pizzazz, 6-foot-5 Cuthbert Collingwood Tinling entered the Hall of Fame in 1986 as a many-faceted benefactor of the game. Witty and literate, a man who had served as a lieutenant colonel in intelligence for the British army during World War II, Tinling, a right-hander, was a good enough player to compete on the English circuit after the war. But it was as an involved bystander that he served the game well, first as a teenager on the Riviera where he, spending winters for reasons of ill health, umpired matches, including some for the great Suzanne Lenglen.

He was master of ceremonies at Wimbledon until one of his careers, that of designer-dressmaker, made him for a time *persona non grata.*

That occurred in 1949 when he scandalously (or so it seemed to the tournament committee) equipped American Gertrude "Gussy" Moran with lace panties that drew hordes of photographers and spectators. Ted made beautiful as well as avant-garde costumes for many female players, including Maureen Connolly, Maria Bueno, Billie Jean King, Margaret Court and Evonne Goolagong, who all won majors in his dresses.

He was couturier for the newly formed Virginia Slims circuit, and later the Slimsies' minister of protocol and emcee, a strong advocate of the women's game. An unmistakable bald-headed beacon, he was of immeasurable value late in life as historian and writer who had observed most of the game's luminaries, and as liaison between the players and Wimbledon. Outspoken, generous in informing and counseling newcomers to the game, Ted could make light of his own death, remarking on one of his last days: "Send me a fax to hell to let me know if Jennifer [Capriati] wins Wimbledon." He was born June 23, 1910, in Eastbourne, England, and died May 23, 1990, in Cambridge, England.

MARY OUTERBRIDGE

United States (1852–86)

Celebrated as the "Mother of Tennis," Mary Ewing Outerbridge was undoubtedly one of the pioneers, but the claims by her adherents that she introduced the game to the U.S. are undocumented. The story is that she, a New Yorker, saw soldiers of the British garrison playing tennis in Bermuda, where she was vacationing in 1874, the year of the game's patenting and early marketing. Intrigued, she is said to have taken a set home where her brother, Emilius Outerbridge, and friends set up a court at the Staten Island Cricket and Baseball Club.

Tennis was indeed introduced to the U.S. at several locations in 1874, the first documented instance in Arizona. Outerbridge was born March 9, 1852, in Philadelphia, died May 3, 1886 (five years after the first U.S. Championships), on Staten Island, and entered the Hall of Fame in 1981.

JIMMY VAN ALEN

United States (1902–91)

James Henry Van Alen, born Sept. 19, 1902, in his beloved Newport, R.I., was intimately involved with tennis as player, organizer and—best known—innovator whose pet idea, the tie-breaker, radically altered the game, making it more televisable in the U.S. As a U.S. singles champ at court tennis in 1933, 1938 and 1940, he was good enough at that abstruse ancestor of lawn tennis to warrant a Hall of Fame spot as a player. He played tennis well enough to have won his blue at his alma mater, Cambridge, appeared in the Wimbledon, French and U.S. Championships, and played in the Newport Casino Invitational, where he had a win over fellow Hall of Famer George Lott.

He would become director of that tournament, a leader in the preservation of the aging wooden Casino (the cradle of U.S. tennis), and, at the instigation of his wife, Candy, the guiding light in founding the Hall of Fame to which he was elected in 1965.

Feeling the game's scoring should be simplified and deuce done away with, he lobbied tirelessly on behalf of his creation, VASSS: Van Alen Streamlined Scoring System. Among the elements were single point scoring and 21-point or 31-point matches (à la table tennis), no-ad (games scored 1-2-3-4, maximum 7-points, sudden death at 3-3), medal play (à la golf, based on single point totals for specific numbers of rounds), and, the most celebrated—tie-breakers.

Unveiled in 1965 at the Casino Pro Championships, which he personally sponsored for $10,000 prize money, the seminal tie-breaker needed retooling. That he did with veteran referee Mike Blanchard. Eventually it became sudden death (best-of-9 points).

Amazingly this breaker was accepted by the USTA, and used in U.S. championship events from 1970 through 1974. Thereafter the USTA embraced the current ITF-approved "lingering death," as Van Alen disparagingly called the best-of-12 point version that requires a 2-point margin for victory, thus can extend into double figures. Between 1970 and 1977, at "Newport Bolshevik" Jimmy's suggestion, red flags were raised wherever a tie-breaker was played at the U.S. Open. Sadly this custom wasn't continued at Flushing Meadow.

A man of old family wealth, Jimmy hoped to give the game a common touch, and became an avuncular, almost cherubic figure in planter's straw hat and burgundy blazer at the Casino. His love for tennis was endless, as well as his delight in shaking up the establishment with his brainstorms. He served in the U.S. Navy during World War II, and died July 3, 1991, in Newport. Jimmy would have enjoyed the irony: That semifinal day at Wimbledon Michael Stich deposed champion Stefan Edberg by winning three breakers while Edberg never lost his serve. Such a match could not have been played during nearly a century before Van Alen.

ADMINISTRATORS

GEORGE ADEE
United States (1874–1948)

George Townsend Adee made his sporting name as an All-American quarterback at Yale in 1894. He was elevated to the Hall of Fame in 1964, for his contributions to tennis on the administrative side. He was president of the USTA four years, 1916–19, and was also a member of the Davis Cup and Amateur Rules committees. A New Yorker, he was an enthusiastic tennis player, good enough to appear six times in the U.S. Championships singles between 1903 and 1909. He served in the U.S. Army in the Spanish-American War and World War I. Born Jan. 4, 1874, in Stonington, Conn., he died July 31, 1948, in New York.

LARRY BAKER
United States (1890–1980)

Lawrence Adams Baker, very active in USTA affairs, was an officer beginning in 1932, and president three years, 1948–50. He was a founder of the National Tennis Foundation, and captained the U.S. Davis Cup team for its 1953 win over Canada at Montreal. He sponsored the Baker Cup, a U.S. vs. Canada event for seniors. Baker was born June 20, 1890, in Lowdensville, S.C., lived in East Hampton, N.Y., and died there Oct. 15, 1980. He entered the Hall of Fame in 1975.

PHILIPPE CHATRIER
France (1926—)

As player, journalist and administrator, Philippe Chatrier, a Parisian, made a tremendous impact on the game, and was instrumental in its growth and success, particularly during the open era. He was a good enough player to win the French junior titles in singles and doubles in 1945, play internationally for France, and later captained the Davis Cup team.

Serving dual roles as president of the French Federation of Tennis (1972–92) and the ITF (1977–91) he was largely responsible for the renaissance of the French Open, placing it on par with the other three majors and overseeing the splendid updating of Stade Roland Garros. He fought valiantly against over-commercialization of the game, and led a campaign to restore tennis to the Olympic Games, a goal realized in 1988 after a 64-year interval.

Championing the Grand Slam concept, he worked hard to ally the four major championships in staying at the pinnacle. He is a member of the International Olympic Committee. An intelligent chronicler of the game, he was a Paris newspaperman, and founded one of the leading magazines of the sport, *Tennis de France*. He was born Feb. 2, 1926, in Paris.

JOE CULLMAN
United States (1912—)

A lifelong love of the game led Joseph Frederick Cullman III to become a working angel in tennis, a moonlighter away from his principal position as chairman and CEO of the Philip Morris Co. As such he benefitted tennis extraordinarily in several ways. He was chairman of the U.S. Open at Forest Hills in 1969 and 1970, formative years, and was instrumental in getting the original Open, 1968, televised.

In 1970, at the behest of another Hall of Fame member, Gladys Heldman, he came to the financial and spiritual rescue of the women, up to then second-class citizens of tournament tennis. With the backing of one of his products, Virginia Slims, a separate women's professional circuit was born. It continues as the Corel Tour.

He was president and chairman of the International Tennis Hall of Fame 1982–88, a period during which the Hall's home, the revered and historic Newport Casino, made a recovery from years of decline, and became a sound and viable institution. A Yale alumnus, he built a tennis complex, the Cullman Center, for his alma mater. A fervent player, he enjoys nothing more than a game on the Casino lawn. Joe is a New Yorker, born there April 9, 1912, and entered the Hall of Fame in 1990.

SLEW HESTER
United States (1912–93)

A fine athlete, a football player at Millsaps College in his native Mississippi, William Ewing Hester won numerous tennis trophies. Among them were U.S. senior doubles titles such as the Grass Court 45s with Alex Wellford in 1957. But, as one of the most thoughtful and forceful USTA presidents, burly Slew made an indelible mark on the game by determining to expand the scope and potential of the U.S. Open by moving the event from Forest Hills after the 1977 Championships.

He took the Open a few miles away to Flushing Meadow and the swiftly constructed, Hester-inspired-and-overseen U.S. National Tennis Center in time for the 1978 Open. There the event annually set tennis attendance records. A gregarious cigar-smoking oilman from Jackson, Hester earned a bronze star while serving in the U.S. Army in World War II.

He was a USTA officer from 1969 to 1977 when he became president for a critical two-year term. Born May 8, 1912, in Hazlehurst, Mass., he was inducted into the Hall of Fame in 1981, and died Feb. 8, 1993, in Jackson, Miss.

LAMAR HUNT
United States (1932—)

A man about Halls of Fame, Texan Lamar Hunt entered the tennis valhalla in 1993, having been inducted previously into the Professional Football Hall of Fame and the Soccer Hall of Fame.

Although he played football—"I sat on the bench"—at Southern Methodist, Hunt, scion of a prominent Dallas oil industry family, made his mark in American and international sport with his organizational and promotional strengths.

He was a leading founder of the American Football League, which eventually merged with the NFL. And with his daughter, Hunt has been credited with the naming of the Super Bowl. He is owner of the Kansas City Chiefs and for a time owned the Dallas Tornados in the North American Soccer League.

It was as a partner in the establishment of World Championship Tennis (WCT)—and later its guiding light—that he was a strong global influence in transforming and professionalizing the tournament game. In 1967, a New Orleans friend, Dave Dixon, enlisted Hunt's aid in forming WCT.

Headquartered in Dallas, WCT hastened the dawn of open tennis with the signing of the elite of the amateurs.

WCT developed a circuit and season of its own, leading the way to increased paydays for the pros that forced the rest of the tennis world to catch up.

Unfortunately (and ungratefully), the Association of Tennis Professionals, in reorganizing the men's tour in 1990, froze WCT out, and Hunt's organization ceased operations after 23 years of raising standards within the professional game. Hunt was born Aug. 2, 1932, in Eldorado, Ark., and lives in Dallas.

PERRY T. JONES
United States (1890–1970)

A powerful figure in making Southern California a tennis vineyard of champions, Perry Thomas Jones oversaw the game from his office at the Los Angeles Tennis Club for well over a quarter-century. As president of the Southern California Association and director of the Pacific Southwest Championships, he was active in the game from bottom to top, singling out promising juniors for attention and travel and making his tournament one of the best in the U.S.

In short, Perry T., or Mr. Jones, as he was called, stood imposingly as Mr. Tennis of the West Coast, an exceptional fund-raiser whose judgment and help forwarded the careers of numerous stars, including Jack Kramer, Billie Jean King and Dennis Ralston.

The last was Alex Olmedo, the Peruvian student at the University of Southern California. Maneuvering controversially, Jones got him, the only non-citizen to play for the U.S., approved for the Davis Cup team in 1958, citing the fact that Peru had no team. Jones, the captain that year, was understandably eager to have Olmedo aboard. Olmedo led the U.S. to the Cup over Australia. Jones also captained the losing 1959 team. He was born June 22, 1890, in Etiwanda, Cal.,

and died Sept. 16, 1970, in Los Angeles. He entered the Hall of Fame in 1970.

ALASTAIR MARTIN
United States (1915—)

A mild yet determined man, Alastair Bradley Martin qualified for 1973 induction to the Hall of Fame on two counts: He was a progressive vice president and president of the USTA during the critical transition period between the amateur and open eras. And he was one of the finest of all court tennis players, U.S. amateur champion in singles eight times, doubles 10 times. He also challenged the great pro Pierre Etchebaster (a fellow Hall of Fame member) for Etchebaster's world title, vainly in 1950 and 1952.

Alastair was a good enough lawn tennis player to have competed in the U.S. Championships at Forest Hills several times before and after World War II. As vice president of the USTA in 1967 and 1968, he worked closely with president Bob Kelleher, advocating, with the British, the revolutionary adoption of open tennis.

He was USTA president in the trying days of 1969–70 as the game became professionalized, and the amateur associations maintained their standing. He founded the Eastern Tennis Patrons in 1951 and served as president of the National Tennis Foundation. A New Yorker, he was born there March 11, 1915, and resides in Katonah, N.Y.

BILL MARTIN
United States (1906—)

A distinguished figure in finance and government when Chairman of the Federal Reserve Board for 20 years (1951–70), William McChesney Martin was long devoted to the game, working behind the scenes to improve its condition in such positions as president of the National Tennis Foundation and the International Tennis Hall of Fame.

In 1992 he was elected honorary chairman of the Hall, and worked diligently to make sure that its home, the historic Newport Casino (imperiled by age and apathy), was preserved and put into fine condition.

Martin married into an honored tennis family, wedding Cynthia Davis, daughter of Dwight Davis, donor of the Cup bearing his name. Like the Davises, he was raised in St. Louis, born there Dec. 17, 1906. He entered the Hall of Fame in 1982 and resides in Washington, D.C.

JULIAN MYRICK
United States (1880–1969)

A New Yorker, though born March 1, 1880, in Murfreesboro, N.C., Julian Southall Myrick was inducted into the Hall of Fame in 1963 on the basis of his administrative ability and contributions to the game in the U.S. Known as "Uncle Mike" to friends and associates, he was president of the USTA 1920–22 and an active committeeman. He was a leader in enlarging the U.S. Championships, influential in construction of the Forest Hills Stadium, at a cost of $300,000, in 1923, and launching the Wightman Cup competition between U.S. and British women, the first edition of which inaugurated the stadium. He died in New York, Jan. 4, 1969.

PATRONS

KING GUSTAV V
Sweden (1858–1950)

A grand patron of the game and an enthusiastic player into his 90s, King Gustav V of Sweden learned to play during a visit to Britain in 1878, and founded his country's first tennis club on his return home. In 1936 he founded the King's Cup. Eventually disbanded during the open era, it was a men's indoor team competition for European countries. He became king on Dec. 8, 1907, ruled for 43 years and was often seen playing friendly events on the Riviera.

Entered under the pseudonym, Mr. G., looking like an aged Mr. Chips in spectacles, white mustache, flannels and straw hat, he frequently took part in handicap tourneys, partnered by famous players such as Suzanne Lenglen. During World War II this widely respected ruler interceded to obtain better treatment for the Nazi-imprisoned Davis Cup stars, Jean Borotra of France and Gottfried von Cramm of Germany, and may have saved their lives.

Gustav was born June 16, 1858, in Drottningholm, Sweden and died Oct. 29, 1950. He was elected to the Hall of Fame in 1980.

ARTHUR NIELSEN
United States (1897–1980)

Arthur Charles Nielsen's name is synonymous with television—the Nielsen Ratings—but he was long an avid player and a generous patron, contributing much time and money to the construction of tennis courts. One such monument to his memory is the Nielsen Center at his alma mater, the University of Wisconsin, where he was captain of the tennis varsity three years, 1916–18.

He continued playing after graduation, teaming with Arthur Nielsen, Jr., to win the U.S. Father and Son doubles titles of 1946 and 1948, and he was good enough to play singles in the U.S. Championships of 1918. A Chicagoan, he was born there, Sept. 5, 1897, and died there, June 1, 1980. He entered the Hall of Fame in 1971.

9

THEY ALSO SERVE

Although a substantial number of the game's all-time elite are to be found in the chapters devoted to the International Tennis Hall of Fame and the Greatest Players (1914–45 and 1946–96), numerous others during 121 years of tournament tennis have made distinctive/unusual marks and contributions. A select number may be found here—such as the eventually unlovable "St. Leger" Goold. Some players may be said to have gotten away with murder, but he is the only Wimbledon finalist to be convicted of same.

Abbreviations used: LH, left-hander; RH, right-hander; B., born; D., died. Denoting tournament finish: RD., round; QF, quarterfinal; SF, semifinal; F, final.

AKHURST, DAPHNE

Daphne Jessie Akhurst Cozens, Australian RH, country's first prolific champ, first female to make World Top Ten (No. 3, 1928), though had short career and life. B. April 22, 1903, d. Jan. 9, 1933, in childbirth. Between 1925 and 1931, won 14 majors, all Australian: five singles, five doubles, four mixed. Last doubles, 1931, won as Mrs. Roy Cozens. French QF; Wimbledon SF, 1928, QF, 1925.

ALVAREZ, LILI DE

Spain's most accomplished female until Arantxa Sanchez Vicario, the chic Lili de Al-

varez, later Comtesse de la Valdene, was World No. 2, 1927 and 1928; No. 3, 1926, No. 8, 1930 and 1931. RH, b. May 9, 1905, Rome. Lost Wimbledon F to Kitty McKane, 1926; to Helen Wills, 1928. French QF, 1927, SF 1930, 1931. Won French doubles, 1929. Lives in Madrid.

AMPON, FELICISIMO

Felicisimo Hermoso Ampon, speedy, popular miniature, 4-foot-11, 100 pounds, smallest world-class man. Philippines' finest, RH, b. Oct. 27, 1920, Manila. Splendid retriever, made mark at French: QF 1952 (beat Tony Trabert), 1953 (beat Budge Patty). Incredible Davis Cup career over

29-year span (played 16)—from Philippines' initial team, 1939, to farewell victory, age 47, 1968. Led team to 22-16 record, was 32-23, singles. Nadir: 6-0, 6-0, 6-0, Cup beating by Frank Parker, U.S., 1946.

AMRITRAJ, VIJAY; ANAND; ASHOK

Three rangy, RH brothers, pros, from India with attacking styles, all born and raised in Madras. Vijay and Anand played Davis Cup together 15 years, led India to two title rounds, 1974 and 1987. All live in Los Angeles.

Vijay Amritraj, b., Dec. 14, 1953, graceful 6-3, superb volleyer, Best World rank, No. 20, 1980. Won 16 singles, 13 doubles pro titles, $1,325,833 career. Winning Bretton Woods, N.H., 1973, saved three match points each vs. Humphrey Hose, Rod Laver, two more in F over Jimmy Connors. QF Wimbledon, U.S., 1973 (beating 2nd seed Laver in latter). Davis Cup: 1970–88, 27-18 singles, 18-10 doubles.

Anand Amritraj, 6-1, b. March 20, 1952. Best World rank, No. 87, 1974. Won 13 pro doubles titles, eight with Vijay, $331,698 career. Davis Cup 1968–88, 12-15 singles, 21-14 doubles.

Ashok Amritraj, 6-1, b. Feb 22, 1957. Best World rank, No. 206, 1976.

ANDERSON, J. O.

Australian Davis Cupper, RH James Outram "Greyhound" Anderson, b. Sept. 17, 1895, Enfield, d. July 19, 1960, Sydney. Best World rank, No. 3, 1923–24. Swift afoot, with husky, damaging forehand, won Australian singles, 1922, 1924, 1925; doubles, 1924. Davis Cup: 1919–25, 20-7 singles, 8-1 doubles. Led Aussies to F, 1922, gave Bill Johnston, U.S., first Cup defeat.

ANDERSON, MAL

Australian Davis Cupper, RH. Malcolm James "Cowboy" Anderson, b. March 5, 1935, Rockhampton. Willowy, 6-1, serve-and-volleyer, came off Queensland ranch. First unseeded player to win

U.S., beat 2nd seed Dick Savitt, 3rd seed Sven Davidson, then 1st seed Ashley Cooper in F. Lost F, 1958, to Cooper. World rank No. 2, 1957 and 1958. Wimbledon QF, 1956, 1958. Lost Australian F, 1958, 1972. Won French doubles, Australian mixed, 1957; Australian doubles, 1973. Davis Cup: 1957–58, 1973 (with 1957 and 1973 winners); 11-3 singles, 2-3 doubles. Turned pro, 1959.

ATKINSON, KATHLEEN

Kathleen Gill Atkinson (b. Nov. 5, 1875, d. April 30, 1957, Maplewood, N.J.) won seven doubles (1897–98, with sister Juliette). In first instance of U.S. sisters clashing in Championships, Juliette beat Kathleen in 1895 SF, 6-1, 6-4. More than a century later, Manuela beat Maggie in Maleeva sisters meeting, QF.

ASBOTH, JOSZEF

Probably Hungary's finest player, Joszef Asboth was clever performer on clay, won French, 1947. Wimbledon SF, 1948. B. Sept. 18, 1917, Szombathely. Davis Cup: 1938–1957; 18-12 singles, 6-5 doubles. World rank, No. 8, 1947–48. Turned pro, 1958.

AUSSEM, CILLY

Until Steffi Graf, Cilly Aussem was Germany's most successful woman. Tiny 5-foot RH baseliner. Won French, Wimbledon, 1931 (latter over Hilde Krahwinkel, only all-German female final). Wimbledon SF, 1930. French SF, 1929, 1930, 1934. Won French mixed, 1930. World rank, No. 7 in 1928, 2 in 1930, 2 in 1931. B. Jan. 4, 1909, Cologne; d. as Countess F. M. della Corte Brae, March 22, 1963, Portofino, Italy.

AUSTIN, BUNNY; JOAN

English brother, sister, RH.

Henry Wilfred "Bunny" Austin liberated male legs, first internationalist to wear shorts in

1932. B. Aug. 26, 1906, London. Smooth ground-stroker, helped Britain win Davis Cup: 1933–36; 36-12 singles. World rank, No. 2 in 1931 and 1938, Top Ten eight other years from 1929. Lost Wimbledon F, 1932, 1938; SF, 1929, 1936, 1937; QF, 1933, 1935, 1939; French F, 1937; SF, 1935; QF, 1934, 1936. US QF, 1939.

Joan Winifred Austin. B. Jan. 23, 1903, London. Lost Wimbledon doubles F, 1923. A liberator herself, first to play on Centre Court without stockings, 1931. Was married to Randolph Lycett, winner Wimbledon doubles, 1921, 1922, 1923.

AYALA, LUIS

Chile's most successful male, Luis Ayala stocky RH, best on clay. B. Sept. 18, 1932, Santiago. Won Italian, 1959. French F, 1958, 1960; SF 1959. Won French mixed, 1956. Wimbledon QF, 1959, 1961. U.S. QF, 1957, 1959. Davis Cup: 1952–57; 27-6 singles, 10-8 doubles. Captained team to F, 1976, lost to Italy. Turned pro, 1961. World rank, No. 5 in 1958, 6 in 1959, 7 in 1960, 7 in 1961.

BADDELEY, HERBERT; WILFRED

English twins, Herbert and Wilfred Baddeley, RH, b. Jan. 11, 1872, Bromley. Made names at Wimbledon. In 1891 Wilfred, 19 years, 5 months, youngest singles champ for almost century, until Boris Becker, younger 19, 1985. Made F six straight years, winning also 1892, 1895. Linked as doubles team, twins made F seven straight years from 1891, winning 1891, 1894, 1895, 1896. In 1895 beat English Doherty brothers for the title, lost it in a reversal, 1897—only brotherly teams to square off for major title. Wilfred d. Jan. 30, 1929; Herbert d. July 20, 1931.

BARKER, SUE

One of last two Brits to make a major impression (along with Virginia Wade), 5-5 blonde Susan Barker, with forceful RH forehand, won French singles, 1976. Had three key singles wins in last British Wightman Cup victories over U.S.,

1974, 1975, 1978 (over Jeanne Evert, Janet Newberry, Tracy Austin). Wimbledon SF, 1977. Won 15 pro singles titles, $878,701. World No. 5, 1976 and 1977. Federation Cup, 1975–82, 15-8 singles, 16-6 doubles; Wightman Cup, 1974–83, 5-13 singles, 4-5 doubles. B. April 19, 1956, Paignton, England. Now a leading BBC telecaster.

BARRETT, ROPER

Herbert Roper Barrett, English RH, b. Nov. 24, 1873, Upton. An original Davis Cupper with losing British, 1900. Also played 1907, 1912, 1913, 1914; 0-2 singles, 4-4 doubles; captained Cup winners of 1933–1936. Had good long run, won Wimbledon doubles, 1909, 1912, 1913. In 1922, age 49, with Arthur Gore, 54, won historic 1st round over Duke of York (future King George VI) and Louis Grieg, only appearance of royalty on court. D. July 27, 1943, Horsham.

BERNARD, MARCEL

French LH, Marcel Bernard had no intention winning French, 1946. He was 32, rusty, planned to play only doubles, but said OK when they wanted to put him in the draw—startled everyone, including himself, by making F, beating favored Jaroslav Drobny, 5 sets. Also won doubles with Yvon Petra, 11 years after first French title, 1935, mixed with Lolette Payot. Davis Cup: 1935–56; 13-8 singles, 16-5 doubles. World rank, No. 5, 1946. B. May 18, 1914, La Madeleine, France, d. April 29, 1994.

BOLLETTIERI, NICK

Most renowned coach, effervescent Nicholas James Bollettieri, b. July 31, 1931, Pelham, N.Y., runs assembly line for champs, Bollettieri Tennis Academy, Bradenton, Fla. Ex–U.S. Army paratrooper, graduate of Spring Hill (Ala.), became teaching pro, 1958. Among pupils to make pro Top Ten: Andre Agassi, Jimmy Arias, Carling Bassett, Jim Courier, Aaron Krickstein, Monica Seles, Mary Pierce, Iva Majoli.

BOLTON, NANCYE

Nancye Meredith Wynne Bolton, RH Australian, career extended around World War II. B. June 10, 1916, Melbourne, prodigious winner of Australian titles (record 20 until topped by Margaret Court—6 singles, 10 doubles, 4 mixed). First Aussie woman in U.S. F, lost to Alice Marble, 1938. Won first Aussie title, 1936, last, 1952, both doubles. Won record 10 doubles (left court) with Thelma Coyne Long, first singles, 1937. Beat Long for singles title, 1940, again for title, 1951. Wimbledon QF, 1947. U.S. SF, 1947. Australian F, 1936, 1949; SF, 1938, 1950, 1952; QF, 1939. World rank, No. 10, 1938; No. 4, 1947, 1948, 1949.

BOOTHBY, PENELOPE

Penelope Dora Harvey Boothby, later Mrs. A. C. Geen, leading English player of her day. Won Wimbledon singles, 1909, doubles, 1913. But poor Dora, twice singles finalist, only double-bagel victim, losing 1911 title to Dorothea Douglass Chambers, 6-0, 6-0—two weeks after Chambers double-bageled her at Beckenham. RH, b. Aug. 2, 1881, Finchley, d. Feb. 22, 1970, London.

BOUMAN, KEA

Only Netherlander to win major women's singles, RH Katerina Cornelia "Kea" Bouman took French, 1927, also French doubles, 1929, Olympic bronze (mixed with Henk Timmer), 1924. Lauded by Bill Tilden as "very strong with good serve, hard forehand, excellent footwork." B. Nov. 23, 1903 in Almeto, quit to marry Swiss oarsman Alexander Tiedemann, 1931. World Nos. 9 and 8, 1927 and 1928, respectively.

BOWREY, LESLEY; BILL

Australian husband, wife, RH, scored singularly year of marriage, 1968, he winning Australian, she Italian.

Lesley Rosemary Turner Bowrey, b. Aug. 16, 1942, Sydney, had the stronger record, 12 major titles, including two French singles, 1963, 1965, all four major doubles. World rank, No. 2, 1963; No. 3, 1964, 1965; Top Ten four other years. Played for Australian Federation Cup winners, 1964, 1965; record: 7-2 singles, 8-3 doubles.

William Walter "Tex" Bowrey, b. Dec. 25, 1943, Sydney. Australian QF, 1965, 1967. U.S. QF, 1966. Doubles F Wimbledon, 1966; Australian, U.S., 1967, with Owen Davidson. Davis Cup: 1968, 1969; 2-2 singles, lost F, 1968.

BOYD, ESNA

Try, try again and again did Aussie Esna Boyd—does the sixth time never fail? Lost first five Australian singles finals, 1922–26, at last won, 1927, 5-7, 6-1, 6-2, over Sylvia Harper, then lapsed to second place again, 1927. One-sided RH, relied on strong flat forehand. B. 1901, Melbourne, d. 1962.

BRUGUERA, SERGI

Big, strong (6-2, 170), fast, ungainly Spanish RH (2-handed backhand) baseliner. Won French singles, 1993, 1994, SF 1995, with heavy, murderous topspin. World No. 4, 1993, 1994. Olympic silver medal, 1996. Davis Cup: 1990–96; 11-9 singles, 2-1 doubles. Turned pro 1988. Won 14 singles, 3 doubles pro titles, $9,520,901 through 1996. B. Jan. 16, 1971, Barcelona.

BUCHHOLZ, BUTCH

Man-about-every-phase of the game, Earl Henry "Butch" Buchholz, Jr., willowy 6-2 RH out of St. Louis was World No. 5, U.S. No. 3, 1960; Davis Cupper, 1959–60; barnstorming pro (U.S. Pro champ, 1962); Commissioner World Team Tennis, 1976–78, Executive Director ATP, 1981–82, and founder-operator of prime attraction Lipton Championships, since 1985, Key Biscayne, Fla. Had volley, has vision, uncommon tennis leader. B. Sept. 16, 1940, St. Louis. Right hand men at Lipton, brother Clifford Buchholz (ex–U.S. No. 18, 1966), son Trey Buchholz.

BUNDY, DOROTHY

Dorothy May "Dodo" Bundy Cheney, a most enduring champ, flowing from teens into superseniors. American RH, B. Sept. 1, 1916, Los Angeles, grew up in Santa Monica. Won Australian, 1938—keeps winning. First U.S. title, 1941, Indoor doubles, with Pauline Betz. Most recent, 1996, 80 Clay, Hart Court singles. End of '96, record total 270 U.S. senior titles, from 40s age group up (45, 50, 55, 60, 65, 70, 75, 80); beginning 1957. Hard Court-40 singles, 13 straight years. Included, 24 U.S. Senior Grand Slams: Grass, Clay, Hard, Indoor singles/doubles within calendar year, five in 70-singles, 1986, 1987, 1988, 1989, 1992, three in 75-singles, 1993, 1994, 1995. Great genes: Mother, Hall of Famer May Sutton Bundy, won Wimbledon, 1904; father, Tom Bundy, U.S. doubles champ, 1912, 1913, 1914.

CAPRIATI, JENNIFER

Jennifer Marie Capriati, American prodigy, RH with two-fisted backhand, b. March 29, 1976, New York, grew up in Florida. Attracted great attention as youngest pro finalist, making debut at 13 years, 11 months, Boca Raton, Fla., 1990, losing F to Gabriela Sabatini. Made numerous "youngest" marks: Federation Cupper (and winner), 1990; Wightman Cupper (and winner), 1989; Wimbledon SF, 1991; in U.S. Top Three (No. 3 in 1990, 2 in 1991, 2 in 1992, 2 in 1993). World rank (No. 8 in 1990, 6 in 1991, 7 in 1992, 9 in 1993). Olympic gold medalist, singles, 1992. Powerful 5-7 groundstroker, dethroned two major champs, 1991—Martina Navratilova, Wimbledon; Sabatini, U.S. Six career singles titles, $1,721,154 through 1996. Disenchantment with tennis, personal problems removed her 1994–95. Comeback, 1996, F Chicago, ended year No. 24.

CARILLO, MARY

Mary Jean Carillo Bowden, LH, b. March 15, 1957, New York. Played women's tour, collaborated with John McEnroe, his first major title, French mixed, 1977. Best known as tennis telecaster, ESPN, CBS, HBO, refreshingly informative, uninhibited style. Husband, Bill Bowden, teaching pro; 2 children.

CASH, PAT

Powerful Aussie RH (6-0, 185), career shortened by injuries. Strong server, excellent volleyer, Patrick Hart Cash hit high points: won Wimbledon singles 1987; led Davis Cup victories, 1983, 1986, and to F 1990; lost sensational Australian F, 1987–88. Won Cup clinchers over Sweden both years; in 1986, beat Stefan Edberg and, stirringly from 0-2 in sets, Mikael Pernfors. Davis Cup: 1983–90; 23-7 singles, 8-3 doubles. World Nos. 8 and 7, 1984 and 1987, respectively. B. May 27, 1965, Melbourne. Turned pro 1982. Won 6 singles, 10 doubles pro titles, $1,788,926 through 1996.

CHANG, MICHAEL

Diminutive (5-7), tenacious Michael Chang, RH American (two-handed backhand). Tireless retriever. B. Feb. 22, 1972, Hoboken, N.J., of Chinese-American parentage, reared in Southern California. Electrified French, 1989, as youngest male champ, 17, first American victor since 1955 (Tony Trabert). Beat favorite Ivan Lendl from 2-sets down 4th rd., Stefan Edberg in 5-set F. Lost longest major match (5:26) to Edberg, SF, U.S., 1992. Youngest to help U.S. win Davis Cup, 1990. In SF that year (3-2 over Austria at Vienna), won extraordinary deciding match from 2-sets down over Horst Skoff. Turned pro 1988. Twenty-six career singles titles, $13,844,909 through 1996. World rank, No. 5 in 1989, 6 in 1992, 8 in 1993, 6 in 1994, 5 in 1995, 2 in 1996. Australian SF and F, 1995 and 1996; French QF 1990, QF 1991, F 1995; U.S. SF 1992, QF 1993, QF 1995, F 1996. Davis Cup: 1989, 1990, 1996; 6-2 singles. Coached by brother, Carl, who played for U. of California, Berkeley.

COCHELL, EARL

Earl Cochell, RH American, created stir at U.S., Forest Hills, 1951, behaving erratically, disruptively, verbally assaulted referee Ellsworth Davenport, other court officials, while losing 4th rd. to Gardnar Mulloy. USTA reacted by banning him for life, unprecedented penalty. Ban later rescinded but had ended exceptional career of Top Ten amateur. Cochell, U.S. No. 8 in 1947, 6 in 1948, 7 in 1949, 7 in 1950, was no longer ranked, though 1951 play warranted another Top Ten spot. A Californian, won Intercollegiate doubles for USC, 1951. B. May 18, 1922, Sacramento.

COURIER, JIM

James Spencer Courier, ruggedly built 6-1 RH American with two-handed backhand, from Dade City, Fla. Parlayed ferocious groundstrokes to French titles, 1991, 1992; Australian titles, 1992, 1993; U.S. F, 1991. B. Aug. 17, 1970, Sanford, Fla. Helped U.S. win Davis Cup, 1992, 1995. U.S. No. 1, 1991, 1992. Won five singles titles, 1992, had 25-match win streak. Through 1996, won $12,734,485, 19 singles, 5 doubles pro titles. Australian QF in 1994, SF in 1995, QF in 1996; French F in 1993, SF in 1994, QF in 1996; Wimbledon QF in 1991, F in 1993; U.S. SF in 1995. World rank, No. 2 in 1991, 4 in 1992, 3 in 1993, 8 in 1995, 26 in 1996. Davis Cup: 1991, 1992, 1995; 9-7 singles. Turned pro, 1988.

COX, MARK

English LH, Cambridge grad, Mark Cox has niche as first amateur to beat a pro in open competition. Defeated Pancho Gonzalez, Roy Emerson successive April afternoons, gained SF, British Hard Court Championships, Bournemouth 1968, inaugural open. B. July 5, 1943, Leicester. Davis Cup 1967–69, 1973, 1978–79, helped Britain reach F, 1978, 15-6 singles, 8-6 doubles.

DALTON, JUDY

Judith Anne Marshall Tegart Dalton, Australian RH, b. Dec. 12, 1937, Melbourne. Tall, sturdy, excellent doubles player, won all majors—Australian, 1964, 1967, 1969, 1970; French, 1966; Wimbledon, 1969; U.S., 1970, 1971; five with Margaret Court. Wimbledon singles F, 1968. Helped Australia win 1970 Federation Cup, played 1965–67, 1969–70, 6-1 singles, 12-3 doubles. World rank No. 10 in 1967, 7 in 1968, 9 in 1971.

DATE, KIMIKO

Most successful modern-day Japanese, quick 5-4 Kimiko "Kid Butterfly" Date with flat groundies (2-handed backhand), excellent anticipation, natural LH transformed to RH. Surprisingly retired at 26, 1996, ranked World No. 9 (No. 9 in 1994, 4 in 1995). Best win, saved 2 match points over Steffi Graf, 7-6, (9-7), 3-6, 12-10, Federation Cup, 1996, led Japan to SF. Made SF Australian, 1994, French, 1995, Wimbledon, 1996; QF, U.S., 1993 and 1994. B. Sept. 28, 1970, Kyoto. Fed Cup, 1989 and 1996, 9-5 singles, 4-3 doubles. Turned pro 1988, won 7 pro singles titles, $1,974,253 through 1996.

DAVIDSON, OWEN

Owen Keir Davidson, LH Australian ladies man—mixed doubles ace. B. Oct. 4, 1943, Melbourne. Mixed Grand Slam, 1967, with Lesley Turner (Australian), Billie Jean King other three. Won eight major mixed plus two doubles: U.S., with John Newcombe, 1973; Australian, with Ken Rosewall, 1972. Wimbledon SF, 1966. Rookie pro, 1968, played, won first open match over amateur John Clifton, inaugural open, British Hard Court.

DAVIDSON, SVEN

Most prominent Swede prior to Bjorn Borg was Sven Viktor Davidson, RH b. July 13, 1928, Boras, Sweden. First Swede to win majors:

French singles, 1957, after losing 1955 and 1956 F; Wimbledon doubles, 1958, with Ulf Schmidt. World rank No. 3, 1957, in Top Ten six straight years from 1953. Davis Cup: 1950–1961; 39-14 singles, 23-9 doubles.

DMITRIEVA, ANNA

Russian pioneer, Anna Vladimirovna Dmitrieva was first Soviet permitted to play abroad, lost F Wimbledon junior 1956. LH, b. Dec. 16, 1940, Moscow, 5-4, 126. Won Soviet title, 1960 and 1964, also Algerian (over Françoise Durr), 1964, Czechoslovak, Hungarian, 1961 and 1962. Now outstanding Russian broadcaster. Federation Cup, 1968, 1-1 singles.

DRYSDALE, CLIFF

Eric Clifford Drysdale, best South African male, RH, with two-handed backhand. B. May 26, 1941, Nelspruit, Transvaal. Slim 6-2, deceptive groundstroker, good volleyer. First to use double-handed stroke in U.S. F, 1965, lost to Manolo Santana. Career spanned amateur, open eras. Wimbledon, French SF, 1965, 1966, became pro, 1968, WCT "Handsome Eight." U.S. QF, 1968 (beat favorite Rod Laver). Australian QF, 1971. Davis Cup: 1962–67, 1974; 30-12 in singles, helped South Africa win Cup, 1974. Became U.S. citizen. Won five singles, seven doubles (including U.S., 1972), pro titles. World rank, Top Ten five times, 1965, 1966, 1968, 1969, 1971, No. 4, 1965. Davis Cup: 1962–74, helped country win Cup, 1974; 32-12 singles, 3-2 doubles.

DURR, FRANÇOISE

Françoise Durr "Frankie" Browning. Best Frenchwoman since Suzanne Lenglen; last to win her country's singles title, 1967. RH. Deceptive: unorthodox grips, strokes, puffball serve made her seem harmless, but combative nature, pinpoint accuracy atoned for lack of power. B. Dec. 25, 1942, Algiers. Married Boyd Browning,

1975, lives in U.S. Turned pro, 1968, joining first female touring troupe (with Rosie Casals, Ann Jones, Billie Jean King). Excellent volleyer, won 11 majors in doubles, mixed, five straight French doubles (1967–71), a record tied by Martina Navratilova, plus two U.S. World rank, Top Ten nine times, 1965–76, No. 3, 1967. Had 41 career pro titles (8 singles, 33 doubles).

EDMONDSON, MARK

Mark "Eddo" Edmondson, husky 6-1 Aussie RH, longest-shot winner of men's major, Australian, 1976. B. June 28, 1954, Gosford. From obscurity (supported himself as janitor), unseeded, ranked No. 212, won homeland title. Beat all-timers, 2-1 seeds, Ken Rosewall, SF, John Newcombe, F. Thereafter, fine career. Wimbledon SF, 1982. Serve-and-volleyer, best at doubles: won French, 1985, Australian, 1980, 1981. Davis Cup: 1977–85; 11-7 singles, 8-3 doubles, helped win 1983 Cup (4-0 doubles, 2-0 singles). Won 6 singles, 35 doubles pro titles, $1,449,486 prize money. Best World rank, No. 20, 1981.

FERNANDEZ, GIGI

Great U.S. doubles performer, acrobatic volleyer (left court), RH beauty Beatriz Cristina "Gigi" Fernandez won 15 majors, 12 with Natasha Zvereva (4 French, 3 Wimbledon, 3 U.S., 2 Australian, second all-time team total). Also two Olympic golds, 1992, 1996, with Mary Joe Fernandez, no relation. She and Zvereva barely missed Grand Slams, 1993, lost SF, U.S., to Arantxa Sanchez Vicario–Helena Sukova, 1-6, 6-3, 6-4, ending 40-match major streak, and 1994, lost SF, U.S., to Katerina Maleeva–Robin White, 7-6 (7-2), 1-6, 6-3. Wimbledon singles SF, 1994. Best World ranking, No. 22, 1991. B. Feb. 22, 1964, San Juan, P.R. All-American, Clemson, 1983. Federation Cup, 1988, 1990, 1991, 1992, 1994, 1995, 1996; 3-1 singles, 19-1 doubles (won 1990, 1996 Cups). Wightman Cup, 1987–88; 2-0 doubles (won 2 Cups). Turned pro 1983. Through

1996 won 3 singles, 67 doubles pro titles, $4,276,024.

FIBAK, WOJTEK

Best Polish man, Wojtek Fibak, RH, b. Aug. 30, 1952, Poznan. Trained as lawyer. Late starter, first Polish pro, 22, despite opposition of Polish Federation, solid 13-year career. Davis Cup: 1972–92; 19-5 singles, 9-7 doubles. Agile 6-footer, superb volleyer, best at doubles, won 48 pro titles; also 15 singles titles; made $2,725,133. Lost Masters F, 1976. Wimbledon, U.S. QF, 1980; French QF, 1977, 1980. Best World rank, No. 13, 1977. Only Pole to win major: Australian doubles, 1978.

GARRISON, ZINA

Zina Lynna Garrison Jackson, American RH from Houston Public parks, won Olympic gold (doubles with Pam Shriver), bronze (singles), 1988. Gave Chris Evert her last defeat, QF U.S., 1989. First black woman in major F, Wimbledon, 1990, since Althea Gibson won there, 1958. Lost first pro F between two blacks, Largo, Fla., 1988, to childhood pal, Lori McNeil. Aggressive, quick, fine volleyer, b. Nov. 16, 1963, Houston. Married Willard Jackson, 1989. U.S. SF, 1988, 1989; QF, 1987, 1990. Wimbledon SF, 1985; QF, 1985, 1991. World Top Ten, No. 10 in 1983, 9 in 1984, 8 in 1985, 9 in 1987 and 1988, 4 in 1989, 10 in 1990. Turned pro 1982. Federation Cup: 1984–94; 7-4 singles, 14-2 doubles (with winner, 1989 and 1990). Wightman Cup: 1987 and 1988; 3-1 singles, 1-1 doubles (both winners, captain, 1988). Through 1996 won 14 pro singles, 20 doubles titles, $4,587,816.

GERULAITIS, VITAS

Vitas Kevin Gerulaitis, "Lithuanian Lion," speedy, RH, lean 6-footer, determined attacker, only American male to win Italian twice, 1977, 1979. Made French F, 1980. SF or better all majors. Won Australian, 1977. Stunning comeback U.S. SF, 1979, beat Roscoe Tanner from two sets and service break down. Lost F, John McEnroe, first all-American U.S. male F since Tony Trabert over Vic Seixas, 1953. That season won four of 22 tournaments on 75-21 match record. Davis Cup: 1977–80; 11-3 singles (1979, 5-1 for winner, including incredible SF escape from Mark Edmondson at Australia, triple match point at 7-8, 0-40 in 3rd to win, 6-8, 14-16, 10-8, 6-3, 6-3). Lost sensational 1977 5-set Wimbledon SF, Bjorn Borg, 8-6. French SF, 1979; QF, 1982. Wimbledon QF, 1976, 1982. U.S. SF, 1978, 1981. Won Wimbledon doubles, 1975. Lost Masters F, 1979, 1981. Won 27 singles, 9 doubles pro titles, $2,778,748. World Top Ten, 1977–82, No. 4 in 1977 and 1979. B. July 26, 1954, Brooklyn, N.Y., d. Sept. 17, 1994. Father, Vitas, champion of native Lithuania. Sister, Ruta, was on women's pro tour, No. 31, 1980; French QF, 1979.

GIMENO, ANDRES

Spanish RH, Andres Gimeno, oldest male winner French, 34, 1972. Best years as touring pro, from 1960, prior to open era. Graceful, slender 6-2, solid groundstrokes, good serve, competent volley. B. Aug. 3, 1937, Barcelona. Won seven singles, four doubles pro titles. Australian F, 1969; QF, 1959. French SF, 1968; QF, 1969. Wimbledon SF, 1970. Davis Cup: 1958–60, 1972–73; 18-5 singles, 5-5 doubles. World rank, No. 10, 1969, 1970, 1972.

GOMEZ, ANDRES

Lone Ecuadoran to win major, French 1990, 6-4 LH Andres "Gogo" Gomez beat favored Andre Agassi. Made 1984 QF French, Wimbledon, U.S., also French, 1986. Heavy server, sharp volleyer, smart user of spin, all-arounder won 21 singles, 34 doubles (French 1988) pro titles, $4,385,040, retired 1993. B. Feb. 27, 1960, Guayaquil. Davis Cup: 1979–93; 30-12 singles, 13-10 doubles.

GORE, ARTHUR

Arthur William Charles Gore (unrelated to first champ, Spencer Gore). English RH, became Wimbledon's most enduring player, thrice singles victor (1901, 1908, 1909), oldest major male champ last year, 41½. First entered 1888, continued in singles through 1922, age 54 (oldest such), doubles through 1927, totaling 156 matches over record 35 years. Was most productive singles player (64-26), now second to Jimmy Connors (84-17). B. Jan. 2, 1868, Lyndhurst, d. Dec. 1, 1928, London.

GORE, SPENCER

Spencer William Gore, English RH, b. March 10, 1850, Wimbledon; d. April 19, 1906, Ramsgate, England. Game's original champ, Wimbledon, 1877. Lost F, 1878. Ex-rackets champ, not overly taken by tennis.

GOTTFRIED, BRIAN

Brian Edward Gottfried, hard-working, energetic 6-foot RH. Sound groundstrokes, preferred serve-and-volley. B. Jan. 27, 1952, Baltimore, raised in Florida, All-American, Trinity (Tex.), 1971-72, lost F Intercollegiate singles, doubles, 1972. Davis Cup: 1976–82; 6-7 singles, 1-0 doubles (with 1978 winner). QF or better all majors but Aussie, lost F French, 1977, to Guillermo Vilas. Heavy-duty 1977: won 5 of 27 tournaments, 108-23 record. U.S. Top Ten, 11 years, 1972–83, No. 2 in 1977, 3 in 1978. World Top Ten, No. 10 in 1976, 5 in 1977, 7 in 1978. With Raul Ramirez won 39 doubles, including Wimbledon, French, Italian. Won 25 singles, 54 doubles pro titles, $2,782,514.

GOOLD, ST. LEGER

Vere Thomas "St. Leger" Goold, Wimbledon F, 1879, RH. Personal finale, death in prison, was most ignominious for a champ. Won native (Irish) championship, 1879, skilled volleyer. Played as "St. Leger" (pseudonyms not uncommon at time), lost F, Wimbledon, to John Hartley before crowd of 1,100. In 1907, with French wife, Violet Girodin, convicted in French court of murdering Emma Levin, given life sentence. D. Sept. 8, 1909, Devils Island, French Guiana. B. Oct. 2, 1853, Waterford.

GRAEBNER, CAROLE; CLARK

American couple, RH Carole and Clark Graebner, only husband-wife to rank World Top Ten, play major F while married. Fourth couple ranked U.S. Top Ten same years, following Sarah and Elwood Cooke (1940, 1945), Marjorie and John Van Ryn (1930, 1931), Virginia and Frank Kovacs (1941). Teammates, Cleveland, World Team Tennis, 1974. However, during divorce proceedings he, player-coach, traded her to Pittsburgh for Laura DuPont, a unique divestiture.

Carole Caldwell Graebner, b. June 24, 1943, Pittsburgh, grew up in Southern California. Baseliner, good volleyer. U.S., lost F, 1964, to Maria Bueno, 6-1, 6-0 (equaling worst such beating, original F, 1884, Ellen Hansell over Laura Knight). World rank, No. 4 in 1964, 9 in 1965. U.S. Top Ten, 1961–65, 1967, No. 3 in 1964 and 1965. Federation Cup: 1963–66; 2-1 singles, 10-0 doubles (with winner, 1963, 1966). Wightman Cup: 1963–65, 1967, 1971; 2-0 singles, 2-2 doubles (with five winners).

Clark Edward Graebner, b. Nov. 4, 1943, Cleveland, grew up there. Strong, 6-2, serve-and-volleyer. Lost U.S. F, 1967, SF, 1968; Wimbledon SF, 1968. World rank, No. 8 in 1967, 7 in 1968. U.S. Top Ten, 1964, 1966–72, No. 2 in 1968, No. 3 in 1966, 1971. Davis Cup: 1965–68; 9-2 singles; 5-2 doubles (with 1968 winner). Won U.S. Indoor, 1971; Clay, 1966, French doubles, 1966.

GREGORY, COLIN

Covering remarkable spread of almost three decades, Davis Cup career of Dr. John Colin Gregory, English physician, concluded in triumph. He, playing captain, oldest to win Cup match: 48 years,

295 days, with Tony Mottram, beat Josip Pallada–Stevan Laszlo, Yugoslavia, 6-4, 1-6, 9-11, 6-2, 6-2, 1952, Belgrade, making the difference in Brits' 3-2 win. Good-humored Yorkshire RH, b. July 28, 1903, Beverly, took a major 23 years before, Australian singles, 1929; same year lost Wimbledon doubles F. Davis Cup: 1926–52; 13-9 singles, 8-1 doubles. D. Sept. 10, 1959, Wimbledon.

GULLIKSON, TIM; TOM

Identical twins, RH Timothy Ernest, LH Thomas Robert Gullikson, b. Sept. 8, 1951, LaCrosse, Wis., Tom elder by minutes. Graduates, Northern Illinois. Lost Wimbledon F, 1983, first twins in major F since English Baddeleys, 1897. Sturdy, 5-11, 185, attackers, won 10 pro doubles titles together. Tim, best World rank No. 18, 1978, won 4 singles, 16 doubles pro titles, $1,120,570. Tom, best World rank, No. 56, 1981, won 1 singles, 12 doubles pro titles, $889,042. Each won U.S. original, Newport, Tim, 1977, Tom, 1985. Tim, d. May 3, 1996, coached Pete Sampras to six majors. Tom, U.S. Davis Cup captain, 1994— (won, 1995).

HADOW, FRANK

Patrick Francis Hadow, English RH, b. Jan. 24, 1855, Regents Park; d. June 29, 1946, Bridgwater. Loftiest Wimbledon champ: introduced the lob to thwart, bring down volleyer Spencer Gore, defender, second Wimbledon F, 1878. Lost no sets in tourney, played on holiday from his tea plantation in Ceylon. Didn't return to defend, may never have played again.

HAMILTON, GHOST

Irish RH, pale, frail-looking. Gave Willie Renshaw only loss in Wimbledon F, 1890, depriving him of eighth title, RH Willoughby James "Ghost" Hamilton from County Kildare made brief mark. Illness (blood poisoning) prevented him from defending. B. Dec. 8, 1864, Monasterevan, d. Sept. 27, 1943, Dublin.

HARTIGAN, JOAN

An international trail-blazer for Aussie women, tall RH Joan Hartigan reached World Top Ten ranking, No. 8 in 1934 and 9 in 1935, when she reached Wimbledon SF (lost to Helen Jacobs, champ Helen Moody after beating defender Dorothy Round). B. 1912, Sydney, rode puissant forehand from baseline to Australian singles titles, 1934, 1935, 1937; QF, 1937, 1938, 1946; SF, 1939, 1940. Also won mixed, 1937. Married Hugh Bathurst in 1947.

HARTLEY, JOHN

English clergyman, only such to win major, Wimbledon singles 1879 and 1880. Rev. John Thorneycroft Hartley, RH, Oxford grad, extremely steady, unerring, but overwhelmed in 1881 F as Willie Renshaw launched 6-title run. B. Jan. 9, 1849, Tong, England, d. Aug. 21, 1935, Knaresborough, England.

HAWKES, JACK

Unpredictable LH Australian, good twist serve and volley. John Bailey Hawkes won Aussie title 1926, also doubles (left court) with Gerald Patterson, 1922, 1926, 1927. Had 7 match points but lost 1927 F to Patterson. They lost Wimbledon F 1928. World No. 10, 1928. Davis Cup: 1921–23; 6-7 singles, 5-2 doubles. B. June 7, 1899, Geelong, Australia, died there, May 31, 1990.

HEATH, ROD

Wilfrid Rodney Heath, First Australian male champ, RH, won at 21 in hometown, Melbourne, 1905, conquering field of 17 at Warehousemen's Cricket Ground, beating Dr. A. H. Curtis' volleying with forehand drives. Won again, 1910. Davis Cup: 1911, 1912; 1-2 singles. After aviation duty, World War I, lost Wimbledon doubles F, 1919, with Randolph Lycett, SF victim in 1905 Aussie. B. June 15, 1884, Melbourne, d. there Oct. 6, 1936.

HELLWIG, HELEN

Helen Rebecca Hellwig, RH out of Brooklyn, was sixth to win U.S. women's title, 1894, at 20, deposing Aline Terry, 5 sets. She and Juliette Atkinson first team to repeat in women's doubles, 1894 and 1895. Reappeared 12 years later, SF, 1907, QF, 1908, as Mrs. William Pouch. Last played 1916 at 42, had 14-8 U.S. singles record. B. March, 1874, Brooklyn, d. Nov. 26, 1960, New York.

HENKEL, HENNER

The younger of Germany's splendid pre–World War II one-two punch, RH 6-foot Henner Ernst Otto Henkel was dead at 29, a soldier killed on Stalingrad front, Dec. 3, 1944. He and Gottfried von Cramm nearly won Davis Cup, 1937, 3-2 SF loss to U.S. They were World Nos. 3 and 2, won French and U.S. doubles; Henkel won French singles. He was also No. 9 in 1936 and 6 in 1939. Davis Cup: 1935–39; 32-13 singles, 16-4 doubles (also made SF 1935, 1936, 1938). Wimbledon SF, 1938, 1939; QF, 1938. B. Oct. 9, 1915, Posen, Germany.

HILLYARD, BLANCHE BINGLEY

Hardy, enthusiastic Englishwoman, Blanche Bingley Hillyard played first female Wimbledon, 1884, still around 29 years later, 1913, her last of 17. Won 6, a record 14-year spread from 1886 to last, 1900, at 36, second-oldest female champ. RH, b. Nov. 3, 1863, Greenford, d. Aug. 6, 1946, Pulborough. At Wimbledon, 48-18 in singles, record 13 F. Best comeback in F, 1889, beat Lena Rice, 4-6, 8-6, 6-4, from 3-5, 3 match points, 2nd set. Also won three Irish, two German. Her 1912 victim, rookie Bunny Ryan, made Hall of Fame.

HINGIS, MARTINA

Martina II, named for Ms. Navratilova, fulfilled promise envisioned by mother Melanie Molitorova. Extraordinarily poised, thoughtful RH (2-handed backhand) 5-6 strokemaker, Martina Maria Hingis debuted as pro at 14, Zurich, 1994, near home, Trubbach. Ended 1996 at World No. 4: SF, U.S., won first pro singles titles, Filderstadt, Oakland (beat Monica Seles, 6-2, 6-0, F), lost WTA F to Steffi Graf, 5 sets. Won doubles (with Helena Sukova), became Wimbledon's greenest champ, 15, 3 days younger than Lottie Dod, 1887 singles winner. Had 50-16 singles matches, made $1,330,996; represented Switzerland in Olympics, Federation Cup. B. Sept. 30, 1980, Kosice, Czechoslovakia (now Slovakia).

HOMANS, HELEN

Helen Homans, a New Yorker, started as U.S. champ in doubles, 1905, losing singles F, turned it around 1906, winning singles, losing doubles. B. 1878 or 1879, d., as Mrs. McLean, March 29, 1949, age 70, Bronxville, N.Y. Brother, Shep Homans, better known athlete, All-American fullback at Princeton, 1890–91.

IVANISEVIC, GORAN

Spidery yet powerful Croatian, Goran Ivanisevic, 6-5 LH. Huge server, streaky, strong strokes. B. Sept. 13, 1971, Split. Only man from his country to play Wimbledon F: 1992, lost to Andre Agassi; 1994, lost to Pete Sampras. First in major F since fellow townsman, Nikki Pilic, French, 1973. Served Wimbledon record 206 aces, 1992; season total, record 1,603, 1996. Won Olympic bronzes, singles, doubles (with Goran Prpic), 1992. Wimbledon SF, 1990. French QF, 1990, 1992, 1994; Australian QF, 1989, 1994. U.S. SF, 1996. World Top Ten, No. 9 in 1990, 4 in 1992, 7 in 1993, 5 in 1994, 10 in 1995, 4 in 1996. Through 1996 won 17 singles, 7 doubles pro titles, $13,935,780.

JAEGER, ANDREA

Peppery, meteoric 5-3, 105-pound blonde prodigy, Andrea Jaeger was one of youngest ranked in World Top Ten: No. 5 at age 15, 1980. Also No. 6 in 1981, 3 in 1982, 4 in 1983, then virtually finished by injuries like contemporary rival of similar style, Tracy Austin. Fast, competitive, hard-hitting RH (2-handed backhand) baseliner, youngest champ U.S. Clay Court singles, 1981. Lost two major F, to Martina Navratilova: French, 1982 (defeated Chris Evert, SF), Wimbledon, 1983 (defeated Billie Jean King, SF). Both 16, she and Jimmy Arias won French mixed, 1981 (youngest team to win major doubles). Played Federation (1981 winner), 8-1 singles, and Wightman Cups (1980, 1981 winners), 2-1 singles, 1-0 doubles, for U.S. B. June 4, 1965, Chicago, raised Lincolnshire, Ill. Won 14 pro singles titles, $1,379,066. Admirably selfless adult, she fund-raises, operates Silver Lining Ranch for terminally ill kids, Aspen, Colorado.

JEDRZEJOWSKA, JADWIGA

Jadwiga "JaJa" Jedrzejowska, best Polish woman, mouthful for umpires, handful for foes. RH, b. Oct. 15, 1912, Cracow; d. Feb. 28, 1980, Katowice. Married Alfred Gallert, 1947. Only Pole in major singles F. Wimbledon, 1937 (beat Alice Marble, lost F to Dorothy Round, 7-5, 3rd, led, 4-1); U.S., 1937, lost first all-foreign F to Anita Lizana, Chile; French, 1939, won doubles with Simone Mathieu. Husky, good-natured baseliner with battering forehand. World Top Ten, 1936–1939, No. 3 in 1937.

JONES, HENRY

Gamesplaying appealed more than medicine to Dr. Henry Jones, English physician who operated only as a sports scribbler for the *Field* (pen name "Cavendish"). Smitten by lawn tennis, he proposed its introduction at All England Club, helped organize the original Wimbledon, 1877, ran the show as referee. B. Nov. 2, 1831, at London, d. Feb. 10, 1899.

JORDAN, BARBARA; KATHY

American sisters, Barbara and Kathy Jordan, King of Prussia, Pa. RH, All-Americans, Stanford, then winners major titles. Only sisters in major singles F (both in Australian) since Maud and Lillian Watson clashed for first Wimbledon title, 1884. Kathy higher rated.

Barbara Jordan, b. April 2, 1957, Milwaukee. Smooth-stroking serve-and-volleyer. Long-shot winner Australian, 1979 (unseeded, ranked No. 68), only American champ 1970s, beat favorite Hana Mandlikova (1980 and 1987 champ), and Sharon Walsh, won $10,000, high in career $135,534. Only pro singles title; won two doubles, plus major mixed, French, 1983. Best World rank, No. 37, 1980.

Kathryn "KJ" Jordan, b. Dec. 3, 1959, Bryn Mawr, Pa. Willowy, 5-8, attacker, awkward-looking but effective stroker, extreme Western forehand, excellent volleyer. Won Intercollegiate singles, doubles, 1979, then turned pro. QF or better all major singles, doubles. Wimbledon SF, 1984; QF, 1983, beating Chris Evert, 3rd rd., first of two times in 19 years Evert failed to make SF. Lost Australian F, 1983, to Martina Navratilova. Won all major doubles: Australia, U.S., 1981; French, 1980; Wimbledon, 1980, 1985, latter with Liz Smylie, ending Navratilova–Pam Shriver 109-match streak. Won 1 singles, 39 doubles (of 71 F) pro titles, $1,592,111, plus Wimbledon mixed. As rookie, minor circuit, won San Antonio, 1979, through pre-qualifying, qualifying, main draw—13 wins, a record. Federation Cup: 1980–85; 6-3 singles, 17-1 doubles (with 1980 and 1981 winners). Wightman Cup: 1979–80; 1-1 singles, 1-0 doubles (both winners). Best World rank, No. 11 in 1979, 13 in 1980, 10 in 1984.

KAFELNIKOV, YEVGENY

Smooth, confident RH (2 handed backhand), Yevgeny Kafelnikov of Sochi only Russian to win major singles, French, 1996, over Michael Stich. Best of that area since Soviet (Georgian) Alex Metreveli (Wimbledon F, 1973, World No. 9, 1974). World No. 6 in 1995, 3 in 1996. B. Feb.

18, 1974, Sochi, 6-3 blond, prefers baseline, though sharp volleyer. Rare singles-doubles combiner today, also won French doubles, 1996: first to score major double since Ken Rosewall, Australian, 1972, at French since Rosewall, 1968. Davis Cup: 1993–96, 18-5 singles, 6-4 doubles, led homeland to F, 1994–1995. Turned pro 1992, won 11 singles, 15 doubles pro titles, $5,715,734 through 1996.

KELLEHER, BOB

Robert Joseph Kelleher, progressive USTA president—right man at right time—shepherded U.S. into open era, 1968, overcoming past organizational objections to "open" concept, backed British revolt against ITF. B. March 5, 1913, New York. Graduate Williams, Harvard Law ('38). Longtime resident Los Angeles, appointed federal judge, 1970. U.S. Davis Cup captain, 1962–63, won 1963. Good player. Won U.S. Hard Court 45s doubles with Elbert Lewis, 1958, 1960, 1962. Wife, Gracyn Wheeler Kelleher (1914–80), U.S. No. 5, 1941.

KINGSCOTE, ALGIE

Algernon Robert Fitzhardinge "Algie" Kingscote, World War I hero, English RH, journeyed Down Under in 1919 to play in Britain's losing Davis Cup cause, but won Australian singles. Wimbledon SF, 1919, QF, 1920, 1921 (lost in 5 to champ Bill Tilden, '20). Sound all-around. World No. 5 in 1919, 3 in 1920. Davis Cup: 1914, 1924; 7-6 singles, 2-2 doubles. B. 1888, India.

KORMOCZI, SUZI

Hungary's best woman, Suzi Kormoczi was persistent baseliner, patient pursuing success. RH, b. Aug. 25, 1924, Budapest. First entered French, 1947, won 1958, oldest champ, almost 34. Oldest champ Italian, 1960. Wimbledon SF, 1958; French F, 1959, SF, 1956, 1961. World Top Ten seven times, 1953, 1955, 1956, 1958, 1959, 1960, 1961, No. 2 in 1958.

KRAJICEK, RICHARD

A fabulous 1996 fortnight was his: Wimbledon's second unseeded champ, Richard Krajicek, Netherlands' only winner of a men's major. Gangling 6-5 RH, he ranked No. 13 coming in, had a case to dissent to non-seed but let his racket be his bombastic mouthpiece, especially with serve, backhand. Romped on loss of one set, ended No. 1 Pete Sampras' 25-match Big W streak, QF, took F from Mal Washington fast. B. Dec. 6, 1971, Rotterdam, parents defected from Czechoslovakia. Australian SF, 1992; French QF, 1996. Davis Cup: 1991–95; 4-6 singles, 1-0 doubles. World No. 10 in 1992, 11 in 1995, 7 in 1996. Won 10 singles, 3 doubles pro titles, $5,050,775 through 1996.

KRIEK, JOHAN

Swift, compact, fine volleying 5-8 RH, Johan Christian Kriek reached peak on Down Under grass, won Australian, 1981, 1982; SF, 1984, QF, 1983, 1985. South African farm boy by birth, April 5, 1958, Pongola, became U.S. citizen, 1982. French SF, 1986; Wimbledon QF, 1982; U.S. SF, 1980, QF, 1978, 1979. Won 14 pro singles titles (including South African, 1983, U.S. Indoor over John McEnroe, 1982), 8 doubles, $2,381,844. Best World Rank, No. 12 in 1981, 13 in 1982 and 1984.

KRISHNAN, RAMANATHAN; RAMESH

Father, son, Ramanathan and Ramesh Krishnan, possibly India's best. Unique, both helping homeland to Davis Cup finales, reaching QF, Wimbledon. RH, clever, deceptive. Born, raised in Madras.

Ramanathan Krishnan, b. April 11, 1932, World Top Ten, 1959–62, No. 6 in 1961. Davis Cup: 18 years, 1953–69, 1976; 50-20 singles, 19-9 doubles; led India to finale, 1966. Wimbledon SF, 1960, 1961.

Ramesh Krishnan, b. June 5, 1961, pro since 1976, best World rank, No. 24 in 1980. QF, Wimbledon, 1986; U.S., 1981, 1987. Davis Cup: 11 years between 1978 and 1992; 23-19 singles, 6-2 doubles (won 5 of 8 singles, leading India to 1987 F). Won 8 singles, 1 doubles pro titles, $1,235,548.

LANGRISHE, MAY

Mary Isabella Langrishe, original female champ—and youngest, 14, to win national title. Won her own, Irish, 1879 (the inaugural, Dublin's Fitzwilliam Club, first to welcome women). RH, b. Dec. 31, 1864, Ireland. Beat D. Meldon, 6-2, 0-6, 8-6, to rule field of seven. Also won first female doubles title, Northern Championship, Manchester, England, 1882, with older sister. D. Jan. 24, 1939.

LARCOMBE, ETHEL

English RH Ethel Warneford Thomson Larcombe jolted Charlotte Cooper Sterry's hopes of 7th Wimbledon title, beat her in 1912 F. Played at both ends of World War I, losing Wimbledon singles, doubles F, 1914, doubles F, 1919, 1920. Won Irish (1912), Scottish (1910) titles. Fine athlete, won All England badminton singles 1900, 1901, 1903, 1904, 1906, doubles 1902, 1904, 1906, mixed 1903, 1906. Married Dudley Larcombe, 1906. B. June 8, 1879, Islington, d. Aug. 11, 1965, Budleigh Salterton. Became teaching pro, 1922.

LAWFORD, HERBERT

Herbert Fortescue Lawford, English RH innovator, Wimbledon champ, 1887. Introduced topspin—known as "Lawford Stroke"—around 1880, first of his six years in title round. B. May 15, 1851, Bayswater; d. April 20, 1925, Dess, Scotland.

LIZANA, ANITA

Chilean RH Anita Lizana, a significant blip—played U.S. Championships once, 1937,

and won, over Pole Jadwiga Jedrzejowska, first all-foreign F. First Latin American to win a major. B. 1915, Santiago, married Ronald Ellis, settled in England. Wimbledon QF, 1936 (led champ Helen Jacobs, 4-2, 30-0 in 3rd) and 1937. Solid groundstroker with good passing shots, drop shot, admirable footwork. World rank, No. 8 in 1936, 1 in 1937.

LONG, THELMA

Thelma Dorothy Coyne Long, sturdy Australian RH, b. Oct. 14, 1918, Sydney. Had one of longest careers, fine volleyer, winning first of record 12 Australian doubles, 1936, last, 1958. Also won singles, 1952, 1954, mixed four times; French mixed, 1956—total 19 majors. Australian F, 1940, 1951, 1955, 1956; SF, 1947, 1949. World rank, No. 7, 1952.

MAIN, LORNE

Lorne Garnet Main, inadvertent father of rare two-way, two-handed style, both forehand and backhand. Foremost proponent today, Monica Seles. "Seemed natural to me as a boy since I was a baseball switch-hitter." Canadian RH, 5-8, 145, b. July 9, 1930, Vancouver. Davis Cup: 1949–55. No. 1, Canada, 1951–54. Biggest title, Monte Carlo, 1954. Davis Cup, 1949–55, 10-11 singles, 4-3 doubles.

LOWE, GORDON; ARTHUR

Francis Gordon Lowe, English RH, won last pre–World War I Australian, 1915. B. June 21, 1884, Edgbaston, Cambridge grad, d. May 17, 1972, London. Davis Cup: 1921–25; 8-6 singles. Brother, RH Arthur Holden Lowe, b. Jan. 29, 1886, Edgbaston, Oxford grad, d. Oct. 22, 1958, London. Also British Davis Cup: 1911–19; 0-5 singles. Both World Top Ten, 1914: Arthur No. 7, Gordon No. 8. At ages 37 and 35, became fourth of five sets of brothers in Wimbledon doubles F, lost, 1921.

MAHONY, HAROLD

Tall, quick-tempered RH Irishman Harold Segerson Mahony won Wimbledon, 1896, unseating Wilfred Baddeley, a fleeting success before Doherty brothers took over. B. Feb. 13, 1867, Edinburgh, d. June 27, 1904, Caragh Hill, Ireland.

MALEEVA, MANUELA; KATERINA; MAGDALENA

Internationally most exceptional trio of sisters ever, clearly greatest in Bulgaria annals. All three—baselining RH with two-handed backhands, born and brought up in Sofia—played for Bulgaria in Federation Cup, Olympics. Mother, Yulia Berberian, champion of Bulgaria nine years; father, Gyorgy Maleev, Olympic basketball player, 1956. Unique accomplishments: Katerina, Manuela in World Top Ten together, 1990, have been in QF every major, together at French, 1990, only sisters to do so. Manuela's 1992 U.S. QF win over Maggie (winner over Martina Navratilova) first such sisterly encounter since 1897 champ Juliette Atkinson beat sibling, Kathleen, SF. Manuela, Katerina in 1988 U.S. QF, first sisters there since Atkinsons. Manuela in U.S. QF five times, 1990 by beating Navratilova.

Manuela Maleeva Fragniere, 5-8, b. Feb. 14, 1967. Won rain-delayed Italian, 1984, three wins last day, F over Chris Evert. Won Olympic bronze, singles, 1988. Married Swiss tennis coach François Fragniere, 1987, became a citizen, played Federation Cup, 1992 Olympics for Switzerland. Through 1994 retirement had 19 singles, 5 doubles pro titles, $3,034,945. World Top Ten, 1984–92, No. 6 in 1984 and 1988. Federation Cup, 1984–87, 1989, 1991–92, 21-5 singles, 7-10 doubles.

Katerina Maleeva, 5-6, b. May 7, 1969, won Japan Open, 1987. Through 1996 had 12 singles, 5 doubles pro titles, $1,936,887. Best World rank, No. 6, 1990. Federation Cup, 1984–89, 1991–95, 20-9 singles, 9-13 doubles.

Magdalena "Maggie" Maleeva, 5-6, b. April 1, 1975, won first pro title, San Marino, 1992.

Through 1996 won 6 singles, 2 doubles pro titles, $1,533,159. Best World rank, No. 6, 1995. Federation Cup, 1991–95, 7-2 singles, 3-3 doubles.

MARTINEZ, CONCHITA

Only Spanish woman to win Wimbledon, 1994, thwarted Martina Navratilova's bid for 10th title in F with topspinning groundies, backhand passers. Quick, 5-7 RH, top-notch performer all majors: SF Australian, 1995, 1996; French, 1994, 1996; Wimbledon, 1993; U.S., 1995, 1996. Won record three straight Italian, 1994–96. Best year, 1995. Won six singles titles. With Arantxa Sanchez Vicario, made Spain dominant in Federation Cup, played 1988–96, won 1991, 1993–1995; 36-7 singles, 15-5 doubles. Olympic silver, 1992, bronze, 1996 (doubles with Sanchez Vicario). B. April 16, 1972, Monzon, Spain. Turned pro 1988. World Top Ten 1991–96; No. 4 in 1993, 3 in 1994, 2 in 1995, 4 in 1996. Won 28 singles, 5 doubles pro titles, $6,149,266 through 1996.

MATHIEU, SIMONE PASSEMARD

Following Suzanne Lenglen, Simone Passemard Mathieu was best French woman prior to World War II. B. Jan. 11, 1908, Neuilly-sur-Seine; was a heroine in the Resistance during the war; d. Jan. 7, 1980, Paris. Married Rene Mathieu, 1925. Steady, accurate, maintained consistently high level. Won French, 1938, 1939, after losing F, 1932, 1933, 1936, 1937. Wimbledon SF, 1930, 1931, 1932, 1934, 1936, 1937; QF, 1933, 1935, 1938, 1939. U.S. QF, 1938. Also won nine major doubles (three Wimbledon, 1933, 1934, 1937, six French, 1933, 1934, 1936, 1937, 1938, 1939, record until Martina Navratilova's seven). World Top Ten 11 straight years from 1929, No. 3 in 1932.

MAYER, SANDY; GENE

American brothers, Sandy and Gene Mayer, RH, winners of major doubles, one together (French, 1979, only brothers to do so), first brothers to win major since Bob and Howard Kinsey, U.S., 1924. Also only brothers to rank together U.S. Top Ten, 1983 (Gene higher, 4-8), World Top Fifteen, 1981 (Gene higher, 7-14), and make Wimbledon QF open era. Family total, 65 pro singles, doubles titles. Stanford grads, All-Americans.

Alexander "Sandy" Mayer, b. April 5, 1952, Flushing, N.Y., sleek 5-10 attacker, excellent volleyer, won Intercollegiate singles, 1973, doubles, 1972, 1973. Wimbledon SF, 1973 (rookie pro beat top seed Ilie Nastase, 4th rd., huge upset); QF, 1978, 1983. Won Wimbledon doubles, 1975. Best World rank, No. 14, 1981. Won 11 singles, 24 doubles pro titles, $1,057,783.

Eugene Mayer, b. April 11, 1956, New York, slender 6-footer, rare unorthodox style: both-handed backhand, forehand. Solid groundstroker, good volleyer. Davis Cup: 1982–83; helped win 1982 (3-1, singles). Wimbledon QF, 1980, 1982; U.S. QF, 1982. World Top Ten 1980–84, No. 4 in 1980, winning five titles. Won 14 singles, 16 doubles pro titles, $1,381,562.

McATEER, MYRTLE

Myrtle McAteer from Pittsburgh was in three U.S. women's F, winning singles, 1900, doubles, 1899 and 1901. Lost F doubles, 1900, mixed 1901. After losing singles title in 5-set battle with Bessie Moore, didn't play again. No details known on b. or d. U.S. singles record (5-1).

McGRATH, VIV

Vivian "Viv" McGrath, pronounced "Mc-Graw," Australian original: RH, introduced two-handed backhand to international game, considered strongest pre-war shot among Aussies. B. Feb. 17, 1916, Mudgee; d. 1978, Buradee. Called "Wonder Boy," at 16, beat World No. 1 Ellie Vines, QF, Australian, 1933. Won that title, 1937, over another rising double-hander, Jack Bromwich. Also Australian SF, 1934, 1935, 1939, 1940; QF, 1932, 1936, 1938. Wimbledon QF, 1935, 1937. Youngest Aussie Davis Cupper:

1933–37; 11-12 singles, 1-2 doubles (4-4 singles, 1933, as team lost European Zone F, 3-2, at Britain, eventual winner). World No. 8 in 1935, 10 in 1936. Unable to regain form after army service in war.

McGREGOR, KEN

Ex–Australian rules football star, 6-3, 180-pound RH Kenneth Bruce McGregor, b. June 2, 1929, Adelaide, teamed with Frank Sedgman to revive Aussie fortunes. They took Davis Cup from U.S., 1950, 4-1; he upset Ted Schroeder first day. Repeated as Cup-winning singles-doubles pair, 1951 and 1952. Three straight Aussie singles F, won last, 1952, over world No. 1 Sedgman. Lost Wimbledon F, 1951. Smashing serve-and-volleyer. With Sedgman made only male doubles Grand Slam 1951, ending Bromwich-Quist's 8-straight grip at Aussie. They won all but U.S. in 1952. Davis Cup: 1950–52; 4-3 singles, 2-0 doubles. World Top Ten No. 8 in 1950, 7 in 1951, 3 in 1952. Turned pro with Sedgman 1953.

MECIR, MILOSLAV

Slovak RH (2-handed backhand) Miloslav "Gattone" Mecir (Big Cat), 6-3, 180, was Czechoslovakia's best, 1985–89. Quick, clever, deceptively mixed speeds, spins, angles. Took Olympic gold, singles, 1988. Davis Cup: 1983–89; 18-8 singles, 5-1 doubles. Lost F, U.S., 1986; Australian, 1989; QF U.S. and Australian, 1987. Wimbledon SF, QF, 1988, 1986; French SF, 1987. Turned pro 1982. B. May 19, 1964, Bojnice, Czechoslovakia, career ended 1991 by back problems. Won 10 singles, 9 doubles pro titles, $2,632,538.

METREVELI, ALEXANDER

Foremost Soviet man, Alexander Metreveli gained prominence open era, beating Pancho Gonzalez, Wimbledon, 1968. Georgian RH, b. Feb. 11, 1944, Tblisi. Atypical Soviet, serve-and-volleyer, poised 5-10. Only USSR male in major

F, until Yevgeny Kafelnikov (French 1996), lost Wimbledon, 1973. Also, with Olga Morozova, lost F Wimbledon mixed, 1968, 1970. In career overlapping amateur, open eras, QF or better all majors. Davis Cup standout, 14 years, spanning 1963 to 1980, one of select few to have played 100 matches or more (56-14, singles; 24-11, doubles). Best World rank, No. 13, 1974. Won eight singles, two doubles pro titles.

MOLESWORTH, MALL

Margaret "Mall" Mutch Molesworth, first Australian women's champ. RH, b. 1894, Brisbane; d. July 9, 1985. Might have exceeded two singles, 1922, 1923; three doubles, 1930, 1933, 1934, had Championships welcomed women prior to 1922, Sydney. Won first title at 27, with complete game, feared serve. Remained factor for some time: lost F, 1934 to Joan Hartigan.

MOON, GAR

"New star is born—it's a Moon!" declared an Aussie newspaper when Edgar Moon, Queensland RH, beat 1922 Wimbledon champ Gerald Patterson, 1st rd. Australian, 1926. He won title, 1930, over Harry Hopman, beating future champ Jack Crawford, SF, won Aussie doubles with Crawford, 1932. Strong groundies, all-round game. Davis Cup, 1930, 4-0 in singles. B. Dec. 3, 1904, Forest Hill, Australia, d. May 26, 1976.

MOROZOVA, OLGA

Preeminent Soviet woman, Olga Morozova, RH, b. Feb. 22, 1949, Moscow. Unusual Soviet, preferred serve-and-volley. Quick, athletic, 5-7. Only USSR female in Wimbledon F, 1974, (beat defender Billie Jean King, QF). QF or better all majors. Won 15 singles, 11 doubles pro titles. World Top Ten, 1973–76, No. 4 in 1974. Federation Cup. First Soviet winner of a U.S. title—Indoor doubles, 1973, with compatriot Marina Kroshina. Federation Cup, 1968, 1978–80, 8-3 singles, 4-2 doubles.

MOTTRAM, TONY; JOY; BUSTER; LINDA

Internationalist English family: father, Tony; mother, Joy; son, Buster; daughter, Linda. All RH.

Anthony John Mottram, b. June 8, 1920, Coventry. Davis Cup: 1947–1955; 25-13 singles, 11-7 doubles. Wimbledon QF, 1948; lost doubles F, 1947. Best Brit immediate post-war.

Joy Gannon Mottram, b. March 21, 1928, Enfield. Wightman Cup: 1947–52, 0-1 singles, 0-3 doubles. Won German, 1954. Wimbledon 3rd rd., 1946, 1947, 1949. French QF, 1952.

Christopher John "Buster" Mottram, b. April 25, 1955, Kingston, lanky 6-3, free-swinging big hitter. Wimbledon 4th rd., 1982; French 4th rd., 1977. Davis Cup: 1975–83; 27-8 singles, 4-2 doubles (high point, 1978, led Britain to first Davis Cup finale since 1937, 8-2 singles, 1-0 doubles). Won two singles, five doubles pro titles, about $500,000. Best World rank, No. 19 in 1982.

Linda Mottram, b. May 17, 1957, Wimbledon. Played Wimbledon six straight years from 1974, lost 3rd rd., 1975. Won German Indoor, 1976.

MUSTER, THOMAS

Muscular "Moo Man," bellowing bovine noises as he belts at the baseline, Austrian Thomas Muster, 5-11 LH, seems indestructible in body and spirit. Sovereign of the soil, strongman of the '90s on clay, won French singles, 1995, Italian, 1990, 1995, 1996. Astoundingly rehabbed left knee, which had been wrecked in 1989 auto accident, to reappear as a winner in 1990, rack up 37 of 42 career singles titles, 1990–96. Huge year, 1995: won 12 titles on 86-18 (40 straight on clay), saved match points in five wins (beat Boris Becker, Monte Carlo F, from 2 sets, 2 match points down). On dirt won 40 titles, 392-100 matches (.797). World No. 7 in 1990, 9 in 1994, 3 in 1995, 5 in 1996; 6 week sojourn at No. 1, 1996. Davis Cup: 1984–96; 33-7 singles, 9-9 doubles, nearly beat U.S. single-handed, 1990 SF (3-2). Australian SF, 1989, QF, 1984; French SF,

1990; U.S. QF, 1993, 1994, 1996. Also won one pro doubles title, $9,474,064 through 1996. B. Oct. 2, 1967, Liebnitz.

NA, HU

When she defected to the U.S. in 1982, she became the first Chinese pro. Slim, 5-8, RH, a serve-and-volleyer. B. April 16, 1963, Chengdu, No. 1 Peoples Republic. Federation Cup: 1981–82; 1-0 singles, 1-2 doubles. Best World rank, No. 58 in 1987. High point, five wins at Wimbledon, 1985, qualifying, reaching 3rd rd. Won one pro title, doubles, $213,220. U.S. citizen, 1989.

NOAH, YANNICK

Yannick Simone Camille Noah, b. May 18, 1960, Sedan, France. Foremost Frenchman in accomplishment, popularity since Four Musketeers, attained all-time renown with countrymen winning French, 1983 (over Mats Wilander), first male title for Frenchman since Marcel Bernard, 1946. Imposing physical specimen, 6-4, 190, RH. Davis Cup hero: 1978–90; 26-15 singles, 13-7 doubles. Led French (6-2, singles; 2-2 doubles) to first Cup F in 49 years, 1982, lost to U.S.; as non-playing captain to first Cup in 59 years, 3-1 over U.S., 1991, also 1996, 3-2 over Sweden. Son of Cameroonian father, French mother, discovered in Yaounde, Cameroon, 1971, recommended to French Federation for development by touring Arthur Ashe. Appealing net-rushing gambler, leaping volleyer, big server. World Top Ten, 1982–87, No. 4 in 1983, 1986. Australian SF, 1990; QF, 1987. French QF, 1981, 1982, 1984, 1987. U.S. QF, 1982, 1984. Won Palm Springs, 1982, ending Ivan Lendl's 44-match streak. Won French doubles, 1984. Over 12 years won 23 singles, 16 doubles pro titles, $3,295,395.

NUSSLEIN, HANS

Extraordinary German Hans "Hanne" Nusslein, perhaps best until Boris Becker, was largely unnoticed as pro trouper, no amateur background. Finest years 1930s. Beat Bill Tilden numerous times, won World Pro title, 1933, 1936, 1937, 1938, U.S. Pro, 1934, French Pro, 1937, 1938. Excellent groundstrokes. RH, b. March 31, 1910, Nuremberg, d. June 28, 1991, Altenkirchen.

O'HARA WOOD, ARTHUR; PAT

Australian brothers, Arthur and Pat O'Hara Wood, RH, both winners homeland's singles title, only brothers to do so. First brothers to win majors since Dohertys, 1906, Wimbledon.

Dr. Arthur Holroyd O'Hara Wood, b. 1890, Melbourne, d. Oct. 4 or 6, 1918, with Royal Air Force, World War I, shot down over St. Quentin, France. Melbourne physician with all-round game. Defeated future Hall of Famer Gerald Patterson, 1914 F, then went to war.

Patrick O'Hara Wood also served, Aussie army, survived to win Australian twice, 1920, 1923, plus four Aussie doubles, Wimbledon doubles and, with Suzanne Lenglen, mixed, 1922. Short, quick, consistent, effortless strokemaker. Davis Cup: 1922, 1924; 9-5 singles, 8-1 doubles, helped Australia gain F both years. B. April 30, 1891. Melbourne; d. there, Dec. 3, 1961. World rank No. 7, 1922. Wife, Meryl Waxman O'Hara Wood, won Australian doubles, 1926, 1927.

OKKER, TOM

Flying Dutchman Tom Samuel Okker, Netherlands' finest male. RH, b. Feb. 22, 1944, Amsterdam. Slight (5-9, 145), speedy, excellent volleyer, one of five men to win more than 100 pro titles (30 singles, record 78 doubles.) Lost F first U.S. Open, 1968, to amateur Arthur Ashe, taking $14,000 first prize. Made SF all majors: Australian, U.S., 1971; French, 1969; Wimbledon, 1978. Made doubles F all majors, won French, 1973, with John Newcombe; U.S., 1976, with Marty Riessen. World Top Ten five times between 1968 and 1973, No. 5 in 1968 and 1969. Davis Cup: 1964–81; 10-13 singles, 5-7 doubles.

O'NEIL, CHRIS

Tall Aussie Chris O'Neil, 5-11, RH, longest shot to win women's major, Australian, 1978. Unseeded, ranked No. 111, she went through weak field, beat No. 68 Betsy Nagelsen in F, 6-3, 7-6, winning $6,000. Only pro title. B. March 19, 1956, Newcastle, serve-and-volleyer. Highest World rank, No. 80, 1978.

ORANTES, MANOLO

Manuel "Manolo" Orantes, stocky, prestidigitating, gracious Spanish LH, master of spin and placement. Won U.S., 1975, sensationally, beating ex-champ Ilie Nastase, 2-1 seeds Guillermo Vilas, defender Jimmy Connors, in succession. Great SF comeback over Vilas: 4-6, 1-6, 6-2, 7-5, 6-4, from 0-5, three match points, then 5-1, two match points 4th. B. Feb. 6, 1949, Granada. Davis Cup: 1967–80; 39-19 singles, 21-8 doubles, helped Spain to finale, 1967. Career, 16 years, spanned amateur, open eras. Won 32 singles, 24 doubles pro titles, including Masters, 1976, U.S. Pro, 1977, 1978, $1,338,601. World Top Ten 1975–77, No. 4 in 1976.

PAILS, DINNY

First of Aussie post-war-developed champs, RH Denis Robert Pails, b. March 4, 1921, at Nottingham, England, won Australian, 1947. Wimbledon SF, 1947, QF, 1946. Davis Cup: 1946–47; 3-5 singles. Turned pro with Jack Kramer, 1947. World No. 6, 1947.

PALFREY, POLLY; LEE; MIANNE; SARAH; JOEY

Five remarkable Bostonians, Palfrey sisters—Joey, Lee, Mianne, Polly, Sarah—all won U.S. junior titles. Sarah won 18 majors, made the Hall of Fame. All RH, b. in Boston, except Sarah, born in Sharon, Mass.

Margaret Germaine "Polly" Palfrey Woodrow, b. Oct. 7, 1906. Won one junior: 18-doubles, 1924, with Fanny Curtis.

Elizabeth Howland "Lee" Palfrey Fullerton, b. Jan. 14, 1909; d. Jan. 5, 1987. Won one junior: 18-Indoor doubles, 1926, with Midge Morrill.

Sarah Hammond Palfrey Fabyan Cooke Danzig, b. Sept. 18, 1912, d. Feb. 27, 1996. Won 13 juniors: 18-singles, 1928, 1929, 1930; 18-doubles, 1926, 1928, 1929, with Mianne; 18-Indoor singles, 1927, 1928, 1930; 18-Indoor doubles, 1927, 1928, 1929, with Mianne, 1930, with Joey.

Mary Ann "Mianne" Palfrey Dexter, b. March 6, 1911, d. Nov. 2, 1993. Won 7 juniors: 18-Indoor singles, 1929; 18-doubles, 1926, 1928, 1929, with Sarah; 18-Indoor doubles, 1927, 1928, 1929, with Sarah. Also won adult U.S. Indoor singles, 1930.

Joanna "Joey" Oakes Palfrey Brown, b. Jan. 30, 1915. Won one junior: 18-Indoor doubles, 1930, with Sarah.

PANATTA, ADRIANO

Best Italian open era, Adriano Panatta, RH, b. July 9, 1950, Rome. Slick 6-foot god at Il Foro Italico, Rome, responding winningly to feverish chants, "AD-REE-ANNO!" Strong serve, whipping forehand, called "Goaltender" for brilliant volleying saves. Spectacular 1976: won Italian, French, 45-15 match record, led Italy to lone Davis Cup (10-1 singles; 5-1 doubles). Also to F, 1977, 1979, 1980. Cup record: 1970–83; 37-26 singles; 27-10 doubles, one of few to play 100 matches. Match point escapes in big titles, 1976: 11, vs. Kim Warwick, Italian; 1, Pavel Hutka, French. Best World rank, No. 7, 1976. Won 10 singles, 18 doubles pro titles, $776,187. Younger brother, Claudio Panatta (b. Feb. 2, 1960, Rome) played Davis Cup, pro tour.

PARKE, JIM

Sturdy Irish RH James Cecil Parke, the man of 1912 Australian season, won singles title, backboned Davis Cup upset for Britain, stunning Norman Brookes, Rod Heath. Beat U.S. champs

Maurice McLoughlin, Dick Williams in losing Cup defense, 1913. World No. 4 in 1913, 6 in 1914. Also rugby international for Ireland, 1913–18. B. July 26, 1881, Clones County, Ireland, d. Feb. 27, 1946, Llandudno, Wales.

PENROSE, BERYL

Made brief mark, 1955. Won Australian (upset Thelma Long, 6-4, 6-3), German, made QF Wimbledon, ranked World No. 8. Tall, slender RH, b. 1930, Sydney.

PETRA, YVON

Yvon François Marie Petra, French RH, at 6-5 tallest winner major singles, Wimbledon, 1946, a surprise, rising above 5th seed to beat 3rd Geoff Brown. B. March 8, 1916, Cholon, Indochina, d. Sept. 12, 1984, Paris. Won French doubles twice, 1938, 1946. Davis Cup: 1937–39, 1946–47; 11-3 singles, 4-4 doubles, led France to SF, 1946. French army, wounded, POW in World War II. Turned pro, 1948. Strong server, last man to win a major Wimbledon in long trousers. World rank, No. 4 in 1946.

PIERCE, MARY

Among all-time hardest hitters, baselining RH with 2-handed backhand, Mary Caroline Pierce, a 3-way split personality. B. Jan. 15, 1975, Montreal, of French mother, U.S. father, raised in Florida, plays Federation Cup for France. Holds U.S., Canadian, French passports. Junoesque blonde, 5-11, glamorized return of the tennis dress. Won Australian, 1995, lost F, 1997. Lost French F, 1994, made QF U.S., 1994, Wimbledon, 1996, ranked No. 5, 1994–95. Coached by demanding father, Jim Pierce, until obtaining restraining order, 1993. Turned pro 1989, won 7 singles titles, $2,337,870.

PILIC, NIKKI

Nikola "Nikki" Pilic, slim 6-3 Croat, LH, from Split, former Yugoslavia's best of post-war (until another Split lefty, Goran Ivanisevic), country's first pro athlete, 1968, with WCT "Handsome Eight." Cause of famous Wimbledon boycott, 1973: most ATP colleagues walked out, protesting Wimbledon honoring his suspension by Yugoslav Federation. Solidarity on Pilic's behalf established year-old union. B. Aug. 27, 1939, Split. Big serve, forehand. French F, 1973 (second oldest finalist), QF, 1967. Wimbledon SF, 1967. U.S. QF, 1973. Won U.S. doubles, 1970. World rank, No. 7 in 1967. Davis Cup: 11 years between 1961 and 1977; 27-12 singles, 11-12 doubles. Won 4 singles, 7 doubles pro titles. Became German citizen, captain Davis Cup team, winner 1988, 1989, 1993.

PIM, JOSHUA

His cup runneth over with Wimbledon titles—singles, 1893, 1894, doubles, 1890, 1893. Ireland's Dr. Joshua Pim, mustachioed physician with daring netside manner, delighted in difficult volleys. Four-year rivalry with Wilfred Baddeley resulted in two F lost, 1891, 1892, then the titles. After that, retirement to medicine, with a brief losing comeback in a Davis Cup weekend for Britain in Boston, 1902. B. May 20, 1869, Bray, Ireland, d. April 15, 1942, Dublin.

RAHIM, HAROON

Foremost player of Pakistan, Haroon Rahim, RH, b. Nov. 12, 1949, Lahore, one of 14 children. Quick, fine volleying All-American, Intercollegiate doubles champ, UCLA, 1971. For years youngest ever Davis Cupper, 15 years, 109 days, 1965 against South Vietnam (beat Vo Van Bay, 6-1 in 5th). Several greener lads, all insignificant otherwise, have lowered the mark since 1990, the youngest Laith Azoni of Jordan, 14 years, 136 days, in 1992 against Singapore. Haroon beat Tom Gorman in closest match ever, 6-7 (3-5), 7-6

(5-1), 7-6 (5-4), Pennsylvania Grass, 1970. Won one singles, six doubles pro titles. Best World rank, No. 49, 1976.

RAMIREZ, RAUL

Raul Carlos Ramirez, Mexico's premier player open era, got tennis education in U.S. All-American, USC, combined with Brian Gottfried in superb doubles team (39 titles). RH, b. June 20, 1953, Ensenada. Quick 6-footer, improviser fond of attack, splendid volleyer. Mexican Davis Cup: 1971–82; 22-8 singles, 14-5 doubles. Thorn in U.S. side: won four singles, two doubles in two 3-2 wins, 1975, 1976. Beat Roscoe Tanner, Jimmy Connors, decisive matches. QF or better all majors but Aussie. Won Italian, 1975 (beat defender Bjorn Borg, Ilie Nastase, Manolo Orantes). World Top Ten, No. 5 in 1976, 8 in 1977, 8 in 1978. Won 17 singles, 62 doubles pro titles, $2,213,671.

REDL, HANS

Austrian Hans Redl, RH (subsequently only-hander) of extraordinary grit. B. Jan. 19, 1914, Vienna, d. May 26, 1976. Davis Cup, Austria, 1937, then Germany, 1938, 1939, when his country was annexed. Lost left arm, World War II, fighting with German army in Russia. Amazingly resumed play at upper level, Davis Cup, Austria, 1948–55. Cup record: 2-2 singles with both arms; 3-10 singles, 3-8 doubles, with one arm. Reached 4th rd. Wimbledon, 1947. Because of him, rules amended to permit one-armed players to make service toss with racket.

REID, KERRY

Among very best Aussies, Kerry Anne Meville Reid won homeland singles, Jan. 1977, her 11th try; made F, 1970, also U.S. F, 1972. All-rounder with strong forehand, volley, World Top Ten 11 years: 1966, 1967, 1969–74, 1977–79, No. 5, 1971–73. SF all majors: Australian, 1966, 1967, 1969, 1973, 1974, Dec.-1977; French, 1967; Wimbledon, 1974; U.S., 1966, 1974. Met American husband Grover "Raz" Reid as teammates on Boston Lobsters, WTT, married 1975. Won 10 singles, 10 doubles (Australian, Dec.-1977; Wimbledon, 1978) pro titles, $750,000. An original Long Way Baby of women's pro tour, 1970. Federation Cup, 1967–79, 20-4 singles, 17-6 doubles (won one Cup, four F). B. Aug. 7, 1947, Mosman, Australia, lives in U.S.

REITANO, MARY

Tiniest Australian champ, 5-2 RH Mary Carter Reitano won under maiden name (1956), married (1959). Saved match point over Thelma Long, 3-6, 6-2, 9-7, in 1956 F; beat all-timer Margaret Court, 16, 2nd rd., 1959, last defeat for Court in nationals until 1968. B. Nov. 29, 1934, Sydney, had solid all-court game.

RICE, HORRIE

Longest-running Australian, LH Horace M. Rice, played first interstate match for New South Wales at 22, 1894, last at 53, 1925. Won Australian singles at 35, 1907, lost F 1910, 1911, 1915. Made SF, 1920, 1923, last at age 51. Won doubles, 1915. Davis Cup rookie at 39, 1913, 0-2 singles. Eager retriever, distinctive in white knickers, long black sox. Sliced serve, strong backhand, hit with same face of racket as forehand, described admiringly by Tony Wilding: "peculiar, one of his own; for ugliness and effectiveness combined I have never seen anything to approach it." B. Sept. 5, 1873.

RICE, LENA

With luck Irish Helena Bertha Grace "Lena" Rice might have been second woman to win successive Wimbledons. Served at 5-3, 40-15 and advantage, 3 match points, 2nd set, lost 1889 F to Blanche Bingley Hillyard, 4-6, 8-6, 6-4. Did win,

1890. RH, b. June 21, 1866, Newinn; d. there, June 21, 1907.

RICHARDS, RENÉE

American LH, 6-1, ophthalmological surgeon, b. Richard Raskind, Aug. 19, 1934, New York. Graduate Yale, Rochester Medical. Unique: Played U.S. as amateur male (1955, 1956, 1957, 1960), pro female (1977–81). Lost F U.S. doubles, 1977, with Bettyann Stuart. Strong server, clever tactician. Following 1975 sex change surgery, sought to play women's pro tour, faced opposition, resorted to courts of law to gain entry. New York Supreme Court ruling, August 1977, cleared way to enter WTA, USTA events. Age 43, lost 1st rd., U.S., 1977, to Wimbledon champ Virginia Wade, reached 3rd rd., 1979, lost to Chris Evert. Reasonable pro career, five years, winning one singles title. Returned to medicine. Best World rank, No. 22, 1977.

RICHEY, NANCY; CLIFF

American brother and sister, Nancy and Cliff Richey, RH, out of San Angelo, Tex. Attained highest standing for such a family pair. Unique: both held No. 1 U.S., rank, she 1964, 1965, 1968, 1969; he, 1970. Both won U.S. Clay Court singles, 1966, played Davis/Federation/Wightman Cup. Careers spanned amateur, open eras.

Nancy Ann Richey (Mrs. Kenneth Gunter, 1970–75), b. Aug. 23, 1942, San Angelo, Tex. Powerful baseliner despite slight physique (5-6, 130), and good volleyer, winning doubles, Australian, Wimbledon, 1966; U.S., 1965, 1966. Best on clay, winning first French Open, 1968, over Ann Jones, record six straight U.S. Clay Courts (33 straight matches) from 1963. Tough on grass, too, winning Australian, 1967, making U.S. F, 1966, 1969; SF, 1968; QF, 1964, 1965, 1966, 1969. U.S. Top Ten, 16 years, 1960–76. World Top Ten, 11 years spanning 1963 to 1975, No. 3, 1968, 1972; No. 4, 1967, 1969, 1970. Federation Cup: 1964, 1968–69; 10-1 singles, 4-1 doubles (with '69 winner). Wightman Cup: 1962–70, 9-7

singles, 3-2 doubles (with eight winners). One of greatest comebacks, rebounded from 1-5, match point, 2nd set, to win 12 straight games, beat Billie Jean King, 4-6, 7-5, 6-0, SF New York International, 1968, and won title.

George Clifford Richey, Jr., b. Dec. 31, 1946, San Angelo, Tex. Quick, stocky (5-7, 170), scrappy, hard worker, strong groundstroker, good volleyer. Led U.S. to 1970 Davis Cup over Germany; also played 1966–67, 10-3 singles. Biggest season, 1970, won eight titles (including U.S. Clay), 93-19 record, SF, French, US; World rank, No. 7. Took U.S. No. 1 rank by narrowest margin: 1-point victory—beating No. 2 Stan Smith in 5-4 5th set tie-breaker, Pacific Coast SF—decided order of rank.

ROBB, MURIEL

An intruding champ, 1902 Wimbledon, English RH Muriel Evelyn Robb interrupted title monopolies of Charlotte Sterry, Blanche Hillyard, Dorothea Douglass Chambers, beating Sterry in F. Had brief British celebrity, won Irish, Scottish titles (1901), Welsh (1899). RH, b. May 13, 1878, Newcastle upon Tyne; d. there, Feb. 12, 1907.

ROSE, MERV

Canny Aussie 6-foot LH Mervyn Gordon "Rosie" Rose, had complete game, strong volleys, flourished in singles on clay (won French, Italian, 1958) or grass (Australian, 1954). Also Australian F, 1953; Wimbledon SF, 1952, 1953, 1958, QF, 1954, 1957; U.S. SF, 1952. World Top Ten 1953–55, 1957, 1958, No. 3 in 1958. Won the three major grass doubles: Australian, 1954, Wimbledon, 1954, U.S., 1952 and 1953 (with Vic Seixas wrecked double Grand Slam bid of Frank Sedgman–Ken McGregor, 1952 U.S. F). Davis Cup: 1951–52; 0-2 singles, 1-0 doubles. Turned pro, 1958. B. Jan. 23, 1930, Coffs Harbour, Australia.

RUZICI, VIRGINIA

Romania's standout woman, Virginia Ruzici, b. Jan. 31, 1955, Cimpa-Turzil, grew up in

Bucharest. Lissome, 5-8, RH, baseliner with lusty forehand. Won French singles, doubles, 1978. QF or better all majors. Won U.S. Clay, 1982. Federation Cup. Over 13-year career won 14 singles, 8 doubles pro titles, $1,184,228. Best World rank: No. 11 in 1980 and 12, 1978, 1982. Federation Cup, 1973–77, 1980–81, 1983, 12-6 singles, 8-4 doubles.

SABATINI, GABRIELA

Argentina's Gabriela Sabatini, RH, finest Latin American female since Maria Bueno. Tall, 5-9, dark-haired beauty, the "Divine Argentine." Powerful topspin, groundstroker, showed attacking qualities to win U.S., 1990, over defender Steffi Graf, reach Wimbledon F, 1991. B. May 16, 1970, Buenos Aires, lives in Florida, where spent formative years. Won Olympic silver, singles, 1988, runner-up to Graf. First impact at 14: three-match day at rain-compressed Hilton Head, 1985, beat Pam Shriver, Manuela Maleeva, lost F, Chris Evert. Won Italian, 1988, 1989, 1991, 1992. SF all majors. Painful loss to Graf, Wimbledon F, 1990, led 3rd set, 6-5, 30-15. Australian SF, 1992, QF, 1991. French SF, 1985, 1987, 1989, 1991, 1992. Wimbledon SF, 1986, 1990, 1992, QF, 1987. U.S. F, 1988; SF, 1989; QF, 1987, 1991, 1992. World Top Ten, 1986–92, No. 3 in 1988, 1989, 1991. Retired after 1996 with 27 singles, 14 doubles pro titles, $8,185,849.

SANCHEZ, EMILIO; JAVIER

Probably most accomplished family combination ever at uppermost level: brothers of Arantxa Sanchez Vicario, RH from Barcelona. Both represented Spain, Davis/Federation Cup, Emilio in Olympics.

Emilio Sanchez, quick, smooth-stroking 5-10, b. May 29, 1965, Madrid. Won Italian, 1991. Excellent at doubles. With Sergio Casal won U.S., 1988; Italian and French, 1990; Olympic silver medal, 1988. Davis Cup: 1984–95; 18-14 singles, 14-9 doubles. Through 1996 had 15 singles, 50 doubles pro titles (44 with Casal, 3 with brother Javier), $5,303,210. Best World rank, No. 8, 1990.

Javier Sanchez, speedy, 5-10, b. Feb. 1, 1968, Pamplona. Consistent winner singles, doubles. U.S. QF, 1991, 1996. Davis Cup: 1987–89; 3-2 singles. Through 1996 had 4 singles, 20 doubles (3 with brother Emilio) career titles, $3,455,007. Best World rank, No. 23, 1994.

JIRO SATOH

Highest ranking Japanese ever—yet tragic. World No. 3, 1933, also No. 9, 1931, 5-5 RH Jiro Satoh killed himself at age 26, having thrice led Japan to Cup SF. B. Jan. 5, 1908, Tokyo, all-rounder, nifty touch. Adept on clay, grass: French SF, 1931, 1933; Wimbledon SF, 1933, QF, 1931; Australian SF, 1932. Lost Wimbledon doubles F, 1933. Had wins over Hall of Famers Jack Crawford, Fred Perry, Elly Vines. Despondent over 3-2 loss to Australia, 1933, feeling pressure of leading team—"I would have been unable to help . . ." said suicide note—he leaped from shipboard into Strait of Malacca, April 5, 1934, on the way to Cup opener in England. Davis Cup: 1931–33; 14-4 singles, 8-2 doubles.

SAWAMATSU, KAZUKO; JUNKO

Sisters, Kazuko and Junko Sawamatsu, RH, first Japanese women to make mark pro tour. Federation Cup together, 1970, 1971. Kazuko only Japanese woman to win major, Wimbledon doubles, 1975. Both made Australian QF: Junko, 1973, Kazuko, 1975.

Kazuko Sawamatsu, sturdy 5-7, b. Jan. 5, 1951, Nishinomiya. Solid groundstroker, won Swiss, 1972. Australia SF, 1973 (beat Virginia Wade); QF, 1975. French QF, 1975. Won Japan National, 1967, 1972; Wimbledon, French Junior, 1969. In one-time unseeded partnership with Japanese-American Ann Kiyomura, won Wimbledon; QF, 1970, with sister.

Junko Sawamatsu, b. April 10, 1948, Nishinomiya. Daughter, Naoko Sawamatsu (RH with two-handed backhand, b. March 23, 1973, Nishinomiya), is on pro tour, best World rank, No. 17, 1995.

SCOTT, GENE

Protean New York RH Eugene Lytton Scott, 6-1, 165, made U.S. Top Ten, 1962–64, 1967, 1968, No. 4 in 1963. Unseeded, reached U.S. SF, 1967. Davis Cup: 1963–65; 3-0 singles, 1-0 doubles. Varsity letterman (hockey, soccer, tennis, track) at Yale ('60). Virginia Law ('65). Founder-publisher-columnist *Tennis Week* newspaper, 1974. Founder Kremlin Cup, Moscow (ATP Tour), 1990. B. Dec. 27, 1937, New York.

SEARS, EVELYN

Evelyn Georgianna Sears of Waltham, Mass., Longwood Cricket Club member, first LH to win U.S. titles, singles 1907, doubles 1908. Didn't venture to Philadelphia until '07, won impressively at 32, losing no sets, 17 games in 5 matches. Lost challenge round, 1908. Tried again, 1916, made SF. Good bloodline, cousin of initial U.S. champ, Richard Sears. B. March 9, 1875, Waltham, d. there, Nov. 10, 1966.

SHIMIDZU, ZENZO

Zenzo "Shimmy" Shimidzu, first Japanese of note, attained highest male level. B. March 25, 1891, Tokyo; d. April 12, 1977, Amagaski City, Japan. Self-taught, 5-6, quick-footed, unorthodox RH, weird stroker, heavy topspin; same face of racket, forehand, backhand, yet effective on grass. Lost Wimbledon F (all-comers), 1920, to champ Bill Tilden; SF, 1921, to Manuel Alonso. With Ichiya Kumagae (b. Sept. 10, 1891; d. Aug. 16, 1968) in Japan's Davis Cup debut—and zenith—1921, upset Australia, entered F vs. U.S., Forest Hills; astoundingly Shimidzu came within two points, 3rd set, of beating Tilden, losing, 5-7, 4-6, 7-5, 6-2, 6-1. Davis Cup: 1921–25; 9-8 singles, 3-5 doubles. Working in the U.S., Shimidzu (No. 7, 1922) and Kumagae (No. 5 in 1916, 6 in 1918, 3 in 1919, 4 in 1920, 7 in 1921) had U.S. rankings. World rank, No. 9 in 1920, 4 in 1921.

SHRIVER, PAM

Pamela Howard "Pam" Shriver, RH American, extraordinary early splash in singles, but her place in history is in doubles, including Olympic gold medal (alongside Zina Garrison), 1988. Joined with Martina Navratilova as all-time team: 1981–87, they won record 20 majors (tying Louise Brough–Margaret duPont), Grand Slam in 1984, 79 titles altogether. Their record 109-match win streak ended 1985. B. July 4, 1962, Baltimore, grew up in Lutherville, Md. Rangy 6-footer, expert serve-and-volleyer, fine smash, lob. As amateur, went to F, first U.S., 1978. First to do so since Anita Lizana, champ, 1937. Was youngest finalist at 16 years, 2 months. Only amateur U.S. female finalist open era. Wimbledon SF, 1981, 1987, 1988. U.S. SF, 1982, 1983; QF, 1980, 1984, 1985, 1986, 1987. Turned pro, 1979. Through 1996, won $5,448,646, 21 singles, 93 doubles pro titles, one of five women to win more than 100 overall. U.S. Top Tenner 12 times between 1978 and 1992, No. 3 in 1984 and 1988. World Top Ten nine times, 1980–88, No. 4 in 1983, 1984, 1985, 1987.

SIROLA, ORLANDO

Gaunt, towering Italian RH Orlando Sirola was tallest (6-6) to play in Davis Cup finale (1960, 1961), major finals (won French doubles, 1959, lost Wimbledon, 1956, with Nicola Pietrangeli) until 6-6 Todd Martin was in Cup F, 1995 and Australian F, 1994. B. April 30, 1928, Fiume, d. Nov. 13, 1995, Bologna. Self-taught, late starter, 1950. Huge serve, overhead, good volleyer, streaky. Joined Cup team, 1953, with Pietrangeli, 1955, playing, winning as pair most doubles in Cup history (34-8) through 1963. Among most active Cuppers: 22-25 singles, 35-8 doubles. High point, 1960 SF, 3-2 comeback from 0-2 over U.S.: won pivotal doubles, 13-11, 4th, over Butch Buchholz–Chuck McKinley, decider in singles over Barry MacKay, 9-7, 6-3, 8-6.

SPERLING, HILDE

Tall, slim RH Hilde Krahwinkel Sperling was strong presence for decade, World Top Ten 10 straight years, 1930–39. Won three straight French, 1935–37, tying Helen Moody's 1928–30 run, equalled by Monica Seles, 1990–92. Lost only all-German female Wimbledon F to Cilly Aussem, 1931, also F to Helen Jacobs, 1936. B. March 26, 1908, Essen, Germany, became Danish citizen (marrying Svend Sperling, 1933), d. March 7, 1981, Halsingborg, Sweden.

STERRY, CHARLOTTE

English RH, consistent factor at Wimbledon over extraordinary period of 18 years and two centuries. Attained record 8 straight F (1895–92). Won 4 (1895, 1896, 1898, 1901), lost 3 (1897, 1899, 1900) as Charlotte Reinagle Cooper. As Mrs. Rex Sterry won 2 (1901, 1908), lost 3 (1902, 1904, 1912), last at age 41. Lost doubles F 1913. Her record eclipsed in 1990: Martina Navratilova appeared in 9th straight final. Won Olympic singles, 1900, first woman gold medalist any sport. Won Scottish (1895), Irish (1895, 1898) titles. B. Sept. 22, 1870, Ealing; d. Oct. 10, 1966, Helensburgh, Scotland.

STICH, MICHAEL

Spindly 6-4 RH, fluid stroker, attacker with big serve, Michael Stich dethroned countryman Boris Becker, Wimbledon, 1991, only all-German male F. Also QF, 1993. Lost F U.S. 1994, French, 1996. SF French, 1991. Davis Cup: 1990–95; 21-9 singles, 13-2 doubles. Led Germany to 1993 Cup, 3-2 over Australia with rare triple, won both singles, doubles. World No. 4 in 1991, 2 in 1993, 9 in 1994. Turned pro 1988. Won 18 singles, 9 doubles pro titles, $12,158,416 through 1996. B. Oct. 18, 1968, Pinneberg, Germany.

STOVE, BETTY

Netherlands' Betty Flippina Stove, 6-foot RH, her country's foremost woman since 1920s. Powerful server, fine volleyer, erratic. Only Hollander in Wimbledon F, 1977 (lost to Virginia Wade), and won most major doubles (nine): three U.S., 1972, with Françoise Durr; 1977, with Martina Navratilova; 1979, with Wendy Turnbull; Wimbledon, French, 1972, with Billie Jean King. Plus two U.S., Wimbledon mixed, with Frew McMillan. Rarity: lost all three Wimbledon F, 1977. B. June 24, 1945, Rotterdam. Federation Cup: 1966–76; 20-4 singles, 20-8 doubles. World Top Ten, No. 7 in 1976, 8 in 1977, 7 in 1978.

SUK/SUKOVA, VERA; HELENA; CYRIL

Great name in Czechoslovak game. Mother, Vera; son, Cyril; daughter, Helena, all RH, major champions played for country in Federation and Davis Cup. Only mother, daughter in major singles F, World Top Ten. Father, Cyril Suk, was president Czechoslovak Federation.

Vera Puzejova Sukova, b. June 13, 1931, Uherske Hradiste; d. May 13, 1982, Prague. Married Suk, 1961. Unimpressive serve, strokes, but strong, persistent, competitive. Stolid baseliner, fine passing shots: French SF, 1957, losing to champ Shirley Bloomer, 6-4, 3rd; QF, 1959, 1960, 1963, 1964. Unseeded, had stunning Wimbledon, 1962, beat 6th, 2nd, 3rd seeds—defender Angela Mortimer, Darlene Hard, ex-champ Maria Bueno—lost F to Karen Susman. Also QF, U.S., 1962. World rank, No. 6 in 1957, 5 in 1962, 10 in 1963. Was Czechoslovak national coach, early tutor of Martina Navratilova.

Helena Sukova, b. Feb. 23, 1965, Prague. At 6-2 tallest ever female player of consequence, until 6-3 Lindsay Davenport won Olympic gold, 1996. Standout serve-and-volleyer, possessing sound groundies. QF or better, all majors. Ended Navratilova's record 74-match streak, Grand Slam bid, SF, Australian, 1984, lost F, Chris Evert. Also Australian, 1989, lost F, Steffi Graf. Beat Evert, U.S. SF, 1986, lost F to Navratilova. Wimbledon

QF, 1985, 1988. French SF, 1986; QF, 1988. U.S. SF, 1987; QF, 1984, 1985, 1989. World rank, Top Ten, 1984–89, No. 5 in 1985. Superior at doubles, won 12 majors: Australian, 1990, 1992; French, 1990; Wimbledon, 1987, 1989, 1990, 1996, last with half-her-age Martina Hingis, 15; U.S., 1985, 1993. Also French mixed, 1991, with Suk, only brother-sister to win; Wimbledon, 1994; U.S., 1993. Missed Grand Slam with Jana Novotna, 1990, lost U.S. F to Martina Navratilova–Gigi Fenandez, 6-2, 6-4. Federation Cup all-timer, 1981–96, 42-11 singles, 12-5 doubles (with four winners, 1983–85, 1988). Through 1996 won 10 singles, 65 doubles pro titles, $5,946,064. Olympic silver, doubles, 1988, 1996, with Novotna.

Cyril Suk, b. Jan. 19, 1967, Prague. Quick, clever, 5-11, singles (best World rank, No. 184, 1988) overshadowed by doubles expertise. Davis Cup: 1992–96; 6-3 doubles. Through 1996, won $1,592,430, 15 pro doubles titles plus French mixed with sister, 1991.

SUSMAN, KAREN

Lovely, free-flowing, 5-7 brilliant RH serve-and-volleyer out of Chula Vista, Calif., Karen Janice Hantze was 1961 unseeded surprise champ at Wimbledon, 18, alongside Billie Jean Moffitt (King), 17: youngest doubles winners. Again surprising, 1962, as Mrs. Rod Susman seeded 8th, won singles, repeated with BJ in doubles. Didn't defend, gave birth to daughter. She and King also won U.S. doubles, 1964. Wimbledon QF, 1961; U.S. QF, 1959, 1964. World Top Ten No. 10 in 1961, 4 in 1962, 8 in 1964; U.S. Top Ten, 1959–62, 1964, No. 2, 1960–62. Wightman Cup, 1960–62, 1965, 3-3 singles, 3-0 doubles (won 3 Cups). Federation Cup, 1964: 1-0 doubles. Won 13 singles titles. B. Dec. 11, 1942, San Diego.

TAPSCOTT, BILLIE

South African Ruth Daphne "Billie" Tapscott, b. May 31, 1903, Kimberly; d. 1970. Emancipated female legs, shocked Wimbledon, 1927, appearing without stockings. "It's just the way we do it at home." With bared gams, made QF, probably inspired Joan Austin Lycett, first bold peeler of hose for Centre Court match, 1931, as stockings went way of corsets. RH, won South African, 1930. Married South African player Collin John James Robbins, 1930.

TEACHER, BRIAN

Long-armed lightning server from San Diego, 6-3½ RH Brian David Teacher seized his monumental prize, Australian singles, 1980, on cruise control, lost three sets, beat homeboy Kim Warwick quick in F. QF Australian, Wimbledon, 1982. UCLA grad, 4 years All-American. Best World Rank, No. 12 in 1980, 16 in 1981. Won eight singles, 17 doubles pro titles, $1,426,244. B. Dec. 23, 1954, San Diego.

TERRY, ALINE

Mystery woman of U.S. Championships. Came from Princeton, N.J., to become fifth to win singles, doubles titles, 1893. Lost both, 1894, singles in 5-set challenge round struggle with Helen Hellwig. Never heard from again. Age unknown, no details b. or d. Called "lithe, feline, leaped at balls like a tiger" by champ Juliette Atkinson.

TIRIAC, ION

First prominent Romanian open era, Ion Ioan Tiriac, b. May 9, 1939, Brasov. Hulking, glowering, ungainly 6-foot RH, excellent athlete, fierce competitor, played Olympic ice hockey prior late start in tennis. Career, almost two decades, spanned amateur, open era. Shrewd polyglot, tactician. "I am best tennis player who cannot play tennis." Davis Cup: 1959–77; led way for protégé Ilie Nastase. Together carried Romania to three F, all lost to U.S.: 1969, 1971, 1972. Sixth in all-time Cup matches played, 109 (40-28, singles: 30-11, doubles). Highest World rank No. 72, 1974 (best years pre-computer). Won 2 singles, 27 doubles pro titles. Entrepreneur in variety of businesses, has a hand in tennis operating tournaments, managed champs Guillermo Vilas, Boris Becker.

TODD, PAT

Mary Patricia Canning Todd, 5-8 California RH, says she "got by on a backhand and guts," made fine immediate post-war record. Won French singles, 1947. Lost F, 1950, played despite blood poisoning, 3 sets to Doris Hart, then hospitalized. World Top Ten, 1946–52, No. 4 in 1950, No. 5, 1946–49, 1952. Wimbledon SF, 1948–50, 1952, QF, 1947. U.S. SF, 1946, 1948, QF, 1945, 1947, 1949, 1950. Only winner over Mo Connolly three times, 1952. Won French doubles, mixed, 1948. Might have had triple, defaulted SF to champ-to-be Nelly Landry, France: referee unfairly advanced starting time to "now" while she ate lunch. Wightman Cup, 1947–51, 4-1 doubles (won Cup every year). B. July 22, 1922, San Francisco.

TRUMAN, CHRIS

Darling of homeland fans from teenage years onward, English 6-foot blonde RH Christine Clara Truman won 1959 French singles at 18, youngest until Steffi Graf, 1987. Had won their hearts beating Althea Gibson, Dorothy Knode, winning doubles, 1958 Wightman Cup victory over U.S., 4-3. She, as Mrs. Gerry Janes, and sister, Nell Truman, won decisive doubles in 4-3 win, 1968. World Top Ten, 1957–61, 1965, No. 2 in 1959. Heartbreaker: 1961 Wimbledon F loss to Angela Mortimer, 4-6, 6-4, 7-5; made SF, 1957, 1960, 1965, was 34-14 there. Federation Cup, 1963, 1965, 1968, 6-3 singles, 2-2 doubles. Wightman Cup, 1957–71, 6-12 singles, 5-4 doubles (won 3 Cups). B. Feb. 16, 1941, Loughton, England.

TURNBULL, WENDY

All-time Aussie Wendy May "Rabbit" Turnbull, 5-3 RH was noted for speed, exceptional volley. Only woman of her country other than Margaret Court and Evonne Goolagong to make three major singles F: Australian, 1980, French, 1979, U.S., 1977. Won 9 major doubles: French, 1979; Wimbledon, 1978; U.S., 1979, 1982, plus five mixed. Upset No. 2 Martina Navratilova,

U.S. SF, 1977, lost F to Chris Evert. World Top Ten 1977–80, 1982–84, No. 6 in 1977, 1979, 1983. Fed Cup, 1977–88, most Aussie wins, 17-8 singles, 29-8 doubles (lost 4 F). Australian SF, 1981, 1984, QF, 1980–81; French QF, 1980; Wimbledon QF, 1979–81, U.S. SF, 1978, 1984, QF, 1986. Won 7 singles, 10 doubles pro titles, $2,769,024. B. Nov. 25, 1952, Brisbane. Olympic bronze, 1988, doubles with Liz Smylie.

ULRICH, EINER; TORBEN; JORGEN

Davis Cup workhorses for Denmark. Father, Einer, two sons, Torben and Jorgen Ulrich, all b. in Copenhagen, played 218 Cup matches between 1924 and 1978.

Einer Ulrich, RH, b. May 6, 1896. Davis Cup: 1924–38; 23-23 singles, 16-12 doubles.

Torben Ulrich, free-spirited, bearded LH, b. Oct. 4, 1928; family's most prominent, strong serve, delicate touch. Career spanned amateur, open eras, 4th rd. French, 1959; 3rd rd., U.S., 1969, at 40. Davis Cup: 1948–61, 1964–68, 1978; one of few in over 100 matches; 31-35 singles, 15-21 doubles. Oldest of all Cuppers, 48 years, 11 months, 1978.

Jorgen Ulrich, RH. b. Aug. 21, 1935. Davis Cup: 1955, 1958–71; 18-18 singles, 8-10 doubles—3-3 with Torben.

WASHINGTON, MAL; MASHISKA; MASHONA; MICHEALA

Exceptional siblings from Swartz Creek, Mich., all RH (2-handed backhand), three currently on pro tour, coached by father, William Washington.

MaliVai Onyeaka, b. June 20, 1969, Glen Cove, N.Y., sinewy 5-11, well-rounded game, first black U.S. Davis Cupper since Arthur Ashe, 1993, 1996 (2-2 singles). Unseeded, made Wimbledon F, 1996, incredible SF comeback from 1-5 in the 5th over Todd Martin, 5-7, 6-4, 6-7 (6-8), 6-3, 10-8. Australian QF, 1994. Olympic QF, 1996. Best World rank, No. 13, 1992. All-American, U. of Michigan, 1987 and 1988. Won 4 pro singles titles, $2,000,000 through 1996.

Mashiska Isabelita, b. Dec. 19, 1974, Flint, Mich., 5-11. All-American, Michigan State, 1994. World No. 611, 1996.

Mashona Lakuta, b. May 31, 1976, Flint, Mich. Won U.S. 18 Indoor singles, 1992. World ranking No. 150, 1996.

Micheala Bharati, b. Jan. 27, 1966, Carbondale, Ill. Played one year as pro. World ranking No. 81, 1984.

WATSON, MAUD

First lady of Wimbledon, Englishwoman; Maud Edith Eleanor Watson, 19, won intramural battle, becoming pioneer among major champs, beat sister, Lillian Mary Watson, 26, as Wimbledon introduced female tourney (13 entered), 1884. Also won Irish, 1884, 1985; Welsh, 1887. RH, b. Oct. 9, 1864, Harrow; d. June 6, 1946, Charmouth. Lillian b. Sept. 17, 1857, Harrow; d. May 27, 1918, Berkswell, England.

WEIR, REGINALD

Racial pioneer, New York physician, Dr. Reginald S. Weir, overcame early discrimination to win U.S. titles. Though Althea Gibson received much attention entering Forest Hills, 1950, Weir RH, was first black to play national championship sanctioned by USTA: U.S. Indoor, 1948, New York, 7th Regt. Armory. Also first to win U.S. title, Senior Indoor singles, 1956, 1957, 1959 (doubles, 1961, 1962), at 7th Regt., gratifying turnaround where he'd been refused entry U.S. Junior Indoor, 1929. Beat Ed Tarangioli, 5-7, 6-3, 6-1, first title. B. 1911; d. Aug. 21, 1987, Fairlawn, N.J.

THE WOODIES

Todd Andrew Woodbridge, b. April 2, 1971, Sydney; Mark Raymond Woodforde (left court),

b. Sept. 23, 1965, Adelaide: extraordinary Aussie doubles team, best of post–John Newcombe–Tony Roche, John McEnroe–Peter Fleming eras. Won seven majors together, four straight Wimbledon (1993–96), longest run there since Doherty brothers' five (1897–1901); U.S., 1995–96; Australian, 1992. Also won World Doubles, 1992, 1996, 41 pro titles. Davis Cup together, 1993–96, 7-2; singles: Woodbridge, 3-2, Woodforde, 3-9.

Woodforde, slim 6-2, LH redhead, also won U.S., with J. McEnroe, 1989; U.S., Australian mixed, 1992; Wimbledon mixed, 1993; French mixed, 1995; 4 singles titles (highest World Rank, No. 27, 1996), $5,560,554 through 1996. Woodbridge, 5-10, RH, also won Australian mixed, 1993; French mixed, 1992; Wimbledon mixed, 1994; U.S. mixed, 1990, 1993; 1 singles title (highest World Rank, No. 34, 1995), $4,833,829 through 1996.

ZVEREVA, NATALIA

Mother Freedom of Soviet tennis, demanded full prize money, 1989, at a time country's players received meager subsidy from federation out of money they won. Risky business then, earned public disapproval—but got her way, benefitting colleagues. Nimble, sharp volleying RH Belarussian, leggy 5-8, b. April 16, 1971, Minsk. Became doubles great (right court), won 17 majors, 12 with Gigi Fernandez (4 French, 3 U.S., 3 Wimbledon, 2 Australian), second all-time team total. They narrowly missed Grand Slams, 1993, lost SF, U.S. to Arantxa Sanchez Vicario–Helena Sukova, 1-6, 6-3, 6-4, ending 40-match major streak, and 1994, lost SF, U.S., to Katerina Maleeva–Robin White, 7-6 (7-2), 1-6, 6-3. First Soviet to win major, French with Larisa Savchenko (Neiland), 1989. Lost singles F, French, 1988, made QF all majors: Australian, 1995, French, 1992, Wimbledon, 1990, 1992, 1993; U.S., 1993. World No. 7 in 1988, 10 in 1994. Federation Cup (USSR/Belarus), 1986–96, 23-11 singles, 18-4 doubles. Olympics, QF, 1988, 3rd rd., 1992. Turned pro, 1988. Through 1996 won 6 singles, 63 pro doubles titles, $5,386,043.

10

TENNIS LINGO

Ace: An outright winning serve, either hit so hard or placed so accurately that the receiver has no chance of returning the ball, which sails past him untouched or barely touched.

Advantage: The point following deuce. The umpire generally calls the name of the player holding advantage (example, "Advantage Graf") whether he is server or receiver. Also called ad in informal play; ad-in is the score called when the server has the advantage; ad-out refers to the advantage being held by the receiver; ad-court refers to the left court, from which the advantage is always played.

Age-group tennis: Diaper-to-doomsday competition is available in the U.S., where sectional and national championships are determined for males and females of practically every age. It starts with the 14s (for those 14 years and under), and continues through the 16s and 18s. After that come the adult tournaments. Then, for older adults, the 30s, 35s, 40s, 50s, 55s, 60s, 65s. Then, the "Super Seniors"—70s, 75s, 80s, 85s. These are contested on four surfaces; grass, clay, hard, indoor.

All: The score is even. It can be 15-all, 30-all in a game; or 2-all, 3-all in set score.

Alley: A 4½-foot-wide addition to the singles court on both sides in order to provide space for doubles play. This area, widening the court by nine feet, is in use during play following the serve.

Amateur: One who plays the game with no monetary reward involved, although some living expenses may be reimbursed. Prior to the advent of open tennis and the prize-money boom in 1968, the word was much abused. Amateurs at top tournaments were frequently referred to as "Shamateurs": players who accepted compensation under the well-known table and did not take checks or report their earnings as income. Alleged amateurs at the top sometimes earned more than the few outright touring professionals. "Pro" was considered a dirty word in most tennis circles until open tennis and a flood of prize money made the profession respectable. There was a semantic problem with "amateur" in the countries of eastern Europe when they formed the Communist bloc. Their state-supported players were labeled "amateurs" but were pros in everything but name. They were permitted to keep prize money in varying amounts, and depending on the outlook of the national federation. In some cases—notably that of the USSR—players had to turn prize money over to the national federation, and then were granted subsidies. This ended in 1990, largely due to the complaints of Soviet players Andrei Chesnokov and Natalia Zvereva, who lobbied publicly to keep the money they earned.

Ambies: Those aberrational few of bisockual habits—the ambidextrous. Unable to tolerate backhands, they switch racket from hand to hand, swatting only forehands. Two most notable were right-handers: Italian Giorgio de Stefani (1904–1992) and American Beverly Baker Fleitz (born March 13, 1930). De Stefani, a Davis Cupper, was World No. 9, 1934, when he may have blotted a Grand Slam for Fred Perry (who won the other three majors), beating him at the French. Fleitz was No. 1 in the U.S., No. 4 in the World, 1959, lost the Wimbledon final that year, only such creature to fly so high. At Wimbledon, 1972, two ambies clashed in the only major backhands-banned battle, Lita Liem, Indonesia, beating Marijke Schaar, Netherlands, 7-5, 7-9, 6-3, a first-rounder.

As far as is known there have been four other ambies in the tournament game: Brits Herbert Chipp, a Wimbledon semifinalist in 1884, Edith Shackle, also an 1880s Wimbledonian, and Indonesian Mrs. R. M. Sugiarto in the early 1970s. The rock-and-rolling Luke Jensen, who won the French doubles with brother Murph Jensen in 1993, is ambidextrous, too. But he plays his strokes as a right-hander with two-handed backhand, changing racket hands only on serve, confusing foes uniquely with left and right-handed deliveries—a switch-pitcher?

American Formation: *See* I Formation.

American twist: A top-spinning serve that takes a high bounce and can present difficulties for the receiver, particularly on grass, where the bounce is tricky. It was originated by Holcombe Ward, a Harvard man, and developed by him with his college friend, Dwight Davis, around the turn of the century. Their use of the stroke during the first Davis Cup match in 1900 was a revelation to their English opponents, whom they baffled and beat. *See* Kicker.

Approach shot: A drive followed to the net.

Around the post: A stroke hit by a player drawn so wide that it goes into the opposing court without clearing the net. In this rare case the shot is within the rules even if the flight of the ball is not higher than the net.

ATA: American Tennis Association. Founded in 1916, a time when tournament tennis was restricted to whites in the U.S., to provide sectional and national championships for blacks. The most famous ATA champs were Althea Gibson, who broke the color barrier in major events by entering the U.S. Championships in 1950, and Arthur Ashe. The organization continues to hold tournaments, open to all.

ATP: Association of Tennis Pros, an organization of male touring pros comparable to a union, embracing most of the leading pros. Founded in 1972, it has been influential in governing tournament conditions, conduct, prize-money amounts, and structure. Rebelling against the ITF and the MIPTC in 1989, and led by executive director Hamilton Jordan, the ATP took over organization and control of the men's worldwide circuit, with the exception of the four majors (Australian, French, Wimbledon, U.S.). After 20 years beneath the umbrella of the Grand Prix, it became in 1990 the ATP Tour.

ATP Tour: Since 1990 the men's professional circuit has been under the jurisdiction of the ATP Tour, with the exception of the Grand Slams (or four majors—Australian, French, Wimbledon, U.S.). This tour follows the same path as the Grand Prix, replacing it. The top eight finishers, on a point system, qualify for cash bonuses and a year-climaxing tournament called the ATP World Championship, formerly the Masters.

Davis Cup: The first U.S. team comprised (from left) Malcolm Whitman, Dwight Davis and Holcombe Ward. (USTA)

Australian Formation: *See* I Formation.

Avon Circuit: A series of women's prize money tournaments that operated from 1979 through 1982, sponsored by Avon cosmetics between the sponsorship of Virginia Slims (1970–78 and 1983–94).

Backhand: The stroke from the side of the body opposite the normal serving side—from the left for the right-handed and from the right for the left-handed.

Bagel, Bagel job: A shutout set, 6-0. The loser's score looks like a bagel. A double bagel or triple bagel could be a shutout match. A golden bagel is a very unusual love set in which the loser is limited to zero points. Two Hall of Famers had the golden touch: Hazel Wightman blitzed a Miss Huiskamp, 6-0, 6-0, winning all 48 points during the Washington State tourney of 1910; Pauline Betz won all 24 first-set points in winning the 1943 Tri-State title over Catherine Wolf, 6-0, 6-2.

Also used as a verb: to bagel, or shut out. The term was coined by Eddie Dibbs, a leading American player, in 1973.

Ball: The bouncing object hit back and forth over the net by the players. It is two-and-a-half inches in diameter and two ounces in weight. Balls are pressurized, with the pressure varying slightly according to national origin. The American ball is generally livelier and more in use for the power game popular in the United States. The European ball is usually lower pressure, easier to control, yet harder to hit for an outright winning point. The nap of the ball also varies, depending on the surface on which it is played. It is thick for abrasive surfaces such as concrete and asphalt, medium for clay and indoor, and light for grass. Balls were uniformly white until 1972 when yellow, offering increased visibility, began to take over.

Ball boy, girl: Youngsters who retrieve balls during tournament matches. Must be as unobtrusive as possible in retrieving balls and throwing to server. For the U.S. Open there are tryouts (minimum age 14), with candidates tested for throwing arm, speed, agility, and knowledge of tennis. They are paid the prevailing minimum wage, receive free uniforms, and get a chance to see the matches free.

Baseline: The court's back line, joining the sidelines, from which the serve is delivered.

Baseliner: A player who hangs back at the rear of the court, generally quite steady, keeping the ball in play with groundstrokes.

Bell Cup: A team competition between Australian and U.S. women, named for the donor, cosmetic manufacturer Jesse Bell, and held for three years, 1971, 1973, 1974. Australia won two of the matches. Discontinued.

Big Four: The major championships—Australian, French, Wimbledon, U.S. Also called the Grand Slams because winning all four within a calendar year constitutes a Grand Slam. Came to be called the Big Four because only those countries had won the Davis Cup for the first 73 years of its existence. Then South Africa (1974), Sweden (1975), Italy (1976), Czechoslovakia (1980) and Germany (1988) joined the club.

Big W: Wimbledon championships. *See* Wimbledon.

Break: A service break or loss of a service game. If the server loses the game, he or she is broken, sometimes in spirit as well as in fact.

Break point: Potentially the last point of a game being won by the receiver. If the receiver wins it, he breaks. If the server wins it, he prolongs the game and may eventually pull it out. Obviously a critical point. The following are break points (with the server's score first): 0-40, 15-40, 30-40, advantage out.

Breaker: Short for tie-breaker or tie-break. *See* Tie-breaker.

Breakfast at Wimbledon: A repast for American televiewers since 1979 when NBC first provided live coverage of the Big W, arriving at 9 a.m. on the East Coast, earlier in the West.

Roscoe Tanner saved the day, and concept, for nervous network officials, worried whether anyone would watch at that hour. He pushed Bjorn Borg for five exciting sets before losing at 6-4. The promo come-on, "Breakfast at Wimbledon," was coined by Bob Basche, then of NBC Sports.

Cannonball: An extraordinarily swift serve. Maurice McLoughlin, who won the U.S. title in 1912 and 1913, was the first of the cannonballing big servers. Bill Tilden, Gerald Patterson and Ellsworth Vines were known for their cannonballs. Pancho Gonzalez was said to be the fastest in his day, clocked at 117 MPH. Later, in the 1960s, Englishman Mike Sangster was timed at 154 MPH. Colin Dibley, an Aussie, was clocked at 148 MPH, American Roscoe Tanner at 140 in 1974—all those times with wooden rackets in serving demonstrations. Timing devices have changed, presumably more sophisticated, and even with the high-tech thundersticks of today in the hands of such bombers as Goran Ivanisevic, Pete Sampras, Boris Becker, Michael Stich, seemingly producing the highest speeds, the clockings don't register as high. But today's timing is done in actual matches, and the serve must be in play. Thus the ATP and WTA recognize only speeds documented within the last decade. The respective records: English lefty Greg Rusedski's 139.8 MPH zinger at Beijing (no Chinese home run that), an ace on match point against Jean Philippe Fleurian in 1996; flogging Dutchwoman, 6-foot-3 right-hander "Big Bad Brenda" Schultz's 121.8 MPH ace against Martina Hingis at the 1996 Australian Open.

Carry: *See* Double hit.

Centre Court: This is the cathedral of tennis, a stadium with roofing above most seats surrounding the principal court at Wimbledon, a structure much like an Elizabethan theater. On this grass court the championship finals are played along with the most important matches of the Wimbledon fortnight. It was built in 1922 to hold 14,000 spectators, 1,500 of them on each side in the open standing-room areas. That capacity was increased to about 15,000 in 1979. However, the imposition of stricter crowd control in Britain, following soccer stadium disasters, eliminated standing room in 1991, and lowered Centre Court capacity, 13,107 as of 1992. Center court can also mean the main court in any tennis complex.

Challenge Round: A type of final once common to tennis, particularly the Davis Cup, and now out of use, whereby the champion was privileged to stand aside the following year, waiting for a challenger to be determined by an elimination "all-comers" tournament. Then the challenger would face the reigning champion for the title. This format was discarded by the U.S. Championships for men after 1911, women after 1918, by Wimbledon after 1921, and by the Davis Cup in 1972. That year the Cup-holding U.S. played through the tournament along with the other nations entered, reached the final against Romania, and retained the title.

Change game, Changeover: At the completion of each odd game of a match, beginning with the first game, the players change sides in order to equalize playing conditions—sun, wind, court surface, etc.

Chip: *See* Dink.

Choking: What a player is doing who can't perform to his normal ability when the going gets rough and the pressure is on. Most players recognize that it can happen to the best of them, and they are not ashamed to admit it. Also called gagging.

Chip and charge: Attacking tactic—following a sliced approach to the net.

Chop: A severe, slicing stroke that imparts underspin.

Computer Rankings: A separate rating system used by male (ATP) and female (WTA) professional tours in both singles and doubles, based on data of results in tournament play. Rankings, revised and released at regular intervals, are used to determine who gets into which tournaments, and who is seeded. Data covers performance over the 12-month period preceding the release of rankings. The computers began making their printout pronouncements in 1973. The WTA changed its system in 1997 to a calendar year proposition, rankings beginning anew with each season.

Corel Tour: Corel, a Canadian software company, took over sponsorship of the women's professional tour in 1996, following Kraft, a subsidiary of Philip Morris.

Court: The surface on which the game is played. A tennis court can be surfaced with anything from anthill grit (in Australia) to dried cow dung (in India) to wood, clay, grass, linoleum, canvas, concrete, asphalt or synthetic carpets. The dimensions are always the same: 78 feet long and 27 feet wide (36 feet wide for doubles). The game began on grass courts in England. That is an uncommon surface now, although the biggest tournament of all, Wimbledon, is still a grass event.

Court speed: The "fastest" courts are those producing quick, low bounces, such as grass or wood, smooth, hard surfaces such as canvas stretched over wood or concrete, or concrete itself, or similar compositions such as asphalt. The "slowest" courts are those producing high, lazy bounces and are usually clay or a similar soft surface, most often a gritty substance spread over earth. Power players favor fast surfaces where serve-and-volley tactics are rewarded, while retrievers and baseliners favor slow surfaces, which allow them more time to make a stroke. Indoor play, without wind resistance, is generally faster than outdoor, usually taking place on synthetic carpets. Outdoors, a damp court of clay or grass generally plays slower. Manufacturers of synthetic carpets can change the speed, as can manufacturers of outdoor hard courts by altering the texture, following the principle that the smoother a court the faster it plays. As of 1988, the Big Four were played on three different surfaces: U.S. and Australia on hard courts, Wimbledon on grass, French on clay. All but the French, the premier clay-court event in the world, favor power players. U.S. titles are de-

termined on three surfaces: indoor, clay, and hard court (the U.S. Open), although a few grass-court titles remain, such as the Boys' and Girls' International 18s at Philadelphia.

Crosscourt: Diagonal shot across the court from the left or the right.

Cyclops: Electric eye device to judge service line. Calls faults with a shrill beep. Introduced at Wimbledon, 1980, continues in use there, numerous other tournaments. Invented by Margaret Parnis of England and Bill Carlton of Malta.

Davis Cup: Men's competition for teams representing nations throughout the world. It was originated at Boston's Longwood Cricket Club in 1900 by Dwight Filley Davis, who was a student at Harvard and played on the first team, competing against leading players from Great Britain. The Americans won in the inaugural year and have won a record 32 times through 1996. The competition has broadened from those two countries in 1900 to more than 125 in 1996, and is played over the course of 9 or 10 months. Only 16 countries actually compete annually for the Cup now, in a section called the World Group, instituted in 1981. The remainder play annually in geographically separated zones (European, African, American, Asian-Oceanian), and hope for promotion to the World Group through a system of relegation of first-round losers in the uppermost group. In 1987, losing in the first round to Paraguay, and then the relegation match to Germany, the U.S. was demoted to the American Zone for 1988. For the first time the U.S. was unable to compete for the Cup. Beating Peru and Argentina in 1988, the U.S. won the American Zone and was reinstated to the World Group in 1989.

The format is for four-man teams to meet in a best-of-five match series (formally called a tie) over three days (four singles, one doubles). Two singles the first day, doubles the second, two singles the third with the opponents reversed. Two men must play two singles each. The doubles team may be made up of any combination among the four players. The country with choice of ground selects the site and surface, usually a "home-court advantage." All matches are best-of-five sets. Since 1989, tie-breakers have been used, except for the ultimate fifth set. Referee and umpires are neutrals. Only nine countries have won: U.S., leading Australia, 32-26, as well as Britain (9), France (7), Sweden (5), Germany (3), South Africa (1) and Italy (1).

Default: Termination of a match in a way other than being played to completion. This can take one of three forms. Walkover: a match that is never begun and is awarded to the victor because the loser concedes beforehand, either by not showing up or informing the referee/supervisor of an inability or unwillingness to begin at the appointed time. In keeping statistics, no win or loss is recorded for an advance by walkover. Retirement: a player quits because of inability (illness, injury) or unwillingness to continue a match that has begun. The score up to that moment is recorded, along with a victory for the person still ready to play, a loss for the retiree. Disqualification: violation of rules of conduct to the point of expulsion, voluntary or involuntary. An example of the former was Jeff Tarango's well-publicized 1995 walkout at Wimbledon during a third-round match against Alex Mronz, who led, 7-6, 3-1, thus disqualifying himself. Examples of the latter vary. One was John McEnroe's obscene tirades at the 1990 Australian Open while playing a fourth rounder against Mikael Pernfors, culminating in the third of three separate code violations; McEnroe thus suffered a mandatory putout by Supervisor Ken Farrar. McEnroe, leading 6-1, 4-6, 7-5, 2-5, didn't want to leave. Another was Andre Agassi's prompt and correct eviction by supervisor Mark Darby from Indianapolis, 1996, after directing unacceptably abusive language at umpire Dana Loconto during a second round match he led, 6-1, 2-3, against Daniel Nestor. It was only the first violation, but deemed sufficiently reprehensible by Darby, despite Agassi's protests. Another was Shuzo Matsuoka's case of severe cramps while playing Petr Korda at the U.S. Open of 1995, responsible for his fourth set dis-

qualification for three time violations. With Matsuoka writhing on court, hoping to recover and resume, the supervisor had no choice but to put the clock on him and tick off his exceeding of the time limitions between points until three such violations had been reached. In each case the opponent was awarded victory by the score at the time of default, whether ahead or behind.

Deuce: A game or set score meaning the opponents are even at a certain point. The deuce factor provides that games and sets can go on and on. In a game the score is deuce at 40-all or three points each. To win, a player must take two straight points from deuce. The first point after deuce is advantage, and the score keeps reverting to deuce unless one player wins the two straight points. A set is deuced when the score becomes five games apiece. To win the set, a player must be two games ahead, thus winning two straight games from 5-all, 6-all, 7-all, etc. The longest deuce set ever played was 49-47 during the longest match ever played: Dick Leach and Dick Dell beat Tom Mozur and Len Schloss, 3-6, 49-47, 22-20—147 games—in the 1967 Newport (R.I.) Invitation. This was prior to adoption of the tie-breaker—death to deuce sets—played at six games all.

Nobody is sure about the longest of deuce games, but there have been some dandies. Most prominent was the dazzling one of 13 deuces, 20 minutes, in the 1995 Wimbledon final, served and lost by Arantxa Sanchez Vicario to Steffi Graf, although Arantxa had eight game points. It was the 11th game of the third set, tipping the match toward Graf, who won, 4-6, 6-1, 7-5. Virginia Wade served and lost a 21-deuce, 22-minute game to Billie Jean King in the semis of the 1970 Italian Open, despite having 16 game points, to lose the second set. King won 3-6, 7-5, 6-3. Marcelo Filippini served and lost a 28-deuce, 20-minute game to Alberto Berasategui at Casablanca in 1996, and the match, 6-2, 6-3.

Dink: A softly sliced stroke intended to fall in the forecourt, between the net and service line at a net-rusher's feet. Also called a chip.

Donkeys: Once fashionable term for consistent losers when the pro tour was principally an odyssey of one-night stands. Coiner was probably Pancho Segura.

Double Chrissie: Rare bird, player who emulates Chris Evert not only with two-handed backhand but also two-handed forehand. Lorne Main, a Canadian Davis Cupper, on scene in the 1940s and '50s, is believed to have been first such; Monica Seles is the most successful. In between a handful have doubled up, such as Japanese Federation Cupper Akiko Kijimuta, U.S. Davis Cuppers Jim Pugh and Gene Mayer. Best of the early specimens was Hall of Famer Frew McMillan. First American of this ilk: Bill Lenoir, No. 13 in the U.S. in 1962.

Double fault: When the server misses with both serves, thus losing the point.

Double hit: Striking the ball twice during the same stroke, a misfortune that used to mean automatic loss of the point but now only if judged "intentional." Also called a carry.

Doubles: A team game with two players on each side of the net.

Down-the-line: A shot along either sideline.

Down Undertakers: Sometimes called Godfather Hopman's Aussie Mafia, they buried the rest of the male world. Most successful tennis mob ever, led and motivated by Australian Davis Cup captain Harry Hopman, dominant from 1950 (Cup-grabbers Frank Sedgman and Ken McGregor) for almost a quarter-century through 1973, with John Newcombe's U.S. triumph and his and Rod Laver's Davis Cup heist. Starting with Sedgman's Aussie titles, 1949 and 1950, the gang accounted for 62 major singles: Sedgman (5), McGregor (1), Ken Rosewall (8), Lew Hoad (4), Mervyn Rose (2), Ashley Cooper (4), Mal Anderson (1), Rod Laver (11), Neale Fraser (3), Roy Emerson (12), Bill Bowrey (1), Newcombe (7), Tony Roche (1) and Fred Stolle (2).

Draw: The lineup for a customary elimination tournament. Names of the non-seeded players are drawn blindly, usually from a cup, and placed in the order drawn, from top to bottom on a bracketed draw sheet that indicates who opposes whom.

Drop shot: A softly hit shot, intentionally aimed to barely clear the net in order to win a point outright, or to pull the opponent in close.

Elbow: Getting the elbow is choking or tightening up at a critical point, a bad reaction to pressure. However, "tennis elbow" is an actual physical affliction, a painful malfunctioning of the elbow that strikes not only tennis players. Chinese cooks have reported a similar malady they call "wok elbow." Physicians have not found a sure cure for what they call "lateral epicondylitis."

Error: A mistake that loses a point during a rally, such as hitting the ball out or into the net.

Fast court: *See* Court Speed.

Fault: Failing to put the ball into play with the serve, either by serving into the net or beyond the confines of the service court. It is also a fault to step on the baseline while serving or to swing and miss the ball altogether. One fault isn't disastrous, but two lose the point.

Federation/Fed Cup: An annual worldwide women's team competition among nations comparable to the Davis Cup for men, which began in 1963, honoring the 50th anniversary of the founding of the ITF (International Tennis Federation). In 1995 the name was shortened to Fed Cup and the format was lengthened, from best-of-three match series (two singles and a doubles) played in one day to best-of-five over three days, identical to Davis Cup. Until 1995 the entire competition was limited to one week at one location. Now, like Davis Cup, they are played on a home-or-away basis with only members of the eight-country World Group eligible to win the Cup. Other nations (more than 80 in 1996) play in lesser zones, striving to move up to the top level.

The U.S. leads in Cups won (15), followed by Australia (7), Czechoslovakia (5), Germany (2), Spain (4), South Africa (1).

Fifteen: The first point either player or side wins.

First Ten or Top Ten: Select groups worldwide and nationally. The ATP and WTA issue computerized worldwide rankings weekly. (*See* Computer Rankings).Countries issue Top Ten rankings at the end of each year for play in that year, some based on computerized data, some based on the outlook of ranking committees. In the U.S. this began in 1894 for men when Bob Wrenn was No. 1, and in 1913 for women with Mary K. Browne at the top. In 1895 the USTA published retroactive rankings for 1885 through 1893, collected as consensus from various sources. Prior to the advent of the computers in 1973, informal world rankings were based on the judgment of various journalists covering the sport. In the U.S. rankings, the most frequent Top Ten residents have been Jimmy Connors (20 times between 1971 and 1991, 8 times at No. 1) and Chris Evert (19 times between 1971 and 1989, No. 1 6 times). Bill Tilden and Martina Navratilova were No. 1 12 times each.

On the worldwide ATP computer, Connors has ranked No. 1 in the year-end rankings five times and was in the Top Ten every year from 1973 through 1988. The WTA computer over the same period has listed Navratilova No. 1 seven times and in the Top Ten every year between 1975 and 1994.

Flinders Park: Location of Australia's National Tennis Center in Melbourne, site of the Australian Open since newly opened in 1988. The main stadium features a retractable roof so there's never a total wipeout by weather. Courts are hard surface, replacing grass, which had been traditional since 1905. Named for Capt. Matthew Flinders of the British navy, an explorer of the territory in the late eighteenth century. His connection with tennis seems only that he traveled a

lot, and may have swung a cat o' nine tails as a both-handed backhand.

Flushing Meadow: A public park, site of the U.S. Open, held there for the first time in 1978. It is named the USTA National Tennis Center, and is located in the borough of Queens in New York City. The principal court, Louis Armstrong Stadium, was the largest tennis arena in the world, seating 19,500. The courts are hard, an asphalt composition called DecoTurf. A new 23,500-seat principal stadium, named Arthur Ashe Stadium, was under construction in 1996, to be opened at the 1997 Open. *See* U.S. Open.

Foot fault: An infraction by the server, stepping on the baseline or serving from the wrong side of the center line. On a first serve it isn't serious. On the second it's a double fault and loss of point.

Forehand: The stroke hit from the right side of the body for a right-hander, and the left for a left-hander.

Forest Hills: Scene of the U.S. National Championships (from 1968 called the U.S. Open) for 63 years until the event moved to Flushing Meadow in 1978. Although the championship was played at the West Side Tennis Club, the tournament was generally referred to as Forest Hills, the residential section of the New York borough of Queens where the club is situated. The men's tournament moved from its original site, the Casino at Newport, R.I., to Forest Hills in 1915 and was played there every year through 1977 with the exception of 1921–23, when it was shifted to Germantown Cricket Club at Philadelphia while the Forest Hills Stadium was constructed on the West Side grounds. The women's tournament moved there from the Philadelphia Cricket Club in 1921. This stadium was opened in 1923 by the inaugural Wightman Cup match between the U.S. and Great Britain, and became one of the world's great tennis arenas, whose record crowd was 16,253 for the 1976 finals. The tournament was played on grass at Forest Hills until 1975, when clay courts were installed for the Open. *See* U.S. Open.

Foro Italico: Scene of the Italian Championships in Rome. A bastion of marble and pines alongside the Tiber, it is the world's most handsome setting for an important event and was built as Foro Mussolini during the dictator's reign in 1935.

Forty: The score for three points won by a side.

Game: The contest within a set and a match. One player serves throughout a game. To win a game, the player must win four points, unless the score is three points apiece, known as deuce. Then the player must get two points ahead of his opponent to win the game. The points in a game are called 15, 30, 40 and game—in that order. To win a set, the player must win six games, unless the score is five games apiece. Then it is a deuce set, and the player must take two straight games from deuce to win. In most cases a tie-breaker game is played to determine the winner of a set at six games apiece. *See* Tie-breaker.

Grand Masters: A prize-money tournament circuit inaugurated in 1973 for the cream of the crocks—ex-champs over 45—by Cincinnati businessman Al Bunis. Dealing in nostalgia and featuring such yet imposing players as Pancho Gonzalez, Frank Sedgman and Torben Ulrich, it was a financial success. Sedgman won the championship tournament in 1975, 1977 and 1978, Ulrich in 1976, and Sven Davidson in 1979. Ken Rosewall had the greatest fortune, winning in 1982, and 1985 through 1989. After that the Grand Masters was discontinued, but had spawned such other enterprises for elders as the ATP Senior Tour and the Legends.

Grand Prix: Between 1970 and 1989, this was the worldwide tournament structure for men. Conceived by Hall of Famer Jack Kramer, it embraced all the consequential tournaments, offering points for each win, cash bonuses for the leading finishers, and spots in the season-climaxing tournament, the Masters, for the top eight fin-

ishers. This system has continued as the ATP Tour, begun in 1990, excluding the majors (Australian, French, Wimbledon, U.S.). The ATP World Championship replaces the Masters.

Grand Slam: The rare feat of winning the four major championships (Australian, French, Wimbledon, U.S.) all in the same year. Don Budge did it in 1938, Maureen Connolly in 1953, Rod Laver in 1962 and 1969, Margaret Smith Court in 1970, Steffi Graf in 1988. Grand Slams have also been made in doubles: Frank Sedgman and Ken McGregor, 1951; Martina Navratilova and Pam Shriver, 1984; Maria Bueno (with two partners, Christine Truman and Darlene Hard), 1960. And mixed doubles: Margaret Smith and Ken Fletcher, 1963; Owen Davidson (with two partners, Lesley Turner and Billie Jean King), 1967.

Grand Slam Cup: An event initiated in 1990 by the ITF for the 16 top male finishers in the four majors/Grand Slams (Australian, French, Wimbledon, U.S.). Played at the close of the season, it is the richest of all tournaments, offering a $6-million purse with a maximum $2 million for the victor. It has been played in Munich from 1990 through 1995, in Hanover in 1996, and has been won by Pete Sampras, David Wheaton, Michael Stich, Petr Korda, Magnus Larsson, Goran Ivanisevic and Boris Becker, respectively.

Grand Slams: The four major tournaments (Australian, French, Wimbledon, U.S.). In recent years it has become popular to refer to any of the majors as a Grand Slam tournament. Formerly the usage was Big Four. Put four Grand Slams together in one year and you have a feat called the Grand Slam.

Grip: The method of holding the racket. Also the wrapping around the handle—often leather stripping—to make the hand's (hands') grip surer. Basic grips are the Eastern, Western and Continental, but there are also numerous (but slight) variations adapted by individual players. Until the arrival of Chris Evert, Jimmy Connors and Bjorn Borg in the early 1970s, two-handed strokes were rare. But those three influenced so many players with their two-handed backhand baseball grip that one-handed backhands now are rare. Left-handed Monica Seles, gripping the racket with both hands on both sides, may be an influence, too. Pancho Segura of Ecuador, right-handed, was one of the earlier two-fisted strokesmen in the 1940s, his shot a forehand. Vivian McGrath, a right-handed Australian Davis Cup player and champion of his country in 1937, at age 20, was the first to use a two-handed backhand at the world-class level.

Groundstroke: A stroke hit after the ball bounces, usually from the backcourt. Also called groundies.

Gut: Animal intestines used to string rackets. The best gut comes from cows.

Hacker: An ordinary player—a term applying to most of us; the tennis equivalent of the golfing duffer. Also used in good-natured ribbing by the pros.

Half volley: The stroke by which the ball is blocked as soon as it hits the ground. Like trapping a baseball.

Hall of Fame: Located at the Newport Casino, Newport, R.I., the International Tennis Hall of Fame was established as a valhalla for all-time greats of the game as well as a museum of tennis history and memorabilia. It was founded in 1953, conceived by tennis innovator Jimmy Van Alen as the National Tennis Hall of Fame, and until 1975 it enshrined only Americans. That year the name and scope went worldwide as the International Tennis Hall of Fame with the induction of Englishman Fred Perry. The first class of inductees was tapped in 1955.

Handsome Eight: The appellation given his World Championship Tennis troupe by promoter Dave Dixon, who raided the traditional game as seldom before, turning five outstanding amateurs professional in 1968: Cliff Drysdale, South Africa; Wimbledon and U.S. champ John Newcombe, Australia; Nikki Pilic, Yugoslavia;

Tony Roche, Australia; Roger Taylor, England. To those he added established pros Pierre Barthes, France; Butch Buchholz and Dennis Ralston, U.S. These signings, depleting the amateur ranks, hastened the advent of open tennis that year. Roche, a rugged type, joked that in handsomeness he ranked 15th among the eight.

Hard court: This term can be confusing because in the U.S. "hard court" means concrete, asphalt or similar paving, such as U.S. Open courts at Flushing Meadow, while in Europe, Australia and most other countries, the term applies to clay courts. Beginning in 1948 the USTA held a U.S. Hard Court Championships for men and women. This ran through 1969 and has been played sporadically since. *See* Court speed.

Heater: A muscular serve.

Hopman Cup: Annual international team competition honoring late Australian Davis Cup captain, Harry Hopman, held in Perth. Latest approved by ITF after eight years as exhibition. Format—best-of-three match ties (men's and women's singles, mixed doubles). First official winner, 1997, U.S. (Chanda Rubin, Justin Gimelstob), 2-1 over South Africa (Amanda Coetzer, Wayne Ferreira).

Houston Nine: The original Long Way Babies of the Virgina Slims tour, rebels who defied suspensions by their national associations to play the $7,500 tour inaugural at Houston: Peaches Bartkowicz, Rosie Casals, Judy Tegart Dalton, Billie Jean King, Julie Heldman, Kerry Melville, Kristy Pigeon, Nancy Richey, Valerie Ziegenfuss. Casals beat Dalton in the final, 5-7, 6-1, 7-5.

I Formation: An unorthodox doubles alignment with the netman standing in the service court directly ahead of his partner, the server, instead of in the adjoining court. The purpose is to confuse the receiver. Also called the tandem formation, as well as the Australian formation (in the U.S.) and the American formation (in Australia).

In the zone: A state of great confidence when one is playing sensationally, even above expected ability, as "I'm sure in the zone today."

From *The Twilight Zone,* a television program about other-worldly behavior and situations.

IPA: Independent Players' Association, an organization founded in opposition to the ATP by Bill Riordan, tournament promoter and then-manager of Jimmy Connors. Connors appeared to be the only member of his private union, of which nothing has been heard since 1975.

ITF: International Tennis Federation (originally the International Lawn Tennis Federation). Since 1913 it has been the world governing body of tennis, embracing the amateur bodies of more than 100 countries. The ITF has little control over professional tennis but does have the major championships (Australian, French, Wimbledon, U.S.) beneath its umbrella, and it administers the Davis Cup, Federation Cup, Hopman Cup, Grand Slam Cup and Olympic competitions as well as a worldwide network of junior and senior events.

Jag: A verb coined by Aussies meaning "to hit the ball unstylishly but somehow getting it over the net," as in Rod Laver remarking, "I just made up my mind to jag a few, keep it in play, until I found my timing."

Johnston Award: An award presented by the USTA since 1947, memorializing Bill Johnston (1894–1946), the competitive but gracious U.S. champion of 1915 and 1919, and standout Davis Cupper of the 1920s. Johnston gave one of his cups for such a purpose, though not suggesting that it be named for him. It was intended to honor an active American male player who exemplified sportsmanship as Johnston had. The last person to fit that description was Tim Mayotte of Springfield, Mass., in 1988. But apparently the present scene is so devoid of such that the USTA desperately has been handing it out to admirable but long-retired players, several of them non-Americans.

Junkballer: Player using a variety of speeds, spins, change-of-pace, soft stuff—a mixture of "junk," ("garbage")—usually intended to throw off a superior, hard-hitting foe. A standout, Julie Heldman, No. 5 in the world, 1974, called herself "Junkball Julie," and relished driving opponents to distraction. An outstanding junk-balling feat was Michael Chang's fourth-round befuddlement of favorite Ivan Lendl at the French, 1989 (en route to the title), his repertory of trash including an underhand serve.

Kicker: An American twist serve taking a high bounce to the right if served by a right-hander and to the left if served by a left-hander. *See* American Twist.

Kill: To put a ball away, usually by hitting an overhead smash that blasts the ball well out of the opponent's reach.

King's Cup: An indoor team competition for European nations, along the lines of the Davis Cup. It was named for the 1936 donor, King Gustav V of Sweden, the tennis fanatic who played into his nineties. Discontinued.

Kooyong: A private club in Melbourne, Australia, whose stadium, built in 1927 (and enhanced by auxiliary stands), held the third-largest crowds in tennis history, 22,000 for the Australian-U.S. Davis Cup finale in 1957. Most frequent site of the grass-based Australian Championships until 1988 when the event moved across town to the newly built National Tennis Centre and hard courts. An Aboriginal word, kooyong means "haunt of the wild fowl," and a few wildly foul tennis players were seen and heard over the years.

Kraft Tour: From 1990 through 1994, the women's professional circuit, including the four majors (Australian, French, Wimbledon, U.S.), was under the sponsorship banner of Kraft Foods. Corel stepped into that role in 1996. Top 16 finishers in a points system qualify for cash bonuses and a year-climaxing playoff at New York's Madison Square Garden.

Let: The signal for a replay. If a serve hits the top of the net and proceeds into the proper service court, the serve is replayed. If a point is interrupted or interfered with in any way (such as a ball from a nearby court rolling through), let is called, and the point is replayed.

Liner: A shot landing on or touching a line. It is a good shot.

Line judge: A court official who judges whether a shot is out or in play. Sometimes known as line umpire or linesman/lineswoman. To indicate "out" an arm-extended signal and vocal call are given ("Fault!" if it is a service line call). On a shot close to the line a "safe" signal—hands extended parallel to the court—is given to indicate that the ball is in play. A "skeleton crew" of six may officiate, with a chair umpire covering service line, baselines, and center and sidelines the length of the court. Eleven make up a full officiating crew: umpire, net judge, two baseline judges, six (three at either end) for side and center lines, one to handle both service lines. A crew can be expanded to 14 with the addition of another service-line judge and two foot-fault judges.

Lingering death: The most common tie-breaker based on Jimmy Van Alen's original theme, but adhering to the deuce principle of winning only if ahead by two or more points. The goal is to reach 7 points, but the winner must be two points ahead; thus at 6 points–all the tie-breaker could continue indefinitely. This form is usually called the 12-point tie-breaker, a misnomer since it may stretch well beyond 12. *See* Tie-breaker.

Lob: A high, arching stroke meant either as a defensive shot (enabling the hitter to regain position) or to go over the head of an opponent at net. Frank Hadow, the Wimbledon champion in 1878, is generally credited with originating this stroke.

Long Way Babies: The women of the early days of the women's pro tour, with the name taken from the sales pitch, "You've Come a Long Way, Baby!," of the sponsor, Virginia Slims cigarettes. Their formative days were chronicled in Grace Lichtenstein's 1974 book, *A Long Way, Baby. See* Houston Nine.

Longwood: Longwood Cricket Club is the oldest significant tennis club in the U.S., dating from 1877 (although the New Orleans Lawn Tennis Club, 1876, is the oldest). Located in the Boston suburb of Chestnut Hill, Longwood has been the scene of top-flight tennis almost since its beginning. The first Davis Cup tie was played there in 1900, the U.S. Doubles Championships from 1917 through 1967, the U.S. Pro from 1964 to date. Among members were such tennis pioneers as Dwight Davis, donor of the Davis Cup; Hazel Wightman, donor of the Wightman Cup; Richard Sears, first U.S. champion; Dr. James Dwight, "Father of the Game" in the U.S. Courts are grass, hard and clay.

Love: A zero score. A love game is a blitz, with the winner taking four straight points. A love set is six games to none (*See* Bagel Job). Probably derived from the French word l'oeuf, meaning the egg—and implying the old goose egg.

Lucky loser: A player who loses in the quallies (qualifying tournament), yet gets into the main draw because a vacancy opens through a withdrawal. The lucky loser filling such a vacancy is the loser in the quallies with the highest computer ranking. In earlier days of the open era such a winning loser was genuinely lucky since he/she was picked at random from a hat containing the names of all the defeated. Rarest of the rare is a lucky loser who actually slips into the tournament and wins it; Swiss Heinz Gunthardt (ranked No. 218) was the first into the select group of such improbable champs, winning Springfield (Mass.) in 1978. Joining him: German Werner Zirngibl (206) at Brussels, 1978; American Billy Scanlon (101) at Maui, 1978; Spaniard Francisco Clavet (148) at Hilversum (Neth.), 1990; Argentine Christian Miniussi (116) at São Paulo, 1991.

Majors: Each year there are only four major championships, the cornerstones of the game: the Australian Open, French Open, Wimbledon and the U.S. Open. Also known as the Big Four, originally because only Australia, France, Britain and the U.S. had won the Davis Cup. Often called the Grand Slams, a carelessness of language because a Grand Slam is not a single championship but the rare feat of winning all four within a calendar year, first accomplished in singles by Don Budge in 1938.

Masters:　The climax of the tennis year was the eight-man Masters playoff among the top eight finishers in the Grand Prix. Begun in 1970 at Tokyo, where Stan Smith won, the Masters moved from city to city, settling in New York in 1977, and stayed at Madison Square Garden through 1989 when the Masters, under that name, was discontinued. The format went on as the ATP Tour World Championship in Frankfurt, Germany, in 1990. Ivan Lendl won the Masters five times (1981, 1982, 1985, 1986, 1987) and Ilie Nastase four (1971, 1972, 1973, 1975).

Match:　The overall contest. It may be a best-of-three-sets match or a best-of-five-sets match, meaning one player must win either two sets or three sets to be the victor. The number of matches needed to win a tournament is determined by the size of the draw in a conventional elimination tournament, or by whatever rules prevail, as in a round-robin or medal-play event.

Match point:　The point prior to completion of a match. The player in the lead needs only one more point to win. This can be a very dramatic spot, and sometimes the player behind in the score saves numerous match points and goes on to victory. Pancho Gonzalez saved seven match points in a dramatic five-set victory over Charlie Pasarell during the 1969 Wimbledon, the longest match ever played there: 22-24, 1-6, 16-14, 6-3, 11-9—112 games.

MIPTC:　Men's International Professional Tennis Council, a board of control for the male pro tournament game. Formed in 1974, it governed the men's game through 1989 with representation from the ATP, ITF and tournament directors. Abandoned in 1990 when the ATP Tour supplanted the Grand Prix.

Mixed doubles:　Doubles with one male and one female on each side.

Moonball:　A high, floating groundstroke used in baseline rallying to slow down the pace.

It's not as high as a lob and is usually hit with topspin. It is most associated with a leading American, Harold Solomon, who hit them forever and who coined the term in 1972 when his moonballing epic, a marathon victory over Guillermo Vilas during the French Open, consumed more than five hours.

Net:　The webbed barrier dividing the court at middle and over which the ball is to be hit. At the center point it is three feet high and at either end three-and-a-half feet.

Net cord:　A shot that hits the top of the net and drops into the opposite court. Also, the cord or wire cable that supports a net.

Net judge:　An official seated at one end of the net, usually below the umpire's chair, to detect lets on serve. During the serve he rests one hand on the net cord to feel whether the ball hits the top of the net. If it does, he calls "Net!" and the serve is replayed as a let if the ball lands in the proper court.

Net rusher:　An attacking player who follows his serve to the net and continually seeks the closeup position to make winning volleys.

Newport Casino:　Oldest of the world's active tournament grounds. The Casino was built in Newport (R.I.) by the wealthy publisher of the *New York Herald,* James Gordon Bennett, an angry reaction to his being tossed out of the Reading Room, the town's most fashionable club of the time. Seems Bennett dared the star of his polo team, a Capt. Candy, to ride into the club to liven things up. Candy complied, resulting in the expulsion of his boss. Although considered a polo pony's posterior by his former fellow members, Bennett had the last horse laugh, hiring renowned architect Stanford White to design the new club that would become the cradle of American tournament tennis, playing host to the first U.S. Championships (for men only) on its grass courts in 1881. The tourney site through 1914, it remains a busy club and location of the International Tennis Hall of Fame. Prominent tournament tennis has continued on the grass, including a men's amateur event from 1915 through 1967, and professional tournaments since 1965, recently an ATP Tour stopover, the last American pro tourney on grass.

No-ad: A form of scoring originated by Jimmy Van Alen that eliminates deuce and replaces love-15-30-40 with 0-1-2-3. The maximum points for a game are seven. At 3-3 (normally deuce) the next point is game point for both sides, with the receiver having choice of courts. No-ad has been used by World Team Tennis and the National Collegiate Athletic Association. *See* VASSS.

No-brainer: A wildly improbable shot or performance, as in Jimmy Connors' "God, what a no-brainer!" after being served out of Wimbledon by Kevin Curren (33 aces) in 1983.

Not up: The call when a player hits the ball just as it has bounced the second time on a close play. Usually the net judge makes the ruling, but if there are no officials, it is up to the offending player to call it against himself and accept loss of the point.

NTL: National Tennis League, an organization formed by George MacCall in 1967 to promote professional tournaments. Under contract were Rod Laver, Ken Rosewall, Pancho Gonzalez, Andres Gimeno, Fred Stolle, Roy Emerson, Billie Jean King, Rosie Casals, Ann Jones and Françoise Durr. By 1970 NTL had been put out of business and absorbed by rival WCT.

Open: A tournament that may be entered by both amateurs and professionals, generally offering prize money. Not until 1968 did the ITF permit opens. The first, the British Hard Court Championships, was won by pro Ken Rosewall and amateur Virginia Wade. Now all the leading national title events are open.

Overhead: A stroke, usually a smash, executed like a serve by raising the racket above the head and swinging down hard.

Passing shot: A ball hit past the opposing netman on either side beyond his reach.

Philadelphia Cricket Club: This private club in the Philadelphia suburb of Chestnut Hill was the site of the U.S. Women's Championships from inception in 1887 through 1920. In 1921 the tournament moved to Forest Hills, and in 1978 to Flushing Meadow.

Placement: A shot aimed at a particular sector and hit so well that the opponent can't touch it.

Poach: In doubles, a net player, hoping to make a winning volley, crosses in front of his partner.

Point: The smallest unit of scoring. A game is won by a player winning four points, except in the case of deuce. The first point of a game is called 15, the second 30, the third 40, and the fourth is game. At 40-all the score is deuce. Each point is begun with the serve, and one player serves an entire game. In keeping score, the server's score is called first—e.g., in 15-40, 15 is the server, and 40 is the receiver.

Professional: A player who plays prize-money events for money or a teacher who gives tennis lessons for money.

Pusher: A player who hopes to wear down the opponent by maddeningly returning everything with soft looping strokes. A pusher hangs back at the baseline, a good retriever, patiently waiting for a big hitter to blow his cool and the match. Also known as a pooper, puddler, or puffball artist.

Quallies: The qualifying tournament preceding every professional tournament. The rewards for winners (qualifiers) are spots in the main draw. Entrance is based on computer ranking.

Qualifier: One who wins the required number of matches in a qualifying tournament to be admitted to the main draw. Most celebrated qualifier was John McEnroe, then an 18-year-old amateur at Wimbledon in 1977. He won three qualifying matches to enter the main draw, and won five more matches to reach the semis. Occasionally a qualifier even wins the tournament—

26 of them on the ATP Tour beginning with No. 226 ranked Argentine Jose-Luis Clerc at Florence in 1978. Longest-shot was Senegalese Yahiya Doumbia, No. 453, winning Lyon in 1988, and as the only repeater, No. 282, winning Bordeaux in 1995. The women's longest-shots were Italian Gloria Pizzichini, No. 150, winning Bol (Croatia) in 1996, and Swede Catrin Jexel, No. 146, winning Hong Kong in 1982. Quallies for the four majors, and some other tournaments, offer prize money.

Racket: The implement used in hitting the ball. Originally the frame—handle and relatively oval head—was made of wood, and remained that way for nearly a century. Metal began making serious inroads with the introduction of the Wilson "steelie," T2000, in 1967, notably in the right hand of Billie Jean King, winning the U.S. title. Conceived by French great, Hall of Famer René Lacoste, the steelie was given its greatest prominence a few years after King by Jimmy Connors, who won almost all of his male-record 109 titles with it. Steel had been used sporadically in the early days of the game, and the durable Dayton Steel racket, with steel strings, enjoyed some popularity in the 1920s and '30s. Aluminum made a hit in 1968 as Arthur Ashe used the Head "snowshoe" to win the U.S. Open. Others took up that metal including Rod Laver. A high-tech breakthrough was scored in 1976 by ski designer and tennis enthusiast Howard Head, introducing for Prince a revolutionary composition model with abnormally oversized head and much more hitting area. Wood's days were numbered then, and all sorts of high-tech materials were introduced, such as graphite, magnesium, boron, fiberglass. Rackets grew in head size, frame thickness and strength. Players hit with more power and speed. Not until 1981 did the ITF decide that rules should be made governing racket size. It was then decreed that it must not exceed 32 inches from bottom of handle to top of head, or 12½ inches in overall width. The strung surface must not exceed 15½ inches in overall length and 11½ inches in overall width. The best strings are made of cow's intestines, but synthetics are efficient, cheaper, more widely used.

Rally: An exchange of shots during a point. Originally called "rest." The shortest would be two shots, return of serve and a reply by the server. While seldom does anybody keep track, there have obviously been tremendous and tedious bids for longest. Probably most dramatic and widely seen of modern-day rallies was the 19-stroke all-court set-point duel of Pete Sampras and Andre Agassi in the 1995 U.S. Open final, ended by Pete's roaring backhand that gave him the opening set. But that was a midget compared with some that have been recorded: 643 strokes, a point lasting 29 minutes, committed indoors by point-winning Vicki Nelson-Dunbar over Jean Hepner in a 6-hour, 31-minute first-rounder (the female record), won by Nelson-Dunbar, 6-4, 7-6 (13-11), Richmond (Va), 1984; Dick Gaines taking a 670-stroke, 16-minute marathon from Tony Vincent during the 1953 Canadian Championships, but losing the match; the USTA reporting in June of 1995 that Ken Graham and Bob Migliorini played a 45-minute point in an unfinished (2-hour time limit) USTA League match at Trumbull, Conn. All that for one point—but who's counting?

Riordan circuit: The first viable indoor circuit for men in the U.S., organized by the late Bill Riordan, dynamic promoter from Salisbury, Md., and then manager of Jimmy Connors. He started in earnest in 1964 by transferring the nearly defunct U.S. Indoor Championships from New York to Salisbury, where it became a thriving event. He expanded to eight tournaments by 1975, its last year. A combative type, Riordan fought the growth of WCT and the ATP; founded his own players' organization, called the IPA (Independent Players' Association); and kept his series of winter tournaments going as a one-man operation under the aegis of the USTA that he called the Independent circuit but was generally known as the Riordan circuit. *See* IPA.

Referee: The official in charge of tournament play, making the draw, scheduling of matches, interpreting the rules and adjudicating disputes between players and umpires.

Roland Garros: The 17,000-seat stadium and tennis complex in Paris where the French Championships has been played yearly since 1928. Built primarily for the first French defense of the Davis Cup that year, it was named for a heroic French aviator killed in World War I. Surface is clay. In 1968 the French was the first major open. Although the tournament dates to 1891, it did not become an international championship, welcoming non-French citizens, until 1925. A secondary stadium, seating 10,000 and named for the luminous Suzanne Lenglen, was opened in 1995. The grounds can accommodate more than 30,000, and one-day (33,583) and tournament (384,092) attendance records were set in 1996, testimony of its preeminence among the country's sporting occasions.

Rubber: An individual singles or doubles match in a team competition such as Davis Cup or Wightman Cup. The usage is British and European.

Scrambler: A player who hustles for every point and manages to get the ball back somehow, though probably not very stylishly. A dogged retriever, usually a pusher, a grubber.

Seeding: The deliberate (instead of chance) placing of certain strong players so that they will not meet in the earlier rounds of an elimination tournament. It was introduced to major tennis at Wimbledon in 1924 in modified form when it was attempted to widely separate leading players of different countries. In 1927 Wimbledon adopted a formal, pre-published seeding list of eight men and women in singles, one in each quarter, with René Lacoste and Helen Wills Moody accorded top seeds by committee judgement (as well as four seeded teams in doubles). The U.S. followed suit that year, with Bill Tilden and Wills at the top of a domestic list, although adding a foreign seeded list of eight headed by Lacoste and Betty Nuthall. The U.S. continued home and foreign seeding until integrating the two in 1956. Seeding lists were enlarged over the year so that now 16 is the standard number at the majors in all five events. Seeded players (those judged by a tournament committee or according to computerized rankings to be the leaders on the basis of performance and ability) are listed in numbered order prior to the draw. Then the seeds are separated by being planted in positions specified by tournament regulations. Thus the top two entrants, Nos. 1 and 2, are located at opposite ends of the draw, and if the seeding runs true, they will meet in the final.

Service or serve: The act of putting the ball into play and beginning a point by hitting the ball from the baseline diagonally over the net and into the opponent's service court. Any motion (underhand, sidearm, or whatever) is permissible. However, the overhead stroke is nearly universal.

Service break: Winning the opponent's service.

Service court(s): There are two, since the server alternates from the right to the left side of the court with each point. The service courts are bounded by the sidelines, the net, and the service line, which is 21 feet from the net; they are divided from one another by the center line. Each court is 13½ feet wide by 21 feet deep.

Service winner: An unreturnable serve, though not an ace.

Set: The third-highest unit of scoring. The winner of six games takes the set, except when the score is 5-all in games. Then it is a deuce set, and the winner must win by two games, unless tie-breakers are used, usually at 6-all in games. In that case one tie-breaker game decides the outcome of the set, whose score would be 7-6.

Set point: The point prior to the completion of a set. The player needs only one more point to win the set. But the player behind may still save the set point and go on to win the set himself, thanks to the deuce factor.

Sitter: An easy opportunity; a ball softly hit close to the net and well within reach, which can be smashed away for a point.

Slice: Hitting under the ball, which produces underspin and a low bounce.

Slims Circuit: The first notable attempt to bring women into the prize-money era of tennis was made successfully by Gladys Heldman, publisher of *World Tennis* magazine, who in 1970 began forming a circuit for the women separate from that of the men and backed by Virginia Slims cigarettes (a product of Philip Morris), a sponsorship lasting through 1978, and returning in 1983. Although Kraft Foods (a Philip Morris subsidiary) took over tour sponsorship, 1990–94, Slims maintained a presence, particularly as sponsor of the season-closing Championships at New York's Madison Square Garden, 1979–94. In 1995, Corel became the Championships sponsor. In 1996, Corel assumed tour sponsorship, Chase that of the Championships. With Heldman as the organizational wizard and Billie Jean King as spokeswoman and all-conquering champion, the women's game took off in 1971. By going it alone, the women no longer played second racket to the men in cash or publicity, and their prize money rose dramatically.

Slow court: *See* Court speed.

Smash: An overhead stroke brought down hard like a serve.

Spikes: Spiked shoes with ⅜-inch metal spikes were in common usage years ago when grass-court tennis was preeminent, usually on wet courts to aid footing. Their last notable appearance was on the feet of Rod Laver, completing his 1969 Grand Slam with a U.S. Open final victory over sneaker-shod Tony Roche at damp and mushy Forest Hills.

Spin: Pronounced rotation of the ball according to how it is struck by the racket, and divided into three categories: topspin (overspin); slice (underspin); and sidespin. For topspin the racket brushes the ball from low to high produc-ing a high bouncing ball, enabling one to hit the ball harder and still keep it deep but within the court. For slice the racket brushes from high to low, producing a low bounce. A serving slice is a chop, causing the ball to bounce to the receiver's right if server is right-handed and to the left if server is left-handed. For sidespin the racket brushes across the ball on either side, producing a bounce to the left if ball is struck on the right side, and vice versa.

Sudden death: A tie-breaker of definite length, either 9-point or 13-point, settled by a sudden-death point when the score is 4-4, or 6-6. It was conceived by Jimmy Van Alen. *See* Tie-breaker.

Supervisor: The person in charge of officiating at an ATP Tour or major tournament. Working in cooperation with the referee, the supervisor is the highest court of appeal, levying fines, if need be, and issuing or approving disqualifications by umpire or referee.

Supreme Court: The trade name for a synthetic carpet court favored for a majority of professional indoor tournaments.

Tandem Formation: *See* I Formation.

Thirty: The second point scored within a game, following 15, preceding 40.

Throat: The thin part of the racket between the handle and the head, when rackets were wood. Now it's an open triangular throat.

Tie: A team match between countries, such as Davis Cup or Federation Cup. It is an old expression, used mainly in Britain and Europe, seldom in the U.S. In the Davis Cup, a tie is composed of five rubbers. *See* Rubber.

Tie-breaker, Tie-break: An overtime game to end a set at 6 games–all, rather than continuing in a theoretically interminable deuce set in which one side must be ahead by two games to win a set that has been tied at 5 games–all. It's another scoring innovation—the most revolutionary rules change in the game's first century—

from the fertile mind of the late Jimmy Van Alen, sometimes called the "Newport Bolshevik." He unveiled it at the pro tourney he sponsored at the Newport (R.I.) Casino in 1965 as a feature of his radical scoring plan, VASSS. Mike Davies defeated Ken Rosewall, 5-points-to-3 in the initial breaker. This evolved to the Sudden Death, best-of-9-points breaker, in use at the U.S. Open between 1970 and 1974, on the Virginia Slims circuit and in U.S. colleges for a time. Following the U.S. in adopting the breaker were Australia and Italy in 1971, France in 1973 and Wimbledon in 1972, although Wimbledon cautiously put it into effect at 8 games–all. That lasted until 1979. Those three majors, as well as Italy and most other countries, didn't approve of Sudden Death, however, and were using the ITF's variation devised by Peter John on Van Alen's theme, the so-called 12-point tie-break, in universal use today. This version is actually "Lingering Death," as Van Alen called it. Although generally won by the first side to reach 7 points, it could theoretically run interminably since a two-point margin is required. The longest thus has lingered 50 points (a 26-24 breaker won by Jan Gunnarson and Michael Mortensen over John Frawley and Victor Pecci at Wimbledon in 1985). Among the major championships, the U.S. is alone in settling all sets by tie-breaker at 6 games–all. The other three revert to conventional deuce sets for the ultimate set (fifth for men, third for women). For a brief time WCT used a Sudden Death best-of-13 point breaker.

This is the tie-breaker format: After one side serves the first point from the right court, serve alternates for two-point sequences, each beginning from the left court. Players change ends at every six-point juncture. The score of a tie-breaker set is 7-6. Only two matches at the U.S. Open have been totally tie-breakered, both female: Steffi Graf over Pam Shriver 7-6 (7-4), 6-7 (4-7), 7-6 (7-4), quarters, 1985; Gigi Fernandez over Leila Meskhi, 7-6 (7-1), 6-7 (3-7), 7-6 (7-2), fourth round, 1991. The closest consequential matches ending with a two-point margin (7-5 fifth-set breakers) were the 1972 WCT final in Dallas, Rosewall over Rod Laver, and the 1988 Masters at New York, Boris Becker over Ivan Lendl. The closest consequential match in the "sudden death" days with a one-point margin (5-4 fifth-set breaker) was the 1970 Pacific Coast semifinal at Berkeley, Cliff Richey over Stan Smith. Scoring the last point—simultaneous match point—with a diving volley, Richey not only won the match, 7-6 (5-2), 6-7 (2-5), 6-4, 4-6, 7-6 (5-4), but barely (by a single point!) assured himself of the No. 1 U.S. ranking over No. 2 Smith as the season concluded. Because of the similarity of their records for the year, the outcome of that meeting was to determine No. 1.

Topspin: An overspin produced by brushing the ball from low to high. This enables one to hit the ball very hard and high over the net and still keep it in court. It creates a high bounce, and also a ball difficult to volley. Originated by Englishman Herbert Lawford in the early days of the game, helping him to gain the Wimbledon final six times, and win in 1887. Called the "Lawford stroke" during the 1880s in the U.S. and "lift" in Europe. *See* Spin.

Top Ten: *See* First Ten.

Tournament: The basic form of competition. The most common is a single-elimination tournament with a minimum of eight entries. Departure of losers cuts the field in half at each round as a tournament narrows to two entries in the final. The world's four premier tournaments—Wimbledon and the Australian, U.S. and French Opens—normally have draws of 128 men and women, with seven rounds of play. Sometimes, as at the ATP Tour World Championships, a round-robin system is used with members of four-man groups playing one another for the right to enter the semis. It is possible to lose a round-robin match and win the title, done several times.

Tree-ing: A fantastic performance where everything goes right—"He was tree-ing: I couldn't get into it." Particularly serving overpoweringly. "The guy was serving from a tree."

U.E.: Dreaded initials for unforced error, a loss of a point on a shot that should have been put in play.

Umpire: The official in charge of a match, keeping and calling score, usually from a high chair at one end of the net.

U.S. Open: *See* Forest Hills and Flushing Meadow.

U.S. Pro Championships: Longest running tournament for male professionals, won at its launching in 1927 by Vinnie Richards on the clay of long-since vanished Notlek Tennis Club in Manhattan. The purse was $2,000, half of it won by Richards for his victory over Howard Kinsey. Largely unnoticed and unsuccessful during the heyday of amateurism, it was played all over the country, indoors and out, until moving to its present location, Longwood Cricket Club in Boston, in 1964, where it has prospered and was the fountainhead for the solid growth of the pro game. In Boston it has been played outdoors, on grass (1964–68), synthetic carpet (1969–73), clay (1974–91) and hard court, from 1992. Pancho Gonzalez won a record eight times between 1953 and 1961, all in Cleveland. Rod Laver won five times, between 1964 and 1969, all in Boston. Prize money rose from $10,000 (first prize $2,200) in 1964 to $400,000 in 1992 (first prize $50,000).

USTA: The United States Tennis Association (formerly U.S. Lawn Tennis Association), the governing organization of amateur tennis in the United States. It also operates the U.S. Open. Founded in 1881 as the U.S. National Lawn Tennis Association, it embraces seventeen sectional associations from New England to Southern California, with about 450,000 members. In 1975 the "L" was dropped from the association abbreviation as dated, since so little tennis is now played on grass.

VASSS: Van Alen Streamlined Scoring System. Devised by Jimmy Van Alen, who was anxious to make the game more readily understood by the general public and to eliminate long drawn-out matches. VASSS replaced love-15-30-40 with 0-1-2-3 and eliminated deuce altogether. He devised the tie-breaker to avoid deuce sets. In VASSS no-ad the first player to win four points wins the game. In VASSS single-point the scoring is changed altogether. The first player to reach 31 points wins the set, with the tie-breaker to be used if the score reaches 30-30. Few tournaments have adopted Van Alen's system, although World Team Tennis and the National Collegiate Athletic Association did use no-ad.

Volley: To hit the ball during play before it touches the ground, usually at the net.

WCT: World Championship Tennis. This most ambitious and successful organization to promote professional tennis was formed in late 1967 by Dave Dixon of New Orleans in partnership with Dallas sportsman–oil millionaire Lamar Hunt. Dixon signed eight players. (*See* Handsome Eight.) The firm was in business, though shakily, and Hunt and his nephew, Al Hill, Jr., bought out Dixon after a few months' operation and huge losses. Gradually, under director Mike Davies, the concept of the World Championship of Tennis developed—a series of tournaments throughout the world involving most of the leading men and pointing to playoffs in May among the top eight finishers in singles and doubles. Ken Rosewall won the first WCT playoff over Rod Laver in Dallas in 1971 and collected the $50,000 first prize. WCT broadened its operations by constructing tennis resorts (Lakeway World of Tennis outside Austin, Tex., and Peachtree World of Tennis outside Atlanta), marketing tennis clothing, and opening tennis academies. ATP Tour squeezed WCT out of a business it led in creating, and, sadly John McEnroe's victory over Brad Gilbert in 1989 was farewell to WCT and its trailblazing championship.

West Side Tennis Club: A private club founded in 1892 when situated on Central Park West between 88th and 89th Streets (hence the name), it occupied two subsequent Manhattan locations before moving to Forest Hills, Queens, in 1913. There it became the scene of big-time tennis, the U.S. Championships for 63 years prior to 1978. *See* Forest Hills.

White City: A club in Sydney, Australia, where the second-largest crowd in tennis history, 25,578, attended the Australia-U.S. Davis Cup finale in 1954. The tournament courts were grass, but some have been paved to conform to the hard courts of the Aussie circuit in line with those for the Open at Flinders Park.

Wide: To be out of the court on either side, thus a loss of a point.

Wightman Cup: The annual women's team competition between Great Britain and the U.S. begun in 1923. The format: best-of-seven matches—five singles and two doubles. The Cup was donated by Mrs. Hazel Hotchkiss Wightman of Boston (1886–1974), winner of a record 45 U.S. titles in singles and doubles. She played in the first Cup match, won by the U.S., 7-0. The series was discontinued after 1989, the U.S. leading, 51-10.

Wild card: A gift of admission to a tournament main draw from the tournament manager to a player who wouldn't otherwise be accepted. A pre-determined number of slots in a draw are reserved for wild cards. A wild card may be granted for a variety of reasons. It may go to a once prominent name (usually a gate attraction) whose computer ranking doesn't warrant admission, or to a star who decides to enter at the last minute. Or to a local attraction, or perhaps as a favor to a player who has helped the tournament in the past, or is on the way up. A player is limited in the number of wild cards permitted. Under ATP rules, however, a player over 30 who has won at least one major may accept unlimited wild cards. Wild cards are also issued for qualifying tournaments. A spectacular wild carding was that of then No. 174-ranked Jimmy Connors at the U.S. Open of 1991. Jimmy, in on a pass, romped to the semifinals.

Wimbledon: The game's leading tournament, considered by many the world championship. Entitled formally, and simply, The Lawn Tennis Championships. Played on the grounds of the All England Lawn Tennis & Croquet Club in the London suburb of Wimbledon. Between the tourney's 1877 inception and 1921, the Championships was played at the "old Wimbledon" on Worple Road. The "new Wimbledon," the present complex, was opened on Church Road in 1922. Grass has always been the surface. The tournament, begun as an amateur event, has been open to pros as well since 1968. Championships are decided in men's and women's singles and doubles, mixed doubles, junior boys and girls singles and doubles, veterans (45s and 35s) doubles. Always a sellout, the tournament draws well over 400,000 for 13 days. The single-day record: 39,813 in 1986 (a world high). The grounds embrace the renowned Centre Court stadium, holding 13,107, and smaller stadia at Courts 1, 2, 3, 13, 14. There are 17 courts. A new 10,000-seat Court 1 stadium opens in 1997. The historic, cozy Court 1, tucked into the west wall of Centre Court, was razed in 1996.

Winner: A shot hit for an outright point. Also called a placement.

WIPTC: Women's International Professional Tennis Council, a board of control for the female pro tournament game. Formed in 1975, it seeks to regulate schedules, conditions of play, and conduct. It is made up of representatives of the ITF, WTA, and various tournaments. *See* MIPTC.

World Cup: An annual team competition between Australia and U.S. male pros, begun in 1970 in Boston. The event had been played at Hartford, Conn., since 1972, and Australia led, 5-4, following a 6-1 victory in 1978. Discontinued after the 1980 meeting, with U.S. leading, 6-5.

World Team Cup: An ATP Tour competition for eight male teams annually at the Rochusclub, Dusseldorf, selections based on computer rankings of singles players, two per team. After the seven top-ranked teams are selected, a wild card is given an eighth. The teams are divided into two groups for round-robin play, best of three matches, two singles and a doubles. Best team in each group meets in the final. Begun in 1978 as Nations Cup, the name changed in 1982.

WTA: The Women's Tennis Association, an organization of the leading female pros, similar to a union and comparable to the ATP. Billie Jean King was the guiding light in the 1973 founding, and she was the first president.

World Team Tennis, Team Tennis: City team franchises, the foundation of major pro sports in the U.S., came to tennis with the establishment of WTT (World Team Tennis), which lasted for five years, folding because of large financial losses after the 1978 season. Founded by Dennis Murphy, Jordan Kaiser and Larry King (then husband of Billie Jean King), WTT operated with 16 cities between Boston and Honolulu in 1974, a high point, and involved most of the game's leading players during its lifespan. They were well paid to ignore the summer season and play team tennis, a new concept in which teams had both male and female players. It was single-set tennis, five sets (men's and women's singles and doubles plus mixed doubles) constituting a match, the score based on total games won. Fearing the summer competition, the ITF (International Tennis Federation) railed against WTT, and the French Open barred players from the league in 1974, one of whom, Jimmy Connors of Baltimore (who won the other three majors) thus being deprived of a chance at a Grand Slam. A feature of the first season was the unprecedented appearance of women coaching professional teams containing men. Billie Jean King led the Philadelphia

Freedoms, Rosie Casals the Detroit Loves. Billie Jean King revived the concept modestly under the masthead of Team Tennis in 1981, with a shorter season, lesser players, although Connors and Martina Navratilova came aboard in 1991 with Los Angeles and Atlanta respectively. In 1992 Team Tennis resumed the name World Team Tennis. These were the championship rounds:

1974	Denver d. Philadelphia, 27-21, 28-24
1975	Pittsburgh d. Oakland-San Francisco, 25-26, 28-25, 21-14
1976	New York d. Oakland-San Francisco, 31-23, 29-21, 31-13
1977	New York d. Phoenix, 27-22, 28-17
1978	Los Angeles d. Boston, 24-21, 30-20, 26-27, 28-25
1981	Los Angeles finished first
1982	Dallas finished first
1983	Chicago d. Los Angeles, 26-20
1984	San Diego d. Long Beach, 30-13
1985	San Diego d. St. Louis, 25-24
1986	San Antonio d. Sacramento, 25-23
1987	Charlotte d. San Antonio, 25-20
1988	Charlotte d. New Jersey, 27-22
1989	San Antonio d. Sacramento, 27-25
1990	Los Angeles d. Raleigh, 27-16
1991	Atlanta d. Los Angeles, 27-16
1992	Atlanta d. Newport Beach, 30-17
1993	Wichita d. Newport Beach, 26-23
1994	New Jersey d. Idaho, 28-25
1995	New Jersey d. Atlanta, 28-20
1996	St. Louis d. Delaware, 27-16

APPENDIX A:
RULES

EXPLANATORY NOTE: *The following Rules and Cases and Decisions are the official Code of the International Tennis Federation, of which the United States Tennis Association is a member. USTA Comments have the same weight and force in USTA tournaments as do ITF Cases and Decisions.*

When a match is played without officials the principles and guidelines set forth in the USTA Publication, The Code, shall apply in any situation not covered by the rules.

Except where otherwise stated, every reference in these Rules to the masculine includes the feminine gender.

THE SINGLES GAME
RULE 1 • The Court

The court shall be a rectangle 78 feet (23.77 m.) long and 27 feet (8.23 m.) wide.

USTA COMMENT: *See Rule 34 for a doubles court.*

It shall be divided across the middle by a net suspended from a cord or metal cable of a maximum diameter of one-third of an inch (0.8 cm.), the ends of which shall be attached to, or pass over, the tops of two posts, which shall be not more than 6 inches (15 cm.) square or 6 inches (15 cm.) in diameter. These posts shall not be higher than 1 inch (2.5 cm.) above the top of the net cord. The centres of the posts shall be 3 feet

(0.914 m.) outside the court on each side and the height of the posts shall be such that the top of the cord or metal cable shall be 3 feet 6 inches (1.07 m.) above the ground.

When a combined doubles (see Rule 34) and singles court with a doubles net is used for singles, the net must be supported to a height of 3 feet 6 inches (1.07 m.) by means of two posts, called "singles sticks," which shall be not more than 3 inches (7.5 cm.) square or 3 inches (7.5 cm.) in diameter. The centres of the singles sticks shall be 3 feet (0.914 m.) outside the singles court on each side.

The net shall be extended fully so that it fills completely the space between the two posts and shall be of sufficiently small mesh to prevent the ball passing through. The height of the net shall be 3 feet (0.914 m.) at the centre, where it shall be held down taut by a strap not more than 2 inches (5 cm.) wide and completely white in colour. There shall be a band covering the cord or metal cable and the top of the net of not less than 2½ inches (5 cm.) nor more than 2½ inches (6.3 cm.) in depth on each side and completely white in colour.

There shall be no advertisement on the net, strap, band or singles sticks.

The lines bounding the ends and sides of the Court shall respectively be called the base-lines and the side-lines. On each side of the net, at a distance of 21 feet (6.40 m.) from it and parallel with it, shall be drawn the service-lines. The space on each side of the net between the service-line and the side-lines shall be divided into two equal parts called the service-courts by the centre service-line, which must be 2 inches (5 cm.) in width, drawn half-way between, and parallel with, the side-lines. Each base-line shall be bisected by an imaginary continuation of the centre service-line to a line 4 inches (10 cm.) in length and 2 inches (5 cm.) in width called the centre mark drawn inside the Court, at right angles to and in contact with such base-lines. All other lines shall be not less than 1 inch (2.5 cm.) nor more than 2 inches (5 cm.) in width except the base-line, which may be not more than 4 inches (10 cm.) in width, and all measurements shall be made to the outside of the lines. All lines shall be of uniform colour.

If advertising or any other material is placed at the back of the court, it may not contain white, or yellow. A light colour may only be used if this does not interfere with the vision of the players.

If advertisements are placed on the chairs of the Linesmen sitting at the back of the court, they may not contain white, or yellow. A light colour may only be used if this does not interfere with the vision of the players.

ITF NOTE: *In the case of the Davis Cup or other Official Championships of the International Tennis Federation, there shall be a space behind each base-line of not less than 21 feet (6.4 m.), and the sides of not less than 12 feet (3.66 m.). The chairs of the linesmen may be placed at the back of the court within the 21 feet or at the side of the court within the 12 feet, provided they do not protrude into that area more than 3 feet (0.914 m.).*

USTA COMMENT: *An approved method for obtaining proper net tautness is this: Loosen the center strap; tighten the net cord until it is approximately 40 inches above the ground, being careful not to overtighten the net; tighten the center strap until the center of the net is 36 inches above the ground. These measurements should always be made before the first match of the day.*

RULE 2 • Permanent Fixtures

The permanent fixtures of the Court shall include not only the net, posts, singles sticks, cord or metal cable, strap and band, but also, where there are any such, the back and side stops, the stands, fixed or movable seats and chairs round the Court, and their occupants, all other fixtures around and above the Court, and the Umpire, Net-cord Judge, Foot-fault Judge, Linesmen and Ball Boys when in their respective places.

ITF NOTE: *For the purpose of this Rule, the word "Umpire" comprehends the Umpire, the persons entitled to a seat on the Court, and all those persons designated to assist the Umpire in the conduct of a match.*

RULE 3 • The Ball

The ball shall have a uniform outer surface and shall be white or yellow in colour. If there are any seams, they shall be stitchless.

The ball shall be more than two and a half inches (6.35 cm.) and less than two and five-eighths inches (6.67 cm.) in diameter, and more than two ounces (56.7 grams) and less than two and one-sixteenth ounces (58.5 grams) in weight.

The ball shall have a bound of more than 53 inches (135 cm.) and less than 58 inches (147 cm.) when dropped 100 inches (254 cm.) upon a concrete base.

The ball shall have a forward deformation of more than 0.220 of an inch (0.56 cm.) and less than 0.290 of an inch (0.74 cm.) and a return deformation of more than 0.350 of an inch (0.89 cm.) and less than 0.425 of an inch (1.08 cm.) at 18 lb. (8.165 kg.) load. The two deformation figures shall be the averages of three individual readings along three axes of the ball and no two individual readings shall differ by more than 0.030 of an inch (0.08 cm.) in each case.

For play above 4,000 feet (1219 m.) in altitude above sea level, two additional types of ball may be used. The first type is identical to those described above except that the bound shall be more than 48 inches (121.92 cm.) and less than 53 inches (135 cm.) and the ball shall have an internal pressure that is greater than the external pressure. This type of tennis ball is commonly known as a pressurized ball. The second type is identical to those described above except that they shall have a bound of more than 53 inches (135 cm.) and less than 58 inches (147 cm.) and shall have an internal pressure that is approximately equal to the external pressure and have been acclimatized for 60 days or more at the altitude of the specific tournament. This type of tennis ball is commonly known as a zero-pressure or non-pressurized ball.

RULE 4 • The Racket

Rackets failing to comply with the following specifications are not approved for play under the Rules of Tennis:

(a) The hitting surface of the racket shall be flat and consist of a pattern of crossed strings connected to a frame and alternately interlaced or bonded where they cross; and the stringing pattern shall be generally uniform, and in particular not less dense in the centre than in any other area. The strings shall be free of attached objects and protrusions other than those utilized solely and specifically to limit or prevent wear and tear or vibration and which are reasonable in size and placement for such purposes.

(b) The frame of the racket shall not exceed 32 inches (81.28 cm.) in overall length, including the handle and 12½ inches (31.75 cm.) in overall width. The strung surface shall not exceed 15½ inches (39.37 cm.) in overall length, and 11½ inches (29.21 cm.) in overall width.

(c) The frame, including the handle, shall be free of attached objects and devices other than those utilized solely and specifically to limit or prevent wear and tear or vibration, or to distribute weight. Any objects and devices must be reasonable in size and placement for such purposes.

(d) The frame, including the handle and the strings, shall be free of any device which makes it possible to change materially the shape of the racket, or to change the weight distribution, during the playing of a point.

The International Tennis Federation shall rule on the question of whether any racket or prototype complies with the above specifications or is otherwise approved, or not approved, for play. Such ruling may be undertaken on its own initiative, or upon application by any party with a bona fide interest therein, including any player, equipment manufacturer or National Association or members thereof. Such rulings and applications shall be made in accordance with the applicable Review and Hearing Procedures of the International Tennis Federation, copies of which may be obtained from the office of the Secretary.

Case 1. Can there be more than one set of strings on the hitting surface of a racket?

Decision. No. The rule clearly mentions a pattern, and not patterns, of crossed strings.

Case 2. Is the stringing pattern of a racket considered to be generally uniform and flat if the strings are no more than one plane?

Decision. No.

Case 3. Can a vibration dampening device be placed on the strings of a racket and if so, where can it be placed?

Decision. Yes; but such devices may only be placed outside the pattern of crossed strings.

RULE 5 • Server and Receiver

The players shall stand on opposite sides of the net; the player who first delivers the ball shall be called the Server, and the other the Receiver.

Case 1. Does a player, attempting a stroke, lose the point if he crosses an imaginary line in the extension of the net,

(a) before striking the ball,

(b) after striking the ball?

Decision. He does not lose the point in either case by crossing the imaginary line and provided he does not enter the lines bounding his opponent's Court (Rule 20 (e)). In regard to hindrance, his opponent may ask for the decision of the Umpire under Rules 21 and 25.

Case 2. The Server claims that the Receiver must stand within the lines bounding his Court. Is this necessary?

Decision. No. The Receiver may stand wherever he pleases on his own side of the net.

RULE 6 • Choice of Ends and Service

The choice of ends and the right to be Server or Receiver in the first game shall be decided by toss. The player winning the toss may choose or require his opponent to choose:

(a) The right to be Server or Receiver, in which case the other player shall choose the end; or

(b) The end, in which case the other player shall choose the right to be Server or Receiver.

USTA COMMENT: *These choices should be made promptly after the toss and are irrevocable, except that if the match is postponed or suspended before the start of the match. See Case 1 below.*

Case 1. Do players have the right to new choices if the match is postponed or suspended before it has started?

Decision. Yes. The toss stands, but new choices may be made with respect to service and end.

RULE 7 • The Service

The service shall be delivered in the following manner. Immediately before commencing to serve, the Server shall stand with both feet at rest behind (i.e. further from the net than) the baseline, and within the imaginary continuations of the centre-mark and side-line. The Server shall then project the ball by hand into the air in any direction and before it hits the ground strike it with his racket, and the delivery shall be deemed to have been completed at the moment of the impact of the racket and the ball. A player with the use of only one arm may utilize his racket for the projection.

USTA COMMENT: *The service begins when the Server takes a ready position (i.e., both feet at rest behind the baseline) and ends when his racket makes contact with the ball, or when he misses the ball in attempting to serve it.*

Case 1. May the Server in a singles game take his stand behind the portion of the base-line between the side-lines of the Singles Court and the Doubles Court?

Decision. No.

USTA COMMENT: *The Server may stand anywhere in back of the baseline between the imaginary extensions of the center mark and the singles sideline.*

Case 2. If a player, when serving, throws up two or more balls instead of one, does he lose that service?

Decision. No. A let should be called, but if the Umpire regards the action as deliberate he may take action under Rule 21.

USTA COMMENT: *There is no restriction regarding the kind of services which may be used; that is, the player may use an underhand or overhand service at his discretion.*

RULE 8 • Foot Fault

(a) The Server shall throughout the delivery of the service:

(i) Not change his position by walking or running. The Server shall not by slight movements of the feet which do not materially affect the location originally taken up by him, be deemed "to change his position by walking or running."

(ii) Not touch, with either foot, any area other than that behind the base-line within the imaginary extensions of the centre mark and side-lines.

(b) The word "foot" means the extremity of the leg below the ankle.

USTA COMMENT: *This rule covers the most decisive stroke in the game, and there is no justification for its not being obeyed by players and enforced by officials. No official has the right to instruct any umpire to disregard violations of it. In a non-officiated match, the Receiver, or his partner, may call foot faults after all efforts (appeal to the server, request for an umpire, etc.) have failed and the foot faulting is so flagrant as to be clearly perceptible from the Receiver's side.*

It is improper for any officials to warn a player that he is in danger of having a foot fault called on him. On the other hand, if a player, in all sincerity, asks for an explanation of how he foot faulted, either the line Umpire or the Chair Umpire should give him that information.

RULE 9 • Delivery of Service

(a) In delivering the service, the Server shall stand alternately behind the right and left Courts beginning from the right in every game. If service from a wrong half of the Court occurs and is undetected, all play resulting from such wrong service or services shall stand, but the inaccuracy of station shall be corrected immediately it is discovered.

(b) The ball served shall pass over the net and hit the ground within the Service Court which is diagonally opposite, or upon any line bounding such Court, before the Receiver returns it.

USTA COMMENT: *See Rule 18.*

RULE 10 • Service Fault

The Service is a fault:

(a) if the Server commits any breach of Rules 7, 8 or 9(b);

(b) if he misses the ball in attempting to strike it;

(c) if the ball served touches a permanent fixture (other than the net, strap or band) before it hits the ground.

Case 1. After throwing a ball up preparatory to serving, the Server decides not to strike at it and catches it instead. Is it a fault?

Decision. No.

USTA COMMENT: *As long as the Server makes no attempt to strike the ball, it is immaterial whether he catches it in his hand or on his racket or lets it drop to the ground.*

Case 2. In serving in a singles game played on a Doubles Court with doubles posts and singles sticks, the ball hits a singles stick and then hits the ground within the lines of the correct Service Court. Is this a fault or a let?

Decision. In serving it is a fault, because the singles stick, the doubles post, and that portion of the net, or band between them are permanent fixtures. (Rules 2 and 10, and note to Rule 24.).

USTA COMMENT: *The significant point governing Case 2 is that the part of the net and band "outside" the singles sticks is not part of the net over which this singles match is being played. Thus such a serve is a fault under the provisions of Article (c) above... By the same token, this would be a fault also if it were a singles game played with permanent posts in the singles position. (See Case 1 under Rule 24 for difference between "service" and "good return" with respect to a ball's hitting a net post.)*

USTA COMMENT: *In a non-officiated singles match, each player makes calls for all balls landing on, or aimed at, his side of the net. In doubles, normally the Receiver's partner makes the calls with respect to the service line, with the Receiver calling the side and center lines, but either partner may have the call on any ball he clearly sees out.*

RULE 11 • Second Service

After a fault (if it is the first fault) the Server shall serve again from behind the same half of the Court from which he served that fault, unless the service was from the wrong half, when, in accordance with Rule 9, the Server shall be entitled to one service only from behind the other half.

Case 1. A player serves from a wrong Court. He loses the point and then claims it was a fault because of his wrong station.

Decision. The point stands as played and the next service should be from the correct station according to the score.

Case 2. The point score being 15 all, the Server, by mistake, serves from the left-hand Court. He wins the point. He then serves again from the right-hand Court, delivering a fault. This mistake in station is then discovered. Is he entitled to the previous point? From which Court should be next serve?

Decision. The previous point stands. The next service should be from the left-hand Court, the score being 30/15, and the Server has served one fault.

RULE 12 • When to Serve

The Server shall not serve until the Receiver is ready. If the latter attempts to return the service, he shall be deemed ready. If however, the Receiver signifies that he is not ready, he may not claim a fault because the ball does not hit the ground within the limits fixed for the service.

USTA COMMENT: *The Server must wait until the Receiver is ready for the second service as well as the first, and if the Receiver claims to be not ready and does not make any effort to return a service, the Server's claim for the point may not be honored even though the service was good. However, the Receiver, having indicated he is ready, may not become unready unless some outside interference takes place.*

RULE 13 • The Let

In all cases where a let has to be called under the rules, or to provide for an interruption to play, it shall have the following interpretations:

(a) When called solely in respect of a service that one service only shall be replayed.

(b) When called under any other circumstance, the point shall be replayed.

Case 1. A service is interrupted by some cause outside those defined in Rule 14. Should the service only be replayed?

Decision. No, the whole point must be replayed.

USTA COMMENT: *If a delay between first and second serves is caused by the Receiver, by an official or by an outside interference the whole point shall be replayed; if the delay is caused by the Server, the Server has one serve to come. A spectator's outcry (of "out," "fault" or other) is not a valid basis for replay of a point, but action should be taken to prevent a recurrence.*

USTA COMMENT: *Case 1 refers to a second serve, and the decision means that if the interruption occurs during delivery of the second service, the Server gets two serves. Example: On a second service a linesman calls "fault" and immediately corrects it, the Receiver meanwhile having let the ball go by. The Server is entitled to two serves, on this ground: The corrected call means that the Server has put the ball into play with a good service, and once the ball is in play and a let is called, the point must be replayed. Note, however, that if the serve is an unmistakable ace—that is, the Umpire is sure the erroneous call had no part in the Receiver's inability to play the ball—the point should be declared for the Server.*

Case 2. If a ball in play becomes broken, should a let be called?

Decision. Yes.

USTA COMMENT: *A ball shall be regarded as having become "broken" if, in the opinion of the Chair Umpire, it is found to have lost compression to the point of being unfit for further play, or unfit for any reason, and it is clear the defective ball was the one in play.*

RULE 14 • The "Let" in Service

The service is a let:

(a) If the ball served touches the net, strap or band, and is otherwise good, or, after touching the net, strap or band, touches the Receiver or anything which he wears or carries before hitting the ground.

(b) If a service or a fault is delivered when the Receiver is not ready (see Rule 12).

In case of a let, that particular service shall not count, and the Server shall serve again, but a service let does not annul a previous fault.

RULE 15 • Order of Service

At the end of the first game the Receiver shall become Server, and the Server Receiver, and so on alternately in all the subsequent games of a match. If a player serves out of turn, the player who ought to have served shall serve as soon as the mistake is discovered, but all points scored before such discovery shall be reckoned. If a game shall have been completed before such discovery, the order of service remains as altered. A fault served before such discovery shall not be reckoned.

RULE 16 • When Players Change Ends

The players shall change ends at the end of the first, third and every subsequent alternate game of each set, and at the end of each set unless the total number of games in such set is even, in which case the change is not made until the end of the first game of the next set.

If a mistake is made and the correct sequence is not followed the players must take up their correct station as soon as the discovery is made and follow their original sequence.

RULE 17 • The Ball in Play

A ball is in play from the moment at which it is delivered in service. Unless a fault or a let is called it remains in play until the point is decided.

USTA COMMENT: *A point is not decided simply when, or because, a good shot has clearly passed a player, or when an apparently bad shot passes over a baseline or sideline. An outgoing ball is still definitely in play until it actually strikes the ground, backstop or a permanent fixture (other than the net, posts, singles sticks, cord or metal cable, strap or band), or a player. The same applies to a good ball, bouncing after it has landed in the proper court. A ball that becomes imbedded in the net is out of play.*

Case 1.   A player fails to make a good return. No call is made and the ball remains in play. May his opponent later claim the point after the rally has ended?

Decision.   No. The point may not be claimed if the players continue to pay after the error has been made, provided the opponent was not hindered.

USTA COMMENT: *To be valid, an out call on A's shot to B's court, that B plays, must be made before B's shot has either gone out of play or has been hit by A. See Case 3 under Rule 29.*

USTA COMMENT: *When a ball is hit into the net and the player on the other side, thinking the ball is coming over,*

strikes at it and hits the net he loses the point if his touching the net occurs while the ball is still in play.

RULE 18 • Server Wins Point

The Server wins the point:

(a) If the ball served, not being a let under Rule 14, touches the Receiver or anything which he wears or carries, before it hits the ground;

(b) If the Receiver otherwise loses the point as provided by Rule 20.

RULE 19 • Receiver Wins Point

The Receiver wins the point:

(a) If the Server serves two consecutive faults;

(b) If the Server otherwise loses the point as provided by Rule 20.

RULE 20 • Player Loses Point

A player loses the point if:

(a) He fails, before the ball in play has hit the ground twice consecutively, to return it directly over the net (except as provided in Rule 24(a) or (c)); or

(b) He returns the ball in play so that it hits the ground, a permanent fixture, or other object, outside any of the lines which bound his opponent's Court (except as provided in Rule 24(a) or (c)); or

USTA COMMENT: *A ball hitting a scoring device or other object attached to a net post results in loss of point to the striker.*

(c) He volleys the ball and fails to make a good return even when standing outside the Court; or

(d) In playing the ball he deliberately carries or catches it on his racket or deliberately touches it with his racket more than once; or

USTA COMMENT: *Only when there is a definite "second push" by the player does his shot become illegal, with consequent loss of point. The word "deliberately" is the key word in this rule. Two hits occurring in the course of a single continuous swing are not deemed a double hit.*

(e) He or his racket (in his hand or otherwise) or anything which he wears or carries touches the net, posts, singles sticks, cord or metal cable, strap or band, or the ground within his opponent's Court at any time while the ball is in play; or

USTA COMMENT: Touching a pipe support that runs across the court at the bottom of the net is interpreted as touching the net; See USTA Comment under Rule 23.

(f) He volleys the ball before it has passed the net; or

(g) The ball in play touches him or anything that he wears or carries, except his racket in his hand or hands; or

USTA COMMENT: This loss of point occurs regardless of whether the player is inside or outside the bounds of his court when the ball touches him.

(h) He throws his racket at and hits the ball; or

(i) He deliberately and materially changes the shape of his racket during the playing of the point.

Case 1. In serving, the racket flies from the Server's hand and touches the net before the ball has touched the ground. Is this a fault, or does the player lose the point?

Decision. The Server loses the point because his racket touches the net while the ball is in play (Rule 20(e)).

Case 2. In serving, the racket flies from the Server's hand and touches the net after the ball has touched the ground outside the proper court. Is this a fault, or does the player lose the point?

Decision. This is a fault because the ball was out of play when the racket touched the net.

Case 3. A and B are playing against C and D, A is serving to D, C touches the net before the ball touches the ground. A fault is then called because the service falls outside the Service Court. Do C and D lose the point?

Decision. The call "fault" is an erroneous one. C and D had already lost the point before "fault" could be called, because C touched the net while the ball was in play (Rule 20(e)).

Case 4. May a player jump over the net into his opponent's Court while the ball is in play and not suffer penalty?

Decision. No. He loses the point (Rule 20(e)).

Case 5. A cuts the ball just over the net, and it returns to A's side. B, unable to reach the ball, throws his racket and hits the ball. Both racket and ball fall over the net on A's Court. A returns the ball outside of B's Court. Does B win or lose the point?

Decision. B loses the point (Rule 20(e) and (h)).

Case 6. A player standing outside the service Court is struck by a service ball before it has touched the ground. Does he win or lose the point?

Decision. The player struck loses the point (Rule 20(g)), except as provided under Rule 14(a).

Case 7. A player standing outside the Court volleys the ball or catches it in his hand and claims the point because the ball was certainly going out of court.

Decision. In no circumstances can he claim the point:

(1) If he catches the ball he loses the point under Rule 20(g).

(2) If he volleys it and makes a bad return he loses the point under Rule 20(c).

(3) If he volleys it and makes a good return, the rally continues.

RULE 21 • Player Hinders Opponent

If a player commits any act which hinders his opponent in making a stroke; then, if this is deliberate, he shall lose the point or if involuntary, the point shall be replayed.

USTA COMMENT: "Deliberate" means a player did what he intended to do, although the resulting effect on his opponent might or might not have been what he intended. Example: A player, after his return is in the air, gives advice to his partner in such a loud voice that his opponent is hindered. "Involuntary" means a non-intentional act such as a hat blowing off or a scream resulting from a sudden wasp sting.

Case 1. Is a player liable to a penalty if in making a stroke he touches his opponent?

Decision. No, unless the Umpire deems it necessary to take action under Rule 21.

Case 2. When a ball bounds back over the net, the player concerned may reach over the net in order to play the ball. What is the ruling if the player is hindered from doing this by his opponent?

Decision. In accordance with Rule 21, the Umpire may either award the point to the player hindered, or order the point to be replayed. (See also Rule 25).

Case 3. Does an involuntary double hit constitute an act which hinders an opponent within Rule 21?

Decision. No.

USTA COMMENT: *Upon appeal by a competitor that the server's action in discarding a "second ball" after a rally has started constitutes a distraction (hindrance), the Umpire, if he deems the claim valid, shall require the server to make some other and satisfactory disposition of the ball. Failure to comply with this instruction may result in loss of point(s) or disqualification.*

RULE 22 • Ball Falls on Line

A ball falling on a line is regarded as falling in the Court bounded by that line.

USTA COMMENT: *In a non-officiated singles match, each player makes the call on any ball hit toward his side of the net, and if a player cannot call a ball out with surety he should regard it as good. See paragraph 7 of The Code and the last USTA Comment under Rule 10.*

RULE 23 • Ball Touches Permanent Fixtures

If the ball in play touches a permanent fixture (other than the net, posts, singles sticks, cord or metal cable, strap or band) after it has hit the ground, the player who struck it wins the point; if before it hits the ground, his opponent wins the point.

Case 1. A return hits the Umpire or his chair or stand. The player claims that the ball was going into Court.

Decision. He loses the point.

USTA COMMENT: *A ball in play that after passing the net strikes a pipe support running across the court at the base of the net is regarded the same as a ball landing on clear ground. See also Rule 20(e).*

RULE 24 • A Good Return

It is a good return:

(a) If the ball touches the net, posts, singles sticks, cord or metal cable, strap or band, provided that it passes over any of them and hits the ground within the Court; or

(b) If the ball, served or returned, hits the ground within the proper Court and rebounds or is blown back over the net, and the player whose turn it is to strike reaches over the net and plays the ball, provided that he does not contravene Rule 20(e), and that the stroke be otherwise good; or

(c) If the ball is returned outside the posts, or singles sticks, either above or below the level of the top of the net, even though it touches the posts or singles sticks, provided that it hits the ground within the proper Court; or

(d) If a player's racket passes over the net after he has returned the ball, provided the ball passes the net before being played and is properly returned; or

(e) If a player succeeds in returning the ball, served or in play, which strikes a ball lying in the Court.

USTA COMMENT: *Paragraph (e) of the rule refers to a ball lying on the court at the start of the point, as a result of a service let or fault, or as a result of a player dropping it. If a ball in play strikes a rolling or stationary "foreign" ball that has come from elsewhere after the point started, a let should be played. See Case 7 under Rule 25 and note that it pertains to an object other than a ball that is being used in the match.*

ITF NOTE: *In a singles match, if, for the sake of convenience, a doubles court is equipped with singles sticks for the purpose of a singles game, then the doubles posts and those portions of the net, cord or metal cable and the band outside such singles sticks shall at all times be permanent fixtures, and are not regarded as posts or parts of the net of a singles game.*

A return that passes under the net cord between the singles stick and adjacent doubles post without touching either net cord, net or doubles post and falls within the court, is a good return.

USTA COMMENT: *But in doubles this would be a "through"—Loss of point.*

Case 1. A ball going out of Court hits a net post or singles stick and falls within the lines of the opponent's Court. Is the stroke good?

Decision. If a service: no, under Rule 10(c). If other than a service: yes, under Rule 24 (a).

Case 2. Is it good return if a player returns the ball holding his racket in both hands?

Decision. Yes.

Case 3. The service, or ball in play, strikes a ball lying in the Court. Is the point won or lost thereby?

USTA COMMENT: *A ball that is touching a boundary line is considered to be "lying in the court."*

Decision. No. Play must continue. If it is not clear to the Umpire that the right ball is returned a let should be called.

Case 4. May a player use more than one racket at any time during play?

Decision. No; the whole implication of the Rules is singular.

Case 5. May a player request that a ball or balls lying in his opponent's Court be removed?

Decision. Yes, but not while a ball is in play.

USTA COMMENT: *This request must be honored.*

RULE 25 • Hindrance of a Player

In case a player is hindered in making a stroke by anything not within his control, except a permanent fixture of the Court, or except as provided for in Rule 21, a let shall be called.

Case 1. A spectator gets into the way of a player, who fails to return the ball. May the player then claim a let?

Decision. Yes, if in the Umpire's opinion he was obstructed by circumstances beyond his control, but not if due to permanent fixtures of the Court or the arrangements of the ground.

Case 2. A player is interfered with as in Case No. 1, and the Umpire calls a let. The Server had previously served a fault. Has he the right to two services?

Decision. Yes: as the ball is in play, the point, not merely the stroke, must be replayed as the Rule provides.

Case 3. May a player claim a let under Rule 25 because he thought his opponent was being hindered, and consequently did not expect the ball to be returned?

Decision. No.

Case 4. Is a stroke good when a ball in play hits another ball in the air?

Decision. A let should be called unless the other ball is in the air by the act of one of the players, in which case the Umpire will decide under Rule 21.

Case 5. If an Umpire or other judge erroneously calls "fault" or "out," and then corrects himself, which of the calls shell prevail?

Decision. A let must be called unless, in the opinion of the Umpire, neither player is hindered in his game, in which case the corrected call shall prevail.

Case 6. If the first ball served—a fault—rebounds, interfering with the Receiver at the time of the second service, may the Receiver claim a let?

Decision. Yes. But if he had an opportunity to remove the ball from the Court and negligently failed to do so, he may not claim a let.

Case 7. Is it a good stroke if the ball touches a stationary or moving object on the Court?

Decision. It is a good stroke unless the stationary object came into Court after the ball was put into play in which case a let must be called. If the ball in play strikes an object moving along or above the surface of the Court a let must be called.

Case 8. What is the ruling if the first service is a fault, the second service correct, and it becomes necessary to call a let either under the provision of Rule 25 or if the Umpire is unable to decide the point?

Decision. The fault shall be annulled and the whole point replayed.

USTA COMMENT: *See Rule 13 with its USTA Comments.*

RULE 26 • Score in a Game

If a player wins his first point, the score is called 15 for that player; on winning his second point, the score is called 30 for that player; on winning his third point, the score is called 40 for that player, and the fourth point won by a player is scored game for that player except as below:

If both players have won three points, the score is called deuce; and the next point won by a player is scored advantage for that player. If the same player wins the next point, he wins the game; if the other player wins the next point the score is again called deuce; and so on, until a player wins the two points immediately following the score at deuce, when the game is scored for that player.

USTA COMMENT: *In a non-officiated match the Server should announce, in a voice audible to his opponent and spectators, the set score at the beginning of each game, and point scores as the game goes on. Misunderstandings will be avoided if this practice is followed.*

RULE 27 • Score in a Set

(a) A player (or players) who first wins six games wins a set; except that he must win by a margin of two games over his opponent and where necessary a set is extended until this margin is achieved.

(b) The tie-break system of scoring may be adopted as an alternative to the advantage set system in paragraph (a) of this Rule provided the decision is announced in advance of the match. In this case, the following Rules shall be effective:

The tie-break shall operate when the score reaches six games all in any set except in the third or fifth set of a three set or five set match respectively when an ordinary advantage set shall be played, unless otherwise decided and announced in advance of the match.

The following system shall be used in a tie-break game:

Singles

(i) A player who first wins seven points shall win the game and the set provided he leads by a margin of two points. If the score reaches six points all the game shall be extended until this margin has been achieved. Numerical scoring shall be used throughout the tie-break game.

(ii) The player whose turn it is to serve shall be the server for the first point. His opponent shall be the server for the second and third points and thereafter each player shall serve alternately for two consecutive points until the winner of the game and set has been decided.

(iii) From the first point, each service shall be delivered alternately from the right and left courts, beginning from the right court. If service from a wrong half of the court occurs and is undetected, all play resulting from such wrong service or services shall stand, but the inaccuracy of station shall be corrected immediately it is discovered.

(iv) Players shall change ends after every six points an at the conclusion of the tie-break game.

(v) The tie-break game shall count as one game of the ball change, except that, if the balls are due to be changed at the beginning of the tie-break, the change shall be delayed until the second game of the following set.

Doubles

In doubles the procedure for singles shall apply. The player whose turn is to serve shall be the server for this point. Thereafter each player shall serve in rotation for two points, in the same order as previously in that set, until the winners of the game and set have been decided.

Rotation of Service

The player (or pair in the case of doubles) whose turn it was to serve first in the tie-break game shall receive service in the first game of the following set.

Case 1. At six all the tie-break is played, although it has been decided and announced in advance of the match that an advantage set will be played. Are the points already played counted?

Decision. If the error is discovered before the ball is put in play for the second point, the first point shall count but the error shall be corrected immediately. If the error is discovered after the ball is put in play for the second point the game shall continue as a tie-break game.

Case 2. At six all, an advantage game is played, although it has been decided and announced in advance of the match that a tie-break will be played. Are the points already played counted?

Decision. If the error is discovered before the ball is put in play for the second point, the first point shall be counted but the error shall be corrected immediately. If the error is discovered after the ball is put in play for the second point an advantage set shall be continued. If the score thereafter reaches eight games all or a higher even number, a tie-break shall be played.

Case 3. If during a tie-break in a singles or doubles game, a player serves out of turn, shall the order of service remain as altered until the end of the game?

Decision. If a player has completed his turn of service the order of service shall remain as altered. If the error is discovered before a player has completed his turn of service the order of service shall be corrected immediately and any points already played shall count.

RULE 28 • Maximum Number of Sets

The maximum number of sets in a match shall be 5, or, where women take part, 3.

RULE 29 • Role of Court Officials

In matches where an Umpire is appointed, his decision shall be final; but where a Referee is appointed, an appeal shall lie to him from the decision of an Umpire on a question of law, and in all such cases the decision of Referee shall be final.

In matches where assistants to the Umpire are appointed (Linesmen, Net-cord Judges, Foot-fault Judges) their decisions shall be final on questions of fact except that if in the opinion of an Umpire a clear mistake has been made he shall have the right to change the decision of an assistant or order a let to be played. When such an assistant is unable to give a decision he shall indicate this immediately to the Umpire who shall give a decision. When an Umpire is unable to give a decision on a question of fact he shall order a let to be played.

In Davis Cup matches or other team competitions where a Referee is on Court, any decision can be changed by the Referee, who may also instruct an Umpire to order a let to be played.

The Referee, in his discretion, may at any time postpone a match on account of darkness or the condition of the ground or the weather. In any case of postponement the previous score and previous occupancy of Courts shall hold good, unless the Referee and the players unanimously agree otherwise.

USTA COMMENT: *See second USTA Comment under Rule 30.*

Case 1. The Umpire orders a let, but a player claims that the point should not be replayed. May the Referee be requested to give a decision?

Decision. Yes. A question of tennis law, that is an issue relating to the application of specific facts, shall first be determined by the Umpire. However, if the Umpire is uncertain or if a player appeals from his determination, then the Referee shall be requested to give a decision, and his decision is final.

Case 2. A ball is called out, but a player claims that the ball was good. May the Referee give a ruling?

Decision. No. This is a question of fact, that is an issue relating to what actually occurred during a specific incident, and the decision of the on-court officials is therefore final.

Case 3. May an Umpire overrule a Linesman at the end of a rally if, in his opinion, a clear mistake has been made during the course of a rally?

Decision. No, unless in his opinion the opponent was hindered. Otherwise an Umpire may only overrule a Linesman if he does so immediately after the mistake has been made.

USTA COMMENT: *See Rule 17, Case 1.*

Case 4. A Linesman calls a ball out. The Umpire was unable to see clearly, although he thought the ball was in. May he overrule the Linesman?

Decision. No. An Umpire may only overrule if he considers that a call was incorrect beyond all reasonable doubt. He may only overrule a ball determined good by a Linesman if he has been able to see a space between the ball and the line; and he may only overrule a ball determined out, or a fault, by a Linesman if he has seen the ball hit the line, or fall inside the line.

Case 5. May a Linesman change his call after the Umpire has given the score?

Decision. Yes. If a Linesman realizes he has made an error, he may make a correction provided he does so immediately.

Case 6. A player claims his return shot was good after a Linesman called "out." May the Umpire overrule the Linesman?

Decision. No. An Umpire may never overrule as a result of a protest or an appeal by a player.

RULE 30 • Continuous Play and Rest Periods

Play shall be continuous from the first service until the match is concluded, in accordance with the following provisions:

(a) If the first service is a fault, the second service must be struck by the Server without delay.

The Receiver must play to the reasonable pace of the Server and must be ready to receive when the Server is ready to serve.

When changing ends, a maximum of one minute thirty seconds shall elapse from the moment the ball goes out of play at the end of the game to the time the ball is struck for the first point of the next game.

The Umpire shall use his discretion when there is interference which makes it impractical for play to be continuous.

The organizers of international circuits and team events recognized by the ITF may determine the time allowed between points, which shall not at any time exceed 25 seconds.

(b) Play shall never be suspended, delayed or interfered with for the purpose of enabling a player to recover his strength, breath, or physical condition.

However, in the case of accidental injury, the Umpire may allow a one-time three minute suspension for that injury.

The organizers of international circuits and team events recognized by the ITF may extend the one-time suspension period from three minutes to five minutes.

(c) If, through circumstances outside the control of the player, his clothing, footwear or equipment (excluding racket) becomes out of adjustment in such a way that it is impossible or undesirable for him to play on, the Umpire may suspend play while the maladjustment is rectified.

USTA COMMENT: *Loss of, or damage to, a contact lens or eyeglasses shall be treated as equipment maladjustment. All players must follow the same rules with respect to sus-*

pending play, even though in misty, but playable, weather a player who wears glasses may be handicapped.

(d) The Umpire may suspend or delay play at any time as may be necessary and appropriate.

USTA COMMENT: *When a match is resumed after a suspension of more than ten minutes, it is permissible for the players to engage in a re-warm-up that may be of the same duration as that at the start of the match. The preferred method is to warm-up with other used balls and then insert the match balls when play starts. If the match balls are used in the re-warm-up, then the next ball change will be two games sooner. There shall be no re-warm-up after an authorized intermission or after a suspension of ten minutes or less.*

(e) After the third set, or when women take part the second set, either player is entitled to a rest, which shall not exceed 10 minutes, or in countries situated between latitude 15 degrees north and latitude 15 degrees south, 45 minutes and furthermore, when necessitated by circumstances not within the control of the players, the Umpire may suspend play for such a period as he may consider necessary. If play is suspended and is not resumed until a later day the rest may be taken only after the third set (or when women take part the second set) of play on such a later day, completion of an unfinished set being counted as one set.

If play is suspended and is not resumed until 10 minutes have elapsed in the same day, the rest may be taken only after three consecutive sets have been played without interruption (or when women take part two sets), completion of an unfinished set being counted as one set.

Any nation and/or committee organizing a tournament, match or competition, other than the International Tennis Championships (Davis Cup and Federation Cup), is at liberty to modify this provision or omit it from its regulations provided this is announced before the event commences.

(f) A tournament committee has the discretion to decide the time allowed for a warm-up period prior to a match but this may not exceed five minutes and must be announced before the event commences.

USTA COMMENT: *When there are no ball persons this time may be extended to 10 minutes.*

(g) When approved point penalty and non-accumulative point penalty systems are in operation, the Umpire shall make his decisions within the terms of those systems.

(h) Upon violation of the principle that play shall be continuous the Umpire may, after giving due warning, disqualify the offender.

RULE 31 • Coaching

During the playing of a match in a team competition, a player may receive coaching from a captain who is sitting on the court only when he changes ends at the end of a game, but not when he changes ends during a tie-break game.

A player may not receive coaching during the playing of any other match.

After due warning an offending player may be disqualified. When an approved point penalty system is in operation, the Umpire shall impose penalties according to that system.

Case 1. Should a warning be given, or the player be disqualified, if the coaching is given by signals in an unobtrusive manner?

Decision. The Umpire must take action as soon as he becomes aware that coaching is being given verbally or by signals. If the Umpire is unaware that coaching is being given, a player may draw his attention to the fact that advice is being given.

Case 2. Can a player receive coaching during an authorized rest period under Rule 30(e), or when play is interrupted and he leaves the court?

Decision. Yes. In these circumstances, when the player is not on the court, there is no restriction on coaching.

ITF NOTE: *The word "coaching" includes any advice or instruction.*

RULE 32 • Changing Balls

In cases where balls are to be changed after a specified number of games, if the balls are not changed in the correct sequence, the mistake shall be corrected when the player, or pair in the case of doubles, who should have served with new balls is next due to serve. Thereafter the balls shall be changed so that the number of games between changes shall be that originally agreed.

THE DOUBLES GAME

RULE 33

The above Rules shall apply to the Doubles Game except as below.

RULE 34 • The Doubles Court

For the Doubles Game, the Court shall be 36 feet (10.97 m.) in width, i.e. 4½ feet (1.37 m.) wider on each side than the Court for the Singles Game, and those portions of the singles side-lines which lie between the two service-lines shall be called the service side-lines. In other respects, the Court shall be similar to that described in Rule 1, but the portions of the singles side-lines between the base-line and service-line on each side of the net may be omitted if desired.

USTA COMMENT: *The Server has the right in doubles to stand anywhere back of the baseline between the center mark imaginary extension and the doubles sideline imaginary extension.*

RULE 35 • Order of Service in Doubles

The order of serving shall be decided at the beginning of each set as follows:

The pair who have to serve in the first game of each set shall decide which partner shall do so and the opposing pair shall decide similarly for the second game. The partner of the player who served in the first game shall serve in the third; the partner who served in the second game shall serve in the fourth, and so on in the same order in all the subsequent games of a set.

Case 1.   In doubles, one player does not appear in time to play, and his partner claims to be allowed to play single-handed against the opposing players. May he do so?

Decision.   No.

RULE 36 • Order of Receiving in Doubles

The order of receiving the service shall be decided at the beginning of each set as follows:

The pair who have to receive the service in the first game shall decide which partner shall receive the first service, and that partner shall continue to receive the first service in every odd game throughout that set. The opposing pair shall likewise decide which partner shall receive the first service in the second game and that partner shall continue to receive the first service in every even game throughout that set. Partners shall receive the service alternately throughout each game.

Case 1.   Is it allowable in doubles for the Server's partner or the Receiver's partner to stand in a position that obstructs the view of the Receiver?

Decision.   Yes. The Server's partner or the Receiver's partner may take any position on his side of the net in or out of the Court that he wishes.

RULE 37 • Service Out of Turn in Doubles

If a partner serves out of his turn, the partner who ought to have served shall serve as soon as the mistake is discovered, but all points scored, and any faults served before such discovery, shall be reckoned. If a game shall have been completed before such discovery, the order of service remains as altered.

USTA COMMENT: *For an exception to Rule 37, see Case 3 under Rule 27.*

RULE 38 • Error in Order of Receiving in Doubles

If during a game the order of receiving the service is changed by the Receivers it shall remain as altered until the end of the game in which the mistake is discovered, but the partners shall resume their original order of receiving in the next game of that set in which they are Receivers of the service.

RULE 39 • Service Fault in Doubles

The service is a fault as provided for by Rule 10, or if the ball touches the Server's partner or anything which he wears or carries; but if the ball served touches the partner of the Receiver, or anything which he wears or carries, not being a let under Rule 14(a) before it hits the ground, the Server wins the point.

RULE 40 • Playing the Ball in Doubles

The ball shall be struck alternately by one or other player of the opposing pairs, and if a player touches the ball in play with his racket in contravention of this Rule, his opponents win the point.

USTA COMMENT: *This means that, in the course of making one return, only one member of a doubles team may hit the ball. If both of them hit the ball, either simultaneously or consecutively, it is an illegal return. The partners themselves do not have to "alternate" in making returns. Mere clashing of rackets does not make a return illegal unless it is clear that more than one racket touched the ball.*

ITF NOTE: *Except where otherwise stated, every reference in these rules to the masculine includes the feminine gender.*

APPENDIX B:
RECORDS

UNITED STATES CHAMPIONSHIPS

The United States Championships, now called the U.S. Open, held at the U.S. National Tennis Center, Flushing Meadow, New York, had separate beginnings for men and women. The first Championships, men only, was staged at the Newport Casino in 1881, and held there through 1914. The doubles championship was played along with the singles between 1881 and 1886. From 1887 through 1914, sectional doubles tournaments, East and West, sometimes North and South as well, were staged at various locations, with the winners playing off for the title at Newport.

In 1915 the men's singles moved to the West Side Tennis Club, Forest Hills, New York, as did the doubles final for sectional winners. In 1917 the men's doubles championship, a complete tournament, was installed at the Longwood Cricket Club, Boston, and remained there through 1967, with two exceptions (1934 at Germantown Cricket Club, Philadelphia, and 1942 through 1945 at Forest Hills, during World War II).

The men's singles departed briefly from Forest Hills for a three-year stay at Germantown

Cricket, 1921 through 1923, and thereafter was staged at West Side where the newly constructed Stadium was ready in 1924.

The women's championships in singles and doubles began in 1887 at the Philadelphia Cricket Club (but the 1887–88 doubles were not considered championship events) and remained there through 1920, along with the mixed doubles, begun in 1892. In 1921 the women's singles and doubles moved to Forest Hills, but as an event prior to and separate from the men's championship, while the mixed doubles moved to Longwood to be played concurrently with the men's doubles.

In 1935 the men's and women's singles championships were united at Forest Hills while the women's doubles moved to Longwood as part of the U.S. Doubles with men's and mixed events.

During World War II (1942–45) all five events—men's and women's singles and doubles and mixed—were played at Forest Hills. In 1946 the men's and women's doubles returned to Longwood but the mixed remained at West Side until 1967 when it was played again at Longwood.

In 1968, with the advent of open tennis, the Championships, an amateur event closed to professionals since inception, was moved to Longwood where men's and women's singles and doubles and mixed were played as amateur events in 1968–69. Forest Hills thus became the scene of the first U.S. Open in 1968, and remained so until the move to Flushing Meadow in 1978. Men's and women's singles and doubles and mixed were thereby open to professionals and amateurs alike, and prize money was offered from 1968 on, originally $100,000, escalating to $10,893,890 in 1996. Singles first prize was $14,000 for men and $6,000 for women in 1968, escalating to $600,000 each in 1996. Prize money for men and women has been equal since 1973. The original amateurs-only event was abandoned in Boston after 1969, eliminating the confusion of two U.S. championships on successive dates on the calendar.

The Championships began on grass courts and continued that way until 1975 when the Forest Hills surface was changed to clay. The present surface at Flushing Meadow is hard, an asphalt composition. Night play began with the installation of floodlights in 1975 at Forest Hills. Prior to establishment of the U.S. Open, the Championships was often referred to as the U.S. Nationals or merely the Nationals.

The following is a list of champions and finalists in men's and women's singles and doubles, and champions in mixed doubles. The challenge round system was in force from 1884 through 1911 for the men's singles, and from 1888 through 1919 for the women's singles. This meant that the defending champion played only one match, waiting for a challenger to emerge from an all-comers tournament. When the champion did not defend, the winner of the all-comers became champion.

Separate U.S. Championships have been determined on clay, hard and indoor courts at various locations for men and women, but only the men's Clay Court has been held annually to date since inception. The Indoor championships, begun at New York's Seventh Regiment Armory in 1898

for men and 1907 for women, both have been discontinued, after 1988 and 1987 respectively. The Clay Court began for men at Omaha, Neb., in 1910, for women (joining the men) at Pittsburgh in 1912. The latter was discontinued after 1986. The Hard Court, begun for men and women at San Francisco in 1948, stopped after 1971. It was restored in 1988, and discontinued again after 1993 and 1994 respectively, seemingly redundant since the foremost championship, the Open at Flushing, is played on identical courts.

The original Championships venue at Newport held about 4,000. Temporary stands at Forest Hills could accommodate about 10,000. Later the concrete horseshoe stadium, opened in 1923, seated 15,000, although a record 16,253 crowded in for the Jimmy Connors–Bjorn Borg final of 1976. Floodlights were installed in 1975 and the attendance record, 218,480 for 19 sessions, was set in 1977. With 21,000-seat Louis Armstrong Stadium available at Flushing in 1978, and 25 sessions becoming the norm, attendance soared. The single-session record, 21,863, was for the afternoon, Aug. 27, 1990, while the afternoon-night record, 41,012 (21,185-19,865) was Aug. 27, 1996. The 1993 Open drew a record 534,274.

In 1970 the USTA approved use of a tie-breaker to conclude sets that reached 6-6 in games. Between 1970 and 1974 the system was "sudden death," best-of-nine points. Thereafter the ITF tie-breaker has been used, a theoretically best-of-12 points (meaning the first to reach seven but with the stipulation that it must be won by a margin of two points, thus possibly "lingering death").

MEN'S SINGLES

YEAR	
1881	Richard Sears d. William Glyn 6-0, 6-3, 6-2
1882	Richard Sears d. Clarence Clark 6-1, 6-4, 6-0
1883	Richard Sears d. James Dwight 6-2, 6-0, 9-7
1884	Richard Sears d. Howard Taylor 6-0, 1-6, 6-0, 6-2
1885	Richard Sears d. Godfrey Brinley 6-3, 4-6, 6-0, 6-3
1886	Richard Sears d. R. Livingston Beeckman 4-6, 6-1, 6-3, 6-4
1887	Richard Sears d. Henry Slocum 6-1, 6-3, 6-2
1888	Henry Slocum d. Howard Taylor 6-4, 6-1, 6-0
1889	Henry Slocum d. Quincy Shaw 6-3, 6-1, 4-6, 6-2

1890	Oliver Campbell d. Henry Slocum 6-2, 4-6, 6-3, 6-1
1891	Oliver Campbell d. Clarence Hobart 2-6, 7-5, 7-9, 6-1, 6-2
1892	Oliver Campbell d. Fred Hovey 7-5, 3-6, 6-3, 7-5
1893	Robert Wrenn d. Fred Hovey 6-4, 3-6, 6-4, 6-4
1894	Robert Wrenn d. Manliffe Goodbody 6-8, 6-1, 6-4, 6-4
1895	Fred Hovey d. Robert Wrenn 6-3, 6-2, 6-4
1896	Robert Wrenn d. Fred Hovey 7-5, 3-6, 6-0, 1-6, 6-1
1897	Robert Wrenn d. Wilberforce Eaves 4-6, 8-6, 6-3, 2-6, 6-2
1898	Malcolm Whitman d. Dwight Davis 3-6, 6-2, 6-2, 6-1
1899	Malcolm Whitman d. Parmly Paret 6-1, 6-2, 3-6, 7-5
1900	Malcolm Whitman d. Bill Larned 6-4, 1-6, 6-2, 6-2
1901	Bill Larned d. Beals Wright 6-2, 6-8, 6-4, 6-4
1902	Bill Larned d. Reggie Doherty 4-6, 6-2, 6-4, 8-6
1903	Laurie Doherty d. Bill Larned 6-0, 6-3, 10-8
1904	Holcombe Ward d. Bill Clothier 10-8, 6-4, 9-7
1905	Beals Wright d. Holcombe Ward 6-2 6-1, 11-9
1906	Bill Clothier d. Beals Wright 6-3, 6-0, 6-4
1907	Bill Larned d. Bob LeRoy 6-2, 6-2, 6-4
1908	Bill Larned d. Beals Wright 6-1, 6-2, 8-6
1909	Bill Larned d. Bill Clothier 6-1, 6-2, 5-7, 1-6, 6-1
1910	Bill Larned d. Tom Bundy 6-1, 5-7, 6-0, 6-8, 6-1
1911	Bill Larned d. Maurice McLoughlin 6-4, 6-4, 6-2
1912	Maurice McLoughlin d. Wallace Johnson 3-6, 2-6, 6-2, 6-4, 6-2
1913	Maurice McLoughlin d. Dick Williams 6-4, 5-7, 6-3, 6-1
1914	Dick Williams d. Maurice McLoughlin 6-3, 8-6, 10-8
1915	Bill Johnston d. Maurice McLoughlin 1-6, 6-0, 7-5, 10-8
1916	Dick Williams d. Bill Johnston 4-6, 6-4, 0-6, 6-2, 6-4
1917	R. Lindley Murray d. Nathaniel Niles 5-7, 8-6, 6-3, 6-3
1918	R. Lindley Murray d. Bill Tilden 6-3, 6-1, 7-5
1919	Bill Johnston d. Bill Tilden, 6-4, 6-4, 6-3
1920	Bill Tilden d. Bill Johnston 6-1, 1-6, 7-5, 5-7, 6-3
1921	Bill Tilden d. Wallace Johnson 6-1, 6-3, 6-1
1922	Bill Tilden d. Bill Johnston 4-6, 3-6, 6-2, 6-3, 6-4
1923	Bill Tilden d. Bill Johnston 6-4, 6-1, 6-4
1924	Bill Tilden d. Bill Johnston 6-1, 9-7, 6-2
1925	Bill Tilden d. Bill Johnston 4-6, 11-9, 6-3, 4-6, 6-3
1926	René Lacoste d. Jean Borotra 6-4, 6-0, 6-4
1927	René Lacoste d. Bill Tilden 11-9, 6-3, 11-9
1928	Henri Cochet d. Francis Hunter 4-6, 6-4, 3-6, 7-5, 6-3
1929	Bill Tilden d. Francis Hunter 3-6, 6-3, 4-6, 6-2, 6-4
1930	John Doeg d. Frank Shields 10-8, 1-6, 6-4, 16-14
1931	Ellsworth Vines d. George Lott 7-9, 6-3, 9-7, 7-5
1932	Ellsworth Vines d. Henri Cochet 6-4, 6-4, 6-4
1933	Fred Perry d. Jack Crawford 6-3, 11-13, 4-6, 6-0, 6-1
1934	Fred Perry d. Wilmer Allison 6-4, 6-3, 3-6, 1-6, 8-6
1935	Wilmer Allison d. Sidney Wood 6-2, 6-2, 6-3
1936	Fred Perry d. Don Budge 2-6, 6-2, 8-6, 1-6, 10-8
1937	Don Budge d. Gottfried von Cramm 6-1, 7-9, 6-1, 3-6, 6-1
1938	Don Budge d. Gene Mako 6-3, 6-8, 6-2, 6-1
1939	Bobby Riggs d. Welby Van Horn 6-4, 6-2, 6-4
1940	Don McNeill d. Bobby Riggs 4-6, 6-8, 6-3, 6-3, 7-5
1941	Bobby Riggs d. Frank Kovacs 5-7, 6-1, 6-3, 6-3
1942	Ted Schroeder d. Frank Parker 8-6, 7-5, 3-6, 4-6, 6-2
1943	Joe Hunt d. Jack Kramer 6-3, 6-8, 10-8, 6-0
1944	Frank Parker d. Bill Talbert 6-4, 3-6, 6-3, 6-3
1945	Frank Parker d. Bill Talbert 14-12, 6-1, 6-2
1946	Jack Kramer d. Tom Brown 9-7, 6-3, 6-0
1947	Jack Kramer d. Frank Parker 4-6, 2-6, 6-1, 6-0, 6-3
1948	Richard "Pancho" Gonzalez d. Eric Sturgess 6-2, 6-3, 14-12

1949	Richard "Pancho" Gonzalez d. Ted Schroeder 16-18, 2-6, 6-1, 6-2, 6-4
1950	Art Larsen d. Herbie Flam 6-3, 4-6, 5-7, 6 4, 6-3
1951	Frank Sedgman d. Vic Seixas 6-4, 6-1, 6-1
1952	Frank Sedgman d. Gardnar Mulloy 6-1, 6-2, 6-3
1953	Tony Trabert d. Vic Seixas 6-3, 6-2, 6-3
1954	Vic Seixas d. Rex Hartwig 3-6, 6-2, 6-4, 6-4
1955	Tony Trabert d. Ken Rosewall 9-7, 6-3, 6-3
1956	Ken Rosewall d. Lew Hoad 4-6, 6-2, 6-3, 6-3
1957	Mal Anderson d. Ashley Cooper 10-8, 7-5, 6-4
1958	Ashley Cooper d. Mal Anderson 6-2, 3-6, 4-6, 10-8, 8-6
1959	Neale Fraser d. Alex Olmedo 6-3, 5-7, 6-2, 6-4
1960	Neale Fraser d. Rod Laver 6-4, 6-4, 9-7
1961	Roy Emerson d. Rod Laver 7-5 6-3, 6-2
1962	Rod Laver d. Roy Emerson 6-2, 6-4, 5-7, 6-4
1963	Rafael Osuna d. Frank Froehling III 7-5, 6-4, 6-2
1964	Roy Emerson d. Fred Stolle 6-4, 6-1, 6-4
1965	Manuel Santana d. Cliff Drysdale 6-2, 7-9, 7-5, 6-1
1966	Fred Stolle d. John Newcombe 4-6, 12-10, 6-3, 6-4
1967	John Newcombe d. Clark Graebner 6-4, 6-4, 8-6
1968	Arthur Ashe d. Bob Lutz 4-6, 6-3, 8-10, 6-0, 6-4
1968*	Arthur Ashe d. Tom Okker 14-12, 5-7, 6-3, 3-6, 6-3
1969	Stan Smith d. Bob Lutz 9-7, 6-3, 6-1
1969*	Rod Laver d. Tony Roche 7-9, 6-1, 6-2, 6-2
1970	Ken Rosewall d. Tony Roche 2-6, 6-4, 7-6 (5-2), 6-3
1971	Stan Smith d. Jan Kodes 3-6, 6-3, 6-2, 7-6 (5-3)
1972	Ilie Nastase d. Arthur Ashe 3-6, 6-3, 6-7 (1-5), 6-4, 6-3
1973	John Newcombe d. Jan Kodes 6-4, 1-6, 4-6, 6-2, 6-3
1974	Jimmy Connors d. Ken Rosewall 6-1, 6-0, 6-1
1975	Manuel Orantes d. Jimmy Connors 6-4, 6-3, 6-3
1976	Jimmy Connors d. Bjorn Borg 6-4, 3-6, 7-6 (11-9), 6-4
1977	Guillermo Vilas d. Jimmy Connors 2-6, 6-3, 7-6 (7-4), 6-0
1978	Jimmy Connors d. Bjorn Borg 6-4, 6-2, 6-2
1979	John McEnroe d. Vitas Gerulaitis 7-5, 6-3, 6-3
1980	John McEnroe d. Bjorn Borg 7-6 (7-4), 6-1, 6-7 (5-7), 5-7, 6-4
1981	John McEnroe d. Bjorn Borg 4-6, 6-2, 6-4, 6-3
1982	Jimmy Connors d. Ivan Lendl 6-3, 6-2, 4-6, 6-4
1983	Jimmy Connors d. Ivan Lendl 6-3, 6-7 (2-7), 7-5, 6-0
1984	John McEnroe d. Ivan Lendl 6-3, 6-4, 6-1
1985	Ivan Lendl d. John McEnroe 7-6 (7-1), 6-3, 6-4
1986	Ivan Lendl d. Miloslav Mecir 6-4, 6-2, 6-0
1987	Ivan Lendl d. Mats Wilander 6-7 (7-9), 6-0, 7-6 (7-4), 6-4
1988	Mats Wilander d. Ivan Lendl 6-4, 4-6, 6-3, 5-7, 6-4
1989	Boris Becker d. Ivan Lendl 7-6 (7-2), 1-6, 6-3, 7-6 (7-4)
1990	Pete Sampras d. Andre Agassi 6-4, 6-3, 6-2
1991	Stefan Edberg d. Jim Courier 6-2, 6-4, 6-0
1992	Stefan Edberg d. Pete Sampras 3-6, 6-4, 7-6 (7-5), 6-2
1993	Pete Sampras d. Cedric Pioline 6-4, 6-4, 6-3
1994	Andre Agassi d. Michael Stich 6-1, 7-6 (7-5), 7-5
1995	Pete Sampras d. Andre Agassi 6-4, 6-3, 4-6, 7-5
1996	Pete Sampras d. Michael Chang 6-1, 6-4, 7-6 (7-3)

Open champions. In 1968 and 1969 both Amateur and Open Championships were held. Thereafter there was only the Open as principal Championship.

WOMEN'S SINGLES

YEAR

1887	Ellen Hansell d. Laura Knight 6-1, 6-0
1888	Bertha Townsend d.Ellen Hansell 6-3, 6-5
1889	Bertha Townsend d. Lida Voorhees 7-5, 6-2
1890	Ellen Roosevelt d. Bertha Townsend 6-2, 6-2
1891	Mabel Cahill d. Ellen Roosevelt 6-4, 6-1, 4-6, 6-3
1892	Mabel Cahill d. Elisabeth Moore 5-7, 6-3, 6-4, 4-6, 6-2
1893	Aline Terry d. Augusta Schultz 6-1, 6-3
1894	Helen Hellwig d. Aline Terry 7-5, 3-6, 6-0, 3-6, 6-3
1895	Juliette Atkinson d. Helen Hellwig 6-4, 6-1, 6-2
1896	Elisabeth Moore d. Juliette Atkinson 6-4, 4-6, 6-2, 6-2
1897	Juliette Atkinson d. Elisabeth Moore 6-3, 6-3, 4-6, 3-6, 6-3
1898	Juliette Atkinson d. Marion Jones 6-3, 5-7, 6-4, 2-6, 7-5
1899	Marion Jones d. Maud Banks 6-1, 6-1, 7-5
1900	Myrtle McAteer d. Edith Parker 6-2,6-2, 6-0
1901	Elisabeth Moore d. Myrtle McAteer 6-4, 3-6, 7-5, 2-6, 6-2
1902	Marion Jones d. Elisabeth Moore 6-1, 1-0 default
1903	Elisabeth Moore d. Marion Jones 7-5, 8-6
1904	May Sutton d. Elisabeth Moore 6-1, 6-2
1905	Elisabeth Moore d. Helen Homans 6-4, 5-7, 6-1
1906	Helen Homans d. Maud Barger Wallach 6-4, 6-3
1907	Evelyn Sears d. Carrie Neely 6-3, 6-2
1908	Maud Barger Wallach d. Evelyn Sears 6-2, 1-6, 6-3
1909	Hazel Hotchkiss d. Maud Barger Wallach 6-0, 6-1
1910	Hazel Hotchkiss d. Louise Hammond 6-4, 6-2
1911	Hazel Hotchkiss d. Florence Sutton 8-10, 6-1, 9-7
1912	Mary K. Browne d. Eleonora Sears 6-4, 6-2
1913	Mary K. Browne d. Dorothy Green 6-2, 7-5
1914	Mary K. Browne d. Marie Wagner 6-2, 1-6, 6-1
1915	Molla Bjurstedt d. Hazel Hotchkiss Wightman 4-6, 6-2, 6-0
1916	Molla Bjurstedt d. Louise Hammond Raymond 6-0, 6-1
1917	Molla Bjurstedt d. Marion Vanderhoef 4-6, 6-0, 6-2
1918	Molla Bjurstedt d. Eleanor Goss 6-4, 6-3
1919	Hazel Hotchkiss Wightman d. Marion Zinderstein 6-1, 6-2
1920	Molla Bjurstedt Mallory d. Marion Zinderstein 6-3, 6-1
1921	Molla Bjurstedt Mallory d. Mary K. Browne 4-6, 6-4, 6-2
1922	Molla Bjurstedt Mallory d. Helen Wills 6-3, 6-1
1923	Helen Wills d. Molla Bjurstedt Mallory 6-2, 6-1
1924	Helen Wills d. Molla Bjurstedt Mallory 6-1, 6-3
1925	Helen Wills d. Kitty McKane 3-6, 6-0, 6-2
1926	Molla Bjurstedt Mallory d. Elizabeth Ryan 4-6, 6-4, 9-7
1927	Helen Wills d. Betty Nuthall 6-1, 6-4
1928	Helen Wills d. Helen Jacobs 6-2, 6-1
1929	Helen Wills Moody d. Phoebe Holcroft Watson 6-4, 6-2
1930	Betty Nuthall d. Anna McCune Harper, 6-1, 6-4
1931	Helen Wills Moody d. Eileen Bennett Whittingstall 6-4, 6-1
1932	Helen Jacobs d. Carolin Babcock 6-2, 6-2
1933	Helen Jacobs d. Helen Wills Moody 8-6, 3-6, 3-0, default
1934	Helen Jacobs d. Sarah Palfrey Fabyan 6-1, 6-4
1935	Helen Jacobs d. Sarah Palfrey Fabyan 6-2, 6-4
1936	Alice Marble d. Helen Jacobs 4-6, 6-3, 6-2
1937	Anita Lizana d. Jadwiga Jedrzejowska 6-4, 6-2
1938	Alice Marble d. Nancye Wynne 6-0, 6-3
1939	Alice Marble d. Helen Jacobs 6-0, 8-10, 6-4
1940	Alice Marble d. Helen Jacobs 6-2, 6-3
1941	Sarah Palfrey Cooke d. Pauline Betz 7-5, 6-2
1942	Pauline Betz d. Louise Brough 4-6, 6-1, 6-4
1943	Pauline Betz d. Louise Brough 6-3, 5-7, 6-3
1944	Pauline Betz d. Margaret Osborne 6-3, 8-6
1945	Sarah Palfrey Cooke d. Pauline Betz 3-6, 8-6, 6-4
1946	Pauline Betz d. Doris Hart 11-9, 6-3
1947	Louise Brough d. Margaret Osborne duPont 8-6, 4-6, 6-1
1948	Margaret Osborne duPont d. Louise Brough 4-6, 6-4, 15-13
1949	Margaret Osborne duPont d. Doris Hart 6-4, 6-1
1950	Margaret Osborne duPont d. Doris Hart 6-3, 6-3
1951	Maureen Connolly d. Shirley Fry 6-3, 1-6, 6-4
1952	Maureen Connolly d. Doris Hart 6-3, 7-5
1953	Maureen Connolly d. Doris Hart 6-2 6-4
1954	Doris Hart d. Louise Brough 6-8, 6-1, 8-6
1955	Doris Hart d. Pat Ward 6-4, 6-2
1956	Shirley Fry d. Althea Gibson 6-3, 6-4
1957	Althea Gibson d. Louise Brough 6-3, 6-2
1958	Althea Gibson d. Darlene Hard 3-6, 6-1, 6-2
1959	Maria Bueno d. Christine Truman 6-1, 6-4
1960	Darlene Hard d. Maria Bueno 6-4, 10-12, 6-4
1961	Darlene Hard d. Ann Haydon 6-3, 6-4
1962	Margaret Smith d. Darlene Hard 9-7, 6-4
1963	Maria Bueno d. Margaret Smith 7-5, 6-4
1964	Maria Bueno d. Carole Caldwell Graebner 6-1, 6-0
1965	Margaret Smith d. Billie Jean Moffitt 8-6, 7-5
1966	Maria Bueno d. Nancy Richey 6-3, 6-1
1967	Billie Jean Moffitt King d. Ann Haydon Jones 11-9, 6-4
1968	Margaret Smith Court d. Maria Bueno 6-2, 6-2
1968*	Virginia Wade d. Billie Jean Moffitt King 6-4, 6-2
1969	Margaret Smith Court d. Virginia Wade 4-6, 6-3, 6-0
1969*	Margaret Smith Court d. Nancy Richey 6-2, 6-2
1970	Margaret Smith Court d. Rosie Casals 6-2, 2-6, 6-1
1971	Billie Jean Moffitt King d. Rosie Casals 6-4, 7-6 (5-2)
1972	Billie Jean Moffitt King d. Kerry Melville 6-3, 7-5
1973	Margaret Smith Court d. Evonne Goolagong 7-6 (5-2), 5-7, 6-2
1974	Billie Jean Moffitt King d. Evonne Goolagong 3-6, 6-3, 7-5
1975	Chris Evert d. Evonne Goolagong 5-7, 6-4, 6-2
1976	Chris Evert d. Evonne Goolagong 6-3, 6-0
1977	Chris Evert d. Wendy Turnbull 7-6 (5-3), 6-2
1978	Chris Evert d. Pam Shriver 7-5, 6-4
1979	Tracy Austin d. Chris Evert Lloyd 6-4, 6-3
1980	Chris Evert d. Hana Mandlikova 5-7, 6-1, 6-1
1981	Tracy Austin d. Martina Navratilova 1-6, 7-6 (7-4), 7-6 (7-1)
1982	Chris Evert d Hana Mandlikova 6-3, 6-1
1983	Martina Navratilova d. Chris Evert 6-1, 6-3
1984	Martina Navratilova d. Chris Evert Lloyd 4-6, 6-4, 6-4
1985	Hana Mandlikova d. Martina Navratilova 7-6 (7-3), 1-6, 7-6 (7-2)
1986	Martina Navratilova d. Helena Sukova 6-3, 6-2
1987	Martina Navratilova d. Steffi Graf 7-6 (7-4), 6-1
1988	Steffi Graf d. Gabriela Sabatini 6-3, 3-6, 6-1
1989	Steffi Graf d. Martina Navratilova 3-6 7-5, 6-1
1990	Gabriela Sabatini d. Steffi Graf 6-2, 7-6 (7-4)
1991	Monica Seles d. Martina Navratilova 7-6 (7-1), 6-1
1992	Monica Seles d. Arantxa Sanchez Vicario 6-3, 6-3
1993	Steffi Graf d. Helena Sukova 6-3, 6-3
1994	Arantxa Sanchez Vicario d. Steffi Graf 1-6, 7-6 (7-3), 6-4
1995	Steffi Graf d. Monica Seles 7-6 (8-6), 0-6, 6-3
1996	Steffi Graf d. Monica Seles 7-5, 6-4

Open champions. In 1968 and 1969 both Amateur and Open Championships were held. Thereafter there was only the Open as principal Championship.

MEN'S DOUBLES

YEAR

1881	Clarence Clark–Fred Taylor d. Alexander Van Rensselaer–Arthur Newbold 6-5, 6-4, 6-5
1882	Richard Sears–James Dwight d. Crawford Nightingale–George Smith 6-2, 6-4, 6-4
1883	Richard Sears–James Dwight d. Alexander Van Rensselaer–Arthur Newbold 6-0, 6-2, 6-2
1884	Richard Sears–James Dwight d. Alexander Van Rensselaer–Walter Berry 6-4, 6-1, 8-10, 6-4
1885	Richard Sears–Joseph Clark d. Henry Slocum–Percy Knapp 6-3, 6-0, 6-2
1886	Richard Sears–James Dwight d. Howard Taylor–Godfrey Brinley 7-5, 5-7, 7-5, 6-4
1887	Richard Sears–James Dwight d. Howard Taylor–Henry Slocum 6-4, 3-6, 2-6, 6-3, 6-3
1888	Oliver Campbell–Valentine Hall d. Clarence Hobart–Edward MacMullen 6-4, 6-2, 6-4
1889	Henry Slocum–Howard Taylor d. Valentine Hall–Oliver Campbell 14-12, 10-8, 6-4
1890	Valentine Hall–Clarence Hobart d. John Carver–John Ryerson 6-3, 4-6, 6-2, 2-6, 6-3
1891	Oliver Campbell–Bob Huntington d. Valentine Hall–Clarence Hobart 6-3, 6-4, 8-6
1892	Oliver Campbell–Bob Huntington d. Valentine Hall–Edward Hall 6-4, 6-2, 4-6, 6-3
1893	Clarence Hobart–Fred Hovey d. Oliver Campbell–Bob Huntington 6-4, 6-4, 4-6, 6-2
1894	Clarence Hobart–Fred Hovey d. Carr Neel–Sam Neel 6-3, 8-6, 6-1
1895	Malcolm Chace–Robert Wrenn d. Clarence Hobart–Fred Hovey 7-5, 6-1, 8-6
1896	Carr Neel–Sam Neel d. Robert Wrenn–Malcolm Chace 6-3, 1-6, 6-1, 3-6, 6-1
1897	Leo Ware–George Sheldon d. Harold Mahony–Harold Nisbet 11-13, 6-2, 9-7, 1-6, 6-1
1898	Leo Ware–George Sheldon d. Holcombe Ward–Dwight Davis 1-6, 7-5, 6-4, 4-6, 7-5
1899	Holcombe Ward–Dwight Davis d. Leo Ware–George Sheldon 6-4, 6-4, 6-3
1900	Holcombe Ward–Dwight Davis d. Fred Alexander–Ray Little 6-4, 9-7, 12-10
1901	Holcombe Ward–Dwight Davis d. Leo Ware–Beals Wright 6-3, 9-7, 6-1
1902	Reggie Doherty–Laurie Doherty d. Holcombe Ward–Dwight Davis 11-9, 12-10, 6-4
1903	Reggie Doherty–Laurie Doherty d. Kreigh Collins–Harry Waidner 7-5, 6-3, 6-3
1904	Holcombe Ward–Beals Wright d. Kreigh Collins–Ray Little 1-6, 6-2, 3-6, 6-4, 6-1
1905	Holcombe Ward–Beals Wright d. Fred Alexander–Harold Hackett 6-2, 6-1, 6-3
1906	Holcombe Ward–Beals Wright d. Fred Alexander–Harold Hackett 6-3, 3-6, 6-3, 6-3
1907	Fred Alexander–Harold Hackett d. Nat Thornton–Wylie Grant 6-2, 6-1, 6-1
1908	Fred Alexander–Harold Hackett d. Ray Little–Beals Wright 6-1, 7-5, 6-2
1909	Fred Alexander–Harold Hackett d. Maurice McLoughlin–George Janes 6-4, 6-4, 6-0
1910	Fred Alexander–Harold Hackett d. Tom Bundy–Trowbridge Hendrick 6-1, 8-6, 6-3
1911	Ray Little–Gus Touchard d. Fred Alexander–Harold Hackett 7-5, 13-15, 6-2, 6-4
1912	Maurice McLoughlin–Tom Bundy d. Ray Little–Gus Touchard 3-6, 6-2, 6-1, 7-5
1913	Maurice McLoughlin–Tom Bundy d. John Strachan–Clarence Griffin 6-4, 7-5, 6-1
1914	Maurice McLoughlin–Tom Bundy d. George Church–Dean Mathey 6-4, 6-2, 6-4
1915	Bill Johnston–Clarence Griffin d. Maurice McLoughlin–Tom Bundy 2-6, 6-3, 6-4, 3-6, 6-3
1916	Bill Johnston–Clarence Griffin d. Maurice McLoughlin–Ward Dawson 6-4, 6-3, 5-7, 6-3
1917	Fred Alexander–Harold Throckmorton d. Harry Johnson–Irving Wright 11-9, 6-4, 6-4
1918	Bill Tilden–Vinnie Richards d. Fred Alexander–Beals Wright 6-3, 6-4, 3-6, 2-6, 6-2
1919	Norman Brookes–Gerald Patterson d. Bill Tilden–Vinnie Richards 8-6, 6-3, 4-6, 4-6, 6-2
1920	Bill Johnston–Clarence Griffin d. Willis Davis–Roland Roberts 6-2, 6-2, 6-3
1921	Bill Tilden–Vinnie Richards d. Dick Williams–Watson Washburn 13-11, 12-10, 6-1
1922	Bill Tilden–Vinnie Richards d. Gerald Patterson–Pat O'Hara Wood 4-6, 6-1, 6-3, 6-4
1923	Bill Tilden–Brian Norton d. Dick Williams–Watson Washburn 3-6, 6-2, 6-3, 5-7, 6-2
1924	Howard Kinsey–Robert Kinsey d. Gerald Patterson–Pat O'Hara Wood 7-5, 5-7, 7-9, 6-3, 6-4
1925	Dick Williams–Vinnie Richards d. Gerald Patterson–John Hawkes 6-2, 8-10, 6-4, 11-9
1926	Dick Williams–Vinnie Richards d. Bill Tilden–Al Chapin 6-4, 6-8, 11-9, 6-3
1927	Bill Tilden–Francis Hunter d. Bill Johnston–Dick Williams 10-8, 6-3, 6-3
1928	George Lott–John Hennessey d. Gerald Patterson–John Hawkes 6-2, 6-1, 6-2
1929	George Lott–John Doeg d. Berkeley Bell–Lewis White 10-8, 16-14, 6-1
1930	George Lott–John Doeg d. John Van Ryn–Wilmer Allison 8-6, 6-3, 4-6, 13-15, 6-4
1931	Wilmer Allison–John Van Ryn d. Greg Mangin–Berkeley Bell 6-4, 8-6, 6-3
1932	Ellsworth Vines–Keith Gledhill d. Wilmer Allison–John Van Ryn 6-4, 6-3, 6-2
1933	George Lott–Lester Stoefen d. Frank Shields–Frank Parker 11-13, 9-7, 9-7, 6-3
1934	George Lott–Lester Stoefen d. Wilmer Allison–John Van Ryn 6-4, 9-7, 3-6, 6-4
1935	Wilmer Allison–John Van Ryn d. Don Budge–Gene Mako 6-4, 6-2, 3-6, 2-6, 6-1
1936	Don Budge–Gene Mako d. Wilmer Allison–John Van Ryn 6-4, 6-2, 6-4
1937	Gottfried von Cramm–Henner Henkel d. Don Budge–Gene Mako 6-4, 7-5, 6-4
1938	Don Budge–Gene Mako d. Adrian Quist–John Bromwich 6-3, 6-2, 6-1
1939	Adrian Quist–John Bromwich d. Jack Crawford–Harry Hopman 8-6, 6-1, 6-4
1940	Jack Kramer–Ted Schroeder d. Gardnar Mulloy–Henry Prusoff 6-4, 8-6, 9-7
1941	Jack Kramer–Ted Schroeder d. Wayne Sabin–Gardnar Mulloy 9-7, 6-4, 6-2
1942	Gardnar Mulloy–Bill Talbert d. Ted Schroeder–Sidney Wood 9-7, 7-5, 6-1
1943	Jack Kramer–Frank Parker d. Bill Talbert–David Freeman 6-2, 6-4, 6-4
1944	Don McNeill–Bob Falkenburg d. Bill Talbert–Francisco "Pancho" Segura 7-5, 6-4, 3-6, 6-1
1945	Gardnar Mulloy–Bill Talbert d. Bob Falkenburg–Jack Tuero 12-10, 8-10, 12-10, 6-2
1946	Gardnar Mulloy–Bill Talbert d. Don McNeill–Frank Guernsey 3-6, 6-4, 2-6, 6-3, 20-18
1947	Jack Kramer–Ted Schroeder d. Bill Talbert–Bill Sidwell 6-4, 7-5, 6-3
1948	Gardnar Mulloy–Bill Talbert d. Frank Parker–Ted Schroeder 1-6, 9-7, 6-3, 3-6, 9-7

1949	John Bromwich–Bill Sidwell d. Frank Sedgman–George Worthington 6-4, 6-0, 6-1

1949 John Bromwich–Bill Sidwell d. Frank Sedgman–George Worthington 6-4, 6-0, 6-1

1950 John Bromwich–Frank Sedgman d. Bill Talbert–Gardnar Mulloy 7-5, 8-6, 3-6, 6-1

1951 Ken McGregor–Frank Sedgman d. Don Candy–Mervyn Rose 10-8, 6-4, 4-6, 7-5

1952 Mervyn Rose–Vic Seixas d. Ken McGregor–Frank Sedgman 3-6, 10-8, 10-8, 6-8, 8-6

1953 Rex Hartwig–Mervyn Rose d. Gardnar Mulloy–Bill Talbert 6-4, 4-6, 6-2, 6-4

1954 Vic Seixas–Tony Trabert d. Lew Hoad–Ken Rosewall 3-6, 6-4, 8-6, 6-3

1955 Kosei Kamo–Atsushi Miyagi d. Gerald Moss–Bill Quillian 6-2, 6-3, 3-6, 1-6, 6-4

1956 Lew Hoad–Ken Rosewall d. Ham Richardson–Vic Seixas 6-2, 6-2, 3-6, 6-4

1957 Ashley Cooper–Neale Fraser d. Gardnar Mulloy–J. Edward "Budge" Patty 4-6, 6-3, 9-7, 6-3

1958 Alex Olmedo–Ham Richardson d. Sammy Giammalva–Barry MacKay 3-6, 6-3, 6-4, 6-4

1959 Neale Fraser–Roy Emerson d. Alex Olmedo–Earl "Butch" Buchholz 3-6, 6-3, 5-7, 6-4, 7-5

1960 Neale Fraser–Roy Emerson d. Rod Laver–Bob Mark 9-7, 6-2, 6-4

1961 Chuck McKinley–Dennis Ralston d. Rafael Osuna–Antonio Palafox 6-3, 6-4, 2-6, 13-11

1962 Rafael Osuna–Antonio Palafox d. Chuck McKinley–Dennis Ralston 6-4, 10-12, 1-6, 9-7, 6-3

1963 Chuck McKinley–Dennis Ralston d. Rafael Osuna–Antonio Palafox 9-7, 4-6, 5-7, 6-3, 11-9

1964 Chuck McKinley–Dennis Ralston d. Graham Stilwell–Mike Sangster 6-3, 6-2, 6-4

1965 Roy Emerson–Fred Stolle d. Frank Froehling III–Charlie Pasarell 6-4, 10-12, 7-5, 6-3

1966 Roy Emerson–Fred Stolle d. Clark Graebner–Dennis Ralston 6-4, 6-4, 6-4

1967 John Newcombe–Tony Roche d. Bill Bowrey–Owen Davidson 6-8, 9-7, 6-3, 6-3

1968 Bob Lutz–Stan Smith d. Bob Hewitt–Ray Moore 6-4, 6-4, 9-7

1968* Bob Lutz–Stan Smith d. Arthur Ashe–Andres Gimeno 11-9, 6-1, 7-5

1969 Dick Crealy–Allan Stone d. Bill Bowrey–Charlie Pasarell 9-11, 6-3, 7-5

1969* Ken Rosewall–Fred Stolle d. Charlie Pasarell–Dennis Ralston 2-6, 7-5, 13-11, 6-3

1970 Pierre Barthes–Nikki Pilic d. Roy Emerson–Rod Laver 6-3, 7-6 (5-4), 4-6, 7-6 (5-2)

1971** John Newcombe–Roger Taylor d. Stan Smith–Erik van Dillen 6-7, 6-3, 7-6 (5-4), 4-6, 5-3

1972 Cliff Drysdale–Roger Taylor d. Owen Davidson–John Newcombe 6-4, 7-6 (5-3), 6-3

1973 Owen Davidson–John Newcombe d. Rod Laver–Ken Rosewall 7-5, 2-6, 7-5, 7-5

1974 Bob Lutz–Stan Smith d. Pat Cornejo–Jaime Fillol 6-3, 6-3

1975 Jimmy Connors–Ilie Nastase d. Tom Okker–Marty Riessen 6-4, 7-6

1976 Tom Okker–Marty Riessen d. Paul Kronk–Cliff Letcher 6-4, 6-4

1977 Bob Hewitt–Frew McMillan d. Brian Gottfried–Raul Ramirez 6-4, 6-0

1978 Bob Lutz–Stan Smith d. Marty Riessen–Sherwood Stewart 1-6, 7-5, 6-3

1979 John McEnroe–Peter Fleming d. Bob Lutz–Stan Smith 6-2, 6-4

1980 Bob Lutz–Stan Smith d. Peter Fleming–John McEnroe 7-5, 3-6, 6-1, 3-6, 6-3

1981 Peter Fleming–John McEnroe d. Heinz Gunthardt–Peter McNamara (walkover)

1982 Kevin Curren–Steve Denton d. Victor Amaya–Hank Pfister 6-2, 6-7 (4-7), 5-7, 6-2, 6-4

1983 Peter Fleming–John McEnroe d. Fritz Buehning–Van Winitsky 6-3, 6-4, 6-2

1984 John Fitzgerald–Tomas Smid d. Stefan Edberg–Anders Jarryd 7-6, 6-3, 6-3

1985 Ken Flach–Robert Seguso d. Henri Leconte–Yannick Noah 6-7 (5-7), 7-6 (7-1), 7-6 (8-6), 6-0

1986 Andres Gomez–Slobodan Zivojinovic d. Joakim Nystrom–Mats Wilander 4-6, 6-3, 6-3, 4-6, 6-3

1987 Stefan Edberg–Anders Jarryd d. Ken Flach–Robert Seguso 7-6 (7-1), 6-2, 4-6, 5-7, 7-6 (7-2)

1988 Sergio Casal–Emilio Sanchez d. Rick Leach–Jim Pugh, (walkover)

1989 John McEnroe–Mark Woodforde d. Ken Flach–Robert Seguso 6-4, 4-6, 6-3, 6-3

1990 Pieter Aldrich–Danie Visser d. Paul Annacone–David Wheaton 6-2, 7-6 (7-3), 6-2

1991 John Fitzgerald–Anders Jarryd d. Scott Davis–David Pate 6-3, 3-6, 6-3, 6-3

1992 Jim Grabb–Richey Reneberg d. Kelly Jones–Rick Leach 3-6, 7-6 (7-2), 6-3, 6-3

1993 Ken Flach–Rick Leach d. Martin Damm–Karel Novacek 6-7 (3-7), 6-4, 6-2

1994 Jacco Eltingh–Paul Haarhuis d. Todd Woodbridge–Mark Woodforde 6-3, 7-6 (7-1)

1995 Todd Woodbridge–Mark Woodforde d. Alex O'Brian–Sandon Stolle 6-3, 6-3

1996 Todd Woodbridge–Mark Woodforde d. Paul Haarhuis–Jacco Eltingh 4-6, 7-6 (7-5), 7-6 (7-2)

Open champions. In 1968 and 1969 both Amateur and Open Championships were held. Thereafter there was only the Open as principal Championships.

**At nightfall, by mutual agreement, a tie-breaker was played to decide the title, Newcombe-Taylor winning 5-points-to-3.*

WOMEN'S DOUBLES

YEAR

1889 Margarette Ballard–Bertha Townsend d. Marion Wright–Laura Knight 6-0, 6-2

1890 Ellen Roosevelt–Grace Roosevelt d. Bertha Townsend–Margarette Ballard, 6-1, 6-2

1891 Mabel Cahill–Emma Leavitt Morgan d. Grace Roosevelt–Ellen Roosevelt 2-6, 8-6, 6-4

1892 Mabel Cahill–Adeline McKinlay d. Helen Day Harris–Amy Williams 6-1, 6-3

1893 Aline Terry–Hattie Butler d. Augusta Shultz–Stone 6-4, 6-3

1894 Helen Hellwig–Juliette Atkinson d. Annabella Wistar–Amy Williams 6-4, 8-6, 6-2

1895 Helen Hellwig–Juliette Atkinson d. Elisabeth Moore–Amy Williams 6-2, 6-2, 12-10

1896 Elisabeth Moore–Juliette Atkinson d. Annabella Wistar–Amy Williams 6-4, 9-7

1897 Juliette Atkinson–Kathleen Atkinson d. Mrs. F Edwards–Elizabeth Rastall 6-2, 6-1, 6-1

1898 Juliette Atkinson–Kathleen Atkinson d. Marie Wimer–Carrie Neely 6-1, 2-6, 4-6, 6-1, 6-2

1899 Jane Craven–Myrtle McAteer d. Maud Banks–Elizabeth Rastall 6-1, 6-1, 7-5

1900 Edith Parker–Hallie Champlin d. Marie Wimer–Myrtle McAteer 9-7, 6-2, 6-2

1901 Juliette Atkinson–Myrtle McAteer d. Marion Jones–Elisabeth Moore, default

1902 Juliette Atkinson–Marion Jones d. Maud Banks–Nona Closterman 6-2, 7-5

1903 Elisabeth Moore–Carrie Neely d. Miriam Hall–Marion Jones 4-6, 6-1, 6-1

1904 May Sutton–Miriam Hall d. Elisabeth Moore–Carrie Neely 3-6, 6-3, 6-3

1905 Helen Homans–Carrie Neely d. Marjorie Oberteuffer–Virginia Maule 6-0, 6-1

1906 Ann Burdette Coe–Ethel Bliss Platt d. Helen Homans–Clover Boldt 6-4, 6-4

1907 Marie Wimer–Carrie Neely d. Edna Wildey–Natalie Wildey 6-1, 2-6, 6-4

1908 Evelyn Sears–Margaret Curtis d. Carrie Neely–Marion Steever 6-3, 5-7, 9-7

1909 Hazel Hotchkiss–Edith Rotch d. Dorothy Green–Lois Moyes 6-1, 6-1

1910 Hazel Hotchkiss–Edith Rotch d. Adelaide Browning–Edna Wildey 6-4, 6-4

1911 Hazel Hotchkiss–Eleonora Sears d. Dorothy Green–Florence Sutton 6-4, 4-6, 6-2

1912 Dorothy Green–Mary K. Browne d. Maud Barger Wallach–Mrs. Frederick Schmitz 6-2, 5-7, 6-0

1913 Mary K. Browne–Louise Riddell Williams d. Dorothy Green–Edna Wildey 12-10, 2-6, 6-3

1914 Mary K. Browne–Louise Riddell Williams d. Louise Hammond Raymond–Edna Wildey 8-6, 6-2

1915 Hazel Hotchkiss Wightman–Eleonora Sears d. Helen Homans McLean–Mrs. George L. Chapman 10-8, 6-2

1916 Molla Bjurstedt–Eleonora Sears d. Louise Hammond Raymond–Edna Wildey 4-6, 6-2, 10-8

1917 Molla Bjurstedt–Eleonora Sears d. Phyllis Walsh–Grace Moore LeRoy 6-2, 6-4

1918 Marion Zinderstein–Eleanor Goss d. Molla Bjurstedt–Mrs. Johan Rogge 7-5, 8-6

1919 Marion Zinderstein–Eleanor Goss d. Eleanora Sears–Hazel Hotchkiss Wightman 10-8, 9-7

1920 Marion Zinderstein–Eleanor Goss d. Eleanor Tennant–Helen Baker 13-11, 4-6, 6-3

1921 Mary K. Browne–Louise Riddell Williams d. Helen Gilleaudeau–Aletta Bailey Morris 6-3, 6-2

1922 Marion Zinderstein Jessup–Helen Wills d. Edith Sigourney–Molla Bjurstedt Mallory 6-4, 7-9, 6-3

1923 Kitty McKane–Phyllis Howkins Covell d. Hazel Hotchkiss Wightman–Eleanor Goss 2-6, 6-2, 6-1

1924 Hazel Hotchkiss Wightman–Helen Wills d. Eleanor Goss–Marion Zinderstein Jessup 6-4, 6-3

1925 Mary K. Browne–Helen Wills d. May Sutton Bundy–Elizabeth Ryan 6-4, 6-3

1926 Elizabeth Ryan–Eleanor Goss d. Mary K. Browne–Charlotte Hosmer Chapin 3-6, 6-4, 12-10

1927 Kitty McKane Godfree–Ermyntrude Harvey d. Betty Nuthall–Joan Fry 6-1, 4-6, 6-4

1928 Hazel Hotchkiss Wightman–Helen Wills d. Edith Cross–Anna McCune Harper 6-2, 6-2

1929 Phoebe Holcroft Watson–Peggy Michell d. Phyllis Howkins Covell–Dorothy Shepherd Barron 2-6, 6-3, 6-4

1930 Betty Nuthall–Sarah Palfrey d. Edith Cross–Anna McCune Harper 3-6, 6-3, 7-5

1931 Betty Nuthall–Eileen Bennett Whittingstall d. Helen Jacobs–Dorothy Round 6-2, 6-4

1932 Helen Jacobs–Sarah Palfrey d. Marjorie Morrill Painter–Alice Marble 8-6, 6-1

1933 Betty Nuthall–Freda James d. Helen Wills Moody–Elizabeth Ryan (default)

1934 Helen Jacobs–Sarah Palfrey d. Carolin Babcock–Dorothy Andrus 4-6, 6-3, 6-4

1935 Helen Jacobs–Sarah Palfrey Fabyan d. Carolin Babcock–Dorothy Andrus 6-4, 6-2

1936 Marjorie Gladman Van Ryn–Carolin Babcock d. Helen Jacobs–Sarah Palfrey Fabyan 9-7, 2-6, 6-4

1937 Sarah Palfrey Fabyan–Alice Marble d. Marjorie Gladman Van Ryn–Carolin Babcock 7-5, 6-4

1938 Sarah Palfrey Fabyan–Alice Marble d. Simone Passemard Mathieu–Jadwiga Jedrzejowska 6-8, 6-4, 6-3

1939 Sarah Palfrey Fabyan–Alice Marble d. Kay Stammers–Freda James Hammersley 7-5, 8-6

1940 Sarah Palfrey Fabyan–Alice Marble d. Dorothy Bundy–Marjorie Gladman Van Ryn 6-4, 6-3

1941 Sarah Palfrey Fabyan–Margaret Osborne d. Dorothy Bundy–Pauline Betz 3-6, 6-1, 6-4

1942 Louise Brough–Margaret Osborne d. Pauline Betz–Doris Hart 2-6, 7-5, 6-0

1943 Louise Brough–Margaret Osborne d. Pauline Betz–Doris Hart 6-4, 6-3

1944 Louise Brough–Margaret Osborne d. Pauline Betz–Doris Hart 4-6, 6-4, 6-3

1945 Louise Brough–Margaret Osborne d. Pauline Betz–Doris Hart 6-3, 6-3

1946 Louise Brough–Margaret Osborne d. Patricia Canning Todd–Mary Arnold Prentiss 6-1, 6-3

1947 Louise Brough–Margaret Osborne d. Patricia Canning Todd–Doris Hart 5-7, 6-3, 7-5

1948 Louise Brough–Margaret Osborne duPont d. Patricia Canning Todd–Doris Hart 6-4, 8-10, 6-1

1949 Louise Brough–Margaret Osborne duPont d. Doris Hart–Shirley Fry 6-4, 10-8

1950 Louise Brough–Margaret Osborne duPont d. Doris Hart–Shirley Fry 6-2, 6-3

1951 Shirley Fry–Doris Hart d. Nancy Chaffee–Patricia Canning Todd 6-4, 6-2

1952 Shirley Fry–Doris Hart d. Louise Brough–Maureen Connolly 10-8, 6-4

1953 Shirley Fry–Doris Hart d. Louise Brough–Margaret Osborne duPont 6-2, 7-9, 9-7

1954 Shirley Fry–Doris Hart d. Louise Brough–Margaret Osborne duPont 6-4, 6-4

1955 Louise Brough–Margaret Osborne duPont d. Doris Hart–Shirley Fry 6-3, 1-6, 6-3

1956 Louise Brough–Margaret Osborne duPont d. Betty Rosenquest Pratt–Shirley Fry 6-3, 6-0

1957 Louise Brough–Margaret Osborne duPont d. Althea Gibson–Darlene Hard 6-2, 7-5

1958 Jeanne Arth–Darlene Hard d. Althea Gibson–Maria Bueno 2-6, 6-3, 6-4

1959 Jeanne Arth–Darlene Hard d. Maria Bueno–Sally Moore 6-2, 6-3

1960 Maria Bueno–Darlene Hard d. Ann Haydon–Deidre Catt 6-1, 6-1

1961 Darlene Hard–Lesley Turner d. Edda Buding–Yola Ramirez 6-4, 5-7, 6-0

1962 Darlene Hard–Maria Bueno d. Karen Hantze Susman–Billie Jean Moffitt 4-6, 6-3, 6-2

1963 Robyn Ebbern–Margaret Smith d. Darlene Hard–Maria Bueno 4-6, 10-8, 6-3

1964 Billie Jean Moffitt–Karen Hantze Susman d. Margaret Smith–Lesley Turner 3-6, 6-2, 6-4

1965 Carole Caldwell Graebner–Nancy Richey d. Billie Jean Moffitt–Karen Hantze Susman 6-4, 6-4

1966 Maria Bueno–Nancy Richey d. Billie Jean Moffitt King–Rosie Casals 6-3, 6-4

1967 Rosie Casals–Billie Jean Moffitt King d. Mary Ann Eisel–Donna Floyd Fales 4-6, 6-3, 6-4

1968 Maria Bueno–Margaret Smith Court d. Virginia Wade–Joyce Barclay Williams 6-3, 7-5

1968* Maria Bueno–Margaret Smith Court d. Billie Jean Moffitt King–Rosie Casals 4-6, 9-7, 8-6

1969 Virginia Wade–Margaret Smith Court d. Mary Ann Eisel Curtis–Valerie Ziegenfuss 6-1, 6-3

1969* Francoise Durr–Darlene Hard d. Margaret Smith Court–Virginia Wade 0-6, 6-4, 6-4

1970 Margaret Smith Court–Judy Tegart Dalton d. Rosie Casals–Virginia Wade 6-3, 6-4

1971 Rosie Casals–Judy Tegart Dalton d. Gail Sherriff Chanfreau–Francoise Durr 6-3, 6-3

1972 Francoise Durr–Betty Stove d. Margaret Smith Court–Virginia Wade 6-3, 1-6, 6-3

1973 Margaret Smith Court–Virginia Wade d. Billie Jean Moffitt King–Rosie Casals 3-6, 6-3, 7-5

1974	Rosie Casals–Billie Jean Moffit King d. Francoise Durr–Betty Stove 7-6 (5-4), 6-7 (2-5), 6-4
1975	Margaret Smith Court–Virginia Wade d. Billie Jean Moffitt King–Rosie Casals 7-5, 2-6, 7-6 (7-5)
1976	Delina Boshoff–Ilana Kloss d. Olga Morozova–Virginia Wade 6-1, 6-4
1977	Martina Navratilova–Betty Stove d. René Richards–Bettyann Grubb Stuart 6-1, 7-6
1978	Billie Jean Moffitt King–Martina Navratilova d. Kerry Melville Reid–Wendy Turnbull 7-6 (9-7), 6-4
1979	Betty Stove–Wendy Turnbull d. Billie Jean Moffitt King–Martina Navratilova 7-5, 6-3
1980	Billie Jean Moffitt King–Martina Navratilova d. Pam Shriver–Betty Stove 7-6 (7-2), 7-5
1981	Anne Smith–Kathy Jordan d. Rosie Casals–Wendy Turnbull 6-3, 6-3
1982	Rosie Casals–Wendy Turnbull d. Sharon Walsh–Barbara Potter 6-4, 6-4
1983	Pam Shriver–Martina Navratilova d. Rosalyn Fairbank–Candy Reynolds 6-7 (4-7), 6-1, 6-3
1984	Pam Shriver–Martina Navratilova d. Anne Hobbs–Wendy Turnbull 6-2, 6-4
1985	Claudia Kohde Kilsch–Helena Sukova d. Martina Navratilova–Pam Shriver 6-7, 6-2, 6-3
1986	Martina Navratilova–Pam Shriver d. Hana Mandlikova–Wendy Turnbull 6-4, 3-6, 6-3
1987	Martina Navratilova–Pam Shriver d. Kathy Jordan–Elizabeth Sayers Smylie 5-7, 6-4, 6-2
1988	Beatriz "Gigi" Fernandez–Robin White d. Patty Fendick–Jill Hetherington 6-4, 6-1
1989	Hana Mandlikova–Martina Navratilova d. Mary Joe Fernandez–Pam Shriver 5-7, 6-4, 6-4
1990	Beatriz "Gigi" Fernandez–Martina Navratilova d. Jana Novotna–Helena Sukova 6-2, 6-4
1991	Pam Shriver–Natalia Zvereva d. Jana Novotna–Larisa Savchenko 6-4, 4-6, 7-6 (7-5)
1992	Beatriz "Gigi" Fernandez–Natalia Zvereva d. Jana Novotna–Larisa Savchenko Neiland 7-6 (7-4), 6-1
1993	Arantxa Sanchez Vicario–Helena Sukova d. Amanda Coetzer–Ines Gorrochategui 6-4, 6-2
1994	Arantxa Sanchez Vicario–Jana Novotna d. Katerina Maleeva–Robin White 6-3, 6-3
1995	Beatriz "Gigi" Fernandez–Natalia Zvereva d. Brenda Schultz McCarthy–Rennae Stubbs 7-5, 6-3
1996	Natalia Zvereva–Beatriz "Gigi" Fernandez d. Jana Novotna–Arantxa Sanchez Vicario 1-6, 6-1, 6-4

Open champions. In 1968 and 1969 both Amateur and Open Championships were held. Thereafter there was only the Open as principal Championship.

MIXED DOUBLES

YEAR	
1892	Mabel Cahill–Clarence Hobart d. Elisabeth Moore–Rod Beach 5-7, 6-1, 6-4
1893	Ellen Roosevelt–Clarence Hobart d. Ethel Bankson–Robert Willson, Jr. 6-1, 4-6, 10-8, 6-1
1894	Juliette Atkinson–Edwin Fischer d. Mrs. McFadden–Gustav Remack, Jr. 6-3, 6-2, 6-1
1895	Juliette Atkinson–Edwin Fischer d. Amy Williams–Mantle Fielding 4-6, 8-6, 6-2
1896	Juliette Atkinson–Edwin Fischer d. Amy Williams–Mantle Fielding 6-2, 6-3, 6-3
1897	Laura Henson–D. L. Magruder d. Maud Banks–B. L. C. Griffiths 6-4, 6-3, 7-5
1898	Carrie Neely–Edwin Fischer d. Helen Chapman–J. A. Hill 6-2, 6-4, 8-6

1899	Elizabeth Rastall–Albert Hoskins d. Jennie Craven–James Gardner 6-4, 6-0, default
1900	Margaret Hunnewell–Alfred Codman d. T. Shaw–George Atkinson 11-9, 6-3, 6-1
1901	Marion Jones–Raymond Little d. Myrtle McAteer–Clyde Stevens 6-4, 6-4, 7-5
1902	Elisabeth Moore–Wylie Grant d. Elizabeth Rastall–Albert Hoskins 6-2, 6-1
1903	Helen Chapman–Harry Allen d. Carrie Neely–W. H. Rowland 6-4, 7-5
1904	Elisabeth Moore–Wylie Grant d. May Sutton–Trevanion Dallas 6-2, 6-1
1905	Augusta Schultz Hobart–Clarence Hobart d. Elisabeth Moore–Edward Dewhurst 6-2, 6-4
1906	Sarah Coffin–Edward Dewhurst d. Margaret Johnson–Wallace Johnson 6-3, 7-5
1907	May Sayers–Wallace Johnson d. Natalie Wildey–W. Morris Tilden 6-1, 7-5
1908	Edith Rotch–Nat Niles d. Louise Hammond–Raymond Little 6-4, 4-6, 6-4
1909	Hazel Hotchkiss–Wallace Johnson d. Louise Hammond–Raymond Little 6-2, 6-0
1910	Hazel Hotchkiss–Joseph Carpenter, Jr. d. Edna Wildey–Herbert M. Tilden 6-2, 6-2
1911	Hazel Hotchkiss–Wallace Johnson d. Edna Wildey–Herbert M. Tilden 6-4, 6-4
1912	Mary K. Browne–Dick Williams d. Eleanora Sears–Bill Clothier 6-4, 2-6, 11-9
1913	Mary K. Browne–Bill Tilden d. Dorothy Green–C. S. Rogers 7-5, 7-5
1914	Mary K. Browne–Bill Tilden d. Margarette Myers–J. R. Rowland 6-1, 6-4
1915	Hazel Hotchkiss Wightman–Harry Johnson d. Molla Bjurstedt–Irving Wright 6-0, 6-1
1916	Eleanora Sears–Willis Davis d. Florence Ballin–Bill Tilden 6-4, 7-5
1917	Molla Bjurstedt–Irving Wright d. Florence Ballin–Bill Tilden 10-12, 6-1, 6-3
1918	Hazel Hotchkiss Wightman–Irving Wright d. Molla Bjurstedt–Fred Alexander 6-2, 6-4
1919	Marion Zinderstein–Vinnie Richards d. Florence Ballin–Bill Tilden 2-6, 11-9, 6-2
1920	Hazel Hotchkiss Wightman–Wallace Johnson d. Molla Bjurstedt Mallory–Craig Biddle 6-4, 6-3
1921	Mary K. Browne–Bill Johnston d. Molla Bjurstedt Mallory–Bill Tilden 3-6, 6-4, 6-3
1922	Molla Bjurstedt Mallory–Bill Tilden d. Helen Wills–Howard Kinsey 6-4, 6-3
1923	Molla Bjurstedt Mallory–Bill Tilden d. Kitty McKane–John Hawkes 6-3, 2-6, 10-8
1924	Helen Wills–Vinnie Richards d. Molla Bjurstedt Mallory–Bill Tilden 6-8, 7-5, 6-0
1925	Kitty McKane–John Hawkes d. Ermyntrude Harvey–Vinnie Richards 6-2, 6-4
1926	Elizabeth Ryan–Jean Borotra d. Hazel Hotchkiss Wightman–René Lacoste 6-4, 7-5
1927	Eileen Bennett–Henri Cochet d. Hazel Hotchkiss Wightman–René Lacoste 6-2, 0-6, 6-2
1928	Helen Wills–John Hawkes d. Edith Cross–Gar Moon, 6-1, 6-3
1929	Betty Nuthall–George Lott d. Phyllis Howkins Covell–Henry "Bunny" Austin 6-3, 6-3
1930	Edith Cross–Wilmer Allison d. Marjorie Morrill–Frank Shields 6-4, 6-4
1931	Betty Nuthall–George Lott d. Anna McCune Harper–Wilmer Allison 6-3, 6-3
1932	Sarah Palfrey–Fred Perry d. Helen Jacobs–Ellsworth Vines 6-3, 7-5
1933	Elizabeth Ryan–Ellsworth Vines d. Sarah Palfrey–George Lott 11-9, 6-1
1934	Helen Jacobs–George Lott d. Elizabeth Ryan–Les Stoefen 4-6, 13-11, 6-2

1935	Sarah Palfrey Fabyan–Enrique Maier d. Kay Stammers–Roderick Menzel 6-3, 3-6, 6-4
1936	Alice Marble–Gene Mako d. Sarah Palfrey Fabyan–Don Budge 6-3, 6-2
1937	Sarah Palfrey Fabyan–Don Budge d. Sylvie Jung Henrotin–Yvon Petra 6-2, 8-10, 6-0
1938	Alice Marble–Donald Budge d. Thelma Coyne–John Bromwich 6-1, 6-2
1939	Alice Marble–Harry Hopman d. Sarah Palfrey Fabyan–Elwood Cooke 9-7, 6-1
1940	Alice Marble–Bobby Riggs d. Dorothy Bundy–Jack Kramer 9-7, 6-1
1941	Sarah Palfrey Cooke–Jack Kramer d. Pauline Betz–Bobby Riggs 4-6, 6-4, 6-4
1942	Louise Brough–Ted Schroeder d. Patricia Canning Todd–Alejo Russell 3-6, 6-1, 6-4
1943	Margaret Osborne–Bill Talbert d. Pauline Betz–Francisco "Pancho" Segura, 10-8, 6-4
1944	Margaret Osborne–Bill Talbert d. Dorothy Bundy–Don McNeill 6-2, 6-3
1945	Margaret Osborne–Bill Talbert d. Doris Hart–Bob Falkenburg 6-4, 6-4
1946	Margart Osborne–Bill Talbert d. Louise Brough–Robert Kimbrell 6-3, 6-4
1947	Louise Brough–John Bromwich d. Gertrude "Gussy" Moran–Francisco "Pancho" Segura 6-3, 6-1
1948	Louise Brough–Tom Brown d. Margaret Osborne duPont–Bill Talbert 6-4, 6-4
1949	Louise Brough–Eric Strugess d. Margaret Osborne duPont–Bill Talbert 4-6, 6-3, 7-5
1950	Margaret Osborne duPont–Ken McGregor d. Doris Hart–Frank Sedgman 6-4, 3-6, 6-3
1951	Doris Hart–Frank Sedgman d. Shirley Fry–Mervyn Rose 6-3, 6-2
1952	Doris Hart–Frank Sedgman d. Thelma Coyne Long–Lew Hoad 6-3, 7-5
1953	Doris Hart–Vic Seixas d. Julia Sampson–Rex Hartwig 6-2, 4-6, 6-4
1954	Doris Hart–Vic Seixas d. Margaret Osborne duPont–Ken Rosewall 4-6, 6-1, 6-1
1955	Doris Hart–Vic Seixas d. Shirley Fry–Gardnar Mulloy 7-5, 5-7, 6-2
1956	Margaret Osborne duPont–Ken Rosewall d. Darlene Hard–Lew Hoad 9-7, 6-1
1957	Althea Gibson–Kurt Nielsen d. Darlene Hard–Bob Howe 6-3, 9-7
1958	Margaret Osborne duPont–Neale Fraser d. Maria Bueno–Alex Olmedo 6-4, 3-6, 9-7
1959	Margaret Osborne duPont–Neale Fraser d. Janet Hopps–Bob Mark 7-5, 13-15, 6-2
1960	Margaret Osborne duPont–Neale Fraser d. Maria Bueno–Antonio Palafox 6-3, 6-2
1961	Margaret Smith–Bob Mark d. Darlene Hard–Dennis Ralston (default) Ralston under suspension.
1962	Margaret Smith–Fred Stolle d. Lesley Turner–Frank Froehling III 7-5, 6-2
1963	Margaret Smith–Ken Fletcher d. Judy Tegart–Ed Rubinoff 3-6, 8-6, 6-2
1964	Margaret Smith–John Newcombe d. Judy Tegart–Ed Rubinoff 10-8, 4-6, 6-3
1965	Margaret Smith–Fred Stolle d. Judy Tegart–Frank Froehling III 6-2, 6-2
1966	Donna Floyd Fales–Owen Davidson d. Carol Hanks Aucamp–Ed Rubinoff 6-1, 6-3
1967	Billie Jean Moffitt King–Owen Davidson d. Rosemary Casals–Stan Smith 6-3, 6-2
1968	Mary Ann Eisel–Peter Curtis d. Tory Ann Fretz–Robert Perry 6-4, 7-5
1969	Patti Hogan–Paul Sullivan d. Kristy Pigeon–Terry Addison 6-4, 2-6, 12-10
1969*	Margaret Smith Court–Marty Riessen d. Francoise Durr–Dennis Ralston 7-5, 6-3

1970	Margaret Smith Court–Marty Riessen d. Judy Tegart Dalton–Frew McMillan 6-4, 6-4
1971	Billie Jean Moffitt King–Owen Davidson d. Betty Stove–Rob Maud, 6-3, 7-5
1972	Margaret Smith Court–Marty Riessen d. Rosie Casals–Ilie Nastase 6-3, 7-5
1973	Billie Jean Moffitt King–Owen Davidson d. Margaret Smith Court–Marty Riessen 6-3, 3-6, 7-6
1974	Pam Teeguarden–Geoff Masters d. Chris Evert–Jimmy Connors 6-1, 7-6
1975	Rosemary Casals–Dick Stockton d. Billie Jean Moffitt King–Fred Stolle 6-3, 7-6
1976	Billie Jean Moffitt King–Phil Dent d. Betty Stove–Frew McMillan 3-6, 6-2, 7-6
1977	Betty Stove–Frew McMillan d. Billie Jean Moffitt King–Vitas Gerulaitis 6-2, 3-6, 6-3
1978	Betty Stove–Frew McMillan d. Billie Jean Moffitt King–Ray Ruffels 6-3, 7-6
1979	Greer Stevens–Bob Hewitt d. Betty Stove–Frew McMillan 6-3, 7-5
1980	Wendy Turnbull–Marty Riessen d. Betty Stove–Frew McMillan 7-5, 6-2
1981	Anne Smith–Kevin Curren d. JoAnne Russell–Steve Denton 6-4, 7-6 (7-4)
1982	Anne Smith–Kevin Curren d. Barbara Potter–Ferdi Taygan 6-7, 7-6 (7-4), 7-6 (7-5)
1983	Elizabeth Sayers–John Fitzgerald d. Barbara Potter–Ferdi Taygan 3-6 6-3, 6-4
1984	Manuela Maleeva–Tom Gullikson d. Elizabeth Sayers–John Fitzgerald 2-6, 7-5, 6-4
1985	Martina Navratilova–Heinz Gunthardt d. Elizabeth Sayers Smylie–John Fitzgerald 6-3, 6-4
1986	Raffaella Reggi–Sergio Casal d. Martina Navratilova–Peter Fleming 6-4, 6-4
1987	Martina Navratilova–Emilio Sanchez d. Betsy Nagelsen–Paul Annacone 6-4, 6-7 (6-8), 7-6 (14-12)
1988	Jana Novotna–Jim Pugh d. Elizabeth Sayers Smylie–Patrick McEnroe 7-5, 6-3
1989	Robin White–Shelby Cannon d. Meredith McGrath–Rick Leach 3-6, 6-2, 7-5
1990	Elizabeth Sayers Smylie–Todd Woodbridge d. Natalia Zvereva–Jim Pugh 6-4, 6-2
1991	Manon Bollegraf–Tom Nijssen d. Arantxa Sanchez Vicario–Emilio Sanchez 6-2, 7-6 (7-2)
1992	Nicole Provis–Mark Woodforde d. Helena Sukova–Tom Nijssen 4-6, 6-3, 6-3
1993	Helena Sukova–Todd Woodbridge d. Martina Navratilova–Mark Woodforde 6-3, 7-6 (8-6)
1994	Elna Reinach–Patrick Galbraith d. Jana Novotna–Todd Woodbridge 6-2, 6-4
1995	Meredith McGrath–Matt Lucena d. Gigi Fernandez–Cyril Suk 6-4, 6-4
1996	Lisa Raymond–Patrick Galbraith d. Manon Bollegraf–Rick Leach 7-6 (8-6), 7-6 (7-4)

Open champions. In 1969 both Amateur and Open Championships were held. Thereafter there was only the Open as principal Championship.

ALL-TIME UNITED STATES CHAMPIONSHIPS RECORDS

Most men's singles: 7—Dick Sears, 1881–87; Bill Larned, 1901–02, 1907–11; Bill Tilden, 1920–25, 1929

Most men's doubles: 6—Sears, 1882–87; Holcombe Ward, 1899–01, 1904–06

Most men's mixed: 4—Edwin Fischer, 1894–96, 1908; Wallace Johnson, 1907, 1909, 1911, 1920; Tilden, 1913–14, 1922–23; Bill Talbert, 1943–46; Owen Davidson, 1966–67, 1971, 1973; Marty Riessen 1969–70, 1972, 1980

Most men's altogether: 16—Tilden, 1913–30 (7 singles, 5 doubles, 4 mixed)

Most women's singles: 8—Molla Bjurstedt Mallory, 1915–18, 1920–22, 1926

Most women's doubles: 13—Margaret Osborne duPont, 1941–50, 1955–1957

Most women's mixed: 9—duPont, 1943–46, 1950, 1956, 1958–60

Most women's altogether: 25—duPont, 1941–60 (3 singles, 13 doubles, 9 mixed)

Most men's doubles, team: 5—James Dwight and Sears, 1882–84, 1886–87

Most women's doubles, team: 12—Louise Brough and duPont, 1942–50, 1955–1957

Most mixed doubles, team: 4—duPont and Talbert, 1943–46

YOUNGEST CHAMPIONS

Women's singles: Tracy Austin, 1979, 16 years, 9 months
Women's doubles: May Sutton, 1904, 17 years, 11 months
Women's mixed: Manuela Maleeva Fragniere, 1984, 17 years, 7 months
Men's singles: Pete Sampras, 1990, 19 years, 1 month
Men's doubles: Vinnie Richards, 1918, 15 years, 4 month
Men's mixed: Vinnie Richards, 1919, 16 years, 3 months

OLDEST CHAMPIONS

Men's singles: Bill Larned, 1911, 38 years, 8 months
Men's doubles: Bob Hewitt, 1977, 37 years, 8 months
Men's mixed: Bob Hewitt, 1979, 39 years, 8 months
Women's singles: Molla Bjurstedt Mallory, 1926, 42 years, 5 months
Women's doubles: Hazel Hotchkiss Wightman, 1928, 41 years, 8 months
Women's mixed: Margaret Osborne duPont, 1960, 42 years, 5 months

INDIVIDUAL SINGLES CAREER RECORDS

MEN

Tournaments played: 28—Vic Seixas, 1940–43, 1946–69
Matches played: 115—Jimmy Connors, 1970–89, 1991–92
Matches won: 98—Jimmy Connors, 1970–89, 1991–92
Matches won consecutively: 42—Bill Tilden, 1920 through 3rd rd., 1926, lost quarters to Henri Cochet
Match winning percentage: 1.000—Dick Sears 18-0, 1881–87; .910, Bill Tilden 71-7, 1916–1927, 1929–30

WOMEN

Tournaments played: 21—Martina Navratilova, 1972–93
Matches played: 113—Chris Evert, 1971–89
Matches won: 101—Evert, 1971–89
Matches won consecutively: 46—Helen Wills Moody, 1923–25, 1927–29, 1931, 1933 through semis, lost final to Helen Jacobs
Match winning percentage: .962—Moody (51-2), 1922–25, 1927–29, 1931, 1933

BEST SEASONS (MEN'S SINGLES) OPEN ERA

TOURNAMENTS			MATCHES		MAJORS WON
NO.	W	LF	W	L	
Guillermo Vilas, 1977					
33	17	4*	145	14	Fr, U.S.
Rod Laver, 1969					
32	17	2	106	16	Grand Slam
Jimmy Connors, 1974					
21	15	2	99	4	Aus, Wim, U.S.
Ilie Nastase, 1973					
31	15	3	118	17	Fr
Ivan Lendl, 1982					
23	15	4	107	9	none
John McEnroe, 1984					
15	13	2	82	3	Wim, U.S.
Bjorn Borg, 1979					
19	12	1	93	6	Fr, Wim
Jimmy Connors, 1976					
23	13	4	100	12	U.S.
Bjorn Borg, 1979					
19	12	3	93	6	Fr, Wim
Pete Sampras, 1994					
18	10	1	77	12	Aus, Wim
Arthur Ashe, 1975					
29	9	5	108	23	Wim
Ivan Lendl, 1986					
15	9	3	74	6	Fr, U.S.
Bjorn Borg, 1980					
13	8	3	68	6	Fr, Wim
Mats Wilander, 1988					
15	6	0	53	11	Aus, Fr, U.S.
Boris Becker, 1989					
13	6	2	64	8	Wim, U.S.

Also reached two finals that were not played

BEST SEASONS (WOMEN'S SINGLES), OPEN ERA

TOURNAMENTS			MATCHES		MAJORS WON
NO.	W	LF	W	L	
Margaret Court, 1970					
27	21	2	104	6	Grand Slam
Margaret Court, 1973					
25	18	1	102	6	Aus, Fr, U.S.
Billie Jean King, 1971					
31	17	6	112	13	Wim, U.S.
Chris Evert, 1974					
23	16	5	100	7	Fr, Wim
Martina Navratilova, 1983					
17	16	0	86	1	Aus, Wim, U.S.
Martina Navratilova, 1982					
18	15	2	90	3	Fr, Wim
Steffi Graf, 1989					
16	14	2	86	2	Aus, Wim, U.S.
Martina Navratilova, 1984					
15	13	1	78	2	Fr, Wim, U.S.
Steffi Graff, 1988					
14	11	2	72	3	Grand Slam
Monica Seles, 1992					
15	10	4	70	5	Aus, Fr, U.S.
Monica Seles, 1991					
16	10	6	74	6	Aus, Fr, U.S.
Steffi Graf, 1995					
11	9	0	47	2	Fr, Wim, U.S.
Steffi Graf, 1996					
11	7	1	54	4	Fr, Wim, U.S.

LONGEST MATCHES (TOTAL GAMES)

Men's singles: 100 games—F. D. Robbins d. Dick Dell 22-20, 9-7, 6-8, 8-10, 6-4, 1st rd., 1969

Men's doubles: 105 games—Marcelo Lara–Joaquin Loyo-Mayo d. Luis Garcia–Manuel Santana 10-12, 24-22, 11-9, 3-6, 6-2, 3rd rd., 1966. 105 games, Cliff Drysdale–Ray Moore d. Ronnie Barnes–Roy Emerson 29-31, 8-6, 3-6, 8-6, 6-2, quarters, 1967

Women's singles: 51 games—Juliette Atkinson d. Marion Jones 6-3, 5-7, 6-4, 2-6, 7-5. Challenge round, 1898

Women's doubles: 48 games—Mrs. George L. Chapman–Marion Chapman (mother-daughter) d. Dorothy Green Briggs–Corinne Stanton Henry 10-8, 6-8, 9-7, 1st. rd., 1922

Mixed doubles: 71 games—Margaret Osborne duPont–Bill Talbert d. Gertrude "Gussy" Moran–Bob Falkenburg 27-25, 5-7, 6-1, semis, 1948

LONGEST MATCH (PLAYING TIME)

Men's singles: 5 hours 26 minutes—Stefan Edberg d. Michael Chang 6-7 (3-7), 7-5, 7-6, (7-3), 5-7, 6-4, semis, 1992

Women's singles: 2 hours 42 minutes—Tracy Austin d. Martina Navratilova, 1-6, 7-6 (7-4), 7-6 (7-1), final, 1981

LONGEST TIE-BREAKERS

Men's singles: 20-18, third set, Goran Ivanisevic d. Daniel Nestor, 6-4, 7-6 (7-5), 7-6 (20-18), 1st rd., 1993

Women's singles: 13-11, second set, Hana Mandlikova d. Nathalie Herreman, 6-3, 6-7 (11-13), 6-2, 2nd rd., 1987

BIGGEST UPSETS

Men: Aleksandr Volkov (No. 52) d. first-seeded Stefan Edberg (Wimbledon champ), 6-3, 7-6 (7-1), 6-2, 1st rd., 1990

Women: Andrea Leand (amateur, no ranking, first pro tourney) d. second-seeded Andrea Jaeger, 1-6, 7-5, 6-3, 2nd rd., 1981

BEST COMEBACKS

Men: Manolo Orantes d. Guillermo Vilas, 4-6, 1-6, 6-2, 7-5, 6-4, semis, 1975. From 0-2, third; saved 5 match points, fourth, 3 at 0-5, 2 at 5-1. Rod Laver d. Butch Buchholz, 4-6, 5-7, 6-4, 6-2, 7-5, semis, 1960. Saved 3 match points. Boris Becker d. Derrick Rostagno, 1-6, 6-7 (1-7), 6-3, 7-6 (8-6), 6-3, 2nd rd., 1989. Saved 2 match points from 6-4 in tie-breaker.

Women: Chris Evert d. Mary Ann Eisel, 4-6, 7-6 (5-1), 6-1, 2nd rd., 1971. Saved 6 match points, Eisel serving at 6-5, 40-0, and 3 ads, second. Molla Mallory d. Elizabeth Ryan, 4-6, 6-4, 9-7, final, 1926. From 0-4, third, and 6-7, match point. Betty Nuthall d. Alice Marble, 8-10, 6-0, 7-5, quarters, 1933. From 5-1, 40-15 down, saved 3 match points.

U.S. NATIONAL INTERCOLLEGIATE CHAMPIONS

MEN'S SINGLES

YEAR	PLAYER	COLLEGE
1883	Joseph Clark (spring)	Harvard
1883	Howard Taylor (fall)	Harvard
1884	Percy Knapp	Yale
1885	Percy Knapp	Yale
1886	Godfrey Brinley	Trinity (CT)
1887	Philip Sears	Harvard
1888	Philip Sears	Harvard
1889	Bob Huntingdon	Yale
1890	Fred Hovey	Harvard
1891	Fred Hovey	Harvard
1892	Bill Larned	Cornell
1893	Malcolm Chace	Brown
1894	Malcolm Chace	Yale
1895	Malcolm Chace	Yale
1896	Malcolm Whitman	Harvard
1897	Samuel Thomson	Princeton
1898	Leo Ware	Harvard
1899	Dwight Davis	Harvard
1900	Ray Little	Princeton
1901	Fred Alexander	Princeton
1902	Bill Clothier	Harvard
1903	Ed Dewhurst	Pennsylvania
1904	Bob LeRoy	Columbia
1905	Ed Dewhurst	Pennsylvania
1906	Bob LeRoy	Columbia
1907	George Peabody "Peabo" Gardner	Harvard
1908	Nat Niles	Harvard
1909	Wallace Johnson	Pennsylvania
1910	Reuben Holden	Yale
1911	Edward Whitney	Harvard
1912	George Church	Princeton
1913	Dick Williams	Harvard
1914	George Church	Princeton
1915	Dick Williams	Harvard
1916	Colket Caner	Harvard
1917–18	Not held; World War I	
1919	Chuck Garland	Yale
1920	Maxwell Banks	Yale
1921	Phil Neer	Stanford
1922	Lucien Williams	Yale
1923	Carl Fischer	Philadelphia Osteopathic
1924	Wallace Scott	Washington
1925	Edward Chandler	California
1926	Edward Chandler	California
1927	Wilmer Allison	Texas
1928	Julius Seligson	Lehigh
1929	Berkeley Bell	Texas
1930	Cliff Sutter	Tulane
1931	Keith Gledhill	Stanford
1932	Cliff Sutter	Tulane
1933	Jack Tidball	UCLA
1934	Gene Mako	USC
1935	Wilbur Hess	Rice
1936	Ernie Sutter	Tulane
1937	Ernie Sutter	Tulane
1938	Frank Guernsey	Rice
1939	Frank Guernsey	Rice
1940	Don McNeill	Kenyon
1941	Joe Hunt	U.S. Naval Academy
1942	Ted Schroeder	Stanford
1943	Francisco "Pancho" Segura	Miami (FL)
1944	Francisco "Pancho" Segura	Miami (FL)
1945	Francisco "Pancho" Segura	Miami (FL)
1946	Bob Falkenburg	USC
1947	Gardner Larned	William & Mary

1948	Harry Likas	San Francisco
1949	Jack Tuero	Tulane
1950	Herbie Flam	UCLA
1951	Tony Trabert	Cincinnati
1952	Hugh Stewart	USC
1953	Ham Richardson	Tulane
1954	Ham Richardson	Tulane
1955	Jose Aguero	Tulane
1956	Alex Olmedo	USC
1957	Barry MacKay	Michigan
1958	Alex Olmedo	USC
1959	Whitney Reed	San Jose State
1960	Larry Nagler	UCLA
1961	Allen Fox	UCLA
1962	Rafael Osuna	USC
1963	Dennis Ralston	USC
1964	Dennis Ralston	USC
1965	Arthur Ashe	UCLA
1966	Charlie Pasarell	UCLA
1967	Bob Lutz	USC
1968	Stan Smith	USC
1969	Joaquin Loyo-Mayo	USC
1970	Jeff Borowiak	UCLA
1971	Jimmy Connors	UCLA
1972	Dick Stockton	Trinity (TX)
1973	Alex Mayer	Stanford
1974	John Whitlinger	Stanford
1975	Billy Martin	UCLA
1976	Bill Scanlon	Trinity (TX)
1977	Matt Mitchell	Stanford
1978	John McEnroe	Stanford
1979	Kevin Curren	Texas
1980	Robert Van't Hof	USC
1981	Tim Mayotte	Stanford
1982	Mike Leach	Michigan
1983	Greg Holmes	Utah
1984	Mikael Pernfors	Georgia
1985	Mikael Pernfors	Georgia
1986	Dan Goldie	Stanford
1987	Andrew Burrow	Miami (FL)
1988	Robbie Weiss	Pepperdine
1989	Donni Leaycraft	LSU
1990	Steve Bryan	Texas
1991	Jared Palmer	Stanford
1992	Alex O'Brien	Stanford
1993	Chris Woodruff	Tennessee
1994	Mark Merklein	Florida
1995	Sargis Sargsian	Arizona State
1996	Cecil Mamiit	USC

WOMEN'S SINGLES

YEAR	PLAYER	COLLEGE
1958	Darlene Hard	Pomona
1959	Donna Floyd	William & Mary
1960	Linda Vail	Oakland City College
1961	Tory Fretz	Occidental
1962	Roberta Alison	Alabama

1963	Roberta Alison	Alabama
1964	Jane Albert	Stanford
1965	Mimi Henreid	UCLA
1966	Cecilia Martinez	San Francisco State
1967	Patsy Rippy	Odessa (TX) JC
1968	Emilie Burrer	Trinity (TX)
1969	Emilie Burrer	Trinity (TX)
1970	Laura DuPont	North Carolina
1971	Pam Richmond	Arizona State
1972	Janice Metcalf	Redlands
1973	Janice Metcalf	Redlands
1974	Carrie Meyer	Marymount
1975	Stephanie Tolleson	Trinity (TX)
1976	Barbara Hallquist	USC
1977	Barbara Hallquist	USC
1978	Stacy Margolin	USC
1979	Kathy Jordan	Stanford
1980	Wendy White	Rollins College
1981	Anna Maria Fernandez	USC
1982	Alycia Moulton	Stanford
1983	Beth Herr	USC
1984	Lisa Spain	Georgia
1985	Linda Gates	Stanford
1986	Patty Fendick	Stanford
1987	Patty Fendick	Stanford
1988	Shaun Stafford	Florida
1989	Sandra Birch	Stanford
1990	Debbie Graham	Stanford
1991	Sandra Birch	Stanford
1992	Lisa Raymond	Florida
1993	Lisa Raymond	Florida
1994	Angela Lettiere	Georgia
1995	Keri Phebus	UCLA
1996	Jill Crayba	Florida

MEN'S DOUBLES

YEAR	PLAYERS	COLLEGE
1883	Joseph Clark–Howard Taylor (spring)	Harvard
1883	Howard Taylor–Palmer Presbrey (fall)	Harvard
1884	Percy Knapp–William Thorne	Yale
1885	Percy Knapp–Arthur Shipman	Yale
1886	Percy Knapp–William Thacher	Yale
1887	Philip Sears–Quincy Shaw	Harvard
1888	Valentine Hall–Oliver Campbell	Columbia
1889	Oliver Campbell–Alfred Wright	Columbia
1890	Quincy Shaw–Sam Chase	Harvard
1891	Fred Hovey–Robert Wrenn	Harvard
1892	Robert Wrenn–Fred Winslow	Harvard
1893	Malcolm Chace–Clarence Budlong	Brown
1894	Malcolm Chace–Arthur Foote	Yale
1895	Malcolm Chace–Arthur Foote	Yale
1896	Leo Ware–William Scudder	Harvard
1897	Leo Ware–Malcolm Whitman	Harvard
1898	Leo Ware–Malcolm Whitman	Harvard
1899	Holcombe Ward–Dwight Davis	Harvard

1900	Fred Alexander–Ray Little	Princeton
1901	Howard Plummer–Sam Russell	Yale
1902	Bill Clothier–Edgar Leonard	Harvard
1903	Fred Colston–Edwin Clapp	Yale
1904	Karl Behr–George Bodman	Yale
1905	Ed Dewhurst–Henry Register	Pennsylvania
1906	Harold Wells–Alfred Spaulding	Yale
1907	Nathaniel Niles–Alfred Dabney	Harvard
1908	Herbert Tilden–Alex Thayer	Pennsylvania
1909	Wallace Johnson–Alex Thayer	Pennsylvania
1910	Dean Mathey–Burnham Dell	Princeton
1911	Dean Mathey–Charles Butler	Princeton
1912	George Church–Winifred Mace	Princeton
1913	Watson Washburn–Joe Armstrong	Harvard
1914	Dick Wiliams–Richard Harte	Harvard
1915	Dick Williams–Richard Harte	Harvard
1916	Colket Caner–Richard Harte	Harvard
1917–18	Not held; World War I	
1919	Chuck Garland–Ken Hawkes	Yale
1920	Amos Wilder–Lee Wiley	Yale
1921	J. Brooks Fenno–Bill Fiebleman	Harvard
1922	Jim Davies–Phil Neer	Stanford
1923	Lew White–Louis Thalheimer	Texas
1924	Lew White–Louis Thalheimer	Texas
1925	Gervais Hills–Gerald Stratford	California
1926	Edward Chandler–Tom Stow	California
1927	John Van Ryn–Ken Appel	Princeton
1928	Ralph McElvenny–Alan Herrington	Stanford
1929	Benjamin Gorchakoff–Arthur Kussman	Occidental
1930	Dolf Muehleisen–Bob Muench	California
1931	Bruce Barnes–Karl Kamrath	Texas
1932	Keith Gledhill–Joe Coughlin	Stanford
1933	Joe Coughlin–Sam Lee	Stanford
1934	Gene Mako–Phil Castlen	USC
1935	Paul Newton–Richard Bennett	California
1936	Bennett Dey–Bill Seward	Stanford
1937	Richard Bennett–Paul Newton	California
1938	Joe Hunt–Lewis Wetherell	USC
1939	Doug Imhoff–Bob Peacock	California
1940	Larry Dee–Jim Wade	Stanford
1941	Charles Olewine–Charles Mattmann	USC
1942	Ted Schroeder–Larry Dee	Stanford
1943	John Hickman–Walt Driver	Texas
1944	John Hickman–Felix Kelly	Texas
1945	Francisco "Pancho" Segura–Tom Burke	Miami (FL)
1946	Bob Falkenburg–Tom Falkenburg	USC
1947	Sam Match–Bobby Curtis	Rice
1948	Fred Kovaleski–Bernard "Tut" Bartzen	William & Mary
1949	Jim Brink–Fred Fisher	Washington
1950	Herbie Flam–Gene Garrett	UCLA
1951	Earl Cochell–Hugh Stewart	USC
1952	Hugh Ditzler–Clif Mayne	California
1953	Larry Huebner–Bob Perry	UCLA
1954	Ron Livingston–Bob Perry	UCLA
1955	Francisco Contreras–Joaquin Reyes	USC
1956	Francisco Contreras–Alex Olmedo	USC
1957	Crawford Henry–Ron Holmberg	Tulane
1958	Ed Atkinson–Alex Olmedo	USC
1959	Crawford Henry–Ron Holmberg	Tulane
1960	Larry Nagler–Allen Fox	UCLA
1961	Rafael Osuna–Ramsey Earnhart	USC
1962	Rafael Osuna–Ramsey Earnhart	USC
1963	Rafael Osuna–Dennis Ralston	USC
1964	Bill Bond–Dennis Ralston	USC
1965	Arthur Ashe–Ian Crookenden	UCLA
1966	Ian Crookenden–Charlie Pasarell	UCLA
1967	Bob Lutz–Stan Smith	USC
1968	Bob Lutz–Stan Smith	USC
1969	Joaquin Loyo-Mayo–Marcelo Lara	USC
1970	Pat Cramer–Luis Garcia	Miami (FL)
1971	Jeff Borowiak–Haroon Rahim	UCLA
1972	Alex Mayer–Roscoe Tanner	Stanford
1973	Alex Mayer–Jim Delaney	Stanford
1974	Jim Delaney–John Whitlinger	Stanford
1975	Bruce Manson–Ken "Butch" Walts	USC
1976	Peter Fleming–Ferdi Taygan	UCLA
1977	Bruce Manson–Chris Lewis	USC
1978	John Austin–Bruce Nichols	UCLA
1979	Eric Iskersky–Ben McKown	Trinity (TX)
1980	Mel Purcell–Rodney Harmon	Tennessee
1981	David Pate–Karl Richter	TCU
1982	Peter Doohan–Pat Serrett	Arkansas
1983	Ole Malmqvist–Allen Miller	Georgia
1984	Jerome Jones–Kelly Jones	Pepperdine
1985	Carlos DiLaura–Kelly Jones	Pepperdine
1986	Rick Leach–Tim Pawsat	USC
1987	Rick Leach–Scott Melville	USC
1988	Patrick Galbraith–Brian Garrow	UCLA
1989	Eric Amend–Byron Black	USC
1990	Doug Eisenman–Matt Lucena	California
1991	Matt Lucena–Bengt Pedersen	California
1992	Alex O'Brien–Chris Cocotos	Stanford
1993	David Blair–Mark Merklein	Florida
1994	Laurent Miquelard–Joc Simmons	Mississippi State
1995	Mahesh Bhupathi–Ali Hamedeh	Mississippi
1996	Justin Gimelstob–Srdjan Muskatirovic	UCLA

WOMEN'S DOUBLES

YEAR	PLAYERS	COLLEGE
1958	Sue Metzger–Erika Puetz Webster	St. Mary's (IN)-Notre Dame
1959	Joyce Pniewski–Phyllis Saganski	Michigan State
1960	Susan Butt–Linda Vail	British Columbia–Oakland City
1961	Tory Fretz–Mary Sherar	Occidental–Yakima Valley
1962	Linda Yeomans–Carol Hanks	Stanford
1963	Roberta Alison–Justina Bricka	Alabama-Washington (MO)
1964	Connie Jaster–Carol Loop	Cal State (L.A.)
1965	Nancy Falkenburg–Cynthia Goeltz	Mary Baldwin
1966	Yale Stockwell–Libby Weiss	USC
1967	Jane Albert–Julie Anthony	Stanford
1968	Emilie Burrer–Becky Vest	Trinity (TX)

1969	Emilie Burrer–Becky Vest	Trinity (TX)
1970	Pam Farmer–Connie Capozzi	Odessa (TX) JC
1971	Pam Richmond–Peggy Michel	Arizona State
1972	Pam Richmond–Peggy Michel	Arizona State
1973	Cathy Beene–Linda Rupert	Lamar
1974	Ann Lebedeff–Karen Reinke	San Diego State
1975	JoAnne Russell–Donna Stockton	Trinity (TX)
1976	Susie Hagey–Diane Morrison	Stanford
1977	Jodi Applebaum–Terry Saiganik	Miami (FL)
1978	Sherry Acker–Judy Acker	Florida
1979	Kathy Jordan–Alycia Moulton	Stanford
1980	Trey Lewis–Anne White	USC
1981	Alycia Moulton–Caryn Copeland	Stanford
1982	Heather Ludloff–Lynn Lewis	UCLA
1983	Louise Allen–Gretchen Rush	Trinity (TX)
1984	Elise Burgin–Linda Gates	Stanford
1985	Leigh Ann Eldredge–Linda Gates	Stanford
1986	Lise Gregory–Ronni Reis	Miami (FL)
1987	Katrina Adams–Diana Donnelly	Northwestern
1988	Allyson Cooper–Stella Sampras	UCLA
1989	Jackie Holden–Claire Pollard	Mississipi State
1990	Meredith McGrath–Teri Whitlinger	Stanford
1991	Jillian Alexander–Nicole Arendt	Florida
1992	Mamie Ceniza–Iwalina McCalla	UCLA
1993	Alex Creek–Michelle Oldham	Arizona
1994	Rebecca Jensen–Nora Koves	Kansas
1995	Keri Phebus–Susie Starrett	UCLA
1996	Stephanie Nickitas–Dawn Booth	Florida

U.S. INTERSCHOLASTIC CHAMPIONS

BOYS

YEAR	PLAYER	SCHOOL
1891	Robert Wrenn	Cambridge Latin (MA)
1892	Malcolm Chace	Univ. Grammar (RI)
1893	Clarence Budlong	Providence (RI)
1894	Gordon Parker	Tutor (NY)
1895	Leo Ware	Roxbury Latin (MA)
1896	Rex Fincke	Hotchkiss (CT)
1897	Rex Fincke	Hotchkiss (CT)
1898	Beals Wright	Hopkinson (MA)
1899	Beals Wright	Hopkinson (MA)
1900	Irving Wright	Hopkinson (MA)
1901	Edward Larned	Lawrenceville (NJ)
1902	Hendricks Whitman	Noble & Greenough (MA)
1903	Karl Behr	Lawrenceville (NJ)
1904	Nathaniel Niles	Boston Latin (MA)
1905	Nathaniel Niles	Volkmann (MA)
1906	J. Allen Ross	Hyde Park (IL)
1907	Wallace Johnson	Haverford (PA)
1908	Dean Mathey	Pingry (PA)
1909	Maurice McLoughlin	San Francisco (CA)
1910	Edwin Whitney	Stone's (MA)
1911	George Church	Irving (MA)
1912	Clifton Herd	Exeter (NH)
1913	Colket Caner	St. Mark's (MA)

1914	Leonard Beekman	Pawling (NY)
1915	Harold Throckmorton	Woodridge (NY)
1916–22	Not held	
1923	John Whitbeck	Loomis (CT)
1924	Horace Orser	Stuyvesant (NY)
1925-35	Not held	
1936	Robert Low	Choate (CT)
1937	William Gillespie	Scarborough (RI)
1938	Jack Kramer	Montebello (CA)
1939	Ted Olewine	Santa Monica (CA)
1940	Bob Carothers	Coronado (CA)
1941	Vic Seixas	Penn Charter (PA)
1942	Bob Falkenburg	Fairfax (CA)
1943	Chuck Oliver	Perth Amboy (NJ)
1944	Bernard "Tut" Bartzen	San Angelo (TX)
1945	Herbie Flam	Beverly Hills (CA)
1946	Hugh Stewart	South Pasadena (CA)
1947	Herb Behrens	Fort Lauderdale (FL)
1948	Gil Bogley	Landon (MD)
1949	Keston Deimling	Oak Park (IL)
1950	Ham Richardson	Univ. High, Baton Rouge (LA)
1951	Herb Browne	Dreher (SC)
1952	Ed Rubinoff	Miami Beach (FL)
1953	Mike Green	Miami Beach (FL)
1954	Greg Grant	South Pasadena (CA)
1955	Crawford Henry	Grady (GA)
1956	Clarence Slodge	Highland Park (TX)
1957	Earl "Butch" Buchholz, Jr. John Burroughs	St. Louis (MO)
1958	Ray Senkowski	Hamtramck (MI)
1959	Bill Lenoir	Tucson (AR)
1960	Bill Lenoir	Tucson (AR)
1961	Arthur Ashe	Sumner, St. Louis (MO)
1962	Jackie Cooper	St. Xavier, Louisville (KY)
1963	Mike Belkin	Miami Beach (FL)
1964	Bob Goeltz	Landon (MD)
1965	Bob Goeltz	Landon (MD)
1966	Bob Goeltz	Landon (MD)
1967	Zan Guerry	Baylor (TN)
1968	Charlie Owens	Tuscaloosa (AL)
1969	Fred McNair	Landon (MD)
1970	Harold Solomon	Springbrook (CT)
1971	John Whitlinger	Shattuck (WI)
1972	Bill Matyastik	Univ. High (LA)
1973	Dave Parker	Galesburg (IL)
1974	Chris Delaney	Georgetown (MD)
1975	Pem Guerry	Baylor (TN)
1976	Jim Hodges	Landon (MD)
1977	Jay Lapidus	Lawrenceville (NJ)
1978	Jeff Turpin	St. Mark's (TX)
1979	Mike DePalmer	Bradenton Acad. (FL)
1980	Mike DePalmer	Bradenton Acad. (FL)
1981	Chris Kennedy	Ravencroft (NC)
1982	John Zahurak	Calvert Hall (MD)
1983	Bryan Shelton	Randolph School (AL)
1984	Ashley Rhoney	S. Caldwell (NC)
1985	Al Parker	Pinewood Christian (GA)
1986	Jim Courier	St. Stephen's, Bradenton (FL)

1987	Jack Frierson	Vista (CA)
1988	John Yancey	Liggett (MI)
1989	William Webb	Durham (NC)
1990	Chris Woodruff	Bearden (TN)
1991	Craig Baskin	Walker School (GA)
1992	Jim Thomas	Canton Catholic (IA)
1993	Brook Blain	West Bloomfield (MI)
1994	Sam Schroerlucke	North Springs (GA)
1995	Joey Pitts	Lovett (GA)
1996	Marko Cerenko	Marist (CA)

GIRLS

YEAR	PLAYER	SCHOOL
1968	Linda Tuero	St. Martin's (LA)
1969	Connie Capozzi	Hillsdale (OH)
1970–77	Not held	
1978	Mary Lou Piatek	Whiting (IN)
1979	Connie Yowell	St. Marks (TX)
1980	Beverly Bowes	Evan Junior (TX)
1981	Gretchen Rush	St. Stephen's, Bradenton (FL)
1982	Beverly Bowes	St. Mary's Hall (TX)
1983	Juliet Kaczmarek	St. Mary's Hall (TX)
1984	Trisha Laux	Marist (GA)
1985	Jennifer Young	Bradenton Acad. (FL)
1986	Jennifer Young	Bradenton Acad. (FL)
1987	Jennifer Young	Spanish River H.S., Boca Raton (FL)
1988	Audra Keller	Bartlett (TN)
1989	Lihini Weerasuriya	Bradenton Acad.(FL)
1990	Tracee Lee	Punahou (HI)
1991	Jean Okada	Lahaina Luna (HI)
1992	Angela Nelson	Highland (UT)
1993	Angela Nelson	Highland (UT)
1994	Tu Dong	Wilson (CA)
1995	Pilar Montgomery	Santa Barbara (CA)
1996	Whitney Wells	Fresno (CA)

WIMBLEDON

Considered the championships of Great Britain, but generally known by the word Wimbledon (the London suburb in which this, the original tennis championships, has always taken place), the event is officially entitled the Lawn Tennis Championships. Since the beginning, 1877, it has been played on the grounds of the All England Lawn Tennis and Croquet Club, starting at the Worple Road ground and moving in 1922 to the present location on Church Road.

The first Centre Court held about 4,500. The present Centre has held as many as 16,000 with standing liberally allowed. But current law limits it to 13,120 seats. The record one-day attendance, 39,813, on the grounds (a tennis record), was June 26, 1986, while the tourney high was 411,270 for 13 days, 1988.

The surface has always been grass. The challenge round system was in force, 1878 for men's singles and 1885 for women's singles through 1921, and men's doubles 1885 through 1921. This meant that the defending champion played only one match, waiting for a challenger to emerge from the all-comers tournament. When the champion didn't defend, the winner of the all-comers became champion.

In 1972 the tie-breaker was adopted, but, more conservatively, at 8-8 in games until 1979, when Wimbledon conformed with the rest of the world at 6-6, but never in the ultimate fifth set for men, third for women.

In 1968 the tournament was opened to professionals and amateurs alike, and prize money offered, originally $63,000, escalating to $8,855,410 in 1996. Singles first prize was $4,800 for men, $1,800 for women in 1968, escalating to $609,160 and $547,150, respectively, in 1996.

MEN'S SINGLES

YEAR	
1877	Spencer Gore d. William Marshall 6-1, 6-2, 6-4
1878	Frank Hadow d. Spencer Gore 7-5, 6-1, 9-7
1879	John Hartley d. Vere "St. Leger" Goold 6-2, 6-4, 6-2
1880	John Hartley d. Herbert Lawford 6-3, 6-2, 2-6, 6-3
1881	Willie Renshaw d. John Hartley 6-0, 6-1, 6-1
1882	Willie Renshaw d. Ernest Renshaw 6-1, 2-6, 4-6, 6-2, 6-2
1883	Willie Renshaw d. Ernest Renshaw 2-6, 6-3, 6-3, 4-6, 6-3
1884	Willie Renshaw d. Herbert Lawford 6-0, 6-4, 9-7
1885	Willie Renshaw d. Herbert Lawford 7-5, 6-2, 4-6, 7-5
1886	Willie Renshaw d. Herbert Lawford 6-0, 5-7, 6-3, 6-4
1887	Herbert Lawford d. Ernest Renshaw 1-6, 6-3, 3-6, 6-4, 6-4
1888	Ernest Renshaw d. Herbert Lawford 6-3, 7-5, 6-0
1889	Willie Renshaw d. Ernest Renshaw 6-4, 6-1, 3-6, 6-0
1890	Willoughby Hamilton d. Willie Renshaw 6-8, 6-2, 3-6, 6-1, 6-1
1891	Wilfred Baddeley d. Joshua Pim 6-4, 1-6, 7-5, 6-0
1892	Wilfred Baddeley d. Joshua Pim 4-6, 6-3, 6-3, 6-2
1893	Joshua Pim d. Wilfred Baddeley 3-6, 6-1, 6-3, 6-2
1894	Joshua Pim d. Wilfred Baddeley 10-8, 6-2, 8-6
1895	Wilfred Baddeley d. Wilberforce Eaves 4-6, 2-6, 8-6, 6-2, 6-3
1896	Harold Mahony d. Wilfred Baddeley 6-2, 6-8, 5-7, 8-6, 6-3
1897	Reggie Doherty d. Harold Mahony 6-4, 6-4, 6-3
1898	Reggie Doherty d. Laurie Doherty 6-3, 6-3, 2-6, 5-7, 6-1

1899	Reggie Doherty d. Arthur Gore 1-6, 4-6, 6-3, 6-3, 6-3
1900	Reggie Doherty d. Sidney Smith 6-8, 6-3, 6-1, 6-2
1901	Arthur Gore d. Reggie Doherty 4-6, 7-5, 6-4, 6-4
1902	Laurie Doherty d. Arthur Gore 6-4, 6-3, 3-6, 6-0
1903	Laurie Doherty d. Frank Riseley 7-5, 6-3, 6-0
1904	Laurie Doherty d. Frank Riseley 6-1, 7-5, 8-6
1905	Laurie Doherty d. Norman Brookes 8-6, 6-2, 6-4
1906	Laurie Doherty d. Frank Riseley 6-4, 4-6, 6-2, 6-3
1907	Norman Brookes d. Arthur Gore 6-4, 6-2, 6-2
1908	Arthur Gore d. Herbert Roper Barrett 6-3, 6-2, 4-6, 3-6, 6-4
1909	Arthur Gore d. Josiah Ritchie 6-8, 1-6, 6-2, 6-2, 6-2
1910	Tony Wilding d. Arthur Gore 6-4, 7-5, 4-6, 6-2
1911	Tony Wilding, d. Herbert Roper Barrett 6-4, 4-6, 2-6, 6-2 (retired)
1912	Tony Wilding d. Arthur Gore 6-4, 6-4, 4-6, 6-4
1913	Tony Wilding d. Maurice McLoughlin 8-6, 6-3, 10-8
1914	Norman Brookes d. Tony Wilding 6-4, 6-4, 7-5
1915–18	Not held; World War I
1919	Gerald Patterson d. Norman Brookes 6-3, 7-5, 6-2
1920	Bill Tilden d. Gerald Patterson 2-6, 6-3, 6-2, 6-4
1921	Bill Tilden d. Brian (Babe) Norton 4-6, 2-6, 6-1, 6-0, 7-5
1922	Gerald Patterson d. Randolph Lycett 6-3, 6-4, 6-2
1923	Bill Johnston d. Francis Hunter 6-0, 6-3, 6-1
1924	Jean Borotra d. René Lacoste 6-1, 3-6, 6-1, 3-6, 6-4
1925	René Lacoste d. Jean Borotra 6-3, 6-3, 4-6, 8-6
1926	Jean Borotra d. Howard Kinsey 8-6, 6-1, 6-3
1927	Henri Cochet d. Jean Borotra 4-6, 4-6, 6-3, 6-4, 7-5
1928	René Lacoste d. Henri Cochet 6-1, 4-6, 6-4, 6-2
1929	Henri Cochet d. Jean Borotra 6-4, 6-3, 6-4
1930	Bill Tilden d. Wilmer Allison 6-3, 9-7, 6-4
1931	Sidney Wood d. Frank Shields (walkover)
1932	Ellsworth Vines d. Henry "Bunny" Austin 6-4, 6-2, 6-0
1933	Jack Crawford d. Ellsworth Vines 4-6, 11-9, 6-2, 2-6, 6-4
1934	Fred Perry d. Jack Crawford 6-3, 6-0, 7-5
1935	Fred Perry d. Gottfried von Cramm 6-2, 6-4, 6-4
1936	Fred Perry d. Gottfried von Cramm 6-1, 6-1, 6-0
1937	Don Budge d. Gottfried von Cramm 6-3, 6-4, 6-2
1938	Don Budge d. Henry "Bunny" Austin 6-1, 6-0, 6-3
1939	Bobby Riggs d. Elwood Cooke 2-6, 8-6, 3-6, 6-3, 6-2
1940–45	Not held; World War II
1946	Yvon Petra d. Geoff Brown 6-2, 6-4, 7-9, 5-7, 6-4
1947	Jack Kramer d. Tom Brown 6-1, 6-3, 6-2
1948	Bob Falkenburg d. John Bromwich 7-5, 0-6, 6-2, 3-6, 7-5
1949	Ted Schroeder d. Jaroslav Drobny 3-6, 6-0, 6-3, 4-6, 6-4
1950	J. Edward "Budge" Patty d. Frank Sedgman 6-1, 8-10, 6-2, 6-3
1951	Dick Savitt d. Ken McGregor 6-4, 6-4, 6-4
1952	Frank Sedgman d. Jaroslav Drobny 4-6, 6-2, 6-3, 6-2
1953	Vic Seixas d. Kurt Nielsen 9-7, 6-3, 6-4
1954	Jaroslav Drobny d. Ken Rosewall 13-11, 4-6, 6-2, 9-7
1955	Tony Trabert d. Kurt Nielsen 6-3, 7-5, 6-1
1956	Lew Hoad d. Ken Rosewall 6-2, 4-6, 7-5, 6-4
1957	Lew Hoad d. Ashley Cooper 6-2, 6-1, 6-2
1958	Ashley Cooper d. Neale Fraser 3-6, 6-3, 6-4, 13-11
1959	Alex Olmedo d. Rod Laver 6-4, 6-3, 6-4
1960	Neale Fraser d. Rod Laver 6-4, 3-6, 9-7, 7-5
1961	Rod Laver d. Chuck McKinley 6-3, 6-1, 6-4
1962	Rod Laver d. Marty Mulligan 6-2, 6-2, 6-1
1963	Chuck McKinley d. Fred Stolle 9-7, 6-1, 6-4
1964	Roy Emerson d. Fred Stolle 6-4, 12-10, 4-6, 6-3
1965	Roy Emerson d. Fred Stolle 6-2, 6-4, 6-4

1966	Manuel Santana d. Dennis Ralston 6-4, 11-9, 6-4
1967	John Newcombe d. Wilhelm Bungert 6-3, 6-1, 6-1
1968	Rod Laver d. Tony Roche 6-3, 6-4, 6-2
1969	Rod Laver d. John Newcombe 6-4, 5-7, 6-4, 6-4
1970	John Newcombe d. Ken Rosewall 5-7, 6-3, 6-2, 3-6, 6-1
1971	John Newcombe d. Stan Smith 6-3, 5-7, 2-6, 6-4, 6-4
1972	Stan Smith d. Ilie Nastase 4-6, 6-3, 6-3, 4-6, 7-5
1973	Jan Kodes d. Alex Metreveli 6-1, 9-8 (7-5), 6-3
1974	Jimmy Connors d. Ken Rosewall 6-1, 6-1, 6-4
1975	Arthur Ashe d. Jimmy Connors 6-1, 6-1, 5-7, 6-4
1976	Bjorn Borg d. Ilie Nastase 6-4, 6-2, 9-7
1977	Bjorn Borg d. Jimmy Connors 3-6, 6-2, 6-1, 5-7, 6-4
1978	Bjorn Borg d. Jimmy Connors 6-2, 6-2, 6-3
1979	Bjorn Borg d. Roscoe Tanner 6-7 (4-7), 6-1, 3-6, 6-3, 6-4
1980	Bjorn Borg d. John McEnroe 1-6, 7-5, 6-3, 6-7 (16-18), 8-6
1981	John McEnroe d. Bjorn Borg 4-6, 7-6 (7-1), 7-6 (7-4), 6-4
1982	Jimmy Connors d. John McEnroe 3-6, 6-3, 6-7 (2-7), 7-6 (7-5), 6-4
1983	John McEnroe d. Chris Lewis 6-2, 6-2, 6-2
1984	John McEnroe d. Jimmy Connors 6-1, 6-1, 6-2
1985	Boris Becker d. Kevin Curren 6-3, 6-7 (4-7), 7-6 (7-3), 6-4
1986	Boris Becker d. Ivan Lendl 6-4, 6-3, 7-5
1987	Pat Cash d. Ivan Lendl 7-6 (7-5), 6-2, 7-5
1988	Stefan Edberg d. Boris Becker 4-6, 7-6 (7-2), 6-4, 6-2
1989	Boris Becker d. Stefan Edberg 6-0, 7-6 (7-1), 6-4
1990	Stefan Edberg d. Boris Becker 6-2, 6-2, 3-6, 3-6, 6-4
1991	Michael Stich d. Boris Becker 6-4, 7-6 (7-4), 6-4
1992	Andre Agassi d. Goran Ivanisevic 6-7 (8-10), 6-4, 6-4, 1-6, 6-4
1993	Pete Sampras d. Jim Courier 7-6 (7-3), 7-6 (8-6), 4-6, 6-3
1994	Pete Sampras d. Goran Ivanisevic 7-6 (7-2), 7-6 (7-5), 6-0
1995	Pete Sampras d. Boris Becker 6-7 (5-7), 6-2, 6-4, 6-2
1996	Richard Krajicek d. MaliVai Washington 6-3, 6-4, 6-3

WOMEN'S SINGLES

YEAR	
1884	Maud Watson d. Lillian Watson 6-8, 6-3, 6-3
1885	Maud Watson d. Blanche Bingley 6-1, 7-5
1886	Blanche Bingley d. Maud Watson 6-3, 6-3
1887	Lottie Dod d. Blanche Bingley Hillyard 6-2, 6-0
1888	Lottie Dod d. Blanche Bingley Hillyard 6-3, 6-3
1889	Blanche Bingley Hillyard d. Helena Rice 4-6, 8-6, 6-4
1890	Helena Rice d. M. Jacks 6-4, 6-1
1891	Lottie Dod d. Blanche Bingley Hillyard 6-2, 6-1
1892	Lottie Dod d. Blanche Bingley Hillyard 6-1, 6-1
1893	Lottie Dod d. Blanche Bingley Hillyard 6-8, 6-1, 6-4
1894	Blanche Bingley Hillyard d. Edith Austin 6-1, 6-1
1895	Charlotte Cooper d. Helen Jackson 7-5, 8-6
1896	Charlotte Cooper d. Alice Simpson Pickering 6-2, 6-3
1897	Blanche Bingley Hillyard d. Charlotte Cooper 5-7, 7-5, 6-2
1898	Charlotte Cooper d. Louise Martin 6-4, 6-4
1899	Blanche Bingley Hillyard d. Charlotte Cooper 6-2, 6-3
1900	Blanche Bingley Hillyard d. Charlotte Cooper 4-6, 6-4, 6-4
1901	Charlotte Cooper Sterry d. Blanche Bingley Hillyard 6-2, 6-2
1902	Muriel Robb d. Charlotte Cooper Sterry 7-5, 6-1
1903	Dorothea Douglass d. Ethel Thomson 4-6, 6-4, 6-2
1904	Dorothea Douglass d. Charlotte Cooper Sterry 6-0, 6-3
1905	May Sutton d. Dorothea Douglass 6-3, 6-4
1906	Dorothea Douglass d. May Sutton 6-3, 9-7

1907	May Sutton d. Dorothea Douglass Chambers 6-1, 6-4
1908	Charlotte Cooper Sterry d. Agnes Morton 6-4, 6-4
1909	Dora Boothby d. Agnes Morton 6-4, 4-6, 8-6
1910	Dorothea Douglass Chambers d. Dora Boothby 6-2, 6-2
1911	Dorothea Douglass Lambert Chambers d. Dora Boothby 6-0, 6-0
1912	Ethel Thomson Larcombe d. Charlotte Cooper Sterry 6-3, 6-1
1913	Dorothea Douglass Chambers d. Winifred Slocock McNair 6-0, 6-4
1914	Dorothea Douglass Chambers d. Ethel Thomson Larcombe 7-5, 6-4
1915–18	Not held; World War I
1919	Suzanne Lenglen d. Dorothea Douglass Chambers 10-8, 4-6, 9-7
1920	Suzanne Lenglen d. Dorothea Douglass Chambers 6-3, 6-0
1921	Suzanne Lenglen d. Elizabeth Ryan 6-2, 6-0
1922	Suzanne Lenglen d. Molla Bjurstedt Mallory 6-2, 6-0
1923	Suzanne Lenglen d. Kitty McKane 6-2, 6-2
1924	Kitty McKane d. Helen Wills 4-6, 6-4, 6-4
1925	Suzanne Lenglen d. Joan Fry 6-2, 6-0
1926	Kitty McKane Godfree d. Lili de Alvarez 6-2, 4-6, 6-3
1927	Helen Wills d. Lili de Alvarez 6-2, 6-4
1928	Helen Wills d. Lili de Alvarez 6-2, 6-3
1929	Helen Wills d. Helen Jacobs 6-1, 6-2
1930	Helen Wills Moody d. Elizabeth Ryan 6-2, 6-2
1931	Cilly Aussem d. Hilde Krahwinkel 6-2, 7-5
1932	Helen Wills Moody d. Helen Jacobs 6-3, 6-1
1933	Helen Wills Moody d. Dorothy Round 6-4, 6-8, 6-3
1934	Dorothy Round d. Helen Jacobs 6-2, 5-7, 6-3
1935	Helen Wills Moody d. Helen Jacobs 6-3, 3-6, 7-5
1936	Helen Jacobs d. Hilde Krahwinkel Sperling 6-2, 4-6, 7-5
1937	Dorothy Round d. Jadwiga Jedrzejowska 6-2, 2-6, 7-5
1938	Helen Wills Moody d. Helen Jacobs 6-4, 6-0
1939	Alice Marble d. Kay Stammers 6-2, 6-0
1940–45	Not held; World War II
1946	Pauline Betz d. Louise Brough 6-2 6-4
1947	Margaret Osborne d. Doris Hart 6-2, 6-4
1948	Louise Brough d. Doris Hart 6-3, 8-6
1949	Louise Brough d. Margaret Osborne duPont 10-8, 1-6, 10-8
1950	Louise Brough d. Margaret Osborne duPont 6-1, 3-6, 6-1
1951	Doris Hart d. Shirley Fry 6-1, 6-0
1952	Maureen Connolly d. Louise Brough 7-5, 6-3
1953	Maureen Connolly d. Doris Hart 8-6, 7-5
1954	Maureen Connolly d. Louise Brough 6-2, 7-5
1955	Louise Brough d. Beverly Baker Fleitz 7-5, 8-6
1956	Shirley Fry d. Angela Buxton 6-3, 6-1
1957	Althea Gibson d. Darlene Hard 6-3, 6-2
1958	Althea Gibson d. Angela Mortimer 8-6, 6-2
1959	Maria Bueno d. Darlene Hard 6-4, 6-3
1960	Maria Bueno d. Sandra Reynolds 8-6, 6-0
1961	Angela Mortimer d. Christine Truman 4-6, 6-4, 7-5
1962	Karen Hantze Susman d. Vera Sukova 6-4, 6-4
1963	Margaret Smith d. Billie Jean Moffitt 6-3, 6-4
1964	Maria Bueno d. Margaret Smith 6-4, 7-9, 6-3
1965	Margaret Smith d. Maria Bueno 6-4, 7-5
1966	Billie Jean Moffitt King d. Maria Bueno 6-3, 3-6, 6-1
1967	Billie Jean Moffitt King d. Ann Haydon Jones 6-3, 6-4
1968	Billie Jean Moffitt King d. Judy Tegart 9-7, 7-5
1969	Ann Haydon Jones d. Billie Jean Moffitt King 3-6, 6-3, 6-2
1970	Margaret Smith Court d. Billie Jean Moffitt King 14-12, 11-9
1971	Evonne Goolagong d. Margaret Smith Court 6-4, 6-1
1972	Billie Jean Moffitt King d. Evonne Goolagong 6-3, 6-3

1973	Billie Jean Moffitt King d. Chris Evert 6-0, 7-5
1974	Chris Evert d. Olga Morozova 6-0, 6-4
1975	Billie Jean Moffitt King d. Evonne Goolagong Cawley 6-0, 6-1
1976	Chris Evert d. Evonne Goolagong Cawley 6-3, 4-6, 8-6
1977	Virginia Wade d. Betty Stove 4-6, 6-3, 6-1
1978	Martina Navratilova d. Chris Evert 2-6, 6-4, 7-5
1979	Martina Navratilova d. Chris Evert Lloyd 6-4, 6-4
1980	Evonne Goolagong Cawley d. Chris Evert Lloyd 6-1, 7-6 (7-4)
1981	Chris Evert Lloyd d. Hana Mandlikova 6-2, 6-2
1982	Martina Navratilova d. Chris Evert Lloyd 6-1, 3-6, 6-2
1983	Martina Navratilova d. Andrea Jaeger 6-0, 6-3
1984	Martina Navratilova d. Chris Evert Lloyd 7-6 (7-5), 6-2
1985	Martina Navratilova d. Chris Evert Lloyd 4-6, 6-3, 6-2
1986	Martina Navratilova d. Hana Mandlikova 7-6 (7-1), 6-3
1987	Martina Navratilova d. Steffi Graf 7-5, 6-3
1988	Steffi Graf d. Martina Navratilova 5-7, 6-2, 6-1
1989	Steffi Graf d. Martina Navratilova 6-2, 6-7 (1-7), 6-1
1990	Martina Navratilova d. Zina Garrison 6-4, 6-1
1991	Steffi Graf d. Gabriela Sabatini 6-4, 3-6, 8-6
1992	Steffi Graf d. Monica Seles 6-2, 6-1
1993	Steffi Graf d. Jana Novotna 7-6 (8-6), 1-6, 6-4
1994	Conchita Martinez d. Martina Navratilova 6-4, 3-6, 6-3
1995	Steffi Graf d. Arantxa Sanchez Vicario 4-6, 6-1, 7-5
1996	Steffi Graf d. Arantxa Sanchez Vicario 6-3, 7-5

MEN'S DOUBLES

YEAR	
1884	Willie Renshaw–Ernest Renshaw d. Ernest Lewis–Edward Williams 6-3, 6-1, 1-6, 6-4
1885	Willie Renshaw–Ernest Renshaw d. Claude Farrar–Arthur Stanley 6-3, 6-3, 10-8 (challenge round instituted)
1886	Willie Renshaw–Ernest Renshaw d. Claude Farrar–Arthur Stanley 6-3, 6-3, 4-6, 6-3
1887	Herbert Wilberforce–Patrick Bowes Lyon d. James Crisp–Barratt Smith 7-5, 6-3, 6-2
1888	Willie Renshaw–Ernest Renshaw d. Herbert Wilberforce–Patrick Bowes Lyon 2-6, 1-6, 6-3, 6-4, 6-3
1889	Willie Renshaw–Ernest Renshaw d. Ernest Lewis–George Hillyard 6-4, 6-4, 3-6, 0-6, 6-1
1890	Joshua Pim–Frank Stoker d. Ernest Lewis–George Hillyard 6-0, 7-5, 6-4
1891	Wilfred Baddeley–Herbert Baddeley d. Joshua Pim–Frank Stoker 6-1, 6-3, 1-6, 6-2
1892	Ernest Lewis–Harry Barlow d. Wilfred Baddeley–Herbert Baddeley 4-6, 6-2, 8-6, 6-4
1893	Joshua Pim–Frank Stoker d. Ernest Lewis–Harry Barlow 4-6, 6-3, 6-1, 2-6, 6-0
1894	Wilfred Baddeley–Herbert Baddeley d. Harry Barlow–Charles Martin 5-7, 7-5, 4-6, 6-3, 8-6
1895	Wilfred Baddeley–Herbert Baddeley d. Ernest Lewis–Wilberforce Eaves 8-6, 5-7, 6-4, 6-3
1896	Wilfred Baddeley–Herbert Baddeley d. Reggie Doherty–Harold Nisbet 1-6, 3-6, 6-4, 6-2, 6-1
1897	Reggie Doherty–Laurie Doherty d. Wilfred Baddeley–Herbert Baddeley 6-4, 4-6, 8-6, 6-4
1898	Reggie Doherty–Laurie Doherty d. Harold Nisbet–Clarence Hobart 6-4, 6-4, 6-2
1899	Reggie Doherty–Laurie Doherty d. Harold Nisbet–Clarence Hobart 7-5, 6-0, 6-2
1900	Reggie Doherty–Laurie Doherty d. Herbert Roper Barrett–Harold Nisbet 9-7, 7-5, 4-6, 3-6, 6-3
1901	Reggie Doherty–Laurie Doherty d. Dwight Davis–Holcombe Ward 4-6, 6-2, 6-3, 9-7

1902	Sidney Smith–Frank Riseley d. Reggie Doherty–Laurie Doherty 4-6, 8-6, 6-3, 4-6, 11-9	
1903	Reggie Doherty–Laurie Doherty d. Sidney Smith–Frank Risely 6-4, 6-4, 6-4	
1904	Reggie Doherty–Laurie Doherty d. Sidney Smith–Frank Riseley 6-1, 6-2, 6-4	
1905	Reggie Doherty–Laurie Doherty d. Sidney Smith–Frank Riseley 6-2, 6-4, 6-8, 6-3	
1906	Sidney Smith–Frank Riseley d. Reggie Doherty–Laurie Doherty 6-8, 6-4, 5-7, 6-3, 6-3	
1907	Norman Brookes–Tony Wilding d. Beals Wright–Karl Behr 6-4, 6-4, 6-2	
1908	Tony Wilding–Josiah Ritchie d. Arthur Gore–Herbert Roper Barrett 6-1, 6-2, 1-6, 1-6, 9-7	
1909	Arthur Gore–Herbert Roper Barrett d. Stanley Doust–Harry Parker 6-2, 6-1, 6-4	
1910	Tony Wilding–Josiah Ritchie d. Arthur Gore–Herbert Roper Barrett 6-1, 6-1, 6-2	
1911	Andre Gobert–Max Decugis d. Tony Wilding–Josiah Ritchie 9-7, 5-7, 6-3, 2-6, 6-2	
1912	Herbert Roper Barrett–Charles Dixon d. Andre Gobert–Max Decugis 3-6, 6-3, 6-4, 7-5	
1913	Herbert Roper Barrett–Charles Dixon d. Friedrich Rahe–Heinrich Kleinschroth 6-2, 6-4, 4-6, 6-2	
1914	Norman Brookes–Tony Wilding d. Herbert Roper Barrett–Charles Dixon 6-1, 6-1, 5-7, 8-6	
1915–18	Not held; World War I	
1919	Ronald Thomas–Pat O'Hara Wood d. Randolph Lycett–Rodney Heath 6-4, 6-2, 4-6, 6-2	
1920	Dick Williams–Chuck Garland d. Algernon Kingscote–James Parke 4-6, 6-4, 7-5, 6-2	
1921	Randolph Lycett–Max Woosnam d. Arthur Lowe–Frank Lowe 6-3, 6-0, 7-5	
1922	James Anderson–Randolph Lycett d. Gerald Patterson–Pat O'Hara Wood 3-6, 7-9, 6-4, 6-3, 11-9	
1923	Leslie Godfree–Randolph Lycett d. Manuel de Gomar–Eduardo Flaquer 6-3, 6-4, 3-6, 6-3	
1924	Frank Hunter–Vinnie Richards d. Dick Williams–Watson Washburn 6-3, 3-6, 8-10, 8-6, 6-3	
1925	Jean Borotra–René Lacoste d. John Hennessey–Ray Casey 6-4, 11-9, 4-6, 1-6, 6-3	
1926	Jacques Brugnon–Henri Cochet d. Howard Kinsey–Vinnie Richards 7-5, 4-6, 6-3, 6-2	
1927	Frank Hunter–Bill Tilden d. Jacques Brugnon–Henri Cochet 1-6, 4-6, 8-6, 6-3, 6-4	
1928	Jacques Brugnon–Henri Cochet d. Gerald Patterson–John Hawkes 13-11, 6-4, 6-4	
1929	Wilmer Allison–John Van Ryn d. Colin Gregory–Ian Collins 6-4, 5-7, 6-3, 10-12, 6-4	
1930	Wilmer Allison–John Van Ryn d. John Doeg–George Lott 6-3, 6-3, 6-2	
1931	George Lott–John Van Ryn d. Jacques Brugnon–Henri Cochet 6-2, 10-8, 9-11, 3-6, 6-3	
1932	Jean Borotra–Jacques Brugnon d. Fred Perry–Pat Hughes 6-0, 4-6, 3-6, 7-5, 7-5	
1933	Jean Borotra–Jacques Brugnon d. Ryosuki Nunoi–Jiro Satoh 4-6, 6-3, 6-3, 7-5	
1934	George Lott–Les Stoefen d. Jean Borotra–Jacques Brugnon 6-2, 6-3, 6-4	
1935	Jack Crawford–Adrian Quist d. Wilmer Allison–John Van Ryn 6-3, 5-7, 6-2, 5-7, 7-5	
1936	Pat Hughes–Charles Tuckey d. Charles Hare–Frank Wilde 6-4, 3-6, 7-9, 6-1, 6-4	
1937	Don Budge–Gene Mako d. Pat Hughes–Charles Tuckey 6-0, 6-4, 6-8, 6-1	
1938	Don Budge–Gene Mako d. Henner Henkel–Georg von Metaxa 6-4, 3-6, 6-3, 8-6	
1939	Elwood Cooke–Bobby Riggs d. Charles Hare–Frank Wilde 6-3, 3-6, 6-3, 9-7	
1940–45	Not held; World War II	
1946	Tom Brown–Jack Kramer d. Geoff Brown–Dinny Pails 6-4, 6-4, 6-2	
1947	Bob Falkenburg–Jack Kramer d. Tony Mottram–Bill Sidwell, 8-6, 6-3, 6-3	
1948	John Bromwich–Frank Sedgman d. Tom Brown–Gardnar Mulloy 5-7, 7-5, 7-5, 9-7	
1949	Richard "Pancho" Gonzalez–Frank Parker d. Gardnar Mulloy–Ted Schroeder 6-4, 6-4, 6-2	
1950	John Bromwich–Adrian Quist d. Geoff Brown–Bill Sidwell 7-5, 3-6, 6-3, 3-6, 6-2	
1951	Ken McGregor–Frank Sedgman d. Jaroslav Drobny–Eric Sturgess 3-6, 6-2, 6-3, 3-6, 6-3	
1952	Ken McGregor–Frank Sedgman d. Vic Seixas–Eric Sturgess 6-3, 7-5, 6-4	
1953	Lew Hoad–Ken Rosewall d. Rex Hartwig–Mervyn Rose 6-4, 7-5, 4-6, 7-5	
1954	Rex Hartwig–Mervyn Rose d. Vic Seixas–Tony Trabert 6-4, 6-4, 3-6, 6-4	
1955	Rex Hartwig–Lew Hoad d. Neale Fraser–Ken Rosewall 7-5, 6-4, 6-3	
1956	Lew Hoad–Ken Rosewall d. Nicola Pietrangeli–Orlando Sirola 7-5, 6-2, 6-1	
1957	J. Edward "Budge" Patty–Gardnar Mulloy d. Neale Fraser–Lew Hoad 8-10, 6-4, 6-4, 6-4	
1958	Sven Davidson–Ulf Schmidt d. Ashley Cooper–Neale Fraser 6-4, 6-4, 8-6	
1959	Roy Emerson–Neale Faser d. Rod Laver–Bob Mark 8-6, 6-3, 14-16, 9-7	
1960	Rafael Osuna–Dennis Ralston d. Mike Davies–Bobby Wilson 7-5, 6-3, 10-8	
1961	Roy Emerson–Neale Fraser d. Bob Hewitt–Fred Stolle 6-4, 6-8, 6-4, 6-8, 8-6	
1962	Bob Hewitt–Fred Stolle d. Boro Jovanovic–Nikki Pilic 6-2, 5-7, 6-2, 6-4	
1963	Rafael Osuna–Antonio Palafox d. Jean-Claude Barclay–Pierre Darmon 4-6, 6-2, 6-2, 6-2	
1964	Bob Hewitt–Fred Stolle d. Roy Emerson–Ken Fletcher 7-5, 11-9, 6-4	
1965	John Newcombe–Tony Roche d. Ken Fletcher–Bob Hewitt 7-5, 6-3, 6-4	
1966	Ken Fletcher–John Newcombe d. Bill Bowrey–Owen Davidson 6-3, 6-4, 3-6, 6-3	
1967	Bob Hewitt–Frew McMillan d. Roy Emerson–Ken Fletcher 6-2, 6-3, 6-4	
1968	John Newcombe–Tony Roche d. Ken Rosewall–Fred Stolle 3-6, 8-6, 5-7, 14-12, 6-3	
1969	John Newcombe–Tony Roche d. Tom Okker–Marty Riessen 7-5, 11-9, 6-3	
1970	John Newcombe–Tony Roche d. Ken Rosewall–Fred Stolle 10-8, 6-3, 6-1	
1971	Roy Emerson–Rod Laver d. Arthur Ashe–Dennis Ralston 4-6, 9-7, 6-8, 6-4, 6-4	
1972	Bob Hewitt–Frew McMillan d. Stan Smith–Eric van Dillen 6-2, 2-6, 9-7	
1973	Jimmy Connors–Ilie Nastase d. John Cooper–Neale Fraser 3-6, 6-3, 6-4, 8-9 (3-7), 6-1	
1974	John Newcombe–Tony Roche d. Bob Lutz–Stan Smith 8-6, 6-4, 6-4	
1975	Vitas Gerulaitis–Alex Mayer d. Colin Dowdeswell–Allan Stone 7-5, 8-6, 6-4	
1976	Brian Gottfried–Raul Ramirez d. Ross Case–Geoff Masters 3-6, 6-3, 8-6, 2-6, 7-5	
1977	Geoff Masters–Ross Case d. John Alexander–Phil Dent 6-3, 6-4, 3-6, 8-9 (4-7), 6-4	
1978	Bob Hewitt–Frew McMillan d. Peter Fleming–John McEnroe 6-1, 6-4, 6-2	
1979	Peter Fleming–John McEnroe d. Brian Gottfried–Raul Ramirez 4-6, 6-4, 6-2, 6-2	
1980	Peter McNamara–Paul McNamee d. Bob Lutz–Stan Smith 7-6 (7-5), 6-3, 6-7 (4-7), 6-4	

1981	Peter Fleming–John McEnroe d. Bob Lutz–Stan Smith 6-4, 6-4, 6-4
1982	Peter McNamara–Paul McNamee d. Peter Fleming–John McEnroe 6-3, 6-2
1983	Peter Fleming–John McEnroe d. Tim Gullikson–Tom Gullikson 6-4, 6-3, 6-4
1984	Peter Fleming–John McEnroe d. Patrick Cash–Paul McNamee 6-2, 5-7, 6-2, 3-6, 6-3
1985	Heinz Gunthardt–Balazs Taroczy d. Patrick Cash–John Fitzgerald 6-4, 6-3, 4-6, 6-3
1986	Joakim Nystrom–Mats Wilander d. Gary Donnelly–Peter Fleming 7-6 (7-4), 6-3, 6-3
1987	Ken Flach–Robert Seguso d. Sergio Casal–Emilio Sanchez 3-6, 6-7 (6-8), 7-6 (7-3), 6-1, 6-4
1988	Ken Flach–Robert Seguso d. John Fitzgerald–Anders Jarryd 6-4, 2-6, 6-4, 7-6 (7-3)
1989	John Fitzgerald–Anders Jarryd d. Rick Leach–Jim Pugh 3-6, 7-6 (7-4), 6-4, 7-6 (7-4)
1990	Rick Leach–Jim Pugh d. Pieter Aldrich–Danie Visser 7-6 (7-5), 7-6 (7-4), 7-6 (7-5)
1991	John Fitzgerald–Anders Jarryd d. Javier Frana–Leonardo Lavalle 6-3, 6-4, 6-7 (7-9), 6-1
1992	John McEnroe–Michael Stich d. Jim Grabb–Richey Reneberg 5-7, 7-6 (7-5), 3-6, 7-6 (7-5), 19-17
1993	Todd Woodbridge–Mark Woodforde d. Grant Connell–Pat Galbraith 7-5, 6-3, 7-6 (7-4)
1994	Todd Woodbridge–Mark Woodforde d. Grant Connell–Pat Galbraith 7-6 (7-3), 6-3, 6-1
1995	Todd Woodbridge–Mark Woodforde d. Rick Leach–Scott Melville 7-5, 7-6 (10-8), 7-6 (7-5)
1996	Todd Woodbridge–Mark Woodforde d. Byron Black–Grant Connell 4-6, 6-1, 6-3, 6-2

WOMEN'S DOUBLES

YEAR	
1913	Winifred Slocock McNair–Dora Boothby d. Charlotte Cooper Sterry–Dorothea Douglass Chambers 4-6, 2-4, retired
1914	Agnes Morton–Elizabeth Ryan d. Edith Boucher Hannam–Ethel Thomson Larcombe 6-1, 6-3
1915–18	Not held; World War I
1919	Suzanne Lenglen–Elizabeth Ryan d. Dorothea Douglass Chambers–Ethel Thomson Larcombe 4-6, 7-5, 6-3
1920	Suzanne Lenglen–Elizabeth Ryan d. Dorothea Douglass Chambers–Ethel Thomson Larcombe 6-4, 6-0
1921	Suzanne Lenglen–Elizabeth Ryan d. Geraldine Ramsey Beamish–Irene Bowder Peacock 6-1, 6-2
1922	Suzanne Lenglen–Elizabeth Ryan d. Kitty McKane–Margaret McKane Stocks 6-0, 6-4
1923	Suzanne Lenglen–Elizabeth Ryan d. Joan Austin–Evelyn Colyer 6-3, 6-1
1924	Hazel Hotchkiss Wightman–Helen Wills d. Phyllis Howkins Covell–Kitty McKane 6-4, 6-4
1925	Suzanne Lenglen–Elizabeth Ryan d. Kathleen Lidderdale Bridge–Mary Hart McIlquham 6-2, 6-2
1926	Mary K. Browne–Elizabeth Ryan d. Kitty McKane Godfree–Evelyn Colyer 6-1, 6-1
1927	Helen Wills–Elizabeth Ryan d. Bobbie Heine–Irene Bowder Peacock 6-3, 6-2
1928	Peggy Saunders–Phoebe Holcroft Watson d. Eileen Bennett–Ermyntrude Harvey 6-2, 6-3
1929	Peggy Saunders Michell–Phoebe Holcroft Watson d. Phyllis Howkins Covell–Dorothy Shepherd Barron 6-4, 8-6
1930	Helen Wills Moody–Elizabeth Ryan d. Edith Cross–Sarah Palfrey 6-2, 9-7
1931	Dorothy Shepherd Barron–Phyllis Mudford d. Doris Metaxa–Josane Sigart 3-6, 6-3, 6-4
1932	Doris Metaxa–Josane Sigart d. Helen Jacobs–Elizabeth Ryan 6-4, 6-3

1933	Simone Passemard Mathieu–Elizabeth Ryan d. Freda James–Adeline "Billie" Yorke 6-2, 9-11, 6-4
1934	Simone Passemard Mathieu–Elizabeth Ryan d. Dorothy Andrus–Sylvie Jung Henrotin 6-3, 6-3
1935	Freda James–Kay Stammers d. Simone Passemard Mathieu–Hilde Krahwinkel Sperling 6-1, 6-4
1936	Freda James–Kay Stammers d. Sarah Palfrey Fabyan–Helen Jacobs 6-2, 6-1
1937	Simone Passemard Mathieu–Adeline "Billie" Yorke d. Phyllis Mudford King–Elsie Goldsack Pittman 6-3, 6-3
1938	Sarah Palfrey Fabyan–Alice Marble d. Simone Passemard Mathieu–Adeline "Billie" Yorke 6-2, 6-3
1939	Sarah Palfrey Fabyan–Alice Marble d. Helen Jacobs–Adeline "Billie" Yorke 6-1, 6-0
1940–45	Not held; World War II
1946	Louise Brough–Margaret Osborne d. Pauline Betz–Doris Hart 6-3, 2-6, 6-3
1947	Doris Hart–Pat Canning Todd d. Louise Brough–Margaret Osborne 3-6, 6-4, 7-5
1948	Louise Brough–Margaret Osborne duPont d. Doris Hart–Pat Canning Todd 6-3, 3-6, 6-3
1949	Louise Brough–Margaret Osborne duPont d. Gertrude "Gussy" Moran–Patricia Canning Todd 8-6, 7-5
1950	Louise Brough–Margaret Osborne duPont d. Shirley Fry–Doris Hart 6-4, 5-7, 6-1
1951	Shirley Fry–Doris Hart d. Louise Brough–Margaret Osborne duPont 6-3, 13-11
1952	Shirley Fry–Doris Hart d. Louise Brough–Maureen Connolly 8-6, 6-3
1953	Shirley Fry–Doris Hart d. Maureen Connolly–Julia Sampson 6-0, 6-0
1954	Louise Brough–Margaret Osborne duPont d. Shirley Fry–Doris Hart 4-6, 9-7, 6-3
1955	Angela Mortimer–Anne Shilcock d. Shirley Bloomer–Pat Ward 7-5, 6-1
1956	Angela Buxton–Althea Gibson d. Fay Muller–Daphne Seeney 6-1, 8-6
1957	Althea Gibson–Darlene Hard d. Mary Bevis Hawton–Thelma Coyne Long 6-1, 6-2
1958	Maria Bueno–Althea Gibson d. Margaret Osborne duPont–Margaret Varner 6-3, 7-5
1959	Jeanne Arth–Darlene Hard d. Beverly Baker Fleitz–Christine Truman 2-6, 6-2, 6-3
1960	Maria Bueno–Darlene Hard d. Sandra Reynolds–Renee Schuurman 6-4, 6-0
1961	Karen Hantze–Billie Jean Moffitt d. Jan Lehane–Margaret Smith 6-3, 6-4
1962	Billie Jean Moffitt–Karen Hantze Susman d. Sandra Reynolds Price–Renee Schuurman 5-7, 6-3, 7-5
1963	Maria Bueno–Darlene Hard d. Robyn Ebbern–Margaret Smith 8-6, 9-7
1964	Margaret Smith–Lesley Turner d. Billie Jean Moffitt–Karen Hantze Susman 7-5, 6-2
1965	Maria Bueno–Billie Jean Moffitt d. Francoise Durr–Jeanine Lieffrig 6-2, 7-5
1966	Maria Bueno–Nancy Richey d. Margaret Smith–Judy Tegart 6-3, 4-6, 6-4
1967	Rosie Casals–Billie Jean Moffitt King d. Maria Bueno–Nancy Richey 9-11, 6-4, 6-2
1968	Rosie Casals–Billie Jean Moffitt King d. Francoise Durr–Ann Haydon Jones 3-6, 6-4, 7-5
1969	Margaret Smith Court–Judy Tegart d. Patti Hogan–Margaret "Peggy" Michel 9-7, 6-2
1970	Rosie Casals–Billie Jean Moffitt King d. Francoise Durr–Virginia Wade 6-2, 6-3
1971	Rosie Casals–Billie Jean Moffitt King d. Margaret Smith Court–Evonne Goolagong 6-3, 6-2
1972	Billie Jean Moffitt King–Betty Stove d. Judy Tegart Dalton–Francoise Durr 6-2, 4-6, 6-3

1973 Rosie Casals–Billie Jean Moffitt King d. Francoise Durr–Betty Stove 6-1, 4-6, 7-5

1974 Evonne Goolagong–Margaret "Peggy" Michel d. Helen Gourlay–Karen Krantzcke 2-6, 6-4, 6-3

1975 Ann Kiyomura–Kazuko Sawamatsu d. Francoise Durr–Betty Stove 7-5, 1-6, 7-5

1976 Chris Evert–Martina Navratilova d. Billie Jean Moffitt King–Betty Stove 6-1, 3-6, 7-5

1977 Helen Gourlay Cawley–JoAnne Russell d. Martina Navratilova–Betty Stove 6-3, 6-3

1978 Kerry Melville Reid–Wendy Turnbull d. Mima Jausovec–Virginia Ruzici 4-6, 9-8 (12-10), 6-3

1979 Billie Jean Moffitt King–Martina Navratilova d. Betty Stove–Wendy Turnbull 5-7, 6-3, 6-2

1980 Kathy Jordan–Anne Smith d. Rosie Casals–Wendy Turnbull 4-6, 7-5, 6-1

1981 Martina Navratilova–Pam Shriver d. Kathy Jordan–Anne Smith 6-3, 7-6 (8-6)

1982 Martina Navratilova–Pam Shriver d. Kathy Jordan–Anne Smith 6-4, 6-1

1983 Martina Navratilova–Pam Shriver d. Rosie Casals–Wendy Turnbull 6-2, 6-2

1984 Martina Navratilova–Pam Shriver d. Kathy Jordan–Anne Smith, 6-3, 6-4

1985 Kathy Jordan–Elizabeth Sayers Smylie d. Martina Navratilova–Pam Shriver 5-7, 6-3, 6-4

1986 Martina Navratilova–Pam Shriver d. Hana Mandlikova–Wendy Turnbull 6-1, 6-3

1987 Claudia Kohde-Kilsch–Helena Sukova d. Betsy Nagelsen–Elizabeth Sayers Smylie 7-5, 7-5

1988 Steffi Graf–Gabriela Sabatini d. Larisa Savchenko–Natalia Zvereva 6-1, 3-6, 12-10

1989 Jana Novotna–Helena Sukova d. Larisa Savchenko–Natalia Zvereva 6-1, 6-2

1990 Jana Novotna–Helena Sukova d. Kathy Jordan–Elizabeth Sayers Smylie 6-3, 6-4

1991 Larisa Savchenko–Natalia Zvereva d. Beatriz "Gigi" Fernandez–Jana Novotna 6-4, 3-6, 6-4

1992 Beatriz "Gigi" Fernandez–Natalia Zvereva d. Jana Novotna–Larisa Savchenko Neiland 6-4, 6-1

1993 Beatriz "Gigi" Fernandez–Natalia Zvereva d. Jana Novotna–Larisa Sarchenko Neiland 6-4, 6-7 (4-7), 6-4

1994 Beatriz "Gigi" Fernandez–Natalia Zvereva d. Jana Novotna–Arantxa Sanchez Vicario 6-4, 6-1

1995 Jana Novotna–Arantxa Sanchez Vicario d. Beatriz "Gigi" Fernandez–Natasha Zvereva 5-7, 7-5, 6-4

1996 Martina Hingis–Helena Sukova d. Meredith McGrath–Larisa Savchenko Neiland 5-7, 7-5, 6-1

MIXED DOUBLES

YEAR

1913 Agnes Daniell Tuckey–Hope Crisp d. Ethel Thomson Larcombe–James Parke 3-6, 5-3 (retired)

1914 Ethel Thomson Larcombe–James Parke d. Marguerite Broquedis–Tony Wilding 4-6, 6-4, 6-2

1915–18 Not held; World War I

1919 Elizabeth Ryan–Randolph Lycett d. Dorothea Douglass Chambers–Albert Prebble 6-0, 6-0

1920 Suzanne Lenglen–Gerald Patterson d. Elizabeth Ryan–Randolph Lycett 7-5, 6-3

1921 Elizabeth Ryan–Randolph Lycett d. Phyllis Howkins–Max Woosnam 6-3, 6-1

1922 Suzanne Lenglen–Pat O'Hara Wood d. Elizabeth Ryan–Randolph Lycett 6-4, 6-3

1923 Elizabeth Ryan–Randolph Lycett d. Dorothy Shepherd Barron–Lewis Deane 6-4, 7-5

1924 Kitty McKane–J. Brian Gilbert d. Dorothy Shepherd Barron–Leslie Godfree 6-3, 3-6, 6-3

1925 Suzanne Lenglen–Jean Borotra d. Elizabeth Ryan–Umberto de Morpurgo 6-3, 6-3

1926 Kitty McKane Godfree–Leslie Godfree d. Mary K. Browne–Howard Kinsey 6-3, 6-4

1927 Elizabeth Ryan–Frank Hunter d. Kitty McKane Godfree–Leslie Godfree 8-6, 6-0

1928 Elizabeth Ryan–Pat Spence d. Daphne Akhurst–Jack Crawford 7-5, 6-4

1929 Helen Wills–Frank Hunter d. Joan Fry–Ian Collins 6-1, 6-4

1930 Elizabeth Ryan–Jack Crawford d. Hilde Krahwinkel–Daniel Prenn 6-1, 6-3

1931 Anna McCune Harper–George Lott d. Joan Ridley–Ian Collins 6-3, 1-6, 6-1

1932 Elizabeth Ryan–Enrique Maier d. Josane Sigart–Harry Hopman 7-5, 6-2

1933 Hilde Krahwinkel–Gottfried von Cramm d. Mary Heeley–Norman Farquharson 7-5, 8-6

1934 Dorothy Round–Ryuki Miki d. Dorothy Shepherd Barron–Henry "Bunny" Austin 3-6, 6-4, 6-0

1935 Dorothy Round–Fred Perry d. Nell Hall Hopman–Harry Hopman 7-5, 4-6, 6-2

1936 Dorothy Round–Fred Perry d. Sarah Palfrey Fabyan–Don Budge 7-9, 7-5, 6-4

1937 Alice Marble–Don Budge d. Simone Passemard Mathieu–Yvon Petra 6-4, 6-1

1938 Alice Marble–Don Budge d. Sarah Palfrey Fabyan–Henner Henkel 6-1, 6-4

1939 Alice Marble–Bobby Riggs d. Nina Brown–Frank Wilde 9-7, 6-1

1940–45 Not held; World War II

1946 Louise Brough–Tom Brown d. Dorothy Bundy–Geoff Brown 6-4, 6-4

1947 Louise Brough–John Bromwich d. Nancye Wynne Bolton–Colin Long 1-6 6-4 6-2

1948 Louise Brough–John Bromwich d. Doris Hart–Frank Sedgman 6-2, 3-6, 6-3

1949 Sheila Piercey Summers–Eric Sturgess d. Louise Brough–John Bromwich 9-7, 9-11, 7-5

1950 Louise Brough–Eric Sturgess d. Pat Canning Todd–Geoff Brown 11-9, 1-6, 6-4

1951 Doris Hart–Frank Sedgman d. Nancye Wynne Bolton–Mervyn Rose 7-5, 6-2

1952 Doris Hart–Frank Sedgman d. Thelma Coyne Long–Enrique Morea 4-6, 6-3, 6-4

1953 Doris Hart–Vic Seixas d. Shirley Fry–Enrique Morea 9-7, 7-5

1954 Doris Hart–Vic Seixas d. Margaret Osborne duPont–Ken Rosewall 5-7, 6-4, 6-3

1955 Doris Hart–Vic Seixas d. Louise Brough–Enrique Morea 8-6, 2-6, 6-3

1956 Shirley Fry–Vic Seixas d. Althea Gibson–Gardnar Mulloy 2-6, 6-2, 7-5

1957 Darlene Hard–Mervyn Rose d. Althea Gibson–Neale Fraser 6-4, 7-5

1958 Lorraine Coghlan–Bob Howe d. Althea Gibson–Kurt Nielsen 6-3, 13-11

1959 Darlene Hard–Rod Laver d. Maria Bueno–Neale Fraser 6-4, 6-3

1960 Darlene Hard–Rod Laver d. Maria Bueno–Bob Howe 13-11, 3-6, 8-6

1961 Lesley Turner–Fred Stolle d. Edda Buding–Bob Howe 11-9, 6-2

1962 Margaret Osborne duPont–Neale Fraser d. Ann Haydon–Dennis Ralston 2-6, 6-3, 13-11

1963 Margaret Smith–Ken Fletcher d. Darlene Hard–Bob Hewitt 11-9, 6-4

1964 Lesley Turner–Fred Stolle d. Margaret Smith–Ken Fletcher 6-4, 6-4

1965 Margaret Smith–Ken Fletcher d. Judy Tegart–Tony Roche 12-10, 6-3

1966 Margaret Smith–Ken Fletcher d. Billie Jean Moffitt King–Dennis Ralston 4-6, 6-3, 6-3

1967 Billie Jean Moffitt King–Owen Davidson d. Maria Bueno–Ken Fletcher 7-5, 6-2

1968	Margaret Smith Court–Ken Fletcher d. Olga Morozova–Alex Metreveli 6-1, 14-12
1969	Ann Haydon Jones–Fred Stolle d. Judy Tegart–Tony Roche 6-3, 6-2
1970	Rosie Casals–Ilie Nastase d. Olga Morozova–Alex Metreveli 6-3, 4-6, 9-7
1971	Billie Jean Moffitt King–Owen Davidson d. Margaret Smith Court–Marty Riessen 3-6, 6-2, 15-13
1972	Rosemary Casals–Ilie Nastase d. Evonne Goolagong–Kim Warwick 6-4, 6-4
1973	Billie Jean Moffitt King–Owen Davidson d. Janet Newberry–Raul Ramirez 6-3, 6-2
1974	Billie Jean Moffitt King–Owen Davidson d. Lesley Charles–Mark Farrell 6-3, 9-7
1975	Margaret Smith Court–Marty Riessen d. Betty Stove–Allan Stone 6-4, 7-5
1976	Francoise Durr–Tony Roche d. Rosemary Casals–Dick Stockton 6-3, 2-6, 7-5
1977	Greer Stevens–Bob Hewitt d. Betty Stove–Frew McMillan 3-6, 7-5, 6-4
1978	Betty Stove–Frew McMillan d. Billie Jean Moffitt King–Ray Ruffels 6-2, 6-2
1979	Greer Stevens–Bob Hewitt d. Betty Stove–Frew McMillan 7-5, 7-6 (9-7)
1980	Tracy Austin–John Austin d. Dianne Fromholtz–Mark Edmondson 4-6, 7-6 (8-6), 6-3
1981	Betty Stove–Frew McMillan d. Tracy Austin–John Austin 4-6, 7-6 (7-2), 6-3
1982	Anne Smith–Kevin Curren d. Wendy Turnbull–John Lloyd 2-6, 6-3, 7-5
1983	Wendy Turnbull–John Lloyd b. Billie Jean Moffitt King–Steve Denton 6-7 (5-7), 7-6 (7-5), 7-5
1984	Wendy Turnbull–John Lloyd d. Kathy Jordan–Steve Denton 6-3, 6-3
1985	Martina Navratilova–Paul McNamee d. Elizabeth Sayers Smylie–John Fitzgerald 7-5, 4-6, 6-2
1986	Kathy Jordan–Ken Flach d. Martina Navratilova–Heinz Gunthardt 6-3, 7-6 (9-7)
1987	Jo Durie–Jeremy Bates d. Nicole Provis–Darren Cahill 7-6 (12-10), 6-3
1988	Zina Garrison–Sherwood Stewart d. Gretchen Rush Magers–Kelly Jones 6-1, 7-6 (7-3)
1989	Jana Novotna–Jim Pugh d. Jenny Byrne–Mark Kratzmann 6-4, 5-7, 6-4
1990	Zina Garrison–Rick Leach d. Elizabeth Sayers Smylie–John Fitzgerald 7-5, 6-2
1991	Elizabeth Sayers Smylie–John Fitzgerald d. Natalia Zvereva–Jim Pugh 7-6 (7-4), 6-2
1992	Larisa Savchenko Neiland–Cyril Suk d. Miriam Oremans–Jacco Eltingh 7-6 (7-2), 6-2
1993	Martina Navratilova–Mark Woodforde d. Manon Bollegraf–Thomas Nijssen 6-3, 6-4
1994	Helena Sukova–Todd Woodbridge d. Lori McNeil–Todd Jason Middleton 3-6, 7-5, 6-3
1995	Martina Navratilova–Jonathan Stark d. Beatriz "Gigi" Fernandez–Cyril Suk 6-4, 6-4
1996	Helena Sukova–Cyril Suk d. Larisa Savchenko Neiland–Mark Woodforde 1-6, 6-3, 6-2

ALL-TIME WIMBLEDON CHAMPIONSHIP RECORDS

Most men's singles: 7—Willie Renshaw, 1881–86, 1889

Most men's doubles: 8—Reggie Doherty, 1897–1901, 1903–05 Laurie Doherty, 1897–1901, 1903–05

Most men's, mixed: 4—Ken Fletcher, 1963, 1965–66, 1968 Owen Davidson, 1967, 1971, 1973–74

Most men's altogether: 13—Laurie Doherty, 1897–1905 (5 singles, 8 doubles)

Most women's singles: 9—Martina Navratilova, 1978–79, 1982–87, 1990

Most women's doubles: 12—Elizabeth Ryan, 1914, 1919–23, 1925–27, 1930, 1933–34

Most women's mixed: 7—Elizabeth Ryan, 1919, 1921, 1923, 1927–28, 1930, 1932

Most women's altogether: 20—Billie Jean Moffitt King, 1961–79 (6 singles, 10 doubles, 4 mixed)

Most men's doubles, team: 8—Reggie and Laurie Doherty, 1897–1901, 1903–1905

Most women's doubles, team: 6—Suzanne Lenglen and Elizabeth Ryan, 1919–23, 1925

Most mixed doubles, team: 4—Margaret Smith Court and Ken Fletcher, 1963, 1965–1966, 1968; Billie Jean King and Owen Davidson, 1967, 1971, 1973–74

YOUNGEST CHAMPIONS

Men's singles: Boris Becker, 1985, 17 years, 7 months

Men's doubles: Dennis Ralston, 1960, 17 years, 10 months

Men's mixed: Rod Laver, 1959, 20 years, 10 months

Women's singles: Lottie Dod, 1887, 15 years, 9 months, 12 days

Women's doubles: Martina Hingis, 1996, 15 years, 9 months, 9 days

Women's mixed: Tracy Austin, 1980, 17 years, 7 months

OLDEST CHAMPIONS

Men's singles: Arthur Gore, 1909, 41 years, 6 months

Men's doubles: Gardnar Mulloy, 1957, 43 years, 8 months

Men's mixed: Sherwood Stewart, 1988, 42 years, 1 month

Women's singles: Charlotte Cooper Sterry, 1908, 37 years, 9 months

Women's doubles: Elizabeth Ryan, 1934, 42 years, 5 months

Women's mixed: Margaret Osborne duPont, 1962, 44 years, 4 months

INDIVIDUAL CAREER SINGLES RECORDS

MEN

Tournaments played: 29—Arthur Gore, 1888–1922

Matches played: 102—Jimmy Connors, 1972–89, 1991–92

Matches won: 84—Jimmy Connors, 1972–89, 1991

Matches won consecutively: 41—Bjorn Borg, 1976 through semis, 1981, lost final to John McEnroe

Match winning percentage: .927—Bjorn Borg (51-4), 1973–81

WOMEN

Tournaments played: 24—Blanche Bingley Hillyard, 1884–89, 1891–94, 1897, 1899–1902, 1904–10, 1912–13

Matches played: 132—Martina Navratilova, 1973–94

Matches won: 119—Martina Navratilova

Matches won consecutively: 50—Helen Wills Moody, 1927–30, 1932–33, 1935, 1938

Match winning percentage: 1.000—Suzanne Lenglen (28-0), 1919–23, 1925–26; .982, Helen Wills Moody (55-1), 1924, 1927–30, 1932–33, 1935, 1938

LONGEST MATCHES (TOTAL GAMES)

Men's singles: 112 games—Richard "Pancho" Gonzalez d. Charlie Pasarell 22-24, 1-6, 16-14, 6-3, 11-9, 1st rd., 1969

Men's doubles: 98 games—Nikki Pilic–Gene Scott d. Cliff Richey–Torben Ulrich 19-21, 12-10, 6-4, 4-6, 9-7, 1st rd., 1966

Women's singles: 58 games—Chanda Rubin d. Patricia Hy-Boulais, 7-6 (7-4), 6-7 (5-7), 17-15, 2nd rd., 1996

Women's doubles: 48 games—Pat Brazier–Christabel Wheatcroft d. Mildred Nonwiler–Betty Soames 11-9, 5-7, 9-7, 1st rd., 1933. 48 games,

Svetlana Cherneva–Larisa Savchenko (Neiland) d. Catherine Tanvier–Chris Evert Lloyd 3-6, 7-6, 14-12, 3rd rd., 1984.

Mixed doubles: 77 games—Brenda Schultz (McCarthy)–Michiel Schapers d. Andrea Temesvari–Tom Nijssen 6-3, 5-7, 29-27, 1st rd., 1991

LONGEST MATCHES (PLAYING TIME)

Men: 5 hours, 12 minutes—Richard "Pancho" Gonzalez d. Charlie Pasarell, 22-24, 1-6, 16-14, 6-3, 11-9. 1st rd., 1969 (over two days)

Women: 3 hours, 45 minutes—Chanda Rubin d. Patricia Hy-Boulais, 7-6 (7-4), 6-7 (5-7), 17-15. 2nd rd., 1996

LONGEST TIE-BREAKERS

Men's singles: 20-18, third set, Bjorn Borg d. Premjit Lall, 6-3, 6-4, 9-8 (20-18), 1st rd., 1973. Doug Flach (qualifier ranked No. 281 in the world) defeated 3rd-seeded Andre Agassi, 2-6, 7-6 (7-1), 6-4, 7-6 (7-4), 1996.

Women's singles: 15-13, second set, Virginia Wade d. Jo Durie, 3-6, 7-6 (15-13), 6-2. 1st rd., 1982

BIGGEST UPSETS

Men: Peter Doohan (No. 70) d. first-seeded Boris Becker (defending champ), 7-6 (7-4), 4-6, 6-2, 6-4. 2nd rd., 1987

Women: Lori McNeil (No. 22) d. first-seeded Steffi Graf (defending champ), 7-5, 7-6 (7-5). 1st rd., 1994

BEST COMEBACKS

Men: Henri Cochet d. Bill Tilden, 3-6, 4-6, 7-5, 6-4, 6-3, semi, 1927. From 1-5, 15-all, third; and 3-2, a break down, fifth. Cochet d. Jean Borotra, 4-6, 4-6, 6-3, 6-4, 7-5. Final, 1927. Saved 6 match points, 1 at 2-5, 5 at 5-3, fifth. Richard "Pancho" Gonzalez d. Charlie Pasarell, 22-24, 1-6, 16-14, 6-3, 11-9, 1st rd., 1969. Saved 7 match points, fifth, twice serving out of 0-40.

Women: Helga Schultz d. Jeanine Lieffrig, 4-6, 11-9, 12-10. From 3-5, second; saved 11 match points, third. 1st rd., 1966. Blanche Bingley Hillyard d. Lena Rice, 4-6, 8-6, 6-4. Final, 1889. Saved 3 match points, Rice serving, 5-3, 40-15 and ad, second set.

AUSTRALIAN CHAMPIONSHIPS

Inaugurated at the Warehousemen's Grounds in Melbourne in 1905, the Australian Championships rotated thereafter among principal cities Down Under until 1972, when an uninterrupted run began in Melbourne. It was always played on grass until the permanent National Tennis Centre site at Flinders Park in Melbourne opened with hard courts and a 15,000-seat retractable-roof stadium in 1988. With the construction of the 12,000-seat concrete horseshoe stadium at Kooyong in 1927, Melbourne became the most successful host. Stadia rising at White City in Sydney (1922) and Memorial Drive in Adelaide (1920) were other prominent sites.

Kooyong's record attendance of 140,000 for its last year, 1987, was quickly passed by Flinders Park, where the record, 388,602, was set in 1996. The record for one session on the grounds, 27,168, was the afternoon of Jan. 17, 1996; 12,625 for the night session made it a day-night record, 39,793. The night record, 14,067, was set by the Mark Philippoussis–Pete Sampras third-rounder, Jan. 20, 1996, and the stadium record, 15,925, for the men's semis, was set Jan. 26, 1996.

Two championships were held in 1977 when the event was moved from January to December, and none in 1986 to readjust back to January. Three separate women's tourneys were held, 1980–82.

In 1969, Australia was the last of the majors to be opened to amateurs and professionals alike and offer prize money, originally $25,000, accelerating to $6,526,520 in 1996. Originally, first prize was $5,000 for men, $1,500 for women, accelerating to $410,620 and $329,615, respectively, in 1996. The tie-breaker was adopted in 1971, one year after the U.S., but not in force for the ultimate set, fifth for men, third for women.

MEN'S SINGLES

YEAR	
1905	Rodney Heath d. A. H. Curtis 4-6, 6-3, 6-4, 6-4
1906	Tony Wilding d. Francis Fisher 6-0, 6-4, 6-4
1907	Horace Rice d. Harry Parker 6-3, 6-4, 6-4
1908	Fred Alexander d. Alfred Dunlop 3-6, 3-6, 6-0, 6-2, 6-3
1909	Tony Wilding d. Ernie Parker 6-1, 7-5, 6-2
1910	Rodney Heath d. Horace Rice 6-4, 6-3, 6-2
1911	Norman Brookes d. Horace Rice 6-1, 6-2, 6-3
1912	James Parke d. Alfred Beamish 3-6, 6-3, 1-6, 6-1, 7-5
1913	Ernie Parker d. Harry Parker 2-6, 6-1, 6-3, 6-2
1914	Arthur O'Hara Wood d. Gerald Patterson 6-4, 6-3, 5-7, 6-1
1915	Gordon Lowe d. Horace Rice 4-6, 6-1, 6-1, 6-4
1916–18	Not held; World War I
1919	Algernon Kingscote d. Eric Pockley 6-4, 6-0, 6-3
1920	Pat O'Hara Wood d. Ron Thomas 6-3, 4-6, 6-8, 6-1, 6-3
1921	Rhys Gemmell d. Alf Hedemann 7-5, 6-1, 6-4
1922	James Anderson d. Gerald Patterson 6-0, 3-6, 3-6, 6-3, 6-2
1923	Pat O'Hara Wood d. Bert St. John 6-1, 6-1, 6-3
1924	James Anderson d. Bob Schlesinger 6-3, 6-4, 3-6, 5-7, 6-3
1925	James Anderson d. Gerald Patterson 11-9, 2-6, 6-2, 6-3
1926	John Hawkes d. Jim Willard 6-1, 6-3, 6-1
1927	Gerald Patterson d. John Hawkes 3-6, 6-4, 3-6, 18-16, 6-3
1928	Jean Borotra d. R. O. "Jack" Cummings 6-4, 6-1, 4-6, 5-7, 6-3
1929	Colin Gregory d. Bob Schlesinger 6-2, 6-2, 5-7, 7-5
1930	Gar Moon d. Harry Hopman 6-3, 6-1, 6-3

1931	Jack Crawford d. Harry Hopman 6-4, 6-2, 2-6, 6-1
1932	Jack Crawford d. Harry Hopman 4-6, 6-3, 3-6, 6-3, 6-1
1933	Jack Crawford d. Keith Gledhill 2-6, 7-5, 6-3, 6-2
1934	Fred Perry d. Jack Crawford 6-3, 7-5, 6-1
1935	Jack Crawford d. Fred Perry 2-6, 6-4, 6-4, 6-4
1936	Adrian Quist d. Jack Crawford 6-2, 6-3, 4-6, 3-6, 9-7
1937	Vivian McGrath d. John Bromwich 6-3, 1-6, 6-0, 2-6, 6-1
1938	Don Budge d. John Bromwich 6-4, 6-2, 6-1
1939	John Bromwich d. Adrian Quist 6-4, 6-1, 6-3
1940	Adrian Quist d. Jack Crawford 6-3, 6-1, 6-2
1941–45	Not held; World War II
1946	John Bromwich d. Dinny Pails 5-7, 6-3, 7-5, 3-6, 6-2
1947	Dinny Pails d. John Bromwich 4-6, 6-4, 3-6, 7-5, 8-6
1948	Adrian Quist d. John Bromwich 6-4, 3-6, 6-3, 2-6, 6-3
1949	Frank Sedgman d. John Bromwich 6-3, 6-3, 6-2
1950	Frank Sedgman d. Ken McGregor 6-3, 6-4, 4-6, 6-1
1951	Dick Savitt d. Ken McGregor 6-3, 2-6, 6-3, 6-1
1952	Ken McGregor d. Frank Sedgman 7-5, 12-10, 2-6, 6-2
1953	Ken Rosewall d. Mervyn Rose 6-0, 6-3, 6-4
1954	Mervyn Rose d. Rex Hartwig 6-2,0-6, 6-4, 6-2
1955	Ken Rosewall d. Lew Hoad 9-7, 6-4, 6-4
1956	Lew Hoad d. Ken Rosewall 6-4, 3-6, 6-4, 7-5
1957	Ashley Cooper d. Neale Fraser 6-3, 9-11, 6-4, 6-2
1958	Ashley Cooper d. Mal Anderson 7-5, 6-3, 6-4
1959	Alex Olmedo d. Neale Fraser 6-1, 6-2, 3-6, 6-3
1960	Rod Laver d. Neale Fraser 5-7, 3-6, 6-3, 8-6, 8-6
1961	Roy Emerson d. Rod Laver 1-6, 6-3, 7-5, 6-4
1962	Rod Laver d. Roy Emerson 8-6, 0-6, 6-4 6-4
1963	Roy Emerson d. Ken Fletcher 6-3, 6-3, 6-1
1964	Roy Emerson d. Fred Stolle 6-3, 6-4 6-2
1965	Roy Emerson d. Fred Stolle 7-9, 2-6, 6-4 7-5 6-1
1966	Roy Emerson d. Arthur Ashe 6-4, 6-8, 6-2, 6-3
1967	Roy Emerson d. Arthur Ashe 6-4, 6-1, 6-4
1968	Bill Bowrey d. Juan Gisbert 7-5, 2-6, 9-7, 6-4
1969	Rod Laver d. Andres Gimeno 6-3, 6-4, 7-5
1970	Arthur Ashe d. Dick Crealy 6-4, 9-7, 6-2
1971	Ken Rosewall d. Arthur Ashe 6-1, 7-5, 6-3
1972	Ken Rosewall d. Mal Anderson 7-6 (7-2), 6-3, 7-5
1973	John Newcombe d. Onny Parun 6-3, 6-7, 7-5, 6-1
1974	Jimmy Connors d. Phil Dent 7-6 (9-7), 6-4, 4-6, 6-3
1975	John Newcombe d. Jimmy Connors 7-5, 3-6, 6-4, 7-6 (9-7)
1976	Mark Edmondson d. John Newcombe 6-7, 6-3, 7-6 6-1
1977	(January) Roscoe Tanner d. Guillermo Vilas 6-3, 6-3, 6-3
1977	(December) Vitas Gerulaitis d. John Lloyd 6-3, 7-6, 5-7 3-6, 6-2
1978	Guillermo Vilas d. John Marks 6-4, 6-4, 3-6, 6-3
1979	Guillermo Vilas d. John Sadri 7-6 (7-4), 6-3, 6-2
1980	Brian Teacher d. Kim Warwick 7-5, 7-6 (7-4), 6-3
1981	Johan Kriek d. Steve Denton 6-2, 7-6 (7-1), 6-7 (1-7), 6-4
1982	Johan Kriek d. Steve Denton 6-3, 6-3, 6-2
1983	Mats Wilander d. Ivan Lendl 6-1, 6-4, 6-4
1984	Mats Wilander d. Kevin Curren 6-7 (5-7), 6-4, 7-6 (7-3), 6-2
1985	Stefan Edberg d. Mats Wilander 6-4, 6-3, 6-3
1986	Not held due to change in dates
1987	Stefan Edberg d. Pat Cash 6-3, 6-4, 3-6, 5-7, 6-3
1988	Mats Wilander d. Pat Cash 6-3, 6-7 (3-7), 3-6, 6-1, 8-6
1989	Ivan Lendl d. Miloslav Mecir 6-2, 6-2, 6-2
1990	Ivan Lendl d. Stefan Edberg 4-6, 7-6 (7-3), 5-2 (retired)
1991	Boris Becker d. Ivan Lendl 1-6, 6-4, 6-4, 6-4
1992	Jim Courier d. Stefan Edberg 6-3, 3-6, 6-4 6-2
1993	Jim Courier d. Stefan Edberg 6-2, 6-1, 2-6, 7-5
1994	Pete Sampras d. Todd Martin 7-6 (7-4), 6-4, 6-4
1995	Andre Agassi d. Pete Sampras 4-6, 6-1, 7-6 (8-6), 6-4
1996	Boris Becker d. Michael Chang 6-2, 6-4, 2-6, 6-2
1997	Pete Sampras d. Carlos Moya 6-2, 6-3, 6-3

WOMEN'S SINGLES

YEAR

1922	Mall Molesworth d. Esna Boyd 6-3, 10-8
1923	Mall Molesworth d. Esna Boyd 6-1, 7-5
1924	Sylvia Lance d. Esna Boyd 6-3, 3-6, 8-6
1925	Daphne Akhurst d. Esna Boyd 1-6, 8-6, 6-4
1926	Daphne Akhurst d. Esna Boyd 6-1, 6-3
1927	Esna Boyd d. Sylvia Lance Harper 5-7, 6-1, 6-2
1928	Daphne Akhurst d. Esna Boyd 7-5, 6-2
1929	Daphne Akhurst d. Louie Bickerton 6-1, 5-7, 6-2
1930	Daphne Akhurst d. Sylvia Lance Harper 10-8, 2-6, 7-5
1931	Coral McInnes Buttsworth d. Marjorie Cox Crawford 1-6, 6-3, 6-4
1932	Coral McInnes Buttsworth d. Kathrine Le Mesurier 9-7, 6-4
1933	Joan Hartigan d. Coral McInnes Buttsworth 6-4, 6-3
1934	Joan Hartigan d. Mall Molesworth 6-1, 6-4
1935	Dorothy Round d. Nancy Lyle 1-6, 6-1, 6-3
1936	Joan Hartigan d. Nancye Wynne 6-4, 6-4
1937	Nancye Wynne d. Emily Hood Westacott 6-3, 5-7, 6-4
1938	Dorothy Bundy d. Dorothy Stevenson 6-3, 6-2
1939	Emily Hood Westacott d. Nell Hall Hopman 6-1, 6-2
1940	Nancye Wynne d. Thelma Coyne 5-7, 6-4, 6-0
1941–45	Not held; World War II
1946	Nancye Wynne Bolton d. Joyce Fitch 6-4, 6-4
1947	Nancye Wynne Bolton d. Nell Hall Hopman 6-3, 6-2
1948	Nancye Wynne Bolton d. Marie Toomey 6-3, 6-1
1949	Doris Hart d. Nancye Wynne Bolton 6-3, 6-4
1950	Louise Brough d. Doris Hart 6-4, 3-6, 6-4
1951	Nancye Wynne Bolton d. Thelma Coyne Long 6-1, 7-5
1952	Thelma Coyne Long d. Helen Angwin 6-2, 6-3
1953	Maureen Connolly d. Julia Sampson 6-3, 6-2
1954	Thelma Coyne Long d. Jenny Staley 6-3, 6-4
1955	Beryl Penrose d. Thelma Coyne Long 6-4, 6-3
1956	Mary Carter d. Thelma Coyne Long 3-6, 6-2, 9-7
1957	Shirley Fry d. Althea Gibson 6-3, 6-4
1958	Angela Mortimer d. Lorraine Coghlan 6-3, 6-4
1959	Mary Carter Reitano d. Renee Schuurman 6-2, 6-3
1960	Margaret Smith d. Jan Lehane 7-5, 6-2
1961	Margaret Smith d. Jan Lehane 6-1, 6-4
1962	Margaret Smith d. Jan Lehane 6-0, 6-2
1963	Margaret Smith d. Jan Lehane 6-2, 6-2
1964	Margaret Smith d. Lesley Turner, 6-3, 6-2
1965	Margaret Smith d. Maria Bueno 5-7, 6-4, 5-2 (retired)
1966	Margaret Smith d. Nancy Richey (walkover)
1967	Nancy Richey d. Lesley Turner 6-1, 6-4
1968	Billie Jean Moffitt King d. Margaret Smith 6-1, 6-2
1969	Margaret Smith Court d. Billie Jean Moffitt King 6-4, 6-1
1970	Margaret Smith Court d. Kerry Melville 6-1, 6-3
1971	Margaret Smith Court d. Evonne Goolagong 2-6, 7-6 (7-0), 7-5
1972	Virginia Wade d. Evonne Goolagong 6-4, 6-4
1973	Margaret Smith Court d. Evonne Goolagong 6-4, 7-5
1974	Evonne Goolagong d. Chris Evert 7-6 (7-5), 4-6, 6-0

1975	Evonne Goolagong d. Martina Navratilova 6-3, 6-2

1975   Evonne Goolagong d. Martina Navratilova 6-3, 6-2

1976   Evonne Goolagong d. Renata Tomanova 6-2, 6-2

1977   (January) Kerry Melville Reid d. Dianne Fromholtz Balestrat 7-5, 6-2

1977   (December) Evonne Goolagong Cawley d. Helen Gourlay Cawley 6-3, 6-0

1978   Chris O'Neil d. Betsy Nagelsen 6-3, 7-6

1979   Barbara Jordan d. Sharon Walsh 6-3, 6-3

1980   Hana Mandlikova d. Wendy Turnbull 6-0, 7-5

1981   Martina Navratilova d. Chris Evert Lloyd 6-7 (4-7), 6-4, 7-5

1982   Chris Evert Lloyd d. Martina Navratilova 6-3, 2-6, 6-3

1983   Martina Navratilova d. Kathy Jordan 6-2, 7-6 (7-5)

1984   Chris Evert Lloyd d. Helena Sukova 6-7 (4-7), 6-1, 6-3

1985   Martina Navratilova d. Chris Evert Lloyd 6-2, 4-6, 6-2

1986   Not held due to change in dates

1987   Hana Mandlikova d. Martina Navratilova 7-5, 7-6 (7-2)

1988   Steffi Graf d. Chris Evert 6-1, 7-6 (7-3)

1989   Steffi Graf d. Helena Sukova 6-4, 6-4

1990   Steffi Graf d. Mary Joe Fernandez 6-3, 6-4

1991   Monica Seles d. Jana Novotna 5-7, 6-3, 6-1

1992   Monica Seles d. Mary Joe Fernandez 6-2, 6-3

1993   Monica Seles d. Steffi Graf 4-6, 6-3, 6-2

1994   Steffi Graf d. Arantxa Sanchez Vicario 6-0, 6-2

1995   Mary Pierce d. Arantxa Sanchez Vicario, 6-3, 6-2

1996   Monica Seles d. Anke Huber 6-4, 6-1

1997   Martina Hingis d. Mary Pierce 6-2, 6-2

MEN'S DOUBLES

YEAR

1905   Randolph Lycett–Tom Tachell d. E. T. Barnard–B. Spence 11-9, 8-6, 1-6, 4-6, 6-1

1906   Rodney Heath–Tony Wilding d. Harry Parker–C. C. Cox 6-2, 6-4, 6-2

1907   Bill Gregg–Harry Parker d. Horace Rice–George Wright 6-2, 3-6, 6-2, 6-2

1908   Fred Alexander–Alfred Dunlop d. G. G. Sharp–Tony Wilding 6-3, 6-2, 6-1

1909   J. P. Keane–Ernie Parker d. L. Crooks–Tony Wilding 1-6, 6-1, 6-1, 9-7

1910   Ashley Campbell–Horace Rice d. Rodney Heath–J. L. O'Dea 6-3, 6-3, 6-2

1911   Rodney Heath–Randolph Lycett d. J. J. Addison–Norman Brookes 6-2, 7-5, 6-0

1912   James Parke–Charles Dixon d. Alfred Beamish–Gordon Lowe 6-4, 6-4, 6-2

1913   Alf Hedemann–Ernie Parker d. Harry Parker–Roy Taylor 8-6, 4-6, 6-4, 6-4

1914   Ashley Campbell–Gerald Patterson d. Rodney Heath–Arthur O'Hara Wood 7-5, 3-6, 6-3, 6-3

1915   Horace Rice–Clarrie Todd d. Gordon Lowe–Bert St. John 8-6, 6-4, 7-9, 6-3

1916–18   Not held; World War 1

1919   Pat O'Hara Wood–Ron Thomas d. James Anderson–Arthur Lowe 7-5, 6-1, 7-9, 3-6, 6-3

1920   Pat O'Hara Wood–Ron Thomas d. Horace Rice–R. Taylor 6-1, 6-0, 7-5

1921   S. H. Eaton–Rhys Gemmell d. N. Brearley–E. Stokes 7-5, 6-3, 6-3

1922   John Hawkes–Gerald Patterson d. James Anderson–Norman Peach 8-10, 6-0, 6-0, 7-5

1923   Pat O'Hara Wood–Bert St. John d. Dudley Bullough–Horace Rice 6-4, 6-3, 3-6, 6-0

1924   James Anderson–Norman Brookes d. Gerald Patterson–Pat O'Hara Wood 6-2, 6-4, 6-3

1925   Pat O'Hara Wood–Gerald Patterson d. James Anderson–Fred Kalms 6-4, 8-6, 7-5

1926   John Hawkes–Gerald Patterson d. James Anderson–Pat O'Hara Wood 6-1, 6-4, 6-2

1927   John Hawkes–Gerald Patterson d. Pat O'Hara Wood–Ian McInnes 8-6, 6-2, 6-1

1928   Jean Borotra–Jacques Brugnon d. Jim Willard–Gar Moon 6-2, 4-6, 6-4, 6-4

1929   Jack Crawford–Harry Hopman d. R. O. "Jack" Cummings–Gar Moon 6-1, 6-8, 4-6, 6-1, 6-3

1930   Jack Crawford–Harry Hopman d. John Hawkes–Tim Fitchett 8-6, 6-1, 2-6, 6-3

1931   Charles Donohoe–Ray Dunlop d. Jack Crawford–Harry Hopman 8-6, 6-2, 5-7 7-9, 6-4

1932   Jack Crawford–Gar Moon d. Harry Hopman–Gerald Patterson 12-10, 6-3, 4-6 6-4

1933   Keith Gledhill–Ellsworth Vines d. Jack Crawford–Gar Moon 6-4, 10-8, 6-2

1934   Fred Perry–Pat Hughes d. Adrian Quist–Don Turnbull 6-8, 6-3, 6-4, 3-6, 6-3

1935   Jack Crawford–Viv McGrath d. Pat Hughes–Fred Perry 6-4, 8-6, 6-2

1936   Adrian Quist–Don Turnbull d. Jack Crawford–Viv McGrath 6-8, 6-2 6-1, 3-6, 6-2

1937   Adrian Quist–Don Turnbull d. John Bromwich–Jack Harper 6-2, 9-7, 1-6, 6-8, 6-4

1938   John Bromwich–Adrian Quist d. Gottfried von Cramm–Henner Henkel 7-5, 6-4, 6-0

1939   John Bromwich–Adrian Quist d. Don Turnbull–Colin Long 6-4, 7-5, 6-2

1940   John Bromwich–Adrian Quist d. Jack Crawford–Viv McGrath 6-3, 7-5, 6-1

1941–45   Not held; World War II

1946   John Bromwich–Adrian Quist d. Max Newcombe–Len Schwartz 6-3, 6-1, 9-7

1947   John Bromwich–Adrian Quist d. Frank Sedgman–George Worthington 6-1, 6-3, 6-1

1948   John Bromwich–Adrian Quist d. Frank Sedgman–Colin Long 1-6, 6-8, 9-7, 6-3, 8-6

1949   John Bromwich–Adrian Quist d. Geoff Brown–Bill Sidwell 1-6, 7-5, 6-2, 6-3

1950   John Bromwich–Adrian Quist d. Eric Sturgess–Jaroslav Drobny 6-3, 5-7 4-6, 6-3, 8-6

1951   Ken McGregor–Frank Sedgman d. John Bromwich–Adrian Quist 11-9, 2-6, 6-3, 4-6, 6-3

1952   Ken McGregor–Frank Sedgman d. Don Candy–Mervyn Rose 6-4, 7-5, 6-3

1953   Lew Hoad–Ken Rosewall d. Don Candy–Mervyn Rose 9-11, 6-4, 10-8, 6-4

1954   Rex Hartwig–Mervyn Rose d. Neale Fraser–Clive Wilderspin 6-3, 6-4, 6-2

1955   Vic Seixas–Tony Trabert d. Lew Hoad–Ken Rosewall 6-3, 6-2, 2-6, 3-6, 6-1

1956   Lew Hoad–Ken Rosewall d. Don Candy–Mervyn Rose 10-8, 13-11, 6-4

1957   Neale Fraser–Lew Hoad d. Mal Anderson–Ashley Cooper 6-3, 8-6, 6-4

1958   Ashley Cooper–Neale Fraser d. Roy Emerson–Bob Mark 7-5, 6-8, 3-6, 6-3, 7-5

1959   Rod Laver–Bob Mark d. Don Candy–Bob Howe 9-7, 6-4, 6-2

1960   Rod Laver–Bob Mark d. Roy Emerson–Neale Fraser 1-6, 6-2, 6-4, 6-4

1961   Rod Laver–Bob Mark d. Roy Emerson–Marty Mulligan 6-3, 7-5, 3-6, 9-11, 6-2

1962   Roy Emerson–Neale Fraser d. Bob Hewitt–Fred Stolle 4-6, 4-6, 6-1, 6-4, 11-9

1963   Bob Hewitt–Fred Stolle d. Ken Fletcher–John Newcombe 6-2, 3-6, 6-3, 3-6, 6-3

1964   Bob Hewitt–Fred Stolle d. Roy Emerson–Ken Fletcher 6-4, 7-5, 3-6, 4-6, 14-12

1965	John Newcombe–Tony Roche d. Roy Emerson–Fred Stolle 3-6, 4-6, 13-11, 6-3, 6-4
1966	Roy Emerson–Fred Stolle d. John Newcombe–Tony Roche 7-9, 6-3, 6-8, 14-12, 12-10
1967	John Newcombe–Tony Roche d. Bill Bowrey–Owen Davidson 3-6, 6-3, 7-5, 6-8, 8-6
1968	Dick Crealy–Allan Stone d. Terry Addison–Ray Keldie 10-8, 6-4, 6-3
1969	Roy Emerson–Rod Laver d. Ken Rosewall–Fred Stolle 6-4, 6-4 (shortened by agreement)
1970	Bob Lutz–Stan Smith d. John Alexander–Phil Dent 8-6, 6-3, 6-4
1971	John Newcombe–Tony Roche d. Tom Okker–Marty Riessen 6-2, 7-6
1972	Owen Davidson–Ken Rosewall d. Ross Case–Geoff Masters 3-6, 7-6, 6-2
1973	Mal Anderson–John Newcombe d. John Alexander–Phil Dent 6-3, 6-4, 7-6
1974	Ross Case–Geoff Masters d. Syd Ball–Bob Giltinan 6-7, 6-3, 6-4
1975	John Alexander–Phil Dent d. Bob Carmichael–Allan Stone 6-3, 7-6
1976	John Newcombe–Tony Roche d. Ross Case–Geoff Masters 7-6, 6-4
1977	(January) Arthur Ashe–Tony Roche d. Charlie Pasarell–Erik van Dillen 6-4, 6-4
1977	(December) Ray Ruffels–Allan Stone d. John Alexander–Phil Dent 7-6, 7-6
1978	Wojtek Fibak–Kim Warwick d. Paul Kronk–Cliff Letcher 7-6, 7-5
1979	Peter McNamara–Paul McNamee d. Paul Kronk–Cliff Letcher 7-6, 6-2
1980	Mark Edmondson–Kim Warwick d. Peter McNamara–Paul McNamee 7-5, 6-4
1981	Mark Edmondson–Kim Warwick d. Hank Pfister–John Sadri 6-3, 6-7, 6-3
1982	John Alexander–John Fitzgerald d. Andy Andrews–John Sadri 6-4, 7-6
1983	Mark Edmondson–Paul McNamee d. Steve Denton–Sherwood Stewart 6-3, 7-6
1984	Mark Edmondson–Sherwood Stewart d. Joakim Nystrom–Mats Wilander 6-2, 6-2, 7-5
1985	Paul Annacone–Christo Van Rensburg d. Mark Edmondson–Kim Warwick 3-6, 7-6, 6-4, 6-4
1986	Not held due to change in dates
1987	Stefan Edberg–Anders Jarryd d. Peter Doohan–Laurie Warder 6-4, 6-4, 7-6 (7-3)
1988	Rick Leach–Jim Pugh d. Jeremy Bates–Peter Lundgren 6-3, 6-2, 6-3
1989	Rick Leach–Jim Pugh d. Darren Cahill–Mark Kratzmann 6-4, 6-4, 6-4
1990	Pieter Aldrich–Danie Visser d. Grant Connell–Glenn Michibata 6-4, 4-6, 6-1, 6-4
1991	Scott Davis–David Pate d. Patrick McEnroe–David Wheaton 6-7 (4-7), 7-6 (10-8), 6-3 7-5
1992	Todd Woodbridge–Mark Woodforde d. Kelly Jones–Rick Leach 6-4, 6-3, 6-4
1993	Danie Visser–Laurie Warder d. John Fitzgerald–Anders Jarryd 6-4, 6-3, 6-4
1994	Jacco Eltingh–Paul Haarhuis d. Byron Black–Jonathan Stark 6-7 (3-7), 6-3, 6-4, 6-3
1995	Jared Palmer–Richey Reneberg d. Mark Knowles–Daniel Nestor 6-3, 3-6, 6-3, 6-2
1996	Stefan Edberg–Petr Korda d. Alex O'Brien–Sebastian Lareau 7-5, 7-5, 4-6, 6-1
1997	Todd Woodbridge–Mark Woodforde d. Sebastien Lareau–Alex O'Brien 4-6, 7-5, 7-5, 6-3

WOMEN'S DOUBLES

YEAR	
1922	Esna Boyd–Marjorie Mountain d. Floris St. George–Lorna Utz 1-6, 6-4, 7-5

1923	Esna Boyd–Sylvia Lance d. Mall Molesworth–H. Turner 6-1, 6-4
1924	Daphne Akhurst–Sylvia Lance d. Kathrine LeMesurier–Meryl Waxman Lister O'Hara Wood 7-5, 6-2
1925	Sylvia Lance Harper–Daphne Akhurst d. Esna Boyd–Kathrine LeMesurier 6-4, 6-3
1926	Meryl Waxman Lister O'Hara Wood–Esna Boyd d. Daphne Akhurst–Marjorie Cox 6-3, 6-8, 8-6
1927	Meryl Waxman Lister O'Hara Wood–Louie Bickerton d. Esna Boyd–Sylvia Lance Harper 6-3, 6-3
1928	Dahpne Akhurst–Esna Boyd d. Kathrine LeMesurier–Dorothy Weston 6-3, 6-1
1929	Daphne Akhurst–Louie Bickerton d. Sylvia Lance Harper–Meryl Waxman Lister O'Hara Wood 6-2, 3-6, 6-2
1930	Mall Molesworth–Emily Hood d. Marjorie Cox–Sylvia Harper 6-3, 0-6, 7-5
1931	Daphne Akhurst Cozens–Louie Bickerton d. Nell Lloyd–Lorna Utz 6-0, 6-4
1932	Coral McInnes Buttsworth–Marjorie Cox d. Kathrine LeMesurier–Dorothy Weston 6-2, 6-2
1933	Mall Molesworth–Emily Hood Westacott d. Joan Hartigan–Marjorie Gladman Van Ryn 6-3, 6-2
1934	Mall Molesworth–Emily Hood Westacott d. Joan Hartigan–Ula Valkenburg 6-8, 6-4, 6-4
1935	Evelyn Dearman–Nancy Lyle d. Louie Bickerton–Nell Hall Hopman 6-3, 6-4
1936	Thelma Coyne–Nancye Wynne d. May Blick–Katherine Woodward 6-2, 6-4
1937	Thelma Coyne–Nancye Wynne d. Nell Hall Hopman–Emily Hood Westacott 6-2, 6-2
1938	Thelma Coyne–Nancye Wynne d. Dorothy Bundy–Dorothy Workman 9-7, 6-4
1939	Thelma Coyne–Nancye Wynne d. May Hardcastle–Emily Hood Westacott 7-5, 6-4
1940	Thelma Coyne–Nancye Wynne d. Joan Hartigan–Emily Niemeyer 7-5, 6-2
1941–45	Not held; World War II
1946	Joyce Fitch–Mary Bevis d. Nancye Wynne Bolton–Thelma Coyne Long 9-7, 6-4
1947	Thelma Coyne Long–Nancye Wynne Bolton d. Mary Bevis–Joyce Fitch 6-3, 6-3
1948	Thelma Coyne Long–Nancye Wynne Bolton d. Mary Bevis–Pat Jones 6-3, 6-3
1949	Thelma Coyne Long–Nancye Wynne Bolton d. Doris Hart–Marie Toomey 6-0, 6-1
1950	Louise Brough–Doris Hart d. Nancye Wynne Bolton–Thelma Coyne Long 6-2, 2-6, 6-3
1951	Thelma Coyne Long–Nancye Wynne Bolton d. Joyce Fitch–Mary Bevis Hawton 6-2, 6-1
1952	Thelma Coyne Long–Nancye Wynne Bolton d. Allison Burton Baker–Mary Bevis Hawton 6-1, 6-1
1953	Maureen Connolly–Julia Sampson d. Mary Bevis Hawton–Beryl Penrose 6-4, 6-2
1954	Mary Bevis Hawton–Beryl Penrose d. Hazel Redick-Smith–Julia Wipplinger 6-3, 8-6
1955	Mary Bevis Hawton–Beryl Penrose d. Nell Hall Hopman–Gwen Thiele 7-5, 6-1
1956	Mary Bevis Hawton–Thelma Coyne Long d. Mary Carter–Beryl Penrose 6-2, 5-7, 9-7
1957	Althea Gibson–Shirley Fry d. Mary Bevis Hawton–Fay Muller 6-2, 6-1
1958	Mary Bevis Hawton–Thelma Coyne Long d. Lorraine Coghlan–Angela Mortimer 7-5, 6-8, 6-2
1959	Renee Schuurman–Sandra Reynolds d. Lorraine Coghlan–Mary Carter Reitano 7-5, 6-4
1960	Maria Bueno–Christine Truman d. Lorraine Coghlan Robinson–Margaret Smith 6-2, 5-7, 6-2
1961	Mary Carter Reitano–Margaret Smith d. Mary Bevis Hawton–Jan Lehane 6-4, 3-6, 7-5
1962	Margaret Smith–Robyn Ebbern d. Darlene Hard–Mary Carter Reitano 6-4, 6-4
1963	Margaret Smith–Robyn Ebbern d. Jan Lehane–Lesley Turner 6-1, 6-3

1964	Judy Tegart Dalton–Lesley Turner d. Robyn Ebbern–Margaret Smith 6-4, 6-4
1965	Margaret Smith–Lesley Turner d. Robyn Ebbern–Billie Jean Moffitt King 1-6, 6-2, 6-3
1966	Carole Caldwell Graebner–Nancy Richey d. Margaret Smith–Lesley Turner 6-4, 7-5
1967	Lesley Turner–Judy Tegart Dalton d. Lorraine Coghlan Robinson–Evelyn Terras 6-0, 6-2
1968	Karen Krantzcke–Kerry Melville d. Judy Tegart Dalton–Lesley Turner 6-4, 3-6, 6-2
1969	Margaret Smith Court–Judy Tegart Dalton d. Rosie Casals–Billie Jean Moffitt King 6-4, 6-4
1970	Margaret Smith Court–Judy Tegart Dalton d. Karen Krantzcke–Kerry Melville 6-3, 6-1
1971	Margaret Smith Court–Evonne Goolagong d. Jill Emmerson–Lesley Hunt 6-0, 6-0
1972	Kerry Harris–Helen Gourlay d. Patricia Coleman–Karen Krantzcke 6-0, 6-4
1973	Margaret Smith Court–Virginia Wade d. Kerry Harris–Kerry Melville 6-4, 6-4
1974	Evonne Goolagong–Margaret "Peggy" Michel d. Kerry Harris–Kerry Melville 7-5, 6-3
1975	Evonne Goolagong–Margaret "Peggy" Michel d. Margaret Smith Court–Olga Morozova 7-6, 7-6
1976	Evonne Goolagong–Helen Gourlay d. Lesley Turner Bowrey–Renata Tomanova 8-1 (one pro set by mutual agreement)
1977	(January) Dianne Fromholtz–Helen Gourlay Cawley d. Betsy Nagelsen–Kerry Melville Reid 5-7, 6-1, 7-5
1977	(December) Evonne Goolagong Cawley–Helen Gourlay Cawley and Mona Schallau Guerrant–Kerry Melville Reid shared title due to rained-out final
1978	Betsy Nagelsen–Renata Tomanova d. Naoko Sato–Pam Whytcross 7-5, 6-2
1979	Judy Chaloner–Dianne Evers d. Leanne Harrison–Marcella Mesker 6-1, 3-6, 6-0
1980	Martina Navratilova–Betsy Nagelsen d. Ann Kiyomura–Candy Reynolds 6-4, 6-4
1981	Kathy Jordan–Anne Smith d. Martina Navratilova–Pam Shriver 6-2, 7-5
1982	Martina Navratilova–Pam Shriver d. Claudia Kohde Kilsch–Eva Pfaff 6-4, 6-2
1983	Martina Navratilova–Pam Shriver d. Anne Hobbs–Wendy Turnbull 6-4, 6-7, 6-2
1984	Martina Navratilova–Pam Shriver d. Claudia Kohde Kilsch–Helena Sukova 6-3, 6-4
1985	Martina Navratilova–Pam Shriver d. Claudia Kohde Kilsch–Helena Sukova 6-3, 6-4
1986	Not held due to change in dates
1987	Martina Navratilova–Pam Shriver d. Zina Garrison–Lori McNeil, 6-1, 6-0
1988	Martina Navratilova–Pam Shriver d. Chris Evert–Wendy Turnbull 6-0, 7-5
1989	Martina Navratilova–Pam Shriver d. Patty Fendick–Jill Hetherington 3-6, 6-3, 6-2
1990	Jana Novotna–Helena Sukova d. Patty Fendick–Mary Joe Fernandez 7-6 (7-5), 7-6 (8-6)
1991	Patty Fendick–Mary Joe Fernandez d. Beatriz "Gigi" Fernandez–Jana Novotna 7-6 (7-4), 6-1
1992	Arantxa Sanchez Vicario–Helena Sukova d. Mary Joe Fernandez–Zina Garrison 6-4, 7-6 (7-3)
1993	Beatriz "Gigi" Fernandez–Natalia Zvereva d. Pam Shriver–Elizabeth Sayers Smylie 6-4, 6-3
1994	Beatriz "Gigi" Fernandez–Natalia Zvereva d. Patty Fendick–Meredith McGrath 6-3, 4-6, 6-4
1995	Jana Novotna–Arantxa Sanchez Vicario d. Beatriz "Gigi" Fernandez–Natalia Zvereva 6-3, 6-7 (3-7), 6-4
1996	Chanda Rubin–Arantxa Sanchez Vicario d. Lindsay Davenport–Mary Joe Fernandez 7-5, 2-6, 6-4
1997	Martina Hingis–Natalia Zvereva d. Lindsay Davenport–Lisa Raymond 6-2, 6-2

MIXED DOUBLES

YEAR	
1922	Esna Boyd–John Hawkes d. Lorna Utz–H. S. Utz 6-1, 6-1
1923	Sylvia Lance–Horace Rice d. Mall Molesworth–Bert St. John 2-6, 6-4, 6-4
1924	Daphne Akhurst–John Willard d. Esna Boyd–Gar Hone 6-3, 6-4
1925	Daphne Akhurst–John Willard d. Sylvia Lance Harper–Bob Schlesinger 6-4 6-4
1926	Esna Boyd–John Hawkes d. Daphne Akhurst–Jim Willard 6-2, 6-4
1927	Esna Boyd–John Hawkes d. Youtha Anthony–Jim Willard 6-1, 6-3
1928	Daphne Akhurst–Jean Borotra d. Esna Boyd–John Hawkes, default
1929	Daphne Akhurst–Gar Moon d. Marjorie Cox–Jack Crawford 6-0, 7-5
1930	Nell Hall–Harry Hopman d. Marjorie Cox–Jack Crawford 11-9, 3-6, 6-3
1931	Marjorie Cox Crawford–Jack Crawford d. Emily Hood Westacott–Aubrey Willard 7-5, 6-4
1932	Marjorie Cox Crawford–Jack Crawford d. Meryl Waxman O'Hara Wood–Jiro Satoh 6-8, 8-6, 6-3
1933	Marjorie Cox Crawford–Jack Crawford d. Marjorie Gladman Van Ryn–Ellsworth Vines 3-6, 7-5, 13-11
1934	Joan Hartigan–Gar Moon d. Emily Hood Westacott–Ray Dunlop 6-3, 6-4
1935	Louie Bickerton–Christian Boussus d. Mrs. Bond–Vernon Kirby 1-6, 6-3, 6-3
1936	Nell Hall Hopman–Harry Hopman d. May Blick–Abe Kay 6-2, 6-0
1937	Nell Hall Hopman–Harry Hopman d. Dorothy Stevenson–Don Turnbull 3-6, 6-3, 6-2
1938	Margaret Wilson–John Bromwich d. Nancye Wynne–Colin Long 6-3, 6-2
1939	Nell Hall Hopman–Harry Hopman d. Margaret Wilson–John Bromwich 6-8, 6-2, 6-3
1940	Nancye Wynne–Colin Long d. Nell Hall Hopman–Harry Hopman 7-5, 2-6, 6-4
1941–45	Not held; World War II
1946	Nancye Wynne Bolton–Colin Long d. Joyce Fitch–John Bromwich 6-0, 6-4
1947	Nancye Wynne Bolton–Colin Long d. Joyce Fitch–John Bromwich 6-3, 6-3
1948	Nancye Wynne Bolton–Colin Long d. Thelma Coyne Long–Bill Sidwell 7-5, 4-6, 8-6
1949	Doris Hart–Frank Sedgman d. Joyce Fitch–John Bromwich 6-1, 5-7, 12-10
1950	Doris Hart–Frank Sedgman d. Joyce Fitch–Eric Sturgess 8-6, 6-4
1951	Thelma Coyne Long–George Worthington d. Clare Proctor–Jack May 6-4, 3-6
1952	Thelma Coyne Long–George Worthington d. Gwen Thiele–Tom Warhurst 9-7, 7-5
1953	Julia Sampson–Rex Hartwig d. Maureen Connolly–Hamilton Richardson 6-4, 6-3
1954	Thelma Coyne Long–Rex Hartwig d. Beryl Penrose–John Bromwich 4-6, 6-1, 6-2
1955	Thelma Coyne Long–George Worthington d. Jenny Staley–Lew Hoad 6-2, 6-1
1956	Beryl Penrose–Neale Fraser d. Mary Bevis Hawton–Roy Emerson 6-2, 6-4
1957	Fay Muller–Mal Anderson d. J. Langley–Billy Knight 7-5, 3-6, 6-1
1958	Mary Bevis Hawton–Bob Howe d. Angela Mortimer–Peter Newman 9-11, 6-1, 6-2
1959	Sandra Reynolds–Bob Mark d. Renee Schuurman–Rod Laver 4-6, 13-11, 6-1
1960	Jan Lehane–Trevor Fancutt d. Mary Carter Reitano–Bob Mark 6-2, 7-5
1961	Jan Lehane–Bob Hewitt d. Mary Carter Reitano–John Pearce 9-7, 6-2
1962	Lesley Turner–Fred Stolle d. Darlene Hard–Roger Taylor 6-3, 9-7

1963 Margaret Smith–Ken Fletcher d. Lesley Turner–Fred Stolle 7-5, 5-7, 6-4

1964 Margaret Smith–Ken Fletcher d. Jan Lehane–Mike Sangster 6-3, 6-2

1965 Margaret Smith–John Newcombe shared title with Robyn Ebbern–Owen Davidson; final not played

1966 Judy Tegart–Tony Roche d. Robyn Ebbern–Bill Bowrey 6-1, 6-3

1967 Lesley Turner–Owen Davidson d. Judy Tegart–Tony Roche 9-7, 6-4

1968 Billie Jean Moffitt King–Dick Crealy d. Margaret Smith Court–Allan Stone (walkover)

1969 Margaret Smith Court–Marty Riessen shared title with Ann Haydon Jones–Fred Stolle (final not played)

1970–86 Not held

1987 Zina Garrison–Sherwood Stewart d. Anne Hobbs–Andrew Castle 3-6, 7-6 (7-5), 6-3

1988 Jana Novotna–Jim Pugh d. Martina Navratilova–Tim Gullikson 5-7, 6-2, 6-4

1989 Jana Novotna–Jim Pugh d. Zina Garrison–Sherwood Stewart 6-3, 6-4

1990 Natalia Zvereva–Jim Pugh d. Zina Garrison–Rick Leach 4-6, 6-2, 6-3

1991 Jo Durie–Jeremy Bates d. Robin White–Scott Davis 2-6, 6-4, 6-4

1992 Nicole Provis–Mark Woodforde d. Arantxa Sanchez Vicario–Todd Woodbridge 6-3, 4-6, 11-9

1993 Arantxa Sanchez Vicario–Todd Woodbridge d. Zina Garrison Jackson–Rick Leach 7-5, 6-4

1994 Larisa Savchenko Neiland–Andrei Olhovskiy d. Helena Sukova–Todd Woodbridge 7-5, 6-7 (0-7), 6-2

1995 Natalia Zvereva–Rick Leach d. Beatriz "Gigi" Fernandez–Cyril Suk 7-6 (7-4), 6-7 (3-7), 6-4

1996 Larisa Savchenko Neiland–Mark Woodforde d. Nicole Arendt–Luke Jensen 4-6, 7-5, 6-0

1997 Manon Bollegraf–Rick Leach d. Larisa Savchenko Neiland–John Laffnie de Jager 6-3, 6-7 (5-7), 7-5

ALL-TIME AUSTRALIAN CHAMPIONSHIP RECORDS

Most men's singles: 6—Roy Emerson, 1961, 1963–67

Most men's doubles: 10—Adrian Quist, 1936–40, 1946–50

Most men's mixed: 4—Colin Long, 1940, 1946–48; Harry Hopman, 1930, 1936–37, 1939

Most men's altogether: 13—Quist, 1936–50 (3 singles, 10 doubles)

Most women's singles: 11—Margaret Smith Court, 1960–66, 1969–71, 1973

Most women's doubles: 12—Thelma Coyne Long, 1936–40, 1947–49, 1951–52, 1956, 1958

Most women's mixed: 4—Nell Hall Hopman, 1930, 1936–37, 1939; Nancye Wynne Bolton, 1940, 1946–48; Thelma Coyne Long, 1951–52, 1954–55

Most women's altogether: 21—Court, 1960–75 (11 singles, 8 doubles, 2 mixed)

Most men's doubles, team: 8—Quist and John Bromwich, 1938–40, 1946–50

Most women's doubles, team: 10—Long and Bolton, 1936–40, 1947–49, 1951–52

Most mixed doubles, team: 4—Nell and Harry Hopman, 1930, 1936–37, 1939; Bolton and Colin Long, 1940–48

YOUNGEST CHAMPIONS

Men's singles: Ken Rosewall, 1953, 18 years, 2 months

Men's doubles: Lew Hoad–Ken Rosewall, 1953, 18 years, 2 months (Hoad 19 days younger)

Men's mixed: Tony Roche, 1966, 20 years, 8 months

Women's singles: Martina Hingis, 1997, 16 years, 4 months

Women's doubles: Thelma Coyne (Long), 1936, 17 years, 7 months

Women's mixed: Jan Lehane, 1960, 18 years, 6 months

OLDEST CHAMPIONS

Men's singles: Ken Rosewall, 1972, 37 years, 2 months

Men's doubles: Norman Brookes, 1924, 46 years, 2 months

Men's mixed: Sherwood Stewart, 1987, 40 years, 7 months

Women's singles: Thelma Coyne Long, 1954, 35 years, 7 months

Women's doubles: Thelma Coyne Long, 1956, 37 years, 7 months

Women's mixed: Thelma Coyne Long, 1955, 36 years, 7 months

INDIVIDUAL CAREER SINGLES RECORDS

MEN

Tournaments played: 19—Jack Crawford, 1927–37, 1939–40, 1946–51

Matches played: 67—Stefan Edberg, 1983–96

Matches won: 56—Stefan Edberg

Matches won consecutively: 27—Roy Emerson, 1963 through 2nd rd., 1969, lost 3rd rd. to Rod Laver

Match winning percentage: .836—Stefan Edberg (56-11)

WOMEN

Tournaments played: 14—Margaret Smith Court, 1959–66, 1968–71, 1973, 1975

Matches played: 63—Margaret Smith Court

Matches won: 60—Margaret Smith Court

Matches won consecutively: 38—Margaret Smith Court, 1960–68, lost final to Billie Jean King

Match winning percentage: 1.000—Monica Seles (28-0); .952—Margaret Smith Court (60-3)

LONGEST MATCHES (TOTAL GAMES)

Men's singles: 94 games—Dennis Ralston d. John Newcombe, 19-17, 20-18, 4-6, 6-4, quarters, 1970

Men's doubles: 94 games—Max Senior–Paul Avery d. Warren Jacques–Cedric Mason, 4-6, 18-16, 7-9, 17-15, 2-0, retired, 1st rd., 1968

Women's singles: 48 games—Chanda Rubin d. Arantxa Sanchez Vicario, 6-4, 2-6, 16-14, quarters, 1996

Women's doubles: 42 games—Linda Gates–Alycia Moulton d. Katerina Maleeva–Manuela Maleeva, 4-6, 6-2, 13-11, 2nd rd., 1985; 42 games, Lise Gregory–Manon Bollegraf d. Elise Burgin–Roslyn Fairbank Nideffer, 5-7, 6-4, 11-9, 3rd rd., 1991

Mixed doubles: 47 games—Joe-Anne Faull–Jason Stoltenberg d. Paula Smith–Mike Bauer, 7-6 (7-5), 4-6, 13-11, 1st rd., 1988

LONGEST MATCH (PLAYING TIME)

Men's singles: 5 hours, 11 minutes—Boris Becker d. Omar Camporese, 7-6 (7-4), 7-6 (7-5), 0-6, 4-6, 14-12, 3rd rd., 1991

Men's doubles: 5 hours, 29 minutes—Pieter Aldrich–Danie Visser d. Scott Davis–Bob Van't Hof, 6-4, 4-6, 7-6 (7-4), 4-6, 23-21 (last set took 2 hours, 53 minutes), quarters, 1990

Women's singles: 3 hours, 33 minutes—Chanda Rubin d. Arantxa Sanchez Vicario, 6-4, 2-6, 16-14, quarters, 1996

LONGEST TIE-BREAKERS

Men's singles: 17-15, third set, Omar Camporese d. Lars Wahlgren, 6-4, 6-2, 7-6 (17-15), 3rd rd., 1992

Women's singles: 15-13, first set, Silke Meier d. Jane Taylor, 7-6 (15-13), 2-6, 6-2, 1st rd., 1995

Men: Mark Edmondson (No. 212) d. first-seeded Ken Rosewall, 6-1, 2-6, 6-2, 6-4, second-seeded John Newcombe, 6-7, 6-3, 7-6, 6-2, in succession to win title, 1976.

Women: Ninth-seeded Helena Sukova d. first-seeded Martina Navratilova, 1-6, 6-3, 7-5, ending 74-match winning streak, breaking last leg of a prospective Grand Slam, semis, 1984 (after beating fifth-seeded Claudia Kohde Kilsch and third-seeded Pam Shriver).

BEST COMEBACKS

Men: Rod Laver d. Neale Fraser, 5-7, 3-6, 6-3, 8-6, 8-6, final, 1960, from 4-5, 30-40, match point, fourth. Won on 7th match point. In semi, Laver d. Roy Emerson, 4-6, 6-1, 9-7, 3-6, 7-5, winning last four games from 5-3 down. Emerson was twice 2 points from victory on serve. Stefan Edberg d. Wally Masur, 6-7 (4-7), 2-6, 7-6 (7-4), 6-4, 6-2, quarters, 1985. Saved 2 match points, 4-5, third.

Women: Mall Molesworth d. Sylvia Lance, 3-6, 6-4, 8-6, semis, 1923. Saved match point, third. Daphne Akhurst d. Esna Boyd, 1-6, 8-6, 6-4, final, 1925, from 4-1 down, third.

FRENCH CHAMPIONSHIPS

The French Championships dates back to 1891 (men) and 1897 (women), but only since 1925 has it been open to players besides French citizens or residents. Then it became the fourth of the major international championships, considered the world clay championship, the European surface on which it has always been played.

A national event in France, the "World's Hard Court (clay in the continental vernacular) Championships" was held in the Paris area between 1912 and 1923, abandoned in 1924 in favor of the Olympics, and then abandoned altogether as the French decided to welcome foreigners. The first outsiders to win a French title were Americans Vinnie Richards and Howard Kinsey, in the doubles of 1926. The most successful of the French-only days were Max Decugis, who won the singles eight times (1903–04, 1907–09, 1912–14), and Cecilia Masson, who won six singles titles (1897–1900, 1902–03).

In 1925, a Grand Slam became possible, though the concept didn't seem feasible until 1933, when Jack Crawford added the French and Wimbledon to his Australian title; nobody had come close to winning the first two until Crawford. In 1925 and 1927, the Championships was staged at Stade Français in St. Cloud, and in 1926 at the Racing Club of Paris, both holding no more than 5,000. But in 1928, the present home, Stade Roland Garros, seating 10,000, was built, and the tournament has been played there since.

While Australia and Wimbledon shut down during World War II, the French received permission from the Nazi occupation authority to resume in 1942. Obviously, only French citizens played until the first postwar tourney in 1946.

In 1968, the French was the first of the majors to become open to amateurs and professionals alike and offer prize money, originally $25,000, escalating to $10,707,560 in 1996. First prize was $3,000 for men, $1,000 for women, escalating respectively to $690,400 and $644,000 in 1996. As the site constantly improved and grew over the last decade, Court Central was enlarged to hold 17,000, and in 1995 the Suzanne Lenglen Court, holding 10,000, opened. A record single-day crowd, 33,583, appeared May 19, 1996. The French was the last major to adopt the tie-breaker, 1973.

MEN'S SINGLES

YEAR	
1925	René Lacoste d. Jean Borotra 7-5, 6-1, 6-4
1926	Henri Cochet d. René Lacoste 6-2, 6-4, 6-3
1927	René Lacoste d. Bill Tilden 6-4, 4-6, 5-7, 6-3, 11-9
1928	Henri Cochet d. René Lacoste 5-7, 6-3, 6-1, 6-3
1929	René Lacoste d. Jean Borotra 6-3, 2-6, 6-0, 2-6, 8-6
1930	Henri Cochet d. Bill Tilden 3-6, 8-6, 6-3, 6-1
1931	Jean Borotra d. Christian Boussus 2-6, 6-4, 7-5, 6-4
1932	Henri Cochet d. Giorgio de Stefani 6-0, 6-4, 4-6, 6-3
1933	Jack Crawford d. Henri Cochet 8-6, 6-1, 6-3
1934	Gottfried von Cramm d. Jack Crawford 6-4, 7-9, 3-6, 7-5, 6-3
1935	Fred Perry d. Gottfried von Cramm 6-3, 3-6, 6-1, 6-3
1936	Gottfried von Cramm d. Fred Perry 6-0, 2-6, 6-2, 2-6, 6-0
1937	Henner Henkel, d. Henry "Bunny" Austin 6-1, 6-4, 6-3
1938	Don Budge d. Roderich Menzel 6-3, 6-2, 6-4
1939	Don NcNeill d. Bobby Riggs 7-5, 6-0, 6-3
1940–45	Not held; World War II
1946	Marcel Bernard d. Jaroslav Drobny 3-6, 2-6, 6-1, 6-4, 6-3
1947	Joszef Asboth d. Eric Sturgess 8-6, 7-5, 6-4
1948	Frank Parker d. Jaroslav Drobny 6-4, 7-5, 5-7, 8-6
1949	Frank Parker d. J. Edward "Budge" Patty 6-3, 1-6, 6-1, 6-4
1950	J. Edward "Budge" Patty d. Jaroslav Drobny 6-1, 6-2, 3-6, 5-7, 7-5
1951	Jaroslav Drobny d. Eric Sturgess 6-3, 6-3, 6-3
1952	Jaroslav Drobny d. Frank Sedgman 6-2, 6-0, 3-6, 6-4
1953	Ken Rosewall d. Vic Seixas 6-3, 6-4, 1-6, 6-2
1954	Tony Trabert d. Arthur Larsen 6-4, 7-5, 6-1
1955	Tony Trabert d. Sven Davidson 2-6, 6-1, 6-4, 6-2
1956	Lew Hoad d. Sven Davidson 6-4, 8-6, 6-3

1957	Sven Davidson d. Herbie Flam 6-3, 6-4, 6-4
1958	Mervyn Rose d. Luis Ayala 6-3, 6-4, 6-4
1959	Nicola Pietrangeli d. Ian Vermaak 3-6, 6-3, 6-4, 6-1
1960	Nicola Pietrangeli d. Luis Ayala 3-6, 6-3, 6-4, 3-6, 6-3
1961	Manuel Santana d. Nicola Pietrangeli 4-6, 6-1, 3-6, 6-0, 6-2
1962	Rod Laver d. Roy Emerson 3-6, 2-6, 6-3, 9-7, 6-2
1963	Roy Emerson d. Pierre Darmon 3-6, 6-1, 6-4, 6-4
1964	Manuel Santana d. Nicola Pietrangeli 6-3, 6-1, 4-6, 7-5
1965	Fred Stolle d. Tony Roche 3-6, 6-0, 6-2, 6-3
1966	Tony Roche d. Istvan Gulyas 6-1, 6-4, 7-5
1967	Roy Emerson d. Tony Roche 6-1, 6-4, 2-6, 6-2
1968	Ken Rosewall d. Rod Laver 6-3, 6-1, 2-6, 6-2
1969	Rod Laver d. Ken Rosewall 6-4, 6-3, 6-4
1970	Jan Kodes d. Zeljko Franulovic 6-2, 6-4, 6-0
1971	Jan Kodes d. Ilie Nastase 8-6, 6-2, 2-6, 7-5
1972	Andres Gimeno d. Patrick Proisy 4-6, 6-3, 6-1, 6-1
1973	Ilie Nastase d. Nikki Pilic 6-3, 6-3, 6-0
1974	Bjorn Borg d. Manuel Orantes 2-6, 6-7 (1-7), 6-0, 6-1, 6-1
1975	Bjorn Borg d. Guillermo Vilas 6-2, 6-3, 6-4
1976	Adriano Panatta d. Harold Solomon 6-1, 6-4, 4-6, 7-6 (7-3)
1977	Guillermo Vilas d. Brian Gottfried 6-0, 6-3, 6-0
1978	Bjorn Borg d. Guillermo Vilas 6-1, 6-1, 6-3
1979	Bjorn Borg d. Victor Pecci 6-3, 6-1, 6-7 (6-8), 6-4
1980	Bjorn Borg d. Vitas Gerulaitis 6-4, 6-1, 6-2
1981	Bjorn Borg d. Ivan Lendl 6-1, 4-6, 6-2, 3-6, 6-1
1982	Mats Wilander d. Guillermo Vilas 1-6, 7-6 (8-6), 6-0, 6-4
1983	Yannick Noah d. Mats Wilander 6-2, 7-5, 7-6 (7-3)
1984	Ivan Lendl d. John McEnroe 3-6, 2-6, 6-4, 7-5, 7-5
1985	Mats Wilander d. Ivan Lendl 3-6, 6-4, 6-2, 6-2
1986	Ivan Lendl d. Mikael Pernfors 6-3, 6-2, 6-4
1987	Ivan Lendl d. Mats Wilander 7-5, 6-2, 3-6, 7-6 (7-3)
1988	Mats Wilander d. Henri Leconte 7-5, 6-2, 6-1
1989	Michael Chang d. Stefan Edberg 6-1, 3-6, 4-6, 6-4, 6-2
1990	Andres Gomez d. Andre Agassi 6-3, 2-6, 6-4, 6-4
1991	Jim Courier d. Andre Agassi 3-6, 6-4, 2-6, 6-1, 6-4
1992	Jim Courier d. Petr Korda 7-5, 6-2, 6-1
1993	Sergi Bruguera d. Jim Courier 6-4, 2-6, 6-2, 3-6, 6-3
1994	Sergi Bruguera d. Alberto Berasategui 6-3, 7-5, 2-6, 6-1
1995	Thomas Muster d. Michael Chang 7-5, 6-2, 6-4
1996	Yevgeny Kafelnikov d. Michael Stich 7-6 (7-4), 7-5, 7-6 (7-4)

WOMEN'S SINGLES

YEAR

1925	Suzanne Lenglen d. Kitty McKane 6-1, 6-2
1926	Suzanne Lenglen d. Mary K. Browne 6-1, 6-0
1927	Kea Bouman d. Irene Bowder Peacock 6-2, 6-4
1928	Helen Wills d. Eileen Bennett 6-1, 6-2
1929	Helen Wills d. Simone Passemard Mathieu 6-3, 6-4
1930	Helen Wills Moody d. Helen Jacobs 6-2, 6-1
1931	Cilly Aussem d. Betty Nuthall 8-6, 6-1
1932	Helen Wills Moody d. Simone Passemard Mathieu 7-5, 6-1
1933	Margaret Scriven d. Simone Passemard Mathieu 6-2, 4-6, 6-4
1934	Margaret Scriven d. Helen Jacobs 7-5, 4-6, 6-1
1935	Hilde Krahwinkel Sperling d. Simone Passemard Mathieu 6-2, 6-1
1936	Hilde Krahwinkel Sperling d. Simone Passemard Mathieu 6-3, 6-4
1937	Hilde Krahwinkel Sperling d. Simone Passemard Mathieu 6-2, 6-4
1938	Simone Passemard Mathieu d. Nelly Adamson Landry 6-0, 6-3

1939	Simone Passemard Mathieu d. Jadwiga Jedrzejowska 6-3, 8-6
1940-45	Not held; World War II
1946	Margaret Osborne d. Pauline Betz 1-6, 8-6, 7-5
1947	Pat Canning Todd d. Doris Hart 6-3, 3-6, 6-4
1948	Nelly Adamson Landry d. Shirley Fry 6-2, 0-6, 6-0
1949	Margaret Osborne duPont d. Nelly Adamson 7-5, 6-2
1950	Doris Hart d. Patricia Canning Todd 6-4, 4-6, 6-?
1951	Shirley Fry d. Doris Hart 6-3, 3-6, 6-3
1952	Doris Hart d. Shirley Fry 6-4, 6-4
1953	Maureen Connolly d. Doris Hart 6-2, 6-4
1954	Maureen Connolly d. Ginette Bucaille 6-4, 6-1
1955	Angela Mortimer d. Dorothy Head Knode 2-6, 7-5, 10-8
1956	Althea Gibson d. Angela Mortimer 6-0, 12-10
1957	Shirley Bloomer d. Dorothy Head Knode 6-1, 6-3
1958	Suzi Kormoczi d. Shirley Bloomer 6-4, 1-6, 6-2
1959	Christine Truman d. Suzi Kormoczi 6-4, 7-5
1960	Darlene Hard d. Yola Ramirez 6-3, 6-4
1961	Ann Haydon d. Yola Ramirez 6-2, 6-1
1962	Margaret Smith d. Lesley Turner 6-3, 3-6, 7-5
1963	Lesley Turner d. Ann Haydon Jones 2-6, 6-3, 7-5
1964	Margaret Smith d. Maria Bueno 5-7, 6-1, 6-2
1965	Lesley Turner d. Margaret Smith 6-3 6-4
1966	Ann Haydon Jones d. Nancy Richey 6-3, 6-1
1967	Françoise Durr d. Lesley Turner 4-6, 6-3, 6-4
1968	Nancy Richey d. Ann Haydon Jones 5-7, 6-4, 6-1
1969	Margaret Smith Court d. Ann Jones 6-1, 4-6, 6-3
1970	Margaret Smith Court d. Helga Niessen 6-2, 6-4
1971	Evonne Goolagong d. Helen Gourlay 6-3, 7-5
1972	Billie Jean Moffitt King d. Evonne Goolagong 6-3, 6-3
1973	Margaret Smith Court d. Chris Evert 6-7 (5-7), 7-6 (8-6), 6-4
1974	Chris Evert d. Olga Morozova 6-1, 6-2
1975	Chris Evert d. Martina Navratilova 2-6, 6-2, 6-1
1976	Sue Barker d. Renata Tomanova 6-2, 0-6, 6-2
1977	Mima Jausovec d. Florenta Mihai 6-2, 6-7 (5-7), 6-1
1978	Virginia Ruzici d. Mima Jausovec 6-2, 6-2
1979	Chris Evert Lloyd d. Wendy Turnbull 6-2, 6-0
1980	Chris Evert Lloyd d. Virginia Ruzici 6-0, 6-3
1981	Hana Mandlikova d. Sylvia Hanika 6-2, 6-4
1982	Martina Navratilova d. Andrea Jaeger 7-6 (8-6), 6-1
1983	Chris Evert Lloyd d. Mima Jausovec 6-1, 6-2
1984	Martina Navratilova d. Chris Evert Lloyd 6-3, 6-1
1985	Chris Evert Lloyd d. Martina Navratilova 6-3, 6-7 (4-7), 7-5
1986	Chris Evert Lloyd d. Martina Navratilova 2-6, 6-3, 6-3
1987	Steffi Graf d. Martina Navratilova 6-4, 4-6, 8-6
1988	Steffi Graf d. Natalia Zvereva 6-0, 6-0
1989	Arantxa Sanchez Vicario d. Steffi Graf 7-6 (8-6), 3-6, 7-5
1990	Monica Seles d. Steffi Graf 7-6 (8-6), 6-4
1991	Monica Seles d. Arantxa Sanchez Vicario 6-3, 6-4
1992	Monica Seles d. Steffi Graf 6-2, 3-6, 10-8
1993	Steffi Graf d. Mary Joe Fernandez 4-6, 6-2, 6-4
1994	Arantxa Sanchez Vicario d. Mary Pierce 6-4, 6-4
1995	Steffi Graf d. Arantxa Sanchez Vicario 7-5, 4-6, 6-0
1996	Steffi Graf d. Arantxa Sanchez Vicario 6-3, 6-7 (4-7), 10-8

MEN'S DOUBLES

YEAR

| 1925 | Jean Borotra–René Lacoste d. Henri Cochet–Jacques Brugnon 7-5, 4-6, 6-3, 2-6, 6-3 |

1926	Vinnie Richards–Howard Kinsey d. Henri Cochet–Jacques Brugnon 6-4, 6-1, 4-6, 6-4
1927	Henri Cochet–Jacques Brugnon d. Jean Borotra–René Lacoste 2-6, 6-2, 6-0, 1-6, 6-4
1928	Jean Borotra–Jacques Brugnon d. Henri Cochet–René de Buzelet 6-4, 3-6, 6-2, 3-6, 6-4
1929	René Lacoste–Jean Borotra d. Henri Cochet–Jacques Brugnon 6-3, 3-6, 6-3, 3-6, 8-6
1930	Henri Cochet–Jacques Brugnon d. Harry Hopman–Jim Willard 6-3, 9-7, 6-3
1931	George Lott–John Van Ryn d. Vernon Kirby–Norman Farquharson 6-4, 6-3, 6-4
1932	Henri Cochet–Jacques Brugnon d. Christian Boussus–Marcel Bernard 6-4, 3-6, 7-5, 6-3
1933	Pat Hughes–Fred Perry d. Adrian Quist–Viv McGrath 6-2, 6-4, 2-6, 7-5
1934	Jean Borotra–Jacques Brugnon d. Jack Crawford–Viv McGrath 11-9, 6-3, 2-6, 4-6, 9-7
1935	Jack Crawford–Adrian Quist d. Viv McGrath–Don Turnbull 6-1, 6-4, 6-2
1936	Jean Borotra–Marcel Bernard d. Charles Tuckey–Pat Hughes 6-2, 3-6, 9-7, 6-1
1937	Gottfried von Cramm–Henner Henkel d. Norman Farquharson–Vernon Kirby 6-4, 7-5, 3-6, 6-1
1938	Bernard Destremau–Yvon Petra d. Don Budge–Gene Mako 3-6, 6-3, 9-7, 6-1
1939	Don McNeill–Charles Harris d. Jean Borotra–Jacques Brugnon 4-6, 6-4, 6-0, 2-6, 10-8
1940–45	Not held; World War II
1946	Marcel Bernard–Yvon Petra d. Enrique Morea–Francisco "Pancho" Segura 7-5, 6-3, 0-6, 1-6, 10-8
1947	Eustace Fannin–Eric Sturgess d. Tom Brown–Billy Sidwell 6-4, 4-6, 6-4, 6-3
1948	Lennart Bergelin–Jaroslav Drobny d. Harry Hopman–Frank Sedgman 8-6, 6-1, 12-10
1949	Richard "Pancho" Gonzalez–Frank Parker d. Eustace Fannin–Eric Sturgess 6-3, 8-6, 5-7, 6-3
1950	Bill Talbert–Tony Trabert d. Jaroslav Drobny–Eric Sturgess 6-2, 1-6, 10-8, 6-2
1951	Ken McGregor–Frank Sedgman d. Gardnar Mulloy–Dick Savitt 6-2, 2-6, 9-7, 7-5
1952	Ken McGregor–Frank Sedgman d. Gardnar Mulloy–Dick Savitt 6-3, 6-4, 6-4
1953	Lew Hoad–Ken Rosewall d. Mervyn Rose–Clive Wilderspin 6-2, 6-1, 6-1
1954	Vic Seixas–Tony Trabert d. Lew Hoad–Ken Rosewall 6-4, 6-2, 6-1
1955	Vic Seixas–Tony Trabert d. Nicola Pietrangeli–Orlando Sirola 6-1, 4-6, 6-2, 6-4
1956	Don Candy–Robert Perry d. Ashley Cooper–Lew Hoad 7-5, 6-3, 6-3
1957	Mal Anderson–Ashley Cooper d. Don Candy–Mervyn Rose 6-3, 6-0, 6-3
1958	Ashley Cooper–Neale Fraser d. Bob Howe–Abe Segal 3-6, 8-6, 6-3, 7-5
1959	Orlando Sirola–Nicola Pietrangeli d. Roy Emerson–Neale Fraser 6-3, 6-2, 14-12
1960	Roy Emerson–Neale Fraser d. Jose-Luis Arilla–Andres Gimeno 6-2, 8-10, 7-5, 6-4
1961	Roy Emerson–Rod Laver d. Bob Howe–Bob Mark 3-6, 6-1, 6-1, 6-4
1962	Roy Emerson–Neale Fraser d. Wilhelm Bungert–Christian Kuhnke 6-3, 6-4, 7-5
1963	Roy Emerson–Manuel Santana d. Gordon Forbes–Abe Segal 6-2, 6-4, 6-4
1964	Roy Emerson–Ken Fletcher d. John Newcombe–Tony Roche 7-5, 6-3, 3-6, 7-5
1965	Roy Emerson–Fred Stolle d. Ken Fletcher–Bob Hewitt 6-8, 6-3, 8-6, 6-2
1966	Clark Graebner–Dennis Ralston d. Ilie Nastase–Ion Tiriac 6-3, 6-3, 6-0

1967	John Newcombe–Tony Roche d. Roy Emerson–Ken Fletcher 6-3, 9-7, 12-10
1968	Ken Rosewall–Fred Stolle d. Roy Emerson–Rod Laver 6-3, 6-4, 6-3
1969	John Newcombe–Tony Roche d. Roy Emerson–Rod Laver 4-6, 6-1, 3-6, 6-4, 6-4
1970	Ilie Nastase–Ion Tiriac d. Arthur Ashe–Charles Pasarell 6-2, 6-4, 6-3
1971	Arthur Ashe–Marty Riessen d. Tom Gorman–Stan Smith 6-8, 4-6, 6-3, 6-4, 11-9
1972	Bob Hewitt–Frew McMillan d. Patricio Cornejo–Jaime Fillol 6-3, 8-6, 3-6, 6-1
1973	John Newcombe–Tom Okker d. Jimmy Connors–Ilie Nastase 6-1, 3-6, 6-3, 5-7, 6-4
1974	Dick Crealy–Onny Parun d. Stan Smith–Bob Lutz 6-3, 6-2, 3-6, 5-7, 6-1
1975	Brian Gottfried–Raul Ramirez d. John Alexander–Phil Dent 6-2, 2-6, 6-2, 6-4
1976	Fred McNair–Sherwood Stewart d. Brian Gottfried–Raul Ramirez 7-6 (8-6), 6-3, 6-1
1977	Brian Gottfried–Raul Ramirez d. Wojtek Fibak–Jan Kodes 7-6, 4-6, 6-3, 6-4
1978	Gene Mayer–Hank Pfister d. Jose Higueras–Manuel Orantes 6-3, 6-2, 6-2
1979	Gene Mayer–Alex Mayer d. Ross Case–Phil Dent 6-4, 6-4, 6-4
1980	Victor Amaya–Hank Pfister d. Brian Gottfried–Raul Ramirez 1-6, 6-4, 6-4, 6-3
1981	Heinz Gunthardt–Balazs Taroczy d. Terry Moor–Eliot Teltscher 6-2, 7-6, 6-3
1982	Sherwood Stewart–Ferdi Taygan d. Hans Gildemeister–Belus Prajoux 7-5, 6-3, 1-1, (retired)
1983	Anders Jarryd–Hans Simonsson d. Mark Edmondson–Sherwood Stewart 7-6 (7-4), 6-4, 6-2
1984	Henri Leconte–Yannick Noah d. Pavel Slozil–Tomas Smid 6-4, 2-6, 3-6, 6-3, 6-2
1985	Mark Edmondson–Kim Warwick d. Schlomo Glickstein–Hans Simonsson 6-3, 6-4, 6-7, 6-3
1986	John Fitzgerald–Tomas Smid d. Stefan Edberg–Anders Jarryd 6-3, 4-6, 6-3, 6-7 (4-7), 14-12
1987	Anders Jarryd–Robert Seguso d. Guy Forget–Yannick Noah 6-7, 6-7, 6-3, 6-4, 6-2
1988	Andres Gomez–Emilio Sanchez d. John Fitzgerald–Anders Jarryd 6-3, 6-7 (8-10), 6-4, 6-3
1989	Jim Grabb–Patrick McEnroe d. Mansour Bahrami–Eric Winogradsky 6-4, 2-6, 6-4, 7-6 (7-5)
1990	Sergio Casal–Emilio Sanchez d. Goran Ivanisevic–Petr Korda 7-5, 6-3
1991	John Fitzgerald–Anders Jarryd d. Rick Leach–Jim Pugh 6-0, 7-6 (7-2)
1992	Jakob Hlasek–Marc Rosset d. David Adams–Andrei Olhovskiy 7-6 (7-4), 6-7 (3-7), 7-5
1993	Luke Jensen–Murphy Jensen d. Marc Goellner–David Prinosil 6-4, 6-7 (4-7), 6-4
1994	Byron Black–Jonathan Stark d. Jan Apell–Jonas Bjorkman 6-4, 7-6 (7-5)
1995	Jacco Eltingh–Paul Haarhuis d. Nicklas Kulti–Magnus Larsson 6-7 (3-7), 6-4, 6-1
1996	Yevgeny Kafelnikov–Daniel Vacek d. Guy Forget–Jakob Hlasek 6-2, 6-3

WOMEN'S DOUBLES

YEAR	
1925	Suzanne Lenglen–Didi Vlasto d. Evelyn Colyer–Kitty McKane 6-1, 9-11, 6-2
1926	Suzanne Lenglen–Didi Vlasto d. Evelyn Colyer–Kitty McKane Godfree 6-1, 6-1
1927	Irene Bowder Peacock–Esther "Bobbie" Heine d. Peggy Saunders–Phoebe Holcroft Watson 6-2, 6-1

1928	Phoebe Watson–Eileen Bennett d. Suzanne Deve–Sylvia Lafaurie 6-0, 6-2
1929	Lili de Alvarez–Kea Bouman d. Esther "Bobbie" Heine–Alida Neave 7-5, 6-3
1930	Helen Wills Moody–Elizabeth Ryan d. Simone Barbier–Simone Passemard Mathieu 6-3, 6-1
1931	Eileen Bennett Whittingstall–Betty Nuthall d. Cilly Aussem–Elizabeth Ryan 9-7, 6-2
1932	Helen Wills Moody–Elizabeth Ryan d. Betty Nuthall–Eileen Bennett Whittingstall 6-1, 6-3
1933	Simone Passemard Mathieu–Elizabeth Ryan d. Sylvie Jung Henrotin–Colette Rosambert 6-1, 6-3
1934	Simone Passemard Mathieu–Elizabeth Ryan d. Helen Jacobs–Sarah Palfrey 3-6, 6-4, 6-2
1935	Margaret Scriven–Kay Stammers d. Ida Adamoff–Hilde Krahwinkel Sperling 6-4, 6-0
1936	Simone Passemard Mathieu–Adeline "Billie" Yorke d. Susan Noel–Jadwiga Jedrzejowska 2-6, 6-4, 6-4
1937	Simone Passemard Mathieu–Adeline "Billie" Yorke d. Dorothy Andrus–Sylvia Jung Henrotin 3-6, 6-2, 6-2
1938	Simone Passemard Mathieu–Adeline "Billie" Yorke d. Arlette Halff–Nelly Adamson Landry 6-3, 6-3
1939	Simone Passemard Mathieu–Jadwiga Jedrzejowska d. Alice Florian–Hella Kovac 7-5, 7-5
1940–45	Not held; World War II
1946	Louise Brough–Margaret Osborne d. Pauline Betz–Doris Hart 6-4, 0-6, 6-1
1947	Louise Brough–Margaret Osborne d. Doris Hart–Patricia Canning Todd 7-5, 6-2
1948	Doris Hart–Patricia Canning Todd d. Shirley Fry–Mary Arnold Prentiss 6-4, 6-2
1949	Margaret Osborne duPont–Louise Brough d. Joy Gannon–Betty Hilton 7-5, 6-1
1950	Doris Hart–Shirley Fry d. Louise Brough–Margaret Osborne duPont 1-6, 7-5, 6-2
1951	Doris Hart–Shirley Fry d. Beryl Bartlett–Barbara Scofield 10-8, 6-3
1952	Doris Hart–Shirley Fry d. Hazel Redick-Smith–Julie Wipplinger 7-5, 6-1
1953	Doris Hart–Shirley Fry d. Maureen Connolly–Julia Sampson 6-4, 6-3
1954	Maureen Connolly–Nell Hall Hopman d. Maude Galtier–Suzanne Schmitt 7-5, 4-6, 6-0
1955	Beverly Baker Fleitz–Darlene Hard d. Shirley Bloomer–Pat Ward 7-5, 6-8, 13-11
1956	Angela Buxton–Althea Gibson d. Darlene Hard–Dorothy Head Knode 6-8, 8-6, 6-1
1957	Shirley Bloomer–Darlene Hard d. Yola Ramirez–Rosie Reyes 7-5, 4-6, 7-5
1958	Rosie Reyes–Yola Ramirez d. Mary Bevis Hawton–Thelma Coyne Long 6-4, 7-5
1959	Sandra Reynolds–Renee Schuurman d. Yola Ramirez–Rosie Reyes 2-6, 6-0, 6-1
1960	Maria Bueno–Darlene Hard d. Pat Ward Hales–Ann Haydon 6-2, 7-5
1961	Sandra Reynolds–Renee Schuurman d. Maria Bueno–Darlene Hard (walkover)
1962	Sandra Reynolds Price–Renee Schuurman d. Justina Bricka–Margaret Smith 6-4, 6-4
1963	Ann Haydon Jones–Renee Schuurmann d. Robyn Ebbern–Margaret Smith 7-5, 6-4
1964	Margaret Smith–Lesley Turner d. Norma Baylon–Helga Schultze 6-3, 6-1
1965	Margaret Smith–Lesley Turner d. Françoise Durr–Jeanine Lieffrig 6-3, 6-1
1966	Margaret Smith–Judy Tegart d. Jill Blackman–Fay Toyne 4-6, 6-1, 6-1
1967	Françoise Durr–Gail Sherriff d. Annette Van Zyl–Pat Walkden 6-2, 6-2
1968	Françoise Durr–Ann Haydon Jones d. Rosie Casals–Billie Jean Moffitt King 7-5, 4-6, 6-4
1969	Françoise Durr–Ann Haydon Jones d. Margaret Smith–Nancy Richey 6-0, 4-6, 7-5
1970	Gail Sherriff Chanfreau–Françoise Durr d. Rosie Casals–Billie Jean Moffitt King 6-1, 3-6, 6-3
1971	Gail Sherriff Chanfreau–Françoise Durr d. Helen Gourlay–Kerry Harris 6-4, 6-1
1972	Billie Jean Moffitt King–Betty Stove d. Winnie Shaw–Christine Truman 6-1, 6-2
1973	Margaret Smith Court–Virginia Wade d. Françoise Durr–Betty Stove 6-2, 6-3
1974	Chris Evert–Olga Morozova d. Gail Sherriff Chanfreau–Katja Ebbinghaus 6-4, 2-6, 6-1
1975	Chris Evert–Martina Navratilova d. Julie Anthony–Olga Morozova 6-3, 6-2
1976	Fiorella Bonicelli–Gail Sherriff Lovera d. Kathleen Harter–Helga Niessen Masthoff 6-4, 1-6, 6-3
1977	Regina Marsikova–Pam Teeguarden d. Rayni Fox–Helen Gourlay 5-7, 6-4, 6-2
1978	Mima Jausovec–Virginia Ruzici d. Lesley Turner Bowrey–Gail Sherriff Lovera 5-7, 6-4, 8-6
1979	Betty Stove–Wendy Turnbull d. Françoise Durr–Virginia Wade 3-6, 7-5, 6-4
1980	Kathy Jordan–Anne Smith d. Ivanna Madruga–Adriana Villagran 6-1, 6-0
1981	Rosalyn Fairbank–Tayna Harford d. Candy Reynolds–Paula Smith 6-1, 6-3
1982	Martina Navratilova–Anne Smith d. Rosie Casals–Wendy Turnbull 6-3, 6-4
1983	Rosalyn Fairbank–Candy Reynolds d. Kathy Jordan–Anne Smith 5-7, 7-5, 6-2
1984	Martina Navratilova–Pam Shriver d. Claudia Kohde Kilsch–Hana Mandlikova 5-7, 6-3, 6-2
1985	Martina Navratilova–Pam Shriver d. Claudia Kohde Kilsch–Helena Sukova 4-6, 6-2, 6-2
1986	Martina Navratilova–Andrea Temesvari d. Steffi Graf–Gabriela Sabatini 6-1, 6-2
1987	Martina Navratilova–Pam Shriver d. Steffi Graf–Gabriela Sabatini 6-2, 6-1
1988	Martina Navratilova–Pam Shriver d. Claudia Kohde Kilsch–Helena Sukova 6-2, 7-5
1989	Larisa Savchenko–Natalia Zvereva d. Steffi Graf–Gabriela Sabatini 6-4, 6-4
1990	Jana Novotna–Helena Sukova d. Larisa Savchenko–Natalia Zvereva 6-4, 7-5
1991	Beatriz "Gigi" Fernandez–Jana Novotna d. Larisa Savchenko–Natalia Zvereva 6-4, 6-0
1992	Beatriz "Gigi" Fernandez–Natalia Zvereva d. Conchita Martinez–Arantxa Sanchez Vicario 6-3, 6-2
1993	Beatriz "Gigi" Fernandez–Natalia Zvereva d. Larisa Savchenko Neiland–Jana Novotna 6-3, 7-5
1994	Beatriz "Gigi" Fernandez–Natalia Zvereva d. Lindsay Davenport–Lisa Raymond 6-2, 6-2
1995	Beatriz "Gigi" Fernandez–Natalia Zvereva d. Jana Novotna–Arantxa Sanchez Vicario 6-7 (6-8), 6-4, 7-5
1996	Lindsay Davenport–Mary Joe Fernandez d. Beatriz "Gigi" Fernandez–Natalia Zvereva 6-2, 6-1

MIXED DOUBLES

YEAR

1925	Suzanne Lenglen–Jacques Brugnon d. Didi Vlasto–Henri Cochet 6-2, 6-2
1926	Suzanne Lenglen–Jacques Brugnon d. Mme. LeBesnerais–Jean Borotra 6-4, 6-3
1927	Marguerite Broquedis Bordes–Jean Borotra d. Lili de Alvarez–Bill Tilden 6-4, 2-6, 6-2
1928	Eileen Bennett–Henri Cochet d. Helen Wills–Frank Hunter 3-6, 6-3 6-3
1929	Eileen Bennett–Henri Cochet d. Helen Wills–Frank Hunter 6-3, 6-2

1930	Cilly Aussem–Bill Tilden d. Eileen Bennett·Whittingstall–Henri Cochet 6-4, 6-4
1931	Betty Nuthall–Pat Spence d. Dorothy Shepherd Barron–Henry "Bunny" Austin 6-3, 5-7, 6-3
1932	Betty Nuthall–Fred Perry d. Helen Wills Moody–Sidney Wood 6-4, 6-2
1933	Margaret Scriven–Jack Crawford d. Betty Nuthall–Fred Perry 6-2, 6-3
1934	Colette Rosambert–Jean Borotra d. Elizabeth Ryan–Adrian Quist 6-2, 6-4
1935	Lolette Payot–Marcel Bernard d. Sylvie Jung Henrotin–Martin Legeay 4-6, 6-2 6-4
1936	Adeline "Billie" York–Marcel Bernard d. Sylvie Jung Henrotin–Martin Legeay 7-5, 6-8 6-3
1937	Simone Passemard Mathieu–Yvon Petra d. Marie Luise Horn–R. Journu 7-5, 7-5
1938	Simone Passemard Mathieu–Dragutin Mitic d. Nancye Wynne–Christian Boussus 2-6, 6-3, 6-4
1939	Sarah Palfrey Fabyan–Elwood Cooke d. Simone Passemard Mathieu–Franjo Kukuljevic 4-6, 6-1, 7-5
1940–45	Not held; World War II
1946	Pauline Betz–J. Edward "Budge" Patty d. Dorothy Bundy–Tom Brown 7-5, 9-7
1947	Sheila Piercey Summers–Eric Sturgess d. Jadwiga Jedrzejowska–Christian Caralulis 6-0, 6-0
1948	Patricia Canning Todd–Jaroslav Drobny d. Doris Hart–Frank Sedgman 6-3, 3-6, 6-3
1949	Sheila Piercey Summers–Eric Sturgess d. Jean Quertier–Gerry Oakley 6-1, 6-1
1950	Barbara Scofield–Enrique Morea d. Pat Canning Todd–Bill Talbert (walkover)
1951	Doris Hart–Frank Sedgman d. Thelma Coyne Long–Mervyn Rose 7-5, 6-2
1952	Doris Hart–Frank Sedgman d. Shirley Fry–Eric Sturgess 6-8, 6-3, 6-3
1953	Doris Hart–Vic Seixas d. Maureen Connolly–Mervyn Rose 4-6, 6-4, 6-0
1954	Maureen Connolly–Lew Hoad d. J. Patorni–Rex Hartwig 6-4, 6-3
1955	Doris Hart–Gordon Forbes d. Jenny Staley–Luis Ayala 5-7, 6-1, 6-2
1956	Thelma Coyne Long–Luis Ayala d. Doris Hart–Bob Howe 4-6, 6-4, 6-1
1957	Vera Puzejova–Jiri Javorsky d. Edda Buding–Luis Ayala 6-3, 6-4
1958	Shirley Bloomer–Nicola Pietrangeli d. Lorraine Coghlan–Bob Howe 9-7, 6-8, 6-2
1959	Yola Ramirez–Billy Knight d. Renee Schuurman–Rod Laver 6-4, 6-4
1960	Maria Bueno–Bob Howe d. Ann Haydon–Roy Emerson 1-6, 6-1, 6-2
1961	Darlene Hard–Rod Laver d. Vera Puzejova–Jiri Javorsky 6-0, 2-6, 6-3
1962	Renee Schuurman–Bob Howe d. Lesley Turner–Fred Stolle 3-6, 6-4, 6-4
1963	Margaret Smith–Ken Fletcher d. Lesley Turner–Fred Stolle 6-1, 6-2
1964	Margaret Smith–Ken Fletcher d. Lesley Turner–Fred Stolle 6-3, 4-6, 8-6
1965	Margaret Smith–Ken Fletcher d. Maria Bueno–John Newcombe 6-4, 6-4
1966	Annette Van Zyl–Frew McMillan d. Ann Haydon Jones–Clark Graebner 1-6, 6-3, 6-2
1967	Billie Jean Moffitt King–Owen Davidson d. Ann Haydon Jones–Ion Tiriac 6-3, 6-1
1968	Françoise Durr–Jean Claude Barclay d. Billie Jean Moffitt King–Owen Davidson 6-1, 6-4
1969	Margaret Smith Court–Marty Riessen d. Françoise Durr–Jean Claude Barclay 6-3, 6-2
1970	Billie Jean Moffitt King–Bob Hewitt d. Françoise Durr–Jean Claude Barclay 3-6, 6-4, 6-2

1971	Françoise Durr–Jean Claude Barclay d. Winnie Shaw–Tomas Lejus 6-2, 6-4
1972	Evonne Goolagong–Kim Warwick d. Françoise Durr–Jean Claude Barclay 6-2, 6-4
1973	Françoise Durr–Jean Claude Barclay d. Betty Stove–Patrice Dominguez 6-1, 6-4
1974	Martina Navratilova–Ivan Molina d. Rosie Reyes Darmon–Marcelo Lara 6-3, 6-3
1975	Fiorella Bonicelli–Tom Koch d. Pam Teeguarden–Jaime Fillol 6-4, 7-6
1976	Ilana Kloss–Kim Warwick d. Delina Boshoff–Colin Dowdeswell 5-7, 7-6, 6-2
1977	Mary Carillo–John McEnroe d. Florenta Mihai–Ivan Molina 7-6, 6-3
1978	Renata Tomanova–Pavel Slozil d. Virginia Ruzici–Patrice Dominguez 7-6 (retired)
1979	Wendy Turnbull–Bob Hewitt d. Virginia Ruzici–Ion Tiriac 6-3, 2-6, 6-3
1980	Anne Smith–Billy Martin d. Renata Tomanova–Stanislav Birner 2-6, 6-4, 8-6
1981	Andrea Jaeger–Jimmy Arias d. Betty Stove–Fred McNair 7-6, 6-4
1982	Wendy Turnbull–John Lloyd d. Claudia Monteiro–Cassio Motta 6-2, 7-6
1983	Barbara Jordan–Eliot Teltscher d. Lesley Allen–Charles Strode 6-2, 6-3
1984	Anne Smith–Dick Stockton d. Anne Minter–Laurie Warder 6-2, 6-4
1985	Martina Navratilova–Heinz Gunthardt d. Paula Smith–Francisco Gonzalez 2-6, 6-3, 6-2
1986	Kathy Jordan–Ken Flach d. Rosalyn Fairbank–Mark Edmondson 3-6, 7-6 (7-3), 6-3
1987	Pam Shriver–Emilio Sanchez d. Lori McNeil–Sherwood Stewart 6-3, 7-6 (7-4)
1988	Lori McNeil–Jorge Lozano d. Brenda Schultz–Michiel Schapers 7-5, 6-2
1989	Manon Bollegraf–Tom Nijssen d. Arantxa Sanchez Vicario–Horacio de la Pena 6-3, 6-7 (3-7), 6-2
1990	Arantxa Sanchez Vicario–Jorge Lozano d. Nicole Provis–Danie Visser 7-6 (7-5), 7-6 (10-8)
1991	Helena Sukova–Cyril Suk d. Caroline Vis–Paul Haarhuis 3-6, 6-4, 6-1
1992	Arantxa Sanchez Vicario–Mark Woodforde d. Lori McNeil–Bryan Shelton 6-2, 6-3
1993	Eugenia Maniokova–Andrei Olhovskiy d. Elna Reinach–Danie Visser 6-2, 4-6, 6-4
1994	Kristie Boogert–Menno Oosting d. Larisa Savchenko Neiland–Andrei Olhovskiy 7-5, 3-6, 7-5
1995	Larisa Savchenko Neiland–Mark Woodforde d. Jill Hetherington–John-Laffnie de Jager 7-6 (10-8), 7-6 (7-4)
1996	Patricia Tarabini–Javier Frana d. Nicole Arendt–Luke Jensen 6-2, 6-2

ALL-TIME FRENCH CHAMPIONSHIP RECORDS

(Only since 1925, when championships were opened to non-French.)

Most men's singles: 6—Bjorn Borg, 1974–75, 1978–81

Most men's doubles: 6—Roy Emerson, 1960–65

Most men's mixed: 3—Ken Fletcher, 1963–65

Most men's altogether: 9—Henri Cochet, 1926–32 (4 singles, 3 doubles, 2 mixed)

Most women's singles: 7—Chris Evert, 1974–75, 1979–80, 1983, 1985–86

Most women's doubles: 7—Martina Navratilova, 1975, 1982, 1984–88

Most women's mixed: 4—Margaret Smith Court, 1963–65, 1969

Most women's altogether: 13—Court, 1962–66, 1969–70, 1973 (5 singles, 4 doubles, 4 mixed)

Most men's doubles, team: 3—Cochet and Jacques Brugnon, 1927, 1930, 1932

Most women's doubles, team: 4—Doris Hart and Shirley Fry, 1950–53; Martina Navratilova and Pam Shriver, 1984–85, 1987–88; Beatriz "Gigi" Fernandez and Natalia Zvereva, 1992–95

Most mixed doubles, team: 3—Françoise Durr and Jean Claude Barclay, 1968, 1971, 1973; Court and Fletcher, 1963–65

YOUNGEST CHAMPIONS

Men's singles: Michael Chang, 1989, 17 years, 4 months

Men's doubles: Lew Hoad–Ken Rosewall, 1953, 18 years, 7 months (Lew Hoad 19 days younger)

Men's mixed: Jimmy Arias, 1981, 16 years, 8 months

Women's singles: Monica Seles, 1990, 16 years 6 months

Women's doubles: Natalia Zvereva, 1989, 18 years, 2 months

Women's mixed: Andrea Jaeger, 1981, 15 years, 11 months

OLDEST CHAMPIONS

Men's singles: Andres Gimeno, 1972, 34 years, 10 months

Men's doubles: Jacques Brugnon, 1934, 39 years

Men's mixed: Bob Hewitt, 1979, 39 years, 5 months

Women's singles: Suzi Kormoczi, 1958, 33 years, 9 months

Women's doubles: Elizabeth Ryan, 1934, 42 years, 3 months

Women's mixed: Thelma Coyne Long, 1956, 38 years

INDIVIDUAL CAREER SINGLES RECORDS

MEN

Tournaments played: 20—François Jauffret, 1961–80; Ben Berthet, 1929–55; Antoine Gentien, 1929–53

Matches played: 75—Guillermo Vilas, 1972–89

Matches won: 58—Guillermo Vilas

Matches won consecutively: 28—Bjorn Borg, 1978–81

Match winning percentage: .961—Bjorn Borg (49-2), 1973–1976, 1978–81

WOMEN

Tournaments played: 19—Andree Varin, 1932–64; Anne-Marie Simon Seghers, 1937–66

Matches played: 82—Steffi Graf, 1983–96

Matches won: 73—Steffi Graf

Matches won consecutively: 29—Chris Evert, 1974–75, 1979, 1980 through quarters, 1981, lost semis to Hana Mandlikova

Match winning percentage: 1.000—Helen Wills Moody (20-0), 1928–30, 1932; .938, Monica Seles (30-2), 1989–92, 1996

LONGEST MATCHES (TOTAL GAMES)

Men's singles: 76 games—Eric Sturgess d. Ken McGregor, 10-8, 7-9, 8-6, 5-7, 9-7, semis, 1951

Men's doubles: 81 games—Gordon Forbes–Russell Seymour d. Merv Rose–George Worthington, 11-13, 6-1, 7-5, 4-6, 15-13, 2nd rd., 1952

Women's singles: 56 games—Kerry Melville (Reid) d. Pam Teeguarden, 9-7, 4-6, 16-14, 3rd rd., 1972

Women's doubles: 50 games—Beverly Baker Fleitz–Darlene Hard d. Shirley Bloomer (Brasher)–Pat Ward (Hale), 7-5, 6-8, 13-11, final, 1955

Mixed doubles: 48 games—Rosie Reyes Darmon–Bob Howe d. Marina Tshuvirina–Teimuraz Kakulia, 5-7, 10-8, 10-8, 1st rd., 1972. 48 games, Lucia Bassi–Francisco Contreras d. Edda Buding–Ingo Buding, 10-12, 9-7, 6-4, 2nd rd., 1960

LONGEST MATCH (PLAYING TIME)

Men's singles: 5 hours, 2 minutes—Ronald Agenor d. David Prinosil, 6-7 (4-7), 6-7 (2-7), 6-3, 6-4, 14-12, 2nd rd., 1994

Women's singles: 4 hours, 7 minutes—Virginia Buisson d. Noelle van Lottum, 6-7 (3-7), 7-5, 6-2, 1st rd., 1996

LONGEST TIE-BREAKERS

Men's singles: 12-10, second set—Bohdan Ulihrach d. Andrei Medvedev, 6-3, 6-7 (10-12), 6-1, 6-4, 2nd rd., 1996

Women's singles: 12-10, 2nd set—Gabriela Sabatini d. Jana Novotna, 5-7, 7-6 (12-10), 6-0, Quarters, 1991

BIGGEST UPSETS

Men: 15th seed Michael Chang d. first-seeded Ivan Lendl (3-time champ on a 28-match streak), 4-6, 4-6, 6-3, 6-3, 6-3, 4th rd., 1989; Christophe Roger-Vasselin (No. 230, wild card) d. first-seeded Jimmy Connors, 6-4, 6-4, 7-6 (7-5), quarters, 1983; Stephane Huet (No. 297), qualifier, first tour match) d. seventh-seeded Lendl, 3-6, 7-5, 6-0, 7-6 (7-2), 1st rd., 1993.

Women: Kathy Horvath (No. 33) d. first-seeded Martina Navratilova, 6-4, 0-6, 6-3 (only loss of year for defending champ, ending 39-match streak), quarters, 1983; Arantxa Sanchez Vicario (No. 22) d. third-seeded Chris Evert (7-time champ, last of 78 matches, 6 losses in Paris), 6-3, 7-6 (7-4), 3rd rd., 1988.

BEST COMEBACKS

Men: Ivan Lendl d. John McEnroe, 3-6, 2-6, 6-4, 7-5, 7-5, final, 1984. From breaks down, 1-2 and 2-3, fourth. Held serve to 4-3 from 15-40, fourth, ended 42-match McEnroe streak. Robert Haillet d. Budge Patty, 5-7, 7-5, 10-8, 4-6, 7-5, 4th rd., 1958. From 5-0, 40-0 down, fifth, saved a 4th match point at 5-4. René Lacoste d. Bill Tilden, 6-4, 4-6, 5-7, 6-3, 11-9, final, 1927. Saved 2 match points, Tilden serving at 9-8, 40-15.

Women: Chanda Rubin d. Jana Novotna, 7-6 (10-8), 4-6, 8-6, 3rd rd., 1995. From 0-5, 0-40, third. Saved 9 match points: 5 to 1-5, 1 to 5-2, 3 to 5-5. Saved 2 set points, tie-breaker. Mary Joe Fernandez d. Gabriela Sabatini, 1-6, 7-6 (7-4), 10-8, quarters, 1993. From 5-1, 40-30 down, match point, second. Saved 3 more match points at 5-3.

ITALIAN CHAMPIONSHIPS

Welcoming non-citizens for the first time in 1930, the Italian Championships became an important international stopover, soon ranking behind the French in Europe. The tournament, always on clay, began in Milan, then shifted in 1935 to its permanent site in Rome, the handsome marble Foro Italico (originally named Foro Mussolini, honoring the country's dictator). As punishment for Italy's role as an Axis member during World War II, the ITF barred the Italian from resuming international status until 1950.

For seven years the women's tournament lost stature, banished from Rome to be played at smaller venues, in Perugia (1980–84), Taranto (1985), abandoned altogether in 1986. It made a comeback to Rome in 1987, the women's tournament occupying the first week, the men's the second, as the event enlarged to a fortnight.

The tournament became open to pros and amateurs alike in 1969. The tie-breaker was adopted in 1971. One peculiar trans-Atlantic match was played in 1976 when the men's doubles final, rained out in Rome, took place later in the year at Houston.

MEN'S SINGLES

YEAR	
1930	Bill Tilden d. Umberto de Morpurgo 6-1, 6-1, 6-2
1931	Pat Hughes d. Henri Cochet 6-4, 6-3, 6-2
1932	Andre Merlin d. Pat Hughes 6-1, 5-7, 6-0, 8-6
1933	Emanuele Sertorio d. Martin Legeay 6-3, 6-1, 6-3
1934	Giovanni Palmieri d. Giorgio de Stefani 6-3, 6-0, 7-5
1935	Wilmer Hines d. Giovanni Palmieri 6-3, 10-8, 9-7
1936–49	Not held
1950	Jaroslav Drobny d. Bill Talbert 6-4, 6-3, 7-9, 6-2
1951	Jaroslav Drobny d. Gianni Cucelli 6-3, 10-8, 6-0
1952	Frank Sedgman d. Jaroslav Drobny 7-5, 6-3, 1-6, 6-4
1953	Jaroslav Drobny d. Lew Hoad 6-2, 6-1, 6-2
1954	J. Edward "Budge" Patty d. Enrique Morea 11-9, 6-4, 6-4
1955	Fausto Gardini d. Giuseppe Marlo 6-1, 1-6, 3-6, 6-6, (retired)
1956	Lew Hoad d. Sven Davidson 7-5, 6-2, 6-0
1957	Nicola Pietrangeli d. Giuseppe Merlo 8-6, 6-2, 6-4
1958	Mervyn Rose d. Nicola Pietrangeli 5-7, 8-6, 6-4, 1-6, 6-2
1959	Luis Ayala d. Neale Fraser 6-3, 3-6, 6-3, 6-3
1960	Barry MacKay d. Luis Ayala 7-5, 7-5, 0-6, 0-6, 6-1
1961	Nicola Pietrangeli d. Rod Laver 6-8, 6-1, 6-1, 6-2
1962	Rod Laver d. Roy Emerson 6-2, 1-6, 3-6, 6-3, 6-1
1963	Marty Mulligan d. Boro Jovanovic 6-2, 4-6, 6-3, 8-6
1964	Jan-Erik Lundquist d. Fred Stolle 1-6, 7-5, 6-3, 6-1
1965	Marty Mulligan d. Manuel Santana 1-6, 6-4, 6-3, 6-1
1966	Tony Roche d. Nicola Pietrangeli 11-9, 6-1, 6-3
1967	Marty Mulligan d. Tony Roche 6-3, 0-6, 6-4, 6-1
1968	Tom Okker d. Bob Hewitt 10-8, 6-8, 6-1, 1-6, 6-0
1969	John Newcombe d. Tony Roche 6-3, 4-6, 6-2, 5-7, 6-3
1970	Ilie Nastase d. Jan Kodes 6-3, 1-6, 6-3, 8-6
1971	Rod Laver d. Jan Kodes 7-5, 6-3, 6-3
1972	Manuel Orantes d. Jan Kodes 4-6, 6-1, 7-5, 6-2
1973	Ilie Nastase d. Manuel Orantes 6-1, 6-1, 6-1
1974	Bjorn Borg d. Ilie Nastase 6-3, 6-4, 6-2
1975	Raul Ramirez d. Manuel Orantes 7-6, 7-5, 7-5
1976	Adriano Panatta d. Guillermo Vilas 2-6, 7-6 (7-5), 6-2, 7-6 (7-1)
1977	Vitas Gerulaitis d. Antonio Zugarelli 6-2, 7-6 (7-2), 3-6, 7-6 (7-1)
1978	Bjorn Borg d. Adriano Panatta 1-6, 6-3, 6-1, 4-6, 6-3
1979	Vitas Gerulaitis d. Guillermo Vilas 6-7 (4-7), 7-6 (7-0), 6-7 (5-7), 6-4, 6-2
1980	Guillermo Vilas d. Yannick Noah 6-0, 6-4, 6-4
1981	Jose Luis Clerc d. Victor Pecci 6-3, 6-4, 6-0
1982	Andres Gomez d. Eliot Teltscher 6-2, 6-3, 6-2
1983	Jimmy Arias d. Jose Higueras 6-2, 6-7 (3-7), 6-1, 6-4
1984	Andres Gomez d. Aaron Krickstein 2-6, 6-1, 6-2, 6-2
1985	Yannick Noah d. Miloslav Mecir 6-3, 3-6, 6-2, 7-6 (7-4)
1986	Ivan Lendl d. Emilio Sanchez 7-5, 4-6, 6-1, 6-1
1987	Mats Wilander d. Martin Jaite 6-3, 6-4, 6-4
1988	Ivan Lendl d. Guillermo Perez-Roldan 2-6, 6-4, 6-2, 4-6, 6-4
1989	Alberto Mancini d. Andre Agassi 6-3, 4-6, 2-6, 7-6 (7-2), 6-1
1990	Thomas Muster d. Andrei Chesnokov 6-1, 6-3, 6-1
1991	Emilio Sanchez d. Alberto Mancini 6-3, 6-1, 3-0, (retired)
1992	Jim Courier d. Carlos Costa 7-6 (7-3), 6-0, 6-4
1993	Jim Courier d. Goran Ivanisevic 6-1, 6-2, 6-2
1994	Pete Sampras d. Boris Becker 6-1, 6-2, 6-2
1995	Thomas Muster d. Sergi Bruguera 3-6, 7-6 (7-5), 6-2, 6-3
1996	Thomas Muster d. Richard Krajicek 6-2, 6-4, 3-6, 6-3

WOMEN'S SINGLES

YEAR	
1930	Lili de Alvarez d. Lucia Valerio 3-6, 8-6, 6-0
1931	Lucia Valerio d. Dorothy Andrus 2-6, 6-2, 6-2
1932	Ida Adamoff d. Lucia Valerio 6-4, 7-5
1933	Elizabeth Ryan d. Ida Adamoff 6-1, 6-1
1934	Helen Jacobs d. Lucia Valerio 6-3, 6-0
1935	Hilde Krahwinkel Sperling d. Lucia Valerio 6-4, 6-1
1936–49	Not held
1950	Annelies Ullstein Bossi d. Joan Curry 6-4, 6-4
1951	Doris Hart d. Shirley Fry 6-3, 8-6
1952	Susan Partridge d. Betty Harrison 6-3, 7-5
1953	Doris Hart d. Maureen Connolly 4-6, 9-7, 6-3
1954	Maureen Connolly d. Pat Ward 6-3, 6-0
1955	Pat Ward d. Erika Vollmer 6-4, 6-3
1956	Althea Gibson d. Suzi Kormoczi 6-3, 7-5
1957	Shirley Bloomer d. Dorothy Head Knode 1-6, 9-7, 6-2
1958	Maria Bueno d. Lorraine Coghlan 3-6, 6-3, 6-3
1959	Christine Truman d. Sandra Reynolds 6-0, 6-1
1960	Suzi Kormoczi d. Ann Haydon 6-4, 4-6, 6-1
1961	Maria Bueno d. Lesley Turner 6-4, 6-4
1962	Margaret Smith d. Maria Bueno 8-6, 5-7, 6-4
1963	Margaret Smith d. Lesley Turner 6-3, 6-4
1964	Margaret Smith d. Lesley Turner 6-1, 6-1
1965	Maria Bueno d. Nancy Richey 6-1, 1-6, 6-3
1966	Ann Haydon Jones d. Annette van Zyl 8-6, 6-1
1967	Lesley Turner d. Maria Bueno 6-3, 6-3
1968	Lesley Turner Bowrey d. Margaret Smith Court 2-6, 6-2, 6-3
1969	Julie Heldman d. Kerry Melville 7-5, 6-4
1970	Billie Jean Moffitt King d. Julie Heldman 6-1, 6-3
1971	Virginia Wade d. Helga Niessen Masthoff 6-4, 6-4
1972	Linda Tuero d. Olga Morozova 6-4, 6-3
1973	Evonne Goolagong d. Chris Evert 7-6 (8-6), 6-0
1974	Chris Evert d. Martina Navratilova 6-3, 6-3
1975	Chris Evert d. Martina Navratilova 6-1, 6-0
1976	Mima Jausovec d. Lesley Hunt 6-1, 6-3
1977	Janet Newberry d. Renata Tomanova 6-3, 7-6 (7-5)
1978	Regina Marsikova d. Virginia Ruzici 7-5, 7-5
1979	Tracy Austin d. Sylvia Hanika 6-4, 1-6, 6-3
1980	Chris Evert Lloyd d. Virginia Ruzici 5-7, 6-2, 6-2
1981	Chris Evert Lloyd d. Virginia Ruzici 6-1, 6-2
1982	Chris Evert Lloyd d. Hana Mandlikova 6-0, 6-3
1983	Andrea Temesvari d. Bonnie Gadusek 6-1, 6-0
1984	Manuela Maleeva d. Chris Evert Lloyd 6-3, 6-3
1985	Raffaela Reggi d. Vicki Nelson 6-4, 6-4
1986	Not held
1987	Steffi Graf d. Gabriela Sabatini 7-5, 4-6, 6-0
1988	Gabriela Sabatini d. Helen Kelesi 6-1, 6-7 (4-7), 6-1
1989	Gabriela Sabatini d. Arantxa Sanchez 6-2, 5-7, 6-4
1990	Monica Seles d. Martina Navratilova 6-1, 6-1
1991	Gabriela Sabatini d. Monica Seles 6-3, 6-2
1992	Gabriela Sabatini d. Monica Seles 7-5, 6-4

1993	Conchita Martinez d. Gabriela Sabatini 7-5, 6-1
1994	Conchita Martinez d. Martina Navratilova 7-6 (7-5), 6-4
1995	Conchita Martinez d. Arantxa Sanchez Vicario 6-3, 6-1
1996	Conchita Martinez d. Martina Hingis 6-2, 6-3

MEN'S DOUBLES

YEAR

1930	Wilbur Coen–Bill Tilden d. Umberto de Morpurgo–Placido Gaslini 6-0, 6-3
1931	Alberto DelBono–Pat Hughes d. Henri Cochet–Andre Merlin 3-6, 8-6, 4-6, 6-4, 6-3
1932	Pat Hughes–Giorgio de Stefani d. J. Bonte–Andre Merlin 6-2, 6-2, 6-4
1933	Jean Lesuer–Martin Legeay d. Giovanni Palmieri–Emanuele Sertorio 6-2, 6-4, 6-2
1934	Giovanni Palmieri–George Lyttleton Rogers d. Pat Hughes–Giorgio de Stefani 3-6, 6-4, 9-7, 0-6, 6-2
1935	Jack Crawford–Viv McGrath d. Jean Borotra–Jacques Brugnon 4-6, 4-6, 6-4, 6-2, 6-2
1936–49	Not held
1950	Bill Talbert–Tony Trabert d. J. Edward "Budge" Patty–Billy Sidwell 6-3, 6-1, 4-6, 5-5 (ret.)
1951	Jaroslav Drobny–Dick Savitt d. Gianni Cucelli–Marcello Del Bello 6-2, 7-9, 6-3, 6-3
1952	Jaroslav Drobny–Frank Sedgman d. Gianni Cucelli–Marcello Del Bello 3-6, 7-5, 3-6, 6-3, 6-2
1953	Lew Hoad–Ken Rosewall d. Jaroslav Drobny–J. Edward "Budge" Patty 6-2, 6-4, 6-2
1954	Jaroslav Drobny–Enrique Morea d. Vic Seixas–Tony Trabert 6-4, 0-6, 3-6, 6-3, 6-4
1955	Art Larsen–Enrique Morea d. Nicola Pietrangeli–Orlando Sirola 6-1, 6-4, 4-6, 7-5
1956	Jaroslav Drobny–Lew Hoad d. Nicola Pietrangeli–Orlando Sirola 11-9, 6-2, 6-3
1957	Neale Fraser–Lew Hoad d. Nicola Pietrangeli–Orlando Sirola 6-1, 6-8, 6-0, 6-2
1958	Anton Jancso–Kurt Nielsen d. Luis Ayala–Don Candy 8-10, 6-3, 6-2, 1-6, 9-7
1959	Roy Emerson–Neale Fraser d. Nicola Pietrangeli–Orlando Sirola 8-6, 6-4, 6-4
1960	Nicola Pietrangeli–Orlando Sirola vs. Roy Emerson–Neale Fraser 3-6, 7-5, 7-5, 2-6, 11-11 (darkness, shared title)
1961	Roy Emerson–Neale Fraser d. Nicola Pietrangeli–Orlando Sirola 6-2, 6-4, 11-9
1962	Neale Fraser–Rod Laver d. Ken Fletcher–John Newcombe 11-9, 6-2, 6-4
1963	Bob Hewitt–Fred Stolle d. Nicola Pietrangeli–Orlando Sirola 6-3, 6-3, 6-1
1964	Bob Hewitt–Fred Stolle d. Tony Roche–John Newcombe 7-5, 6-2, 2-6, 8-6
1965	Tony Roche–John Newcombe vs. Ronnie Barnes–Tom Koch 1-6, 6-4, 2-6, 12-10 (shared title)
1966	Roy Emerson–Fred Stolle d. Nicola Pietrangeli–Cliff Drysdale 6-4, 12-10, 6-3
1967	Bob Hewitt–Frew McMillan d. Bill Bowrey–Owen Davidson 6-3, 2-6, 6-3, 9-7
1968	Tom Okker–Marty Riessen d. Allan Stone–Nicky Kalogeropoulos 6-3, 6-4, 6-2
1969	Tony Roche–John Newcombe vs. Tom Okker–Marty Riessen 6-4, 1-6, (suspended, unfinished)
1970	Ilie Nastase–Ion Tiriac d. Bill Bowrey–Owen Davidson 0-6, 10-8, 6-3, 6-8, 6-1
1971	Tony Roche–John Newcombe d. Andres Gimeno–Roger Taylor, 6-4, 6-4
1972	Ilie Nastase–Ion Tiriac d. Lew Hoad–Frew McMillan 3-6, 3-6, 6-4, 6-3, 5-3, retired

1973	John Newcombe–Tom Okker d. Ross Case–Geoff Masters 6-3, 6-2, 6-4
1974	Brian Gottfried–Raul Ramirez d. Juan Gisbert–Ilie Nastase 6-3, 6-2, 6-3
1975	Brian Gottfried–Raul Ramirez d. Jimmy Connors–Ilie Nastase 6-4, 7-6, 2-6, 6-1
1976	Brian Gottfried–Raul Ramirez d. Geoff Masters–John Newcombe, 7-6, 5-7, 6-3, 3-6, 6-3
1977	Brian Gottfried–Raul Ramirez d. Fred McNair–Sherwood Stewart 7-6 (7-2), 6-7 (6-8), 7-5
1978	Victor Pecci–Belus Prajoux d. Jan Kodes–Tomas Smid 6-7, 7-6, 6-1
1979	Peter Fleming–Tomas Smid d. Jose-Luis Clerc–Ilie Nastase 4-6, 6-1, 7-5
1980	Mark Edmondson–Kim Warwick d. Balazs Taroczy–Eliot Teltscher 7-6, 7-6
1981	Hans Gildemeister–Andres Gomez d. Bruce Manson–Tomas Smid 7-5, 6-2
1982	Heinz Gunthardt–Balazs Taroczy d. Wojtek Fibak–John Fitzgerald 6-4, 4-6, 6-3
1983	Francisco Gonzalez–Victor Pecci d. Jan Gunnarsson–Mike Leach 6-2, 6-7 (5-7), 6-4
1984	Ken Flach–Robert Seguso d. John Alexander–Mike Leach 3-6, 6-3, 6-4
1985	Anders Jarryd–Mats Wilander d. Ken Flach–Robert Seguso 4-6, 6-3, 6-2
1986	Guy Forget–Yannick Noah d. Mark Edmondson–Sherwood Stewart 7-6 (7-5), 6-2
1987	Guy Forget–Yannick Noah d. Miloslav Mecir–Tomas Smid 6-2, 6-7 (2-7), 6-3
1988	Jorge Lozano–Todd Witsken d. Anders Jarryd–Tomas Smid 6-3, 6-3
1989	Jim Courier–Pete Sampras d. Danilo Marcelino–Mauro Menezes 6-4, 6-3
1990	Sergio Casal–Emilio Sanchez d. Jim Courier–Marty Davis 7-6 (7-2), 7-5
1991	Omar Camporese–Goran Ivanisevic d. Luke Jensen–Laurie Warder 6-2, 6-3
1992	Jakob Hlasek–Marc Rosset d. Wayne Ferreira–Mark Kratzmann 6-4, 3-6, 6-1
1993	Jacco Eltingh–Paul Haarhuis d. Wayne Ferreira–Mark Kratzmann 6-4, 7-6
1994	Yevgeny Kafelnikov–David Rikl d. Wayne Ferreira–Javier Sanchez 6-1, 7-5
1995	Cyril Suk–Daniel Vacek d. Jan Apell–Jonas Bjorkman 6-3, 6-4
1996	Byron Black–Grant Connell d. Libor Pimek–Byron Talbot 6-2, 6-3

WOMEN'S DOUBLES

YEAR

1930	Lili de Alvarez–Lucia Valerio d. Claude Anet–M. Neufeld 7-5, 5-7, 8-6
1931	Anna Luzzatti–Rosetta Gagliardi Prouse d. Dorothy Andrus Burke–Lucia Valerio 6-3, 1-6, 6-3
1932	Colette Rosambert–Lolette Payot d. Dorothy Andrus Burke–Lucia Valerio 7-5, 6-3
1933	Ida Adamoff–Dorothy Andrus Burke d. Elizabeth Ryan–Lucia Valerio 6-2, 1-6, 6-4
1934	Helen Jacobs–Elizabeth Ryan d. Ida Adamoff–Dorothy Andrus Burke 7-5, 9-7
1935	Evelyn Dearman–Nan Lyle d. Cilly Aussem–Elizabeth Ryan 6-2, 6-4
1936–49	Not held
1950	Jean Quertier–Jean Walker-Smith d. Betty Hilton–Kay Tuckey 1-6, 6-3, 6-2
1951	Shirley Fry–Doris Hart d. Louise Brough–Thelma Coyne Long 6-1, 7-5

1952   Nell Hall Hopman–Thelma Coyne Long d. Nicla Migliori–V. Tonilli 6-2, 6-8, 6-1

1953   Maureen Connolly–Julia Sampson d. Shirley Fry–Doris Hart 6-8, 6-4, 6-4

1954   Pat Ward–Elaine Watson d. Nelly Adamson–Ginette Bucaille 3-6, 6-3, 6-4

1955   Christiane Mercellis–Pat Ward d. Fay Muller–Beryl Penrose 6-4, 10-8

1956   Mary Bevis Hawton–Thelma Coyne Long d. Angela Buxton–Darlene Hard 6-4, 6-8, 9-7

1957   Mary Bevis Hawton–Thelma Coyne Long d. Yola Ramirez–Rosie Reyes 6-1, 6-1

1958   Shirley Bloomer–Christine Truman d. Mary Bevis Hawton–Thelma Coyne Long 6-3, 6-2

1959   Yola Ramirez–Rosie Reyes d. Maria Bueno–Janet Hopps 4-6, 6-4, 6-4

1960   Margaret Hellyer–Yola Ramirez d. Shirley Bloomer Brasher–Ann Haydon 6-4, 6-4

1961   Jan Lehane–Lesley Turner d. Mary Carter Reitano–Margaret Smith 2-6, 6-1, 6-1

1962   Maria Bueno–Darlene Hard d. Silvana Lazzarino–Lea Pericoli 6-4, 6-4

1963   Robyn Ebbern–Margaret Smith d. Silvana Lazzarino–Lea Pericoli 6-2, 6-3

1964   Lesley Turner–Margaret Smith d. Silvana Lazzarino–Lea Pericoli 6-1, 6-2

1965   Madonna Schacht–Annette van Zyl d. Silvana Lazzarino–Lea Pericoli 2-6, 6-2, 12-10

1966   Norma Baylon–Annette van Zyl d. Ann Haydon Jones–Liz Starkie 6-3, 1-6, 6-2

1967   Rosie Casals–Lesley Turner d. Silvana Lazzarino–Lea Pericoli 7-5, 7-5

1968   Margaret Smith Court–Virginia Wade d. Annette van Zyl–Pat Walkden 6-2, 7-5

1969   Françoise Durr–Ann Haydon Jones d. Rosie Casals–Billie Jean Moffitt King 6-3, 3-6, 6-2

1970   Rosie Casals–Billie Jean Moffitt King d. Françoise Durr–Virginia Wade 6-2, 3-6, 9-7

1971   Helga Niessen Masthoff–Virginia Wade d. Lesley Turner–Helen Gourlay 5-7, 6-2, 6-2

1972   Lesley Hunt–Olga Morozova d. Gail Sherriff Chanfreau–Rosalba Vido 6-3, 6-4

1973   Olga Morozova–Virginia Wade d. Martina Navratilova–Renata Tomanova 3-6, 6-2, 7-5

1974   Chris Evert–Olga Morozova d. Helga Niessen Masthoff–Heidi Orth (walkover)

1975   Chris Evert–Martina Navratilova d. Sue Barker–Glynis Coles 6-1, 6-2

1976   Delina Boshoff–Ilana Kloss d. Mariana Simionescu–Virginia Ruzici 6-1, 6-2

1977   Brigitte Cuypers–Marise Kruger d. Bunny Bruning–Sharon Walsh 3-6, 7-5, 6-2

1978   Mima Jausovec–Virginia Ruzici d. Florenta Mihai–Betsy Nagelsen 6-2, 2-6, 7-5

1979   Betty Stove–Wendy Turnbull d. Evonne Goolagong–Kerry Melville Reid 6-3, 6-4

1980   Hana Mandlikova–Renata Tomanova d. Ivanna Madruga–Adriana Villigran 6-4, 6-4

1981   Candy Reynolds–Paula Smith d. Chris Evert Lloyd–Virginia Ruzici 7-5, 6-1

1982   Kathy Horvath–Yvonne Vermaak d. Billie Jean Moffitt King–Ilana Kloss 2-6, 6-4, 7-6

1983   Virginia Ruzici–Virginia Wade d. Ivanna Madruga Osses–Catherine Tanvier 6-3, 2-6, 6-1

1984   Iva Budarova–Marcela Skuherska d. Kathy Horvath–Virginia Ruzici 7-6, 1-6, 6-4

1985   Sandra Cecchini–Raffaela Reggi d. Patricia Murgo–Barbara Romano 1-6, 6-4, 6-3

1986   Not held

1987   Martina Navratilova–Gabriela Sabatini d. Claudia Kohde Kilsch–Helena Sukova 6-4, 6-1

1988   Jana Novotna–Catherine Suire d. Jenny Byrne–Janine Thompson 6-3, 4-6, 7-5

1989   Liz Sayers Smylie–Janine Thompson d. Manon Bollegraf–Mercedes Paz 6-4, 6-3

1990   Helen Kelesi–Monica Seles d. Laura Garrone–Laura Golarsa 6-3, 6-4

1991   Jennifer Capriati–Monica Seles d. Nicole Provis–Elna Reinach 7-5, 6-2

1992   Monica Seles–Helena Sukova d. Katerina Maleeva–Barbara Rittner 6-1, 6-2

1993   Jana Novotna–Arantxa Sanchez Vicario d. Mary Joe Fernandez–Zina Garrison Jackson 6-4, 6-2

1994   Beatriz "Gigi" Fernandez–Natalia Zvereva d. Gabriela Sabatini–Brenda Schultz-McCarthy 6-1, 6-3

1995   Beatriz "Gigi" Fernandez–Natalia Zvereva d. Conchita Martinez–Patricia Tarabini 3-6, 7-6 (7-3), 6-4

1996   Arantxa Sanchez Vicario–Irina Spirlea d. Beatriz "Gigi" Fernandez–Martina Hingis 6-4, 3-6, 6-3

MIXED DOUBLES

YEAR

1930   Lili de Alvarez–Umberto Morpurgo d. Lucia Valerio–Pat Hughes 4-6, 6-4, 6-2

1931   Lucia Valerio–Pat Hughes d. Dorothy Andrus Burke–Alberto Del Bono 6-0, 6-1

1932   Lolette Payot–J. Bonte d. Dorothy Andrus Burke–Alberto Del Bono 6-1, 6-2

1933   Dorothy Andrus Burke–Martin Legeay d. Y. Orlandini–E. Gabrowitz 6-4, 6-3

1934   Elizabeth Ryan–Henry Culley d. Rollin Couquerque–Franjo Puncec 6-1, 6-3

1935   Jadwiga Jedrzejowska–Harry Hopman d. Evelyn Dearman–Pat Hughes 6-3, 1-6, 6-3

1936–49 Not held

1950   Gertrude "Gussy" Moran–Adrian Quist divided title with Annelies Ullstein Bossi–Gianni Cucelli 6-3, 1-1 unfinished

1951   Shirley Fry–Felicisimo Ampon d. Doris Hart–Lennart Bergelin 8-6, 3-6, 6-4

1952   Arvilla McGuire–Kurt Nielsen d. M.J. de Riba–E. Migone 4-6, 6-3, 6-3

1953   Doris Hart–Vic Seixas d. Maureen Connolly–Mervyn Rose 6-4, 6-4

1954   Maureen Connolly–Vic Seixas divided title with Barbara Kimbrell–Tony Trabert 3-6, 11-9, 3-3 unfinished

1955   Pat Ward–Enrique Morea divided title with Beryl Penrose–Mervyn Rose not played

1956   Thelma Coyne Long–Luis Ayala d. Shirley Bloomer–Giorgio Facchini 6-4, 6-3

1957   Thelma Coyne Long–Luis Ayala d. Shirley Bloomer–Bob Howe 6-1, 6-1

1958   Shirley Bloomer–Giorgio Facchini d. Thelma Coyne Long–Luis Ayala 4-6, 6-2, 9-7

1959   Rosie Reyes–Francisco "Pancho" Contreras d. Yola Ramirez–Billy Knight 9-7, 6-1

1960   Not held

1961   Margaret Smith–Roy Emerson d. Jan Lehane–Bob Hewitt 6-1, 6-1

1962   Lesley Turner–Fred Stolle d. Madonna Schacht–Sven Davidson 6-4, 6-1

1963   Not held

1964   Margaret Smith–John Newcombe d. Maria Bueno–Tom Koch 3-6, 7-5, 6-2

1965   Carmen Coronado–Edison Mandarino d. Elena Subirats–Vicente Zarazua 6-1, 6-1

1966   Not held

1967   Lesley Turner–Bill Bowrey d. Françoise Durr–Frew McMillan 6-2, 7-5

1968*   Margaret Smith Court–Marty Riessen d. Virginia Wade–Tom Okker 8-6, 6-3

Discontinued after 1968

DAVIS CUP

The sporting vision of a 20-year-old Harvard student from St. Louis, Dwight Filley Davis (1879–1945), burgeoned from a modest start to encompass the world in a celebrated international team competition that would eventually bear his name. The Davis Cup, a large, pedestaled and ornately decorated 217-ounce sterling bowl, was originally entitled the International Lawn Tennis Challenge Trophy. But only Britain (known as the British Isles) challenged, launching the event in 1900 on the grass of Davis' Boston club, Longwood Cricket Club. A total of 124 countries from all continents were involved in 1996, a number that would have gratified Davis, who felt Cup play could promote friendship and understanding among nations.

It was a time when college men of the Northeast dominated the American game. Davis, as U.S. captain and No. 2–ranked nationally, enlisted schoolmates Malcolm Whitman (No. 1) and Holcombe Ward (No. 9) to complete the home side for a fairly routine 3-0 victory over the invaders. For the first three years of the competition (1900, 1902, 1903), the same two countries entered, but in 1904 Belgium and France signed on (the U.S. dropped out). Belgium beat France for the right to challenge Britain, the 1903 winner over the U.S. Australia entered in 1905 and would become the most prolific winner other than the U.S.; they played under the banner of Australasia until 1923 because of a partnership with New Zealand, which entered separately in 1924.

Davis commissioned the Cup from Boston jeweler Shreve, Crump & Low. It was designed by Rowland Rhodes, and crafted by William Morton and Warren Peckman at the William B. Durgin Co. in Concord, N.H. The price was "about $1,000, but it would cost almost $200,000 to duplicate today," says Kevin Jenness of Shreve's. Since the names of players of both final-round teams are engraved on the trophy (first on the bowl, then on an accompanying tray, now on silver tablets attached to two subsequently added circular bases), a search for more space is unending. Another base is imminent.

By 1923, when 17 nations entered, it was necessary to divide the world into two zones, American and European. In 1955 an Eastern Zone was added, and in 1966 the European Zone was split into sections A and B. In 1967 the American Zone was split into North and South sections.

In 1981 the World Group of 16 countries was instituted. Only those 16 are eligible annually to compete for the Cup itself. Remaining countries engage in zonal competition with the possibility of being promoted to the World Group the following year, replacing four first-round World Group losers who are relegated to zonal play.

It became necessary to divide the world into zones for preliminary tournaments to determine one challenger for the championship nation. The champion was required to play only the title match—the Challenge Round—the following year against the winner of the preliminary tournament. That system was changed in 1972, when all nations were required to play in the eliminations in their respective zones: American (North and South sections), European (A and B sections) and Eastern. That year the Cup-defending U.S. reached the final against Romania in Bucharest and won, 3-2.

A total of 124 nations have appeared in the competition, but only nine have won the Cup: the U.S. (31 times), Australia (26), Britain (9), France (7), Sweden (5), Germany (3), Italy (1), South Africa (1), Czechoslovakia (1). Nine nations besides the nine winners have qualified for the Challenge Round and/or Final: Romania (3 times), India (2), Spain (2), Belgium (1), Japan (1), Mexico (1), Chile (1), Switzerland (1) and Argentina (1).

The competition was confined to amateurs until 1969, when certain professionals, those with ties to their national federations, became eligible. In 1973 it became a truly open event, with all players welcome, and Australia won with possibly the strongest team ever, a group of pros who had been away from Davis Cup for years: Rod Laver, Ken Rosewall, John Newcombe, Mal Anderson.

The format for a match (or tie) is four singles and one doubles, a best-of-five series over three days. A team may be composed of no more than four players. Two players are nominated for singles and the No. 1 computer-ranked player of each country faces the No. 2 on the first day with the opponents reversed on the third day. A draw determines who plays the first match each day.

Nations visit one another for matches, a scheduling formula determining which of two opponents has choice of ground.

Through 1996 the competition had been held 85 times, the annual flow interrupted only by two world wars and a hiatus in 1901 and 1910.

TITLE-ROUND STANDINGS

	FINAL ROUNDS		(SINCE 1972)		TOTAL	
	W	L	W	L	W	L
United States	24	24	7	3	31	27
Australia	22	15	4	2	26	17
Britain	9	7	0	1	9	8
France	6	3	2	1	8	4
Italy	0	2	1	3	1	5
Sweden	0	0	6	5	6	5
South Africa	0	0	1	0	1	0
Romania	0	2	0	1	0	3
Spain	0	2	0	0	0	2
India	0	1	0	2	0	3
Belgium	0	1	0	0	0	1
Japan	0	1	0	0	0	1
Mexico	0	1	0	0	0	1
Germany	0	1	4	1	4	2
Czechoslovakia	0	0	1	1	1	1
Chile	0	0	0	1	0	1
Argentina	0	0	0	1	0	1
Switzerland	0	0	0	1	0	1
Russia	0	0	0	2	0	2

Davis Cup Championship Rounds

CHALLENGE ROUNDS

YEAR

1900　United States d. British Isles 3-0 (Boston)
Malcolm Whitman d. Arthur Gore 6-1, 6-3, 6-2
Dwight Davis d. Ernest Black 4-6, 6-2, 6-4, 6-4
Holcombe Ward–Dwight Davis d. Ernest Black–Herbert Roper Barrett 6-4, 6-4, 6-4
Malcolm Whitman vs. Ernest Black (not played)
Dwight Davis vs. Arthur Gore 9-7, 9-9 (unfinished)

1901　Not held

1902　United States d. British Isles 3-2 (Brooklyn, N.Y.)
Reggie Doherty (B) d. Bill Larned 2-6, 3-6, 6-3, 6-4, 6-4
Malcolm Whitman (US) d. Joshua Pim 6-1, 6-1, 1-6, 6-0

Bill Larned d. Joshua Pim 6-3, 6-2, 6-3
Malcolm Whitman d. Reggie Doherty 6-1, 7-5, 6-4
Reggie Doherty–Laurie Doherty (B) d. Holcombe Ward–Dwight Davis 3-6, 10-8, 6-3, 6-4

1903　British Isles d. United States 4-1 (Boston)
Laurie Doherty (B) d. Robert Wrenn 6-0, 6-3, 6-4
Bill Larned (US) d. Reggie Doherty (walkover, injury)
Reggie Doherty–Laurie Doherty d. Robert Wrenn–George Wrenn 7-5, 9-7, 2-6, 6-3
Laurie Doherty d. Bill Larned 6-3, 6-8, 6-0, 2-6, 7-5
Reggie Doherty d. Robert Wrenn 6-4, 3-6, 6-3, 6-8, 6-4

1904　British Isles d. Belgium 5-0 (Wimbledon)
Laurie Doherty d. Paul de Borman 6-4, 6-1, 6-1
Frank Riseley d. Willie Lemaire de Warzee 6-1, 6-4, 6-2
Reggie Doherty–Laurie Doherty d. Paul de Borman–Willie Lemaire de Warzee 6-0, 6-1, 6-3
Laurie Doherty d. Willie Lemaire de Warzee (walkover)
Frank Riseley d. Paul de Borman 4-6, 6-2, 8-6, 7-5

1905　British Isles d. United States 5-0 (Wimbledon)
Laurie Doherty d. Holcombe Ward 7-9, 4-6, 6-1, 6-2, 6-0
Sidney Smith d. Bill Larned 6-4, 6-4, 5-7, 6-4
Reggie Doherty–Laurie Doherty d. Holcombe Ward–Beals Wright 8-10, 6-2, 6-2, 4-6, 8-6
Sidney Smith d. Bill Clothier 4-6, 6-1, 6-4, 6-3
Laurie Doherty d. Bill Larned 6-4, 2-6, 6-8, 6-4, 6-2

1906　British Isles d. United States 5-0 (Wimbledon)
Sidney Smith d. Raymond Little 6-4, 6-4, 6-1
Laurie Doherty d. Holcombe Ward 6-2, 8-6, 6-3
Reggie Doherty–Laurie Doherty d. Holcombe Ward–Raymond Little 3-6, 11-9, 9-7, 6-1
Sidney Smith d. Holcombe Ward 6-1, 6-0, 6-4
Laurie Doherty d. Raymond Little 3-6, 6-3, 6-8, 6-1, 6-3

1907　Australasia d. British Isles 3-2 (Wimbledon)
Norman Brookes (A) d. Arthur Gore 7-5, 6-1, 7-5
Tony Wilding d. Herbert Roper Barrett 1-6, 6-4, 6-3, 7-5
Arthur Gore–Herbert Roper Barrett (B) d. Norman Brookes–Tony Wilding 3-6, 4-6, 7-5, 6-2, 13-11
Norman Brookes d. Herbert Roper Barrett 6-2, 6-0, 6-3
Arthur Gore (B) d. Tony Wilding 3-6, 6-3, 7-5, 6-2

1908　Australasia d. United States 3-2 (Melbourne)
Norman Brookes (A) d. Fred Alexander 5-7, 9-7, 6-2, 4-6, 6-3
Beals Wright (US) d. Tony Wilding 3-6, 7-5, 6-3, 6-1
Norman Brookes–Tony Wilding (A) d. Beals Wright–Fred Alexander 6-4, 6-2, 5-7, 1-6, 6-4
Tony Wilding d. Fred Alexander 6-3, 6-4, 6-1
Beals Wright d. Norman Brookes 0-6, 3-6, 7-5, 6-2, 12-10

1909　Australasia d. United States 5-0 (Sydney)
Norman Brookes d. Maurice McLoughlin 6-2, 6-2, 6-4
Tony Wilding d. Melville Long 6-2, 7-5, 6-1
Norman Brookes–Tony Wilding d. Maurice McLoughlin–Melville Long 12-10, 9-7, 6-3
Norman Brookes d. Melville Long 6-4, 7-5, 8-6
Tony Wilding d. Maurice McLoughlin 3-6, 8-6, 6-2, 6-3

1910　No competition

1911　Australasia d. United States 5-0 (Christchurch, New Zealand)
Norman Brookes d. Beals Wright 6-4, 2-6, 6-3, 6-3
Rod Heath d. Bill Larned 2-6, 6-1, 7-5, 6-2
Norman Brookes–Alfred Dunlop d. Beals Wright–Maurice McLoughlin 6-4, 5-7, 7-5, 6-4
Norman Brookes d. Maurice McLoughlin 6-4, 3-6, 4-6, 6-3, 6-4
Rod Heath d. Beals Wright (walkover)

1912　British Isles d. Australasia 3-2 (Melbourne)

James Parke (B) d. Norman Brookes 8-6, 6-3, 5-7, 6-2

Charles Dixon d. Rodney Heath 5-7, 6-4, 6-4, 6-4

Norman Brookes–Alfred Dunlop (A) d. Cecil Parke–Alfred Beamish 6-4, 6-1, 7-5

James Parke d. Rodney Heath 6-2, 6-4, 6-4

Norman Brookes (A) d. Charles Dixon 6-2, 6-4, 6-4

1913   United States d. British Isles 3-2 (Wimbledon)

James Parke (B) d. Maurice McLoughlin 8-10, 7-5, 6-4, 1-6, 7-5

Dick Williams (US) d. Charles Dixon 8-6, 3-6, 6-2, 1-6, 7-5

Harold Hackett–Maurice McLoughlin d. Herbert Roper Barrett–Charles Dixon 5-7, 6-1, 2-6, 7-5, 6-4

Maurice McLoughlin d. Charles Dixon 8-6, 6-3, 6-2

James Parke (B) d. Dick Williams 6-2, 5-7, 5-7, 6-4, 6-2

1914   Australasia d. United States 3-2 (Forest Hills)

Tony Wilding (A) d. Dick Williams 7-5, 6-2, 6-3

Maurice McLoughlin (US) d. Norman Brookes 17-15, 6-3, 6-3

Norman Brookes–Tony Wilding d. Maurice McLoughlin–Tom Bundy 6-3, 8-6, 9-7

Norman Brookes d. Dick Williams 6-1, 6-2, 8-10, 6-3

Maurice McLoughlin d. Tony Wilding 6-2, 6-3, 2-6, 6-2

1915–18 Not held, World War I

1919   Australasia d. British Isles 4-1 (Sydney)

Gerald Patterson (A) d. Arthur Lowe 6-4, 6-3, 2-6, 6-3

Algernon Kingscote (B) d. Jim Anderson 7-5, 6-2, 6-4

Norman Brookes–Gerald Patterson d. Algernon Kingscote–Alfred Beamish 6-0, 6-0, 6-2

Gerald Patterson d. Algernon Kingscote 6-4, 6-4, 8-6

Jim Anderson d. Arthur Lowe 6-4, 5-7, 6-3, 4-6, 12-10

1920   United States d. Australasia 5-0 (Auckland)

Bill Tilden d. Norman Brookes 10-8, 6-4, 1-6, 6-4

Bill Johnston d. Gerald Patterson 6-3, 6-1, 6-1

Bill Tilden–Bill Johnston d. Norman Brookes–Gerald Patterson 4-6, 6-4, 6-0, 6-4

Bill Tilden d. Gerald Patterson 5-7, 6-2, 6-3, 6-3

Bill Johnston d. Norman Brookes 5-7, 7-5, 6-3, 6-3

1921   United States d. Japan 5-0 (Forest Hills)

Bill Johnston d. Ichiya Kumagae 6-2, 6-4, 6-2

Bill Tilden d. Zenzo Shimidzu 5-7, 4-6, 7-5, 6-2, 6-1

Dick Williams–Watson Washburn d. Zenzo Shimidzu–Ichiya Kumagae 6-2, 7-5, 4-6, 7-5

Bill Tilden d. Ichiya Kumagae 9-7, 6-4, 6-1

Bill Johnston d. Zenzo Shimidzu 6-3, 5-7, 6-2, 6-4

1922   United States d. Australasia 4-1 (Forest Hills)

Bill Tilden d. Gerald Patterson 7-5, 10-8, 6-0

Bill Johnston d. Jim Anderson 6-1, 6-2, 6-3

Gerald Patterson–Pat O'Hara Wood (A) d. Bill Tilden–Vinnie Richards 6-3, 6-0, 6-4

Bill Johnston d. Gerald Patterson 6-2, 6-2, 6-1

Bill Tilden d. Jim Anderson 6-4, 5-7, 3-6, 6-4, 6-2

1923   United States d. Australia 4-1 (Forest Hills)

Jim Anderson (A) d. Bill Johnston 4-6, 6-2, 2-6, 7-5, 6-2

Bill Tilden d. John Hawkes 6-4, 6-2, 6-1

Bill Tilden–Dick Williams d. Jim Anderson–John Hawkes 17-15, 11-13, 2-6, 6-3, 6-2

Bill Johnston d. John Hawkes 6-0, 6-2, 6-1

Bill Tilden d. Jim Anderson 6-2, 6-3, 1-6, 7-5

1924   United States d. Australia 5-0 (Philadelphia)

Bill Tilden d. Gerald Patterson 6-4, 6-2, 6-2

Vincent Richards d. Pat O'Hara Wood 6-3, 6-2, 6-4

Bill Tilden–Bill Johnston d. Gerald Patterson–Pat O'Hara Wood 5-7, 6-3, 6-4, 6-1

Bill Tilden d. Pat O'Hara Wood 6-2, 6-1, 6-1

Vincent Richards d. Gerald Patterson 6-3, 7-5, 6-4

1925   United States d. France 5-0 (Philadelphia)

Bill Tilden d. Jean Borotra 4-6, 6-0, 2-6, 9-7, 6-4

Bill Johnston d. René Lacoste 6-1, 6-1, 6-8, 6-3

Vincent Richards–Dick Williams d. René Lacoste–Jean Borotra 6-4, 6-4, 6-3

Bill Tilden d. René Lacoste 3-6, 10-12, 8-6, 7-5, 6-2

Bill Johnston d. Jean Borotra 6-1, 6-4, 6-0

1926   United States d. France 4-1 (Philadelphia)

Bill Johnston d. René Lacoste 6-4, 0-6, 6-0

Bill Tilden d. Jean Borotra 6-2, 6-3, 6-3

Dick Williams–Vincent Richards d. Henri Cochet–Jacques Brugnon 6-4, 6-4, 6-2

Bill Johnston d. Jean Borotra 8-6, 6-4, 9-7

René Lacoste (F) d. Bill Tilden 4-6, 6-4, 8-6, 8-6

1927   France d. United States 3-2 (Philadelphia)

René Lacoste (F) d. Bill Johnston 6-3, 6-2, 6-2

Bill Tilden (US) d. Henri Cochet 6-4, 2-6, 6-2, 8-6

Bill Tilden–Frank Hunter (US) d. Jean Borotra–Jacques Brugnon 3-6, 6-3, 6-3, 4-6, 6-0

René Lacoste d. Bill Tilden 6-3, 4-6, 6-3, 6-2

Henri Cochet d. Bill Johnston 6-4, 4-6, 6-2, 6-4

1928   France d. United States 4-1 (Paris)

Bill Tilden (US) d. René Lacoste 1-6, 6-4, 6-4, 2-6, 6-3

Henri Cochet (F) d. John Hennessey 5-7, 9-7, 6-3, 6-0

Henri Cochet–Jean Borotra d. Bill Tilden–Frank Hunter 6-4, 6-8, 7-5, 4-6, 6-2

Henri Cochet d. Bill Tilden 9-7, 8-6, 6-4

René Lacoste d. John Hennessey 4-6, 6-1, 7-5, 6-3

1929   France d. United States 3-2 (Paris)

Jean Borotra (F) d. George Lott 6-1, 3-6, 6-4, 7-5

Henri Cochet (F) d. Bill Tilden 6-3, 6-1, 6-2

John Van Ryn–Wilmer Allison (US) d. Henri Cochet–Jean Borotra 6-1, 8-6, 6-4

Bill Tilden (US) d. Jean Borotra 4-6, 6-1, 6-4, 7-5

Henri Cochet d. George Lott 6-1, 3-6, 6-0, 6-3

1930   France d. United States 4-1 (Paris)

Bill Tilden (US) d. Jean Borotra 2-6, 7-5, 6-4, 7-5

Henri Cochet (F) d. George Lott 6-4, 6-2, 6-2

Henri Cochet–Jacques Brugnon d. Wilmer Allison–John Van Ryn 6-3, 7-5, 1-6, 6-2

Jean Borotra d. George Lott 5-7, 6-3, 2-6, 6-2, 8-6

Henri Cochet d. Bill Tilden 4-6, 6-3, 6-1, 7-5

1931   France d. Great Britain 3-2 (Paris)

Henri Cochet d. Henry "Bunny" Austin 3-6, 11-9, 6-2, 6-4

Fred Perry (B) d. Jean Borotra 4-6, 10-8, 6-0, 4-6, 6-4

Henri Cochet–Jacques Brugnon d. Pat Hughes–Charles Kingsley 6-1, 5-7, 6-3, 8-6

Henry "Bunny" Austin (B) d. Jean Borotra 7-5, 6-3, 3-6, 7-5

Henri Cochet d. Fred Perry 6-4, 1-6, 9-7, 6-3

1932   France d. United States 3-2 (Paris)

Jean Borotra (F) d. Ellsworth Vines 6-4, 6-2, 3-6, 6-4

Henri Cochet (F) d. Wilmer Allison 5-7, 7-5, 7-5, 6-2

Wilmer Allison–John Van Ryn (US) d. Henri Cochet–Jacques Brugnon 6-3, 11-13, 7-5, 4-6, 6-4

Jean Borotra d. Wilmer Allison 1-6, 3-6, 6-4, 6-2, 7-5

Ellsworth Vines (U.S.) d. Henri Cochet 4-6, 0-6, 7-5, 8-6, 6-2

1933   Great Britain d. France 3-2 (Paris)

Henry "Bunny" Austin (B) d. Andre Merlin 6-3, 6-4, 6-0

Fred Perry (B) d. Henri Cochet 8-10, 6-4, 8-6, 3-6, 6-1

Jean Borotra–Jacques Brugnon (F) d. Pat Hughes–Harold Lee 6-3, 8-6, 6-2

Henri Cochet (F) d. Henry "Bunny" Austin 5-7, 6-4, 4-6, 6-4, 6-4

Fred Perry d. Andre Merlin 4-6, 8-6, 6-2, 7-5

1934   Great Britain d. United States 4-1 (Wimbledon)

Henry "Bunny" Austin (B) d. Frank Shields 6-4, 6-4, 6-1

Fred Perry (B) d. Sidney Wood 6-1, 4-6, 5-7, 6-0, 6-3

George Lott–Lester Stoefen (US) d. Pat Hughes–Harold Lee 7-5, 6-0, 4-6, 9-7

Fred Perry d. Frank Shields 6-4, 4-6, 6-2, 15-13

Henry "Bunny" Austin d. Sidney Wood 6-4, 6-0, 6-8, 6-3

1935   Great Britain d. United States 5-0 (Wimbledon)

Henry "Bunny" Austin d. Wilmer Allison 6-2, 2-6, 4-6, 6-3, 7-5

Fred Perry d. Don Budge 6-0, 6-8, 6-3, 6-4

Pat Hughes–Charles Tuckey d. Wilmer Allison–John Van Ryn 6-2, 1-6, 6-8, 6-3, 6-3

Bunny Austin d. Don Budge 6-2, 6-4, 6-8, 7-5

Fred Perry d. Wilmer Allison 4-6, 6-4, 7-5, 6-3

1936   Great Britain d. Australia 3-2 (Wimbledon)

Henry "Bunny" Austin (B) d. Jack Crawford 4-6, 6-3, 6-1, 6-1

Fred Perry (B) d. Adrian Quist 6-1, 4-6, 7-5, 6-2

Jack Crawford–Adrian Quist d. Pat Hughes–Charles Tuckey 6-4, 2-6, 7-5, 10-8

Adrian Quist (A) d. Henry "Bunny" Austin 6-4, 3-6, 7-5, 6-2

Fred Perry d. Jack Crawford 6-2, 6-2, 6-3

1937   United States d. Great Britain 4-1 (Wimbledon)

Henry "Bunny" Austin (B) d. Frank Parker 6-3, 6-2, 7-5

Don Budge (US) d. Charlie Hare 15-13, 6-1, 6-2

Don Budge–Gene Mako d. Charles Tuckey–Frank Wilde 6-3, 7-5, 7-9, 12-10

Frank Parker d. Charlie Hare 6-2, 6-4, 6-2

Don Budge d. Henry "Bunny" Austin 8-6, 3-6, 6-4, 6-3

1938   United States d. Australia 3-2 (Philadelphia)

Bobby Riggs (US) d. Adrian Quist 4-6, 6-0, 8-6, 6-1

Don Budge (US) d. John Bromwich 6-2, 6-3, 4-6, 7-5

Adrian Quist–John Bromwich (A.) d. Don Budge–Gene Mako 0-6, 6-3, 6-4, 6-2

Don Budge d. Adrian Quist 8-6, 6-1, 6-2

John Bromwich (A) d. Bobby Riggs 6-4, 4-6, 6-0, 6-2

1939   Australia d. United States 3-2 (Haverford, Pa.)

Bobby Riggs (US) d. John Bromwich 6-4, 6-0, 7-5

Frank Parker (US) d. Adrian Quist 6-3, 2-6, 6-4, 1-6, 7-5

Adrian Quist–John Bromwich d. Jack Kramer–Joe Hunt 5-7, 6-2, 7-5, 6-2

Adrian Quist d. Bobby Riggs 6-1, 6-4, 3-6, 3-6, 6-4

John Bromwich d. Frank Parker 6-0, 6-3, 6-1

1940–45   Not held, World War II

1946   United States d. Australia 5-0 (Melbourne)

Ted Schroeder d. John Bromwich 3-6, 6-1, 6-2, 0-6, 6-3

Jack Kramer d. Dinny Pails 8-6, 6-2, 9-7

Jack Kramer–Ted Schroeder d. John Bromwich–Adrian Quist 6-2, 7-5, 6-4

Gardnar Mulloy d. Dinny Pails 6-3, 6-3, 6-4

Jack Kramer d. John Bromwich 8-6, 6-4, 6-4

1947   United States d. Australia 4-1 (Forest Hills)

Jack Kramer (US) d. Dinny Pails 6-2, 6-1, 6-2

Ted Schroeder (US) d. John Bromwich 6-4, 5-7, 6-3, 6-4

John Bromwich–Colin Long (A) d. Jack Kramer–Ted Schroeder 6-4, 2-6, 6-2, 6-4

Ted Schroeder d. Dinny Pails 6-3, 8-6, 4-6, 9-11, 10-8

Jack Kramer d. John Bromwich 6-3, 6-2, 6-2

1948   United States d. Australia 5-0 (Forest Hills)

Frank Parker d. Bill Sidwell 6-4, 6-4, 6-4

Ted Schroeder d. Adrian Quist 6-3, 4-6, 6-0, 6-0

Bill Talbert–Gardnar Mulloy d. Bill Sidwell–Colin Long 8-6, 9-7, 2-6, 7-5

Ted Schroeder d. Bill Sidwell 6-2, 6-1, 6-1

Frank Parker d. Adrian Quist 6-2, 6-2, 6-3

1949   United States d. Australia 4-1 (Forest Hills)

Ted Schroeder (US) d. Bill Sidwell 6-1, 5-7, 4-6, 6-2, 6-3

Richard "Pancho" Gonzalez (US) d. Frank Sedgman 8-6, 6-4, 9-7

Bill Sidwell–John Bromwich (A) d. Bill Talbert–Gardnar Mulloy 3-6, 4-6, 10-8, 9-7, 9-7

Ted Schroeder d. Frank Sedgman 6-4, 6-3, 6-3

Richard "Pancho" Gonzalez d. Bill Sidwell 6-1, 6-3, 6-3

1950   Australia d. United States 4-1 (Forest Hills)

Frank Sedgman (A) d. Tom Brown 6-0, 8-6, 9-7

Ken McGregor (A) d. Ted Schroeder 13-11, 6-3, 6-4

Frank Sedgman–John Bromwich d. Ted Schroeder–Gardnar Mulloy 4-6, 6-4, 6-2, 4-6, 6-4

Frank Sedgman d. Ted Schroeder 6-2, 6-2, 6-2

Tom Brown (US) d. Ken McGregor 9-11, 8-10, 11-9, 6-1, 6-4

1951   Australia d. United States 3-2 (Sydney)

Vic Seixas (US) d. Mervyn Rose 6-3, 6-4, 9-7

Frank Sedgman d. Ted Schroeder 6-4, 6-3, 4-6, 6-4

Ken McGregor–Frank Sedgman d. Ted Schroeder–Tony Trabert 6-2, 9-7, 6-3

Ted Schroeder (US) d. Mervyn Rose 6-4, 13-11, 7-5

Frank Sedgman d. Vic Seixas 6-4, 6-2, 6-2

1952   Australia d. United States 4-1 (Adelaide)

Frank Sedgman d. Vic Seixas 6-3, 6-4, 6-3

Ken McGregor d. Tony Trabert 11-9, 6-4, 6-1

Ken McGregor–Frank Sedgman d. Vic Seixas–Tony Trabert 6-3, 6-4, 1-6, 6-3

Frank Sedgman d. Tony Trabert 7-5, 6-4, 10-8

Vic Seixas (US) d. Ken McGregor 6-3, 8-6, 6-8, 6-3

1953   Australia d. United States 3-2 (Melbourne)

Lew Hoad (A) d. Vic Seixas 6-4, 6-2, 6-3

Tony Trabert (US) d. Ken Rosewall 6-3, 6-4, 6-4

Vic Seixas–Tony Trabert (US) d. Rex Hartwig–Lew Hoad 6-2, 6-4, 6-4

Lew Hoad d. Tony Trabert 13-11, 6-3, 2-6, 3-6, 7-5

Ken Rosewall d. Vic Seixas 6-2, 2-6, 6-3, 6-4

1954   United States d. Australia 3-2 (Sydney)

Tony Trabert (US) d. Lew Hoad 6-4, 2-6, 12-10, 6-3

Vic Seixas (US) d. Ken Rosewall 8-6, 6-8, 6-4, 6-3

Vic Seixas–Tony Trabert d. Lew Hoad–Ken Rosewall 6-2, 4-6, 6-2, 10-8

Ken Rosewall (A) d. Tony Trabert 9-7, 7-5, 6-3

Rex Hartwig (A) d. Vic Seixas 4-6, 6-3, 6-2, 6-3

1955   Australia d. United States 5-0 (Forest Hills)

Ken Rosewall d. Vic Seixas 6-3, 10-8, 4-6, 6-2

Lew Hoad d. Tony Trabert 4-6, 6-3, 6-3, 8-6

Lew Hoad–Rex Hartwig d. Tony Trabert–Vic Seixas 12-14, 6-4, 6-3, 3-6, 7-5

Lew Hoad d. Vic Seixas 7-9, 6-1, 6-4, 6-4

Ken Rosewall d. Ham Richardson 6-4, 3-6, 6-1, 6-4

1956   Australia d. United States 5-0 (Adelaide)

Lew Hoad d. Herbie Flam 6-2, 6-3, 6-3

Ken Rosewall d. Vic Seixas 6-1, 6-4, 4-6, 6-1

Lew Hoad–Ken Rosewall d. Sammy Giammalva–Vic Seixas 1-6, 6-1, 7-5, 6-4

Ken Rosewall d. Sammy Giammalva 4-6, 6-1, 8-6, 7-5

Lew Hoad d. Vic Seixas 6-2, 7-5, 6-3

1957   Australia d. United States 3-2 (Melbourne)

Mal Anderson (A) d. Barry MacKay 6-3, 7-5, 3-6, 7-9, 6-3

Ashley Cooper (A) d. Vic Seixas 3-6, 7-5, 6-1, 1-6, 6-3

Mal Anderson–Mervyn Rose d. Barry MacKay–Vic Seixas 6-4, 6-4, 8-6

Vic Seixas (US) d. Mal Anderson 6-3, 4-6, 6-3, 0-6, 13-11

Barry MacKay (US) d. Ashley Cooper 6-4, 1-6, 4-6, 6-4, 6-3

1958 United States d. Australia 3-2 (Brisbane)

Alex Olmedo (US) d. Mal Anderson 8-6, 2-6, 9-7, 8-6

Ashley Cooper (A) d. Barry MacKay 4-6, 6-3, 6-2, 6-4

Alex Olmedo–Ham Richardson (A) d. Mal Anderson–Neale Fraser 10-12, 3-6, 16-14, 6-3, 7-5

Alex Olmedo d. Ashley Cooper 6-3, 4-6, 6-4, 8-6

Mal Anderson d. Barry MacKay 7-5, 13-11, 11-9

1959 Australia d. United States 3-2 (Forest Hills)

Neale Fraser (A) d. Alex Olmedo 8-6, 6-8, 6-4, 8-6

Barry MacKay (US) d. Rod Laver 7-5, 6-4, 6-1

Neale Fraser–Roy Emerson d. Alex Olmedo–Earl "Butch" Buchholz 7-5, 7-5, 6-4

Alex Olmedo (US) d. Rod Laver 9-7, 4-6, 10-8, 12-10

Neale Fraser d. Barry MacKay 8-6, 3-6, 6-2, 6-4

1960 Australia d. Italy 4-1 (Sydney)

Neale Fraser (A) d. Orlando Sirola 4-6, 6-3, 6-3, 6-3

Rod Laver (A) d. Nicola Pietrangeli 8-6, 6-4, 6-3

Neale Fraser–Roy Emerson d. Nicola Pietrangeli–Orlando Sirola 10-8, 5-7, 6-2, 6-4

Rod Laver d. Orlando Sirola 9-7, 6-2, 6-3

Nicola Pietrangeli (I) d. Neale Fraser 11-9, 6-3, 1-6, 6-2

1961 Australia d. Italy 5-0 (Melbourne)

Roy Emerson d. Nicola Pietrangeli 8-6, 6-4, 6-0

Rod Laver d. Orlando Sirola 6-1, 6-4, 6-3

Neale Fraser–Roy Emerson d. Nicola Pietrangeli–Orlando Sirola 6-2, 6-3, 6-4

Rod Laver d. Nicola Pietrangeli 6-3, 3-6, 4-6, 6-3, 8-6

Roy Emerson d. Orlando Sirola 6-3, 6-3, 4-6, 6-2

1962 Australia d. Mexico 5-0 (Brisbane)

Rod Laver d. Rafael Osuna 6-2, 6-1, 7-5

Neale Fraser d. Tony Palafox 7-9, 6-3, 6-4, 11-9

Roy Emerson–Rod Laver d. Rafael Osuna–Tony Palafox 7-5, 6-2, 6-4

Neale Fraser d. Rafael Osuna 3-6, 11-9, 6-1, 3-6, 6-4

Rod Laver d. Tony Palafox 6-1, 4-6, 6-4, 8-6

1963 United States d. Australia 3-2 (Adelaide)

Dennis Ralston (US) d. John Newcombe 6-4, 6-1, 3-6, 4-6, 7-5

Roy Emerson (A) d. Chuck McKinley 6-3, 3-6, 7-5, 7-5

Chuck McKinley–Dennis Ralston d. Roy Emerson–Neale Fraser 6-3, 4-6, 11-9, 11-9

Roy Emerson (A) d. Dennis Ralston 6-2, 6-3, 3-6, 6-2

Chuck McKinley d. John Newcombe 10-12, 6-2, 9-7, 6-2

1964 Australia d. United States 3-2 (Cleveland)

Chuck McKinley (US) d. Fred Stolle 6-1, 9-7, 4-6, 6-2

Roy Emerson (A) d. Dennis Ralston 6-3, 6-1, 6-2

Chuck McKinley–Dennis Ralston (US) d. Roy Emerson–Fred Stolle 6-4, 4-6, 4-6, 6-3, 6-4

Fred Stolle d. Dennis Ralston 7-5, 6-3, 3-6, 9-11, 6-4

Roy Emerson d. Chuck McKinley 3-6, 6-2, 6-4, 6-4

1965 Australia d. Spain 4-1 (Sydney)

Fred Stolle (A) d. Manuel Santana 10-12, 3-6, 6-1, 6-4, 7-5

Roy Emerson (A) d. Juan Gisbert 6-3, 6-2, 6-2

John Newcombe–Tony Roche d. Jose Luis Arilla–Manuel Santana 6-3, 4-6, 7-5, 6-2

Manuel Santana (S) d. Roy Emerson 2-6, 6-3, 6-4, 15-13

Fred Stolle d. Juan Gisbert 6-2, 6-4, 8-6

1966 Australia d. India 4-1 (Melbourne)

Fred Stolle (A) d. Ramanathan Krishnan 6-3, 6-2, 6-4

Roy Emerson (A) d. Jaidip Mukerjea 7-5, 6-4, 6-2

Ramanathan Krishnan–Jaidip Mukerjea (I) d. John Newcombe–Tony Roche 4-6, 7-5, 6-4, 6-4

Roy Emerson d. Ramanathan Krishnan 6-0, 6-2, 10-8

Fred Stolle d. Jaidip Mukerjea 7-5, 6-8, 6-3, 5-7, 6-3

1967 Australia d. Spain 4-1 (Brisbane)

Roy Emerson (A) d. Manuel Santana 6-4, 6-1, 6-1

John Newcombe (A) d. Manuel Orantes 6-3, 6-3, 6-2

John Newcombe–Tony Roche d. Manuel Santana–Manuel Orantes 6-4, 6-4, 6-4

Manuel Santana (S) d. John Newcombe 7-5, 6-4, 6-2

Roy Emerson d. Manuel Orantes 6-1, 6-1, 2-6, 6-4

1968 United States d. Australia 4-1 (Adelaide)

Clark Graebner (US) d. Bill Bowrey 8-10, 6-4, 8-6, 3-6, 6-1

Arthur Ashe d. Ray Ruffels 6-8, 7-5, 6-3, 6-3

Bob Lutz–Stan Smith d. John Alexander–Ray Ruffels 6-4, 6-4, 6-2

Clark Graebner d. Ray Ruffels 3-6, 8-6, 2-6, 6-3, 6-1

Bill Bowrey (A) d. Arthur Ashe 2-6, 6-3, 11-9, 8-6

1969 United States d. Romania 5-0 (Cleveland)

Arthur Ashe d. Ilie Nastase 6-2, 15-13, 7-5

Stan Smith d. Ion Tiriac 6-8, 6-3, 5-7, 6-4, 6-4

Bob Lutz–Stan Smith d. Ilie Nastase–Ion Tiriac 8-6, 6-1, 11-9

Stan Smith d. Ilie Nastase 4-6, 4-6, 6-4, 6-1, 11-9

Arthur Ashe d. Ion Tiriac 6-3, 8-6, 3-6, 4-0 (default)

1970 United States d. Germany 5-0 (Cleveland)

Arthur Ashe d. Wilhelm Bungert 6-2, 10-8, 6-2

Cliff Richey d. Christian Kuhnke 6-3, 6-4, 6-2

Bob Lutz–Stan Smith d. Christian Kuhnke–Wilhelm Bungert 6-3, 7-5, 6-4

Cliff Richey d. Wilhelm Bungert 6-4, 6-4, 7-5

Arthur Ashe d. Christian Kuhnke 6-8, 10-12, 9-7, 13-11, 6-4

1971 United States d. Romania 3-2 (Charlotte, N.C.)

Stan Smith (US) d. Ilie Nastase 7-5, 6-3, 6-1

Frank Froehling (US) d. Ion Tiriac 3-6, 1-6, 6-1, 6-3, 8-6

Ilie Nastase–Ion Tiriac (R) d. Stan Smith–Erik van Dillen 7-5, 6-4, 8-6

Stan Smith d. Ion Tiriac 8-6, 6-3, 6-0

Ilie Nastase (R) d. Frank Froehling 6-3, 6-1, 4-6, 6-4

FINAL ROUNDS

YEAR

1972 United States d. Romania 3-2 (Bucharest)

Stan Smith (US) d. Ilie Nastase 11-9, 6-2, 6-3

Ion Tiriac (R) d. Tom Gorman 4-6, 2-6, 6-4, 6-3, 6-2

Stan Smith–Erik van Dillen d. Ilie Nastase–Ion Tiriac 6-2, 6-0, 6-3

Stan Smith d. Ion Tiriac 4-6, 6-2, 6-4, 2-6, 6-0

Ilie Nastase (R) d. Tom Gorman 6-1, 6-2, 5-7, 10-8

1973* Australia d. United States 5-0 (Cleveland)

John Newcombe d. Stan Smith 6-1, 3-6, 6-3, 3-6, 6-4

Rod Laver d. Tom Gorman 8-10, 8-6, 6-8, 6-3, 6-1

John Newcombe–Rod Laver d. Erik van Dillen–Stan Smith 6-1, 6-2, 6-4

John Newcombe d. Tom Gorman 6-2, 6-1, 6-3

Rod Laver d. Stan Smith 6-3, 6-4, 3-6, 6-2

First Open Davis Cup

1974　South Africa d. India (default—Indian government ordered team not to play, a protest against the South African government's policy of apartheid. The South African team was Bob Hewitt, Frew McMillan, Ray Moore, and Rob Maud. The Indian team was Vijay Amritraj, Anand Amritraj, Jasjit Singh, and Sashi Menon.)

1975　Sweden d. Czechoslovakia 3-2 (Stockholm)

Bjorn Borg d. Jiri Hrebec 6-1, 6-3, 6-0

Jan Kodes (C) d. Ove Bengtson 4-6, 6-2, 7-5, 6-4

Bjorn Borg–Ove Bengtson d. Jan Kodes–Vladimir Zednik 6-4, 6-4, 6-4

Bjorn Borg d. Jan Kodes 6-4, 6-2, 6-2

Jiri Hrebec (C) d. Ove Bengtson 1-6, 6-3, 6-1, 6-4

1976　Italy d. Chile 4-1 (Santiago)

Corrado Barazzutti (I) d. Jaime Fillol 7-5, 4-6, 7-5, 6-1

Adriano Panatta (I) d. Patricio Cornejo 6-3, 6-1, 6-3

Adriano Panatta–Paolo Bertolucci d. Patricio Cornejo–Jaime Fillol 3-6, 6-2, 9-7, 6-3

Adriano Panatta d. Jaime Fillol 8-6, 6-4, 3-6, 10-8

Belus Prajoux (C) d Antonio Zugarelli 6-4, 6-4, 6-2

1977　Australia d. Italy 3-1 (Sydney)

Tony Roche (A) d. Adriano Panatta 6-3, 6-4, 6-4

John Alexander (A) d. Corrado Barazzutti 6-4, 8-6, 4-6, 6-2

Adriano Panatta–Paolo Bertolucci (I) d. John Alexander–Phil Dent 6-4, 6-4, 7-5

John Alexander d. Adriano Panatta 6-4, 4-6, 2-6, 8-6, 11-9

Tony Roche vs. Corrado Barazzutti 12-12 (unfinished)

1978　United States d. Great Britain 4-1 (Rancho Mirage, Cal.)

John McEnroe (US) d. John Lloyd 6-1, 6-2, 6-2

Christopher "Buster" Mottram (B) d. Brian Gottfried 4-6, 2-6, 10-8, 6-4, 6-3

Stan Smith–Bob Lutz d. David Lloyd–Mark Cox 6-2, 6-2, 6-3

John McEnroe d. Christopher "Buster" Mottram 6-2, 6-2, 6-1

Brian Gottfried d. John Lloyd 6-1, 6-2, 6-4

1979　United States d. Italy 5-0 (San Francisco)

Vitas Gerulaitis d. Corrado Barazzutti 6-3, 3-2 (default, injury)

John McEnroe d. Adriano Panatta 6-2, 6-3, 6-4

Stan Smith–Bob Lutz d. Paolo Bertolucci–Adriano Panatta 6-4, 12-10, 6-2

John McEnroe d. Antonio Zugarelli 6-4, 6-3, 6-1

Vitas Gerulaitis d. Adriano Panatta 6-1, 6-3, 6-3

1980　Czehoslovakia d. Italy 4-1 (Prague)

Tomas Smid (C) d. Adriano Panatta 3-6, 3-6, 6-3, 6-4, 6-4

Ivan Lendl (C) d. Corrado Barazzutti 4-6, 6-1, 6-1, 6-2

Ivan Lendl–Tomas Smid d. Paolo Bertolucci–Adriano Panatta 3-6, 6-3, 3-6, 6-3, 6-4

Corrado Barazzutti d. Tomas Smid 3-6, 6-3, 6-2

Ivan Lendl d. Gianni Ocleppo 6-3, 6-3

WORLD GROUP: FINAL ROUND

1981　United States d. Argentina 3-1 (Cincinnati)

John McEnroe (US) d. Guillermo Vilas 6-3, 6-2, 6-2

Jose-Luis Clerc (A) d. Roscoe Tanner 7-5, 6-3, 8-6

Peter Fleming–John McEnroe d. Jose-Luis Clerc–Guillermo Vilas 6-3, 4-6, 6-4, 4-6, 11-9

John McEnroe d. Jose-Luis Clerc 7-5, 5-7, 6-3, 3-6, 6-3

Roscoe Tanner vs. Guillermo Vilas (suspended at 11-10, first set)

1982　United States d. France 4-1 (Grenoble)

John McEnroe (US) d. Yannick Noah 12-10, 1-6, 3-6, 6-2, 6-3

Gene Mayer (US) d. Henri Leconte 6-2, 6-2, 7-9, 6-4

Peter Fleming–John McEnroe d. Henri Leconte–Yannick Noah 6-3, 6-4, 9-7

Yannick Noah d. Gene Mayer 6-1, 6-0

John McEnroe d. Henri Leconte 6-2, 6-3

1983　Australia d. Sweden 3-2 (Melbourne)

Mats Wilander (S) d. Pat Cash 6-3, 4-6, 9-7, 6-3

John Fitzgerald (A) d. Joakim Nystrom 6-4, 6-2, 4-6, 6-4

Mark Edmondson–Paul McNamee (A) d. Anders Jarryd–Hans Simonsson 6-4, 6-4, 6-2

Pat Cash d. Joakim Nystrom 6-4, 6-1, 6-1

Mats Wilander d. John Fitzgerald 6-8, 6-0, 6-1

1984　Sweden d. United States 4-1 (Goteborg, Sweden)

Mats Wilander (S) d. Jimmy Connors 6-1, 6-3, 6-3

Henrik Sundstrom (S) d. John McEnroe 13-11, 6-4, 6-3

Stefan Edberg–Anders Jarryd d. Peter Fleming–John McEnroe 7-5, 5-7, 6-2, 7-5

John McEnroe d. Mats Wilander 6-3, 5-7, 6-3

Henrik Sundstrom d. Jimmy Arias 3-6, 8-6, 6-3

1985　Sweden d. Germany 3-2 (Munich)

Mats Wilander (S) d. Michael Westphjal 6-3, 6-4, 10-8

Boris Becker (G) d. Stefan Edberg 6-3, 3-6, 7-5, 8-6

Joakim Nystrom–Mats Wilander d. Boris Becker–Andreas Maurer 6-4, 6-2, 6-1.

Boris Becker d. Mats Wilander 6-3, 2-6, 6-3, 6-3

Stefan Edberg d. Michael Westphal 3-6, 7-5, 6-4, 6-3

1986　Australia d. Sweden 3-2 (Melbourne)

Pat Cash (A) d. Stefan Edberg 13-11, 13-11, 6-4

Mikael Pernfors (S) d. Paul McNamee 6-3, 6-1, 6-3

Pat Cash–John Fitzgerald d. Stefan Edberg–Anders Jarryd 6-3, 6-4, 4-6, 6-1

Pat Cash d. Mikael Pernfors 2-6, 4-6, 6-3, 6-4, 6-3

Stefan Edberg d. Paul McNamee 10-8, 6-4

1987　Sweden d. India 5-0 (Goteborg, Sweden)

Mats Wilander d. Ramesh Krishnan 6-4, 6-1, 6-3

Anders Jarryd d. Vijay Amritraj 6-3, 6-3, 6-1

Joakim Nystrom–Mats Wilander d. Anand Amritraj–Vijay Amritraj 6-3, 3-6, 6-1, 6-2

Anders Jarryd d. Ramesh Krishnan 6-4, 6-3

Mats Wilander d. Vijay Amritraj 6-2, 6-0

1988　Germany d. Sweden 4-1 (Goteborg, Sweden)

Carl-Uwe Steeb (G) d. Mats Wilander 8-10, 1-6, 6-2, 6-4, 8-6

Boris Becker (G) d. Stefan Edberg 6-3, 6-1, 6-4

Boris Becker–Eric Jelen d. Stefan Edberg–Anders Jarryd 3-6, 2-6, 7-5, 6-3, 6-2

Stefan Edberg d. Carl-Uwe Steeb 6-4 8-6

Patrick Kuhnen d. Kent Carlsson (walkover)

1989*　Germany d. Sweden 3-2 (Stuttgart, Germany)

Mats Wilander (S) d. Carl-Uwe Steeb 5-7, 7-6 (7-0), 6-7 (4-7), 6-2, 6-3

Boris Becker (G) d. Stefan Edberg 6-2, 6-2, 6-4

Boris Becker–Eric Jelen d. Jan Gunnarson–Anders Jarryd 7-6 (8-6), 6-4, 3-6, 6-7 (4-7), 6-4

Boris Becker d. Mats Wilander 6-2, 6-0, 6-2

Stefan Edberg d. Carl-Uwe Steeb 6-2, 6-4

1990　United States d. Australia 3-2 (St. Petersburg, Fla.)

Andre Agassi (US) d. Richard Fromberg 4-6, 6-2, 4-6, 6-2, 6-4

Michael Chang (US) d. Darren Cahill 6-2, 7-6 (7-4), 6-0

Rick Leach–Jim Pugh (US) d. Pat Cash–John Fitzgerald 6-4, 6-2, 3-6, 7-6 (7-2)

Darren Cahill d. Andre Agassi 6-4, 4-6 (retired)

Richard Fromberg d. Michael Chang 7-5, 2-6, 6-3

1991　France d. United States 3-1 (Lyon)

Andre Agassi (US) d. Guy Forget 6-7 (7-9), 6-2, 6-1, 6-2

Henri Leconte (F) d. Pete Sampras 6-4, 7-5, 6-4

*First use of tie-breaker in Davis Cup.

Guy Forget–Henri Leconte d. Ken Flach–Robert Seguso 6-1, 6-4, 4-6, 6-2

Guy Forget d. Pete Sampras 7-6 (8-6), 3-6, 6-3, 6-4

Leconte vs. Agassi (not played)

1992   United States d. Switzerland 3-1 (Fort Worth, Tex.)

Andre Agassi (US) d. Jakob Hlasek 6-1, 6-2, 6-2

Marc Rosset (S) d. Jim Courier 6-3, 6-7 (9-11), 3-6, 6-4, 6-4

John McEnroe–Pete Sampras d. Jakob Hlasek–Marc Rosset 6-7 (5-7), 6-7 (7-9), 7-5, 6-1, 6-2

Jim Courier d. Jakob Hlasek 6-3, 3-6, 6-3, 6-4

Agassi vs. Rosset (not played)

1993   Germany d. Australia 4-1 (Dusseldorf)

Michael Stich (G) d. Jason Stoltenberg 6-7 (2-7), 6-3, 6-1, 4-6, 6-3

Richard Fromberg (A) d. Marc Goellner 3-6, 5-7, 7-6 (10-8), 6-2, 9-7

Michael Stich–Patrick Kuhnen d. Todd Woodbridge–Mark Woodforde 7-6 (7-4), 4-6, 6-3, 7-6 (7-4)

Michael Stich   d. Richard Fromberg 6-4, 6-2, 6-2

Marc Goellner d. Jason Stoltenberg 6-1, 6-7 (2-7), 7-6 (7-3)

1994   Sweden d. Russia 4-1 (Moscow)

Stefan Edberg (S) d. Alexander Volkov 6-4, 6-2, 6-7 (2-7), 0-6, 8-6

Magnus Larsson (S) d. Yevgeny Kafelnikov 6-0, 6-2, 3-6, 2-6, 6-3

Jan Apell–Jonas Bjorkman d. Yevgeny Kafelnikov–Andrei Olhovskiy 6-7 (4-7), 6-2, 6-3, 1-6, 8-6

Yevgeny Kafelnikov d. Stefan Edberg 4-6, 6-4, 6-0

Magnus Larsson d. Alexander Volkov 7-6 (7-4), 6-4

1995   United States d. Russia 3-2 (Moscow)

Pete Sampras (US) d. Andrei Chesnokov 3-6, 6-4, 6-3, 6-7 (5-7), 6-4

Yevgeny Kafelnikov (R) d. Jim Courier 7-6 (7-1), 7-5, 6-3

Pete Sampras–Todd Martin d. Yevgeny Kafelnikov–Olhovskiy 7-5, 6-4, 6-3

Pete Sampras d. Yevgeny Kafelnikov 6-2, 6-4, 7-6 (7-4)

Andrei Chesnokov d. Jim Courier 6-7 (1-7), 7-5, 6-0

1996   France d. Sweden 3-2 (Malmo, Sweden)

Cedric Pioline (F) d. Stefan Edberg 6-3, 6-4, 6-3

Thomas Enqvist (S) d. Arnaud Boetsch 6-4, 6-3, 7-6 (7-2)

Guy Forget–Guillaume Raoux d. Jonas Bjorkman–Nicklas Kulti 6-3, 1-6, 6-3, 6-3

Thomas Enqvist d. Cedric Pioline 3-6, 6-7 (8-10), 6-4, 6-4, 9-7

Arnaud Boetsch d. Nicklas Kulti 7-6 (7-2), 2-6, 4-6, 7-6 (7-5), 10-8

ALL-TIME DAVIS CUP RECORDS

INDIVIDUAL

Most Cup-winning years: 8—Roy Emerson, Australia, 1959–67

Most years in challenge round and/or final: 11—Bill Tilden, U.S., 1920–30

Most years played: 21—Torben Ulrich, Denmark, 1948–68, 1978

Most matches played: 164—Nicola Pietrangeli, Italy, 1954–72

Most singles played: 110—Nicola Pietrangeli

Most singles won: 78—Nicola Pietrangeli

Most doubles played: 54—Nicola Pietrangeli

Most doubles won: 42—Nicola Pietrangeli

Most singles and doubles altogether: 164—Nicola Pietrangeli

Most singles and doubles won altogether: 120—Nicola Pietrangeli

Most consecutive singles wins: 33—Bjorn Borg, Sweden, 1973–79

Longest singles: 100 games—Harry Fritz, Canada, d. Jorge Andrew, Venezuela, 16-14, 11-9, 9-11, 4-6, 11-9. American Zone, 2nd rd., Caracas, 1982.

Longest doubles: 122 games—Stan Smith and Erik van Dillen, U.S., d. Jaime Fillol and Patricio Cornejo, Chile, 7-9, 37-39, 8-6, 6-1, 6-3; zone match, Little Rock, Ark., 1973

Best record in challenge round and/or finals: 7-0 in singles, 5-0 in doubles—Laurie Doherty, Britain, 1902–06

Most Cups won as captain: 16—Harry Hopman, Australia, 1938–67

Youngest player: Laith Azoni, Jordan, 1992, 14 years, 135 days, vs. Singapore

Oldest player: Torben Ulrich, Denmark, 1978, 48 years, 11 months, vs. Belgium

Oldest winner: Colin Gregory, Britain, 1952, 48 years, 295 days, vs. Yugoslavia, with Tony Mottram, d. Stevan Laszlo–Josip Pallada, 6-4, 1-6, 9-11, 6-2, 6-2

Biggest upsets: Dan Nestor (No. 238), Canada, d. Stefan Edberg (No. 1), Sweden, 4-6, 6-3, 1-6, 6-3, 6-4, 1992, Vancouver; Hugo Chapacu (No. 282), Paraguay, d. Jimmy Arias (No. 54), U.S., 6-4, 6-1, 5-7, 3-6, 9-7, from 1-5, saving 3 match points in 5th, 1987, Asuncion.

Best comebacks: Wilmer Allison, U.S., d. Giorgio deStefani, Italy, 4-6, 7-9, 6-4, 8-6, 10-8, 1930, Paris, from 2-4, 4th, 1-5, 5th, saving 18 match points; Barry MacKay, U.S., d. Nicola Pietrangeli, Italy, 8-6, 3-6, 8-10, 8-6, 13-11, 1960, Perth, Australia, from 5-3 down, 5th, saving 8 match points; Andrei Chesnokov, Russia, d. Michael Stich, Germany, 6-4, 1-6, 1-6, 6-3, 14-12, 1995, Moscow. Stich, serving at 7-6, 5th, held 9 match points.

TEAM

Most Cups won: 31—United States

Most ties won: 183—U.S.

Most consecutive Cups won: 7—U.S., 1920–26

Most consecutive ties won: 17—U.S., 1968–73

U.S. DAVIS CUP RECORDS

INDIVIDUAL

Most Cup-winning years: 7—Bill Tilden, 1920–26; Stan Smith, 1968–72, 1978–79

Most years played: 12—John McEnroe, 1978–92

Most ties played: 30—John McEnroe, 1978–92

Most singles played: 49—John McEnroe, 1978–91

Most singles won: 41—John McEnroe, 1978–91

Most doubles played: 24—John Van Ryn

Most doubles won: 22—John Van Ryn

Most singles and doubles played altogether: 69—John McEnroe, 1978–92

Most singles and doubles won altogether: 59—John McEnroe, 1978–92

Most consecutive singles won: 16—Bill Tilden, 1920–27

Best winning percentage, 25 or more wins, singles and doubles altogether: .903—John Van Ryn, 29 wins, 3 losses

Best doubles team record: 14-1—John McEnroe–Peter Fleming

Best winning percentage, singles, 15 or more wins: 1.000—Bernard Bartzen, 1952–61, 15 wins

Most Cups won as captain: 6—Dick Williams, 1921–26

Most matches won as captain: 17—Tom Gorman, 1986–92

PLAYERS WITH MORE THAN 100 DAVIS CUP MATCHES

MATCHES	W-L	SINGLES W-L	DOUBLES W-L	TIES
Nicola Pietrangeli, Italy (1954–72)				
164	120-44	78-32	42-12	66
Ilie Nastase, Romania (1966–85)				
146	109-37	74-22	35-15	52
Jacques Brichant, Belgium (1949–65)				
120	71-49	52-27	19-22	42
Manolo Santana, Spain (1958–73)				
120	92-28	69-17	23-11	46
Tomas Koch, Brazil (1962–81)				
118	74-44	46-32	28-12	44

Jose-Edison Mandarino, Brazil (1961–76)				
109	68-41	41-31	27-10	43

Ion Tiriac, Romania (1959–77)
| 109 | 70-39 | 40-28 | 30-11 | 43 |

Kurt Nielsen, Denmark (1948–62)
| 106 | 57-49 | 44-27 | 13-22 | 37 |

Alex Metreveli, U.S.S.R. (1963–79)
| 105 | 80-25 | 56-14 | 24-11 | 38 |

Wilhelm Bungert, Germany (1958–71)
| 102 | 67-35 | 53-26 | 14-9 | 43 |

Ulf Schmidt, Sweden (1955–64)
| 102 | 66-36 | 44-25 | 22-11 | 39 |

Torben Ulrich, Denmark (1948–77)
| 102 | 46-56 | 31-35 | 15-21 | 40 |

Philippe Washer, Belgium (1946–61)
| 102 | 66-36 | 46-18 | 20-18 | 39 |

Gottfried Von Cramm, Germany (1932–53)
| 101 | 82-19 | 58-10 | 24-9 | 37 |

Ramanathan Krishnan, India (1953–70)
| 100 | 71-29 | 52-20 | 19-9 | 45 |

Adriano Panatta, Italy (1970–83)
| 100 | 64-36 | 37-26 | 27-10 | 38 |

FEDERATION CUP

In response to a growing interest in a worldwide women's team competition similar to the men's Davis Cup, the International Tennis Federation put the Federation Cup into play in 1963, marking the ITF's 50th birthday. Sixteen countries entered the competition that year in London at Queen's Club, and the United States edged Australia for the Cup, 2-1, as Billie Jean King and Darlene Hard beat Margaret Court and Lesley Turner in the decisive doubles, 3-6, 13-11, 6-3.

In 1995, the name was changed to Fed Cup, and a Davis Cup–style format was adopted, a best-of-five match series of four singles, one doubles, played in the home country of one of the opponents. Only members of the World Group of eight countries are eligible to compete for the Cup itself, while other countries are involved in playoffs for a chance to enter the top group.

Prior to 1995, the competition of one-day, best-of-three match series was conducted at one site with all entrants in a one-week tournament. The Federation Cup was confined to amateurs until 1969, when it became an open event. The competition eventually grew to more than 32 countries.

Prize money has been offered since 1976. Only six countries have won the Cup: U.S. (15 times), Australia (7), South Africa (1), Czechoslovakia (5), Germany (2), Spain (4).

TITLE-ROUND STANDINGS

	W	L
United States	15	8
Australia	7	10
Czechoslovakia	5	1
Germany	2	4
Spain	4	3
South Africa	1	1
Netherlands	0	1
USSR	0	2
Great Britain	0	4

FED CUP FINAL ROUND RESULTS

YEAR	
1963	United States d. Australia 2-1 (London)
	Margaret Smith (A) d. Darlene Hard 6-3, 6-0
	Billie Jean Moffitt d. Lesley Turner 5-7, 6-0, 6-3
	Darlene Hard–Billie Jean Moffitt d. Margaret Smith–Lesley Turner 3-6, 13-11, 6-3
1964	Australia d. United States 2-1 (Philadelphia)
	Margaret Smith d. Billie Jean Moffitt 6-2, 6-3
	Lesley Turner d. Nancy Richey 7-5, 6-1
	Billie Jean Moffitt–Karen Susman (US) d. Margaret Smith–Lesley Turner 4-6, 7-5, 6-1
1965	Australia d. United States 2-1 (Melbourne)
	Lesley Turner d. Carole Caldwell Graebner 6-3, 2-6, 6-3
	Margaret Smith d. Billie Jean Moffitt 6-4, 8-6
	Billie Jean Moffitt–Carole Caldwell Graebner (US) d. Margaret Smith–Judy Tegart 7-5, 4-6, 6-4
1966	United States d. Germany 3-0 (Turin)
	Julie Heldman d. Helga Niessen 4-6, 7-5, 6-1
	Billie Jean Moffitt King d. Edda Buding 6-3, 3-6, 6-1
	Carole Caldwell Graebner–Billie Jean Moffitt King d. Helga Schultze–Edda Buding 6-4, 6-2
1967	United States d. Great Britain 2-0 (Berlin)
	Rosie Casals d. Virginia Wade 9-7, 8-6
	Billie Jean Moffitt King d. Ann Jones 6-3, 6-4
	Doubles match called at set-all
1968	Australia d. Netherlands 3-0 (Paris)
	Kerry Melville d. Marijke Jansen 4-6, 7-5, 6-3
	Margaret Smith Court d. Astrid Suurbeek 6-1, 6-3
	Margaret Smith Court–Kerry Melville d. Astrid Suurbeek–Lidy Venneboer 6-3, 6-8, 7-5
1969	United States d. Australia 2-1 (Athens)
	Nancy Richey d. Kerry Melville 6-4, 6-3
	Margaret Smith Court (A) d. Julie Heldman 6-1, 8-6
	Jane "Peaches" Bartkowicz–Nancy Richey d. Margaret Smith Court–Judy Tegart 6-4, 6-4
1970	Australia d. Germany 3-0 (Freiburg, West Germany)
	Karen Krantzcke d. Helga Schultze Hoesl 6-2, 6-3
	Judy Tegart Dalton d. Helga Niessen 4-6, 6-3, 6-3

Karen Krantzcke–Judy Dalton d. Helga Hoesl–Helga Niessen 6-2, 7-5

1971   Australia d. Great Britain 3-0 (Perth, Australia)

Margaret Smith Court d. Ann Haydon Jones 6-8, 6-3, 6-2

Evonne Goolagong d. Virginia Wade 6-4, 6-1

Margaret Smith Court–Lesley Hunt d. Virginia Wade–Winnie Shaw 6-4, 6-4

1972   South Africa d. Great Britain 2-1 (Johannesburg)

Virginia Wade (GB) d. Pat Walkden Pretorious 6-3, 6-2

Brenda Kirk d. Winnie Shaw 4-6, 7-5, 6-0

Brenda Kirk–Pat Pretorious d. Winnie Shaw–Virginia Wade 6-1, 7-5

1973   Australia d. South Africa 3-0 (Bad Homburg, West Germany)

Evonne Goolagong d. Pat Walkden Pretorious 6-0, 6-2

Patti Coleman d. Brenda Kirk 10-8, 6-0

Evonne Goolagong–Janet Young d. Brenda Kirk–Pat Pretorious 6-1, 6-2

1974   Australia d. United States 2-1 (Naples, Italy)

Evonne Goolagong d. Julie Heldman 6-1, 7-5

Jeanne Evert (US) d. Dianne Fromholtz 2-6, 7-5, 6-4

Evonne Goolagong–Janet Young d. Julie Heldman–Sharon Walsh 7-5, 8-6

1975   Czechoslovakia d. Australia 3-0 (Aix-en-Provence, France)

Martina Navratilova d. Evonne Goolagong 6-3, 6-4

Renata Tomanova d. Helen Gourlay 6-4, 6-2

Martina Navratilova–Renata Tomanova d. Dianne Fromholtz–Helen Gourlay 6-3, 6-1

1976   United States d. Australia 2-1 (Philadelphia)

Kerry Melville Reid (A) d. Rosie Casals 1-6, 6-3, 7-5

Billie Jean Moffitt King d. Evonne Goolagong 7-6 (7-4), 6-4

Billie Jean Moffitt King–Rosie Casals d. Evonne Goolagong–Kerry Melville Reid 7-5, 6-3

1977   United States d. Australia 2-1 (Eastbourne, England)

Billie Jean Moffitt King d. Dianne Fromholtz 6-1, 2-6, 6-2

Chris Evert d. Kerry Melville Reid 7-5, 6-3

Kerry Melville Reid–Wendy Turnbull (A) d. Chris Evert–Rosie Casals 6-3, 6-3

1978   United States d. Australia 2-1 (Melbourne)

Kerry Melville Reid (A) d. Tracy Austin 6-3, 6-3

Chris Evert d. Wendy Turnbull 3-6, 6-1, 6-1

Chris Evert–Billie Jean Moffitt King d. Wendy Turnbull–Kerry Melville Reid 4-6, 6-1, 6-4

1979   United States d. Australia 3-0 (Madrid)

Tracy Austin d. Kerry Melville Reid 6-3, 6-0

Chris Evert Lloyd d. Dianne Fromholtz 2-6, 6-3, 8-6

Billie Jean Moffitt King–Rosie Casals d. Wendy Turnbull–Kerry Melville Reid 3-6, 6-3, 8-6

1980   United States d. Australia 3-0 (Berlin)

Chris Evert Lloyd d. Dianne Fromholtz 4-6, 6-1, 6-1

Tracy Austin d. Wendy Turnbull 6-2, 6-3

Rosie Casals–Kathy Jordan d. Dianne Fromholtz–Susan Leo 2-6 6-4, 6-4

1981   United States d. Great Britain 3-0 (Tokyo)

Chris Evert Lloyd d. Sue Barker 6-2, 6-1

Andrea Jaeger d. Virginia Wade 6-3, 6-1

Kathy Jordan–Rosie Casals d. Sue Barker–Virginia Wade 6-4, 7-5

1982   United States d. Germany 3-0 (Santa Clara, Cal.)

Chris Evert Lloyd d. Claudia Kohde Kilsch 2-6, 6-1, 6-3

Martina Navratilova d. Bettina Bunge 6-4, 6-4

Martina Navratilova–Chris Evert Lloyd d. Claudia Kohde Kilsch–Bettina Bunge 3-6, 6-1, 6-2

1983   Czechoslovakia d. Germany 2-1 (Zurich, Switzerland)

Helena Sukova (C) d. Claudia Kohde Kilsch 6-4, 2-6, 6-2

Hana Mandlikova (C) d. Bettina Bunge 6-2, 3-0 ret.

Claudia Kohde Kilsch–Eva Pfaff d. Iva Budarova–Marcela Skuherska 3-6 6-2, 6-1

1984   Czechoslovakia d. Australia 2-1 (Sao Paulo, Brazil)

Anne Minter (A) d. Helena Sukova 7-5, 7-5

Hana Mandikova (C) d. Elizabeth Sayers 6-1, 6-0

Hana Mandlikova–Helena Sukova d. Elizabeth Sayers–Wendy Turnbull 6-2, 6-2

1985   Czechoslovakia d. United States 2-1 (Nagoya, Japan)

Hana Mandlikova (C) d. Kathy Jordan 7-5, 6-1

Helena Sukova (C) d. Elise Burgin 6-3, 6-7, 6-4

Elise Burgin–Sharon Walsh d. Regina Marsikova–Andrea Holikova 6-2, 6-3

1986   United States d. Czechoslovakia 3-0 (Prague, Czechoslovakia)

Chris Evert Lloyd d. Helena Sukova 7-5, 7-6 (7-5)

Martina Navratilova d. Hana Mandlikova 7-5, 6-1

Martina Navratilova–Pam Shriver d. Hana Mandlikova–Helena Sukova 6-4, 6-2

1987   Germany d. United States 2-1 (West Vancouver, British Columbia)

Pam Shriver d. Claudia Kohde Kilsch 6-0, 7-6 (7-5)

Steffi Graf d. Chris Evert 6-2, 6-1

Steffi Graf–Claudia Kohde Kilsch d. Chris Evert–Pam Shriver 1-6, 7-5 6-4

1988   Czechoslovakia d. U.S.S.R. 2-1 (Melbourne)

Radka Zrubakova (C) d. Larisa Savchenko 6-1, 7-6 (7-2)

Helena Sukova (C) d. Natalia Zvereva 6-3, 6-4

Larisa Savchenko–Natalia Zvereva d. Jana Novotna–Jana Pospisilova 7-6 (7-5), 7-5

1989   United States d. Spain 3-0 (Tokyo)

Chris Evert d. Conchita Martinez 6-3, 6-2

Martina Navratilova d. Arantxa Sanchez Vicario 0-6, 6-3, 6-4

Zina Garrison–Pam Shriver d. Conchita Martinez–Arantxa Sanchez Vicario 7-5, 6-1

1990   United States d. U.S.S.R. 2-1 (Atlanta)

Jennifer Capriati (US) d. Leila Meskhi 7-6 (13-11), 6-2

Natalia Zvereva (USSR) d. Zina Garrison 6-3, 7-5

Zina Garrison–Beatriz "Gigi" Fernandez d. Natalia Zvereva–Larisa Savchenko 6-4, 6-3

1991   Spain d. United States 2-1 (Nottingham, England)

Jennifer Capriati (US) d. Conchita Martinez 4-6, 7-6 (7-3), 6-1

Arantxa Sanchez Vicario (S) d. Mary Joe Fernandez 6-3, 6-4

Conchita Martinez–Arantxa Sanchez Vicario d. Beatriz "Gigi" Fernandez–Zina Garrison 3-6, 6-1, 6-1

1992   Germany d. Spain 2-1 (Frankfurt)

Steffi Graf d. Arantxa Sanchez Vicario 6-4, 6-2

Anke Huber d. Conchita Martinez 6-3, 6-7 (1-7), 6-1

Arantxa Sanchez Vicario–Martinez (S) d. Huber–Barbara Rittner 6-1, 6-4

1993   Spain d. Australia 3-0 (Frankfurt)

Conchita Martinez d. Michelle Jaggard-Lai 6-0, 6-2

Arantxa Sanchez Vicario d. Nicole Provis 6-2, 6-3

Conchita Martinez–Arantxa Sanchez Vicario d. Liz Sayers Smylie–Rennae Stubbs 3-6, 6-1, 6-3

1994   Spain d. United States 3-0 (Frankfurt)

Conchita Martinez d. Mary Joe Fernandez 6-2, 6-2

Arantxa Sanchez Vicario d. Lindsay Davenport 6-2, 6-1

Conchita Martinez–Arantxa Sanchez Vicario d. Beatriz "Gigi" Fernandez–Mary Joe Fernandez 6-3, 6-4

1995   Spain d. United States 3-2 (Valencia)

Conchita Martinez (S) d. Chanda Rubin 7-5, 7-6 (7-3)

Arantxa Sanchez Vicario (S) d. Mary Joe Fernandez 6-3, 6-2

Conchita Martinez d. Mary Joe Fernandez 6-3, 6-4

Chanda Rubin d. Arantxa Sanchez Vicario 1-6, 6-4, 6-4

Lindsay Davenport–Beatriz "Gigi" Fernandez d. Virginia Ruano Pascual–Maria Antonia Sanchez Lorenzo 6-3, 7-6 (7-3)

1996   United States d. Spain 5-0 (Atlantic City)

Monica Seles d. Conchita Martinez 6-2, 6-4

Lindsay Davenport d. Arantxa Sanchez Vicario 7-5, 6-1

Monica Seles d. Arantxa Sanchez Vicario 3-6, 6-3, 6-1

Lindsay Davenport d. Gala Leon Garcia 7-5, 6-2

Mary Joe Fernandez–Lindsay Davenport d. Gala Leon Garcia–Virginia Ruano Pascual 6-1, 6-4

ALL-TIME FEDERATION CUP RECORDS

INDIVIDUAL

Most Cup-winning years: 7—Billie Jean Moffitt King, U.S. 1963–79

Most years played: 17—Virginia Wade, Britain, 1967–83

Most team ties played: 57—Virginia Wade, Britain

Most singles played: 56—Virginia Wade, Britain

Most singles won: 40—Chris Evert, U.S.

Most singles and doubles played together: 99—Virginia Wade, Britain

Most singles and doubles won together: 66—Virginia Wade, Britain

Most consecutive singles won: 29—Chris Evert Lloyd, U.S., 1977–86

WIGHTMAN CUP

Hoping to stimulate international interest in women's tennis as the Davis Cup did in men's, Hazel Hotchkiss Wightman, an all-time champion from Boston, donated a sterling vase to the USTA as a prize for such a team competition. It was decided to invite Great Britain to challenge for the prize in 1923 to open the new Forest Hills Stadium at the West Side Tennis Club in New York. With Mrs. Wightman as player-captain, the U.S. won the inaugural, 7-0. The rivalry was rewarding to both countries and initially developed into a close competition, an annual match between the two with the prize soon known as the Wightman Cup. The matches were played in even years in Britain and in odd years in the U.S.

Interrupted only by World War II, the series became dominated by the U.S., which mounted a 50-10 record through 1989, when it was mutually agreed to suspend what was no longer a competition.

WIGHTMAN CUP RESULTS

YEAR

1923   United States d. Great Britain 7-0 (Forest Hills)

Helen Wills d. Kitty McKane 6-2, 0-6, 7-5

Molla Bjurstedt Mallory d. M. H. Davey Clayton 6-1, 8-6

Eleanor Goss d. Geraldine Beamish 6-2, 0-6, 7-5

Helen Wills d. M. H. Clayton 6-2, 6-3

Molla Bjurstedt Mallory d. Kitty McKane 6-2, 6-3

Hazel Hotchkiss Wightman–Eleanor Goss d. Kitty McKane–Phyllis Howkins Covell 10-8, 5-7, 6-4

Molla Bjurstedt Mallory–Helen Wills Moody d. Geraldine Beamish–M. H. Clayton 6-3, 6-2

1924   Great Britain d. United States 6-1 (Wimbledon)

Phyllis Howkins Covell d. Helen Wills 6-2, 6-4

Kitty McKane d. Molla Bjurstedt Mallory 6-3, 6-3

Kitty McKane d. Helen Wills 6-2, 6-2

Phyllis Howkins Covell d. Molla Bjurstedt Mallory 6-2, 5-7, 6-3

Geraldine Beamish d. Eleanor Goss 6-1, 8-10, 6-3

Phyllis Howkins Covell–Dorothy Shepherd Barron d. Marion Zinderstein Jessup–Eleanor Goss 6-2, 6-2

Hazel Hotchkiss Wightman–Helen Wills (US) d. Kitty McKane–Evelyn Colyer 2-6, 6-2, 6-4

1925   Great Britain d. United States 4-3 (Forest Hills)

Kitty McKane d. Molla Bjurstedt Mallory 6-4, 5-7, 6-0

Helen Wills (US) d. Joan Fry 6-0, 7-5

Dorothea Douglass Lambert Chambers d. Eleanor Goss 7-5, 3-6, 6-1

Helen Wills (US) d. Kitty McKane 6-1, 1-6, 9-7

Molla Bjurstedt Mallory (US) d. Joan Fry 6-3, 6-0

Dorothea Douglass Lambert Chambers–Ermyntrude Harvey (GB) d. Molla Bjurstedt Mallory–May Sutton Bundy 10-8, 6-1

Kitty McKane–Evelyn Colyer (GB) d. Helen Wills–Mary K. Browne 6-0, 6-3

1926   United States d. Great Britain 4-3 (Wimbledon)

Elizabeth Ryan d. Joan Fry 6-1, 6-3

Kitty McKane Godfree (GB) d. Mary K. Browne 6-1, 7-5

Joan Fry (GB) d. Mary K. Browne 3-6, 6-0, 6-4

Kitty McKane Godfree (GB) d. Elizabeth Ryan 6-1, 5-7, 6-4

Marion Zinderstein Jessup d. Dorothy Shepherd Barron 6-1, 5-7, 6-4

Marion Zinderstein Jessup–Eleanor Goss d. Dorothea Douglass Lambert Chambers–Dorothy Shepherd Barron 6-4, 6-2

Mary K. Browne–Elizabeth Ryan d. Kitty McKane Godfree–Evelyn Colyer 2-6, 6-2, 6-4

1927   United States d. Great Britain 5-2 (Forest Hills)

Helen Wills d. Joan Fry 6-2, 6-0

Molla Bjurstedt Mallory d. Kitty McKane Godfree 6-4, 6-2

Betty Nuthall (GB) d. Helen Jacobs 6-3, 2-6, 6-1

Helen Wills d. Kitty McKane Godfree 6-1, 6-1

Molla Bjurstedt Mallory d. Joan Fry 6-2, 11-9

Gwendolyn Sterry–Betty Hill (GB) d. Eleanor Goss–Charlotte Hosmer Chapin 5-7, 7-5, 7-5

Helen Wills–Hazel Hotchkiss Wightman d. Kitty McKane Godfree–Ermyntrude Harvey 6-4, 4-6, 6-3

1928   Great Britain d. United States 4-3 (Wimbledon)

Helen Wills (US) d. Phoebe Holcroft Watson 6-1, 6-2

Eileen Bennett d. Molla Bjurstedt Mallory 6-1, 6-3

Helen Wills (US) d. Eileen Bennett 6-3, 6-2

Phoebe Holcroft Watson d. Molla Bjurstedt Mallory 2-6, 6-1, 6-2

Helen Jacobs (US) d. Betty Nuthall 6-3, 6-1

Ermyntrude Harvey–Peggy Saunders d. Eleanor Goss–Helen Jacobs 6-4, 6-1

Eileen Bennett–Phoebe Holcroft Watson d. Helen Wills–Penelope Anderson 6-2, 6-1

1929   United States d. Great Britain 4-3 (Forest Hills)

Helen Wills d. Phoebe Holcroft Watson 6-1, 6-4

Helen Jacobs d. Betty Nuthall 7-5, 8-6

Phoebe Holcroft Watson (GB) d. Helen Jacobs 6-3, 6-2

Edith Cross d. Peggy Saunders Michell 6-3, 3-6, 6-3

Helen Wills d. Betty Nuthall 8-6, 8-6

Phoebe Watson–Peggy Michell (GB) d. Helen Wills–Edith Cross 6-4, 6-1

Phyllis Howkins Covell–Dorothy Shepherd Barron (GB) d. Hazel Hotchkiss Wightman–Helen Jacobs 6-2, 6-1

1930   Great Britain d. United States 1-0 (Wimbledon)

Helen Wills Moody (US) d. Joan Fry 6-1, 6-1

Phoebe Holcroft Watson d. Helen Jacobs 2-6, 6-2, 6-4

Helen Wills Moody (US) d. Phoebe Watson 7-5, 6-1

Helen Jacobs (US) d. Joan Fry 6-0, 6-3

Phyllis Mudford d. Sarah Palfrey 6-0, 6-2

Joan Fry–Ermyntrude Harvey d. Sarah Palfrey–Edith Cross 2-6, 6-2, 6-4

Phoebe Holcroft Watson–Kitty McKane Godfree d. Helen Wills Moody–Helen Jacobs 7-5, 1-6, 6-4

1931   United States d. Great Britain 5-2 (Forest Hills, N.Y.)

Helen Wills Moody d. Betty Nuthall 6-4, 6-2

Anna McCune Harper d. Dorothy Round 6-3, 4-6, 9-7

Helen Jacobs d. Phyllis Mudford 6-4, 6-2

Helen Wills Moody d. Phyllis Mudford 6-1, 6-4

Helen Jacobs d. Betty Nuthall 8-6, 6-4

Phyllis Mudford–Dorothy Shepherd Barron (GB) d. Sarah Palfrey–Hazel Hotchkiss Wightman 6-4, 10-8

Betty Nuthall–Eileen Bennett Whittingstall (GB) d. Helen Moody–Anna Harper 8-6, 5-7, 6-3

1932   United States d. Great Britain 4-3 (Wimbledon)

Helen Jacobs d. Dorothy Round 6-4, 6-3

Helen Wills Moody d. Eileen Bennett Whittingstall 6-2, 6-4

Helen Wills Moody d. Dorothy Round 6-2, 6-3

Eileen Bennett Whittingstall (GB) d. Helen Jacobs 6-4, 2-6, 6-1

Phyllis Mudford King (GB) d. Anna McCune Harper 3-6, 6-3, 6-1

Anna McCune Harper–Helen Jacobs d. Peggy Saunders Michell–Dorothy Round 6-4, 6-1

Eileen Whittingstall–Betty Nuthall (GB) d. Helen Wills Moody–Sarah Palfrey 6-3, 1-6, 10-8

1933   United States d. Great Britain 4-3 (Forest Hills)

Helen Jacobs d. Dorothy Round 6-4, 6-2

Sarah Palfrey d. Margaret Scriven 6-3, 6-1

Betty Nuthall (GB) d. Carolin Babcock 1-6, 6-1, 6-3

Dorothy Round (GB) d. Sarah Palfrey 6-4, 10-8

Helen Jacobs d. Margaret Scriven 5-7, 6-2, 7-5

Helen Jacobs–Sarah Palfrey d. Dorothy Round–Mary Heeley 6-4, 6-2

Betty Nuthall–Freda James (GB) d. Alice Marble–Marjorie Gladman Van Ryn 7-5, 6-2

1934   United States d. Great Britain 5-2 (Wimbledon)

Sarah Palfrey d. Dorothy Round 6-3, 3-6, 8-6

Helen Jacobs d. Margaret Scriven 6-1, 6-1

Helen Jacobs d. Dorothy Round 6-4, 6-4

Sarah Palfrey d. Margaret Scriven 4-6, 6-2, 8-6

Betty Nuthall (GB) d. Carolin Babcock 5-7, 6-3, 6-4

Nancy Lyle–Evelyn Dearman (GB) d. Carolin Babcock–Josephine Cruickshank 7-5, 7-5

Helen Jacobs–Sarah Palfrey d. Kitty McKane Godfree–Betty Nuthall 5-7, 6-3, 6-2

1935   United States d. Great Britain 4-3 (Forest Hills)

Kay Stammers (GB) d. Helen Jacobs 5-7, 6-1, 9-7

Dorothy Round (GB) d. Ethel Burkhardt Arnold 6-0, 6-3

Sarah Palfrey Fabyan d. Phyllis Mudford King 6-0, 6-3

Helen Jacobs d. Dorothy Round 6-3, 6-2

Ethel Arnold d. Kay Stammers 6-2, 1-6, 6-3

Helen Jacobs–Sarah Palfrey Fabyan d. Kay Stammers–Freda James 6-3, 6-2

Nancy Lyle–Evelyn Dearman (GB) d. Dorothy Andrus–Carolin Babcock 3-6, 6-4, 6-1

1936   United States d. Great Britain 4-3 (Wimbledon)

Kay Stammers (GB) d. Helen Jacobs 12-10, 6-1

Dorothy Round (GB) d. Sarah Palfrey Fabyan 6-3, 6-4

Sarah Palfrey Fabyan d. Kay Stammers 6-3, 6-4

Dorothy Round (GB) d. Helen Jacobs 6-3, 6-3

Carolin Babcock d. Mary Hardwick 6-4, 4-6, 6-2

Carolin Babcock–Marjorie Gladman Van Ryn d. Evelyn Dearman–Nancy Lyle 6-2, 1-6, 6-3

Helen Jacobs–Sarah Palfrey Fabyan d. Kay Stammers–Freda James 1-6, 6-3, 7-5

1937   United States d. Great Britain 6-1 (Forest Hills)

Alice Marble d. Mary Hardwick 4-6, 6-2, 6-4

Helen Jacobs d. Kay Stammers 6-1, 4-6, 6-4

Helen Jacobs d. Mary Hardwick 2-6, 6-4, 6-2

Alice Marble d. Kay Stammers 6-3, 6-1

Sarah Palfrey Fabyan d. Margot Lumb 6-3, 6-1

Alice Marble–Sarah Palfrey Fabyan d. Evelyn Dearman–Joan Ingram 6-3, 6-2

Kay Stammers–Freda James (GB) d. Marjorie Gladman Van Ryn–Dorothy Bundy 6-3, 10-8

1938   United States d. Great Britain 5-2 (Wimbledon)

Kay Stammers (GB) d. Alice Marble 3-6, 7-5, 6-3

Helen Wills Moody d. Margaret Scriven 6-0, 7-5

Sarah Palfrey Fabyan d. Margot Lumb 5-7, 6-2, 6-3

Alice Marble d. Margaret Scriven 6-3, 3-6, 6-0

Helen Wills Moody d. Kay Stammers 6-2, 3-6, 6-3

Alice Marble–Sarah Palfrey Fabyan d. Margot Lumb–Freda James 6-4, 6-2

Evelyn Dearman–Joan Ingram (GB) d. Helen Wills Moody–Dorothy Bundy 6-2, 7-5

1939   United States d. Great Britain 5-2 (Forest Hills)

Alice Marble d. Mary Hardwick 6-3, 6-4

Kay Stammers (GB) d. Helen Jacobs 6-2, 1-6, 6-3

Valerie Scott (GB) d. Sarah Palfrey Fabyan 6-3, 6-4

Alice Marble d. Kay Stammers 3-6, 6-3, 6-4

Helen Jacobs d. Mary Hardwick 6-2, 6-2

Dorothy Bundy–Mary Arnold d. Betty Nuthall–Nina Brown 6-3, 6-1

Alice Marble–Sarah Palfrey Fabyan d. Kay Stammers–Freda James Hammersley 7-5, 6-2

1940–45 Not held, World War II

1946   United States d. Great Britain 7-0 (Wimbledon)

Pauline Betz d. Jean Bostock 6-2, 6-4

Margaret Osborne d. Jean Bostock 6-1, 6-4

Margaret Osborne d. Kay Stammers Menzies 6-3, 6-2

Louise Brough d. Joan Curry 8-6, 6-3

Pauline Betz d. Kay Menzies 6-4, 6-4

Margaret Osborne–Louise Brough d. Jean Bostock–Mary Halford 6-2, 6-1

Pauline Betz–Doris Hart d. Betty Passingham–Molly Lincoln 6-1, 6-3

1947   United States d. Great Britain 7-0 (Forest Hills)

Margaret Osborne d. Jean Bostock 6-4, 2-6, 6-2

Louise Brough d. Kay Stammers Menzies 6-4, 6-2

Doris Hart d. Betty Hilton 4-6, 6-3, 7-5

Louise Brough d. Jean Bostock 6-4, 6-4

Margaret Osborne d. Kay Menzies 7-5, 6-2

Doris Hart–Pat Canning Todd d. Joy Gannon–Jean Quertier 6-1, 6-2

Margaret Osborne–Louise Brough d. Jean Bostock–Betty Hilton 6-1, 6-4

1948   United States d. Great Britain 6-1 (Wimbledon)

Margaret Osborne duPont d. Jean Bostock 6-4, 8-6

Louise Brough d. Betty Hilton 6-1, 6-1

Margaret Osborne DuPont d. Betty Hilton 6-3, 6-4

Louise Brough d. Jean Bostock 6-2, 4-6, 7-5

Doris Hart d. Joy Gannon 6-1, 6-4

Louise Brough–Margaret Osborne DuPont d. Kay Stammers Menzies–Betty Hilton 6-2, 6-2

Jean Bostock–Molly Lincoln Blair (GB) d. Doris Hart–Pat Canning Todd 6-3, 6-4

1949   United States d. Great Britain 7-0 (Haverford, Pa.)

Doris Hart d. Jean Walker Smith 6-3, 6-1

Margaret Osborne duPont d. Betty Hilton 6-1, 6-3

Doris Hart d. Betty Hilton 6-1, 6-3

Margaret Osborne DuPont d. Jean Smith 6-4, 6-2

Beverly Baker d. Jean Quertier 6-4, 7-5

Doris Hart–Shirley Fry d. Jean Quertier–Molly Lincoln Blair 6-1, 6-2

Gertrude "Gussy" Moran–Pat Canning Todd d. Betty Hilton–Kay Tuckey 6-4, 8-6

1950   United States d. Great Britain 7-0 (Wimbledon)

Margaret Osborne duPont d. Betty Hilton 6-3, 6-4

Doris Hart d. Joan Curry 6-2, 6-4

Louise Brough d. Betty Hilton 2-6, 6-2, 7-5

Margaret Osborne DuPont d. Jean Walker-Smith 6-3, 6-2

Louse Brough d. Jean Smith 6-0, 6-0

Pat Canning Todd–Doris Hart d. Jean Walker-Smith–Jean Quertier 6-2, 6-3

Louise Brough–Margaret Osborne DuPont d. Betty Hilton–Kay Tuckey 6-2, 6-0

1951   United States d. Great Britain 6-1 (Chestnut Hill, Mass.)

Doris Hart d. Jean Quertier 6-4, 6-4

Shirley Fry d. Jean Walker-Smith 6-1, 6-4

Maureen Connolly d. Kay Tuckey 6-1, 6-3

Doris Hart d. Jean Walker-Smith 6-4, 2-6, 7-5

Jean Quertier (GB) d. Shirley Fry 6-3, 8-6

Pat Canning Todd–Nancy Chaffee d. Pat Ward–Joy Gannon Mottram 7-5, 6-3

Shirley Fry–Doris Hart d. Jean Quertier–Kay Tuckey 6-3, 6-3

1952   United States d. Great Britain 7-0 (Wimbledon)

Doris Hart d. Jean Quertier–Rinkel 6-3, 6-3

Maureen Connolly d. Jean Walker-Smith 3-6, 6-1, 7-5

Doris Hart d. Jean Walker-Smith 7-5, 6-2

Maureen Connolly d. Jean Quertier–Rinkel 9-7, 6-2

Shirley Fry d. Susan Partridge 6-0, 8-6

Shirley Fry–Doris Hart d. Helen Fletcher–Jean Quertier–Rinkel 8-6, 6-4

Louise Brough–Maureen Connolly d. Joy Gannon Mottram–Pat Ward 6-0, 6-3

1953   United States d. Great Britain 7-0 (Rye, N.Y.)

Maureen Connolly d. Angela Mortimer 6-1, 6-1

Doris Hart d. Helen Fletcher 6-4, 7-5

Shirley Fry d. Jean Quertier–Rinkel 6-2, 6-4

Maureen Connolly d. Helen Fletcher 6-1, 6-1

Doris Hart d. Angela Mortimer 6-1, 6-1

Maureen Connolly–Louise Brough d. Angela Mortimer–Anne Shilcock 6-2, 6-3

Doris Hart–Shirley Fry d. Jean Quertier–Rinkel–Helen Fletcher 6-2, 6-1

1954   United States d. Great Britain 6-0 (Wimbledon)

Maureen Connolly d. Helen Fletcher 6-1, 6-3

Doris Hart d. Anne Shilcock 6-4, 6-1

Doris Hart d. Helen Fletcher 6-1, 6-8, 6-2

Louise Brough d. Angela Buxton 8-6, 6-2

Maureen Connolly d. Anne Shilcock 6-2, 6-2

Louise Brough–Margaret Osborne duPont d. Angela Buxton–Pat Hird 2-6, 6-4, 7-5

Helen Fletcher–Anne Shilcock vs. Shirley Fry–Doris Hart (not played)

1955   United States d. Great Britain 6-1 (Rye, N.Y)

Angela Mortimer (GB) d. Doris Hart 6-4, 1-6, 7-5

Louise Brough d. Shirley Bloomer 6-2, 6-4

Louise Brough d. Angela Mortimer 6-0, 6-2

Dorothy Head Knode d. Angela Buxton 6-3, 6-3

Doris Hart d. Shirley Bloomer 7-5, 6-3

Louise Brough–Margaret Osborne duPont d. Shirley Bloomer–Pat Ward 6-3, 6-3

Doris Hart–Shirley Fry d. Angela Mortimer–Angela Buxton 3-6, 6-2, 7-5

1956   United States d. Great Britain 5-2 (Wimbledon)

Louise Brough d. Angela Mortimer 3-6, 6-4, 7-5

Shirley Fry d. Angela Buxton 6-2, 6-8, 7-5

Louise Brough d. Angela Buxton 3-6, 6-3, 6-4

Shirley Bloomer (GB) d. Dorothy Head Knode 6-4, 6-4

Angela Mortimer (GB) d. Shirley Fry 6-4, 6-3

Dorothy Knode–Beverly Baker Fleitz d. Shirley Bloomer–Pat Ward 6-1, 6-4

Louise Brough–Shirley Fry d. Angela Buxton–Angela Mortimer 6-2, 6-2

1957   United States d. Great Britain 6-1 (Sewickley, Pa.)

Althea Gibson d. Shirley Bloomer 6-4, 4-6, 6-2

Dorothy Head Knode d. Christine Truman 6-2, 11-9

Ann Haydon (GB) d. Darlene Hard 6-3, 3-6, 6-4

Dorothy Knode d. Shirley Bloomer 5-7, 6-1, 6-2

Althea Gibson d. Christine Truman 6-4, 6-2

Althea Gibson–Darlene Hard d. Shirley Bloomer–Sheila Armstrong 6-3, 6-4

Louise Brough–Margaret Osborne duPont d. Anne Shilcock–Ann Haydon 6-4, 6-1

1958   Great Britain d. United States 4-3 (Wimbledon)

Althea Gibson (US) d. Shirley Bloomer 6-3, 6-4

Christine Truman d. Dorothy Head Knode 6-4, 6-4

Dorothy Knode (US) d. Shirley Bloomer 6-4, 6-2

Christine Truman d. Althea Gibson 2-6, 6-3, 6-4

Ann Haydon d. Mimi Arnold 6-3, 5-7, 6-3

Christine Truman–Shirley Bloomer d. Karol Fageros–Dorothy Knode 6-2, 6-3

Althea Gibson–Janet Hopps (US) d. Anne Shilcock–Pat Ward 6-4, 3-6, 6-3

1959   United States d. Great Britain 4-3 (Sewickley, Pa.)

Beverly Baker Fleitz d. Angela Mortimer 6-2, 6-1

Christine Truman (GB) d. Darlene Hard 6-4, 2-6, 6-3

Darlene Hard d. Angela Mortimer 6-3, 6-8, 6-4

Beverly Fleitz d. Christine Truman 6-4, 6-4

Ann Haydon (GB) d. Sally Moore 6-1, 6-1

Darlene Hard–Jeanne Arth d. Shirley Bloomer Brasher–Christine Truman 9-7, 9-7

Ann Haydon–Angela Mortimer (GB) d. Janet Hopps–Sally Moore 6-2, 6-4

1960   Great Britain d. United States 4-3 (Wimbledon)

Ann Haydon d. Karen Hantze 2-6, 11-9, 6-1

Darlene Hard (US) d. Christine Truman 4-6, 6-3, 6-4

Darlene Hard (US) d. Ann Haydon 5-7, 6-2, 6-1

Christine Truman d. Karen Hantze 7-5, 6-3

Angela Mortimer d. Janet Hopps 6-8, 6-4, 6-1

Karen Hantze–Darlene Hard (US) d. Ann Haydon–Angela Mortimer 6-0, 6-0

Christine Truman–Shirley Bloomer Brasher d. Janet Hopps–Dorothy Head Knode 6-4, 9-7

1961   United States d. Great Britain 6-1 (Chicago)

Karen Hantze d. Christine Truman 7-9, 6-1, 6-1

Billie Jean Moffitt d. Ann Haydon 6-4, 6-4

Karen Hantze d. Ann Haydon 6-1, 6-4

Christine Truman (GB) d. Billie Jean Moffitt 6-3, 6-2

Justina Bricka d. Angela Mortimer 10-8, 4-6, 6-3

Karen Hantze–Billie Jean Moffitt d. Christine Truman–Deidre Catt 7-5, 6-2

Margaret Osborne duPont–Margaret Varner d. Angela Mortimer–Ann Haydon (default)

1962   United States d. Great Britain 4-3 (Wimbledon)

Darlene Hard d. Christine Truman 6-2, 6-2

Ann Haydon (GB) d. Karen Hantze Susman 10-8, 7-5

Deidre Catt (GB) d. Nancy Richey 6-1, 7-5

Darlene Hard d. Ann Haydon 6-3, 6-8, 6-4

Karen Susman d. Christine Truman 6-4, 7-5

Margaret Osborne duPont–Margaret Varner d. Deidre Catt–Elizabeth Starkie 6-3, 2-6, 6-2

Christine Truman–Ann Haydon (GB) d. Darlene Hard–Billie Jean Moffitt 6-4, 6-3

1963   United States d. Great Britain 6-1 (Cleveland)

Ann Haydon Jones (GB) d. Darlene Hard 6-1, 0-6, 8-6

Billie Jean Moffitt d. Christine Truman 6-4, 19-17

Nancy Richey d. Deidre Catt 14-12, 6-3

Darlene Hard d. Christine Truman 6-3, 6-0

Billie Jean Moffitt d. Ann Jones 6-4, 4-6, 6-3

Darlene Hard–Billie Jean Moffitt d. Christine Truman–Ann Jones 4-6, 7-5, 6-2

Nancy Richey–Donna Floyd Fales d. Deidre Catt–Elizabeth Starkie 6-4, 6-8, 6-2

1964   United States d. Great Britain 5-2 (Wimbledon)

Nancy Richey d. Deidre Catt 4-6, 6-4, 7-5

Billie Jean Moffitt d. Ann Haydon Jones 4-6, 6-2, 6-3

Carole Caldwell d. Elizabeth Starkie 6-4, 1-6, 6-3

Nancy Richey d. Ann Jones 7-5, 11-9

Billie Jean Moffitt d. Deidre Catt 6-3, 4-6, 6-3

Deidre Catt–Ann Jones (GB) d. Carole Caldwell–Billie Jean Moffitt 6-3, 4-6, 6-0

Angela Mortimer–Elizabeth Starkie (GB) d. Nancy Richey–Donna Floyd Fales 2-6, 6-3, 6-4

1965   United States d. Great Britain 5-2 (Cleveland)

Ann Haydon Jones (GB) d. Billie Jean Moffitt 6-2, 6-4

Nancy Richey d. Elizabeth Starkie 6-1, 6-0

Carole Caldwell Graebner d. Virginia Wade 3-6, 10-8, 6-4

Billie Jean Moffitt d. Elizabeth Starkie 6-3, 6-2

Ann Jones (GB) d. Nancy Richey 6-4, 9-7

Carole Graebner–Nancy Richey d. Nell Truman–Elizabeth Starkie 6-1, 6-0

Billie Jean Moffitt–Karen Hantze Susman d. Ann Jones–Virginia Wade 6-3, 8-6

1966   United States d. Great Britain 4-3 (Wimbledon)

Ann Haydon Jones (GB) d. Nancy Richey 2-6, 6-4, 6-3

Billie Jean Moffitt King d. Virginia Wade 6-2, 6-3

Winnie Shaw (GB) d. Mary Ann Eisel 6-3, 6-3

Nancy Richey d. Virginia Wade 2-6, 6-2, 7-5

Billie Jean King d. Ann Jones 5-7, 6-2, 6-3

Ann Jones–Virginia Wade (GB) d. Billie Jean King–Jane Albert 7-5, 6-2

Nancy Richey–Mary Ann Eisel d. Rita Bentley–Elizabeth Starkie 6-1, 6-2

1967   United States d. Great Britain 6-1 (Cleveland)

Billie Jean Moffitt King d. Virginia Wade 6-3, 6-2

Nancy Richey d. Ann Haydon Jones 6-2, 6-2

Christine Truman (GB) d. Rosie Casals 3-6, 7-5, 6-1

Nancy Richey d. Virginia Wade 3-6, 8-6, 6-2

Billie Jean King d. Ann Jones 6-1, 6-2

Rosie Casals–Billie Jean King d. Ann Jones–Virginia Wade 10-8, 6-4

Mary Ann Eisel–Carole Caldwell Graebner d. Winnie Shaw–Joyce Barclay Williams 8-6, 12-10

1968   Great Britain d. United States 4-3 (Wimbledon)

Nancy Richey (US) d. Christine Truman Janes 6-1, 8-6

Virginia Wade d. Mary Ann Eisel 6-0, 6-1

Jane "Peaches" Bartkowicz (US) d. Winnie Shaw 7-5, 3-6, 6-4

Mary Ann Eisel (US) d. Christine Janes 6-4, 6-3

Virginia Wade d. Nancy Richey 6-4, 2-6, 6-3

Virginia Wade–Winnie Shaw d. Nancy Richey–Mary Ann Eisel 5-7, 6-4, 6-3

Nell Truman–Christine Janes d. Stephanie DeFina–Kathy Harter 6-3, 2-6, 6-3

1969   United States d. Great Britain 5-2 (Cleveland)

Julie Heldman d. Virginia Wade 3-6, 6-1, 8-6

Nancy Richey d. Winnie Shaw 8-6, 6-2

Jane "Peaches" Bartkowicz d. Christine Truman Janes 8-6, 6-0

Christine Janes–Nell Truman (GB) d. Mary Ann Eisel Curtis–Valerie Ziegenfuss 6-1, 3-6, 6-4

Virginia Wade (GB) d. Nancy Richey 6-3, 2-6, 6-4

Julie Heldman d. Winnie Shaw 6-3, 6-4

Julie Heldman–Jane "Peaches" Bartkowicz d. Winnie Shaw–Virginia Wade 6-4, 6-2

1970   United States d. Great Britain 4-3 (Wimbledon)

Billie Jean Moffitt King d. Virginia Wade 8-6, 6-4

Ann Haydon Jones (GB) d. Nancy Richey 6-3, 6-2

Julie Heldman d. Joyce Barclay Williams 6-3, 6-2

Virginia Wade (GB) d. Nancy Richey 6-3, 6-2

Billie Jean King d. Ann Jones 6-4, 6-2

Ann Jones–Joyce William (GB) d. Mary Ann Eisel Curtis–Julie Heldman 6-3, 6-2

Billie Jean King–Jane "Peaches" Bartkowitz d. Virginia Wade–Winnie Shaw 7-5, 6-8, 6-2

1971   United States d. Great Britain 4-3 (Cleveland)

Chris Evert d. Winnie Shaw 6-0, 6-4

Virginia Wade (GB) d. Julie Heldman 7-5, 7-5

Joyce Barclay Williams (GB) d. Kristy Pigeon 7-5, 3-6, 6-4

Mary Ann Eisel Curtis–Valerie Ziegenfuss d. Christine Truman Janes–Nell Truman 6-1, 6-4

Valerie Ziegenfuss d. Winnie Shaw 6-4, 4-6, 6-3

Chris Evert d. Virginia Wade 6-1, 6-1

Virginia Wade–Joyce Williams (GB) d. Carole Caldwell Graebner–Chris Evert 10-8, 4-6, 6-1

1972   United States d. Great Britain 5-2 (Wimbledon)

Joyce Barclay Williams (GB) d. Wendy Overton 6-3, 3-6, 6-3

Chris Evert d. Virginia Wade 6-4, 6-4

Chris Evert–Patti Hogan d. Winnie Shaw–Nell Truman 7-5, 6-4

Patti Hogan d. Corinne Molesworth 6-8, 6-4, 6-2

Chris Evert d. Joyce Williams 6-2, 6-3

Virginia Wade (GB) d. Wendy Overton 8-6, 7-5

Valerie Ziegenfuss–Wendy Overton d. Virginia Wade–Joyce Willams 6-3, 6-3

1973   United States d. Great Britain 5-2 (Brookline, Mass.)

Chris Evert d. Virginia Wade 6-4, 6-2

Patti Hogan d. Veronica Burton 6-4, 6-3

Linda Tuero d. Glynis Coles 7-5, 6-2

Virginia Wade–Glynis Coles (GB) d. Chris Evert–Marita Redondo 6-3, 6-4

Chris Evert d. Veronica Burton 6-3, 6-0

Virginia Wade (GB) d. Patti Hogan 6-2, 6-2

Patti Hogan–Jeanne Evert d. Lindsey Beaven–Lesley Charles 6-3, 4-6, 8-6

1974   Great Britain d. United States 6-1, (Queensferry, North Wales)

Virginia Wade d. Julie Heldman 5-7, 9-7, 6-4

Glynis Coles d. Janet Newberry 4-6, 6-1, 6-3

Sue Barker d. Jeanne Evert 4-6, 6-4, 6-1

Lesley Charles–Sue Barker d. Janet Newberry–Betsy Nagelsen 4-6, 6-, 6-1

Glynis Cole d. Julie Heldman 6-0, 6-4

Virginia Wade d. Janet Newberry 6-1, 6-3

Julie Heldman–Mona Schallau (US) d. Virginia Wade–Glynis Coles 7-5, 6-4

1975   Great Britain d. United States 5-2 (Cleveland)

Virginia Wade d. Mona Schallau 6-2, 6-2

Chris Evert (US) d. Glynis Coles 6-4, 6-1

Sue Barker d. Janet Newberry 6-4, 7-5

Virginia Wade–Ann Haydon Jones d. Janet Newberry–Julie Anthony 6-2, 6-3

Chris Evert d. Virginia Wade 6-3, 7-6

Glynis Coles d. Mona Schallau 6-3, 7-6

Glynis Coles–Sue Barker d. Chris Evert–Mona Schallau 7-5, 6-4

1976   United States d. Great Britain 5-2 (Wimbledon)

Chris Evert d. Virginia Wade 6-2, 3-6, 6-3

Sue Barker (GB) d. Rosie Casals 1-6, 6-3, 6-2,

Terry Holladay d. Glynis Coles 3-6, 6-1, 6-4

Chris Evert–Rosie Casals d. Virginia Wade–Sue Barker 6-0, 5-7, 6-1

Virginia Wade (GB) d. Rosie Casals 3-6, 9-7, ret.

Chris Evert d. Sue Barker 2-6, 6-2, 6-2

Ann Kiyomura–Mona Schallau Guerrant d. Sue Mappin–Lesley Charles 6-2, 6-2

1977   United States d. Great Britain 7-0 (Oakland)

Chris Evert d. Virginia Wade 7-5, 7-6

Billie Jean Moffitt King d. Sue Barker 6-1, 6-4

Rosie Casals d. Michele Tyler 6-2, 3-6, 6-4

Billie Jean King–Jo Anne Russell d. Sue Mappin–Lesley Charles 6-0, 6-1

Billie Jean Moffitt King d. Virginia Wade 6-4, 3-6, 8-6

Chris Evert d. Sue Barker 6-1, 6-2

Chris Evert–Rosie Casals d. Virginia Wade–Sue Barker 6-2, 6-4

1978   Great Britain d. United States 4-3 (London)

Chris Evert (US) d. Sue Barker 6-2, 6-1

Michele Tyler d. Pam Shriver 5-7, 6-3, 6-3

Virginia Wade d. Tracy Austin 3-6, 7-5, 6-3

Billie Jean Moffitt King–Tracy Austin (US) d. Sue Mappin–Anne Hobbs 6-2, 4-6, 6-2

Chris Evert (US) d. Virginia Wade 6-0, 6-1

Sue Barker d. Tracy Austin 6-3, 3-6, 6-0

Virginia Wade–Sue Barker d. Chris Evert–Pam Shriver 6-0, 5-7, 6-4

1979   United States d. Great Britain 7-0 (Palm Beach, Fla.)

Chris Evert Lloyd d. Sue Barker 7-5, 6-2

Kathy Jordan d. Anne Hobbs 6-4, 6-7, 6-2

Tracy Austin d. Virginia Wade 6-1, 6-4

Tracy Austin–Ann Kiyomura d. Jo Durie–Debbie Jevans 6-3, 6-1

Tracy Austin d. Sue Barker 6-4, 6-2

Chris Evert Lloyd d. Virginia Wade 6-1, 6-1

Chris Evert Lloyd–Rosie Casals d. Virginia Wade–Sue Barker 6-0, 6-1

1980   United States d. Great Britain 5-2 (London)

Chris Evert Lloyd d. Sue Barker 6-1 6-2

Anne Hobbs d. Kathy Jordan 4-6, 6-4, 6-1

Andrea Jaeger d. Virginia Wade 3-6, 6-3, 6-2

Rosie Casals–Chris Evert Lloyd d. Glynis Coles–Anne Hobbs 6-3, 6-3

Chris Evert Lloyd d. Virginia Wade 7-5, 3-6, 7-5

Sue Barker d. Andrea Jaeger 5-7, 6-3, 6-3

Kathy Jordan–Anne Smith d. Sue Barker–Virginia Wade 6-4, 7-5

1981   United States d. Great Britain 7-0 (Chicago)

Tracy Austin d. Sue Barker 7-5, 6-3

Andrea Jaeger d. Anne Hobbs 6-0, 6-0

Chris Evert Lloyd d. Virginia Wade 6-1, 6-3

Andrea Jaeger–Pam Shriver d. Anne Hobbs–Jo Durie 6-1, 6-3

Tracy Austin d. Virginia Wade 6-3, 6-1

Chris Evert Lloyd d. Sue Barker 6-3, 6-0

Chris Evert Lloyd–Rosie Casals d. Glynis Coles–Virginia Wade 6-3, 6-3

1982   United States d. Great Britain 6-1 (London)

Barbara Potter d. Sue Barker 6-2, 6-2

Anne Smith d. Virginia Wade 3-6, 7-5, 6-3

Chris Evert Lloyd d. Jo Durie 6-2, 6-2

Jo Durie–Anne Hobbs d. Rosie Casals–Anne Smith 6-3, 2-6, 6-2

Barbara Potter d. Jo Durie 5-7, 7-6, 6-2

Chris Evert Lloyd d. Sue Barker 6-4, 6-3

Barbara Potter–Sharon Walsh d. Sue Barker–Virginia Wade 2-6, 6-4, 6-4

1983   United States d. Great Britain 6-1 (Williamsburg, Va.)

Martina Navratilova d. Sue Barker 6-2, 6-0

Kathy Rinaldi d. Virginia Wade 6-2, 6-2

Pam Shriver d. Jo Durie 6-3, 6-2

Sue Barker–Virginia Wade d. Candy Reynolds–Paula Smith 7-5, 3-6, 6-1

Pam Shriver d. Sue Barker 6-0, 6-1

Martina Navratilova d. Jo Durie 6-3, 6-3

Martina Navratilova–Pam Shriver d. Annabel Croft–Jo Durie 6-2, 6-1

1984   United States d. Great Britain 5-2 (London)

Chris Evert Lloyd d. Anne Hobbs 6-2, 6-2

Annabel Croft d. Alycia Moulton 6-1, 5-7, 6-4

Jo Durie d. Barbara Potter 6-3, 7-6

Chris Evert Lloyd–Alycia Moulton d. Virginia Wade–Amanda Brown 6-2, 6-2

Barbara Potter d. Anne Hobbs 6-1, 6-3

Chris Evert Lloyd d. Jo Durie 7-6, 6-1

Barbara Potter–Sharon Walsh d. Jo Durie–Anne Hobbs 7-6, 4-6, 9-7

1985   United States d. Great Britain 7-0 (Williamsburg, Va.)

Chris Evert Lloyd d. Jo Durie 6-2, 6-3

Kathy Rinaldi d. Anne Hobbs 7-5, 7-5

Pam Shriver d. Annabel Croft 6-0, 6-0

Betsy Nagelsen–Anne White d. Annabel Croft–Virginia Wade 6-4, 6-1

Pam Shriver d. Jo Durie 6-4, 6-4

Chris Evert Lloyd d. Annabel Croft 6-3, 6-0

Chris Evert Lloyd–Pam Shriver d. Jo Durie–Anne Hobbs 6-3, 6-7, 6-2

1986   United States d. Great Britain 7-0 (London)

Kathy Rinaldi d. Sara Gomer 6-3, 7-6

Stephanie Rehe d. Annabel Croft 6-3, 6-1

Bonnie Gadusek d. Jo Durie 6-2, 6-4

Bonnie Gadusek–Kathy Rinaldi d. Annabel Croft–Sara Gomer 6-3, 5-7, 6-3

Bonnie Gadusek d. Anne Hobbs 2-6, 6-4, 6-4

Kathy Rinaldi d. Jo Durie 6-4, 6-2

Elise Burgin–Anne White d. Jo Durie–Anne Hobbs 7-6, 6-3

1987   United States d. Great Britain 5-2 (Williamsburg, Va.)

Zina Garrison d. Anne Hobbs 7-5, 6-2

Lori McNeil d. Sara Gomer 6-2, 6-1

Pam Shriver d. Jo Durie 6-1, 7-5

Beatriz "Gigi" Fernandez–Robin White d. Sara Gomer–Clare Wood 6-4, 6-1

Pam Shriver d. Anne Hobbs 6-4, 6-3

Jo Durie d. Zina Garrison 7-6, 6-3

Jo Durie–Anne Hobbs d. Zina Garrison–Lori McNeil 0-6, 6-4, 7-5

1988   United States d. Great Britain 7-0 (London)

Zina Garrison d. Jo Durie 6-2, 6-4

Patty Fendick d. Monique Javer 6-2, 6-1

Lori McNeil d. Sara Gomer 6-7, 6-4, 6-4

Lori McNeil–Betsy Nagelsen d. Sara Gomer–Julie Salmon 6-3, 6-2

Zina Garrison d. Claire Wood 6-3, 6-2

Lori McNeil d. Jo Durie 6-1, 6-2

Beatriz "Gigi" Fernandez–Zina Garrison d. Jo Durie–Clare Wood 6-1, 6-3

1989   United States d. Great Britain 7-0 (Williamsburg, Va.)

Lori McNeil d. Jo Durie 7-5, 6-1

Jennifer Capriati d. Clare Wood 6-0, 6-0

Mary Joe Fernandez d. Sara Gomer 6-1, 6-2

Mary Joe Fernandez–Betsy Nagelsen d. Sara Gomer–Clare Wood 6-2 7-6

Lori McNeil d. Sara Gomer 6-4, 6-2

Mary Joe Fernandez d. Jo Durie 6-1, 7-5

Patty Fendick–Lori McNeil d. Jo Durie–Anne Hobbs 6-3, 6-3

ALL-TIME WIGHTMAN CUP RECORDS

INDIVIDUAL

Most Cup-winning years: 11—Helen Jacobs, U.S., 1927–39; , 1971–85

Most years played: 21—Virginia Wade, Britain, 1965–85

Most singles played: 35—Virginia Wade, Britain

Most singles won: 26—Chris Evert, U.S.

Most doubles played: 20—Virginia Wade, Britain

Most doubles won: 10—Louise Brough, U.S., 1946–57

Most singles and doubles together: 55—Virginia Wade, Britain

Most singles and doubles won together: 34—Chris Evert, U.S.

Most consecutive singles won: 26—Chris Evert, U.S.

Best winning percentage, 15 or more wins, singles and doubles altogether: 1.000—Chris Evert, U.S., 26 wins, 0 losses.

Best winning percentage, doubles, 5 or more wins: 1.000—Louise Brough, U.S., 10 wins, 0 losses

Best doubles team record: 7-0—Margaret Osborne duPont and Louise Brough, U.S., 1946–57

Longest singles: 46 games—Billie Jean Moffitt King, U.S., d. Christine Truman, 19-17, 6-4, 1963

Longest doubles: 40 games—Hazel Hotchkiss Wightman and Eleanor Goss, U.S., d. Kitty McKane and Phyllis Howkins Covell, 10-8, 5-7, 6-4, 1923

Most Cups won by captain: 12—Hazel Hotchkiss Wightman, 1923–48

GRAND PRIX MASTERS/ATP WORLD CHAMPIONSHIP

The Grand Prix Masters was a playoff for the top eight players at the end of a year-long series of Grand Prix tournaments. The players earned the right to play the Masters by accumulating points in tournaments throughout the year. It became a prestigious event from the time the first Masters was played under the sponsorship of Pepsi in 1970. Commercial Union sponsored the Grand Prix and the Masters from 1972 through 1976, and then Colgate, 1977–79, Volvo from 1980 to 1984, and Nabisco from 1985 to 1989. When the MIPTC (Men's International Professional Tennis Council) disbanded at the end of 1989, the ATP (Association of Tennis Professionals) took over their own tour with IBM as the sponsor from 1990 to 1992. When that transition occurred, the ATP moved the eight-player, round-robin event from Madison Square Garden in New York (where it had been since 1977) to the Festhalle in Frankfurt.

Meanwhile, Colgate established the Colgate International Series for women in 1976. This meant that the women had their own Grand Prix, and when the top eight women assembled in Palm Springs for the Colgate Series Championship, the tournament was a female version of the Masters.

In 1981 Toyota replaced Colgate as the primary sponsor for the women's tour and in 1981 and 1982 they held the year-end championship. The top eight players of the year continued to compete in a round-robin, eight-player format. In 1982 the top 16 were invited for a conventional, single elimination event.

MEN

YEAR	
1970	(Tokyo) Stan Smith won a round-robin among six players with 4-1 record ($15,000)
1971	(Paris) Ilie Nastase won a round-robin among seven players with 6-0 record ($15,000)
1972	(Barcelona) Ilie Nastase ($15,000) d. Stan Smith ($10,000) 6-3, 6-2, 3-6, 2-6, 6-3
1973	(Boston) Ilie Nastase ($15,000) d. Tom Okker ($10,000) 6-3, 7-5, 4-6, 6-3

1974	(Melbourne) Guillermo Vilas ($40,000) d. Ilie Nastase ($17,500) 7-6, 6-2, 3-6, 3-6, 6-4
1975	(Stockholm) Ilie Nastase ($40,000) d. Bjorn Borg ($20,000) 6-2, 6-2, 6-1
1976	(Houston) Manuel Orantes ($42,000) d. Wojtek Fibak ($20,000) 5-7, 6-2, 0-6, 7-6 (7-1), 6-1
1977	(New York) Jimmy Connors ($100,000) d. Bjorn Borg ($64,000) 6-4, 1-6, 6-4
1978	(New York) John McEnroe ($100,000) d. Arthur Ashe ($64,000) 6-7, 6-3, 7-5
1979	(New York) Bjorn Borg ($100,000) d. Vitas Gerulaitis ($64,000) 6-2, 6-2
1980	(New York) Bjorn Borg ($100,000) d. Ivan Lendl ($64,000) 6-4, 6-2, 6-2
1981	(New York) Ivan Lendl ($100,000) d. Vitas Gerulaitis ($50,000) 6-7 (5-7), 2-6, 7-6 (8-6), 6-2, 6-4
1982	(New York) Ivan Lendl ($100,000) d. John McEnroe ($60,000) 6-4, 6-4, 6-2
1983	(New York) John McEnroe ($100,000) d. Ivan Lendl ($60,000) 6-3, 6-4, 6-4
1984	(New York) John McEnroe ($100,000) d. Ivan Lendl ($60,000) 7-5, 6-0, 6-4
1985	(New York) Ivan Lendl ($100,000) d. Boris Becker ($70,000) 6-2, 7-6 (7-1), 6-3
1986	(New York) Ivan Lendl ($210,000) d. Boris Becker ($110,000) 6-4, 6-4, 6-4
1987	(New York) Ivan Lendl ($210,000) d. Mats Wilander ($90,000) 6-2, 6-2, 6-3
1988	(New York) Boris Becker ($285,000) d. Ivan Lendl ($135,000) 5-7, 7-6 (7-5), 3-6, 6-2, 7-6 (7-5)
1989	(New York) Stefan Edberg ($285,000) d. Boris Becker ($165,000) 4-6, 7-6 (8-6), 6-3, 6-1
1990	(Frankfurt) Andre Agassi ($950,000) d. Stefan Edberg ($400,000) 5-7, 7-6 (7-5), 7-5, 6-2
1991	(Frankfurt) Pete Sampras ($1,020,000) d. Jim Courier ($395,000) 3-6, 7-6 (7-5), 6-3, 6-4
1992	(Frankfurt) Boris Becker ($1,090,000) d. Jim Courier ($465,000) 6-4, 6-3, 7-5
1993	(Frankfurt) Michael Stich ($1,240,000) d. Pete Sampras ($610,000) 7-6 (7-3), 2-6, 7-6 (9-7), 6-2
1994	(Frankfurt) Pete Sampras ($1,225,000) d. Boris Becker ($665,000) 4-6, 6-3, 7-5, 6-4
1995	(Frankfurt) Boris Becker ($1,225,000) d. Michael Chang ($575,000) 7-6 (7-3), 6-0, 7-6 (7-5)
1996	(Hanover) Pete Sampras ($1,340,000) d. Boris Becker ($640,000) 3-6, 7-6 (7-5), 7-6 (7-4), 6-7 (11-13), 6-4

WTA CHAMPIONSHIPS

The Women's Tennis Association season-concluding playoffs are best known as the Virginia Slims Championships (the original sponsorship, 1972–78 and 1983–94), but have also operated under other sponsorships, such as Avon (1979–82), Corel (1995), and Chase (1996—).

In the fall of 1970 a breakaway group of nine women, including ringleaders Billie Jean King and Rosie Casals, guided by Gladys Heldman, founder-publisher of *World Tennis* magazine, were determined to establish pro tennis with decent prize money for women. Virginia Slims put up prize money for the first small tournament, Houston ($7,500), and the Houston Nine (Casals, King, Valerie Ziegenfuss, Nancy Richey, Kristy Pigeon, Judy Tegart Dalton, Kerry Melville, Julie Heldman, Peaches Bartkowicz) bucked their national associations by going on their own. Casals won $1,700, over Dalton, 5-7, 6-1, 7-5, and in effect a genuine professional tour for women was launched. A Slims winter circuit followed in 1971, and the playoffs for leaders in a points system was instituted in 1972 on clay at Boca Raton, Fla., with the 32 top players. An amateur, Chris Evert, won, and turned down the $12,000 first prize. After 1973 it became an indoor event, played principally in California until settling into New York's Madison Square Garden in 1979. It has taken various forms—round robin, double-elimination—but since 1983 has been a straight elimination tourney for the top 16 women and 8 doubles teams. In 1984, the singles final became the only best-of-five set test for women.

VIRGINIA SLIMS CHAMPIONSHIPS

YEAR	
1972	(Boca Raton, Fla.) Chris Evert d. Kerry Melville Reid 7-5, 6-4
1973	(Boca Raton, Fla.) Chris Evert d. Nancy Richey 6-3, 6-3
1974	(Los Angeles) Evonne Goolagong d. Chris Evert 6-3, 6-4
1975	(Los Angeles) Chris Evert d. Martina Navratilova 6-4, 6-2
1976	(Los Angeles) Evonne Goolagong d. Chris Evert 6-3, 5-7, 6-3
1977	(New York) Chris Evert d. Sue Barker 2-6, 6-1, 6-1
1978	(Oakland) Martina Navratilova d. Evonne Goolagong 7-6, 6-4

AVON CHAMPIONSHIPS

YEAR	
1979	(New York) Martina Navratilova d. Tracy Austin 6-3, 3-6, 6-2
1980	(New York) Tracy Austin d. Martina Navratilova 6-2, 2-6, 6-2
1981	(New York) Martina Navratilova d. Andrea Jaeger 6-3, 7-6 (7-3)
1982	(New York) Sylvia Hanika d. Martina Navratilova 1-6, 6-3, 6-4

VIRGINIA SLIMS CHAMPIONSHIPS

YEAR	
1983	(New York) Martina Navratilova d. Chris Evert 6-2, 6-0
1984	(New York) Martina Navratilova d. Chris Evert Lloyd 6-3, 7-5, 6-1
1985	(New York) Martina Navratilova d. Helena Sukova 6-3, 7-5, 6-4
1986	(spring) (New York) Martina Navratilova d. Hana Mandlikova 6-2, 6-0, 3-6, 6-1
1986	(fall) (New York) Martina Navratilova d. Steffi Graf 7-6 (7-1), 6-3, 6-2
1987	(New York) Steffi Graf d. Gabriela Sabatini 4-6, 6-4, 6-0, 6-4

1988	(New York) Gabriela Sabatini d. Pam Shriver 7-5, 6-2, 6-2
1989	(New York) Steffi Graf d. Martina Navratilova 6-4, 7-5, 2-6, 6-2
1990	(New York) Monica Seles d. Gabriela Sabatini 6-4, 5-7, 3-6, 6-4, 6-2
1991	(New York) Monica Seles d. Martina Navratilova 6-4, 3-6, 7-5, 6-0
1992	(New York) Monica Seles d. Martina Navratilova 7-5, 6-3, 6-1
1993	(New York) Steffi Graf d. Arantxa Sanchez Vicario 6-1, 6-4, 3-6, 6-1
1994	(New York) Gabriela Sabatini d. Lindsay Davenport 6-3, 6-3, 6-4

COREL CHAMPIONSHIPS
YEAR	
1995	(New York) Steffi Graf d. Anke Huber 6-1, 2-6, 6-1, 4-6, 6-3

CHASE CHAMPIONSHIPS
YEAR	
1996	(New York) Steffi Graf d. Martina Hingis 6-3, 4-6, 6-0, 4-6, 6-0

COLGATE SERIES/TOYOTA SERIES CHAMPIONS (WOMEN)

In the early years of the Virginia Slims Tour, another compatible tour sprang up: the Colgate Series (1976) followed by the Toyota Series (1979), also with season ending playoffs for leading tour players. This tour stopped operating after 1982.

YEAR	
1976	(Palm Springs, Cal.) Chris Evert d. Françoise Durr 6-1, 6-2
1977	(Palm Springs, Cal.) Chris Evert d. Billie Jean King 6-2, 6-2
1978	(Palm Springs, Cal.) Chris Evert d. Martina Navratilova 6-3, 6-3
1979	(Landover, Md.) Martina Navratilova d. Tracy Austin 6-2, 6-1
1980	(Landover, Md.) Tracy Austin d. Andrea Jaeger 6-2, 6-2
1981	(East Rutherford, N.J.) Tracy Austin d. Martina Navratilova 2-6, 6-4, 6-2
1982	(East Rutherford, N.J.) Martina Navratilova d. Chris Evert Lloyd 4-6, 6-1, 6-2

GRAND SLAM CUP

The Grand Slam Cup was organized by the ITF in 1990 to compete with the ATP Championship as a year-end attraction, continuing the divisive rivalry of the two bodies. Containing a similar cast of players, it brings together in Munich the top 16 in finishers during the four majors. It offers $6 million in prize money, and the largest first prize (varying according to a bonus scheme). The winners the first three years (Pete Sampras, David Wheaton, Michael Stich) got a flat $2 million each.

YEAR	
1990	Pete Sampras ($2,000,000) d. Brad Gilbert ($1,000,000) 6-3, 6-4, 6-2
1991	David Wheaton ($2,000,000) d. Michael Chang ($1,000,000) 7-5, 6-2, 6-4

1992	Michael Stich ($2,000,000) d. Michael Chang ($1,000,000) 6-2, 6-3, 6-2
1993	Petr Korda ($1,625,000) d. Michael Stich ($812,500) 2-6, 6-4, 7-6 (7-5), 2-6, 11-9
1994	Magnus Larrson ($1,500,000) d. Pete Sampras ($750,000) 7-6 (8-6), 4-6, 7-6 (7-5), 6-4
1995	Goran Ivanisevic ($1,625,000) d. Todd Martin ($812,500) 7-6 (7-4), 6-3, 6-4
1996	Boris Becker ($1,875,000) d. Goran Ivanisevic ($812,500) 6-3, 6-4, 6-4

WORLD CHAMPIONSHIP TENNIS

World Championship Tennis (WCT), Dallas-based, was the first solid promoter of the open era. The 1967 brainchild of Dave Dixon of New Orleans soon had to be bailed out and taken over by his partners Lamar Hunt and Al Hill, Jr., in Dallas. Dixon and aide Bob Briner hastened the advent of opens by skimming the cream of amateurism late in 1967, signing John Newcombe, Tony Roche, Cliff Drysdale, Nikki Pilic and Roger Taylor to pro contracts. Adding pros Dennis Ralston, Pierre Barthes, Butch Buchholz to the mix called the "Handsome Eight," WCT began as a small circuit in 1968, but expanded under the guidance of Hunt and his director, Mike Davies, to a global operation, attracting TV and substantial sponsorship dollars. The tour climaxed with the season-ending playoffs for the eight top finishers in Dallas. Starting in 1971 with an astounding first prize of $50,000, by far the richest (won by Ken Rosewall), it became a focal point of the year every May through 1989. WCT alternately battled and integrated with the ITF's Grand Prix circuit until 1990. That year the Grand Prix and WCT were killed by Hamilton Jordan, new executive director of the ATP, who rearranged the male tennis firmament in establishing the ATP Tour.

WCT FINALS
YEAR	
1971	Ken Rosewall d. Rod Laver 6-4, 1-6, 7-6, 7-6
1972	Ken Rosewall d. Rod Laver 4-6, 6-0, 6-3, 6-7, 7-6
1973	Stan Smith d. Arthur Ashe 6-3, 6-3, 4-6, 6-4
1974	John Newcombe d. Bjorn Borg 4-6, 6-3, 6-2, 6-3
1975	Arthur Ashe d. Bjorn Borg 3-6, 6-4, 6-4, 6-0
1976	Bjorn Borg d. Guillermo Vilas 1-6, 6-1, 7-5, 6-1
1977	Jimmy Connors d. Dick Stockton 6-7, 6-1, 6-4, 6-3
1978	Vitas Gerulaitis d. Eddie Dibbs 6-3, 6-2, 6-1

1979 John McEnroe d. Bjorn Borg 7-5, 4-6, 6-2, 7-6
1980 Jimmy Connors d. John McEnroe 2-6, 7-6, 6-1, 6-2
1981 John McEnroe d. Johan Kriek 6-1, 6-2, 6-4
1982 Ivan Lendl d. John McEnroe 6-2, 3-6, 6-3, 6-3
1983 John McEnroe d. Ivan Lendl 6-2, 4-6, 6-3, 6-7, 7-6
1984 John McEnroe d. Jimmy Connors 6-1, 6-2, 6-3
1985 Ivan Lendl d. Tim Mayotte 7-6, 6-4, 6-1
1986 Anders Jarryd d. Boris Becker 6-7, 6-1, 6-1, 6-4
1987 Miloslav Mecir d. John McEnroe 6-0, 3-6, 6-2, 6-2
1988 Boris Becker d. Stefan Edberg 6-4, 1-6, 7-5, 6-2
1989 John McEnroe d. Brad Gilbert 6-3, 6-3, 7-6

UNITED STATES TENNIS ASSOCIATION RANKINGS

Every year the United States Tennis Association, formerly the U.S. Lawn Tennis Association, releases annual rankings for the leading male and female players in the country. Until 1969, these rankings included only amateur players, but when open tennis arrived in 1968, bringing the pros and amateurs together under the same roof, it was inevitable that the American rankings would soon include all players.

USTA Men's Rankings

# Indicates foreign citizens residing in the U.S.

* Indicates tie

1885

1. Richard Sears
2. James Dwight
3. Walter Berry
4. Godfrey Brinley
5. Joseph Clark
6. Alex Moffat
7. Livingston Beeckman
8. Howard Taylor
9. Fred Mansfield
10. Percy Knapp

1886

1. Richard Sears
2. James Dwight
3. Livingston Beeckman
4. Howard Taylor
5. Joseph Clark
6. Henry Slocum
7. Godfrey Brinley
8. Fred Mansfield
9. Alex Moffat
10. Richard Conover

1887

1. Richard Sears
2. Henry Slocum
3. Livingston Beeckman
4. Howard Taylor
5. Joseph Clark
6. Fred Mansfield
7. Philip Sears
8. Godfrey Brinley
9. Edward P. MacMullen
10. Quincy Shaw

1888

1. Henry Slocum
2. Howard Taylor
3. James Dwight
4. Joseph Clark
5. Charles Chase
6. Philip Sears
7. Edward P. MacMullen
8. Oliver Campbell
9. Livingston Beeckman
10. Fred Mansfield

1889

1. Henry Slocum
2. Quincy Shaw
3. Oliver Campbell
4. Howard Taylor
5. Charles Chase
6. Joseph Clark
7. Percy Knapp
8. Bob Huntington
9. Philip Sears
10. Fred Mansfield

1890

1. Oliver Campbell
2. Bob Huntington
3. Percy Knapp
4. Henry Slocum
5. Fred Hovey
6. Clarence Hobart
7. Philip Sears
8. Howard Taylor
9. Charles Chase
10. Valentine Hall

1891

1. Oliver Campbell
2. Clarence Hobart
3. Bob Huntington
4. Fred Hovey
5. Edward Hall
6. Valentine Hall
7. Philip Sears
8. Samuel Chase
9. Charles Lee
10. Marmaduke Smith

1892

1. Oliver Campbell
2. Edward Hall
3. Percy Knapp
4. Clarence Hobart
5. Fred Hovey
6. Bill Larned
7. Malcolm Chace
8. Robert Wrenn
9. Richard Stevens
10. Charles Hubbard

1893

1. Robert Wrenn
2. Clarence Hobart
3. Fred Hovey
4. Malcolm Chace
5. Bill Larned
6. Edward Hall
7. Richard Stevens
8. Arthur Foote
9. John Howland
10. Clarence Budlong

1894

1. Robert Wrenn
2. Bill Larned
3. Manliffe Goodbody
4. Fred Hovey
5. Malcolm Chace
6. Clarence Hobart
7. Richard Stevens
8. Clarence Budlong
9. Arthur Foote
10. Gordon Parker

1895

1. Fred Hovey
2. Bill Larned
3. Malcolm Chace
4. John Howland
5. Robert Wrenn
6. Carr Neel
7. Clarence Hobart
8. Richard Stevens
9. Arthur Foote
10. Clarence Budlong

1896

1. Robert Wrenn
2. Bill Larned
3. Carr Neel
4. Fred Hovey
5. Edwin Fischer
6. George Wrenn
7. Richard Stevens
8. Malcolm Whitman
9. Leo Ware
10. George Sheldon

1897

1. Robert Wrenn
2. Bill Larned
3. # Wilberforce Eaves
4. # Harold Nisbet
5. Harold Mahony
6. George Wrenn
7. Malcolm Whitman
8. Kreigh Collins
9. Edwin Fischer
10. William Bond

1898

1. Malcolm Whitman
2. Leo Ware
3. William Bond
4. Dwight Davis
5. Clarence Budlong
6. Edwin Fischer
7. George Wrenn
8. Richard Stevens
9. Stephen Millett
10. George Belden

1899

1. Malcolm Whitman
2. Dwight Davis
3. Bill Larned
4. Parmly Paret
5. Kreigh Collins
6. George Wrenn
7. Leo Ware
8. Beals Wright
9. Holcombe Ward
10. Bob Huntington

1900

1. Malcolm Whitman
2. Dwight Davis
3. Bill Larned
4. Beals Wright
5. Kreigh Collins
6. George Wrenn
7. Holcolmbe Ward
8. Leo Ware
9. John Allen
10. Ray Little

1901

1. Bill Larned
2. Beals Wright
3. Dwight Davis
4. Leo Ware
5. Clarence Hobart
6. Ray Little
7. Holcolmbe Ward
8. Kreigh Collins
9. Edwin Fischer
10. Bill Clothier

1902

1. Bill Larned
2. Malcolm Whitman
3. Beals Wright
4. Holcolmbe Ward
5. Bill Clothier
6. Leo Ware
7. Ray Little
8. Harold Hackett
9. Clarence Hobart
10. Kreigh Collins

1903

1. Bill Larned
2. Holcolmbe Ward
3. Bill Clothier
4. Beals Wright
5. Kreigh Collins
6. Edward Larned
7. Harry Allen
8. Edgar Leonard
9. Richard Carleton
10. Ken Horton

1904

1. Holcombe Ward
2. Bill Clothier
3. Bill Larned
4. Beals Wright
5. Kreigh Collins
6. Ray Little
7. Fred Alexander
8. Richard Stevens
9. Alphonzo Bell
10. Edgar Leonard

1905

1. Beals Wright
2. Holcombe Ward
3. Bill Larned
4. Bill Clothier
5. Fred Alexander
6. Clarence Hobart
7. Richard Stevens
8. Kreigh Collins
9. Ray Little
10. Fred Anderson

1906

1. Bill Clothier
2. Bill Larned
3. Beals Wright
4. Fred Alexander
5. Karl Behr
6. Ray Little
7. Harold Hackett
8. Fred Anderson
9. Ed Dewhurst
10. Irving Wright

1907

1. Bill Larned
2. Beals Wright
3. Karl Behr
4. Ray Little
5. Bob LeRoy
6. Clarence Hobart
7. Edward Larned
8. Robert Seaver
9. Irving Wright
10. Fred Colston

1908

1. Bill Larned
2. Beals Wright
3. Fred Alexander
4. Bill Clothier
5. Ray Little
6. Bob LeRoy
7. Nat Emerson
8. Nat Niles
9. Wallace Johnson
10. Richard Palmer

1909

1. Bill Larned
2. Bill Clothier
3. Wallace Johnson
4. Nat Niles
5. Ray Little
6. Maurice McLoughlin
7. Melville Long
8. Karl Behr
9. Edward Larned
10. Bob LeRoy

1910

1. Bill Larned
2. Tom Bundy
3. Beals Wright
4. Maurice McLoughlin
5. Melville Long
6. Nat Niles
7. Gus Touchard
8. Theodore Pell
9. Fred Colston
10. Carlton Gardner

1911

1. Bill Larned
2. Maurice McLoughlin
3. Tom Bundy
4. Gus Touchard
5. Melville Long
6. Nat Niles
7. Theodore Pell
8. Ray Little
9. Karl Behr
10. Walter Hall

1912

1. Maurice McLoughlin
2. Dick Williams
3. Wallace Johnson
4. Bill Clothier
5. Nat Niles
6. Tom Bundy
7. Karl Behr
8. Ray Little
9. George "Peabo" Gardner
10. Gus Touchard

1913

1. Maurice McLoughlin
2. Dick Williams
3. Bill Clothier
4. Bill Johnston
5. Theodore Pell
6. Nat Niles
7. Wallace Johnson
8. Gus Touchard
9. George "Peabo" Gardner
10. John Strachan

1914

1. Maurice McLoughlin
2. Dick Williams
3. Karl Behr
4. R. Lindley Murray
5. Bill Clothier
6. Bill Johnston
7. George Church
8. Fred Alexander
9. Watson Washburn
10. Elia Fottrell

1915

1. Bill Johnston
2. Dick Williams
3. Maurice McLoughlin
4. Karl Behr
5. Theodore Pell
6. Nat Niles
7. Clarence Griffin
8. Watson Washburn
9. George Church
10. Walter Hall

1916

1. Dick Williams
2. Bill Johnston
3. George Church
4. R. Lindley Murray
5. # Ichiya Kumagae
6. Clarence Griffin
7. Watson Washburn
8. Wallace Davis
9. Joseph Armstrong
10. Dean Mathey

1917

No rankings, World War I

1918

1. R. Lindley Murray
2. Bill Tilden
3. Fred Alexander
4. Walter Hall
5. Walter Hayes
6. Nat Niles
7. # Ichiya Kumagae
8. Chuck Garland
9. Howard Voshell
10. Theodore Pell

1919

1. Bill Johnston
2. Bill Tilden
3. # Ichiya Kumagae
4. R. Lindley Murray
5. Wallace Johnson
6. Dick Williams
7. Roland Roberts
8. Chuck Garland
9. Walter Hayes
10. Watson Washburn

1920

1. Bill Tilden
2. Bill Johnston
3. Dick Williams
4. # Ichiya Kumagae
5. Willis Davis
6. Clarence Griffin
7. Watson Washburn
8. Chuck Garland
9. Nat Niles
10. Wallace Johnson

1921

1. Bill Tilden
2. Bill Johnston
3. Vinnie Richards
4. Wallace Johnson
5. Watson Washburn
6. Dick Williams
7. # Ichiya Kumagae
8. Howard Voshell
9. Larry Rice
10. Nat Niles

1922

1. Bill Tilden
2. Bill Johnston
3. Vinnie Richards
4. Dick Williams
5. Wallace Johnson
6. Bob Kinsey
7. # Zenzo Shimidzu
8. Howard Kinsey
9. Frank Hunter
10. Watson Washburn

1923

1. Bill Tilden
2. Bill Johnston
3. Dick Williams
4. Vinnie Richards
5. Frank Hunter
6. Howard Kinsey
7. Carl Fischer
8. # Brian "Babe" Norton
9. Harvey Snodgrass
10. Bob Kinsey

1924

1. Bill Tilden
2. Vinnie Richards
3. Bill Johnston
4. Howard Kinsey
5. Wallace Johnson
6. Harvey Snodgrass
7. John Hennessey
8. # Brian "Babe" Norton
9. George Lott
10. Clarence Griffin

1925

1. Bill Tilden
2. Bill Johnston
3. Vinnie Richards
4. Dick Williams
5. # Manuel Alonso
6. Howard Kinsey
7. # Takeichi Harada
8. Cranston Holman
9. # Brian "Babe" Norton
10. Wray Brown

1926

1. Bill Tilden
2. # Manuel Alonso
3. # Takeichi Harada
4. Bill Johnston
5. Ed Chandler
6. Lewis White
7. Al Chapin
8. # Brian "Babe" Norton
9. George Lott
10. George King

1927

1. Bill Tilden
2. Frank Hunter
3. George Lott
4. # Manuel Alonso
5. John Hennessey
6. John Van Ryn
7. Arnold Jones
8. John Doeg
9. Lewis White
10. Cranston Holman

1928

1. Bill Tilden
2. Frank Hunter
3. George Lott
4. John Hennessey
5. Wilmer Allison
6. John Van Ryn
7. Fred Mercur
8. John Doeg
9. Julius Seligson
10. Frank Shields

1929

1. Bill Tilden
2. Frank Hunter
3. John Doeg
4. George Lott
5. John Van Ryn
6. Fred Mercur
7. Wilmer Allison
8. Wilbur Coen
9. Berkeley Bell
10. Greg Mangin

1930

1. John Doeg
2. Frank Shields
3. Wilmer Allison
4. Sidney Wood
5. Cliff Sutter
6. Greg Mangin
7. George Lott
8. Ellsworth Vines
9. John Van Ryn
10. Bryan "Bitsy" Grant

1931

1. Ellsworth Vines
2. George Lott
3. Frank Shields
4. John Van Ryn
5. John Doeg
6. Cliff Sutter
7. Sidney Wood
8. Keith Gledhill
9. Wilmer Allison
10. Berkeley Bell

1932

1. Ellsworth Vines
2. Wilmer Allison
3. Cliff Sutter
4. Sidney Wood
5. Frank Shields
6. Lester Stoefen
7. Greg Mangin
8. Keith Gledhill
9. John Van Ryn
10. David Jones

1933

1. Frank Shields
2. Wilmer Allison
3. Lester Stoefen
4. Cliff Sutter
5. Greg Mangin
6. Sidney Wood
7. Bryan "Bitsy" Grant
8. Frank Parker
9. Keith Gledhill
10. George Lott

1934

1. Wilmer Allison
2. Sidney Wood
3. Frank Shields
4. Frank Parker
5. Lester Stoefen
6. George Lott
7. Berkeley Bell
8. Cliff Sutter
9. Don Budge
10. Bryan "Bitsy" Grant

1935

1. Wilmer Allison
2. Don Budge
3. Bryan "Bitsy" Grant
4. Frank Shields
5. Sidney Wood
6. Greg Mangin
7. Frank Parker
8. Gilbert Hall
9. Wilmer Hines
10. Berkeley Bell

1936

1. Don Budge
2. Frank Parker
3. Bryan "Bitsy" Grant
4. Bobby Riggs
5. Greg Mangin
6. John Van Ryn
7. John McDiarmid
8. Charlie Harris
9. Joe Hunt
10. Arthur Hendrix

1937

1. Don Budge
2. Bobby Riggs
3. Frank Parker
4. Bryan "Bitsy" Grant
5. Joe Hunt
6. Wayne Sabin
7. Hal Surface
8. Gene Mako
9. Don McNeill
10. John Van Ryn

1938

1. Don Budge
2. Bobby Riggs
3. Gene Mako
4. Sidney Wood
5. Joe Hunt
6. Bryan "Bitsy" Grant
7. Elwood Cooke
8. Frank Parker
9. Gilbert Hunt
10. Frank Kovacs

1939

1. Bobby Riggs
2. Frank Parker
3. Don McNeill
4. Welby Van Horn
5. Wayne Sabin
6. Elwood Cooke
7. Bryan "Bitsy" Grant
8. Gardnar Mulloy
9. Gilbert Hunt
10. Henry Prusoff

1940

1. Don McNeill
2. Bobby Riggs
3. Frank Kovacs
4. Joe Hunt
5. Frank Parker
6. Jack Kramer
7. Gardnar Mulloy
8. Henry Prusoff
9. Elwood Cooke
10. Ted Schroeder

1941

1. Bobby Riggs
2. Frank Kovacs
3. Frank Parker
4. Don McNeill
5. Ted Schroeder
6. Wayne Sabin
7. Gardnar Mulloy
8. Bryan "Bitsy" Grant
9. Jack Kramer
10. Bill Talbert

1942

1. Ted Schroeder
2. Frank Parker
3. Gardnar Mulloy
4. # Francisco "Pancho" Segura
5. Bill Talbert
6. Sidney Wood
7. Seymour Greenberg
8. George Richards
9. Vic Seixas
10. Ladislav Hecht

1943

1. Joe Hunt
2. Jack Kramer
3. # Francisco "Pancho" Segura
4. Bill Talbert
5. Seymour Greenberg
6. Sidney Wood
7. Bob Falkenburg
8. Frank Parker
9. Jim Brink
10. Jack Tuero

1944

1. Frank Parker
2. Bill Talbert
3. # Francisco "Pancho" Segura
4. Don McNeill
5. Seymour Greenberg
6. Bob Falkenburg
7. Jack Jossi
8. Charles Oliver
9. Jack McManis
10. Gilbert Hall

1945

1. Frank Parker
2. Bill Talbert
3. # Francisco "Pancho" Segura
4. Elwood Cooke
5. Sidney Wood
6. Gardnar Mulloy
7. Frank Shields
8. Hal Surface
9. Seymour Greenberg
10. Jack McManis

1946

1. Jack Kramer
2. Ted Schroeder
3. Frank Parker
4. Tom Brown
5. Gardnar Mulloy
6. Bill Talbert
7. Don McNeill
8. Bob Falkenburg
9. Eddie Moylan
10. # Francisco "Pancho" Segura

1947

1. Jack Kramer
2. Frank Parker
3. Ted Schroeder
4. Gardnar Mulloy
5. Bill Talbert
6. # Francisco "Pancho" Segura
7. Bob Falkenburg
8. Eddie Moylan
9. Earl Cochell
10. Seymour Greenberg

1948

1. Richard "Pancho" Gonzalez
2. Ted Schroeder
3. Frank Parker
4. Bill Talbert
5. Bob Falkenburg
6. Earl Cochell
7. Vic Seixas
8. Gardnar Mulloy
9. Herbie Flam
10. Harry Likas

1949

1. Richard "Pancho" Gonzalez
2. Ted Schroeder
3. Bill Talbert
4. Frank Parker
5. Gardnar Mulloy
6. Art Larsen
7. Earl Cochell
8. Sam Match
9. Eddie Moylan
10. Herbie Flam

1950

1. Art Larsen
2. Herbie Flam
3. Ted Schroeder
4. Gardnar Mulloy
5. Bill Talbert
6. Dick Savitt
7. Earl Cochell
8. Vic Seixas
9. Tom Brown
10. Sam Match

1951

1. Vic Seixas
2. Dick Savitt
3. Tony Trabert
4. Herbie Flam
5. Bill Talbert
6. Art Larsen
7. Ted Schroeder
8. Gardnar Mulloy
9. Ham Richardson
10. J. Edward "Budge" Patty

1952

1. Gardnar Mulloy
2. Vic Seixas
3. Art Larsen
4. Dick Savitt
5. Herbie Flam
6. Bill Talbert
7. Ham Richardson
8. Tom Brown
9. Noel Brown
10. Harry Likas

1953

1. Tony Trabert
2. Vic Seixas
3. Art Larsen
4. Gardnar Mulloy
5. Straight Clark
6. Ham Richardson
7. Bernard "Tut" Bartzen
8. Tom Brown
9. Noel Brown
10. Grant Golden

1954

1. Vic Seixas
2. Tony Trabert
3. Ham Richardson
4. Art Larsen
5. Gardnar Mulloy
6. Tom Brown
7. Eddie Moylan
8. Bernard "Tut" Bartzen
9. Bill Talbert
10. Gilbert Shea

1955

1. Tony Trabert
2. Vic Seixas
3. Art Larsen
4. Bernard "Tut" Bartzen
5. Eddie Moylan
6. Gilbert Shea
7. Ham Richardson
8. Herbie Flam
9. Sammy Glammalva
10. Tom Brown

1956

1. Ham Richardson
2. Herbie Flam
3. Vic Seixas
4. Eddie Moylan
5. Bernard "Tut" Bartzen
6. Bob Perry
7. Sammy Giammalva
8. Art Larsen
9. Gilbert Shea
10. Grant Golden

1957

1. Vic Seixas
2. Herbie Flam
3. Dick Savitt
4. Gilbert Shea
5. Barry MacKay
6. Ron Holmberg
7. Tom Brown
8. Whitney Reed
9. Bernard "Tut" Bartzen
10. William Quillian

1958

1. Ham Richardson
2. # Alex Olmedo
3. Barry MacKay
4. Bernard "Tut" Bartzen
5. Herbie Flam
6. Dick Savitt
7. Sammy Giammalva
8. Vic Seixas
9. Earl "Butch" Buchholz, Jr.
10. Tom Brown

1959

1. # Alex Olmedo
2. Bernard "Tut" Bartzen
3. Barry MacKay
4. Ron Holmberg
5. Dick Savitt
6. Earl "Butch" Buchholz, Jr.
7. Mike Franks
8. Noel Brown
9. Whitney Reed
10. Vic Seixas

1960

1. Barry MacKay
2. Bernard "Tut" Bartzen
3. Earl "Butch" Buchholz, Jr.
4. Chuck McKinley
5. Dennis Ralston
6. Jon Douglas
7. Ron Holmberg
8. Whitney Reed
9. Donald Dell
10. Chris Crawford

1961

1. Whitney Reed
2. Chuck McKinley
3. Bernard "Tut" Bartzen
4. Jon Douglas
5. Donald Dell
6. Frank Froehling III
7. Ron Holmberg
8. Allen Fox
9. Jack Frost
10. Bill Bond

1962

1. Chuck McKinley
2. Frank Froehling III
3. Ham Richardson
4. Allen Fox
5. Jon Douglas
6. Whitney Reed
7. Donald Dell
8. Gene Scott
9. Marty Riessen
10. Charlie Pasarell

1963

1. Chuck McKinley
2. Dennis Ralston
3. Frank Froehling III
4. Gene Scott
5. Marty Riessen
6. Arthur Ashe
7. Ham Richardson
8. Allen Fox
9. Tom Edlefsen
10. Charlie Pasarell

1964

1. Dennis Ralston
2. Chuck McKinley
3. Arthur Ashe
4. Frank Froehling III
5. Gene Scott
6. Ron Holmberg
7. Ham Richardson
8. Allen Fox
9. Clark Graebner
10. Marty Riessen

1965

1. Dennis Ralston
2. Arthur Ashe
3. Cliff Richey
4. Chuck McKinley
5. Charlie Pasarell
6. Ham Richardson
7. # Mike Belkin
8. Marty Riessen
9. Ron Holmberg
10. Tom Edlefsen

1966

1. Dennis Ralston
2. Arthur Ashe
3. Clark Graebner
4. Charlie Pasarell
5. Cliff Richey
6. Ron Holmberg
7. Marty Riessen
8. Frank Froehling III
9. Vic Seixas
10. Chuck McKinley

1967

1. Charlie Pasarell
2. Arthur Ashe
3. Cliff Richey
4. Clark Graebner
5. Marty Riessen
6. Ron Holmberg
7. Stan Smith
8. Allen Fox
9. Gene Scott
10. Bob Lutz

1968

1. Arthur Ashe
2. Clark Graebner
3. Stan Smith
4. Cliff Richey
5. Bob Lutz
6. Ron Holmberg
7. Charlie Pasarell
8. Jim Osborne
9. Jim McManus
10. Gene Scott

1969

1. Stan Smith
2. Arthur Ashe
3. Cliff Richey
4. Clark Graebner
5. Charlie Pasarell
6. Bob Lutz
7. Tom Edlefsen
8. Roy Barth
9. Jim Osborne
10. Jim McManus

1970

1. Cliff Richey
2. Stan Smith
3. Arthur Ashe
4. Clark Graebner
5. Bob Lutz
6. Tom Gorman
7. Jim Osborne
8. Jim McManus
9. Barry MacKay
10. Charlie Pasarell

1971

1. Stan Smith
2. Cliff Richey
3. Clark Graebner
4. Tom Gorman
5. Jimmy Connors
6. Erik van Dillen
7. Frank Froehling III
8. Roscoe Tanner
9. Alex Olmedo
10. Harold Solomon

All-American Ranking, 1970–71

*(In 1970 and 1971 contract pro-
fessionals were not included in the
traditional rankings. In those years
an additional All-American ranking
was made to include professionals
of every status.)*

1970

1. Cliff Richey
2. Stan Smith
3. Marty Riessen
4. Arthur Ashe
5. Dennis Ralston
6. Richard "Pancho" Gonzalez
7. Clark Graebner
8. Bob Lutz
9. Tom Gorman
10. Earl " Butch" Buchholz, Jr.

1971

1. Stan Smith
2. Arthur Ashe
3. Marty Riessen
4. Cliff Richey
5. Clark Graebner
6. Tom Gorman
7. Jimmy Connors
8. Erik van Dillen
9. Frank Froehling III
10. Bob Lutz

1972

1. Stan Smith
2. Tom Gorman
3. Jimmy Connors
4. Dick Stockton
5. Roscoe Tanner
6. Harold Solomon
7. Erik van Dillen
8. Clark Graebner
9. Richard "Pancho" Gonzalez
10. Brian Gottfried

1973

1. * Jimmy Connors
   * Stan Smith
3. Arthur Ashe
4. Tom Gorman
5. Cliff Richey
6. Charlie Pasarell
7. Marty Riessen
8. Erik van Dillen
9. Brian Gottfried
10. Bob Lutz

1974

1. Jimmy Connors
2. Stan Smith
3. Marty Riessen
4. Roscoe Tanner
5. Arthur Ashe
6. Tom Gorman
7. Dick Stockton
8. Harold Solomon
9. Charlie Pasarell
10. Jeff Borowiak

1975

1. Arthur Ashe
2. Jimmy Connors
3. Roscoe Tanner
4. Vitas Gerulaitis
5. Eddie Dibbs
6. Brian Gottfried
7. Harold Solomon
8. Bob Lutz
9. Cliff Richey
10. Dick Stockton

1976

1. Jimmy Connors
2. Eddie Dibbs
3. Arthur Ashe
4. Harold Solomon
5. Brian Gottfried
6. Roscoe Tanner
7. Dick Stockton
8. Stan Smith
9. Vitas Gerulaitis
10. Bob Lutz

1977

1. Jimmy Connors
2. Brian Gottfried
3. Vitas Gerulaitis
4. Eddie Dibbs
5. Dick Stockton
6. Harold Solomon
7. Stan Smith
8. Roscoe Tanner
9. Bob Lutz
10. John McEnroe

1978

1. Jimmy Connors
2. Vitas Gerulaitis
3. Brian Gottfried
4. Eddie Dibbs
5. John McEnroe
6. Alex "Sandy" Mayer
7. Roscoe Tanner
8. Harold Solomon
9. Arthur Ashe
10. Dick Stockton

1979

1. John McEnroe
2. Jimmy Connors
3. Roscoe Tanner
4. Vitas Gerulaitis
5. Arthur Ashe
6. Eddie Dibbs
7. Harold Solomon
8. Peter Fleming
9. Gene Mayer
10. Brian Gottfried

1980

1. John McEnroe
2. Jimmy Connors
3. Gene Mayer
4. Vitas Gerulaitis
5. Harold Solomon
6. Brian Gottfried
7. Eddie Dibbs
8. Roscoe Tanner
9. Eliot Teltscher
10. Stan Smith

1981

1. John McEnroe
2. Jimmy Connors
3. Gene Mayer
4. Brian Teacher
5. Vitas Gerulaitis
6. Eliot Teltscher
7. Roscoe Tanner
8. Brian Gottfried
9. Bill Scanlon
10. Mel Purcell

1982

1. Jimmy Connors
2. John McEnroe
3. Vitas Gerulaitis
4. Gene Mayer
5. Alex "Sandy" Mayer
6. Johan Kriek
7. Eliot Teltscher
8. Brian Teacher
9. Steve Denton
10. Brian Gottfried

1983

1. John McEnroe
2. Jimmy Connors
3. Jimmy Arias
4. Gene Mayer
5. Bill Scanlon
6. Eliot Teltscher
7. Johan Kriek
8. Alex "Sandy" Mayer
9. Brian Teacher
10. Brian Gottfried

1984

1. John McEnroe
2. Jimmy Connors
3. Johan Kriek
4. Eliot Teltscher
5. Jimmy Arias
6. Aaron Krickstein
7. Vitas Gerulaitis
8. Gene Mayer
9. Brad Gilbert
10. Mark Dickson

1985

1. John McEnroe
2. Jimmy Connors
3. Kevin Curren
4. Tim Mayotte
5. Johan Kriek
6. Paul Annacone
7. Brad Gilbert
8. Eliot Teltscher
9. Scott Davis
10. Greg Holmes

1986

1. Jimmy Connors
2. John McEnroe
3. Brad Gilbert
4. Tim Mayotte
5. Kevin Curren
6. Robert Seguso
7. Aaron Krickstein
8. Johan Kriek
9. David Pate
10. Tim Wilkison

1987

1. Jimmy Connors
2. John McEnroe
3. Tim Mayotte
4. Brad Gilbert
5. David Pate
6. Eliot Teltscher
7. Paul Annacone
8. Jimmy Arias
9. Kevin Curren
10. Andre Agassi

1988

1. Andre Agassi
2. Jimmy Connors
3. John McEnroe
4. Tim Mayotte
5. Aaron Krickstein
6. Kevin Curren
7. Brad Gilbert
8. Michael Chang
9. Robert Seguso
10. Dan Goldie

1989

1. John McEnroe
2. Brad Gilbert
3. Michael Chang
4. Andre Agassi
5. Aaron Krickstein
6. Tim Mayotte
7. Jay Berger
8. Jimmy Connors
9. Kevin Curren
10. Jim Courier

1990

1. Andre Agassi
2. Pete Sampras
3. Brad Gilbert
4. John McEnroe
5. Jay Berger
6. Michael Chang
7. Jim Courier
8. David Wheaton
9. Aaron Krickstein
10. Richey Reneberg

1991

1. Jim Courier
2. Pete Sampras
3. Andre Agassi
4. Michael Chang
5. David Wheaton
6. Derrick Rostagno
7. Jimmy Connors
8. Brad Gilbert
9. John McEnroe
10. Richey Reneberg

1992

1. Jim Courier
2. Pete Sampras
3. Michael Chang
4. Andre Agassi
5. Ivan Lendl
6. John McEnroe
7. Aaron Krickstein
8. MaliVai Washington
9. David Wheaton
10. Brad Gilbert

1993

1. Pete Sampras
2. Jim Courier
3. Andre Agassi
4. Michael Chang
5. Todd Martin
6. MaliVai Washington
7. Ivan Lendl
8. Richey Reneberg
9. Brad Gilbert
10. Aaron Krickstein

1994

1. Pete Sampras
2. Andre Agassi
3. Todd Martin
4. Jim Courier
5. Michael Chang
6. MaliVai Washington
7. Ivan Lendl
8. Richey Reneberg
9. David Wheaton
10. Aaron Krickstein

1995

1. Andre Agassi
2. Pete Sampras
3. Michael Chang
4. Jim Courier
5. Todd Martin
6. MaliVai Washington
7. Patrick McEnroe
8. Richey Reneberg
9. David Wheaton
10. Aaron Krickstein

1996

1. Pete Sampras
2. Michael Chang
3. Andre Agassi
4. Todd Martin
5. MaliVai Washington
6. Jim Courier
7. Richey Reneberg
8. Alex O'Brien
9. Chris Woodruff
10. Vince Spadea

USTA Women's Rankings

1913

1. Mary K. Browne
2. Ethel Sutton Bruce
3. Florence Sutton
4. Helen Homans McLean
5. Louise Riddell Williams
6. Marie Wagner
7. Dorothy Green Briggs
8. Edith Rotch
9. Anita Myers
10. Gwendolyn Rees

1914

1. Mary K. Browne
2. Florence Sutton
3. Marie Wagner
4. Louise Hammond Raymond
5. Edith Rotch
6. Eleonora Sears
7. Louise Riddell Williams
8. Sarita Van Vliet Wood
9. Mrs. H. Niemeyer
10. Sara Livingston

1915

1. Molla Bjurstedt
2. Hazel Hotchkiss Wightman
3. Helen Homans McLean
4. Florence Sutton
5. Maud Barger Wallach
6. Marie Wagner
7. Anita Myers
8. Sara Livingston
9. Clare Cassel
10. Eleonora Sears

1916

1. Molla Bjurstedt
2. Louise Hammond Raymond
3. Evelyn Sears
4. Anita Myers
5. Sara Livingston
6. Marie Wagner
7. Adelaide Browning Green
8. Martha Guthrie
9. Eleonora Sears
10. Maud Barger Wallach

1917

No rankings

1918

1. Molla Bjurstedt
2. Hazel Hotchkiss Wightman
3. Adelaide Browning Green
4. Eleanor Goss
5. Marie Wagner
6. Carrie Neely
7. Corinne Gould
8. Helene Pollak
9. Edith Handy
10. Clare Cassel

1919

1. Hazel Hotchkiss Wightman
2. Eleanor Goss
3. Molla Bjurstedt Mallory
4. Marion Zinderstein
5. Helen Baker
6. Louise Hammond Raymond
7. Helen Gilleaudeau
8. Marie Wagner
9. Corinne Gould
10. Helene Pollak

1920

1. Molla Bjurstedt Mallory
2. Marion Zinderstein
3. Eleanor Tennant
4. Helen Baker
5. Eleanor Goss
6. Louise Hammond Raymond
7. Helene Pollak Falk
8. Edith Sigourney
9. Florence Ballin
10. Marie Wagner

1921

1. Molla Bjurstedt Mallory
2. Mary K. Browne
3. Marion Zinderstein Jessup
4. May Sutton Bundy
5. Eleanor Goss
6. Helen Gilleaudeau
7. Anne Sheafe Cole
8. Leslie Bancroft
9. Louise Hammond Raymond
10. Margaret Grove

1922

1. Molla Bjurstedt Mallory
2. Leslie Bancroft
3. Helen Wills
4. Marion Zinderstein Jessup
5. May Sutton Bundy
6. Martha Bayard
7. Helen Gilleaudeau
8. Mollie Thayer
9. Marie Wagner
10. Florence Ballin

1923

1. Helen Wills
2. Molla Bjurstedt Mallory
3. Eleanor Goss
4. Lillian Scharman
5. Helen Gilleaudeau Lockhorn
6. Mayme MacDonald
7. Edith Sigourney
8. Leslie Bancroft
9. Martha Bayard
10. Helen Hooker

1924

1. Helen Wills
2. Mary K. Browne
3. Molla Bjurstedt Mallory
4. Eleanor Goss
5. Marion Zinderstein Jessup
6. Martha Bayard
7. Mayme MacDonald
8. Anne Sheafe Cole
9. Mollie Thayer
10. Leslie Bancroft

1925

1. Helen Wills
2. Elizabeth Ryan
3. Molla Bjurstedt Mallory
4. Marion Zinderstein Jessup
5. Eleanor Goss
6. Mary K. Browne
7. Martha Bayard
8. May Sutton Bundy
9. Charlotte Hosmer
10. Edith Sigourney

1926

1. Molla Bjurstedt Mallory
2. Elizabeth Ryan
3. Eleanor Goss
4. Martha Bayard
5. Charlotte Hosmer Chapin
6. Betty Corbiere
7. Margaret Blake
8. Penelope Anderson
9. Edna Hauselt Roeser
10. Ellis Endicott

1927

1. Helen Wills
2. Molla Bjurstedt Mallory
3. Charlotte Hosmer Chapin
4. Helen Jacobs
5. Eleanor Goss
6. Betty Corbiere
7. Penelope Anderson
8. Margaret Blake
9. Edna Hauselt Roeser
10. Alice Francis

1928

1. Helen Wills
2. Helen Jacobs
3. Edith Cross
4. Molla Bjurstedt Mallory
5. May Sutton Bundy
6. Marjorie Morrill
7. Marjorie Gladman
8. Anna McCune Harper
9. Charlotte Hosmer Chapin
10. Betty Corbiere

1929

1. Helen Wills Moody
2. Helen Jacobs
3. Edith Cross
4. Sarah Palfrey
5. Anna McCune Harper
6. Mary Greef
7. Eleanor Goss
8. Ethel Burkhardt
9. Marjorie Gladman
10. Josephine Cruickshank

1930

1. Anna McCune Harper
2. Marjorie Morrill
3. Dorothy Weisel
4. Virginia Hilleary
5. Josephine Cruickshank
6. Ethel Burkhardt
7. Marjorie Gladman Van Ryn
8. Sarah Palfrey
9. Mary Greef
10. Edith Cross

1931

1. Helen Wills Moody
2. Helen Jacobs
3. Anna McCune Harper
4. Marion Zinderstein Jessup
5. Mary Greef
6. Marjorie Morrill
7. Sarah Palfrey
8. Marjorie Gladman Van Ryn
9. Virginia Hilleary
10. Dorothy Andrus Burke

1932

1. Helen Jacobs
2. Anna McCune Harper
3. Carolin Babcock
4. Marjorie Morrill Painter
5. Josephine Cruickshank
6. Virginia Hilleary
7. Alice Marble
8. Marjorie Gladman Van Ryn
9. Virginia Rice
10. Marjorie Sachs

1933

1. Helen Jacobs
2. Helen Wills Moody
3. Alice Marble
4. Sarah Palfrey
5. Carolin Babcock
6. Josephine Cruickshank
7. Maud Rosenbaum Levi
8. Marjorie Gladman Van Ryn
9. Virginia Rice
10. Agnes Sherwood Lamme

1934

1. Helen Jacobs
2. Sarah Palfrey Fabyan
3. Carolin Babcock
4. Dorothy Andrus
5. Maude Rosenbaum Levi
6. Jane Sharp
7. Marjorie Morrill Painter
8. Mary Greef Harris
9. Marjorie Sachs
10. Catherine Wolf

1935

1. Helen Jacobs
2. Ethel Burkhardt Arnold
3. Sarah Palfrey Fabyan
4. Carolin Babcock
5. Marjorie Gladman Van Ryn
6. Gracyn Wheeler
7. Mary Greef Harris
8. Agnes Lamme
9. Dorothy Andrus
10. Catherine Wolf

1936

1. Alice Marble
2. Helen Jacobs
3. Sarah Palfrey Fabyan
4. Gracyn Wheeler
5. Carolin Babcock
6. Helen Pedersen
7. Marjorie Gladman Van Ryn
8. Dorothy Bundy
9. Katherine Winthrop
10. Mary Greef Harris

1937

1. Alice Marble
2. Helen Jacobs
3. Dorothy Bundy
4. Marjorie Gladman Van Ryn
5. Gracyn Wheeler
6. Sarah Palfrey Fabyan

7. Dorothy Burke Andrus
8. Helen Pedersen
9. Carolin Babcock Stark
10. Katherine Winthrop

1938

1. Alice Marble
2. Sarah Palfrey Fabyan
3. Dorothy Bundy
4. Barbara Winslow
5. Gracyn Wheeler
6. Dorothy Workman
7. Margaret Osborne
8. Helen Pedersen
9. Virginia Wolfenden
10. Katherine Winthrop

1939

1. Alice Marble
2. Helen Jacobs
3. Sarah Palfrey Fabyan
4. Helen Bernhard
5. Virginia Wolfenden
6. Dorothy Bundy
7. Dorothy Workman
8. Pauline Betz
9. Katherine Winthrop
10. Mary Arnold

1940

1. Alice Marble
2. Helen Jacobs
3. Pauline Betz
4. Dorothy Bundy
5. Gracyn Wheeler Kelleher
6. Sarah Palfrey Cooke
7. Virginia Wolfenden
8. Helen Bernhard
9. Mary Arnold
10. Hope Knowles

1941

1. Sarah Palfrey Cooke
2. Pauline Betz
3. Dorothy Bundy
4. Margaret Osborne
5. Helen Jacobs
6. Helen Bernhard
7. Hope Knowles
8. Mary Arnold
9. Virginia Wolfenden Kovacs
10. Louise Brough

1942

1. Pauline Betz
2. Louise Brough
3. Margaret Osborne
4. Helen Bernhard
5. Mary Arnold

6. Doris Hart
7. Pat Canning Todd
8. Helen Pedersen Rihbany
9. Madge Harshaw Vosters
10. Katherine Winthrop

1943

1. Pauline Betz
2. Louise Brough
3. Doris Hart
4. Margaret Osborne
5. Dorothy Bundy
6. Mary Arnold
7. Dorothy Head
8. Helen Bernhard
9. Helen Pedersen Rihbany
10. Katherine Winthrop

1944

1. Pauline Betz
2. Margaret Osborne
3. Louise Brough
4. Dorothy Bundy
5. Mary Arnold
6. Doris Hart
7. Virginia Wolfenden Kovacs
8. Shirley Fry
9. Pat Canning Todd
10. Dorothy Head

1945

1. Sarah Palfrey Cooke
2. Pauline Betz
3. Margaret Osborne
4. Louise Brough
5. Pat Canning Todd
6. Doris Hart
7. Shirley Fry
8. Mary Arnold Prentiss
9. Dorothy Bundy
10. Helen Pedersen Rihbany

1946

1. Pauline Betz
2. Margaret Osborne
3. Louise Brough
4. Doris Hart
5. Pat Canning Todd
6. Dorothy Bundy Cheney
7. Shirley Fry
8. Mary Arnold Prentiss
9. Virginia Wolfenden Kovacs
10. Dorothy Head

1947

1. Louise Brough
2. Margaret Osborne duPont
3. Doris Hart
4. Pat Canning Todd
5. Shirley Fry
6. Barbara Krase
7. Dorothy Head
8. Mary Arnold Prentiss
9. Gertrude "Gussy" Moran
10. Helen Pedersen Rihbany

1948

1. Margaret Osborne duPont
2. Louise Brough
3. Doris Hart
4. Gertrude "Gussy" Moran
5. Beverly Baker
6. Pat Canning Todd
7. Shirley Fry
8. Helen Pastall Perez
9. Virginia Wolfenden Kovacs
10. Helen Pedersen Rihbany

1949

1. Margaret Osborne duPont
2. Louise Brough
3. Doris Hart
4. Pat Canning Todd
5. Helen Pastall Perez
6. Shirley Fry
7. Gertrude "Gussy" Moran
8. Beverly Baker Beckett
9. Dorothy Head
10. Barbara Scofield

1950

1. Margaret Osborne duPont
2. Doris Hart
3. Louise Brough
4. Beverly Baker
5. Pat Caning Todd
6. Nancy Chaffee
7. Barbara Scofield
8. Shirley Fry
9. Helen Pastall Perez
10. Maureen Connolly

1951

1. Maureen Connolly
2. Doris Hart
3. Shirley Fry

4. Nancy Chaffee Kiner
5. Pat Canning Todd
6. Beverly Baker Fleitz
7. Dorothy Head
8. Betty Rosenquest Pratt
9. Magda Rurac
10. Mercedes "Baba" Madden Lewis

1952

1. Maureen Connolly
2. Doris Hart
3. Shirly Fry
4. Louise Brough
5. Nancy Chaffee Kiner
6. Anita Kanter
7. Pat Canning Todd
8. Mercedes "Baba" Madden Lewis
9. Althea Gibson
10. Julie Sampson

1953

1. Maureen Connolly
2. Doris Hart
3. Shirley Fry
4. Louise Brough
5. Margaret Osborne duPont
6. Helen Pastall Perez
7. Althea Gibson
8. Mercedes "Baba" Madden Lewis
9. Anita Kanter
10. Julie Sampson

1954

1. Doris Hart
2. Louise Brough
3. Beverly Baker Fleitz
4. Shirley Fry
5. Betty Rosenquest Pratt
6. Barbara Breit
7. Darlene Hard
8. Lois Felix
9. Helen Pastall Perez
10. Barbara Scofield Davidson

1955

1. Doris Hart
2. Shirley Fry
3. Louise Brough
4. Dorothy Head Knode
5. Beverly Baker Fleitz
6. Barbara Scofield Davidson
7. Barbara Breit
8. Althea Gibson
9. Darlene Hard
10. Dorothy Bundy Cheney

1956

1. Shirley Fry
2. Althea Gibson
3. Louise Brough
4. Margaret Osborne duPont
5. Betty Rosenquest Pratt
6. Dorothy Head Knode
7. Darlene Hard
8. Karol Fageros
9. Janet Hopps
10. Miriam Arnold

1957

1. Althea Gibson
2. Louise Brough
3. Dorothy Head Knode
4. Darlene Hard
5. Karol Fageros
6. Miriam Arnold
7. Jeanne Arth
8. Sally Moore
9. Janet Hopps
10. Mary Ann Mitchell

1958

1. Althea Gibson
2. Beverly Baker Fleitz
3. Darlene Hard
4. Dorothy Head Knode
5. Margaret Osborne duPont
6. Jeanne Arth
7. Janet Hopps
8. Sally Moore
9. Gwyneth Thomas
10. Mary Ann Mitchell

1959

1. Beverly Baker Fleitz
2. Darlene Hard
3. Dorothy Head Knode
4. Sally Moore
5. Janet Hopps
6. Karen Hantze
7. Barbara Green Weigandt
8. Karol Fageros
9. Miriam Arnold
10. Lois Felix

1960

1. Darlene Hard
2. Karen Hantze
3. Nancy Richey
4. Billie Jean Moffitt
5. Donna Floyd
6. Janet Hopps
7. Gwyneth Thomas
8. Vicki Palmer
9. Kathy Chabot
10. Carol Hanks

1961

1. Darlene Hard
2. Karen Hantze
3. Billie Jean Moffitt
4. Kathy Chabot
5. Justina Bricka
6. Gwyneth Thomas
7. Marilyn Montgomery
8. Judy Alvarez
9. Carole Caldwell
10. Donna Floyd

1962

1. Darlene Hard
2. Karen Hantze Susman
3. Billie Jean Moffitt
4. Carole Caldwell
5. Donna Floyd Fales
6. Nancy Richey
7. Vicki Palmer
8. Gwyneth Thomas
9. Justina Bricka
10. Judy Alvarez

1963

1. Darlene Hard
2. Billie Jean Moffitt
3. Nancy Richey
4. Carole Caldwell
5. Gwyneth Thomas
6. Judy Alvarez
7. Carol Hanks
8. Tory Fretz
9. Donna Floyd Fales
10. Julie Heldman

1964

1. Nancy Richey
2. Billie Jean Moffitt
3. Carole Caldwell Graebner
4. Karen Hantze Susman
5. Carol Hanks Aucamp
6. Jane Albert
7. Julie Heldman
8. Justina Bricka
9. Tory Fretz
10. Mary Ann Eisel

1965

1. * Nancy Richey
   * Billie Jean Moffitt
3. Carole Caldwell Graebner
4. Jane Albert
5. Mary Ann Eisel
6. Carol Hanks Aucamp
7. Kathy Harter
8. Julie Heldman
9. Tory Fretz
10. Donna Floyd Fales

1966

1. Billie Jean Moffitt King
2. Nancy Richey
3. Rosie Casals
4. Tory Fretz
5. Jane "Peaches" Bartkowicz
6. Mary Ann Eisel
7. Donna Floyd Fales
8. Carol Hanks Aucamp
9. Stephanie DeFina
10. Fern "Peachy" Kellmeyer

1967

1. Billie Jean Moffitt King
2. Nancy Richey
3. Mary Ann Eisel
4. Jane "Peaches" Bartkowicz
5. Rosie Casals
6. Carole Caldwell Graebner
7. Stephanie DeFina
8. Kathy Harter
9. Lynne Abbes
10. Vicky Rogers

1968

1. Nancy Richey
2. Julie Heldman
3. Vicky Rogers
4. Mary Ann Eisel
5. Kathy Harter
6. Kristy Pigeon
7. Jane "Peaches" Bartkowicz
8. Linda Tuero
9. Stephanie DeFina
10. Patti Hogan

1969

1. Nancy Richey
2. Julie Heldman
3. Mary Ann Eisel Curtis
4. Jane "Peaches" Bartkowicz
5. Patti Hogan
6. Kristy Pigeon
7. Betty Ann Grubb
8. Denise Carter
9. Valerie Ziegenfuss
10. Linda Tuero

1970

1. Billie Jean Moffitt King
2. Rosie Casals
3. Nancy Richey Gunter
4. Mary Ann Eisel Curtis
5. Patti Hogan
6. Jane "Peaches" Bartkowicz

7. Valerie Ziegenfuss
8. Kristy Pigeon
9. Stephanie DeFina Johnson
10. Denise Carter Triolo

1971

1. Billie Jean Moffitt King
2. Rosie Casals
3. Chris Evert
4. Nancy Richey Gunter
5. Mary Ann Eisel
6. Julie Heldman
7. Jane "Peaches" Bartkowicz
8. Linda Tuero
9. Patti Hogan
10. Denise Carter Triolo

1972

1. Billie Jean Moffitt King
2. Nancy Richey Gunter
3. Chris Evert
4. Rosie Casals
5. Wendy Overton
6. Patti Hogan
7. Linda Tuero
8. Julie Heldman
9. Pam Teeguarden
10. Janet Newberry

1973

1. Billie Jean Moffitt King
2. Chris Evert
3. Rosie Casals
4. Nancy Richey Gunter
5. Julie Heldman
6. Pam Teeguarden
7. Kristien Kemmer
8. Janet Newberry
9. Valerie Ziegenfuss
10. Wendy Overton

1974

1. Chris Evert
2. Billie Jean Moffitt King
3. Rosie Casals
4. Nancy Richey Gunter
5. Julie Heldman
6. Kathy Kuykendall
7. Pam Teeguarden
8. Valerie Ziegenfuss
9. Jeanne Evert
10. Marcie Louie

1975

1. Chris Evert
2. Nancy Richey Gunter
3. Julie Heldman
4. Wendy Overton
5. Marcie Louie

---

6. Mona Schallau
7. Kathy Kuykendall
8. Janet Newberry
9. Terry Holladay
10. Rosie Casals

1976

1. Chris Evert
2. Rosie Casals
3. Nancy Richey Gunter
4. Terry Holladay
5. Marita Redondo
6. Mona Schallau Guerrant
7. Kathy May
8. JoAnne Russell
9. Janet Newberry
10. Kathy Kuykendall

1977

1. Chris Evert
2. Billie Jean Moffitt King
3. Rosie Casals
4. Tracy Austin
5. JoAnne Russell
6. Kathy May
7. Terry Holladay
8. Kristien Kemmer Shaw
9. Janet Newberry
10. Laura DuPont

1978

1. Chris Evert
2. Billie Jean Moffitt King
3. Tracy Austin
4. Rosie Casals
5. Pam Shriver
6. Marita Redondo
7. Kathy May Teacher
8. Anne Smith
9. JoAnne Russell
10. Jeanne DuVall

1979

1. Martina Navratilova
2. Chris Evert Lloyd
3. Tracy Austin
4. Billie Jean Moffitt King
5. Kathy Jordan
6. Ann Kiyomura
7. Caroline Stoll
8. Kathy May Teacher
9. Kate Latham
10. Terry Holladay

1980

1. Tracy Austin
2. Chris Evert Lloyd
3. Martina Navratilova
4. Andrea Jaeger
5. Billie Jean Moffitt King

---

6. Pam Shriver
7. Kathy Jordan
8. # Bettina Bunge
9. Terry Holladay
10. Mary Lou Piatek

1981

1. Chris Evert Lloyd
2. Tracy Austin
3. Martina Navratilova
4. Andrea Jaeger
5. Pam Shriver
6. Barbara Potter
7. # Bettina Bunge
8. Kathy Jordan
9. Mary Lou Piatek
10. Pam Casale

1982

1. Martina Navratilova
2. Chris Evert Lloyd
3. Andrea Jaeger
4. Tracy Austin
5. Pam Shriver
6. Barbara Potter
7. Billie Jean Moffitt King
8. Anne Smith
9. Zina Garrison
10. Kathy Rinaldi

1983

1. Martina Navratilova
2. Chris Evert Lloyd
3. Andrea Jaeger
4. Pam Shriver
5. Tracy Austin
6. Zina Garrison
7. Kathy Jordan
8. Kathy Rinaldi
9. Kathy Horvath
10. Bonnie Gadusek

1984

1. Martina Navratilova
2. Chris Evert Lloyd
3. Pam Shriver
4. Kathy Jordan
5. Zina Garrison
6. Bonnie Gadusek
7. Barbara Potter
8. Pam Casale
9. Lisa Bonder
10. Kathy Rinaldi

1985

1. Martina Navratilova
2. Chris Evert Lloyd
3. Pam Shriver
4. Bonnie Gadusek
5. Zina Garrison
6. Kathy Rinaldi

---

7. Kathy Jordan
8. Barbara Potter
9. Stephanie Rehe
10. Marcie Louie

1986

1. Martina Navratilova
2. Chris Evert Lloyd
3. Pam Shriver
4. Kathy Rinaldi
5. Zina Garrison
6. Kathy Jordan
7. Bonnie Gadusek
8. Stephanie Rehe
9. Lori McNeil
10. Robin White

1987

1. Martina Navratilova
2. Chris Evert
3. Pam Shriver
4. Zina Garrison
5. Lori McNeil
6. Mary Joe Fernandez
7. Barbara Potter
8. Kate Gompert
9. Elly Hakami
10. Kathy Jordan

1988

1. Martina Navratilova
2. Chris Evert
3. Pam Shriver
4. Zina Garrison
5. Mary Joe Fernandez
6. Lori McNeil
7. Barbara Potter
8. Stephanie Rehe
9. Patty Fendick
10. Susan Sloane

1989

1. Martina Navratilova
2. Zina Garrison
3. Chris Evert
4. Mary Joe Fernandez
5. Pam Shriver
6. Gretchen Rush Magers
7. Patty Fendick
8. Beatriz "Gigi" Fernandez
9. Amy Frazier
10. Susan Sloane

1990

1. Martina Navratilova
2. Mary Joe Fernandez
3. Jennifer Capriati
4. Zina Garrison
5. Amy Frazier
6. Meredith McGrath

7. Gretchen Rush Magers
8. Patty Fendick
9. Beatriz "Gigi" Fernandez
10. Susan Sloane

1991

1. Martina Navratilova
2. Jennifer Capriati
3. Mary Joe Fernandez
4. Zina Garrison
5. Amy Frazier
6. Lori McNeil
7. Beatriz "Gigi" Fernandez
8. Mary Pierce
9. Pam Shriver
10. Marianne Werdel

1992

1. Martina Navratilova
2. Jennifer Capriati
3. Mary Joe Fernandez
4. Lori McNeil
5. Amy Frazier
6. Zina Garrison Jackson
7. Beatriz "Gigi" Fernandez
8. Pam Shriver
9. Patty Fendick
10. Ann Grossman

1993

1. Martina Navratilova
2. Jennifer Capriati
3. Mary Joe Fernandez
4. Zina Garrison Jackson
5. Lindsay Davenport
6. Lori McNeil
7. Patty Fendick

8. Pam Shriver
9. Kimberly Po
10. Ann Grossman

1994

1. Lindsay Davenport
2. Martina Navratilova
3. Chanda Rubin
4. Amy Frazier
5. Ginger Helgeson
6. Zina Garrison Jackson
7. Lori McNeil
8. Ann Grossman
9. Beatriz "Gigi" Fernandez
10. Marianne Werdel

1995

1. Mary Joe Fernandez
2. Lindsay Davenport
3. Chanda Rubin
4. Amy Frazier
5. Lisa Raymond
6. Zina Garrison Jackson
7. Marianne Werdel Witmeyer
8. Lori McNeil
9. Lindsay Lee
10. Patty Fendick

1996

1. Monica Seles
2. Lindsay Davenport
3. Chanda Rubin
4. Mary Joe Fernandez
5. Meredith McGrath
6. Jennifer Capriati
7. Kimberly Po
8. Amy Frazier
9. Linda Wild
10. Lisa Raymond

WORLD RANKINGS

World rankings are delightfully controversial because there is no official basis for the ranking. Since 1973 the ATP (Association of Tennis Professionals) and WTA (Women's Tennis Association) have rated *their* flocks weekly by computer. Rankings used in the seasonal summaries (1973–96) are those held by the specified players at the time of the tournament in question. ATP and WTA rankings are those at the conclusion of specified years.

National associations/federations have ranked their own players for years, by committee judge-ment, beginning with the USTA's first Top Tens in 1885 (men) and 1913 (women).

Pre-computer world rankings, a matter of judgement, usually made by respected tennis journalists, have appeared since 1913 (men), and 1921, plus 1925 onward (women). We have used those of the well-traveled authorities of London's *Daily Telegraph* (with time out for World Wars I and II): Wallis Myers, 1913–38; John Olliff, 1939–51; Lance Tingay, 1952–67. Rankings since the advent of the open era are those of Bud Collins of the *Boston Globe* and NBC.

*Indicates tie

Men

1913

1. Tony Wilding, New Zealand
2. * Norman Brookes, Australia
   * Maurice McLoughlin, U.S.
4. Jim Cecil Parke, Ireland
5. Dick Williams, U.S.
6. Percy Dixon, England
7. Otto Froitzheim, Germany
8. Stanley Doust, Australia
9. André Gobert, France
10. Max Decugis, France

1914

1. Maurice McLoughlin, U.S.
2. * Norman Brookes, Australia
   * Tony Wilding, New Zealand
4. Otto Froitzheim, Germany
5. Dick Williams, U.S.
6. Jim Cecil Parke, Ireland
7. Arthur Lowe, England
8. F. Gordon Lowe, England
9. Heinrich Kleinschroth, Germany
10. Max Decugis, France

1919

1. * Gerald Patterson, Australia
   * Bill Johnston, U.S.
3. André Gobert, France

4. Bill Tilden, U.S.
5. Norman Brookes, Australia
6. Algernon Kingscote, England
7. Dick Williams, U.S.
8. Percival Davson, England
9. Willis Davis, U.S.
10. William Laurentz, France

1920

1. Bili Tilden, U.S.
2. Bill Johnston, U.S.
3. Algernon Kingscote, England
4. Jim Cecil Parke, Ireland
5. André Gobert, France
6. Norman Brookes, Australia
7. Dick Williams, U.S.
8. William Laurentz, France
9. Zenzo Shimidzu, Japan
10. Gerald Patterson, Australia

1921

1. Bill Tilden, U.S.
2. Bill Johnston, U.S.
3. Vinnie Richards, U.S.
4. Zenzo Shimidzu, Japan
5. Gerald Patterson, Australia
6. James Anderson, Australia
7. Brian "Babe" Norton, S. Africa
8. Manuel Alonso, Spain
9. Dick Williams, U.S.
10. André Gobert, France

1922

1. Bill Tilden, U.S.
2. Bill Johnston, U.S.
3. Gerald Patterson, Australia
4. Vinnie Richards, U.S.
5. Jim Anderson, Australia
6. Henri Cochet, France
7. Pat O'Hara Wood, Australia
8. Dick Williams, U.S.
9. Algernon Kingscote, England
10. André Gobert, France

1923

1. Bill Tilden, U.S.
2. Bill Johnston, U.S.
3. Jim Anderson, Australia
4. Dick Williams, U.S.
5. Frank Hunter, U.S.
6. Vinnie Richards, U.S.
7. Brian "Babe" Norton, S. Africa
8. Manuel Alonso, Spain
9. Jean Washer, Belgium
10. Henri Cochet, France

1924

1. Bill Tilden, U.S.
2. Vinnie Richards, U.S.
3. Jim Anderson, Australia
4. Bill Johnston, U.S.
5. René Lacoste, France
6. Jean Borotra, France
7. Howard Kinsey, U.S.
8. Gerald Patterson, Australia
9. Henri Cochet, France
10. Manuel Alonso, Spain

1925

1. Bill Tilden, U.S.
2. Bill Johnston, U.S.
3. Vinnie Richards, U.S.
4. René Lacoste, France
5. Dick Williams, U.S.
6. Jean Borotra, France
7. Gerald Patterson, Australia
8. Manuel Alonso, Spain
9. Brian "Babe" Norton, S. Africa
10. Takeichi Harada, Japan

1926

1. René Lacoste, France
2. Jean Borotra, France
3. Henri Cochet, France
4. Bill Johnston, U.S.
5. Bill Tilden, U.S.
6. Vinnie Richards, U.S.
7. Takeichi Harada, Japan
8. Manuel Alonso, Spain
9. Howard Kinsey, U.S.
10. Jacques Brugnon, France

1927

1. René Lacoste, France
2. Bill Tilden, U.S.
3. Henri Cochet, France
4. Jean Borotra, France
5. Manuel Alonso, Spain
6. Frank Hunter, U.S.
7. George Lott, U.S.
8. John Hennessey, U.S.
9. Jacques Brugnon, France
10. Jan Kozeluh, Czechoslovakia

1928

1. Henri Cochet, France
2. René Lacoste, France
3. Bill Tilden, U.S.
4. Frank Hunter, U.S.
5. Jean Borotra, France
6. George Lott, U.S.
7. Henry "Bunny" Austin, England
8. John Hennessey, U.S.
9. Umberto de Morpurgo, Italy
10. John Hawkes, Australia

1929

1. Henri Cochet, France
2. René Lacoste, France
3. Jean Borotra, France
4. Bill Tilden, U.S.
5. Frank Hunter, U.S.
6. George Lott, U.S.
7. John Doeg, U.S.
8. John Van Ryn, U.S.
9. Henry "Bunny" Austin, England
10. Umberto de Morpurgo, Italy

1930

1. Henri Cochet, France
2. Bill Tilden, U.S.
3. Jean Borotra, France
4. John Doeg, U.S.
5. Frank Shields, U.S.
6. Wilmer Allison, U.S.
7. George Lott, U.S.
8. Umberto de Morpurgo, Italy
9. Christian Boussus, France
10. Henry "Bunny" Austin, England

1931

1. Henri Cochet, France
2. Henry "Bunny" Austin, England
3. Ellsworth Vines, U.S.
4. Fred Perry, England
5. Frank Shields, U.S.
6. Sidney Wood, U.S.
7. Jean Borotra, France
8. George Lott, U.S.
9. Jiro Satoh, Japan
10. John Van Ryn, U.S.

1932

1. Ellsworth Vines, U.S.
2. Henri Cochet, France
3. Jean Borotra, France
4. Wilmer Allison, U.S.
5. Cliff Sutter, U.S.
6. Daniel Prenn, Germany
7. Fred Perry, England
8. Gottfried von Cramm, Germany
9. Henry "Bunny" Austin, England
10. Jack Crawford, Australia

1933

1. Jack Crawford, Australia
2. Fred Perry, England
3. Jiro Satoh, Japan
4. Henry "Bunny" Austin, England
5. Ellsworth Vines, U.S.
6. Henri Cochet, France
7. Frank Shields, U.S.
8. Sidney Wood, U.S.
9. Gottfried von Cramm, Germany
10. Lester Stoefen, U.S.

1934

1. Fred Perry, England
2. Jack Crawford, Australia
3. Gottfried von Cramm, Germany
4. Henry "Bunny" Austin, England
5. Wilmer Allison, U.S.
6. Sidney Wood, U.S.
7. Roderich Menzel, Czechoslovakia
8. Frank Shields, U.S.
9. Giorgio de Stefani, Italy
10. Christian Boussus, France

1935

1. Fred Perry, England
2. Jack Crawford, Australia
3. Gottfried von Cramm, Germany
4. Wilmer Allison, U.S.
5. Henry "Bunny" Austin, England
6. Don Budge, U.S.
7. Frank Shields, U.S.
8. Viv McGrath, Australia
9. Christian Boussus, France
10. Sidney Wood, U.S.

1936

1. Fred Perry, England
2. Gottfried von Cramm, Germany
3. Don Budge, U.S.
4. Adrian Quist, Australia
5. Henry "Bunny" Austin, England
6. Jack Crawford, Australia
7. Wilmer Allison, U.S.
8. Bryan "Bitsy" Grant, U.S.
9. Henner Henkel, Germany
10. Viv McGrath, Australia

1937

1. Don Budge, U.S.
2. Gottfried von Cramm, Germany
3. Henner Henkel, Germany
4. Henry "Bunny" Austin, England
5. Bobby Riggs, U.S.
6. Bryan "Bitsy" Grant, U.S.
7. Jack Crawford, Australia
8. Roderich Menzel, Czechoslovakia
9. Frank Parker, U.S.
10. Charlie Hare, England

1938

1. Don Budge, U.S.
2. Henry "Bunny" Austin, England
3. John Bromwich, Australia
4. Bobby Riggs, U.S.

5. Sidney Wood, U.S.
6. Adrian Quist, Australia
7. Roderich Menzel, Czechoslovakia
8. Jiro Yamagishi, Japan
9. Gene Mako, U.S.
10. Franjo Puncec, Yugoslavia

1939

1. Bobby Riggs, U.S.
2. John Bromwich, Australia
3. Adrian Quist, Australia
4. Franjo Puncec, Yugoslavia
5. Frank Parker, U.S.
6. Henner Henkel, Germany
7. Don McNeill, U.S.
8. Elwood Cooke, U.S.
9. Welby Van Horn, U.S.
10. Joe Hunt, U.S.

1946

1. Jack Kramer, U.S.
2. Ted Schroeder, U.S.
3. Jaroslav Drobny, Czechoslovakia
4. Yvon Petra, France
5. Marcel Bernard, France
6. John Bromwich, Australia
7. Tom Brown, U.S.
8. Gardnar Mulloy, U.S.
9. Frank Parker, U.S.
10. Geoff Brown, Australia

1947

1. Jack Kramer, U.S.
2. Ted Schroeder, U.S.
3. Frank Parker, U.S.
4. John Bromwich, Australia
5. Jaroslav Drobny, Czechoslovakia
6. Dinny Pails, Australia
7. Tom Brown, U.S.
8. J. Edward "Budge" Patty, U.S.
9. Jozsef Asboth, Hungary
10. Gardnar Mulloy, U.S.

1948

1. Frank Parker, U.S.
2. Ted Schroeder, U.S.
3. Richard "Pancho" Gonzalez, U.S.
4. John Bromwich, Australia

5. Jaroslav Drobny, Czechoslovakia
6. Eric Sturgess, S. Africa
7. Bob Falkenburg, U.S.
8. Jozsef Asboth, Hungary
9. Lennart Bergelin, Sweden
10. Adrian Quist, Australia

1949

1. Richard "Pancho" Gonzalez, U.S.
2. Ted Schroeder, U.S.
3. Bill Talbert, U.S.
4. Frank Sedgman, Australia
5. Frank Parker, U.S.
6. Eric Sturgess, S. Africa
7. Jaroslav Drobny, Czechoslovakia
8. J. Edward "Budge" Patty, U.S.
9. Gardnar Mulloy, U.S.
10. Billy Sidwell, Australia

1950

1. J. Edward "Budge" Patty, U.S
2. Frank Sedgman, Australia
3. Art Larsen, U.S.
4. Jaroslav Drobny, Egypt
5. Herbie Flam, U.S.
6. Ted Schroeder, U.S.
7. Vic Seixas, U.S.
8. Ken McGregor, Australia
9. Bill Talbert, U.S.
10. Eric Sturgess, S. Africa

1951

1. Frank Sedgman, Australia
2. Dick Savitt, U.S.
3. Jaroslav Drobny, Egypt
4. Vic Seixas, U.S.
5. Tony Trabert, U.S.
6. Ted Schroeder, U.S.
7. Ken McGregor, Australia
8. Herbie Flam, U.S.
9. Art Larsen, U.S.
10. Mervyn Rose, Australia

1952

1. Frank Sedgman, Australia
2. Jaroslav Drobny, Egypt
3. Ken McGregor, Australia
4. Mervyn Rose, Australia
5. Vic Seixas, U.S.

6. Herbie Flam, U.S.
7. Gardnar Mulloy, U.S.
8. Eric Sturgess, S. Africa
9. Dick Savitt, U.S.
10. *Ken Rosewall, Australia
*Lew Hoad, Australia

1953

1. Tony Trabert, U.S.
2. Ken Rosewall, Australia
3. Vic Seixas, U.S.
4. Jaroslav Drobny, Egypt
5. Lew Hoad, Australia
6. Mervyn Rose, Australia
7. Kurt Nielsen, Denmark
8. J. Edward "Budge" Patty, U.S.
9. Sven Davidson, Sweden
10. Enrique Morea, Argentina

1954

1. Jaroslav Drobny, Egypt
2. Tony Trabert, U.S.
3. Ken Rosewall, Australia
4. Vic Seixas, U.S.
5. Rex Hartwig, Australia
6. Mervyn Rose, Australia
7. Lew Hoad, Australia
8. J. Edward "Budge" Patty, U.S.
9. Art Larsen, U.S.
10. * Enrique Morea, Argentina
*Ham Richardson, U.S.
*Sven Davidson, Sweden

1955

1. Tony Trabert, U.S.
2. Ken Rosewall, Australia
3. Lew Hoad, Australia
4. Vic Seixas, U.S.
5. Rex Hartwig, Australia
6. J. Edward "Budge" Patty, U.S.
7. Ham Richardson, U.S.
8. Kurt Nielson, Denmark
9. Jaroslav Drobny, Egypt
10. *Sven Davidson, Sweden
*Mervyn Rose, Australia

1956

1. Lew Hoad, Australia
2. Ken Rosewall, Australia

3. Ham Richardson, U.S.
4. Vic Seixas, U.S.
5. Sven Davidson, Sweden
6. Neale Fraser, Australia
7. Ashley Cooper, Australia
8. Dick Savitt, U.S.
9. Herbie Flam, U.S.
10. * J. Edward "Budge" Patty, U.S.
* Nicola Pietrangeli, Italy

1957

1. Ashley Cooper, Australia
2. Mal Anderson, Australia
3. Sven Davidson, Sweden
4. Herbie Flam, U.S.
5. Neale Fraser, Australia
6. Mervyn Rose, Australia
7. Vic Seixas, U.S.
8. J. Edward "Budge" Patty, U.S.
9. Nicola Pietrangeli, Italy
10. Dick Savitt, U.S.

1958

1. Ashley Cooper, Australia
2. Mal Anderson, Australia
3. Mervyn Rose, Australia
4. Neale Fraser, Australia
5. Luis Ayala, Chile
6. Ham Richardson, U.S.
7. Nicola Pietrangeli, Italy
8. Ulf Schmidt, Sweden
9. Barry MacKay, U.S.
10. Sven Davidson, Sweden

1959

1. Neale Fraser, Australia
2. Alex Olmedo, Peru
3. Nicola Pietrangeli, Italy
4. Barry MacKay, U.S.
5. Rod Laver, Australia
6. Luis Ayala, Chile
7. Roy Emerson, Australia
8. Bernard "Tut" Bartzen, U.S.
9. Ramanathan Krishnan, India
10. Ian Vermaak, S. Africa

1960

1. Neale Fraser, Australia
2. Rod Laver, Australia

3. Nicola Pietrangeli, Italy
4. Barry MacKay, U.S.
5. Earl "Butch" Buchholz, Jr., U.S.
6. Roy Emerson, Australia
7. Luis Ayala, Chile
8. Ramanathan Krishnan, India
9. Jan-Erik Lundquist, Sweden
10. Dennis Ralston, U.S.

1961

1. Rod Laver, Australia
2. Roy Emerson, Australia
3. Manolo Santana, Spain
4. Nicola Pietrangeli, Italy
5. Chuck McKinley, U.S.
6. Ramanathan Krishnan, India
7. Luis Ayala, Chile
8. Neale Fraser, Australia
9. Jan-Erik Lundquist, Sweden
10. Ulf Schmidt, Sweden

1962

1. Rod Laver, Australia
2. Roy Emerson, Australia
3. Manolo Santana, Spain
4. Neale Fraser, Australia
5. Chuck McKinley, U.S.
6. Rafael Osuna, Mexico
7. Marty Mulligan, Australia
8. Bob Hewitt, Australia
9. Ramanathan Krishnan, India
10. Wilhelm Bungert, Germany

1963

1. Rafael Osuna, Mexico
2. Chuck McKinley, U.S.
3. Roy Emerson, Australia
4. Manolo Santana, Spain
5. Fred Stolle, Australia
6. Frank Froehling III, U.S.
7. Dennis Ralston, U.S.
8. Boro Jovanovic, Yugoslavia
9. Mike Sangster, England
10. Marty Mulligan, Australia

1964

1. Roy Emerson, Australia
2. Fred Stolle, Australia
3. Jan-Erik Lundquist, Sweden
4. Wilhelm Bungert, Germany
5. Chuck McKinley, U.S.
6. Manolo Santana, Spain
7. Nicola Pietrangeli, Italy
8. Christian Kuhnke, Germany
9. Dennis Ralston, U.S.
10. Rafael Osuna, Mexico

1965

1. Roy Emerson, Australia
2. Manolo Santana, Spain
3. Fred Stolle, Australia
4. Cliff Drysdale, S. Africa
5. Marty Mulligan, Australia
6. Jan-Erik Lundquist, Sweden
7. Tony Roche, Australia
8. John Newcombe, Australia
9. Dennis Ralston, U.S.
10. Arthur Ashe, U.S.

1966

1. Manolo Santana, Spain
2. Fred Stolle, Australia
3. Roy Emerson, Australia
4. Tony Roche, Australia
5. Dennis Ralston, U.S.
6. John Newcombe, Australia
7. Arthur Ashe, U.S.
8. Istvan Gulyas, Hungary
9. Cliff Drysdale, S. Africa
10. Ken Fletcher, Australia

1967

1. John Newcombe, Australia
2. Roy Emerson, Australia
3. Manolo Santana, Spain
4. Marty Mulligan, Australia
5. Tony Roche, Australia
6. Bob Hewitt, S. Africa
7. Nikki Pilic, Yugoslavia
8. Clark Graebner, U.S.
9. Arthur Ashe, U.S.

10. * Jan Leschley, Denmark
    * Wilhelm Bungert, Germany
    * Cliff Drysdale, S. Africa

1968

1. Rod Laver, Australia
2. Arthur Ashe, U.S.
3. Ken Rosewall, Australia
4. Tony Roche, Australia
5. Tom Okker, Netherlands
6. John Newcombe, Australia
7. Clark Graebner, U.S.
8. Dennis Ralston, U.S.
9. Cliff Drysdale, S. Africa
10. Richard "Pancho" Gonzalez, U.S.

1969

1. Rod Laver, Australia
2. Tony Roche, Australia
3. John Newcombe, Australia
4. Ken Rosewall, Australia
5. Tom Okker, Netherlands
6. Richard "Pancho" Gonzalez, U.S.
7. Stan Smith, U.S.
8. Arthur Ashe, U.S.
9. Cliff Drysdale, S. Africa
10. Andres Gimeno, Spain

1970

1. John Newcombe, Australia
2. Ken Rosewall, Australia
3. Tony Roche, Australia
4. Rod Laver, Australia
5. Ilie Nastase, Romania
6. Tom Okker, Netherlands
7. Cliff Richey, U.S.
8. Stan Smith, U.S.
9. Arthur Ashe, U.S.
10. Andres Gimeno, Spain

1971

1. John Newcombe, Australia
2. Stan Smith, U.S.
3. Ken Rosewall, Australia
4. Rod Laver, Australia
5. Jan Kodes, Czechoslovakia

6. Arthur Ashe, U.S.
7. Ilie Nastase, Romania
8. Tom Okker, Netherlands
9. Cliff Drysdale, S. Africa
10. Marty Riessen, U.S.

1972

1. Stan Smith, U.S.
2. Ken Rosewall, Australia
3. Ilie Nastase, Romania
4. Rod Laver, Australia
5. Arthur Ashe, U.S.
6. John Newcombe, Australia
7. Bob Lutz, U.S.
8. Tom Okker, Netherlands
9. Marty Riessen, U.S.
10. Andres Gimeno, Spain

1973

1. Ilie Nastase, Romania
2. John Newcombe, Australia
3. Stan Smith, U.S.
4. Rod Laver, Australia
5. Ken Rosewall, Australia
6. Jimmy Connors, U.S.
7. Tom Okker, Netherlands
8. Jan Kodes, Czechoslovakia
9. Arthur Ashe, U.S.
10. Manolo Orantes, Spain

1974

1. Jimmy Connors, U.S.
2. Guillermo Vilas, Argentina
3. John Newcombe, Australia
4. Bjorn Borg, Sweden
5. Rod Laver, Australia
6. Ilie Nastase, Romania
7. Ken Rosewall, Australia
8. Stan Smith, U.S.
9. Manolo Orantes, Spain
10. Arthur Ashe, U.S.

1975

1. Arthur Ashe, U.S.
2. Bjorn Borg, Sweden
3. Manolo Orantes, Spain
4. Jimmy Connors, U.S.
5. Ilie Nastase, Romania
6. Guillermo Vilas, Argentina
7. Rod Laver, Australia
8. Raul Ramirez, Mexico

9. John Alexander, Australia
10. Ken Rosewall, Australia

1976

1. Jimmy Connors, U.S.
2. Bjorn Borg, Sweden
3. Ilie Nastase, Romania
4. Manolo Orantes, Spain
5. Adriano Panatta, Italy
6. Harold Solomon, U.S.
7. Raul Ramirez, Mexico
8. Roscoe Tanner, U.S.
9. Eddie Dibbs, U.S.
10. Wojtek Fibak, Poland

1977

1. Bjorn Borg, Sweden
2. Guillermo Vilas, Argentina
3. Jimmy Connors, U.S.
4. Vitas Gerulaitis, U.S.
5. Brian Gottfried, U.S.
6. Manolo Orantes, Spain
7. Dick Stockton, U.S.
8. Eddie Dibbs, U.S.
9. Ilie Nastase, Romania
10. Raul Ramirez, Mexico

1978

1. Bjorn Borg, Sweden
2. Jimmy Connors, U.S.
3. John McEnroe, U.S.
4. Vitas Gerulaitis, U.S.
5. Eddie Dibbs, U.S.
6. Guillermo Vilas, Argentina
7. Brian Gottfried, U.S.
8. Raul Ramirez, Mexico
9. Harold Solomon, U.S.
10. Arthur Ashe, U.S.

1979

1. Bjorn Borg, Sweden
2. John McEnroe, U.S.
3. Jimmy Connors, U.S.
4. Vitas Gerulaitis, U.S.
5. Roscoe Tanner, U.S.
6. Guillermo Vilas, Argentina
7. Harold Solomon, U.S.
8. Jose Higueras, Spain
9. Victor Pecci, Paraguay
10. Wojtek Fibak, Poland

1980

1. Bjorn Borg, Sweden
2. John McEnroe, U.S.
3. Jimmy Connors, U.S.

4. Ivan Lendl, Czechoslovakia
5. Gene Mayer, U.S.
6. Guillermo Vilas, Argentina
7. Jose-Luis Clerc, Argentina
8. Vitas Gerulaitis, U.S.
9. Harold Solomon, U.S.
10. Brian Gottfried, U.S.

1981

1. John McEnroe, U.S.
2. Bjorn Borg, Sweden
3. Jimmy Connors, U.S.
4. Ivan Lendl, Czechoslovakia
5. Jose-Luis Clerc, Argentina
6. Guillermo Vilas, Argentina
7. Gene Mayer, U.S.
8. Eliot Teltscher, U.S.
9. Peter McNamara, Australia
10. Roscoe Tanner, U.S.

1982

1. Jimmy Connors, U.S.
2. Ivan Lendl, Czechoslovakia
3. John McEnroe, U.S.
4. Mats Wilander, Sweden
5. Guillermo Vilas, Argentina
6. Vitas Gerulaitis, U.S.
7. Jose-Luis Clerc, Argentina
8. Yannick Noah, France
9. Johan Kriek, U.S.
10. Jose Higueras, Spain

1983

1. John McEnroe, U.S.
2. Mats Wilander, Sweden
3. Jimmy Connors, U.S.
4. Yannick Noah, France
5. Ivan Lendl, Czechoslovakia
6. Jimmy Arias, U.S.
7. Jose Higueras, Spain
8. Jose-Luis Clerc, Argentina
9. Bill Scanlon, U.S.
10. Guillermo Vilas, Argentina

1984

1. John McEnroe, U.S.
2. Ivan Lendl, Czechoslovakia

3. Jimmy Connors, U.S.
4. Mats Wilander, Sweden
5. Andres Gomez, Ecuador
6. Henrik Sundstrom, Sweden
7. Aaron Krickstein, U.S.
8. Anders Jarryd, Sweden
9. Joakim Nystrom, Sweden
10. Pat Cash, Australia

1985

1. Ivan Lendl, Czechoslovakia
2. Boris Becker, Germany
3. Mats Wilander, Sweden
4. John McEnroe, U.S.
5. Stefan Edberg, Sweden
6. Jimmy Connors, U.S.
7. Yannick Noah, France
8. Anders Jarryd, Sweden
9. Kevin Curren, U.S.
10. Joakim Nystrom, Sweden

1986

1. Ivan Lendl, Czechoslovakia
2. Boris Becker, Germany
3. Stefan Edberg, Sweden
4. Mats Wilander, Sweden
5. Joakim Nystrom, Sweden
6. Miloslav Mecir, Czechoslovakia
7. Yannick Noah, France
8. Henri Leconte, France
9. Andres Gomez, Ecuador
10. Brad Gilbert, U.S.

1987

1. Ivan Lendl, Czechoslovakia
2. Mats Wilander, Germany
3. Stefan Edberg, Sweden
4. Pat Cash, Australia
5. Miloslav Mecir, Czechoslovakia
6. Boris Becker, Germany
7. Jimmy Connors, U.S.
8. Tim Mayotte, U.S.
9. John McEnroe, U.S.
10. Brad Gilbert, U.S.

1988

1. Mats Wilander, Sweden
2. Stefan Edberg, Sweden
3. Boris Becker, Germany
4. Ivan Lendl, Czechoslovakia
5. Andre Agassi, U.S.,
6. Miloslav Mecir, Czechoslovakia
7. Jimmy Connors, U.S.
8. Tim Mayotte, U.S.
9. Pat Cash, Australia
10. Jakob Hlasek, Switzerland

1989

1. Boris Becker, Germany
2. Ivan Lendl, Czechoslovakia
3. Stefan Edberg, Sweden
4. John McEnroe, U.S.
5. Michael Chang, U.S.
6. Brad Gilbert, U.S.
7. Aaron Krickstein, U.S.
8. Jay Berger, U.S.
9. Andre Agassi, U.S.
10. Jimmy Connors, U.S.

1990

2. * Stefan Edberg, Sweden
2. * Ivan Lendl, Czechoslovakia
2. * Pete Sampras, U.S.
4. Andre Agassi, U.S.
5. Boris Becker, Germany
6. Thomas Muster, Austria
7. Andres Gomez, Ecuador
8. Brad Gilbert, U.S.
9. Michael Chang, U.S.
10. John McEnroe, U.S.
* No number 1

1991

1. Stefan Edberg, Sweden
2. Michael Stich, Germany
3. Jim Courier, U.S.
4. Boris Becker, Germany
5. Guy Forget, France
6. Pete Sampras, U.S.
7. Ivan Lendl, Czechoslovakia
8. Andre Agassi, U.S.
9. Petr Korda, Czechoslovakia
10. Karel Novacek, Czechoslovakia

1992

1. Jim Courier, U.S.
2. Stefan Edberg, Sweden
3. Andre Agassi, U.S.
4. Pete Sampras, U.S.
5. Michael Chang, U.S.
6. Goran Ivanisevic, Yugoslavia
7. Peter Korda, Czechoslovakia
8. Boris Becker, Germany
9. Wayne Ferreira, S. Africa
10. Ivan Lendl, Czechoslovakia

1993

1. Pete Sampras, U.S.
2. Jim Courier, U.S.
3. Sergi Bruguera, Spain
4. Stefan Edberg, Sweden
5. Michael Stich, Germany
6. Thomas Muster, Austria
7. Andrei Medvedev, Ukraine
8. Michael Chang, U.S.
9. Goran Ivanisevic, Yugoslavia
10. Cedric Pioline, France

1994

1. Pete Sampras, U.S.
2. Andre Agassi, U.S.
3. Sergi Bruguera, Spain
4. Boris Becker, Germany
5. Todd Martin, U.S.
6. Goran Ivanisevic, Croatia
7. Alberto Berasategui, Spain
8. Stefan Edberg, Sweden
9. Michael Stich, Germany
10. Michael Chang, U.S.

1995

1. Pete Sampras, U.S.
2. Andre Agassi, U.S.
3. Thomas Muster, Austria
4. Boris Becker, Germany
5. Michael Chang, U.S.
6. Jim Courier, U.S.
7. Yevgeny Kafelnikov, Russia
8. Goran Ivanisevic, Croatia
9. Thomas Enqvist, Sweden

10. Wayne Ferreira, S. Africa

1996

1. Pete Sampras, U.S.
2. Michael Chang, U.S.
3. Yevgeny Kafelnikov, Russia
4. Richard Krajicek, Netherlands
5. Boris Becker, Germany
6. Thomas Muster, Austria
7. Goran Ivanisevic, Croatia
8. Andre Agassi, U.S.
9. Jim Courier, U.S.
10. MaliVai Washington, U.S.

Women

1921

1. Suzanne Lenglen, France
2. Molla Bjurstedt Mallory, U.S.
3. Mary K. Browne, U.S.
4. Elizabeth Ryan, U.S.
5. Kitty McKane, England
6. May Sutton Bundy, U.S.
7. Irene Peacock, India
8. Winifred Beamish, England
9. Eleanor Goss, U.S.
10. Marion Zinderstein Jessup, U.S.

1925

1. Suzanne Lenglen, France
2. Helen Wills, U.S.
3. Kitty McKane, England
4. Elizabeth Ryan, U.S.
5. Molla Bjurstedt Mallory, U.S.
6. Eleanor Goss, U.S.
7. Dorothea Douglass Chambers, England
8. Joan Fry, England
9. Marguerite Billout, France
10. Marion Zinderstein Jessup, U.S.

1926

1. Suzanne Lenglen, France
2. Kitty McKane Godfree, England
3. Lili de Alvarez, Spain

4. Molla Bjurstedt Mallory, U.S.
5. Elizabeth Ryan, U.S.
6. Mary K. Browne, U.S.
7. Joan Fry, England
8. Phoebe Holcroft Watson, England
9. Marion Zinderstein Jessup, U.S.
10. Didi Vlasto, France

1927

1. Helen Wills, U.S.
2. Lili de Alvarez, Spain
3. Elizabeth Ryan, U.S.
4. Molla Bjurstedt Mallory, U.S.
5. Kitty McKane Godfree, England
6. Betty Nuthall, England
7. Esther "Bobbie" Heine, S. Africa
8. Joan Fry, England
9. Kea Bouman, Netherlands
10. Charlotte Hosmer Chapin, U.S.

1928

1. Helen Wills, U.S.
2. Lili de Alvarez, Spain
3. Daphne Akhurst, Australia
4. Eileen Bennett, England
5. Phoebe Holcroft Watson, England
6. Elizabeth Ryan, U.S.
7. Cilly Aussem, Germany
8. Kea Bouman, Netherlands
9. Helen Jacobs, U.S.
10. Esna Boyd, Australia

1929

1. Helen Wills Moody, U.S.
2. Phoebe Holcroft Watson, England
3. Helen Jacobs, U.S.
4. Betty Nuthall, England
5. Esther "Bobby" Heine, S. Africa
6. Simone Passemard Mathieu, France
7. Eileen Bennett, England
8. Paula von Reznicek, Germany
9. Peggy Saunders Michell, England
10. Elsie Goldsack, England

1930

1. Helen Wills Moody, U.S.
2. Cilly Aussem, Germany
3. Phoebe Holcroft Watson, England
4. Elizabeth Ryan, U.S.
5. Simone Passemard Mathieu, France
6. Helen Jacobs, U.S.
7. Phyllis Mudford, England
8. Lili de Alvarez, Spain
9. Betty Nuthall, England
10. Hilde Krahwinkel, Germany

1931

1. Helen Wills Moody, U.S.
2. Cilly Aussem, Germany
3. Eileen Bennett Whittingstall, England
4. Helen Jacobs, U.S.
5. Betty Nuthall, England
6. Hilde Krahwinkel, Germany
7. Simone Passemard Mathieu, France
8. Lili de Alvarez, Spain
9. Phyllis Mudford, England
10. Elsie Goldsack Pittman, England

1932

1. Helen Wills Moody, U.S.
2. Helen Jacobs, U.S.
3. Simone Passemard Mathieu, France
4. Lolette Payot, Switzerland
5. Hilde Krahwinkel, Germany
6. Mary Heeley, England
7. Eileen Bennett Whittingstall, England
8. Marie Luise Horn, Germany
9. Kay Stammers, England
10. Josane Sigart, Belgium

1933

1. Helen Wills Moody, U.S.
2. Helen Jacobs, U.S.
3. Dorothy Round, England
4. Hilde Krahwinkel, Germany

5. Margaret Scriven,
England
6. Simone Passemard
Mathieu, France
7. Sarah Palfrey, U.S.
8. Betty Nuthall, England
9. Lolette Payot,
Switzerland
10. Alice Marble, U.S.

1934

1. Dorothy Round,
England
2. Helen Jacobs, U.S.
3. Hilde Krahwinkel
Sperling, Germany
4. Sarah Palfrey, U.S.
5. Margaret Scriven,
England
6. Simone Passemard
Mathieu, France
7. Lolette Payot,
Switzerland
8. Joan Hartigan,
Australia
9. Cilly Aussem,
Germany
10. Carolin Babcock, U.S.

1935

1. Helen Wills Moody,
U.S.
2. Helen Jacobs, U.S.
3. Kay Stammers,
England
4. Hilde Krahwinkel
Sperling, Germany
5. Sarah Palfrey Fabyan,
U.S.
6. Dorothy Round,
England
7. Mary Arnold, U.S.
8. Simone Passemard
Mathieu, France
9. Joan Hartigan,
Australia
10. Margaret "Peggy"
Scriven, England

1936

1. Helen Jacobs, U.S.
2. Hilda Krahwinkel
Sperling, Germany
3. Dorothy Round,
England
4. Alice Marble, U.S.
5. Simone Passemard
Mathieu, France
6. Jadwiga
Jedrzejowska, Poland
7. Kay Stammers,
England
8. Anita Lizana, Chile
9. Sarah Palfrey Fabyan,
U.S.
10. Carolin Babcock, U.S.

1937

1. Anita Lizana, Chile
2. Dorothy Round Little,
England
3. Jadwiga
Jedrzejowska, Poland
4. Hilde Krahwinkel
Sperling, Germany
5. Simone Passemard
Mathieu, France
6. Helen Jacobs, U.S.
7. Alice Marble, U.S.
8. Marie Luise Horn,
Germany
9. Mary Hardwick,
England
10. Dorothy Bundy, U.S.

1938

1. Helen Wills Moody,
U.S.
2. Helen Jacobs, U.S.
3. Alice Marble, U.S.
4. Hilde Krahwinkel
Sperling, Germany
5. Simone Passemard
Mathieu, France
6. Jadwiga
Jedrzejowska, Poland
7. Sarah Palfrey Fabyan,
U.S.
8. Esther "Bobbie" Heine
Miller, S. Africa
9. Kay Stammers,
England
10. Nancye Wynne,
Australia

1939

1. Alice Marble, U.S.
2. Kay Stammers,
England
3. Helen Jacobs, U.S.
4. Hilde Krahwinkel
Sperling, Germany
5. Simone Passemard
Mathieu, France
6. Sarah Palfrey Fabyan,
U.S.
7. Jadwiga
Jedrzejowska, Poland
8. Mary Hardwick,
England
9. Valerie Scott, England
10. Virginia Wolfenden, U.S.

1946

1. Pauline Betz, U.S.
2. Margaret Osborne,
U.S.
3. Louise Brough, U.S.
4. Doris Hart, U.S.
5. Pat Canning Todd,
U.S.
6. Dorothy Bundy, U.S.

7. Nelly Adamson Landry,
France
8. Kay Stammers
Menzies, England
9. Shirley Fry, U.S.
10. Virginia Wolfenden
Kovacs, U.S.

1947

1. Margaret Osborne
duPont, U.S.
2. Louise Brough, U.S.
3. Doris Hart, U.S.
4. Nancye Wynne Bolton,
Australia
5. Pat Canning Todd,
U.S.
6. Sheila Piercey
Summers, S. Africa
7. Jean Bostock, England
8. Barbara Krase, U.S.
9. Betty Hilton, England
10. Magda Rurac,
Romania

1948

1. Margaret Osborne
duPont, U.S.
2. Louise Brough, U.S.
3. Doris Hart, U.S.
4. Nancye Wynne Bolton,
Australia
5. Pat Canning Todd,
U.S.
6. Jean Bostock, England
7. Sheila Piercey
Summers, S. Africa
8. Shirley Fry, U.S.
9. Magda Rurac,
Romania
10. Nelly Adamson Landry,
France

1949

1. Margaret Osborne
duPont, U.S.
2. Louise Brough, U.S.
3. Doris Hart, U.S.
4. Nancye Wynne Bolton,
Australia
5. Pat Canning Todd,
U.S.
6. Betty Hilton, England
7. Sheila Piercey
Summers, S. Africa
8. Annelies Ullstein
Bossi, Italy
9. Joan Curry, England
10. Jean Walker-Smith,
England

1950

1. Margaret Osborne
duPont, U.S.
2. Louise Brough, U.S.

3. Doris Hart, U.S.
4. Pat Canning Todd,
U.S.
5. Barbara Scofield, U.S.
6. Nancy Chaffee, U.S.
7. Beverly Baker, U.S.
8. Shirley Fry, U.S.
9. Annelies Ullstein
Bossi, Italy
10. Maria Weiss, Argentina

1951

1. Doris Hart, U.S.
2. Maureen Connolly,
U.S.
3. Shirley Fry, U.S.
4. Nancy Chaffee Kiner,
U.S.
5. Jean Walker-Smith,
England
6. Jean Quertier, England
7. Louise Brough, U.S.
8. Beverly Baker Fleitz,
U.S.
9. Pat Canning Todd,
U.S.
10. Kay Tuckey Maule,
England

1952

1. Maureen Connolly,
U.S.
2. Doris Hart, U.S.
3. Louise Brough, U.S.
4. Shirley Fry, U.S.
5. Pat Canning Todd,
U.S.
6. Nancy Chaffee Kiner,
U.S.
7. Thelma Coyne Long,
Australia
8. Jean Walker-Smith,
England
9. Jean Quertier-Rinkel,
U.S.
10. Dorothy Head Knode,
U.S.

1953

1. Maureen Connolly,
U.S.
2. Doris Hart, U.S.
3. Louise Brough, U.S.
4. Shirley Fry, U.S.
5. Margaret Osborne
duPont, U.S.
6. Dorothy Head Knode,
U.S.
7. Suzi Kormoczi,
Hungary
8. Angela Mortimer,
England
9. Helen Fletcher,
England
10. Jean Quertier-Rinkel,
England

1954

1. Maureen Connolly, U.S.
2. Doris Hart, U.S.
3. Beverly Baker Fleitz, U.S.
4. Louise Brough, U.S.
5. Margaret Osborne duPont, U.S.
6. Shirley Fry, U.S.
7. Betty Rosenquest Pratt, U.S.
8. Helen Fletcher, England
9. Angela Mortimer, England
10. * Ginette Bucaille, France
    * Thelma Coyne Long, Australia

1955

1. Louise Brough, U.S.
2. Doris Hart, U.S.
3. Beverly Baker Fleitz, U.S.
4. Angela Mortimer, England
5. Dorothy Head Knode, U.S.
6. Barbara Breit, U.S.
7. Darlene Hard, U.S.
8. Beryl Penrose, Australia
9. Pat Ward, England
10. * Suzi Kormoczi, Hungary
    * Shirley Fry, U.S.

1956

1. Shirley Fry, U.S.
2. Althea Gibson, U.S.
3. Louise Brough, U.S.
4. Angela Mortimer, England
5. Suzi Kormoczi, Hungary
6. Angela Buxton, England
7. Shirley Bloomer, England
8. Pat Ward, England
9. Betty Rosenquest Pratt, Jamaica
10. *Margaret Osborne duPont, U.S.
    *Darlene Hard, U.S.

1957

1. Althea Gibson, U.S.
2. Darlene Hard, U.S.
3. Shirley Bloomer, England
4. Louise Brough, U.S.

5. Dorothy Head Knode, U.S.
6. Vera Puzejova, Czechoslovakia
7. Ann Haydon, England
8. Yola Ramirez, Mexico
9. Christine Truman, England
10. Margaret Osborne duPont, U.S.

1958

1. Althea Gibson, U.S.
2. Suzi Kormoczi, Hungary
3. Beverly Baker Fleitz, U.S.
4. Darlene Hard, U.S.
5. Shirley Bloomer, England
6. Christine Truman, England
7. Angela Mortimer, England
8. Ann Haydon, England
9. Maria Bueno, Brazil
10. Dorothy Head Knode, U.S.

1959

1. Maria Bueno, Brazil
2. Christine Truman, England
3. Darlene Hard, U.S.
4. Beverly Baker Fleitz, U.S.
5. Sandra Reynolds, S. Africa
6. Angela Mortimer, England
7. Ann Haydon, England
8. Suzi Kormoczi, Hungary
9. Sally Moore, U.S.
10. Yola Ramirez, Mexico

1960

1. Maria Bueno, Brazil
2. Darlene Hard, U.S.
3. Sandra Reynolds, S. Africa
4. Christine Truman, England
5. Suzi Kormoczi, Hungary
6. Ann Haydon, England
7. Angela Mortimer, England
8. Jan Lehane, Australia
9. Yola Ramirez, Mexico
10. Renee Schuurman, S. Africa

1961

1. Angela Mortimer, England
2. Darlene Hard, U.S.
3. Ann Haydon, England
4. Margaret Smith, Australia
5. Sandra Reynolds, S. Africa
6. Yola Ramirez, Mexico
7. Christine Truman, England
8. Suzi Kormoczi, Hungary
9. Renee Schuurman, S. Africa
10. Karen Hantze, U.S.

1962

1. Margaret Smith, Australia
2. Maria Bueno, Brazil
3. Darlene Hard, U.S.
4. Karen Hantze Susman, U.S.
5. Vera Puzejova Sukova, Czechoslovakia
6. Sandra Reynolds Price, S. Africa
7. Lesley Turner, Australia
8. Ann Haydon, England
9. Renee Schuurman, S. Africa
10. Angela Mortimer, England

1963

1. Margaret Smith, Australia
2. Lesley Turner, Australia
3. Maria Bueno, Brazil
4. Billie Jean Moffitt, U.S.
5. Ann Haydon Jones, England
6. Darlene Hard, U.S.
7. Jan Lehane, Australia
8. Renee Schuurman, S. Africa
9. Nancy Richey, U.S.
10. Vera Puzejova Sukova, Czechoslovakia

1964

1. Margaret Smith, Australia
2. Maria Bueno, Brazil
3. Lesley Turner, Australia
4. Carole Caldwell Graebner, U.S.
5. Helga Schultze, Germany
6. Nancy Richey, U.S.
7. Billie Jean Moffitt, U.S.

8. Karen Hantze Susman, U.S.
9. Robyn Ebbern, Australia
10. Jan Lehane, Australia

1965

1. Margaret Smith, Australia
2. Maria Bueno, Brazil
3. Lesley Turner, Australia
4. Billie Jean Moffitt King, U.S.
5. Ann Haydon Jones, England
6. Annette Van Zyl, S. Africa
7. Christine Truman, England
8. Nancy Richey, U.S.
9. Carole Caldwell Graebner, U.S.
10. Françoise Durr, France

1966

1. Billie Jean Moffitt King, U.S.
2. Margaret Smith, Australia
3. Maria Bueno, Brazil
4. Ann Haydon Jones, England
5. Nancy Richey, U.S.
6. Annette Van Zyl, S. Africa
7. Norma Baylon, Argentina
8. Françoise Durr, France
9. Rosie Casals, U.S.
10. Kerry Melville, Australia

1967

1. Billie Jean Moffitt King, U.S.
2. Ann Haydon Jones, England
3. Françoise Durr, France
4. Nancy Richey, U.S.
5. Lesley Turner, Australia
6. Rosie Casals, U.S.
7. Maria Bueno, Brazil
8. Virginia Wade, England
9. Kerry Melville, Australia
10. Judy Tegart, Australia

1968

1. Billie Jean Moffitt King, U.S.
2. Virginia Wade, England
3. Nancy Richey, U.S.

4. Margaret Smith Court,
   Australia
5. Maria Bueno, Brazil
6. Ann Haydon Jones,
   England
7. Judy Tegart, Australia
8. Lesley Turner Bowrey,
   Australia
9. Annette Van Zyl
   duPlooy, S. Africa
10. Rosie Casals, U.S.

1969

1. Margaret Smith Court,
   Australia
2. Ann Haydon Jones,
   England
3. Billie Jean Moffitt King,
   U.S.
4. Nancy Richey, U.S.
5. Julie Heldman, U.S.
6. Rosie Casals, U.S.
7. Kerry Melville,
   Australia
8. Mary Ann Eisel, U.S.
9. Virginia Wade, England
10. Lesley Turner Bowrey,
    Australia

1970

1. Margaret Smith Court,
   Australia
2. Billie Jean Moffitt King,
   U.S.
3. Rosie Casals, U.S.
4. Nancy Richey, U.S.
5. Virginia Wade, England
6. Helga Niessen
   Masthoff, Germany
7. Ann Haydon Jones,
   England
8. Kerry Melville,
   Australia
9. Karen Krantzcke,
   Australia
10. Françoise Durr, France

1971

1. Billie Jean Moffitt King,
   U.S.
2. Evonne Goolagong,
   Australia
3. Margaret Smith Court,
   Australia
4. Rosie Casals, U.S.
5. Kerry Melville,
   Australia
6. Françoise Durr, France
7. Virginia Wade, England
8. Helga Niessen
   Masthoff, Germany
9. Judy Tegart, Australia
10. Chris Evert, U.S.

1972

1. Billie Jean Moffitt King,
   U.S.
2. Margaret Smith Court,
   Australia
3. Nancy Richey Gunter,
   U.S.
4. Chris Evert, U.S.
5. Virginia Wade, England
6. Evonne Goolagong,
   Australia
7. Rosie Casals, U.S.
8. Kerry Melville,
   Australia
9. Françoise Durr, France
10. Olga Morozova,
    U.S.S.R.

1973

1. Margaret Smith Court,
   Australia
2. Billie Jean Moffitt King,
   U.S.
3. Evonne Goolagong,
   Australia
4. Chris Evert, U.S.
5. Rosie Casals, U.S.
6. Virginia Wade, England
7. Kerry Melville,
   Australia
8. Nancy Richey Gunter,
   U.S.
9. Julie Heldman, U.S.
10. Helga Niessen
    Masthoff, Germany

1974

1. Billie Jean Moffitt King,
   U.S.
2. Evonne Goolagong,
   Australia
3. Chris Evert, U.S.
4. Virginia Wade, England
5. Julie Heldman, U.S.
6. Rosie Casals, U.S.
7. Kerry Melville,
   Australia
8. Olga Morozova,
   U.S.S.R.
9. Lesley Hunt, Australia
10. Françoise Durr, France

1975

1. Chris Evert, U.S.
2. Billie Jean Moffitt King,
   U.S.
3. Evonne Goolagong,
   Australia
4. Martina Navratilova,
   Czechoslovakia
5. Virginia Wade, England
6. Margaret Smith Court,
   Australia
7. Olga Morozova,
   U.S.S.R.

8. Nancy Richey Gunter,
   U.S.
9. Françoise Durr, France
10. Rosie Casals, U.S.

1976

1. Chris Evert, U.S.
2. Evonne Goolagong,
   Australia
3. Virginia Wade, England
4. Martina Navratilova,
   (defected to U.S.)
5. Sue Barker, England
6. Betty Stove,
   Netherlands
7. Dianne Fromholtz,
   Australia
8. Mima Jausovec,
   Yugoslavia
9. Rosie Casals, U.S.
10. Françoise Durr, France

1977

1. Chris Evert, U.S.
2. Billie Jean Moffitt King,
   U.S.
3. Virginia Wade, England
4. Martina Navratilova,
   (awaiting U.S.
   citizenship)
5. Sue Barker, England
6. Wendy Turnbull,
   Australia
7. Betty Stove,
   Netherlands
8. Rosie Casals, U.S.
9. Dianne Fromholtz,
   Australia
10. Kerry Melville Reid,
    Australia

1978

1. Martina Navratilova,
   Czechoslovakia
2. Chris Evert, U.S.
3. Evonne Goolagong,
   Australia
4. Virginia Wade, England
5. Billie Jean Moffitt King,
   U.S.
6. Tracy Austin, U.S.
7. Pam Shriver, U.S.
8. Virginia Ruzici,
   Romania
9. Wendy Turnbull,
   Australia
10. Kerry Melville Reid,
    Australia

1979

1. Martina Navratilova,
   U.S.
2. Tracy Austin, U.S.
3. Chris Evert Lloyd, U.S.

4. Evonne Goolagong,
   Australia
5. Billie Jean Moffitt King,
   U.S.
6. Wendy Turnbull,
   Australia
7. Dianne Fromholtz,
   Australia
8. Kerry Melville Reid,
   Australia
9. Virginia Wade, England
10. Regina Marsikova,
    Czechoslovakia

1980

1. Chris Evert Lloyd, U.S.
2. Tracy Austin, U.S.
3. Martina Navratilova,
   U.S.
4. Hana Mandlikova,
   Czechoslovakia
5. Andrea Jaeger, U.S.
6. Evonne Goolagong,
   Australia
7. Billie Jean Moffitt King,
   U.S.
8. Wendy Turnbull,
   Australia
9. Pam Shriver, U.S.
10. Virginia Ruzici,
    Romania

1981

1. Tracy Austin, U.S.
2. Martina Navratilova,
   U.S.
3. Chris Evert Lloyd, U.S.
4. Hana Mandlikova,
   Czechoslovakia
5. Pam Shriver, U.S.
6. Andrea Jaeger, U.S.
7. Sylvia Hanika,
   Germany
8. Mima Jausovec,
   Yugoslavia
9. Barbara Potter, U.S.
10. Virginia Ruzici,
    Romania

1982

1. Martina Navratilova,
   U.S.
2. Chris Evert Lloyd, U.S.
3. Andrea Jaeger, U.S.
4. Barbara Potter, U.S.
5. Hana Mandlikova,
   Czechoslovakia
6. Tracy Austin, U.S.
7. Wendy Turnbull,
   Australia
8. Sylvia Hanika,
   Germany
9. Pam Shriver, U.S.
10. Bettina Bunge,
    Germany

1983

1. Martina Navratilova, U.S.
2. Chris Evert Lloyd, U.S.
3. Pam Shriver, U.S.
4. Andrea Jaeger, U.S.
5. Jo Durie, England
6. Wendy Turnbull, Australia
7. Hana Mandlikova, Czechoslovakia
8. Andrea Temesvari, Hungary
9. Sylvia Hanika, Germany
10. Kathy Jordan, U.S.

1984

1. Martina Navratilova, U.S.
2. Chris Evert Lloyd, U.S.
3. Hana Mandlikova, Czechoslovakia
4. Helena Sukova, Czechoslovakia
5. Manuela Maleeva, Bulgaria
6. Pam Shriver, U.S.
7. Claudia Kohde Kilsch, Germany
8. Zina Garrison, U.S.
9. Wendy Turnbull, Australia
10. Carling Bassett, Canada

1985

1. Martina Navratilova, U.S.
2. Chris Evert Lloyd, U.S.
3. Hana Mandlikova, Czechoslovakia
4. Claudia Kohde Kilsch, Germany
5. Pam Shriver, U.S.
6. Zina Garrison, U.S.
7. Helena Sukova, Czechoslovakia
8. Steffi Graf, Germany
9. Kathy Rinaldi, U.S.
10. Gabriela Sabatini, Argentina

1986

1. Martina Navratilova, U.S.
2. Chris Evert Lloyd, U.S.
3. Steffi Graf, Germany
4. Helena Sukova, Czechoslovakia
5. Pam Shriver, U.S.
6. Hana Mandlikova, Czechoslovakia
7. Claudia Kohde Kilsch, Germany

8. Gabriela Sabatini, Argentina
9. Lori McNeil, U.S.
10. Manuela Maleeva, Bulgaria

1987

1. Steffi Graf, Germany
2. Martina Navratilova, U.S.
3. Chris Evert, U.S.
4. Pam Shriver, U.S.
5. Hana Mandlikova, Czechoslovakia
6. Gabriela Sabatini, Argentina
7. Helena Sukova, Czechoslovakia
8. Manuela Maleeva Fragniere, Bulgaria
9. Lori McNeil, U.S.
10. Zina Garrison, U.S.

1988

1. Steffi Graf
2. Martina Navratilova, U.S.
3. Gabriela Sabatini, Argentina
4. Chris Evert, U.S.
5. Pam Shriver, U.S.
6. Natalia Zvereva, Russia
7. Manuela Maleeva Fragniere, Bulgaria
8. Helena Sukova, Czechoslovakia
9. Zina Garrison, U.S.
10. Katerina Maleeva, Bulgaria

1989

1. Steffi Graf, Germany
2. Martina Navratilova, U.S.
3. Arantxa Sanchez Vicario, Spain
4. Gabriela Sabatini, Argentina
5. Monica Seles, Yugoslavia
6. Zina Garrison, U.S.
7. Chris Evert, U.S.
8. Helena Sukova, Czechoslovakia
9. Manuela Maleeva Fragniere, Bulgaria
10. Mary Joe Fernandez, U.S.

1990

1. Monica Seles, Yugoslavia
2. Gabriela Sabatini, Argentina

3. Steffi Graf, Germany
4. Martina Navratilova, U.S.
5. Jennifer Capriati, U.S.
6. Arantxa Sanchez Vicario, Spain
7. Mary Joe Fernandez, U.S.
8. Katerina Maleeva, Bulgaria
9. Manuela Maleeva Fragniere, Switzerland
10. Zina Garrison, U.S.

1991

1. Monica Seles, Yugoslavia
2. Steffi Graf, Germany
3. Gabriela Sabatini, Argentina
4. Martina Navratilova, U.S.
5. Jennifer Capriati, U.S.
6. Arantxa Sanchez Vicario, Spain
7. Jana Novotna, Czechoslovakia
8. Mary Joe Fernandez, U.S.
9. Manuela Maleeva Fragniere, Switzerland
10. Conchita Martinez, Spain

1992

1. Monica Seles, Yugoslavia
2. Steffi Graf, Germany
3. Arantxa Sanchez Vicario, Spain
4. Jennifer Capriati, U.S.
5. Martina Navratilova, U.S.
6. Gabriela Sabatini, Argentina
7. Mary Joe Fernandez, U.S.
8. Conchita Martinez, Spain
9. Manuela Maleeva Fragniere, Switzerland
10. Anke Huber, Germany

1993

1. Steffi Graf, Germany
2. Arantxa Sanchez Vicario, Spain
3. Martina Navratilova, U.S.
4. Monica Seles, Yugoslavia
5. Jana Novotna, Czechoslovakia

6. Conchita Martinez, Spain
7. Mary Joe Fernandez, U.S.
8. Gabriela Sabatini, Argentina
9. Jennifer Capriati, U.S.
10. Anke Huber, Germany

1994

1. Arantxa Sanchez Vicario, Spain
2. Steffi Graf, Germany
3. Conchita Martinez, Spain
4. Martina Navratilova, U.S.
5. Mary Pierce, France
6. Gabriela Sabatini, Argentina
7. Lindsay Davenport, U.S.
8. Kimiko Date, Japan
9. Jana Novotna, Czechoslovakia
10. Anke Huber, Germany

1995

1. Steffi Graf, Germany
2. Arantxa Sanchez Vicario, Spain
3. Conchita Martinez, Spain
4. Mary Pierce, France
5. Kimiko Date, Japan
6. Monica Seles, U.S.
7. Mary Joe Fernandez, U.S.
8. Magdalena Maleeva, Bulgaria
9. Jana Novotna, Czech Republic
10. Gabriela Sabatini, Argentina

1996

1. Steffi Graf, Germany
2. Monica Seles, U.S.
3. Arantxa Sanchez Vicario, Spain
4. Conchita Martinez, Spain
5. Lindsay Davenport, U.S.
6. Jana Novotna, Czech Republic
7. Kimiko Date, Japan
8. Martina Hingis, Switzerland
9. Anke Huber, Germany
10. Chanda Rubin, U.S.

MISCELLANEOUS ALL-TIME RECORDS

MEN • Singles

MATCH

Aces: 54—Gary Muller vs. Peter Lundgren, Wimbledon qualifying, Roehampton, 1993
44—Mark Philippoussis vs. Byron Black, Kuala Lumpur, 1995
43—Steve Warner vs. Matt Anger, Wimbledon qualifying, Roehampton, 1989
41—Goran Ivanisevic vs. Yevgeny Kafelnikov, Grand Slam Cup, 1995
40—Bryan Shelton vs. Paolo Cane, Australian Open, 1991
39—Goran Ivanisevic vs. Yevgeny Kafelnikov, Grand Slam Cup, 1996
38—Marc Rosset vs. Jordi Arrese, Olympic final, 1992; Ivanisevic, Croatia, vs. Leander Paes, India, Davis Cup, New Delhi, 1995
37—Ivanisevic vs. Andre Agassi, Wimbledon final, 1992 (served 206 aces, a record for one tournament)

Double faults: 29—Gerald Patterson vs. Jack Hawkes, Australian final, 1927
26—Marc Rosset vs. Michael Joyce, Wimbledon, 1995
25—Goran Ivanisevic, Croatia, vs. Leander Paes, India, Davis Cup, New Delhi, 1995

Foot faults: 26—Stefan Edberg vs. Aaron Krickstein, U.S. Open, 1983

SEASON

Aces: 1,603—Goran Ivanisevic, 1996

Fastest serve: 139.8 MPH—Greg Rusedski vs. Jean-Philippe Fleurian, Beijing, 1996

Double faults: 421—Michael Stich, 1993

Winning streaks: 98—Bill Tilden, 1924–25
92—Don Budge, 1937–38
50—Guillermo Vilas, 1977
49—Bjorn Borg, 1978
44—Ivan Lendl, 1981–82
42—John McEnroe, 1984

Losing streak: 20—Garry Donnelly, 1986–87

Tournaments played: 40—Ross Case; Onny Parun, 1973
39—Dick Crealy, 1974
38—Bob Carmichael, Frew McMillan, 1973
37—Onny Parun, 1972; Colin Dibley, Ray Moore, 1973; Dick Crealy, 1975
36—Gerald Battrick, 1973; Barry Phillips-Moore, 1974; Ray Moore, 1975; Javier Sanchez, 1994
35—Phil Dent, 1971; Brian Gottfried, Dick Crealy, 1973; Harold Solomon, 1974 and 1975; Javier Sanchez, 1995

Tournaments won: 17—Rod Laver (of 32), 1969
17—Guillermo Vilas (of 33), 1977
15—Ivan Lendl (of 23), 1982; Ilie Nastase (of 31), 1973

Matches played: 159—Guillermo Vilas, 1977
142—Ivan Lendl, 1980
135—Ilie Nastase, 1973
123—Arthur Ashe, 1975

Matches won: 145—Vilas (of 159), 1977
118—Nastase (of 135), 1973
113—Lendl (of 142), 1980
107—Lendl (of 116), 1982
106—Laver (of 122), 1969

Match winning percentage: .987 (78-1)—Bill Tilden, 1925
.965 (82-3)—McEnroe, 1984

CAREER

Tournaments played: 410—Jimmy Connors, 1970–96
348—Ivan Lendl, 1978–94

Finals: 163—Jimmy Connors, 1971–89
146—Ivan Lendl, 1978–94

Tournaments won: 109—Jimmy Connors, 1970–89
94—Ivan Lendl, 1980–94
77—John McEnroe, 1978–92
62—Bjorn Borg, 1974–81
62—Guillermo Vilas, 1973–86
57—Ilie Nastase, 1970–81
54—Rod Laver, 1968–73

Matches played: 1,622—Jimmy Connors, 1970–96
1,310—Ivan Lendl, 1978–94

Matches won: 1,337—Jimmy Connors, 1970–96
1,072—Ivan Lendl, 1978–94

MEN • Doubles

SEASON

Tournaments played: 41—Libor Pimek, 1994

Tournaments won: 17—John McEnroe, 1979
15—Bob Hewitt, Frew McMillan, both 1977

Matches played: 86—John McEnroe, 1979

Matches won: 83—John McEnroe, 1979

Tournaments played, team: 19—Peter Fleming–John McEnroe, 1979

Tournaments won, team: 15—Peter Fleming–John McEnroe, 1979
13, Bob Hewitt–Frew McMillan, 1977

Matches played team: 78—Peter Fleming–John McEnroe, 1979

Matches won, team: 74—Peter Fleming–John McEnroe, 1979

CAREER

Finals: 125—Tom Okker, 1968–80
119—Frew McMillan, 1968–81

Tournaments won: 78—Tom Okker, 1968–80
77—John McEnroe, 1978–92
74—Frew McMillan, 1968–81
66—Peter Fleming, 1978–87
65—Bob Hewitt, 1968–80
62—Raul Ramirez, 1973–83

Tournaments won, team: 57—Peter Fleming–John McEnroe; Bob Hewitt–Frew McMillan
44—Sergio Casal–Emilio Sanchez
41—Todd Woodbridge–Mark Woodforde
39—Brian Gottfried–Paul Ramirez
34—Bob Lutz–Stan Smith

MEN • Overall (Singles and Doubles together)

SEASON

Singles and doubles tournaments played: 44—Guillermo Vilas, 1977
43—John McEnroe, 1979

Singles and doubles tournaments won: 27—John McEnroe (10-17), 1979
23—Ilie Nastase, (15-8), 1973; Rod Laver (17-6), 1969
21—Guillermo Vilas (17-4), 1977

Singles and doubles matches played: 221—Guillermo Vilas, 1977 (159-62)
192—John McEnroe, 1979 (106-86)

Singles and doubles matches won: 187—Guillermo Vilas, 1977 (145 singles, 42 doubles)
177—John McEnroe, 1979 (94 singles, 83 doubles)

CAREER

Singles and doubles tournaments won: 152—John McEnroe (77-75), 1978–92
128—Jimmy Connors (109-19), 1972–89
108—Ilie Nastase (57-51) 1968–81
108—Tom Okker (30-78), 1968–80
100—Stan Smith (39-61), 1968–80; Ivan Lendl (94-6), 1978–94

WOMEN • Singles

MATCH

Aces: 22—Brenda Schultz-McCarthy vs. Iva Majoli, Birmingham (Eng), 1994
17—Brenda Schultz-McCarthy vs. Audra Keller, U.S. Open, 1995 (served 62 aces, a record for one tournament); Brenda Schultz-McCarthy vs. Arantxa Sanchez Vicario, Chase Championships, New York, 1996

16—Brenda Schultz-McCarthy vs. Monica Seles, Wimbledon, 1989

Fastest serve: 121.8 MPH—Brenda Schultz-McCarthy vs. Martina Hingis, Australian Open, 1996

Double faults: 19—Debbie Graham vs. Martina Navratilova, Oakland, 1994
18—Gabriela Sabatini vs. Kimiko Date, Lipton, 1995

SEASON

Winning streaks: 158—Helen Wills Moody, 1926–33
111—Alice Marble, 1938–40
74—Martina Navratilova, 1984
66—Steffi Graf, 1990
58—Martina Navratilova, 1986–87
55—Chris Evert, 1974
54—Margaret Smith Court, 1972–73; Martina Navratilova, 1983–84

Consecutive singles finals reached: 23—Martina Navratilova, 1983–84 (won 22)
22—Steffi Graf, 1989–90 (won 18)

Tournaments played: 32—Rosie Casals, 1971
31—Billie Jean King, 1971
30—Kim Steinmetz, 1985
29—Camille Benjamin, 1985
28—Camille Benjamin, 1986

Tournaments won: 21—Margaret Smith Court, 1970
18—Margaret Smith Court, 1973
17—Billie Jean King, 1971
16—Chris Evert, 1974–1975; Martina Navratilova, 1983

Matches played: 126—Billie Jean King, 1971
116—Rosie Casals, 1971
110—Margaret Smith Court, 1970
108—Margaret Smith Court, 1973; Chris Evert, 1974
103—Martina Navratilova, 1981
102—Martina Navratilova, 1979

Matches won: 112—Billie Jean King, 1971
104—Margaret Smith Court, 1970
102—Margaret Smith Court, 1973
100—Chris Evert, 1974
90—Martina Navratilova, 1979

Match winning percentage: 1.000 (45-0)—Alice Marble, 1939, 1940 (Suzanne Lenglen and Helen Wills Moody also had undefeated seasons, but fewer matches)
.981 (86-1)—Martina Navratilova, 1983

CAREER

Tournaments played: 380—Martina Navratilova, 1973–94
304—Rosie Casals, 1968–82
303—Chris Evert, 1969–89
291—Pam Shriver, 1978–96
283—Zina Garrison Jackson, 1981–96
216—Billie Jean King, 1968–83
197—Steffi Graf, 1982–96
130—Margaret Smith Court, 1968–77

Tournaments won: 167—Martina Navratilova, 1973–94
157—Chris Evert, 1970–89
102—Steffi Graf, 1982–96
79—Margaret Smith Court, 1968–77
67—Billie Jean King, 1968–83
55—Virginia Wade, 1968–78

Matches played: 1,650—Martina Navratilova
1,455—Chris Evert
1,168—Virginia Wade
914—Steffi Graf
892—Margaret Smith Court
891—Pam Shriver
857—Zina Garrison Jackson
826—Billie Jean King
824—Rosie Casals
821—Gabriela Sabatini
700—Arantxa Sanchez Vicario

Matches won: 1,438—Martina Navratilova
1,309—Chris Evert
839—Virginia Wade
820—Steffi Graf
789—Margaret Smith Court
677—Billie Jean King
632—Gabriela Sabatini
621—Pam Shriver
588—Zina Garrison Jackson

534—Arantxa Sanchez Vicario

WOMEN • Doubles

SEASON

Tournaments played: 31—Rosie Casals, 1979
30—Rosie Casals, 1980, 1982
28—Rosie Casals, 1971, 1981
26—Billie Jean King, 1971; Lori McNeil, 1985–87; Jana Novotna, 1987
25—Lori McNeil, 1984–86
24—Lori McNeil, 1988
23—Martina Navratilova, 1975

Tournaments won: 21—Billie Jean King, 1971; Rosie Casals, 1971
14—Martina Navratilova, 1982
13—Pam Shriver, 1982 and 1983; Rosie Casals, 1970, 1973

Matches played: 99—Rosie Casals, 1982
96—Rosie Casals, 1981
89—Rosie Casals, 1971
85—Billie Jean King, 1971
84—Arantxa Sanchez Vicario, 1992
83—Natalia Zvereva, 1991
82—Gigi Fernandez, 1991

Matches won: 82—Rosie Casals, 1971
80—Billie Jean King, 1971
74—Rosie Casals, 1981, 1982; Gigi Fernandez, 1995
73—Arantxa Sanchez Vicario, 1992
72—Gigi Fernandez, 1993
71—Arantxa Sanchez Vicario, 1994
70—Natalia Zvereva, 1991

Winning streak, team: 109—Martina Navratilova–Pam Shriver, 1984–85

Matches played, team: 78—Rosie Casals–Billie Jean King, 1971
58—Rosie Casals–Billie Jean King, 1969
56—Martina Navratilova–Pam Shriver, 1982

Matches won, team: 73—Rosie Casals–Billie Jean King, 1971
54, Martina Navratilova–Pam Shriver, 1982

Tournaments played, team: 24—Rosie Casals–Billie Jean King, 1971
17—Rosie Casals–Billie Jean King, 1969
16—Rosie Casals–Billie Jean King, 1973
14—Martina Navratilova–Pam Shriver, 1982

Tournaments won, team: 19—Rosie Casals–Billie Jean King, 1971
12—Martina Navratilova–Pam Shriver, 1982
11—Martina Navratilova–Pam Shriver, 1983–84
10—Rosie Casals–Billie Jean King, 1973

CAREER

Tournaments played: 381—Rosie Casals, 1968–91
286—Martina Navratilova, 1973–94
266—Pam Shriver, 1978–96
263—Zina Garrison Jackson, 1978–96
239—Gigi Fernandez, 1983–96
216—Billie Jean King, 1968–90

Tournaments won: 162—Martina Navratilova
112—Rosie Casals
106—Pam Shriver
101—Billie Jean King

Matches played: 1,111—Martina Navratilova
1,125—Rosie Casals
921—Pam Shriver
806—Gigi Fernandez
725—Billie Jean King

Matches won: 989—Martina Navratilova
856—Rosie Casals
764—Pam Shriver
634—Gigi Fernandez
611—Billie Jean King

Tournaments played, team: 101—Martina Navratilova–Pam Shriver
98—Rosie Casals–Billie Jean King

Tournaments won, team: 79—Martina Navratilova–Pam Shriver
56—Rosie Casals–Billie Jean King

Matches won, team: 390 (of 415)—Martina Navratilova–Pam Shriver
294 (of 335)—Rosie Casals–Billie Jean King

WOMEN • Overall
(Singles and Doubles Together)

SEASON

Singles and doubles tournaments played: 60—Rosie Casals, 1971
57—Billie Jean King, 1971
56—Rosie Casals, 1979
55—Rosie Casals, 1980
48—Martina Navratilova, 1975
45—Margaret Smith Court, 1970
44—Jana Novotna, 1987

Singles and doubles tournaments won: 38—Billie Jean King (17-21), 1971
29—Margaret Smith Court (21-8), 1970; Martina Navratilova (15-14), 1982; Martina Navratilova (16-13), 1983
26—Margaret Smith Court (18-8), 1973
25—Margaret Smith Court (14-11), 1969
23—Rosie Casals (2-21), 1971

Singles and doubles matches played: 210—Billie Jean King, 1971
205—Rosie Casals, 1971
167—Sanchez Vicario, 1992
166—Margaret Smith Court, 1970
165—Martina Navratilova, 1982
161—Arantxa Sanchez Vicario, 1994
157—Margaret Smith Court, 1973

Singles and doubles matches won: 192—Billie Jean King (of 210), 1971
169—Rosie Casals (of 205), 1971
158—Martina Navratilova (of 165), 1982
150—Margaret Smith Court (of 166), 1970
145—Arantxa Sanchez Vicario (of 161), 1994
144—Margaret Smith Court (of 157), 1973
139—Arantxa Sanchez Vicario (of 167), 1992

CAREER

Singles and doubles tournaments played: 685—Rosie Casals
666—Martina Navratilova
567—Rosie Casals
546—Zina Garrison Jackson
504—Pam Shriver
472—Gigi Fernandez
442—Chris Evert
432—Billie Jean King
231—Margaret Smith Court

Singles and doubles tournaments won: 329—Martina Navratilova
189—Chris Evert
168—Billie Jean King
127—Margaret Smith Court
123—Rosie Casals

Singles and doubles matches played: 2,761—Martina Navratilova
1,949—Rosie Casals
1,875—Chris Evert
1,812—Pam Shriver
1,551—Billie Jean King
892—Margaret Smith Court

Singles and doubles matches won: 2,427—Martina Navratilova
1,631—Chris Evert
1,385—Pam Shriver
1,384—Rosie Casals
1,288—Billie Jean King

LONGEST MATCHES

Men's singles: 126 games—Roger Taylor, Britain, d. Wieslaw Gasiorek, Poland, 27-29, 31-29, 6-4. King's Cup match, Warsaw, 1966

Men's doubles: 147 games—Dick Leach, Arcadia, Calif., and Dick Dell, Bethesda, Md., d. Len Schloss, Baltimore, and Tom Mozur, Sweetwater, Tenn., 3-6, 49-47, 22-20. Second round, Newport (R.I.) Casino Invitation, 1967

Women's singles: 62 games—Kathy Blake, Pacific Palisades, Calif., d. Elena Subirats, Mexico, 12-10, 6-8, 14-12. First round, Piping Rock Invitation, Locust Valley, N.Y., 1966

Women's doubles: 81 games—Nancy Richey, San Angelo, Tex., and Carole Graebner, New York, d. Carol Hanks and Justina Bricka, both St. Louis, 31-33, 6-1, 6-4. Semifinal, Eastern Grass Championship, South Orange, N.J., 1964

Mixed doubles: 77 games—Brenda Schultz and Michiel Schapers, Netherlands, d. Andrea Temesvari, Hungary, and Tom Nijssen, Netherlands, 6-3, 5-7, 29-27, first round, Wimbledon, 1991

LONGEST MATCHES (PLAYING TIME)

Men: 6 hours, 32 minutes—John McEnroe, U.S., d. Mats Wilander, Sweden, 9-7, 6-2, 15-17, 3-6, 8-6, Davis Cup, quarters, St. Louis, 1982

Women: 6 hours, 31 minutes—Vicki Nelson-Dunbar d. Jean Hepner, 6-4, 7-6 (13-11), Richmond, Va., 1st rd., 1984 (tie-breaker alone lasted 1 hour, 47 minutes, one point of which lasted 29 minutes, a rally of 643 strokes)

LONGEST SETS

Men's singles: 70 games—John Brown, Australia, d. Bill Brown, Omaha, Neb., 36-34, 6-1, 3rd rd., Heart of America tourney, Kansas City, Mo., 1968

Men's doubles: 96 games—Dick Dell and Dick Leach d. Len Schloss and Tom Mozur, 3-6, 49-47, 22-20 (see above)

Women's singles: 36 games—Billie Jean King, U.S., d. Christine Truman, Britain, 6-4, 19-17, Wightman Cup, Cleveland, 1963

Women's doubles: 64 games—Nancy Richey and Carole Graebner d. Carol Hanks and Justina Bricka, 31-33, 6-1, 6-4 (see above)

Mixed doubles: 77 games—see previous, longest matches

52 games—Margaret Osborne DuPont, Wilmington, Del., and Bill Talbert, N.Y., d. Gertrude "Gussy" Moran, Santa Monica, Cal., and Bob Falkenburg, Los Angeles, 27-25, 5-7, 6-1, semifinal, U.S. Championships, Forest Hills, N.Y.

LONGEST TIE-BREAKS

Men's singles: 24-22—First set, Aki Rahunen, Finland, d. Peter Nyborg, Denmark, 7-6, 2-6, 6-3, 1st rd., qualifying Copenhagen Open, 1992

Men's doubles: 26-24—Fourth set, Jan Gunnarson, Sweden, and Michael Mortensen, Denmark, d. John Frawley, Australia, and Victor Pecci, Paraguay, 6-4, 6-4, 3-6, 7-6, 1st rd., Wimbledon, 1985

Women's singles: 19-17—First set, Pat Medrado, Brazil, d. Laura Arraya (Gildemeister), 7-6, 6-7, 6-1, round-robin, São Paulo, Brazil, 1981

Women's doubles: 20-18—Third set, Rosie Casals, Sausalito, Calif., and Kathy Horvath, Largo, Fla., d. Sandy Collins, Odessa, Tex., and Beth Herr, Dayton, Ohio, 5-7, 6-1, 7-6, 2nd rd., Amelia Island, Fla., 1984

Mixed doubles: 18-16—Third set, Marcie Louie, San Francisco, and Andy Lucchesi, San Mateo, Cal., d. Diane Desfor, Long Beach, Calif., and Horace Reid, New York, 6-2, 6-7, 7-6, 2nd rd., U.S. Open, Flushing Meadow, N.Y., 1978

CHAMPIONSHIPS

These records pertain to the major titles, the Big Four championships of Australia, France, Wimbledon, and the United States, with years between first and last championship indicated.

Most men's singles: 12—Roy Emerson, 1961–67 (6 Aus., 2 Fr., 2 Wim., 2 U.S.)

Most men's doubles: 17—John Newcombe, 1965–76 (5 Aus., 3 Fr., 6 Wim., 3 U.S.)

Most men's mixed: 8—Vic Seixas, 1953–56 (1 Fr., 4 Wim., 3 U.S.); Frank Sedgman, 1949–52 (2 Aus., 2 Fr., 2 Wim., 2 U.S.)

Most men's altogether: 28—Roy Emerson, 1959–71

Most women's singles: 24—Margaret Smith Court, 1960–73 (11 Aus., 4 Fr., 2 Wim. 7 U.S.)

Most women's doubles: 31—Martina Navratilova (8 Aus., 7 Fr., 7 Wim., 9 U.S.)

Most women's mixed: 19—Margaret Smith Court, 1961–75 (2 Aus., 4 Fr., 5 Wim., 8 U.S.)

Most women's altogether: 62—Margaret Smith Court, 1960–75

Most men's doubles, team: 12—John Newcombe and Tony Roche, 1965–75 (4 Aus., 2 Fr., 5 Wim., 1 U.S.)

Most women's doubles, team: 20—Margaret Osborne duPont and Louise Brough, 1942–57 (3 Fr., 5 Wim., 12 U.S.); Martina Navratilova and Pam Shriver, 1982–89 (7 Aus., 4 Fr., 5 Wim., 4 U.S.)

Most mixed doubles, team: 10—Margaret Smith Court and Ken Fletcher, 1963–68 (2 Aus., 3 Fr., 4 Wim., 1 U.S.)

PRIZE MONEY

Figures, as of close of 1996 season, are based on recognized tournament prize money and do not include exhibitions or endorsements.

Men's season high: $5,415,066—Pete Sampras, 1995

Women's season high: $2,665,706—Steffi Graf, 1996

Men's career high: $25,562,347—Pete Sampras

Women's career high: $20,344,061—Martina Navratilova

Men's tournament high: $2,000,000—Pete Sampras, 1990 Compaq Grand Slam Cup, Munich; David Wheaton, 1991 Compaq Grand Slam Cup, Munich; Michael Stich, 1992 Compaq Grand Slam Cup, Munich.

Women's tournament high: $600,000—Steffi Graf, 1996 U.S. Open, Flushing Meadow, N.Y.

CAREER PRIZE MONEY LEADERS

MEN

1.	Pete Sampras	1988–96	$25,562,347
2.	Boris Becker	1984–96	$21,966,402
3.	Ivan Lendl	1978–94	$21,262,417
4.	Stefan Edberg	1984–96	$20,630,941
5.	Goran Ivanisevic	1988–96	$13,995,780
6.	Michael Chang	1988–96	$13,744,809
7.	Andre Agassi	1986–96	$12,801,331
8.	John McEnroe	1978–94	$12,539,827
9.	Jim Courier	1988–96	$12,471,985
10.	Michael Stich	1988–96	$12,158,416
11.	Thomas Muster	1985–96	$9,474,064
12.	Jimmy Connors	1972–96	$8,841,070
13.	Sergi Bruguera	1988–96	$8,520,901
14.	Mats Wilander	1982–96	$7,976,256
15.	Petr Korda	1987–96	$7,524,226
16.	Guy Forget	1982–96	$5,817,843
17.	Yevgeny Kafelnikov	1992–96	$5,715,734
18.	Jakob Hlasek	1983–96	$5,521,725
19.	Brad Gilbert	1982–95	$5,507,745
20.	Wayne Ferreira	1989–96	$5,472,573

WOMEN

1.	Martina Navratilova	1973–96	$20,344,061
2.	Steffi Graf	1982–96	$19,846,316
3.	Arantxa Sanchez Vicario	1985–96	$11,632,976
4.	Monica Seles	1989–96	$8,960,490
5.	Chris Evert	1973–89	$8,896,195
6.	Gabriela Sabatini	1985–96	$8,785,850
7.	Jana Novotna	1987–96	$6,572,665
8.	Conchita Martinez	1988–96	$6,349,266
9.	Helena Sukova	1983–96	$5,946,064
10.	Zina Garrison-Jackson	1982–96	$5,448,686
11.	Pam Shriver	1979–97	$5,384,316
12.	Natalia Zvereva	1988–96	$5,336,043
13.	Gigi Fernandez	1983–96	$4,226,024
14.	Mary Joe Fernandez	1986–96	$4,134,754
15.	Hana Mandlikova	1978–87	$3,340,959
16.	Manuela Maleeva Fragniere	1988–92	$3,244,811
17.	Larisa Savchenko Neiland	1988–96	$3,226,139
18.	Lori McNeil	1983–96	$3,176,429
19.	Wendy Turnbull	1975–89	$2,769,024
20.	Anke Huber	1989–96	$2,708,585

WTA Year-End Computer Top 10 1973–96

1973

1. Margaret Smith Court
2. Billie Jean Moffitt King
3. Evonne Goolagong Cawley
4. Chris Evert
5. Rosie Casals
6. Virginia Wade
7. Kerry Melville
8. Nancy Richey Gunter
9. Julie Heldman
10. Helga Niessen Masthoff

1974

1. Billie Jean Moffitt King
2. Evonne Goolagong Cawley
3. Chris Evert
4. Virginia Wade
5. Julie Heldman
6. Rosie Casals
7. Kerry Melville
8. Olga Morozova
9. Lesley Hunt
10. Françoise Durr

1975

1. Chris Evert
2. Billie Jean Moffitt King
3. Evonne Goolagong Cawley
4. Martina Navratilova
5. Virginia Wade
6. Margaret Smith Court
7. Olga Morozova
8. Nancy Richey Gunter
9. Françoise Durr
10. Rosie Casals

1976

1. Chris Evert
2. Evonne Goolagong Cawley
3. Virginia Wade
4. Martina Navratilova
5. Sue Barker
6. Betty Stove
7. Dianne Fromholtz
8. Mima Jausovec
9. Rosie Casals
10. Françoise Durr

1977

1. Chris Evert
2. Billie Jean Moffitt King
3. Martina Navratilova

4. Virginia Wade
5. Sue Barker
6. Rosie Casals
7. Betty Stove
8. Dianne Fromholtz
9. Wendy Turnbull
10. Kerry Melville Reid

1978

1. Martina Navratilova
2. Chris Evert
3. Evonne Goolagong Cawley
4. Virginia Wade
5. Billie Jean Moffitt King
6. Tracy Austin
7. Wendy Turnbull
8. Kerry Melville Reid
9. Betty Stove
10. Dianne Fromholtz

1979

1. Martina Navratilova
2. Chris Evert Lloyd
3. Tracy Austin
4. Evonne Goolagong Cawley
5. Billie Jean Moffitt King
6. Dianne Fromholtz
7. Wendy Turnbull
8. Virginia Wade
9. Kerry Melville Reid
10. Sue Barker

1980

1. Chris Evert Lloyd
2. Tracy Austin
3. Martina Navratilova
4. Hana Mandlikova
5. Evonne Goolagong Cawley
6. Billie Jean Moffitt King
7. Andrea Jaeger
8. Wendy Turnbull
9. Pam Shriver
10. Greer Stevens

1981

1. Chris Evert Lloyd
2. Tracy Austin
3. Martina Navratilova
4. Andrea Jaeger
5. Hana Mandlikova
6. Sylvia Hanika
7. Pam Shriver
8. Wendy Turnbull
9. Bettina Bunge
10. Barbara Potter

1982

1. Martina Navratilova
2. Chris Evert Lloyd

3. Andrea Jaeger
4. Tracy Austin
5. Wendy Turnbull
6. Pam Shriver
7. Hana Mandlikova
8. Barbara Potter
9. Bettina Bunge
10. Sylvia Hanika

1983

1. Martina Navratilova
2. Chris Evert Lloyd
3. Andrea Jaeger
4. Pam Shriver
5. Sylvia Hanika
6. Jo Durie
7. Bettina Bunge
8. Wendy Turnbull
9. Tracy Austin
10. Zina Garrison

1984

1. Martina Navratilova
2. Chris Evert Lloyd
3. Hana Mandlikova
4. Pam Shriver
5. Wendy Turnbull
6. Manuela Maleeva
7. Helena Sukova
8. Claudia Kohde Kilsch
9. Zina Garrison
10. Kathy Jordan

1985

1. Martina Navratilova
2. Chris Evert Lloyd
3. Hana Mandlikova
4. Pam Shriver
5. Claudia Kohde Kilsch
6. Steffi Graf
7. Manuela Maleeva
8. Zina Garrison
9. Helena Sukova
10. Bonnie Gadusek

1986

1. Martina Navratilova
2. Chris Evert Lloyd
3. Steffi Graf
4. Hana Mandlikova
5. Helena Sukova
6. Pam Shriver
7. Claudia Kohde Kilsch
8. Manuela Maleeva
9. Kathy Rinaldi
10. Gabriela Sabatini

1987

1. Steffi Graf
2. Martina Navratilova
3. Chris Evert

4. Pam Shriver
5. Hana Mandlikova
6. Gabriela Sabatini
7. Helena Sukova
8. Manuela Maleeva
9. Zina Garrison
10. Claudia Kohde Kilsch

1988

1. Steffi Graf
2. Martina Navratilova
3. Chris Evert
4. Gabriela Sabatini
5. Pam Shriver
6. Manuela Maleeva Fragniere
7. Natalia Zvereva
8. Helena Sukova
9. Zina Garrison
10. Barbara Potter

1989

1. Steffi Graf
2. Martina Navratilova
3. Gabriela Sabatini
4. Zina Garrison
5. Arantxa Sanchez Vicario
6. Monica Seles
7. Conchita Martinez
8. Helena Sukova
9. Manuela Maleeva Fragniere
10. Chris Evert

1990

1. Steffi Graf
2. Monica Seles
3. Martina Navratilova
4. Mary Joe Fernandez
5. Gabriela Sabatini
6. Katerina Maleeva
7. Aranxta Sanchez Vicario
8. Jennifer Capriati
9. Manuela Maleeva Fragniere
10. Zina Garrison

1991

1. Monica Seles
2. Steffi Graf
3. Gabriela Sabatini
4. Martina Navratilova
5. Aranxta Sanchez Vicario
6. Jennifer Capriati
7. Jana Novotna
8. Mary Joe Fernandez
9. Conchita Martinez
10. Manuela Maleeva Fragniere

1992

1. Monica Seles
2. Steffi Graf
3. Gabriela Sabatini
4. Arantxa Sanchez Vicario
5. Martina Navratilova
6. Mary Joe Fernandez
7. Jennifer Capriati
8. Conchita Martinez
9. Manuela Maleeva Fragniere
10. Jana Novotna

1993

1. Steffi Graf
2. Arantxa Sanchez Vicario
3. Martina Navratilova
4. Conchita Martinez
5. Gabriela Sabatini
6. Jana Novotna
7. Mary Joe Fernandez
8. Monica Seles
9. Jennifer Capriati
10. Anke Huber

1994

1. Steffi Graf
2. Arantxa Sanchez Vicario
3. Conchita Martinez
4. Jana Novotna
5. Mary Pierce
6. Lindsay Davenport
7. Gabriela Sabatini
8. Martina Navratilova
9. Kimiko Date
10. Natalia Zvereva

1995

1. Steffi Graf and Monica Seles
2. Conchita Martinez
3. Arantxa Sanchez Vicario
4. Kimiko Date
5. Mary Pierce
6. Magdalena Maleeva
7. Gabriela Sabatini
8. Mary Joe Fernandez
9. Iva Majoli
10. Anke Huber

1996

1. Steffi Graf
2. Arantxa Sanchez Vicario and Monica Seles
3. Jana Novotna
4. Martina Hingis
5. Conchita Martinez

6. Anke Huber
7. Iva Majoli
8. Kimiko Date
9. Lindsay Davenport
10. Barbara Paulus

ATP Tour Year-End Computer Top 10 1973–96

1973

1. Ilie Nastase
2. John Newcombe
3. Jimmy Connors
4. Tom Okker
5. Stan Smith
6. Ken Rosewall
7. Manuel Orantes
8. Rod Laver
9. Jan Kodes
10. Arthur Ashe

1974

1. Jimmy Connors
2. John Newcombe
3. Bjorn Borg
4. Rod Laver
5. Guillermo Vilas
6. Tom Okker
7. Arthur Ashe
8. Ken Rosewall
9. Stan Smith
10. Ilie Nastase

1975

1. Jimmy Connors
2. Guillermo Vilas
3. Bjorn Borg
4. Arthur Ashe
5. Manuel Orantes
6. Ken Rosewall
7. Ilie Nastase
8. John Alexander
9. Roscoe Tanner
10. Rod Laver

1976

1. Jimmy Connors
2. Bjorn Borg
3. Ilie Nastase
4. Manuel Orantes
5. Raul Ramirez
6. Guillermo Vilas
7. Adriano Panatta
8. Harold Solomon
9. Eddie Dibbs
10. Brian Gottfried

1977

1. Jimmy Connors
2. Guillermo Vilas

3. Bjorn Borg
4. Vitas Gerulaitis
5. Brian Gottfried
6. Eddie Dibbs
7. Manuel Orantes
8. Raul Ramirez
9. Ilie Nastase
10. Dick Stockton

1978

1. Jimmy Connors
2. Bjorn Borg
3. Guillermo Vilas
4. John McEnroe
5. Vitas Gerulaitis
6. Eddie Dibbs
7. Brian Gottfried
8. Raul Ramirez
9. Harold Solomon
10. Corrado Barazzutti

1979

1. Bjorn Borg
2. Jimmy Connors
3. John McEnroe
4. Vitas Gerulaitis
5. Roscoe Tanner
6. Guillermo Vilas
7. Arthur Ashe
8. Harold Solomon
9. Jose Higueras
10. Eddie Dibbs

1980

1. Bjorn Borg
2. John McEnroe
3. Jimmy Connors
4. Gene Mayer
5. Guillermo Vilas
6. Ivan Lendl
7. Harold Solomon
8. Jose-Luis Clerc
9. Vitas Gerulaitis
10. Eliot Teltscher

1981

1. John McEnroe
2. Ivan Lendl
3. Jimmy Connors
4. Bjorn Borg
5. Jose-Luis Clerc
6. Guillermo Vilas
7. Gene Mayer
8. Eliot Teltscher
9. Vitas Gerulaitis
10. Peter McNamara

1982

1. John McEnroe
2. Jimmy Connors
3. Ivan Lendl

4. Guillermo Vilas
5. Vitas Gerulaitis
6. Jose-Luis Clerc
7. Mats Wilander
8. Gene Mayer
9. Yannick Noah
10. Peter McNamara

1983

1. John McEnroe
2. Ivan Lendl
3. Jimmy Connors
4. Mats Wilander
5. Yannick Noah
6. Jimmy Arias
7. Jose Higueras
8. Jose-Luis Clerc
9. Kevin Curren
10. Gene Mayer

1984

1. John McEnroe
2. Jimmy Connors
3. Ivan Lendl
4. Mats Wilander
5. Andres Gomez
6. Anders Jarryd
7. Henrik Sundstrom
8. Pat Cash
9. Eliot Teltscher
10. Yannick Noah

1985

1. Ivan Lendl
2. John McEnroe
3. Mats Wilander
4. Jimmy Connors
5. Stefan Edberg
6. Boris Becker
7. Yannick Noah
8. Anders Jarryd
9. Miloslav Mecir
10. Kevin Curren

1986

1. Ivan Lendl
2. Boris Becker
3. Mats Wilander
4. Yannick Noah
5. Stefan Edberg
6. Henri Leconte
7. Joakim Nystrom
8. Jimmy Connors
9. Miloslav Mecir
10. Andres Gomez

1987

1. Ivan Lendl
2. Stefan Edberg
3. Mats Wilander
4. Jimmy Connors

5. Boris Becker
6. Miloslav Mecir
7. Pat Cash
8. Yannick Noah
9. Tim Mayotte
10. John McEnroe

1988

1. Mats Wilander
2. Ivan Lendl
3. Andre Agassi
4. Boris Becker
5. Stefan Edberg
6. Kent Carlsson
7. Jimmy Connors
8. Jakob Hlasek
9. Henri Leconte
10. Tim Mayotte

1989

1. Ivan Lendl
2. Boris Becker
3. Stefan Edberg
4. John McEnroe
5. Michael Chang
6. Brad Gilbert
7. Andre Agassi
8. Aaron Krickstein
9. Alberto Mancini
10. Jay Berger

1990

1. Stefan Edberg
2. Boris Becker
3. Ivan Lendl
4. Andre Agassi
5. Pete Sampras
6. Andres Gomez
7. Thomas Muster
8. Emilio Sanchez
9. Goran Ivanisevic
10. Brad Gilbert

1991

1. Stefan Edberg
2. Jim Courier
3. Boris Becker
4. Michael Stich
5. Ivan Lendl
6. Pete Sampras
7. Guy Forget
8. Karel Novacek
9. Petr Korda
10. Andre Agassi

1992

1. Jim Courier
2. Stefan Edberg
3. Pete Sampras
4. Goran Ivanisevic
5. Boris Becker

6. Michael Chang
7. Petr Korda
8. Ivan Lendl
9. Andre Agassi
10. Richard Krajicek

1993

1. Pete Sampras
2. Michael Stich
3. Jim Courier
4. Sergi Bruguera
5. Stefan Edberg
6. Andrei Medvedev
7. Goran Ivanisevic
8. Michael Chang
9. Thomas Muster
10. Cedric Pioline

1994

1. Pete Sampras
2. Andre Agassi
3. Boris Becker
4. Sergi Bruguera
5. Goran Ivanisevic
6. Michael Chang
7. Stefan Edberg
8. Alberto Berasategui
9. Michael Stich
10. Todd Martin

1995

1. Pete Sampras
2. Andre Agassi
3. Thomas Muster
4. Boris Becker
5. Michael Chang
6. Yevgeny Kafelnikov
7. Thomas Enqvist
8. Jim Courier
9. Wayne Ferreira
10. Goran Ivanisevic

1996

1. Pete Sampras
2. Michael Chang
3. Yevgeny Kafelnikov
4. Goran Ivanisevic
5. Thomas Muster
6. Boris Becker
7. Richard Krajicek
8. Andre Agassi
9. Thomas Enqvist
10. Wayne Ferreira

ITF WORLD CHAMPIONS

Since 1978 the ITF has crowned world champions in men's and women's singles. Until 1992 these were subjective, chosen by committees. That year a computerized ranking was adopted.

MEN

1978	Bjorn Borg, Sweden
1979	Bjorn Borg, Sweden
1980	Bjorn Borg, Sweden
1981	John McEnroe, U.S.
1982	Jimmy Connors, U.S.
1983	John McEnroe, U.S.
1984	John McEnroe, U.S.
1985	Ivan Lendl, Czechoslovakia
1986	Ivan Lendl, Czechoslovakia
1987	Ivan Lendl, Czechoslovakia
1988	Mats Wilander, Sweden
1989	Boris Becker, Germany
1990	Ivan Lendl, Czechoslovakia
1991	Stefan Edberg, Sweden
1992	Jim Courier, U.S.
1993	Pete Sampras
1994	Pete Sampras
1995	Pete Sampras
1996	Pete Sampras

WOMEN

1978	Chris Evert Lloyd, U.S.
1979	Martina Navratilova, Czechoslovakia
1980	Chris Evert Lloyd, U.S.
1981	Chris Evert Lloyd, U.S.
1982	Martina Navratilova, U.S.
1983	Martina Navratilova, U.S.
1984	Martina Navratilova, U.S.
1985	Martina Navratilova, U.S.
1986	Martina Navratilova, U.S.
1987	Steffi Graf, Germany
1988	Steffi Graf, Germany
1989	Steffi Graf, Germany
1990	Steffi Graf, Germany
1991	Monica Seles, Yugoslavia
1992	Monica Seles, Yugoslavia
1993	Steffi Graf, Germany
1994	Arantxa Sanchez Vicario, Spain
1995	Steffi Graf, Germany
1996	Steffi Graf, Germany

THE GRAND SLAMS

First to win a Grand Slam—the championships of Australia, France, Britain (Wimbledon) and the United States in the same calendar year—was Don Budge of the U.S. Then came Maureen Connolly of the U.S. in 1953 and Rod Laver of Australia, in 1962 as an amateur, again in 1969 when the Slam first became open to all competitors. In 1970 Margaret Smith Court of Australia made the second female Slam and in 1988 Steffi Graf of Germany became the fifth to claim a Slam.

Slams have also been made in doubles by Frank Sedgman and Ken McGregor of Australia in 1951; Martina Navratilova and Pam Shriver of the U.S. in 1984; and in mixed doubles by Margaret Smith (Court) and Ken Fletcher in 1963. A Slam in doubles with two partners was made by Maria Bueno in 1960, and in mixed by Owen Davidson of Australia in 1967.

The complete record of all Grand Slams follows:

Singles

DON BUDGE, 1938

Australian, at Memorial Drive, Adelaide—d. Les Hancock, 6-2, 6-3, 6-4; Harold Whillans, 6-1, 6-0, 6-1; Len Schwartz, 6-4, 6-3, 10-8; Adrian Quist , 5-7, 6-4, 6-1, 6-2; John Bromwich, 6-4, 6-2, 6-1.

French at Roland Garros, Paris—d. Antoine Gentien, 6-1, 6-2, 6-4; Ghaus Mohammed, 6-1, 6-1, 5-7, 6-0; Franjo Kukuljevic, 6-2, 8-6, 2-6, 1-6, 6-1; Bernard Destremau, 6-4, 6-3, 6-4; Josip Pallada, 6-2, 6-3, 6-3; Roderich Menzel, 6-3, 6-2, 6-4.

British, at Wimbledon, London—d. Kenneth Gandar Dower, 6-2, 6-3, 6-3; Henry Billington, 7-5, 6-1, 6-1; George Lyttleton Rogers, 6-0, 7-5, 6-1; Ronald Shayes, 6-3, 6-4, 6-1; Franz Cejnar, 6-3, 6-0, 7-5; Henner Henkel, 6-2, 6-4, 6-0; Henry "Bunny" Austin, 6-1, 6-0, 6-3.

United States, at Forest Hills, New York—d. Welby Van Horn, 6-0, 6-0, 6-1; Bob Kamrath, 6-3, 7-5, 9-7; Charles Hare, 6-3, 6-4, 6-0; Harry Hopman, 6-3, 6-1, 6-3; Sidney Wood, 6-3, 6-3, 6-3; Gene Mako, 6-3, 6-8, 6-2, 6-1.

MAUREEN CONNOLLY, 1953

Australian at Kooyong, Melbourne—d. Carmen Boreilli, 6-0, 6-1; Alison Burton Baker, 6-1, 6-0; Pam Southcombe, 6-0, 6-1; Mary Bevis Hawton, 6-2, 6-1; Julie Sampson, 6-3, 6-2.

French, at Roland Garros, Paris—d. Christine Mercelis, 6-1, 6-3; Raymonde Verber Jones, 6-3, 6-1; Susan Partridge Chatrier, 3-6, 6-2, 6-2; Dorothy Head Knode, 6-3, 6-3; Doris Hart, 6-2, 6-4.

British, at Wimbledon, London—d. D. Killian, 6-0, 6-0; J. M. Petchell, 6-1, 6-1; Anne Shilcock, 6-0, 6-1; Erika Vollmer, 6-3, 6-0; Shirley Fry, 6-1, 6-1; Doris Hart, 8-6, 7-5.

United States, at Forest Hills, New York—d. Jean Fallot, 6-1, 6-0; Pat Stewart, 6-3, 6-1; Jeanne Arth, 6-1, 6-3; Althea Gibson, 6-2, 6-3; Shirley Fry, 6-1, 6-1; Doris Hart, 6-2, 6-4.

ROD LAVER, 1962

Australian, at White City, Sydney—d. Fred Sherriff, 8-6, 6-2, 6-4; Geoff Pares, 10-8, 18-16, 7-9, 7-5; Owen Davidson, 6-4, 9-7, 6-4; Bob Hewitt, 6-1, 4-6, 6-4, 7-5; Roy Emerson, 8-6, 0-6, 6-4, 6-4.

French, at Roland Garros, Paris—d. Michele Pirro, 6-4, 6-0, 6-2; Tony Pickard, 6-2, 9-7, 4-6, 6-1; Sergio Jacobini, 4-6, 6-3, 7-5, 6-1; Marty Mulligan, 6-4, 3-6, 2-6, 10-8, 6-2; Neale Fraser, 3-6, 6-3, 6-2, 7-5; Roy Emerson, 3-6, 2-6, 6-3, 9-7, 6-2.

British, at Wimbledon, London—d. Naresh Kumar, 7-5, 6-1, 6-2; Tony Pickard, 6-1, 6-2, 6-2; Whitney Reed, 6-4, 6-1, 6-4; Pierre Darmon, 6-3, 6-2, 13-11; Manolo Santana, 14-16, 9-7, 6-2, 6-2; Neale Fraser, 10-8, 6-1, 7-5; Marty Mulligan, 6-2, 6-2, 6-1.

United States, at Forest Hills, New York—d. Eleazar Davidman, 6-3, 6-2, 6-3; Eduardo Zuleta, 6-3, 6-3, 6-1; Bodo Nitsche, 9-7, 6-1, 6-1; Antonio Palafox, 6-1, 6-2, 6-2; Frank Froehling, 6-3, 13-11, 4-6, 6-3; Rafe Osuna, 6-1, 6-3, 6-4; Roy Emerson, 6-2, 6-4, 5-7, 6-4.

ROD LAVER, 1969

Australian, at Milton Courts, Brisbane—d. Massimo di Domenico, 6-2, 6-2, 6-3; Roy Emerson, 6-2, 6-3, 3-6, 9-7; Fred Stolle, 6-4, 18-16, 6-2; Tony Roche, 7-5, 22-20, 9-11, 1-6, 6-3; Andres Gimeno, 6-3, 6-4, 7-5.

French, at Roland Garros, Paris—d. Koji Watanabe, 6-1, 6-1, 6-1; Dick Crealy, 3-6, 7-9, 6-2, 6-2, 6-4; Pietro Marzano, 6-1, 6-0, 8-6; Stan Smith, 6-4, 6-2, 6-4; Andres Gimeno, 3-6, 6-3, 6-4, 6-3; Tom Okker, 4-6, 6-0, 6-2, 6-4; Ken Rosewall, 6-4, 6-3, 6-4.

British, at Wimbledon, London—d. Nicola Pietrangeli, 6-1, 6-2, 6-2; Premjit Lall, 3-6, 4-6, 6-3, 6-0, 6-0; Jan Leschly, 6-3, 6-3, 6-3; Stan Smith, 6-4, 6-2, 7-9, 3-6, 6-3; Cliff Drysdale, 6-4, 6-2, 6-3; Arthur Ashe, 2-6, 6-2, 9-7, 6-0; John Newcombe, 6-4, 5-7, 6-4, 6-4.

United States, at Forest Hills, New York—d. Luis Garcia, 6-2, 6-4, 6-2; Jaime Pinto-Bravo, 6-4, 7-5, 6-2; Jaime Fillol, 8-6, 6-1, 6-2; Dennis Ralston, 6-4, 4-6, 4-6, 6-2, 6-3; Roy Emerson, 4-6-8-6, 13-11, 6-4; Arthur Ashe, 8-6, 6-3, 14-12; Tony Roche, 7-9, 6-1, 6-2, 6-2.

MARGARET SMITH COURT, 1970

Australian, at White City, Sydney—d. R. Langsford, 6-0, 6-0, K. Wilkinson, 6-0, 6-1; Evonne Goolagong, 6-3, 6-1; Karen Krantzke, 6-1, 6-3; Kerry Melville, 6-3, 6-1.

French, at Roland Garros, Paris—d. Marijke Jansen Schaar, 6-1, 6-1; Olga Morozova, 3-6, 8-6, 6-1; Lesley Hunt, 6-2, 6-1; Rosie Casals, 7-5, 6-2; Julie Heldman, 6-0, 6-2; Helga Niessen, 6-2, 6-4.

British, at Wimbledon, London—d. Sue Alexander, 6-0, 6-1, Maria Guzman, 6-0, 6-1; Vlasta Vopickova, 6-3, 6-3; Helga Niessen, 6-8, 6-0, 6-0; Rosie Casals, 6-4, 6-1; Billie Jean King, 14-12, 11-9.

United States, at Forest Hills, New York—Pam Austin, 6-1, 6-0; Patti Hogan, 6-1, 6-1; Pat Faulkner, 6-0, 6-2; Helen Gourlay, 6-2, 6-2; Nancy Richey, 6-1, 6-3; Rosie Casals, 6-2, 2-6, 6-1.

STEFFI GRAF, 1988

Australian, at Flinders Park, Melbourne—d. Amy Jonsson, 6-3, 6-1; Janine Thompson, 6-0, 6-1; Cammy MacGregor, 6-1, 6-2; Catarina Lindqvist, 6-0, 7-5; Hana Mandlikova, 6-2, 6-2; Claudia Kohde Kilsch, 6-2, 6-3; Chris Evert, 6-1, 7-6 (7-3).

French, at Roland Garros, Paris—d. Natalie Guerree, 6-0, 6-4, Ronni Reis, 6-1, 6-0; Susan Sloane, 6-0, 6-1; Nathalie Tauziat, 6-1, 6-3; Bettina Fulco, 6-0, 6-1; Gabriela Sabatini, 6-3, 7-6 (7-3); Natalia Zvereva, 6-0, 6-0.

British, at Wimbledon, London—d. Hu Na, 6-0, 6-0; Karine Quentrec, 6-2, 6-0; Terry Phelps, 6-3, 6-1; Mary Joe Fernandez, 6-2, 6-2; Pascale Paradis, 6-3, 6-1; Pam Shriver, 6-1, 6-2; Martina Navratilova, 5-7, 6-2, 6-1.

United States, at Flushing Meadow, New York—d. Elizabeth Minter 6-1, 6-1; Manon Bollegraf, 6-1, 6-0; Nathalie Herreman, 6-0, 6-1; Patty Fendick, 6-4, 6-2; Katerina Maleeva, 6-3, 6-0; Chris Evert, default (illness); Gabriela Sabatini, 6-3, 3-6, 6-1.

Doubles

FRANK SEDGMAN–KEN McGREGOR, 1951

Australian, at White City, Sydney—d. Don Rocavert–Jim Gilchrist, 6-1, 6-3, 13-11; John Mehaffey–Clive Wilderspin, 6-4, 6-4, 6-3; Merv Rose–Don Candy, 8-6, 6-4, 6-3; Adrian Quist–John Bromwich, 11-9, 2-6, 6-3, 4-6, 6-3.

French, at Roland Garros, Paris—d. Antoine Gentien–Pierre Grandquillot, 6-0, 6-0, 6-0; Biddy Bergamo–Beppe Merlo, 6-2, 7-5, 6-1; Bob Abdesselam–Paul Remy, 6-2, 6-2, 4-6, 6-3; Merv Rose–Ham Richardson, 6-3, 7-5, 6-2; Gardnar Mulloy–Dick Savitt, 6-2, 6-9, 9-7, 7-5.

British, at Wimbledon, London—d. Vladimir Petrovic–P. Milojkovic, 6-1, 6-1, 6-3; Raymundo Deyro–Gene Garrett, 6-4, 6-4, 6-3; Bernard Destremau–Torsten Johansson, 3-6, 6-3, 6-2, 9-7; Gianni Cucelli–Marcello del Bello, 6-4, 7-5, 16-14; Budge Patty–Ham Richardson, 6-4, 6-2, 6-3; Eric Sturgess–Jaroslav Drobny, 3-6, 6-2, 6-3, 3-6, 6-3.

United States, at Longwood Cricket Club, Boston—d. Harrison Rowbotham–Sumner Rodman, 6-2, 6-3, 6-3; Dave Mesker–Ed Wesely, 6-1, 6-1, 6-4; Earl Cochell–Ham Richardson, default; Budge Patty–Tony Trabert, 6-3, 6-1, 6-4; Don Candy–Merv Rose, 10-8, 4-6, 6-4, 7-5 (final-round match played at Forest Hills, moved from Boston due to heavy rains).

MARTINA NAVRATILOVA–PAM SHRIVER, 1984

French, at Roland Garros, Paris—d. Heather Crowe–Kim Steinmetz, 6-2, 6-1; Carling Bassett–Andrea Temesvari, 6-4, 6-2; Sandy Collins–Alycia Moulton, 6-2, 6-4; Brenda Remilton–Naoko Sato, 6-2, 6-2; Kathleen Horvath–Virginia Ruzici, 6-0, 7-6; Claudia Kohde Kilsch–Hana Mandlikova, 5-7, 6-3, 6-2.

British, at Wimbledon, London—d. Pam Casale–Lucia Romanov, 6-1, 6-1; Peanut Louie–Heather Ludloff, 6-4, 6-1; Lisa Bonder–Susan Mascarin, 6-0, 6-0; Claudia Kohde Kilsch–Hana Mandlikova, 6-7 (1-7), 6-4, 6-2; Jo Durie–Ann Kiyomura Hayashi, 6-3, 6-3; Kathy Jordan–Anne Smith, 6-3, 6-4.

United States, at Flushing Meadow, New York—d. Jennifer Mundel–Felicia Raschiatore, 6-2, 6-1; Leslie Allen–Kim Shaefer, 6-1, 7-6 (7-4); Rosalyn Fairbank–Candy Reynolds, 6-3, 6-4; Betsy Nagelsen–Anne White, 6-4, 7-5; Anne Hobbs–Wendy Turnbull, 6-2, 6-4.

Australian, at Kooyong Stadium, Melbourne—d. Rosalyn Fairbank–Candy Reynolds, 7-6, 6-4; Jennifer Mundel–Yvonne Vermaak, 6-2, 6-1; Carling Bassett–Zina Garrison, 6-2, 6-0; Chris Evert Lloyd–Wendy Turnbull, 6-4, 6-3; Claudia Kohde Kilsch–Helena Sukova, 6-3, 6-4.

MARIA BUENO (WITH TWO PARTNERS), 1960

(Maria Bueno began the Slam by winning the Australian with Christine Truman and completed it with Darlene Hard at the French, Wimbledon and U.S.)

Australian, at Milton Courts, Brisbane—Christine Truman–Bueno d. Val Craig–Hortense Saywell, 6-2, 6-1; Betty Holstein–Sapphire Shipton, 6-3, 6-4; Fay Muller–Mary Bevis Hawton, 6-4, 11-9; Margaret Smith–Lorraine Coghlan Robinson, 6-3, 5-7, 6-2.

French, at Roland Garros, Paris—Darlene Hard–Bueno d. Jacqueline Kermina–Pierette Seghers, 6-2, 6-2; Jacqueline Rees Lewis–Jacqueline Morales, 6-2, 6-0; Josette Billaz–Suzanne Le Besnerais, 6-4, 6-4; Mary Bevis Hawton–Jan Lehane, 6-3, 7-5; Pat Ward Hales–Ann Haydon, 6-2, 7-5.

British, at Wimbledon, London—Hard–Bueno d. Myrtle Cheadle–Gem Hoahing, 6-1, 6-2; Pat Hird–Caroline Yates Bell, 6-2, 7-5; Edda Buding–Vera Puzejova, 6-2, 6-3; Karen Hantze–Janet Hopps, 3-6, 6-1, 6-4; Renee Schuurman–Sandra Reynolds, 6-4, 6-0.

United States, at Longwood Cricket Club, Boston—Hard–Bueno d. Lorraine Carder–Polly Knowlton, 6-1, 7-5; Linda Vail–Marilyn Montgomery, 6-1, 7-5; Carol Loop–Carole Wright, 6-2, 6-4; Mary Bevis Hawton–Jan Lehane, 8-6, 6-4; Ann Haydon–Deidre Catt, 6-1, 6-1.

Mixed Doubles

MARGARET SMITH COURT–KEN FLETCHER, 1963

Australian, at Memorial Drive, Adelaide—d. Faye Toyne–Bill Bowrey, 6-2, 6-2; Jill Blackman–Roger Taylor, 6-3, 6-3; Liz Starkie–Mark Cox, 7-5, 6-4; Lesley Turner–Fred Stolle, 7-5, 5-7, 6-4.

French, at Roland Garros, Paris—d. C. Rouire–M. Lagard, 6-2, 6-1; Marie Dusapt–Ion Tiriac, 6-0, 6-2; Mary Habicht–Peter Strobl, 6-3, 6-0; Margaret Hunt–Cliff Drysdale, 7-5, 4-6, 6-1; Judy Tegart–Ed Rubinoff, 6-3, 6-1; Lesley Turner–Fred Stolle, 6-1, 6-2.

British, at Wimbledon, London—d. Judy Tegart–Ed Rubinoff, 6-2, 6-2; Judy Alvarez–John Fraser, 6-2, 9-7; Yola Ramirez Ochoa–Alfonso Ochoa, 6-4, 6-1; Rene Schuurman–Wilhelm Bungert, 6-2, 6-1; Ann Jones–Dennis Ralston, 6-1, 7-5; Darlene Hard–Bob Hewitt, 11-9, 6-4.

United States, at Forest Hills, New York—d. Heidi Schildnecht–Peter Scholl, 6-2, 6-3; Jill Rook Mills–Alan Mills, 6-4, 3-6, 6-1; Robyn Ebbern–Owen Davidson, 6-2, 6-2; Billie Jean Moffitt–Donald Dell, 5-7, 8-6, 6-4; Judy Tegart–Ed Rubinoff, 3-6, 8-6, 6-2.

OWEN DAVIDSON (WITH TWO PARTNERS), 1967

(Davidson began his Slam by winning the Australian with Lesley Turner, then completed the next three legs with Billie Jean Moffitt King.)

Australian, at Memorial Drive, Adelaide—Lesley Turner–Davidson d. Melba Foster–Brenton Higgins, 7-1, 7-5; Margaret Starr–Paul McPherson, 6-2, 6-4; Jan Lehane O'Neill–Ray Ruffels, 7-5, 6-4; Judy Tegart–Tony Roche, 9-7, 6-4.

French, at Roland Garros, Paris—Billie Jean Moffitt King–Davidson d. Maria Zuleta–Eduardo Zuleta, 6-2, 6-4; Pat Walkden–Colin Stubs, 6-2, 2-6, 6-3; Trudy Groenman–Tom Okker, 6-1, 6-2; Christine Truman–Bob Howe, 6-2, 6-4; Ann Haydon Jones–Ion Tiriac, 6-3, 6-1.

British, at Wimbledon, London—King-Davidson d. Betty Stove–Bob Howe, 6-1, 6-1; Ingrid Lofdahl–Patricio Cornejo, 6-4, 6-1; Mr. and Mrs. John Cottrill, 6-4, 6-1; Annette van Zyl–Frew McMillan, 6-3, 3-6, 6-1; Maria Bueno–Ken Fletcher, 7-5, 6-2.

United States, at Longwood Cricket Club, Boston—King-Davidson d. Joyce Barclay Williams–George Seewagen, Jr., 6-4, 6-4; Donna Floyd Fales–Paul Sullivan, 6-2, 6-2; Mary Ann Eisel–Peter Curtis, 6-4, 6-3; Kristy Pigeon–Terry Addison, 6-4, 6-4; Rosie Casals–Stan Smith, 6-3, 6-2.

ALL-TIME MAJOR CHAMPIONS

The following is based on the four major championships—Australian, French, Wimbledon and U.S. The dates indicate years of first and last championships. In the Overall section, the numbers reflect totals in singles, doubles and mixed matches.

Overall

MEN

AUST.	FR.	WIM.	U.S.	S-D-M	TOTAL
Roy Emerson, 1959–71					
6-3-0	2-6-0	2-3-0	2-4-0	12-16-0	28
John Newcombe, 1965–76					
2-5-0	0-3-0	3-6-0	2-3-1	7-17-1	25
Frank Sedgman, 1949–52					
2-2-2	0-2-2	1-3-2	2-2-2	5-9-8	22
Bill Tilden, 1913–30					
—	0-0-1	3-1-0	7-5-4	10-6-5	21
Rod Laver, 1959–71					
3-4-0	2-1-1	4-1-2	2-0-0	11-6-3	20
John Bromwich, 1938–50					
2-8-1	0-0-0	0-2-2	0-3-1	2-13-4	19
Neale Fraser, 1957–62					
0-3-1	0-3-0	1-2-1	2-3-3	3-11-5	19
Jean Borotra, 1925–36					
1-1-1	1-5-2	2-3-1	0-0-1	4-9-5	18
Fred Stolle, 1962–69					
0-3-1	1-2-0	0-2-3	1-3-2	2-10-6	18
Ken Rosewall, 1953–72					
4-3-0	2-2-0	0-2-0	2-2-1	8-9-1	18
Adrian Quist, 1936–50					
3-10-0	0-2-0	0-1-0	0-1-0	3-14-0	17
John McEnroe, 1977–92					
0-0-0	0-0-1	3-5-0	4-4-0	7-9-1	17
Jack Crawford, 1929–35					
4-4-3	1-1-1	1-1-1	0-0-0	6-6-5	17
Laurie Doherty, 1897–06					
—	—	5-8-0	1-2-0	6-10-0	16
Henri Cochet, 1926–32					
—	4-3-2	2-2-0	1-0-1	7-5-3	15
Vic Seixas, 1952–56					
0-1-0	0-2-1	1-0-4	1-2-3	2-5-8	15
Bob Hewitt, 1961–79					
0-2-1	0-1-2	0-5-2	0-1-1	0-9-6	15
Reggie Doherty, 1897–05					
—	4-8-0	0-2-0	4-10-0	14	
Fred Perry, 1933–36					
1-1-0	1-1-1	3-0-2	3-0-1	8-2-4	14
Don Budge, 1936–38					
1-0-0	1-0-0	2-2-2	2-2-2	6-4-4	14

AUST.	FR.	WIM.	U.S.	S-D-M	TOTAL
Tony Roche, 1965–76					
0-4-1	1-2-0	0-5-0	0-1-0	1-12-1	14
Willie Renshaw, 1880–1889					
—	7-7-0	—	7-7-0	14	
Lew Hoad, 1953–57					
1-3-0	1-1-1	2-3-0	0-1-0	4-8-1	13
Mark Woodforde, 1992–96					
0-1-2	0-0-1	0-4-1	0-3-1	0-8-5	13
Richard Sears, 1881–87					
—	—	7-6-0	13		
Jacques Brugnon, 1925–34					
0-1-0	0-5-2	0-4-0	0-0-0	0-10-2	12
George Lott, 1928–34					
0-0-0	0-1-0	0-2-1	0-5-3	0-8-4	12
Owen Davidson, 1966–74					
0-1-1	0-0-1	0-0-4	0-1-4	0-2-10	12
Ken Fletcher, 1963–68					
0-0-2	0-1-3	0-1-4	0-0-1	0-2-10	12
Todd Woodbridge, 1992–96					
0-1-1	0-0-1	0-4-1	0-2-2	0-7-5	12
Tony Wilding, 1906–14					
2-1-0	4-4-0	—	6-5-0	11	
Bjorn Borg, 1975–81					
0-0-0	6-0-0	5-0-0	0-0-0	11-0-0	11
Jimmy Connors, 1973–83					
1-0-0	0-0-0	2-1-0	5-1-0	8-2-0	10
René Lacoste, 1925–29					
—	3-2-0	2-1-0	2-0-0	7-3-0	10
Jack Kramer, 1940–47					
—	1-2-0	2-4-1	3-6-1	10	
Tony Trabert, 1950–55					
0-1-0	2-3-0	1-0-0	2-1-0	5-5-0	10
Frew McMillan, 1967–81					
0-0-0	0-1-1	0-3-2	0-1-2	0-5-5	10
Gerald Patterson, 1914–27					
1-5-0	—	2-0-1	0-1-0	3-6-1	10

WOMEN

AUST.	FR.	WIM.	U.S.	S-D-M	TOTAL
Margaret Smith Court, 1960–75					
11-8-2	5-4-4	3-2-5	5-5-8	24-19-19	62
Martina Navratilova, 1974–95					
3-8-0	2-7-2	9-7-3	4-9-2	18-31-7	56
Billie Jean Moffitt King, 1961–81					
1-0-1	1-1-2	6-10-4	4-5-4	12-16-11	39
Margaret Osborne duPont, 1941–60					
—	2-3-0	1-5-1	3-13-9	6-21-10	37
Louise Brough, 1942–57					
1-1-0	0-3-0	4-5-4	1-12-4	6-21-8	35
Doris Hart, 1948–55					
1-1-2	2-5-3	1-4-5	2-4-5	6-14-15	35
Helen Wills Moody, 1923–38					
—	8-3-1	7-4-2	19-9-3	31	
Elizabeth Ryan, 1914–34					
—	0-4-0	0-12-7	0-1-2	0-17-9	26
Steffi Graf, 198?–96					
4-0-0	5-0-0	7-1-0	5-0-0	21-1-0	22
Pam Shriver, 1981–91					
0-7-0	0-4-1	0-5-0	0-5-0	0-21-1	22
Darlene Hard, 1958–69					
—	1-3-2	0-4-3	2-6-0	3-15-5	21
Suzanne Lenglen, 1919–26					
—	2-2-2	6-6-3	0-0-0	8-8-5	21
Chris Evert, 1974–86					
2-0-0	7-2-0	3-1-0	6-0-0	18-3-0	21
Nancye Wynne Bolton, 1935–52					
6-10-4	0-0-0	0-0-0	0-0-0	6-10-4	20

Maria Bueno, 1958–68
| 0-1-0 | 0-1-1 | 3-5-0 | 4-4-0 | 7-11-1 | 19 |

Thelma Long, 1936–58
| 2-12-4 | 0-0-1 | 0-0-0 | 0-0-0 | 2-12-5 | 19 |

Sarah Palfrey Cooke, 1930–45
| — | 0-0-1 | 0-2-0 | 2-9-4 | 2-11-5 | 18 |

Alice Marble, 1936–39
| — | — | 1-2-3 | 4-4-4 | 5-6-7 | 18 |

Hazel Hotchkiss Wightman, 1909–28
| — | — | 0-1-0 | 4-6-6 | 4-7-6 | 17 |

Shirley Fry, 1950–57
| 1-1-0 | 1-4-0 | 1-3-1 | 1-4-0 | 4-12-1 | 17 |

Natalia Zvereva, 1989–96
| 0-2-2 | 0-5-0 | 0-4-0 | 0-4-0 | 0-15-2 | 17 |

Gigi Fernandez, 1988–96
| 0-2-0 | 0-5-0 | 0-3-0 | 0-5-0 | 0-15-0 | 15 |

Daphne Akhurst, 1924–31
| 5-5-4 | 0-0-0 | 0-0-0 | — | 5-5-4 | 14 |

Evonne Goolagong Cawley, 1971–80
| 4-4-0 | 1-0-1 | 2-1-0 | 0-0-0 | 7-5-1 | 13 |

Lesley Turner, 1961–67
| 0-3-2 | 2-2-0 | 0-1-2 | 0-1-0 | 2-7-4 | 13 |

Simone Passemard Mathieu, 1933–39
| — | 2-6-2 | 0-3-0 | 0-0-0 | 2-9-2 | 13 |

Molla Bjurstedt Mallory, 1915–26
| — | 0-0-0 | 0-0-0 | 8-2-3 | 8-2-3 | 13 |

Mary K. Browne, 1912–26
| — | — | 0-1-0 | 3-5-4 | 3-6-4 | 13 |

Juliette Atkinson, 1895–1902
| | | | 3-7-3 | 3-7-3 | 13 |

Helena Sukova, 1987–96
| 0-2-0 | 0-1-1 | 0-4-1 | 0-2-1 | 0-9-3 | 12 |

Rosie Casals, 1967–82
| 0-0-0 | 0-0-0 | 0-5-2 | 0-4-1 | 0-9-3 | 12 |

Françoise Durr, 1967–76
| 0-0-0 | 1-5-3 | 0-0-1 | 0-2-0 | 1-7-4 | 12 |

Maureen Connolly, 1951–54
| 1-1-0 | 2-1-1 | 3-0-0 | 3-0-0 | 9-2-1 | 12 |

Althea Gibson, 1956–58
| 0-1-0 | 1-1-0 | 2-3-0 | 2-0-1 | 5-5-1 | 11 |

Anne Smith, 1980–84
| 0-1-0 | 0-2-2 | 0-1-1 | 0-1-2 | 0-5-5 | 10 |

Men's Doubles

	AUST.	FR.	WIM.	U.S.	TOTAL
John Newcombe–Tony Roche, 1965–76					
	4	2	5	1	12
John Bromwich–Adrian Quist, 1938–50					
	8	—	1	1	10
Laurie Doherty–Reg Doherty, 1897–1905					
	—	—	8	2	10

Women's Doubles

	AUST.	FR.	WIM.	U.S.	TOTAL	
Louise Brough–Margaret Osborne duPont, 1942–57						
	—	3	5	12	20	
Martina Navratilova–Pam Shriver, 1981–89						
	7	4	5	4	20	
Gigi Fernandez–Natalia Zvereva, 1992–96						
	2	4	3	3	12	

Mixed Doubles

	AUST.	FR.	WIM.	U.S.	TOTAL
Margaret Smith Court–Ken Fletcher, 1963–68					
	2	3	4	1	10

U.S. PRO CHAMPIONSHIPS

Although there were earlier instances of professional tournaments offering prize money, particularly in France and Britain, with teaching professionals/coaches as entries, the U.S. Pro Championships stands as the oldest continous such event. It began in 1927 on courts of the small, since vanished, Notlek Tennis Club on the West Side of Manhattan, starring the newly avowed touring pros, Vinnie Richards and Howard Kinsey, from the Pyle troupe, and was filled out by teaching pros, playing for a $2000 purse. Richards won first prize, $1,000. The tournament, never very healthy financially, somehow kept going, often changing surfaces and locations, surviving indoors (1955–62) in Cleveland as the "World Pro Championships."

In 1963 at Forest Hills it went bankrupt (only Pancho Gonzalez, who negotiated a prior guarantee, got paid), and seemed finished at last. But in 1964 the tournament was revived at Boston's Longwood Cricket Club through the efforts of Ed Hickey, public relations officer for the sponsoring New England Merchants Bank, and John Bottomley, Longwood president, with an assist from ex-promoter, Jack Kramer, and has thrived thereafter at that location.

YEAR	WINNER	RUNNER-UP	SCORE
1927	Vincent Richards	Howard Kinsey	11-9, 6-4, 6-3
1928	Vincent Richards	Karel Kozeluh	8-6, 6-3, 0-6, 6-2
1929	Karel Kozeluh	Vincent Richards	6-4, 6-4, 4-6, 4-6, 7-5
1930	Vincent Richards	Karel Kozeluh	2-6, 10-8, 6-3, 6-4
1931	Bill Tilden	Vincent Richards	7-5, 6-2, 6-1
1932	Karel Kozeluh	Hans Nusslein	6-2, 6-2, 7-5
1933	Vincent Richards	Frank Hunter	6-3, 6-0, 6-2
1934	Hans Nusslein	Karel Kozeluh	6-4, 6-2, 1-6, 7-5
1935	Bill Tilden	Karel Kozeluh	0-6, 6-1, 6-4, 0-6, 6-4
1936	Joseph Whalen	Charles Wood	4-6, 4-6, 6-3, 6-2, 6-4
1937	Karel Kozeluh	Bruce Barnes	6-2, 6-3, 4-6, 4-6, 6-1
1938	Fred Perry	Bruce Barnes	6-3, 6-2, 6-4
1939	Ellsworth Vines	Fred Perry	8-6, 6-8, 6-1, 20-18
1940	Don Budge	Fred Perry	6-3, 5-7, 6-4, 6-3
1941	Fred Perry	Dick Skeen	6-4, 6-8, 6-2, 6-3
1942	Don Budge	Bobby Riggs	6-2, 6-2, 6-2
1943	Lt. Bruce Barnes	John Nogrady	6-1, 7-9, 7-5, 4-6, 6-3
1944	Not Held		
1945	Welby Van Horn	John Nogrady	6-4, 6-2, 6-2
1946	Bobby Riggs	Don Budge	6-3, 6-1, 6-1
1947	Bobby Riggs	Don Budge	3-6, 6-3, 10-8, 4-6,6-3
1948	Jack Kramer	Bobby Riggs	14-12, 6-2, 3-6, 7-5
1949	Bobby Riggs	Don Budge	9-7, 3-6, 6-3, 6-3
1950	Pancho Segura	Frank Kovacs	6-4, 1-6, 8-6, 4-4 retired
1951	Pancho Segura	Pancho Gonzalez	6-3, 6-4, 6-2
1952	Pancho Segura	Pancho Gonzalez	3-6, 6-4, 3-6, 6-4, 6-0
1953	Pancho Gonzalez	Don Budge	4-6, 6-4, 7-5, 6-2
1954	Pancho Gonzalez	Frank Sedgman	6-3, 9-7, 3-6, 6-2

1955	Pancho Gonzalez	Pancho Segura	21-16, 19-21, 21-8, 20-22, 21-19*
1956	Pancho Gonzalez	Pancho Segura	21-15, 13-21, 21-14, 22-20*
1957	Pancho Gonzalez	Pancho Segura	6-3, 3-6, 7-5, 6-1
1958	Pancho Gonzalez	Lew Hoad	3-6, 4-6, 14-12, 6-1, 6-4
1959	Pancho Gonzalez	Lew Hoad	6-4, 6-2, 6-4
1960	Alex Olmedo	Tony Trabert	7-5, 6-4
1961	Pancho Gonzalez	Frank Sedgman	6-3, 7-5
1962	Butch Buchholz	Pancho Segura	6-4, 6-3, 6-4
1963	Ken Rosewall	Rod Laver	6-4, 6-2, 6-2
1964	Rod Laver	Pancho Gonzalez	4-6, 6-3, 7-5, 6-4
1965	Ken Rosewall	Rod Laver	6-4, 6-3, 6-3
1966	Rod Laver	Ken Rosewall	6-4, 4-6, 6-2, 8-10, 6-3
1967	Rod Laver	Andres Gimeno	4-6, 6-4, 6-3, 7-5
1968	Rod Laver	John Newcombe	6-4, 6-4, 9-7
1969	Rod Laver	John Newcombe	7-5, 6-2, 4-6, 6-1
1970	Tony Roche	Rod Laver	3-6, 6-4, 1-6, 6-2, 6-2
1971	Ken Rosewall	Cliff Drysdale	6-4, 6-3, 6-0
1972	Bob Lutz	Tom Okker	6-4, 2-6, 6-1, 6-4
1973	Jimmy Connors	Arthur Ashe	6-3, 4-6, 6-4, 3-6, 6-2
1974	Bjorn Borg	Tom Okker	7-6 (7-3), 6-1, 6-1
1975	Bjorn Borg	Guillermo Vilas	6-3, 6-4, 6-2
1976	Bjorn Borg	Harold Solomon	6-7 (3-7), 6-4, 6-1, 6-2
1977	Manuel Orantes	Eddie Dibbs	7-6 (7-3), 7-5, 6-4
1978	Manuel Orantes	Harold Solomon	6-4, 6-3
1979	Jose Higueras	Hans Gildemeister	6-3, 6-1
1980	Eddie Dibbs	Gene Mayer	6-2, 6-1
1981	Jose-Luis Clerc	Hans Gildemeister	0-6, 6-3, 6-2
1982	Guillermo Vilas	Mel Purcell	6-4, 6-0
1983	Jose-Luis Clerc	Jimmy Arias	6-3, 6-1
1984	Aaron Krickstein	Jose-Luis Clerc	7-6 (7-2), 3-6, 6-4
1985	Mats Wilander	Martin Jaite	6-2, 6-4
1986	Andres Gomez	Martin Jaite	7-5, 6-4
1987	Mats Wilander	Kent Carlsson	7-6 (7-5), 6-1
1988	Thomas Muster	Lawson Duncan	6-2, 6-2
1989	Andres Gomez	Mats Wilander	6-1, 6-4
1990	Martin Jaite	Libor Nemecek	7-5, 6-3
1991	Andres Gomez	Andrei Cherkasov	7-5, 6-3
1992	Ivan Lendl	Richey Reneberg	6-3, 6-3
1993	Ivan Lendl	Todd Martin	5-7, 6-3, 7-6 (7-4)
1994	Ivan Lendl	MaliVai Washington	7-5, 7-6 (7-5)
1995	not completed, rain		
1996	not played		

*VASSS Scoring

ONE-NIGHT STANDS OF THE BYGONE PROS

Until the dawn of open tennis in 1968, the usual format for the handful of playing pros—outlaws beyond the boundaries of traditional amateur tourneys—was a tour of one-night stands, indoors on a portable canvas court, across the U.S., and sometimes other countries as well. The champion of the previous tour went head-to-head against a challenger, most often the leading amateur who had turned pro, as during the winter of 1934, when rookie Ellsworth Vines, 23, brought down the biggest name, Bill Tilden, 41, by 47 matches to 26.

After resisting promoters for several years, Tilden finally turned pro in 1931, having failed to extricate the Davis Cup from France or win a long-desired eighth U.S. title. He then toured victoriously against the Czech master, Karel Kozeluh, and repeated the next winter against German Hans Nusslein. Nusslein had the edge in 1933, but since Tilden had the drawing power he was the rookie Vines' opponent. Vines' triumphant campaign over Tilden, his senior by 18 years, left him in charge to fend off the next rookie, Fred Perry, 1937–38. Tilden stuck around, as did a few others, to play secondary roles.

Whoever the promoter, he lured the leading amateur with a guarantee against a percentage of gate receipts, making a similar type of deal with the champion, and generally paying the others' salaries. It all began in November 1926 as promoter Charles C. Pyle transformed the first troupe—Suzanne Lenglen, Mary K. Browne, Vinnie Richards, Howard Kinsey, Harvey Snodgrass, Paul Feret—from amateurs to pros en masse, principally to capitalize on Lenglen's gate appeal on a North American tour. The last challenge tour, 1963, was Australian-dominated as pros Ken Rosewall and Lew Hoad personally guaranteed 1962 Grand Slammer Rod Laver $110,000 over three years to give up his amateur status, and put them back in business.

Although the pros grew slightly in numbers and began leaning toward tournament formats in 1964, hastening the day of opens, tours continued into 1968, but merely as exhibitions, lacking the king-of-the-hill aspect. Pancho Gonzalez, challenger, and loser, in his first tour against player-promoter Jack Kramer, 1949–50, was relegated to the scrap heap. But he got a second chance when Kramer retired from the court, and became the most successful king-of-the-canvas.

These were the best-documented tours:

1926–27—Suzanne Lenglen d. Mary K. Browne, 38-0
1928—Karel Kozeluh d. Vinnie Richards, 13-7
1931—Bill Tilden d. Karel Kozeluh, 27-6; Bill Tilden d. Vinnie Richards, 12-1
1932—Bill Tilden d. Hans Nusslein and Vinnie Richards
1933—Hans Nusslein d. Bill Tilden
1934—Ellsworth Vines d. Bill Tilden, 47-26
1935—Ellsworth Vines d. Lester Stoefen, Bruce Barnes, Bill Tilden and others
1936—Bill Tilden d. Bruce Barnes and others; Ellsworth Vines d. Lester Stoefen, Bill Tilden and others; Ethel Burkhardt Arnold d. Jane Sharp
1937—Ellsworth Vines d. Fred Perry, 32-29
1938—Ellsworth Vines d. Fred Perry, 48-35

1939—Don Budge d. Ellsworth Vines, 21-18; Don Budge d. Fred Perry, 18-11
1941—Don Budge d. Bill Tilden, 51-7; Alice Marble d. Mary Hardwick, 17-3
1942—Don Budge won a round-robin tour with a 54-18 record, 15-10 over Bobby Riggs. Others: Bobby Riggs, 36-36; Frank Kovacs, 25-26; Fred Perry, 23-30
1946-47—Bobby Riggs d. Don Budge, 23-21
1947-48—Jack Kramer d. Bobby Riggs, 69-20
1949-50—Jack Kramer d. Richard "Pancho" Gonzalez, 96-27
1950-51—Jack Kramer d. Francisco "Pancho" Segura, 64-28; Pauline Betz d. Gertrude "Gussy" Moran
1953—Jack Kramer d. Frank Sedgman, 54-41; Francisco "Pancho" Segura d. Ken McGregor
1954—Richard "Pancho" Gonzalez d. Frank Sedgman and Francisco "Pancho" Segura, round-robin
1955-56—Richard "Pancho" Gonzalez d. Tony Trabert, 74-27
1957—Richard "Pancho" Gonzalez d. Ken Rosewall, 50-26
1957-58—Richard "Pancho" Gonzalez d. Lew Hoad, 51-36
1959—Richard "Pancho" Gonzalez d. Lew Hoad, Mal Anderson and Ashley Cooper, round-robin
1958-59—Althea Gibson d. Karol Fageros, 114-4
1959-60—Richard "Pancho" Gonzalez d. Alex Olmedo, Ken Rosewall and Francisco "Pancho" Segura, round-robin
1961—Richard "Pancho" Gonzalez leading winner in tour involving Butch Buchholz, Barry MacKay, Andres Gimeno, Lew Hoad, Alex Olmedo, Frank Sedgman, Tony Trabert, Ashley Cooper
1963—Ken Rosewall, Rod Laver finished 1-2 on tour also including Luis Ayala, Butch Buchholz, Andres Gimeno, Barry MacKay

OLYMPIC GAMES

Although tennis could hardly be termed a staple of the Olympic Games—having disappeared from the Olympic calendar for 64 years—it is very much back in the lineup of medal sports.

First played when the Games were revived in Athens in 1896, tennis was a fixture on the program through the 1924 edition in Paris—when the Americans swept all five events on the program.

Friction arose after 1924 between the Olympic Committee and the International Tennis Federation. It centered on the definition of amateurism and it led to the absence of tennis—except as a demonstration sport in Mexico City in 1968 and Los Angeles in 1984—until ITF president Philippe Chatrier led the successful drive toward return of the sport to the 1988 Olympics in Seoul, Korea.

Players from the United States have won three gold medals in men's singles, three in women's singles, two in men's doubles, four in women's doubles and one in mixed doubles.

The restoration of tennis has not been greeted wholeheartedly by the top players, since the regular season is more crowded with events than in 1924. As a rule, the women have been stronger

supporters. Steffi Graf, having won the four majors in 1988, completed a "golden slam" or "quintessential quintuple" with her unique feat of appending the gold medal, beating third-seeded Gabriela Sabatini. Graf was upset in the 1992 final by the youngest gold medalist, third-seeded Jennifer Capriati, 16, and was kept out of the 1996 games by injury. Lindsay Davenport, seeded ninth, perpetrated another upset that year, beating third-seeded Arantxa Sanchez Vicario. Top-seeded Monica Seles had been beaten in the quarters by Jana Novotna.

Miloslav Mecir was the third-seeded victor over top-seeded Stefan Edberg and second-seeded Tim Mayotte in 1988. Barcelona in 1992 presented the long-shot special: unseeded Marc Rosset (who'd beaten top-seeded Jim Courier), served 38 aces and outlasted 16th-seeded Jordi Arrese. In 1996, first-seeded Andre Agassi came through a field diluted by the absence of the year's four major champs.

1896, ATHENS

Men's singles—John Pius Boland (Great Britain/ Ireland) d. Dionysius Kasdaglis (Greece) 7-5, 6-4, 6-1

Men's doubles—John Pius Boland (Great Britain/Ireland)–Fritz Traun (Germany) d. Dionysius Kasdaglis–Demetrios Petrokokkinos (Greece) 6-2, 6-4

1900, PARIS

Men's singles—Laurie Doherty (Great Britain) d. Harold Segerson Mahony (Great Britain/Ireland) 6-4, 6-2, 6-3

Women's singles—Charlotte Cooper (Great Britain) d. Helene Prevost (France) 6-1, 6-4

Men's doubles—Reggie Doherty–Laurie Doherty (Great Britain) d. Basil de Garmendia (U.S.)–Max Decugis (France) 6-1, 6-1, 6-0

Mixed doubles—Charlotte Cooper–Reggie Doherty (Great Britain) d. Helene Prevost (France)–Harold Segerson Mahony (Ireland) 6-2, 6-4

1904, ST. LOUIS

Men's singles—Beals Wright (U.S.) d. Robert LeRoy (U.S.) 6-4, 6-4

Men's doubles—Edgar Welch Leonard–Beals Wright (U.S.) d. Alphonzo Bell–Robert LeRoy (U.S.) 6-4, 6-4, 6-2

1908, LONDON

Men's singles—Josiah Ritchie (Great Britain) d. Otto Froitzheim (Germany) 7-5, 6-3, 6-4

Women's singles—Dorothea Douglass Chambers (Great Britain) d. Penelope Dora Boothby (Great Britain) 6-1, 7-5

Men's doubles—George Whiteside Hillyard–Reggie Doherty (Great Britain) d. Josiah George Richie–James Cecil Parke (Great Britain/Ireland) 9-7, 7-5, 9-7

1908, LONDON (INDOOR)

Men's singles—Arthur Wentworth Gore (Great Britain) d. George Caridia (Great Britain) 6-3, 7-5, 6-4

Women's singles—Gladys Eastlake-Smith (Great Britain) d. Angela Greene (Great Britain) 6-2, 4-6, 6-0

Men's doubles—Arthur Wentworth Gore–Herbert Roper Barrett (Great Britain) d. George Mieville Simond–George Caridia (Great Britain) 6-2, 2-6, 6-3, 6-3

1912, STOCKHOLM

Men's singles—Charles Winslow (South Africa) d. Harold Kitson (South Africa) 7-5, 4-6, 10-8, 8-6

Women's singles—Marguerite Broquedis (France) d. Dora Koring (Germany) 4-6, 6-3, 6-4

Men's doubles—Charles Winslow–Harold Kitson (South Africa) d. Felix Pipes–Arthur Zborzil (Austria) 4-6, 6-1, 6-2, 6-2

Mixed doubles—Dora Koring–Heinrich Schomburg (Germany) d. Sigrid Fick–Gunnar Setterwall (Sweden) 6-4, 6-0

1912, STOCKHOLM (INDOOR)

Men's singles—Andre Gobert (France) d. Charles Percy Dixon (Great Britain) 8-6, 6-4, 6-4

Women's singles—Edith Hannam (Great Britain) d. Sofia Castenschiold (Denmark) 6-4, 6-3

Men's doubles—Andre Gobert–Maurice Germot (France) d. Gunnar Setterwall–Carl Kempe (Sweden) 14-12, 6-2, 6-4

Mixed doubles—Edith Hannam–Charles Percy Dixon (Great Britain) d. Helen Aitchison–Herbert Roper Barrett (Great Britain) 6-4, 3-6, 6-2

1920, ANTWERP

Men's singles—Louis Raymond (South Africa) d. Ichiya Kumagae (Japan) 5-7, 6-4, 7-5, 6-4

Women's singles—Suzanne Lenglen (France) d. Dorothy Holman (Great Britain) 6-3, 6-0

Men's doubles—Noell Turnbull (South Africa)–Max Woosnam (Great Britain) d. Seiichiro Kashio–Ichiya Kumagae (Japan) 6-2, 5-7, 7-5, 7-5

Women's doubles—Kitty McKane–Winifred McNair (Great Britain) d. Geraldine Beamish–Dorothy Holman (Great Britain) 8-6, 6-4

Mixed doubles—Suzanne Lenglen–Max Decugis (France) d. Kitty McKane–Max Woosnam (Great Britain) 6-4, 6-2

1924, PARIS

Men's singles—Vinnie Richards (U.S.) d. Henri Cochet (France) 6-4, 6-4, 5-7, 4-6, 6-2

Women's singles—Helen Wills (U.S.) d. Didi Vlasto (France) 6-2, 6-2

Men's doubles—Frank Hunter–Vinnie Richards (U.S.) d. Jacques Brugnon–Henri Cochet (France) 4-6, 6-2, 6-3, 2-6, 6-3

Women's doubles—Hazel Hotchkiss Wightman–Helen Wills (U.S.) d. Kitty McKane–Phyllis Howkins Covell (Great Britain) 7-5, 8-6

Mixed doubles—Hazel Hotchkiss Wightman–Dick Williams (U.S.) d. Marion Zinderstein Jessup–Vinnie Richards (U.S.) 6-2, 6-3

1988, SEOUL

Men's singles—Miloslav Mecir (Czechoslovakia) d. Tim Mayotte (U.S.) 3-6, 6-2, 6-4, 6-2

Women's singles—Steffi Graf (Germany) d. Gabriela Sabatini (Argentina) 6-3, 6-3

Men's doubles—Ken Flach–Robert Seguso (U.S.) d. Sergio Casal–Emilio Sanchez (Spain), 6-3, 6-4, 6-7 (5-7), 6-7 (1-7), 9-7

Women's doubles—Zina Garrison–Pam Shriver (U.S.) d. Jana Novotna–Helena Sukova (Czechoslovakia) 4-6, 6-2, 10-8

1992, BARCELONA

Men's singles—Marc Rosset (Switzerland) d. Jordi Arrese (Spain) 7-6 (7-2), 6-4, 3-6, 4-6, 8-6

Women's singles—Jennifer Capriati (U.S.) d. Steffi Graf (Germany) 3-6, 6-3, 6-4

Men's doubles—Boris Becker–Michael Stich (Germany) d. Wayne Ferreira–Piet Norval (South Africa) 7-6 (7-5), 4-6, 7-6 (7-5), 6-3

Women's doubles—Beatriz "Gigi" Fernandez–Mary Joe Fernandez (U.S.) d. Conchita Martinez–Arantxa Sanchez Vicario (Spain) 7-5, 2-6, 6-2

1996, ATLANTA

Men's singles—Andre Agassi (U.S.) d. Sergi Bruguera (Spain) 6-2, 6-3, 6-1

Women's singles—Lindsay Davenport (U.S.) d. Arantxa Sanchez Vicario (Spain) 7-6 (8-6), 6-2

Men's doubles—Todd Woodbridge–Mark Woodforde (Australia) d. Tim Henman–Neil Broad (Great Britain) 6-4, 6-4, 6-2

Women's doubles—Mary Joe Fernandez–Beatriz "Gigi" Fernandez (U.S.) d. Jana Novotna–Helena Sukova (Czechoslovakia) 7-6 (8-6), 6-4

INDEX

Amritraj, Vijay, 249, 278, 282, **520;** 1987 Davis Cup, 300

Amritraj, Vijay–Stockton, Dick: 1977 WCT title, 233

Anderson, J.O. ("Greyhound"), 33, 34, **520;** 1925 Australian Championships, 35

Anderson, Mal, **520;** 1957 U.S. Championships: vs. Cooper, 148; 1958 U.S. Championships: vs. Cooper, 151; 1959 turns pro, 153

Andersson, Birger, 220

Anger, Matt, 295

Anna Karenina (Tolstoy), 13

Annacone, Paul, 281, 293

Antonitsch, Alex, 322

Antonoplis, Lea, 223

Apartheid, 188, 193, 210, 214, 219, 311, 379-80

Apell, Jan–Bjorkman, Jonas: 1994 Davis Cup, 357, 358

Apey, Pato, 290

Appel, Ellie Vessies, 230

Approach shot: defined, 548

Arias, Jimmy: 1983 King of Italy, 275; 1983 U.S. Open, 276; 1990 vs. Muster, 321

Armstrong, Gerry, 323, 450

Army & Navy, tennis announced in, 3

Around the post: defined, 548

Arraya, Pablo, 308

Arrese, Jordi, 343

Arriens, Carsten: 1995 racket incident, 449

The Art of Lawn Tennis (Tilden), 9

Asboth, Josef, **520;** 1947 French Championships, 124

Ashe, Arthur, *178,* **377-80,** *378;* 1965 U.S. Championships, 168; 1968 amateur status, 178, 378; 1968 Davis Cup, 182-83; 1968 Man of the Year, 182; 1968 U.S. Amateur Championships, 182; 1968 U.S. Open: first, 181, 378; 1969 season, 186-87; 1970 Australian Championships, 192; 1971 French Open, 195; 1972 WCT "winter championship," 203; 1973 South African Open, 210, 379-80; 1973 WCT tour, 205; 1975 attempt at WCT-Masters double, 218; 1975 Masters: default at, 219, 448; 1975 season and earnings, 216; 1975 Wimbledon: vs. Connors, 216-17; 1975 win and earnings record, 218; 1976 chronic heel injury, 225;

1978 Grand Prix Masters: vs. McEnroe, 241; 1978 heel surgery shortens season, 241-42; 1979 U.S. Indoor, health concerns, 246; 1992 AIDS announcement, 338; 1993 death of, 351; causes supported by, 380; Davis cup play by, 379

Ashe-Gimeno: 1968 U.S. Open longest match, 181

Ashe-Okker: 1973 South African Open, 210, 380

Association of Tennis Professionals (ATP), **548;** 1973, 205; computer rankings, 662-63; formation of, 203, 417; officials disqualify Agassi, 370; opposed to World Team Tennis, 207; and Pilic Affair, 207; Riordan antitrust suit against, 211-12, 217; and self-managed men's tour, 313, 321-22; World Championship, 635

ATA. *See* American Tennis Association

Atkinson, Juliette Paxton, **454**

Atkinson, Kathleen, 454, **520**

ATP. *See* Association of Tennis Professionals

ATP Tour, **548**

ATP World Championships, 635-36. *See also* Grand Prix Masters

Aussem, Cilly, **520;** vs. Krahwinkel, 48

Austin, Bunny, 54, **520;** 1931 Davis Cup: vs. Shields, 47; 1932 Wimbledon: vs. Vines, 48; 1933 fashion change, 52, 53; 1935 Davis Cup, 57; 1936 Wimbledon, 59; on Vines, 48

Austin, Joan, **520-21**

Austin, Tracy, *231, 246, 263,* **454-55;** 1977 Wimbledon, 230; 1977 youngest in U.S. Top Ten, 234, 455; 1978 season, 243-44; 1978 Virginia Slims: vs. Navratilova, 243; 1979 Rome: vs. Evert, 247; 1979 U.S. Open: youngest-ever U.S. champion, 250-51; 1979 win record, 245; 1981 summer circuit, 264; 1981 U.S. Open: vs. Navratilova, 264, 455; 1981 Wimbledon: vs. Shriver, 263; 1983 season, 272; on King, 269

Austin, Tracy–Austin, John: 1980 Wimbledon, 252

Australasia, defined, 17, 621

Australia: 1958 pro tour, 152-53; air travel to, 123

Australian Championships, **606-12;** 1927 first season at Kooyong,

42; all-time records, 611; best comebacks, 612; biggest upsets, 612; career singles records, 611; early, 22; longest matches, 611; longest tie-breakers, 611; men's doubles records, 608-9; men's singles records, 606-7; mixed doubles records, 610-11; oldest champions, 611; prize money at, 606; women's doubles records, 609-10; women's singles records, 607-8; youngest champions, 611

Australian formation. *See* I formation

Automated line-calling, 447-48

Avon Championships, 244-45, 636

Avon Circuit, **550**

Ayala, Luis, 148, 151, 155, 178, **521**

Ayala-Ziegenfuss: 1968 Bournemouth, 179

B

Babcock, Carolin, 50

Backhand: of Budge, 65; defined, 550; two-handed: of Borg, 384; of Drysdale, 168; of Evert, 400; of McGrath, 52, 53

Baddeley, Herbert, **521**

Baddeley, Wilfred, 14, 380, **521**

Bagel: defined, 550

Bagel job: defined, 550

Bagnal-Wild, R.B., 7

Bailey, Ella Wilkin, 8

Baker, Larry, **515**

Ballestrat, Dianne Fromholtz. *See* Fromholtz, Dianne

Ball(s): changing during match, 582-83; defined, 550; dimensions of, 570; in doubles play, 584; for high-altitudes, 571; in play: in singles, 575, 577-78; shortage of: during World War II, 74; touches fixtures, 577; yellow, 294

Ball boy (girl), defined, 550

"Ballboy of Lyon." *See* Cochet, Henri

Barazzutti, Corrado, 226, 248; 1976 Davis Cup, 226; 1980 Davis Cup, 256

Barclay, Ian, 305

Barger, Maud. *See* Wallach, Maud Barger

Barker, Sue, **521;** 1976 Wightman Cup, French and German Opens, 228; 1977 Virginia Slims, 234

Barker–Schallau Guerrant: 1978 Wimbledon, 242

Boshoff, Delina ("Linky"), 228

Bottomley, John, 166, 667

Bouman, Kea, **522**

"Bouncing Czech." *See* Kodes, Jan

"Bounding Basque from Biarritz." *See* Borotra, Jean

Bournemouth: 1968 first open tournament, 178-79, 432

Boussus, Christian, 43

Bowden, Mary Carillo. *See* Carillo (Bowden), Mary

Bowrey, Bill ("Tex"), **522**

Bowrey, Lesley Turner, **522;** 1963 French Championships, 162; 1964 doubles near Grand Slam, 166; 1967, 173

Bowron, Bertie, 449

"Boy Boppers." *See* Smith-Lutz

Boyd, Esna, **522;** 1927 Australian Championships, 42

Break: defined, 550

Break point, defined, 550

Breakfast at Wimbledon, **550**

Bricka, Justina, 159

Briner, Bob: on open tennis, 176

Brinker, Mrs. Norman. *See* Connolly, Maureen

Brinker, Norman, 140

Bromwich, John ("Jack"), **456-57;** 1937 Australian Championship, 61; 1939 Australian Championship, 68, 69; 1946 Australian Championship, 120; on Budge, 65

Bromwich-Quist, 457, 489; 1939 Davis Cup, 69; 1949 Australian Championships, 129

Brookes, Norman, 16, 26, **83-85,** *84;* 1907 Wimbledon, 17, 84; 1914 Wimbledon, 19, 84; serve and volley of, 84

Brough, Louise, *128, 385,* **385-86;** 1942 U.S. Championships, 75; 1947 U.S. Championships, 124; 1948 Wimbledon, U.S. triples, 128; 1949 Wimbledon, 130; 1950 Australian Championships, 132; 1950 U.S. Championships: vs. Gibson, 133-34, 403; 1955 Wimbledon: vs. Fleitz, 145; 1957 U.S. Championships: vs. Gibson, 148-49; Wimbledon career, 385

Brough-Hart: 1950 Australian, 132

Brough-Osborne (duPont), 386, 395; 1945 doubles titles, 79; 1946 French, Wimbledon, and U.S. Doubles, 122; 1948 Wimbledon, 128; 1949 Wimbledon, 130;

1954 Wimbledon, 143; 1955 U.S. title, 145; 1957 U.S. Doubles, 149

Brown, Geoff: 1946 Wimbledon, 120-21

Brown, Tom, 75

Browne, Mary K., *21,* 28, 38, 39, 40, *458;* 1926 season, 40

Browning, Françoise (Frankie) Durr. *See* Durr (Browning), Françoise (Frankie)

Brugnon, Jacques ("Toto"), 33-34, 48, **458-59;** 1977 at Wimbledon Centenary, 230

Bruguera, Sergi, 324, *347,* **522;** 1993 French Open: vs. Courier, 346-47; 1994 French Open: vs. Courier, vs. Berasategui, 354; 1996 Olympic Games, 370

Brunetti, Michele, 448

Buchholz, Butch, **522;** as pro, 156, 161, 169

Budge, Don, 55, *58, 61,* 64, *65,* **85-87,** *86;* 1935 Davis Cup, 57; 1935 and Queen Mary, 57; 1936 U.S. Championships: vs. Perry, 59-60, 85; 1936 Wimbledon: vs. Perry, 85; 1937 Davis Cup: vs. von Cramm, 62-63, 85; 1937 U.S. Championships: vs. von Cramm, 63; 1937 Wimbledon triple, 62; 1938 first Grand Slam, 64-66, *65,* 86, 664; 1939 pro debut, 70, 86; 1942 pro season: Riggs rivalry and, 74; compared with Chang, 323; and Graf, 305-6; on Mako, 65, 477; on Tilden, 73-74; on von Cramm, 62

Buehning, Fritz, 277

Bueno, Maria, *169,* **386-87,** *387;* 1959 Wimbledon, U.S. titles, 154, 387; 1961 contracts hepatitis, 158; 1963 U.S. Championships: vs. Smith, 163; 1964 Wimbledon, U.S. Championships, 166, 387; 1965 season, 168; 1966 U.S. Championships: vs. Richey and Casals, 172

Bueno-Hard, 387; 1960 doubles Grand Slam, 155

Bueno-Gibson: 1958 Wimbledon, 152, 387

Buller, C. F., 10

Bundy, May Sutton, 16, *17, 20,* **459-60;** 1907 Wimbledon, 17, 459

Bundy (Cheney), Dorothy ("Dodo"), **523;** 1938 Australian Championships, 66

Bunge, Bettina, 272

Bungert, Wilhelm, 163, 165, 193

Burke, Albert, 48

Burke, Edmund, 48

Burke, Thomas, 48

Burnett, Brian, 267

Burto, Veronica, 210

Buttsworth, Coral, 47, 50, 52

Buxton, Angela, 146

C

Caesar's Palace matches. *See* Heavyweight Championship of Tennis

Cahill, Darren, 313, 322

Cahill, Mabel, 13, **460**

Cairnes, J.J., 13

Caldwell, Carole. *See* Graebner, Carole Caldwell

"California Comet." *See* McLoughlin, Maurice

Camp Apache (Arizona Territory), 8

Campbell, Oliver Samuel, 13, *453,* **460**

Canadian Championships, early, 22-23

Canadian Lawn Tennis Association (Toronto), 23

Cancellotti, Francesco, 275

Cane, Paolo: 1987 Wimbledon: vs. Lendl, 304

Canning, Mary Patricia (Pat). *See* Todd, Pat

Cannonball: defined, 551; first, 19

Cano, Ricardo, 233

Capriati, Jennifer, 321, *321, 340,* **523;** 1989 Wightman Cup, 316; 1990 Federation Cup, 322; 1990 French Open: vs. Seles, 323; 1990 pro debut, 321; 1990 season, 321; 1991 Federation Cup, 332; 1991 U.S. Open: vs. Seles, 332-33; 1991 Wimbledon: vs. Navratilova, 331; 1992 Olympic gold medal: vs. Graf, 339, 343, 669

Capriati-King: 1990 "Virginia Slims of Capriati," 321

Caratti, Cristiano, 333

Career earnings. *See* Prize money; specific individuals by name

Career singles records: Australian Championships, 611; French Championships, 617; miscellaneous, 658-61; U.S. Championships, 594; Wimbledon, 605

Carillo (Bowden), Mary, **523**

Down Undertakers, **554**

Down-the-line, defined, 554

Draw, defined, 554

Dress, tennis. *See* Tennis attire

Drobny, Jaroslav, 66, *141,* **393-95,** *395;* 1951 French Championships: vs. Sturgess, 134; 1953 Wimbledon epic match: vs. Patty, 140-41, *141,* 394-95; 1954 Wimbledon: vs. Rosewall, 143, 395; during World War II, 393-94

Drop shot, defined, 554

Drysdale, Cliff, **525;** 1965 U.S. Championships: vs. Santana, 168; as ATP president, 203

duPont, Margaret Osborne, **395-96,** *396;* 1945 U.S. Championships, 78; 1946 French Championships, 121; 1947 Wimbledon, 124; 1948 U.S. Championships, 128, 396; 1949 French Championships, 129; 1949 U.S. Championships, 130; Wightman Cup record, 396

duPont-Brough. *See* Brough-Osborne (duPont)

Durie, Jo, 264, 274

Durr (Browning), Françoise (Frankie), **525;** 1967 French Championships, 173; 1969 U.S. Open doubles, 188

Durr-Sherriff: 1967 French Championships, 173; 1971 French Open, 198

Dwight, James, 8, 9, 12, **466-67;** and Davis Cup, 9; visits Europe, 9

E

Earnshill, as test site for lawn tennis, 4

Eaves, Wilburforce, 14

Edberg, Stefan, 278, *308, 337,* **396-98,** *398;* 1983 U.S. Open, 449; 1984 Davis Cup, 283, 397; 1985 Australian Open: vs. Wilander, 285, 289, 397; 1985 Davis Cup: vs. Westphal, 289, 397; 1987 titles, 303-4; 1988 Wimbledon: vs. Becker, 313; 1989 French Open: vs. Chang, 317-18; 1989 Wimbledon: vs. Becker, 318; 1989 win record, 316; 1990 Australian Open: injured vs. Lendl, 323; 1990 No. 1 ranking, 327; 1990 U.S. Open: vs. Volkov, 327; 1990 Wimbledon: vs. Lendl, vs. Becker, 326-27; 1991 earnings and win record, 330, 344; 1991 U.S. Open: vs. Courier, 335;

1992 U.S. Open: vs. Chang, vs. Sampras, 344; 1993 Australian Open: vs. Courier, 346; 1993 U.S. Open, 349-50; 1994 Davis Cup, 358, 397; 1996 Davis Cup, 373, 397-98; on Chang, 317; on Connors, 335

Edmondson, Mark, **525;** 1976 Australian Open, 224; 1982 Wimbledon, 270

The Education of a Tennis Player (Collins), 510

Edwards, Eddie, 270

Edwards, Vic, 198, 221, 406-7

"Egg ball," 46

Elbow, defined, 554

Electronic line-calling devices, 447-48

Electronic scoreboard: installed at Wimbledon (1929), *43*

Elizabeth, Queen (Great Britain), *123,* 125

Elizabeth II, Queen (Great Britain): at Wimbledon Centenary, 230

Emerson, Roy ("Emmo"), 165, *165,* **398-99,** *399;* 1959, 153; 1961 Australian Championships, 157; 1961 U.S. Championships: vs. Osuna and Laver, 159; 1962 U.S. Championships: vs. Laver, 160; 1963 Australian, French Championships, 162; 1964 LTAA suspension, 164; 1964 near Grand Slam, Davis Cup, 164, 165, 398; 1965 Australian Championships, near Grand Slam, 167; 1965 Davis Cup, 168; 1966 Australian Championship, 170; 1966 Wimbledon injury, 170; 1967 Davis Cup, 175-76; 1967 turns pro, 176; 1972 World Cup, 200, 399; on injury, 399

Emerson-Fletcher, 165

Emerson-Fraser, 155

Emerson-Stolle: 1965 U.S. Doubles, 168; 1966 Australian Championships, 170; 1979 U.S. Open play, 251

"Emmo." *See* Emerson, Roy

Ends: change of, rules for, 7, 575; choice of, rules for, 572

England, early lawn tennis in, 1-8

Enqvist, Thomas, 364, 370; 1996 Davis Cup: vs. Pioline, 373

Equipment: early sales of, 3

Error: defined. *See* Elbow; unforced (U.E.): defined, 566

Estep, Mike, 279, 301

Etchebaster, Pierre, **509**

"The Eternal Second." *See* Vilas, Guillermo

Evans, Richard: on Emerson injury at Wimbledon, 170

Everett, Harris, 75

Evert, Chris, 190, 198-99, *211, 243, 257, 265,* **400-402,** *401;* 1971 U.S. Open, 400; 1971 Virginia Slims, 197; 1971 Wightman Cup, 198-99; 1972 No. 3 U.S. ranking, 204; 1972 Wightman Cup, 204; 1973 U.S. Clay, 210; 1973 vs. Navratilova, 208-9; 1973 Wightman Cup, 210; 1973 win record, 210; 1974 as president of WTA, 215; 1974 No. 1 U.S. ranking, 214; 1974 U.S. Open: vs. Goolagong, 215, 400; 1974 Wimbledon: vs. Hunt, 214-15; 1975 season and earnings, 216, 221; 1975 U.S. Clay Court, 222; 1975 U.S. Open, 221, 401; 1976 36-match streak, 227-28; 1976 team and tournament play, 227; 1976 Wightman Cup, 228; 1977 earnings and ranking, 234; 1977 Federation Cup, 234; 1977 Wimbledon, 230; 1977 win record, 234; 1978 awards and win record, 244, 400; 1978 Wimbledon: vs. Navratilova, 242; 1979 Avon series, 246-47; 1979 clay court streak ends, 247; 1979 French Open, 247-48; 1979 marries Lloyd, 245; 1979 season, 246; 1979 U.S. Clay Court, 249; 1980 Italian, French, U.S. Clay, 256; 1980 U.S. Open: vs. Austin, vs. Mandlikova, 256-57; 1980 Wightman Cup: vs. Wade, 257; 1980 win record, 252; 1981 U.S. Open: vs. Navratilova, 264; 1981 Wimbledon: vs. Mandlikova, 264; 1981 win record, 264-65; 1982 Australian Open, 270; 1982 U.S. Open: vs. Gadusek, 269; 1982 vs. Jaeger, 268; 1982 Wimbledon: vs. King, 269; vs. King, vs. Navratilova, 269; 1982 winning streak, 270; 1983 U.S. Open: vs. Navratilova, 274; 1983 win record, 273, 275; 1984 Australian Open: vs. Sukova, 279, 284; 1984 U.S. Open: vs. Navratilova, 284; 1984 win record, 279, 284; 1985 Australian Open: vs. Navratilova, 292; 1985 French Open: vs. Navratilova, 290; 1986 Federation Cup, 296; 1986 French Open, 292; 1986 U.S. Open: vs. Navratilova, 294; 1986 Wimbledon, 294; 1987 U.S. Open: vs.

McNeil, 303; 1988 Australian indoor-outdoor: vs. Graf, 309; 1988 U.S. Open, 310; 1989 Federation Cup, 315, 401; 1989 final U.S. Open: vs. Garrison, 320; 1989 season, 315; 1989 Wimbledon: vs. Graf, 318; on Austin, 455; on Austin's U.S. Open, 251; and Navratilova, 400; as pro, 401

Evert, Jack, 77

Evert, Jeanne, 215

Evert, Jimmy, 75, 257

Evert Lloyd, Chris. *See* Evert, Chris

Evert-Casals: 1977, 234; 1980 Wightman Cup, 257

Evert-Navratilova: 1976 Wimbledon, 228

Evonne! On the Move (Collins and Goolagong), 510

F

Fabyan, Sarah Palfrey. *See* Cooke, Sarah Palfrey

Fageros, Karol, 152

Fairbank, Rosalyn (Ros), 268, 290, 310

Falkenburg, Bob: 1947, 125; 1948 Davis Cup: vs. Bromwich, 127

Family Circle Cup, 210

Farrar, Ken, 323, 450

Fast court. *See* Court speed

Fault: defined, 554; double, 554; foot, 555, 572-73; service, 573

Faunce, Johnny, 74

Federation Cup (now Fed Cup), **554-55, 628-30;** 1963 inaugural, 163; 1995 name change, 365, 628; all-time records, 630; final round results, 628-30; title round standings, 628

Fendick, Patty, 311

Feret, Paul, 38

Fernandez, Gigi, **525-26**

Fernandez, Gigi–Garrison: 1990 Federation Cup, 322

Fernandez, Gigi–Zvereva: 1992 doubles titles, 343; 1993 near Grand Slam, 351

Fernandez, Mary Joe, *295;* 1985 U.S. Open, 286, 291; 1986 U.S. Open, 294; 1990 Australian Open, 323; 1990 U.S. Open: vs. Sabatini, 328; 1992 Australian Open, 340; 1993 French Open: vs. Graf, vs. Sabatini, 347; 1996 Fed Cup, 372-73; 1996 Olympic Games, 370

Fernandez-Fernandez: 1992 Olympic gold, 343; 1996 Fed Cup, 373

Ferreira, Wayne: 1996 Olympic Games, 370

Ferreira, Wayne–Norval, Piet: 1992 Olympic Games, 343

Ferrier, Gerrard le, 49

Fibak, Wojtek, 225, **526**

Fibak-Meiler: 1976 WCT doubles, 226

Field, The: rules announced in, 6; tennis described in, 4, 6

"Fiery Fred." *See* Stolle, Fred

Fifteen, defined, 555

Fillol, Jaime, 208, 220

Fines, 449-50

First Ten, defined, 555

Fishbach, Mike, 236

Fitzgerald, John, 298, 300

Fitzgerald-Jarryd: 1991 three-major year, 336

Fitzwilliam Club (Dublin), 13

Fixtures: court, 570, 577

Flach, Doug: 1996 Wimbledon: vs. Agassi, 370

Flach, Ken: 1985 U.S. Open hair trouble, 286

Flach-Seguso: 1985 doubles record, 286; 1988 Olympic gold, 309; 1988 Wimbledon, 312

Flam, Herb: 1951 Wimbledon: vs. Savitt, 134

Fletcher, Ken: 1963 Australian Championship, 162; 1963 mixed doubles Grand Slam, 665; 1964 LTAA suspension, 164, 165

Flinders Park (Melbourne, Australia), 308, 311, **555,** 606

Flushing Meadow Park (New York), 236-37, *237,* **555,** 585, 586; Hester and, 231

"Flying Dutchman." *See* Okker, Tom

Foot fault, 7, 555, 572-73

Forehand: defined, 555; two-fisted, 438

Forest Hills (New York), 19, **555,** 586; 1920 plane crash, 28; 1977 last U.S. Open held at, 231-32; construction of, 31; demise of grass at, 215, 217, 586; first men's U.S. Championships, 34; night play at, 217, 222, 586; opened with Wightman Cup matches, *31,* 31-32

Forget, Guy: 1991 Davis Cup, 336; 1992 Wimbledon, 341

Forget-Hlasek: 1990 ATP Tour, 322

Forget-Leconte: 1991 Davis Cup, 336

Foro Italico (Rome), **556,** 617

Forty, defined, 556

Four Musketeers, 33-34, 82, 88, 459. *See also* Borotra, Jean; Brugnon, Jacques ("Toto"); Cochet, Henri; Lacoste, (Jean) René; 1926 U.S. Championships, 39; 1928 Davis Cup, 43

Fragniere, Manuela Maleeva. *See* Maleeva Fragniere, Manuela

Frana, Javier, 308

Frank, Mike: State Department tour, 159

Fraser, Neale, *150, 156,* **468;** 1957 Australian Championships, 147; 1959 Davis Cup: vs. McKay, 154; 1959 U.S. Championships: vs. Olmedo, 153; 1960 Wimbledon, U.S. Championships, 155-56, **468;** 1973 Davis Cup, 208; 1986 Davis Cup, 298; 1990 Davis Cup, 322

"Fraulein Forehand." *See* Graf, Steffi

French and Co., 3

French Championships, **612-17;** 1968 first open, 179-80; 1978 golden anniversary, 237-38; all-time records, 616; best comebacks, 617; biggest upsets, 617; individual career singles records, 617; longest matches, 617; men's doubles records, 613-14; men's singles records, 612-13; mixed doubles records, 615-16; oldest champions, 617; prize money at, 612; women's doubles records, 614-15; women's singles records, 613

French Federation: proposes registered players, 155

French Pro: 1966 Rosewall, 172

French Tennis Federation: 1974 bars World Team Tennis players, 211

Froehling, Frank, III: 1963 U.S. Championships: vs. Osuna, 163; 1971 Davis Cup: vs. Tiriac, 199

Fromberg, Richard, 350

Fromholtz, Dianne, 215, 234, 247; 1988 Flinders Park baptism: vs. Wood, 311

Fry, Joan, 35

Fry, Shirley, *147, 402,* **402-3;** 1951 French Championships, 136; 1955 U.S. Championships, 146;

1956 U.S. Championships: vs. Gibson, 146

Fry-Hart. *See* Hart-Fry

Fuller, William "Pop," 51

G

Gadusek, Bonnie, 269, 272

Gagging. *See* Choking

Game: change: defined, 551; defined, 555; scoring in, 579-80

The Game of Doubles in Tennis (Talbert and Old), 501

The Game of Singles in Tennis (Talbert and Old), 501

Gardini, Fausto: 1955 Italian Championships: vs. Merlo, 144

Garland, Chuck, **468-69**

Garrison, Zina, **526;** 1987 U.S. Open: vs. McNeil, 302-3; 1988 U.S. Open: vs. Navratilova, 310; 1990 Reebok contract for, 326; 1990 Wimbledon: vs. Seles, vs. Graf, vs. Navratilova, 325-26; 1995 Birmingham, 365-66; on Gibson, 326

Garrone, Laura, 286

Gasiorek, Wieslaw, 172

"Gattone." *See* Mecir, Miloslav

Gaudenzi, Andrea: 1996 Olympic Games, 370

Gem, Harry, 5

Gemmel, Rhys, 30

George V, King (Great Britain), 26, 30, 38, 55

George VI, King (Great Britain), 39-40, *123,* 124

Gerken, Barbara, 264

Germains Lawn Tennis, 6

German Championships, early, 22

Germantown Cricket Club (Philadelphia), 585

Gerulaitis, Vitas ("Broadway"), *248,* **526;** 1977 Italian Open, 233; 1977 Wimbledon: vs. McEnroe, 230; 1978 prize money, 241; 1979 Davis Cup, 251; 1979 Italian Open: vs. Vilas, 247; 1979 U.S. Open: vs. Tanner, 250; 1981 Melbourne Indoor walkout, 450

Gibson, Althea, *133,* 149, *149,* **403-4,** *404;* 1950 U.S. Championships, 133-34, 403; 1956 French, Italian titles, 146, 404; 1957 U.S. Championships: vs. Brough, 148-49; 1957 Wightman

Cup team, 403; 1958 turns pro, 404; and Palfrey Cooke, 91

Gilbert, Brad, 290, 293, 298, 319, 322, 350; as Agassi's coach, 356, 360, 377

Gimeno, Andres, **526;** 1968 Wimbledon, U.S. Open, 180, 181; 1972 French Open, 200-201

Gisbert, Juan: 1967 Davis Cup, 167; 1972 Davis Cup, 202; 1975 Masters, 219

Gledhill, Keith, *52,* 74

Glyn, William E., 9

Gobert, Andre: 1911: and Decugis, 23

Godfree, Kitty McKane, 30, *31,* 32, 36, 46, **92-93,** *93;* 1924 Wimbledon: vs. Wills, 34, 92; 1926 Wimbledon, 39; on Lenglen, 26; in Olympics, 93

Godfree, Leslie, 30

Godwin, Neville: 1996 Wimbledon, 370

Goellner, Marc, 350

Golarsa, Laura, 318, 321

"Golden Slam," 669

Gomer, Sarah, 291

Gomez, Andres, **526;** 1984 win record, 278; 1986 Davis Cup, 298; 1990 French Open: vs. Agassi, 324-25; 1990 Italian Open: vs. Muster, 321

Gonzalez, Pancho, *127,* 128, *186,* **404-6,** *405,* 668; 1948 U.S. Championships, 128; 1949 U.S. Championships: vs. Schroeder, 130, 405; 1949 turns pro, 131, 405; 1954 second life, 143, 405; 1958 pro tour: vs. Hoad, 152; 1962 pro retirement, 161; 1968 Bournemouth: vs. Cox, 179; 1968 U.S. Open: first, 181; 1969 top money winner, 186; 1969 Wimbledon: vs. Pasarell, 186, 405; 1970 U.S. Open, 192; 1971 Pacific Southwest Open, 196; 1972 Des Moines Indoor, 200, 406; on Hoad, 412; serve of, 48, 406

Gonzalez-Parker: 1949 French and Wimbledon doubles, 129, 130

Good return, 577-78

Goodbody, Manliffe, 14

Goolagong, Evonne, *195, 253,* 400, **406-8,** *407;* 1971 French Open, Wimbledon, 407; 1971 season, 198; 1971 Wimbledon, 198; 1972 Wimbledon: vs. Evert, 204, 408; 1973 Federation Cup, Bonne Bell Cup, 210; 1973 South African Open, 210; 1974

U.S. Open: vs. Evert, vs. King, 215; 1974 Virginia Slims, 215; 1974 vs. Evert, 214; 1975 Australian Open, 221; 1976 win record, 227; 1977 fall comeback, 235; 1980 Wimbledon comeback: vs. Evert, 256, 407

Goolagong-Gourlay: 1976 Australian Open, 227

Goolagong-Michel: 1974 doubles titles, 214; 1975 Australian Open, 221

Goold, V. "St. Leger," 11, 519, **527**

Gore, Arthur, 14, 40, **527**

Gore, Spencer, 10, **527;** 1877 Wimbledon: vs. W. C. Marshall, 7; on tennis, 11

"Gorgeous Gaby." *See* Sabatini, Gabriela

"Gorgeous Gussy." *See* Moran, Gertrude

"Gorgo." *See* Gonzalez, Pancho

Gorman, Tom, 195, 202, 208

Goss, Eleanor, 32, 36, 40

Gottfried, Brian, 206, **527;** 1977 win record, 233

Gottfried-Ramirez: 1974 Italian Open, 213; 1975 win record, 219; 1976 titles, 226; 1977 Italian, French Opens, 226; 1978 decline, 242

Gourlay, Helen: 1971 French Open, 198; 1977 Wimbledon doubles, 231

Grabb, Jim, 320, 342

Graebner, Carole Caldwell, **527;** 1964 U.S. Championships: vs. Bueno, 166

Graebner, Clark, 169, **527;** 1967 and steel racket, 174; 1968 Davis Cup, 182; 1971 U.S. Indoor, 195; 1972 vs. Nastase, 449

Graebner-Bowrey: 1969 U.S. Clay, 188

Graf, Peter, 306, 310, 409

Graf, Steffi, *302, 309, 363,* **408-10,** *410;* 1985 U.S. Open, 285, 291; 1986 Federation Cup, 296; 1986 U.S. Open: vs. Navratilova, 296; 1986 winning streak, 293, 294; 1987 Federation Cup, 302; 1987 French Open: vs. Navratilova, 301; 1987 International Players Championship: vs. Navratilova, 301; 1987 Italian Open, 301; 1987 U.S. Open: vs. McNeil, vs. Navratilova, 303; 1987 Virginia Slims: vs. Sabatini, 301; 1987 Wimbledon: vs. Shriver, vs.

Hart-Fry, 402-3, 411; 1951 doubles sweep, 136; 1952 season, 139; 1954, 143

Hart-Sedgman: 1951 mixed doubles sweep, 136; 1952 season, 138

Hart-Seixas: 1954 doubles titles, 143

Hartigan, Joan, 52, 55, 58, **528**

Hartley, John, 11, **528**

Har-Tru, 217

Hartwig, Rex, *138;* 1955 Davis Cup doubles, 144

Hawkes, Jack (John), 33, 40, **528**

Haydon, Ann. *See* Jones, Ann Haydon

Haynie, Sandra, 242

Head, Howard, 229

Heater, defined, 557

Heath, Rodney, 22, **528**

Heathcote, Charles, 10

Heathcote, J. M., 6

Heavyweight Championship of Tennis: 1975 Connors vs. Laver, 216; 1976 Connors vs. Orantes, 224

Heldman, Gladys, 140, **511-12;** and Women's International Tennis Federation, 203, 208, 209; as women's prize money promoter, 190, 197, 203, 636

Heldman, Julie, *187;* 1969 Federation Cup, 188; 1969 Wightman Cup, Italian Ch., 188; 1973 U.S. Open: King default, 209, 448; 1974 Bonne Bell Cup, 215

Heldman, Julius: on Vines, 47

Helena Victoria, Princess, *61*

Hellwig, Helen, **529**

Helmuth, J. F., 12

Henessey, John, 35

Henkel, Henner, **529;** 1935 Davis Cup, 57; 1937 French Championships, 62

Henman, Tim: 1995 disqualification, 450

Herrera, Luis, 341

Herrick, Myron T., 43

Hester, Slew (William E.), *239,* **516;** and Flushing Meadow, 231, 237

Hewitt, Bob, **471-72;** 1964 LTAA suspension, 164-65; 1967 Davis Cup injury, 175

Hewitt-McMillan, 471, 480-81; 1967 Wimbledon, 174; 1972 French Open, 201; 1974 WCT doubles, 213; 1975 Mexican playoff, 219; 1977 U.S. Open, Masters, 233; 1978 seven-title season, 242

Heyman, Allan, 197, 201

Hickey, Ed, 166, 667

Higueras, Jose, 275; on Chang, 317

Hill, Al, Jr., 176

Hillyard, Blanche Bingley, 11, 12, **529**

Hillyard, George, 37

Hindrance of opponent: deliberate vs. involuntary, 576-77

Hindrance of player, 578-79

Hingis, Martina, **529;** 1996 ATP World Championship: vs. Graf, 373; 1996 U.S. Open: vs. Graf, 372

Hingis-Sukova: 1996 Wimbledon, 372

History of Forest Hills, A (Minton), 54, 69

History of Lawn Tennis in Pictures (Tingay), 513

Hit, double, 554

Hitler, Adolf, telephones von Cramm, 62

Hlasek, Jakob, 322; 1992 Davis Cup, 337

Hoad, Lew, *138,* **412-13,** *413;* 1953 Davis Cup: vs. Trabert, 412; 1955 Davis Cup doubles, 144; 1955 near Grand Slam, 146; 1956 Davis Cup, 147; 1956 season: vs. Rosewall, 145-46, 413; 1957 turns pro, 147-48; 1957 Wimbledon: vs. Cooper, 148; 1958 pro tour: vs. Gonzalez, 152

Hoad-Hartwig: 1955 Davis Cup: vs. Seixas-Trabert, 144

Hoad-Rosewall: 1953 triple doubles titles, 140, 412-13

Hobart, Clarence, 14, *453*

Holmes, Elisabeth. *See* Moore, Bessie

Holmes, Greg: 1983 U.S. Open, 276

Holmes, Norman: conduct violation, 448

Holt, Richard, 268

Homans, Helen, **529**

Hood (Westacott), Emily. *See* Westacott, Emily Hood

Hopman, Harry ("Hop") (Henry Christian), 47, 57, 68, 271, **472,** 557; on Laver, 418

Hopman, Nell Hall, 57, 68

Hopman Cup, **557**

Horvath, Kathy: 1983 French Open: vs. Navratilova, 271, 273; 1983 season, 272, 275

Hotchkiss, Hazel. *See* Wightman, Hazel Hotchkiss

Houston Nine, 191, 511-12, **557,** 636

Hovey, Fred, 14, **473**

Hoyle, Fred, 259

Huber, Anke: 1995 WTA Tour Championships, 364; 1996 Australian Open: vs. Seles, 368; 1996 Olympic Games, 370

Hughes, George, 54

Hughes, Pat: 1935 Davis Cup, 57

"Human Catapult." *See* Patterson, Gerald

Hunt, Jacque Virgil, 77

Hunt, Joe, **473;** 1943 U.S. Championships, 76, 416; 1944 vs. Schroeder, 77; death of, 76, 77, 473

Hunt, Lamar, 176, 201, **516-17**

Hunt, Lesley, 198; 1974 Wimbledon: vs. Evert, 214-15

Hunt, Ward, 3

Hunter, Frank, 29, 32, 34, 41, 43, 48, **474**

Hurlingham, Club, 6

Hutka, Pavel, 224

I

I formation, 557

"Ice Maiden." *See* Evert, Chris

Il Foro Italico, 131

In the zone, defined, 557-58

Independent Players' Association (IPA), 558

"Independent pros": 1970 indoor circuit, 195

Individual career singles records: Australian Championships, 611; French Championships, 617; miscellaneous, 658-61; U.S. Championships, 594; Wimbledon, 605

Ings, Richard, 305

Innovators, in Hall of Fame, 513-15

Instruction, during match, 582

International competition: post World War II, 123-24, 131

International Lawn Tennis Challenge Trophy. *See* Davis Cup

International Lawn Tennis Federation (ILTF). *See also* International Tennis Federation (ITF); founding of, 20-21

WTA, 209; 1973 U.S. Open walkoff, 209; 1973 vs. Riggs, 204-5, *205*, 414; 1973 Wimbledon triple, 209; 1974 U.S. Open: vs. Goolagong, 215; 1975 Wimbledon: ties with Ryan, 221; 1976 Federation Cup, 228; 1977 season, 234, 235; on 1978 Dallas Virginia Slims, 243; 1980 Top Ten ranking, 257; 1982 Edgbaston Cup: vs. Fairbank, 268; 1982 Wimbledon: vs. Austin, vs. Evert, 268-69; 1982 Wimbledon 100 singles award, 268; 1983 Wimbledon: vs. Jaeger, 273-74, 415; 1990 coach for Navratilova, 325; 1990 last pro appearance, 321; 1996 Fed Cup captain, 372; on Bueno, 387; on Mandlikova, 479; walkouts by, 448; Wimbledon record, 414

King-Casals: 1968 Wimbledon, 181; 1971 Virginia Slims tournaments, 197

King-Stove: 1976 Wimbledon, 228

King's Cup, 137, **558;** 1966 longest match on record, 172

Kingscote, Algie (Algernon), 30, **531;** 1919 Davis Cup, 26

Kinsey, Bob: 1926 Wimbledon "cripple," 39

Kinsey, Howard, 38, 612

Kirby, Vernon, 55

Kirmayr, Carlos, 328

Kleinschroth, Heinrich, 22

Kloss, Ilana, 228

Klosterkemper, Horst, 448

Knapp, Barbara, 403

Knight, Laura, 13

Knowles, Mark, 351

Kodes, Jan: 1970 French Open, 192; 1971 French Open: vs. Nastase, 195; 1971 U.S. Open, 195-96; 1973 U.S. Open, 208; 1973 Wimbledon, 207; 1974 conduct violation, 448

Koestler, Arthur, 70-71

Kohde Kilsch, Claudia, 279

Kohde Kilsch–Sukova: 1985 Wimbledon, 286

Kooyong Stadium (Melbourne), 42, 123; audience capacity at, 606; construction of, **558**

Korda, Petr, 322, 373; 1992 French Open: vs. Courier, 341

Korff, John, 332

Kormoczi, Suzi, **531**

Kovacs, Frank, *72;* 1941 U.S. Championships: vs. Riggs, 73; 1942 pro debut, 74

Kozeluh, Karel, *42,* 48, 668; 1928 pro matches, 44; 1929 U.S. Pro Championships, 45; 1931 pro tour, 48; 1932 pro tour, 50; 1935 pro tour, 58; 1937 first "open," 64

Kraft Tour, **558**

Krahwinkel, Hilde. *See* Sperling, Hilde Krahwinkel

Krajicek, Richard, 355, *366,* **531;** 1996 Wimbledon: vs. Sampras, 369; vs. Washington, 366, 369, 370

Kramer, Jack, *120, 123, 126,* **416-18,** *417;* 1943 U.S. Championships, 75-76, 416; 1946 Davis Cup, 122-23; 1946 U.S. Nationals, 120, 122; 1946 Wimbledon, 120, 121; 1947 pro debut, 125-26, 417; 1947 U.S. Championships pre-pro scare, 125; 1947 Wimbledon, U.S. Championships and Davis Cup, 124-25; 1950 pro tour: vs. Segura, 134; 1952 as promoter, 139, 417; 1953 vs. Sedgman, 141; 1954 retires from play, 143; 1957 signs Hoad, 147-48; 1959 as promoter, 152-53; 1960 raid on amateurs, 157; 1962 retires as promoter, 161; 1964 reenlisted, 166; 1970 Grand Prix idea, 189, 417; on Hoad vs. Gonzalez, 148; as promoter, 448

Krickstein, Aaron: 1983 Israel title, 277; 1983 U.S. Open, 276; 1985 Davis Cup, 289; 1990 Davis Cup, 322; 1991 U.S. Open: vs. Connors, 335

Kriek, Johan, *266,* **531;** 1980 U.S. Open: vs. Borg, 254; 1981 Australian Open, 261; 1982 Australian Open, 266

Krishnan, Ramanathan, 170, **531-32;** 1987 Davis Cup, 300

Krishnan, Ramesh, 170, 261, 316, **531-32;** 1987 Davis Cup, 300

Kuhn, Ferdinand: on Perry vs. Crawford (1934), 54

Kuhnen, Patrik, 312, 350

Kuhnke, Christian, 193

Kulti, Nicklas, 337; 1996 Davis Cup: vs. Boetsch, 373

Kuykendall, Kathy, 210, 223

L

Lacoste, (Jean) René, *33, 38,* 44, **96-97,** *97;* 1924, 33; 1925 Davis

Cup: vs. Tilden, 35-36; 1925 Wimbledon, 35, 96; 1926 U.S. Championships, 39; 1927 season: vs. Tilden, 41, 96; 1928 Davis Cup: vs. Tilden, 43, 97; death of, 373; and steel racket, 174; on Tilden, 43, 44; U.S. Championships (1926), *38*

Ladbrokes: on Becker, 288

Ladies' tennis, introduction of, 8

"Lady Tennis." *See* Wightman, Hazel Hotchkiss

Lakhta Lawn Tennis Club, 13

Lall, Premjit: 1969 Wimbledon, 185

Lambert Chambers, Dorothea Douglass. *See* Chambers, Dorothea Douglass (Mrs. Robert Lambert Chambers)

Lance, Sylvia, 34, 42

Landry, Nelly Adamson: 1948 French Championships, 128

Laney, Al, **512;** on Crawford, 91; on great Cup theft, 453; on Kramer vs. Budge, 127; on Suzanne Lenglen, 28; on Tilden, 34, 64

Langrishe, May, 12, 13, **532**

Lara, Marcelo, 220

Larcombe, Ethel, **532**

Larned, Bill, 14, 16, *22,* 44, **476;** singles record of, 18

Larsen, Art ("Tappy"), 132, *132,* 135, **476-77**

Larsson, Magnus: 1991 French Open: vs. Courier, 334; 1993 U.S. Open, 350; 1994 Davis Cup, 357, 358; 1994 Grand Slam Cup, 357

Lavalle, Leo, 298

Laver, Rod, *154, 160, 184,* **418-20,** *420;* 1959, 153, 418; 1960 season, 154, 156; 1962 first Grand Slam, 160, 664; 1962 Grand Slam, 160; 1962 lured to pro ranks, 162, 164, 419, 668; 1962 U.S. Championships: vs. Emerson, 160; 1964 U.S. Pro Championships at Longwood, 166, 419; 1968 Bournemouth, 179; 1968 Wimbledon: vs. Roche, 180; 1969 Australian Championship: vs. Roche, 184-85; 1969 Grand Slam, 184-85, 419, 665; 1969 U.S. Open: vs. Tony Roche, 185; 1970 prize winnings, 190; 1970 Tennis Champions Classic, 193; 1971 as first career millionaire, 196, 419; 1971 Tennis Champions Classic, 196; 1972 WCT final: vs. Rosewall, 200; 1973 Davis Cup, 208, 419; 1974 prize money, 213; 1975 "Heavy-weight" challenge: vs. Connors, 216; on Emerson, 399; on Gonzalez, 404-5; Grand Slam record, 664-65; on Santana, 436; self-assessment, 185

Laver-Newcombe: 1973 Davis Cup, 200

"Law and order," 447-50

Lawford, Herb, 8; 1884 Wimbledon: vs. Dwight, 9

Lawn tennis: first clubs for, 6; first public exhibition of, 4; international growth of, 13; need to standardize, 12; origin of, 2-3. *See also* Tennis; patent for, *5, 6*

Lawn Tennis Association (LTA), formed, 8

Lawn Tennis Association of Australia (LTAA): 1964 suspends five players, 164-65

Lawn Tennis Association of Britain (LTAB): 1967 denounces shamateurism, 172-73

Lawn Tennis Championships (Great Britain). *See* Wimbledon

Lawn Tennis (Dwight), 9

Lawn Tennis Tournaments (Dodgson), 7

Leach, Dick–Dell, Dick: vs. Schloss, Len–Mozur, Tom: 1967 longest tournament match, 175

Leach, Rick, 322

Leach, Rick–Pugh, Jim: 1990 Davis Cup, 322

Leamington Club, 4

Leand, Andrea, 264, 272

"Leaning Tower of Pizzazz." *See* Tinling, Ted

Leconte, Henri, 286, 312; 1985 Wimbledon, 287; 1991 Davis Cup, 336

Lee, Harold, 54

Lendl, Ivan, *278, 287,* 351-52, **420-21,** *421;* 1980 Canadian Open, 254; 1980 Davis Cup, 255-56, 420; 1980 U.S. Open, 254; 1981 French Open: vs. Borg, 258-59; 1981 season, 261-62; 1982 tour record, 266-67; 1982 U.S. Open, 271; 1983 U.S. Open, 276-77; 1984 French Open: vs. McEnroe, 280-81, 421; 1984 U.S. Open: vs. McEnroe, 282, 420; 1985 Australian Open, 289; 1985 Masters, 290; 1985 top ATP computer rankings, 285; 1985 U.S. Open: vs. Connors, vs. McEnroe, 288-89; 1985 Wimbledon, 286;

1985 win record, 289; 1986 French Open: vs. Pernfors, 294; 1986 Masters: vs. Becker, 293; 1986 U.S. Open: vs. Mecir, 297-98; 1986 Wimbledon: vs. Becker, 295; 1986 win and earnings record, 298; 1987 French Open: vs. Wilander, 304; 1987 Masters, 305; 1987 near Grand Slam, 299; 1987 U.S. Open: vs. Wilander, 305; 1987 Wimbledon: vs. Cane, 304; 1987 win record, 299; 1988 slip from No. 1, 307; 1988 U.S. Open: vs. Wilander, 313; 1988 Wimbledon, 312; 1989 Australian Open, 316; 1989 earnings and win record, 314, 320; 1989 U.S. Open: vs. Becker, 319; 1990 Australian Open: vs. Edberg, 323; 1990 U.S. Open: vs. Sampras, 327; 1990 Wimbledon: "Zazrany," 326; 1992 1,000th tour victory, 344; 1992 Top Ten ranking, 338; 1994 retirement, 351-52; grass aversion, 267, 295; and Wimbledon, 421; on Wimbledon victory tradition, 305

Lenglen, Charles, 25

Lenglen, Suzanne, 21, 25-26, *37,* **97-99,** *98;* 1919 Wimbledon: vs. Lambert Chambers, 25-26, 87; 1921 U.S. Championships default, 28, 98, 448; 1922 Wimbledon: vs. Mallory, 30; 1923 Wimbledon, 32; 1924 Wimbledon singles loss, 34; 1926 Cannes: vs. Wills, *36,* 36-38, 98; 1926 turns pro, *37,* 38-39; 1926 Wimbledon mix-up, 98; appeal of, 25-26, 28, 98; death of, 66, 98

Lenglen-Borotra: 1925 Wimbledon, 35

Lenglen-Ryan: 1925 Wimbledon, 35

Leschly, Jan, 174

Let: defined, 559; rules for, 574

Letts, John, 311

Lewis, Chris: 1983 Wimbledon, 276

Licensing Corporation of America: USTA signs with, 173

Lieberman, Nancy, 273

Liess, Zenda, 228

Lindqvist, Catarina, 311

Line: ball falling on, 577

Line judge, defined, 559

Line-calling devices: electronic, 447-48

Liner, defined, 559

"Lingering death," 222, 515; defined, 559, 586; *See also* Tie-breaker, tie-break

"Lingo": tennis, 547-68

Little, Dorothy Round. *See* Round, Dorothy

"Little Miss Poker Face." *See* Wills Moody, Helen

"Little Mo." *See* Connolly, Maureen ("Little Mo")

Lizana, Anita, **532;** 1937 U.S. Championships, 63-64

Lloyd, Chris Evert. *See* Evert, Chris

Lloyd, John, 240, 402

Lob, defined, 559

Locanto, Dana, 370, 447

Logan, Bonnie, 210

Long, Melville, 18

Long, Thelma, **532;** 1952 Australian Championships, 139

Long matches: Australian Championships, 611; Boetsch vs. Kulti, 373; Chang at 1989 French Open, 317; French Championships, 617; Gerulaitis vs. Vilas, 247; Gonzalez vs. Pasarell, 186, 405-6; Graf vs. Sanchez Vicario, 368; Leach-Dell, 175; Lendl vs. Wilander, 304, 305; Matuszewski vs. Denton, 286; McEnroe vs. Wilander, 271; miscellaneous, 660; Noah vs. Smith, 311-12; Robbins vs. Dell, 188; Seles vs. Sabatini, 328; Smith-van Dillen vs. Fillol-Cornejo, 208; U.S. Championships, 595; Wilson-Cox vs. Pasarell-Graebner, 183; Wimbledon, 605-6

Long tennis *(Longue paume),* 4

Long Way Babies, 512, 559

Longest sets, 660

Longest tie-breakers: Australian Championships, 611; French Championships, 617; miscellaneous, 660; U.S. Championships, 595; Wimbledon, 606

Longwood Cricket Club (Boston), 10, *10,* **559,** 585; Davis Cup at, 14-15, 621; U.S. Pro Championships at, 166, 667

Loser, lucky, defined, 559

Lott, George, 44-45, 54, **477;** 1930 Davis Cup, 46; turns pro, 58

Lott-Van Ryn: 1931 French and Wimbledon, 502

Louis Armstrong Stadium (National Tennis Center), 237

Louis Harris survey: on tennis as spectator sport, 211

Love, defined, 559

"Lovebird double," 215, 245; revisited, 265-66

Lovera, Mme. *See* Sherriff, Gail

Lowe, Arthur, **532**

Lowe, Gordon, 23, **532**

LTA. *See* Lawn Tennis Association (LTA)

LTAA. *See* Lawn Tennis Association of Australia (LTAA)

Lucky loser, defined, 559

Lundgren, Peter, 305

Lundquist, Jan Erik, 165

Lutz, Bob, *227;* 1970 Davis Cup, 193; 1972 U.S. Pro Championship, 201

Lycett, Mrs. Randolph. *See* Austin, Joan

Lycett, Randolph, 29, 30

Lyle, Nancy, 56

M

Macaulay, Duncan: on Cochet, 41; on Crawford, 52; on Four Musketeers, 34; on Lenglen, 30; on postwar Wimbledon, 121; on postwar women's tennis, 121; on Ryan, 55

MacCall, George, 175, 176, 208

Maciel, Pancho, 298

MacKay, Barry, 153, *154;* 1960 Rome, U.S. Indoor titles, 155; as pro, 156, 169

Madison Square Garden (New York): 1926 pro tour debut, 38-39; 1947 Kramer pro debut vs. Riggs, 125; 1968 International: Richey vs. King, 183; Virginia Slims at, 636

Mahony, Harold, 14, **533**

Main, Lorne Garnet, **532**

Majoli, Iva, 362, 365; 1996 Olympic Games, 370

Majors, **559-60.** *See also* Grand Slam

Major's Game of Lawn Tennis, The, tennis described in, 3

Mako, Gene, *61,* **477-78;** 1938 U.S. Championships: vs. Budge, 65

Malaga, Robert, 173

Maleeva, Katerina, 285-86, **533**

Maleeva, Magdalena ("Maggie"), **533;** 1992 U.S. Open: vs. Navratilova, 343

Maleeva Fragniere, Manuela, **533;** 1984 Italian Open: vs. Evert,

279; 1992 U.S. Open: vs. Maggie Maleeva, 343

Mallory, Molla (Mrs. Franklin Mallory), *20, 29,* 44, *99,* **99-100;** 1921 U.S. Championships, 28; vs. Lenglen, 28, 98, 99; 1922 U.S. Championships: vs. Wills, 30; 1926 U.S. title: record win, 39, 100

Mancini, Alberto, 317

Mandela, Nelson, 380

Mandlikova, Hana, *291,* **478-79;** 1980 Australian Open, 253; 1980 U.S. Open: vs. Evert, 257; 1981 French Open, 263; 1981 Wimbledon, 263-64; 1982 U.S. Open, 269; 1984 vs. Navratilova, 283; 1985 season, 292; 1985 U.S. Open, 291-92, 478; 1986 Federation Cup, 296; 1986 Wimbledon, 294-95; 1987 U.S. Open conduct, 450

Mandlikova-Sukova: 1984 Federation Cup, 284

Mansfield, Fred, 16

Marble, Alice, 50, 67, **100-102,** *101,* 401; 1932 U.S. Championships, 50; 1933 heat exhaustion, 101; 1936 U.S. Championships, 60; 1938 U.S. Championships, 66-67, 101; 1939 Wimbledon triple, 67-68, 101; 1940 U.S. Championships triple-tripler, 72; 1941 pro debut, 73, 102; 1949 U.S. triple, 70

Maria, Pascal, 448

Marshall, Julian, 2

Marshall, William, 10

Marsikova, Regina, 244

Martin, Alastair Bradley, **517;** on Laver, 185

Martin, Bill, **517-18**

Martin, Todd: 1994 Australian Open, 353; 1994 Davis Cup, 357; 1994 U.S. Open: vs. Agassi, 355; 1996 Davis Cup, 373; 1996 Wimbledon, 370

"Martina Navratilova Night," 357

Martinez, Conchita, **533;** 1989 season, 316; 1993 Federation Cup, 351; 1994 Federation Cup, 358; 1994 Wimbledon: vs. Navratilova, vs. McNeil, 355; 1995 French Open: vs. Graf, 361; 1995 Wimbledon, 363

Mary, Queen (Great Britain), 26, 30, 38, 55; and Budge "wave," 57

Marylebone Cricket Club (MCC), rules of for lawn tennis, 6

Masson, Cecilia, 612

Masters. *See also* Grand Prix Masters; defined, 560

Masthoff, Helga Niessen. *See* Niessen, Helga

Masur, Wally, 300, 312, 350

Match, defined, 560

Match Play and the Spin of the Ball (Tilden), 111

Match point, defined, 560

Matches: longest: Australian Championships, 611; French Championships, 617; miscellaneous, 660; U.S. Championships, 595; Wimbledon, 605-6

Mathey, Dean, *22*

Mathieu, Simone Passemard, 45, **533;** 1935 French Championships, 57; 1938 French Championships triple, 66

Matuszewski, Richard: 1985 U.S. Open: vs. Denton, 286

Maureen Connolly Brinker Cup, 389

Maureen Connolly Brinker Indoor, 204

May, Kathy, 229

Mayer, Gene (Eugene), 264, 277, **533-34**

Mayer, Sandy, **533-34**

Mayer, Sandy–Gerulaitis: 1975 Wimbledon, 219

Mayer, Sandy–Meyer, Gene: 1979 French Open, 248

Mayotte, Tim, 263; 1982 Wimbledon, 270; 1985 Wimbledon, 287; 1986 Davis Cup, 298; 1987 Davis Cup, 299; 1988 Wimbledon, 312; on 1993 U.S. Open, 350

McAteer, Myrtle, **534**

McDowell, Fran, 342

McEnroe, John, *240, 250, 260, 280, 292,* **421-24,** *423;* 1977 Wimbledon, 230; 1978 Davis Cup, 240, 422; 1978 Grand Prix Masters: vs. Connors, vs. Ashe, 240-41; 1978 Grand Prix record, 240; 1978 Stockholm: vs. Borg, 240; 1979 pre-Wimbledon press, 248; 1979 U.S. Open: vs. Nastase, 249-50; 1979 WCT final, 246; 1979 win record, 245, 251; 1980 season, 255; 1980 U.S. Open: vs. Borg, 252, 255; vs. Lendl, vs. Connors, 254-55; 1980 Wimbledon: vs. Borg, 251-52, 253-54, 423; 1981 Davis Cup: vs. Vilas, vs. Clerc, 262; 1981 U.S. Open: vs. Borg, 261; vs. Gerulaitis,

Mottram, Tony (Anthony John), **535**

Mozur, Tom, 175

Mr. G. *See* Gustav V, King

Mronz, Alex, 358

Mudford, Phyllis, 46

Mukerjea, Jaidip, 170

Mulligan, Marty: 1964 LTAA suspension, 164

Mulligano, Martino. *See* Mulligan, Marty

Mulloy, Gardnar, *122, 137,* **483-84;** on Cooper vs. Anderson, 151; during World War II, 75

Mulloy-Patty: 1957 Wimbledon title, 148

Mulloy-Talbert. *See* Talbert-Mulloy

Murphy, Dennis, 207

Murray, (Robert) Lindley, 23, 27, 484

"Muscles." *See* Rosewall, Ken

Muster, Thomas ("Moo Man"), **535-36;** 1988 Australian Open, 311; 1989 accident, 317, 321; 1990 Davis Cup, 322; 1990 return to competition, 321; 1993 U.S. Open, 350; 1994 U.S. Open, 355; 1995 French Open: vs. Kafelnikov, vs. Chang, 361; 1996 French Open: vs. Stich, 369; walkouts, 449-50

"Mutt & Jeff" match, 52

My Life with the Pros (Collins), 510

Myers, A. T., 11

Myers, Wallis, 41

Myrick, Julian, 32, 52, **518**

N

Na, Hu, **536**

Nagelson, Betsy–Annacone: 1987 U.S. Open, 301

Nahant (Mass.) tournament, 8-9

Najuck, Roman, 48

Nantclwyd, as test site for lawn tennis, 4

Nastase, Ilie, *202,* **424-26,** *425;* 1970 U.S. Indoor, 193, 425; 1971 Davis Cup, 199; 1971 earnings, 197; 1971 French Open: vs. Kodes, 195; 1971 Grand Prix Masters, 196; 1972 U.S. Open: vs. Ashe, 201; 1972 Wimbledon: vs. Smith, 201; 1973 No. 1 ranking, 206, 425; 1973 U.S. Open, 207-8; 1975 Canadian Open, 219, 449; 1975 Masters: "Nasty" conduct at, 219, 448; 1976 Davis Cup behavior, 226; 1976 win

record, 225-26; 1977 and spaghetti racket, 236; 1979 U.S. Open conduct, 249-50, 449; conduct violations, 425, 449; temperament, 449

Nastase-Connors: 1973 Wimbledon, 207

National Championships (U.S.). *See also* U.S. Championships (now U.S. Open); inaugural, 12

National Singles and Doubles (Longwood): 1969, 184, 586

National Tennis Center (Flushing, New York), 231, 236-37, *237,* 585

National Tennis League (NTL), **561;** 1967 formation, 172, 176; 1970 vs. ITF, 189

Nations Cup (ATP), 220

Navratilova, Martina, *222, 245, 259, 273, 339,* 351, 352, 400, **426-28,** *428;* 1973 vs. Evert, 208-9, 426; 1974 vs. Evert, 214; 1975 announces defection, 221; 1975 win record, Federation Cup play, 221; 1976 U.S. Open, 228; 1977 Virginia Slims, 234; 1978 Virginia Slims season, 242; 1978 Wimbledon: vs. Evert, 242; on 1978 Wimbledon win, 242; 1979 Avon series, 246; 1979 mother at Wimbledon, 249-50; 1981 receives U.S. citizenship, 258; 1981 U.S. Open: vs. Evert, vs. Austin, 264; 1981 win record, 258, 264; 1982 French Open: vs. Jaeger, 268; 1982 U.S. Open: vs. Shriver, 269; 1982 Wimbledon: vs. Evert, 269; 1982 win record, 266, 267, 268; 1983 Australian Open, 274-75; 1983 marred by single loss: French Open: vs. Horvath, 271, 272-73; 1983 U.S. Open: vs. Evert, 274, 427; 1983 Wimbledon: vs. Jaeger, 274; 1983 win and earnings record, 272; 1984 Australian Open: vs. Sukova, 284, 427; 1984 doubles Grand Slam, 279, 427, 665; 1984 French Open, 283; 1984 near Grand Slam singles season, 278, 283-84; 1984 U.S. Open: vs. Sabatini, vs. Evert, 284; 1984 Wimbledon, 283-84; 1985 Australian Open: vs. Mandlikova, vs. Evert, 292; 1985 eyeglasses improve win record, 290; 1985 French Open: vs. Evert, 290; 1985 Wimbledon four in a row, 291; 1985 win record, 290; 1986 earnings, 298; 1986 Federation Cup, 296, 428; 1986 U.S. Open: vs. Evert, 294; vs. Graf, 293, 296; vs. Sukova, 296-97; 1986

Virginia Slims, 293; 1986 Wimbledon: vs. Mandlikova, 294-95; 1987 Australian Open, 301; 1987 French Open: vs. Graf, 301; 1987 season, 298, 301; 1987 U.S. Open: vs. Graf, 300-301, 303; 1987 U.S. Open triple, 301, 427; 1987 Wimbledon: vs. Evert, vs. Graf, 301-2; 1988 season, 308, 309; 1988 U.S. Open: vs. Garrison, 310; 1988 Wimbledon: vs. Graf, 309-10; 1989 Wimbledon and U.S. Open: vs. Graf, 318; 1990 Wimbledon, 325; vs. Garrison, 326, 426; 1991 U.S. Open, 332; vs. Seles, 333; 1991 Wimbledon: vs. Capriati, 331; 1991 win record, 329; 1992 Caesars Palace: vs. Connors, 338-39; 1992 Chicago: vs. Novotna, 338; 1992 season, 338; 1992 U.S. Open: vs. Maggie Maleeva, 343; 1993 Wimbledon: vs. Novotna, 348; 1994: vs. Sanchez Vicario, 357; 1994 "Martina Navratilova Night," 357, 426; 1994 Oakland: vs. Sanchez Vicario, 357, 428; 1994 singles retirement, 351, 352; 1994 Wimbledon: vs. Martinez, 355, 427; compared with Wills Moody, 326; conditioning regimen, 279; on Evert, 290, 320; on Seles' grunting, 342

"Navratilova Night," 357

Navratilova-King: 1978 U.S. Open, 242; 1979 Wimbledon, 249

Navratilova-Sanchez: 1987 U.S. Open, 301

Navratilova-Shriver, 427; 1981 11-title year, 258; 1983 three majors plus, 275; 1984 Grand Slam, 279, 665; 1985 end of streak, 286; 1986 Federation Cup, 292, 296; 1987 U.S. Open, 301; 1988 season, 308-9; 1991 Virginia Slims, 333

Naylor-Leyland, Major, 4

Neighborhood Club (West Newton, Mass.): 1895: British at, 14

Nelson, Judy, 284, 329

Nestor, Daniel, 370

Net: defined, 560

Net cord, defined, 560

Net judge, defined, 560

Net rusher, defined, 560

New Orleans Lawn Tennis Club, 10

Newberry, Janet: 1976 U.S. Open, 228; 1977 Italian Open, 235

Newcombe, John, *173, 206,* **428-30,** *430;* 1963 Davis Cup, 164; 1967

Palfrey (Fabyan Cooke Danzig), Sarah Hammond. *See* Cooke, Sarah Palfrey

Palfrey (Fullerton), Lee (Elizabeth Howland), **537**

Palfrey (Woodrow), Polly (Margaret Germaine), **537**

Palmer, Jared, 357, 358

Panatta, Adriano, **537**; 1976 Davis Cup, 226; 1976 French, Italian Opens, 224; 1977 Davis Cup, 233; 1978 Italian semi, 449; 1978 U.S. Open: vs. Connors, 238-39; 1980 Davis Cup, 256

Parche, Guenther, 346, 409, 438

Pare, Emmett, 48

Paris: 1968 trouble in, 179-80; 1984 McEnroe in, 280

Parke, Jim, **537-38**

Parker, Frank, *61*, 76, *78*, **486**; 1937 Davis Cup, 63; 1941 U.S. Clay, 73; 1943 U.S. Championships, 76; 1944 U.S. Championships, 76; 1945 U.S. Championships, 77-78; 1947 U.S. Championships: vs. Kramer, 125; 1949 French Championships, 129

Parkhomenko, Svetlana, 301

Partridge, Susan. *See* Chatrier, Susan Partridge

Parun, Onny, 206, 213

Pasarell, Charlie: 1967 vs. Ashe, 175; 1967 Wimbledon, 173; 1969 Wimbledon: vs. Gonzalez, 186

Pasquale, Claudia, 268

Passemard, Simone. *See* Mathieu, Simone Passemard

Passing shot, defined, 561

"Pasta Kid." *See* Bertolucci, Paolo

Pate, Walter, *61*

Patent, for lawn tennis, *5*, 6

"Patriotic Tournaments": 1917, 23

Patterson, Gerald, *30*, **487**; 1919 Wimbledon: vs. Brookes, 26; 1922 Wimbledon, 30; 1927 Australian Championships, 42

Patterson–O'Hara Wood: 1922 Davis Cup, 31

Pattison, Andrew, 206, 208

Patty, Budge, 132, *141*, **487-88**; 1950 French Championships, 132; 1953 Wimbledon epic match: vs. Drobny, 140-41, *141*, 488

Paulus, Barbara, 373

Pearl Harbor, 74

Pecci, Victor: 1979 French Open, 248; 1987 Davis Cup, 299, 300

Pell, Teddy, **488**

"Pelota," 4, 6

Pena, Horacio de la, 304

Penrose, Beryl, 145, **538**

Perez-Roldan, Guillermo, 308

Permanent fixtures, of court, 570, 577

Pernfors, Mikael: 1986 Davis Cup, 298; 1986 French Open, 294

Perry, Fred, 47, *51, 58, 106*, **106-7**, *581*; 1929 Wimbledon, 44; 1933 Davis Cup: vs. Merlin, 53, 107; 1933 U.S. Championships: vs. Crawford, 52, 107; 1934 championship year, 53-54; 1934 U.S. Championships, 55; 1934 Wimbledon: vs. Crawford, 54; 1935 Australian Championships vs. de Stefani, 56; 1935 Forest Hills injury, 57; 1935 French Championships, 56, 107; 1935 Wimbledon, 57; 1936 U.S. Championships: vs. Budge, 59-60; 1936 turns pro, 58; 1936 Wimbledon, 58, 59; 1937 pro tour: vs. Vines and Tilden, 64, 107; on Borg, 238; on de Stefani, 56; on von Cramm and Becker, 288

Peru: Olmedo visit, 153

Petra, Yvon, **538**; 1940s French titles, 71; 1946 Wimbledon, 120-21

Pettit, Tom, 14, **509**

Pfau, Zeno, 286

Pfister, Hank, 253

Phelan, Dick: on Kramer, 152-53

Philadelphia Cricket Club, 13, **561**, 585; as women's championship host, 20

Philadelphia Freedoms, 214

Philippoussis, Mark: 1996 Australian Open: vs. Sampras, vs. Woodforde, 367, 606

Philips-Moore, Barry, 236

Piatek, Mary Lou. *See* Daniels, Mary Lou Piatek

Pierce, Jim, 360

Pierce, Mary, *360*, **538**; 1993 Virginia Slims semifinal: vs. Sanchez Vicario, 351; 1994 French Open: vs. Sanchez Vicario, 353-54; 1995 Australian Open, 359-60

Pietrangeli, Nicky, **488-89**; 1960 French singles title, 155; 1961 French Championships, 157-58; 1976 Davis Cup, 226; Davis Cup career, 488

Pilic, Nikki, **538**; 1967 turns pro, 176; 1967 Wimbledon, 173; 1973 suspension of, 207

Pilic-Barthes: 1970 U.S. Open, 192

Pim, Joshua, 14, 380, **538**

Pioline, Cedric: 1993 U.S. Open: vs. Courier, vs. Sampras, 349; 1996 Davis Cup: vs. Edberg, vs. Enqvist, 373

"Pits of the world," 259, 423, 450

Pittsburgh Triangles, 214

Placement, defined, 561

Play, continuous, 581-82

Player. *See also* Receiver; *See also* Server; hindering of opponent by, 576-77; hindrance of by opponent, 578-79; and point, 575-76; registered: defined by ITF, 178

Playing for Life (Trabert), 501

Poach, defined, 561

Pohmann, Hans, 226

Point(s): defined, 561; match, 560; winning and losing of: rules for, 575-76

Pooper. *See* Pusher

Porwik, Claudia, 321

Practical Lawn Tennis (Dwight), 9

Pratt, Betty, *187*

Pressurized ball, 571

Prince racket, 229

Princes Club, 6

Prize money, **661**; 1926 pro tour, 39; 1937 pro tour for Perry vs. Vines, 64; 1939 pro tour Budge debut, 70; 1969 open era escalation, 183, 184; 1970 $200,000 barrier, 190, 211; 1970 escalation in, 189-90; 1970 Grand Prix, 189; 1970 men's vs. women's, 190, 191; 1971 first millionaire, 196; 1972 upward spiral, 200; 1973 Nastase, 206; 1974 men's season's, 213; 1977 tennis millionaires, 233; 1978 ATP "official money" list, 241; for Australian Championships, 606; for French Championships, 612; for Grand Slam Cup, 637; leaders in, 661; in open era, 586; for U.S. Championships, 586; for Virginia Slims, 636; for Wimbledon, 599; for World Championship Tennis (WCT), 637

"Pro Council." *See* Men's International Professional Tennis Council

Professional: contract: defined by ITF, 178; defined, 561; independent, 194-95; at Olympics, 306; teaching: defined by ITF, 178; vs. amateur, 150, 152-53, 157, 172-73, 194-95, 457-548; 1968,

205; on Wimbledon wager, 67, 68

Rinaldi, Kathy, 263; 1981 French Open, Wimbledon, 263; 1985 Wimbledon, 291

Riordan, Bill: files antitrust suit, 211-12, 217, 390; and ITF-WCT agreement, 201; split with Connors, 216, 218, 390

Riordan Circuit, 195, 200, 205-6, **562.** *See also* Independent Players' Association (IPA)

Riviera, tennis at, 21

Roark, Mrs. Aidan. *See* Wills Moody, Helen

Robb, Muriel, **540**

Robertson, Max: on Brough vs. Fleitz, 145; on Savitt, 134; on Wills Moody vs. Jacobs, 56

Robinson, Adeline, 13

Roche, Tony, **493;** 1965 French Championships, 167; 1966 Italian, French Championships, 171; 1967 season, 173, 174; 1967 turns pro, 176; 1969 Australian Championships: vs. Laver, 176, 184-85; 1969 U.S. Open: vs. Laver, 185; 1977 Davis Cup, 233

Roche-Newcombe. *See* Newcombe-Roche

"Rocket." *See* Laver, Rod

"Rockhampton Rocket." *See* Laver, Rod

Roger-Vasselin, Christophe, *236, 275*

Roland Garros, 43, **563,** 612; 1968 first open, 179-80; 1979 expansion, 247, 515; as World War II concentration camp, 70-71

Rollinson, Sue, 263

Romance of Wimbledon, The (Olliff), 124

Romania: 1969 Davis Cup play, 187-88; 1972 Davis Cup play, 202

Rome. *See* Italian Championships

Roosevelt, Ellen Crosby, 13, **493-94**

Roosevelt, Grace (Mrs. Appleton Clark), 13, 494

Roosevelt, Theodore, 1

Rose, Merv, **540;** 1954 Australian Championships, 142; 1958 Italian, French Championships, 151

Rosewall, Ken, 140, *146,* 412, **430-32,** *431;* 1953 Australian, French Championships, 140; 1954 Wimbledon, 143; 1956 Davis Cup, 147; 1956 season: vs. Hoad, 145-46, 431; 1956 turns pro, 146,

431; 1956 U.S. Championships: vs. Hoad, 145-46; 1962 lackluster pro year, 162; 1968 Bournemouth, French, 179-80; 1970 U.S. Open, 192; 1971 Australian Championships, 194, 197; 1971 earnings, 196; 1971 WCT final, 196; 1972 Australian Open, 200; 1972 WCT final: vs. Laver, 200; 1974 Wimbledon, U.S. Open: vs. Connors, 212; 1975 World Cup, 220

Rosset, Marc: 1992 Davis Cup, 337; 1992 Olympic tournament: vs. Arrese, 343, 669

Rostagno, Derrick: 1989 U.S. Open: vs. Becker, 319

Rotation of service: during tie-break, 580

Round: challenge: defined, 551

Round, Dorothy (Mrs. Douglas Little), *109,* **109-10;** 1934 Wimbledon, 54-55, 109; 1935 Australian Championships, 56; 1937 Wimbledon, 63, 109

Royalty and Lawn Tennis (Tingay), 513

Rubber, defined, 563

Rubin, Chanda: 1996 Australian Open: vs. Sanchez Vicario, 367-68

Rules, **569-84;** for doubles game, 579, 583-84; for early tennis, 6; in early women's competition, 13; for singles game, 569-83

Rush, Gretchen, 269

Rusher, net, 560

Russel, JoAnne—Gourlay Cawley, Helen: 1977 Wimbledon, 231-32

Russia: lawn tennis in, 13

Russian Championships: 1913, 21-22

Ruzici, Virginia, 228, 244, **540-41**

Ryan, Elizabeth ("Bunny"), 21, 28, 32, 34, 39, **494;** 1924 Wimbledon doubles, 55; 1926 Wightman Cup, 40; 1977 at Wimbledon Centenary, 230; 1979 death of, 249, 494

Ryan-Mathieu: 1934 Wimbledon, 55

S

Sabatini, Gabriela, 284, *328,* **541;** 1984 U.S. Open, 284; 1985 French Open, 285, 290; 1985 season, 290; 1988 U.S. Open: vs. Graf, 310; 1988 win record, 309; 1989 U.S. Open, 318; 1990 U.S. Open: vs. M. Fernandez, vs.

Graf, 328; 1990 Virginia Slims: vs. Seles, 328; 1991 duel for No. 1, 331; 1991 Wimbledon: vs. Graf, 331-32; 1992 French Open: vs. Seles, 340; 1993 French Open: vs. M.J. Fernandez, 347; 1994 U.S. Open, 356; 1994 Virginia Slims: vs. Davenport, 357

Sampras, Pete, *312, 349, 363, 371,* **432-34,** *434;* 1989 U.S. Open: vs. Wilander, 319, 433; 1990 Grand Slam Cup, 322, 433; 1990 U.S. Open, 432; vs. Agassi, 327-28, 335; vs. McEnroe, 327-28; 1991 Davis Cup: vs. Forget, 336, 433; 1992 U.S. Open: vs. Edberg, 344; 1993 ATP Tour finals: vs. Stich, 351; 1993 season, 346; 1993 U.S. Open: vs. Pioline, 349; 1993 Wimbledon: vs. Courier, vs. Agassi, 347-48; 1994 ATP Tour Championship: vs. Agassi, vs. Becker, 357; 1994 Australian Open: vs. Martin, 353; 1994 French Open: vs. Courier, 354; 1994 U.S. Open, 355; 1994 Wimbledon: vs. Ivanisevic, 354; 1995 Australian Open: vs. Courier, vs. Agassi, 360-61; 1995 Davis Cup: vs. Chesnokov, 364, 365, 433-34; vs. Kafelnikov, 365; 1995 Davis Cup triple, 364-65; 1995 No. 1 ranking, 365; 1995 on Tim Gullikson, 361; 1995 rivalry with Agassi, 358; 1995 U.S. Open: vs. Courier, vs. Agassi, 363; 1995 Wimbledon (third in a row): vs. Ivanisevic, vs. Becker, 362; 1996 ATP World Championship: vs. Becker, 373; 1996 Australian Open: vs. Philippoussis, 367, 606; 1996 French Open: vs. Courier, vs. Kafelnikov, 368-69, 433; 1996 U.S. Open: vs. Chang, vs. Corretja, 371-72, 432, 434; 1996 Wimbledon: vs. Krajicek, 369, 432-33; on Agassi, 376

Sampras-Martin: 1995 Davis Cup, 365

Sampson, Julie, *138*

Sanchez, Emilio, 313, 316, 327, 343, **541**

Sanchez, Javier, 316, **541**

Sanchez Vicario, Arantxa, 309, *315, 353,* **434-36,** *435;* 1989 French Open: vs. Graf, 314, 316-17, 435; 1991 French Open: vs. Seles, 331; 1992 French Open: vs. Graf, 340; 1993 Federation Cup, 351; 1993 Virginia Slims semifinal: vs. Pierce, 351; 1994: vs. Williams, vs. Navratilova,

Shorts, 50, 52, 53, 55, 125

Shot: approach, 548; passing, 561

Shriver, Pam, *243*, **542;** 1978 season, 243, 244; 1979 U.S. Open, 250; 1982 U.S. Open: vs. Navratilova, 269; 1984 Grand Slam, 665; 1987 Canadian Open: vs. Evert, vs. Garrison, 302; 1987 Wimbledon: vs. Graf, 302; 1988 win record, 309; on Graf, 302

Shriver-Garrison: 1988 Olympic gold, 309

Simionescu, Mariana, 254

Singles: rules for, 569-83; scoring tie-break in, 579-80

Singles records: Grand Slam, 664-65; individual career: Australian Championships, 611; French Championships, 617; miscellaneous, 658-61; U.S., 594-95; Wimbledon, 605; men's, 18; all-time major, 666; Australian Championships, 606-7; French Championships, 612-13; Italian Championships, 618; miscellaneous, 658; U.S. Championships, 586-87; Wimbledon, 599-600; women's: all-time major, 666-67; Australian Championships, 607-8; French Championships, 613; Italian Championships, 618-19; miscellaneous, 658-59; title records, 66; U.S. Championships, 588; Wimbledon, 600-601

Sirola, Orlando, **542-43;** 1960 Davis Cup: vs. MacKay, 156

Sitter, defined, 564

Skeen, Dick, 74

Skoff, Horst, 322

Slice, defined, 564

Slims Circuit, **564**

Slocum, Henry Warner, **499**

Slow court. *See* Court speed

Smash, defined, 564

Smid, Tom, 256

Smidl, Robert, 75

Smith, Anne: 1978 Dallas Virginia Slims, 243; 1981 U.S. Open, 264

Smith, Margaret. *See* Court, Margaret Smith

Smith, Paula, 284

Smith, Red, 125

Smith, Roger, 350; 1988 Australian Open: vs. Smith, 311-12

Smith, Sid, 16

Smith, Stan, *196, 227,* **442-43,** *442;* 1969 National Singles, 184; 1969 No. 1 ranking, 186; 1970 Grand Prix Masters, 194; 1970 Pacific Coast Championships:

vs. Richey, 193; 1971 earnings, 196-97; 1971 U.S. Open: vs. Kodes, 442-43; 1971 Wimbledon: vs. Newcombe, 195; 1972 Davis Cup: vs. Nastase, 202, 442; 1972 Wimbledon: vs. Nastase, 201, 442-43; 1973 Davis Cup, 208; 1973 No. 1 U.S. ranking with Connors, 206; 1973 WCT tour, 205

Smith-Lutz, 442-43; 1968 Davis Cup, 182; 1968 U.S. Open, 181; 1970 Davis Cup, 193; 1973 WCT doubles, 205; 1974 U.S. Open, 212; 1978 U.S. Open, Davis Cup, 242

Smith-van Dillen: 1972 Davis Cup, 203; 1973 Davis Cup, 208

Smylie, Liz Sayers. *See* Sayers, Liz

Snodgrass, Fred, 38

Solomon, Harold ("Solly"), *225;* 1972 Davis Cup, 202; 1976 French Open, 224-25; 1976 Italian: vs. Panatta, 449

South Africa, 188, 193, 210, 214, 219, 220, 311

Soweto exhibition: Ashe at, 210

"Spaghetti" ("double-strung") racket, 229, 235-36, *236*

Speed, of court, 552

Sperling, Hilde Krahwinkel, 48, **543;** 1935 French Championships, 57; 1936 French Championships, 59; 1937 French Championships, 61

Sphairistike, 6

"Spider Man." *See* Froehling, Frank, III

Spikes, defined, 564

Spin, defined, 564

Spirlea, Irina: 1995 Palermo conduct, 450

Sponsors: Avon, 244-45; Chase, 636; Clairol Crown, 247; Colgate-Palmolive, 225, 251, 635; Commercial Union Assurance, 197, 635; Corel, 636; Family Circle Cup, 210; L'Eggs World Series, 221; Lipton Tea, 274; Louisiana Pacific, 289; Nabisco, 290, 635; Pepsico, 189; Philip Morris, 185; Virginia Slims, 191, 209, 244, 512; Reebok, 326; Toyota, 635; Volvo, 251, 635

Srejber, Milan, 322

Stade Français (St. Cloud), 612

Stade Roland Garros. *See* Roland Garros

Stafford, Shaun, 357

Stammers, Kay, 56

Stancin, Margaret, 448

Stark, Jonathan, 357

Steeb, Charlie, 313, 319

Stefanki, Larry, 342

Steiner, Charlie, 259

Steinmetz, Kim, 310

Sterry, Charlotte, **543**

Stevens, Greer-Hewitt: 1979 U.S. Open, 251

Stewart, Sherwood–McNair, Freddie: 1975 Masters, 219; 1976 No. 1 doubles ranking, 226

Stich, Michael, *336,* **543;** 1991 Wimbledon: vs. Edberg, vs. Becker, 334-35; 1992 Grand Slam Cup: vs. Chang, 344; 1993 ATP Tour finals: vs. Sampras, 351; 1993 Davis Cup, 350; 1994 U.S. Open: vs. Agassi, 355-56; 1996 French Open: vs. Muster, vs. Stich, 369

Stich-Kuhnen: 1993 Davis Cup, 350

Stockings, 45

Stockton, Dick, 212, 232, 267

Stoefen, Les, 54, 58

Stolle, Fred ("Fiery Fred"), *170,* **499;** 1963 Wimbledon, 163; 1964 LTAA suspension, 164; 1964 U.S. Championships, Davis Cup: vs. Ralston, 165; 1965 French Championships, 167; 1966 late bloomer, 169-70; 1966 U.S. Championships, 499; on attitude, 262

Stoltenberg, Jason, 350, 369

Stone, Allan–Dowdeswell, Colin: 1975 Wimbledon, 219

Stove, Betty, **543;** 1972 triple titles, 204; 1977 U.S. Open, 235; 1977 Wimbledon, 230

Stove-McMillan: 1978 two-title year, 242

Stove-Turnbull: 1979 French Open, 248; 1979 U.S. Open, 251

Strandlund, Maria, 311

Streisand, Barbra, 348

Strings, spaghetti racket, 235

Strougal, Lubomir, 249

Stuart, Bettyann Grubb, 235

Studenikova, Katarina: 1996 Wimbledon: vs. Seles, 370

Sturgess, Eric: 1947 French Championships, 124

Stvanice Stadium (Prague), 292

Subirats, Elena, 172

Sudden death, 222; defined, 564, 586

Suk, Cyril, **543-44**

Sukova, Helena, *279,* 284, *297,* **543-44;** 1984 Australian Open: vs.

Evert, 284; vs. Navratilova, 278, 284; 1986 U.S. Open: vs. Evert, vs. Navratilova, 296-97; 1989 Australian Open: vs. Navratilova, 316; 1993 U.S. Open: vs. Navratilova, vs. Graf, 350

Sukova, Vera Puzejova, **543;** 1962 Wimbledon, 161; 1963 French Championships, 162

Sullivan Award: for Don Budge, 63

Summerhayes, Martha, 8

Sundstrom, Henrik, 278, 283

"Sunshine Supergirl." *See* Goolagong, Evonne

"Superbrat." *See* McEnroe, John

Supervisor: defined, 564; role of, 448

Supreme Court, defined, 564

Susman, Karen Hantze, *158,* **544;** 1962 Wimbledon, 161; 1964 U.S. Championships, 166

Suspensions, for poor conduct: 1976 Nastase, 226; 1986 McEnroe, 297

Sutter, Cliff: 1932 U.S. Championships: vs. Vines, 50

Sutton, May. *See* Bundy, May Sutton

Svensson, Jonas, 312

Swardt, Mariaan de, 364

Sweden: 1975 first Davis Cup, 218; 1984 Davis Cup sweep, 278, 283; 1988 "Swedish" slam, 306-7; 1994 fifth Davis Cup, 357-58

Synthetic clay, 217

T

Talbert, Bill, *122,* 250, 449, **500-501;** 1943 U.S. Championships, 76; 1944 U.S. Championships, 76; 1945 long set vs. Parker, 78

Talbert-Mulloy, 500; 1946 U.S. doubles, 122

Tandem formation. *See* I formation

Tanner, Roscoe, *213;* 1977 Australian Open, 231; 1979 U.S. Open: net-snapping serve, 250; 1979 Wimbledon: vs. Borg, 248; 1980 U.S. Open: vs. Borg, 254; 1981 U.S. Open: vs. Borg, 261; on Borg, 261; on Connors, 218

Tapscott, Billie, 45, **544**

Tarango, Benedicte, 359, 448

Tarango, Jeff, *359;* 1995 Wimbledon walkoff, 358-59, 448, 450

Taroczy, Balazs, 278

Tauziat, Nathalie, 342

Taylor, Fred, 9

Taylor, Howard, 12

Taylor, Roger, 172, 173, 176

Teacher, Brian, **544;** 1980 Australian Open, 252

Teaching professional: defined by ITF, 178

"Team Navratilova," 273

Team Tennis (World Team Tennis), 560

"Teen Angel." *See* Borg, Bjorn

Tegart, Judy. *See* Dalton, Judy Tegart

TEL (Tennis Electronics Line) system, 447

Television: tennis and, 69, 197, 200, 216, 231

Teltscher, Eliot, 270, 289

Temesvari, Andrea: 1983 Italian Open, U.S. Clay Court, 275

Tennant, Eleanor "Teach," 139, 388

Tenney, Robin, 210

Tennis: age-group: defined, 547; early. *See* Lawn tennis; early strokes in, 10; etymology of, 1; first televised: in U.S., 69; long *(longue paume),* 4; origins of, 1-9; patent notice, *5;* popularity of, 205, 211; pro vs. amateur, 457-548; women's, 8

Tennis attire: of Agassi, 324, 327, 333, 334; Bermuda shorts as, 50; of Casals, 462; of de Alvarez, Bennett, and Nuthall, 46; of "Gorgeous Gussy" Moran, 128-29, *129;* Lacoste and, 97; of Lenglen, 26, 97; sans stockings, 45; shorts as, 50, 52, 53, 55, 125; Tinling and, 128-29, 514-15

Tennis ball. *See* Ball(s)

"Tennis bum," 119

Tennis Champions Classic, 193

Tennis clubs: early, 9-10

Tennis elbow. *See* Elbow

Tennis Electronics Line (TEL) system, 447

Tennis Observed (Trabert), 501

Tennis Origins and Mysteries (Whitman), 2

Tennis racket. *See* Racket

Tennis terms: defined, 547-68

Terry, Aline, **544**

Thirty, defined, 564

Thomas, C. E., 2

Thompson, Gloria: 1943 U.S. Championships, 76

Throat, defined, 564

Throckmorton, Harold, 27, 452

Tie, defined, 564

Tie-breaker, tie-break: 1970 U.S. Open adopts 9-point sudden death, 192-93, 196; 1975 U.S. Open adopts 12-point lingering death, 222; defined, 564-65, 586; Jimmy Van Alen and, 175, 514-15. *See also* Van Alen Streamlined Scoring System (VASSS); longest: Australian Championships, 611; French Championships, 617; miscellaneous, 660; U.S. Championships, 595; Wimbledon, 606

Tiedemann, Mrs. Alexander. *See* Bouman, Kea

Tilden, Bill ("Big Bill"), 23, *27, 33, 44,* **110-12,** *111;* 1919 U.S. Championships: vs. Johnston, 26-27, 110; 1920 Davis Cup, *27,* 28; 1920 U.S. Championships, 27-28; vs. Johnston, 27-28; 1920 Wimbledon, 27, 110; vs. Shimidzu and Patterson, 27; 1921 Davis Cup, 29-30; 1921 U.S. Championships, 30; 1921 Wimbledon: vs. Norton, 28-29; 1922 U.S. Championships: vs. Johnston, 30-31; 1923 Davis Cup, 33; 1923 U.S. Nationals, 32; 1924 Davis Cup, 34; 1924 U.S. Championships, 34; 1925 Davis Cup: vs. Musketeers, 35-36; 1925 U.S. Finals: vs. Johnston, 35; 1926 Davis Cup: ends singles streak, 40; 1926 U.S. Championships: Cochet vs., 39; 1927 U.S. Championships: vs. Lacoste, 41; 1927 Wimbledon: vs. Cochet, 40-41; 1928 French Championships: vs. Lacoste, 43; 1929 U.S. Championships, 44; 1930 Davis Cup: final appearance, 46; 1930 European tour, 45; 1930 turns pro, 45-46, 668; 1930 U.S. Championships: vs. Doeg, 46; 1930 Wimbledon: vs. Borotra and Allison, 45, 110; 1931 pro debut, 48, 112; 1932 pro season, 50; 1933 pro season, 53; 1934 vs. Vines, vs. Cochet, 55; 1935 vs. Lott, 58; 1937 as Davis Cup coach for Germany, 63; 1937 vs. Perry, 64; 1941 vs. Budge, 73-74; on Brookes, 85; on Budge, 87; death of, 112; and USTA conflict, 34, 42-43, 111

Tilden-Johnston: 1920 Davis Cup, 28; 1924 Davis Cup, 34

Tilden-Williams: 1923 Davis Cup, 33

Tingay, Lance, **513;** on Bueno, 155; on Connolly, 139, 142, 389; on Drobny, 143; on Falkenburg vs. Bromwich, 127; on Hoad vs. Cooper, 148; on Laver, 180; on

Patty, 132; on Schroeder, 130; on Seixas, 140

Tinling, Ted, **513-14;** and Bueno, 386; and Casals, 462; on David Gray, 511; and Goolagong, 198; on McEnroe's trophies, 270; shocks Wimbledon with lace panties, 128-29

Tiriac, Ion, 424, **544-45;** 1968 French Championships: vs. Laver, 180; 1969 Davis Cup, 187; 1971 Davis Cup: vs. Froehling, 199; 1977 coaches Vilas, 231; on Becker, 287

Titanic, and Dick Williams, 116

"To cough and quit," 28

Todd, Pat Canning, **545;** 1947 French Championships, 124

Tolstoy, Leo, 13

Tomanova, Renata, 221

Top Ten, 565; 1930, 46; ATP, 662-63; defined, 555; WTA, 661-62

Topspin: defined, 565. *See also* Spin; Herb Lawford and, 532; Johnston and, 95; Laver and, 418

Toulmin, Mrs. Harry. *See* Townsend, Bertha

Tournament(s): age-group, 457; defined, 565; early control of, 7; Nahant, 8-9

Townsend, Bertha, 13, **501**

Toyota Series Championships, 637

Trabert, Tony, *144, 227, 443,* **443-44;** 1953 U.S. Championships: vs. Seixas, 141; 1954 Davis Cup, 143; 1954 French Championships, 142, 443; 1955 French, Wimbledon, and U.S. titles, 144, 443; 1975 Davis Cup, 219; on Chang, 317

Tree-ing, defined, 565

Triple-triplers: in majors, 72

Truman, Christine (Chris), **545;** 1958 Wightman Cup: vs. Gibson, 152; 1961 Wimbledon: vs. Mortimer, 158; 1968 Wightman Cup, 183

Truman, Nell: 1968 Wightman Cup, 183

Truman-Truman: 1968 Wightman Cup, 183

Tuckey, Charles: 1935 Davis Cup, 57

Turnbull, Wendy May ("Rabbit"), **545;** 1977 U.S. Open, 234-35; 1984 Federation Cup, 284

Turner, Lesley. *See* Bowrey, Lesley Turner

Turville, Ed, 162, 193, 199

TV. *See* Television

Twist: American: defined, 548; early, 15

U

U.E., defined, 566

Ulrich, Einer, **545**

Ulrich, Jorgen, **545**

Ulrich, Torben, **545**

Umpire: defined, 566; vs. Tennis Electronics Line (TEL) system, 447

Umpires, 447-50

United States. *See also* U.S.; championship records, 586-95; Davis Cup records, 627; early tennis in, 8-9

United States Lawn Tennis Association (USLTA). *See* United States Tennis Association (USTA)

United States Tennis Association (USTA), **566, 638-48;** and National Tennis Center, 236-37, *237;* and open tennis, 150, 155, 162, 173, 183-84; vote for, 177; rankings: All-American (1970-1971), 642; men's, 638-43; women's, 643-48; and Richards case, 223; suspends Betz, 124; Tilden's feud with, 34, 42-43; on Virginia Slims Circuit, 208; during World War II, 74

Unprofessional conduct. *See by specific individual, e.g., McEnroe, John*

Upsets: Australian Championships, 612; biggest: Australian Championships, 612; French Championships, 617; U.S. Championships, 595; Wimbledon, 606; French Championships, 617; U.S. Championships, 595; Wimbledon, 606

U.S. Amateur Championships: 1968 Ashe at, 182

U.S. Championships (now U.S. Open), **585-95.** *See also* Flushing Meadow Park (New York); Forest Hills (New York); 1968 first open, 181-82; 1996 seeding controversy, 371; all-time records, 593-94; attendance at, 586; best comebacks, 595; biggest upsets, 595; early, 11-12; individual career records, 594; longest matches, 188, 595; longest tie-breakers, 595; men's doubles records, 589-90; men's singles records, 586-87; mixed doubles records, 592-93; oldest champions, 594;

unseeded champions, 355; women's, first, 13; women's doubles records, 580-92; women's singles records, 588; youngest champions, 594

U.S. Clay Court, 74-75, 586

U.S. Indoor Championships, 586; 1971 promotion, 195

U.S. Intercollegiate Championship: Segura and, 75

U.S. Interscholastic Champions, 598-99

U.S. National Intercollegiate Champions, 595-98

U.S. National Lawn Tennis Association: formation of, 12

U.S. National Lawn Tennis Association (USNLTA), 9. *See also* United States Tennis Association (USTA)

U.S. Open. *See also* Flushing Meadow; *See also* Forest Hills; 1968 first open at Forest Hills, 181-82; 1977 last open held at Forest Hills, 231-32

U.S. Pro Championships, **566, 667-68.** *See also* Professional competition; 1927 inaugural, 42, 492; 1928, 44; 1929, 45; 1931, 48; 1939, 70; 1940, 72; 1943 Ft. Knox, 76; 1946 Riggs vs. Budge, 122; 1948 Kramer at, 126-27; 1950 Segura at, 134; 1951, 137; 1952 Segura vs. Gonzalez, 139; 1953 Gonzalez at, 142; 1954, 143; 1958 Gonzalez vs. Hoad, 152; 1959, 154; 1961, 159; 1962, 161; 1964 revival of, 166; 1965 Rosewall at, 169; 1966 Laver vs. Rosewall, 172

U.S. Summer Circuit: 1969, 184

USTA. *See* United States Tennis Association (USTA)

USTA National Tennis Center. *See* Flushing Meadow Park (New York)

V

Vacek, Daniel, 373

Van Alen, Candy: and National Tennis Hall of Fame, 451, 514

Van Alen, Jimmy, **514-15;** 1965 hosts pro tournament, 169; death of, 334, 515; and Newport Casino, 451; and VASSS, 169, 175, 192, 451, 514, 566

Van Alen Streamlined Scoring System (VASSS), 169, 192-93, 514, **566**

van Dillen, Erik, 202, 203